E-COMMERCE LAW

The Legal Compliance Handbook for Online Business

Tom James, J.D.

E-COMMERCE LAW

The Legal Compliance Handbook for Online Business

Tom James, J.D.

Echion Publishing
Plymouth, Minn.

Echion, LLC
P.O. Box 46162
Plymouth, MN 55446

www.echionllc.com

First printing.

Published in Plymouth, Minnesota
Printed in the United States of America

ISBN-13: 978–1–946397–06–5
Library of Congress Control Number:

10 9 8 7 6 5 4 3 2 1

Table of Contents

Table of Abbreviations

AAA: American Arbitration Association
ACH: Automated Clearing House
ACLU: American Civil Liberties Union
ACMLA: Association of Composers and Publishers of Latin American Music
ACPA: Anticybersquatting Consumer Protection Act
ADA: Americans with Disabilities Act
ADEA: Age Discrimination in Employment Act
ADR: alternative dispute resolution
AIPA: American Inventors Protection Act
APR: annual percentage rate
ASCAP: American Society of Composers, Authors and Publishers
ASCII: American Standard Code for Information Interchange
AVI: Audio Video Interleave
BATF: Bureau of Alcohol, Tobacco and Firearms
BFPV: bona fide purchaser for value
BHCA: Bank Holding Company Act
BMI: Broadcast Music Incorporated
BSA: Bank Secrecy Act
CD-ROM: compact disc- read-only memory
CFR: Code of Federal Regulations
CAN-SPAM Act: Controlling the Assault of Nonsolicited Pornography and Marketing Act
CD: compact disc
CDA: Communications Decency Act
CEO: chief executive officer
CFAA: Computer Fraud and Abuse Act
CFO: chief financial officer
CFTC: Commodity Futures Trading Commission
CGL: Comprehensive General Liability
CISA: Cybersecurity Information Sharing Act
CISG: U.N. Convention on Contracts for the International Sale of Goods
COBRA: Comprehensive Omnibus Budget Reconciliation Act
COPA: Child Online Protection Act
COPPA: Children's Online Privacy Protection Act
CPAA: Classics Protection and Access Act
CPOEA: Child Protection and Obscenity Enforcement Act
CPR: International Institute for Conflict Prevention and Resolution
CPTR Rule: Credit Practices Trade Regulation Rule
Credit CARD Act: Credit Card Accountability, Responsibility and Disclosure Act
CRFA: Consumer Review Fairness Act
CRRA: California Resale Royalty Act
CSS: Cascading Style Sheets
CVC: card verification code
CVV: card verification value
DHS: U.S. Department of Homeland Security
DHHS: U.S. Department of Health and Human Services
DMCA: Digital Millennium Copyright Act
DNS: domain name system or server
DPO: direct public offering
DPPA: Driver's Privacy Protection Act
DPRA: Digital Performance Right in Sound Recordings Act
DRM: digital rights management
DSHEA: Dietary Supplements Health and Education Act
DVD: digital versatile disc
EBSA: Employee Benefits Security Administration

ECC: UN Convention on the Use of Electronic Communications in International Contracts
ECOA: Equal Credit Opportunity Act
ECPA: Electronic Communications Privacy Act
EEA: Economic Espionage Act
EEOC: Equal Employment Opportunity Commission
EFT: electronic funds transfer
EFTA: Electronic Funds Transfer Act
EPA: Equal Pay Act
EPPA: Employee Polygraph Protection Act
ERISA: Employee Retirement Income Security Act
E-SIGN Act: Electronic Signatures in Global and National Commerce Act
EU: European Union
EULA: end user license agreement
FACTA: Fair and Accurate Credit Transactions Act
FBI: Federal Bureau of Investigation
FCC: Federal Communications Commission
FCBA: Fair Credit Billing Act
FCPA: Foreign Corrupt Practices Act
FCRA: Fair Credit Reporting Act
FDA: Food and Drug Administration
FDCPA: Fair Debt Collection Practices Act
FDD: Financial Disclosure Document
FinCEN: Financial Crimes Enforcement Network
FLSA: Fair Labor Standards Act
FMLA: Family and Medical Leave Act
FOIA: Freedom of Information Act
FPR: financial performance representations disclosure
FRB: Federal Reserve Board
FTC: Federal Trade Commission
FTC Act: Federal Trade Commission Act
FTP: File Transfer Protocol
GATT: General Agreement on Tariffs and Trade
GDPR: General Data Protection Regulation
GINA: Genetic Information Nondiscrimination Act
GLBA: Gramm-Leach-Bliley Act
GNU: GNU ("GNU's Not Unix!") Project
GP: general partnership
GS: Goods and Services
GUID: globally unique identifier
HIPAA: Health Insurance Portability and Accountability Act
HITECH Act: Health Information Technology for Economic and Clinical Health Act
HTML: Hypertext Markup Language
HTTP: Hypertext Transfer Protocol
HTTPS: Hypertext Transfer Protocol Secure
IC: International Class
ICANN: Internet Corporation for Assigned Names and Numbers
ICC: International Chamber of Commerce
ICCPR: International Covenant on Civil and Political Rights
ICE: Immigration and Customs Enforcement
IDS: intrusion detection system
IM: instant messaging
IP: Internet Protocol
IPS: intrusion prevention system
IRS: Internal Revenue Service
ISP: Internet Service Provider
ISSN: International Standard Serial Number
ITFA: Internet Tax Freedom Act
JPEG: Joint Photographic Experts Group
LCIA: London Court of International Arbitration
LLC: limited liability company
LLP: limited liability partnership
LP: limited partnership
MAC: media access control
MLC: mechanical licensing collective
MIT: Massachusetts Institute of Technology
MP3: Moving Picture Experts Group Layer-3 Audio (audio file format/extension)
MPEG: Moving Picture Experts Group
MRI: magnetic resonance imaging
MWMA: Musical Works Modernization Act
NASD: National Association of Securities Dealers

NIPRCC: National Intellectual Property Rights Coordination Center
NLRA: National Labor Relations Act
NSMIA: National Securities Markets Improvement Act
OSHA: 1. Occupational Safety and Health Act; 2. Occupational Safety and Health Administration
PBS: Public Broadcasting Service
PCI: Payment card industry
PCI DSS: Payment Card Industry Security Standards Council Data Security Standard
PCI SSC: Payment Card Industry Security Standards Council
PDA: personal digital assistant
PDF: Portable Document Format
PETA: People for the Ethical Treatment of Animals
PIN: personal identification number
PIPEDA: Personal Information Protection and Electronic Documents Act
PO: Post Office
POS: point of sale
PROTECT Act: Prosecutorial Remedies and Other Tools to End the Exploitation of Children Today Act
PRS: Performing Rights Society
PSLRA: Private Securities Litigation Reform Act
RICO: Racketeer Influenced and Corrupt Organizations Act
ROSCA: Restore Online Shoppers' Confidence Act
SAFE WEB Act: Undertaking Spam, Spyware and Fraud Enforcement with Enforcers Beyond Borders Act
SAQ: Self-Assessment Questionnaire
SBCTEA: Sonny Bono Copyright Term Extension Act
SCMS: Serial Copy Management System
SEC: Securities Exchange Commission
SESAC: Society of European Stage Authors and Composers
SLAPP: strategic lawsuit against public participation
SLUSA: Securities Litigation Uniform Standards Act
SM: service mark
SMS: short message service
SMTP: Simple Mail Transfer Protocol
SOPIPA: Student Online Personal Information Protection Act
SOX Act: Sarbanes-Oxley Act
SPEECH Act: Securing the Protection of Our Enduring and Established Constitutional Heritage Act
SQL: Structured Query Language
SSID: service set identifier
SSL: Secure Sockets Layer
SSO: sequence, structure and organization
TARR: Trademark Applications and Registrations Retrieval
TCPA: Telephone Consumer Protection Act
TDR: Trademark Document Retrieval
TEAS: Trademark Electronic Application System
TEAS RF: TEAS—Reduced Fee
TESS: Trademark Electronic Search System
TILA: Truth in Lending Act
TLD: top-level domain
TLS: Transport Layer Security
TM: trademark
TMEP: Trademark Manual of Examining Procedures
TRIPS Agreement: Agreement on Trade-Related Aspects of Intellectual Property
TRO: temporary restraining order
TSDR: Trademark Status and Document Retrieval
TSR: Telemarketing Sales Rule
TTAB: United States Trademark Trial and Appeals Board
U.C.C.: Uniform Commercial Code
UCC: Universal Copyright Convention
UCITA: Uniform Computer Information Transactions Act

UDRP: Uniform Domain Name Dispute Resolution Policy
UDTPA: Uniform Deceptive Trade Practices Act
UETA: Uniform Electronic Transactions Act
UFMJRA: Uniform Foreign Money Judgments Recognition Act
UFOC: Uniform Franchise Offering Circular
UN: United Nations
UPS: United Parcel Service
URAA: Uruguay Round Agreements Act
URL: Uniform Resource Locator
U.S. United States
USA FREEDOM Act: Uniting and Strengthening America by Fulfilling Rights and Ensuring Effective Discipline Over Monitoring Act
USA PATRIOT Act: Uniting and Strengthening America by Providing Appropriate Tools Required to Intercept and Obstruct Terrorism Act
U.S.C.: United States Code
USERRA: Uniformed Services Employment and Reemployment Rights Act
USPTO: United States Patent and Trademark Office
USSR: Union of Soviet Socialist Republics
UTSA: Uniform Trade Secrets Act
VARA: Visual Artists Rights Act
VAT: Value-Added Tax
VoIP: Voice over Internet Protocol
VPA: Volunteer Protection Act
WARN Act: Worker Adjustment and Retraining Notification Act
WAV: Windows Wave
WIPO: World Intellectual Property Organization
WIPO Performances and Phonograms Treaty: WIPO Convention for the Protection of Producers of Phonograms Against Unauthorized Duplication of Their Phonograms
WMA: Windows Media Audio
WMV: Windows Media Video
WSA: Webcaster Settlement Act
WTO: World Trade Organization.

Preface

E-commerce is a shorthand expression for electronic commerce. It encompasses any sale, license, lease, rental or other transfer of a product, service or property interest, whether tangible or intangible, that is conducted, advertised or facilitated using an online service. It also refers to the conduct of some or all of a business's operations online. It is not a discrete, compartmentalized field of study like contract, tort, intellectual property, business, or constitutional law. It is all of those things—and more. Unfortunately, a book of this size cannot provide in-depth coverage of every aspect of every possible legal topic a business may encounter when it engages in e-commerce. Nor can it take the place of an attorney. What it can and does provide is a means for identifying and understanding the issues that may arise in the course of doing business online.

This book has been written for readers of average intelligence and education. While it is anticipated that it will be useful to attorneys who advise e-commerce business owners, it is written in plain English and concepts are explained in such a way that an advanced degree is not necessary to understand them.

The book provides general information and commentary about the law, not legal advice. While I am an attorney, I am not your attorney. Neither your acquisition of this book nor your reading of it creates an attorney-client relationship between us. You should hire a licensed attorney if you need legal advice.

Laws are always changing, especially the ones relating to the Internet. Consequently, no assurance can be made that the information in this book will still be current by the time you acquire it. It is a good idea to keep informed about new developments in this area of the law. If you have a question or need specific legal advice, you should consult an attorney.

A reference to the laws of a particular country does not imply anything about the laws of other countries. While an effort has been made to indicate the range and variety of laws in different countries, the focus of much of this book is largely on U.S. law. An omission of a reference to differences between U.S. law and the laws of another country does not imply that they are the same.

All of the examples in this book are hypothetical. Any similarity to any person, whether living or dead, or to any past, present or future legal entity, is purely coincidental.

The author has made a conscious effort to employ both masculine and feminine pronouns. In all events, and unless the context clearly indicates otherwise, the masculine includes the feminine; the feminine includes the masculine; and the use of either pronoun includes transsexuals, bisexuals, asexuals, and every other variant that has been or may in the future be used in the taxonomy of human beings.

The book is divided into five parts. Part I deals with the business aspects of e-commerce—choosing and creating a business entity, raising capital, managing the business, transferring stock and other kinds of interests, hiring and managing employees, franchising, combinations in restraint of trade, antitrust and unfair competition laws. The legal considerations involved in terminating a business are also explained.

Part II covers the law of commercial transactions in the online context. Particular attention is given to credit and debit card processing standards and data security requirements. Sales, use and other kinds of taxes are also explained.

Part III describes the legal limitations on website content. This includes advertising; spam, spyware and other kinds of computer crime and abuse; trade disparagement; and other kinds of content regulations in the United States and around the world. Also included are chapters on child-directed websites, adult websites with sexually explicit content, liability for user-provided content, and privacy rights.

Part IV covers the various kinds of intellectual property rights that may be involved in the operation of an ecommerce business—copyrights, trademarks, patents, trade secrets, information, ideas—with an emphasis on acquiring usage rights and licensing.

Part V provides some tools for tackling the complicated problems of jurisdiction and conflicts of laws in interstate and international e-commerce transactions. The book concludes with a look at the UDRP procedure for resolving domain name disputes and some other promising methods of resolving online legal disputes without going to court.

A bibliography, topical index and tables of abbreviations, statutes and cases are included.

Introduction

The Internet has unlocked exciting new opportunities for business. Unlike traditional brick-and-mortar businesses, anyone can start an online business, usually for little more than the cost of an Internet connection, domain name registration, and web hosting. Many people have. In North America alone, there are over a million e-commerce businesses, and the number is growing all the time. What began as an information-sharing system for academics has evolved into the most powerful tool for transacting business the world has ever known.

The Internet has also vastly expanded the geographic territory of the average business. Historically, businesses were limited to a single geographic area of trade. Only the most successful businesses could expand into new sales territories. Doing so typically involved the establishment of satellite offices or franchises, neither of which the average small business could afford. Only the most amply capitalized ventures could afford to invest in national or international advertising or conduct mail order campaigns. These methods still continue to be employed by large companies, but the Internet now makes it possible for small and mid-size firms to compete for sales in the global market, too, and at a fraction of the cost. International trade law has suddenly become relevant to a vastly greater number of people than it once was.

A spirit of freedom permeates Internet culture. The fight for Net neutrality—the idea that the Internet should be available for anyone to use, free from efforts to control it—reflects that spirit. It is part of a broader reverence for freedoms of conscience and expression in general. The United States Supreme Court has declared that the right to freedom of speech enshrined in the First Amendment of the American constitution is such a fundamental right that it is protected by both the First and the Fourteenth Amendments. It is not an absolute right, however. The same constitution that protects it also empowers Congress to pass laws protecting copyrights and to regulate interstate commerce. Moreover, the Supreme Court has created a few exceptions of its own, holding that the First Amendment does not provide any protection at all for obscenity and certain other categories of speech. And some categories of speech are more constitutionally protected than others. In particular, government is allowed considerably more room to regulate commercial speech than political or religious speech.

The Internet is not quite the Wild Frontier of free expression people imagine it to be. There are many restrictions, emanating from many different sources, on what may be published and how transactions may be conducted online. Failing to recognize them puts website owners and online service providers at serious risk of being sued, or worse, going to jail. Copyright infringement filings in federal court, for example, have skyrocketed since the advent of the Internet. Untold numbers of people – estimated to be in the thousands – have received cease and desist letters or have been sued for large sums of money for publishing things to their websites or blogs. Many of these people honestly believed their activities were protected by the First

Amendment, or they erroneously believed the material was in the public domain or that their publication of it was fair use. Website owners are increasingly coming under attack for trademark infringement or dilution, as well. Recent developments in data privacy and sales tax law have also added layers of complexity to legal compliance.

Although the Internet facilitates the sharing of ideas and creative expression, it also facilitates infringement of intellectual property rights. It facilitates exchanges of money and personal information, but it also facilitates invasions of privacy, identity theft, and crime. It facilitates quicker, simpler methods of resolving disputes, but it also generates complicated jurisdiction and conflicts of laws issues. Starting and running an e-commerce business is simple, but the legal issues are not. They are not insurmountable, though. Understanding the "rules of the road" makes it possible to structure operations in a way that minimizes legal costs and reduces the risk of incurring liability when doing business online.

PART I. BUSINESS LAW

Chapter 1. Starting a Business

Selecting a Business Entity

The first step in starting a business is to decide on the kind of business entity to create. The five most common kinds are:

- Sole proprietorship
- General partnership
- Limited partnership
- Corporation
- Limited liability company.

SOLE PROPRIETORSHIP

A sole proprietorship is a business that is owned and operated by only one individual. It is not a separate legal entity. It may be operated under an assumed name, but the use of an assumed name is not enough to create a separate legal entity.

A sole proprietorship has the advantage of being less expensive to create and manage than other kinds of business entities inasmuch as it is not actually a business entity at all. Because it is not a business entity, organizational documents do not need to be drafted or filed in order to establish one. It also has the advantage of tax simplicity. Profits and losses are reported directly on the proprietor's individual income tax return using Schedule C. A separate income tax filing for the business is neither necessary nor permitted.

A sole proprietorship is not the ideal business entity for raising capital, however. A sole proprietor cannot issue stock or sell interests in the company like corporations and limited liability companies (LLCs) can. And lenders may be reluctant to extend credit.

The most significant disadvantage of sole proprietorships is that owners are personally liable for the debts and obligations of the business. They are also personally liable for any actionable civil wrongs (torts and breaches of contract) committed during the course of the operation of the business. This means that creditors may seek to satisfy judgments against the business by garnishing the proprietor's personal income, attaching his personal bank account, proceeding against his personal property, and so on. By the same token, creditors may levy on business property and accounts that have been set up in the business's name to satisfy the proprietor's personal debts. It is for this reason that most people choose not to operate their businesses as sole proprietorships.

GENERAL PARTNERSHIP

A partnership is a contractual association of two or more people as joint principals in a business. Unlike other kinds of business entities, a writing is not required. A partnership may be implied by conduct or its existence may be inferred from an oral or written agreement.

While general partnerships are easy to form, the ease of creation comes with a high degree of risk. In a general partnership, each partner is personally liable for the debts, obligations and civil wrongs of the business, including those incurred or committed by other partners in the course of the business. This means that all of the partners are jointly and severally liable for the negligence, debts, obligations and liabilities that other partners incur in the course of the partnership business.

Although a general partnership is easier and less expensive to establish than a corporation, this kind of entity is not recommended for businesses that might want to raise capital at some point. Investors will not often want to put themselves at risk of personal liability for the debts and acts of the partnership or of other partners acting on its behalf.

Management of a partnership can also be a problem, especially for two-member partnerships. If a two-member partnership agreement requires unanimous agreement on major decisions, then disagreements result in stalemates. Yet, if unanimous agreement is not required, then either partner would have the right to make any decision unilaterally. The drawback to entrusting one person with power without any need to consult the other person should be obvious to anyone who has ever been in any kind of relationship with another person.

Partnerships—especially those with few members—are often breeding grounds for discontent and resentment. After a partnership has been operating for a while, it is not uncommon for one or more partners to begin to feel that they are contributing more of their time, effort, services, money, goodwill, etc. than others are. Since business partners owe fiduciary duties of loyalty, candor and fair dealing to each other, this can result in more than just hurt feelings and lost friendships. It can—and often does—result in litigation.

Partnerships do not have the advantage of perpetual duration that corporations have. In the absence of a carefully worded partnership agreement, general partnerships are at risk of automatic dissolution anytime a partner dies, becomes incapacitated, or leaves the partnership.

The principal advantage of a partnership is that profits and losses pass through to the partners. Double taxation, which can be a problem for corporations, is not an issue for partnerships because profits are not taxed at the partnership level. Moreover, the pass-through can be useful for high-income earners because losses may be used to offset other income and thereby reduce individual income tax liability. The value of this benefit, however, needs to be weighed against the fact that partners are personally liable for partnership debts and obligations. Incurring a large debt to a creditor may reduce tax liability but the partner will owe money to a private creditor in an amount that might very well exceed the tax savings.

LIMITED PARTNERSHIP

A limited partnership is a partnership in which one or more partners have managerial powers and one or more do not. The partner(s) with managerial powers are called *general* partners. Those who contribute capital but do not have managerial powers are called *limited* partners. General partners are personally liable for the debts and obligations of the partnership; limited partners are not. Creditors may not seek to satisfy judgments against a limited partnership by garnishing a limited partner's wages, attaching his personal bank account, proceeding against his nonbusiness property, etc.

This kind of entity is attractive to investors and high-income individuals seeking to shelter income from taxes. It allows pass-through of profits and losses without putting the limited partners at risk of personal liability. A limited partner's liability is limited to the amount of her investment. It is not as advantageous for the general partners, though, as they remain personally liable for partnership debts and obligations.

A limited partnership can be more expensive to establish and maintain than a sole proprietorship or general partnership. Unlike general partnerships, a limited partnership cannot arise by conduct. A written agreement is required. It must be created formally, in a way that is similar to (but not completely the same as) the way a corporation is formed.

A limited partner may become personally liable for partnership debts and obligations if he becomes too involved in the management or operation of the business.

Limited Liability Partnership

A limited liability partnership (LLP) is a partnership in which a partner is not personally liable for the negligent acts and omissions of other partners, although she may be personally liable for her own negligent acts and omissions. Some states limit the use of this kind of entity to certain licensed professionals (such as attorneys), and may require that the partnership maintain liability insurance for each partner.

Joint Venture

A joint venture is a project on which two or more people or organizations work together. It is similar to a partnership only in the sense that it involves two persons or business entities working together pursuant to a contract. Unlike a partnership, though, it is limited to a single project and/or a finite period of time.

A joint venture is not a separate legal entity. It is simply a contractual arrangement between two businesses. Each business retains ownership of its own assets. Profits are taxed to each entity separately. The rights and obligations of participants in a joint venture are determined primarily by the contract between them.

Increasingly, businesses seeking to collaborate on a project or to engage in an activity together are forming separate business entities for that purpose rather than structuring the arrangement as a joint venture. Due to its flexibility and ease of formation, the LLC is often the entity of choice for this purpose.

CORPORATION

A corporation is an entity that is treated as a completely separate legal person, distinct from any of its owners. It is similar to a limited partnership without general partners. A corporation can sue and be sued, enter into contracts and own property as if it were a natural person. It is managed by a board of directors.

Owners of interests in a corporation are called *shareholders*. The corporation may elect to either reinvest profits in the business or distribute them to shareholders in the form of dividends.

Profits are allocated to shareholders in proportion to the number of shares owned. Shareholders may or may not have the right to participate in the election of directors and other major corporate decisions, depending on the class of stock they own. Some classes of stock have voting rights; others do not.

Directors appoint officers for the day-to-day management of a corporation's business affairs. Directors and officers owe fiduciary duties to the corporation and shareholders. These include duties of undivided loyalty, candor, good faith, and care. Among other things, this means that directors and officers must avoid self-dealing, waste of corporate assets, and mismanagement of the corporation. Shareholders may enforce these duties by filing a shareholder derivative lawsuit.

The most significant advantage of corporations over proprietorships and partnerships is that the owners of the business (shareholders) are not personally liable for the debts and obligations of the corporation. As a separate legal entity, the corporation is responsible for its own debts and obligations. Shareholders are not personally liable for a corporation's debts and obligations. This characteristic of corporations is sometimes referred to as the *corporate veil*. The shelter from the risk of personal liability that the corporate veil provides generally makes corporations more attractive to investors than other kinds of entities.

Creditors of the corporation cannot proceed against a shareholder's property to satisfy corporate debts, nor may they proceed against corporate-owned property to satisfy a shareholder's personal debt. A shareholder's creditors may proceed against the shareholder's stock to satisfy the shareholder's personal debt, though. Since a share of stock in a corporation represents an ownership interest, shares of stock are items of personal property belonging to the shareholder. Just as creditors may garnish money in a debtor's personal bank account, so they may proceed against shares of stock for the satisfaction of a shareholder's debt.

Next to protection from personal liability for corporate debts and obligations, perpetual duration is probably the most significant advantage of incorporation. Sole proprietorships and partnerships dissolve when the proprietors or partners die or become legally incapacitated. A corporation does not dissolve when a shareholder dies or becomes incapacitated

Another significant advantage of incorporation is that capital can by raised by selling shares of stock rather than attempting to borrow money. Also, except in the case of closely held corporations, ownership interests are easily transferable.

Because a corporation is a separate taxable entity, it generally must pay taxes on any profits it makes. When it distributes those profits to shareholders (in the form of dividends), the shareholders must also pay tax on them. If the corporation keeps the profit in the business rather than distributing it to shareholders, then there is a tax savings. If the corporation distributes any of the profits to shareholders, however, then the corporation and the shareholder who receives a dividend will each be taxed on the same earnings. For this reason, corporations (or at least those which the Internal Revenue Code classifies as "C" corporations) have the advantage of lower tax rates but the disadvantage of double taxation.

Another significant disadvantage of corporations is that they can be more expensive, complicated and time-consuming to establish and maintain than other kinds of business entities. Even for a small business, some legal and accounting fees typically will need to be incurred. Statutes impose requirements like periodic meetings of the board of directors and shareholders, documentation of meetings and resolutions, and periodic filings of various kinds with an office of the state of incorporation. As a corporation grows, it may become necessary to comply with detailed regulations established by the Securities Exchange Commission (SEC) and other regulatory agencies. These requirements can be onerous. Meanwhile, small businesses must incur the expense of complying with ongoing recordkeeping, meetings and reporting requirements dictated by state corporations laws and federal and state tax laws. Failure to do so can have serious consequences, including the loss of immunity from personal liability for the corporation's debts and obligations.

The benefit of immunity from personal liability may be lost if the corporation is not managed and run like one. If, for example, a person were to set up a one-person corporation and then disregard state corporations laws (such as the requirement to hold regular meetings and maintain specified kinds of records), then a court or taxing authority might rule that the corporation is just a shell. If that happens, then the corporate form is disregarded and the business will be treated as a sole proprietorship. This could also happen if a business manager commingles corporate and personal accounts and records. Depositing both business and personal receipts into the same account, or withdrawing funds from a business account for personal purposes are examples. In these situations, courts describe the purported corporation as being nothing more than a sole proprietor's alter ego. They will then "lift the corporate veil" to impose personal liability on the proprietor for the corporation's debts and obligations.

Tax laws impose some limitations on debt financing by corporations. If it is anticipated that capital will be raised by incurring debt rather than by selling equity shares, then consideration should be given to one of the other forms of business entity. If capital will be raised by selling equity ownership interests in the business, then a corporation or LLC would be preferable to a sole proprietorship or partnership.

Closely Held Corporations

A *closely held corporation* is one that is owned by a small number of people. To ensure retention of control, stock shares are, by agreement, subject to restrictions on transfer. They are not publicly traded. Definitions vary, but in many states a corporation must have no more than thirty-five members in order to be classified as closely held.

Closely held corporations typically are an outgrowth of a desire to keep a business in the family, but there can be other motivations. A business founded by individuals who are committed to a particular business philosophy or manner of doing business, for example, might wish to avoid the risk of ownership and control of the business falling into the hands of people who do not share their philosophy or methods.

Closely held corporations allow owners and founders greater control over their businesses. Without the need to account to public shareholders, managers of closely held corporations have more freedom to try new ideas and take on high-risk projects.

The principal disadvantage of closely held corporations as compared to other kinds of corporations is that it is not possible to raise capital by making public offerings of stock. Restrictions on transfer of shares can also create problems. If, as is often the case, shareholders interested in selling their shares must give the corporation an opportunity to buy them out, there is a risk that the corporation might not pay them a fair price. Determining a fair price is problematic. "Fair market value" means the price a willing buyer would pay a willing seller if neither is under any legal compulsion or restriction. Since there is no market for the shares of stock in a closely held corporation, that measure cannot be used.

Nonprofit Corporations

A corporation that is established and operated for charitable, educational, civic, religious or certain other public interest purposes may apply to the Internal Revenue Service (IRS) for recognition as a nonprofit organization that is exempt from federal income taxes.

S Corporations

If a corporation meets certain requirements, it may elect to be treated as an *S corporation* for federal income tax purposes. When this election is made, the corporation's income will not be taxed at the entity level. Instead, profits and losses pass through to the shareholders as if the entity were a partnership. Shareholders are responsible for the tax due on any profits that are passed through to them. The election is made by filing IRS Form 2553. It requires unanimous shareholder consent. All shareholders must sign and file. C corporations are corporations that have not elected S corporation tax treatment. S corporations avoid the problem of double taxation, but they may not be as attractive to investors as C corporations are.

To qualify as an S corporation, a corporation must be a domestic (U.S.) corporation with only one class of stock. This can be a problem, as some venture capital investors refuse to accept common stock in return for their investments, insisting instead on preferred or convertible stock, or some other kind of security. In addition, a business entity cannot be a shareholder in an S corporation, yet some investment firms are organized as corporations. Moreover, some venture capital firms are prohibited from investing in pass-through entities.

S corporations are subject to a number of other restrictions: They cannot have more than 100 shareholders. No stock may be owned by a nonresident alien. Insurance companies and certain kinds of financial institutions cannot elect S corporation status. Domestic international sales corporations may not make this election, either.

Not all states recognize a federal S corporation election for purposes of state income taxation. Some require all corporations, even S corporations, to pay state income tax on profits earned by the corporation even if not distributed to shareholders. That is to say, in some states, S corporations do not avoid the problem of double taxation when it comes to liability for state income taxes.

LIMITED LIABILITY COMPANY

A limited liability company (LLC) is similar to an S corporation in some ways. Like any corporation, it is a legal entity with an existence separate and distinct from the individuals who own or operate it. Also like a corporation, it has both managers and investors. Like an S corporation, an LLC is not taxed at the entity level; rather, profits and losses pass through to the individual owners of the company.

In an LLC, the people who own interests in the company are called *members*, not shareholders. Unlike an S corporation, an LLC may have any number of members. Most states permit one-person LLCs, as well. Some members may have managerial power; some may have a right to a share of the earnings but no managerial power; and some may have both managerial powers and a right to a share of the earnings. (A member's share of ownership is usually called a membership interest, but some operating agreements may refer to it as a "share.")

In most states, an LLC is easier to establish, manage and run than a corporation is. Of course, the individuals who establish an LLC may make it more complicated if they wish—and some have. Even so, state laws typically impose more flexible meetings requirements and require fewer periodic reports and filings than are required of corporations.

Like the shareholders of a corporation, the owners of interests in an LLC are not personally liable for the company's debts and obligations. Creditors may not proceed against property or accounts owned by an LLC to satisfy a member's personal debts and obligations, either. There is one important difference, though. When a shareholder's creditor seizes stock, it stands in the shoes of the stockholder. It receives any dividends the corporation might pay to shareholders and it may exercise the shareholder's voting rights. This is not true of LLC membership interests. A creditor who proceeds against an LLC membership interest does not thereby acquire the right to vote or otherwise participate in the management of the company. State laws limit the rights of creditors who proceed against an LLC membership interest to one or more of the following:

- charging order
- foreclosure of the membership interest
- court order dissolving the LLC.

A *charging order* is a court order requiring the LLC make any distributions to which the member would otherwise be entitled to the creditor instead of to the member. In most states, a charging order is a creditor's exclusive remedy. When a charging order is in place, any distributions of profit or income the LLC would otherwise send to the member must go instead to the creditor, but the member retains voting and managerial rights. This prevents creditors from voting for distributions to themselves. Some jurisdictions allow a creditor to foreclose on a member's interest if the debt is not satisfied through the charging order, but even in these states the creditor does not acquire voting rights. Only a small minority of states allow a creditor to take the more extreme step of obtaining a court order for the dissolution of an LLC in which a debtor has an interest.

Some states, either by statute or judicial decision, authorize a broader range of collection remedies for creditors of single-member LLCs than for creditors of multimember LLCs. Other states have gone the other way, enacting statutes expressly stating that the rules limiting creditor remedies to a charging order also apply to single-member LLCs. Still other states have not addressed the question whether single-member and multiple-member LLCs should be treated differently for purposes of enforcing creditor rights.

For federal income tax purposes, a domestic LLC with more than one member will be treated as a partnership unless it elects to be treated as a corporation. A one-member LLC will be treated as a disregarded entity (i.e., a sole proprietorship) for federal income tax purposes unless it elects to be treated as a corporation. An election to be treated as a corporation for tax purposes is made with Form 8832. Qualifying LLCs that do not elect to be treated as C corporations avoid the double taxation problem. Profits and losses pass through to the members; they are not taxed at the entity level. An LLC may also elect to be treated as an S corporation for federal income tax purposes.

State laws and federal tax regulations prohibit banks, insurance companies and certain other kinds of businesses from setting themselves up as LLCs. There are special rules for foreign LLCs.

It is important to distinguish between how an LLC is treated for federal income tax purposes and how it is treated for purposes of other kinds of taxes. An LLC may be treated as a disregarded entity for federal income tax purposes, yet treated as a separate entity for purposes of employment taxes and excise taxes. And although the federal government allows pass-through of income for federal tax purposes, a few states impose state income taxes at the entity level on LLCs. Other states follow the federal tax treatment.

It is easier to qualify as an LLC than as an S corporation. Corporations, partnerships and trusts can be members of an LLC. An LLC can offer more than one kind of share or equity interest, such as "common" and "preferred." An LLC may have any number of members; it is not limited to one hundred. And an LLC may have wholly owned subsidiaries.

On the other hand, an LLC does not always have the advantage of perpetual duration that corporations have. In many states, an LLC is dissolved if a member dies, becomes incapacitated or retires; the remaining members must close the business. This result can sometimes be avoided by including appropriate language in the operating agreement, however.

Another drawback is that members are considered self-employed, so they must pay self-employment taxes (Social Security, Medicare) when they receive distributions.

All other things being equal, an LLC should be as attractive to potential investors as a limited partnership or S corporation is. Some venture funds are prohibited from investing in pass-through entities, however.

An LLC is the only form of business entity which, if managed properly, offers all four of the following advantages:

- limited personal liability for company obligations
- pass-through of profits and losses for tax purposes
- protection against creditors acquiring voting rights
- high level of flexibility in structuring and managing the organization.

COMPARISON OF BUSINESS ENTITIES

Personal Liability

Sole proprietors and general partners are personally liable for business debts and obligations. Partners in an LLP are personally liable for their own negligence but not for that of the other partners. Limited partners are not personally liable for business debts and obligations. Shareholders in corporations and LLCs generally are not personally liable for business debts and obligations, although there are some exceptions to this rule.

Capital

Corporations, limited partnerships and LLCs can raise capital by selling shares or interests. In sole proprietorships and general partnerships, participants contribute assets or make loans to the business. The limited liability feature of corporations, limited partnerships and LLCs makes them more attractive to investors.

Management

Sole proprietorships are managed by the proprietor. General partners have managerial rights and duties, which may be defined or restricted by agreement. Limited partners do not participate in management. LLCs are managed by elected managers or by the members directly, as provided in the agreement. In a corporation, shareholders vote for directors, who are responsible for major decisions concerning the corporation. Directors appoint officers to manage the day-to-day operations of the business.

Income Tax

C corporations are taxed at the entity level and at the shareholder level (when cash dividends are paid, for example). For S corporations and other business entities, income passes through to participants (shareholders, LLC members, etc.) and is taxed at the individual level only. An LLC may elect either corporate or pass-through treatment. Partnerships must file information returns.

Cost

Sole proprietorships are the least expensive to form. LLCs are relatively inexpensive, involving a filing fee and possible legal fees for drafting organizational documents. Partnerships also involve legal fees and a filing fee, and may also require other kinds of filings and fees. Corporations generally are the most expensive to form, involving a filing fee and legal fees for drafting articles, bylaws, resolutions, and in some cases, shareholder agreements. There are also filings, fees, and mailing costs associated with stock offerings.

Complexity

Sole proprietorships are the easiest to form and manage. Corporations and limited partnerships are the most complicated. General partnerships and LLCs vary in difficulty, depending on how much planning and negotiation goes into the agreement.

Personal Guarantees

Since the dot-com bubble burst in the early 2000s, many lenders have become more reluctant to extend credit to e-commerce businesses than they previously were. Many now require an individual to give a personal guarantee for a business loan. If this is expected to be a significant problem, then consideration should be given to whether the organization should be set up in a way that enables capital to be raised by selling shares of equity ownership either instead of or in addition to borrowing money from lenders.

Designations

Sole proprietorships may be operated in the name of the proprietor. If an assumed business name is desired, it may be designated by the business name standing alone. A "d/b/a" (doing business as) identifier may be used to refer to the proprietor by name. For example, if John Doe is selling produce under the name Amazing Pomegranates, then he may be identified as John

Doe, d/b/a Amazing Pomegranates. Other kinds of businesses are designated by the business name followed by an abbreviation signifying the kind of entity it is.

GP = general partnership
LP = limited partnership
LLP = limited liability partnership
LLC = limited liability company
Inc. (or "Corp.") = corporation.

State laws often regulate business type designations. For example, some states require that the "LLC" designation be included in the business name wherever the LLC's name is displayed. It is important to abide by these rules. An improper or confusing use of a designation can amount to fraud. An "Ltd." designation for an LLC, for example, might lead an investor to mistakenly believe she is acquiring an interest in a limited partnership. Designating an LLC as an "LLP" could mislead customers into believing the company has liability insurance for each of its partners. Some corporations, largely for historical reasons, continue to use "Company" or "Co." With the growing popularity of LLCs, though, using "Corp." or "Inc." to designate a corporation is the better practice.

Organizational Documents

No organizational documents need to be drafted for a sole proprietorship. No organizational documents are required for a general partnership, either. A general partnership may arise by conduct even if no written agreement is in place. A written partnership agreement is strongly recommended, though. At a minimum, it should address:

- rights and obligations of each partner
- nature and amount of each partner's capital contribution, if any
- how capital will be raised in the future and how it will affect partnership interests
- distribution of profits and losses
- allocation of managerial responsibilities
- what will happen in the event of a partner's resignation, incapacitation or death
- transfers and transferability of partnership interests
- dissolution of the partnership
- dispute resolution.

In the absence of an agreement otherwise, profits, losses and management rights are presumed to be divided equally among all partners in a general partnership. If a different kind of distribution is desired, then it should be spelled out clearly in the partnership agreement.

Limited partnerships require a written agreement.

The organizational documents for an LLC typically include Articles of Organization and an Operating Agreement, although some states only mandate the filing of Articles. A considerable amount of flexibility exists when drafting an LLC operating agreement. For example, it can create managerial positions and delegate to those who fill them specific areas of responsibility for managing the business. When this is done, the LLC will resemble a corporation. Alternatively, it can simply leave it up to the members to manage the business directly, in which case day-to-day management will resemble that of a partnership. Some states may require an LLC to designate specified kinds of officers, such as a chief manager and a treasurer. Even in these states, though, offices often are permitted to be filled by the same person.

The principal organizational document of a corporation is the Articles of Incorporation. Other documents that may be necessary or desirable include bylaws, shareholder agreements, resolutions and minutes of meetings.

At a minimum, a corporation's or LLCs organizational documents should address:

- business name
- business purpose(s)
- names and addresses of the incorporators or founding members
- titles of managerial offices
- rights and obligations of managers
- capital contributions
- types of stock or membership interests that may be issued
- amount of stock or membership interests that may be issued
- distributions
- rights and obligations of shareholders/members
- transferability of interests or shares
- dissolution.

In most states, a business may be established for "any lawful purpose." The managers of a corporation are called directors and officers. LLCs might call them governors and managers, respectively. Managerial titles for officers and managers typically include at least the following: president (sometimes called the "chief executive officer" (CEO) or "chief manager"), vice president, secretary and treasurer. Additional offices may be created. In addition to the foregoing matters, an LLC agreement should explain the relationship of capital contribution to membership interest.

It is important for organizational documents to address removal and succession issues, too. What happens if an interest owner dies, becomes incapacitated, or resigns? This and related issues are especially important in the case of closely held corporations, where shareholders often are also directors, officers and/or employees of the corporation. What happens to the shares of an employee or officer who is fired or quits? What happens if a shareholder files for bankruptcy or if a shareholder, partner or member of an entity that is jointly owned by spouses files for a divorce?

The rights of minority shareholders are an important concern in closely held corporations. If the agreement requires an outgoing shareholder to sell only to the corporation or other shareholders, then what, if anything, will prevent majority shareholders from "squeezing out" minority shareholders, such as by offering a buyout in an amount grossly disproportionate to the value of the business? How will value be determined? Since the stock in a closely held corporation cannot be publicly traded, fair market value (what a willing buyer would pay a willing seller in an arms-length transaction) is not an available measure.

Founders of a business often enter into contribution agreements to address the nature and amount of each individual's initial contribution. Typically a separate *operating agreement* addresses the management and operation of the organization, but contribution agreements and operating agreements are sometimes combined in a single document. In any event, a contribution agreement may obligate an investor to transfer property or money in a specified amount or value to the company in exchange for a part ownership interest and/or a right to share in profits. A contribution agreement that provides for a contribution of property typically includes a provision containing a warranty of ownership and freedom from liens or other encumbrances. A contribution of property usually is made subject to the condition that it may only be used in ways and for purposes specifically authorized by the agreement.

Care should be exercised when drafting agreements that contemplate a contribution of intellectual property rights. A well-drafted contribution agreement should be very clear about which existing and to-be-created intellectual property rights are covered by the agreement, and which rights in existing and to-be-created intellectual property the contributor retains. Otherwise, disputes are likely to arise over such things as whether the owner assigned title or only granted a license to use the property; whether the owner granted all rights or only some (e.g., distribution rights vs. right to make derivative works), and the like.

Application to Create a Business Entity

To create a corporation, it is necessary to apply to the appropriate division of state government (typically, the secretary of state) for a certificate of incorporation. Many states require Articles of Incorporation to be filed along with the application. Some impose additional requirements in the application process, as well, such as that the corporation must identify its initial board of directors, issue initial stock, and such.

LLPs and LLCs also must file an application with a state office. Some states may require LLPs to maintain liability insurance in a specified amount for each partner.

Whenever filing with a state office is required, a filing fee generally will be required, too. The amount varies depending on the type of filing and the state.

Tax Identification Number

Most businesses will need to register with federal, state and/or local taxing authorities. In some states, this process is combined with, or is part of, the business registration. In others, it is a separate process. It is fairly common for a state to require a business registration to be filed with the secretary of state and a tax identification number to be obtained from the department of revenue.

Business Registration

Most states require companies that do business in the state to register with a state office for state tax purposes. It some states, this process is combined with the application to establish a business entity; in others, they are separate procedures. In some states, a business registration application may be combined with an application for a state tax identification number.

Many states require a corporation with a principal place of business in a different state or country to register as a foreign corporation if it transacts a significant amount of business within the state. For the purpose of these kinds of state laws, a foreign corporation is usually defined to mean any corporation that is not organized under the laws of the state in question. For example, a Delaware corporation and a Russian corporation are both "foreign corporations" for purposes of California law.

ASSUMED NAME REGISTRATION

In addition to establishing a business and registering it with a state office, a state may require a business entity to register the company's business name with a state office. This generally will not be necessary in the case of a sole proprietorship that is operated under the proprietor's personal name. If a business intends to operate or market goods or services under a trade name, though, then it may need to file a fictitious business name statement or apply for an assumed name certificate of some kind. Different requirements apply in different jurisdictions.

Sometimes a state or local law will require notice of an assumed name to be published in an approved periodical (such as a newspaper of general circulation) for a specified period of time or in a specified number of issues. These requirements, too, vary from place to place.

A few states require an LLC to publish an announcement of the LLC's formation in a newspaper.

Licenses and Permits

A federal, state or local government may require a license or permit to engage in business. In addition, special kinds of licenses or permits may be required for certain kinds of businesses and professions. The kinds of licenses and permits that may be required vary by jurisdiction (federal, state, locality) and by the kind of industry or business.

A license or permit from the U.S. government may be required if the business is involved in activities that are supervised or regulated by a federal agency, such as radio broadcasting, aviation, maritime transportation, interstate transportation of animals or plants, and so on.

State requirements vary widely. Links to state business license and permit requirements are provided at the Small Business Administration website. Businesses in countries outside of the United States must comply with the licensing and permit requirements of those countries.

Zoning

Zoning ordinances are laws that municipalities (cities, counties, etc.) enact to regulate land use. They specify the kinds of activities and structures that are allowed in defined areas within the territory over which the regulating entity has jurisdiction.

Zoning laws divide a geographic area into zones, establish categories of activity, and then specify the zones in which each category of activity may be carried out and in which particular kinds of structures are or are not permitted. The main categories are commercial, residential and industrial, and to a lesser extent, agricultural, historic and aesthetic. Subcategories are often created, too. For example, a commercial zone might be further divided into areas where retail businesses are or are not permitted; where office buildings are or are not permitted; and where both are permitted. Restaurants might be allowed in some commercial zones but not others. Theaters or other entertainment services may be permitted in some zones but not others. And so on. Sometimes the specifications are quite detailed.

Zones permitting more than one kind of activity may be established (e.g., commercial-residential). A zoning regulation may also provide exceptions for specified types of activities which otherwise would be prohibited within a particular kind of zone. Certain kinds of home businesses are often (but not always) allowed in areas that are zoned residential These kinds of regulations may impose restrictions, though, such as the portion of the home that may be used for business purposes, whether and what kind of signage is allowed, parking restrictions, etc. Some kinds of home businesses may be prohibited altogether.

Building, fire, housing, safety and other codes and state laws also regulate land use. In addition, property may be subject to restrictive covenants imposed by the land developer or, in the case of leased property, the landlord. These may also restrict signage, aesthetics, parking, etc. In the case of residential property, they may require compliance with the dictates of a homeowners' or condominium association. These often impose more onerous requirements and restrictions than zoning ordinances do. Finally, new construction may need to comply with federal requirements imposed by the Americans with Disabilities Act of 1990[1] (ADA) and modifications may need to be made to existing structures, in some cases, to make them accessible to disabled persons

Even in areas zoned commercial, or residential with a home business exception, a permit will usually be required. And even in areas zoned commercial or commercial-residential, a sign permit may be required.

If a particular use or structure is not authorized by a zoning law, a person may apply for a variance. This involves making a request to the relevant regulatory authority to allow a particular use or structure despite the fact that a zoning law prohibits it.

Zoning laws are land use regulations, not tort laws. They apply only to businesses that are physically present on the land. They cannot be enforced against a business that does not have a physical presence in the geographic area to which the regulation applies. Electrons alone do not count as a physical presence. Liability for violating a zoning ordinance cannot be predicated solely on a company's Internet transmissions into a zone from a location outside of it.

Chapter 2. Capital

An e-commerce business, like any other business, will need capital, both to get started and to operate. *Capital* is a broad term that can include anything of value—money, tangible property, intangible property, or a combination of one or more of those things.

The two ways of raising capital are equity and debt. *Equity* involves the grant of an ownership interest in a business in exchange for a contribution of capital. *Debt* refers to a contribution of capital to a business with the expectation that it will be repaid or returned, usually but not always with interest.

Equity

Ownership interests in a business are called *equity shares.* In a corporation, they may be referred to as "shares of stock," or simply "stock." In LLCs and partnerships, they are usually called interests, although some companies use the term "share" instead. An equity share entitles the owner to a share of the profits, but not to the return of the capital contributed.

Common stock is a kind of equity share in a corporation. It entitles the owner to a share of the corporation's profits. Profits are usually distributed in the form of dividends to shareholders. A share of stock entitles the owner to share in the market value of the corporation, as reflected in the stock's sale price. The owner of common stock also is entitled to a share of the corporation's assets in the event the corporation is dissolved.

Ownership of common stock entails some risk. The market value of a share of stock can go down as well as up. A shareholder's liability is limited to the extent of his investment (the price he paid for the stock). Creditors cannot reach his personal assets for the satisfaction of corporate debts. Nevertheless, if a corporation's stock becomes worthless, then the stockholder loses the money he invested in the stock. Unlike a loan, an investment in stock does not entitle the investor to a return of his contribution.

Common stock usually entitles its owner to vote in elections of directors and on any other matters as to which shareholders are entitled to vote. A corporation may issue different classes of common stock, though—including voting vs. nonvoting classes—unless the articles, bylaws or an enforceable agreement otherwise provide.

> **Example.** The original founders of Infinity, Inc. wish to maintain some continuing control over the corporation, so the organizational documents provide for three classes of stock. A share of Class *A* stock entitles its owner to ten votes. A share of Class *B* stock entitles its owner to only one vote. A share of Class *C* stock entitled its owner to no votes. Shares of Class *A* stock are issued to the founders; Class *B* stock is issued to the public; and Class *C* stock is issued to investment firms.

Preferred stock is another kind of equity share in a corporation. Preferred stock is usually nonvoting, but has priority over common stock in dividend payments and in the distribution of assets when a corporation is dissolved. Preferred stock holders have rights to fixed dividends and a fixed percentage of the corporation's assets upon liquidation.

Debt

The other way for a company to raise capital is by borrowing money. Rights and obligations of creditors differ substantially from those of shareholders. The interest of a creditor in a company to which it lends money is limited to the amount of the loan. Unlike an equity investor, a creditor is not entitled to share in the profits or the increased value of business assets except to the extent of the amount the creditor invested in (loaned to) the company. Nor does the amount of a creditor's interest decrease when the company experiences losses. When a company borrows money, it usually issues the lender an instrument representing the amount of the debt, such as a bond, note or debenture. Debt instruments take priority over both common and preferred stock. If the corporation is dissolved and its assets are liquidated, the proceeds will first be applied to repayment of debt, then to owners of preferred stock, and lastly to owners of common stock.

Unlike shareholders, lenders are entitled only to the return of the amount of the loan and, in the case of interest-bearing loans, interest.

Like any other loan agreement, a debt instrument may impose conditions on the borrower. For example, it may impose limits on the amount of debt the corporation may take on or how much stock it may issue.

Debt *vs.* Equity

From the corporation's point of view, the advantages of issuing equity shares as a means of raising capital include::

- no financial obligation to repay the amount contributed to the business
- no obligation to pay interest
- flexibility to either distribute profits to owners or reinvest them in the business.

Disadvantages of issuing equity shares include:

- greater control over the business by investors (via the right to vote for directors)
- dilution of voting power as more shares are issued.

From an investor's point of view, the primary advantage of equity is that the return is potentially greater than the amount of the investment and interest. The primary disadvantage is that there is a risk of losing the amount invested.

Advantages of debt, from the corporation's point of view, include:

- attractive to risk-averse investors
- no dilution of voting power
- no sharing of profits.

Disadvantages of debt, for a corporation (advantages, for investors) include:

- lender-imposed restrictions and conditions
- interest
- priority of debt instrument holders over shareholders in the event of dissolution.

Initial Contributions

The organizing documents should describe any capital that will be contributed to the business initially and identify who will be contributing it.

Contributions of intellectual property (such as a patent, copyright, trademark, trade secret) or of an interest in intellectual property are common in e-commerce businesses. These may take the form of either a grant of a license to the business or a transfer of title to the intellectual property. If a license is involved, the license agreement should address the following questions:

(a) Is it exclusive or nonexclusive?
(b) Is it revocable? If so, on what grounds?
(c) What is the duration of the license?
(d) Are transfers and sublicensing permitted? If so, on what terms?
(e) Does the license include the right to use updates, enhancements and modifications that are subsequently developed by the licensor?
(f) May the licensee make derivative works? If so, who will own rights in them?
(g) What uses are authorized?
(h) What uses are prohibited?
(i) What is the geographic scope of the license?
(j) What is the value of the property, and how was value determined?
(k) What happens if the licensor resigns or is removed from the business? For example, will the license remain in effect? On what terms?
(l) What effect will a breach of a license agreement have? For example, it might be prudent for a company to have a means of protecting its business in the event the licensor-member fails to maintain or update the contributed software as agreed.

If it is anticipated that intellectual property (such as software) will be developed by participants in the business, then the organizational documents should address the respective rights of the company and such participants in these items of intellectual property.

Intellectual property is not the only kind of intangible property that may be contributed as capital to a company. A contractual right to receive royalties or other payments from a third party may be assigned to a business, for example. Organizers of a business should exercise due diligence to ensure that such rights are, in fact, valuable and assignable and that all necessary procedures for effecting an assignment have been followed.

Issuing Securities

Issuing stock is the principal way that corporations raise capital. Because the issuance of more shares of stocks dilutes the ownership interests of existing shareholders, existing shareholders have a right to protect their interests by purchasing newly issued shares of stock before the corporation offers them to the public at large. This is called a *preemptive* right.

After the Stock Market Crash of 1929, Congress passed laws regulating both the issuance and the sale of publicly traded stock and other securities. It also created the SEC, charging it with responsibility for interpreting and enforcing these laws. States have also enacted laws regulating the issuance and sale of securities. These state laws are known as blue sky laws. A primary purpose of all of these laws is to protect the public from making bad investment decisions on the basis of misinformation about a company and/or the value of its securities.

DEFINITION OF SECURITY

Securities regulations do not just apply to corporations, and they are not limited to shares of stock. The definition of a security is broad enough to include many kinds of capital-raising instruments, including:

- Stock
- Bond
- Note
- Debenture
- Evidence of indebtedness
- Treasury stock
- Security future
- Security-based swap
- Certificate of interest or participation in any profit-sharing agreement
- Collateral trust certificate
- Preorganization certificate or subscription
- Transferable share
- Investment contract
- Voting trust certificate
- Certificate of deposit for a security
- Fractional undivided interest in oil, gas, or other mineral rights
- Put, call, straddle, option, or privilege on any security, certificate of deposit, or group or index of securities (including any interest therein or based on the value thereof)
- Put, call, straddle, option, or privilege entered into on a national securities exchange relating to foreign currency
- Any interest or instrument commonly known as a "security"
- Any certificate of interest or participation in, temporary or interim certificate for, receipt for, guarantee of, or warrant or right to subscribe to or purchase, any of the above
- Certificate of interest or participation in an oil, gas or mineral royalty or lease.[2]

In some cases, a business plan might even come within the definition.

Currency is excluded from the definition. Notes, drafts, bills of exchange and banker's acceptances maturing in less than nine months at the time of issuance or renewal are also excluded.

Because it includes investment contracts, the scope of the federal definition is quite broad—broad enough to include not only corporations, but also limited partnerships and some LLCs. This is because the U.S. Supreme Court has interpreted *investment contract* as including any agreement involving an investment of money in a common enterprise with an expectation of profits produced by the efforts of others.[3] A limited partnership or LLC in which person *A* contributes capital and the business is managed by person *B*, and person *A* has a right to share in the profits generated by person *B*'s (and/or other people's) efforts would be an investment contract, and therefore a security.

For purposes of this definition, the commonality of the enterprise may be horizontal, vertical, or both. Horizontal commonality may exist when investors pool their resources. A shareholder in a corporation, for example, pools its investment funds with those of other shareholders, so a corporation has horizontal commonality. Vertical commonality is demonstrated by showing that an investor's fortunes are dependent on the efforts and success of the sellers or promoters of the investment.

THE SECURITIES ACT OF 1933

The Securities Act of 1933 is a federal law regulating the issuance of securities by a business. It requires a business that issues a security to provide truthful, accurate information about it. It also requires certain businesses to register a security with the SEC before issuing it. When this requirement applies, a very detailed registration statement must be filed with the SEC. The kinds of information required to be disclosed include financial data; information about the principals of the business; the business's managerial structure; any risks to the business's assets or income (including, for example, pending litigation, regulatory action, tax lien, etc.), and other matters. An issuer must also provide potential investors a prospectus containing this information (or a summary of it) prior to issuing the security.

Businesses are liable for any material misrepresentations or omissions in a registration statement or prospectus. A fact is material if it would have an effect on a reasonably prudent investor's decision about whether to invest or not. Such misrepresentations and omissions may subject a business to criminal penalties. In addition, a misled investor may rescind the sale and seek a refund.

Exemptions

Compliance with SEC registration and prospectus requirements can be expensive. A number of exemptions are available, though, including:

(a) charitable organizations
(b) government-issued securities
(c) banks and certain other institutions regulated by other laws
(d) securities issued in connection with certain corporate reorganizations
(e) commercial paper with a maturity date of less than nine months
(f) securities exchanges with the business's existing security holders
(g) securities issued to finance the purchase of railroad equipment
(h) annuities and certain other products issued by insurance companies

(i) Tier 1 Regulation A[4] issuances of up to $20,000,000 in a twelve-month period, provided a sufficient offering circular is distributed, filed and qualified by the SEC and state authorities

(j) Tier 2 Regulation A issuances of up to $50,000,000 in a twelve-month period, provided an audited offering circular is distributed, filed and qualified by the SEC

(k) offerings of up to $5,000,000 in a twelve-month period solely to accredited investors,[5] provided they are not advertised or solicited

(l) purely local offerings, restricted to purchase by residents of the same state as the business, with resale to nonresidents barred for six months

(m) Regulation D[6] offers for small amounts of money or in a limited manner

(n) resales where there is adequate public information about the issuer; the seller has held the securities for at least a year; the sales are in limited amounts in unsolicited brokers' transactions; and the SEC is given notice

(o) resales of securities that are not of the same class as those listed on national exchanges or quoted in a U.S. automated interdealer quotation system, if the buyer knows the seller is relying on the Rule 144A[7] exemption

(p) Rule 701 sales of securities to compensate employees, consultants and advisors. A number of conditions and restricts apply.

A significant difference between Tier 1 and Tier 2 issuances under Regulation A is that Tier 1 issuances are not subject to the ongoing SEC reporting obligations that Tier 2 and nonexempt issuances are. Nonexempt, publicly traded companies are subject to more frequent SEC reporting requirements than are issuers of Tier 1 and Tier 2 securities. Tier 1 and Tier 2 offerings are subject to "bad actor "disqualification rules.

Regulation D offers different kinds of exemptions:

(a) Rule 504[8] offerings of up to $5,000,000 in any twelve-month period by a noninvestment company that are not advertised or solicited. To qualify, the issuer must advise investors that they may not be able to resell the securities for at least a year unless the issuer registers the resale. Investment companies, companies that are already Securities Exchange Act reporting companies, blank check companies, companies that do not have a business plan, companies with a business plan to engage in a merger or acquisition with an unidentified company, and companies disqualified by a "bad actor" are not eligible.

(b) Rule 506(b)[9] safe harbor. This exemption applies to an offering, in any amount, that is not generally advertised or solicited. To qualify for this exemption, purchasers must be either accredited or sophisticated nonaccredited investors. Sales can be made to any number of accredited investors, but to no more than thirty-five nonaccredited investors. The company must give any nonaccredited investors disclosure documents that generally contain the same type of information as provided in registered offerings. The company is not required to provide specified disclosure documents to accredited investors, but, if it does provide information to accredited investors, it must also make this information available to the nonaccredited investors as well. A "bad actor" will disqualify a business from claiming this exemption.

(c) Rule 506(c) offerings exclusively to accredited investors.

Businesses claiming one of these exemptions must file Form D with the SEC within fifteen days after the issuance.

The SEC's Crowdfunding Regulation allows certain companies to sell securities through crowdfunding, provided the sales take place online through an SEC-registered intermediary. A maximum of $1,070,000 may be raised this way during a 12–month period. There are limitations on the amount that individual investors can invest this way. Specified disclosures must be made to investors, the intermediary facilitating the offering, and the SEC. Securities purchased this way are restricted; they cannot be resold for one year. A "bad actor" will disqualify a business from claiming this exemption.

A "bad actor" is an issuer, director, officer, partner, managing member, beneficial owner of 20% or more of a corporation's voting stock, promoter or paid solicitor in connection with the issuance, who has violated securities regulations or certain other laws, or who has had certain kinds of actions taken against him.

These rules are subject to a variety of exceptions and qualifications. In addition, the "bad actor" rule is subject to limitations on the lookback period.

An exemption from federal registration requirements does not necessarily exempt a business from state securities registration requirements. And an exemption from registration does not exempt a business from liability for fraud and misrepresentation in connection with the issuance of a security.

THE SARBANES-OXLEY ACT

The Sarbanes-Oxley Act[10] (SOX Act) imposes strict recordkeeping and reporting requirements on publicly traded companies and, to a lesser extent, on certain companies that are not publicly traded. Most of these are intended to ensure the accuracy and reliability of a company's reports and financial statements. For example, CEOs and CFOs of publicly traded companies must certify the accuracy of reports that are filed with the SEC, and directors, officers, and shareholders owning at least 10% of the company's stock must report their dealings in the company's shares within two days after the transaction. For more information about securities trading, see Chapter 6.

BLUE SKY LAWS

States also regulate securities. Like their federal counterparts, state laws typically prohibit misrepresentations and material omissions in securities offerings and sales. They also require certain issuers to register their offerings and disclose specified financial information, to the end of ensuring that potential investors have access to verifiable information about a company before making the decision to invest in it. Blue sky laws also usually include licensing requirements for brokers, brokerage firms, and investment advisors. The Uniform Securities Act is a model code of state blue sky laws. It has been adopted in several, but not all, states.

The ability of states to regulate with respect to securities issued by businesses that are registered on a national exchange (New York Stock Exchange, American Stock Exchange), or that qualify for Nasdaq inclusion, is preempted by federal law. State regulation of private offerings that come within the Rule 506 exemption is also preempted. States can and do regulate other kinds of exempt offerings, though.

MATERIAL MISREPRESENTATIONS

Not every misrepresentation or omission in connection with the issuance of securities is a violation of securities laws. Only misrepresentations and omissions of material facts are. A fact is deemed to be material only if a reasonably prudent investor would consider it important to an investment decision.

While it is impossible to construct a comprehensive list of every kind of fact that would be deemed to be material if misrepresented or concealed, here are some examples that would probably qualify:

- managerial conflicts of interest
- nature or amount of manager compensation and/or benefits
- experience, expertise and integrity of management
- existence of a pending lawsuit
- revocation of a license
- loan default
- dispute with a major customer
- adverse profitability or feasibility report
- cessation of diminution of business operations
- significant change in type of business operation
- marketing problems
- product's quantifiable performance or quality rating
- impact of competition on sales
- nature and amount of capital
- aggregate amount of accounts payable
- collectability of accounts receivable.

This is not an exhaustive list. Because materiality determinations depend on all the facts and circumstances, they must be made on a case-by-case basis.

REINING IN SECURITIES LITIGATION

An investor who has been misled about the profitability of a business may file a civil action for damages. This puts an issuer at risk of being sued whenever the company turns out to be less profitable than expected, if the issuer or seller made more optimistic predictions about a company's future than turned out to be warranted. To protect businesses from crippling amounts of litigation of this kind (known as strike suits), Congress enacted the Private Securities Litigation Reform Act[11] (PSLRA) and the Securities Litigation Uniform Standards Act[12] (SLUSA).

The PSLRA provides safe harbors against those strike suits that are "shareholder derivative actions begun with [the] hope of winning large attorney fees or private settlements, and with no intention of benefiting [the] corporation on behalf of which [the] suit is theoretically brought."[13]

SLUSA prohibits certain kinds of class actions when they are based on state law protections against misrepresentations and material omissions of fact or the use of a manipulative device or contrivance in connection with the sales of certain kinds of securities.

While these laws provide some protection from liability for "hyping" a company, its product, or a security in order to encourage purchases of a security, they do not eliminate the anti-fraud provisions of securities laws. Liability may still attach for those who make material misrepresentations of fact or who omit material facts.

ONLINE SECURITIES TRANSACTIONS

Securities laws and regulations apply to stock offerings made via the Internet as well as to offerings made by mail or other means. This includes the disclosure, registration, and anti-fraud requirements of the Securities Acts, any applicable blue sky laws, and the regulations issued pursuant to them.

Where a federal securities law or regulation requires information to be disclosed to investors, potential investors or shareholders, the information may be sent by means of email transmission if the recipient has specifically consented to email delivery of such information. An issuer or trader transmitting information by means of email must obtain the affirmative consent of the recipient to receive such information by email and must inform the recipient of the right to revoke consent at any reasonable time before the delivery. If the recipient does not consent, or if the recipient timely revokes consent once given, then the information must be delivered by regular mail.

Issuers using electronic means of disclosing information must create and implement a systematic method of assuring that the information has been properly delivered. Merely posting the information to a public website is not enough. The issuer must either (1) deliver the information by regular mail or, if the recipient has consented to it, email; or (2) deliver (by regular mail or, if the recipient has consented to it, email) a link that will take the recipient to the website where the information is posted. Information posted to a website for this purpose must remain accessible for as long as any delivery requirement applies. Issuers must make paper versions available in cases of computer incompatibility, computer system failure, or a user's withholding or revocation of consent to email delivery.

Some email systems have a confirmation-of-receipt feature and/or a confirmation of opening feature. Use of these features is recommended inasmuch as they can generate evidence of compliance with a delivery/disclosure requirement.

The SEC has taken the position that a user of an Internet-based securities purchasing system may be deemed to be a securities dealer if the user posts quotations simultaneously on both the buyer and seller bulletin boards with respect to a security. As such, the user may be required to register as a broker-dealer under all applicable securities laws.

DIRECT PUBLIC OFFERINGS

Historically, public stock offerings involved a chain of intermediaries—underwriters, dealers, brokers. They still can. The Internet, however, makes it possible for an issuer to make offers to the public without using intermediaries. These kinds of offerings are known as direct public offerings, or DPOs. Issuers must take care to comply with securities laws and regulations in connection with DPOs, including all disclosure requirements. False or misleading representations about the profitability of the company and its securities must be avoided.

The issuer must also comply with "quiet period" statutes, laws prohibiting issuers from touting a security during preregistration periods. A company should wait until the quiet period is over and the registration is effective before providing a link to the prospectus for potential investors. Companies intending to make a public offering should also be aware that a website may violate this kind of law if, before the quiet period has ended, it displays or distributes information that a potential investor might consider to be part of the prospectus or registration statement, even if that is not what the company intended.

THE SECURITIES EXCHANGE ACT OF 1934

The Securities Exchange Act of 1934 regulates dealings in securities after they are initially issued. Stock trading is discussed in Chapter 6.

Chapter 3. Management

Businesses need to be managed in a way that complies with both their organizational documents and applicable laws. Laws vary from state to state. Nevertheless, thanks to model and uniform laws there are some similarities. The Uniform Law Commission has promulgated a number of uniform laws for the operation and management of different kinds of business entities. Most jurisdictions have adopted its Uniform Partnership Act, and nearly one-half have adopted the Uniform Limited Partnership Act. About one-third have adopted the Uniform Limited Liability Company Act, but only a few have adopted the Uniform Unincorporated Nonprofit Association Act. The American Bar Association's Model Business Corporation Act has been enacted in about one-half of American jurisdictions. Even in states that have not enacted a model or uniform law in its entirety, substantial portions may have been adopted. Despite all of this, there are still some significant variations. Delaware and Nevada laws are notably more favorable to businesses and their managers than the laws of other states are.

For the management of any business in any state, legal compliance requires consideration of both the organizational documents and applicable statutes. Many statutory provisions contain language like "unless otherwise provided in the articles" (or some other organizational document). When this is the case, the statute provides the default rule that applies when the company has not addressed a particular matter in its organizational documents, but a business is free to adopt a different rule for the management of the company. Other statutes state a mandatory rule that cannot be waived by agreement. These kinds of statutes override contrary or inconsistent provisions in an organizational document, resolution, etc.

Directors

Directors are the top tier of management. In LLCs and other noncorporate organizations they may be called something else, such as "governors." Whatever they are called, their purpose is to oversee the officers of an organization and make major decisions about and for the organization. Principal functions of a board of directors include planning, organization, operations, oversight and compensation.

Planning means developing market positioning strategy, deciding how to allocate resources, and the like. *Organization* involves appointing officers, evaluating their performances, forming and appointing members to committees, and succession planning. *Operations* includes reviewing progress toward goals; and reviewing and approving acquisitions, divestitures, capital expenditures, new ideas and strategies. *Oversight* entails performing or reviewing audits to ensure compliance with government regulations, including the SOX Act; addressing conflict of interest issues and the like. *Compensation* involves reviewing and approving executive compensation, particularly amounts paid to the CEO and any outside directors.

A corporation's directors are elected or appointed in accordance with the organization's bylaws. Shareholders with voting rights vote for directors, usually at their annual meeting.

An *inside director* is one who is also an officer, employee or shareholder of the corporation. Venture capital investors commonly condition their investments in a corporation on the right to participate in managing the corporation, usually by being a member of the board of directors. Outside directors have no stake or interest in the corporation. They are usually appointed to a board because they possess some special knowledge or business expertise

Officers

Officers are appointed by the directors to manage the daily operations of the company. They have the power to legally bind the corporation to agreements and normally have at least some amount of discretionary decision-making power as well.

The number and titles of officers in an organization should be specified in organizational documents. Sometimes a state statute will require at least one officer. Some require more. The most common offices are the chief executive officer (called the "president" or "chief manager" in some organizations); vice president; treasurer; and secretary. An organization may have other kinds of officers besides just these, and it may have more than one of a particular kind of officer. For example, it is common for a large company to have several different vice presidents, each with responsibility for a different facet of the company's operations, or to designate officers according to their areas of responsibility rather than by one of the traditional titles—Communications Officer, Technology Officer, Chief Information Security Officer, etc.

The CEO acts under the direction of the board of directors, but otherwise has general responsibility for making major decisions, entering into and approving contracts, and taking other actions on behalf of the company.

Officers have both contractual and implied legal obligations to act on behalf of the corporation for the benefit of the shareholders. They generally are not personally liable for lawful acts that they perform on behalf of the corporation, but like directors, they owe fiduciary duties of undivided loyalty, due care, candor and good faith to the company and its shareholders.

An officer may be held personally liable for making an unlawful payment of a dividend. An officer with power to pay wages, or to pay withholding and sales taxes, may be held personally liable for paying them if he neglects to cause the company to do so.

A person's legal status as an officer is not controlled entirely by designations in the organizational documents. Whether the articles, bylaws or other documents expressly describe the person as an officer or not, a court may attribute officer status to an individual who has been assigned executive functions and high-level decision-making authority.

Shareholders

Shareholders do not have managerial powers, but they may have the right to vote on some important matters affecting the company, such as:

- Election of directors
- Matters as to which directors have a conflict of interest
- Amendments to the articles of incorporation

- Mergers
- Sales of substantially all of the corporation's assets
- Dissolution.

Shareholders do not have a right to vote on managerial decisions that arise during the ordinary day-to-day conduct of the company's business. They may vote to make recommendations to the directors about how to manage the company, but these recommendations are not binding on directors. Voting occurs at an annual meeting. It may also occur at specially called meetings, provided notice and other procedural requirements are met. Voting may be in person or by proxy.

The managers of a corporation, and others, may send out solicitations to shareholders prior to a meeting. The solicitations ask shareholders to allow them to vote at the meeting on the shareholder's behalf. That is to say, they ask shareholders to vote by proxy, authorizing the person making the solicitation to vote their shares for them at the meeting. This kind of request is called a proxy solicitation.

A company that is registered with the SEC is not permitted to send proxy solicitations to shareholders unless it sends a proxy statement to them prior to the meeting for which the proxy is sought. The information contained in the statement must be filed with the SEC before soliciting a shareholder vote on the election of directors or the approval of other corporate action. A proxy statement must include an extensive amount of detail not only about the matters on which shareholders will be voting at the meeting, but also about the company and its financial condition. Strict compliance with SEC regulations is required. Solicitations must disclose all important facts about the issues on which shareholders are asked to vote.

The information in a proxy statement must be truthful, which is to say it must be neither false nor misleading. SEC regulations provide the following examples of statements that are likely to result in a finding of a misleading proxy solicitation: predictions as to specific future market values; material that impugns character, integrity or personal reputation; unsupported charges of improper, illegal or immoral conduct or associations; failure to identify proxy material in a way that clearly distinguishes it from another person's soliciting material; claims made prior to a meeting regarding the results of a solicitation. This is not an exhaustive list.

Shareholders may bring lawsuits against directors and officers either in their own right or on behalf of the corporation. A lawsuit brought by shareholders on behalf of the corporation against directors or officers for malfeasance, mismanagement or other breaches of their obligations to the corporation are called shareholder derivative suits. Because these kinds of lawsuits are easily abused for their nuisance value, Congress has imposed severe limitations on them. The PSLRA limits damages and attorney fee awards; provides some safe harbors for management; authorizes the imposition of sanctions for frivolous lawsuits; and prohibits any discovery until after any motions to dismiss are heard. A claim alleging a false or misleading statement was made in connection with a securities transaction, in violation of Section 10(b), must be pleaded with particularity. To survive a motion to dismiss, the facts pleaded must be such that, if true, would give rise to a strong inference of scienter (knowledge of wrongdoing) on the part of the person making the statement.

Issuing stock to raise capital is discussed in Chapter 2. Stock transfers are discussed in Chapter 6.

Fiduciary Duties

In addition to contractual and statutory obligations, the directors and officers of a company have certain legal obligations that are implied by law even if they are not set forth in any statute or contract. These legal obligations are called fiduciary duties.

A fiduciary is a person who has undertaken to act for and on behalf of another, in circumstances giving rise to a relationship of trust and confidence. Trustees are fiduciaries. Agents are fiduciaries of their principals. Partners are each other's fiduciaries. Directors, officers and other control persons of business entities are also fiduciaries. Employees who are officers of a company are fiduciaries. Lower level employees may be fiduciaries, too, but courts generally apply a more lenient standard to them. A court might impose a strong fiduciary duty on an employee who undertakes a specific contractual obligation of a kind that involves a high level of trust or confidence, though.

A fiduciary has an implied duty to act at all times for the benefit and in the interest of the principal. This requires the exercise of the highest standards of integrity and prudence. In addition to whatever express promises they have undertaken (such as in a partnership agreement or trust instrument), fiduciaries have the following duties:

- Good faith and fair dealing
- Undivided loyalty
- Care
- Candor.

The duty of loyalty means that a fiduciary must place the interests of the principal above the fiduciary's own personal or other business interests. Directors and officers must place the interests of the corporation and the shareholders above their own personal interests. Partners must place the interests of the partnership ahead of their own interests. Fiduciaries may not engage in self-dealing, such as acquiring an actual or potentially conflicting interest in property. They may not usurp a business opportunity for the company to their own personal gain, such as by buying property the company has an interest in acquiring. They must avoid any conflicts of interest between the interests of the company and its owners, on one hand, and their personal and other business interests, on the other. A fiduciary must refrain from using business property for her own personal profit or advantage without fully disclosing how she will benefit and obtaining the informed consent of each of the other owners of the business. Fiduciaries may not use their positions of trust, confidence and inside knowledge to further their own private interests or approve an action that will provide them with a personal benefit, not even if the personal benefit consists solely of the fiduciary's continued employment by the company. A director or officer may not arrange for a loan from the company with interest lower than the market rate. Fiduciaries are not prohibited from taking action from which they derive an incidental benefit, however, provided the action primarily benefits the company or its other owners.

Serving as a director for two competing businesses can give rise to a conflict of interest, potentially breaching a director's fiduciary duty of undivided loyalty. Even if no breach of fiduciary duty to either company is found to exist in a particular case, the arrangement may violate antitrust laws. See Chapter 7.

The duty of care requires fiduciaries to act in a reasonably prudent manner in conducting the responsibilities that have been entrusted to them. For business managers, this includes both a responsibility to avoid mismanagement and waste of company funds or assets, and a responsibility to refrain from doing things that would deprive the company of profit or other advantage. But it requires more than just refraining from doing bad things. It also entails a responsibility to make an affirmative effort to do good things for the company. Managers must inform themselves about what alternatives are available to the company and then prudently weigh the advantages and disadvantages of an action before taking it. They may rely on input from advisers and employees, but only if they consider it critically and do not simply accept the information unquestioningly. A fiduciary who is entrusted with the responsibility of keeping a company's business records may have an implied obligation to implement appropriate audit procedures to ensure proper accounting and preservation of business assets.

Courts apply a presumption, known as the business judgment rule, that the directors of a business act on an informed basis, in good faith and in the honest belief that the actions they take are in the best interests of the company. Judges generally try to avoid second guessing the wisdom of business managers' decisions. They will not hold a business manager personally liable for a company's losses just because his decisions did not turn out to be good ones. All that is required is reasonable care and a good faith belief that a decision was in the company's best interest.

The duty of candor is more stringent. Fiduciaries must make full disclosure of all reasonably known risks and potential benefits of a particular action. This obligation applies to every kind of activity in which a fiduciary may engage—operations, finance, contracts, loans, assets, etc. The utmost candor is also required when there are potential conflicts of interest in a business dealing.

A fiduciary is prohibited from profiting or benefitting from the fiduciary relationship if (a) there is a conflict between the duty to the principal and the fiduciary's own interest; (b) there is conflict between the duty to the principal and a duty to another; or (c) the fiduciary profits or receives a benefit on account of his position without the principal's knowledge and consent.

Some states exempt lower level officers (those who perform purely ministerial functions and have no discretionary authority), but this exemption does not apply if the officer has any amount of decision-making power.

The duty of good faith requires fiduciaries to refrain from acting for improper purposes or in ways that produce grossly inequitable results. This means more than simply refraining from violating the law. For business managers, it means acting for the purpose of advancing the best interests of the company and its shareholders. Many courts treat this as an aspect of the duties of loyalty and care rather than as an independent obligation.

A person who owes a fiduciary to a subsidiary company also owes fiduciary duties to the parent company.

Depending on the circumstances, remedies for breach of a fiduciary duty may include:

- Injunction
- Damages
- Restitution
- Rescission
- Disgorging profits.

THE BUSINESS JUDGMENT RULE

Although business managers (such as partners, directors and officers) have fiduciary obligations, courts try to avoid micromanaging businesses. If a corporation could be sued every time a shareholder believed better management decisions could have been made, there would be a logjam in the courts. To prevent this, courts have developed what is known as the business judgment rule. Where it has not been established by case law, it has been created by statute.

The business judgment rule is a legal presumption that business managers make their decisions on an informed basis, in good faith, and with an honest belief that the decision is in the company's best interest. In other words, it is a presumption that managers exercised their business judgment in the best interests of the company. It says, in essence, that a court generally will not substitute its own judgment for that of a business manager in the absence of evidence of fraud, self-dealing, conflict of interest, bad faith or lack of due care. Directors normally cannot be sued simply for making a poor business decision that results in a loss for the company.

In most states, *due care* means the exercise of such care, including reasonable inquiry, as an ordinarily prudent, similarly situated individual would exercise under similar circumstances. In several states fiduciaries are entitled to rely on reports and advice from attorneys, accountants, business analysts and other professionals, if the reliance is in good faith and the fiduciary is not aware of any circumstances that would render the advice invalid, inapplicable or untrustworthy.

The business judgment rule is most useful as a defense against claims of mismanagement and waste arising from a fiduciary's poor judgment. Courts are not as deferential to directors or other fiduciaries when self-dealing is involved, or when a fiduciary clearly has put personal interests ahead of those of the business or its shareholders.

The Sarbanes-Oxley Act

The SOX Act was enacted in response to the Enron, WorldCom, and other corporate and accounting failures that severely harmed investors near the beginning of the millennium. It imposes strict controls on recordkeeping and reporting to improve the accuracy and reliability of a company's records and reports. It also includes other provisions that are intended to protect investors from fraudulent or unethical practices on the part of the company's managers.

While many provisions apply only to publicly traded companies, some apply to private companies, too. A private company that has filed a registration in preparation for an initial public offering must comply with the SOX Act even if the filing is subsequently withdrawn. Private companies with registered debt securities also need to comply with many of the SOX Act's provisions. The SOX Act's prohibition against knowingly destroying, falsifying or concealing records to obstruct, impede or influence a federal investigation or bankruptcy proceeding is generally applicable to everyone. Severe penalties are provided for this crime.

Of the provisions specifically applicable only to publicly traded companies, Title III is probably the one with the most significant implications for officers and directors. It imposes individual responsibility on senior executives for the accuracy and completeness of the company's financial reports. It also requires the board of directors and executive managers to attest to the authenticity, content, and accuracy of the financial reports that the company issues. A company's principal officers (typically the CEO and CFO) must certify and approve the integrity of their company financial reports on a quarterly basis.

Title IV requires internal controls for assuring the accuracy of financial reports and disclosures and mandates both audits and reports on those controls. It requires inclusion of an internal control report in a company's annual reports. This report states that management is responsible for maintaining an "adequate internal control structure" and it must include management's assessment of the control structure's effectiveness. It must be generated from truthful, factual data, with strict access and process safeguards in place, and with management-authored documentation supporting the existence of safeguards and adherence to them. Any loss of data from a critical system must be logged. Issuers are required to publish information in their annual reports concerning the scope and adequacy of the internal control structure and procedures for financial reporting. This statement must also assess the effectiveness of such internal controls and procedures.

Material changes in financial condition must be timely reported. Enhanced reporting requirements exist for certain financial transactions, including stock transactions with officers, off-balance-sheet transactions, and pro forma figures.

To further ensure accuracy and reliability, the Act requires periodic external audits. A publicly traded company must have an independent audit committee, and auditors must actually be independent. They must not provide bookkeeping, financial information system design, appraisal, valuation, legal, or any other service to the company that they may be called upon to audit at some point. Log collection and monitoring systems must provide an audit trail of all access and activity to sensitive business information.

Publicly traded companies are not allowed to make personal loans to directors or executive officers of the company. They must disclose whether they have adopted a code of corporate ethics or not. If they haven't, they must explain why not.

Finally, the Act prohibits a company from retaliating against any person for providing a law enforcement officer truthful information relating to a possible federal offense (a violation of the SOX Act, the Occupational Safety and Health Act[14] (OSHA) or the Employee Retirement Income Security Act[15] (ERISA), for example). When charged under the SOX Act, retaliation is a crime, punishable by up to ten years imprisonment.

Although the SOX Act principally applies to publicly traded companies, it provides useful guideline for best practices for any company. Moreover, even if compliance with a particular provision is not legally mandated, lenders, investors and insurers may include SOX-compliant governance and recordkeeping requirements in their contracts with a business.

Insurance

Managing risks is one of the responsibilities of any business owner. A business that owns property—office, warehouse, equipment, machinery, vehicles, and/or product inventory—may wish to obtain fire and casualty insurance to cover potential loss or damage to the property. Liability insurance may be prudent, too, if the company's products and/or services—or a defect in them—could potentially result in significant damage or harm to another person. An e-commerce business should review the policy carefully to ensure its activities will be covered. Some insurance companies offer policies and/or riders specifically for online business activities.

E-commerce businesses should also consider insurance for certain uniquely Internet-related risks, such as security breaches, computer viruses, loss of data, service outages, unauthorized access to a customer's online account information, and the like.

The Volunteer Protection Act

The Volunteer Protection Act[16] (VPA) grants some immunity from liability for individuals who commit torts in the course of performing volunteer work for nonprofit organizations. A *volunteer* is an individual who performs services for a nonprofit organization or governmental entity and does not receive payment of more than $500 per year (whether cash or any other thing of value), plus expenses. Some exception to VPA immunity apply:

(a) It does not cover acts that are not within the scope of the volunteer's responsibilities.
(b) It does not protect a volunteer who engages in activities or practices for which a license, certification or other authority is required if the volunteer did not have such license, certification or authority at the time she engaged in the act or practice.
(c) Willful or criminal misconduct is not covered.
(d) Gross negligence and reckless misconduct are not covered.
(e) Harm resulting from a conscious, flagrant indifference to the rights or safety of another person is not covered.
(f) Harm resulting from the operation of a motor vehicle or other craft or vessel for which a state requires the owner to have an operator's license or maintain insurance is not covered.
(g) Crimes of violence, sexual offenses, hate crimes, and international terrorism are not covered.
(h) Civil rights violations are not covered.
(i) Harm resulting from acts committed under the influence of alcohol or drugs is not covered.
(j) The VPA does not immunize a volunteer from liability to the nonprofit organization or government entity for which she volunteers.

Exceptions and limitations that apply only if a state has enacted them include:

(a) The organization must adhere to risk management procedures, including training.
(b) The organization must provide a financially secure source of recovery for individuals who suffer harm as a result of a volunteer's actions (e.g., insurance).
(c) State and local government officers may bring actions against the organization.

The immunity does not protect an organization from liability. It only protects individual volunteers. State laws may treat nonprofit organizations the same as employers for purposes of vicarious liability.

The VPA preempts inconsistent state laws. State laws giving volunteers greater protection than what the VPA provides remain effective. A state may opt-out of VPA applicability by enacting appropriate legislation.

Chapter 4. Employment

Many e-commerce businesses are run by a small handful of people who either do all the work of the business themselves or periodically contract with others for the completion of individual projects on an as-needed basis. When a business is doing well enough to hire employees, it must comply with myriad federal and state labor and employment laws.

The Fair Labor Standards Act

The Fair Labor Standards Act[17] (FLSA) imposes wage, hour, overtime, child labor, record-keeping, and other obligations on employers. Unless specifically exempted, the Act protects:

(a) employees of businesses with at least two employees and annual volume of sales or business done of at least $500,000
(b) employees of schools, preschools, hospitals, businesses providing medical or nursing care for residents, and government agencies with at least two employees
(c) domestic service workers (such as home health aides, full-time babysitters, gardeners, cooks) who earn at least $1,900 from one employer in a given year or who work more than eight hours per week
(d) employees who are engaged in the production of goods for commerce
(e) employees who are engaged in interstate commerce.

Courts have interpreted *interstate commerce* very broadly. As a result, nearly every employer in the United States is subject to FLSA requirements unless specifically exempted.

The U.S. Department of Labor provides a free online tool to assist employers in determining which major federal laws apply to them. Called the FirstStep Employment Law Advisor, it may be accessed at www.dol.gov/elaws/firststep.

Hiring

During the hiring process, an employer attempts to gather as much information as it can about a prospective employee's education, experience, references, and other qualifications for employment. An employer should also strive to ascertain whether the individual is subject to a noncompete or other agreements that may affect his ability to accept employment or that may limit the scope of what he can do for the company.

If an on-site interview of candidates is conducted prior to the hiring decision, it may be prudent to have the interviewee sign an agreement not to disclose any information about the company, its employees, or the interviewee's impressions of the company for a specified period of time.

Sharing employee information with other companies for the purpose of either keeping wages low or implementing an agreement to refrain from hiring each other's employees (called a *poaching agreement*) is unlawful. Wage-fixing, like price-fixing, is a combination in restraint of trade prohibited by antitrust laws. Poaching agreements restrict employee mobility and are considered an anticompetitive practice.

MEDICAL AND GENETIC INFORMATION

Employers are generally permitted to ask prospective employees about their backgrounds, but federal law prohibit an employer from asking for medical information until after it has offered a person a job. Employers generally may not ask for an employee's genetic information at all. This includes family medical history. The Genetic Information Nondiscrimination Act[18] generally restricts employers from requesting, requiring, or purchasing genetic information. This includes conducting an Internet search in a way that is likely to result in obtaining genetic information, as well as other methods of acquiring the information. Further, employers must keep any genetic information they do happen to acquire about applicants or employees confidential.

CREDIT REPORTS

Under the Fair Credit Reporting Act[19] (FCRA), an employer wishing to obtain an applicant's credit report must comply with the following requirements:

(1) Give the applicant prior written notice that a credit report will be requested;
(2) Obtain the applicant's written consent;
(3) Identify itself to the consumer reporting agency ("credit bureau");
(4) Certify to the credit bureau the purpose for which the information is sought and that it will not be used for any other purpose;
(5) Certify to the credit bureau that it has given the applicant the required notice and obtained the applicant's written consent;
(6) Certify to the credit bureau that it will give the applicant a copy of the report and a written summary of consumer rights before taking adverse action on the basis of the report.

The written summary of rights must comply with Consumer Financial Protection Bureau (CFPB) requirements. A form is available for download from the CFPB website.

If an applicant is denied employment on the basis of a credit report—or if any adverse action is taken against an employee on the basis of a credit report—then the employer must give the applicant a copy of the report and a written summary of consumer rights.

BACKGROUND CHECKS

Additional requirements apply when an employer requests a background check that will include more than just the applicant's credit report. Under the FCRA, an employer wishing to request a background check that includes information about the applicant's reputation, character and/or mode of living must give the applicant notice that this kind of information will be sought. The notice must be in writing and must be provided either before or within three days after ordering the report. It must: (1) notify the applicant that an investigative report including information about the applicant's character, general reputation, personal characteristics, and mode of living, whichever are applicable, may be made; and (2) inform the applicant of his right to request a complete and accurate written disclosure of the nature and scope of the investigation requested and the written summary of consumer rights.

The notice must be in a stand-alone document containing no other information. Including the notice in an employment application or employee handbook is not enough. The employer must certify to the company or agency performing the background check that it has made these disclosures and that it will comply with the applicant's request for a complete written disclosure of the nature and scope of the investigation and summary of consumer rights if such a request is made. An employer has five days to comply if an applicant makes such a request.

Although prospective employees are not legally required to give their permission, an employer is free to reject applicants who withhold permission.

If an employer decides to take an adverse action against an applicant or employee because of something in a background check, it must first inform the applicant that the action is being considered and provide a copy of the report to the applicant. It must also provide the applicant with the summary of consumer rights.

After taking an adverse employment action, an employer must inform the applicant or employee of each of the following facts:

(a) The action was taken because of information in the report;
(b) The name, address and telephone number of the company that sold the report;
(c) The company selling the report did not make the decision and cannot give specific reasons for it;
(d) The applicant/employee has a right to dispute the accuracy or completeness of the report and to get an additional free report from the reporting company within sixty days.

If the applicant exercises her right to dispute information in the report and the investigative company makes a requested change, the applicant may ask the investigative company to send a copy of the corrected report to the employer.

Selecting applicants or employees upon whom to perform background checks on the basis of their membership in a protected class is unlawful discrimination.

Criminal History

Employers need to be cautious about how they use information gleaned from background checks. During the hiring process, both overt discrimination and facially neutral discrimination having a disparate impact on a protected class are illegal. According to the U.S. Equal Employment Opportunity Commission (EEOC), a policy or practice that excludes everyone with any kind of criminal record from employment is never job-related or consistent with business necessity and therefore will violate Title VII of the federal Civil Rights Act,[20] except in those rare instances where an exclusion of this kind is required by law. Employers should not automatically disqualify any applicant who has a criminal record.

An employer generally may not base a decision to deny employment on an applicant's criminal record unless it gives due consideration to the nature of the crime, the time elapsed, and the nature of the job. For the same reason, employers need to be cautious about how they advertise job openings. Saying that only those with "clean" criminal records need apply is very likely to trigger a claim of "disparate impact" discrimination.

Some states provide even greater protections to prospective employees than what are provided by federal law. For example, a number of states prohibit employers from even asking potential employees about their criminal histories, at least during the initial application process. Some of these states permit inquiries into criminal history at later stages in the hiring process, though.

MINORS

The FLSA sets the minimum age for employment in the United States at fourteen. Further, fourteen and fifteen year olds may only be employed during certain hours. Children under eighteen years of age may not be employed in hazardous occupations.

These rules do not apply to child actors, newspaper delivery persons, children doing work on a parent's farm, or children making evergreen wreaths at home.

The rule that children to whom the FLSA applies may not be employed in hazardous occupations is also subject to some exceptions. Fourteen- and fifteen-year-olds with proper certification and training, or who are enrolled in a bona fide vocational agriculture program, may work in a hazardous occupation, under close supervisions and other specified conditions. Sixteen- and seventeen-year old apprentices and student-learners are permitted to work in specified hazardous occupations, under certain conditions. Fourteen- and fifteen-year- olds may be employed in an approved school-administered work-study or work experience program during school hours.

CITIZENSHIP

Under federal law, an employer must determine whether an individual is eligible to work in the United States before hiring the person. Form I-9 is used for this purpose. To be eligible, a person must be a citizen or national of the United States; a lawful permanent resident; or an alien who is authorized to work in the United States. Hiring a person who does not fall into one of these categories is a crime.

The U.S. immigration system involves several categories of visa preferences. The EB series, popularly known as a green card, is for permanent worker visa preference categories. It allows a person to live and work permanently in the United States. Eligibility for lawful permanent resident status may be based on several different things, including, e.g., extraordinary knowledge or ability. Other common categories of eligibility include: manager of a multinational business, investor of $1,000,000 or more ($500,000, in some cases) in a targeted U.S. business enterprise, physician (subject to some conditions), journalist coming to work in American media, family or spousal relationship to a U.S. citizen or lawful permanent resident, certain asylees and refugees, abuse or human trafficking victims, and U.S. State Department "diversity lottery" winners. This is not an exhaustive list.

An HB-1 visa is a temporary work permit that is granted to skilled workers in specialty occupations who are sponsored by U.S. companies. HB-1 visa holders do not have job mobility.

More information about these and other categories of visas may be found at the U.S. Citizenship and Immigration Services website, https://www.uscis.gov/.

MILITARY SERVICE MEMBERS AND VETERANS

Under the Uniformed Services Employment and Reemployment Rights Act[21] (USERRA), certain persons who serve in the armed forces have a right to reemployment with the employer for whom they were working at the time they entered the service. This includes those called up from the reserves or National Guard. The cumulative length of time that an individual may be absent from work for military duty and retain reemployment rights is five years. There are exceptions to the five-year limit, including initial enlistments lasting more than five years, periodic National Guard and Reserve training duty, and involuntary active duty extensions and recalls, especially during a time of national emergency. Reemployment protection does not depend on the timing, frequency, duration, or nature of an individual's service as long as the basic eligibility criteria are met.

USERRA provides additional protections for disabled veterans, requiring employers to make reasonable efforts to accommodate the disability. Service members convalescing from injuries received during service or training may have up to two years from the date of completion of service to return to their jobs or apply for reemployment.

Reemployed service members must be assigned the job they would have had if they had not been absent for military service, with the same seniority, status and pay, as well as other rights and benefits determined by seniority. USERRA also requires that reasonable efforts (such as training or retraining) be made to enable returning service members to refresh or upgrade their skills to help them qualify for reemployment, or to provide alternative reemployment positions if the service member cannot qualify for the job to which USERRA would otherwise require him to be returned. USERRA also provides that while an individual is performing military service, he is deemed to be on a furlough or leave of absence and is entitled to the same rights (other than accumulation of seniority) that employees who are on nonmilitary leaves of absence enjoy.

Service members must provide an employer with advance written or oral notice of military duty unless giving notice is impossible, unreasonable, or precluded by military necessity.

Discrimination

Federal, state and local laws have been enacted to protect employees from discrimination in hiring, firing, promotion, discipline, and the terms and conditions of employment. Primary sources of federal laws prohibiting employment discrimination are the Civil Rights Act, as amended (Title VII); the ADA; the Age Discrimination in Employment Act[22] (ADEA); the Pregnancy Discrimination Act;[23] and the Genetic Information Nondiscrimination Act. State and local statutes and ordinances similar to the federal laws exist in most jurisdictions.

PROTECTED CLASSES

Not every kind of discrimination is unlawful; only discrimination on the basis of membership in certain kinds of classes of people is. Protected classes under federal laws include race, color, national origin, sex, religion, disability, age, pregnancy, and genetic information (including family medical history).

Sexual orientation and gender identity discrimination are not explicitly prohibited by federal statutory law yet. Employers need to be aware, however, that the EEOC has interpreted these forms of discrimination as potentially coming within the meaning of sex discrimination. The EEOC is the agency that is charged with responsibility for enforcing federal employment discrimination laws. While its interpretations are not binding on courts, they are applied by the EEOC during agency investigations and proceedings. Courts tend to give EEOC interpretations great weight.

State statutes often identify additional protected classes. Roughly half of the states and the District of Columbia have expressly added sexual orientation to the list of protected classes. Several states have also added gender identity to the list. Minnesota and some other states have added marital status, receipt of public assistance, family status, and membership or activity in a local commission to the list of protected classes.[24] This is not an exhaustive list of the additional protected classes that states have created.

Many municipalities (cities and counties) have also enacted ordinances prohibiting employment discrimination. Often, these mirror federal and state prohibitions. Sometimes, though, a municipal ordinance specifies additional protected classes that would not otherwise be covered by applicable state or federal law.

A business with employees, or one that is planning to hire an employee, should familiarize itself with all applicable antidiscrimination laws—federal, state and local.

APPLICABILITY OF FEDERAL LAWS

The EEOC enforces Title VII of the Civil Rights Act and the ADA, which cover all private employers, state and local governments, and educational institutions that employ fifteen or more individuals. The ADEA covers all private employers with twenty or more employees. The Equal Pay Act[25] (EPA) covers all employers who are covered by the FLSA, that is to say, virtually all employers.

GOVERNMENT CONTRACTS

Additional nondiscrimination and affirmative action requirements apply to certain federal contractors under Executive Order 11246, Section 503 of the Rehabilitation Act,[26] and the Vietnam Era Veterans' Readjustment Assistance Act.[27] These programs prohibit discrimination and require affirmative action with regard to race, sex, ethnicity, religion, disability, and veterans' status. The Office of Federal Contract Compliance Programs (OFCCP) administers them.

Similar provisions exist in state laws pertaining to contracts with state governments.

THEORIES OF LIABILITY

Employment discrimination may be established by proof of discriminatory motive, disparate impact, or harassment.

Discriminatory motive may consist of either discrimination against an individual on the basis of the individual's membership in a protected class, or systematic discrimination against the protected class (such as a company policy against hiring Muslims). It may be proven by direct or circumstantial evidence. An employer's statement to a white male that he need not apply for a position because the business is only looking for a woman or a member of a racial minority would be direct evidence of discriminatory motive. An example of circumstantial evidence might be an employer's pattern of hiring the most qualified candidate for a position but breaking that pattern when a black woman is the most qualified candidate. Of course, this is not the only way that discriminatory motive may be proven.

An employer may be liable for employment discrimination if an action has a disparate impact on members of a protected class, even if there was no discriminatory motive. To prevail using a disparate impact theory, it is necessary to prove: (1) an employer's policy or action has a different impact on members of a protected class than on members of a different protected class; and (2) the action or policy is not justified by business necessity.

> **Example.** An e-book seller specifies a minimum height requirement for its employees. Statistically, men are taller than women, so the requirement has a disparate impact on women. Since it is not necessary to be tall to sell e-books, the requirement is not justified by business necessity. An employer who denies a female applicant a position on this basis would be at great risk of being sued for employment discrimination.

Subjecting people to different disqualifying criteria depending on their race, national origin, color, sex, religion, disability, age (over thirty-nine vs. under forty) or genetic information is overt discrimination. Even an apparently neutral employment qualification, though, can be discriminatory if it has a disparate impact on some members of a protected class. According to the EEOC, "[n]ational data supports a finding that criminal record exclusions have a disparate impact based on race and national origin [and] provides a basis for the Commission to investigate Title VII disparate impact charges challenging criminal record exclusions."[28] Furthermore, the EEOC has declared that a policy or practice that excludes anyone with any kind of criminal record from employment is never job-related or consistent with business necessity and therefore will always violate Title VII of the federal Civil Rights Act, except in those rare instances where the exclusion is required by federal law.

Agencies responsible for the enforcement of state employment discrimination laws have adopted similar policies.

Job announcements may violate employment discrimination laws if they state qualifications which, if applied, would have a disparate impact on members of a protected class. Saying that persons with criminal records need not apply is very likely to trigger a claim of "disparate impact" discrimination.

Employment discrimination may also be established by proof of harassment on the basis of membership in a protected class. This may be proven with evidence of direct harassment (threats, offensive remarks, demeaning jokes, quid pro quo requests for sexual favors, etc.) of an employee referencing the employee's membership in a protected class It may also be proven with evidence that an employer created, contributed to, or unreasonably tolerated a hostile work environment for a member of a protected class. While sexual harassment is the most common variety of this kind of claim, the rule also applies to other protected classes. For example, an employer's tolerance of racist jokes in the workplace could subject him to liability for racial harassment. Nor is the prohibition only for the benefit of women and minorities. An employer who tolerates a workplace in which women regularly make misandric jokes or derogatory or humiliating remarks about men could be liable for sexual harassment even if all the male employees in the workplace are heterosexual and white.

Harassment can take many different forms—inappropriate physical contact; inappropriate oral or written communications, email messages, postings to Internet forums, etc.

Employers are not only potentially responsible for their own personal acts of harassment, but also for the harassing acts of other employees. The potential for liability is very strong if an employer acquires actual knowledge of it but fails to do anything. In some cases, liability may attach even if the employer had no knowledge of such acts. For this reason, it is important for an employer not only to avoid doing things that create a hostile work environment, but also to take proactive steps to prevent other employees from doing things that may cause such an environment to develop. Recommended proactive steps could include such things as:

(a) Have a written anti-harassment policy in place that includes specific behavioral guidelines.
(b) Adopt workplace rules that are consistent with the anti-harassment policy.
(c) Implement a harassment and discrimination reporting system that employees can use.
(d) Have more than one alternative method of reporting. Consider, for example, what an employee should do if the allegation of harassment is against the person to whom harassment reports are made.
(e) Use uniform reporting procedures and forms.
(f) Train the people to whom complaints are reported on how to appropriately investigate and evaluate complaints.
(g) Promptly and fully investigate all complaints, with detailed documentation.
(h) Maintain the confidentiality of complaints.
(i) Provide updates to the complainant throughout the investigation. It is not necessary to reveal all details of the investigation, however.
(j) Take appropriate remedial action against the offender if a an improper, discriminatory or harassing act is determined to have occurred.
(k) Document all remedial actions.
(l) Provide anti-harassment training for all employees.
(m) Monitor employee emails and company-owned bulletin boards and forums.
(n) Monitor employee use of Internet websites where user content may be contributed, such as blogs, Facebook and other social media websites.

Monitoring employee emails and Internet use is important because even an employee's sending or posting of an off-color joke via the Internet exposes the employer to potential sexual harassment liability for creating a hostile work environment if another employee finds it offensive.

Taking these steps can go a long way toward preventing an employer's liability for the harassing and discriminatory conduct of its employees. An employer may assert as a defense to liability the fact that it took appropriate and diligent measures to discover and eliminate harassment in the workplace upon learning about it.

DEFENSES

Defenses to employment discrimination vary depending on the kind of liability theory that is invoked. A nondiscriminatory business justification will suffice as a defense in most cases, unless it is simply a pretext for discrimination. In a very limited number of situations, an employer is allowed to use race, sex, religion or membership in some other protected class as an explicit condition of employment, provided it is a bona fide occupational qualification. A movie producer, for example, may discriminate against white actors when casting for the part of a black character in a movie. A Catholic church may legitimately refuse to hire a Jewish rabbi for the position of priest. Courts construe this exception narrowly, however.

REASONABLE ACCOMMODATIONS

Most employment discrimination laws only prohibit discrimination against members of protected classes. The ADA goes further, not only prohibiting discrimination against disabled persons, but also requiring certain businesses to make reasonable accommodations for disabled employees, clients, and customers, unless doing so would result in undue hardship for the business. The ADA applies both to employers and to places of public accommodation.

Courts are not in agreement about whether a web site is a place of public accommodation. In *National Association for the Blind v. Scribd*[29] a court held that an online digital library must provide an optional aural interface for sight-impaired users because a web site is a place of public accommodation. In *Access Now, Inc. v. Southwest Airlines Co.*[30] a court held that an airline company need not take steps to enable sight-impaired purchasers to have access to exclusively online ticket deals because a web site is not a place of public accommodation.

RETALIATION

Retaliating against an employee for reporting or filing a claim of unlawful employment discrimination is prohibited. An employer who does so may be liable for damages and attorney fees. In many jurisdictions, a retaliation claim may succeed even if the underlying harassment or discrimination complaint turns out to have been unfounded.

It is also unlawful for an employer to discriminate against an employee for filing a complaint with the employer or with the Department of Labor alleging a violation of the FLSA, or for participating in a legal proceeding under the FLSA.

EQUAL PAY

The Equal Pay Act prohibits discrimination on the basis of sex by paying wages to employees in an establishment at a rate less than the rate paid to employees of the opposite sex in the establishment for equal work on jobs the performance of which requires equal skill, effort, and responsibility, and which are performed under similar working conditions.

Exceptions exist for unequal payments that are made pursuant to a seniority system, merit system, a system which measures earnings by quantity or quality of production, or a differential that is based on any factor other than sex.

An employer may not reduce any employee's wage in order to bring itself into compliance with the EPA.

Polygraph Tests

The Employee Polygraph Protection Act[31] (EPPA) limits private employer use of lie detector tests either for pre-employment screening of job applicants or for testing current employees during the course of employment. Polygraph tests are only permitted under limited circumstances and subject to certain restrictions.

Contracts

Employment contracts may be either written or oral. In a number of states, contractual terms may be implied by conduct even if there is no written or oral agreement. Having a written contract in place is usually a good idea, as it can remove uncertainty about the terms of the agreement. This helps prevent misunderstandings and disputes from arising in the future. A written employment agreement is also a useful interpretive guide for resolving disagreements about the parties' respective rights and obligations.

EMPLOYMENT AT WILL

At common law, employment is at will unless the parties agree otherwise. This means that the employment may be terminated by either the employer or the employee at any time for any reason or for no reason at all without liability to the other. This is still the general rule.

From an employer's perspective, ease of hiring and hiring employees can be important. Any business has an obvious interest in ensuring that unproductive and/or harmful employees can be removed as quickly as possible, without risk of liability. To minimize the risk of a finding that employment is not at will, an employer should avoid using language in contracts, employee handbooks and other documents to the effect that the employment is for a specified term, or that employees may only be fired for specified reasons. To that end, including a statement that the employment is at will in all of these kinds of documents may help.

Employers who wish to preserve the right to terminate employment at will must conform their conduct to that of an at-will employer. Even if a contract expressly provides that employment is at will, subsequently stating or acting as if an employee may be fired only for good cause may result in a court finding that the contract was subsequently modified to become a "termination for cause only" contract. There have been cases where courts have held that an employer did not have a right to terminate an employee at will because the employer had adopted a stated policy or practice of firing employees only for cause, or where the employer had interpreted and applied such contracts as requiring cause for termination.

Legislatures and courts have carved out some exceptions to the employment-at-will doctrine. These are discussed later in this chapter.

CONTRACT TERMS

An employment contract should cover at least the following topics:

- Hours
- Compensation (wage/salary)
- Benefits (health plan, 401k, etc.)
- Job title/classification
- Responsibilities
- Permanent vs. temporary

- Duration (if it is not a permanent hire)
- Termination (at will vs. for cause)

Other clauses that can be of particular importance to e-commerce businesses include: nondisclosure agreements; noncompete agreements; nonsolicitation agreements; assignments of intellectual property; and forfeiture clauses. Other standard contract terms—e.g., forum selection, choice of law, arbitration, etc.—can also be important.

Nondisclosure Agreements

An employment contract may require employees to refrain from disclosing trade secrets and/or other specified kinds of information. The contract may provide that this obligation survives the termination of the employment relationship. These clauses generally are enforceable, provided the kinds of information to which the obligation applies is specified in the contract and they are reasonable in scope. A provision prohibiting an employee from using publicly available information or information acquired before the employment began is not reasonable in scope.

Recognizing the public interests in freedom to work and in reducing monopolistic tendencies, courts have held that employees have a right to use skills and general knowledge they acquire during the course of an employment after the employment terminates. The line between general knowledge and skills, on one hand, and knowhow that is protected as a trade secret is not always clear. Accordingly, the more specific the contract is on this point, the better.

Unlike noncompete agreements, nondisclosure agreements do not need to be limited to a short period of time. In fact, a nondisclosure agreement that is limited to a short period will undermine a company's claim of having taken reasonable measures to protect a trade secret. In one case, for example, a court held that a nondisclosure agreement that only required nondisclosure for a ten-year period was not a reasonable measure to protect a trade secret.

In some states, a court may invoke the "inevitable disclosure" doctrine to enjoin a departing employee from accepting employment at a competing business if there is a high probability that the employee will inevitably use trade secret or sensitive business information to benefit the new employer, whether intentionally or inadvertently This may be done even if there is no noncompete agreement, and even if there is no evidence of actual or threatened disclosure. The more similar the two businesses are, the higher the probability of a finding that disclosure is inevitable. California has rejected the "inevitable disclosure" doctrine, but it is followed in some other states.[32]

Noncompete Agreements

An employment contract may contain a provision prohibiting the employee from competing with the employer's business—during the employment, following the employment, or both—either by starting a competing business or by accepting employment with a competing business. This kind of provision is called a noncompete agreement. While they are most commonly found in employment contracts, the term is broad enough to cover any agreement by one party to refrain from entering into, starting, or working for a similar business, trade or profession in competition against the other party.

Companies may reasonably be concerned about an employee using or disclosing to a business competitor a trade secret, confidential information, or knowhow that the employee acquired or developed during the employment. This might include the company's customer database; salary information; marketing methods; production and design materials; inventions; software programs; new product ideas, plans and release dates, and so on. A former employee can put a company at a competitive disadvantage if she brings these things to a competitor after leaving the company. While a nondisclosure agreement goes part of the way toward preventing this from happening, a noncompete provision adds further protection. It also helps protect a company's investment in training its employees.

Under early common law, noncompete agreements were considered an unenforceable restraint of trade. Today, they are enforceable in a number of states, at least to some extent, provided they are limited in scope. California is not one of these states. California Business and Professions Code Section 16600 preserves the early common law view of noncompete agreements as restraints of trade, and prohibits the courts of that state from enforcing them.

California courts consider the public policy reflected in this statute to be so strong that it overrides the usual conflicts-of-laws principle in favor of enforcing contractual choice-of-law provisions. In *Application Group, Inc. v. Hunter Group, Inc.*[33] an employee of a Maryland-based company signed an employment contract containing a noncompete clause. The contract also contained a choice-of-law provision specifying that it was to be governed by Maryland law. Later, the employee left and went to work for an employer in California. The California employer filed suit in a California court to invalidate the noncompete clause. The California court ruled in favor of the California employer, holding that California's strong interest in enabling California businesses to hire employees of their choosing outweighed the conflicts-of-laws principle that choice-of-law clauses in private contracts are enforceable. Although the clause was enforceable under Maryland law, it would not be enforced in California.

Noncompete provisions in some other kinds of contracts are enforceable in California. A clause in a contract that prohibits the seller of a business or its goodwill from competing against the buyer in a specified geographic area is enforceable. They can also be enforceable in partnership and LLC agreements, provided they are reasonably limited in scope.

Hawaii prohibits high-tech companies from requiring employees to sign noncompete agreements. In many other states, the general rule is that noncompete agreements are enforceable if they are reasonable and supported by consideration. The employer's interests must be balanced against the public interest in receiving the employee's services and the right of individuals to work for a living. Courts strike this balance by declining to enforce a noncompete agreement that is unreasonable. A noncompete agreement usually will be considered reasonable if:

(a) It is no greater in scope than necessary to protect a legitimate business interest employer;
(b) It does not impose an undue hardship on the employee; and
(c) It is not contrary to the public interest.

Legitimate business interests include things like the protection of trade secrets, confidential information, and goodwill. An employer's interest in receiving the benefit of the services it has invested time and resources in training an employee to perform is also legitimate. For legal purposes, a simple desire to restrict ordinary competition is not considered a legitimate business interest, however.

To be considered reasonable in scope, a restriction must be appropriately limited as to:

- Time
- Geographic territory
- Type of business.

What is considered an appropriate length of time and geographic scope is a highly fact-specific determination. Of course, a restriction that forever bars competition anywhere in the universe is likely to be considered unreasonable. A few states, by statute or judicial decision, have specified a time limit, such as one year, beyond which a restriction will be deemed unreasonable. In most states, though, the reasonableness of the scope of a restriction must be decided by courts on a case-by-case basis, occasionally with the guidance of an on-point judicial precedent. Although it is not a rule of law, it may be said that it is likely to be difficult to persuade a court that a restriction of more than two years is reasonable.

Some courts have noted that because Internet commerce changes rapidly, it may not be reasonable to restrict an employee from working for another Internet company for as long a period of time as is permitted in other industries. These courts have held that a noncompete provision for a year or more is unreasonable in the Internet industry. Other courts disagree.

Courts in some states, such as New York,[34] hold that a noncompete agreement will not be enforced in cases where an employer terminates an employee without cause.

Some states permit courts to edit a noncompete agreement to make it reasonable. Others hold that if the clause is not enforceable as drafted, then it cannot be enforced at all. To reduce the risk of complete nonenforcement, language could be included in the contract to authorize a court to reform the noncompete clause if it is found to be unreasonable.

Nonsolicitation and Antipiracy Agreements

In the employment context, a nonsolicitation agreement is a contract in which an employee agrees not to solicit the employer's other employees or its customers, prospective customers, partners or companies with which the company does business. Like noncompete agreements, the contract may provide that the obligation survives termination of the employment relationship. The term can also refer to an agreement between two companies that neither one will hire away the other's employee(s).

An antipiracy agreement is a contract in which an employee agrees not to solicit the employer's employees.

The legal principles governing these kinds of contracts are not significantly different from those governing noncompete agreements.

Assignments of Intellectual Property

All expressive works created by an employee during the course and within the scope of employment are works made for hire. As such, the employer owns the copyright in them. This is not true of other kinds of intellectual property, such as inventions.

Under the "hired to invent" doctrine, which some but not all states have adopted, an employer acquires ownership rights in an invention the employee was hired to invent for the employer. Even in states that have adopted this rule, however, it will not necessarily apply to inventions an employee was not expressly hired to invent.

If the "hired to invent" doctrine does not apply, and no contract provides otherwise, then the employee retains ownership of his invention. If, however, the invention is created within the scope of the employment while using the employer's facilities, equipment or resources, then the employer has an implied nonexclusive license to exploit it. This is called a *shop right*. An employer's shop right exists even if the employee has not expressly granted the employer a license to use the invention, and even if the employee was not hired for the purpose of inventing things. Shop rights last for the duration of a patent. They cannot be transferred except in connection with a sale of the employer's business.

Shop rights are most commonly invoked as a defense when an employee develops an improvement to an employer's machinery, product, business method, etc., and then obtains a patent on it after leaving the employment. If an employee (or former employee) sues the employer for patent infringement, the employer may assert shop rights as a defense.

Many companies would rather own inventions created by their employees than merely hold a license to use them. This way, the employer can claim ownership rights in any patents that are obtained for them. If a valid assignment has been made by the employee, then the employee will be liable for patent infringement if the employer secures a patent and the inventor-employee exploits the invention without a license from the employer. An employment contract containing an assignment of rights to inventions to be developed by the employee, or a provision to the effect that the employer owns any inventions created by the employee during the course of employment, is usually enforceable, at least if it specifies inventions that are created using the employer's facilities, equipment or resources.

California and some other states have enacted statutes to protect employee rights to inventions they create. California Labor Code Section 2870 declares that a provision in an employment contract purporting to require an employee to assign his rights to an invention to the employer is against public policy, and therefore unenforceable, if:

(a) The invention was created on the employee's own time;
(b) None of the employer's facilities, equipment, resources or trade secrets were used;
(c) It does not relate to the employer's business or its actual or anticipated research and development activities; and
(d) It does not result from work performed for the employer.

Contracts between universities (and other postsecondary and graduate schools) and faculty often provide that an invention created by a faculty member is the property of the school. Many schools impose this requirement on students, too. Often, the contract gives the faculty or student inventor a right to a percentage royalty. The contract usually contains some exceptions to the school's ownership rights which, when applicable, permit a faculty member or student to retain ownership. Even when an exception applies, though, the contract may authorize the school to use student and faculty inventions royalty-free for research and teaching. The specific contours of these rights and obligations are largely a matter of contract, which may include a school's handbook, intellectual property policy, or the like, to which the student or teacher most likely will have assented at some point.

A contract may define the term *invention* more broadly than patent law does, and may include an assignment of all trade secrets, knowhow, formulae and data associated with the invention. Contracts assigning an employee's rights to both ideas and inventions to the employer are not uncommon. An employee's use of an idea in violation of the terms of an employment contract may result in liability for breach of contract even if the idea is not protectable as such under patent, copyright, trade secret, or other law.

The contract may require an employee to disclose all inventions to the company and to maintain adequate records of the invention process. It may also provide that the employee's obligations with respect to ideas and inventions survive the termination of the employment relationship. When such language is included in the contract, an employee may not exploit an idea conceived during the employment even if the employee did not develop it during the employment.

The interpretation and enforceability of intellectual property assignment clauses in contracts is a matter of state law. State laws vary. Nevertheless, protection of employee rights and promotion of job mobility are dominant themes in many court decisions in this area. Accordingly, many courts tend to construe intellectual assignment clauses narrowly, if possible. For this reason, employers should make these clauses as specific as possible. To protect itself from the possibility that an employee may exploit an idea for a competing product line, for example, a company may want to ensure that the assignment covers not only inventions, patents and copyrights, but also ideas for products, trademarks, and ideas for trademarks.[35]

Forfeiture Clauses

A forfeiture clause in an employment contract is one that provides that specified kinds of compensation or benefits are forfeited if the employee leaves and works for a different company in the same industry. They are often used in conjunction with a noncompete provision, typically providing for forfeiture of benefits earned or paid during a specified period of time (during the last year of employment, for example) in the event the employee breaches the noncompete agreement. If an employee breaches the noncompete agreement, and the forfeiture provision so provides, then the employee is not entitled to receive the specified kinds of compensation that were earned during the specified period and will have to pay back any such compensation that was received during that period.

Forfeitures of salary are not enforceable. Forfeitures of other kinds of compensation (e.g., bonuses, stock options, severance pay, pensions, etc.) are, at least in most states. The rationale for this distinction is that benefits on top of a living wage are just extras; they are not necessary to survival like wages and salary are. When a forfeiture clause is limited to kinds of compensation other than salary, they do not leave an employee impoverished. They also do not prohibit employment. So long as forfeitures are limited to forms of compensation other than salaries and wages, they are not considered an unreasonable restraint.

EMPLOYEE HANDBOOKS

An employee handbook may be viewed as embodying an implied contract between the employer and each employee, at least when there has been conduct consistent with that. A few states reject this view, instead regarding a handbook as providing only precatory guidance unless the parties have signaled their assent to its binding nature. In any event, employee handbooks are extremely useful, so an employer should take steps to generate evidence of the employee's awareness of the handbook and agreement to be bound by it. This might be done by obtaining an employee's written agreement to be bound by it, as opposed to simply mentioning that one exists. Written agreement to it may be obtained, for example, by including a provision in the employment contract specifying that the parties agree to be bound by it and that its terms are incorporated into the contract by reference.

The employment contract should address matters specific to a particular employee—such as date of hire, position, duration of employment, rate of pay, and the employee's assent to the company's employment policies, as set out in the Employee Handbook. The Employee Handbook should address matters applicable throughout the company. Subjects typically covered in an employee handbook include:

- Hours
- Performance reviews
- Raises
- Bonuses
- Expense reimbursements
- Tuition assistance
- Insurance
- Promotions and transfers
- Holidays
- Vacations
- Sick leave
- Family and medical leave
- Parental and adoption leave
- Funeral leave
- Jury duty
- Payroll reporting
- Employee benefits
- Equal employment opportunity statement
- Disabilities and requesting accommodations
- Harassment policy
- Internet use policy
- Communications policy
- Authorized and unauthorized uses of company property
- Accident reporting and procedures
- Privacy
- Security
- Nondisclosure requirements

- Noncompete provisions
- Client confidentiality
- Substance abuse
- Smoking
- Dress code.

This is not an exhaustive list.

Hours

The FLSA restricts the hours of work for fourteen- and fifteen-year- olds. Minors under the age of sixteen working in a business solely owned or operated by their parents or by persons standing in place of their parents can work any time of day and for any number of hours. There is no maximum limit on the number of hours an adult may work per week.

There is no federal law requiring an employer to give employees meal or rest breaks. Some state laws require employers to give their employees these breaks. Such provisions are also common in collective bargaining agreements and other employment contracts. And certain employees may have a right to request periodic breaks as an accommodation for a disability if it qualifies as "reasonable" under the ADA. There is no federal requirement that all employees must be given breaks, though.

Under the FLSA, employers must provide break time and space for nursing mothers to express breast milk. This obligation continues for one year after the child's birth. If the employer compensates other employees for break time, then it must also compensate a nursing mother for break time that is spent breastfeeding. If the employer does not compensate any employees for break time, then it does not have to compensate a nursing mother for break time spent breastfeeding.

State laws may provide greater protections to employees than are provided by federal law.

Compensation

The kinds and amounts of compensation an employee receives normally are negotiated between an employer and an employee, or between the employer and a union or other bargaining agent for the employee. There are some legal constraints, however.

MINIMUM WAGE

Compensation of employees is largely, but not entirely, a matter of contract between an employer and an employee. Statutes at both the federal and state levels impose minimum requirements on employers pertaining to wages. As of 2017, the federal minimum wage for nonexempt employees is $7.25 per hour. State minimum wage laws may provide for a higher amount.

A special rule applies to employees who are under the age of twenty. Under the Youth Minimum Wage Program, employees under the age of twenty may be paid as little as $4.25 per hour for their first ninety consecutive days of employment with the same employer, as long as their work does not displace other workers. After ninety consecutive days of employment, or when the worker reaches age twenty (whichever comes first), the worker must receive at least the federal minimum wage.

Employers of tipped employees (i.e., those who customarily and regularly receive more than $30 a month in tips) may consider such tips as part of their wages, but they must pay a direct wage of at least $2.13 per hour if they claim a tip credit. They must also meet certain other requirements.

The FLSA allows the employment of certain individuals at wage rates below the statutory minimum wage under certificates issued by the Department of Labor, namely:

(a) student learners (vocational education students)
(b) full time students in retail or service establishments, agriculture, or institutions of higher education
(c) individuals whose earning or productive capacities for the work to be performed are impaired by physical or mental disabilities, including those related to age or injury.

Nonprofit organizations and governments may contract with individuals for unpaid full- or part-time placement ("unpaid internships") without violating federal or state minimum wage or overtime laws. A for-profit business may offer an unpaid internship only if:

(a) It includes training;
(b) It benefits the intern;
(c) It does not displace regular employees;
(d) The intern is closely supervised by existing staff;
(e) The intern is not entitled to a job after the internship is over;
(f) Both the company and the intern understand that the intern is not entitled to wages; and
(g) The employer does not derive immediate advantage from the intern's contributions and employer operations may actually be impeded.

Other exemptions from federal minimum wage laws exist for:

- Salaried executive, administrative, and professional employees
- Outside salespersons
- Certain amusement or recreational establishment employees
- Camp employees
- Certain seasonal establishment employees
- Certain religious or nonprofit educational conference center employees
- Fishing operation workers
- Certain agricultural workers
- Employees of local or regional newspapers with a circulation of less than 4,000
- Certain telephone company switchboard operators
- Seamen on foreign vessels
- Babysitters
- Companionship providers for the elderly or disabled
- Certain crime investigators

- Homeworkers making wreaths
- Newspaper delivery persons
- Farm workers on certain small farms.

The exemption for salaried executive, administrative, and professional employees also includes teachers and academic administrative personnel in elementary or secondary schools, and certain skilled computer professionals. The exemption for companion care providers does not include employees of an agency or other third party employer.

Many states have enacted minimum wage laws, too. When an employer is subject to both state and federal minimum wage requirements, the employee is entitled to a minimum wage pursuant to the applicable higher standard.

PREVAILING WAGE

The Davis-Bacon Act[36] requires contractors and subcontractors engaged in federally financed and assisted construction projects to pay prevailing wages and fringe benefits to the laborers and mechanics they employ. The McNamara-O'Hara Service Contract Act[37] requires payment of prevailing wages and fringe benefits to service employees of contractors and subcontractors furnishing services to federal government agencies. Most states have enacted comparable laws for employers that contract with the state. The prevailing wage is the hourly wage, usual benefits and overtime paid to the majority of workers, laborers, and mechanics within the relevant local area. It is established by regulatory agencies for each trade and occupation employed in the performance of public work, as well as by state departments of labor (or the equivalent).

OVERTIME PAY

The FLSA requires most employers in the United States to pay their employees at least one and one-half their regular rate for hours worked beyond forty in a workweek ("overtime pay.")

Exemptions from the federal overtime pay requirement exist for:

- Salaried executive, administrative, and professional employees
- Computer programmers, computer systems analysts, software engineers, or employees doing other similar work, who are paid at least $27.63 per hour
- Outside salespersons
- Commissioned employees of retail or service establishments who average at least one-and-a-half times the minimum wage for each hour worked
- Car, truck, trailer, farm implement, boat, or aircraft salespersons employed by nonmanufacturing establishments primarily engaged in selling these items to ultimate purchasers
- Car, truck, or farm implement mechanics or parts clerks employed by nonmanufacturing establishments primarily engaged in selling these items to ultimate purchasers (motor vehicle dealerships)
- Certain amusement or recreational establishment employees
- Camp employees
- Certain seasonal establishment employees

- Certain employees of national parks, forests and wildlife refuges
- Certain religious or nonprofit educational conference center employees
- Fishing operation workers
- Certain agricultural workers and product buyers
- Employees of local or regional newspapers with a circulation of less than 4,000
- Certain telephone company switchboard operators
- Seamen
- Babysitters
- Individuals who are employed by elderly persons or persons with disabilities to provide companionship services
- Certain crime investigators
- Homeworkers making wreaths
- Newspaper delivery persons
- Farmworkers
- Railroad and air carrier employees, taxi drivers, certain employees of motor carriers, and local delivery employees paid on approved trip rate plans
- Announcers, news editors, and chief engineers of certain nonmetropolitan broadcasting stations
- Domestic service employees solely employed by the individual, family, or household receiving services (not an agency or other third party employer) who reside in the private home where they provide services
- Motion picture theater employees
- Certain airline employees
- Firefighters and police officers working in small public fire or police departments
- Certain forestry employees
- Fruit & vegetable transportation employees
- Houseparents in nonprofit educational institutions
- Livestock auction workers
- Local delivery drivers and driver's helpers
- Employees of small lumber operations
- Sugar processing employees.

The exemption for salaried executive, administrative, and professional employees also includes teachers and academic administrative personnel in elementary or secondary schools, and certain skilled computer professionals. The exemption for companion care providers does not include employees of an agency or other third party employer.

A partial exemption from the overtime pay requirement exists for police, fire fighters, and hospital and nursing home employees, in some circumstances. Hospitals and residential care facilities that have agreements with their employees that they will work fourteen-day periods instead of seven-day workweeks do not have to comply with the standard overtime rule. By agreement with their employees, nursing care facilities may choose to adopt either the regular overtime rule or the "8 and 80" system. The "8 and 80" system allows an employer to pay overtime at time-and-a-half for hours worked over eight in a day or hours worked over eighty in a fourteen-day period, whichever results in the greater number of overtime hours.

Partial exemptions also exist for employees engaged in certain operations on agricultural commodities and employees of certain bulk petroleum distributors.

An employer of an individual who does not have a high school diploma is only required to pay minimum wage, not overtime pay, for the time the employee spends in employer-mandated remedial reading or training in other basic skills that are not specific to the job. This exemption may only be invoked for up to ten hours of training per workweek.

The FLSA does not require premium pay for weekend, night or holiday work, except that any hours in excess of a forty-hour workweek—whether on a weekday, weeknight, weekend, or holiday—must be paid at time-and-a-half unless an exemption applies.

Some states have enacted overtime pay requirements, too. Where an employee is subject to both state and federal overtime laws, the employee is entitled to overtime according to the higher applicable standard.

WAGE GARNISHMENTS

Creditors may garnish an employee's wages to satisfy a debt. 15 U.S.C. § 1673 sets the maximum amount that may be garnished from wages. An employer may not fire an employee solely because the employee's wages are being garnished. Doing so is a federal crime.

COLLECTIVE BARGAINING AGREEMENTS

Collective bargaining agreements for unionized employees often provide benefits and protections beyond those required by law. The National Labor Relations Act[38] (NLRA) expressly excludes supervisory employees (management) from its coverage, however. Accordingly, they are excluded from the protections of a collective bargaining agreement and their contracts need to be negotiated separately and independently. Compensation and other contract terms for managerial employees who are not covered by a collective bargaining agreement are negotiated individually with the company. The employment contract for an officer or other managerial employee typically will include provisions for a base salary; bonuses (usually based on performance); and benefits, which may include health insurance, life insurance, retirement plan, flex spending account, employee stock ownership, severance package, etc.

STOCK OPTIONS AND PROFIT SHARING

To attract talent, to provide employees with an incentive to do good work for the company, and to reduce employee turnover, many companies provide or offer employees an opportunity to participate in the company's profits. This can be a way of attracting talented employees when a business does not have the necessary cash flow to pay a higher salary. A company might also offer other kinds of benefits, too, such as a company car, phone, a dental plan, a legal indemnification plan, etc. Provided they are reasonable in amount, a company generally may deduct these as business expenses.

Employee stock options are a kind of call option. Specifically, an employee stock option is an employee benefit which gives an employee the right, but not the obligation, to acquire stock (or some other representation of a share in the ownership of a business) for an agreed-upon price. When a corporation grants an employee a stock option, it obligates itself to buy the specified number of shares of stock on the open market and sell them to the employee at the price established in the contract (called the exercise price, or strike price). Normally, this is the market price of the stock at the time the option is granted. When offered to all (or a large number) of a company's employees, stock options and other profitsharing plans have been found to enhance a corporation's performance. Offering stock options only to the top executives generally does not. This is why many companies set up profitsharing plans in which all of their employees may participate.

A stock option plan generally includes the grant, the exercise price, a vesting date, and an expiration date.

The grant specifies the number and kind of shares to which the employee is entitled. The vesting date is the date that the option matures and the employee may choose to act. An employee who exercises the right may either sell the stock or hold onto it and sell it later. Plans typically impose a waiting period before stocks acquired pursuant to the plan may be sold. The expiration date is the date past which the employee no longer has the right to exercise the option.

Stock option agreements typically include restrictions on transfer. They may also establish company repurchase rights in specified circumstances.

A drawback to using stock options as a form of employee compensation is that they must be valued for tax and SEC reporting purposes. Since stock values change rapidly and often, that can be complicated. Backdating transactions for the purpose of affecting the reported value of a stock option may be a form of securities fraud if it is done for a nefarious reason, such as to hide expenses.

OTHER EMPLOYEE BENEFITS

ERISA regulates employers who offer pension or welfare benefit plans for their employees. Title I of ERISA is administered by the Employee Benefits Security Administration (EBSA) (formerly the Pension and Welfare Benefits Administration) and imposes a wide range of fiduciary, disclosure, and reporting requirements on fiduciaries of pension and welfare benefit plans and on others having dealings with these plans. These provisions preempt many similar state laws. Under Title IV, certain employers and plan administrators must fund an insurance system to protect certain kinds of retirement benefits, with premiums paid to the federal government's Pension Benefits Guaranty Corporation.

EBSA also administers reporting requirements for continuation of health care provisions, required under the Comprehensive Omnibus Budget Reconciliation Act[39] (COBRA) and the health care portability requirements on group plans under the Health Insurance Portability and Accountability Act[40] (HIPAA).

Leave

FAMILY AND MEDICAL LEAVE

The Family and Medical Leave Act[41] (FMLA) requires certain employers to offer eligible employees up to twelve weeks of unpaid leave each year for the birth and care of a newborn child, for placement with the employee of a child for adoption or foster care, or for the serious illness of the employee or the employee's child, spouse, or parent. Up to twenty-six weeks of leave may be taken to care for a military service member who was injured in combat.

Employers who are subject to the FMLA must display a notice advising employees of their rights in the workplace. They must also provide them with information about their rights under the Act when they are hired.

The Act applies to every private employer with fifty or more employees.[42] An employee is eligible for FMLA leave, however, only if the employee meets the following requirements:

(a) works at a location where the company employs at least fifty employees within seventy-fives miles;

(b) has worked for the employer for at least twelve months during the preceding six years;[43]

(c) has put in at least 1,250 hours during the preceding twelve months.

An exception to the second and third requirements exists for individuals whose employment was interrupted by military service. Special rules apply to airline flight crew and local school employees.

Employees generally must request leave thirty days in advance when the need for leave is foreseeable. In all other cases, they must give notice as soon as practicable. An employer must notify an employee when it designates the employee's leave as FMLA leave and the amount of leave that will be deducted from the employee's FMLA entitlement. When an employee requests FMLA leave due to his or her own serious health condition or a covered family member's serious health condition, the employer may require certification in support of the leave from a health care provider. An employer may also require second or third medical opinions (at the employer's expense) and periodic recertification of a serious health condition.

An employer must maintain an employee's health benefits while the employee is on FMLA leave. All benefits an employee had accrued prior to taking FMLA leave must be restored upon the employee's return. An employee must be restored to the same job or to a job that is equivalent to the one she had before taking leave. It need not be a completely identical job, but it must be a job with equivalent pay, benefits, and other terms and conditions (including shift and location). It must have the same or equivalent pay premiums, such as a shift differential, and the same opportunity for overtime. An employee is entitled to any unconditional pay increases and bonuses that occurred while he or she was on FMLA leave, such as cost of living increases. Pay increases conditioned upon seniority, length of service, or work performed are required only if employees taking the same type of leave for non-FMLA reasons receive the increases. If an employee does not meet a specific goal for earning a bonus because of taking FMLA leave, the employer only needs to pay the bonus if employees taking the same type of leave for non-FMLA reasons receive it. An employee's use of FMLA leave cannot be counted against the employee under a no-fault attendance policy. It is unlawful for an employer to interfere with, restrain, or deny the exercise of or the attempt to exercise any right provided by the FMLA. It is also unlawful for an employer to discharge or discriminate against any individual for opposing any practice, or because of involvement in any proceeding, related to the FMLA

An employee on FMLA leave is not protected from actions that would have affected the employee even if FMLA had not been taken. For example, if overtime for all employees has been decreased in the employee's absence, the employee would not be entitled to return to work with the original overtime hours.

An employer may not lay off an employee who is on FMLA leave unless the employer can demonstrate that the employee would not have been employed at the time of reinstatement irrespective of whether leave had been taken or not.

A special rule applies to key employees. A *key employee* is a salaried employee who is among the highest-paid 10% of all of the employer's employees within a seventy-five-mile radius. Employers do not have any greater right to refuse FMLA leave to a key employee than to other employees. An employer may have a right to refuse to reinstate a key employee following FMLA leave, however. To preserve this right, the employer must give two notifications to the employee, one near the beginning of the leave and one at the end. The employer must:

(1) Make a determination that "substantial and grievous economic injury" to the company's operations will occur if the employee is restored to his position after taking leave;
(2) Notify the employee that he is a key employee and that restoration will be denied;
(3) Give the employee a reasonable opportunity to return to work anyway;
(4) Make another "substantial and grievous economic injury" determination at the time the employee seeks to return to work after the leave;
(5) Notify the employee of its decision to deny reinstatement and the reason for the denial.

"Substantial and grievous injury" is a difficult standard to meet. The injury must be one that would be caused by the employee's restoration upon returning from leave, not injury caused by the employee's absence. A claim that an employee is "too important" or valuable, or that the company "cannot afford" to allow him to go on leave, is not a valid reason for denying FMLA leave. Moreover, minor inconveniences consequent to reinstating an employee do not qualify as grievous injury. "Substantial and grievous injury" is a more stringent standard than the "undue hardship" exception to an employer's obligation to accommodate a disabled employee's disability under the ADA.

DISABILITY LEAVE

While the ADA does not specifically require employers to grant employees leave to accommodate disabilities, an employer may be required to grant a leave request if it is a reasonable accommodation for a disability and does not cause the employer undue hardship.

MILITARY LEAVE

USERRA allows employees who become active duty military to maintain their employment while they are on active military duty for an extended time. (See above.) They are entitled to paid military leave if, while on leave, their military compensation is less than the employee's pay. All employers must comply with USERRA.

JURY DUTY

The federal Jury System Improvements Act[44] prohibits all private employers from disciplining or firing any permanent employee who properly takes time off for federal jury duty. An employer may ask an employee to provide prompt notification of the need for jury duty leave, and may ask for proof of jury duty. Insurance and other benefits must continue while the employee is on jury duty, and employees must be reinstated to their positions without loss of seniority when they return. A company may request a postponement of an employee's jury duty if the employee's absence creates an undue hardship.

Every state except Montana requires employers to give employees time off when summoned for jury duty in a state or local court. Most prohibit employers from disciplining or firing an employee for missing work when summoned to serve on a jury. Most states only mandate unpaid leave, but a few states require paid jury duty leave. Several states prohibit employers from requiring employees to take vacation, sick, or other kinds of leave when called for jury duty. Some allow an employer to setoff from wages any compensation the employee receives for serving on a jury.

VOTING LEAVE

Most states require private employers to give employees time off to vote. In a number of states, the employer must pay the employee for this time. Even states that do not give employees voting leave rights have laws protecting them from employer influence, interference or intimidation with respect to their political opinions or their right to vote.

WORKERS' COMPENSATION LEAVE

Workers' compensation leave must be granted after an employee injury.

RELIGION LEAVE

Title VII of the Civil Rights Act protects employees from religious discrimination. In general, this means, among other things, that an employer with at least fifteen employees may be required to allow an employee to take leave for purposes of religious observation, if requested as a religious accommodation. An employer does not have to accommodate an employee's religious beliefs or practices if doing so would cause undue hardship to the employer. An accommodation may cause undue hardship if it is costly, compromises workplace safety, decreases workplace efficiency, infringes on the rights of other employees, or requires other employees to do more than their share of potentially hazardous or burdensome work.

COURT LEAVE

About one-half of the states have laws requiring employers to give employees time off to serve as witnesses, attend or prepare for court hearings.

OTHER KINDS OF LEAVE

Most states have laws comparable to the federal laws giving employees a right to certain kinds of leave. These laws often provide greater protections to employees than federal laws do. Some states, for example, extend family medical leave provisions similar to those in the FMLA to smaller employers. Some offer new parents more time to care for a newborn child. A few mandate some amount of employer-paid sick leave. Some establish a right to a kind of leave that federal laws do not mandate. For example, some states mandate a specified amount of unpaid time off to attend a child's school activities.

Collective bargaining and other employment contracts may provide more protections for employees than either state or federal laws do. And while no federal law mandates vacation, sick or other kinds of leave besides the ones described above, certain kinds of leave provisions are sometimes required to be included in contracts between a business and the federal government. The same is true of certain contracts between a private business and a state government.

Records

Every employer covered by the FLSA must keep records for each of its covered employees, as set forth in U.S. Department of Labor regulations. These must include accurate information about the employee and data about the hours worked and the wages earned, including:

- Full name
- Address, including zip code
- Birth date, if younger than nineteen
- Sex
- Occupation
- Time and day of week when employee's workweek begins
- Total wages paid each pay period
- Date of payment and the pay period covered by the payment.

The employee's name should be the same as it is listed for Social Security purposes. On the same record should be listed the employee's identifying symbol or number if such is used in place of name on any time, work, or payroll records.

For all employees other than salaried executive, administrative or professional employees (which includes teachers and academic administrative personnel in elementary and secondary schools) or outside sales employees who are exempt from FLSA minimum wage and overtime requirements, the following additional records must be maintained:

- Hours worked each day and total hours worked each workweek
- Basis on which employee's wages are paid (e.g., "$9 per hour," "$440 a week," "piecework")
- Regular hourly pay rate
- Total daily or weekly straight time earnings
- Total overtime earnings for the workweek
- All additions to or deductions from the employee's wages.

Payroll records, collective bargaining agreements, sales and purchase records must be preserved for at least three years. Records on which wage computations are based should be retained for two years (time cards and piece work tickets, wage rate tables, work and time schedules, and records of additions to or deductions from wages).

The EEOC and the Federal Trade Commission (FTC) also require certain records to be maintained. The EEOC requires all employment and personnel records (including both accepted and rejected applications for employment) to be kept for at least one year after the later of the date the record was made or the date a personnel action was taken. Educational institutions and public employers must keep these records for two years. A company that has 150 or more employees must maintain the records for two years if the company has a contract with the federal government of at least $150,000. If an employee files a charge of discrimination, then records must be maintained at least until the case is concluded.

When an employer makes a decision to dispose of records, the disposal must be performed securely. Throwing papers in a dumpster is not a secure method of disposal. Secure methods of disposal might include burning, pulverizing, or shredding paper documents. Digitally stored records must be disposed of in a way that causes the files to be unreadable and not capable of being reconstructed.

Safety and Health

OSHA requires employers to protect their employees from recognized hazards that are causing or are likely to cause death or serious physical harm. It is administered either by the Occupational Safety and Health Administration (also called OSHA) or by states pursuant to an OSHA-approved plan. About half of the states have OSHA-approved plans. State plans may cover a broader range of workplace hazards than OSHA regulations do.

Companies wishing to employ homeworkers in the manufacture of clothing, accessories or jewelry must provide written assurances to the Department of Labor that they will comply with FLSA requirements, including minimum wage and overtime pay laws. Home manufacture of women's clothing is prohibited unless age, disability, or a need to care for a disabled individual in the home prevents a worker from adjusting to factory work. A special certificate must be obtained.

POSTERS

Employers must display the general FLSA poster regarding employee rights, including minimum wage requirements, in their workplaces. Employers having workers who are employed under special minimum wage certificates authorized by the FLSA must display the Employee Rights for Workers with Disabilities Paid at Special Minimum Wages poster. An EPPA Notice must be displayed where employees and prospective employees can see it. Employers covered by OSHA must display the OSHA poster. Employers covered by the FMLA must display an FMLA poster. Agricultural employers must display the Migrant and Seasonal Agricultural Workers Protection Act[45] poster; and they must post the Employee Rights Under the H-2A Program poster if they hire temporary agricultural workers with H-2A visas.

An employer must provide the "Your Rights Under USERRA" Notice to all persons with rights protected by USERRA. Some businesses may be required to display the "Equal Employment Opportunity Is The Law" poster and a Pay Transparency Nondiscrimination Provision Notice. Additional poster requirements apply to federal contractors.

The FirstStep Poster Advisor, http://webapps.dol.gov/elaws/posters.htm, is a free online tool the U.S. Department of Labor provides to help businesses ascertain which posters they need. Posters may be downloaded at https://www.dol.gov/whd/resources/posters.htm. They are also available from commercial vendors.

Termination

The employment relationship may be terminated by either party at any time unless one of the following applies:

(a) The contract provides otherwise;
(b) It is public employment;
(c) The termination is discriminatory;
(d) The termination violates a whistleblower protection law;
(e) The termination is retaliatory;
(f) The termination is for the employee's refusal to take a polygraph test;
(g) The termination is against public policy.

Public employees are not at-will employees. They are generally protected by civil service statutes which require a showing of good cause before they may be fired. These statutes typically also provide detailed protections against other kinds of adverse employment actions, as well, such as suspension, demotion, reduction in pay, and various other kinds of disciplinary actions. Because a governmental body (state or federal) is the employer, employment decisions affecting a public employee are state action. As such, they must comply with First Amendment, Due Process and other constitutional requirements. Governmental bodies have greater power to regulate the speech and conduct of public employees than that of private individuals, but the power is not absolute.

If the employees of a company are unionized, then the terms and conditions of employment are specified in a collective bargaining agreement. Union contracts often contain provisions limiting an employer's power to terminate employees at will, such as a prohibition against termination except for good cause, a bona fide reduction in force, or the like.

Under the federal Employee Polygraph Protection Act, an employer may not fire an employee for refusing to take a polygraph test. Many states have enacted similar laws.

Whistleblower protection statutes prohibit firing an employee for reporting OSHA violations to the appropriate state or federal authority. There are also laws and court precedents in some states that bar an employer from firing an employee for other kinds of whistle blowing, such as reporting that the employer is engaged in illegal dumping of toxic materials, or other activity that is harmful to the public interest.

State and federal laws prohibit firing an employee on the basis of race, sex, or other protected classification. These laws also prohibit firing an employee in retaliation for complaining about discrimination.

The Immigration Reform and Control Act[46] prohibits employers from firing employees on the basis of their alien status if the employee is legally eligible for employment in the United States.

Courts and legislatures in several states have recognized a public policy exception to employment-at-will contracts in certain other situations, too. The public policy exception to employment at will has been held to prohibit termination of an employee for such things as:

(a) refusing to commit an illegal act
(b) exercising a legal right, such as the right to take a specified kind of leave
(c) performing an important civic obligation, such as preventing a violent crime in progress.

Courts in different states vary with respect to the extent to which they recognize these exceptions and how they interpret and apply them.

To avoid claims of unlawful termination, documenting the reasons for termination is a good idea (provided the reasons are legitimate, of course).

The Worker Adjustment and Retraining Notification Act[47] (WARN Act) requires employers to provide written notice sixty days in advance of covered plant closings or mass layoffs. This notice must be provided to either affected workers or their representatives (e.g., a labor union); to the State dislocated worker unit; and to the appropriate unit of local government. The WARN Act applies to employers with 100 or more full-time employees. A full-time employee is defined as one who works more than twenty hours per week and for at least six of the preceding twelve months. A plant closing occurs when an employment site is shut down and results in an employment loss of fifty or more full-time employees during any thirty-day period. A mass layoff is a layoff that results in an employment loss during any thirty-day period for at least 500 full-time employees, or for 50–499 full-time employees if they make up at least a third of the employer's active workforce. Notice is also required if the number of employment losses for two or more groups of workers, each of which is less than the minimum number needed to trigger notice, reaches the threshold level, during any ninety-day period, of either a plant closing or mass layoff. "Employment loss" refers only to long-term layoffs. Terminations for cause, voluntary quits, retirements, and short-term layoffs (under six months) are not considered employment losses. An employer is permitted to give less than sixty days notice in some circumstances. The notice is not required at all if the facility or project was a temporary one and the employees were hired with the understanding that their employment would be limited to the duration of the facility or project. Penalties for violating the WARN Act include back pay; civil penalties; attorney fees and costs.

An employment contract or a state law may also impose termination notice obligations.

Some provisions in an employment contract end when the employment terminates; others may survive. Care should be taken to ensure that the contract provides for the survival of important obligations (e.g., nondisclosure, noncompete, nonsolicitation, and forfeiture clauses) that relate, in whole or in part, to post-termination conduct.

Conducting exit interviews is a good idea. It may be prudent for an employer to require an employee to participate in one prior to departure from the company. It is an opportunity to require the employee to return company property, change passwords and disable access to company accounts, as well as to give the employee information about unemployment insurance, retirement plans, pensions, health plans, and so on.

It can be a good idea to have the employee sign a separation agreement covering these and other matters. Appropriate subjects for a separation agreement may include such things as severance pay, nondisparagement (employee agrees not to say bad things about the company), nondisclosure; noncompete, nonsolicitation, and other matters. It can also be a good idea to include a provision containing a release from any existing or future claims against the company.

Large companies often include a generous severance package in executive employment agreements. These packages, called "golden parachutes," are intended to encourage some amount of risk-taking. The idea is that a CEO or other high-level executive will be apt to make bolder decisions without the fear of being fired and left in a ruined financial condition hanging over his head.

Eligibility requirements for unemployment benefits vary by state, but in every state a person must have been employed for a specified period of time in order to qualify. In addition, the employee must not be at fault for the unemployment. An employee who quits without good cause is not eligible. What qualifies as good cause varies by state. An employee who is fired for misconduct usually is not eligible, either. Other grounds for denial of a claim include such things as refusing suitable work; being unavailable for suitable work; or the unemployment resulted from a labor dispute. Not all of these are valid grounds for denial of a claim in every state. Individual state laws vary. An employee has a right to appeal a denial of unemployment benefits. If an employee is fired for misconduct, the employer has the burden of proving that the termination was for misconduct as defined in applicable state law. If an employee quits, then the employee has the burden of proving that it was for good cause

Employee Speech

The First Amendment protects individuals against governmentally imposed restrictions on speech. It does not forbid a private company from imposing restrictions on their employees' speech. Unless an employment contract provides otherwise, a private employer may discipline or fire an employee for speech that would be constitutionally protected if the restriction was imposed by a government entity or official. The speech of public employees, on the other hand, is constitutionally protected, provided it is about a matter of public concern.

Because employees are agents of their employers, people to whom an employee communicates a statement may mistakenly believe it to be one that is made on behalf of the employer. This can sometimes be embarrassing or problematic for a business. For this reason, an employer may find it prudent to include a "Blogging and Comments" policy in its employee handbook (or directly in the employment contact if it does not incorporate a handbook by reference) to require employees to include a disclaimer to the effect that the views the employee expresses are her own and not those of the company.

NATIONAL LABOR RELATIONS ACT

An employer's power to control an employee's speech activities is not absolute. The NLRA guarantees employees the right to organize and to bargain collectively with their employers or to refrain from such activities. The Act, which generally applies to all employers involved in interstate commerce, implements the national labor policy of assuring free choice and encouraging collective bargaining as a means of maintaining industrial peace. The NLRA also extends rights to employers, protecting commercial interests against unfair actions committed by labor organizations, and extends rights to labor organizations, protecting organizational and collective bargaining representative interests against unfair actions committed by employers.

The NLRA also prohibits an employer from restricting an employee's right to talk about wages or working conditions with other employees. Also, an employer may not prohibit an employee from telling other people who his employer is. Thus, an employer cannot restrict an employee's right to post comments about wages and working conditions to social media or a blog. The Act does not protect an employee from being terminated or disciplined for merely griping about the employer, the company, or the job, if the complaint is not about wages or working conditions.

The NLRA only provides protection for concerted activity by multiple employees. Posting to a website or blog to which no coworkers are connected does not qualify for NLRA protection. An employer may lawfully discipline or fire an employee for complaining on her own behalf without any intended or actual group action to improve working conditions.

The NLRA does not protect employees from being fired or disciplined for making threats of physical violence. And the NLRA does not protect an employee from being fired or disciplined for making a statement that constitutes a violation of the employment agreement. For example, if an employment contract prohibits an employee from disclosing trade secrets, then the NLRA does not prohibit the employer from firing or disciplining the employee for doing that.

The NLRA does not apply to certain categories of employees. Agricultural workers, domestic servants, the spouse of an employer, and supervisory employees are excluded from its protections. Thus, the NLRA does not protect the speech activities of a company's president or other managerial officers.

WHISTLEBLOWER PROTECTIONS

In some circumstances, employees are protected from retaliatory action for reporting illegal, unethical or other improper activity, or unsafe or unhealthy conditions. The SOX Act makes it a crime to knowingly retaliate against any person, including interfering with the person's employment, for providing law enforcement any truthful information relating to any federal offense. The FLSA prohibits employers from firing an employee in retaliation for the employee testifying against the employer in a trial or hearing. The False Claims Act[48] prohibits employers from retaliating against employees who report or disclose fraud in the employer's dealings in connection with a federal contract. OSHA and other federal statutes provide whistleblower protections in other circumstances, as well.

At the state level, laws prohibit terminating an employee in retaliation for disclosing any activity that is dangerous to the public. Some states have extended whistleblower protections to employees who disclose illegal conduct, whether it is dangerous or not. Others have not.[49]

State and federal laws imposing obligations on employers for the protection of employees, such as occupational safety and anti-discrimination laws—typically prohibit an employer from retaliating against an employee for reporting a violation.

Employee Privacy Rights

The increased use of the Internet in workplaces has brought the subject of employee privacy rights to the fore. To what extent may an employer access or demand to know the content of an employee's email and Internet postings? Of course, an employer may fire an at-will employee who refuses to allow access to his email and disclose all of his Internet activity. The more difficult question is: May an employee sue for invasion of privacy if the employer accesses and views the employee's email without the employee's permission?

A common law cause of action for invasion of privacy might be difficult to sustain if the employer provides the email account and server on which email messages are stored. A cause of action for invasion of privacy requires proof of both a subjective and an objectively reasonable expectation of privacy. Even if the employee subsequently moves an email message from the server to a personal password-protected folder, the fact that the message was, at one time, on a server that the employer could access makes an employee's expectation of privacy in the email unreasonable. Even in the unlikely event a court were to find that an employee had a reasonable expectation of privacy in email messages sent or received on company equipment using a company-provided email account, it is not likely to find an employer's reading of employee emails to be "highly offensive" if the employer's purpose is to prevent illegal, harassing, discriminatory or unprofessional activity.

The fact that an employee uses company-provided equipment to send and receive email messages is not necessarily dispositve of the privacy issue. An employee may have a reasonable expectation of privacy in email messages sent and received to and from the employee's personal email account (such the employee's own Yahoo! email account) on a company-provided computer, at least where the employee has not knowingly saved her account password or copies of the messages to the hard drive of the company's computer.[50]

The Electronic Communications Privacy Act[51] (ECPA) establishes some protections for email messages and other electronic communications. Its requirements are enforceable criminally and civilly. Title I prohibits the intentional interception of an electronic communication and also prohibits the disclosure or use of an electronic communication that is known to have been intercepted in violation of the ECPA. Title II (also known as the Stored Communications Act) prohibits unauthorized access to a stored communication. It also prohibits unauthorized disclosure of the content of a stored communication.

Under the ECPA, a communication is capable of being intercepted only while it is in transit. Accordingly, accessing email messages residing on a server cannot violate Title I, but might violate Title II. Thus, accessing email messages which have been sent and received by a mail server but not yet opened by the recipient would not violate Title I but could violate Title II.

There are three major exceptions to the ECPA:

(a) The sender or the recipient of the communication consents.
(b) Interception by means of a device provided by a communications provider or subscriber and done in the interceptor's ordinary course of business is permitted, provided the interception is not by surreptitious means.
(c) Providers of communications services may acquire information in the ordinary course of business. For example, Internet Service Providers (ISPs) are allowed to monitor activity to ensure adequate service.

The consent exception allows an employer to intercept, access, use and divulge electronic communications intended for the employee, but only if the employee who gives consent is a user of the electronic service. If an employer obtains Employee *A*'s consent to use Employee *A*'s password to gain access to Employee *B*'s password-protected website, the requisite consent will not exist unless Employee *A* has actually used the password to access the website. Until that happens, Employee *A* is not a user of the electronic communication service.[52]

An employer invoking the business extension exception is only allowed to intercept long enough to determine if the communication is employment-related. Once it is determined that the communication is personal, the employer must cease any further interception.

Some courts have held that an employer that provides the computers, terminals and software that enable employees to send and receive electronic communications is a provider of communication services and therefore is exempt from the ECPA.[53] Other courts have come to the opposite conclusion. If an employer is uncertain whether this exception applies or not, obtaining employee consent to the employer's access and interception of electronic communications might be a good idea.

The ECPA does not preempt state laws that provide greater protection of employee privacy. Some states—California, Illinois, and others—have enacted privacy laws that require the consent of all parties to the communication. Some states require an employer to give an employee advance notice before monitoring electronic communications. This might be done by including an appropriate provision in a written policy or handbook that is distributed to employees.

Some states have gone in the opposite direction, granting greater protection to employers than to employees. Nebraska, for example, gives employers the right to intercept, disclose, and use electronic communications in the ordinary course of business.

Consent may be either express or implied. Consent to the interception, access to, or use or disclosure of an employee's email message may be implied if the employer has given the employee prior notice that it will monitor the employee's Internet usage and email.

Provisions an employer could consider including in an employment contract (or in an employee handbook that is incorporated by reference into an employment contract) to reduce the risk of liability for violating employee privacy rights include:

(a) agreement that employee email messages, voicemail messages and other Internet communications during company time, on company-provided equipment, and/or using a company-provided service (such as an employer-provided email account), are not private, and may be monitored, intercepted, accessed, used and disclosed by the employer
(b) agreement that employee email messages, voicemail messages and other Internet communications on company-provided equipment are not private, and may be monitored, intercepted, accessed, used and disclosed by the employer even if the employee uses a personal web-based account or a third party service (such as Yahoo!) to send or receive them
(c) agreement that email messages, voicemail messages and other Internet communications sent or received on company-provided equipment—whether using a company-provided email (or other electronic communications) account or a personal web-based email (or other) account or one provided by a service provider other than the employer (such as Yahoo!)—may be stored on the equipment and the employer has a right to access, use and disclose them even if the employee uses a password or access code that is kept secret from the employer and is not stored on company equipment
(d) notice that the contents of email and other electronic communications may be forensically retrieved and read by the company
(e) agreement that agents and employees of the company may access and disclose an employee's electronic communications for any lawful purpose
(f) description of how an employee's online activities may be monitored
(g) notice and agreement that employees may use company-provided equipment only for conducting company business, and that any communications using such equipment—whether they are sent, received or stored using a company-provided service, on one hand, or a third party service (such as Yahoo!), on the other—are the property of the company

(h) notice and agreement that employees are not permitted to use company-provided equipment or services to access Internet websites for purposes unrelated to company business

(i) agreement that employees may not use company-provided equipment or services to send, receive or post discriminatory or offensive material, or to access web sites containing such material

(j) notice that employees are prohibited from accessing other employees' email, voicemail or other electronically stored documents except for a legitimate business purpose.

Be sure to define what the "legitimate business purposes" are. These might include such things as performance of an employment duty when the employee in question is not available to do it; investigation into possible criminal activity, security violations or violations of company policy; compliance with a subpoena; recovery from system failures; business emergency. Others should be added, as appropriate.

Provisions like the ones described above serve two purposes: (1) they make it difficult for an employee to credibly claim he had a reasonable expectation of privacy in electronic communications; and (2) they establish a consent defense.

Courts generally agree that they are effective for this purpose, even as applied to an employee's communications with the employee's attorney. In *Stengart v. Loving Care Agency*,[54] however, the New Jersey Supreme Court suggested, in dictum, that the confidentiality of certain kinds of communications is so important that not even a bulletproof employment contract would give an employer a right to access and read them. That case involved a company that accessed and read communications between an employee and her attorney. The reasoning of this case arguably could be applied to any relationship in which client communications are legally protected—attorney-client, doctor-patient, psychotherapist-client, accountant-client, clergy-penitent. It is not clear how influential the *Stengart* dictum is or will be in other jurisdictions. Many courts continue to analyze cases involving these kinds of communications no differently from the way they analyze cases involving other kinds of communications. To these courts, provisions like the ones listed above either prevent a finding that the employee's expectation of privacy was reasonable or operate as a waiver of the confidentiality of any messages communicated in the indicated ways. It is possible, however, that even these courts might refuse to enforce a contract that is so broadly worded that it is not justified by any legitimate business need or interest, such as a clause purportedly giving an employer a right to intercept, access and disclose email messages that the employee sends or receives on the employee's own time using the employee's own equipment and the employee's personal email account.

Including language permitting employees to occasionally use company-provided equipment or services to send personal messages can be problematic from a legal point of view. It may result in a court finding the contract to be ambiguous about whether such messages are company property or an employee's personal property.[55] Many courts construe employment contracts narrowly and against the employer. Employers therefore have a motivation to ensure that provisions like these are comprehensive, detailed and clear.

For more information about the ECPA, see Chapter 17.

Because public employers are state actors, they need to be more cautious about monitoring employee email and Internet activity. A public employer who violates a public employee's privacy rights may be liable to the employee for violating the employee's constitutional rights in a Section 1983 lawsuit. Public employees have a reasonable expectation of privacy in their workplace computers and email, but the employer may have a legitimate reason to intrude on this privacy in some circumstances. Courts apply a balancing test to determine whether a public employer's intrusion on a public employee's privacy is justified by a legitimate purpose.

Employers have broader freedom to monitor employee activity in the United States than in European countries. In Europe, an employer who monitors employee email or Internet activity without prior notice to the employee may be liable for violation of the employee's privacy rights in the European Court of Human Rights.

Vicarious Liability

Employees are agents. As such, their employers are vicariously liable for conduct occurring during the course and within the scope of the employment. For example, if an employee infringes a copyright or defames someone while conducting the employer's business, the employer may be held liable for it. Accordingly, an employer should implement supervisory measures to reduce the risk that an employee will engage in actionable misconduct while on the job. Among other things, this could include imposing controls on an employee's access and use of the Internet. Specific prohibitions against activities that increase the risk of liability could be included in the employment contract and/or employee handbook. These might include restrictions against copying and pasting material from other websites (high potential for copyright infringement), cyberstalking, posting defamatory content, browsing adult websites and so on.

Printing and distributing an Internet Use Policy and training employees to understand and follow it can help reduce the risk of liability.

Filtering software and regular oversight of employee online activity can help, too. Monitoring of employee email and Internet use is not only important to reduce the risk of liability for sexual harassment or other kinds of employment discrimination, but also to prevent employees from committing crimes and torts, misappropriating the company's trade secrets or other intellectual property, and the like. An employer should give notice and secure an employee's consent to such monitoring, preferably as part of the contract of employment, or in an Internet Use Policy that is incorporated into such a contract by reference.

An employer normally is not liable for an employee's crimes unless the employer directed or ratified the employee's criminal activity.

Fiduciary Duties

As agents of their employers, employees owe an implied fiduciary duty of loyalty to their employers. This means that an employee has a legal obligation to act for the employer's benefit in all matters connected to the employment.

An employee may not compete with the employer, use work time to further the employee's own interests, or solicit the employer's customers or employees for his own or another person's competing business prior to leaving the employment. An employee may not misappropriate confidential information or trade secrets of the employer by sharing them with others. An employee must account for profits and deal fairly with the employer in all transactions between them. An employee must try to avoid conflicts of interest and must disclose their existence to the employer. Information adverse to the employer's interests must also be disclosed, if it becomes known to the employee. Some duties continue to exist even after the employment is terminated. A former' employee's use of information gained during the employment to benefit a competing business may be a breach of fiduciary duty, for example.

Despite these obligations, most courts hold that it is not a breach of fiduciary duties to seek employment with a competitor or to start up a competing business while still employed, provided the employee does not (a) solicit the employer's customers or other employees to leave the company; (b) use company time to prepare to compete or to work for a competitor; or (c) actually start competing or working for a competitor while still employed. So long as the employee does not do any of these things, she also does not have a fiduciary duty to disclose to her employer that she is preparing to work for a competitor or to start a competing business.

At least one court has held that an employee does not breach the fiduciary duty to disclose adverse information by failing to tell the employer about another employee who is preparing to work for a competitor or to start a competing business.[56]

Employees also have a fiduciary duty to act with reasonable care on the employer's behalf, in accordance with industry standards.

An employment contract can impose stricter obligations upon an employee than fiduciary duties would otherwise require. For example, an employer may include a noncompete agreement in the employment contract. Provided it is reasonably limited in scope temporally and geographically, these kinds of agreements usually are enforceable.

Independent Contractors

Many of the legal obligations and liabilities a company incurs when it hires an employee do not apply when it uses an independent contractor instead. A company does not have to withhold and pay taxes on payments made to independent contractors. An employer is bound by contracts entered into by its employees and is liable for torts committed by them within the scope and course of the employment. A business normally is not bound by contracts entered into by an independent contractor when the business is not a party to the contract. An independent contractor owes implied duties of good faith and fair dealing, but it does not owe fiduciary duties to the business with which it contracts. And except when a business induces, facilitates or incurs contributory liability for them in some other way, it normally is not liable for torts committed by independent contractors, either.

The label that a business attaches to a worker is not determinative for legal purposes. The IRS and courts will examine the level of control and independence to determine whether a particular worker is an employee or an independent contractor. The more control a business has over a worker, the more likely the worker is to be classified as an employee rather than an independent contractor. Factors relevant to this determination include:

(a) the extent to which the company controls what the worker does and how the worker does her job
(b) the extent of the company's right to control the worker
(c) how the worker is paid (upon completion of a job vs. wage or salary)
(d) whether the company reimburses expenses
(e) whether the company or the worker provides tools, equipment, and the like
(f) whether benefits like health and/or retirement plan, vacation pay, etc. are provided

(g) whether the work performed is a key aspect of the business
(h) whether the relationship will continue after the completion of a single task or not
(i) the terms of the agreement between the parties.

No single factor is determinative.

Because of the increased responsibilities and potential liabilities that a business takes on when it has employees, care should be taken to preserve the independent status of nonemployees with whom a business contracts. Resellers of a company's products or services are at particular risk of being classified as agents or employees. For this reason, a contract with a reseller should prohibit the reseller from holding himself out to others as an agent or employee of the business. The relationship should be terminated immediately if the reseller engages in any conduct to suggest the existence of an employment or agency relationship with the business.

An independent contractor may be an individual or a business entity. *Outsourcing*, whereby a business subcontracts some of its operations to another business, is an example of an independent contractor relationship. *Offshoring* involves moving all or a portion of a company's operations to a different country. To the extent the operations are performed by a separate legal entity (e.g., a subsidiary corporation), the arrangement is essentially a form of outsourcing. These practices enable companies to access cheap labor and fewer regulatory compliance requirements. With the advent of the Internet and e-commerce, a large and growing number of companies are outsourcing and offshoring.

Employment Taxes

A business must withhold federal and state income taxes, pay Social Security and Medicare taxes, and pay unemployment taxes on compensation paid to its permanent employees. Employers must withhold Social Security and Medicare taxes from the employee and pay a matching amount. Unemployment taxes are reported and paid separately from federal income tax, Social Security and Medicare taxes.

The amounts to withhold and pay are determined by using the information on the employee's W-4 Form and withholding tables provided by federal and state taxing authorities. The amounts withheld must be deposited with the taxing authority. At the end of the year, an employer must report all wages, tips, and other compensation paid to each employee (a) to whom remuneration, including both cash and noncash payments, totaled $600 or more for the year; or (b) for whom any income, Social Security or Medicare tax was withheld during the year (or would have been withheld but for the fact that the employee claimed exemption from withholding or claimed more than one withholding allowance). The W-2 Form is used for this purpose. A copy must be provided to the employee, as well. Form W-3 is used to transmit W-2 forms to the Social Security Administration.

Employers must pay federal and state unemployment taxes for each employee from company funds. They may not withhold it from employee pay or require employees to pay it.

A permanent employee is one who is hired directly by the company. A person who is employed by an employment agency that farms employees out to other companies on a contract basis is called a *temporary* worker. Since it is the employment agency that pays temporary workers, it is the employment agency that is responsible for withholding and paying taxes.

Withholding taxes are not imposed on payments made to independent contractors, but a business must file a Form 1099–MISC for every independent contractor that is paid more than $600 in a calendar year. A copy must be provided to the contractor, as well.

The IRS is not required to accept a company's classifications of its workers at face value. The nature of the relationship of the parties, not the label the parties affix to it, is determinative. If the IRS determines an "independent contractor" is really more like an employee, then it may treat the person as a permanent employee for tax purposes. If a "temporary" worker works for the same company for months, the IRS may classify the employee as a permanent employee of the company rather than as an employee of the employment agency.[57] Either of these determinations can have serious financial consequences for the company, including liability to the workers and liability to the IRS for back employment taxes, penalties and interest—even if the worker has already paid the taxes in full.

A company that is unsure about whether a worker is an employee or an independent contractor may file Form SS-8 to request a determination from the IRS.

IRS Publication 15, *Employer's Tax* Guide, and Publication 15–A, *Employer's Supplemental Tax Guide*, explain employment tax requirements in more detail.

Chapter 5. Franchises

A franchise is a contractual arrangement in which an established business—usually one with a strong or well-known brand—authorizes another person to sell its products or services. It has the following characteristics:

- Substantial association with a trademark
- Marketing plan, community of interest or significant control
- Payment of a fee.

The fee may take the form of a flat fee, a royalty, or a combination of both. The terms the parties use to describe the fee are ("assistance fee," "consulting fee," etc.) are not controlling. What matters is whether the fee must be paid in order to qualify for the right to operate, or to continue operating, the business. Under the FTC's Franchise Rule,[58] payments totaling less than $570 during the first six months are exempt; such payments will not result in a finding of a payment of a fee for purposes of determining whether the arrangement is a franchise or not. State laws typically have similar laws exempting de minimis fee payments. Payment of a bona fide wholesale price for goods for resale does not qualify as a payment of fee for purposes of determining whether an arrangement is a franchise, either, provided the purchaser is not required to buy more than what a reasonable businessperson would buy for inventory.

"Substantial association with a trademark" usually takes the form of a license to the franchisee to use the franchisor's trademark(s). A trademark license is not a sine qua non for a franchise, however. Courts have found a franchise to exist even where the franchisor had not granted a license to the franchisee to use a trademark. In most cases, though, the "substantial association with a trademark" element is satisfied by a company's grant of a trademark license.

The "marketing plan" factor is the most important of the three. In most states, a franchise will not be found to exist unless the arrangement is set up in a way that gives the alleged franchisor the right to prescribe a marketing plan for the alleged franchisee. To support a finding of a franchise on this basis, the alleged franchisor must exert a substantial amount of control over the alleged franchisee's operation. Merely making a few suggestions about a small number of aspects of an alleged franchisee's operation of the business will not suffice.

Factors that are considered in determining whether a marketing plan has been prescribed include such things as:

- whether the alleged franchisor provides an operations manual and/or promotional material
- whether the alleged franchisor provides training and/or sets training standards
- how much freedom the alleged franchisee has to make decisions without needing the alleged franchisor's approval.

Some states apply a "community of interest" test rather than a "marketing plan" test. These states require interdependent and continuing financial interests between the parties before a franchise relationship will be found to exist. Relevant factors include such things as::

- the amount of revenue attributable to the alleged franchisor's goods or services
- the amount of time spent dealing in the alleged franchisor's goods or services
- the length of the parties' business relationship
- the grant of a geographically limited sales territory
- the grant and use of a trademark license
- the proportion of the alleged franchisee's advertising expenditures for the alleged franchisor's products or services
- the proportion of the alleged franchisee's personnel that concentrate on marketing the alleged franchisor's goods or services
- the nature and extent of the parties' contractual obligations
- investments in inventory and facilities
- investment in goodwill
- the nature and extent of services provided by the alleged franchisor to the alleged franchisee.

The FTC applies a third standard: whether the alleged franchisor exerts significant control over the alleged franchisee's operations, or provides significant assistance with respect to the method of operation of the business. Relevant indicia of significant control include such things as:

- Specifying site design or appearance
- Providing an operations manual
- Designating hours of operation
- Specifying production techniques
- Requiring participation in promotional campaigns
- Conducting training programs
- Imposing required accounting methods.

New York only requires two things: (a) payment of a fee, and (b) either substantial association with a trademark or a marketing plan.

The label the parties give to their contract is not controlling. A contract that the parties denominate a "trademark license agreement" may be treated in law as establishing a franchise if the necessary elements of a franchise exist under applicable law. Because franchises are subject to strict regulatory requirements and enforcement, care needs to be taken when drafting documents—especially trademark licenses—to ensure they will not accidentally result in the establishment of a franchise.

Unlike a partnership, a franchisor and a franchisee do not owe fiduciary duties to each other. Franchisees normally are not considered agents or employees of the franchisor. Thus, a franchisor generally is not vicariously liable for the acts or omissions of their franchisees. A claim based on vicarious liability might succeed, though, in the rare case where a franchisor exerts supervisory control over the day-to-day operations of a particular franchise location.

Disclosure Requirements

The FTC's Franchise Rule requires a franchisor to provide prospective franchisees with a Financial Disclosure Document (FDD). It must contain a wide range of information about such things as the franchisor's officers and directors, history of litigation, bankruptcies, parent and affiliate organizations, in addition to the franchisor's financial statements and specific details about the obligations of the parties to the franchise contract. As detailed as this document is, it does not satisfy more extensive state law disclosure requirements. For this reason, most franchisors choose to use the Uniform Franchise Offering Circular (UFOC), which is acceptable in all registration states.

A franchisor must give the UFOC to the prospective franchisee at their first face-to-face meeting to discuss sale of a franchise, or ten business days before the franchisee signs an agreement or pays money to the franchisor, whichever is earlier. The franchisor must furnish a copy of the franchise agreement at least five business days before the prospective franchisee signs the agreement or pays money to the franchisor. It must not have any terms, or portions of terms, left blank.

A franchisor generally may not provide information to a franchisee from which a range of sales, income or profit may be ascertained unless it makes a financial performance representations disclosure (FPR) in its FDD. In the absence of an FPR, a franchisor may only refer prospective franchisees to existing franchisees and to the franchisee's advisors to find this information

The FTC enforces the Franchise Rule with injunctions and cease and desist orders. The FTC may also pursue civil and criminal penalties. Officers, directors and people with controlling interests in the franchisor may be held individually liable for violations. There is no private right of action to enforce the Franchise Rule.

Registration

Franchises do not need to be registered with the FTC. Registration may be required at the state level, though. States with registration requirements include California, New York and a number of others. A person wishing to sell a franchise in one of these states must register prior to selling.

Registration entails filing the UFOC and paying a fee. It is usually valid for one year. In some states, annual renewals are required. Periodic reports may also be required. Several states also require a franchisor to file detailed information about the individuals who will be selling franchises on the franchisor's behalf in the state. If any material facts change after a UFOC has been filed, then the franchisor must file an amendment to update it.

Advertising Franchise Offers

The FTC and state agencies regulate advertisements of franchise offers. Some states require franchisors to file copies of advertisements with the state before publishing them. The FTC may bring an enforcement action against a franchise offeror if the advertisement contains false or misleading representations. States also have this power. An advertisement may not characterize the franchise as a safe investment or suggest that state registration means the state has approved it.

Business Opportunity and Seller-Assisted Marketing Plans

Business opportunity sales and seller-assisted marketing plans are subject to the FTC's Business Opportunity Rule[59] and similar state laws and regulations. These impose disclosure and registration requirements similar to those that exist for franchises. In some cases, a franchise arrangement might also come within the definition of a seller-assisted marketing plan or business opportunity sale. To avoid duplicative filings, a state may provide an exemption for franchises that are in compliance with the FTC's Franchise Rule. Disclosure requirements for business opportunity offerings are discussed in Chapter 15.

Rights of Franchisees and Franchisors

Nearly half of the states have enacted laws governing the rights and obligations of franchisors and franchisees. Some of these apply generally to all kinds of franchises; others are specific to particular industries—automobile dealerships; alcoholic beverage distributorships; etc. A principal objective of these laws is to protect franchisees from some of the consequences of the imbalance of power between franchisors and franchisees. They tend to focus on protecting franchisees from unscrupulous franchisors.

These laws typically prohibit a franchisor from terminating a franchise agreement except for good cause, which may include the franchisee's:

- Insolvency
- Bankruptcy
- Abandonment of operations
- Conviction of a crime related to the franchise operations
- Material breach of the franchise agreement.

Typically, the franchisor must give written notice a specified number of days in advance of the termination. In the case of a breach of the franchise agreement, these laws typically require the franchisor to give the franchisee an opportunity to cure the default.

A few states prohibit discrimination by a franchisor against similarly situated franchisees.

Several states restrict a franchisor's right to refuse to renew a franchise, either treating a refusal to renew as a termination or imposing statutory conditions on a franchisor's refusal to renew (such as a requirement of advance notice or waiver of noncompete provisions). Some states require a franchisor to repurchase a franchisee's assets upon termination or nonrenewal, under some circumstances.

Some states allow private causes of action as well as enforcement by a state agency in cases involving a franchisor's violation of a franchisee's rights under state law.

In California, Minnesota and several other states, a franchisor may not refuse to allow the franchisee to transfer the franchise unless the franchisor has good cause for the refusal. These states often give the franchisor a right of first refusal to purchase the franchise before the franchisee transfers it to another.

SALES TERRITORIES

Franchise contracts typically grant the franchisee a right to operate only within a specified territory. They also usually contain nonexclusivity provisions reserving to the franchisor the right to distribute its goods and services through other channels. Some states restrict a franchisor's encroachment on a franchisee's sales territory, that is, the use of distribution channels other than the franchisee in a way that diminishes the franchisee's market share.

In *Scheck v. Burger King*[60] a court held that a franchisor does not necessarily have a right to distribute its products or services using an outlet in close proximity to the franchisee's location unless the right to do so is expressly retained in the contract. This is true, the court held, even if the contract is clear that the franchise and associated licenses are nonexclusive. Courts often resolve ambiguities in a contract against the party who was primarily responsible for drafting it. In most cases, that would be the franchisor. A franchisor's encroachment on a franchisee's sales territory may be a breach of the implied covenants of good faith and fair dealing.

For these reasons, franchises are not a natural fit for e-commerce. Unless the franchise agreement expressly permits it, a franchisee who sells the franchised products or services to customers that are outside the franchisee's sales territory may be in breach of the franchise contract. By the same token, a franchisor who establishes a web site and proceeds to take online orders from customers in the franchisee's sales territory may be liable for encroachment. A franchise agreement should be drafted in a way that addresses the rights and obligations of the parties with respect to online sales.

MODIFICATIONS

Modifications of franchise agreements generally are governed by the same legal principles that apply to the modification of any contract. Modifications normally must be supported by new consideration, and contract clauses requiring all modifications to be in writing normally are enforceable.

California requires a franchisor to register a proposed modification with the state and to provide a written disclosure statement to the franchisee at least five days before the modification is signed. Registration of a modification is not required if it does not substantially and adversely impact the franchisee's rights, obligations, benefits or privileges under the franchise agreement. Even if a modification does adversely impact a franchise, registration is not required if it is executed within a year of the original franchise agreement, does not waive any of the franchisee rights that are protected by California law, and the franchisee either receives the complete modification at least five days prior to signing it or is given a right to rescind it within five days of signing it. To qualify for this exemption from registration, the modification must either be: (a) made in connection with the resolution of a bona fide dispute between the parties, and not offered on a systemwide basis; or (b) offered on a voluntary basis to fewer than 25% of the franchisees in the system within any twelve-month period. California's registration and disclosure requirements are triggered only if the modification is a material one. A change that is made in accordance with a discretionary power expressly reserved to the franchisor under the franchise agreement is not a material modification of the agreement.

As with other kinds of contracts, there are circumstances in which a party to a franchise contract may be estopped from denying the validity of an unwritten modification even though the contract says that all modifications must be in writing. In *Ralph's Distributing Company v. AMF, Inc.*,61 for example, it was held that an unwritten modification of a franchise agreement may occur where a franchisee detrimentally relies on the franchisor's conduct subsequent to the agreement. In that case, a snowmobile franchise agreement was silent as to whether the franchisee's salea territory was exclusive or not. There was evidence that once the franchisor designated a distributor for a territory, it would not assign other distributors to the same area. The franchisee expended considerable money on promotional activities in reliance on an expectation that his sales territory was exclusive. Under these circumstances, the court held that the franchisee was entitled to rely on his reasonable expectation that the franchise agreement had been modified to include an exclusivity provision and that the franchisor would not assign other franchisees to his territory.

Most courts require more than proof of conduct consistent with a modification to support a claim of an unwritten modification that is based solely on conduct. These courts require, in addition, proof that the franchisor unequivocally intended to modify the franchise agreement. In *Haynes Trane Service Agency, Inc. v. American Standard, Inc.*[62] the Tenth Circuit Court of Appeals considered a franchisee's claim that an expressly at-will franchise contract had been modified into one allowing termination only for cause. There was no written modification. Instead, the franchisee sought to prove modification by course of conduct alone. The court held that evidence of a franchisor's pattern of citing a cause when terminating a franchise was not sufficient to prove the franchisor had an unequivocal intention to change its at-will franchise contracts into "termination for cause only" contracts. The court observed that it might have ruled differently had there been evidence of an intended policy to terminate only for cause, such as testimony that the franchisor believed it was contractually required to terminate only for cause.

Franchise contracts that are otherwise subject to the statute of frauds normally may be modified only in writing. Nevertheless, a court may bar a party from asserting the statute of frauds as a defense if it finds the party waived the right, or that the parties partially or fully performed the purported modification, or that grounds for the application of the estoppel doctrine exist. Grounds for applying the estoppel doctrine exist when a party makes a statement or engages in conduct that induces detrimental reliance of the part of the other party to the contract.

Franchise contracts sometimes provide that the franchisor may make changes to the franchise operation manual. This kind of clause is usually enforceable. In some situations, however, a court may be reticent to enforce such a unilateral change where it clearly benefits the franchisor to the franchisee's detriment.

WAIVER

A franchisor who fails to exercise a right promptly upon learning of a breach that triggers the right runs the risk of a subsequent court ruling that he has waived the right.

> **Example**. The franchise agreement requires the franchisee to make monthly payments to the franchisor. It further provides that failure to comply with this requirement is grounds for termination of the franchise. Despite this requirement, the franchisee is often a couple of weeks late with payments. The franchisor accepts them anyway. At some point, the franchisor decides it wants to assign part of the franchisee's exclusive territory to someone else. To get out of the original contract with the original franchisee, the franchisor terminates it on the grounds that the franchisee breached the contractual agreement to make timely monthly payments. If the case goes to court, the franchisor might be held to have waived the right to enforce strict compliance with the thirty-day requirement.

A *waiver* is the intentional relinquishment or abandonment of a known right. It occurs when a party knowingly fails to enforce a term of a contract or performs its obligations under the contract knowing that the other party has failed to perform. Temporary forbearance is not usually enough to establish waiver. If, upon receiving the first late payment, the franchisor in the Example had told the franchisee that it would accept an untimely payment "this one time but not in the future," then a court would be less likely to find that a waiver had occurred. A waiver may not be retractable if the other party has materially changed its position in reliance on it.

ESTOPPEL

Estoppel is an equitable defense that may be asserted to prevent a party to litigation from asserting an otherwise applicable defense, where allowing the defense to be asserted would be unjust. A court may hold that a party whose conduct (or inaction) induces reasonable reliance to the detriment of the other party is estopped from asserting certain kinds of defenses.

> **Example.** To celebrate a Super Bowl victory, fans loot a local 6–Eleven franchisee's establishment, making off with and/or destroying the store's entire inventory. Although the written franchise agreement says franchisees are responsible for the costs of restocking inventories, a 6–Eleven representative tells the franchisee it will reimburse the franchisee for these restocking costs. The franchisee proceeds to spend a considerable amount of his own money restocking the store's inventory. He submits the bill to the 6–Eleven franchisor. The franchisor refuses to pay, citing the terms of the written franchise agreement. The franchisee sues to enforce the oral promise. Although the contract or an applicable statute of frauds requires modifications to be in writing, a court might hold that 6–Eleven is estopped from asserting the defense. Of course, the franchisee will still need to prove that the oral promise was made.

RESTRICTIONS ON MODIFICATIONS AND WAIVERS

Franchise agreements may—and often do—include a clause that reads something like this:

> This Agreement is the entire agreement between the parties and supersedes all prior agreements between the parties regarding the subject matter of this agreement. It may be modified only by a writing signed by both parties. No waiver, amendment, release, or modification of this Agreement shall be established orally or by conduct, custom, or course of dealing, but solely by a written document signed by both parties.

Courts are split on the enforceability of this kind of provision in a franchise contract. In some states, courts generally enforce them. Courts in other states generally ignore them. Courts in most states take a middle ground, deciding the issue according to the facts and equities on a case-by-case basis. New York is representative of this approach. New York courts generally will enforce these clauses, but they recognize two exceptions: (a) where there has been partial performance that is unequivocally referable to an oral modification; or (b) where it is appropriate to apply the doctrine of equitable estoppel.[63] Under this approach, mere acquiescence in the other party's conduct that is not compliant with a term of the original contract is not enough to establish part performance that is unequivocally referable to a modification. In *KBQ, Inc. v. E.I. du Pont de Nemours & Co.*[64] a federal district court, applying Delaware law, held that the fact that a franchisor gave the franchisee opportunities to cure defects and spoke of a "long-term relationship" was not unequivocally referable to a modification of an expressly at-will franchise agreement into a "termination for cause only" agreement.

The principal takeaway from all of this is that a franchisor seeking to protect itself from claims of unwritten modifications or waivers should not stop at including a "no unwritten modifications or waivers" clause in the franchise agreement. It should also adopt a policy of ensuring that all modifications are, in fact, in writing. Any variance from the terms of a written contract that is not intended to serve as a modification should also be in writing, and should expressly state that the variance is a one-time forbearance that is not intended to modify the terms of the contract. These practices can help generate evidence that a franchisor established a course of conduct of requiring modifications to be in writing. For their part, franchisees should always get a franchisor's promises and representations in writing. And of course, both franchisors and franchisees should strive to act in conformity with the terms of their written contracts and forbearances.

RENEWAL

Renewal rights are not implied. They exist only if the agreement expressly provides for them. If a franchise agreement states that the franchisee has a right to renew, then a court will presume that the terms of the renewal franchise are the same as the existing franchise. A new agreement that materially changes the terms of an existing franchise agreement may be treated as a refusal to renew or a termination of the existing franchise, and the beginning of a new franchise. Substituting a nonexclusive franchise agreement for an exclusive one is an example.

Franchise agreements often contain a clause stating that when the term of a franchise expires, the franchisee will sign the franchisor's then current form of franchise agreement. They sometimes add that the agreement may contain terms that are materially different from the terms of this agreement. Although this kind of clause is not illegal, courts tend to be reluctant to require franchisees to sign a franchisor's then-current franchise agreement when it contains material changes that the franchisor unilaterally makes. This kind of clause might be unenforceable if the franchisor attempts to use it to bind the franchisee to onerous or unfair terms. Unduly burdensome and unfair new terms may breach the covenants of good faith and fair dealing that are implied by law in the original franchise agreement. Courts are not in agreement about this. In any case, a growing number of courts consider franchise agreements to be adhesion contracts. As such, enforcement of some of the terms (or in some cases, the entire contract) may be denied on the grounds of unconscionability if there was no negotiation and the terms are unduly onerous and unfair to a franchisee.

In addition to the common law doctrines of implied covenants and unconscionability, some states have enacted laws expressly regulating the right to renew a franchise. A Delaware law, for example, prohibits franchisors from including provisions in a franchise agreement that permit unjust renewal terms. Delaware law also does not allow a franchisor to unjustly refuse to renew the franchise of a franchisee with whom the franchisor has been dealing for two years or more. Wisconsin Statutes Section 135.03 (2017) is also exemplary. It provides that no franchisor "may terminate, cancel, fail to renew or substantially change the competitive circumstances of a dealership agreement without good cause. The burden of proving good cause is on the grantor." Tennessee requires a franchisor to give advance notice of an intention to refuse renewal, and requires a franchisor to have good cause for nonrenewal. Several other states have enacted other kinds of statutes protective of franchisees with respect to renewal rights.

A number of states require franchisors to deal with all of their franchisees in the same way, including with respect to renewal rights.

COVENANTS NOT TO COMPETE

The majority rule is that a noncompete clause in a franchise agreement is generally enforceable insofar as it restricts the franchisee from competing against the franchisor during the term of the franchise. Courts are split as to whether such clauses remain enforceable as a bar to competition after the franchise has ended. Several states require noncompete covenants to be reasonably limited as to duration and geographic scope. Among these states, some courts will reform an agreement that is defective in this respect to bring it into compliance; others will simply refuse enforcement of the noncompete covenant altogether. A few states have enacted statutes imposing specific restrictions and requirements on the use of noncompete clauses in franchise agreements.

ANTITRUST CONSIDERATIONS

Although there is earlier contradictory case law, more recent decisions hold that requiring franchisees to purchase supplies exclusively from the franchisor or from a source the franchisor approves does not violate antitrust laws. A small number of states, however, have adopted laws limiting a franchisor's right to require this.

MISCELLANEOUS RESTRICTIONS

A number of other restrictions and limitations are imposed on franchises. For example, clauses in franchise agreements purporting to require the use of an out-of-state forum for the resolution of disputes are unenforceable in some states, either by statute or judicial decision. Some states make it illegal for a franchisor to restrict free association among franchisees or to prohibit participation in a trade association. A person who is thinking about acquiring a franchise, or an e-commerce business that is considering the idea of offering franchises, should consult an attorney with knowledge and experience in franchise law.

Multi-Level Marketing

Multi-level marketing (MLM) is often mischaracterized as a form of franchising. Franchising and MLM are both distribution methods for a company's line of products or services, but they are structured differently. A franchisee is a business entity; MLM participants are independent sales representatives. Franchisees earn money by making direct sales to customers in their sales territory. MLM participants do, too, but they are not usually limited to a defined territory.

MLM participants are not employees. They have no base wage or salary. Their earnings depend entirely on the amount of revenue they raise by selling the product or service in question. A company that uses this method marketing does not directly recruit or hire a sales force. It relies on its existing sales force to recruit new salespeople. This process results in multiple levels of distributors along different down-lines. (A "down-line" is participant's network of her recruits, recruits of those recruits, and so on.)

Pyramid schemes require members to pay a fee to join to receive fees from other people they recruit to join. Because these schemes exploit people's mistaken belief that it is possible to get rich quick without actually performing a valuable service or selling a useful product, they are deemed inherently unfair and deceptive. As such, they are unlawful under the Federal Trade Commission Act[65] (FTC Act) and state laws.

MLM is not illegal per se, but it is an unlawful trade practice if the arrangement is structured like a pyramid scheme. For purposes of the FTC Act, an unlawful MLM structure is "characterized by the payment by participants of money to the company in return for which they receive (1) the right to sell a product and (2) the right to receive in return for recruiting other participants into the program rewards which are unrelated to the sale of the product to ultimate users."[66] Having a real product or service to sell does not necessarily make an MLM arrangement lawful. The determinative question is whether participants' earnings are based primarily on the number of distributors they recruit and their sales to these new recruits or whether they are based on sales to people outside the plan who intend to use the product or service. The defining characteristic of a pyramid scheme is a promise (express or implied) that a large profit may be made primarily by recruiting others to join the program rather than from (or only secondarily from) sales of actual products or services to members of the public.

Pyramid schemes often are set up to make it appear as if the purpose is to sell products to the public, when in reality the only significant market for the products is other participants in the program. Two common indicia of an unlawful pyramid scheme in disguise are inventory loading and the existence of few, if any, unconditional sales to members of the public. Inventory loading occurs when the arrangement requires new recruits to buy a large number of products at inflated prices. These kinds of arrangements garner rich rewards for the people at the top of the pyramid but leave the people at the bottom with depleted bank accounts and an inventory of products they can't sell. The more an MLM arrangement is structured to actually sell products or services to members of the public, without requiring these members of the public to pay anything extra or to join the MLM program, the more likely it is to be classified as a lawful MLM arrangement. The fact that participants primarily earn money by making commissions on sales to the public rather than by recruiting new MLM participants is another characteristic of a lawful MLM enterprise. Put another way, an MLM compensation structure that incentivizes participants to buy product and to recruit additional participants to buy product in order to advance in the marketing program rather than in response to consumer demand in the marketplace is likely to be an unlawful MLM program.

MLM offers must comply with truth-in-advertising requirements. Earnings claims may not be made unless the person making them complies with the FTC's substantiation requirements. If the arrangement amounts to an offer of a business opportunity, then the company must comply with the FTC's Business Opportunity Rule. See Chapter 15.

PONZI SCHEMES

A Ponzi scheme is an investment scheme in which a promoter persuades people to invest by promising sizable returns on their investments. The promise is kept only by obtaining money from new investors. Typically, no actual product or service is sold. These schemes collapse when not enough new investors can be found to ensure the existing ones receive their promised or expected returns. When this happens, most of the investors will not be able to recoup their losses. Many states make them illegal for this reason. Under the FTC Act, they are an unfair trade practice.

Chapter 6. Transfers of Business Interests

Ownership interests in a business are property. As such, they are capable of being transferred, although a contract or law may restrict certain kinds of transfers in some circumstances.

Transfers of Stock and Other Securities

Ownership interests in corporations are represented by shares of stock. A transfer of ownership of a corporation is accomplished by transferring shares of stock.

Congress has passed laws regulating transfers of stock. The SEC interprets and enforces these laws. States have also enacted laws regulating the issuance and sale of securities. These are known as blue sky laws. A principal purpose of all of these laws is to protect the public from making bad investment decisions on the basis of misinformation about a company or the value of its securities.

The Securities Exchange Act of 1934[67] regulates the trading of securities after they have been issued. It applies to buyers, sellers, dealers, brokers, brokerage firms, securities associations, national exchanges, and other entities that are involved in investor-to-investor sales. Among other things, the 1934 Act imposes the following requirements:

(a) Issuers whose securities are traded on a public exchange must register with the SEC, as must those who deal in such securities—brokers and national exchanges.
(b) Sellers of securities must make full disclosure of all pertinent, material information to potential buyers.
(c) Businesses must disclose information to their existing shareholders about the business's performance and of any changes in risk.

Section 10(b) is arguably the most important provision of the 1934 Act. It prohibits fraud in connection with the trading of securities:

> It shall be unlawful for any person, directly or indirectly, by the use of any means or instrumentality of interstate commerce or of the mails, or of any facility of any national securities exchange … [t]o use or employ, in connection with the purchase or sale of any security registered on a national securities exchange or any security not so registered, or any securities-based swap agreement any manipulative or deceptive device or contrivance in contravention of such rules and regulations as the [SEC] may prescribe as necessary or appropriate in the public interest or for the protection of investors.[68]

The antifraud provision of the Act applies to purchases and sales of securities whether they are traded on a public exchange or not.

RULE 10b-5

The SEC has adopted a regulation implementing Section 10(b). Known as Rule 10b-5,[69] it provides as follows:

> It shall be unlawful for any person, directly or indirectly, by the use of any means or instrumentality of interstate commerce, or of the mails or of any facility of any national securities exchange,
> (a) To employ any device, scheme, or artifice to defraud,
> (b) To make any untrue statement of a material fact or to omit to state a material fact necessary in order to make the statements made, in the light of the circumstances under which they were made, not misleading, or
> (c) To engage in any act, practice, or course of business that operates or would operate as a fraud or deceit upon any person,
> in connection with the purchase or sale of any security.

Rule 10b-5 has been construed as prohibiting any kind of activity or scheme that might deceive investors. Attempts to manipulate the market price of stock in order to make a profit on a resulting upturn or downturn in the market price usually come within the meaning of Rule 10b-5, particularly where the manipulation involves distributing or publishing materially false information about a company or a security.

Pump and dump is a colloquial expression for a kind of securities fraud in which a person makes false, misleading or grossly exaggerated statements about a company in which the person owns stock. Once the person has succeeded in boosting the stock price ("pump"), he sells his shares ("dump"), usually making a profit in the process.

Insider Trading

Rule 10b-5–1[70] defines securities trading by certain persons on the basis of material nonpublic information about the security or the issuer of the security as a kind of manipulative and deceptive device that the 1934 Securities Exchange Act and Rule 10b-5 prohibit. This applies to persons for whom such trading is a breach of a duty of trust or confidence that is owed, directly, indirectly or derivatively, to (a) the issuer of the security, (b) the shareholders of the issuer of the security, or (c) the source of the information.

There are two theories of insider trading liability: the classical theory and the misappropriation theory.

The classical theory, first articulated in *Chiarella v. United States*,[71] holds that a classic corporate insider (director or officer) who owes fiduciary duties to the corporation and its shareholders has a duty either to abstain from trading or to disclose such information before trading. This duty arises when a party to a securities transaction has information that the other party is entitled to know because of a fiduciary or similar relationship of trust and confidence between them, such as the relationship between the shareholders of a corporation and insiders who have obtained confidential information by reason of their position with the corporation. The duty to disclose or abstain arises in this kind of relationship because of the need to prevent a corporate insider from taking unfair advantage of shareholders.

Under the classical theory, people who do not have a fiduciary or similar relationship of trust with shareholders do not have the duty to disclose or abstain. Thus, in *Chiarella*, the Supreme Court held that a person who acquires inside information solely by virtue of his employment at a printing company that contracts with a corporation to print the corporation's financial reports does not have the Rule 10b-5 duty to disclose or abstain. A person who is employed by an independent printing company rather than by the corporation owes no fiduciary or other duties to the corporation's shareholders.

The classical duty to disclose or abstain is not limited to directors and officers. It also applies to temporary insiders. This includes anybody who has entered into a confidential relationship in the conduct of the business of the enterprise and is given access to information solely for corporate purposes. Examples of temporary insiders are the issuing corporation's attorney, accountant, underwriter, and consultants. A person who has entered into a confidentiality agreement that includes an agreement not to trade in the company's securities is also a temporary insider to whom the duty to disclose or abstain applies.

Corporate insiders who do not themselves trade on inside information, but who "tip" others to do so, may be guilty of insider trading. A tippee who trades on such information knowing that his source's disclosure of such information breaches a duty also violates the federal securities laws. Not only are insiders forbidden by their fiduciary relationship from personally using undisclosed corporate information to their advantage, but they also may not give such information to an outsider for the same improper purpose of exploiting the information for their personal gain. A tippee assumes a fiduciary duty to the shareholders of a corporation not to trade on material nonpublic information when the tippee's acquisition of material nonpublic information from an insider was a breach of the insider's fiduciary duty to shareholders and the tippee knows or should know it was a breach. On the other hand, a tippee's liability, being derived from that of the insider, does not breach a fiduciary duty to the shareholders if the insider does not personally benefit from the use of the information. Courts are split as to whether the tipper is also not liable in the absence of personal benefit.

The misappropriation theory does not require the existence of a fiduciary or other relationship between the shareholders of the issuing corporation and the person who is trading in the corporation's securities. The case establishing this basis of liability is *United States v. O'Hagan*.[72] An attorney for a law firm that was handling a tender offer for a company planning a takeover of a corporation acquired confidential information about the planned takeover and, on that basis, bought stock in the target corporation. Since he was not a director, officer or an attorney for the target corporation, he owed no fiduciary or other duty to its shareholders. The Court held that he was nevertheless guilty of securities fraud because he had misappropriated confidential information in breach of the law firm's fiduciary duty owed to the source of the information, namely, the company that was planning the takeover. In short, a person who has access to information as to which he owes someone a duty to keep secret is subject to the "disclose or abstain" duty if the information would affect the market price of the securities he trades were it to be revealed

Rule 10b-5–2[73] identifies some situations in which breach of a duty of confidence or trust will constitute misappropriation of confidential information triggering the duty to disclose or abstain. These include:

(a) There is an agreement to maintain information in confidence;

(b) The person communicating the material nonpublic information and the person to whom it is communicated have a history, pattern, or practice of sharing confidences, such that the recipient of the information knows or reasonably should know that the person communicating the information expects that the recipient will maintain its confidentiality; or

(c) A person receives or obtains such information from a spouse, parent, child, or sibling.

A person who receives or obtains the information from a spouse, parent, child or sibling and neither knows nor reasonably should know that the person communicating the information expected it to be kept confidential has no duty of trust or confidence with respect to the information.

Nonpublic information is material if it could affect a reasonable person's investment decision. Examples of information that might be considered material in some cases include: earnings information; mergers, acquisitions, tender offers, joint ventures, or changes in assets; new products or discoveries; developments regarding customers or suppliers; changes in control or in management; change in auditors or auditor notification that the issuer may no longer rely on an auditor's audit report; events regarding the issuer's securities—e.g., defaults on senior securities, calls of securities for redemption, repurchase plans, stock splits or changes in dividends, changes to the rights of security holders, public or private sales of additional securities; and bankruptcies or receiverships.

Rule 10b-5–1 provides that a person trades "on the basis of" material nonpublic information if the person is aware of the material nonpublic information when making the purchase or sale. The rule also sets forth several affirmative defenses or exceptions to liability. Insider trading is permitted when it is clear that the information is not a factor in the decision to trade, such as when trades are made pursuant to a pre-existing plan, contract, or instruction that was made in good faith. This provision makes it possible for insiders to avoid charges of insider trading by creating trading plans that set a specific date or price at which to effect a purchase of sale. For example, insiders who want to purchase or sell shares throughout the year may set up a 10b-5–1 plan and purchase a fixed number of shares on specified dates, such as the first of each month. Similarly, if an insider wishes to trade a large amount of stock, he may set up a plan that liquidates a specified number of shares of stock each month over the course of the upcoming year. Because these transactions are automatic, any inside information the insider possesses is not a factor in the decision to trade. The insider cannot be charged with illegal insider trading, as long as the plan was established at a time when material nonpublic information was not known.

A person does not necessarily have to violate a fiduciary duty in order to be guilty of securities fraud. In *SEC v. Dorozhko* [74] the Second Circuit Court of Appeals held that trading in securities with inside information acquired by hacking into the corporation's computer system is deceptive and therefore may qualify as securities fraud even though it doesn't come within either the classical or misappropriation theories of insider trading liability.

Engaging in insider trading or fraud in connection with the purchase or sale of a security may result in an SEC enforcement action, criminal penalties and civil liability for damages to the seller or purchaser involved in the fraudulent transaction.

BLUE SKY LAWS

State laws, like federal laws, typically prohibit misrepresentations and material omissions in connection with purchases and sales of securities.

The National Securities Markets Improvement Act[75] (NSMIA) exempts certain securities from state regulation of securities transactions. The exemption applies to businesses that are registered on a national exchange (New York Stock Exchange, American Stock Exchange) or that are qualified for Nasdaq inclusion. The NSMIA effectively preempts state regulation of sales of publicly traded securities.

MATERIAL MISREPRESENTATIONS

Not every misrepresentation or omission in connection with securities trading is a violation of securities laws. Only misrepresentations and omissions of material facts are. A fact is material only if a reasonably prudent investor would consider it important to an investment decision.

Some examples of things that are likely to be found to be material facts:

- Managerial conflicts of interest
- Nature or amount of manager compensation and/or benefits
- Experience, expertise and integrity of management
- Existence of a pending lawsuit
- Revocation of license
- Loan default
- Dispute with a major customer
- Adverse profitability or feasibility report
- Cessation of diminution of business operations
- Significant change in type of business operation
- Marketing problems
- Product's quantifiable performance or quality rating
- Impact of competition on sales
- Nature and amount of capital
- Aggregate amount of accounts payable
- Collectability of accounts receivable

This is not an exhaustive list.

Reining in Securities Litigation

An investor who has been misled about the profitability of a business may file a civil action for damages. If a seller has made optimistic predictions about a company's future that turn out to be wrong, the seller is at risk of being sued.

Congress recognized that it is natural and expected for the seller of a product to present it in a positive way. The PSLRA and SLUSA were enacted to protect stock traders from crippling amounts of litigation of this kind (called strike suits). The PSLRA provides safe harbors against strike suits that are "shareholder derivative actions begun with [the] hope of winning large attorney fees or private settlements, and with no intention of benefiting [the] corporation on behalf of which [the] suit is theoretically brought." SLUSA prohibits certain kinds of class actions when they are based on a state's statutory or common law protections against misrepresentations and material omissions of fact or the use of a manipulative device or contrivance in connection with the sale or purchase of certain kinds of securities.

While these laws provide some protection from liability for "hyping" a company, its product, or a security in order to encourage purchases of a security, they do not eliminate the anti-fraud provisions of securities laws. Liability may still attach for making material misrepresentations of fact or omitting material facts.

THE SARBANES-OXLEY ACT

Publicly traded companies must comply with the SOX Act. Most significantly, CEOs and CFOs of public companies must certify specified kinds of reports that are filed with the SEC. Directors, officers and shareholders owning at least 10% of the company's stock must report their dealings in the company's shares within two days after the transaction. And public companies may not make personal loans to directors and officers.

ONLINE SECURITIES TRADING

Online securities trading is not exempt from security regulations.

Where a federal securities law or regulation requires information to be disclosed to investors, potential investors or shareholders, the information may be sent by email if the recipient has specifically consented to email delivery of such information. The offeror must obtain the affirmative consent of the recipient to receive such information by email and must inform the recipient of the right to revoke consent at any reasonable time before the delivery. If the recipient does not consent, or if the recipient timely revokes consent once given, then the information must be delivered by regular mail.

Some email systems have a confirmation-of-receipt feature and/or a confirmation of opening feature. Use of these features is recommended, inasmuch as they can generate evidence of compliance with a delivery/disclosure requirement.

The SEC has taken the position that a user of an Internet-based securities purchasing system may be deemed to be a securities dealer if the user posts quotations simultaneously on both the buyer and seller bulletin boards with respect to a security. As such, the user may be required to register as a broker-dealer under the federal securities laws.

INVESTMENT ACCOUNTS

Online financial institutions—banks, investment funds, and the like—generally do not hold any tangible property for their clients. Rather than storing tangible dollar bills, a bank will set up an account and enter into an agreement with the customer to return the amount deposited, sometimes with interest, at such times as the customer may direct. Likewise, an investment business will not likely use its client's funds to immediately purchase a stock certificate for the client. Rather, such businesses typically maintain fungible, pooled accounts for multiple clients, and will add and subtract market gains and losses to each individual client's ledger in proportion to the client's investment in the stock.

Both kinds of arrangements usually work smoothly, but what happens if the financial institution becomes insolvent and is not able to meet its obligations to its clients? For banks, the problem is largely prevented by banking regulations imposing strict capital adequacy and deposit insurance requirements. The issue can, and does, arise in the case of investment companies, though. The answer depends largely on whether the interest in an investment account is deemed a proprietary interest or a contractual one. If it is considered a proprietary interest, then ownership of the customer's funds (or the customer's interest in a fund) does not vest in the investment company (or other holder of customer funds); the company is essentially only a trustee or bailee of another person's property, not the legal or beneficial title holder. Among other things, this means the customer's investment would not be subject to the claims of the company's creditors. A creditor generally may not levy on one person's property to satisfy another person's debt. By contrast, if the customer's interest is characterized as contractual rather than proprietary, then the customer would be on the same footing as any other ordinary creditor of the company.

Early English common law held that interests in fungible accounts could only be contractual, not proprietary. The modern approach, however, is to treat an investor in a fungible investment fund as having a pro rata proprietary interest in the pooled investment fund. Under this approach, the intermediary (the investment company) owns the underlying interest (usually stock in a company), but the customer does not. The customer does, however, have a proprietary interest in the pooled account the intermediary has established for its customers.

Linking to Broker-Dealers

Merely providing a link to a securities broker-dealer should not be considered a form of participation in securities trading, and should not result in the owner of the linking website being treated as a broker-dealer for purposes of securities regulations. Participating in the broker-dealer's business to any greater extent than that could, though. A linking website owner who does not wish to be subject to securities regulations should avoid handling customer funds or securities; should not effect clearance of trades; and should not loan customers funds to make purchases of securities.

Charging a small flat fee for an order placed by following a link on the website is permissible, so long as the amount does not vary based on the number of shares, the value of the securities, or whether the trade is completed or not.

INTERNATIONAL SECURITIES REGULATION

The Organization for Economic Cooperation and Development is a coalition of nations working on solutions to economic, social, and governance problems raised by a global economy. Member countries are required to accede to its Code of Liberalization of Capital Movements, which aims to implement a progressive relaxation of restrictions on the movement of capital between countries. The goal is to allow residents of different country to invest in companies in other countries, i.e., foreign securities trading.

The Council of Europe's Convention on Insider Trading authorizes a member country's securities regulation agency to request the assistance of another country's securities regulation agency in investigating conduct that would be considered insider trading if committed in the requesting country. The Convention has been ratified in the United Kingdom and a few other European countries.

Although the United States has not ratified the Convention on Insider Trading, the SEC has entered into Memorandums of Understanding with their counterparts in other countries for the exchange of information and mutual cooperation in the investigation of securities violations. In addition, the International Organization of Securities Commissions, of which the United States is a member, has a Multilateral Memorandum of Understanding that encourages cooperation among securities regulators in different countries.

Bulk Transfers

A bulk transfer is a sale of all or a substantial portion of a company's supplies or inventory to a single buyer, other than in the ordinary course of business. Unlike stock transfers, a bulk transfer conveys title to property owned by the company, not ownership of the company itself. If Company *A* borrows money (to acquire inventory or for other purposes), then sells everything to Company *B*, creditors and taxing authorities will be left with nothing upon which to levy for the payment of money owed to them.

Bulk sales statutes were enacted to prevent, or at least remove the benefit from, the practice of selling a company's entire inventory to defeat the claims of creditors who would otherwise be able to seize the goods to satisfy debts. Prior to the enactment of these statutes, the only remedy an unsecured creditor had in these situations was to seek a court order voiding the transfer on the basis that it was fraudulent conveyance. In many cases, however, the transfer was not fraudulent. Bulk sales were often at arm's length for adequate consideration given. Bulk transfer laws, patterned on Article 6 of the Uniform Commercial Code (U.C.C.), sought to protect creditors and buyers by requiring a bulk seller to prepare an affidavit listing all of its creditors. If the buyer did not complete the registration process for the bulk sale (which might involve filing the affidavit with a government office, for example), the seller's creditors could obtain a declaration that the sale was invalid and take possession of the goods or obtain judgment for any proceeds the buyer received from subsequent sales of the goods.

Although U.C.C. Article 6 was initially adopted in every state, in one form or another, most states have since repealed it. The Uniform Law Commission has recommended repeal because there is no longer much need for it inasmuch as Article 9 now provides a means for suppliers to perfect security interests in inventory and other personal property. A few states still have bulk transfer laws, however. California is such a state.

The California Bulk Sales Law defines a bulk sale as any sale of over half of a company's inventory and equipment outside the ordinary course of business, as measured by the fair market value on the date of the bulk sale agreement. The law applies to sellers of inventory (such as retail businesses) who are located in California. It only applies to bulk sales of assets with a net value between $10,000 and $5 million. The buyer is required to publish, record and deliver to the appropriate county tax assessor a notice of the proposed sale at least twelve business days prior to the sale. The notice must include:

(a) a statement that a bulk sale is pending
(b) all business names and addresses used by the seller and the buyer within the past three years
(c) location and general description of assets to be sold
(d) location and expected date of the bulk sale
(e) whether the bulk sale is a small cash sale.

In the case of a small cash sale (one in which the net asset value is under $2 million), the notice must also provide the name and address of the person with whom claims may be filed and state the last day on which claims may be filed. The last day on which claims may be filed must be the business day before the sale date.

The notice must be filed with the recorder in the county where the seller is located and in every county in which tangible assets for sale are located. It must be published in a newspaper of general circulation. And it must be delivered by registered or certified mail to the tax assessor in the county which in tangible assets for sale are located.

If the buyer fails to provide proper notice, the transfer is valid but the buyer becomes liable to creditors for damages to each creditor for the difference between a creditor's total claim and the amount the creditor could have recovered if the buyer had complied with the notice requirements.

The buyer must place in escrow an amount sufficient to cover any tax liability the seller might owe to the state until the seller produces a receipt from the State Board of Equalization affirming that all taxes have been paid or until the Board issues a Certificate of Tax Clearance. If the buyer fails to comply with the notice requirements and the seller has failed to pay taxes in full, the buyer may be liable for any unpaid taxes. A lien may be imposed on any personal property conveyed. A bulk sale may trigger additional tax obligations.

If the buyer is purchasing the business and the business has employees, the buyer must place in escrow an amount sufficient to pay contributions, interest and/or penalties due or owing by the seller for unemployment compensation insurance benefits or disability insurance. As with sales and use tax, the amount withheld is released upon issuance of a Tax Clearance Certificate. A buyer who fails to withhold sufficient funds may be personally liable for these payments.

Additional requirements relating to the payment of creditors apply to small cash sales. A small cash sale is a sales of assets with a net value of $10,000 to $2,000,000 on the date of the Agreement. In these cases, the n otice must include a statement that a bulk sale is pending; the names and addresses used by the seller and the buyer in the past three years; a description and the location of the assets to be sold; the location and expected date of the bulk sale; the fact that the bulk sale is a small-cash sale; the name and address of the person with whom to file claims; and the last day to file claims, which must be the business day before the sale date.

As noted, most states have repealed their bulk transfer laws.

Antitrust Laws

When transferring ownership of a business, care should be taken to ensure that the transaction does not run afoul of antitrust laws, particularly Sherman Act provisions relating to monopolies and anticompetitive combinations and Clayton Act provisions regulating mergers and acquisitions. See Chapter 7.

Chapter 7. Unfair Competition

It's a jungle out there.
—Peter Parker

Owning and operating a business enterprise is like a sport. Sport teams win by scoring points; businesses win by scoring customers. Consumers usually have multiple options for their purchasing decisions, so companies must expend energy persuading them to deal with them rather than others. In sports, competition incentivizes individuals to improve their skills and abilities. In the business world, it incentivizes people and companies to innovate and to improve their products and services. It can also operate as a check against price gouging. As with sporting competitions, though, rules of fair play are necessary to ensure that the benefits of competition are not thwarted.

Efforts to establish rules of fair play in the business world began centuries ago. Early English statutes recognized three kinds of activities that could not be countenanced: forestalling, regrating, and engrossing. *Forestalling* referred to attempts to eliminate competition prior to the opening of the marketplace. This might be done by buying up all competing goods before they reach the marketplace and then, having established control over the supply, exacting a high price for them. It might also be done by more direct methods, such as convincing competitors to stay away from the marketplace. *Regrating* referred to what is now known as retailing. Early English lawmakers were concerned that this practice would drive prices up because every successive seller will need to make a profit. *Engrossing* referred to cornering the market, i.e., buying up all goods of a particular kind and then reselling them. Like forestalling, gaining control over the supply enabled a merchant to exact a higher price. Early English statutes also sought to forbid conspiracies and agreements to fix prices or to acquire monopoly power. Although these early regulations were subsequently repealed, one principle has survived: Agreements to fix prices or to control the market are unenforceable restraints of trade. The modern common law doctrine of unfair competition is an outgrowth of that principle.

Judges developed the law of unfair competition on a case-by-case basis, guided by precedent and their own senses of justice and fair play. Some kinds of business practices came to be deemed categorically unfair, such as trade libel (making false statements about a competitor or the competitor's products and services); palming off (representing one's goods to be those of a competitor); trademark infringement; unauthorized disclosure or use of a trade secret; inducing a third party or an employee of a competitor to breach the person's contract with the competitor; agreements between competitors in restraint of trade; monopolization of the entire supply of a commodity; price-fixing agreements between two or more competitors to shut out other competitors. Contracts to increase price, limit supply or control a market are also forms of unfair competition recognized in the common law.

The universe of activities that qualify as unfair competition is not a closed set. The common law is always developing and evolving. Even today, a court may determine that a particular business practice is unfair to competition even though it does not come within one of the established categories. To the frustration of business managers and advisors, it is an elastic concept as to which no one so far has been able to formulate a single, noncircular definition. It can be any conduct on the part of a business that tends unnecessarily or unjustly to injure another in his business. It is for a judge to decide what is just or unjust. In other words, unfair competition ultimately is whatever a judge says it is, subject to the approval or disapproval of a reviewing court or a controlling legislative body.

In addition to the common law, statutes at both the federal and state levels regulate unfair competition. Primary among the federal enactments are the Sherman Act,[76] the Clayton Act,[77] the Lanham Act,[78] and the FTC Act. These laws are enforced by the U.S. Department of Justice and the FTC. In some situations, a private right of action to enforce certain provisions of these laws may be available, too. The principal objective of these laws is to prevent businesses from creating barriers to entry into a market or engaging in other activities that lessen or discourage competition or unfairly harm a competitor's interests.

The FTC Act simply states: "Unfair methods of competition ... are hereby declared unlawful"[79] and gives the FTC power to enforce this provision. Congress's use of broad, undefined terms in this enactment was deliberate.

> The committee [considered] whether it would attempt to define the many and variable unfair practices which prevail in commerce and to forbid their continuance or whether it would, by a general declaration condemning unfair practices, leave it to the commission to determine what practices were unfair. It concluded that the latter course would be the better, [because] there were too many unfair practices to define, and after writing 20 of them into the law it would be quite possible to invent others.[80]

Although not exhaustive, here is a partial list of examples of conduct that courts have found to be forms of unfair competition:

(a) sale of rebuilt, refurbished, reconditioned, or used products as new
(b) sale of finished products made from used materials as new
(c) misrepresentation of the nature, quality, purity, origin, source, properties or manufacture of goods
(d) packaging in a manner that deceives consumers about quantity, weight or volume
(e) tactics to persuade a consumer that the terms of an offer are more advantageous than they really are
(f) misstatement of the regular price of a "sale" item
(g) misrepresentation of the seller's identity
(h) copying the trade dress of a competitor's product
(i) adopting a trade name confusingly similar to a competitor's
(j) bad faith threats of legal action, such as for an unfounded patent infringement claim
(k) use of concealed subsidiaries to obtain business that the company otherwise would not be able to get

(l) bribery
(m) schemes involving chance or lottery distribution of goods
(n) paying unnecessarily excessive prices for materials for the purpose of eliminating competitors who depend on the same sources of supply.

Sometimes a specific statute supplants a particular application of the common law cause of action for unfair competition. The Uniform Trade Secrets Act (UTSA), for example, expressly preempts common law unfair competition claims that are based on misappropriation of a trade secret. Even when a statute of this kind has been enacted, however, common law claims for other kinds of unfair competition may still be asserted.

Some kinds of unfair competition—trademark infringement, misappropriation of information, use or disclosure of trade secrets, false advertising, and trade disparagement, for example—are addressed in other chapters of this book.

Interference with Contract

Procuring or inducing the breach of a contract between other people may result in liability for damages for the breach. The elements of a cause of action for interference with contract are:

(a) existence of a contract
(b) knowledge of the contract
(c) intentional procurement of a breach
(d) absence of justification
(e) causation of damage
(f) damage.

This cause of action may be invoked to redress unfair competition that involves a company's meddling with a competitor's beneficial contract with a third party. It may also be used to redress unfair competition involving a company's exertion of influence on a competitor's employee. Paying an employee of one's competitor to reveal the competitor's trade secret in breach of a confidentiality agreement between the competitor and the employee is an example. Promising higher returns of income to a merchant if she breaches an exclusive dealing agreement she has with a competing company is another example.

Interference with a Prospective Business Relationship

Interference with someone else's prospective business advantage can expose a person to liability for damages. Unlike interference with contract, this kind of claim requires no proof of any actual contract. Instead, a right of recovery exists upon proof of all of the following elements:

(a) intentional interference with an existing or potential business or economic relationship
(b) for an improper purpose or by improper means
(c) causation
(d) damage.

The interference must be wrongful (tortious). Merely persuading a consumer who is considering buying from Company *A* to buy from Company *B* instead is not unfair.

This cause of action is most often asserted against employees and former employees who divert customers and/or potential customers away from their employers or former employers either to their own competing business or to a new employer's competing business, where doing so violates the employment contract and/or the employee's implied fiduciary duty of loyalty. The cause of action is not limited to claims against employees, though. A business might incur liability, for example, if it reaches out to known customers or potential customers of a competitor and gives them false or misleading information about the competitor or the competitor's products and services to deter them from dealing with the competitor.

Deep Linking

Deep linking means linking to a page within a website in a way that bypasses the website's home page. Because it is not often likely to result in consumer confusion, deep-linking is not often likely to result in liability for trademark infringement.[81] In some circumstances, though, it may be a form of unfair competition. For example, the owner of a website that sells information to its users (such as a news service) may be guilty of unfair competition if it links to an informational page on another information-selling site directly, rather than sending its users to the other site's home page first. Because customers bypass the other site's home page, its "number of hits" data will not accurately reflect the number of visitors to the site, making it appear to be less popular than it is and less likely to achieve a high ranking in search engine results. If the other site has advertising on its home page, the practice may also deprive the other site's owner of advertising revenue.

Deep-linking may also result in liability for trespass to chattel, if it decreases the value or speed of the deep-linked site. At least one court has ruled that increased load on a server due to an increased number of visitors to the deep-linked page may qualify as an injury to chattel (the server) sufficient to sustain a cause of action against the deep-linker for trespass to chattel.

The Terms of Use of many websites explicitly prohibit or restrict deep-linking. Deep-linking in violation of such a term may result in liability for breach of contract. Before deep-linking to another web page, a website owner should review the site's Terms of Use very carefully. Of course, the safest course would be to obtain the website owner's permission to deep-link to a page within the site before doing so.

Monopolization and Combinations in Restraint of Trade

There is no law against becoming a monopoly naturally as a consequence of having a superior product, business acumen, or simply by historical accident. The general consensus among policy makers, though, is that the acquisition of monopoly power is not something to be encouraged. The existence of competing businesses in a market sector serves the public interest by encouraging innovation and the continual improvement of products and services. It also tends to keep prices reasonable. Assuming consumers have a need for a particular product, a business that acquires monopoly power over sales of the product may exact whatever price it pleases without having to worry about being undercut by competitors with better products or lower prices.

The Sherman Act makes it unlawful for businesses to work together to quell competition or for a business to attempt, conspire to, or actually monopolize any part of interstate or foreign commerce.

> **[Sec. 1]** Every contract, combination in the form of trust or otherwise, or conspiracy, in restraint of trade or commerce among the several States, or with foreign nations, is declared to be illegal. Every person who shall make any contract or engage in any combination or conspiracy hereby declared to be illegal shall be deemed guilty of a felony, and, on conviction thereof, shall be punished by fine not exceeding $100,000,000 if a corporation, or, if any other person, $1,000,000, or by imprisonment not exceeding ten years, or by both said punishments, in the discretion of the court.
> **[Sec. 2]** Every person who shall monopolize, or attempt to monopolize, or combine or conspire with any other person or persons, to monopolize any part of the trade or commerce among the several States, or with foreign nations, shall be deemed guilty of a felony, and, on conviction thereof, shall be punished by fine not exceeding $100,000,000 if a corporation, or, if any other person, $1,000,000, or by imprisonment not exceeding ten years, or by both said punishments, in the discretion of the court.[82]

Sherman Act violations are also punishable civilly. Treble damages are sometimes available.

As previously indicated, it is not against the law to acquire monopoly power naturally solely as the result of having a superior product or offering a superior service. The Sherman Act only prohibits acquisitions of monopoly power or attempts to acquire monopoly power in other ways. The two kinds of conduct in connection with monopoly power that are prohibited are (a) intentional or attempted acquisition of monopoly power, and (b) use of monopoly power to create an anticompetitive market in an industry.

In addition to monetary penalties and damages, a court may use its equitable powers to order the breakup of a monopoly when an antitrust violation is found to have occurred.

INTENTIONAL MONOPOLIZATION

A business is guilty of intentional monopolization only if each of these elements is proven:

(a) monopoly power
(b) intent to monopolize[83]
(c) use of anticompetitive methods to acquire or maintain monopoly power.

Monopoly power exists when a business has the power to set prices or exclude competitors in a particular zone of commercial activity. A business may have monopoly power even if it is not the only game in town. A significant market share is highly relevant to monopoly power, though. Businesses with 50% or more market share are at greater risk of being found to have monopoly power than other businesses are.

Courts consider other factors, too, such as barriers to entry for new competitors. In *United States v. Microsoft*,[84] for example, the court found that Microsoft's 95% share of the operating system market, together with the widespread design of applications for compatibility with Windows but not other operating systems, created a significant barrier to entry into the operating system market by new competitors.

For purposes of the Sherman Act, a market (or "zone of commercial activity") includes all products which consumers can reasonably interchange for the same purposes.

Intent to monopolize may be established by proof of either willful acquisition or willful maintenance of monopoly power, i.e., intent to acquire monopoly power or intent to maintain monopoly power after it has been acquired.

Healthy competition is not an anticompetitive method. Taking steps to make a business more profitable by offering a better product or service at a lower price than competing businesses is healthy competition, not anticompetitive. Merely showing that a company adopted measures to reduce costs, improve products and services, and increase sales will not suffice to establish that monopoly power was acquired or is being maintained by anticompetitive methods. If a business employs certain other kinds of methods to achieve monopoly power, such as combinations in restraint of trade or predatory actions to suppress competition, then it may be found to have violated the Sherman Act.

Although patents can give their owners exclusive rights to exploit a particular invention, merely applying for and obtaining a patent is not considered evidence of intent to monopolize. Nor is obtaining a patent considered an anticompetitive method of acquiring monopoly power.

ATTEMPTED MONOPOLIZATION

A business entity may be guilty of violating the Sherman Act if it attempts to acquire monopoly power, whether it is successful or not. To establish a case of attempted monopolization it is necessary to prove three things:

(a) intent to acquire monopoly power
(b) anticompetitive conduct intended to injure actual or potential competition
(c) substantial likelihood of acquiring monopoly power.

Liability for a Sherman Act violation will not be imposed if a company has a legitimate business justification for its action.

The Clayton Act prohibits certain kinds of restraints of trade and anticompetitive actions that are not covered by the Sherman Act. It is enforceable civilly, but not criminally. The civil penalties can be significant, however. Both the U.S. Department of Justice and the FTC enforce it.

The principal objective of the Clayton Act is to curb practices that businesses use to acquire monopoly power. This includes such things as exclusive dealing agreements, tying agreements, price discrimination, and interlocking directorates. The Act also regulates mergers and acquisitions.

The Clayton Act does not apply to services, real estate or intangibles. It only applies to commodities, i.e., products of the kind traditionally sold in brick-and-mortar retail establishments.

COMBINATIONS IN RESTRAINT OF TRADE

The Sherman Act prohibits combinations in restraint of trade. The U.S. Supreme Court has developed two kinds of analyses to give substance to that prohibition. First, certain kinds of concerted activity between businesses are so clearly anticompetitive as to be per se violations of the Sherman Act. Price-fixing and bid rigging are examples. The second kind of analysis is known as the *rule of reason*. This approach requires examining all the facts and circumstances to determine whether a particular action is reasonably necessary to serve some legitimate business purpose other than suppressing competition. In the course of this analysis, the marketwide benefits of the action are weighed against the anticompetitive harm.

Restraints of trade are classified as either horizontal or vertical. A horizontal restraint of trade is one in which business competitors at the same level of the distribution chain act in concert to reduce or eliminate competition. Vertical restraints involve concerted activity by businesses at different levels of the distribution chain.

Price-fixing

Price-fixing is unfair to both competitors and consumers. It puts competitors out of business and it deprives consumers of the benefit of competitive pricing. It is a per se violation of the Sherman Act. It occurs when two or more businesses agree to work together for the purpose of affecting the market price of a commodity.

An agreement between business competitors to sell or buy products or services for a specified price is the most direct form, but it may occur in less direct ways, as well. Artificially reducing the supply of a commodity to drive prices up is another kind of price-fixing. These kinds of price-fixing are horizontal restraints of trade. Price-fixing between noncompeting businesses at different levels of the distribution chain is a vertical restraint of trade. A manufacturer and a retailer setting the price at which the retailer will sell the commodity that the manufacturer supplies is an example. A manufacturer may suggest a retail price, but attempting to exact a commitment from a retailer to sell at that price violates the Sherman Act.

Merely announcing a price or a planned price increase or decrease is not a violation of the Sherman Act. Standing alone, it will not suffice as circumstantial evidence of an agreement to fix prices, either, even if competitors proceed to set their prices at the same level. This kind of behavior is to be expected in a competitive market. When a business learns that a competitor is lowering a price, it may lower its price to remain competitive, not because it has entered into a price-fixing agreement for an anti-competitive purpose. Such an agreement might be inferred, however, if a competitor's conduct is not something that would ordinarily be expected to result naturally from competitive pricing practices.

Unlawful price-fixing agreements need not be in writing. They may be oral, written or inferred from conduct. Communication followed by conduct that would not be expected in a competitive market sometimes suffices as circumstantial evidence of an agreement.

Supply Manipulation

Limiting the supply of a commodity makes it possible to command a higher price for it. If the commodity is material used to produce goods, it can also force competitors to go out of business. Accordingly, agreements to artificially reduce the supply of a particular material or product, or to cut off competitors' sources of supply, violate the prohibition against combinations in restraint of trade. The same may be said of contracts among competitors to restrict exports or imports.

Allocating Markets or Customers

An agreement by business competitors to divide up customers or allocate markets is a per se violation of the Sherman Act.

Boycotts

Acting in concert with a competing business to refuse to sell to or buy from a particular business is usually a violation of the Sherman Act. A unilateral decision to boycott or refuse to deal with a particular third party does not violate the Sherman Act, however.[85]

Trade Association Activities

Because they are groups of business competitors, trade associations are at risk of violating the Sherman Act if they engage in per se horizontal restraints like price-fixing or market allocation. This is why a trade association should not publish a list of suggested prices for goods and services offered or sold by members of the trade. Gathering and reporting statistical data, on the other hand, does not violate the Sherman Act.

Distribution Restraints

Businesses sometimes impose restraints on other businesses with respect to matters other than price. For example, a manufacturer might enter into an agreement with a retailer that restricts the retailer to a particular sales territory. These kinds of vertical restraints are not per se violations of the Sherman Act. Instead, courts apply the rule of reason to determine whether the agreement in a particular case is an unlawful restraint of trade.

Exclusive Dealing Contracts

Exclusive dealing contracts (such as exclusive distributorships and exclusive territory agreements) are not per se violations of the Sherman Act. Under the rule of reason, such an arrangement violates the Sherman Act only if it substantially forecloses competition in a relevant market by significantly reducing the number of outlets available to a competitor to reach prospective consumers. In this connection, courts consider six factors:

(a) degree of exclusivity and the line of commerce impacted by the agreement
(b) substantiality of the percentage of the market foreclosed by the agreement (gauged by the likelihood that competitors will be excluded from competing)
(c) actual anticompetitive effect
(d) whether a legitimate business justification exists
(e) length and irrevocability of the agreement
(f) availability of less restrictive means of achieving the same benefits.

The Clayton Act also restricts exclusive dealing contracts. As with the Sherman Act, not all exclusive dealing contracts are violations. Only agreements that substantially lessen the competition or tend to create a monopoly violate the Clayton Act. Franchise agreements do not violate the Clayton Act.

Franchises

A franchise agreement prohibiting the franchisee from distributing a product at a location other than what is authorized in the franchise agreement does not violate antitrust laws.[86]

Franchise agreements requiring the franchisee to sell only one business's products exclusively and/or to purchase its entire inventory from a single seller do not violate antitrust laws, either.

Tying Agreements

A tying agreement is one in which a buyer is required to buy two products or services together (or one product and one service together) in order to buy either of them from the seller. Some kinds of tying agreements violate the Sherman Act and/or the Clayton Act.

A tying agreement is a per se violation of the Sherman Act if all four of the following elements are proven:

(a) The agreement involves two separate, distinct items (as distinguished from integrated components of the same product or service);
(b) The agreement does not allow purchase of each item separately;
(c) The seller has so much market power as to make the tie-in coercive;
(d) The amount of commerce in the tied product that is affected by the tying agreement is not insubstantial.[87]

Some courts hold that the third element (market power) need not be proven when a case is prosecuted under the Clayton Act rather than the Sherman Act.

The most famous example of a tying agreement that was alleged to have violated the Sherman Act is Microsoft's bundling of its Web browser, Internet Explorer, with its Windows operating system, with a provision in the Windows licensing agreement that forbade licensees from modifying or deleting Internet Explorer from Windows. The U.S. Department of Justice and several states sued Microsoft for violating antitrust laws in various ways, including by having this tying agreement in their Windows license agreement. Ultimately, a consent order was entered. Under the consent order, Microsoft agreed to use a standard licensing agreement that does not include a browser tying agreement.

There is no antitrust violation if a legitimate business justification exists for configuring a product in such a way that it must be used in conjunction with another product. Enhanced quality, performance, speed or accuracy would be examples of business justifications for configuring a product in such a way that it must be used in conjunction with another product.

Price Discrimination

The Clayton Act, as amended by the Robinson-Patman Act,[88] makes it unlawful for a business to discriminate between different purchasers with respect to commodities of like quantity or grade, if doing so may have either of the following effects:

- substantially lessening competition, or tending to create a monopoly
- injuring, destroying or preventing competition with any person who either grants or knowingly receives the benefit of the discrimination.

Price discrimination does not violate the Clayton Act unless sales at the discriminatory prices actually occur. Offering to sell at discriminatory prices is not a violation if no sales at those prices actually take place.

Interlocking Directorates

Interlocking directorates are arrangements in which the same individual (or legal entity) serves on the boards of directors of two or more different corporations. While there is no absolute prohibition against them, they can give rise to significant legal issues. The Clayton Act provides:

> No person shall, at the same time, serve as a director or officer in any two corporations (other than banks, banking associations, and trust companies) that are
> (A) engaged in whole or in part in commerce; and
> (B) by virtue of their business and location of operation, competitors, so that the elimination of competition by agreement between them would constitute a violation of any of the antitrust laws;
> if each of the corporations has capital, surplus and undivided profits aggregating more than $10,000,000.[89]

For purposes of the Act, "person" includes legal entities (e.g., corporations) as well as natural persons. Courts have held that a violation may occur either when the same natural person serves on the boards of competing businesses or when different individual agents of the same corporation serve on the boards of competing businesses. For example, if Officer *A* and Agent *B* of Megabucks Corporation each serve as directors of competing businesses, then there may be a Clayton Act violation—provided their service on these boards is in their capacity as agents of Megabucks rather than in their individual capacities.[90]

The FTC has warned that "coopetition"—marketing or developing products or services together in one market while competing in another—creates a risk of anticompetitive agreements and information sharing that could violate antitrust laws.

The Act provides a safe harbor for smaller businesses. Simultaneous service on the boards of directors of two businesses is not an antitrust violation if:

(a) The competitive sales of either corporation are under $1,000,000;
(b) The competitive sales of either corporation are less than 2% of that year's total sales; or
(c) The competitive sales of each corporation are less than 4% of that corporation's total sales.

Exemption from liability for a violation of the Clayton Act does not exempt a director from liability for breaching legal responsibilities imposed by other laws, such as the fiduciary duty of undivided loyalty to shareholders.

MERGERS AND ACQUISITIONS

Mergers and acquisitions can lead to the acquisition of monopoly power. The Clayton Act attempts to prevent this from happening by prohibiting a business from acquiring the stock or assets of its competitors if doing so will substantially lessen competition or tend to create a monopoly.

Under the Hart-Scott-Rodino Act,[91] businesses that are contemplating mergers worth more than a specified threshold dollar amount must give advance notice of their intention to the FTC and the U.S. Department of Justice. The Department of Justice has veto power over any proposed merger that it determines would violate antitrust laws.

MIXING BANKING AND COMMERCIAL ACTIVITIES

Prior to the Great Depression, banks routinely bought shares in other commercial business enterprises and sat on their boards of directors. Concerns arose, however, that these practices could lead banks to encourage anticompetitive collusion among the selected companies on whose boards of directors they served or with which they were affiliated. To prevent the excessive concentration of economic power, anticompetitive practices, misallocation of credit, and the exposure of federally established safety nets for banks to losses from commercial activities, the Clayton Act implemented prohibitions against interlocking directorates. After the bank failures and stock market crash of 1929, additional federal laws were enacted to create an even stronger wall of separation between banking and commerce. The two principal laws were the Glass-Steagall Act[92] and the Bank Holding Company Act[93] (BHCA).

The Glass-Steagall Act prevented commercial banks from underwriting or distributing securities, or engaging in investment activities on behalf of their customers. At the same time, it prevented investment banks and securities investment firms from taking deposits. It also prevented banks from affiliating or sharing employees with investment firms, and vice versa. The affiliation prohibitions were repealed in 1999, as part of the Gramm-Leach-Bliley Act[94] (GLBA).

The BHCA prohibited bank holding companies from engaging in nonbanking activities, acquiring voting stock in certain kinds of nonbank companies, and acquiring banks in other states. The prohibition against interstate acquisitions has been repealed. Interstate mergers are now permitted, provided the banks are adequately capitalized and managed. They are also subject to concentration limits, states laws, and Community Reinvestment Act[95] evaluations. The GLBA repealed other provisions of the BHCA. Bank holding companies may now own other financial institutions, although they continue to be barred from owning nonfinancial companies.

Unitary thrifts—thrift holding companies that own a single savings bank—may engage in commercial activities. Commercial enterprises may not acquire thrifts.

Private equity firms are not banks. They may acquire interests in nonbank companies.

STATE ANTITRUST LAWS

Antitrust laws have also been enacted at the state level. State attorneys general are responsible for the enforcement of these laws. Private persons injured in their business or property by an antitrust violation may also file civil suits for any provable damages.

The Foreign Corrupt Practices Act

Bribery of government officials to obtain favorable treatment is a crime under the laws of every jurisdiction in the United States. Although the impetus for these laws may have its roots in precepts of civics and morality, they also promote fair competition. The Foreign Corrupt Practice Act[96] (FCPA) extends the prohibition to commercial bribery by American companies in foreign countries.

Specifically, the FCPA makes it a crime to use the mails or any instrumentality of interstate commerce (which includes the Internet) corruptly in furtherance of any offer, payment, promise to pay, or authorization of the payment of money or anything of value to any person, while knowing that all or a portion of it will be offered, given or promised to a foreign official to influence the foreign official in his official capacity, induce the foreign official to do or refrain from doing an act in violation of the official's lawful duty, or to secure an improper advantage in order to assist in obtaining or retaining business for or with, or directing business to, a person. This provision of the Act applies to any person or company, not just to publicly traded corporations. Penalties for violations are severe. They may include imprisonment and fines in the millions of dollars.

What this means, basically, is that American companies and persons acting on their behalf should be careful not to give or promise to give anything of value to foreign officials in exchange for any kind of commercial advantage. They should not pay, offer to pay or authorize, a bribe. They may not make gifts or provide anything else of value to foreign officials to obtain or retain business or secure an advantage. This includes offering lavish entertainment, business opportunities, covering an official's expenses, or making charitable, political or other in-kind contributions.

A company is vicariously liable for any bribery or attempted bribery on the part of its own officers and employees, and it is also vicariously liable for bribery or attempted bribery on the part of its agents, foreign partners, foreign consultants, local contact persons in a foreign country, and the like. This liability may exist even if the company is not aware of such person's conduct.

The definition of *foreign official* is very broad. It includes not only government officials and employees but also the directors, officers and employees of any company in which a foreign government owns an interest; candidates for government office; political parties; officers of political parties; and officials of international organizations like the United Nations (UN) or the World Bank. It also includes family members of any of these persons.

To help enforce compliance with these prohibitions, publicly traded companies and their related entities must comply with specified accounting provisions and maintain an adequate system of internal accounting controls.

The FCPA also prohibits foreign businesses and persons from bribing officials in the United States.

Chapter 8. Dissolution

Going out of business is not often pleasant. Yet, it is estimated that 95% of online businesses fail.[97] Therefore, almost every online business venture will need to know about the laws applicable to terminating a business, even if only for the purpose of winding one up and trying again with another.

Sole Proprietorships

A sole proprietorship may be dissolved at any time by an exercise of the proprietor's will. Inventory is liquidated; creditors are paid off; and any leases, licenses and registrations are cancelled. If the proprietor has incurred a large amount of debt in connection with the business, she may want to look into the possibility of filing for bankruptcy protection. If that option is not pursued, then the proprietor remains personally liable for debts incurred by the business.

Partnerships

A partnership may be dissolved in three ways:

- Voluntary act of a partner
- Judicial decree
- Operation of law.

VOLUNTARY DISSOLUTION

The partnership agreement may specify condition(s) under which the partnership will terminate. If so, then the partnership automatically terminates when the specified condition(s) occurs. Partners may also enter into a separate agreement to dissolve their partnership.

If partners continue to operate the partnership after it is terminated, they become partners at will. Any partner at will may dissolve the partnership at any time. A partner may withdraw from a partnership at any time. A withdrawing partner may be liable for damages, however, if the withdrawal, or the time or manner in which it is effected, breaches a provision in the partnership agreement.

JUDICIAL DISSOLUTION

A partner may commence a legal proceeding to dissolve a partnership if grounds for dissolution exist and the partners have not reached an agreement to dissolve it. Depending on state laws and the language of the partnership agreement, grounds for dissolving a partnership might include:

- Incapacity (serious illness, disability or mental illness)
- Illegal conduct
- Conduct harmful to the partnership or other partners (e.g., fraud, drug or alcohol abuse)
- Business impracticality (when a business is not capable of becoming profitable)
- High level of continuous conflict between partners
- Other grounds.

AUTOMATIC DISSOLUTION

The partnership laws of most states specify circumstances under which a partnership will automatically dissolve by operation of law. These typically include such things as:

- Death of a partner
- Bankruptcy declaration by a partner
- Illegal business operations or activity
- Admission of a new partner without the consent of the other partners.

The admission of a new partner without the consent of the other partners has the effect of terminating the partnership. At the same time, a new partnership consisting of the remaining partners and the new partner is formed. The new partnership so formed assumes the debts of the dissolved one.

If a partnership dissolves as a result of illegal activity on the part of less than all of the partners, the innocent partner(s) may buy out the interest(s) of the offending partner(s) and continue the partnership. An innocent partner might also be able to sue the offending partner for breach of contract or breach of fiduciary duty.

Corporations

VOLUNTARY DISSOLUTION

A corporation may be dissolved voluntarily, if desired. The process may be initiated either by its directors or by its shareholders. Shareholders may do it by voting unanimously to dissolve the corporation. Directors must submit a proposal for dissolution to the shareholders for their vote.

After a formal decision to dissolve is made, the corporation must file articles of dissolution with the secretary of state in the state where it is incorporated. State laws specify the kinds of information that must be included. Typically, this will include, at a minimum, the name of the corporation, the manner in which dissolution was authorized, and the date of dissolution.

The corporation must also contact its creditors and make arrangements for the payment of outstanding debts.

JUDICIAL DISSOLUTION

Shareholders may commence a proceeding to dissolve a corporation in some circumstances, such as:

(a) waste of corporate assets by the directors
(b) conduct by a director that is illegal, fraudulent or oppressive to shareholders
(c) deadlock on the part of shareholders or directors resulting in, or likely to result in, harm to the corporation

WINDING UP

Once the corporation is dissolved, its affairs must be wound up. The corporation must distribute its remaining assets in this order of priority:

(1) creditors
(2) owners of preferred stock
(3) owners of common stock.

Assets are distributed pro rata, i.e., in proportion to the amount or value of a party's interest.

During the winding up period following a dissolution, a corporation may continue to collect debts and discharge liabilities that were incurred prior to the dissolution, but it may not transact any new business.

Assignment for the Benefit of Creditors

An assignment for the benefit of creditors is a vehicle for carrying out the distribution of a company's assets and payment of debts after the decision is made to dissolve the business. The company's assets are transferred to an independent thirty party in trust. The trustee agrees to liquidate them and distribute the proceeds to creditors in accordance with priorities established by law. It is a common law alternative to filing a petition in bankruptcy. It operates in much the same way as a Chapter 7 bankruptcy, but without the formality and expense.

Any kind of business entity may make an assignment for the benefit of creditors. Because sole proprietors are personally liable for business debts, they often opt for a formal bankruptcy proceeding instead. Liquidation in a formal bankruptcy proceeding results in a discharge of liability for most debts. An assignment for the benefit of creditors may be advantageous for a guarantor of a business entity's obligations or a corporate officer who has incurred personal liability for corporate debts. From their point of view, using corporate assets to satisfy the debts may be preferable to having creditors look elsewhere for payment.

When a company enters into an assignment for the benefit of creditors, all of the company's property is transferred to the trustee. This includes both real and personal property, and both tangible and intangible property, such as trademarks and copyrights. Once the assets have been transferred to the trustee, the company no longer has any control over them. Assets sold pursuant to an assignment for the benefit of creditors are sold as is, without warranties.

The trustee (assignee) owes a fiduciary duty to the company's creditors to protect the assets and to administer them fairly. He may be removed by a court for breaching the assignment contract or a fiduciary duty.

Secured creditors are not required to consent to an assignment and they are not barred from enforcing their liens or other security interests. As in a bankruptcy proceeding, the assignee's fees, legal expenses and costs of administration are paid first; then secured creditors; then tax and wage claims. Unsecured debts are paid last. Unlike a bankruptcy, a discharge of all dischargeable debts is not granted at the conclusion of an assignment for the benefit of creditors. There is also no automatic stay of collection actions while the process is underway. As a practical matter, collection efforts are often fruitless inasmuch as the debtor (the company) will have transferred title to its assets to a third party.

An assignment for the benefit of creditors gives creditors grounds for filing an involuntary petition for bankruptcy on the debtor's behalf, if they so choose.

Bankruptcy

If the business has incurred significant debt or liability, filing for bankruptcy protection may be an option to consider. Federal courts have exclusive jurisdiction over proceedings in bankruptcy. A special court has been established exclusively for bankruptcy cases. The two principle objectives of bankruptcy are: (a) to give debtors a fresh start and (b) to ensure that all creditors are treated fairly, with none enjoying unfair advantages over others.

Bankruptcy proceedings are governed by federal law. Principal sources of law are the Bankruptcy Code[98] and regulations promulgated pursuant to it.

Businesses may choose to file under either Chapter 7 or 11. Individuals may choose to file under either Chapter 7 or 13. Special provisions apply in the case of municipal, stockbroker, and railroad bankruptcies.

CHAPTER 7 LIQUIDATION

In a Chapter 7 bankruptcy the debtor's nonexempt assets are sold to pay off debts. To the extent a dischargeable debt is not completely paid off in the bankruptcy, it is discharged, which is to say the judge issues an order declaring that no one may attempt to collect it from the debtor. Chapter 7 petitions may be filed by either business or individual debtors.

The proceeding is commenced by filing a petition with the Bankruptcy Court and paying the required filing fee. The proceeding may be commenced voluntarily by the debtor or it may be commenced involuntarily by a creditor with an unsecured claim of at least $10,000.

The debtor must provide detailed information about assets, income, expenses and other things.

A bankruptcy filing gives rise to an automatic stay of collection activity by creditors. This means that creditors may not initiate a collection action, send a collection letter or do anything else to attempt to collect a debt that is included in the bankruptcy. The stay is temporary, lasting until such time as the court determines the validity of the petition. If the court determines the petition is in proper form and that the filing is valid, it will issue an order for relief. This extends the stay of collection activity for the duration of the bankruptcy proceeding.

After an order for relief is issued, the court will appoint a trustee. The trustee's job is to administer the bankruptcy estate. The trustee represents neither the debtor nor the creditors. Rather, the trustee performs a largely ministerial role for the court.

The court will schedule a meeting of creditors within thirty days of the order for relief. At the meeting, creditors may question the debtor about the debtor's assets, income, liabilities, and financial affairs in general. This is an opportunity for creditors to uncover any attempt on the debtor's part to conceal assets or income. In no-asset and low-asset cases, it is not uncommon for no creditors to appear at the meeting. Nevertheless, it is their right, if they so choose.

After the meeting of creditors, the trustee begins the task of taking possession of the debtor's nonexempt assets. These comprise the "bankruptcy estate." Property acquired after the petition is filed is not part of the bankruptcy estate. Although websites and domain names are not, in themselves, forms of property, their contents may be. Intellectual property, such as copyrights, trademarks, trade secrets and patents can be part of a bankruptcy estate.

The Bankruptcy Code makes certain kinds of transfers by a debtor prior to or during the bankruptcy proceeding voidable by the trustee. They fall into two general categories: preferential and fraudulent. A preferential transfer is one that gives a creditor preferential treatment relative to other creditors. A transfer to a creditor ninety days or less before filing bankruptcy is a voidable preferential transfer. Transfers to insiders (family, relatives, partners, directors, officers) within one year of filing the petition are also voidable preferential transfers. A fraudulent transfer is one made to a third party with the intent to hinder, delay or defraud creditors. It is voidable if made within one year before the petition is filed.

After the trustee gathers the bankruptcy estate, he then sells or disposes of the nonexempt property and distributes the proceeds to creditors. Secured creditors are paid first; anything remaining is distributed to unsecured creditors. The Bankruptcy Code specifies an order of priority for the payment of unsecured creditors. Expenses associated with the bankruptcy are the first priority. These include court costs, attorney fees, trustee fees, and administration expenses. Next in line are various kinds of unsecured claims such as tax debts, wage claims, etc. The claims of general creditors (e.g., credit card companies) are paid last.

A debtor is entitled to keep property to the extent it is covered by an exemption. An exemption is a statutory grant to a debtor of the right to keep an item of property despite the general rule that the debtor's assets are to be liquidated in a bankruptcy proceeding. The Bankruptcy Code offers several exemptions. The homestead exemption is an example. It exempts up to $23,675 in the equity in the debtor's residence and burial plot. Other exemptions exist for a specified amount of value in things like a motor vehicle, jewelry, tools of the trade, life insurance, household goods, prescription health aids, retirement accounts, certain elements of personal injury and wrongful death damage recoveries, damage awards for loss of future earnings needed for support, and support payments (alimony, child support, Social Security benefits, unemployment benefits, public assistance, and the like). There is also a "wildcard" exemption of $250 plus up to $11, 850 of the unused portion of the homestead exemption, which may be applied to any property of the debtor's choosing.

A married couple filing jointly is entitled to twice the amounts of the exemptions.

Exemption amounts are adjusted periodically. Consult the Bankruptcy Code for current amounts.

States provide their own lists of exemptions and specify whether a debtor may or may not elect to use the federal exemptions instead. No debtor may use both federal and state exemptions.

At the conclusion of the proceeding, the judge will determine whether the debtor is entitled to a discharge of all debts (or portions of debts) that are dischargeable in bankruptcy. If the judge grants a discharge, then no one may thereafter take any action against the debtor to collect a debt that was covered by the bankruptcy petition.

Not all debts are dischargeable. Examples of debts that are not dischargeable in bankruptcy include, but are not limited to:

- tax claims (federal, state or local) within three years of the filing of the petition
- alimony, child support, maintenance
- debts arising from claims of willful or malicious injury to person or property
- debts incurred for luxury goods within sixty days before the petition is filed
- certain cash advances using credit cards or a revolving line of credit
- student loans, unless repayment would cause undue hardship.

CHAPTER 11 REORGANIZATION

Instead of liquidating the business and getting out from under debt permanently, a business may opt to continue its operations and obtain only temporary relief from creditors by filing a Chapter 11 petition. Chapter 11 gives a business relief from debt collection activities while the business comes up with a plan for paying its debts (or a portion of its debts).

A Chapter 11 proceeding is commenced by filing a petition, which may be voluntary or involuntary. The filing results in an automatic stay of collection actions. If the court determines the petition is valid, it issues an order for relief.

Unlike in Chapter 7, a creditor committee is appointed. The creditor committee consults with the debtor and trustee about the debtor's plan for repaying creditors. Also unlike a Chapter 7 proceeding, the business may continue to be operated, rather than liquidated, after the petition is filed. The court may appoint a trustee (or "receiver") to oversee the operation of the business if it sees fit to do so.

A business that is continuing to operate in a Chapter 11 proceeding is called a *debtor in possession*. A debtor in possession has the power to void prepetition preferential payments and to cancel prepetition executory contracts. The debtor in possession may also avoid obligations and transfers.

Ultimately, the business files a reorganization plan outlining the specifics of a strategy for overcoming the business's financial difficulties. Creditors have the right to vote to either accept or reject the plan. The court has the power, known as "cramdown" power, to require creditors to accept a plan over their objection, if the court determines the plan is fair, equitable and feasible. Once a plan is approved, all debts are discharged, and the debtor and creditors are bound by the terms of the plan instead.

Small businesses with debts amounting to less than $2,000,000 may elect a "fast track" form of Chapter 11 proceeding that makes creditor committees optional and aims to have a case processed within 160 days or less.

A Chapter 11 proceeding can be converted to a Chapter 7.

CHAPTER 13 PLAN

Chapter 13 provides a means by which individuals can obtain relief from creditor collection actions and enter into a repayment plan. It cannot be used for the discharge of business debt, not even debts incurred by sole proprietors. The automatic stay in a Chapter 13 proceeding does not bar creditors from trying to collect business debts.

PART II. SALES

Chapter 9. Contracts

Every online sale involves a contract, whether it is formalized in a signed writing or not. Because the law of contracts reflects a belief in freedom of contract—i.e., the principle that people should have the power to structure their business relationships with others in whatever way they see fit—these contracts generally are enforceable. Fairness is also a concern, however, especially in contracts between merchants and consumers. And of course, there can be no enforcement of a contract that was never formed in the first place.

Basic Contract Law

FORMATION OF A CONTRACT

The formation of an enforceable contract requires six things:

- offer
- acceptance
- "meeting of the minds"
- consideration
- contractual capacity
- a lawful purpose.

Some kinds of contracts must be in writing; others may be oral or implied by conduct.

Offer and Acceptance

An *offer* is a communication on an intent to enter into a contract with another person. Intent is assessed using an objective standard. A person's subjective intent does not matter. If a reasonable person would interpret a communication as an invitation to enter into a contract, then it is an offer.

> **Example**. Charlie intends to offer to sell encyclopedias to Bob so he sends him an email message containing only the words, "Let's talk." A person may have any number of reasons for wanting to talk to somebody, so a reasonable person would not interpret this communication as an offer. Charlie's subjective intention does not determine whether he has made an offer or not.

An offer must be definite. Advertisements that do nothing more than tout the qualities of a product or service are not offers. Neither are expressions of interest or invitations to negotiate.

Example. Bob sends Charlie the following message, "I am interested in the encyclopedias you sell. What is your price?" A reasonable person would interpret this as information gathering or an invitation to negotiate, not as an offer to buy. Since it is not an invitation to enter into a contract, it is not an offer. If Charlie replies, "Send me $500 and they are yours," then Charlie has made an offer and now it will be up to Bob to decide whether he wants to accept the offer or not.

An *acceptance* is a communication of an intent to agree to the terms of an offer. An objective standard is applied to determine whether an acceptance occurred.

The offeror may specify the manner in which the offer may be accepted, provided the conduct specified as the manner of acceptance can reasonably be interpreted as a communication of intent to accept the offer. An offer that invites acceptance by "doing nothing" would not meet this criterion. It cannot reasonably be interpreted from a person's silence or inaction that the person wants to enter into a contract. On the other hand, a website that invites a user to accept an offer of access to a page by clicking an 'I Agree' button adjacent to a notice that says clicking on the button signals assent to the displayed terms of the offer probably would be interpreted as a communication of intent to accept the offer.

An offer that invites acceptance by performance may be accepted by performance. A website that offers to ship a product if a person makes a payment in a specified amount is an example of an offer that invites acceptance by performance. In this case, acceptance is communicated by sending payment in the amount specified.

The offer also may impose conditions on the acceptance of an offer. For example, an offeror might specify that the offer is only available for a specified period of time. An offeree must comply with those conditions. Otherwise, no contract is formed.

In most jurisdictions, courts hold that offers are subject to the implied condition that the offeror must be alive at the time the offer is accepted. This means that an offer terminates by operation of law if the offeror dies before the offer has been accepted.

Usually an offeror may revoke an offer at any time before it is accepted. There are three exceptions to this:

(a) **Options contract**. An options contract is one that gives one person an option but not an obligation to buy or sell a particular asset at a later date or at an agreed price. They are most often used in securities and commodities trading and in real estate transactions. If the promise to leave the offer open is supported by consideration, then the offeror may not revoke it until the term of the option expires. Most courts hold that the mailbox rule does not apply to option contracts, so an acceptance will not be effective until it is received by the offeror. California and a few other courts, however, hold that the mailbox rule does apply to options contracts. In these states, acceptance is effective as soon as the offeree deposits it in the mail or transmits it.

(b) **Firm offer between merchants**. Between merchants, a signed, written statement that an offer will remain open causes the offer to be irrevocable even if the agreement to keep the offer open is not supported by consideration. If no time period is specified, the offer remains irrevocable for a reasonable time. A state statute may specify a maximum period of time, such as three months, if the agreement doe not specify one.

(c) **Promissory estoppel**. When an offer calls for acceptance by performance but performance is not of a kind that can be completed all at once, the offeror must give the offeror a reasonable time to complete performance. The doctrine of promissory estoppel bars an offeror from denying the existence of a contract where the offeror induced reasonable reliance to the offeree's detriment.

> **Example.** Donald, a domain name owner, has arranged hosting and sends a password and administrator privileges to a designer along with a note reading, "Build my website and I'll pay you a thousand dollars when it's completed." The designer proceeds to purchase image and software licenses to use on the website and spends a considerable amount of time working on it. Before it is done, Donald decides he doesn't want to have a website, after all, so he tells the designer to stop work. He adds that he won't be paying anything because the designer has not yet completed performance. Without an acceptance, he says, there can be no enforceable contract. If the designer sues for breach of contract, a court may hold that Donald is barred from claiming that no contract exists because his conduct in making an offer which, by its terms, could be accepted by performance, induced reasonable reliance to the offeree's detriment.

Generally, acceptance is deemed to occur at the time the offeree initiates the transmission of the acceptance to the offeror. Thus, acceptance occurs at the time the offeree deposits a communication of acceptance in a mailbox (or hands it to a courier for overnight delivery, or faxes it), not when the offeror actually receives the communication. This is known as the *mailbox rule*. The mailbox rule applies only when the offeree uses the method of acceptance specified in the offer or a faster method. If an offeree uses a slower method of communicating acceptance than what is specified in the offer, then acceptance will not be deemed to have occurred until the offeror actually receives the communication. Several courts have held that the mailbox rule applies to email as well as regular mail.

Meeting of the Minds

To form an enforceable contract, the offeree must accept the offer that was made, not a different offer that the offeree wishes had been made.

> **Example**. Alex offers to sell Brunhilda a license to read a digital copy of a romance novel for $1.50. Brunhilda responds: "I accept your offer, but make it a Sarbanes-Oxley auditing software license coupled with a royalty-free right to use a photograph of Prince in my advertising." Alex responds, "No way." He proceeds to sell the novel to someone else. Brunhilda then says, "Okay, forget the SOX software and the Prince photograph. I accept your original offer now. Send me that romance novel." You can probably guess Alex's response. Brunhilda's material alteration of Alex's offer caused Brunhilda's first purported "acceptance" to operate as a rejection and counteroffer. It automatically took Alex's offer off the table. Brunhilda's second purported "acceptance" comes too late. The offer is gone. There is nothing for her to accept at that point.

At common law, a purported acceptance that alters a material term of an offer is a rejection and counteroffer, not an acceptance. The U.C.C., which has been adopted in nearly every state, creates a limited exception to this rule in the case of contracts for the sale of goods. For these kinds of contracts, an acceptance containing additional or different terms may nevertheless operate as an acceptance in some cases. (See below.) The U.C.C. exception does not apply to contracts for the sale, lease or license of services, intangible goods, or real estate interests. For these kinds of contracts, the common law rule that a purported acceptance that materially alters the terms of the offer is a rejection and counteroffer still applies. At common law, no contract is formed by the acceptance of an offer after it has been rejected unless the offeror has since renewed the offer. Of course, if the offeror accepts the offeree's counterproposal, then that acceptance may result in the formation of a contract. That contract, however, would embody the terms of the counterproposal. It would not include the terms of the original offer except to the extent the counterproposal explicitly or implicitly incorporates them into the counteroffer.

In addition to being unequivocal, offers and acceptances must be communicated in sufficiently definite terms to assure that there is a meeting of the minds concerning what has been offered and what has been accepted. It is not possible to enforce a contract unless the intended terms of the contract can be ascertained.

Not every ambiguity in a contract will render it void. The material terms must be sufficiently certain, though. Price, quantity and the kinds of goods that are being sold are material terms in a sales contract.

> **Example 1**. Bob, a mature adult, walks into a fast food restaurant and places an order for "food." When a worker brings him three $7.00 happy meals, Bob refuses them, insisting he wanted a $0.50 hamburger and a $0.10 order of fries instead.

Here, there has been no meeting of the minds regarding either the goods being sold or the quantity. These are material terms in a sales contract. Since there was no meeting of the minds, no contract was formed. Bob does not have to accept and pay for the value meals. The restaurant does not have to sell him a $0.50 hamburger and a $0.10 order of fries.

> **Example 2.** Same as Example 1, except that Bob orders three $7.00 happy meals. Now he refuses to pay because there was no agreement about the design of the bag in which the meals are packed. He wanted one with a clown picture on it, not one with pictures of flowers on it.

Although the parties in Example 2 did not have a meeting of the minds about the bag design, a court probably would hold the agreement is enforceable anyway because bag design is not a material term in an adult fast food purchase agreement.

Agreements to agree generally are too indefinite to be enforceable, either, unless the parties also agree to be bound by the application of a specified objective standard that will result in a sufficiently definite term.

> **Example 3**: Same as Example 2, except that the worker asks, "Would you like to buy a value meal?" and Bob says, "Yes, I will buy three." Prices are posted on a sign that is readable from where Bob is standing when he places the order.

Price is a material term, but neither the worker's offer nor Bob's acceptance addresses it. The sign, however, provides an objective standard by which the price of three value meals may be determined. If, under all the circumstances, it is reasonable for Bob to understand from custom, usage and trade practices that the restaurant's offer is to sell at the prices posted on the sign, the contract should not fail for indefiniteness.

On occasion, a court will supply a "reasonable" material term that has been omitted from an otherwise enforceable agreement. They will not always do this, however, and what a judge thinks is reasonable may not be the same as what a party to the contract thinks is reasonable. Accordingly, it is always a good idea to address all material terms when entering into a contract.

Consideration

To be enforceable, a contract must be supported by consideration. A promise is not enforceable unless the promisee gives, does or refrains from doing something (or promises to give, do or refrain from doing something) in return. In other words, there must be a bargained-for exchange of value or benefit of some kind for each party.

The consideration given by each party need not be equal. A contract for the sale of land, for example, may be enforceable even if the consideration given is only $1. A promise to make a gift, however, is not valid consideration.

Consideration generally must be given in exchange for each party's obligations. Past consideration generally will not support a new promise.

> **Example**. Although not under any contractual obligation to do so, Ross gives Rachel a diamond ring. Rachel is so happy she promises to let Ross use her kitchen to boil cabbage and chicken any time he wants. A few months later, Ross shows up at 3:15 a.m. with cabbage and chicken in hand. Rachel refuses to get out of bed and let him in. Ross will probably lose a breach of contract action against Rachel because Rachel's promise is not supported by consideration. At the time Ross gave her the ring, it was not in exchange for any promise on her part. It was a gift.

The rule that past consideration cannot support a present promise is why, at common law, a modification of an existing contract is not enforceable unless new consideration is given for the modification.

Although a pre-existing obligation normally cannot serve as the consideration for a new promise, courts sometimes enforce a promise made on account of a past detriment suffered by the promisee for the promisor's benefit, in circumstances where refusing to enforce the promise would unjustly enrich the promisor. The clearest case for this is where the consideration a party gives for a new contract is a promise to pay a pre-existing debt despite the fact that it is now barred by a statute of limitations or has been discharged in bankruptcy.

It can be difficult to prevail on a claim of unjust enrichment. Courts are reluctant to consider a person's acceptance of an unrequested service without paying for it to be unjust. If the rule were otherwise, then people could bind each other to contracts simply by officiously performing work for people without having been asked and then arguing that it would be unjust for those people to retain the benefit of the work without paying for it. It is not unjust to accept the benefit of an unrequested, gratuitous performance. Volunteers and officious intermeddlers generally will not prevail on unjust enrichment claims.

Promissory estoppel is an exception to the consideration requirement. If a promise has the effect of inducing a person to do or refrain from doing something, so that the person reasonably relies on the promise to his detriment, then a court might declare that the promisor is barred (estopped) from claiming that the promise is unenforceable. Promissory estoppel may be applied even if the promise was not supported by consideration.

Capacity

A contract is not enforceable against a person who lacks contractual capacity. In most states, a person must be of sufficient age and mental capacity to enter into an enforceable contract. An unemancipated minor may avoid a contract into which she has entered. The only exception is that a contract to provide necessities (e.g., food or clothing) to a minor may be enforced, typically against the parent or another person who is legally responsible for the child's care.

A person who is not mentally capable of understanding the obligations of a contract is not capable of entering into an enforceable contract. A person who knows or has reason to know of the incapacity at the time of contracting may not enforce the contract against the incapacitated person.

Illegality

Contracts to perform illegal acts are not enforceable. Also, if the formation of a particular kind of contract is itself unlawful, then the resulting contract is unenforceable.

The Requirement of a Writing

The general common law rule is that a contract may be written, oral, or implied by conduct. In some circumstances, though, a statute of frauds may require certain kinds of contracts to be in writing. While statutes of frauds vary from state to state, they typically require the following things to be in writing:

(a) real estate sales contracts
(b) contracts that are not capable of being performed in less than one year
(c) surety contracts (where one person acts as guarantor of another person's debt)
(d) prenuptial agreements (and other contracts made in consideration of marriage)
(e) contracts for the sale of goods, or for the "sale or return" of goods, for $500 or more
(f) leases of goods for $1,000 or more.

In most cases, the writing must also be signed by the party against whom enforcement is sought. The U.C.C. creates a limited exception to the signature requirement for certain kinds of contracts between merchants. (See below.)

There are some exceptions to the Statute of Frauds requirement of a writing.

(a) **Admission under oath**. A contract that would normally require a signed writing in order to be enforceable may be enforced despite the absence of a writing against a person who has admitted under oath the existence of the agreement.

(b) **Part performance**. Courts have held that performance of some of the obligations under a contract can make the contract enforceable to the extent of the obligation performed, at least if the performance unequivocally relates to the contract and embarking upon the performance was reasonable under the circumstances. Some courts hold that the executory portion of the contract—i.e., the part of it that has not yet been performed—remains subject to the requirement of a writing. Other courts hold that part performance makes the entire contract enforceable, at least if the conditions for an application of the promissory estoppel doctrine exist.

(c) **Promissory estoppel**. In most states, a person who has reasonably relied on an unenforceable contract to his detriment may invoke the equitable doctrine of promissory estoppel to enforce it anyway. Because it is an equitable defense, principles of equity jurisprudence apply to it. For example, a court might refuse to apply promissory estoppel in a way that benefits a litigant who has "unclean hands."

(d) **Certain surety contracts**. Some courts will enforce a surety contract despite the absence of a writing if it is made primarily for the surety's own economic advantage.

(e) **Implied easements**. Easements arising by operation of law do not need to be in writing.

(f) **Specially manufactured goods**.

(g) **Merchant confirmation rule**.

The merchant confirmation rule and rules pertaining to specially manufactured goods are discussed in connection with contracts for the sale of goods, infra.

The parol evidence rule is often confused with the Statute of Frauds. It is a rule of evidence that bars the use of extrinsic evidence to contradict the terms of a written agreement. It applies to any written contract, whether it is one for which the Statute of Frauds mandates a writing or not. The parol evidence rule does not bar the use of extrinsic evidence to clarify an ambiguous term or to prove that a valid contract was not formed.

Implied Covenants of Good Faith and Fair Dealing

By law, every contract includes implied covenants of good faith and fair dealing whether the contract expressly provides for them or not.

MODIFICATIONS

Once an enforceable contract has been formed, it may not be modified without the consent of both parties. In addition, a modification normally must be supported by new consideration. Some courts will enforce a modification that is not supported by new consideration if the modification merely adapts the contract to unforeseen events that render performance more difficult or costly. Also, the U.C.C. creates an exception for certain contracts for the sales of goods. (See below.)

If the original agreement may be unwritten, then modifications of it may also be unwritten. If a statute of frauds requires the original agreement to be in writing and signed, then modifications must also be in writing and signed. As is the case with any agreement that is subject to a statute of frauds, however, a court may bar a party from asserting the statute of frauds as a defense if an exception to the requirement of a writing exists (e.g., promissory estoppel).

In cases where a modification is not required to be in writing, it may be oral, written, or implied by a course of conduct. To modify on the basis of course of conduct subsequent to the original agreement, the conduct must be inconsistent with the terms of the existing agreement and must unequivocally evidence an intention to modify the contract. The mere fact that a party fails to act in a way that is consistent with the existing terms does not unequivocally evidence an intention to modify the contract. It could simply evidence an intention to breach the contract. There must be some additional, independent evidence that the parties intended the inconsistent performance to become the obligatory performance.

Contracts often contain a clause requiring all modifications to be in writing, and that the writing must be signed by both parties. Most courts enforce these clauses but may deny enforcement in cases where (a) there has been part performance that is unequivocally referable to an oral modification or a modification proven by course of conduct; or (b) the estoppel doctrine applies. Some courts deny, or are inclined to deny, enforcement of this kind of clause in other circumstances, too.

PERFORMANCE AND BREACH

To prevail on a claim for breach of contract, it is necessary to prove four things:

(a) the existence of an enforceable contract
(b) the plaintiff substantially performed obligations under it
(c) the defendant did not substantially perform obligations under it
(d) resulting damage.

Contracts often condition the performance of a specified obligation on either the other party's performance or some other event. When a specified condition fails, the party whose obligation is conditioned on it generally is excused from performing the obligation. On the other hand, the law abhors a forfeiture. When courts are applying common law, they are not inclined to strictly enforce contractual conditions if doing so would result in an unjust forfeiture of value on the part of one of the parties to the contract. If a deficit in one party's performance of an obligation upon which the other party's obligation is conditional is merely technical—if it does not appreciably reduce the other party's benefit of the bargain—a court may relieve the breaching party of the consequences, except to the extent of any provable resulting damage. Put another way, a court may be reluctant to enforce a contract term calling for a forfeiture upon a party's failure to completely perform a specified obligation if the party substantially performed the obligation.

In a similar vein, a court may decline a remedy for a breach that is not material.

Defenses

Of course, it is a defense to an action for breach of contract that a valid contract was never formed. Thus, incapacity, illegality, lack of consideration, or the absence of mutual assent and a "meeting of the minds" are defenses.

Some kinds of conduct can vitiate assent and therefore prevent the formation of a valid contract. Fraud in the inducement is an example. It occurs when the offeror makes a false statement of a material fact (or creates a misimpression by knowingly omitting a material fact) with the intention and effect of inducing the offeree to enter into the contract. Fraud in the factum may also prevent the formation of an enforceable contract. This involves misrepresenting the nature of the document that is being signed. An example would be substituting a contract with terms to which the offeree has not agreed for the one containing terms to which the offeree has agreed, thereby deceiving the offeree into signing a different document that the one he thinks he is signing.

Duress can also vitiate assent. This may include coercing a person to sign a contract by threatening the person with injury, criminal prosecution, bad faith litigation, or economic ruin.

Undue influence occurs where a person uses a position of trust to induce another person to enter into an agreement. This, too, can vitiate assent to a contract.

Mutual mistake of fact is a defense. The mistake must be a material one, and it must be one of fact, not judgment. Estimations of value, for instance, are matters of judgment, not fact. A unilateral mistake may be a defense if the other party knew or should have known of the mistake and did nothing to correct the other party's misunderstanding.

Unconscionability may be a defense in cases where the terms of a contract are grossly unfair to one of the parties, or the procedure for obtaining assent was unfair. A court is most likely to allow this defense when there is a serious imbalance of bargaining power, such as in adhesion contracts (nonnegotiable take-it-or-leave-it contracts). Courts are more likely to refuse to enforce a consumer contract on the basis of unconscionability than a commercial contract between merchants. In lieu of voiding an unconscionable contract altogether, a court may instead elect to reform the contract by either removing the offending terms or rewriting them to make the contract fairer.

If a writing is required, then the Statute of Frauds may be a defense to the enforcement of an oral contract, provided none of the exceptions to the requirement of a writing applies.

Waiver is another potential defense. Waiver is the intentional relinquishment or abandonment of a known right. It occurs when a party knowingly fails to enforce a term of a contract or performs its obligations under the contract knowing that the other party has failed to perform. Temporary forbearance likely will not rise to the level of waiver. A party who accepts a breach of a term on a one-time basis is not likely to be held to have waived it unless the other party relied on the forbearance to his detriment. This result might be forestalled by clearly conveying to the breaching party that the forbearance is a one-time thing and that strict compliance with the terms of the contract will be expected in the future.

Not all waivers are retractable. If retraction would be unjust because the other party has materially changed its position in reasonable reliance on the waiver, courts generally will not give effect to any purported retraction. Clearly conveying to the breaching party that a waiver is a one-time thing and that strict compliance is expected in the future may alter that result, though. A breaching party's reliance on a one-time waiver as a basis for future breaches of the same kind after receiving a notice like this arguably would not be reasonable.

Estoppel is an equitable defense that may be asserted to prevent a party from denying the enforceability of a representation upon which another party has relied to his detriment.

> **Example**. Rapper MJ McLofty signs a contract with Big Man Ltd. committing him to record twelve original songs in the rap genre. Later, McLofty asks if it would be cool if one of the songs could be a cover version of James Taylor's "You've Got a Friend."

A Big Man executive says that will be fine. McLofty proceeds to secure licensing rights and pays a guitarist to perform on the recording. If Big Man later tries to enforce the original agreement, McLofty may be able to assert estoppel as a defense.

To prevail on an estoppel defense, it is necessary to show that the party against whom it is asserted acted (or failed to act) in a way that induced reasonable reliance to the other party's detriment.

Accord and satisfaction is another possible defense. It may be asserted in situations where the parties have accepted a performance, or a substituted performance, as adequate.

Example. Same as above, except that McLofty never asks and Big Man never represents that a cover of a James Taylor song may be recorded in lieu of an original rap song. Instead, McLofty simply presents the James Taylor cover along with eleven original rap songs to Big Man. He explains that he knows he is in breach but he just did not have enough angst in him to come up with twelve original songs. A Big Man executive says, "That's okay. This will fulfill your obligation to us if you agree to assume full responsibility for paying the guitarist." McLofty agrees. If Big Man later attempts to sue him for breach of contract, McLofty may defend on the basis that the parties already settled the dispute.

Impossibility or frustration of purpose may be a defense if an unforeseen circumstance beyond the parties' control makes performance impossible or frustrates the purpose of the contract. At common law, the performance must be literally impossible, not just unexpectedly costly or burdensome. A growing number of courts, however, also recognize commercial impracticability as a defense, excusing performance that would require a party to incur unreasonable cost due to unexpected circumstances beyond the party's control.

The availability of a defense may be impacted by language in the contract. For example, a clause disclaiming oral promises and representations and requiring all modifications to be in writing may make it difficult to prevail on an estoppel claim that is based on an oral promise or representation. Similarly, if a contract details how specified future contingencies will affect the parties' rights and obligations, then the contingency can no longer be treated as unforeseen, so it may be difficult to prevail on an impossibility, frustration of purpose or impracticability defense.

Remedies

The three kinds of damages that may be available for breach of contract, depending on the circumstances, are:

- Compensatory damages
- Consequential damages
- Liquidated damages.

Compensatory damages are intended to give the aggrieved party the benefit of the bargain, i.e., what she would have gained if the contract had been performed, minus the cost she would have incurred had the contract been performed. Consequential damages are reasonably foreseeable losses besides loss of the benefit of the bargain. An award of compensatory damages is the ordinary remedy in breach of contract cases.

Liquidated damages are damages that are awarded pursuant to a contract in which the parties have agreed at the outset what amount will be payable in the event of a breach. If the contract so provides, a party may be limited to the recovery of the amount of liquidated damages set out in the contract, and may be barred from recovering any other or additional compensatory or consequential damages.

Punitive damages generally are not awarded in contract casts.

Normally, an award of damages is the exclusive remedy for breach of contract. In extraordinary cases, though, where an award of damages is not an adequate remedy, a court may grant an equitable remedy of one of the following kinds:

(a) **Specific performance**. This requires the defaulting party to perform an obligation rather than compensate the other party for not doing it. This will be ordered only when the subject matter of the contract is unique and an award of monetary damages would be inadequate. A contract for the sale of land and a contract for the return of a prized family heirloom with incalculable sentimental value are examples of rare situations in which specific performance might be an appropriate remedy.

(b) **Injunction**. An injunction is a court order prohibiting a party from doing something. An injunction is very rarely issued as a remedy for breach of contract.

(c) **Reformation**. This involves the court rewriting a contract to reflect the parties' true intent. It is appropriate in cases where there is a mutual mistake in the wording of a contract.

(d) **Rescission and restitution**. When rescission and restitution are ordered, the contract is declared void and the parties are required to return to each other the benefits they have received under it. It might be an appropriate remedy in cases where a contract has been procured by fraud, for example.

Contracts for Sales and Leases of Goods

In the United States, contracts for the sale of goods are governed by Article 2 of the U.C.C., some version of which has been adopted in every state. Contracts for the lease of goods are governed by Article 2A. Articles 2 and 2A are very similar.

For purposes of the U.C.C., *goods* are tangible things that are moveable at the time they are identified to a contract. Article 2 does not apply to real estate or to copyrights, trademarks, patents, publicity rights, or any other intangibles. It also does not apply to sales of services.

The U.C.C. principles applicable to contracts for the sales of goods are generally consistent with common law contract principles. Important areas where they diverge from the common law are described below.

ACCEPTANCE VARYING OFFER

An acceptance of an offer for the sale of goods may state additional or different terms without being treated as a rejection and counteroffer. Additional terms are treated as proposals for addition, but do not cause what would otherwise be a valid acceptance to be treated as a rejection. The benefit of this rule may be lost, however, if the acceptance is expressly made conditional on the offeror's assent to the additional or different terms.

Proposals for addition to a contract between a merchant and a consumer do not become part of the contract unless the other party assents to the proposed additions.

Proposals for addition to a contract between merchants become part of the contract unless:

(a) The offer expressly limits acceptance to the terms of the offer;
(b) They materially alter the terms of the offer; or
(c) Notification of objection to them has already been given or is given within a reasonable time after notice of them is received.

Conduct by both parties recognizing the existence of a contract may suffice to establish the existence of a contract even though the writings of the parties are not sufficient, standing alone, to establish that a contact has been formed. The terms of the contact consist of those terms on which the writings of the parties agree, together with any supplementary terms dictated by the U.C.C., such as the covenants of honesty in fact and observance of reasonable commercial standards of fair dealing that are implied in every contract for the sale of goods under the U.C.C.

DEFINITENESS

The U.C.C. allows a greater degree of indefiniteness in contracts than the common law does. For example, the absence of a price term in the contract does not necessarily make the contract too indefinite to enforce. A court will supply a reasonable price term if:

(a) Price was completely omitted from the contract;
(b) The contract left the price to be agreed upon by the parties at a later time, and they failed to agree; or
(c) The contract called for the price to be set with reference to a standard to be set by a third party who then fails to do so.

If a time for the performance of an obligation is not specified in the contract, the court will supply a reasonable one. If the contract does not specify a time when payment is due, then it is due at the time and place of delivery. If the place of delivery is not specified, then it is the seller's place of business or, if he has none, then his home. If the goods are identified at some other place, and both parties are aware of it, then that is the place of delivery. Of course, the parties may alter these rules by simply including their desired delivery, time and payment terms in the contract.

CONSIDERATION

No new consideration is needed to modify a contract for the sale or lease of goods. Modifications may be enforceable even if no consideration has been given for them. The same is true of firm offers between merchants. Between merchants, a signed, written statement that an offer will remain open causes the offer to be irrevocable even if the agreement to keep the offer open is not supported by consideration. If no time period is specified, the U.C.C. calls for the offer to remain irrevocable for "a reasonable time," not to exceed three months.

THE REQUIREMENT OF A WRITING

The U.C.C. contains a statute of frauds. It requires contracts for the sale of goods, or for the "sale or return" of goods, for $500 or more to be in writing. Leases of goods for $1,000 or more also must be in writing. Some version of the U.C.C. statute of frauds has been adopted in every state. A recent revision to Article 2 increased the threshold from $500 to $5,000. Very few states have adopted this revision, however.

A writing that incorrectly states an agreed term or omits a term may nevertheless satisfy the requirement of a writing. In such cases, though, the contract is not enforceable beyond the quantity of goods shown in the writing.

The writing generally must be signed by the person against whom enforcement is sought, or that person's agent or broker.

A contract that is required to be in writing and signed, but is not, may nevertheless be enforced (assuming it would otherwise be enforceable) in any of the following circumstances:

(a) The goods are specially manufactured for the buyer, are not suitable for sale to others in the ordinary course of the seller's business, and the seller, before notice of repudiation is received and under circumstances which reasonably indicate that the goods are for the buyer, has made either a substantial beginning of their manufacture or commitments for their procurement;

(b) The buyer or lessee has partially accepted the contract by virtue of retaining some of the goods the seller/lessor has furnished pursuant to the oral contract, in which case the buyer/lessee must pay for the goods that have been accepted but is under no obligation to accept more;

(c) The party against whom enforcement is sought admits in a pleading, testimony or otherwise in court that a contract was made (in which case, the contract is not enforceable beyond the quantity of goods admitted); or

(d) The contract is between merchants and one merchant has sent a confirmation of the contract to the other merchant to which the other merchant has not objected within ten days after receiving it.

The exception listed in paragraph (d) is known as the *merchant confirmation rule*. It means that a merchant may bind another merchant to a contract that neither one has signed by sending the other merchant a letter in confirmation and waiting for the other merchant to fail to object to it. The rule will not be applied, however, unless the receiving merchant knew or had reason to know of the contents of the written confirmation message. The rule does not apply to contracts between merchants and consumers.[99]

A clause in a contact that provides that no modification or rescission of the contract is permitted except in a signed writing generally is enforceable. If it appears in a form contract supplied by a merchant to a consumer, however, it must be separately signed.

IMPLIED COVENANTS

The common law holds that there are implied covenants of good faith and fair dealing in every contract. The U.C.C. adopts a similar but slightly more specific standard. Under the U.C.C., every contract for the sale of good includes an implied covenant of honesty in fact and observance of reasonable commercial standards of fair dealing.

UNCONSCIONABILITY

The U.C.C. does not significantly alter the common law unconscionability doctrine. It makes explicit, however, that a clause limiting consequential damages for personal injury in a contract for the sale of goods to a consumer is prima facie unconscionable. A limitation of damages for commercial loss is not prima facie unconscionable.

PERFORMANCE AND BREACH

The U.C.C. significantly alters common law principles relating to performance and breach. The seller has a right to cure a nonconformity that is not substantial if the time for performance has not expired.

Electronic Contracts

The Electronic Signatures in Global and National Commerce Act[100] (E-SIGN Act) provides that a digital contract is enforceable if both parties agree to an electronic format for their contract. It also provides that an e-signature in a format that both parties have agreed is acceptable is enforceable to the same extent as a pen-and-ink signature is. Unless it comes within one of the categories of documents that are excepted from the Act, an electronically signed digital document (or "record") will be just as legally effective, valid, and enforceable as a paper document with pen-and-ink signatures on it. If a statute of frauds or another law requires a writing or a signature, an electronic record or signature will satisfy the requirement, unless the document or record comes within one of the listed exceptions.

No special technology is required to create a valid electronic signature. Affixing/Inputting one's typewritten name or some other symbol(s) or sound with the intention of denoting one's name in an email message or online form may suffice. While encryption and authentication processes have some benefits, their use is not legally required in order to create a valid and enforceable electronic signature. The key element is intent: it is only necessary that the name, symbol, sound or process is used or affixed for the purpose of signing an electronic document (record). If the intent is there, then it will qualify as an electronic signature.

Parties to a contract may impose their own conditions and specifications regarding how the contract must be signed. In any case, of course, an electronic signature must be logically associated with the record to which it relates.

If a law requires information about a transaction (such as the terms of a contract or other notices and disclosures) to be in writing, an electronic record containing the information will suffice, provided it is capable of being printed or stored by the recipient. In addition, some method of attributing the document to the parties purporting to sign it must be in place. An email or website user account that requires the use of a password to sign in is an example of an attribution mechanism.

Consumers have the right to (a) demand paper instead of electronic documents, (b) withhold consent to receiving electronic communications from a merchant, (c) withdraw consent once given.

Merchants must disclose the following information to a consumer before the consumer signifies consent:

(a) the consumer's right to demand paper instead of electronic documents
(b) the consumer's right to withhold consent to receiving electronic communications from the merchant
(c) the consumer's right to withdraw consent once given
(d) the existence and nature of any conditions, consequences (which may include termination of the parties' relationship, if the merchant so specifies), or fees in the event of such withdrawal
(e) a specification of whether the consent applies only to the particular transaction which gave rise to the obligation to provide the record, or to identified categories of records that may be provided or made available during the course of the parties' relationship
(f) a description of the procedures the consumer must use to withdraw consent
(g) a description of the procedures the consumer must use to update information needed to contact the consumer electronically
(h) how, after the consent, the consumer may obtain a paper copy of an electronic record, and whether any fee will be charged for it
(i) a statement of the hardware and software requirements for access to and retention of the electronic records.

Consent may be given electronically. It must reasonably demonstrate that the consumer can access information in the electronic form that will be used to provide the information that is the subject of the consent. It should be possible to satisfy this requirement by means of an 'I Agree' button in conjunction with a clickwrap agreement that contains provisions (a) describing the hardware and software requirements necessary to access the electronic record; (b) acknowledging that the customer understands those requirements; and (c) affirming that the customer has the required hardware and software to access the record. This is just one method of satisfying the requirement; other methods are possible.

After consent has been obtained, merchants must notify consumers of any change in hardware or software requirements if the change creates a material risk that the consumer will be unable to access or retain a subsequent electronic record that was the subject of the consent. The notification must (a) include a statement of the revised hardware and software requirements for access to and retention of the electronic records and (b) inform the consumer of the consumer's right to withdraw consent without the imposition of any fees for such withdrawal and without the imposition of any condition or consequence that was not disclosed prior to the original consent.

A new consent must be obtained, and it must satisfy the same "reasonable demonstration of ability to access the record" requirement that applies to obtaining an initial consent.

The customer must be offered the option of withdrawing consent. No fee may be charged, and no new conditions or consequences may be imposed for a customer's withdrawal of consent that is due to a merchant's change in hardware or software requirements that creates a material risk that the customer will be unable to access or retain a subsequent electronic record that was the subject of the original consent. If a merchant fails to comply with any of these requirements, then the consumer, at the consumer's option, may elect to treat the failure as a withdrawal of consent without any further action on her part.

A consumer's withdrawal of consent can only operate prospectively, not retroactively. Withdrawal of consent does not affect the legal effectiveness, validity or enforceability of electronic records that have already been provided or made available to the consumer in accordance with E-SIGN Act requirements.

The E-SIGN Act does not apply to:

- wills, codicils, or testamentary trusts
- adoption, divorce or other family law matters
- court orders, notices, briefs, pleadings and other court documents
- notices of cancellation or termination of utility services
- product recall notices
- hazardous materials documents
- secured transactions
- investment securities
- negotiable instruments (promissory notes and drafts)
- bank deposits and collections
- funds transfers
- letters of credit
- bulk transfers and bulk sales (auctions and liquidations of assets)
- warehouse receipts, bills of lading and other documents of title relating to the storage and bailment of goods
- notices of default, acceleration, repossession, foreclosure, or eviction, or the right to cure, under a credit agreement secured by, or a rental agreement for, an individual's primary residence
- notices of cancellation or termination of health insurance or benefits or life insurance benefits (excluding annuities).

The Act *does* apply to transactions governed by Articles 2 or 2A of the U.C.C., i.e., sales or leases of goods.

Failure to comply with the E-SIGN Act does not, in itself, make a contract unenforceable. Nor does it vitiate the validity or effectiveness of any document that is required to be in writing. It simply means that the E-SIGN Act cannot be invoked as the basis for treating the record as a writing. If not preempted, state laws (such as an applicable state law giving legal effect to electronic records as "writings") and statutory and common law exceptions to the requirement of a writing may be invoked to uphold the validity and effectiveness of an electronic record as a "writing" notwithstanding the unavailability of the E-SIGN Act for that purpose.

At the state level, the Uniform Electronic Transactions Act (UETA) provides that contracts that are formed online generally are enforceable to the same extent and in the same way that traditional contracts are. It applies to transactions that both parties agree to conduct by electronic means. As with most other kinds of agreements, an agreement to conduct business by electronic means may be written, oral or implied by the conduct of the parties. UETA does not apply to wills or trusts. Additional exclusions may apply in a particular state. When it applies, it authorizes and gives the same effect to electronic records, documents, contracts and signatures as is given to paper documents and pen-and-ink signatures.

UETA has been adopted in nearly every state. Those states that have not adopted it have enacted other laws authorizing and giving effect to electronic records, documents and signatures when specified conditions are met.

The E-SIGN Act expressly preempts inconsistent state laws except for a state's version of the UETA. A state's enactment of an exception to the scope of UETA is preempted by E-SIGN, however, to the extent the exception either: (a) is inconsistent with the E-SIGN Act, or (b) specifies alternative procedures or requirements that either do not require, or accord greater legal status or effect to, the implementation or application of a specific technology or technical specification for performing the functions of creating, storing, generating, receiving, communicating, or authenticating electronic records. State laws relating to documents that are not covered by E-SIGN, of course, are not preempted. Not being within the coverage of E-SIGN, state regulation of them would not be inconsistent with E-SIGN. E-SIGN would not preempt a state law requiring a will to be on paper and signed manually, for example.

In the European Union (EU), the Directive on Electronic Commerce[101] generally validates electronic contracts as "writings." A number of exceptions are provided for certain kinds of contracts, such as real estate and family law contracts. Merchants must disclose to consumers how to conclude online contracts and how to correct errors in electronic records. A consumer must be able to store and retrieve contracts or they are unenforceable

CLICKWRAP AGREEMENTS

A click on a webpage click-through process may qualify as an electronic signature. A click on an 'I Agree' button after entering information needed to place and fill an order may qualify as a signature on a purchase order, for example. The process in this case is the click-through process, and the purchaser uses it with the intention of associating himself with the record of that process.

Clickwrap agreements are contracts that are formed by clicking on something (usually an 'I Accept' button) that is displayed on an Internet website. They differ from shrinkwrap agreements in that shrinkwrap agreements are set out in the physical packaging or documentation accompanying a product. Courts have held that opening and using a packaged product may bind a consumer to a shrinkwrap agreement that is included in the package. Clickwrap agreements, too, are usually enforceable, at least when there is no ambiguity about the terms to which the user has signaled assent. Courts have held that third parties who use the account of a user who has assented to a clickwrap agreement (such as by clicking the 'I Agree' button) are also bound by the terms of the agreement even if they do not personally click on the button. The person who uses the account of a user who has assented to the agreement is deemed to be a sublicensee of the assenting user. As one court has explained, if the rule were otherwise, then people could circumvent clickwrap agreements simply by having a friend click the 'I Agree' button rather than clicking on it themselves.

Unlike clickwrap agreements, a browsewrap agreement generally is not enforceable. A browsewrap agreement is not really an agreement at all. It is a claimed agreement that is purportedly formed by a user's act of accessing a website on which a statement asserting that use of the site constitutes acceptance of the Terms of Use appears. An example would be a website whose Terms of Use specify that use of the site constitutes acceptance of the Terms of Use, but which does not provide any specific mechanism for signaling assent other than the use of the site alone. Browsewrap agreements are usually held to be unenforceable against users because a legally enforceable contract is not formed unless an offer and acceptance occur—in that order. A pool owner cannot acquire contract rights simply by announcing to people who are already swimming in it that swimming in the pool constitutes acceptance of the terms of a contract that are set out in a document the pool owner keeps in a desk drawer in his office. By the same token, a website owner cannot bind users to conditions of use simply by announcing that their use of the site constitutes acceptance. In short, browsewrap agreements generally are not enforceable because visitors to the website are not given actual or constructive notice of the terms and conditions on their use of the site prior to visiting it.

Once a user has been given notice that use of the website signifies acceptance of the Terms of Use, then the continued use of the website arguably constitutes acceptance of those terms, and therefore may be binding on the user from that point forward Similarly, if a company serves a cease and desist letter on a user informing the user that her continued use of the website will constitute acceptance and bind the user to specified terms and conditions, then any further use of the website by that user from that point forward would make the terms and conditions enforceable against her.

Browsewrap agreements have generated a fair amount of litigation, most often over the question whether a user had adequate notice of the fact that use of the website constitutes acceptance of the terms and conditions. Placing the notice in the Terms of Use themselves, without also placing it anywhere else on the site, may not suffice to bind a user to them except in the rare case where it can be proven that the user actually visited and read the Terms of Use page.

The enforceability of a browsewrap agreement is a fact-specific determination requiring consideration of a variety of factors—whether notice that use of the site constitutes acceptance of the Terms of Use appears on the home page, some other page, or not at all; the font, type size, color, and position of the notice; the number of clicks required to get to the Terms of Use page; etc. A better way to remove any doubt about whether a user accepted the Terms of Use would be to set up the website in such a way that the user is required to take some affirmative step to signal assent to the terms before the user is allowed access to the site (or to a portion of it that the website owner wishes to protect) or to conduct a transaction using the site. A good way to do this is to display the Terms of Use adjacent to a statement like "I agree to these Terms of Use" along with a checkbox or 'I Agree' button that the user must click in order to proceed further. A question-and-answer format may also work—"Do you accept these terms?" followed by 'Yes' and 'No' radio buttons or checkboxes.

Some courts require the button or the sentence accompanying the checkbox to be very specific. Merely positioning the statement, "I agree," next to a checkbox, for example, might be too ambiguous. "By clicking this button, I acknowledge that I have read the above Terms of Use and I agree to these terms" would be better.

A user need not actually have read a clickwrap agreement in order to be bound by its terms. It is enough if the user was given adequate notice and a reasonable opportunity to review the terms before signaling assent. Thus, a clickwrap agreement may be enforceable if an 'I Agree' button is displayed next to an instruction to press the button if the user agrees to terms of a contract which, although not displayed directly adjacent to the button, are accessible by clicking a hypertext link that is placed next to the 'I Agree' button. To avoid claims of unfair surprise (which might support an unconscionability defense), however, the better practice would be to display the terms of the contract directly on the same page as the 'I Agree' button.

Another reason a prudent merchant will specify all the terms and conditions in the initial purchase agreement rather than notifying the buyer of them later is that unilateral modifications of contracts generally are not enforceable unless supported by new consideration.

> **Example.** AI Co., a software vendor, advertises software products for sale on its website. The website is set up so that after a buyer makes a purchase she is taken, for the first time, to a clickwrap page, where she is not permitted to access the software without first clicking the 'I Agree' button. Alternatively, she may purchase a physical copy, which will be delivered to her in a package containing a shrinkwrap agreement. In both cases, the buyer might not be legally bound by new terms that are set out in the clickwrap or shrinkwrap agreement if she did not agree to those terms at the time she made the initial purchase. A court might instead treat the new terms as offers to modify the original purchase agreement. Since the modifications are not supported by new consideration, they are not enforceable.[102]

What could AI Co. have done differently to ensure that the buyer in the Example will be bound by all of the terms of the license? The simplest solution would be to require users to signify assent to all of the terms of the license agreement before the purchase order is placed, not afterward. Many e-commerce websites accomplish this by setting up the website in such a way that an order cannot be placed until the user clicks on an 'I Agree' button signifying assent to all of the licensing terms and conditions to which the product is subject. Failing that, a vendor could at least put the buyer on notice, at the time of purchase, that the product is subject to a license agreement. In *ProCD v. Zeidenberg*[103] the Seventh Circuit Court of Appeals held that a buyer may be bound by the terms of a shrinkwrap or clickwrap agreement that is not delivered to him until after he has already purchased the product, where the vendor informed the purchaser at the time of the purchase that it would be subject to the terms of a license agreement and the vendor gave buyers, upon delivery of the product, the option of either agreeing to the license or canceling the purchase and returning the product.

The different outcomes in *ProCD* and in the Example given in this text may be explained in terms of whether and when a meeting of the minds occurred. In *ProCD*, the seller and buyer both understood, at the time of the purchase, that the software was subject to a license. That the buyer would be bound by the license that would come with the software if he kept it was part of the original deal. In the case illustrated in the Example, the only meeting of the minds that occurred at the time of the purchase was that the vendor would deliver software and the purchaser would pay for it. There was never any meeting of the minds as to whether the product would be subject to a licensing agreement or not: the seller intended to sell a product that was subject to a license; the buyer reasonably believed he was buying a product that was not subject to a license.

In sum, the most prudent approach for a vendor of licensed products like software is to explicitly set forth all the terms of the license on the website and require a potential customer to click an 'I Agree'" button as a condition of completing the purchase. Failing that, the vendor should at least require the customer to click on an 'I Agree' button signifying agreement to be bound by the terms of a license agreement that will accompany the product when it is delivered. If the latter approach is elected, then it would be a good idea to give the customer the option of either keeping and using the product in a manner that complies with the terms of the license or returning it for a refund within a specified time period. This kind of provision will not necessarily forestall an unconscionability claim, but it can help.

UNCONSCIONABILITY

Unconscionability is a potential defense to the enforcement of a contract if either the terms of the contract or the means by which acceptance is procured are so one-sided and unfair as to shock a court's conscience. The former is called *substantive* unconscionability; the latter is called *procedural* unconscionability. Mass market, take-it-or-leave-it consumer contracts in which no negotiation is permitted are most vulnerable to unconscionability claims.

Courts are most inclined to apply the substantive unconscionability doctrine to contract terms the enforcement of which would be contrary to an important public policy of the state. Class action waivers, forum selection clauses and choice-of-law provisions in consumer contracts are particularly vulnerable to attack on substantive unconscionability grounds. For example, a Massachusetts court refused to enforce a class action waiver in a consumer contract because it determined that allowing consumers to file class action lawsuits promoted the important policy of protecting consumers that is embodied in Massachusetts law.[104]

To avoid a finding of procedural unconscionability, and to increase the chances that a clickwrap agreement will be enforceable, website owners should do the following things:

(a) Give the user an opportunity to read the terms of a contract before agreeing to it.

(b) Display the contract terms on the same page as the 'I Agree' (or equivalent) button appears. This helps defend against a claim that the terms of the contract were hidden.

(c) Use plain English, with a minimum of legalese.

(d) Use a readable font and type size, not "fine print."

(e) Make sure the most controversial terms are conspicuously displayed—e.g., capital letters.

(f) Protect business interests, but be reasonable; don't impose unusually onerous and unfair burdens on customers.

(g) Design the site so that the user has to take some affirmative step to accept the terms of the contract, such as pressing an 'I Agree' button.

Giving a purchaser the option of returning a product within a specified period of time after the purchase is neither necessary nor sufficient to ensure enforceability of the purchase agreement, but it can help. Under these circumstances, a purchaser will find it difficult to support a claim that the offer was an unconscionable "take it or leave it" proposition or that there was not adequate time to read the contract.

Finally, caution should be exercised when assisting a customer with an online transaction. A court may refuse to enforce a contract if it finds the process by which it was formed to be unfair or likely to cause the customer to fail to read or understand the terms. If a customer calls the company or visits the company's physical location, and the company then has the customer complete an online order or other clickwrap agreement, the company must ensure that the customer is given enough time to actually read all the terms of the agreement before clicking 'I Agree.' There have been cases where courts have held online sales contracts to be unenforceable because the seller's employee verbally instructed the customer to click the 'I Agree' button without first allowing the customer sufficient time to read all of the terms of the agreement. How much time will be considered sufficient depends on how wordy the agreement is. The lengthier the agreement, the more time the customer should be given to read it.

European Union

The EU has stronger online consumer protections than the United States does. As in many American states, consumer contracts must be drafted in plain, understandable language, and any ambiguities are resolved in the consumer's favor. In addition to imposing these requirements, the Directive on Unfair Terms in Consumer Contracts provides that contractual terms that are unfair to a consumer are unenforceable against the consumer. A contract is unfair if "it causes a significant imbalance in the parties' rights and obligations arising under the contract, to the detriment of the consumer." A court in a European country is more likely than a U.S. court to find a consumer contract to be unfair to the consumer because it contains a waiver or adverse limitation of remedies or because it contains adverse choice-of-law and forum selection clause(s).

To prevent unfair surprise to consumers, EU countries require businesses that sell to consumers who are domiciled in the EU to make full disclosure of the contract terms and the parties' respective obligations under the contract.

THE UNIFORM COMPUTER INFORMATION TRANSACTIONS ACT

The Uniform Computer Information Transactions Act (UCITA) is a controversial model law governing software development, sales, licensing and support. It is essentially an attempt to bring U.C.C. principles relating to the sale of goods to the world of software and website licensing. It is controversial primarily because it contains provisions that are more favorable to software and website content licensors than to consumers and licensees.

UCITA has faced strong opposition from consumer groups in many states because it would generally validate all shrinkwrap and clickwrap agreements and all of the terms in them, such as forum selection and choice-of-law provisions empowering licensors to select the jurisdiction with laws most favorable to their interests, and provisions empowering licensors to terminate or repossess software products in the event of breach, validating license agreements in which licensees are not apprised of the terms until after a purchase, allowing the licensor to unilaterally modify terms of the license without prior individual notice to licensees, disclaiming warranties (including the warranty of merchantability), and permitting contract law instead of copyright law to govern. This is not an exhaustive list of the controversial provisions.

The Act has only been enacted in its entirety in Virginia. Maryland has adopted most of it, but with substantial consumer protection amendments. Software and website licensors might consider choosing Virginia law to govern their license agreements. On the other hand, opposition to UCITA has been so strong that at least one state (Iowa) has gone so far as to enact legislation forbidding courts from enforcing against its residents and businesses any provision in a licensing agreement that specifies the law of a state that has enacted UCITA to govern the agreement. A court may look to the UCITA for guidance, on occasion, but not all do.

ONLINE SALES CONTRACT TERMS

It is not possible to catalog and detail all of the provisions that should go into a particular e-commerce contract. The best that can be done is to identify terms that may be useful to include in a website's Terms of Use, licensing agreement or similar document specifying the terms of use of an e-commerce website and/or the terms applicable to transactions that are conducted on the website. As with any contract, the advice of an attorney is recommended.

Price

Most e-commerce businesses post their prices adjacent to the product description, along with a 'Buy Now' or similar button. To remove any doubts, the contract could provide that prices are as stated on the website, including any updates made to the site up to and including the date a purchase is made. This language will make it easier to change prices while avoiding disputes over which price applies to a sale. If installment payments are permitted, then the seller may wish to require some sort of security to ensure that installment payments are, in fact, made. The interest rate and late fee should be specified. The seller's rights upon the buyer's default should also be specified.

Delivery

A seller may wish to include a clause allowing an extended time period for delivery, even if it is known that delivery will usually only take a day or two. Allowing six to eight weeks, for example, may help protect a seller from a claim of breach if an unexpected delay occurs.

Unless a site sells only digital downloads, shipping and handling rates should be specified. Usually, this will be postage, but a seller may also want to include an additional amount to cover the cost of shipping supplies, freight, and the like. A prudent seller will provide customers a range of faster delivery times (such as Express Mail) and the corresponding rates.

Returns, Refunds, Cancellations

A sales contract should address the seller's and buyer's rights and responsibilities with respect to a buyer's cancellation of a purchase order, return of merchandise, and refunds. For example, a seller who does not want to be bothered with returns may want to include provisions stating that "all sales are final," "all goods are sold as-is," and "no refunds will be made."

Risk of Loss

The contract may specify how the risk of loss will be allocated between the seller and the buyer. A clause placing the risk of loss on the buyer once the seller delivers the product to the post office or other carrier for delivery means the buyer should not have recourse against the seller if the product is lost in transit. In the case of purchases of digital downloads and access to web pages, the provision should make clear that the risk of loss is on the buyer once the product is downloaded or accessed.

Disclaimer of Liability

In the absence of an agreement otherwise, a seller may be liable for consequential damages for losses or harm a product causes the consumer. Disclaimers of liability typically exclude liability for consequential damages.

Disclaimers of liability are enforceable to some extent in most jurisdictions, subject to some exceptions. Courts may refuse to enforce a disclaimer of liability for a seller's intentional wrongdoing. Some courts go even further, refusing to enforce disclaimers of liability for negligence, either. Most states have enacted statutes prohibiting a seller from disclaiming or limiting liability for personal injury resulting from a breach of an implied warranty, at least in situations where the injury occurs while the product is being used for its intended purpose.

Even in the absence of a statute, unconscionability may be a defense to the enforcement of some kinds of disclaimers of liability. Courts are likely to rule that a disclaimer of liability for intentional wrongdoing or willful breaches of contract is unusually unfair and onerous, and therefore unenforceable, in an adhesion contract to which a consumer is a party.

E-commerce businesses may find it useful to include disclaimers of liability for:

(a) computer- and Internet-related issues (making it clear that the company is not responsible for any downtime, disconnections or inability to connect to the website, or problems attributable to the ISP or web host)
(b) the accuracy and functionality of hyperlinks
(c) the representations, advertising, products or services of any other websites or businesses
(d) the content or policies of other websites
(e) the practices of other website owners with respect to the collection of data, or maintenance of data privacy and security
(f) the accuracy of information provided by other websites
(g) the quality, safety, reliability, fitness or merchantability of products or services provided by other companies.

A disclaimer will not always relieve a website operator of its legal obligations. For example, a website operator who displays a link to a website knowing it sells copyright circumvention tools cannot avoid liability under the Digital Millennium Copyright Act[105] (DMCA) by including a disclaimer of responsibility for the content of other websites in the Terms of Use.

Warranties

See infra.

Exclusive Remedies

Sales contracts often contain a provision limiting a seller's responsibility in the event a buyer is not satisfied with a product. These clauses typically limit the seller's obligation to exchanging the product or refunding the purchase price, at the seller's option.

Liquidated Damages

A dollar limitation on the amount of damages that may be recovered from the company is often included in sales contracts.

Indemnification

An indemnification clause requires a party to be responsible for the other party's damage or loss. A seller may want to include a clause stating that the buyer agrees to indemnify the seller for loss or damage that is incurred by the seller as a result of the buyer's negligence or the way the buyer uses the website or uses, stores, resells or receives the goods.

Commercial Use of Website Content

A provision prohibiting users from making commercial use of information or other website content may be useful if the information is valuable or the website content is protected intellectual property.

Intellectual Property Protection

Website owners may wish to include provisions to put users on notice that website content is protected by copyright or other law. The appropriate symbols—©, ®, ™, etc.—should be used If some of the content is owned by a third party, those rights holders and their property should be identified (e.g., "Amazon®, Kindle®, Fire® and all related logos are trademarks of Amazon.com, Inc. or its affiliates.")

The Terms of Use may prohibit users from reproducing, distributing, publicly performing, publicly displaying, digitally transmitting, or modifying (making derivative works from) website content, whether for commercial or noncommercial purposes. If one or more of these uses is permitted, then a provision requiring display of the copyright notice and attribution of the work to the author on all copies would be a good idea.

A website owner may also impose limitations on use, such as restricting the number of copies that may be made. Software vendors, for example, typically limit the number of authorized downloads. The number of devices on which it may be installed may also be specified. Permissible uses may also be specified—e.g., "personal, noncommercial use only." And restrictions against resale, assignment or sublicensing may be imposed.

If the business owns trademarks and/or patents, trademark and/or patent protection provisions may be included. Prohibitions against accessing trade secrets (such as customer databases) and/or unauthorized access to proprietary information (such as digital music or article content to which access is restricted to those users who pay the required fee) may also be included.

Of course, some of these rights are protected by law without need for an express contract. Including them in the Terms of Use, however, helps put users on notice that the fact that content has been made available for viewing does not mean that there is an implied license to copy and distribute it further. In some cases, these provisions may also help defeat a claim of innocent infringement.

If a website deals in intellectual property (such as sales of digital music or books), the Terms of Use should be clear about whether its terms apply to website content, product content or both.

Linking

A provision stating that users may not link to the website without the owner's consent may be worth considering. Depending on the circumstances, a narrower prohibition against linking to the website, or to content within the website, for a commercial purpose may be more appropriate. If the latter alternative is chosen, it might nevertheless be prudent to state that any linking of any kind, commercial or otherwise, is subject to the company's approval.

Prohibitions against deep linking (linking to the site in such a way as to bypass the home page or advertising) may also be included, as may prohibitions against framing (causing the original website's content to be displayed on another website without a user needing to actually visit the original website).

User Content

Websites that display, distribute, perform or transmit user-submitted content (such as comments, music uploads, etc.) should consider including a warranty on the part of the user that the user owns the copyright in the content and/or has the legal right to upload it to the site.

It may be prudent to include a license provision. An assignment provision states that the user assigns all rights, including but not limited to ownership of the copyright, in user-provided content (including email, comments posted to the site, and material uploaded to the site) to the website owner. Astute users and customers may balk at this. In many cases, a license may be all that is really needed, anyway. It is becoming more common for website owners to use the less extreme alternative of providing that the user retains ownership but grants the website owner a nonexclusive license to copy, distribute, display, etc. the work.

Interactive websites (such as sites that have a chat feature or allow users to post comments) may want to establish a set of rules governing online behavior. This might include, for example, prohibitions against posting threatening, harassing, defamatory, infringing or other tortious content; obscene, profane, or sexually explicit content; content the posting of which violates federal or state laws (criminal or civil); or content that violates a person's privacy or publicity rights.

Website owners typically offer users a second chance for less serious violations, reserving the right to terminate or suspend the account of a user for second or subsequent violations. It may be a good idea, however, to allow some room for immediately terminating an account, at least for certain kinds of violations, such as where a user circumvents technological copyright protection measures that have been installed at the website.

Privacy Policy and Data Security

The best practice is to create a separate privacy policy rather than including it in the Terms of Use. The Terms of Use may include a provision stating that the Privacy Policy is incorporated by reference into the Terms of Use, and that the user agrees to be bound by its terms to the same extent as if it were set out in full. Privacy policies and data security are discussed in Chapters 13 and 17.

Dispute Resolution

Litigation can be expensive, so merchants often include some sort of alternative dispute resolution (ADR) clause in their contracts. The most common forms are arbitration and mediation. See Chapter 35.

Attorney Fees

Attorney fees normally are not awarded unless specifically allowed by a statute or contract. Accordingly, some merchants include a provision requiring the prevailing party to pay the other party's attorney fees and costs if a dispute is litigated in court.

Governing Law

This clause specifies which jurisdiction's laws will be applied in the event of a dispute about the interpretation of the contract or the rights and obligations of the parties under it. A website owner may find it convenient to specify the law of her home state. If the laws of other states are more hospitable, however, then the contract may provide that the laws of one of those states apply.

Of course, the enforceability of this kind of provision depends on whether and to what extent courts in other jurisdictions respect them. This could be a problem if, for example, a country has passed a law specifying that the laws of that country apply to any e-commerce-based lawsuit that is filed in that country notwithstanding any contractual agreement to the contrary.

Some courts may refuse to enforce this kind of clause if doing so would be contrary to public policy in the state in which the court sits.

Forum Selection

This clause (sometimes called a "venue" provision") specifies where litigation will be conducted. The seller will want to select a forum that will be within a convenient distance. Some courts have held that requiring a consumer to litigate claims in a distance state to which the parties do not have any significant connection may be unconscionable.

Severability

This clause provides that if a particular provision in the contract is deemed unenforceable, then the remaining provisions will nevertheless be enforceable. This prevents a court from "throwing out the baby with the bathwater" in the event the "bathwater" is not good.

Complete Agreement

This clause asserts that the agreement is the entire agreement, i.e., there are no oral or side agreements.

Modification

A website owner may wish to reserve the right to modify the agreement at any time, without notice. To protect against claims of oral modifications or of special promises made to individual buyers, it may be prudent to state that no modification is effective unless it is either (a) in writing and signed by both parties; or (b) published or displayed on the website, such as in a modified version of the Terms of Use.

Even though the Terms of Use allow a website owner to change the terms without notice, a website owner may find it prudent to post a notice to the website whenever changes to the Terms of Use are made. This will make it more difficult for a user to claim he was not aware of the change or to claim the changed Terms of Use are unconscionable.

Other Provisions

Other provisions may address such things as assignments and whether the terms of the contract are binding on assignees, licensees, and heirs; notices and when they must be served; the terms of contests, sweepstakes and promotions, if any; age requirements; and other matters.

Warranties

Warranties are enforceable promises about a product or service. They may be either express or implied. Implied warranties exist by operation of law in every contract for the sale of goods between a merchant and a consumer, except to the extent they are expressly excluded.

EXPRESS WARRANTIES

It is not necessary to include a warranty of any kind in a contract. If the decision is made to offer a warranty, then the company must be prepared to fulfill the promises that are made in it.

At a minimum, any warranty that is offered should specify at least three things:

(a) the duration (starting date and time period)
(b) the remedy for breach (e.g., repair or replace, at seller's option)
(c) an objective, measurable performance standard.

Sellers should be cautious when making statements about their products. A court may find that a product description in a catalog or a product claim in an advertisement is an express warranty about the product. An express warranty may also arise from a statement made to an individual buyer. Neither a specific intention to create a warranty nor any "magic words" are necessary. Any statement of fact, description of the goods, or promise a seller makes to the buyer which relates to the goods is an express warranty that the goods will conform to the promise, description, or statement of fact. The statement does not need to appear in a sales agreement. A merchant's assertion in an email message to a prospective customer may constitute an express warranty. Providing a sample or model to a buyer creates an express warranty that all of the goods conform to the model or sample.

Only factual statements can give rise to warranties. A seller's opinions, estimation of value or praise for the goods do not give rise to express warranties.

Magnuson-Moss Warranty Act Requirements

A manufacturer or seller that offers a written warranty on a consumer product must comply with the Magnuson-Moss Warranty Act[106] and the rules the FTC has adopted pursuant to it.

These include the FTC's interpretive guidelines, its Rule on Disclosure of Written Consumer Product Warranty Terms[107] ("Disclosure Rule"), Rule on Pre-Sale Availability of Written Warranty Terms[108] ("Pre-Sale Availability Rule"), and the Rule on Informal Dispute Settlement Procedures[109] ("Dispute Resolution Rule.")

The Act does not apply to oral warranties, sales between merchants (e.g., wholesaler's sale to a retailer for resale), sales of nonconsumer products, sales of intangibles (e.g., software licenses), warranties for services, or contracts that contain no written warranty provisions. It does apply to a warranty that covers both the parts used in a repair and the repair, however.

A consumer product is an item of tangible personal property that is normally used for personal, family or household purposes. Thus, software licenses are not within the Act's coverage. Sales of interests in real estate are not covered, either. Sales of industrial machinery are not covered. The applicability of the Act, however, does not depend on how the particular purchaser will use a product. The determinative question is whether the product is normally used for personal, family or household purposes.

When the Act applies and a written warranty is offered on a product that sells to a consumer for at least $10, a warrantor has the following obligations:

(a) to correctly title the warranty as either Full or Limited;
(b) to include all the terms of the warranty in a single, understandable document;
(c) to provide information about what the warranty does and does not cover;
(d) to ensure it is available to a consumer before buying.

If all of the following conditions are met, then it is a full warranty. If any condition is not met, then it is a limited warranty:

(a) The duration of implied warranties is not limited;
(b) Warranty service is provided to anyone who owns the product during the warranty period; that is, coverage is not limited to the original purchaser;
(c) The warranty service is free of charge, including such costs as returning the product or removing and reinstalling the product when necessary;
(d) Either a replacement or a full refund, at the consumer's choice, is provided if, after a reasonable number of tries, the warrantor is unable to repair the product;
(e) Consumers are not required to perform any unreasonable duty as a precondition for receiving service, other than notifying the warrantor that service is needed.

A warrantor may offer a full warranty on some parts of a product and a limited warranty on other parts, so long as the parts to which each warranty applies is made clear. Also, a warrantor may offer one kind of warranty on a product for a specified period of time and then a different kind of warranty thereafter—e.g., a full warranty for the first year and a limited warranty for the second year.

When the Act applies, a warranty generally may not:

(a) disclaim or modify implied warranties
(b) be deceptive or misleading
(c) include tie-in sales provisions.

Disclaimers of Implied Warranties

Implied warranties may not be disclaimed or modified. A limited warranty may limit the duration of implied warranties to the duration of the limited warranty, though. Full warranties may not limit the duration of implied warranties at all.

A manufacturer's warranty and a seller's warranty are two separate things. A seller cannot unilaterally alter the terms of a manufacturer's warranty, and vice versa. In the absence of an agreement otherwise, a seller is not bound by the terms of a manufacturer's warranty. And the fact that a retailer sells a product that comes with a manufacturer's warranty does not mean that the retailer is offering a written warranty. Unless a retailer offers its own warranty to a purchaser, the retailer is not required to comply with the Act. If a retailer offers no written warranty at all, then its contract with the purchaser may include a disclaimer of implied warranties, if any, arising from the contract between the retailer and the purchaser. Such a disclaimer would not have any effect on the manufacturer's warranty.

A merchant who sells a product that comes with a manufacturer's warranty must give the consumer a copy of the manufacturer's warranty.

Deceptive Terms

A written warranty must not contain deceptive or misleading terms. Among other things, this means that offering a "warranty" that doesn't actually cover anything, or that promises something that the warrantor does not intend to provide, is unlawful.

Tie-in Sales Provisions

A tie-in sales provision is a clause in a warranty that requires a consumer to buy specified items or services only from a particular company in order to keep the warranty coverage in effect. These kinds of provisions are unlawful. A warranty may impose a requirement like this only if it gives away the item or service for free.

On the other hand, a warranty may provide that coverage will be denied if damage is caused by the use of items or service purchased from another company.

A company may apply to the FTC for a waiver of the prohibition against tie-in sales clauses. To qualify for the waiver, the applicant must prove that the product will not work properly without the specified item or service.

The Act establishes a private right of action for damages for any consumer who is harmed by a violation. Attorney fees and court costs may be awarded. It also allows a warrantor to include a provision requiring customers to first try to resolve warranty disputes by means of nonbinding arbitration, but only if the arbitration is made available at no cost to the consumer. A merchant who includes this kind of provision in a warranty must keep complete records of all disputes and undergo an annual audit for compliance with FTC requirements.

Required Disclosures

Written warranties on products with a cost to the consumer of more than $15 must address and answer the following questions:

(a) What does the warranty cover/not cover? If not all parts or not all types of defects are covered, the warranty must describe with specificity what is not covered.

(b) What is the period of coverage? If coverage begins at some time other than the purchase date, the time or event that begins the coverage must be specified. The warranty must also explain when coverage ends. Any event triggering warranty termination must be stated.

(c) What will be done to correct a problem? (e.g., repair or replace, a refund, a store credit, etc.). Things that will not be done, and costs that will not be covered, should also be specified (e.g., no consequential or incidental damages). To avoid misunderstanding, and a construction of the contract against the merchant, the specific kinds of costs that are not covered should be clearly spelled out (e.g., towing charges, postage, etc.).

(d) How can the customer get warranty service? (Name and address of company; contact person. A toll-free telephone number may be provided in lieu of an address).

(e) How will state law affect the customer's rights under the warranty? This requirement may be satisfied by including the statement: "This warranty gives you specific legal rights, and you may also have other rights which vary from state to state."

All conditions and limitations must be specified in the written warranty. For example, if the written warranty does not say that a defaced or removed serial number on the product voids the warranty, then it does not void the warranty.

If the warranty limits the duration of an implied warranty, then it must contain the following statement: "Some states do not allow limitations on how long an implied warranty lasts, so the above limitation may not apply to you."

If the warranty disclaims or limits liability for consequential or incidental damages, then it must include the following statement: "Some states do not allow the exclusion or limitation of incidental or consequential damages, so the above limitation or exclusion may not apply to you."

If the warranty restricts who has rights under the warranty, then it must include an explanation of who, specifically, is covered. For example, if a limited warranty is valid only for the first purchaser, then the warranty must say that.

If the warranty requires customers to use a dispute resolution mechanism before suing under the Magnuson-Moss Warranty Act for breach of warranty, then it must include a statement informing consumers that they may sue under state law without first using the mechanism, but that before suing under the Magnuson-Moss Act, they must first try to resolve the dispute through the mechanism. The warranty must also provide information and materials about the dispute resolution mechanism, including the name and address or a toll-free telephone number, or a form for filing a claim.

Format

Written warranties on products with a cost to the consumer of more than $15 must be clear and easy to understand. Here are some pointers from the FTC's guidelines:

Do not include anything other than warranty information in the warranty. Extraneous matter, such as promotional statements, may confuse customers about the purpose of the document. If promotional matter appears on the same page with warranty information, it should be clearly set apart from the warranty, such as by placing a border around it.

TITLE

The warranty must have either the word *full* or the word *limited* in the title. The title of a full warranty should have the following components: (a) the words *full* and *warranty*; (b) the period of coverage; and (c) what parts or problems the coverage includes. If a full warranty does not cover all of the parts or all types of defects, the title should inform consumers of that fact. If listing all the parts or problems would make the title unwieldy, then use a phrase like "certain parts" and then identify what those parts are in the body of the warranty. The title for a limited warranty should include only the phrase "Limited Warranty."

When a full warranty is offered on some parts and a limited warranty is offered on other parts, the entire warranty may simply be titled "Limited Warranty." Alternatively, the full warranty provisions may be set out separately from the limited warranty provisions. The title for the full warranty provisions should be as described above.

When both full and limited warranties are offered, the title of the limited warranty provisions may not be simply "Limited Warranty." It will need to indicate how the time period of the limited portion is related to the time period of the full portion, and which parts or problems are within the coverage of the limited portion.

Titles must be prominent. This may be accomplished by including extra space around them and using larger type.

HEADINGS

The FTC recommends using the questions listed above (e.g., What is the period of coverage?) as headings, adding other headings as needed. Headings consisting only of nouns and noun phrases should be avoided. Don't use numbers.

ORGANIZATION

An effort must be made to fulfill two competing objectives: inclusiveness and brevity. This is something of an art. At a minimum, don't unnecessarily repeat the same information under different headings. If different warranties apply to different component parts, state the terms and conditions applicable to all of them in one place. Then set out the specific conditions that are applicable to some, but not all, parts under separate headings.

CLARITY

Warranties must be written in clear, easy-to-read, understandable language. Here are some suggestions from the FTC:

Use personal pronouns ("we" and "you," not "the buyer" or "the party of the first part").

Be consistent. For example, don't refer to the purchaser as "you" in some places and "the buyer" in other places.

Wherever possible, use the active voice, not the passive voice.

Use verbs, not nominalizations (nouns created from verbs).

Provide concrete examples.

Use short sentences. Aim for under 25 words, on average.

Avoid sentence fragments.

Avoid inserting lengthy parenthetical information into the middle of sentences.

Avoid inserting multiple phrases into a sentence in a way that might confuse readers.

Group related items into lists, but don't do it too often.

Make sure lists are parallel in structure.

Don't break up a list with commentary.

Use simple, everyday language. For example, say "paid," not "compensated."

Use a logical structure.

Avoid legalese, stilted or archaic language. Avoid constructs like "the said party" or "hereinafter."

Avoid big words.

Avoid technical or obscure language.

Explain the meaning of any required terms (e.g., merchantability).

Explain any words or phrases that may be unfamiliar to a consumer.

Explain any provisions that may be confusing to a consumer.

Clarify all ambiguous provisions.

Use an attractive graphic design.

Use at least 8–point type; preferably, 10-point type.

Do not mix serif and sans-serif typefaces.

Use boldface for title, headings, and words and sentences that require emphasis.

Avoid crowded text; for 10-point type, use one to three points of leading between lines of type.

Keep line length short (50–70 characters per line).

Don't overuse capital letters (no more than a few words or a phrase, not an entire paragraph).

Apply only one emphasis technique at a time.

Avoid yellow type or background.

Select a type color that contrasts sharply with the background color.

Avoid patterned backgrounds.

Use colors sparingly (one color, used for emphasis only, is good).

Left-justified is preferable to full-justified.

Leave generous margins.

Add space between paragraphs.

Drawings can be helpful, but they should not replace headings or text.

Don't overuse illustrations.

Don't mix different styles of illustrations (e.g., line drawings and photographs).

Test the warranty on a sample of consumers. Smaller businesses might test it on family and friends.

These are guidelines, not rules having the force of law. The more of them are used, though, the more likely a warranty is to be found to be understandable, easy to read, and clear.

Pro Rata Warranties

A pro rata warranty is one that provides for a refund or credit that decreases according to a formula as the warranty period progresses or as the product is used. If this kind of provision is included, the warranty should include the following information:

(a) the formula the company will use to calculate how much the refund or credit will be at any time during the period of coverage
(b) what the consumer will get (a credit, a refund, or a choice of a credit or a refund)
(c) a statement that the only remedy is a credit toward an identical product, if this is the case
(d) what price the company will use as a basis for calculating the refund or credit (e.g., the original purchase price, the price at the time the product malfunctions, or the price at some other specified time).

Availability Before Purchase

Written warranties on products with a cost to the consumer of more than $15 must be made available to the consumer before the purchase. In advertising, either a full copy of the warranty or information about where the customer may view the warranty prior to purchase must be displayed in proximity to the product description. On the product ordering page, a clearly labeled hyperlink should be placed in close proximity to the description of the warrantied product, such as 'Get warranty information here' to lead to the full text of the warranty The warranty should be displayed on the website in a way that it can be preserved either by downloading or printing so consumers can refer to it after purchase.

Service Contracts

A service contract is an optional agreement for product service that a seller may offer customers if it is so inclined. It provides additional protection beyond what the warranty offers. Warranties come with a product and are included in the purchase price. Service contracts are agreements that are separate from the contract or sale of the product. They are separate either because they are made some time after the sale of the product, or because they cost the customer a fee beyond the purchase price of the product. Some parts of the Magnuson-Moss Warranty Act apply to service contracts.

All of the terms and conditions of any service contract must be in simple and readily understood language. Service contracts are not required to be titled Full or Limited.

The company that makes the service contract is responsible for complying with legal requirements. The seller is responsible only if the seller and the maker of the service contract are one and the same. A seller that makes services contracts on its products may not disclaim or limit implied warranties.

IMPLIED WARRANTIES

Warranty of Merchantability

Every contract for the sale of goods by a merchant to a consumer contains an implied promise that the goods sold:

(a) are fit for the ordinary purposes for which such goods are used
(b) would pass without objection in the trade under the description given in the contract
(c) are adequately packaged, contained, and labeled
(d) conform to any promises or representations of fact made on the container or label

(e) run, within the variations permitted by the agreement, of even kind, quality and quantity within each unit and among all units involved
(f) if fungible, are of fair average quality within the description.

The warranty of merchantability is implied only in contracts between a merchant and a consumer. It does not apply to sales of goods between persons who are merchants with respect to the goods (e.g., a wholesaler selling a product to a retailer for resale). It also does not apply to private sales between nonmerchants.

A merchant is an individual or a business entity that deals in goods of the kind to which a contract relates, or who holds himself out as having knowledge or skill peculiar to the goods or practices involved in the transaction, or to whom such knowledge or skill may be attributed by his employment of an agent, broker or other intermediary who holds himself out as having such knowledge or skill.

Warranty of Fitness for a Particular Purpose

An implied warranty of fitness for a particular purpose arises if, at the time of contracting, the seller knows or has reason to know of a particular purpose for which the buyer requires the goods, and that the buyer is relying on the seller's skill or judgment to select or furnish goods that are suitable for that purpose.

Warranty of Title

Contracts for the sale of goods (and certain other kinds of transactions in goods) contain an implied warranty of title. This means that the seller is deemed to have made an implicit promise to the buyer that the title is good; the transfer is lawful; and that the goods will be delivered free from any lien, encumbrance or security interest of which the buyer has no knowledge at the time he enters into the contract.

Warranty of NonInfringement

A merchant implicitly warrants that the goods will be delivered free of the rightful claim of any third person for infringement or the like.

On the other hand, a buyer who furnishes specifications to the seller must hold the seller harmless against claims that arise out of compliance with the specifications.

Warranties Implied by Conduct or Usage of Trade

The implied warranties described above arise by operation of law irrespective of the parties' conduct or course of dealing. Additional implied warranties may also arise from a party's conduct, the parties' course of dealing, or usage of trade.

Exclusions of Warranties

In many states, warranties may be excluded by express agreement. Selling goods "as is," "with all faults" or other language that calls a buyer's attention to the fact that the goods are being sold without warranties normally will have the effect of excluding implied warranties unless the circumstances indicate otherwise. An implied warranty may also be excluded or modified by course of dealing, course of performance, or usage of trade. Prudent sellers often include in their written sales contracts an exclusion of all express and implied warranties "except as otherwise expressly provided" in the written sales contract.

Under the U.C.C., a disclaimer of the warranty of merchantability in a contract for the sale of goods by a merchant to a consumer must either (a) use the word *merchantability* in the disclaimer or (b) state that the goods are sold "as is" or "with all faults." It must be conspicuous.

Not all states interpret or enforce an "as is" notice as a disclaimer of implied warranties. And not all states enforce disclaimers of implied warranties in consumer sales contracts. Some states allow them but impose additional conditions on enforceability.

Courts vary in their interpretations of the word *conspicuous*. Some hold that it means the disclaimer must be printed in larger and/or different font or color. Others allow additional methods of emphasizing it, such as bolding, italicizing or indenting the provision. In some jurisdictions, courts will take the buyer's experience and sophistication into consideration. In other jurisdictions, the buyer's experience and sophistication are deemed irrelevant.

The warranty of title may be excluded or modified only by specific language or by circumstances which give the buyer reason to know that the seller does not have clear title or that he is purporting to sell only such right or title as he or a third person may have.

Depending on the circumstances, it may be necessary or prudent to include disclaimers of specific kinds of representations, whether or not the contract contains general disclaimers of warranties. Disclaimers like these can be helpful in terms of forestalling claims of fraud or deceptive trade practices. For example, a company offering franchises or other business opportunities might include an earnings disclaimer that:

(a) disclaims any promises or representations about actual or potential future income
(b) disclaims any promises or representations that there will be no losses
(c) denies that any prior successes or results are an indication of future results or successes
(d) disclaims any representations concerning suitability
(e) discloses risks
(f) recommends that qualified professionals assist in the evaluation of any business or financial opportunity.

Other examples of specific disclaimers that may be appropriate in some circumstances:

(a) disclaimer of qualifications to dispense professional advice
(b) web designer's disclaimer of responsibility for a website's legal compliance
(c) no investment recommendation
(d) no responsibility for third-party content.

This is not an exhaustive list.

Disclaimers of facts may be necessary either to ensure that a representation is not deceptive or to minimize the likelihood of confusion with another product, service or business. For example, to avoid confusing consumers, a celebrity fan site might need to include a disclaimer to the effect that it is not the official site of the celebrity. A service business that repairs brand-name products might find it prudent to disclaim affiliation, sponsorship or endorsement by the maker of such products.

Contracts with Advertisers

In addition to contracts with its customers, an e-commerce business that accepts third-party advertising on its website, or that places advertisements on other websites, should have specific, written contracts in place with these vendors and website owners. As is discussed elsewhere in this book, it is possible for a website operator to be held liable for the content of third-party advertising appearing on the site. Contracts with advertisers should include, at a minimum, a definition of acceptable content; the advertiser's representation and warranty that all advertising content it will submit or cause to be displayed is lawful, truthful, and noninfringing; restrictions and limitations on specific kinds of content, such as sexually explicit, child-directed, or other regulated content; and allocation of responsibility for the content (e.g., an indemnification clause).

Credit Sales

Credit sales, as used here, are transactions in which the seller extends credit to the buyer rather than accepting payment in full at the time of purchase. A transaction in which the buyer pays the full price by credit or debit card at the time of purchase is not a credit sale.

Credit sale transactions are not as simple to conduct online as other kinds of sales are. Numerous disclosures are required, some of which are dependent on the consumer's desires at the time of the transaction. The lack of seller-buyer interaction impedes the ability to do things like obtain a buyer's authorization to check a credit report or to perform a credit check while the customer waits. In any event, those merchants who decide to offer credit sales must ensure that if a sale is to an individual for the purchase of consumer goods (products for personal, family or household use), the truth-in-lending disclosures are given as required by 15 U.S.C. § 1638. This means providing the buyer with a statement disclosing all of the following things:

(a) The creditor's identity.
(b) The amount financed. The is the cash price minus down payment and trade-in, plus every other cost or charge besides finance charges, minus any charges which are part of the finance charge but which will be paid by the consumer before or at the time of the consummation of the transaction or which have been withheld from the proceeds of the transaction.
(c) A statement of the consumer's right to obtain, upon written request, a written itemization of the amount financed, along with 'Yes' and 'No' checkboxes for the consumer to initial if an itemization is requested.
(d) The finance charge (unitemized).
(e) The annual percentage rate (APR), if either (i) the amount financed is more than $75 and the finance charge is more than $7.50, or (ii) the amount financed is less than $75.01 and the finance charge is more than $5.
(f) The total of payments (amount financed plus finance charge).
(g) The number, amount, and due dates or periods of payments scheduled to repay the total of payments.
(h) The total sale price. This is the sum of the cash price, additional charges, and finance charge.

(i) Descriptive explanations of the terms *amount financed*, *finance charge*, *annual percentage rate*, *total of payments*, and *total sale price*, as specified by the Bureau of Consumer Financial Protection.

(j) A reference to the amount of the down payment. This should be included in the descriptive explanation of the meaning of *total sale price*.

(k) If the credit is secured by property, a statement that a security interest has been taken in: (i) the property that is purchased as part of the credit transaction, or (ii) property not purchased as part of the transaction, identified by item or type.

(l) A statement of the amount (fixed or percentage) the creditor may impose as a late fee.

(m) A statement indicating whether or not the consumer is entitled to a rebate of any finance charge upon refinancing or prepayment in full pursuant to acceleration or otherwise, if the obligation involves a precomputed finance charge. Include a statement indicating whether or not a penalty will be imposed in those same circumstances if the obligation involves a finance charge computed from time to time by application of a rate to the unpaid principal balance.

(n) A statement that the consumer should refer to the appropriate contract document for any information such document provides about nonpayment, default, the right to accelerate the maturity of the debt, and prepayment rebates and penalties.

An itemization of the amount financed must be provided to the consumer at the time these disclosures are made, if the customer requests it. Any itemization of the amount financed must disclose all of the following:

(a) the amount that is or will be paid directly to the consumer

(b) the amount that is or will be credited to the consumer's account to discharge obligations owed to the creditor

(c) each amount that is or will be paid to third persons on the consumer's behalf, together with an identification of or reference to the third person

(d) the total amount of any charges which are part of the finance charge but which will be paid by the consumer before or at the time of the consummation of the transaction or which have been withheld from the proceeds of the transaction.

The disclosures, including any requested itemization, generally must be made to the consumer before credit is extended. They must be conspicuously segregated from all the other terms and information pertaining to the transaction.

Any retailer who regularly extends or arranges for the extension of credit must comply with the Equal Credit Opportunity Act[110] (ECOA), which makes it unlawful to discriminate against a credit applicant on the basis of race, color, religion, national origin, sex, marital status, age, or receipt of public assistance. Discrimination in retaliation for an applicant's exercise of rights under the ECOA is also prohibited.

It is unlawful to extend credit or increase a credit limit if the company has received the applicant's credit report and it has a fraud alert in it, unless the company uses a reasonable procedure to form a reasonable belief that the company knows the identity of the person applying for the credit. If the person who requested the alert has specified a telephone number to be used for identity verification, then before extending or increasing credit the company must contact the person using that telephone number or use other reasonable measures to verify the person's identity and confirm that the application for credit is not the result of identity theft. If the consumer report includes an extended fraud alert, then calling the indicated telephone number is mandatory.

A company must notify a credit applicant of the company's action on the application within thirty days. If credit is denied or offered on less favorable terms, the company must either (a) give the applicant a written statement of specific reasons for the denial, or (b) give the applicant a written notification of adverse action that informs the applicant of (i) the applicant's right to a statement of reasons within thirty days after receipt by the company of a request made within sixty days after such notification and (ii) the identity of the person or office from which the statement may be obtained.

If credit is denied, in whole or in part, on the basis of information in a credit report, or if credit is granted on less favorable terms, the FCRA requires the company to provide the consumer, in writing or electronically, the following:

(a) notice of the denial or other adverse action to the consumer
(b) notice of the name, address and telephone number of the consumer reporting agency (including a toll-free telephone number established by the agency if the agency compiles and maintains files on consumers on a nationwide basis) that furnished the report
(c) a statement that the consumer reporting agency did not make the decision to take the adverse action and is unable to provide the specific reasons why the adverse action was taken
(d) disclosure of the numerical credit score that was used in making the decision
(e) disclosure of: (i) the range of possible credit scores under the credit scoring model used and (ii) all of the key factors that adversely affected the credit score of the consumer in the model used, the total number of which must not exceed four, unless the number of credit inquiries is one of the factors, in which case the total number must not exceed five
(f) disclosure of the date on which the credit score was created
(g) disclosure of the name of the person or entity that provided the credit score or credit file upon which the credit score was created
(h) notice of the consumer's right to obtain a free copy of a consumer report on the consumer from the consumer reporting agency if requested within sixty days of the denial of credit
(i) notice of the consumer's right to dispute, with the consumer reporting agency, the accuracy or completeness of any information that the agency furnished to the company.

The notices of denial of credit (or other adverse action), contact information for the credit reporting agency, statement that the credit reporting agency did not make the decision and cannot provide the reasons for denial, and the consumer's rights to request a copy of the report and dispute information in it, may be made orally, in writing, or electronically.

Disclosures and requirements additional to those described in the preceding paragraphs apply if the extension of credit is secured by a mortgage or a security interest in real estate.

If consumer credit is denied, in whole or in part, or is offered on less favorable terms, on the basis of information obtained from someone other than a consumer reporting agency, the company must inform the applicant, at the time credit is denied, of the applicant's right to make a written request for the reasons for the adverse action within sixty days. The company must disclose this information when an applicant timely and properly requests it.

If a company denies credit, in whole in part, or is offered on less favorable terms, on the basis of information received from an affiliate, the company must notify the applicant of the denial, and include a statement that the consumer may obtain the information by making a written request within sixty days. If the company receives a timely written request from the applicant, it must disclose to the applicant the nature of the information upon which the denial was based within thirty days after receiving the request. Disclosure is not required, however, if the information relates solely to transactions or experiences between the applicant and the affiliate or is a consumer report.

A company that grants a consumer credit but on materially less favorable terms than the best terms offered to a substantial number of other customers has additional obligations under the Risk-Based Pricing Rule[111] that the FTC and other federal regulatory agencies have established. In particular, the company must either (a) notify customers when they are being offered credit on materially less favorable terms, or (b) disclose to all customers who are granted credit their credit scores.

"Materially less favorable terms" generally means a higher APR. If none, then it means the term that has the most significant financial impact on the consumer and varies based on information in a consumer report. This may be determined by making a direct comparison or by using the 60/40 Credit Score Proxy Method. This involves determining the credit score that 40% of the company's customers who have been granted credit are above and 60% are below. (A representative sample of customers may be used.) If this method is used, then the notice must be sent to applicants whose scores are below the cutoff or for whom no credit score is available. The cutoff must be recalculated every two years. First-time credit grantors can base the cutoff score on market research, third party data, and other sources, but they must calculate their own score within one year. If the company gives its best credit terms to more than 40% of its customers, then it may set the cutoff score based on the approximate percentage of customers to whom the company has not granted credit on the most favorable terms.

If credit arrangements are structured in tiers (e.g., 8% APR in Tier 1, 10% in Tier 2, etc.), then notice must be given to all who are not in the top tier, unless there are more than four tiers, in which case, notice must be given to all except those who are in the first or second tier or any tier that makes up more than 30% but less than 40% of the total tiers.

A risk-based pricing notice must be sent to a customer any time the customer's APR is raised, regardless of prices charged to other customers.

For closed-end credit plans, notice must be given before the consumer becomes contractually obligated. For open-end credit plans, the notice must be given before the person makes the first transaction. Notice may not be given before someone is notified about the decision to extend them credit.

Risk-based pricing notices must be clear and conspicuous. They may be oral, written or electronic. The notice must disclose:

(a) that a consumer report includes information about the consumer's credit history and the type of information included in that history

(b) that the terms offered were based on information from a consumer report

(c) that the terms offered may be less favorable than those offered to consumers with better credit histories
(d) a suggestion that the consumer should make sure the information in their consumer report is accurate
(e) that the consumer has a right to dispute information that is inaccurate
(f) the identity of each consumer reporting agency that furnished a consumer report used in the credit decision
(g) that federal law gives the consumer a right to a free copy of a consumer report from the consumer reporting agency(ies) identified in the notice for sixty days after the consumer got the notice
(h) how to get a consumer report from the consumer reporting agency, with contact information (including a toll free number, where applicable) for the consumer reporting agency
(i) a suggestion that the consumer visit the website of the Consumer Financial Protection Bureau for more information about consumer reports.

Special requirements apply if the company uses credit scores or if credit is secured by real property.

The requirements of the Risk-Based Pricing Rule may be satisfied by giving a credit score notice to every consumer, regardless of the terms on which the company granted them credit. The notice must be in writing and must include the person's credit score and information about credit and credit scores. It must be separate from other information, and clear and conspicuous. It must be sent as soon as practicable after the company requests the credit score from a consumer reporting agency.

The FTC's Credit Practices Trade Regulation Rule[112] (CPTR Rule) also establishes requirements for certain consumer credit sales contracts. It applies to any retailer, finance company, or credit union that offers consumer credit contracts. Civil penalties of up to $41,484 per violation may be assessed for violations. Similar rules have been enacted by other regulatory agencies for banks and other financial institutions.

The CPTR Rule prohibits the following provisions in consumer credit sales contracts:

- Confessions of judgment;
- Waivers of exemption;
- Wage assignments;
- Security interests in household goods.

A confession of judgment is a consent to the entry of judgment against the person giving the consent. It effectively waives a person's right to assert defenses to the other party's complaint in court. Clauses in consumer credit contracts to the effect that the creditor may obtain immediate judgment against the buyer in the event of the buyer's breach, without need for service of process and so on, are unlawful. Repossession provisions are permitted, however.

"Waiver of exemptions" provisions authorize creditors to seize (or threaten to seize) specific possessions or possessions of a specified value even if state law treats them as exempt from seizure. It is unlawful to include this kind of clause in a consumer credit sale contract.

A provision assigning a buyer's wages to the seller/creditor in the event of a default is a wage assignment. Irrevocable assignments of future wages are prohibited in consumer credit sales contracts. The contract may provide for wage assignments that can be revoked at will by the consumer and for assignments of wages already earned at the time of the assignment. Also, a creditor/seller may use payroll deduction plans where consumers choose to pay by regular deductions from paychecks. A payroll deduction plan may provide that if borrowers change employers, final paychecks will be assigned to the seller/creditor to be credited toward balances due on loans, without notice to debtors and without allegations of default or delinquency. Finally, the prohibition against wage assignments does not prohibit garnishment. If a creditor obtains a court judgment against a debtor, the creditor may use wage garnishment to collect the judgment, subject to the consumer protections provided by federal and state laws.

Consumer credit sales contracts may not contain provisions granting the seller/creditor a security interest in the consumer's household goods. Purchase money security interests are allowed, however. A purchase money security interest is a lien that a buyer grants to a creditor to secure the purchase of the particular item the lien encumbers. A purchase money security interest is limited to goods that are purchased with the loan proceeds or with the credit that is advanced for the purchase.

A seller/creditor who requires a cosigner for a sale or for a buyer in default must inform the cosigner of the potential liability involved before the cosigner becomes obligated for the debt. The following statement must be provided to the cosigner:

> **Notice to Cosigner**
> You are being asked to guarantee this debt. Think carefully before you do. If the borrower doesn't pay the debt, you will have to. Be sure you can afford to pay if you have to, and that you want to accept this responsibility.
> You may have to pay up to the full amount of the debt if the borrower does not pay. You may also have to pay late fees or collection costs, which increase this amount.
> The creditor can collect this debt from you without first trying to collect from the borrower. The creditor can use the same collection methods against you that can be used against the borrower, such as suing you, garnishing your wages, etc. If this debt is ever in default, that fact may become a part of your credit record.
> This notice is not the contract that makes you liable for debt.

No other distracting statements may be included in the notice. The notice may not be attached to other documents unless it appears before any other document in the package.

Co buyers, co-borrowers and co-loan-applicants are not cosigners.

"Pyramiding" of late charges is not permitted. A late fee may not be assessed solely on the basis that a previously assessed late fee has not been paid.

These are just the principal highlights of the CPTR Rule. A merchant who extends credit to buyers should review the Rule in its entirety and comply with all of its provisions.

Consumer Leases

The Consumer Leasing Act[113] regulates long-term (over four months) personal property leases to a consumer with a contractual cost of no more than $25,000. It requires disclosure of lease costs and terms and imposes limitations on the size of penalties for delinquency or default and on the size of residual liabilities. Specific requirements are set out in the Federal Reserve Board's Regulation M.[114]

The Act only applies to property that is used primarily for personal, family or household purposes. It generally does not apply to month-to-month or week-to-week leases; leases to organizations or governmental units; leases for business, commercial or agricultural purposes; leases of real property; a lease of personal property incidental to a real property lease; or credit sales.

Post-Transaction Third-Party Sellers

The Restore Online Shoppers' Confidence Act[115] (ROSCA) prohibits e-commerce merchants from passing along their customers' billing information to third-party sellers. In addition, third-party sellers are prohibited from charging or trying to charge a consumer's credit or debit card, bank account or other financial account for any product or service sold in an online transaction unless they comply with both of the following requirements:

(a) Before obtaining the consumer's billing information, the post-transaction third-party seller must clearly and conspicuously disclose to the consumer all material terms of the transaction, including (i) a description of the goods or services being offered, (ii) the fact that the post-transaction third-party seller is not affiliated with the initial merchant, which may include disclosure of the name of the post-transaction third party in a manner that clearly differentiates the post-transaction third-party seller from the initial merchant, and (iii) the cost of the goods or services.

(b) The post-transaction third-party seller must obtain express, informed consent for the charge from the consumer whose credit card, debit card, bank account, or other financial account will be charged, by (i) obtaining from the consumer the full account number of the account to be charged; (ii) obtaining the consumer's name and address and a means to contact the consumer; and (iii) requiring the consumer to perform an additional affirmative action, such as clicking on a confirmation button or checking a box that indicates the consumer's consent to be charged the amount disclosed.

A post-transaction third party seller is a person who (a) sells or offers for sale any good or service on the Internet, (b) solicits the purchase of such goods or services on the Internet through an initial merchant after the consumer has initiated a transaction with the initial merchant, and (c) is not (i) the initial merchant, (ii) a subsidiary or corporate affiliate of the initial merchant, or (iii) a successor of an the initial merchant or of a subsidiary or corporate affiliate of the initial merchant.

Consumer Protection

Most jurisdictions have enacted laws regulating the form and content of contracts pertaining to sales to consumers or to consumers of specified kinds of goods or services. There is also a body of law that exists to protect consumers from business practices which, although not fraudulent, are shoddy or not in consumers' best interests.

PRICE GOUGING

Price gouging is the practice of charging inflated prices for a commodity that is in short supply and/or high demand. Many states prohibit price gouging during a time of emergency, either as a distinct crime or as a violation of the state's prohibition against unfair or deceptive trade practices. Definitions vary, but typically it involves setting a price that is 10% or 15% higher than the price of the same goods immediately price to a declaration of a state of emergency. In California and some other states, it is a crime. In Michigan, charging a consumer a price that is grossly in excess of the price at which similar merchandise or services are being sold is prohibited even if no emergency has been declared. Penalties for price gouging are often severe. Accordingly, online merchants should keep abreast of news events and prices in those states were purchasers of the company's products and services reside.

PROHIBITED SALES

Some kinds of business activities, products, sales and services are prohibited, to varying degrees in different jurisdictions. For example, several states prohibit interstate sales or transportation of wine.

To avoid prosecution, an out-of-state website owner must make a good faith effort to screen out sales to customers in places where the law does not allow sales of the kinds of goods or services the website offers. When regulations conflict, a business might consider establishing separate websites for each jurisdiction with a conflicting regulation. For example, www.puffypants.au could be set up for a company's Australian customers; and www.puffypants.uk, for customers residing in the United Kingdom; and so on. If that is not feasible, then a notice could be placed on the company's website to let customers know that the offers appearing on the website are void where prohibited by law. Whichever method is used, it is still the company's responsibility to ensure that every sale or other contractual transaction with a customer complies with all applicable regulatory laws. For example, if a country's laws require a specified disclosure when selling to a resident of the country, then the disclosure must be made when selling to a resident of that country.

Contracts to engage in illegal activity are unenforceable. For example, a customer who incurs a gambling debt on an online gambling website may not have to pay it if the customer is in a jurisdiction where gambling is illegal.

It is also important to be aware that although certain items may be lawful to sell, it may not be lawful to transport them via the United States Mail. As of 2018, it is a violation of U.S. postal regulations to mail air bags, ammunition, explosives or gasoline. In addition to these, the following items may not be sent internationally using the U.S. Mail: alcoholic beverages, cigarettes, dry ice, nail polish, perfumes, poison, fresh fruit or vegetables. There are also restrictions on what may be mailed into particular countries. A list is available at the U.S.P.S. website.

International Sales Contracts

E-commerce businesses will need to ensure that the contracts into which they enter do not violate the laws of the state, country or other jurisdiction in which the person or company with whom they contract is located. A contract to provide online services to a person who resides in a jurisdiction where those services are illegal is not only unenforceable but it could also result in criminal penalties. A New York court, for example, has held that a foreign website owner that allows New York residents to access its online gambling site may be prosecuted for violating a New York law making it a crime to conduct gambling activities.

Chapter 10. Electronic Payments

At one time, the only method of paying for purchases was with a physical object, i.e., cash, check or money order Some online businesses still offer buyers the option of printing out an order form, filling it in and sending it back to the company by regular mail in an envelope with a check or money order enclosed. Most online shoppers today, however, have neither the desire nor the patience for that. For this reason, nearly every online business has adopted some method of enabling customers to make immediate electronic payments at the time of sale.

The five major categories of electronic payment methods are:

- Credit card
- Gift or prepaid card
- Debit card
- Transfer of bank account funds
- Virtual currency.

Credit Cards

A credit card enables an authorized cardholder to present it (or information from it) to a merchant in lieu of paying cash for a purchase. In represents a contractual promise on the part of the issuer to pay money in the amounts and to the merchants the cardholder specifies. In return, the cardholder promises to pay those amounts back to the issuer, with interest. The issuer is the financial institution that issues the credit card to the cardholder. This institution may be a credit card company that opens accounts and issues cards directly to cardholders (such as American Express or Diner's Club) or it may be a bank or other financial institution that issues cards on behalf of a credit card network like Visa or MasterCard.

When a credit card account is established, the issuer creates an account for the cardholder and grants the cardholder a line of credit. The issuer establishes a credit limit, usually after reviewing the cardholder's credit report. When the cardholder uses the card to make a purchase or to take a cash advance, she is essentially taking out a loan from the issuer. The issuer normally charges interest on the amounts borrowed, and may also charge other kinds of fees, too, such as cash advance fees or late payment fees.

Credit card accounts may or may not be revolving accounts. A revolving account is one that allows the cardholder to carry an unpaid balance from month to month and to pay it in increments over time. A nonrevolving account, or "charge card," requires the cardholder to pay the entire balance at the end of each month. American Express and certain department store payment cards are charge cards.

Most credit card purchases involve at least five parties: the cardholder; the merchant; the issuer; the acquirer; and a credit card association or network. In some cases, the issuer and the credit card association or network are the same. For most revolving credit cards, though, the card is issued by a bank or other financial institution on behalf of a credit card association or network such as Visa or MasterCard. In either case, the credit card association or network sets the credit terms (interest rates, fees, etc.). The issuer is the party responsible for authorizing or declining cardholder credit requests. The acquirer is a financial institution that receives payments from the merchant's customers and transmits them to the issuer for payment. An account that a merchant establishes with an acquirer for this purpose is called a *merchant account*.

Online credit card transactions typically involve two additional parties: a payment processor and a payment gateway. A payment processor is an organization with which an acquirer contracts to process credit card transactions. A payment gateway is the online equivalent of a point-of-sale card-reading machine. It processes payment messages and uses security protocols and encryption to ensure transaction safety. It transmits information that the buyer or someone acting on the buyer's behalf inputs during a credit transaction. It is typically located on the merchant's website, but it may also be hosted on a third-party website.

Additional participants in an online credit card transaction may include a shopping cart software vendor, a Secure Sockets Layer (SSL) certificate issuer, and possibly others. Some issuers also have affinity partners. These are organizations that lend their names to an issuer to attract customers. An affinity partner might be a professional association, a club, a charity, an alumni association, etc. The affinity partner usually gets paid a fee for the use of its name, which is often calculated as a percentage of the balance of each card on which the organization's name appears.

The steps involved in a credit card transaction are:

(1) **Presentment**. The cardholder presents the card to a merchant as payment for a purchase.

(2) **Authorization**. The merchant submits the transaction to the acquirer for authorization. The acquirer sends it to the issuer for authorization. If there is available credit, the issuer reserves an amount for the transaction, reducing the cardholder's available credit accordingly. The issuer then sends an authorization code to the acquirer, who communicates to the merchant that the transaction has been approved. The merchant stores the authorization code with the transaction information. If there is not available credit, then the transaction is denied.

(3) **Batching**. The merchant stores all the approved transactions in a batch and sends them in at one time to the acquirer at the end of each day for payment.

(4) **Clearing and settlement**. The acquirer sends the batch to the credit card network. The credit card network distributes each transaction in the batch to the appropriate issuer for payment. The issuer subtracts its interchange fees, which it shares with the credit card network, from the payments to the card network. The card network then routes the net payment amount to the acquirer. (An interchange fee is a fee that is set by the credit card network, charged to the acquirer, and shared by the issuer and the credit card network.)

(5) **Funding**. The acquirer subtracts a discount fee and pays the remainder to the merchant. The issuer then bills the cardholder. (A discount fee is a fee that is charged to a merchant by the acquirer. This is how an acquirer passes the interchange fee on to the merchant

while at the same time collecting a fee for its processing services and credit card network assessments.)

The Truth in Lending Act[116] (TILA) is a federal statute that aims to promote the informed use of consumer credit by requiring disclosures to consumers about credit terms and the cost of the credit. It also seeks to protect consumers from unfair lending practices. It is implemented by the Federal Reserve Board's Regulation Z.[117] The Act and its implementing regulation apply to any lender that makes funds available to another with the expectation that they will be repaid. A lender may be any individual, entity or organization, including but not limited to a bank or financial institution. The Act and Regulation apply to most kinds of credit transactions, including both closed-end credit (such as installment loans) and open-ended credit (revolving credit accounts, like credit cards and lines of credit). It only applies to consumer credit, however. It does not apply to commercial loans (credit extended primarily for business, agricultural or other commercial purposes) or to credit that is extended to corporations or other legal entities (with the exception of certain trusts). Also, it only applies to small loan amounts, and to home loans. The dividing line between a small and a large loan is adjusted annually.

In a credit card transaction, the card issuer is the lender. Accepting credit card payments does not make a merchant a lender. A card issuer is subject to TILA requirements, but the merchant who accepts the card is not. Of course, a merchant may become a lender in some other way. A business that engages in in-house financing may need to comply with TILA requirements, for example.

The rights and obligations of merchants, issuers, acquirers, cardholders and other parties to a credit transaction are primarily determined by the contractual agreements among them. Federal and state laws impose some limitations on freedom of contract in this area, though. The Credit Card Accountability Responsibility and Disclosure Act[118] (Credit CARD Act) establishes rights for cardholders beyond those that TILA provides. It also imposes additional disclosure requirements on open-ended (revolving) credit lenders, such as credit card issuers. The Act only protects consumers; it does not apply to business and corporate credit cards. Enforcement of antitrust laws is also having an impact on these agreements. Antitrust laws and enforcement actions potentially impact both consumer and business credit transactions.

A merchant who accepts payments by credit card is bound by the terms of the agreement with the acquirer (or a contract with an intermediary between the merchant and the acquirer). The merchant's contract with the acquirer (or an intermediary) normally will include merchant obligations that the credit card network requires acquirers to include in their contracts with merchants. A merchant should read this contract carefully and comply with it. The requirements are very specific and they vary depending on region, merchant category, card program, and a variety of other particulars. It is not possible to list them all here. A few key points are worthy of highlighting, though.

ISSUER OBLIGATIONS

Disclosures

TILA requires open-ended (revolving) credit lenders such as credit card issuers to disclose to borrowers (such as credit card holders) the cost of the credit, including the APR; the methods used to determine finance charges, late fees, over-the-limit fees, annual fees, and other assessments; a standardized set of conditions under which finance charges are imposed; information about grace periods; the borrower's right to dispute charges and the procedure for doing so. Closed-end credit providers and makers of home loans are also required to make certain kinds of disclosures. Under the Credit CARD Act, monthly credit card statements must disclose how long it will take the cardholder to pay off the balance if only minimum payments are made. They also must disclose how much a consumer would have to pay in order to pay off the balance in three years.

Interest

Although disclosure is required, there is no federal limit on the amount of interest that credit card issuers may charge. Interest rates are set by state usury laws. Some states, such as South Dakota, have no ceiling on interest rates and fees.

Additional fees

Credit card agreements with customers typically call for the imposition of a variety of fees for different kinds of customer transactions and behaviors. Late payment fees, over-limit fees, cash advance transaction fees, convenience check fees, returned check fees, fees for transactions in a foreign currency, and membership fees are examples.

LATE FEES

Late fees are capped at $25 unless a cardholder is late more than once in a six-month period.

OVER-LIMIT FEES

Under the Credit CARD Act, over-limit fees may not be charged unless the consumer has opted in to them. Those who opt out will not be charged a fee for going over the limit, but their transactions may be rejected if they do. An over-limit fee may not be more than the amount by which a transaction was over the limit.

Notice of account changes

Credit card issuers must give cardholders at least forty-five days notice before increasing interest rates or making significant changes to the fee structure.

Right to opt out of account changes

Credit card issuers must give cardholders a right to opt out of significant changes to the account terms. By opting out, the cardholder agrees to close the account and pay off balances under the original terms. Credit card companies generally must allow cardholders at least five years to pay the balance.

Universal default

Universal default is the practice of raising interest rates on customers based on their payment records with other creditors. Card issuers may not engage in this practice unless they give customers prior notice that they may do so. If an existing credit card agreement does not provide for it and the credit card company wants to practice it, then it must give customers at least forty-five days notice of the change.

Due dates

The Credit CARD Act requires issuers to provide a cardholder with a statement at least twenty-one days before payment is due. Payment due times may not be set to fall before 5:00 p.m. If a payment is due on a weekend, holiday or a day that the card issuer is closed, then a late fee may not be charged unless the customer also fails to pay on the next day that is not one of those days. Due dates must be the same each month.

Order of application of payments

Credit card issuers often establish different interest rates for different types of credit transactions (purchases, cash advances, balance transfers, ATM withdrawals, and so on). They may allocate the minimum payment to the balances owed on these in any order they wish. For example, a payment from a customer may be applied to the customer's balance on a low interest rate purchase first, leaving other balances to continue to accumulate interest at higher rates. Under the Credit CARD Act, though, any payments in excess of the minimum amount due must be applied to the balance with the highest interest rate first.

Liability for unauthorized charges

Under federal law, a cardholder does not have to pay any charges to a credit card that are made after reporting the card or account information lost or stolen. A consumer's liability for charges incurred before the report is made is limited to $50.[119]

Perks

Different kinds of credit cards provide different benefits to their cardholders. Some offer extended warranties on products purchased with the card, price protection, roadside assistance, rental car discounts, rental car insurance, cell phone replacement, frequent flyer miles, retailer discounts, and the like. These vary widely from card to card.

Offers to young people

Issuers may not establish credit card accounts for people who are under twenty-one years of age unless an adult cosigns or the young person proves she has adequate income to repay credit card debt. There are also restrictions on soliciting people who are under twenty-one to apply for credit cards.

MERCHANT RIGHTS AND OBLIGATIONS

Merchants generally do not contract directly with credit card networks. Instead, they contract with an acquirer, or with an intermediary between an acquirer and the merchant. An acquirer's contract with a credit card network usually will require the acquirer to ensure that participating merchants abide by the standards and practices the card network specifies. The acquirer's contract with the merchant normally will require a merchant to comply with these standards and practices.

Display of logo

An agreement may require a merchant who accepts a network's card to display the network's logo ("acceptance mark") on the merchant's website, and specify how to display it.

Address and telephone number

Agreements typically require a merchant to provide customers with a mailing address and an email address or telephone number for customer inquiries and correspondence. A merchant may be required to display the merchant's country and any export restrictions on the Checkout page and/or a page leading up to it.

Price and other terms

Agreements typically require a merchant to display price and other terms of a transaction, including the timing of billing and fulfillment.

Minimum purchase

At one time, agreements required merchants to accept credit card payments regardless of the amount of the transaction. Because a merchant is assessed transaction fees for every transaction regardless of size, this was an onerous requirement for merchants. The Dodd-Frank Act[120] eases the burden somewhat by giving merchants a right to specify a minimum purchase amount for customers who pay with credit cards. The minimum purchase amount must not be set higher than $10. If a business specifies a minimum for credit card purchases, then it must apply the same minimum to all credit cards regardless of issuer or card network type. The rule applies only to credit cards, however, not to debit cards.

Maximum purchase

Federal law does not address the question of maximum purchase limitations. Credit card agreements often provide that governmental entities and schools may impose maximum limits, but prohibit other merchants from doing so.

Fee caps

Although debit cards are subject to an interchange fee cap, and although the EU and some other countries impose fee caps on credit card transactions, there is currently no fee cap for credit card transactions in the United States.

"Honor all issuers"

Agreements typically require a merchant who accepts a credit card from one issuer to accept the card from all other issuers, too. For example, a merchant who accepts Visa cards issued by Wells Fargo Bank must also accept Visa cards issued by Billy's Bank.

"Honor every kind of card"

Some credit card networks require a merchant who accepts one kind of card in the network to accept other kinds of cards in the network, too. A merchant who has entered into an agreement of this kind to accept a card network's debit cards, for example, would also have to accept the network's credit cards. Due to an antitrust settlement, Visa and MasterCard no longer require merchants in the United States to accept their credit cards solely because they accept their debit cards, or vice versa.

Steering

Because merchants pay higher transaction fees for some cards than for others, they often offer incentives or try to encourage customers to use the payment method that results in a lower fee for the merchant. Because the American Express fee is higher than that for Visa and MasterCard, some merchants refuse to accept American Express. Those who do accept it may be inclined to encourage customers to use different cards or payment methods. American Express has attempted to curb these practices by prohibiting merchants who accept their card from encouraging customers to use a payment method other than American Express. A case asserting that anti-steering provisions in card acceptance agreements violate antitrust laws is pending before the U.S. Supreme Court as this book goes to press.

Cash discounts

The Dodd-Frank Act bars credit card companies from prohibiting merchants from discounting their cards. Discounts are only permitted at the network level. Merchants may discount certain payment methods, such as offering a discount for cash payments but not for credit card payments, but they may not discount prices based on a particular issuer or card type.

Credit surcharges

A merchant might be tempted to charge customers who pay with a credit card an additional fee as a way of recouping credit card transaction costs that the credit card issuer, network and acquirer pass on to the merchant. At one time, credit card networks prohibited merchants from assessing such a surcharge. As part of antitrust settlements, however, Visa and MasterCard have removed surcharge prohibitions from their agreements. The agreements still require a merchant to disclose the surcharge before it is incurred and the amount of any such surcharge must be stated on the receipt.

Even though the prohibition has been removed from credit card agreements, California, New York and a few other states have laws prohibiting merchants from imposing surcharges for a customer's use of a credit card. Minnesota appears to be the only state that expressly allows merchants to impose a surcharge for paying with a credit card.[121] Moreover, the constitutionality of laws prohibiting merchants from adding surcharges for payments with credit cards is dubious. The U.S. Supreme Court has suggested that a law prohibiting credit card surcharges is effectively the same as a law allowing cash discounts, and therefore a law allowing one but not the other is simply a speech regulation. If allowing one phrasing but not the other does not serve any state interest, then this kind of law would seem to violate the First Amendment.[122] The

Supreme Court has not issued a definitive ruling. It remanded the case with instructions to the lower court to consider the constitutionality issue; it did not actually decide it. It is likely, though, that state courts will apply similar reasoning to make a finding of unconstitutionality. Whether state legislators will respond by repealing their laws, amending them to prohibit both surcharges and cash discounts, or doing nothing, is not known. In the meantime, these state anti-surcharge laws remain on the books.

Convenience fees

A convenience fee is a charge for using an alternative payment channel outside a merchant's customary payment channels. As such, it is to be distinguished from a fee charged to a customer simply for using a credit card. Visa's credit card agreement allows a merchant to charge a customer a convenience fee for using a Visa card only if: (a) it is in a card-absent environment (such as an e-commerce website); (b) it is disclosed to the customer before the transaction is completed; (c) the merchant gives the customer an opportunity to cancel; (d) it is a flat amount regardless of the amount of the payment (not a percentage, for example); (e) it is applicable to all forms of payment accepted in the payment channel; (f) it is included as part of the total amount of the transaction; (g) it is not charged by a third party; (h) it is not added to a recurring transaction. A merchant may not charge both a surcharge and a convenience fee for the same transaction.

Refinancing uncollectable debt

An agreement may prohibit a merchant from submitting a request for authorization of a charge to refinance a cardholder's uncollectable debt or a charge arising from a dishonored check.

Illegal or unsavory purposes

Agreements usually prohibit the use of a card for an illegal purpose. Some card agreements also prohibit using the card in connection with a transaction that may damage the goodwill or reputation of the card network or, as the MasterCard agreement puts it, "reflect negatively" on its trademark. According to the card agreement, this includes transactions for the purchase of any material that MasterCard, Inc. "deems unacceptable to sell."

Fraud

A merchant must deposit transactions only for its own business. Depositing transactions for a business that does not have a valid merchant agreement is called *laundering*, which is a form of fraud. Moreover, agreements may prohibit a merchant from submitting a request for authorization of a transaction that the merchant knows or should know is fraudulent or not authorized by the cardholder. Merchants are also barred from colluding with a cardholder for a fraudulent purpose.

Suspicious transactions

Agreements usually require merchants to establish procedures for handling suspicious transactions, including regular employee training in detecting and responding to them. The Visa agreement describes any of the following as suspicious:

- rush orders (might indicate a scheme to fraudulently obtain a product for quick resale)
- random orders, i.e., orders the particulars of which the customer does not seem to care (could indicate the product is intended for resale rather than personal use)
- ship-to address different from billing address, particularly if the ship-to address is a post office box or an office address
- ship-to address in a zip code with a high fraud rate
- customer's uncertainty about her own purported personal information
- hesitation to provide personal information such as the spelling of the customer's family name or of a street or city appearing in the customer's address
- sales that seem too good to be true
- first-time shopper (criminals often try to target merchants they haven't targeted before)
- larger-than-normal order or an order for big-ticket items (stolen accounts have a limited life span, so criminals try to maximize the size of their fraudulent purchases)
- orders for several varieties of the same item
- shipments to a location outside the merchant's country
- customers who use free email account services
- transactions using accounts with similar numbers (could indicate that account numbers have been generated by a computer program)
- orders using different accounts that are shipped to the same address
- multiple transactions on a single card over a short period of time
- multiple transactions and multiple shipping addresses using the same card
- more than two cards used from the same IP address.

A transaction with only one of these risk markers might not be cause for alarm, but two or more may be indicative of a fraud scheme.

"Code 10" calls

A Code 10 authorization request is a telephone call that a merchant places to the issuer to verify a card's validity while simultaneously alerting the issuer of suspicious activity. The merchant is connected with a specialist who advises the merchant on a course of action.

Identity verification

Because the cardholder and the card are not physically present, the risk of fraud is greater for online transactions than for card-present transactions. A card is not scanned into a device in the course of the usual online transaction, so online transactions do not benefit from the added security that chip-embedded smart cards offer. To deter fraud in the online environment, credit card agreements typically require the merchant to collect various kinds of information to ensure that the customer is in physical possession of the card and is an authorized user of it. This may include, in addition to the account number, the expiration date, the billing address for the card account, and the security code. The security code, which may be called a *card verification code* (CVC) or a *card verification value* (CVV or CVV2), is usually printed on the back of the card.

Inclusion of tax

Agreements typically require a merchant to include sales tax or other taxes the merchant is required to collect as part of the transaction amount rather than collecting the tax separately.

Confirmation of purchase

An agreement may require that the merchant's website provide a function for a cardholder to confirm a purchase before the completion of the sale.

Card-present transactions

Requirements for card-present transactions are not identical to requirements for card-absent transactions. For example, a merchant may be required to obtain a cardholder's written signature and/or check an identification card when an unsigned card is presented. In some states, such as California, it is unlawful for a merchant to write down any information from an identification card on a credit card receipt. Some agreements permit merchants only to look at identification cards, not to write down any information from them.

Smart cards

A smart card is a credit card with a readable chip embedded in it. A merchant with a physical location uses a special device to scan the card and read the chip. This way, even if a data thief acquires someone's account information, he will not be able to use it to complete a credit card transaction unless he has the actual card with the chip in it present with him. Merchant agreements may shift the risk of loss to a merchant who accepts a smart card without scanning the chip in it.

Signatures

Historically, agreements required merchants to get signatures from customers who pay for a purchase with a credit card. These agreements were changed to allow merchants to waive the signature requirement for purchases under $50. As this book goes to press, card networks have been announcing plans to eliminate the signature requirement even for purchases over $50, subject to some exceptions. Most agreements require no signature when a personal identification number (PIN) is used.

Holds

Agreements allow merchants, in some circumstances, to request a hold on a cardholder's account for the payment of an anticipated purchase. The amount of the hold is an estimate of what the actual amount will be. If the actual amount ends up being within a specified percentage of the estimated charge (e.g., 15%), then the charge goes through without the merchant having to go back and request a second authorization. The procedure is most often used by hotels, motels, restaurants and rental companies, i.e., situations where consumers customarily run a tab and the final amount is not known until the customer's use of the merchant's service is completed. Different requirements apply to different kinds of merchants and industries.

Recurring transactions

A recurring transaction is one in which a cardholder authorizes a merchant to automatically charge the customer's card account for the recurring or periodic delivery of goods or services. Agreements may require that a receipt for a recurring transaction order be in a specified format. The Visa agreement, for example, requires the initial sales receipt to include: (a) the phrase "recurring transaction;" (b) the frequency of charges; and (c) the duration of time for which the customer has agreed to the periodic charges. Visa has a Visa Account Updater program in which merchants may participate to verify that information on file, including card account number and expiration date, is correct. Visa requires a merchant that is engaged in recurring transactions to keep the cardholder's expiration date on file and include it in all authorization requests and to clearly identify all recurring transactions as such. A merchant may be required to notify a customer a specified number of days in advance before a recurring transaction is charged to their account and may be required to apprise the customer of the amount to be charged. Some states have enacted laws regulating these kinds of arrangements. Depending on the state, such a law may oblige a merchant to do things like obtain the customer's signature, give advance notice a specified number of days before a recurring charge is billed, notify customers of opt-out or cancellation rights, and the like.

Receipt

Agreements typically require a merchant to provide a receipt to the customer unless the customer declines one. Agreements also typically require either the merchant or the acquirer to retain copies of records of receipts for a specified period of time. The Visa agreement, for example, requires receipts or copies of them to be retained for thirteen months. An issuer may require an acquirer or merchant to produce a receipt when a customer disputes a charge. For online transactions, the obligation to provide customers with a receipt might be satisfied by setting up the website to display a printable receipt upon completion of the transaction. Another method would be to send a receipt to the customer's email address. If a receipt is sent to an email address, then care should be taken to comply with data security requirements applicable to transmitting personal and financial information electronically for storage on an email server. Receipts for recurring transactions must have the additional information described above on them. Credit card agreements typically have specified requirements as to the kinds of information that must and must not be included in a receipt. The Visa agreement, for example, requires an online receipt to include: (a) merchant name and location; (b) merchant's website address; (c) transaction date; (d) description of goods or services; (e) transaction amount; (f) payment method used; (g) account number, with all but the last four digits suppressed; (h) transaction type (Purchase vs. Credit); (i) authorization code (which may be required to be suppressed on the receipt). An agreement may recommend or require that a company's cancellations/returns policy be stated on the receipt.

Suppression of sensitive information

Agreements require a merchant to ensure that the expiration date, PIN and security code (CVC, CVV or CVV2) do not appear on a customer's receipt and that the credit card account number is partially suppressed in accordance with state and local laws and acquirer requirements. Suppression of all but the last four digits of an account number is a common requirement.

Record retention

Agreements may require an acquirer and/or merchant to retain records of all credit transactions for a specified period of time. During this time, the issuer may have a right to receive a copy of a transaction receipt upon request.

Data security and privacy

An agreement may require an e-commerce merchant to publish a privacy and/or data security policy to the website. Whether publication of such a policy is required or not, agreements impose a variety of requirements on merchants to protect the privacy and security of information collected from cardholders. These topics are covered in Chapters 13 and 17.

Responsibility for employees

Agreements generally hold a merchant responsible for the conduct of the merchant's employees and agents. They may also require merchants to periodically educate and train employees with respect to the handling of information collected from cardholders.

Delivery

Agreements typically allow a merchant to decide for itself whether and what kinds of restrictions to impose on delivery. Any restrictions on delivery must be clearly stated on the website. If a sales transaction is completed, though, then a merchant usually is required to deliver goods and services to the cardholder at the time of the transaction. For online or other transactions where the card is not present, the merchant should inform the customer of the delivery method and tentative delivery date. An agreement may prohibit a transaction from being deposited until the ordered goods have been shipped or the ordered services have been provided. The agreement may require a merchant to notify the customer if delivery will be made in more than one shipment.

Out of stock items

Agreements may provide that if the ordered product or service is not available at the time of purchase, the merchant must inform the cardholder and obtain the cardholder's agreement to a delayed delivery. If that happens, then the merchant must inform the customer of the expected delivery date. If delivery cannot be made at the time of the transaction or within the agreed time, then the cardholder must be given an opportunity to cancel the transaction. If an item is no longer available at all, a merchant should offer the option of either purchasing a similar item or cancelling the transaction. Another item should not be substituted unless the customer agrees to accept it.

Cancellations, returns, and exchanges

Agreements contain detailed provisions relating to returns, exchanges, and cancellations ("chargebacks.") For more information, see Chapter 11.

Waivers of chargeback rights

The Fair Credit Billing Act[123] (FCBA) gives credit card holders a right to dispute charges on their credit card statements. Accordingly, credit card agreements typically prohibit merchants from requiring a customer to waive the customer's right to dispute charges on his credit card.

OTHER COUNTRIES

Agreements for acquirers and merchants in countries other than the United States contain some of the same terms but also contain some terms that are different from those that apply in the United States. Merchants must take care to ensure that they are in compliance with the applicable terms of their agreements.

PREPAID CARDS, GIFT CARDS AND GIFT CERTIFICATES

A prepaid credit card is a card that entitles the holder to make purchases up to the amount the holder (or someone on the holder's behalf) has paid to purchase the card or has paid into an account that is represented by the card. It is the equivalent of currency, or a savings account, in card form. These cards do not involve an extension of credit. They may say "credit card" on them, and they may even bear the brand of a famous credit card network like Visa or MasterCard, but they are not really credit cards. Since there is no loan, there is nothing to repay. For this reason, the seller of the card may charge a purchasing fee and other kinds of fees, but may not charge interest.

Prepaid cards may be either closed-loop or open-loop. Closed-loop cards are gift cards that are accepted only by a single merchant or a group of affiliated merchants. They usually cannot be reloaded with additional value. Open-loop gift cards are not limited to a single merchant or group of affiliated merchants. They may be used to make purchases from any merchant that accepts credit cards of the kind with which the card is branded. Open-loop gift cards are usually issued by banks and other financial institutions. They are often reloadable.

Although the title of the Credit CARD Act suggests it only applies to credit cards, the Act also contains some provisions relating to prepaid cards, including gift cards and gift certificates that are sold or issued primarily for personal, family, or household use. These provisions apply to prepaid cards and also to all mechanisms that function like prepaid cards whether they are in card form or not. Thus, for example, an electronic promise (a person's commitment, stored in electronic form) to provide payment for goods or services is treated the same as a prepaid card even though it might consist of only a number sequence or a code that may be redeemed for value in an online transaction without a card.[124]

The following are excluded from the Credit CARD Act's "prepaid card" provisions:

- Telephone service cards
- Reloadable cards that are not marketed or labeled as gift cards or gift certificates
- Loyalty, reward, or promotional gift cards The nature of the card—e.g., "reward" or "promotional"—and the expiration date must be disclosed on the front of the card. A toll free number must be displayed somewhere on the card. The issuer must disclose any fees and conditions on or with the card

- Cards that are not marketed to the general public, such as a card representing a tax refund or a card representing a store credit that is issued to a customer upon the customer's return of merchandise
- Cards issued in paper form only
- Cards that are not for a specific value and that are redeemable solely for admission to, or for the acquisition of a specified product or service at or near a specified event or venue.

Five-year expiration

When the Act applies, the expiration date of a prepaid card must not be less than five years from: (a) the date of issuance, in the case of an unloadable card; or (b) the date of the last loading of value to the card, in the case of a reloadable card.

Expiration date disclosures

Either the expiration date or a statement that the card does not expire must be disclosed on the card. If a card is reloadable or has an expiration date of less than seven years from the date of manufacture, then any difference between the expiration of the card and the expiration of the right to use the funds represented by the card must be disclosed. If the card is capable of expiring before the underlying funds do, then the card must disclose a toll free number and, if one is maintained, a website that a consumer may use to obtain a replacement.

Card replacement fee

No fee may be charged to replace an expired card if the underlying funds represented by the card are still usable.

Inactivity, dormancy and service fees

No inactivity or dormancy fee may be imposed on a prepaid card unless there has been no activity for more than a year. Only one fee—whether it is called an inactivity, dormancy or service fee—may be imposed in any month. Fees must be disclosed before or at the time the card is purchased and must appear on the card. The disclosure requirement is satisfied if fee terms and conditions are clearly and legibly visible on the card at the time of purchase.

Other fees

Any other fees, such as issuance or cash-out fees, must be disclosed prior to purchase. These fees do not need to be disclosed on the card, so long as they are disclosed in a document that is furnished before the purchase. A toll free number and a website, if any, that may be contacted for further information about these fees must also be provided.

Clear and conspicuous disclosures

The expiration date and fee disclosures must be clear and conspicuous. They should be in a font and color that contrasts with the background and must not be so small as to be difficult to read.

Debit Cards and Bank Account Transfers

A debit card is one that is associated with the cardholder's deposit account, which is usually a checking or savings account at a bank. It differs from a credit card in that its use results in a deduction of the debit amount from the cardholder's account. A person who uses a credit card undertakes an obligation to repay the amount of the transaction to the card issuer at some time in the future; nothing is deducted from an account.

Debit card transactions may be signature-based or PIN-based. Many cards have both capabilities. Signature-based debit transactions tend to be routed through a credit card network, typically MasterCard or Visa. They are processed in the same basic way that credit cards are, except that the end result is a deduction from the cardholder's checking account instead of a bill. PIN-based debit transactions require the cardholder to enter a PIN—typically required to be four to twelve digits long—at the point of sale (POS). The transaction is routed through electronic funds transfers (EFT) networks such as SHAZAM or STAR, on one hand, or EFT networks at MasterCard, Discover and Visa, such as Interlink, on the other. The PIN-based process uses a single message for authorization, clearing and settlement. Unlike a signature debit, a PIN-based debit transaction results in the customer's checking account being debited immediately, much like an ATM withdrawal. Also like an ATM withdrawal, the issuing bank may charge the customer a fee to make a POS purchase. Because signatures can be forged and PIN-based transactions are more secure, signature debit transactions are riskier for issuers. As a result, fees for these are usually set higher than for PIN-based debit transactions.

Many banks and financial institutions have established websites from which customers may check their account balances and initiate electronic transfers of funds from their accounts. Banks and other financial institutions usually also allow customers to initiate electronic transfers of funds by telephone. In addition, many give their customers the ability to arrange pre-authorized deposits or withdrawals, on either a one-time or a recurring basis. These kinds of transactions do not involve an extension of credit. Only money that is already in the customer's account is transferred; nothing is borrowed.

Electronic check conversion is another method of immediately transferring funds from an account. This involves scanning a paper check to capture account number, routing number and other information needed to convert it into an electronic payment. After the paper check has been scanned for this purpose, it becomes null and void. Since this involves scanning a physical check, it is more useful for brick-and-mortar retail businesses than for e-commerce businesses.

eChecking is yet another method of collecting payments online. An eCheck has the same effect as an electronically converted check but it is created online. There is no scanning of a paper check. Instead, a customer "writes" a check electronically by entering the checking account and routing numbers for his bank account into an online form that a merchant (or an online payment service provider on the merchant's behalf) provides.

The Automated Clearing House (ACH) is a computer-based clearing and settlement facility that processes the exchange of electronic transactions between participating banks and other depository institutions. Rules and regulations for the ACH network are established by the National Automated Clearing House Association and the Federal Reserve Board.

The Electronic Funds Transfer Act[125] (EFTA) and the Federal Reserve Board's Regulation E[126] implementing it are intended to protect consumer rights in connection with electronic funds transfers. They apply to electronic transfers of funds to or from a customer's account at a financial institution. Debit card transactions and online bank account transfers come within their coverage. The EFTA does not apply to credit cards and prepaid cards.

As with credit card transactions, the rights and obligations of the parties to a debit transaction are largely a matter of contract. Merchants should read and comply with these contracts. The obligations these contracts impose on merchants are very specific and differ with respect to region, merchant category, card program, and so on. It is not possible to list them all here. It may be useful to highlight some key provisions, though.

FINANCIAL INSTITUTION OBLIGATIONS

Disclosures

Financial institutions must make an initial disclosure at the time the consumer contracts for the electronic funds transfer service or before the consumer makes his first electronic fund transfer. The disclosure must include information about the limits of the consumer's liability in the event of unauthorized transfers; the telephone number and address of the person or office to receive notifications of unauthorized transfers; the financial institution's business days; the type of electronic fund transfers the consumer may make and any limitations on the frequency and dollar amount of transfers; any fees for electronic fund transfers; a summary of the consumer's right to receipts, periodic statements, and notices regarding pre-authorized transfers; a summary of the consumer's right to stop payment of a pre-authorized electronic funds lo transfer; the circumstances in which the financial institution may disclose confidential information to third parties; error resolution; ATM fees; and disclosures for any new electronic fund transfer service that is added to the customer's account that are subject to different terms and conditions than those set out in the initial disclosures. Disclosures may be in electronic format, if the consumer consents. They may be combined with any disclosures that may be required under TILA or the Truth in Savings Act.[127]

Liability for unauthorized transactions

If a consumer notifies the financial institution of the loss or theft of a debit card (or other access device), or of personally identifying account information (account number, etc.), before unauthorized transactions are conducted, then the consumer is not liable for those transactions. If the consumer notifies the financial institution within two business days of learning of the theft or loss, then the consumer's liability is limited to $50 or the amount of unauthorized transfers that occur before notice to the financial institution, whichever is less. A consumer who waits more than two days to report the theft or loss may be liable for all or a portion of unauthorized transfers that occur before notice is given, up to $500 if notification is given between three and fifty-nine days. If loss is not reported within sixty days, a customer's liability is potentially unlimited. A contract between the financial institution and the consumer may provide greater protection for the consumer, but it may not provide less protection than what the EFTA provides.

Daily limit

The EFTA requires banks to limit the amount of money that may be withdrawn by means of electronic funds transfers from a customer's account during a given time period. Most banks set the limit at $200 or $300 per 24–hour period. The purpose of this rule is to limit a customer's loss in the event a card is lost or stolen.

Notice of account changes

A financial institution must provide a change-in-terms notice at least twenty-one days before the changes take effect.

Error resolution policy

A financial institution must have an error resolution policy and must send periodic notices of it to customers. If a consumer notifies an institution of an error, the institution must investigate and resolve the claim within the timeframes specified in Regulation E.

Statements and receipts

A financial institution must provide customers with documentation of electronic fund transfer transactions, including terminal receipts and monthly statements.

MERCHANT RIGHTS AND OBLIGATIONS

EFT service providers

A business that provides electronic fund transfer services but does not hold the consumer's account is subject to many of the same legal obligations that apply to financial institutions in which a consumer has an account.

Nonexclusivity

Businesses may not require electronic funds transfers as an exclusive method of payment. A business may offer it as an option, but may not require its use. If EFT is offered as a method of payment, then additional payment methods also must be offered. An exception exists for employers. Employers may pay an employee by direct deposit even if the employee would prefer some other method of payment.

Stop payment orders

The EFTA generally does not give consumers the right to stop payment if a purchased product or service is defective or not delivered. If, however, a consumer has arranged recurring automatic payments, the consumer may stop further automatic payments by notifying the company at least three days before the scheduled transfer. The notice may be written or oral. If it is oral, it must be followed up with written notice within fourteen days. A contract or an applicable state law may provide a customer with greater rights to stop payments.

Interchange fee cap

The Dodd-Frank Act requires the interchange fee that issuers charge for electronic debit transactions to be reasonable and proportional to the cost of the transaction to the issuer. The requirement only applies to issuers with assets of at least $10 billion. The Federal Reserve Board, which is tasked with implementing this requirement, has imposed a cap on the per-transaction interchange fee in the amount of 21 cents plus 0.05% of the transaction amount. An additional 1 cent is allowed if the issuer implements specified fraud prevention measures.

Minimum purchase

A merchant has a federally protected right to specify a minimum purchase amount when payment is made with a credit card, but this right does not extend to debit cards. Credit card companies may prohibit merchants from specifying a minimum purchase amount for debit card transactions. The Visa, MasterCard and some other credit card agreements do prohibit merchants from specifying a minimum purchase amount for debit card transactions.

Refinancing uncollectable debt

Some card agreements bar a merchant from submitting a request for authorization of a charge to a customer's credit card to refinance a cardholder's uncollectable debt or charges arising from a dishonored check, but allow debit cards and prepaid cards to be used for this purpose.

PAYMENT PROCESSOR OBLIGATIONS

Payment processing services like PayPal must make clear and conspicuous disclosures of the important terms and conditions of the service to the customer before the customer uses it. This includes, among other things, the funding source for payments (e.g., the fact that money will be withdrawn from the customer's bank account when the service is used); whether and for how long a hold will be placed on funds held in a processing service account; chargeback and dispute resolution rights and procedures.

EUROPEAN UNION

Many EU countries require online debit transactions to be PIN-based.

Virtual Currency

Virtual currency is a medium of exchange that operates likes money but does not have the status of legal tender. It is usually issued and controlled by its developer, and used and accepted among members of a virtual community. Bitcoin is an example. Users access an online computer program that provides them with a virtual "wallet" and enables them to purchase and exchange credits with other Bitcoin users. The credits are purchased with real money (often facilitated by a credit card). Because they are not a real currency, bitcoins are not controlled by a central bank. Their value can change frequently and drastically.

Unlike credit card transactions, Bitcoin transactions cannot be reversed by the purchaser. There is no chargeback system. Of course, the person receiving the funds may voluntarily choose to refund bitcoins if a transaction goes south. In some cases, doing this might be a way of building goodwill or avoiding litigation.

Also unlike credit cards, transactions are stored publicly and permanently on the network. Anyone may view the balance and transactions of any Bitcoin address. The identity of the user behind an address remains unknown, however, until information is revealed during a purchase or in other circumstances. This is why Bitcoin advises using a Bitcoin address only once.

Virtual currency is not legal everywhere. In some countries it is illegal to make a purchase with it, or simply banned altogether. Thailand allows only licensed bitcoin exchanges. Licensees are regulated. A number of countries are either considering or working on establishing some sort of government-controlled virtual currency as a form of legal tender. If that happens, more bans on the use of privately controlled virtual currency are likely to follow.

Bitcoin is not illegal in EU countries. Moreover, the Court of Justice has ruled that exchanging money for units of virtual currency is exempt from value-added tax (VAT) because it is a form of currency, not a commodity. VAT will be due in the normal way from suppliers of any goods or services sold in exchange for virtual currency. Profits and losses on virtual currencies presumably will be subject to capital gains taxes, and earnings from business or employment that are paid in virtual currency presumably will be subject to income taxes, in those jurisdictions where these kinds of taxes are collected. It is not yet clear which, if any, financial and securities regulations apply to issuances and trades of virtual currency in the EU.

There is no law against buying, selling or owning bitcoins in the United States. The federal government has a monopoly on issuing legal tender but private mediums of exchange are not prohibited unless they are designed to appear similar to federally issued tender.

Generally, any transaction that would be illegal if conducted with the use of money is illegal if conducted using virtual currency. For example, 18 U.S.C. § 1960, which was enacted as part of the USA PATRIOT Act,[128] makes it a crime to manage or own an interest in an unlicensed "money transmitting business." The statute defines money transmitting as "transferring funds." *In United States v Murgio*[129] a federal court held that because bitcoins are used as a medium of exchange for the purchase of goods or services, they are a form of money. The Commodity Futures Trading Commission (CFTC) classifies virtual currency as a commodity. The U.S. Treasury classifies Bitcoin as a convertible decentralized virtual currency. It appears the IRS will treat it as property for purposes of capital gains and losses on trades. Since income is taxable whether it is received in the form of money, property or services, earnings that are paid in bitcoins presumably would be taxed in the same way that earnings that are paid with property are.

The Bank Secrecy Act[130] (BSA) requires money services businesses, including money transmitters, to register with the Financial Crimes Enforcement Network (FinCEN), a bureau of the U.S. Treasury Department, and implement an anti-money-laundering program. They must keep detailed records of all customers and cash purchases of negotiable instruments. The BSA also requires certain kinds of reports to be made in specified circumstances. A cash transactions report must be filed whenever the daily aggregate of such purchases or cash transactions by a customer exceeds $10,000. Regardless of the amount of a transaction, a suspicious activity report must be filed whenever a financial institution, including a money services business, becomes aware of a transaction that may signify money laundering, tax evasion, or other possible crimes. A financial institution is not allowed to inform a customer that it is filing a suspicious activity report. Suspicious activity reports are exempt from disclosure under the Freedom of Information Act[131] (FOIA). Persons with an interest in a foreign financial account with an aggregate value of $10,000 must file a foreign financial account report. Financial institutions must keep records of cash purchases of monetary instruments (money orders, cashier's checks, etc.) in the amount of $3,000 or more. Businesses receiving cash payments totaling more than $10,000 must file

IRS/FinCEN Form 8300. Severe penalties are imposed for failure to file a required report, including heavy fines and imprisonment.

According to FinCEN, the BSA applies to virtual currency. It is not entirely clear how and to whom it applies, though. It is clear that money services businesses, including money transmitters, must comply, but are issuers, sellers and buyers of virtual currency in a money services business? FinCEN guidelines[132] attempt to answer this question by distinguishing among three different categories of participants in virtual currency systems: users, exchangers, and administrators. A *user* is a person who buys virtual currency to purchase goods or services. An *exchanger* is a person or company that is in the business of exchanging or transferring virtual currency for either real or virtual currency. An *administrator* is a person or company that is in the business of issuing virtual currency with the authority to redeem (withdraw) it from the system. Users are not considered money services businesses, but exchanges and administrators are. Therefore, exchangers and administrators have to comply with the BSA, but users do not. The category into which investors (people who trade in virtual currency to make a profit rather than to purchase goods or services) fall is not clear. If bitcoins are classified as goods, then investors might be classified as users. If trading in virtual currency is considered a business, then they might be classified as exchangers.

Whether and how the EFTA applies to virtual currency also is not clear. The EFTA defines an electronic funds transfer as "any transfer of funds ... which is initiated [electronically] so as to order, instruct, or authorize a financial institution to debit or credit an account." A financial institution, in turn, is a bank or other person who "holds an account belonging to a consumer."[133] Is a virtual wallet an "account at a financial institution"? If so, does a user's deposit or withdrawal directly to or from his own wallet involve an "order, instruction or authorization" to the provider of the virtual wallet service to do anything?

The SEC has issued a warning that virtual currency may come within the definition of a security if it has the characteristics of an investment contract (investment of money with a reasonable expectation of profit derived from the efforts of others, etc.).[134] As such, offerings may be subject to the same registration and disclosure requirements that publicly traded stocks are. As of the writing of this book, no offering of virtual currency has been registered with the SEC.

Virtual currency is not centrally controlled, so value can and does fluctuate dramatically. Combined with the uncertainty about whether the antifraud provisions of securities regulations apply and the uncertain future of government regulation in this area in general, accepting virtual currency as payment for e-commerce transactions is risky. This does not necessarily mean that an e-commerce business should not consider offering to accept virtual currency to its customers as an alternative method of payment for purchases. It is important to be aware of the risks, though.

Chapter 11. Delivery, Cancellation and Chargebacks

After a product or service is ordered, it must be delivered to the buyer in the manner and within the time frame specified in the contract. If a proper delivery is tendered, then the buyer has an obligation to accept it and pay the contract price. In some circumstances, however, a buyer may have a right to reject a delivery or cancel a purchase altogether.

The parties to a contract generally may structure it in whatever way they wish, but commercial sales are subject to rules for the protection of consumers including the requirement of the FTC Act that merchants may not engage in unfair or deceptive trade practices.

Contracts for the sale of goods are also regulated by state law. In the United States, the primary set of laws governing the rights of buyers and sellers of tangible products is the U.C.C. It has been adopted, with some changes, in every U.S. jurisdiction except Louisiana, American Samoa, Puerto Rico, and certain Indian tribes.

Article 2 deals with contracts for the sale of goods. *Goods* are things that are movable at the time of identification to the contract. Intangible property, such as stock, choses in action, copyrights and so on, are not goods. Services are not goods. Interests in real estate are not goods. Things that become movables when removed from real estate may be goods, though. Growing crops, timber, removable fixtures, oil, gas and other minerals are all goods to which the U.C.C. may apply even if they are affixed to land at the time a contract is formed. A contract for the sale of land along with the crops, timber, fixtures, etc. affixed to it is not subject to U.C.C. Article 2. A contract for the sale of crops, timber, fixtures, etc. that are to be severed and sold separately from the land may be subject to U.C.C. Article 2, though. A contract for the sale of goods that are attached to real estate at the time the contract is formed may be recorded like mortgages and other interests in real property are. This gives real estate buyers (and potential buyers) constructive notice of the rights of the buyer of the goods under the contract.

Delivery

The FTC's Mail, Internet, or Telephone Order Merchandise Trade Regulation Rule[135] ("Mail Order Rule") sets out a merchant's obligations with respect to the delivery of products ordered online, by mail or by telephone. The Rule applies to sales to consumers in which the consumer makes payment before merchandise is shipped. It also applies to sales to consumers in which the consumer applies for in-house credit before the merchandise is shipped, i.e., credit sales.

The Rule provides that if a merchant's advertising or posted contract terms state or imply that the product will be shipped within a specified time, the merchant must have a reasonable basis for stating or claiming that the merchant can ship the product within that time.

If a merchant makes no representation about the time for delivery, then the merchant must have a reasonable basis for believing that it can ship the product within thirty days. In other words, the Mail Order Rule sets a default time limit of thirty days for those situations in which the parties have not agreed otherwise. An additional twenty days is added to the default time period if the sale involves an in-house extension of credit to the buyer, such as a car loan. A credit card payment represents an extension of credit by the card issuer, not by the merchant. Accordingly, the default period for sales is thirty days if a customer pays by credit card.

Representations about delivery times are evaluated by the "reasonable consumer" standard. If a reasonable consumer would interpret a statement as a representation that delivery will be made within a specified time, then it is a representation of delivery time. The statement, "Most orders are shipped within 48 hours," is likely to be understood by consumers as a representation that orders will be shipped within 48 hours. Therefore, it is a representation that orders will be shipped in 48 hours.

A false or unsubstantiated representation in connection with the terms of a sale is an unfair or deceptive trade practice. In addition to injunctive relief, civil penalties of up to $41,484 per violation may be imposed. A seller is responsible to the customer and to the FTC for compliance even if a fulfillment or drop shipping service is used.

CALCULATING THE 30- OR 50-DAY PERIOD

The thirty-day period for delivery begins to run when a merchant receives a properly completed order. An order is "properly completed" when the merchant receives all of the information needed to fill the order, along with the agreed payment. Payment occurs when the merchant receives a check or other payment, or when the customer properly authorizes a credit or debit card charge. In cases where the merchant extends credit to the purchaser, the fifty-day period commences when the customer completes the application for credit. The date on which a check clears or when money is deposited to an account or becomes available for withdrawal is not relevant. If a check bounces or the customer is refused credit, however, then the thirty-day period is stayed. It does not begin to run again until the customer makes a payment that is honored or the merchant receives notice that the customer has been approved for credit.

DELAYED OR IMPOSSIBLE SHIPMENTS

Advertised delivery terms should not be different from the merchant's delivery terms at the time a consumer makes a purchase. If they are, then the merchant must be able to substantiate that he had a reasonable basis for updating the shipping terms.

If, after the customer places an order, the merchant learns that he cannot ship within the stated time (or the default period, if no time was specified), then he must either (a) cancel the order and promptly give the customer a full refund, or (b) promptly notify the customer and seek the customer's consent to a delayed shipment.

The notice must be given within the original stated time period for delivery, if any, or within the original default thirty- or fifty-day period, as applicable. If a merchant does not either ship the product or give notice within this time period, then he must cancel the order and give the customer a prompt refund.

If the merchant gives timely notice but the customer does not agree to a new delivery date, then the merchant must cancel the order and give the customer a prompt refund. If the customer consents to a new delivery time frame, then the merchant must have a reasonable basis for believing that it can ship the product within that time. A representation that the merchant does not know when a delayed shipment can be made also must be substantiated by evidence.

A notice of delay must include:

(a) either: (i) a definite revised shipment date or (ii) a statement that the merchant is unable to provide a revised shipment date, the reason for the delay, and a statement that if the customer agrees to an indefinite delay then the customer may cancel the order at any time until the merchant ships the product
(b) a statement that if the customer chooses not to wait, the customer may cancel the order and obtain a full and prompt refund
(c) a means for the customer to cancel at the merchant's expense (e.g., a link to the appropriate page on the company's website, a prepaid reply card, or a toll free telephone number).

In addition, if the notice provides a revised shipping date of thirty days or less, then it must inform the customer that failure to respond will be treated as consent to the delay. If the revised shipping date is more than thirty days or if the merchant does not specify a revised shipping date, then the notice must inform the customer that unless the customer responds within thirty days the order will be cancelled. A merchant may assume that a customer who does not object to an extension of less than thirty-one days agrees to it, but must obtain express consent to an extension of the delivery time by more than thirty days or for an indefinite period of time.

A customer's failure to respond may be treated as consent to a delay only once. A merchant must obtain the customer's express consent to any further delays. Subject to this qualification, notices of further delay must provide the same information and options as an original notice of delay. Of course, if a customer has agreed to an indefinite revised shipping date pursuant to a timely and proper delay notice, then no further notices of delay are necessary.

Delay notices may be sent via email.

REFUNDS

When a merchant or a customer cancels an order pursuant to these rules, the merchant must notify the customer and send a refund within the time a delay notice would be required. If the customer paid by cash, check, money order, debit or credit card, then the merchant must refund the amount within seven working days after the order is cancelled. If the merchant extended credit to the customer, then it must credit the customer's account or notify the customer that the account will not be charged within one billing cycle after the order is cancelled.

A full refund of the entire amount the customer tendered in payment must be refunded if the merchant is unable to ship any of the ordered merchandise. The merchant must pay any shipping, handling, insurance, or other costs. If some of the merchandise was shipped, then the merchant must refund the difference between the total amount paid and the amount the customer would have paid (including shipping and other charges), according to the merchant's ordering instructions, for the shipped items only.

Credit toward future purchases, credit vouchers, or scrip, may not be substituted for a refund when an order is canceled due to delay. If a customer paid with a coupon or other promotional device, the refund amount must reasonably compensate the customer for the value of the coupon or other device, plus any shipping or other charges the customer paid.

The refund obligations described in this section apply only when the refund is made pursuant to the Mail Order Rule. Refunds given for other reasons (nonconforming goods, breach of warranty of fitness for intended purpose, etc.) are not governed by the Mail Order Rule.

SUBSTITUTIONS

A merchant may not substitute materially different goods for ordered goods unless the buyer expressly consents. A material difference is one that is likely to affect the customer's choice or conduct regarding the merchandise. Any product feature that is expressly mentioned in advertising is material. Differences in design, style, color, fabric, or promoted use also are material.

RECORD-KEEPING

Because of the FTC's substantiation requirement, it is prudent to keep records of representations concerning delivery of merchandise, notices of delays, and dates and times of order fulfillment. Records that should be kept include:

- Substantiation for any representations about delivery
- How inventory is monitored
- How demand is anticipated
- How inventory acquisition is coordinated with demand and cancellations
- Communications with buyers, suppliers and shippers
- Delay notices
- Responses to delay notices
- Records of individual orders
- Scripts of any delay notices given by telephone, along with records of calls.

The records of orders should indicate: the date received; the dates delay notices, if any, were sent; the date of the customer's exercise of a cancellation option, if applicable; the dates of shipments and the merchandise shipped; and the dates of any refunds and the merchandise for which the refund was given;

The limitations period for FTC enforcement is five years. State limitations periods may be longer.

EXCEPTIONS

The Mail Order Rule does not apply to:

- Invoiced shipments
- C.O.D. orders
- Sales on approval
- Negative option sales
- Sales of services
- Sales of plants or growing seeds.

In the case of sales of subscriptions or other serial deliveries, the Mail Order Rule only applies to the first delivery.

The fact that these kinds of transactions are not covered by the Mail Order Rule does not mean that deliveries of them are unregulated. Undue delay in delivering these kinds of things may violate the FTC Act's general prohibition against unfair or deceptive trade practices, a state law, or the terms of a contract

RIGHTS UPON DELIVERY

A *sale* is the passing of title to goods from a seller to a buyer for a price. A contract for a sale is either a present sale or a promise to sell goods at a future time. Under the U.C.C., the time at which purchased goods are identified to the contract greatly impacts the passage of title, and therefore the parties' rights and obligations. *Identification to the contract* means designating the specific goods to be sold. It occurs when the parties say it does. If the parties have not specified in their agreement when identification occurs, then it occurs at the following times:

(a) when the contract is formed, if it is for the sale of goods already existing and identified
(b) when crops are planted, if it is for the sale of growing crops to be harvested within a year or the next normal harvesting season, whichever is longer
(c) at the time of conception, if the contract is for the sale of an animal's unborn young that is to be born within a year after the contract is formed
(d) when goods are shipped, marked, or otherwise designated by the seller as the goods to which the contract refers, if the contract is for the sale of future goods other than crops or unborn young of animals.

In the case of specially manufactured goods (products that are to be made after the contract is formed) and fungible goods (interchangeable goods, such as a shopper's order of "five apples" from a grocer with a large inventory of apples), identification does not occur until the seller ships or designates goods for shipping to the buyer, unless the contract provides otherwise.

Passage of Title

The point at which title to goods passes from a seller to a buyer is important for a number of reasons. Most importantly, a sale does not occur until title passes. In the absence of a sale, there are no implied warranties of merchantability or fitness for a particular purpose. Until title passes to the buyer, the seller's creditors may be able to seize the goods to satisfy debts the seller owes them, but the buyer's creditors cannot. Title can also affect how the risk of loss of the goods is allocated between a buyer and a seller, and whether a buyer has an insurable interest in the goods or not. Unless the parties agree otherwise, title to goods cannot pass to the buyer under a contract for sale before the goods have been identified to the contract.

Identification to the contract is a necessary but not a sufficient condition for the passage of title. Title does not pass to the buyer until the seller completes delivery, unless otherwise agreed.

If the contract calls for the seller to send the goods to the buyer, then title passes upon completion of delivery, even if a document of title is not delivered until later. The question then becomes: Delivery to whom—the shipper (e.g., the U.S. Postal Service, UPS, FedEx, etc.) or the buyer? The answer is: It depends on what the contract says. If it says that the seller's delivery obligation is completely satisfied by getting the goods to the shipper, then title passes to the buyer at the place of shipment. A contract of this kind may be indicated through the use of certain kinds of abbreviations. "F.O.B. [place of shipment]" stands for "free on board" at the designated place of shipment. "F.A.S. [named port]" stands for "free alongside ship" at the designated port. "C.I.F." stands for "cost, freight and insurance." When appended to the contract price, it means the contract price includes the cost of freight and insurance as well as the price of the goods. When any of these designations is used, the seller's delivery obligation is satisfied by delivering them to the shipper.

If, on the other hand, the contract states that the seller's delivery obligation is not satisfied until the goods reach the buyer, then title does not pass to the buyer until the goods are tendered to the buyer at the destination. "F.O.B. [destination]" denotes a contract of this kind. "Ex-ship" also denotes contracts of this kind. A "no arrival, no sale" term in a contract means that the seller must ship conforming goods and tender them on arrival but is under no obligation to ensure that the goods will arrive unless he has caused the nonarrival. If the goods do not arrive, or if they arrive in a damaged state, through no fault of the seller, then the buyer may either treat the contract as avoided or, in the case of damaged goods, pay a reduced amount for the damaged goods, with no further recourse against the seller.

If the contract authorizes the seller to ship the goods to the buyer but does not obligate him to ensure that they arrive at their destination, then title passes to the buyer at the time and place of shipment. If the contract requires delivery at destination, then title passes upon tender of the goods to the buyer at the specified destination. If the contract calls for the buyer to pick up the goods without the seller moving them (such as by shipping them) to or for the buyer, then title passes when the seller delivers a document of title, if the contract calls for one; otherwise, title passes to the buyer at the time the contract is formed.

The parties may alter these rules by agreement. A contract may provide that title passes to the buyer at a time other than delivery, for example. A provision in a sales contract stating that the seller retains title even after delivery, however, will not be given full effect. Instead, it will be construed as retention of a security interest by the seller. A merchant who is interested in retaining title after delivery should lease the goods rather than sell them.

If the contract is silent about when title passes and does not contain terms like F.O.B., etc. then title passes to the buyer at the time and place at which seller completes his performance with reference to the physical delivery of the goods. If the contract is silent about delivery or about the place of delivery, then the place for delivery will be deemed to be the seller's place of business; if there is none, then his residence. In that case, delivery is completed when the seller holds conforming goods for the buyer and gives the buyer any notification reasonably necessary to enable the buyer to take delivery.

A buyer's refusal, rejection or return of goods, whether justified or not, has the effect of re-vesting title in the seller. Title also revests in the seller if the buyer accepts the goods but then justifiably revokes acceptance.

If a seller's title is void, then a buyer does not acquire title. There is no title to pass. A voidable title, by contrast, can pass to a buyer. Title may be voidable where, for example, a person procures ownership by fraud. A defrauded person has a right to rescind the sale, but until he does, the title remains with the defrauder. If the defrauder sells the item to another person before the original fraudulent sale is rescinded, then title passes to the subsequent purchaser, provided the subsequent purchaser neither knows nor has reason to know about the defect in the title at the time of acquiring it.

A purchaser of goods can only acquire whatever title the seller had, unless the purchase is of only a partial interest in the goods, in which case the purchaser acquires only the partial interest. A seller who has voidable title (such as where the seller procured the goods by fraud) has the power to transfer title to a good faith purchaser for value, even if she does not have the right to do so. A good faith purchaser for value (also known as a "bona fide purchaser for value" (BFPV)) is a person who buys without knowledge or constructive notice of the defect or potential defect in the title. A person who entrusts possession of goods to a merchant who deals in goods of that kind gives the merchant power to transfer all of the person's rights to a BFPV, even if the merchant's procurement or sale of the goods violates a contract, and even if it constitutes theft on the part of the merchant. The merchant might be prosecuted for his conduct, but title still passes to the BFPV. Or course, even though a defrauded seller cannot recover the property from the BFPV, he may have recourse against the merchant for the fraud, such as money damages or a constructive trust on property the merchant has acquired with the proceeds of the sale to the BFPV.

Sales on Approval (Free Trials Offers)

Sometimes a merchant will persuade a potential customer to authorize the merchant to send a product on a "free trial" basis or some other kind of arrangement under which the buyer is free to return the product with no obligation to pay for it. The most common such arrangements are consignments, sales on approval, and sale-or-return contracts.

If goods are delivered primarily for the customer's use and the customer is allowed to return them without paying for them even if the goods conform to the contract, the arrangement is called a *sale on approval*. If goods are delivered on these terms but are delivered primarily for resale by the customer, then the arrangement is called a *sale-or-return contract*.

In a sale on approval, title to goods and the risk of loss do not pass the buyer unless and until the buyer signifies approval and acceptance of the goods. A buyer's use of the goods in a way that is consistent with the purpose of the trial does not constitute an implied acceptance. To retain the right to return the goods, however, the buyer must seasonably notify the seller of his election to return them. Retaining the goods without seasonably notifying the seller of the decision to return them constitutes acceptance of the goods. If the goods conform to the contract, then acceptance of any part is acceptance of the whole. A buyer who rightfully chooses to return goods under a sale on approval generally is not responsible for the costs of shipping them back to the seller. The return is at the seller's risk and expense, except that a merchant buyer must follow any reasonable instructions from the seller. Any of the rights and obligations described in this paragraph may be altered by agreement, however.

A sale of goods to a business that deals in goods of the same kind is deemed to be a "sale or return" transaction. These goods are subject to the claims of the buyer's creditors while they are in the buyer's possession. This is true even if the contract reserves title to the person making delivery until the buyer either resells them or pays for them, and regardless of whether the contract describes it as "on consignment." The goods are not subject to the claims of a buyer's creditors, however, if any of the following conditions apply:

(a) the business to which the goods are delivered is generally known by its creditors to be engaged in the business of selling the goods of others

(b) the seller complies with security interest filing requirements
(c) the seller complies with an applicable law, if any, that provides for a consignor's interest to be evidenced by a sign.

Under a "sale or return" contract, the return is at the buyer's expense and risk. The buyer may return the whole lot or any commercial unit of the goods. The buyer's right to return goods is conditioned, however, on the goods still being in substantially their original condition. Also, the buyer must exercise the right to return seasonably. These rights and obligations may be altered by agreement.

Buyer's Right to Inspect Goods

If the contract does not require payment prior to inspection, and does not otherwise provide, the buyer has a right, before payment or acceptance, to inspect the goods. The inspection may be at any reasonable place, in any reasonable manner, and at any reasonable time after the goods have been identified to the contract or tendered or delivered to the buyer. The inspection may occur after the seller has shipped them to the buyer. Inspection is at the buyer's expense, but may be recovered from the seller if the goods are nonconforming and the buyer rejects them. Unless otherwise agreed, the inspection right does not postpone identification of goods to the contract or change the place for delivery for purposes of passing the risk of loss. If compliance with inspection requirements becomes impossible, inspection need only be at a reasonable place and in a reasonable manner, unless the place or method fixed in the contract is clearly intended to be an indispensable condition the failure of which avoids the contract.

If the contract requires payment before the buyer has an opportunity to inspect the goods, a nonconforming delivery does not excuse the buyer from paying for the goods unless the nonconformity is obvious without inspection. Such a payment does not constitute an acceptance of the goods, however, nor does it impair the buyer's right to inspect, to sue for breach of contract, or to pursue any other remedies he may have.

Unless otherwise agreed, a buyer generally does not have a right to inspect goods prior to payment if the contract provides for delivery "C.O.D." or if the contract provides for payment against documents of title (except where such payment is due only after the goods are to become available for inspection).

If a dispute about the conformity of the goods to the contract arises, each party has a right to inspect, test and sample the goods while they are in the other party's possession, to preserve evidence. Reasonable notification must be given. If desired, the parties may agree to the use of a third party to inspect the goods to determine whether they conform to the contract.

If a buyer has examined the goods or a sample of them, or has been given an opportunity to examine them but has refused to do so, then there is no implied warranty with regard to any defects which an examination would have revealed.

Cancellations and Returns

Cancellations of orders and returns of purchased items are a major problem for e-commerce businesses. Over three times as many products bought online are returned as compared to products purchased at brick-and-mortar stores, and only a small fraction of returns of online products are due to the customer's receipt of a damaged or defective product. Part of the explanation for this is that the convenience of online shopping facilitates impulse buying. In addition, online shoppers do not have an opportunity to inspect or "test drive" products that are offered for sale in an online environment the way they can when purchasing merchandise at a brick-and-mortar store. Consequently, some consumers use product return policies to give themselves an opportunity to inspect and try out a product. Companies that offer free shipping on returns are particularly vulnerable to this kind of abuse.

Cancellations and returns create a real dilemma for a business. If they are permitted, then the merchant will not only lose money on sales but will also incur costs like shipping and chargeback fees in addition to the cost of the merchandise itself. In the case of returned merchandise, there may be repackaging costs and losses and expenses in connection with products damaged or destroyed by the purchaser or during transit. A merchant might attempt to recoup costs by raising prices, but higher prices may result in fewer sales. To avoid these problems, a merchant might think about refraining from allowing returns, instead offering all products and services on an "as is" basis. Unfortunately, "as is" notices are not always effective. Worse, they may be too effective, driving away potentially legitimate customers along with the abusive ones. Whether warranted or not, an "as is" notice might give potential buyers the impression that the company does not stand behind its products. Of course, that naturally raises doubts about quality. Since most online businesses do allow returns, and since studies show that an overwhelming majority of online shoppers check a company's returns policy before buying, allowing returns may be necessary in order to remain competitive.

There is no one-size-fits-all solution to this dilemma. A business will need to make its own individual decision about whether and what kind of cancellations/returns policy to adopt.

BUYER'S RIGHT TO REJECT GOODS

Unless the parties have agreed otherwise, if a seller ships goods that are different from what the buyer ordered, or if the time, place or manner of delivery is different from what was agreed, the seller is said to have made a nonconforming delivery. When a seller makes a nonconforming delivery, the buyer has three options:

(a) reject the goods
(b) accept the goods
(c) accept some of the goods and reject the rest.

This rule is known as the *perfect tender rule* because it means the seller must make a delivery of goods that does not differ in any way from what the seller promised.

If a buyer opts to reject goods, then she must notify the seller within a reasonable time. A rejection is not effective unless it is timely communicated to the seller. Also, the buyer must let the seller know of any curable defects in the goods that a reasonable inspection would turn up. If she fails to do so, then she cannot rely on the defect as a justification for rejecting the goods or to establish breach.

If the time for performance has not yet expired, the seller may seasonably notify the buyer of an intention to cure a defective delivery. If he does, then he may make a conforming delivery within the contract time. If the buyer refuses this delivery but the seller has reasonable grounds to believe the delivery would be acceptable, he may seasonably notify the buyer, and he will then have a further reasonable time to substitute a conforming tender.

A merchant buyer's failure to let a merchant seller know of a defect that a reasonable inspection would turn up precludes the merchant buyer from relying on the defect to justify rejection or to establish breach where the seller could have cured the defect if the buyer had timely informed him of it, or where the seller has made a written request for a full and final written statement of all defects from the buyer. (This rule applies to purchases of goods by one merchant from another merchant. Different rules apply to purchases of goods by consumers.)

A buyer who pays for goods without a reservation of rights, despite the fact that defects are apparent on the face of the document, is not entitled to a refund.

Since title to goods revests in the seller when a buyer rejects them, the buyer has no rights of ownership with respect to rejected goods. The buyer may be liable to the seller if he damages them or exercises ownership rights over them at that point. It is the seller's responsibility to retrieve the goods, not the buyer's responsibility to return them. While the goods are in the buyer's possession, however, he must hold them with reasonable care for a sufficient amount of time to permit the seller to retrieve them.

The risk of loss due to causes other than the buyer's negligent or intentional damage to the goods remains with the seller until either cure or acceptance.

If the buyer is also a merchant with respect to the goods, such as a retailer who buys goods for resale, and the seller has an agent or place of business at the buyer's location, then the buyer may return the rejected goods there. Otherwise, a merchant buyer must follow any reasonable instructions from the seller with respect to the goods. If the buyer requests it, the seller must indemnify the buyer for the expenses of complying with the seller's instructions. If the seller refuses to indemnify the buyer, then the seller's instructions are deemed unreasonable.

Whether the buyer is a merchant or not, if the seller does not provide instructions, or if the seller provides unreasonable instructions, then the buyer has three options: (1) store the rejected goods for the seller's account; (2) reship them back to the seller; or (3) resell them for the seller's account with reimbursement. If the goods are perishable or threaten to decline in value speedily, then the merchant buyer (unlike a nonmerchant buyer) has only one option: he must make reasonable efforts to sell them for the seller's account.

When a buyer rightfully rejects or revokes acceptance of goods, the buyer has a security interest in goods in his possession or control for any payments he has made on their price and any expenses reasonably incurred for their inspection, receipt, transportation, care and custody. The buyer may hold such goods and resell them in satisfaction of this security interest. A buyer who rightfully resells rejected goods is entitled to reimbursement from the seller out of the proceeds of the sale for the buyer's reasonable expenses of caring for and selling the goods. The buyer is also entitled to retain a commission on the sale. The amount of the commission is determined by whatever is usual in the trade. If this amount cannot be determined, then the buyer is entitled to a reasonable commission not exceeding 10% of the gross proceeds. The buyer must account to the seller for any excess over the amount of his security interest.

A buyer who, in good faith, exercises the rights outlined above is not liable to the seller for conversion or damage to the goods.

In the case of an installment purchase contract—i.e., one that authorizes the delivery of goods in separate lots to be separately accepted—the buyer may reject any installment that is nonconforming if the nonconformity substantially impairs the value of the installment and cannot be cured or if the nonconformity is a defect in the required documents. If the nonconformity substantially impairs the value of the entire contract, then the seller is in breach of the entire contract, and it is terminated. The seller does not have a right to cure or to require the buyer to accept its assurance that it will cure the defect in this case. The buyer reinstates the contract, however, if he: (a) accepts a nonconforming installment without timely notifying the seller of cancellation; (b) brings an action with respect only to past installments; or (c) demands performance as to future installments. If an installment is nonconforming but does not substantially impair the value of the entire contract, and the seller gives adequate assurance that it will cure the nonconformity, then the buyer must accept that installment.

Several states have enacted laws that modify the U.C.C. rules somewhat. For example, some states require a merchant to accept a return and issue a refund unless the merchant has established a cancellations and returns policy and discloses it to the customer prior to purchase. Under these laws, it does not matter if there is any defect in the merchandise or the delivery. The statute usually requires the customer to return the merchandise within a specified time period (e.g., thirty days) in order to be entitled to a refund.

ACCEPTANCE OF GOODS

Acceptance occurs when a buyer does any of the following things;

(a) signifies to the seller that the goods are conforming, after a reasonable opportunity to inspect them
(b) signifies to the seller that he will take or retain them despite their nonconformity, after a reasonable opportunity to inspect them
(c) fails to make an effective rejection, after a reasonable opportunity to inspect them
(d) performs any act that is inconsistent with the seller's ownership.

A buyer's performance of an act that is inconsistent with the seller' ownership and injurious to the seller's rights is an acceptance only if the seller ratifies it.

Acceptance of a part of any commercial unit is acceptance of the entire unit.

A buyer's acceptance of goods shipped in response to an order has the following consequences:

(a) The buyer must pay for the goods at the contract rate.
(b) The buyer may not change her mind and reject the goods.
(c) The buyer may not revoke the acceptance if she accepted the goods with knowledge of a nonconformity and it would have been unreasonable for her to assume that the seller would cure the nonconformity.
(d) The buyer may revoke the acceptance if she accepted the goods with knowledge of a nonconformity and she reasonably assumed the seller could cure the nonconformity but the seller does not do so.
(e) It does not, by itself, bar the buyer from suing for breach of contract on account of the nonconformity of the goods. The buyer will, however, be barred from any remedy unless she notifies the seller of the breach within a reasonable time after she discovers or should have discovered a breach.

REVOCATION OF ACCEPTANCE

A buyer may revoke acceptance of goods on the basis of a nonconformity that substantially impairs the value of a commercial unit or a lot if (a) the seller has failed to cure the nonconformity, and it was reasonable for the buyer to assume that he would; or (b) the buyer did not discover the nonconformity prior to accepting the goods, and either the seller's assurances induced the buyer to accept the goods or the nonconformity was difficult to discover.

The revocation must occur within a reasonable time after the buyer discovers or should have discovered grounds for it and before any substantial change in the condition of the goods that is not caused by their own defects. It is not effective until the buyer notifies the seller of it.

A buyer who properly revokes acceptance has the same rights and obligations with respect to the goods as she would have if she had rejected them from the outset.

SELLER'S PARTICIPATION IN THIRD PARTY LITIGATION AGAINST BUYER

If the buyer is sued for breach of a warranty (e.g., the warranty of title) or other obligation for which the seller is answerable, the buyer may give the seller notice of the litigation. If the notice is in writing and states that the seller may come in and defend and that if the seller does not do so he will be bound in any action the buyer brings against him by any determination of fact common to the two litigations, then it is binding on the seller.

If a seller breaches the contract by delivering goods that infringe a third party's rights (such as goods that are packaged in a way that infringes a third party's trademark), then the buyer must notify the seller of the litigation within a reasonable time after receiving notice of it or the buyer will be barred from suing the seller on account of any liability established by the litigation. The seller may demand that the buyer turn over control of the litigation, including settlement, to the seller or else be barred from any remedy against the seller. If the demand is in writing, and if the seller agrees to bear all expenses and to satisfy any adverse judgment, then the buyer will be barred from any remedy against the seller if he refuses to comply with the demand.

UNORDERED PRODUCTS OR SERVICES

Because an offer and an acceptance are essential to the formation of a contract, a person who receives unordered merchandise is under no contractual obligation to pay for it. A merchant who sends a person an unrequested product is making a gift.

Sending a person merchandise that the person has not expressly requested is an unfair trade practice in violation of the FTC Act unless the merchandise is clearly identified as a gift, free sample, or the like. It is also an unfair trade practice to try to obtain payment for or the return of the unordered merchandise. This applies to billing for access to a web page that is advertised as "free," too. Billing a website user's credit or debit card or other financial account for accessing a website that is advertised as "free" (or for a "free tour" of the site) is an unfair and deceptive trade practice under the FTC Act. If the U.S. mail is used to ship unordered merchandise, then the sender is also in violation of postal laws. The FTC has taken the position that people who receive unordered merchandise are legally entitled to treat the merchandise as a gift.

NEGATIVE OPTION MARKETING

Negative option marketing is a kind of sales technique in which an offer or agreement to sell or provide product(s) or service(s) contains a provision specifying that the customer's silence or failure to take an affirmative action to reject goods or services or to cancel the agreement constitutes acceptance of the offer. There are four kinds: prenotification, continuity, automatic renewal, and conversion offers.

In a prenotification negative option plan, the seller sends periodic notices offering goods. According to the terms of the plan, if the consumer takes no action then the seller will ship the goods and charge the consumer for them. Book and music clubs often employ this tactic. In a continuity plan, the consumer agrees in advance to receive periodic shipments of goods or provision of services, which they continue to receive and for which they are obligated to pay until they cancel the agreement. An automatic renewal contract is one in which a consumer's contract for a product or service (such as a subscription to a service for a specified period of time) is automatically renewed when it expires and the consumer's credit, debit or other account is charged for it unless the consumer cancels the contract. A conversion offer is one in which the seller ships a product or provides a service to the consumer for a free (or for a nominal fee) trial period, during which the consumer must cancel and/or return the goods or services or else be obligated to pay for the product or service.

ROSCA makes it unlawful to charge or to try to charge a consumer for goods or services sold online by means of a negative option transaction unless all three of the following conditions are satisfied:

(a) the seller clearly and conspicuously discloses all of the material terms of the transaction before collecting billing information from the consumer

(b) the consumer expressly gives informed consent before his credit or debit card, bank account or other financial account is charged for products or services

(c) the seller provides an easy way for a consumer to stop recurring charges from being made to his credit or debit card, bank account or other financial account.

To this, some courts have added that the offer must be understandable by an ordinary consumer.

This law is enforceable by the FTC and by state attorneys general.

Prenotification plans also must comply with the FTC's Prenotification Negative Option Plan Rule.[136] Under this rule, a prenotification negative option plan is an unfair and deceptive trade practice unless it meets both of the following requirements:

(a) Promotional material must clearly and conspicuously disclose the material terms of the plan.

(b) Prior to sending any selection, the seller must send subscribers an announcement identifying the selection and a form clearly and conspicuously (i) disclosing that the subscriber will receive the selection identified in the announcement unless he instructs the seller that he does not want it, (ii) designating a procedure by which the form may be used for the purpose of enabling the subscriber so to instruct the seller, and (iii) specifying either the return date or the mailing date.

The seller must mail the announcement and form either at least twenty days prior to the return date or at least fifteen days prior to the mailing date, or provide a mailing date at least ten days after receipt by the subscriber. Whichever method the seller chooses, it must provide the subscriber with at least ten days in which to mail the form.

Material terms that must be disclosed in promotional material include:

(a) that aspect of the plan under which the subscriber must notify the seller, in the manner provided for by the seller, if he does not wish to purchase the selection
(b) any obligation assumed by the subscriber to purchase a minimum quantity of merchandise
(c) the right of a contract-complete subscriber to cancel his membership at any time
(d) whether billing charges will include an amount for postage and handling
(e) a disclosure indicating that the subscriber will be provided with at least ten days in which to mail any form, contained in or accompanying an announcement identifying the selection, to the seller
(f) a disclosure that the seller will credit the return of any selections sent to a subscriber, and guarantee to the Postal Service or the subscriber postage to return such selections to the seller when the announcement and form are not received by the subscriber in time to afford him at least ten days in which to mail his form to the seller
(g) the frequency with which the announcements and forms will be sent to the subscriber and the maximum number of announcements and forms which will be sent to him during a twelve-month period.

It is also an unfair or deceptive practice for a seller, in connection with the use of any negative option plan, to refuse to credit, for the full invoiced amount, the return of any selection sent to a subscriber, and to guarantee to the Postal Service or the subscriber postage adequate to return the selection to the seller, under any of the following circumstances:

(a) The selection is sent to a subscriber whose form indicating that he does not want to receive the selection was received by the seller by the return date or was mailed by the subscriber by the mailing date.
(b) The form is received by the seller after the return date, but was mailed by the subscriber and postmarked at least three days prior to the return date.
(c) Prior to the date of shipment of such selection, the seller received from a contract-complete subscriber a written notice of cancellation of membership adequately identifying the subscriber. This provision, however, is applicable only to the first selection sent to a canceling contract-complete subscriber after the seller has received written notice of cancellation. After the first selection shipment, all selection shipments thereafter are deemed to be unordered merchandise.
(d) The announcement and form are not received by the subscriber in time to afford him at least ten days in which to mail his form.

The following things are also prohibited unfair or deceptive trade practices:

(a) Failing to notify a subscriber known by the seller to be within any of the circumstances described in paragraphs (a), (b), (c) or (d), above, that if the subscriber elects, the subscriber may return the selection with return postage guaranteed and receive a credit to his account.

(b) Refusing to ship within four weeks after receipt of an order merchandise due subscribers as introductory and bonus merchandise, unless the seller is unable to deliver the merchandise originally offered due to unanticipated circumstances beyond the seller's control and promptly makes a reasonably equivalent alternative offer If, however, the subscriber refuses to accept alternatively offered introductory merchandise, but instead insists upon termination of his membership due to the seller's failure to provide him with his originally requested introductory merchandise, or any portion thereof, the seller must comply with the subscriber's request for cancellation of membership, provided the subscriber returns to the seller any introductory merchandise which already may have been sent.

(c) Failing to terminate promptly the membership of a properly identified contract-complete subscriber upon his written request.

(d) Shipping, without the express consent of the subscriber, substituted merchandise for that ordered by the subscriber.

A contract-complete subscriber is one who has purchased the minimum quantity of merchandise required by the terms of membership in a negative option plan. The return date is the date specified by a seller using a negative option plan as the date by which a form must be received by the seller to prevent shipment of the selection. The mailing date is the time specified by a seller using a negative option plan as the time by or within which a form must be mailed by a subscriber to prevent shipment of the selection.

AUTOMATIC RENEWAL CONTRACTS

A growing number of states are enacting laws to regulate automatic renewal contracts. Most of these laws take the form of a notice requirement, such as a requirement that the merchant give the subscriber clear and conspicuous notice at the time of the contract that the customer's credit or debit card will be automatically billed at specified intervals, or a requirement that the merchant send periodic notices of the right to opt out.

The California statute is one of the tougher ones. It requires a business that makes an automatic renewal or continuous service offer to a consumer to:

(a) Present the terms of the offer in a clear and conspicuous manner before the subscription or purchasing agreement is fulfilled and in visual proximity, or in the case of an offer conveyed by voice, in temporal proximity, to the request for consent to the offer.

(b) Obtain the consumer's affirmative consent to the agreement containing the offer terms before charging the consumer's credit or debit card, or the consumer's account with a third party.

(c) Provide an acknowledgment that includes the offer terms, cancellation policy, and information regarding how to cancel in a manner that is capable of being retained by the consumer. If the offer includes a free trial, the business must also disclose in the acknowledgment how to cancel, and allow the consumer to cancel, before the consumer pays for the goods or services.

(d) Provide a toll free telephone number, email address or a postal address, if the seller directly bills the consumer, or another cost effective, timely, and easy to use mechanism for cancellation that is described in the acknowledgement.

(e) Provide the consumer with a clear and conspicuous notice of change and provide information regarding how to cancel in a manner that is capable of being retained by the consumer, whenever there is a material change in the terms of the offer. The notice describing changes must be given prior to the implementation of the change.

An automatic renewal offer must include a clear and conspicuous disclosure of the following things:

(a) that the subscription or purchasing agreement will continue until the consumer cancels
(b) a description of the cancellation policy that applies to the offer
(c) the recurring charges that will be charged to the consumer's credit or debit card or payment account with a third party as part of the automatic renewal plan or arrangement, and that the amount of the charge may change, if that is the case, and the amount to which the charge will change, if known
(d) the length of the automatic renewal term or that the service is continuous, unless the length of the term is chosen by the consumer
(e) the minimum purchase obligation, if any.

To be "clear and conspicuous" the disclosure must appear in larger type than the surrounding text, or in contrasting type, font, or color to the surrounding text of the same size, or set off from the surrounding text of the same size by symbols or other marks, in a manner that clearly calls attention to the language. For an audio disclosure, "clear and conspicuous" means in a volume and cadence sufficient to be readily audible and understandable.

A number of exemptions are provided for banks and other particular industries.

Violations are not crimes, but civil penalties may be imposed. In addition, the statute provides that products sent by a merchant who has not first obtained the affirmative consent of the recipient are deemed unconditional gifts to the consumer.

To comply with federal and state legal requirements, a website owner might:

(a) Display the offer terms (not a link to them) next to the offer and above an 'I Agree' button.
(b) Display the terms in a type size at least as large as that of the surrounding text.
(c) Display the terms in a font and/or color different from the surrounding text.
(d) Require the user to acknowledge understanding and consent to the terms by clicking the 'I Agree' button before the website can collect any personal or billing information.
(e) Require a second confirmation of agreement to the offer.
(f) Send an email message to the customer when the customer clicks on the 'I Agree' button. The email message should repeat the terms and the fact of the customer's acknowledgement of consent to the terms, describe the cancellation policy, inform the customer how to cancel the agreement, and advise the customer to retain the email for future reference.
(g) Make the cancellation method easy to use.
(h) If changes to the terms are planned, then send customers an email notifying them that changes will be made, the anticipated date they will go into effect, an explanation of what

they are, and how recipients can cancel their subscriptions. The heading of the email should clearly state this it is a notification of changes to the terms.

CANCELLATIONS AND RETURNS POLICY

Many of the rights and obligations of buyers and sellers with respect to a buyer's rejection and/or return of goods may be altered by agreement. Accordingly, it can be a good idea for a commercial website to prepare and publish a Cancellations and Returns Policy.

The FTC Act requires a merchant to disclose any conditions and limitations on cancellations, returns and refunds prior to a purchase. A number of states require e-commerce businesses to disclose their return and refund policy to customers who purchase from them. Not all require that the disclosure be published to the website. Some allow it to be furnished in an email or other written communication to the customer, provided the disclosure occurs before the customer pays for the merchandise. Others require the policy to be prominently displayed at the place of purchase (e.g., a website). California gives merchants three options: (a) display a cancellations and returns policy at the place of purchase; (b) give a full cash refund, store credit or exchange within seven days after the purchase; or (c) allow returns for up to thirty days and give purchasers full cash refunds. Minnesota requires a seller to give a cash refund to a consumer if the goods are acceptable for return unless the seller clearly and conspicuously displays a different cash refund policy, in boldface 14–point type, at the point of purchase.

A merchant who accepts credit card payments may be obligated, by the terms of his merchant account, to disclose cancellation, merchandise and refund policies to the cardholder at or before the time of purchase. Credit card networks impose varying kinds of disclosure requirements depending on whether the transaction is conducted online, in person, or by phone. They may allow a merchant to mail, email or text their return and refund policies to the cardholder when an order is taken by phone. In most cases, the merchant must be able to prove that it provided the disclosure. For this reason, a merchant may find it prudent to obtain documentation of the customer's receipt of the disclosures prior to the purchase. If disclosure is made on the website, the website could be set up in such a way that a customer must take some affirmative step to signify reading, understanding and assenting to it.

For online orders, the Visa agreement requires the merchant's website to communicate its returns/refunds policy to the cardholder either (a) in the sequence of pages before final check-out, with a 'Click to Accept' or other acknowledgement button, checkbox, or location for an electronic signature; or (b) on the checkout screen, near the 'Submit' or 'Click to Accept' button.

Displaying a link to the disclosures may not be enough. Card agreements may specify that a customer must be required to click an 'I Accept' button (or equivalent) for the returns/refunds policy before being permitted to complete a transaction.

A business that does not honor the representations it makes about its return and refund policies risks liability for breach of contract as well as liability for engaging in an unfair or deceptive trade practice in violation of the FTC Act. In the case of transactions for which it receives a credit card payment, the merchant also risks loss of its merchant account and of the right to accept credit cards through that card network.

A cancellations and returns policy should address whether the merchant may charge a restocking fee for returned merchandise to cover the cost of replacing the packaging so the merchandise can be sold again. Some states, such as New York, require a merchant with this term in its cancellations and return policy to notify the purchaser of the restocking fee on returned merchandise prior to the purchase.

Some states have enacted laws requiring certain kinds of sales to be rescindable by the consumer on a "no questions asked" basis regardless of what the merchant's cancellation policy says. Gym memberships and subscription contracts are common targets of this kind of legislation. Other states have not enacted laws of this kind.

A business should never publish statements like "Satisfaction Guaranteed," "Money back guarantee," "Risk-Free Trial Offer," or the like, unless it is prepared to honor them. A cancellations and returns policy that contradicts or qualifies a representation of this kind could constitute a deceptive trade practice, triggering an FTC enforcement action.

NOTIFICATION OF CANCELLED TRANSACTIONS

Regardless of what a merchant's returns policy says, federal law requires a merchant who has accepted a credit card as payment for goods or services to promptly send the card issuer a credit statement if the customer returns the goods or if the merchant forgives a debt for the services that the customer purchased using the card. 15 U.S.C. § 1666e.

EUROPEAN UNION

The Distance Selling Directive requires EU countries to enact laws giving consumers who reside in a EU country a right to cancel distance contracts under certain conditions. A distance contract is a contract that is formed through remote communications rather than face-to-face. Purchases from websites and sales contracts negotiated via email are distance contracts. The Directive does not apply to software licensing.

A merchant must allow a person who resides in an EU country at least seven working days to cancel a distance contract. This is to give the buyer a cooling-off period and an opportunity to inspect the merchandise. A consumer also has a right to cancel the contract if the merchant does not deliver an ordered product within thirty days. If a consumer timely and properly cancels a purchase, the merchant must refund the consumer's payment within thirty days. The merchant may require the customer to pay the postage costs of returning merchandise, but may not assess any other kind of charge against a consumer for timely canceling a purchase.

A merchant who sells to a consumer who resides in an EU country must provide a confirmation disclosure prior to delivery. It must apprise the consumer of the period of time the consumer is allowed to cancel the contract. It must also disclose that the consumer has a right to a refund payable within thirty days. In some jurisdictions, e-commerce businesses must disclose their returns and refunds policy on their websites, too.

These requirements apply to any merchant who sells to a consumer who is domiciled in a EU country, whether the merchant is located in a EU country, the United States, or elsewhere. A merchant may not require a consumer who is domiciled in a EU country to waive these rights.

Chargebacks

The rights and obligations of merchants and buyers are determined by their contracts, as supplemented and modified by the U.C.C. and other laws. A merchant who accepts credit card payments from customers must also comply with credit card network requirements. These are set out in a contract to which a merchant must assent in order to accept payments from customers using the card. They typically include a requirement that the merchant adopt a cancellations and returns policy. Because card networks benefit when customers use their cards to pay, they tend to require merchants to assent to transaction processing procedures that are more favorable to consumers than to merchants. Chargebacks are an example.

A *chargeback* is a reversal of a credit card payment. It originates from the issuer of the card, usually as a result of a cardholder's dispute of a charge appearing on the cardholder's statement. The most common reasons for customer disputes of charges are that ordered merchandise was not received, an ordered service was not performed, or a customer claims that a credit was not applied to her account when it should have been. In some cases, a chargeback may occur because a charge on a cardholder's statement is claimed to be fraudulent or unauthorized.

Chargebacks are popular with some customers who use credit cards to make online purchases because evidence is not usually required in order to cancel a payment. The merchant has the burden of proving that the merchandise or service was properly delivered or provided according to the contract terms. If the merchant is able to prove that, then the disputed payment is made effective. If not, then the charge is removed from the customer's credit card account; the merchant does not get paid for the sale; and the merchant may be required to pay a chargeback fee. In addition, the merchant may be out the cost of the merchandise, inasmuch as merchandise will not necessarily be recovered when a chargeback is allowed.

The chargeback rights of credit card holders vary from those of debit card holders, and they also vary under the laws of different jurisdictions. Some countries require credit card companies to give cardholders chargeback rights. Even in the absence of a statutory enactment, however, most credit card companies have undertaken contractual obligations with their cardholders to offer at least some kind of chargeback right.

PayPal and other online payment systems often have chargeback policies and procedures in place, too. For example, if a buyer makes a complaint that conforming goods were not delivered, PayPal will hold a payment until the dispute is settled. The buyer must lodge the complaint within a specified period of time or PayPal will release the hold on the payment. If the buyer does not lodge the complaint before the seller has taken the money from the buyer's account, then the buyer is out of luck insofar as PayPal is concerned. PayPal cannot place a hold on a payment after it has been taken from the buyer's account.

The typical credit card chargeback process is as follows:

(1) A cardholder contacts the issuer to dispute a charge.

(2) The issuer investigates to determine if the charge is valid. It may request a copy of the sale transaction receipt from the acquirer.

(3) If the issuer believes the charge is valid, it declines the cardholder's dispute. If the issuer believes the charge is not valid, it sends the transaction to the acquirer and charges back the amount of the disputed sale.

(4) The acquirer researches the transaction.

(5) If the acquirer can support the validity of the disputed transaction, the acquirer may resolve the dispute by providing supporting documentation to the issuer. If the acquirer

determines the chargeback is valid, it deducts the amount of the chargeback from the merchant's account and notifies the merchant.

(6) The merchant either accepts the chargeback or fixes the problem (if possible) and resubmits the transaction to the acquirer.

(7) If the acquirer believes the transaction, as resubmitted, is valid, then the acquirer re-presents it to the issuer for payment.

(8) If the issuer accepts the representment, it reposts the transaction to the cardholder's account. If the issuer does not believe the charge is valid, it submits the matter to the credit card network for arbitration.

(9) The credit card network arbitrates the matter and makes a decision whether the chargeback will be allowed or not. In most cases, the arbitrator's decision is final.

Each step has defined time limits with which the acquirer and the merchant must comply.

RECEIPT REQUESTS

When a cardholder disputes a charge, one of the first things an issuer is likely to do is electronically send a request for a copy of the receipt for the disputed transaction ("retrieval request") to the acquirer. If the merchant's acquirer stores the merchant's transaction receipts, then the acquirer will fulfill the copy request. If the merchant stores its own receipts, then the acquirer will forward the request to the merchant. The merchant must then send a copy of the receipt to the acquirer, who sends it on to the issuer.

An acquirer has a specified period of time (e.g., thirty days) to send a copy of the transaction receipt to the issuer. If the acquirer forwards the request to the merchant, the acquirer should inform the merchant how long he has to respond. The merchant must send a copy of the requested receipt to the acquirer within the specified time. The acquirer then sends it to the issuer. The issuer will send it to the cardholder. The concern the cardholder had with the transaction is usually resolved at this point.

When sending a copy of a receipt to the acquirer, a merchant should use a delivery method that provides proof of delivery. If sending by regular mail, use registered or certified mail. If sending it electronically, keep a record of the transmittal.

EXCESSIVE CHARGEBACKS PENALTY

Merchants should monitor chargebacks. A card network may issue warnings to acquirers when a merchant has an excessive number of chargebacks. If chargebacks are not then brought down to an acceptable level, the card network may assess a financial penalty.

A card network may classify some kinds of businesses—gambling, pharmacies, travel services, direct marketers and adult content websites, for example—as high risk, stipulating that they are not entitled to a warning before being assessed a fee for excessive chargebacks.

Card networks may offer fraud or chargeback prevention programs in which merchants and acquirers may participate to reduce liability for chargebacks.

Chapter 12. Collections

In most online transactions, a customer visits a merchant's website, selects items to purchase, completes an order form, and then pays with a credit or debit card. Since payment is made at the time of purchase, no billing statement is sent. The transaction generates no debt. Some merchants, though, find it necessary or desirable to bill a customer for a service or product. If a customer still owes a merchant all or a portion of the purchase price after purchasing a product or service, then the merchant is a creditor, the customer is a debtor, and their legal rights and obligations are dramatically altered. Consumer protection laws give consumer debtors significant levels of protection and creditors must conform their conduct to the requirements of state and federal debt collection laws. Chief among these are the FCBA, the FCRA, the Fair Debt Collection Practices Act[137] (FDCPA), and the Bankruptcy Code.

Billing Disputes

The FCBA gives debtors a right to dispute their bills. The general rule it establishes is that if a debtor sends a written notice that he is disputing the bill, and the creditor receives it within 60 days after sending the bill, then the creditor must do one of the following things within 30 days: (a) acknowledge receipt of the notice; (b) correct the error; or (c) explain why there is no error. If, within those thirty days, the creditor sends an acknowledgement of receipt but does not either correct the error or explain why there is no error, then the creditor must either correct the error or explain why there is no error no later than two complete billing cycles (but in no event more than 90 days) after having received the notice from the debtor. The creditor may not initiate any collection actions until it has complied with this requirement.

After receiving a notice of billing error, the creditor must investigate to determine whether the billing statement contains an error or not. If it does, then the creditor must correct the account statement (including crediting any finance charges on amounts erroneously billed), and send the debtor a notification of correction, along with an explanation of any change in the amount owed. If the creditor determines that there is no error, the creditor must send a written explanation to the debtor stating the reasons why the creditor believes the account statement is correct. If the debtor requests it, the creditor must provide copies of documentary evidence of the debt. This is true even if the creditor admits there is an error.

If the debtor claims that goods were not delivered in accordance with the contract, the creditor must investigate to determine whether they were actually mailed or delivered, and must provide the debtor with a statement of its determination on this issue.

A creditor has to respond to a claimed error only once. If the debtor subsequently sends a notice of error making substantially the same allegation as he did before, the creditor has no obligation to investigate. The creditor may proceed with collection efforts.

The debtor's notice of claimed error must include enough information to enable the creditor to ascertain the debtor's identity and account number. In addition, it must state the amount of the claimed error and set forth a reason for the debtor's belief that the statement contains a billing error.

A billing error may consist of any of the following kinds of things:

- an extension of credit to the debtor that was not made
- an extension of credit to the debtor in a different amount than what the statement shows
- an extension of credit for which the debtor requests clarification, including documentary evidence of it
- a charge for goods or services that were not delivered to the debtor in accordance with the contract terms
- a charge for goods or services that the debtor did not accept
- failure to credit the debtor's account for a payment or other credit to the account
- computational error
- in the case of a credit card or other open-ended credit account, the creditor failed to send a monthly statement containing the information that must be included in such statements under 15 U.S.C. § 1637(b) to the last address the debtor disclosed to the creditor
- any other error described in Bureau of Consumer Financial Protection regulations.

The prohibition against collection actions applies only to the disputed amount. A creditor may proceed with efforts to collect the undisputed portion even before it completes its investigation of the disputed amount. If the creditor sends the debtor an account statement while an investigation of a disputed amount is pending, it must include a statement that the debtor is not required to pay the disputed amount pending the determination of whether the claim of error is valid or not.

If the account is an open-ended consumer credit account, the creditor may not close or restrict it prior to sending an explanation of why the account statement is valid. The creditor may lower the credit limit, though.

After making a determination that there is no error, the creditor must give the debtor either ten days or the same number of days thereafter to make payment as is provided in the parties' agreement for the payment of undisputed amounts, whichever is greater.

A creditor who fails to comply with any of the above requirements forfeits the right to collect up to $50 of the total of the disputed amount and any finance charges on the disputed amount.

Credit Balances

A credit balance is a balance in a consumer's account reflecting an amount the merchant owes to the consumer rather than an amount the consumer owes to the merchant. There are a number of reasons a credit balance may occur. The most common reason is a consumer's overpayment of a bill. The FCBA imposes certain obligations on creditors when a debtor's account has a credit balance.

Whenever a credit balance of more than $1 exists on a customer's account, the merchant must refund it to the customer upon request. If the credit balance has existed for more than six months, the merchant must issue a refund payment whether the customer has requested one or not. The refund may be by check, cash or money order.

A merchant is not required to refund a credit balance if the consumer's current location is unknown and cannot be traced through the person's last known address or telephone number.

Credit Reporting

Reporting or threatening to report unpaid debts to a consumer reporting agency ("credit bureau") may prompt some recalcitrant debtors to pay their bills. In some cases, it can be cheaper and easier than hiring an attorney or a collection agency to try to collect it.

Although reporting unpaid debts to a credit bureau is cheaper than suing to collect a debt, it does not result in an enforceable judgment and it is not free. In order to make a report to a credit bureau, a company must first become a customer. This usually involves entering into a data furnishers or service agreement with a credit bureau. The major credit bureaus are Equifax, Experian, TransUnion, and Innovis. Each bureau establishes its own range of services, account requirements, and fees. Some set a minimum number of debtor accounts that a creditor must have in order to be eligible for an account; others do not. Each credit bureau has a system in place for subscribers to their service to report credit experience with customers. Each credit bureau also establishes its own rules concerning the kinds and amounts of debts that may be reported, and when and how they are to be reported.

Under the FCBA, a creditor may not report the disputed amount of a debt as delinquent to a credit bureau or to anyone else until after the creditor has complied with the requirements for handling disputed charges, as described above, and given the debtor time to pay the disputed amount after the creditor has determined that it is not erroneous. The debtor must be given the same number of days thereafter to make payment as is provided under the credit agreement for the payment of undisputed amounts, but in no event less than ten days. During this time, a creditor may not report or threaten to report adversely on the debtor's credit rating or standing because of the failure to pay the disputed amount unless the creditor has complied with all FCBA requirements and given the debtor the required time to pay the disputed amount.

If, after the creditor determines there is no error, the debtor sends the creditor a notice that the debtor still disputes the amount, then the creditor must include, in any report to a third party, a statement that the amount is in dispute. At the same time, the creditor must notify the debtor of the name and address of each party to whom the creditor is reporting the information. This obligation arises, however, only if the debtor sends the notice to the creditor within the applicable time period for paying the disputed amount.

A creditor who reports a disputed delinquency to a credit bureau or other third party must also report to the third party any subsequent resolution of the dispute.

A creditor who fails to comply with any of the above requirements forfeits the right to collect up to $50 of the total of the disputed amount and any finance charges on the disputed amount.

A company is not required to specify an address for consumers to send notices of inaccurate information. If it does not provide such an address, though, then it violates the FCRA if it sends information to a credit bureau that it knows or has reason to believe is inaccurate. If the company has clearly and conspicuously communicated such an address, then the company's reporting of inaccurate information to a credit bureau violates the FCRA if it sends inaccurate information after having received a properly addressed notification from the consumer that the information is inaccurate. Of course, the fact that knowingly sending false information to a credit bureau does not violate the FCRA does not necessarily mean that the company could not be held liable for defamation.

A company that regularly furnishes information to a credit bureau about transactions with a consumer must promptly notify the credit bureau if it determines that any information it has furnished is incomplete or inaccurate. At the same time, the company must provide the credit bureau with a statement of any corrections and/or additional information required to make the information correct and complete. Once the company has done this, it may not thereafter re-submit the original information to the credit bureau at any time in the future.

If a consumer contacts the company directly to dispute the completeness or accuracy of information the company has furnished to a credit bureau, then the company may not thereafter report the information to any credit bureau unless it includes with the information a notice that it is disputed by the consumer.

If a company regularly reports information about a consumer to a credit bureau, then it must also report any voluntary closure of the account by the consumer.

Reports of collection or other action on delinquent accounts must include the date and year of the delinquency. This information must be provided to the credit bureau not later than ninety days after furnishing information about the collection or other action on the account.

A company must have adequate policies and procedures in place to ensure the accuracy of information it furnishes to credit bureaus. Guidelines for such policies and procedures are set out in the Appendix to 16 C.F.R Part 660.

A company that receives a notice of disputed information in a credit report directly from a consumer must:

(1) Investigate the disputed information.
(2) Review all relevant information the consumer provides with the notice.
(3) Report the results of the investigation to the consumer within the same amount of time that a credit bureau would be required to complete it if the consumer had send the notice of dispute to the credit bureau instead of directly to the company.
(4) Promptly notify each credit bureau to which the company furnished information that the information is inaccurate and provide any needed corrections.

The company need not do these things if it reasonably determines that the dispute is frivolous or irrelevant, either because the consumer has failed to provide sufficient information or because the information the consumer submitted is substantially the same as information the consumer submitted during a previously resolved dispute. If the company determines a dispute is frivolous, it must notify the consumer within five days by mail or any other means authorized by the consumer. The notification must state the reasons for the determination and identify any information required to investigate the disputed information (which may consist of a standardized form describing the general nature of such information).

The statutory duty to investigate when a company receives a dispute notice directly from a consumer does not apply if the dispute is submitted to the company by a credit repair organization on the consumer's behalf.

CREDIT REPORT DISPUTES

When a credit bureau receives a notification from a consumer that the consumer disputes information in her credit report, it must conduct an investigation to determine whether the information is accurate. It must either confirm the accuracy of the information or delete it from the consumer's file within thirty days of receiving the notification. The period is extended by fifteen days if the consumer submits additional relevant information during that period, unless the credit bureau determines during the original time period that the information is inaccurate.

Within five business days after receiving a dispute notification from a consumer, the credit bureau must send the company that furnished the disputed information all relevant information about the dispute that it has received from the consumer. The credit bureau must also send the company any relevant information it thereafter receives from the consumer. The company must investigate and report its determination to the credit bureau within the same time frame. If, after investigation, the credit bureau determines that the information is inaccurate or is not verified by the company that furnished it, it must delete or modify the information as requested by the consumer and notify the consumer and the company that furnished the information that this action has been taken.

Once information has been deleted, it may not be reinserted unless the company furnishing the information certifies that the information is complete and accurate.

The FTC and other regulatory agencies may bring enforcement actions against companies that violate the FCRA. Civil penalties may be imposed. In addition, a consumer may sue a creditor for damages for violations of the FCRA, in some situations.

IDENTIFY THEFT

A company that furnishes information to a credit bureau must have reasonable procedures in place to respond to any notification it receives from a credit bureau relating to identity theft-related information, to prevent the company from refurnishing blocked information.

A company that receives notification from a credit bureau that a debt has resulted from identity theft may not sell, transfer, or place the debt for collection.

If a consumer sends an identity theft notice to the company at the address the company has specified for such notices, the company may not furnish information purporting to relate to the consumer to a credit bureau unless the company later learns or is informed by the consumer that the information is correct.

If the company learns that it has furnished inaccurate information due to identity theft, it must promptly notify each credit bureau of the correct information. Going forward, it must report only complete and accurate information about the consumer.

Unfair Debt Collection Practices

Laws have been enacted at both the federal and state levels to protect debtors from abusive, deceptive and unfair debt collection practices. The FDCPA is the principal federal law on the subject. It applies to the activities of people and businesses that collect debts owed to others. Attorneys and collection agencies must comply with it. The Act does not apply to a company's efforts to collect its own accounts, however. An e-commerce business does not need to worry about complying with the FDCPA when it tries to collect a debt that one of its customers owes the company.

Although the FDCPA does not apply to a creditor's actions to try to collect a debt owed to it, some states have enacted similar laws and some of these laws apply to creditors as well as debt collectors. Florida's Consumer Collection Practices Act is an example. It gives a debtor a right to sue a creditor for actual or statutory damages, punitive damages and attorney fees if the creditor engages in certain kinds of abusive, harassing, unfair, deceptive or misleading practices in an effort to collect a debt.

Examples of prohibited conduct:

- mailing documents with embarrassing words or phrases visible (e.g., a postcard or words written on the outside of the envelope)
- contacting a third party about the debt
- contacting the debtor between 9 p.m. and 8 a.m. without permission
- communicating directly with a debtor known to be represented by an attorney
- communicating or threatening to communicate with an employer before obtaining a judgment on the debt
- reporting or threatening to report a disputed debt to a credit bureau without also disclosing the existence of the dispute
- falsely stating that an attorney is involved
- pretending to be an attorney
- sending communications designed to look like attorney letters or government documents
- pretending to be a police officer or government official
- filing a lawsuit in the wrong venue to inconvenience the debtor
- harassing the debtor about the debt
- harassing the debtor's family about the debt
- using profane, vulgar or abusive language
- using force or violence
- threatening force or violence
- threatening or trying to enforce an uncollectible debt (e.g., a debt that is barred by the statute of limitations).

California's Fair Debt Collection Practices Act is another example. Like the Florida statute, it applies to debt collectors as well as to creditors. It also applies to companies that make forms and tools for debt collection. It contains a long list of prohibited collection activities, such as:

- Contacting an employer for any reason other than to verify employment, to locate the debtor, or to garnish wages. If it is a medical debt, contacting the employer to inquire about health insurance is also prohibited.
- Contacting an employer about garnishing wages before a judgment has been obtained.
- Revealing information about the debt to the debtor's family. This information may be revealed to the debtor's spouse or to a minor debtor's parents, however.

- Publishing the debtor's name in a public place for failing to pay.
- Displaying information about the debt on the outside of an envelope for the purpose of embarrassing the debtor.
- Sending the debtor a postcard.
- Contacting the debtor after receiving a written notice from the debtor's attorney, if the attorney has agreed to talk to creditors on the debtor's behalf. Direct contact may be resumed, though, if the attorney refuses to talk to the collector.
- Commencing a lawsuit against the debtor in the wrong venue or without serving process on the debtor.
- Sending a document that looks like it was sent by a government agency or attorney when it was not.
- Misrepresenting who the creditor is or the person on whose behalf a collector is acting.
- Falsely representing oneself to be an attorney.
- Threatening to file a lawsuit without having any real intention of doing so.
- Falsely pretending to be acting under government authority.
- Threatening to seek attorney fees or recover collection costs when not legally entitled to do so.
- Pretending to be a credit reporting agency.
- Threatening to report the debt to a credit reporting agency without having an actual intention of doing so.
- Sending a letter that looks like it comes from a legal, claims, credit or audit department but that does not actually come from one of these departments.
- Using or threatening to use physical force or criminal tactics to personally harm the debtor or the debtor's property or reputation.
- Accusing the debtor of a crime for not paying the debt.
- Making or threatening to make a defamatory statement about the debtor to someone else.
- Threatening to assign the debt to someone and falsely stating that the debtor will lose any defense to the debt in the process.
- Threatening to have the debtor arrested or to seize property or garnish wages without having both the legal right to do so and an actual intention of doing so.
- Using profane language.
- Calling repeatedly or letting the phone ring repeatedly to annoy the debtor
- Harassing the debtor by calling frequently
- Failing to disclose the creditor's caller identification when calling.

This is not an exhaustive list.

If a creditor violates this law, the debtor may sue for damages, attorney fees and a monetary sanction.

In states that have not enacted fair debt collection practices laws, the common law may provide a remedy. Courts in a number of states recognize a common law cause of action for damages for intentional infliction of emotional distress. A creditor who engages in extreme and outrageous collection methods with the intent to cause or with reckless disregard for the likelihood of causing emotional distress may be liable to the debtor for the debtor's mental anguish. If the debtor suffers physical injury (e.g., a heart attack) attributable to the conduct, then the creditor is liable for that, as well. Some of the conduct described in state fair debt collection practices acts might qualify as "extreme and outrageous." Other kinds of conduct might also qualify. Calling the debtor and deceiving her into calling the creditor back by leaving a message falsely stating that the debtor's spouse or a member of the debtor's family has died or is in the hospital is an example of outrageous collection activity for which the common law would probably allow a debtor to recover damages.

Judgments

Assuming the debt is valid, a company may file a complaint in court and obtain a judgment against the debtor for the unpaid amount of the debt. If the parties have been through arbitration and the company has won an arbitration award, the company may file a petition in court to reduce the award to an enforceable judgment.

Securing a judgment enables a creditor to seize the debtor's assets to satisfy the judgment. The assets may be real or personal property. Although a judgment normally only reaches assets that are located in the territorial jurisdiction of the court in which the judgment is filed, most states and countries have procedures for registering foreign judgments. This way, a judgment issued by a court in one state can be satisfied by seizing assets located in another state or country.

A judgment is usually enforceable for a specified period of time, such as ten years. In most jurisdictions, they are renewable, provided the renewal occurs before the term of the judgment expires. Judgments typically bear interest until satisfied.

Possession of a judgment does not entitle a creditor to simply help himself to the debtor's property. Assets need to be collected through legal process. The writ of execution is the most common postjudgment method. This is basically a court order directing the sheriff of the county in which property is located to seize it. The property might include such things as cash, vehicles, equipment, jewelry, money in a bank account, wages, intangibles (e.g., stocks, certificates of deposit), etc.

Real property may also be seized. In most states, a judgment may be filed with the county recorder's office. Thereafter, it serves as a lien on any real property the debtor owns, or subsequently comes to own, in that county. If the debtor does not pay, then the judgment-creditor may seek to enforce the lien by foreclosing on it. Alternatively, the judgment creditor may wait until the debtor seeks to sell or mortgage the property. Title insurance companies typically will require liens to be paid off first.

A judgment creditor who needs to locate assets upon which to levy may ask the court to issue an order of examination. This kind of order directs a judgment debtor to appear in court and answer questions under oath about the location of assets. If the judgment debtor does not appear or refuses to comply, he may be jailed for contempt. Once the judgment debtor discloses the location of assets, the judgment creditor can ask the court to order him not to move them, and normally may request a writ of execution at that time, if desired.

A judgment debtor may not transfer assets for less than fair market value for the purpose of keeping them out of the reach of a judgment creditor. In these circumstances, the transferee may be made a party to the proceeding and may be ordered to transfer the asset, or its full value, to the creditor.

State laws impose restrictions on what may be seized and/or the amount. For example, states allow garnishment only up to a specified percentage of a debtor's wages. Typically, these are tied to minimum wage laws. Most states also have a homestead exemption statute that protects a debtor's home from being used to satisfy judgments for unsecured debts, at least up to a specified amount. Exemptions in specified amounts may apply to other kinds of property, too. Moreover, compliance with fair debt collections practices laws continues to be required even after a judgment is obtained.

STATUTES OF LIMITATIONS

A *statute of limitations* for debts is the limited time period that a statute allows a creditor to initiate a lawsuit for nonpayment. The time periods vary by type of claim and jurisdiction.

The method of measuring the applicable time period also varies. For ordinary claims for failure to pay for a consumer product, the period of limitations typically is measured from the time a payment is missed. In some states, it is measured from the time of the debtor's last payment. In these states, each successive payment has the effect of extending the period of limitations. There are also states where even a promise to pay an old debt may have the effect of "restarting" the period of limitations. Knowing this, creditors and debt collectors in these states may attempt to persuade a debtor to make even a very small payment, particularly if they know the limitations period is drawing near.

Attempting to collect a debt that is beyond the period of limitations may be an unfair debt collection practice in some states. As such, it might give the debtor and/or a regulatory agency a right to sue.

Bankruptcy

When a debtor files for bankruptcy protection, an automatic stay of collection activity goes into effect. This means that creditors must immediately cease all attempts to collect the debts owed to them. This includes everything—lawsuits, garnishments, collection letters and calls, etc. Knowingly violating a bankruptcy stay is contempt of court. A court may impose sanctions on a creditor who knows of the bankruptcy and continues collection activities anyway. Sanctions may include fines, attorney fees, and damages.

Some kinds of collection actions are not stayed. The IRS may proceed with audits, issue notices of tax deficiency and assessments, and demand payments. Actions to establish parentage and/or to establish, modify or enforce alimony or child support may proceed. Criminal sentences may be imposed and enforced while a bankrupty proceeding is pending. Money may be withheld from income to repay loans from certain trypes of pensions and IRAs. Finally, actions to collect debts incurred after the bankruptcy petition is filed are not stayed.

In some situations, a court may issue an order lifting the stay for a secured creditor.

If a debt is discharged in the bankruptcy, then the debtor is no longer legally obligated to pay it. The bankruptcy court will send a notice to creditors informing them that they should not attempt any further collection. There is a split in the federal circuit courts as to whether a debt collector's attempt to collect a debt that has been discharged in bankruptcy is a violation of the

FDCPA for which a cause of action for damages may be brought. In any case, though, a creditor's or debt collector's attempt to collect a debt that has been discharged in bankruptcy may be punished as contempt of court.

Of course, a debtor may voluntarily reaffirm and pay a debt that has been discharged in bankruptcy. To be enforceable, however, a debt reaffirmation must truly be voluntary.

Chapter 13. Data Security

Data security is of vital importance to businesses that engage in e-commerce. Without adequate data security protections, third parties may gain unauthorized access to a customer's personal information, potentially enabling identity theft. Releasing private information can also cause a customer embarrassment. A person may have legitimate reasons for not wanting others to know about the person's health or financial condition and they may have nothing to do with identity theft. Unauthorized disclosures of customer information can have adverse consequences for a business, too. In addition to bad publicity and loss of customers, there may be liability for negligence, invasion of privacy, and/or breach of contract. Regulatory enforcement actions—and in some cases, criminal proceedings—are also possible.

Data security laws attempt to protect consumers from unauthorized uses of their information, by requiring businesses to implement controls to prevent the information from being disclosed to third parties. For more information about what kinds of information are private, see Chapter 17.

Enforcement of data security laws is usually by regulatory agencies, but in some cases a statute may provide for a private right of action as well. Depending on the circumstances, a data security lapse may also form the basis for a common law negligence cause of action for damages, provided the individual making the claim can prove actual economic loss as a result of the breach. At common law, a business that collects information from a customer has a duty to use reasonable security measures to prevent unauthorized people from accessing it. Merely posting a notice declaring that only authorized users may access data is not enough. Affirmative steps must be taken to prevent access by people who are not inclined to follow instructions. A duty to protect information from disclosure may also arise from contract, including, in some cases, promises set out in a website's Terms of Use.

The FTC Act

The FTC Act prohibits unfair or deceptive acts or practices in or affecting commerce. The FTC has used its power to enforce this provision to impose data security obligations on the owners of e-commerce businesses. An owner of a website that states, in the privacy policy or elsewhere, that the data customers submit will not be shared with others, or gives a similar kind of assurance of privacy or security, must actually maintain an adequate level of security. Otherwise, the company may face a charge of engaging in a deceptive trade practice.

Even if no representation about privacy or security is made, though, collecting personal information from website visitors without protecting it from unauthorized disclosure to others may constitute an unfair trade practice. An act or practice is unfair if each of the following is true:

(a) It causes or is likely to cause substantial injury to consumers.
(b) The injury is not reasonably avoidable by consumers themselves.
(c) The injury is not outweighed by countervailing benefits to consumers or to competition.

The FTC has taken the position that a failure to provide reasonable and appropriate security for consumer information is an unfair trade practice because a data breach is likely to cause substantial injury that is not reasonably avoidable by consumers themselves and an absence of reasonable security measures does not benefit consumers or competition. Given the consequences that can flow from identity theft, it is difficult to argue with the FTC's position.

What the FTC considers reasonable and appropriate may be ascertained from the settlement agreements into which the agency has entered with companies it has alleged to have inadequate security measures. The terms of these settlements are not binding as precedent, but they provide insights into what kinds of security measures the FTC believes are fair to consumers. From these settlements, it is clear that the FTC believes a reasonable data security program should include each of the following elements:

- Identification of protected information
- Assessment of risks and vulnerabilities
- Safeguards
- Contracts with third parties
- Response to detected security breaches
- Review and adjustment.

In some cases, these obligations are also addressed in laws specific to particular types of information and businesses. The requirements of these laws supplement and augment the security measures that are required to comply with the FTC Act. They do not supplant those requirements.

IDENTIFICATION OF INFORMATION

Identifying the information a company has in its possession, or that it may come to have in its possession, which must be protected from unauthorized disclosure is an essential part of any security program. This means performing an inventory of all file cabinets, notes, computers, laptops, mobile devices, flash drives, disks, digital copiers, remote servers, and other equipment to determine where the company stores sensitive data. It is also important to identify all connections to the computers and devices where sensitive information is stored—e.g., Internet, computers at branch offices, computers used by third party service providers and contractors, wireless devices, inventory scanners, digital printers, etc. Information should be inventoried by type, location, and the names of the persons who have access to it.

Device identification must be thorough. Any device that stores protected information, even temporarily, should be identified. The hard drive in a digital copier or printer, for example, stores data about the documents it copies, prints, scans, faxes, or emails. Therefore, measures need to be taken to prevent unauthorized access to this drive, either by remote access or by extraction once the drive has been removed. If feasible, a company should purchase a printer/copier with overwriting and encryption features.

Particular attention should be given to identifying the location and the persons who have access to the principal kinds of information to which security obligations apply:

- Personally identifying information
- Information collected from children under thirteen years of age
- Health and health care information
- Financial information
- Information about publicly traded companies.

Personally Identifying Information

Since the most substantial injury to consumers that may result from a security breach is identity theft, the FTC seeks to ensure that commercial websites protect the personally identifying information of the consumers who visit them. This includes any information that may be used to identify a particular person—name, address, Social Security number, driver license number, date of birth, geographic location, etc. The FTC takes the position that user names, screen names, contact lists, IP addresses and geographic location are also covered by its regulations. According to the FTC, information that may be used to identify a particular device (e.g., an IP address) is "personally identifying information" even if it does not identify any particular human being.

Behavioral advertising (or "targeted marketing") is the practice of tracking an individual's online activities in order to deliver advertising tailored to the person's interests. It is usually accomplished by using cookies. The FTC has taken the position that data collected for purposes of behavioral advertising comes within the meaning of "personally identifying information." As such, a website claiming to maintain the confidentiality, privacy or security of information collected from users must store and transmit any information it collects for purposes of behavioral advertising in a secure way.

Information Collected from Children Under Thirteen

Important restrictions apply to the collection of information from children under thirteen years of ago. See Chapter 18.

Financial Information

The GLBA, also known as the Financial Services Modernization Act, is a federal law intended, among other things, to ensure the privacy and security of information that financial institutions collect from consumers. The FTC has promulgated two key rules to implement it: a Privacy Rule and a Safeguards Rule.[138] These rules apply both to financial institutions and to businesses that receive information from a financial institution. Information about the Privacy Rule may be found in Chapter 17.

For purposes of the Rules, a *financial institution* is a business that is significantly engaged in any of the financial activities described in section 4(k) of the BHCA. Section 4(k) of the BHCA defines financial activities to include any activity that the Federal Reserve Board, by regulation, defines as financial and also a number of specifically identified activities, such as lending, investing or safeguarding money or securities for others, insurance, investment advice, credit counseling, tax preparation, accounting, financial planning, and dealing in securities. This is not an exhaustive list.

"Substantial engagement" is a fact determination that is made on a case-by-case basis. Two factors are particularly important: (a) whether there is a formal arrangement, and (b) how often the business engages in the activity. A business that primarily sells nonfinancial products or services is not "substantially engaged" in financial activities merely because it sometimes informally allows its customers to run a tab. On the other hand, a business that formally extends credit to its customers, such as by issuing its own credit card, is substantially engaged in financial activities. Similarly, a business that only occasionally allows a customer to make payments for nonfinancial products or services on a layaway plan is not significantly engaged in a financial activity. If a business were to regularly engage in a financial activity, then it would be substantially engaged in the financial activity.

The Rules also apply to any company that receives protected information from a financial institution, even if the company is not itself a financial institution.

The Rules only apply to consumer information. A *consumer* is a person who obtains a financial product or service from a financial institution that is to be used primarily for personal, family, or household purposes. A consumer's legal representative is also considered a consumer. Commercial clients—those who purchase products or services for a business purpose—do not come within the protection of the Rules.

The GLBA requires financial institutions to protect the security and confidentiality of their customers' nonpublic personal information, i.e., personally identifiable financial information provided by a consumer to a financial institution, resulting from any transaction with the consumer or any service performed for the consumer, or otherwise obtained by the financial institution. Penalties for noncompliance may be up to $100,000 per violation. States with comparable regulations may impose significant penalties for the same conduct.

Information About Publicly Traded Companies

The SOX Act requires publicly traded companies and any accounting firms that provide auditing services to them to have adequate security controls in place to ensure that financial and other information required to be reported under securities laws is accessed only by those people and systems with a legitimate need for access. A corporate officer must attest to the validity of reported information, requiring safeguards to prevent data tampering.

Health Information

HIPAA establishes data security and privacy rules for individually identifiable health information that is created or received by a "covered entity." Health care providers, health plans, and health care clearinghouses are covered entities. The Act protects all health information that identifies an individual or could be used to identify an individual. This includes an individual's past, present or future physical or mental condition; the provision of health care to the individual; and past, present or future payment for the provision of health care to the individual. The U.S. Department of Health and Human Services (DHHS) has established a HIPAA Privacy Rule[139] to implement HIPAA requirements.

RISK ASSESSMENT

To assess the risks to protected information that a company needs to address, it is necessary to trace information flow: This involves identifying:

(a) the sources from which the company receives information
(b) the mechanisms and means by which information is received
(c) the kinds of information the company collects at each entry point
(d) where the information that is collected at each entry point is kept
(e) who has or could have access to the information
(f) the mechanisms and means the company uses to transmit information.

A company needs to assess the vulnerability of each connection to commonly known or reasonably foreseeable attacks. Depending on a company's circumstances, appropriate assessments may range from having a knowledgeable employee run off-the-shelf security software to having an independent professional conduct a full-scale security audit.

Measures to assess foreseeable risk should consider the possibility of unauthorized access from within the company as well as attacks from outside the company. A business should have measures in place to reduce the risk of either intentional or inadvertent misuse or disclosure of customer information by the company's employees, agents, and persons and businesses with whom the company contracts for goods or services.

For publicly traded companies, the SOX Act requires that both inadvertent and malicious attempts to alter data must be blocked. Accordingly, a publicly traded company needs to consider not only the risk of being hacked but also the risk that an officer, director, employee, agent, or third-party contractor might accidentally erase or alter data. Periodic security audits are necessary.

The GLBA requires financial institutions and companies that receive information from them to have a written plan for protecting customer information from foreseeable threats to security and data integrity. The plan must designate one or more employees to coordinate its information security program and identify and assess the risks to customer information in each relevant area of the company's operations. The plan also must consider and address any unique risks associated with a company's particular business operations—such as the risks that are involved when employees access customer data from their homes or other off-site locations, or when customer data is transmitted electronically outside the company network.

Financial institutions and companies that receive information from them need to assess and address data security risks in relation to customer information in all areas of their operations, including but not necessarily limited to:

- Employee management and training
- Information systems
- Detecting and managing system failures.

Guidance issued by the Federal Financial Institutions Examination Council (FFIEC) requires financial institutions to periodically assess the risks associated with their Internet-based products and services.

SAFEGUARDS

All e-commerce businesses that collect personally identifying information from consumers must have reasonable safeguards in place to prevent unauthorized disclosure of the information to third parties. What is reasonable varies depending on the kind of information, the kind of business, the size of the business, and the kind of activity in which the business is engaged. When a security safeguard is readily available at low cost and is in common use, the FTC is likely to take the position that it is required for every business that collects information from consumers.

Data Security Program

The FTC has taken the position that a failure to create a comprehensive information security program to protect consumers' personal information is an unfair trade practice. Failure to implement reasonable policies and procedures to protect the security of consumers' personal or financial information that a company collects and maintains is also an unfair or deceptive trade practice. Moreover, a comprehensive written program is often a required remediating element in settlement agreements between the FTC and companies charged with engaging in unfair data security practices, as is the designation of an employee or other individual to coordinate and be accountable for the program.

With respect to financial information, the FTC has adopted a Safeguards Rule to implement GLBA requirements for the protection of financial information collected by or received from financial institutions. It requires financial institutions and those who receive information from them to have a written plan for protecting customer information from foreseeable threats to security and data integrity. It must provide for designing, implementing and maintaining a safeguards program to protect customers' financial information, whether the information is collected by the company itself or received from a financial institution. The safeguards must include three kinds of controls: administrative, physical, and technical. Procedural safeguards (such as employee screening and training) are also recommended.

HIPAA requires covered entities to have a data security plan that addresses administrative, physical and technical safeguards of health and health care information. Administrative safeguards are administrative actions, policies and procedures to manage the selection, development, implementation, and maintenance of security measures to protect electronically stored or transmitted health information and to manage employee conduct in relation to the protection of health information. Physical safeguards are physical measures, policies, and procedures to protect electronic information systems and related buildings and equipment from unauthorized access and from natural and environmental hazards. Technical safeguards are the technology and the policy and procedures for its use that protect electronically stored or transmitted health information and control access to it.

Several states have enacted laws requiring businesses that are in possession of personal information to implement and maintain reasonable security procedures and practices. A small but growing number are making specific data security practices obligatory, either through direct statutory enactment or by authorizing a regulatory agency to enact data security regulations. Massachusetts regulations require persons and businesses that own, license, store or maintain personal information about an individual or legal entity that resides in that state to have a comprehensive, written information security program in place and to monitor it periodically.

The regulations contain detailed requirements about what the plan must include.[140] A succession of highly publicized security breaches between 2014 and 2017 make it likely that more jurisdictions will be enacting laws like this in the near future.

A data security program should include controls for:

- System access
- Digital content access
- Physical access
- Portable devices
- Transmissions
- System changes
- Record retention
- Record disposal
- Employee training
- Monitoring and updating.

SYSTEM ACCESS CONTROLS

System access controls are measures that are designed to ensure that only authorized individuals have access to systems containing protected information. They usually include some mechanism for authenticating the identity of individuals with authorization to access the system.

Trusted Persons Only. A reasonable security program will have controls in place to ensure that only trustworthy people are granted access to the company's system. This means that a company should check references and perform background checks before hiring employees who will have access to sensitive data.

Need-to-Know Basis. A company should develop and implement measures to ensure than protected information is accessible only by those employees and individuals with a legitimate business need to access it. This is a reasonable practice for any business, and it is also one of the procedural safeguards prescribed in the Safeguards Rule for financial information that is maintained by or received from a financial institution. The restriction may be implemented by including appropriate language in the employment contract and by distributing passwords and/or other authentication credentials to only those persons with a legitimate business need to know. Also, administrator privileges for a website or computer system should be granted only to those individuals who are responsible for making systemwide changes to the system.

Strong Passwords. Password-protecting personally identifying information is an essential step toward ensuring adequate security, but it may not be enough. The FTC has taken the position that storing personal information in files that may be accessed using weak passwords is not an adequate or reasonable way of protecting the information.

Strength is a function of length, complexity, and randomness. The FTC recommends that companies require passwords at least twelve characters long with a random mix of upper and lower case letters, numerals, and symbols. The following kinds of passwords are inherently weak:

- Words and phrases
- Common numerical strings
- Common alphabetical strings
- Commonly known default passwords
- Weak passwords that are lengthened only by adding a patterned sequence of characters
- Company's name or a brand name
- Default password that comes with a device or software program.

Examples of weak passwords: myaccesscode, Fluffy, 1234, qwerty, password, Apple.

Password Changes. Passwords should be changed, and companies should require employees to change their passwords, in the following circumstances:

(a) when installing new software
(b) immediately following a breach or suspected breach
(c) when establishing multiple accounts
(d) when using multiple applications and programs
(e) periodically, as a matter of course.

Vendor-supplied default passwords should be changed as soon as possible. Different passwords should be used for different accounts.

Account and Password Termination. A company needs to have a procedure in place for making sure that employees who leave the company no longer have access to sensitive information. This includes terminating their user accounts and passwords. An employee's password also should be disabled when the employee undertakes a new position or transfers to a department where the employee no longer needs access to protected information.

Secure Password Storage. If passwords are written down on paper, the paper should be kept in a locked location. If they are stored digitally, then storing them on a device that is not connected to a network is a reasonable method of securing the information, provided the device is physically secured (e.g., locked in a cabinet). Although not required, the FTC recommends using a password management application. Only applications from reputable companies should be used. A strong password should be selected for the master password.

Passwords should not be stored digitally in readable text format. When there is a need to compare a user-entered password with a stored value (such as when a user attempts to log in to a password-protected area, the FTC recommends hashing the passwords for storage. Further, they should be "salted," i.e., random data added to the password for storage The FTC also suggests using slow hash functions.

Secure Transmission of Passwords. Passwords should not be shared by phone, email or text message. Passwords normally should not be transmitted at all. If there is a legitimate need to do so, they should only be sent in a strongly encrypted document.

Password-Activated Screen Savers. Companies should use password-activated screen savers to lock employee computers after a period of inactivity.

Strong User Names. Commonly known user names and IDs should be avoided. Something other than the company's, the user's or a common default name (e.g., 'admin' or 'guest') should be selected. The user name should be different from the password.

Different Credentials for Multiple Users. Every employee should have unique credentials. A third party's multiple users should each have individual credentials. Contracts with employees and third parties should prohibit the sharing of user IDs, passwords and the like with others.

Two-Factor Authentication. A system for verifying or authenticating the identity and qualifications of a user before allowing access to protected information is part of a reasonable security program. Where the system supports it, two-factor authentication is more secure than a password alone, as it requires both the password and an additional piece of information to log in to an account. The second piece could be a code sent to the user's phone, a random number generated by an app, a token, or some other backup protection in the event the password is compromised. Examples of standard customer authentication methods include: passwords; PINs; digital certificates using a public key infrastructure; tokens; transaction profile scripts; and biometric identification.

Guidance issued by the Federal Financial Institutions Examination Council requires the websites of financial institutions that enable customers to make online transfers of funds to require more than a user name and password to authenticate a customer's identity before the customer may gain access to account information or make an online transfer. Multifactor authentication, layered security, or other controls reasonably calculated to mitigate the risks of identity theft or account fraud are needed to protect financial information.

Multiple Login Attempts. A reasonable data security program should provide for suspending or disabling the accounts of users after a reasonable number of unsuccessful login attempts.

Separate Business and Public Networks. Wherever possible, only the company's own computers and devices should have access to the company's network. Wireless routers usually have a mechanism to allow only devices with particular unique Media Access Control (MAC) addresses to access the network. If a company wishes to provide free WiFi for customers, it should set up a second, public network. The public access network should be separate from the network for the company's business devices.

Network Segmentation. Sensitive information should not be stored on computers with an Internet connection unless it is essential for conducting business. If some computers on a network store sensitive information while others do not, consideration should be given to using firewalls to protect the computers with sensitive information. Moreover, not every computer in a company's system needs to be able to communicate with every other one. Particularly sensitive data should be housed offline, or if that is not feasible, then in a separate secure place on the network.

Firewalls. A firewall is software or hardware designed to block others from accessing a computer. A properly configured firewall makes it tougher for hackers to locate a computer and get into programs and files. The FTC considers the use of firewalls or the isolation of systems with sensitive personal information in some other way a readily available, and therefore reasonable, security measure. The FTC particularly recommends that consideration be given to installing a "border" firewall where a company's network connects to the Internet. A border firewall separates a network from the Internet and may prevent an attacker from gaining access to a computer on the network where sensitive information is stored.

Access controls—settings that determine which devices and traffic get through the firewall—should be set to allow only trusted devices with a legitimate business need to access the network through. Access control settings should be reviewed periodically.

Router Setup. Routers need to be set up securely. The name of a router (often called the *service set identifier*, or SSID) is likely to be a standard, default ID assigned by the manufacturer. It should be changed to something unique and not known to others. Some routers offer an option to allow remote access to a router's controls, for purposes such as enabling the manufacturer to provide technical support. Any such remote management features on a router should be turned off. Leaving them turned on increases the risk of being hacked. Once a router has been set up, the administrator should log out promptly, to lessen the risk of somebody piggybacking on the session to gain control of the device.

SQL Injection Attacks. "SQL" stands for Structured Query Language. It is a programming language that is used to communicate with databases. Many of the servers that store data for websites and services use SQL to manage the data in their databases. A SQL injection attack targets this kind of server, using malicious code to get the server to divulge information such as customers' credit card numbers, user names, passwords, or other personally identifying information. It may be done for other malicious purposes, too, such as destroying or tampering with data, voiding transactions, changing balances, or becoming an administrator of the database server. The attack works by exploiting a known SQL vulnerability that allows the SQL server to run malicious code. The hacker inserts malicious commands into an input field that results in the input data being interpreted as part of a SQL query instead of data. A database that is vulnerable to a SQL injection attack is not reasonably secure. Data sanitization and validation are two important precautions. Relatively simple defenses against these attacks are available from various sources. A website may be found to have failed to adopt reasonable security measures if it has not used known methods of preventing SQL injection and cross-site scripting attacks.

Web Application Vulnerabilities. Online applications that a company uses to exchange information with customers may be vulnerable to hacking attacks. Measures should be taken to protect against them.

Downloads. Software programs downloaded to devices that connect to a company's network (computers, smartphones, and tablets) could be used to distribute malware. Therefore, a company should restrict employees' ability to download unauthorized software.

Network Services. Computers on the company's network should be scanned to identify open network services. Unnecessary services should be disabled. For example, if an Internet connection or email service is not needed on a particular computer, the FTC recommends closing the ports to those services on that computer to prevent unauthorized access it.

Child-Directed Websites. See Chapter 18.

Publicly Traded Companies. The SOX Act imposes some additional obligations on publicly traded companies beyond the foregoing safeguards of general applicability. An Internal Controls Report must be included in the company's financial disclosures. It must demonstrate, among other things, that adequate controls are in place to safeguard data residing on computers, network hardware, and any other electronic equipment through which financial data passes. The Act does not give specific details about the kinds of security controls that are required. Whatever controls a company chooses, though, must prevent the destruction, alteration or falsification of records. In addition to encryption and other controls of general applicability, a publicly traded company needs to conduct periodic audits. Accordingly, all access to business records should be logged.

DIGITAL CONTENT CONTROLS

Digital files containing protected information should be encrypted to ensure that only authorized persons are able to read them. *Encryption* means converting text from a readable format to an encoded format. It usually involves the generation of a key by an encryption algorithm which is distributed to authorized users only. Encryption of protected information both while it is being stored and while it is being transmitted is a necessary part of every reasonable and appropriate security program. Storing protected data in clear readable text is a deceptive practice if the website claims to be secure, and it is an unfair practice even if the website does not claim to be secure.

Protected information should be encrypted wherever it is stored, including on the company's computer network and laptops, smartphones and other portable storage devices used by employees.

In addition to safeguards of general applicability, the Safeguards Rule requires financial institutions and companies that receive information from them to use technological measures to protect the information. This includes storing and backing up data in an encrypted format to a password-protected server.

PHYSICAL ACCESS CONTROLS

Physical access controls restrict access to physical locations, including computer facilities, workstations, and computers or other devices containing protected information to only those persons with a legitimate business need to access the information. The purpose of a physical access control is to ensure that only authorized persons are allowed to gain access to areas and devices where information is stored. Examples include: keeping sensitive information in a locked safe; requiring an access code to enter an area where sensitive information may be accessed; ensuring the company's server and computers are in secure locations; and refraining from sending facsimile transmissions to an area in a recipient's office or home where unauthorized individuals might be able to read it. Records should be kept in a locked room or cabinet when unattended.

A company's computers, including portable devices like laptops and smartphones, should be equipped with screen savers that lock the user out after a period of inactivity and require a password to reactivate them. In some circumstances, such as where a customer accesses protected information from a noncompany device, session time limits may also be appropriate.

A company that has devices that collect sensitive information, like PIN pads, should secure them so that identity thieves cannot tamper with them. Also, these items should be inventoried to ensure that they have not been switched.

Any papers or other physical objects containing protected information must be protected from access by unauthorized persons. Passwords and encryption protect digitally stored information, but other methods must be used to protect paper documents. A locked file cabinet, safe or physical storage facility of some kind is needed. Employees should be required to put files away, log off their computers, and lock their file cabinets when they are away from their workstations, and to lock office doors at the end of the day.

A company should limit the instances when employees are away from the office with protected information in their possession. When there is a legitimate need for this, the employee should be required to protect the information from being seen by unauthorized persons and should keep the briefcase or other device in which the information is stored locked and in the employee's possession at all times, if possible.

Physical access controls are also needed when an employee is terminated. A company needs to ensure that terminated employees are not able to gain access to the company's facilities or equipment. This means retrieving keys and identification cards, changing passwords and access codes, and the like. This is usually done as part of the exit interview and check-out routine.

Physical storage areas also need to be protected against damage or destruction from physical hazards like fire or floods. Backup copies of records should be made and maintained securely. Backups and archived data should be stored offline in a physically secure location.

PORTABLE DEVICES

Controls are needed to safeguard protected information that is stored in laptops, smartphones, and other portable devices. This includes: inventorying and tracking such devices; adopting policies on the proper use, storage and disposal of the devices; establishing access controls for the devices (e.g., password protection); and encryption. Controls also should be in place to prevent unauthorized access in the event the device is stolen, borrowed or used by an unauthorized person. Backup storage devices, too, should be encrypted and protected.

A company should assess whether sensitive information really needs to be stored on a laptop or other portable device. If not, a "wiping" program that overwrites data on the laptop should be used to delete it. Deleting files using standard keyboard commands is not sufficient because data may remain on the laptop's hard drive. Wiping programs are available at most office supply stores.

When laptops or other portable devices are used in an office, employees should be required to avoid leaving them unattended, and to store them in a secure place. The FTC suggests that companies consider using cords and locks to secure laptops to employees' desks.

A company should limit the instances when employees are away from the office with protected information in their possession. When there is a legitimate need for this, the employee should be required to protect the information from being seen by unauthorized persons. Information stored on the device should be encrypted and the device should be password-protected. It should have antivirus software installed on it. The FTC recommends that company laptops and portable devices be configured so that users cannot download any software or change the security settings without the company's approval. The FTC also suggests adding an auto-destroy function so that data on a computer that is reported stolen will be destroyed when the thief uses it to try to access the Internet.

A company's employees should be prohibited from leaving their laptops, smartphones or other devices unattended in public. The FTC has charged companies whose employees left laptops unattended in their cars outside of the office with engaging in unfair trade practices, even when the cars were locked.

Controls are also needed to ensure that network access by portable devices is secure. Computers with remote access to the company's network must have appropriate endpoint security. For example, if a company plans to assign login credentials to a customer who can use them to remotely access protected information, the company first needs to assess the security of the customer's computer system. If hackers can access the customer's computer system, then they may be able to gain access to the login credentials and use them to gain access to protected information in the company's system. The FTC has filed "unfair trade practice" charges on the basis of a company's grant of login credentials to a customer to access protected information without first ensuring that the customer used security measures like firewalls and updated antivirus software.

If a company allows employees to use portable devices to remotely access protected information in the company's possession, then it must ensure that those devices are secure. In one case, the FTC charged a company with engaging in an unfair trade practice for allowing employees to access protected information remotely without ensuring that those devices had antivirus programs installed on them.

The FTC recommends that companies that allow employees to access the company's network remotely only allow remote access to information, not storage of the information on a portable device. Under this approach, the information is stored on a secure central computer and the laptops function as terminals that display information from the central computer, but do not store it. The information could be further protected by requiring the use of a token, smart card, thumb print, or other biometric—as well as a password—to access the central computer.

The FTC also considers it an unfair trade practice to fail to impose reasonable limits on remote access. Remote access should be limited to employees and customers who actually need remote access and access should also be limited to what is needed for the particular purpose. Controls might include such things as restricting connections to specified IP addresses or granting temporary, limited access only.

System access controls (strong password, etc.) are needed regardless of the kind of device that is used to access a system.

Some states, such as Massachusetts, require encryption of any consumer's personal information that is stored on laptops or other portable devices.[141]

TRANSMISSION CONTROLS

Controls are needed to protect the integrity of information and to prevent unauthorized access while it is in transit. Controls are also needed to prevent transmissions of information to unauthorized recipients. Encryption is an example of such a control. The FTC has taken the position that the transmission of protected information in unencrypted, readable text is an unfair and deceptive trade practice. Businesses must use industry-tested and accepted encryption methods. Encryption should also be used when sensitive information is sent via email.

If a company plans to have a wireless network, it should acquire a wireless router that has WiFi Protected Access 2 (WPA2) capability and devices that support WPA2. Wireless routers often come with the encryption feature turned off; it may need to be turned on.

Whichever encryption method is used, it must be configured properly. The FTC has charged companies with engaging in unfair trade practices for turning off a critical process in SSL encryption without implementing other compensating security measures. In some cases, for example, companies turned off SSL certificate validation, leaving apps vulnerable to man-in-the-middle attacks, which could allow hackers to decrypt sensitive information the apps transmit.

WiFi hotspots in coffee shops, libraries, airports, hotels, and other public places usually are not secure. To protect information when using wireless hotspots, information should be sent only to websites that are fully encrypted. Look for 'https' on every page. And avoid using mobile apps that require sharing protected information over public WiFi.

The FTC recommends using Transport Layer Security/Secure Sockets Layer (TLS/SSL) encryption, data-at-rest encryption, or an iterative cryptographic hash to protect sensitive information in transit. Secure transmission should be made automatic when collecting information online directly from customers. A company should caution customers against transmitting sensitive data like account numbers via email or in response to an unsolicited email or pop-up message.

A company should take measures to ensure that data that is secure during transmission remains secure after it is received. Data must be stored securely, too.

Care must be taken when responding to email, phone or other communications requesting protected information. A company must attempt to verify that the requester is a person to whom the information may legally be disclosed. It should be office policy to double-check calls from outside the company requesting protected information (account numbers, etc.) by: (1) verifying that disclosure of the information is legally permissible; and (2) contacting the company using a telephone number that is known to be genuine. Due to the prevalence of spoofing, email communications requesting protected information should always be verified by some means other than replying to the email or using links, telephone numbers, websites or other contact information provided in the email message. Instead, use a known telephone number or other known contact information to verify that the source of the request for the information is genuine.

When doing business with other online businesses (e.g., the company's bank), only give sensitive information to websites that use encryption to protect the information as it travels from the company's computer to the other business's server. Look for 'https' at the beginning of the web address in the address bar.

Some states have enacted laws requiring protected information to be encrypted for transmission. Massachusetts regulations require encryption of any consumer's personal information when transmitting it wirelessly or over a public network.[142] A Nevada statute requires companies doing business in the state to encrypt personal information whenever they transmit it to a person outside of the company's secure system.[143]

In addition to security safeguards of general applicability, the FCRA requires credit reporting agencies to take appropriate security precautions to prevent inappropriate disclosures of consumer credit information. To this end, an agency must require prospective recipients of information to identify themselves, state the purpose for requesting the information, and certify that they will not use the information for an unauthorized purpose.

SYSTEM CHANGE CONTROLS

Controls are needed to ensure that safeguards are not compromised during system, application, computer or storage device changes. The SOX Act requires publicly traded companies to have "change management controls" that include reasonable policies and procedures for adding new computers and users, updating software, installing new software, making changes to databases or other data infrastructure components, and keeping records of what was changed, when it was changed, and who changed it.

RECORD RETENTION CONTROLS

Contracts (including merchant card agreements) often require a business to preserve records of customer transactions for a period of time. Laws sometimes require the retention of particular kinds of records for specified periods of time. Even in the absence of a contractual, statutory or regulatory requirement, periodically backing up data and storing it offline is a prudent business practice.

Backing up computer systems is also beneficial because it can provide a solution in the event a computer or a network of computers is the subject of a ransomware attack. Ransomware is a computer program that locks a user out of files that are stored on the computer and then demands payment of money to regain access. In the typical case, this is effected by means of a computer program that encrypts files stored on the computer's hard drive and displays a message on the user's screen that a specified amount of money (the "ransom") must be paid within a specified amount of time or else the encryption key (the key to unlock the files) will be destroyed. Of course, there is no guarantee that the key will work even if the ransom is paid. In some cases, restoring the files from a backup may be the only way to recover from a ransomware attack.

At least three backup copies should be made, each stored in different locations. For example, a company could backup files to: (1) a backup drive in a company office; (2) an off-site backup drive at another physical location (in case a company office burns down, etc.); and (3) backup using a different type of media (CDs, DVDs, or a cloud-based backup system). Backups should be tested regularly to ensure that files really can be restored from them.

Email messages, website files and other data stored on servers or personal computers should also be backed up regularly. This includes, for example, email messages sent and received through a third party service like Yahoo! or Google Mail. The same is true of financial and other business records. Companies should test these systems regularly to ensure that backups are, in fact, being made and that data can be recovered from them.

On the other hand, records that contain protected consumer information should not be retained after they are no longer needed. For example, a business that obtains a consumer credit report will not ordinarily have any legitimate business need to retain it after it finishes evaluating the consumer's credit application, so the company should not retain it unless doing so is necessary to comply with a legal obligation. Credit card account numbers and the like should not be retained any longer than necessary. According to the FTC, a company should not collect sensitive personally identifying information it does not need, and it should store sensitive personally identifying information for only so long as it has a legitimate business need for the information.

The Children's Online Privacy Protection Act[144] (COPPA) prohibits websites and online service providers from retaining personal information collected from a child under the age of thirteen longer than necessary to fulfill the purpose for which it was collected. For other kinds of information, the FTC decides on a case-by-case basis whether a company's retention of a record was for such an unreasonably long period of time as to amount to an unfair trade practice.

Retaining certain kinds of information, such as Social Security numbers, credit card account numbers and expiration dates, longer than necessary to process a transaction is not often likely to be reasonable inasmuch as doing so raises the risk that the information might be accessed and used to commit fraud or identity theft.

Social Security numbers should only be collected and used for required and lawful purposes, such as reporting employment taxes. They should not be used unnecessarily. They should not be put to use as customer identification numbers, for example.

If a company must keep information for business reasons or to comply with a law, it should develop a written records retention policy to identify what information must be kept, how to secure it, how long to keep it, and how to dispose of it securely when it is no longer needed.

Electronic Communications. The ECPA requires electronic communication service providers and remote computing service providers to comply with a governmental entity's request to preserve records and other evidence in the provider's possession for at least ninety days. A governmental entity may extend the required retention period for an additional ninety days by making a renewed request.

Business Information. The SOX Act makes it a crime to knowingly destroy, alter, falsify or conceal records, documents or objects with the intent to obstruct, impede or influence a federal investigation, agency operation or bankruptcy proceeding. Penalties for a violation may include fines and up to twenty years imprisonment. An accountant who knowingly and intentionally fails to maintain all audit and review documents for a period of five years may be fined and imprisoned up to ten years. This provision applies to both private and publicly traded companies.

The Act also establishes strict record retention obligations for publicly traded companies. These apply to all SOX-related business records, including but not limited to financial records and communications. A repository must be created and maintained for the records. The default record retention period is five years. Accounting and auditing entities, however, must retain all documents and data relating to audit reports of companies required to comply with the SOX Act for seven years. SEC Rule 210.2–06[145] requires accountants and audit committees to keep all records, work papers, and other documents including memoranda, correspondence, and communications for seven years. Accordingly, many companies find it prudent to adopt a seven-year retention period for all SOX-related business and financial records. In any event, a company must maintain the security and integrity of the information in records it stores for as long as the SOX Act requires them to be stored. Noncompliance is a crime punishable by fines and imprisonment.

The SOX Act is a bit vague about the kinds of records that must be retained. Potentially any record containing information relevant to a company's financial reporting comes within the coverage of the Act, including email and other electronic communications. As a result, many companies adopt a policy of erring on the side of overinclusiveness, retaining any and every record that might possibly have even the remotest bearing on financial reporting. At a minimum, a company should retain the following kinds of records:

- Contracts
- Insurance policies
- Intellectual property

- Licenses and other intellectual property transactions
- Financial information
- Audit records
- Official correspondence
- Policies and procedures
- Human resources and personnel files
- Any records that must be kept to meet government retention, reporting and compliance requirements
- Any other essential business documents that are used in the course of the business and its management.

If a company permits instant messaging as a means of communication, then instant message logs may also need to be retained. Of course, if a legal proceeding or investigation is pending or reasonably anticipated, then all records containing relevant information or information that may lead to admissible evidence must be retained whether they fit into one of the above categories or not.

The SOX Act does not require certain kinds of records to be retained, and retaining them may actually increase a company's exposure to liability. Documents in this category include personal correspondence and email messages, document drafts, doodles, and the like. These documents should be destroyed unless there is a court order or litigation hold requiring their preservation or they are relevant or may lead to the discovery of admissible evidence in a pending or foreseeable investigation or proceeding.

A company's document retention/destruction policy must be clearly written and effectively communicated to staff with the goal of strict adherence to the law, including but not limited to laws specifying the length of time records must be kept, laws imposing an obligation to preserve evidence, and laws requiring secure disposal of protected information.

To ensure compliance with the SOX Act, a company should have an effective backup and archive solution for electronic records, including but not limited to relevant email communications. To reduce the risk of loss of stored data, a company should ensure that proper care is taken of storage media, that adequate data recovery protocols are in place, and that multiple backups and archives are created and kept in different locations.

Health Records. "Covered entities" (health care providers, health insurance firms, and health care clearing houses) are subject to HIPAA record retention requirements. The preservation period for health and health care records varies between five to six years. There are also statutes that require the retention of such records throughout the life of the patient and for two years after the patient's death. Records of disclosures of protected health and health care information must be kept for three years.

HIPAA also requires covered entities to retain various kinds of documents for the purpose of documenting compliance and to respond to requests. These include such things as policies and procedural documentation (e.g., privacy notices, consents, and other forms); patient requests for access, corrections or records of health information disclosures; documentation relating to the handling of patient or employee complaints; training programs and materials. This is not an exhaustive list.

A covered entity not only must retain health records; it must also make backup copies and establish a disaster recovery and emergency mode operation plan. Among other things, this means it must ensure that emergency access to the information is available. This can be a problem if email messages containing such information are only stored in regular email folders. If the email sever goes down, it will not be possible to access the information in an emergency. For this and other reasons, a covered entity may find it prudent to engage the services of an email archiving service.

Information Collected from Children Under 13. See Chapter 18.

Particular Businesses and Professions. A number of regulatory agencies have enacted rules or regulations requiring the businesses over which they have jurisdiction to preserve documents, including email messages and other electronic documents, for a specified period of time. Licensed stock brokers, for example, must retain records of all communications with clients for a period of at least three years, and in some cases, six years. Record retention regulations exist for businesses in certain other industries, too. In fact, it is probably safe to say that most businesses in most industries are subject to an administrative record retention requirement of one kind or another. To give just one example, SEC and NASD rules require broker/dealer organizations to retain all records, including email messages, pertaining to their trading activity for at least six years.

Administrative regulations vary widely by jurisdiction and industry. Common to nearly all of them, though, are requirements to retain records in an unaltered state; to safeguard them from security threats and unauthorized access; to protect them from being damaged or destroyed; and to make them available to a regulatory authority for auditing.

RECORD DISPOSAL CONTROLS

In general, when a law or regulation requires a business to maintain the privacy or security of information, the business must also take care to dispose of it in a secure way when the time comes. Under the FTC's Disposal Rule,[146] enacted pursuant to the Fair and Accurate Credit Transactions Act[147] (FACTA), special care must be taken to ensure that consumer reports are disposed of securely. The Rule requires any person or business that is in possession of a consumer report (or information from one) for a business purpose to take reasonable measures to protect it from unauthorized access during the disposal of it. The Rule applies to both individuals and to businesses of any kind, not just financial institutions. *Consumer report* includes both credit reports and investigative reports ("background checks.") Financial institutions and businesses that receive information from a financial institution should incorporate disposal procedures and policies into their data security program, as the GLBA Safeguards Rule requires.

Secure disposal of records may include such techniques as:

- burning
- shredding
- erasing data on electronic media or hardware
- hiring a records retention manager to supervise the disposal of records or contracting with an outside records disposal company that has been certified by a recognized industry group.

Records stored on devices also need to be disposed of securely. This includes computers, disks, CDs, magnetic tape, offline storage devices, PDAs, cell phones, and any other electronic media or hardware. When disposing of old computers and portable storage devices, a company should use a "wipe utility" software program for securely erasing data from them. Deleting files using the keyboard or mouse commands usually is not sufficient because the files may continue to exist on the computer's hard drive and often can be easy to retrieve.

Digital printers and copiers may contain protected information, too. When a digitally stored document is sent to a digital printer for printing, the file is copied to the device and remains there until it is either overwritten or the hard drive is removed or destroyed. A computer or digital printer or copier should not be sold, donated or otherwise transferred to a third party with protected information on it. The FTC suggests establishing an office policy of overwriting the hard drive of a printer/copier on a monthly basis.

A company should ensure that employees who work from home follow the same procedures for disposing of sensitive documents and old computers and portable storage devices.

EMPLOYEE TRAINING

A company should require every new employee to sign an agreement to follow the company's confidentiality and security standards for handling sensitive data, and should train employees to maintain the security, confidentiality and integrity of customer information. Ensure that they understand that abiding by the company's data security plan is an essential part of their duties. Regularly remind employees of the company's policy—and any legal requirement—to keep customer information secure and confidential. Update employees about new risks and vulnerabilities. There should be a regular schedule of employee training. Ensure that training includes employees at satellite offices, temporary help, and seasonal workers. If employees do not attend, consider blocking their access to the network.

Training should cover the need to protect passwords and how to do that. Employees should be advised to refrain from sharing them with others or posting them near workstations. Training should cover the possibility that identity thieves may attempt to deceive them into giving out their passwords by impersonating members of the company's IT or support staff. Let employees know that communications requesting passwords are always fraudulent, and that no one should be asking them to reveal their passwords.

Employees should be educated about identity theft and the methods that are used to commit it. Caution them against transmitting sensitive personally identifying data—Social Security numbers, passwords, account information, and the like—via email. Unencrypted email is not a secure way to transmit information. Teach employees about the dangers of spear phishing—emails containing information that makes the emails look legitimate. These emails may appear to come from someone within the company, generally someone in a position of authority, to trick an employee into sharing sensitive information.

Also warn employees about phone phishing. Train them to be suspicious of unknown callers claiming to need account numbers to process an order or asking for customer or employee contact information. Employees should be instructed that the identities of callers who request protected information need to be verified, and to refrain from responding to email messages requesting protected information. A company should consider requiring employees to refer calls or other requests for customer information to designated individuals who have been trained in how the company safeguards personal data and to report suspicious attempts to obtain customer information to designated personnel.

Tell employees about the company's policies regarding keeping information secure and confidential. Post reminders in areas where sensitive information is used or stored, as well as where employees congregate. Employees should be instructed to lock rooms and file cabinets where records are kept.

Make sure the company's policies cover employees who telecommute or access sensitive data from home or an offsite location. Train employees to be mindful of security when they're on the road. They should avoid transmitting protected information via public networks, but they should be instructed that if it becomes necessary to do that, then sensitive customer information must be encrypted when it is transmitted electronically via public networks

Employees should be instructed to never leave a laptop visible in a car, at a hotel luggage stand, or packed in checked luggage unless directed to by airport security. Everyone who goes through airport security should keep an eye on their laptop as it goes on the belt. If an employee must leave a laptop in a car, it should be locked in a trunk. Require employees to notify a supervisor immediately if there is a potential security breach, such as a lost or stolen laptop.

Train employees to spot security vulnerabilities and threats. Tell them how to report suspicious activity. Publicly reward employees who do so. The FTC has video presentations available at their website explaining security vulnerabilities and how to reduce data security risks. Training should also cover policies for responding to security breaches and potential security breaches, and secure disposal of information.

A company should impose disciplinary measures for security policy violations.

MONITORING AND UPDATING

A security program should include monitoring for unauthorized intrusion or access and detection and protection against viruses and other malware or system attacks. Controls may involve logging and audit controls, monitoring web traffic, system activity reviews, an automatic intrusion detection system, and frequently updated antivirus software.

A company should use an intrusion detection system and monitor system logs for suspicious activity. In addition, up-to-date anti-malware programs should be run on individual computers and on servers on the company's network. The websites of software vendors and the U.S. Computer Emergency Readiness Team should be checked regularly for alerts about new vulnerabilities. A company should establish and implement a policy for installing updates and vendor-approved patches to correct problems.

Intrusion detection systems need to be updated frequently to address new types of hacking.

Incoming traffic should be monitored for signs that someone is trying to hack in. Unrecognized new users, multiple login attempts from unknown users or computers, and higher-than-average traffic at unusual times of the day, could be indicators of hacking attempts. Outgoing traffic should also be monitored. Unexpectedly large amounts of data being transmitted from the company's system to an unknown user should be investigated.

Regularly ensure that ports not used for business are closed, and promptly pass along information and instructions to employees regarding any new security risks or possible breaches.

Identity Theft Detection and Mitigation. Pursuant to FACTA, the FTC has issued a Red Flags Rule[148] requiring creditors and financial institutions with covered accounts to implement a written identity theft prevention program that is designed to detect warning signs of identity theft, to prevent it, and to mitigate damage from it. (For a list of examples of red flags, visit the FTC website.) The program must include each of the following:

(a) reasonable policies and procedures to identify the kinds of suspicious activity that could indicate identity theft (red flags)
(b) methods for detecting red flags
(c) response to red flags when they are detected
(d) updates to the program to keep it current.

Covered accounts include checking, savings, credit card and loan accounts and any kind of account a creditor maintains for which there is a reasonably foreseeable risk to customers or to the safety and soundness of the financial institution or creditor from identity theft.

A creditor is any business that (a) bills, defers payment, or extends credit to customers, and (b) regularly uses information from a credit report in connection with a credit transaction, reports information to a credit bureau, or advances funds to customers with the expectation of repayment.

Advancing funds does not include paying incidental expenses in connection with services provided to customers, even if a client is billed for them. Also, merely accepting credit cards as payment for goods or services does not, by itself, make a company a creditor.

OTHER READILY AVAILABLE SECURITY MEASURES

Other security measures the FTC regards as readily available and commonly used, and therefore reasonable, include: practices described in documentation for software manufacturers and developers, and measures recommended by security experts to address risks of a software program collecting sensitive information in an unauthorized manner.

PEER-TO-PEER FILE SHARING

Peer-to-Peer (P2P) technology enables computers using the same or compatible P2P programs to form a network and share digital files directly with other computers on the network. Users can designate the drives and folders where files are shared. BitTorrent is an example. They pose a risk to security because users can accidentally share drives or folders that contain protected information, or share a file with protected information to a shared driver or folder. Further, malware could change the drivers or folders designated for sharing. Once another user has downloaded an inadvertently shared file, it cannot be retrieved or deleted. If there are security vulnerabilities in the P2P software or the network, there may be attacks on other computers in the network. For these reasons, a company should adopt an appropriate P2P policy to minimize these risks. The FTC recommends the following controls:

(a) Eliminate the use of P2P file sharing programs on computers that are used to store or access protected information.
(b) Restrict where files with sensitive information may be saved.

(c) Delete protected information when it is no longer needed.
(d) Use appropriate file-naming conventions.
(e) Monitor the company's network to detect unapproved P2P programs.
(f) Block traffic associated with unapproved P2P file sharing programs at the network perimeter or network firewalls.
(g) Train employees and others who access the company's network about the security risks in using P2P programs.

Eliminating P2P programs may entail using administrative security controls to block access to sites that are used to download P2P programs. Sites may be filtered based on URL, IP address, filename and content. There are also commercial products that are available for this purpose. Controls should also block access to sites that offer free software downloads, inasmuch as these sites often are sources of P2P programs. Administrative security controls may be used to prevent employees from installing unapproved programs on the company's computers.

The FTC also recommends using network monitoring tools and techniques like flow reconstruction to identify whether the company's network has P2P traffic and to determine the nature of files that have been sent to and from the network using P2P file sharing programs. Reviewing records and activity logs may help identify traffic volume spikes that could indicate large files or a large number of small files are being shared.

Another idea is to install data loss prevention tools that inspect files flowing from the network to determine whether they contain certain types of sensitive information, like Social Security numbers. Regularly review the records these tools create to determine whether sensitive information is being exported.

Using application-level encryption to protect the information in files is another useful idea. This type of encryption can help protect files that are shared inadvertently on P2P networks.

Employees should not be permitted to store protected customer information on their personal computers, even if they work remotely. The company should issue company computers for remote workers. Require remote access to proceed only through secure connections to the organization's network, like Virtual Private Network (VPN) software or SSL. This is appropriate for employees who telecommute, or for customers or suppliers who need regular access to the company's system.

Restrict the locations to which work files containing sensitive information may be saved or copied, and permit remote users to access, use or modify the files – but not to download them. Train employees about P2P security risks.

CONTRACTS WITH THIRD PARTIES

Generally, a company should not allow third parties to access customer information. It is becoming increasingly common, however, for businesses to outsource operations that require access to protected information—collections, payroll, customer service, data processing, payment processing, and so on. When this is done, it is necessary to implement measures to reduce the risk that the persons and businesses with whom a company contracts for services will divulge, either intentionally or inadvertently, protected information to unauthorized persons.

Reasonable measures for the protection of information to which a third party has access begin with investigating the third party's data security practices and, if possible, visiting their facilities.

Be candid about security expectations. Take reasonable steps to select service providers that are able to implement appropriate security measures.

Next, put the company's security expectations in writing in contracts with service providers. Contract provisions aimed at preventing intentional misuse or disclosure of information should prohibit disclosure of protected information to others without the prior notification and approval of the company. The authorized uses of the information should be specified in the contract. Any other uses should be prohibited.

Contract provisions aimed at preventing inadvertent misuse or disclosure should require the third party to implement reasonable security measures to prevent unauthorized access to the information. Security expectations should be spelled out explicitly in the contract. The contract should also require the third party to notify the company of any security incidents it experiences, even if the incidents may not have led to an actual compromise of company data.

The company should verify third party compliance with its security obligations. The contract should provide for some mechanism of oversight. Even if it doesn't, the company should take the initiative to check whether the third party is complying with its security obligations.

Third party security also needs to be addressed when a company grants customers or other individuals remote access to the company's computer network. Computers with remote access to the company's network must have appropriate endpoint security. For example, if the company plans to assign login credentials to a customer who can use them to remotely access protected information, then the company first needs to assess the security of the customer's computer system. If hackers can access the customer's computer system, then they may be able to gain access to the login credentials and use them to gain access to protected information in the company's system. The FTC has filed "unfair trade practice" charges on the basis of a company's grant of login credentials to a customer to access protected information without first ensuring that the customer used security measures like firewalls and updated antivirus software.

Encryption should be used if the company allows remote access to the company's computer network by customers, employees or service providers. The FTC recommends requiring .multi-factor authentication for access to the company's network.

COPPA imposes restrictions on the sharing of information collected from children under thirteen years of age. See Chapter 18.

The GLBA Safeguards Rule imposes the following obligations on financial institutions and those who receive information from them:

(a) Select service providers that can maintain appropriate safeguards.
(b) Ensure that contracts with such service providers require them to maintain safeguards.
(c) Oversee such service providers' handling of customer information.

RESPONDING TO SECURITY BREACHES

A reasonable security program needs to address both the prevention of security breaches and the handling of breaches if and when they occur. A company should have a breach response plan in place to reduce the impact of a security breach on the company, employees, and customers. The plan should designate a person within the company to coordinate and implement it. Either this person or another person within the company should be designated as a point person for releasing information about the breach, the company's response to it, and advice to affected persons about how they should respond. The response plan should also include the following measures:

(1) Contact the company's attorney. If the company's attorney does not have expertise in data security and privacy, hire outside legal counsel.
(2) Notify law enforcement immediately.
(3) Verify the types of information compromised, the number of people affected, and whether the company has contact information for those people.
(4) Notify the appropriate persons. Comply with all breach notification laws. These may require notifying some or all of the following: law enforcement, a specified regulatory agency, customers, consumers, credit bureaus, businesses that may be affected by the breach, and/or media. Even in the absence of a specific law, any individual who may be affected by the breach should be notified.
(5) Investigate immediately and take steps to close off existing vulnerabilities or threats to personal information. The steps that should be taken to prevent further data loss will depend on the nature of the breach and the structure of the business.
(6) Compromised computers and equipment should be disconnected from the network immediately. Machines should not be turned off, however, until forensic experts arrive and confirm that they may be turned off.
(7) Secure physical areas potentially related to the breach. Lock them and change access codes, if needed. Ask forensics experts and law enforcement when it is reasonable to resume regular operations.
(8) Assemble a team of experts to participate in the breach response. Depending on the size of the business, they may include forensics, legal, information security, information technology, operations, human resources, communications, investor relations, and management.
(9) Consider hiring independent forensic investigators to help determine the source and scope of the breach. They will capture forensic images of affected systems, collect and analyze evidence, and outline remediation steps.
(10) Closely monitor all entry and exit points, especially those involved in the breach. If possible, put clean machines online in place of affected ones.
(11) Change the credentials and passwords of authorized users.
(12) Remove improperly posted information from the web.
(13) Contact search engines to ensure they do not archive personal information posted in error.
(14) Search for the company's exposed data to make sure that no other websites have saved a copy. If any are found, contact those sites and ask them to remove it.
(15) Interview the people who discovered the breach and anyone else who may know about it.
(16) If the company has a customer service center, make sure the staff knows where to forward information that may aid the investigation of the breach.
(17) Document the investigation of the breach.
(18) Do not destroy evidence.
(19) Fix vulnerabilities

At a minimum, "fixing vulnerabilities" means doing the following things:

(a) If service providers were involved, examine what personal information they can access and decide if their access privileges need to be changed. Also, ensure that service providers are taking the necessary steps to make sure another breach does not occur. If service providers say they have remedied vulnerabilities, verify that they really have fixed things.

(b) Check the company's network segmentation. Work with forensics experts to analyze whether the company's segmentation plan was effective in containing the breach. Make any needed changes.

(c) Check to see if measures such as encryption were enabled. If not, enable them.

(d) Analyze backup or preserved data. Review logs to determine who had access to the data at the time of the breach. Also, analyze who currently has access, determine whether that access is needed, and restrict access if it is not.

(e) Take any remedial measures recommended by the forensic experts as soon as possible.

Notification of security breaches

When security is breached, law enforcement should be contacted immediately to report the situation and the potential risk for identity theft. If the local police are not familiar with investigating information compromises, contact the local office of the Federal Bureau of Investigation (FBI) or the U.S. Secret Service. For incidents involving mail theft, contact the U.S. Postal Inspection Service. When in doubt, a company should err on the side of over-reporting rather than under-reporting.

A company should create a comprehensive communications plan that reaches all affected persons—employees, customers, investors, business partners, and other stakeholders—as well as any agencies, persons and entities the company may be required by law to notify. If a security breach compromises identifying information (e.g., bank or credit card account numbers) obtained from another business, the other business should be notified. If account access information—e.g., credit card or bank account numbers—has been stolen but the account is with an issuer or another third party, then notify the institution that maintains the account so it can monitor the account for fraudulent activity. If the company collects or stores personal information on behalf of other businesses, notify them of the data breach.

If names and Social Security numbers have been stolen, contact the major credit bureaus for additional information or advice. If the compromise may involve a large group of people, advise the credit bureaus if the company is recommending that people request fraud alerts and credit freezes for their files. The major credit bureaus are Equifax, Experian, TransUnion, and .Innovis Consider using letters, websites, and toll free numbers to communicate with people whose information may have been compromised. If the company does not have contact information for all of the affected individuals, it could build an extensive public relations campaign into the communication plan, including press releases or other news media notification.

Consult with law enforcement about the timing of the notice and about what information to include in it so the notice does not impede an investigation.

In general, unless an applicable law provides otherwise, a breach notification should:

(a) Describe what is known about the breach, including: (i) how it happened; (ii) what information was taken; and (iii) how the thieves have used the information, if known.

(b) Describe what actions the company has taken to remedy the situation.

(c) Describe what actions the company is taking to protect individuals, such as offering free credit monitoring services.

(d) Explain how to reach the relevant contact person in the company.

(e) Tell people what steps they can take to prevent and recover from identity theft, given the type of information exposed, and provide relevant contact information. People whose Social Security numbers have been stolen should be advised to contact credit bureaus to ask that fraud alerts or credit freezes be placed on their credit reports and to contact the IRS Identity Protection Specialized Unit at 1–800-908–4490. For more information about appropriate follow-up steps for consumers,, visit https://identitytheft.gov/. The FTC recommends adding this information as an attachment to the breach notification letter.

(f) Provide information about the law enforcement agency that is working on the case, if the law enforcement agency agrees it would be helpful.

(g) Encourage people who discover that their information has been misused to file a complaint with the FTC, using IdentityTheft.gov. This information is entered into the Consumer Sentinel Network, a secure, online database.

(h) Describe how the company will contact consumers in the future. For example, if the company will only contact consumers by mail, then say so. If the company will never call them about the breach, then let them know. This information may help victims avoid phishing scams tied to the breach. Some organizations tell consumers that updates will be posted on their website.

The FTC recommends that companies consider offering at least a year of free credit monitoring or other support such as identity theft protection or identity restoration services, particularly if financial information or Social Security numbers were exposed.

Most states have breach notification laws that specify the information that must be provided in a breach notification. Some also specify things that a company may not include in it.

Notifications should be truthful and should not be misleading. Key details that might help consumers protect themselves and their information should not be omitted, no matter how poorly they may reflect on the company, its security personnel, or its employees. Anticipate questions that people will ask. Then, put top tier questions and clear, plain-language answers on the company's website where they are easy to find.

Early notification is important. People who are notified early may be able to take steps to prevent or limit damage.

Model letters are available from the FTC.

STATE BREACH NOTIFICATION LAWS

Most states and territories have enacted laws requiring notifications to be given, not just to law enforcement, but also to affected persons when security breaches involving personal information occur. Some require that specified regulatory agencies be notified, as well. Nearly every state mandates disclosure to state governmental authorities and affected individuals—and sometimes to the media—of security breaches involving any personally identifiable information that is stored by or for a business. These laws are enforceable by regulatory agencies.

The California breach notification law is an example. It requires a business to immediately disclose a data breach to customers who reside in the state. If the person or business providing the notification was the source of the breach, it must offer to provide appropriate identity theft prevention and mitigation services, if any, at no cost to the affected person for not less than twelve months. A security breach is defined as an unauthorized acquisition of computerized data that compromises the confidentiality or integrity of personal information. For purposes of this law, personal information includes a person's last name and first name (or initial) if it is combined with a Social Security number, driver license number, California Identification Card number, or an account number or credit or debit card number (when the account number is coupled with any required password, security code or access code that permits access to a person's financial account). The California law now also includes compromised medical and health insurance information.

Notification must be given in the most expedient time possible and without unreasonable delay. It may be provided in writing or electronically. If provided electronically, it must comply with the E-SIGN Act. If the cost of providing notice would be over $250,000 or if more than 500,000 notifications would be required, or if contact information is not available, then the company may provide substitute notice. Substitute notice consists of all of the following: (a) email notice, if an email address is available; (b) website notice; and (c) notification sent to major statewide media for publication.

The notification obligation and the obligation to offer free identity theft prevention services are triggered when the security of unencrypted personal information is breached. This gives businesses an incentive to encrypt personal information.

Many states have enacted laws following the basic tenets of the California law. Under these laws, companies must immediately disclose a data breach to customers, usually in writing. The specifics and procedural requirements vary from state to state.

California also provides a statutory cause of action for damages for any data subject who is adversely affected by a breach. A common law cause of action for negligence may also be possible in California and some other states if a user/customer suffers an economic loss as a result of negligent failure to secure the privacy of data or negligent failure to notify the user/customer of a breach of security. The mere risk of being an identity theft victim is not a compensable economic loss, however. Actual damage must be proven. Actual damage may occur where someone did, in fact, exploit the security breach to commit theft of a user's or consumer's money. The California law applies to any business that has customers in California.

Depending on the type of business and the types of information involved in the breach, there may be additional laws or regulations that apply. A company should check applicable state and federal laws and regulations for specific requirements.

PUBLICLY TRADED COMPANIES

The SOX Act requires publicly traded companies to perform periodic audits to ensure that procedures and mechanisms exist for remediating security breaches when they occur. Guidance issued by national banking regulators encourage certain financial institutions to notify customers and the appropriate banking regulator if customer information may have been misused.

HEALTH INFORMATION

Federal laws require notifications of security breaches involving health or health care information. Entities to which HIPAA applies must comply with the HIPAA Breach Notification Rule. Businesses to which HIPAA does not apply must comply with the FTC's Health Breach Notification Rule.

HIPAA BREACH NOTIFICATION RULE

The Health Information Technology for Economic and Clinical Health Act[149] (HITECH Act) requires HIPAA covered entities and their business associates to give notifications following breaches of the security of health information. The notices must be sent to the affected individuals, the covered entity, and the Secretary of Health and Human Services. For a breach affecting more than 500 residents of a state or jurisdiction, the covered entity must provide notice to prominent media outlets serving the state or jurisdiction. Regulations detail additional requirements regarding the form, timing and manner of service of the notice. Covered entities must also report security incidents, i.e., attempted or successful unauthorized access, use, disclosure, modification, or destruction of information or interference with system operations in an information system. Any covered entity that experiences a data security breach must maintain a log of such breaches and submit it annually to the DHHS.

The DHHS has enacted a HIPAA Breach Notification Rule[150] to implement the HITECH Act. It requires HIPAA-covered entities to notify people whose unsecured health information is breached.

Under the Rule, a business associate of a HIPAA-covered entity is also required to provide notifications of breaches, but the obligation is slightly different. A business associate must promptly notify the HIPAA-covered entity when the business associate experiences a security breach. The HIPAA-covered entity must then notify the people affected by the breach. The business associate's notification must be given to the covered entity without unreasonable delay and not more than sixty days from the discovery of the breach. To the extent possible, the business associate should provide the covered entity with the identification of each individual affected by the breach as well as any other available information required to be provided by the covered entity in its notification to affected individuals. A business associate of a HIPAA-covered entity is a business that handles protected health information of HIPAA-covered entities only, not health information from other sources.

The Rule applies only to health information that is not secured through technologies specified by the DHHS. The DHHS has defined unsecured information to include any information that is not encrypted or destroyed.

The HIPAA Breach Notification Rule and associated forms are available at:
hhs.gov/hipaa/for-professionals/breach-notification

THE FTC'S HEALTH BREACH NOTIFICATION RULE

The American Recovery and Reinvestment Act of 2009[151] includes provisions to strengthen privacy and security protections in connection with web-based businesses that deal with health information. The FTC has issued a Health Breach Notification Rule[152] to implement this law. The

Rule requires certain companies that have had a security breach involving health or health care information to provide notifications as specified in the Rule.

The Rule only applies to companies that are not "covered entities" under HIPAA. In case of a security breach, entities covered by HIPAA must comply with the DHHS's HIPAA Breach Notification Rule. The FTC's Health Breach Notification Rule applies only to:

- Vendors of personal health records (PHRs)
- PHR-related entities
- Third party service providers for a vendor of PHRs or for a PHR-related entity.

A *personal health record* (PHR) is an electronic record of identifiable health information on an individual that can include information from multiple sources and that is managed, shared, and controlled by or primarily for the individual. For example, an online service that allows consumers to store and organize medical information in one online location is a vendor of personal health records, unless the service is covered by HIPAA. A *vendor of personal health records* is a person or business that offers or maintains a personal health record.

A PHR-related entity is a business that interacts with a vendor of personal health records either by offering products or services through the vendor's website—even if the site is covered by HIPAA—or by accessing information in a personal health record or sending information to a personal health record. Many businesses that offer web-based apps for health information fall into this category. For example, a business that offers an app that helps consumers manage their medications or lets them upload readings from a device like a pedometer or a blood pressure cuff into a personal health record is a PHR-related entity. On the other hand, if consumers can simply input their own information on the company's site in a way that does not interact with personal health records offered by a vendor—for example, if the site just allows consumers to input their weight each week to track their fitness goals—then the business is not a PHR-related entity. Also, a business is not a PHR-related entity if it is covered by HIPAA.

A business is a third party service provider if it offers services involving the use, maintenance, disclosure, or disposal of health information to vendors of personal health records or PHR-related entities. For example, if a vendor of personal health records hires a business to provide billing, debt collection, or data storage services related to health information, the business is a third party service provider, and is covered by the Rule.

The Rule applies only to health information that is not secured through technologies specified by the DHHS. The DHHS has defined unsecured information to include any information that is not encrypted or destroyed.

The notification obligation arises when there has been an unauthorized acquisition of PHR-identifiable health information that is unsecured and in a personal health record.

An unauthorized acquisition occurs when information is acquired by someone without the affected person's consent. Where there has been unauthorized access, unauthorized acquisition is presumed unless the company can show that it has not taken place or could not reasonably have taken place. For example, if an employee accesses a customer's personal health record without authorization, the Rule presumes that because the data was accessed, it has been "acquired," and the company must follow the breach notification provisions of the Rule. But the presumption may be overcome by establishing and enforcing a company policy that says that if an employee inadvertently accesses a health record, he or she must not read or share the information, must log out immediately, and then must report the access to a supervisor right away. If the employee denies having read or shared the information and the company conducts a reasonable investigation that corroborates the employee's version of events, then the presumption is rebutted and notification is not required. If a laptop containing personal health records is lost and is later recovered, the presumption of unauthorized acquisition may be rebutted if forensic analysis shows that files were not opened, altered, transferred, or otherwise compromised.

PHR-identifiable health information is health information that identifies someone or could reasonably be used to identify someone. A personal health record is an electronic health record that can be drawn from multiple sources and that is managed, shared, and controlled by or primarily for the individual. If a business experiences a breach involving only paper health records, the FTC's Rule does not require any notification. A state law might require notification, however.

Obligations of PHR Vendors and PHR-Related Entities. When a vendor of personal health records (PHRs) or a PHR-related entity experiences a breach, and the Rule applies, notification of the breach must be given to all of the following:

- each affected person
- the FTC
- in some cases, the media.

Notification must be given to each affected person without unreasonable delay and within sixty calendar days after the breach is discovered or reasonably should have been discovered. The timing of the notice to the FTC depends on the number of people affected. If the breach involves the information of 500 people or more, then the FTC must be notified as soon as possible and within ten business days after discovering the breach. The form at www.ftc.gov/tips-advice/business-center/guidance/health-breach-notification-rule must be used to report the breach to the agency. If the breach involves the information of fewer than 500 people, the same form must be used but there is more time to send it in. It must be sent to the FTC within sixty calendar days following the end of the calendar year. Any other breaches during the same calendar year involving fewer than 500 people must also be reported within that time frame.

The media must be notified when at least 500 residents of a particular state, the District of Columbia, or a U.S. territory or possession are affected by a breach. In these cases, the company must notify prominent media outlets serving the relevant locale, including Internet media where appropriate, without unreasonable delay and within sixty calendar days after the breach is discovered. The notice to media is a supplement to the notice to people whose information was breached, not a substitute for individual notices.

Obligations of Third Party Service Providers. A company that is a third party service provider to a vendor of personal health records or a PHR-related entity also has some notification obligations. The Rule requires vendors of PHRs and PHR-related entities who are covered by the Rule to inform third party service providers of this fact. If a third party service provider experiences a breach, it must notify an official designated in its contract with the vendor or PHR-related entity—or if there is no designee, a senior official of the company—without unreasonable delay and within sixty calendar days of discovering the breach. The third party service provider must identify each person whose information may be involved in the breach. The third party service provider must get an acknowledgment that the vendor or PHR-related entity received the notice. They, in turn, must notify the people affected by the breach, the FTC, and in certain cases, the media.

NOTIFICATION METHODS

The best practice in notifying people is to find out from them in advance—perhaps when they sign up for a service—if they would prefer to hear about a security breach by email or by first class mail. If only email addresses are collected from customers, the company might send them a message—or let new customers know when they sign up—that the company intends to contact them by email about any security breaches. If the company plans to use email as the default method, it must give customers the opportunity to choose first class mail notification instead and that option must be clear and conspicuous. If email is a customer's preference, explain how to set up any spam filters so they will get the company's messages.

If the company is unable or fails to contact ten or more people (e.g., because of insufficient or outdated contact information) then it must provide substitute notice through a clear and conspicuous posting for 90 days on the company's home page or a notice in major print or broadcast media where those people likely live. Both of these forms of substitute notice must include a toll free phone number that has to be active for at least 90 days so people can call to find out if their information was affected by the breach.

Contents of Notification. The notice to individuals must be easy to understand and must include the following information:

(a) a brief description of what happened, including the date of the breach (if known) and the date the breach was discovered
(b) the kind of PHR-identifiable health information involved in the breach (e.g., insurance information, Social Security numbers, financial account data, dates of birth, medication information, etc.)
(c) a brief description of the steps the company is taking to investigate the breach, protect against future breaches, and mitigate the harm from the breach
(d) how people can contact the company for more information (including a toll free telephone number, email address, website, or mailing address)
(e) suggested steps people can take to protect themselves (if the breach puts people at risk for identity theft or other possible harm).

The suggested steps for people to take to protect themselves needs to be relevant to the kind of information that was compromised. In some cases, for example, it may be appropriate to refer people to the FTC's identity theft website, www.ftc.gov/idtheft. If the breach involves health insurance information, it may also be appropriate to advice people to contact their health care providers if bills do not arrive on time, in case an identity thief has changed the billing address; to pay attention to the Explanation of Benefit forms from their insurance company to check for irregularities; and to contact their insurance company to notify them of possible medical identity theft or to ask for a new account number. If the breach includes Social Security numbers, it may be appropriate to suggest that people get a free copy of their credit report from www.annualcreditreport.com, monitor it for signs of identity theft, and place a fraud alert on their credit report. They should be advised to contact their local police and, if appropriate, order a credit freeze if they spot suspicious activity. If the breach includes financial information—e.g., a credit card or bank account number—it may be appropriate to suggest that people monitor their accounts for suspicious activity and contact their financial institution about closing any accounts that may have been compromised.

A standard form for notifying the FTC of a breach is available at the FTC website.

Many states have enacted breach notification and/or health breach notification laws. The FTC's Rule preempts contradictory state breach notification laws, but not those that impose additional breach notification requirements that are not in conflict with the FTC's Rule. For example, some state laws require breach notices to include advice on monitoring credit reports or contact information for consumer reporting agencies. While these content requirements are different from the FTC Rule's requirements, they are not contradictory. In this example, a company could comply with both federal and state requirements by including all the information in a single breach notice. The FTC Rule does not require a company to send multiple breach notices to comply with state and federal laws.

The FTC treats each violation of the Rule as an unfair or deceptive act or practice in violation of the FTC Act and regulations enacted pursuant to it. Businesses that violate the Rule may be subject to a civil penalty of up to $41,484 per violation.

PROGRAM REVIEW AND ADJUSTMENT

A data security program should include mechanisms for monitoring and testing the effectiveness of the security controls to make sure they are operating as intended. Periodic adjustments for changing threats, vulnerabilities, business operations and industry trends also need to be made. Sometimes the FTC requires a company to hire an independent, qualified professional for these purposes.

If third party software is used, or if third party software libraries are included in the company's applications, apply patches and updates as they are issued. Outdated software undermines security. This is especially important for antivirus software.

A company must have a process for receiving and addressing reports about security vulnerabilities. Credible security warnings should be heeded and steps should be taken quickly to fix them. Consider a clearly publicized and effective channel (for example, a dedicated email address like security(@)yourcompany.com) for receiving reports and flagging them for security staff.

The GLBA Safeguards Rule requires financial institutions and companies that receive information from them to regularly monitor and test their data security programs, and to evaluate and adjust programs in light of relevant circumstances, including changes in the firm's business or operations, or the results of security testing and monitoring.

Guidance issued by the Federal Financial Institutions Examination Council (FFIEC) recommends that websites of financial institutions measure and evaluate customer awareness, and adjust their data security programs in light of relevant changes in technology, the sensitivity of customer information, and internal or external threats to data.

For publicly traded companies, the SOX Act requires an independent, external SOX auditor to review controls, policies, and procedures. Log collection and monitoring systems must provide an audit trail of all access to and activity with sensitive business information. An audit must check to see that proper controls are in place to prevent data breaches and that procedures and mechanisms exist to remediate security breaches when they occur.

The Obligation to Preserve Evidence

Various laws establish an obligation to preserve everything, including electronic records, that might be relevant evidence in a pending or future investigation or legal proceeding.

SPOLIATION OF EVIDENCE

Spoliating evidence means intentionally or negligently destroying, altering, fabricating, hiding, losing or withholding evidence relevant to a legal proceeding. In many jurisdictions it is a crime if it is done intentionally. In some states, there is a common law obligation to preserve potential evidence, including electronically stored information, as soon as it becomes reasonably foreseeable that the information may be relevant to future litigation. Some states prohibit only intentional spoliation. Other states prohibit negligent spoliation, too, provided the persons sought to be held accountable had a duty to preserve the evidence.

Even in states that do not authorize a tort action, courts may impose sanctions on a party to a proceeding to which the evidence relates if she participated in the spoliation. One such sanction is the spoliation inference. This permits a judge or a jury to draw a negative inference from a party's spoliation of evidence. The reasoning is that it can reasonably be assumed that a person who intentionally conceals, alters or destroys evidence must have something relevant and damaging to hide. A court is not likely to impose this sanction for merely inadvertent or negligent spoliation. Some evidence of bad faith intent must exist. A court may impose stronger sanctions for bad faith spoliation, including dismissal or entry of judgment against the spoliator.

TAMPERING WITH EVIDENCE

Any person—whether engaged in litigation or not—who destroys, alters, falsifies or conceals evidence during a law enforcement or regulatory enforcement investigation may be charged with the crime of tampering with evidence.

OBSTRUCTION OF JUSTICE

A person who alters, falsifies, mutilates, conceals, or destroys evidence knowing that it is relevant to a pending investigation or a judicial, regulatory agency or congressional hearing, and with the intent to impede, obstruct or influence the investigation or proceeding, may be charged with the crime of obstruction of justice.

LEGAL HOLDS

Prohibitions against the destruction, alteration or concealment of potentially relevant evidence or of evidence that could lead to the discovery of admissible evidence in pending or future litigation are called *legal holds.*

Because a business has a duty to preserve relevant information when it learns or reasonably should have learned of a pending or threatened lawsuit, prosecution or regulatory investigation, a business that becomes aware of any such actual or potential investigation or proceeding should promptly inform the custodian(s) of its records of the duty to preserve relevant information. This should also be done when the business anticipates an audit. Notice should be given to every custodian and to every individual with the power to destroy, conceal, alter or manage records.

Notifications of legal holds should be in writing and sent in a way that requires confirmation of receipt. They should explain in detail which records need to be preserved and what needs to be done to preserve them. They should make it clear that normal disposition and processing of records—such as storage, alteration or management of records, or any scheduled destruction, recycling or other disposition of records—is suspended. They should also make it clear that the hold applies to both active records and archived or backup copies of records.

Once a legal hold is in place, all future relevant electronic communications and subsequently created electronic records are also subject to it. This, too, should be made clear in any notification of a legal hold.

The Federal Rules of Civil Procedure and similar state court rules automatically place a legal hold on electronically stored information if the records should be preserved in the anticipation or conduct of litigation. Rule 37(e) leaves questions about which records need to be preserved to courts to decide, as informed by statutes and judicial precedents. What this Rule means is that a person who is a party to litigation, or who reasonably anticipates being a party to litigation in the future, has a duty to preserve all potentially relevant evidence and evidence that could lead to the discovery of admissible evidence, even without a court order. A court may impose sanctions on a party who fails to take reasonable steps to preserve a record that it should have preserved, if the record cannot be restored or replaced through additional discovery.

Rule 37(e) applies to all electronically stored information. This includes email messages, voicemail, temporary files, metadata, and any other kind of stored electronic data. Even deleted electronic data are discoverable under Rule 37(e). The kind of device on which the data are stored does not matter. Data stored in iPhones, Blackberries, PDAs and laptops are no less discoverable than data stored on servers, desktop computers and removable storage devices.

A party who is concerned that another party's continued use of an electronic record may result in its alteration may seek a preservation order prohibiting further use until information from the record can be retrieved and copied.

A company that has an obligation to preserve potential evidence should do each of the following things, either directly or through its attorney:

(a) Serve notice of the litigation hold on its employees and on the custodian(s) of the potential evidence as soon as litigation is reasonably anticipated. If litigation is completely unexpected, then the notice should be served when litigation is commenced.

(b) Periodically reissue notifications of the litigation hold to remind current employees and to ensure that new employees are aware of it.

(c) Identify the key players, i.e., the persons who are likely to have relevant information or records that are likely to lead to the discovery of admissible evidence.

(d) Directly communicate with the key players to ensure that they know and understand their duty to preserve relevant information and records that are likely to lead to the discovery of relevant evidence.

(e) Instruct all employees to produce electronic copies of their relevant active files and to identify, segregate and safely store relevant backup copies, including any files and backup copies that are likely to lead to the discovery of admissible evidence.

A company should track all holds, including dates notifications were sent, the persons to whom they were sent, confirmation receipts, and the contents of the notifications. If the company has an attorney, the attorney should take care of carrying out the legal hold. In some cases, it may be necessary or appropriate for the attorney to actually take physical custody of relevant backup copies in order to safeguard them.

Courts are no longer as willing as they once were to accept ineptness, lack of computer sophistication, or computer crashes as excuses for noncompliance. Today, judges are likely to infer intent to conceal evidence from the fact that a company "lost" records if it does not have backup copies from which to restore them.

Rule 37(e) prohibits a court from dismissing a party's case, entering a default judgment or applying a presumption that the lost information is unfavorable to a party who negligently fails to preserve electronically stored information. A court may apply those sanctions, though, if the failure to preserve evidence was intended to deprive another party of the information in litigation. Sanctions may be even more severe if a party destroys or "loses" electronically stored information in violation of a court order. Violation of a court order is contempt of court. Sanctions for contempt may include imprisonment, a fine, attorney fees, an order barring the introduction of evidence, application of a presumption that the evidence is not favorable to the contemnor, dismissal and/or entry of a default judgment against the contemnor.

Because the duty to preserve evidence includes an obligation to cease routinely scheduled destruction of records, courts generally have not been sympathetic to claims that emails were automatically destroyed by a computer server. Courts may impose sanctions for either negligent or intentional failure to preserve records.

The obligation to preserve records is triggered only when a company knows or should know of a pending or reasonably anticipated future investigation or proceeding. There must be a specific dispute or anticipated proceeding to which the evidence relates. A company is not required to preserve all electronic records that might be relevant to some unspecified, hypothetical future dispute, investigation or proceeding. It is only required to preserve records that may be relevant or likely to lead to admissible evidence in a pending or probable future proceeding.

Rule 26 allows a party who is served a discovery request during litigation to assert, in a motion for a protective order or in response to a motion to compel, that the information sought is electronically stored information from a source that is not reasonably accessible due to undue burden or cost. If that happens, then the court may order discovery from such source only for good cause. A disaster recovery system (such as a backup) probably could qualify as "not reasonably accessible." A court might order production of it anyway, though, if it is the only copy of a relevant record (or a record that may lead to the discovery of admissible evidence) that a party is able to produce.

Reporting Cybersecurity Threats

The Cybersecurity Information Sharing Act[153] (CISA) authorizes any person, organization or governmental unit to exchange information concerning cyberthreat indicators and defensive measures with the federal government. Before sharing such information, however, a private (nongovernmental) entity must remove personal information and personally identifying information about specific individuals.

A *cyberthreat indicator* is any information necessary to identify or describe :

(a) a malicious reconnaissance
(b) a security vulnerability
(c) a method of defeating a security control or exploitation of a security vulnerability
(d) a method of causing a user with legitimate access to an information system or information stored, processed or transmitted on it, to unwittingly enable the defeat of a security control or exploitation of a security vulnerability
(e) a malicious cybercommand and control, the actual or potential harm caused by an incident, and any other attribute of a cybersecurity threat, if disclosure of the attribute is not otherwise prohibited by law.

A defensive measure is an action, device, procedure, signature, technique or other measure applied to an information system or information that is stored on, processed by or transmitted by an information system that detects, prevents or mitigates a known, unknown or suspected cybersecurity threat or security vulnerability.

CISA limits what the federal government may do with information that is obtained in this way. It may be used solely for cybersecurity purposes and law enforcement investigations of threats of physical or economic harm or identity theft. Information obtained pursuant to CISA may not be released in response to a FOIA request.

Persons and entities that supply information to the federal government in compliance with CISA are protected from liability for violating privacy rights on account of the disclosure.

PCI SSC Standards for Credit and Debit Cards

In addition to statutory requirements, businesses that accept credit or debit card payments undertake contractual obligations to implement security measures for the protection of information collected from cardholders. Contracts between card networks and acquirers mandate compliance with security standards developed by the Payment Card Industry Security Standards Council (PCI SSC). Contracts between acquirers and merchants require merchants that accept payment cards to comply with these standards, as well. A small but growing number of states require companies that collect data in connection with the use of a payment card during sales transactions to comply with the current version of the Payment Card Industry Data Security Standard (PCI DSS). Nevada is such a state.[154]

The PCI SSC is an association founded by the major payment card networks (Visa, MasterCard, American Express, Discover Financial Services, and JCB International) to develop and disseminate standards for payment account security. The PCI DSS is chief among these.[155] It applies to all entities that store, process or transmit cardholder data. Compliance with the PCI DSS is enforced by the card networks, not by the PCI SSC directly. Each of the founding card networks has agreed to incorporate the PCI DSS into its data security compliance program.

The six general obligations set forth in the PCI DSS are:

- Establish and maintain secure systems
- Protect cardholder data
- Maintain a vulnerability management program
- Implement strong access control measures
- Monitor and test networks regularly
- Establish and maintain an information security policy.

To meet these requirements, a merchant must:

1. Install and maintain a firewall to protect cardholder data.

Firewalls are devices that control computer traffic allowed into and out of an organization's network, and into sensitive areas within its internal network. Firewall functionality can also appear in other system components. Routers are hardware or software that connect two or more networks. All such networking devices that are used within the cardholder data environment are within the scope of this requirement. Specifically, a merchant must:

(a) Establish and implement firewall and router configuration standards that formalize testing whenever configurations change; that identify all connections between the cardholder data environment and other networks (including wireless) with documentation and diagrams; that document business justification and various technical settings for each implementation; that diagram all cardholder data flows across systems and networks; and stipulate a review of configuration rule sets at least every six months;
(b) Build firewall and router configurations that restrict all traffic, inbound and outbound, from untrusted networks (including wireless) and hosts, and specifically deny all other traffic except for protocols necessary for the cardholder data environment;
(c) Prohibit direct public access between the Internet and any system component in the cardholder data environment;
(d) Install personal firewall software or equivalent functionality on any devices (whether company or employee owned) that connect to the Internet when outside the network (for example, laptops used by employees), and which are also used to access the cardholder data environment; and
(e) Ensure that related security policies and operational procedures are documented, in use, and known to all affected parties.

2. Avoid using vendor-supplied defaults for system passwords and other security parameters.

One method hackers use to access internal networks is to try default passwords or exploits based on default system software settings in a payment card infrastructure. Default passwords and settings for most network devices are widely known. To safeguard against this, a merchant must:

(a) Change all vendor-supplied defaults and remove or disable unnecessary default accounts before installing a system on the network. This includes wireless devices that are connected to the cardholder data environment or are used to transmit cardholder data.

(b) Develop configuration standards for all system components that address all known security vulnerabilities and are consistent with industry-accepted definitions.
(c) Update system configuration standards as new vulnerability issues are identified.
(d) Encrypt all nonconsole administrative access. Consult the PCI SCC for additional requirements when SSL/early TLS is used.
(e) Use strong cryptography for encryption.
(f) Maintain an inventory of system components that are within the scope of PCI DSS compliance.
(g) Ensure that related security policies and operational procedures are documented, in use, and known to all affected parties.

Website hosting service providers must protect each entity's hosted environment and cardholder data.

3. *Protect stored cardholder data.*

Any information that is printed, processed, transmitted or stored in or on a payment card is cardholder data. Businesses that accept payment cards must protect cardholder data and prevent unauthorized use of it.

(a) Do not store any cardholder data unless it is necessary to meet the needs of the business.
(b) Do not store cardholder data longer than is necessary for business, legal or regulatory purposes, as documented in the company's data retention policy.
(c) Purge unnecessary stored data at least quarterly.
(d) Do not store sensitive authentication data after authorization, even after it is encrypted. This includes: (i) the security code (CVC, CVV or CVV2 number) printed on the card, (ii) data stored in a card's magnetic stripe or chip, (iii) PIN;
(e) Render all sensitive authentication data unrecoverable upon completion of the authorization process.
(f) Mask account numbers when displayed so that only authorized people with a legitimate business need can see more than the first six/last four digits. Stricter requirements may apply with respect to particular places on which an account number may be displayed. For example, a card agreement or a state or local law may specify that only the last four digits may be displayed on a receipt.
(g) Render card account numbers unreadable anywhere they are stored. Possible methods: strong encryption, truncation of all but the last four digits; index tokens with securely stored pads, strong one-way hash functions of the entire account number.
(h) Document and implement procedures to protect any keys used for encryption of cardholder data from disclosure and misuse;
(i) Document and implement key management processes and procedures for cryptographic keys used for encryption of cardholder data.
(j) Ensure that related security policies and operational procedures are documented, in use, and known to all affected parties.

The cardholder's name and service code (as distinguished from the security code) may be stored, and do not need to be rendered unreadable unless a contract with a particular network, acquirer or service provider requires it.

4. Encrypt transmissions of cardholder data across open, public networks.

(a) Use strong cryptography and security protocols to safeguard sensitive cardholder data during transmission over open, public networks (e.g. Internet, wireless technologies, cellular technologies, General Packet Radio Service, satellite communications);
(b) Ensure wireless networks transmitting cardholder data or connected to the cardholder data environment use industry best practices to implement strong encryption for authentication and transmission;
(c) Do not send unprotected card account numbers via email, instant messaging, SMS, chat or other end user messaging technologies;
(d) Ensure that related security policies and operational procedures are documented, in use, and known to all affected parties.

5. Protect all systems against malware and regularly update antivirus software or programs.

(a) Use antivirus software on all systems commonly affected by malicious software (particularly personal computers and servers);
(b) For systems not commonly affected by malicious software, perform periodic evaluations to evaluate evolving malware threats and confirm whether such systems continue to not require antivirus software;
(c) Ensure that all antivirus mechanisms are kept current;
(d) Perform periodic scans;
(e) Generate and retain audit logs;
(f) Ensure that antivirus mechanisms are actively running and cannot be disabled or altered by users unless specifically authorized by management on a case-by-case basis for a limited time period;
(g) Ensure that related security policies and operational procedures are documented, in use, and known to all affected parties.

6. Develop and maintain secure systems and applications.

Many vulnerabilities to unauthorized access are eliminated by installing vendor-provided security patches, which perform a quick repair job for a specific piece of programming code.

(a) Ensure that all critical systems have the most recently released software patches to prevent exploitation, and that they are installed within one month of release.
(b) Apply patches to less critical systems as soon as possible, based on a risk-based vulnerability management program.
(c) Establish a process to identify security vulnerabilities, using reputable outside sources, and assign a risk ranking to newly discovered security vulnerabilities.
(d) Develop internal and external software applications including web-based administrative access to applications in accordance with PCI DSS and based on industry best practices.

Incorporate information security throughout the software development life cycle. This applies to all software developed internally as well as bespoke or custom software developed by a third party.

(e) Follow change control processes and procedures for all changes to system components.

(f) Ensure all relevant PCI DSS requirements are implemented on new or changed systems and networks after significant changes.

(g) Prevent common coding vulnerabilities in software development processes by training developers in secure coding techniques and developing applications based on secure coding guidelines, including how sensitive data is handled in memory.

(h) Ensure all public-facing web applications are protected against known attacks, either by performing application vulnerability assessments at least annually and after any changes, or by installing an automated technical solution that detects and prevents web-based attacks (for example, a web-application firewall) in front of public-facing web applications, to continually check all traffic.

(i) Ensure that related security policies and operational procedures are documented, in use, and known to all affected parties.

7. Restrict access to cardholder data by business need to know.

(a) Limit access to system components and cardholder data to only those individuals whose job requires such access;

(b) Establish an access control system for system components that restricts access based on a user's need to know, and is set to "deny all" unless specifically allowed;

(c) Ensure that related security policies and operational procedures are documented, in use, and known to all affected parties.

8. Identify and authenticate access to system components.

This applies to all accounts, including POS accounts, with administrative capabilities, and all accounts with access to stored cardholder data.

(a) Define and implement policies and procedures to ensure proper user identification management for users and administrators on all system components, including the assignment of a unique user name to users before they are allowed to access system components or cardholder data.

(b) Employ at least one of the following methods to authenticate all users: password or passphrase; a token device or smart card; a biometric.

(c) Use strong authentication methods and render all passwords/passphrases unreadable during transmission and storage using strong cryptography.

(d) Secure all individual nonconsole administrative access and all remote access to the cardholder data environment using multifactor authentication. This requires at least two of the three authentication methods described in paragraph (c) above. Using one factor twice—e.g. using two separate passwords—is not considered multifactor authentication. This requirement applies to administrative personnel with nonconsole access to the cardholder data environment from within the business's network, and all remote network access (including for users, administrators, and third parties) originating from outside the business's network).

(e) Develop, implement and communicate authentication policies and procedures to all users.

(f) Do not use group, shared, or generic IDs, or other authentication methods. Service providers with access to customer environments must use a unique authentication credential (such as a password/passphrase) for each customer environment;

(g) Use of other authentication mechanisms such as physical security tokens, smart cards, and certificates must be assigned to an individual account.

(h) All access to any database containing cardholder data must be restricted. All user access must be through programmatic methods; only database administrators can have direct or query access; and application IDs for database applications can only be used by the applications (and not by users or nonapplication processes).

(i) Ensure that related security policies and operational procedures are documented, in use, and known to all affected parties.

9. Restrict physical access to cardholder data.

[Note: For purposes of the following requirements, "onsite personnel" are employees (whether full time, part time, permanent or temporary), contractors, and consultants who are physically present on the company's premises. "Visitors" are vendors and guests that enter the facility for a short duration, usually up to one day. "Media" is all paper and electronic media containing cardholder data.]

(a) Use appropriate facility entry controls (e.g., lock, door key code, etc.) to limit and monitor physical access to systems in the cardholder data environment.

(b) Develop procedures to easily distinguish between onsite personnel and visitors, such as assigning ID badges.

(c) Control physical access to sensitive areas by onsite personnel. Access must be authorized and based on individual job function; access must be revoked immediately upon termination, and all physical access mechanisms, such as keys, access cards, etc. returned or disabled.

(d) Ensure all visitors are authorized before entering areas where cardholder data is processed or maintained, given a physical badge or other identification that expires and identifies visitors as not onsite personnel, and are asked to surrender the physical badge before leaving the facility or at the date of expiration.

(e) Use a visitor log to maintain a physical audit trail of visitor information and activity, including visitor name, company, and the onsite personnel authorizing physical access.

(f) Retain the visitor log for at least three months unless otherwise restricted by law.

(g) Physically secure all media.

(h) Store media backups in a secure location, preferably off site.

(i) Maintain strict control over the internal or external distribution of any kind of media.

(j) Maintain strict control over the storage and accessibility of media.

(k) Destroy media when it is no longer needed for business or legal reasons.

(l) Protect devices that capture payment card data via direct physical interaction with the card from tampering and substitution. This includes periodic inspections of POS device surfaces to detect tampering, and training personnel to be aware of suspicious activity.

(m) Ensure that related security policies and operational procedures are documented, in use, and known to all affected parties.

10. *Track and monitor all access to network resources and cardholder data.*

(a) Implement audit trails to link all access to system components to each individual user.
(b) Implement automated audit trails for all system components for reconstructing the following events: all individual user accesses to cardholder data; all actions taken by any individual with root or administrative privileges; access to all audit trails; invalid logical access attempts; use of and changes to identification and authentication mechanisms (including creation of new accounts, elevation of privileges), and all changes, additions, deletions to accounts with root or administrative privileges; initialization, stopping or pausing of the audit logs; creation and deletion of system-level objects.
(c) Record audit trail entries for all system components for each event, including at a minimum: user identification, type of event, date and time, success or failure indication, origination of event, and identity or name of affected data, system component or resource.
(d) Using time synchronization technology, synchronize all critical system clocks and times and implement controls for acquiring, distributing, and storing time.
(e) Secure audit trails so they cannot be altered.
(f) Review logs and security events for all system components to identify anomalies or suspicious activity. Perform critical log reviews at least daily.
(g) Retain audit trail history for at least one year; at least three months of history must be immediately available for analysis.
(h) Ensure that related security policies and operational procedures are documented, in use, and known to all affected parties.

Service providers must implement a process for timely detection and reporting of failures of critical security control systems.

11. *Regularly test security systems and processes.*

Malicious individuals and researchers are continually discovering vulnerabilities, and they are being introduced by new software. System components, processes, and custom software should be tested frequently to ensure security is maintained over time. Testing of security controls is especially important for any environmental changes such as deploying new software or changing system configurations.

(a) Implement processes to test for the presence of wireless access points and detect and identify all authorized and unauthorized wireless access points on a quarterly basis.
(b) Maintain an inventory of authorized wireless access points and implement incident response procedures in the event unauthorized wireless access points are detected.
(c) Run internal and external network vulnerability scans at least quarterly and after any significant change in the network.

(d) Address vulnerabilities and perform rescans as needed until passing scans are achieved.

(e) After passing a scan for initial PCI DSS compliance, a business must, in subsequent years, complete four consecutive quarters of passing scans. Quarterly external scans must be performed by a PCI SSC approved scanning vendor. Scans conducted after network changes and internal scans may be performed by internal staff.

(f) Develop and implement a methodology for penetration testing that includes external and internal penetration testing at least annually and after any significant upgrade or modification. If segmentation is used to reduce PCI DSS scope, perform penetration tests at least annually to verify the segmentation methods are operational and effective. Service providers using segmentation must confirm PCI DSS scope by performing penetration testing on segmentation controls at least every six months and after making changes to these controls.

(g) Use network intrusion detection and/or intrusion prevention techniques. Monitor all traffic at the perimeter of the cardholder data environment as well as at critical points inside of the cardholder data environment.

(h) Alert personnel to suspected compromises.

(i) Keep IDS/IPS engines, baselines, and signatures up to date.

(j) Deploy a change detection mechanism (for example, file integrity monitoring tools) to alert personnel to unauthorized modification (including changes, additions, and deletions) of critical system files, configuration files or content files. Configure the software to perform critical file comparisons at least weekly.

(k) Implement a process to respond to any alerts generated by the change-detection solution.

(l) Ensure that related security policies and operational procedures are documented, in use, and known to all affected parties.

12. Maintain a policy that addresses information security for all personnel.

(a) Ensure that all employees are aware of the sensitivity of cardholder data and their responsibilities for protecting it.

(b) Establish, publish, maintain, and disseminate a security policy.

(c) Review the security policy at least annually and update when the environment changes.

(d) Implement a risk assessment process that is performed at least annually and upon significant changes to the environment that identifies critical assets, threats, and vulnerabilities, and results in a formal assessment.

(e) Develop usage policies for critical technologies to define their proper use by all personnel. These include remote access, wireless, removable electronic media, laptops, tablets, handheld devices, email and Internet.

(f) Ensure that the security policy and procedures clearly define information security responsibilities for all personnel. Service providers must also establish responsibility for their executive management for the protection of cardholder data and a PCI DSS compliance program.

(g) Assign to an individual or team information security responsibilities.

(h) Implement a formal security awareness program to make all personnel aware of the cardholder data security policy and procedures.

(i) Screen potential personnel prior to hiring to minimize the risk of attacks from internal sources. Screening might include, for example, reviewing previous employment history, and performing criminal record, credit history, and reference checks.
(j) Maintain and implement policies and procedures to manage service providers with whom cardholder data is shared, or that could affect the security of cardholder data.
(k) Implement an incident response plan.
(l) Be prepared to respond immediately to a system breach.

Service providers must acknowledge in writing to customers that they are responsible for the security of cardholder data that they possess or otherwise store, process, or transmit on behalf of the customer, or to the extent they could impact the security of the customer's cardholder data environment. Service providers also must perform and document reviews at least quarterly to confirm personnel are following security policies and operational procedures.

The PCI DSS forgives a company's failure to meet a requirement exactly as stated if it is due to legitimate technical or documented business constraints and the company has sufficiently mitigated the risk associated with the requirement by implementing compensating controls. In order for a compensating control to be considered valid, it must be reviewed by an authorized assessor. A compensating control that is sufficient in one environment may not be sufficient in another.

Each card network has its own program for compliance, validation levels, reporting, and enforcement. These may include provisions for self-assessments and for when a qualified security assessor must be engaged. Typically, either a self-assessment questionnaire or a compliance report prepared by a third party must be filed with the acquirer on a periodic basis (e.g., annually).

The Self-Assessment Questionnaire (SAQ) is a validation tool the PCI SCC has developed for eligible organizations who self-assess their PCI DSS compliance and who are not required to submit a compliance report. Different SAQs are available for various business environments. More information may be found at the PCI SSC website, www.pcisecuritystandards.org. A merchant should consult with the acquirer to determine whether, which and when it should complete an SAQ, and whether a compliance report must be prepared and submitted.

Because PCI compliance is time-consuming and requires some technical proficiency, many merchants engage a third party service to store, process, or transmit cardholder data on their behalf, or to manage components of the customer data environment. A merchant who contracts with a service provider for this purpose should ensure that the contract clearly identifies the services and system components that are included within the scope of the service provider's annual onsite PCI DSS assessment, the specific PCI DSS requirements covered by the service provider, and any requirements which are the responsibility of the service provider's customers to include in their own PCI DSS reviews. If the service provider undergoes its own PCI DSS assessment, the service provider should provide sufficient evidence to the company with which it contracts to verify that the scope of the service provider's PCI DSS assessment covered the services applicable to the company and that the relevant PCI DSS requirements were examined and determined to be in place. The service provider's Attestation of Compliance should include a table that summarizes PCI DSS requirements covered and the specific service(s) assessed. If it does, it may be provided to customers as evidence of the scope of a service provider's PCI DSS assessment. Merchants and service providers must manage and monitor the PCI DSS compliance of all associated third party service providers with access to cardholder data.

European Union

The EU and its member countries have adopted some of the most stringent data privacy and security laws in the world.

The Data Protection Directive[156] addresses the processing (collection, storage, use, disclosure or destruction) of personal data. It applies to any business, governmental entity, organization or individual that handles personal data. "Personal data" is defined broadly to include any information that can be used to link data to a particular individual—address; credit card number; identification number; physical, mental, economic, cultural or social attributes. Member states have enacted laws implementing it.

The Directive establishes a number of privacy rights. These are discussed in Chapter 17. It also requires a company that collects personal information to implement adequate security measures to protect it from being disclosed to others.

A business that collects data must not keep it in a form which permits identification of data subjects for longer than is necessary for the purposes for which the data were collected or for which they are further processed.

The Electronic Privacy Directive of 2002[157] ("ePrivacy Directive") supplements the Data Protection Directive. It protects both natural persons and legal persons (e.g., corporations). In addition to adding new privacy protections (see Chapter 17), it contains a number of new data security requirements. First, it requires businesses that collect or use geolocation data to anonymize it unless the user consents or the data is used to provide value-added services. Web traffic data must be erased or anonymized when it is no longer needed. Electronic communications service providers must protect the security of their services and must inform subscribers whenever there is a particular risk, such as a virus or other malware attack. Retention of data is allowed for billing purposes but only for the period in which collection activity is permitted under an applicable statute of limitations. Retention is also allowed with the user's consent for marketing and value-added purposes, provided the data subject is informed of the purposes and length of time for which the data may be used.

These Directives also contain provisions relating to unsolicited email ("spam.") and the interception of electronic communications. These topics are covered elsewhere.

The Directives apply when the business is located in a EU country or when equipment located in a EU country is used to process data. Businesses located outside the EU that use equipment in a EU country to process data also must comply with them. It appears that any business that transacts online business with a resident of a EU country must comply, inasmuch as the business would be using the customer's computer in the processing of data.

The Directive on Data Protection allows countries to block the transfer of information about its citizens into countries that do not provide adequate privacy and data security protections. Since EU privacy and security protections are stronger than those in the United States, this means that EU countries may block the transfer of information about their citizens to U.S. companies.

The European Union and the United States enacted a set of guidelines to enable U.S. companies to gather and store personal information about their European customers. These guidelines required U.S. companies operating in the EU to disclose how they use personal information, give their European customers a chance to stop their data from being released, and offer a dispute resolution service, among other things. U.S. companies that complied with these requirements would be deemed to be in compliance. A U.S. company could receive the benefit of this safe harbor by self-certifying to the U.S. Department of Commerce that it agreed to be bound by the guidelines. In 2015, however, the European Court of Justice struck down this "safe harbor" framework.

The following year, the U.S. Department of Commerce and the European Commission adopted a new "Privacy Shield" framework, which is intended to create stronger rights in connection with data transfers. The Privacy Shield imposes more stringent requirements on companies handling data, clearer safeguards and transparency obligations pertaining to U.S. government access, more effective protection of individual rights, and an annual joint review mechanism. A Privacy Shield participant must do all of the following:

(a) Include in its privacy policy a declaration of the company's commitment to complying with the Privacy Shield Principles so that the commitment becomes enforceable under U.S. law.
(b) Include in its privacy policy a link to the U.S. Department of Commerce.
(c) Respond promptly to inquiries and requests by the Department of Commerce for information relating to the Privacy Shield Framework.
(d) Limit personal information collection to what is relevant for the purposes of processing.
(e) Comply with the new Data Retention Principle.
(f) When transferring personal information to a third party, comply with Notice and Choice Principles.
(g) Enter into a contract with the third party that provides that such data may only be processed for limited and specified purposes consistent with the consent provided by the individual, and that the recipient will provide the same level of protection as the Principles and will notify the company if it makes a determination that it can no longer meet this obligation.
(h) Include a provision in contracts with third parties that when the third party makes a determination that it can no longer meet its data security obligations, the third party must (i) stop processing data or must take other reasonable and appropriate steps to remediate; (ii) when transferring personal data to a third party acting as an agent, transfer the data only for limited and specified purposes; (iii) ascertain that the agent is obligated to provide at least the same level of privacy protection as is required by the Principles; (iv) take reasonable and appropriate steps to ensure that the agent effectively processes the personal information transferred in a manner consistent with the company's obligations under the Principles; (v) require the agent to notify the company if it makes a determination that it can no longer meet its obligation to provide the same level of protection as is required by the Principles; (vi) upon notice, take reasonable and appropriate steps to stop and remediate unauthorized processing; and (vii) provide a summary or a representative copy of the relevant privacy provisions of its contract with that agent to the Department of Commerce upon request.
(i) Make public any relevant Privacy Shield-related sections of any compliance or assessment report submitted to the FTC if the company becomes subject to an FTC or court order based on noncompliance.

(j) If a company leaves the Privacy Shield Framework, annually certify its commitment to apply the Principles to information received under the Privacy Shield Framework if it chooses to keep such data or provide adequate protection for the information by another authorized means.

GENERAL DATA PROTECTION REGULATION

The General Data Protection Regulation (GDPR), adopted in April, 2016, supersedes the Data Protection Directive and is enforceable beginning May 25, 2018. Among other things, it requires data protection measures to be designed into the development of businesses processes for products and services ("data protection by design and by default.") Privacy settings must be set at a high level by default. The data controller should implement technical and procedural measures to make sure that the processing complies with GDPR requirements. Controllers should also implement mechanisms to ensure that personal data are only processed when necessary for each specific purpose. Encryption and decryption operations must be carried out locally, not by remote service, because both keys and data must remain in the power of the data owner if any privacy is to be achieved. Outsourced data storage on remote clouds is practical and relatively safe, as long as only the data owner, not the cloud service, holds the decryption keys. Data controllers are responsible for implementing effective data security. They must be able to demonstrate that data is being processed in compliance with GDPR requirements even if another person or entity carries out the processing on the controller's behalf. Penalties for violations can be severe.

Pseudonymisation is a process that transforms personal data in such a way that the resulting data cannot be attributed to a specific data subject without the use of additional information. Encryption is an example. In the case of encrypted information, the decryption key is the "additional information." The "additional information" must be kept separately from the pseudonymised data. Pseudonymisation helps controllers and processors meet their data security obligations under the GDPR.

When certain kinds of risks to the rights and freedoms of data subjects occur, data protection impact assessments must be conducted. Risk assessment and mitigation is required. Prior approval of data protection authorities is required for high risks.

If processing is carried out by a controller whose core activities consist of processing operations that require regular and systematic monitoring of the data subjects, a person with expert knowledge of data protection law and practices should assist the controller or processor to monitor internal compliance with the GDPR. This person, called a Data Protection Officer, should be proficient in data security, managing IT processes, and other critical business continuity issues.

A data controller must notify the supervisory authority of any security beach within seventy-two hours after learning of it. Individuals must be notified if adverse impact is determined. Notice need not be given to data subjects if the data controller has implemented proper technical and organizational protection measures that make the personal data unintelligible to those who are not authorized to access it, such as encryption. A data processor must notify the controller immediately upon becoming aware of a security breach.

Finally, the GDPR prohibits personal data from being transferred to countries outside the European Economic Area unless they guarantee the same level of data protection. The European Economic Area includes members of the EU plus a few other European countries.

Penalties for violations of the GDPR can be severe.

Chapter 14. Taxes

E-commerce businesses are not exempt from sales, use, excise and income taxes. The Due Process and Commerce Clauses of the federal constitution impose some limitations on state power to tax interstate transactions, though. State taxes are unconstitutional if they either discriminate against interstate commerce or impose an undue burden on it. Moreover, a state may not impose a tax on a business unless it has a "substantial nexus" with the state. Determining whether and to whom taxes must be paid involves a two-part inquiry: First, it must be determined what kinds of taxes might apply to a particular kind of transaction (e.g., sales, use, or excise). Then it must be determined whether the business has the requisite nexus with the state that imposes the tax.

Sales Tax

A *sales tax* is a consumption tax. It is imposed on purchases or leases of tangible personal property. It may be imposed by a state, a local unit of government, or both. Forty-five states and the District of Columbia impose state sales tax. States without a state sales tax include Alaska, Delaware, Montana, New Hampshire and Oregon.

Many jurisdictions have extended their sales taxes to sales of services, or most commonly, to specified kinds of services. In Minnesota, for example, gym memberships, dry cleaning, garden, hotel, car washing, pet boarding and telecommunication services, among others, may be subject to state sales tax. As budget demands grow, it may be expected that states will bring more and more services into the ambit of their sales tax laws.

Sales tax rates vary widely, ranging from $0 in the five states that have so state sales tax to 7.25% in California. They are usually uniform throughout the state. New Jersey, however, imposes a lower state tax on sales in Salem County. This special tax break is intended to help businesses in that county remain competitive with the border state of Delaware, where there is no sales tax.

In many states, individual cities, boroughs, counties, taxing districts, or other political subdivision also impose taxes on sales. Both state and local sales taxes may be imposed on the same transaction. Local tax rates vary considerably both between states and within a state. It is possible for a sale to be subject to local sales tax but not state tax, and vice versa. Alaska, for example, has no state sales tax but individual municipalities within the state do.

The seller is responsible for collecting sales taxes and remitting them to the appropriate taxing authorities. Most businesses collect the tax from the customer at the time of sale.

GOODS AND SERVICES SUBJECT TO SALES TAX

The kinds of goods and services that are subject to sales tax vary depending on the jurisdiction. In most jurisdictions, the general rule is that all sales of any kind of tangible personal property are taxable unless exempted, while sales of services or intangible personal property are exempt unless specifically made taxable. Of course, an individual state may alter this rule legislatively. States also vary with respect to the taxability of shipping charges.

Digital Downloads

States vary widely with regard to their tax treatment of sales of digital downloads. Some classify them as tangible personal property for tax purposes, making them presumptively taxable. In other states, they are not considered tangible property, and therefore are not subject to sales tax.

Some states impose taxes only on permanent downloads. Others tax both permanent and limited downloads.

In some states, taxability depends on the kind of content that is downloaded. For example, a state might tax sales of ebooks, digital music and digital audiovisual works, while at the same time refraining from imposing taxes on digital photographs. A growing number of states have devised a separate set of rules for determining the taxability of sales of computer software. Others do not distinguish among types of content.

In states where taxability depends on a specified characteristic, a permanent download is more likely to have been made taxable than a limited or temporary one is; and an e-book or digital music or audiovisual file is more likely to have been made taxable than a computer program is. These are just general tendencies, however; this pattern does not apply in every state.

A company that sells digital downloads will need to check with the relevant taxing authority to determine whether and how much sales tax needs to be collected on digital downloads.

Computer Software

Sales of computer software programs have been problematic for sales tax administration because computer programs are intangible. Since sales tax laws traditionally have imposed the tax on "tangible personal property," sales of computer programs would seem to be nontaxable. States have used a variety of approaches to make at least some of these sales taxable.

Computer programs that are sold in a tangible medium (e.g., a CD-ROM) are usually taxable as tangible personal property. In these cases, the entire amount of the sale is taxable. No account is taken of the fact that in reality, the buyer is paying primarily for the program, and is only incidentally paying for the plastic disk and jewel case in which the program is embodied.

In a few states, it is still the rule that software is taxable only if it is sold in a physical medium like a CD-ROM. Many states, however, now tax software programs that are delivered electronically, as well, at least to some extent. These states have taken two different routes to make electronically delivered software taxable. Some have interpreted the meaning of "tangible" very liberally, holding that because the functioning of a computer program (e.g., screen displays) is perceptible, the program is therefore "tangible." Other states have retained the understanding that computer programs are intangible property, but have enacted laws making this particular kind of intangible property taxable in the same way that tangible personal property is. Laws in these states typically declare that sales of computer programs are taxable regardless of whether the delivery is made in a physical medium or electronically.

States that treat computer software as taxable often distinguish between "canned" and custom software. "Canned" software is a computer program that is prewritten. Custom software is a computer program that is sold and written to the specifications of a particular customer. A state may treat canned software as property, while treating custom software as a service. Canned software is more likely to be taxable in these states than custom software is. On the other hand—and in line with the trend toward increasing the number of services that are taxable—a few states impose sales taxes on both canned and custom software.

Software that is not delivered in a tangible medium may also be classified according to whether a purchase involves downloading a copy of it, on one hand, or a right of access to software that is hosted on the seller's or a third party's server, on the other. Hosted software to which a right of access is granted without a right to download and retain a copy is known as "software as a service" (SaS.) In some states, downloaded software files are considered taxable property, while SaS is an untaxable service. In other states, both downloaded and SaS software is taxable. And of course, there are still a few states that treat neither downloaded nor SaS software as taxable.

Finally, some states make a distinction between software which the buyer has the right to use indefinitely and software to which the buyer has only a limited right (such as a five-year license.)

CONSTITUTIONAL LIMITATIONS

The U.S. Supreme Court has held that the Constitution contains an implicit "dormant commerce clause" that prohibits states from imposing taxes or regulating in such a way as to discriminate against or unreasonably burden interstate commerce. In addition, the concept of fundamental fairness embodied in the Due Process Clause requires that some relevant connection must exist between a taxing authority and the person or business sought to be taxed. The net result of the Supreme Court's decisions in this area is that a state sales tax is constitutional only if it meets all of the following requirements:

(a) it relates to an activity that has a substantial nexus with the taxing state
(b) it is fairly apportioned
(c) it does not discriminate against interstate commerce
(d) it is fairly related to the services and benefits provided by the State.[158]

The Internet Tax Freedom Act

The Internet Tax Freedom Act[159] (ITFA) is an attempt to implement the dormant commerce clause by prohibiting discriminatory taxes on e-commerce. It provides that if a state imposes a tax on retail sales of a particular kind of product, then it cannot impose a higher or additional sales tax on e-commerce vendors for sales of that product solely because the transaction is conducted online.

ITFA also prohibits states from imposing taxes on online sellers who do not have a nexus with the state in which the purchaser resides. What this means, generally, is that e-commerce vendors only need to collect and remit sales taxes on sales to purchasers who reside in a state to which the seller has a constitutionally relevant nexus.

ITFA also imposed a moratorium on state and local taxes on charges for Internet access unless the state had already imposed and collected such a tax prior to October 1, 1998. The Trade Facilitation and Trade Enforcement Act[160] made the moratorium permanent.

The Nexus Requirement

States may impose sales taxes on sales that take place within their borders. If a person physically travels to a store in another state to make a purchase, then the buyer is present in the state where the store is located, so the sale is taxable by that state. The presence of both the buyer and the sale transaction in the state provides a sufficient nexus to the state to support a state's imposition of a tx on the sale. But what if the store has set up a website so that a purchase may be made without having to physically travel to the state?

The U.S. Supreme Court has held that imposing taxes on sales to residents of other states imposes a constitutionally impermissible burden on interstate commerce unless the vendor has a substantial nexus to the other state.[161] Merely using an instrumentality of interstate commerce to make a sale to a resident of another state is not enough to establish a nexus to the purchaser's state.[162] The U.S. Mail is an example of an instrumentality of commerce. The fact that a product is ordered from a state and shipped into the state by mail is not enough to establish a substantial nexus with the state. Presumably, merely using the Internet to order and/or deliver products into a state also would not be nexus substantial enough to support a tax imposed by the state into which the product is shipped.

The Court has eschewed any bright-line test for determining whether a nexus is substantial or not. One general rule that has emerged is that payment of sales taxes may be required by states in which the vendor has a physical presence.[163]

While no all-encompassing definition of physical presence exists, and states have established different rules for determining whether it exists, it may be said that the presence of any of the following things in a state will probably qualify as a substantial nexus to the state for Commerce Clause purposes:

- office
- physical storefront
- warehouse
- inventory
- order fulfillment site
- agents, employees or contractors
- trade show with on-site sales
- subsidiary or affiliate having one or more of the above
- delivery into the state using the company's vehicle
- performance of a taxable service within the state
- product installers
- trainers for purchasers of a company's product
- contractors within the state who engage in activities that are intended to establish and maintain a market in the state for sales.

Under the *market maintenance* theory, sales tax jurisdiction may be premised on an out-of-state company's use of in-state employees or independent sales or promotional representatives to establish and maintain a market for sales of the company's products or services in the state.[164] Under this theory, merely advertising in a state does not establish a sufficient nexus, but the presence of an independent contractor within the state who solicits sales on a vendor's behalf does.

SERVERS AND COOKIES

Is the physical location of a server within a state a sufficient physical presence to establish a substantial nexus with the state? An ISP that maintains servers in different states for ease of access by local customers makes ISPs analogous to telecommunications providers or common carriers, the use of which the U.S. Supreme Court has indicated generally will not be sufficient to establish a nexus to a state for Commerce Clause purposes. For this reason, some authorities say that hosting an e-commerce website on a server that is physically located in a state is not, in itself, a sufficient physical presence in the state to establish a nexus.[165] A few states have so provided in their laws, regulations or court decisions. Other states disagree. Still other states have not ruled on the question.

> **Query**. In a state that does not recognize the mere presence of a server as a sufficient nexus, would the fact that the server is used to store files that a vendor sells online as digital downloads make a difference? Could an argument be made that the server is a "warehouse" for digital files?

In a similar vein, a few states have enacted laws making a vendor's placement of a cookie on a computer in the state sufficient to establish the vendor's "physical presence" in the state.

AFFILIATE MARKETING AND "CLICK-THROUGH" NEXUS

One way to market products online is to offer incentives to other website owners to display links to the vendor's website on their websites. Typically, the vendor agrees to pay the website owner a small fee when a user clicks on the link. In some arrangements, compensation is payable only if a sale is made as a result of a click on the link. The amount of compensation may be calculated on the basis of the number of clicks on the link or it may be calculated as a commission on sales generated from clicks. These kinds of arrangements are called *affiliate marketing*. The individual website owners who display the links for the vendor are *affiliates*.

An affiliate is much like an independent sales representative. As such, the market maintenance theory suggests that the affiliate's physical presence in a state, coupled with its "pitching" of the product to potential buyers in the state, will suffice to establish a substantial nexus between the vendor and each state in which the vendor has an affiliate. There is a glitch in this analysis, however. Unlike most sales representatives, an online affiliate rarely has any contact with the people who decide to make a purchase from the vendor, and an affiliate is not often an agent or employee of the vendor. In most cases, an affiliate doesn't even know the identity of the people who click on the links on his website. These aspects of the transaction make an affiliate marketer look more like an advertiser than a sales representative.

The legislatures of a number of states have chosen to resolve this ambiguity in favor of treating affiliates as sales representatives rather than as mere advertisers. In 2008, New York enacted a law requiring out-of-state vendors to collect and remit taxes on sales generated by means of affiliate marketing on the part of an affiliate who is a resident of New York. Amazon.com and Overstock.com, both of which have affiliate programs, challenged the constitutionality of this law. In 2013, the New York Court of Appeals upheld its constitutionality.[166] The U.S. Supreme Court denied certiorari.

Emboldened by the U.S. Supreme Court's denial of certiorari, several state legislatures enacted "affiliate nexus" or "click-through nexus" tax laws, popularly known as "Amazon laws." By 2018, nearly half of the states had enacted such laws. While they vary from state to state in their particulars, they usually exempt pay-per-click, banner, and other advertising arrangements if payment is based solely on the number of clicks. If the arrangement is one that provides for payments to an affiliate only if a sale actually results from a click on a link on the affiliate's website, then the vendor is liable to the state for taxes on sales that result from clicks on links provided by affiliates who reside in the state. Different revenue thresholds apply in different states.

Some states were even bolder, enacting laws that premise nexus on large sales, or a high volume of sales to customers in the state, without requiring that the vendor have any kind of physical presence—affiliate or otherwise—in the state. Other states have only gone so far as to require vendors to notify buyers that they must report and pay state use taxes on their purchases. Another approach, pioneered by the Arizona legislature, is to treat a provider of an online marketplace for third party products as if the provider of the marketplace is the seller of the products, for tax purposes, if the provider has a substantial nexus with the state of Arizona. Thus, for example, if an Arizona man owns a website on which other merchants sell their products, then the Arizona man would be treated as the seller and would be responsible for collecting and remitting tax on all taxable sales.

TAXES BASED ON HIGH SALES VOLUME ("ECONOMIC NEXUS")

In *National Bellas Hess, Inc. v. Illinois Dep't of Revenue*[167] and *Quill Corp. v. North Dakota*,[168] the United States Supreme Court held that the dormant commerce clause forbids states from requiring an out-of-state merchant to collect and remit taxes on sales to residents of the state unless the merchant has a physical presence in the state. This rule has had the effect of making a large number of interstate transactions untaxable because the Internet facilitates electronic sales across state lines without either the seller or the buyer needing to have a physical presence in the other's state. Partly for this reason, and in spite of U.S. Supreme Court precedents, the Ohio Supreme Court, in *Crutchfield Corp. v. Testa*,[169] held that physical presence is not required in the case of a tax on gross revenues from sales within a state that exceed a specified threshold if the tax is called a business privilege tax rather than a sales or use tax.

The case involved a Commerce Clause challenge to Ohio's "bright-line" tax on certain businesses for the privilege of doing business in the state. The tax is assessed on the gross revenues earned by out-of-state businesses on sales to Ohio residents. It only applies to out-of-state businesses with more than $500,000 in revenues from sales to Ohio residents. Instead of calling it a sales or use tax, the Ohio legislature calls it a "business privilege tax." The state assessed the tax on Crutchfield Corp. even though it had no office, warehouse, server or any other physical presence in Ohio. Crutchfield challenged the assessment, arguing that business did not have a sufficient nexus with the state of Ohio to be taxed by that state. The Ohio Supreme Court disagreed, holding that a business privilege tax is not the same as a sales or use tax, and is not subject to the same nexus requirement. Two justices dissented, seeing no constitutionally relevant difference between a tax on gross revenues from sales and a sales or use tax.

Several other states enacted tax laws similar to the one at issue in *Crutchfield*. Some went even further. South Dakota enacted a law imposing use taxes on sales to residents by out-of-state vendors with no physical presence in the state when the vendor makes more than 200 sales or earns more than $100,000 in revenues from goods and services delivered to residents of the state. These laws were enacted with full knowledge of their unconstitutionality under *National Bellas Hess* and *Quill*, for the purpose of giving the Supreme Court an opportunity to overrule those cases. In *South Dakota v. Wayfair, Inc.*[170] the United States Supreme Court availed itself of this opportunity, holding that henceforth a vendor's physical presence in a state, although sufficient to establish a nexus with a state, will no longer be necessary to establish a nexus with a state. The Court eschewed establishing any new bright-line test for nexus, but declared that a business that makes over 200 sales and earns over $100,000 from the delivery of goods and services into a state is purposefully availing itself of the consumer market in that state. That, the Court held, suffices to establish a nexus even if the business has no physical presence there.

Wayfair was decided in June, 2018. Since then, many states have enacted "economic nexus" laws similar to South Dakota's. Although some use the same volume thresholds (200 sales or $100,000 revenues), others specify different amounts. These laws are either slated to go into effect at a specified date in the future or will have already gone into effect by the time this book is published.

Use Tax

A use tax is a tax imposed on the use, consumption or storage of personal property within a state. It is essentially a "backstop" for uncollected sales tax. The two taxes are mutually exclusive. A business that collects and pays sales tax on a sale does not need to collect and remit use tax, and vice versa. Typically, sales taxes are imposed on sales to residents of the state in which the seller is physically present (and collected and remitted by the seller); use taxes are imposed in connection with purchases from out-of-state merchants as to which sales tax has not been paid.

Many states require purchasers to pay use tax on items they use, consume or store in a state but for which the seller did not collect or pay sales tax, if the sale would have been taxable had the purchaser bought it in the state where the purchaser uses, consumes or stores it. In the absence of a nexus between the seller and the state, however, payment of use taxes is solely the purchaser's responsibility, not the seller's. If there is a nexus between a state and the seller, then a state may require a seller to collect the use tax from the buyer and remit it to the state.

States historically have been rather lax in their enforcement of use tax laws. With increasingly more sales being conducted online, however, that trend is changing, at least with respect to e-commerce companies with significant sales volumes. In *Borders Online, LLC v. State Board of Equalization*[171] an out-of-state company had an online presence within a state that imposed a use tax on purchases from out-of-state vendors. The company's website authorized customers to take purchased items to physical stores within the state for refunds and exchanges. It specified a particular chain of stores where this could be done. The court held that a sufficient nexus with the state existed because the company was conducting sales in California. The court reasoned that processing refunds and exchanges is part of a sales transaction, and that an implied agency relationship existed between the online company and the chain of physical stores within the state that were authorized to process refunds and exchanges.

Of course, after *Wayfair*, economic nexus may be asserted as another possible basis for the imposition of an obligation to collect and remit use taxes on the part of out-of-state merchants, provided the relevant volume and/or amount thresholds are met.

Employment Taxes

See Chapter 4.

Income Tax

As with any other kind of income, federal and state income taxes must be paid on income from e-commerce.

State income taxes with any of the following features are unconstitutional:

(a) discriminatory against interstate commerce
(b) not fairly apportioned
(c) not fairly related to services provided by the state
(d) applied to an activity that does not have a substantial nexus to the state.

The performance of income-generating activity within a state by a business, or by an employee or agent on its behalf, may suffice to establish the required nexus. A trademark owner's licensing of the trademark for use in connection with goods or services that are sold in another state, in circumstances where the licensor has a right to inspect and supervise the in-state operations for quality control purposes to protect the goodwill and value of the trademark, may subject the trademark owner to liability for payment of income tax in that state on royalties from purchases of the products or services in that state.

Under federal law, a state is prohibited from imposing income taxes solely on the basis of the solicitation of sales and shipment of tangible personal property into the state.

Some countries, including the United States, allow companies a federal income tax credit for taxes paid to foreign governments. These credits are intended to encourage business expansion into global markets by preventing double taxation of income.

Excise Taxes

Excise taxes are taxes on the consumption of specific goods, services, or activities. They are imposed by both federal and state governments. They are collected by requiring vendors of the item to collect them from buyers and remit them to the taxing authority. For example, an excise tax on smoking is implemented by requiring retailers to collect them from purchasers of tobacco products; an excise tax on fuel consumption is implemented by requiring fuel vendors to collect them from customers who purchase gasoline.

Federal excise taxes are imposed on fuels, heavy vehicles, tires for heavy vehicles, automobiles with low fuel efficiency, air and boat travel and cargo, crude oil, imported petroleum products, fishing equipment, bows and arrows, firearms, vaccines, prescription drugs, wine, beer, distilled spirits, cigarettes and other tobacco products, telephone service, gambling, ozone-depleting chemicals, procurement payments to foreign persons, indoor tanning services, certain medical devices, health insurance plans, certain activities related to health insurance (e.g., failure to maintain insurance) and a number of other products and activities.

States also impose excise taxes. Some of these are imposed on the products or activities on which federal excise taxes are also imposed. Some are unique to the state.

Online sales are subject to excise taxes to the same extent that off-line sales are.

Reporting Obligations

Businesses may be required to file specified kinds of reports with state and federal taxing authorities on a periodic basis. For example, the Jenkins Act[172] requires out-of-state sellers of cigarettes to submit customer information to the taxing authorities of the state in which they sell cigarettes. This helps taxing authorities ensure that purchasers are paying the appropriate taxes. State agencies responsible for collecting sales taxes often require retail businesses to file periodic reports of revenue even if there is no income to report.

The federal Internal Revenue Code requires every American individual, corporation, partnership, LLC or trust to provide timely information regarding their foreign accounts. The penalty for noncompliance is $10,000 for every month a report is late.

Custom Duties and Tariffs

The federal government imposes a custom duty on many kinds of goods when they are imported into the United States. The amount of each custom duty is specified in a list called a tariff. The existence and amount of a custom duty varies depending on the kind of product, the country from which it is imported, and any applicable treaties.

The same goods are subject to the same custom duties whether they are purchased online or off-line. Goods delivered online from overseas, however, are not necessarily subject to the same custom duty as they would be if delivered off-line. Software is an example. A software program is not subject to a custom duty when delivered online from an overseas vender. The same program may be subject to a custom duty, however, if a hard copy is shipped into the United States from another country.

Value-Added Tax (European Union)

The value-added tax (VAT) is a tax on consumer spending in a EU country. It is assessed on sales of all products and services, at a uniform rate throughout the country. To sell to consumers in an EU country, a vendor registers with a VAT authority in any EU country. A tax will then be levied at the rate that is applicable in the country where the customer resides. Suppliers selling to businesses in the EU pay the VAT, too, but must assess it themselves.

The EU classifies all electronically delivered products as services that are subject to the VAT, so sales transactions conducted online are subject to the tax. An online sale of a tangible product that is physically delivered into the EU country is also subject to the tax.

Tax Treaties

Many countries have entered into tax treaties under which a participating country is prohibited from imposing an income tax on foreign companies. A treaty may also impose limits on tax withholdings on payments of dividends, royalties and the like.

PART III. WEBSITE CONTENT

Chapter 15. Advertising

Advertising laws serve the dual purpose of fostering healthy competition and protecting consumers. They protect businesses from losing sales or experiencing other economic loss as a result of a competitor's unscrupulous advertising methods or claims. They protect consumers from being deceived about the nature or quality of products or services they purchase, or the terms of sale. They also protect consumers from intrusive or annoying methods of advertising.

Unfair Competition

Competition generally benefits consumers by incentivizing businesses to improve their goods and services and to offer them at affordable prices. Unfortunately, some unscrupulous businesses use advertising as a vehicle for deceiving consumers into believing their products and services are better than they really are and that competing products and services are worse than they really are. In the long run, a business that implements this strategy without actually improving its products might lose customers. In the meantime, though, business competitors are unjustly harmed. And the increased concentration of market power in one or a small number of firms thwarts competition and its benefits.

FALSE ADVERTISING

A business that suffers economic loss as a result of a competitor's false advertising has a common law cause of action against the competitor for false advertising. The elements are:

(a) merchant's representation about its goods or services
(b) that is likely to mislead or deceive potential buyers
(c) to the likely commercial detriment of another.

The wrong that this tort addresses is the injury to a business competitor that results when a false representation diverts customers to another company. As such, the cause of action belongs to businesses, not to consumers.

Neither actual nor certain harm needs to be proven. Proof that harm is likely to result is all that is required. Appropriate remedies include an injunction and/or money damages. Money damages may include:

(a) lost revenue on sales made at reduced prices, where the reduction was made necessary by the false advertising
(b) the cost of corrective advertising
(c) compensation for damage to goodwill, unless remedied by corrective advertising

(d) lost profits on sales diverted to the false advertiser (but only if the false advertising was in bad faith).

Lanham Act

Although the Lanham Act is primarily concerned with trademarks, Section 43(a) provides a cause of action for false advertising that does not necessarily have to involve a trademark. Recovery is allowed against any person who:

> on or in connection with any goods or services, or any container for goods, uses in commerce any word, term, name, symbol, or device, or any combination thereof, or any false designation of origin, false or misleading description of fact, or false or misleading representation of fact, which
> (A) is likely to cause confusion, or to cause mistake, or to deceive as to the affiliation, connection, or association of such person with another person, or as to the origin, sponsorship, or approval of his or her goods, services, or commercial activities by another person, or
> (B) in commercial advertising or promotion, misrepresents the nature, characteristics, qualities, or geographic origin of his or her or another person's goods, services, or commercial activities.[173]

As the language of the Act shows, recovery is allowed for any "false or misleading representation of fact" whether it relates to the source of advertised goods or services or to their qualities The misrepresentation may be about "the nature, characteristics [or] qualities" of goods or services, not just about their origin. The breadth of this language essentially federalizes the common law cause of action for false advertising, making Section 43(a) a powerful tool for deterring false advertising.

A Section 43(a) claim requires proof of each of the following elements:

(a) false or misleading representation of fact
(b) in a commercial advertisement (or label, etc.) about goods or services (either a company's own products or services or those of a competitor)
(c) that either actually deceives or has a tendency to deceive a substantial number of people to whom the advertisement is communicated
(d) is material (i.e., the representation is about something of importance to potential consumers, such as the origin, nature or quality of goods or services, and has an effect on purchasing decisions)
(e) is about goods or services that are in or affect interstate commerce and
(f) results in injury or likely injury to a business competitor, either by diverting sales or by impairing the goodwill associated with the competitor's goods or services.[174]

A Section 43(a) claim does not always involve the misleading use of another person's trademark, but it can. Some trademark infringement claims also constitute false advertising under Section 43(a). Unlike a trademark infringement claim, though, recovery of damages for a false advertising claim under the Lanham Act requires a finding of actual confusion, not merely a likelihood of confusion. More precisely, it must be proved either that some consumers actually were deceived or that the representation is literally or expressly false. Proof of actual confusion is not required if the representation is literally or expressly false. Proof that some consumers were actually deceived is required if the statement is misleading but not literally or expressly false. Likelihood of confusion will suffice for the issuance of an injunction, but not for the recovery of monetary damages. If the advertiser acted with intent to deceive, then it is presumed that some consumers were actually deceived.

Injunctive relief may be granted without need for proof that the false advertisement diverted sales away from the plaintiff or caused any other actual injury to the plaintiff. It is only necessary to establish a reasonable belief that the plaintiff is likely to be harmed.

Only direct commercial competitors have standing to bring an action for false advertising under the Lanham Act. Consumers do not.

Damages recoverable on a Section 43(a) claim include lost profits on sales that were diverted to the false advertiser; lost profits on sales made at reduced prices as a result of the false advertising; the cost of any corrective advertising that is undertaken in response to the false advertising; and any quantifiable harm to goodwill. If the false advertising was willful or in bad faith, then the false advertiser may be required to turn over to the plaintiff any profits it made on account of the advertisement.

Trade Disparagement

A false statement of fact about a competitor or about a competing product or service may result in liability for trade disparagement. See Chapter 16.

Trademarks in Domain Names and Meta Tags

See Chapters 28 and 29.

Disclaimers of Affiliation, Sponsorship or Endorsement

A false or misleading representation in an advertisement may violate the Lanham Act if it creates (or can be presumed to create) confusion among consumers about the source, sponsorship, affiliation or endorsement of a product or service. Displaying another company's trademark on a web page may be understood by consumers as a representation of affiliation, sponsorship, endorsement by the trademark owner, or in some cases, as a representation that products or services offered on a webpage are manufactured or supplied by the company that owns the trademark. To prevent confusion, it may be necessary to display a disclaimer of ownership of the trademark and of any affiliation, sponsorship or endorsement by the trademark owner. For example, unless it is an Apple-authorized repair service, a computer repair service that advertises that it repairs Apple computers should display a disclaimer of ownership of the trademark and of sponsorship, endorsement and affiliation so that consumers will not mistakenly believe the company is an authorized Apple dealer or repair service.

Commercial Use of a Person's Likeness

See Chapter 17.

Consumer Protection

Laws in most jurisdictions reflect a belief that advertising is of value to the extent it enables consumes to make more informed choices. False or misleading claims about a product or service do not help consumers make more informed decisions. In the long run, natural market forces might put a company that leads its customers astray out of business, but buyers could be harmed in the meantime. Consumer protection laws attempt to preserve the benefits of advertising to consumers while protecting them from harm.

COMMON LAW FRAUD

The oldest consumer protection law is the common law cause of action for fraud. Definitions vary, but most jurisdictions are in agreement that the elements are:

(a) intentional representation or omission
(b) of a material fact
(c) that is false or misleading
(d) with intent to induce
(e) and that actually does induce
(f) justifiable reliance by another person
(g) resulting in economic loss to that person.

Courts in different jurisdictions diverge widely on the question of what justifiable reliance entails. When is a person justified in relying on another person's claim without investigating to determine whether it is true? Do consumers have any duty to investigate advertising claims before deciding to buy? If so, is the duty always present or does it only arise under certain circumstances? Which circumstances, and why? Would it make a difference if a particular consumer happened to have notice of facts that would cause a reasonable person to suspect a statement might not be true? What if a consumer actually knows for certain the statement is false? Should a cause of action still exist, in the interest of preventing injury to other, less informed consumers? Will the fact that a person conducted a negligent investigation prevent a finding of justifiable reliance? Courts in different jurisdictions answer these questions differently.

In many jurisdictions, a person who actually knows, at the time a statement is made, that it is false cannot recover damages for fraud. Courts in these jurisdiction hold that the person's reliance on the statement would not be reasonable under these circumstances. Some courts go further and bar recovery for fraud by a person who, although not having actual knowledge that the statement was false, was aware of facts that would have put a reasonable person on notice that the statement was probably not true. Other courts allow recovery on a fraud claim even though the claimant knew or had reason to know that the statement was false, believing it would be inequitable to allow people to benefit from lying or misrepresenting facts.

Remedies for fraud include injunctive relief and compensatory and punitive damages. In addition, fraud in the procurement of a contract may be asserted as a defense to a contract claim. Courts generally will not enforce contracts that are procured by fraud. If a court orders rescission (cancellation) of a contract that was induced by fraud, it will usually attempt to fashion a remedy that restores the parties to the status quo ante.

NEGLIGENT MISREPRESENTATION

Some, but not all, jurisdictions allow recovery for negligent misrepresentation. In these states, damages may be recoverable against a website owner for publishing false or misleading information even though there is no evidence of any actual intention to deceive anybody.

The elements of a cause of action for negligent misrepresentation are:

(a) failure to exercise reasonable care
(b) in obtaining or communicating information
(c) inducing justifiable reliance
(d) that results in pecuniary loss.

The owner of a commercial website that offers third parties a place to sell their property normally is not under any duty to protect buyers from unscrupulous third party sellers. But if the website owner makes a statement like "All sales are safe," then liability for negligent misrepresentation may arise if the owner fails to check out the sellers to ensure that they are, in fact, trustworthy.

In circumstances where a representation may be construed as a warranty, a negligent misrepresentation may result in liability for breach of contract even if a cause of action for negligent misrepresentation is not viable. It is not often a good idea to publish a statement on a website unless the company either knows it is true or is prepared to accept full financial responsibility in the event it is not.

FRAUD STATUTES

Statutes make fraud both a civil wrong and a crime, with varying particulars and standards of proof. Many different anti-fraud statutes exist. Some address fraud generally, but many more address specific kinds of fraud (insurance fraud, wire fraud, welfare fraud, etc.).

In the United States, the principal, general purpose statute dealing with commercial fraud is the FTC Act. It prohibits "unfair or deceptive acts or practices in or affecting commerce" and entrusts the FTC with the power to enforce this prohibition. The FTC may enforce it administratively, such as by issuing a cease and desist order, requiring a company to publish corrective advertising, notify purchasers of undisclosed information and/or to make specified disclosures in future advertising. The FTC may also require a company to post a bond or even ban the company from a particular industry. The FTC also may commence court proceedings to obtain an injunction, seek monetary redress for consumer injury and/or disgorgement of profits, or to obtain an order imposing civil penalties.

An advertisement is unfair if it:

(a) causes or is likely to cause substantial consumer injury
(b) that is not reasonably avoidable by consumers themselves
(c) and is not outweighed by countervailing benefits to consumers or competition.

An advertisement is deceptive if it:

(a) contains a misrepresentation or omission
(b) that is likely to mislead consumers acting reasonably under the circumstances
(c) to their detriment.

Advertisers are strictly liable for violations of the FTC Act. Neither proof of intent to convey a deceptive claim nor evidence that consumers have actually been misled or injured is required. Unlike an "unfairness" claim, no proof of injury, whether actual or probable, is necessary to support a deception charge. Good faith reliance on the advice of counsel is not a defense to a charge of violating the FTC Act. Deceptive claims are actionable only if they are material to consumers' decisions to buy or use a product or service, however.

The acts and practices to which the FTC Act applies are not limited to advertising. False or deceptive representations appearing on a commercial website (e.g., in a privacy policy) that are material (i.e., important to a consumer's decision to use the website) and likely to mislead a reasonable consumer are also prohibited. A commercial website owner's use or disclosure of a website user's information in a way or for a purpose that is inconsistent with the website's privacy policy may constitute an unfair or deceptive trade practice.

States have enacted laws against unfair or deceptive trade practices, too. These laws typically are patterned on one or more of three model laws: the Uniform Deceptive Trade Practices Act (UDTPA); the Uniform Consumer Sales Practices Act; or the Model Law for State Government. These are sometimes called "baby FTC laws" because they are similar to the FTC Act but are not national in scope. States also have enacted laws to protect consumers from specific kinds of fraudulent or deceptive practices. These laws do not always require proof of intent to deceive. They typically call for enforcement by the state's attorney general or a specified agency, but some also permit consumers to file civil lawsuits to enforce them.

The Computer Fraud and Abuse Act[175] (CFAA) is a U.S. law prohibiting fraudulent and criminal activities involving the use of a computer. Among other things, it prohibits the use of a computer to commit fraud. Both criminal penalties and civil remedies are available to enforce it. The scope of this law is broad. It is not necessary to prove common law fraud in order to prevail on a CFAA claim. It is discussed in Chapter 20.

Advertisements of fraudulent investment schemes are handled by the SEC. See Chapters 2 and 6. The U.S. Department of Justice may prosecute criminally fraudulent activity under statutes prohibiting wire and mail fraud or other federal laws.

In the EU, the Unfair Commercial Practices Directive attempts to protect consumers by prohibiting misleading advertising that has the effect of distorting economic behavior. The Directive also prohibits aggressive commercial practices on an advertiser's behalf.

FALSE STATEMENTS

False statements in advertising are prohibited if they are material, i.e., relevant to the purchasing decision. A statement is false when it is demonstrably incorrect.

One rule of thumb for minimizing the risk of liability for false advertising is to avoid making broad claims unless it is absolutely certain that there could never be any exceptions, keeping in mind that nearly every assertion has exceptions. Words like *always* and *never* should be avoided if there is even a remote possibility that there could be an exception. For example, if a company wishes to retain the right to share its customer database with a new owner if the business is sold at some point, then it should not make a representation that customer information will "never" be shared with a third party. Adding language to limit the scope of the representation can help reduce the risk of liability. "We will never share your information for direct marketing purposes without your consent," for example, would be less risky than "We will never share your information." Even this qualification may not be enough, though. A business will need to consider whether there might ever be a circumstance in which it may be necessary or desirable to disclose information even without consent, such as in response to a subpoena, etc.

MISLEADING REPRESENTATIONS

The FTC Act and other truth in advertising laws require more than literal truth. When language or a depiction says one thing but strongly suggests something else, then both the literal claim and the suggested claim must be true. All of the representations in an advertisement—express and implied—must be true.

> **Example 1**. An advertisement says, "ABC Mouthwash prevents colds." This is an express claim that the mouthwash prevents colds. If the mouthwash does not always prevent colds, or if the advertiser does not have substantiating evidence that it does, then it violates the FTC Act.

> **Example 2**. An advertisement says, "ABC Mouthwash kills germs that cause colds." This statement contains an implied claim that the product will prevent colds. Killing some of the germs that cause colds will not necessarily prevent colds. The advertiser in this case will need substantiation that the product not only kills some of the kinds of germs that cause colds but also that the product prevents colds.

The determinative question is not what an advertisement explicitly states but what impression the advertisement, taken as a whole, conveys to consumers who are acting reasonably under the circumstances An advertisement does not need to mislead a majority of consumers to be found deceptive, however. An act or practice is deceptive if it misleads a significant minority of consumers. In addition, when representations or sales practices are targeted to a specific audience, such as children, the elderly, or the terminally ill, the relevant question is whether it is unfair to, or likely to deceive, a reasonable member of that group, not its impact on the average consumer.

An advertiser may be able to neutralize implied claims by expressly disclaiming them. This is usually done by appending a qualifying limitation to a claim. For example, an advertiser who claims a car averages 28 m.p.g. might try to forestall a charge of making an implied representation that everybody will get that kind of mileage by appending the words, "Your mileage may vary."

A disclaimer may qualify, limit, modify or explain a representation, but a disclaimer that contradicts an express claim is not valid. If the claim, "This snake oil cures diabetes" is false, appending the statement, "This snake oil does not cure diabetes" to it will not prevent the advertisement from violating the FTC Act.

The FTC has taken the position that merely negating an implied representation is not necessarily enough. An advertiser may need to disclose what the truth is, as well. For example, if an advertiser states a car gets 28 miles to the gallon, saying "Your mileage may vary" may not be enough. It may also be necessary to disclose what the actual gas mileage actually is, under the conditions described or depicted in the advertisement.

MANDATORY DISCLOSURES

Disclosure of certain facts is sometimes necessary to prevent an express or implied claim from being deceptive. As at common law, an omission of a material fact may be as fraudulent as a misstatement of fact if lack of the information is likely to mislead a reasonable consumer. For example, a claim that a company is "Number 1" or "the best" may be deceptive and misleading if it does not disclose the fact that the only thing the company is "number 1" or "the best" at is winning beer drinking contests.

Enough information must be disclosed to ensure that the advertisement is not likely to mislead or deceive a reasonable consumer. The FTC may consider an advertisement to be deceptive if it does not disclose a material fact, i.e., a fact that could reasonably be expected to change a consumer's purchasing decision. Information relating to a product's performance, features, safety, effectiveness or price generally is considered material.

A disclosure that is necessary to prevent a claim from being misleading may only qualify or limit the claim. If a disclosure provides information that contradicts a material claim, the disclosure will not be sufficient to prevent the advertisement from being deceptive. Disclosures can prevent a truthful claim from being misleading, but no amount of truthful disclosures can fix a false claim.

Disclosures may also be required for reasons other than to prevent deception. The FTC has used its power to deter unfair trade practices by requiring certain disclosures to be made in the interest of helping consumers make healthier, safer or more intelligent consumption decisions. A number of other state and federal laws have been enacted for this purpose, too. Disclosure requirements of this kind apply to virtually every kind of product or service imaginable—food, cigarettes, toasters, hair dryers, legal services, financial products, email advertisements, etc. In 2017, California even mandated warning notices for guns. An e-commerce business will need to comply with all disclosure requirements that apply to the products or services it sells.

At first blush, mandated disclosures seem to conflict with the constitutional prohibition against compelled speech. In the seminal "compelled speech" case, *Wooley v. Maynard*,[176] the U.S. Supreme Court was called upon to decide whether a state, consistent with the First Amendment, could prosecute an automobile owner for failing to display the state's "Live Free or Die" motto on state-issued license plates. The Court held that requiring a person to display a specified message violates the First Amendment. The Court has since clarified, however, that the right to freedom from compelled speech is much weaker in the context of commercial speech than in other contexts. *Zauderer v. Office of the Disciplinary Counsel of the Supreme Court of Ohio*[177] upheld government-mandated disclosures in attorney advertisements. The Court explained that "warning[s] or disclaimer[s] might be appropriately required … in order to dissipate the possibility of consumer confusion or deception."[178]

A mandated disclosure generally will be upheld if it is factual, uncontroversial, reasonably related to the objective of the regulation, and the regulatory entity has a legitimate interest in the objective sought to be advanced by the regulation. Since governments have a legitimate interest in consumer protection, they have a considerable amount of power to require disclosures in commercial advertisements. This power is not absolute, however. The lax standard of review (similar to the rational basis test) articulated in *Zauderer* applies only if the required disclosure is factual and uncontroversial. Disclosures that require more than "just the facts" are subject to a higher level of scrutiny and are less likely to be constitutional. A state-mandated label warning that "Everyone who smokes will die instantly" or requiring a display of graphic images of the harm that may result from the use of a product are not likely to be constitutional. Requirements like these do more than ensure that factual information is communicated. Not everyone dies instantly from smoking, so a statement that they will is not factual information. A display of graphic images does more than communicate factual information; it evokes an emotional response. Mandating such a display is not likely to withstand a First Amendment challenge.[179]

The "Clear and Conspicuous" Requirement

To be effective, a disclosure must be clear, conspicuous, understandable, and placed in close proximity to the claim it qualifies. The FTC has made it clear that disclaimers that are relegated to a footnote, or that are made to appear in fine print, will not have the intended effect of qualifying or modifying an express claim. Nor will they prevent implied claims from being inferred by consumers. Further, disclaimers must be understandable to an ordinary consumer. In determining the effectiveness of a disclaimer or a qualifying disclosure, the FTC considers:

- Prominence
- Presentation
- Placement
- Proximity.

Prominence is gauged by whether it is displayed in such a way that consumers are likely to notice it, read it, and in the case of advertisements with audio, hear it. *Presentation* refers to the extent to which the qualifying information is presented in language that is easy for the intended audience to understand, does not contradict other things said in the advertisement, and is presented at a time when consumers' attention is not distracted elsewhere. *Placement* relates to the question whether the qualifying information is located in a place and conveyed in a format that consumers are likely to read or, in the case of advertisements with audio, hear. *Proximity* relates to the physical closeness of the qualifying information to the claim being qualified.

In the case of video advertisements, superscripts that are difficult to understand, superimposed over distracting backgrounds, compete with audio elements, or that are placed in parts of the advertisement that are less likely to be remembered have been found to be ineffective in modifying a claim made in the body of the advertisement. Visual disclosures should be displayed long enough and in a format and manner for consumers to notice, read, and understand them. Audio disclosures should be made when a claim is presented in an audible format, and the advertiser should present them in a volume and cadence that ensures consumers can hear and understand them. Written disclosures should be used for written claims.

When practical, advertisers should incorporate relevant limitations and qualifying information into the underlying claim rather than having a separate disclosure statement qualifying the claim. If that is not feasible, then the disclosure should appear in close proximity to the claim. To the extent possible, qualifying claims that are needed to prevent a claim from being deceptive should be positioned in such a way that they appear on the same screen as the claims they qualify, even on mobile devices. Hyperlinks may be useful to tell consumers about less critical terms and conditions of an offer, especially when the information may be extensive, but advertisers should not use hyperlinks to other electronic pages to display key information.

When a video is uploaded to YouTube (or any other website), any required disclosures should be made in the video itself rather than in the description or other text accompanying it. Consumers do not often read the accompanying text when they view videos.

Advertisers should consider how the page is displayed when viewed on different devices. They should design the website so that any necessary disclosures are clear and conspicuous regardless of the device on which they are displayed. Putting a disclosure in a mouse-over link, for example, will not be effective on mobile devices that have no cursor to hover over a link. If qualifying text is lengthy or cannot be displayed on the same screen as the claim it qualifies for some other reason, then it should appear directly below the advertisement, with text or visual cues encouraging consumers to scroll. Reliance should not be placed on scroll bars alone to alert consumers to the existence of additional text. Not all devices display them. In no event should information that is significant to the advertised offer be buried at the end of a long web page that requires consumers to scroll past unrelated information.

Advertisers should also be cognizant of technological limitations. Some browsers or devices might not support certain techniques for displaying disclosures or they might display them in a manner that makes them difficult to read. For example, a disclosure that requires Adobe Flash Player will not be displayed on certain mobile devices. Also, because many users block pop-ups, disclosures should not be placed in them.

Text prompts should be tied to the disclosure to which they refer. General, vague statements like "See below for details" should be avoided. Similarly, when using a hyperlinked disclosure, advertisers should clearly label the hyperlink so it shows the importance, nature and relevance of the information to which it links. Example: "Early cancellation of Internet Service may result in substantial penalties. Click Here." A vague label like "Disclosures" is not enough to direct consumers to important restrictions or qualifications.

A hyperlink should be prominent, near the claim it is qualifying, easily noticeable, understandable, and lead directly to the qualifying information. A user should not be required to search a click-through page or go to other places for the information.

Disclosures should be repeated, as necessary, on lengthy websites and in connection with repeated claims. Disclosures may also have to be repeated if consumers have multiple routes through a website. If a product or service promoted online is intended to be (or can be) purchased from brick-and-mortar stores or from online retailers other than the advertiser itself, then any disclosure necessary to prevent deception or unfair injury should be presented in the advertisement itself.

If possible, design the site in such a way that consumers are not able to proceed further with a transaction (e.g., click forward) without scrolling through the disclosure. Making a disclosure unavoidable increases the likelihood that consumers will see it.

Product disclosures should not be placed in a website's Terms of Use.

SUBSTANTIATION

The FTC requires advertisers to do more than merely refrain from making false or misleading statements. They must, in addition, have a reasonable basis for any objective claims they make in their advertisements. An advertiser must have objective evidence that a claim is true before making it.

First announced in *Pfizer, Inc.*,[180] the substantiation requirement effectively shifts the burden of proof to advertisers to show that their claims are truthful rather than leaving it up to the FTC to demonstrate that a challenged claim is false.

Before making a claim, an advertiser must possess at least the level of substantiation expressly or impliedly claimed in the advertisement. If a claim states or implies a level of performance under specified conditions, then the claim must be substantiated by evidence that the product performs at that level under those conditions. If no specific level of substantiation is claimed, what constitutes a reasonable basis for a claim is determined on a case-by-case basis by analyzing the six *Pfizer* factors:

- Type of claim
- Type of product
- The benefits if the claim is true
- The consequences if the claim is false
- The ease and cost of developing substantiation for the claim
- The level of substantiation experts in the field would agree is reasonable.

Objective claims must be supported by objective evidence. Anecdotal and testimonial evidence may substantiate a person's experience but will not substantiate an objective claim.

The substantiation requirement applies to every kind of advertising, including comparative advertising. For example, a claim that "Our product outlasts Brand *X*" must be substantiated by objective evidence that the product does, in fact, endure longer than Brand *X* products do.

The requirement applies to both express and implied claims. The FTC has used this feature to establish a thirty-day time limit for a merchant's delivery of a product or service when the merchant has made no representation about the time for delivery. Under the Mail Order Rule (which applies to both traditional and online sales), a business that specifies a delivery time in an advertisement must have a reasonable basis for believing it can deliver within that time. If the business makes no statement about the time for delivery, the FTC asserts that it is making an implied claim that delivery will occur within thirty days. Accordingly, if a business says nothing about delivery time, then it must have objective evidence to prove that it has a reasonable basis for believing that it can ship within thirty days.

A higher level of substantiation is required for health, safety and pain relief claims than for other kinds of claims. In part, this is because advertisements for food, drugs, cosmetics and health-related devices and services are subject to a special definition of false advertising. 15 U.S.C. § 55 defines an advertisement of this kind of product as false if it "fails to reveal facts material in the light of such representations or material with respect to consequences which may result from the use of the commodity to which the advertisement relates under the conditions prescribed in said advertisement, or under such conditions as are customary or usual." In other words, advertisements for food, cosmetics and health-related products and services must disclose the possible consequences of using them.

Health, safety, and pain relief claims require competent and reliable scientific evidence, i.e., tests, analyses, research, studies, or other evidence based upon the expertise of professionals in the relevant area, that have been conducted and evaluated in an objective manner by persons qualified to do so, using procedures generally accepted in the profession to yield accurate and reliable results. The requirement is particularly stringent for medical claims, at least one court specifying that placebo-controlled, randomized, double blind studies are needed to support these kinds of claims.

If the Food and Drug Administration (FDA) or another government agency or authoritative body has developed a standard for substantiation, the FTC accords great deference to that standard but is not bound by it. FDA approval is not, by itself, adequate substantiation for all specific claims about a product. The FTC and the FDA generally arrive at the same conclusion when evaluating health claims, but there may be some instances when a carefully qualified health claim in advertising may be permissible under FTC law, in circumstances where it has not been authorized by the FDA for labeling.

The substantiation requirement cannot be avoided by offering a money-back guarantee.

Examples of the kinds of substantiating evidence that are necessary with respect to particular kinds of claims:

(a) "This website is secure" requires evidence that the website has what the FTC believes are reasonable security measures in place;

(b) "Best value" requires objective evidence that a product is worth more than the asking price;

(c) "Scientists agree" requires evidence that the claim has attained the level of scientific consensus (not merely that a few scientists agree)

"PUFFING"

Superlative, extremely general, or inherently preposterous statements are not considered false advertising and they do not require substantiation. Merchants are allowed to engage in a certain amount of "puffing" in their advertisement campaigns. For example, an advertiser is not required to have substantiating evidence for a claim that a particular breakfast cereal is "the greatest thing since sliced bread." An advertiser might be liable to a competitor under the Lanham Act for "puffing" but only if a substantial number of consumers are actually deceived by it.

PARTICULAR KINDS OF PRODUCTS AND CLAIMS

Short of producing a multivolume encyclopedia, it is not possible to catalog all of the disclosure and other advertising laws applicable to each and every kind of product, service and claim. The best that can be done is to provide a representative sampling.

Product Reviews

Product reviews are not subject to the disclosure and other requirements of advertising laws unless payment is received for them. Paid product or service reviews, testimonials and endorsements must comply with the FTC Act. All express and implied representations in paid product or service reviews must be truthful and not misleading, and the reviewer must have substantiation for them.

A paid reviewer's comments about the reviewer's experiences with a product must be truthful. Thus, for example, it would violate the FTC Act for a paid reviewer to write, "I like the flavor of this product" without having actually tasted it. Further, a paid reviewer's opinions must be honest. If a paid review does not like a product, then it would violate the FTC Act for the reviewer to claim, in the review, that she does.

These requirements also apply to product reviews that are posted in user comments on other people's websites or blogs.

Product reviews normally give readers the impression that they reflect the opinion of an objective and disinterested consumer. If that is not the case, then the reviewer must include a disclosure to prevent the review from being deceptive. The disclosure must reveal any information that may be relevant to a consumer's perception of the review as objective and disinterested. Any material relationship that exists between the marketer and the reviewer must be disclosed. This includes any family, employment or financial relationship.

Receiving a payment or a promise of payment for a review suffices to establish a financial relationship with the marketer. Payment may be in cash or in some other form. Furnishing or promising to furnish free product to a person with the hope that the person will write a review is a form of payment. It, too, requires a disclosure. Example: "XYZ Company sent me a free package of their product to review."

A review exchange club, in which people agree to publish reviews of each other's products (e.g., books), is a material relationship even though no money or product changes hands. Participants in such clubs may feel pressure to write positive reviews so that they will get positive reviews in return. Knowing this could affect the weight a consumer assigns to the opinions that are set out in one of these reviews. Therefore, the relationship should be disclosed when such reviews are published.

A business that receives revenue from advertisements or sales of another company's product or service (such as an affiliate in an affiliate marketing program) has a material financial relationship with the company. This relationship extends to employees of the business.

> **Example**. Bob is the owner of BobsBookBlog.com. He enters into an arrangement wherein he displays on his website advertisements containing links to books that are offered for sale on the Amazing.com website. Amazing.com agrees to pay him a specified amount of money for each visit to a book's ordering page on the Amazing.com website that results from a click on the link to the book on the BobsBookBlog.com website. Because this establishes a material financial relationship, any of Bob's reviews of an advertised book on his website must contain a disclosure of the relationship. The same is true if the book review is written by one of Bob's employees for the BobsBookBlog.com website, or if Bob pays an independent contractor to write the review.

The disclosures that are published in conjunction with a paid review must reveal that payment has been received (or promised) for the review. The disclosure must be conspicuous but it need not be elaborate. It may be something as simple as "Paid Review" or "Apex Company sent me Apex brand product to try, and here is my opinion about it...." Of course, if Apex Company provided or promised to provide another kind of payment, such as money, then that fact must be disclosed, too. Example: "People providing reviews on this site and/or about our products or services may receive payment in the form of affiliate commissions or fees, referral fees, promotional goods or materials, or other benefits from us."

To encourage honest reviews, the Consumer Review Fairness Act[181] (CRFA) makes it unlawful for a company to use a standard form contract provision that bars or restricts the ability of a person who is a party to the contract to honestly review the company's products, services, or conduct, or that imposes a penalty or fee against the person based on the content of the review. The Act applies to online reviews, social media posts, uploaded videos, etc., and it covers reviews of a company's customer service as well as product or service reviews.

The CRFA does not apply to contracts with a company's own employees or independent contractors or to any individually negotiated contract. It only applies to contracts that are offered without a meaningful opportunity for the individual to negotiate ("adhesion contracts"). A website's Terms of Use is an example of a standard form contract. A predrafted form that a company requires all product reviewers to sign is also an example of a standard form contract.

A company is allowed to prohibit, reject or remove any review from its website if it contains any of the following:

- Trade secret
- Private information
- Confidential communication
- A person's likeness
- Defamatory content
- Abusive or harassing content
- Obscene content
- Sexually explicit content
- Vulgar content
- False or misleading content
- Unlawful content
- Malicious code
- Material that is inappropriate with respect to race, gender, sexuality, ethnicity, or other intrinsic characteristic
- Material that is unrelated to the company's products or services.

The CRFA also makes it unlawful for a company to use a standard form contract provision that requires a reviewer to give up intellectual property rights to the review, except that a company may require a reviewer to grant the company a nonexclusive license to use the content of the review. Broader grants of intellectual property rights may be included in negotiated contracts and in contracts with employees or independent contractors.

The CRFA is enforceable by the FTC and state attorneys general. A violation of the CRFA is an unfair or deceptive trade practice.

Endorsements and Testimonials

Like product reviews, endorsements and testimonials are advertisements if payment (which may be cash, product, or other value) is received for them. As such, they must comply with all applicable advertising laws. This means they must not be false or misleading. It also means that both the marketer and the endorser must have substantiation for any claims made.

The FTC has issued Endorsement and Testimonial Guides providing guidance on how the FTC applies the FTC Act to endorsements and testimonials in advertisements. For purposes of these Guides, an *endorsement* is any advertising message or depiction of an individual, group or organization that consumers are likely to believe reflects the opinions, beliefs, findings or experiences of a person other than the sponsoring advertiser. The FTC does not distinguish between endorsements and testimonials.

> **Example 1**. An advertisement shows two unidentified men in a laundromat. One says to the other, "I love Brand X. It gets my clothes cleaner than any other brand." A company spokesperson then chimes in, saying, "Yes, it does! Our products are the best!" Because the men are presented as fictional characters, and because consumers are not likely to believe a company spokesperson's statements reflect the beliefs of a person other than the company, the advertisement does not contain an endorsement.

> **Example 2.** The same advertisement in Example 1 shows Johnny Depp using Brand X. Now the advertisement contains an endorsement. Although Mr. Depp says nothing, the depiction of him using the product makes consumers likely to believe that he has a positive opinion about it.

If the advertisement in Example 1 contained an express or implied representation that the two men were actual consumers rather than actors, then consumers may be misled into believing that the men were not paid for their endorsement. To prevent the advertisement from being deceptive, the fact that the persons depicted in the advertisement are paid actors would then need to be clearly and conspicuously disclosed.

A favorable product review is an endorsement if the reviewer receives something of value in exchange for writing or considering writing a review.

An endorsement must reflect the honest opinions, findings, beliefs, or experience of the endorser. Furthermore, it may not convey any express or implied representation that would be deceptive if made directly by the advertiser. The endorsement message need not be phrased in the exact words of the endorser, unless the advertisement affirmatively so represents. However, the endorsement may not be presented out of context or reworded so as to distort in any way the endorser's opinion or experience with the product.

When an advertisement represents that the endorser uses the endorsed product, the endorser must have been a bona fide user of it at the time the endorsement was given.

An advertiser may use an endorsement only so long as it has good reason to believe that the endorser continues to have the views presented. An advertiser may satisfy this obligation by inquiring into the endorser's views at reasonable intervals. The reasonableness of an interval is affected by the emergence of new information about product performance or effectiveness, material alterations in the product, changes in the performance of competitors' products, and the advertiser's contract commitments.

Advertisers are liable for false or unsubstantiated statements made through endorsements, or for failing to disclose material connections between themselves and their endorsers. Endorsers also may be liable for statements made in the course of their endorsements.

> **Example.** DermaGoo, Inc. sends its skin cream to Debbie and asks her to consider reviewing it. She does. After a couple of weeks, she notices her eczema has cleared up. She writes a review that states, "DermaGoo cures eczema!" DermaGoo has never made that claim and there is no evidence to substantiate it. Both Debbie and DermaGoo, Inc. may be charged with violating the FTC Act.

To reduce its exposure to liability for the false or misleading claims that an endorser makes, a company should provide guidance and training to endorsers (including reviewers) concerning the need to ensure that the statements they make are truthful and substantiated. A company also should monitor its reviewers and take steps necessary to stop the continued publication of deceptive representations when they are discovered.

An advertisement employing endorsements by one or more consumers about the performance of an advertised product or service will be interpreted as representing that the product or service is effective for the purpose depicted in the advertisement. Therefore, the advertiser must possess and rely upon adequate substantiation, including, when appropriate, competent and reliable scientific evidence, to support such claims. This obligation is the same whether the claim is made directly or by an endorser.

An advertisement containing an endorsement relating the experience of one or more consumers on a central or key attribute of the product or service will be interpreted as representing that the endorser's experience is representative of what consumers will generally experience. Therefore, an advertiser should possess and rely upon adequate substantiation for this representation. If the advertiser does not have substantiation that the endorser's experience is representative of what consumers will achieve, the advertisement should clearly and conspicuously disclose the generally expected performance in the depicted circumstances, and the advertiser must have adequate substantiation for that representation. Merely disclosing that the depicted results are not typical, or "Your results may vary," is not enough.

Advertisements presenting endorsements by what are represented, directly or by implication, to be actual consumers should utilize actual consumers in both the audio and video. If they are paid actors, then the advertisement needs to clearly and conspicuously disclose that the persons in such advertisements are not actual consumers of the advertised product. Of course, if actual, unpaid consumers are depicted giving their own opinions about a product, then there is no need to disclose anything about them. Further, if they only give their own personal, subjective opinions (as distinguished from something that states or implies an objective fact), then there would be no need for substantiation, either. A consumer's statement that "I like this product" is self-substantiating—unless, of course, she has made contradictory statements elsewhere.

An endorsement by a person who is represented to be an expert must be supported by an actual exercise of that expertise in evaluating product features or characteristics with respect to which the person is expert and which are relevant to an ordinary consumer's use of or experience with the product and available to the ordinary consumer. An endorsement of a prescription medication by a "doctor," for example, would be deceptive if the person portrayed has a doctorate in music appreciation rather than medicine.

An expert evaluation must have included an examination or testing of the product at least as extensive as someone with the same degree of expertise would normally need to conduct in order to support the conclusions presented in the endorsement. To the extent that the advertisement implies that the endorsement was based upon a comparison, the comparison must have been included in the expert's evaluation; and as a result of such comparison, the expert must have concluded that, with respect to those features on which the person is expert and which are relevant and available to an ordinary consumer, the endorsed product is at least equal overall to the competitors' products. Moreover, where the net impression created by the endorsement is that the advertised product is superior to other products with respect to any such feature or features, then the expert must in fact have found such superiority to be a fact.

As with product reviews, when there is a connection between the endorser and the seller of the advertised product that might materially affect the weight or credibility of the endorsement, it must be fully disclosed. Disclosure may not be necessary, though, if the endorser is a celebrity. A reasonable consumer is likely to expect a celebrity to have been paid for an endorsement, so failing to disclose the fact of payment would not be deceptive. Of course, if the celebrity's opinions are presented in a context in which consumers would not expect the celebrity to have received payment for his opinions, then a disclosure may be necessary if payment has, in fact been made. Consumers expect celebrities to have been paid for endorsements that appear in what is clearly an advertisement, but they would not expect a celebrity to have been paid to endorse a product during a news interview or in a social media post. If the celebrity was paid to endorse a product during an interview or in social media, then the fact of payment needs to be disclosed in order to prevent the endorsement from being deceptive. Further, if consumers would reasonably believe that the celebrity's experience is typical, then the advertiser must have substantiating evidence that it is

Disclosures may be necessary when consumers naturally expect the endorser to have been paid but not necessarily in the manner she was paid. Consumers might reasonably expect an expert or celebrity to have been paid for an endorsement in an advertisement, but might not reasonably expect the endorser to be receiving a percentage of revenues from sales of the product or to own shares of stock in the company that makes the product. These facts could materially affect the credibility that consumers attach to the endorsement. Accordingly, the advertisement should clearly and conspicuously disclose any such connection.

As with product reviews, a payment need not be in cash to make an endorsement an advertisement. Even if a marketer tells customers that they are not going to be paid but that they might be featured in advertising, that opportunity might be seen as having value. Accordingly, the fact that customers know this when their opinions are solicited should be disclosed (e.g., "Customers were told in advance that they might be featured in an ad.").

A payment made to a person after the person has spontaneously given an opinion about a product or service need not be disclosed, provided the opinion truly is spontaneous. In this situation, the payment could not possibly have affected the person's opinion, so a reasonable consumer would not expect it to have affected the person's opinion.

Although a depiction of a person using a product may be an implied endorsement of the product, the FTC has taken the position that product placement (paying to have a product appear in unrelated entertainment content) does not, by itself, require disclosure of the payment.

Certifications and Seals of Approval

The same principles that apply to endorsements apply to certifications and seals of approval. All express and implied claims must be true and any material relationship between the merchant and the certifying organization must be disclosed. A relationship is material if it could affect the credibility of the endorsement. A certification or seal of approval does not have the effect of substantiating the claims made in an advertisement.

Affiliate Marketing

Since the affiliate in an affiliate marketing arrangement receives payment or a promise of payment from the marketer for referrals to the marketer's website from the affiliate's website, an affiliate must comply with the requirements for advertisements. The requirements are not a lot different from those applicable to product reviews and endorsements. If an affiliate is entitled to a payment that is tied to clicks on an advertisement displayed on the affiliate's website or in the affiliate's posts, then any reviews or endorsements the affiliate publishes about the advertised product must disclose the relationship. The disclosure might be something like, "I get commissions for purchases made through links in this post." Statements like "Affiliate link" or a 'Buy now' button do not adequately disclose the nature of the relationship.

A company that uses the affiliate model to sell its products is responsible for ensuring that their affiliates do not engage in false advertising or other unfair or deceptive trade practices.

Infomercials and Paid "News Articles"

An article about a product or service that creates a false impression that it is objective reporting when in reality it is an advertisement violates the FTC Act's prohibition against deceptive trade practices. To prevent the presentation of the information from being deceptive, it must be clearly and conspicuously disclosed that the article is an advertisement. Any relationship that would be material to a consumer's purchasing decision must be disclosed, as well. For example, if an "informational" website about certain kinds of products is sponsored by or affiliated with a vendor of those products, then the nature of the relationship must be clearly and conspicuously disclosed on the website. If payment is received from the marketer for publishing the "article," the fact of payment must be disclosed.

Business Opportunities

As explained in Chapter 5, a franchisor must make a variety of disclosures to potential franchisees. Businesses that offer or advertise money-making opportunities must also make a variety of disclosures to potential participants. The FTC's principal concern about these kinds of offers is that they may mislead consumers about their earnings potential. Accordingly, the agency has enacted a Business Opportunity Rule aimed at imposing tight controls on earnings claims.

The Rule defines an earnings claim as "an oral, written or visual representation to a prospective business opportunity purchaser which states a specific level of potential sales, income, gross or net profit for that prospective business opportunity purchaser, or which states other facts which suggest such a specific level."

An offer comes within the coverage of the Business Opportunity Rule if all of the following apply:

(a) It is a solicitation for a new business activity, i.e., it offers an opportunity to engage in a business in which the prospective customer is not already engaged;
(b) The prospective customer is required to make a payment to the seller (or to an affiliate of the seller) for the right to obtain or begin operating the new business activity;
(c) The seller or someone recommended by the seller provides assistance to the buyer.

Assistance may take the form of providing outlets, accounts or customers; promising to buy back goods or services; or providing locations for the use or operation of equipment or other things for which the buyer has paid.

The "required payment" may involve a direct or an indirect payment. The Rule cannot be avoided by structuring the offer in a way that requires payment to a third party instead of to the offeree directly. Nor can the Rule by avoided by purporting to require payment for necessary materials or supplies but not for the business opportunity itself. Payment for materials, equipment, supplies, etc. that are needed to operate the business are considered payment for the business opportunity regardless of how the offer is worded.

The Business Opportunity Rule does not apply if any of the three elements listed above is absent. For example, an offer of general business advice and training is not subject to the Rule, even if payment is required. Since no opportunity for a "new business" is being offered, the first of the three elements is absent.

A business opportunity advertiser that makes an earnings claim should avoid publishing an earnings disclaimer that contradicts the claim. Since both statements cannot be true, a business that publishes both statements would be guilty of engaging in a deceptive trade practice.

A variety of disclosures must accompany a business opportunity earnings claim in order to prevent a finding that the claim is an unfair or deceptive trade practice. The disclosures must be made in a detailed disclosure document at least ten days before the consumer pays any money or legally commits to a purchase. Among other things, the document must include:

(a) the names, addresses, and telephone numbers of other purchasers
(b) a fully audited financial statement of the seller
(c) the background and experience of the business's key executives
(d) the cost of starting and maintaining the business
(e) the responsibilities of the seller and purchaser once the purchase is made
(f) if earnings representations are made, the written basis for these claims, including the number and percentage of owners who have done at least as well as claimed.

For more information, see 16 CFR Part 437.

Marketing business opportunities entails many legal risks. For this reason, attorneys and business advisors often advise against attempting it.

Claims About Results

Testimonial claims about results obtained from a product or service (e.g., "I lost 50 lbs. using this product" or "Ned earns $10,000 per month using our method) are inherently misleading unless everybody who uses the product or service is guaranteed to have the same results. Although these kinds of advertisements might not expressly state that everybody will experience the same results, that is what they imply.

At one time, displaying a disclaimer like "Results are not typical" or "Your results may vary" would prevent a finding that a statement of this kind was misleading. The FTC now requires the disclosure to say more than that. If the results described in an advertisement or testimonial are not typical, then it is necessary to disclose what kinds of results actually are typical.

A business that makes claims about a product or service, or about results obtained from using a product or service, must also be able to substantiate them. This is true whether the claim appears in the main part of the advertisement or in a disclosure made in conjunction with the claim. An advertiser must have evidence to substantiate that a statement or depiction of a consumer's experience with a product or service is typical. Otherwise, it must:

(a) disclose the fact that the results are not guaranteed or typical;
(b) describe what results are, in fact, typical;
(c) maintain evidence to substantiate the original claim, as made; and
(d) maintain evidence to substantiate the claim made in the disclosure about what kinds of results are, in fact, typical.

Warranties and Guarantees

FTC guidelines specify that if an advertisement mentions that a product comes with a guarantee or warranty, the advertisement needs to disclose: (a) any conditions or limits on the guarantee or warranty (such as a time limit or a requirement that the consumer return the product), and (b) how consumers can get the details. Any limitations, conditions, qualifications or exceptions to a company's cancellation, return and/or refund policies must be disclosed, too.

Under the FTC's Pre Sale Availability Rule, an advertisement for a consumer product that is sold in stores for more than $15 must inform consumers that a copy of the warranty is available to read prior to sale at the place where the product is sold. For products priced at $15 or less, the advertisement should inform consumers how to get a copy of the warranty. In online advertising, either a full copy of the warranty or information about where the customer may view the warranty (e.g., a link to a page on which the warranty appears) prior to purchase must be displayed in proximity to the product description. To meet FTC requirements, an advertisement that mentions a warranty on a product that may be purchased online or by mail or telephone must tell consumers how they can view the warranty prior to purchase.

Regardless of the price of a product, phrases like "Satisfaction Guaranteed" or "Money Back Guarantee" should be used only if the advertiser is willing to provide full refunds to customers when they return the merchandise for any reason.

An advertisement of a "lifetime" warranty or guarantee is ambiguous. It could mean the life of the product, the life of the purchaser, or the life of the purchaser for so long as he owns the product. This could be material to the purchasing decision. The advertisement should make it clear to consumers which life measures the warranty's duration.

The Magnuson-Moss Warranty Act and FTC Rules require warranties and claims of "satisfaction guaranteed" and the like to inform consumers of any material conditions or limitations on the offer. For example, a restriction limiting the offer to a specific time period, such as thirty days, is a material condition that should be disclosed. Moreover, the term *guarantee* implicitly represents to consumers that the seller will refund the full purchase price at the purchaser's request. Any conditions or limitations necessary to ensure this representation is not deceptive must be clearly and conspicuously disclosed prior to purchase.

Refunds

Refunds must be given to dissatisfied consumers if the advertiser has made a representation to this effect, such as "Your money back if not satisfied."

Rebates

According to the FTC, rebate promotions should disclose:

(a) the amount of the rebate
(b) the before-rebate cost
(c) any additional terms and conditions
(d) any purchase requirements
(e) any additional fees
(f) when consumers can expect to receive the rebate.

Negative Option Offers

The Negative Option Rule applies to sellers of subscription plans who ship merchandise like books or compact discs to consumers who have agreed in advance to become subscribers. It requires advertisements to clearly and conspicuously disclose material information about the terms of the plan. Once consumers agree to enroll, the company must notify them before shipping to allow them to decline the merchandise. Even if an automatic shipment or continuity program doesn't fall within the specifics of the Rule, companies should be careful to clearly disclose the terms and conditions of the plan before billing consumers or charging their credit cards.

Dry-Testing

Dry-testing refers to the practice of placing an advertisement for a product to see if there is sufficient consumer interest to justify the expense of manufacturing it. The FTC has issued an advisory opinion that such advertisements must clearly disclose to consumers the fact that the merchandise is only planned and may not ever be shipped. If any part of the promotion is later dropped, the merchant must notify subscribers of the fact within a reasonable time after soliciting their subscriptions. If, within a reasonable time after soliciting their subscriptions, the merchant has made no decision to ship the merchandise, it must notify subscribers of this fact and give them the opportunity to cancel and, where payment has been made, make a prompt refund. The merchant can make no substitutions of any merchandise for what the customer ordered.

"Free"

Products or services advertised as "free" must, in fact, be free. For example, advertising a "free tour" of a website and then charging a visitor's credit card for it is a violation of the FTC Act. Any conditions or exceptions to a "free offer," or costs of any kind (e.g., postage) must be clearly and conspicuously disclosed. They must not be hidden from potential buyers.

"Buy One, Get One Free"

A company that offers something for "free" when some other item is purchased must truly offer it for free. It must not mark up the price of the purchased item to cover the cost of the "free" item.

Product Demonstrations

Product demonstrations implicitly represent that the product operates in the way shown under normal conditions and use. This representation must be truthful and substantiated.

Deep Linking

Deep linking is the practice of providing a link to a page within another person's or company's website other than the home page. Because it does not take a user to the other person's or company's home page, it might mislead a user into thinking the page is part of the referring website. Publishing a disclaimer to the effect that clicking the link will take the user to another company's website may help forestall a claim that the website misleads consumers.

Auctions

Advertising nonexistent merchandise through online auction houses is an unfair and deceptive trade practice and also violates a number of other laws.

Comparative Advertising

Claims about the relative quality, price, functionality, or other characteristics of a competitor's products or services are permitted so long as all of the express and implied claims in them are truthful and substantiated with objective evidence.

"Studies prove …"

An advertisement claiming that "studies prove" something about a product must be substantiated by actual studies proving the stated fact. A reference to "studies" also conveys an implicit representation that the studies are methodologically sound. Substantiating evidence for this claim is needed, as well.

"9 out of 10 Dentists [Doctors, Mothers, etc.] …"

A claim that a specified percentage, proportion or number of people with a specified attribute regularly use, recommend or prescribe a product must be substantiated by evidence that the stated number actually do use, recommend or prescribe the product. It might be thought that if the claim is that a specified percentage of "those surveyed" use, recommend or prescribe the product, then there is no problem so long as the advertiser can select a group with opinions and preferences in that proportion. The question, though, is how a reasonable consumer would interpret the claim. An argument could be made that a reasonable consumer would interpret a claim like this as implying the survey sample is randomly selected.

Moreover, an advertisement of this kind may convey an implied claim that the product offers some particular benefit associated with the indicated group. A claim that most dentists recommend a brand of chewing gum for their patients who chew gum, for example, conveys an implied claim that the gum is better for the health of people's teeth than other kinds of gum are. An advertiser making such a claim will need to have evidence substantiating both the literal claim and this implied claim. .

Business Name and Address

Several states require an online merchant to disclose its complete address and any assumed business names it uses. Not all require that the disclosure be published to the website, however. Some permit the disclosure to be made in an email or other written communication to the customer, provided the disclosure occurs before the customer pays for the product or service.

A website that sells to consumers domiciled in the EU must disclose the seller's identity.

Consumer Leases

The Consumer Leasing Act requires certain kinds of disclosures in advertising for leases of products to consumers. Specific requirements are set out in the Federal Reserve Board's Regulation M.

Child-Directed Advertising

Children may have greater difficulty evaluating advertising claims and understanding the nature of the information provided in an advertisement. Sellers should take special care to avoid misrepresenting a product or its performance when advertising to children. The Children's Advertising Review Unit of the Council of Better Business Bureaus has published specific guidelines for children's advertising.

900 Numbers

900 numbers allow the owner of the number to charge callers a per-call or per-minute charge for the call. Congress enacted the Telephone Disclosure and Dispute Resolution Act[182] to protect consumers, who do not always know how much a call to such a service will cost. The FTC's 900-Number Rule[183] implements this law by requiring advertisements of pay-per-call services to disclose the cost of the call. All costs and potential charges must be disclosed. If the caller may be transferred to another pay-per-call service, the advertisement must disclose the cost (and all potential charges) of that call as well.

Advertisements for services that promote sweepstakes or games of chance or provide information about a federal program (but are not sponsored by a federal agency) require additional disclosures. Special requirements apply to advertisements directed to children. See Chapter 18.

Software and Computer-Related Products and Services

The FTC Act and other advertising laws usually apply to advertisements for software and other computer-related products and services. For example, continuing to bill a software licensee's credit card after the license period has expired is an unfair trade practice in violation of the FTC Act.

Attorney Advertising

Attorneys and some other professionals with an Internet presence must comply with state regulations of advertising regarding these professions. Content on attorney websites, for example, must comply with rules of professional responsibility that prohibit misleading statements and require disclosure of the fact that it is an advertisement.

The websites and certain social media posts of professionals are considered forms of advertising. Accordingly, they are subject both to advertising laws and to a state's regulations on attorney (or other professional) advertising. Also, the rules of professional responsibility for attorneys prohibit attorneys from soliciting new clients in certain ways. Some, but not all, jurisdictions make an exception for solicitations of family members, close personal friends, people with whom an attorney has a prior professional relationship, and/or people who have specifically requested information from an attorney. It is not clear whether sending a "friend" request to a person who is not a relative or close personal friend and with whom the professional does not have an existing or prior professional relationship is a "solicitation" for purposes of these rules. If the professional's profile page or status updates contain anything that might be construed as advertising (as many LinkedIn profile pages do), then sending this kind of request might very well be considered a solicitation of clients, potentially in violation of ethics rules.

Professionals also need to ensure that they are not described or designated in a misleading way on websites. Describing oneself on a website or discussion board as a "specialist" or "expert" in a particular field within a profession when one is not, in fact, certified as a specialist in that field, is an example of a misleading statement.

Publishing client endorsements and testimonials can run afoul of ethical rules even if they are literally true and do not violate confidentiality rules. This method of advertising may be misleading because it may imply that similar results are attainable for other clients, too. Winning a tidy settlement on behalf of one client does not necessarily mean that similar victories are achievable for others. The facts of each case are different. Some jurisdictions prohibit attorneys from using testimonials and/or endorsements in their advertising at all. Others permit them but only if certain disclaimers are published along with them. Professionals with profiles on directory sites are responsible for ensuring their profiles comply with ethical requirements.

Environmental Claims

The FTC takes the position that it is deceptive to misrepresent, directly or by implication, that a product, package or service offers a general environmental benefit. Broad claims are difficult or impossible to substantiate. Advertisers need to qualify general environmental benefit claims to prevent deception about the nature of the environmental benefit being asserted. Qualifications must be clear, prominent, understandable, in plain language, in sufficiently large type, and in close proximity to the qualified claim. In addition, they should make clear whether the claims made apply to the product, the packaging, or a component of either.

"BIODEGRADABLE"

An unqualified claim that a product is degradable or biodegradable implies a one-year period for complete decomposition of both the product and the package.

"ENVIRONMENTALLY-FRIENDLY" OR "ECO-FRIENDLY"

This is too general, standing alone, so it must be qualified with more specific information.

"FREE OF"

A product may be advertised as "free of" a specified substance or ingredient if there aren't even trace amounts of it. If it contains any amount of the substance at all, then it may be advertised as "free of" the substance only if:

(a) The product does not have more than trace amounts or background levels of the substance;
(b) The amount of the substance present does not cause harm that consumers typically associate with the substance; and
(c) The substance was not added to the product intentionally.

It is deceptive to claim a product is free of a specified substance if it contains another substance that is just as harmful. It may also be deceptive to claim a product is "free of" a substance if the substance normally is not present in the product category anyway.

"GREEN"

This term is too general, standing alone. It must be qualified with more specific information.

"NONTOXIC"

This term implies a product is safe for both humans and the environment. This requires substantiation by reliable scientific evidence.

"RECYCLABLE"

This term implies that recycling facilities are available to at least 60% of the consumers in communities where a product is sold. If that claim cannot be substantiated, then the advertiser should add a qualifier such as: "This product may not be recyclable in your area." If only a very small number of communities offer recycling for the product category, then the qualifier should be something like: "This product is recyclable only in the few communities that have appropriate recycling programs." The FTC takes the position that even a truthful claim that a material is recyclable is deceptive if it implies a significant environmental benefit that is not significant. For example, saying that garbage bags are recyclable, even if true, apparently is deceitful because it implies this is a significant environmental benefit when the reality is that very few garbage bags are separated from trash for recycling.

"RECYCLED CONTENT"

This term implies that the product is made entirely from materials that have been recovered or diverted from the waste stream. If the product contains some unrecycled content, then an appropriate qualifying statement should be added to the claim. Representing used, reconditioned or remanufactured products as "recycled" is deceptive.

Carbon offset claims should not be advertised if the law already requires the activity that is the basis for the offset.

Appliances and Light Bulbs

Online advertisements of major appliances must include images of the Energy Guide. Online advertisements of light bulbs must include images of the "Lighting Facts" (estimated annual energy cost) labels so website retailers can hyperlink to them or download them. The label for each product must remain on the website for six months after production ends. This requirement only applies to those who advertise these products online with price, terms of sale and ordering information. When the requirement applies, the advertisement must clearly and conspicuously disclose, on the page listing the item, an image of the label in close proximity to its price on each page that contains a detailed description of the product.

Country of Origin Claims

Clothing (textile, wool and fur products) and automobiles advertised or sold in the United States are to be marked or labeled "Made in the U.S.A." if and only if all or virtually all significant parts and processing that go into the product are of U.S. origin. Other countries may have country-of-origin labeling requirements that differ from those of the United States.

Any merchant that advertises its products as "Made in the U.S.A.," whether online or in another medium, is representing to consumers that all or substantially all components and final assembly or processing are of U.S. origin. If more than a negligible portion of the components are of foreign origin, the phrase "Assembled in the U.S.A." may be used in lieu of "Made in the U.S.A.," provided the principal assembly takes place in the United States. The assembly, however, must involve a substantial transformation. Merely fastening components together with a screwdriver or wrench is not likely to result in a "substantial transformation."

A "Made in the U.S.A." claim may be express or implied. It may be implied from the use of American symbols or geographic references, such as the U.S. flag, a U.S. map outline, or references to U.S. locations of headquarters or factories.

Imported goods must be marked with a foreign country of origin.

Misrepresentations about country of origin constitute false advertising. Marketing products in a way that does not comply with the FTC's country-of-origin regulations is a deceptive trade practice. Enforcement is by the FTC. A competitor who is harmed as a result of the violation may sue for damages under the Lanham Act.

Clothing (textile and wool products) advertisements must display, in the description of the product, the country of origin (Made in the U.S.A., Imported, or both).

Clothing

In addition to disclosing the country of origin, clothing advertisements that state or imply anything about fiber content must disclose the generic fiber names (as assigned by the FTC) in order of predominance by weight. This requirement applies to all advertisements. Fibers present in an amount less than 5% may be listed as "other fiber(s)." There is an exception to the 5% requirement for fibers that have a functional significance even in an amount less than 5%.

Unless a product is made directly from bamboo fiber ("mechanically processed bamboo"), it cannot be called bamboo. If a product is not made directly from bamboo fiber, but is a manufactured fiber for which bamboo was the plant source, then it should be labeled and advertised using the generic name for the fiber, such as rayon, or "rayon made from bamboo." Also, as with everything else, taking somebody else's word that a fiber was made from bamboo will not suffice as substantiation.

Jewelry

The FTC has published detailed Guides for jewelry advertisements. They cover claims made for gold, silver, platinum, pewter, diamonds, gemstones, and pearls. They explain how certain common terms may be used, such as when a product may be called gold-plated or when a diamond may be called flawless. They also describe information that sellers should disclose in their ads so that consumers are not misled. For example, sellers of synthetic or imitation gemstones must disclose that the gemstone is not natural, and sellers of pearls need to disclose whether they are cultured or imitation.

Food, Drugs, Cosmetics, and Health-Related Devices and Services

Advertisements of food, drugs, cosmetics or health-related devices or services must disclose any information needed to ensure that the claims made are not deceptive. They must also disclose any information that is material in light of the claims made or suggested in the advertisement, or that are material considering how consumers would customarily use the product. Thus, if an advertisement would be misleading without certain qualifying information, that information must be disclosed. For example, advertisers should disclose information relevant to the limited applicability of an advertised benefit. Similarly, advertising that makes either an express or implied safety representation should include information about any significant safety risks. Even in the absence of affirmative safety representations, advertisers may need to inform consumers of significant safety concerns relating to the use of their product. The relevant statute defines false advertising of these kinds of products and services as including not only false or misleading representations but also a failure to include material information about the consequences that may result from the use of the product or service under normal conditions or under the conditions prescribed in the advertisement.

FOOD

Under the Nutrition Labeling and Education Act[184] and FDA regulations, only FDA-approved nutrient content and health claims may appear on food labels. The FTC applies FDA definitions of *serving size, high fiber, low fat* and other nutrition-related terms to analyze the truthfulness of food advertising. Claims characterizing the level of a nutrient must be consistent with FDA definitions. An unqualified claim of a health benefit associated with a food must be substantiated by evidence of significant scientific agreement that the claim is true. Health claims that are not yet FDA-approved must be adequately qualified so that consumers understand both the extent of the support for the claim and any significant contrary evidence in the scientific community. In many cases, the presence and significance of risk-increasing nutrients must be disclosed to prevent a health claim from being deceptive.

OLEOMARGARINE

A representation that oleomargarine is a dairy product is deemed misleading by law.

DIETARY SUPPLEMENTS

The Dietary Supplements Health and Education Act[185] (DSHEA) requires all statements of nutritional support for dietary supplements to be accompanied by a two-part disclaimer on the product label: that the statement has not been evaluated by the FDA and that the product is not intended to diagnose, treat, cure or prevent any disease. Although the DSHEA does not apply to advertising, there are situations where such a disclosure may be needed in advertising to prevent consumers from being misled about the nature of the product and the extent to which its efficacy and safety have been reviewed by regulatory authorities. For example, a disclosure may be necessary if the text or images in the advertisement lead consumers to believe that the product has undergone the kind of review for safety and efficacy that the FDA conducts on new drugs and has been found to be beneficial for the treatment of disease. Failure to correct those misperceptions may render the advertising deceptive.

On the other hand, a DSHEA disclaimer is not sufficient to "fix" a deceptive claim about the health benefits of a product or about the efficacy of the product in preventing or treating disease. Compliance with the notification and disclaimer provisions of the DSHEA does not constitute authorization of a claim by the FDA. Advertisers should not imply that the FDA has specifically approved any claim on that basis.

Under the DSHEA, supplement marketers are allowed to make two kinds of claims on labeling: (1) health claims specifically authorized by the FDA; and (2) statements of nutritional support. Health claims—representations about the relationship between a nutrient and a disease or health-related condition—are permitted only if they have been authorized by an FDA finding that there is significant scientific agreement to support the claim. The Food and Drug Administration Modernization Act[186] also now allows health claims that are based on authoritative statements from certain federal scientific bodies, such as the National Institutes of Health or the National Academy of Sciences. Aside from these authorized claims, supplement marketers are prohibited from making any labeling claim about the diagnosis, mitigation, treatment or cure of a disease.

In contrast to health claims, structure/function claims, within the broader category of "statements of nutritional support," refer to representations about a dietary supplement's effect on the structure or function of the body for maintenance of good health and nutrition. Structure/function claims are not subject to FDA pre-authorization. A marketer may make these claims in labeling if it notifies the FDA and if it includes a disclaimer that the claim has not been evaluated by the FDA and that the product is not intended to diagnose, mitigate, treat, cure, or prevent disease. The DSHEA also requires that structure/function claims in labeling be substantiated, truthful and not misleading. .

DRUGS AND HEALTH-RELATED PRODUCTS AND SERVICES

Claims about drugs and other health products and services generally must be substantiated by confirming scientific evidence.

If a claim is based only on historical or traditional use, then it must be presented in such a way that consumers understand that the sole basis for the claim is a history of use of the product for a particular purpose. Herbal medicines are an example. The degree of qualification necessary to communicate the absence of scientific substantiation for a traditional use claim will depend in large part on consumer understanding of this category of products. There may be situations where even a carefully qualified "traditional use" is inadequate to substantiate a claim, particularly if there is a substantial risk of injury to consumer health or safety as a consequence of a false claim. For this reason, an advertiser should not suggest, either directly or indirectly, that a supplement product will provide a disease benefit unless there is competent and reliable scientific evidence to substantiate that benefit.

Comfrey advertisements should include a warning that internal use may cause liver damage or death.

St. John's Wort advertisements should include a warning that it can have potentially dangerous interactions for patients taking certain prescription drugs and for pregnant women

Ephedra advertisements should include a warning that it can have dangerous effects on the central nervous system and heart.

Advertisements for bodybuilding supplements with steroids should include a warning that steroid hormones may cause breast enlargement, testicle shrinkage and infertility, increased facial and body hair, voice deepening, and clitoral enlargement in females. Consumers should be advised that "if you are at risk for prostate or breast cancer, you should not use this product."

Advertisements for aspirin should include this disclosure: "Aspirin is not appropriate for everyone, so be sure to talk with your doctor before beginning an aspirin regimen."

Representations about the safety or efficacy of Lasik or any other refractive surgery sometimes may require disclosures of key information about health risks or limitations associated with the surgery to prevent charges of deception. An advertisement making express or implied representations that the procedure is "safe" or "clinically proven to be safe," for example, also should tell consumers that, like any surgery, Lasik or other advertised refractive surgery has risks and potential complications, and that they will be discussed during a surgical consultation prior to the procedure.

Antifreeze

Antifreeze advertisements need to warn consumers that it may be harmful if swallowed.

Safety Claims

Advertisers must have reliable substantiation to support safety and risk-reduction claims and must carefully qualify claims to indicate the level of safety or significant risks.

Credit or Insurance

A company that uses a credit report in connection with the making of a firm offer of credit or insurance must include in each solicitation regarding the transaction the following clear and conspicuous disclosures:

(a) Information contained in the consumer's credit report was used in connection with the transaction;
(b) The consumer received the offer of credit or insurance because the consumer satisfied criteria for creditworthiness or insurability;
(c) If applicable, the credit or insurance may not be extended if, after the consumer responds to the offer, the consumer does not meet the criteria used to select the consumer for the offer or any applicable criteria bearing on creditworthiness or insurability or does not furnish any required collateral;
(d) The consumer has a right to prohibit information contained in the consumer's file with any consumer reporting agency from being used in connection with any credit or insurance transaction that is not initiated by the consumer;
(e) The consumer may exercise the right by notifying a credit reporting agency's notification system.

The disclosure must include the address and toll free telephone number of the appropriate notification system and be presented in such format and in such type size and manner as to be simple and easy to understand.

A company that relies on a credit report in making an offer of credit or insurance to a consumer must maintain on file the criteria used to select the consumer to receive the offer, all criteria bearing on creditworthiness or insurability, as applicable, that are the basis for determining whether or not to extend credit or insurance pursuant to the offer, and any requirement for the furnishing of collateral as a condition of the extension of credit or insurance, for three years after the offer was made.

Credit Repair

The Credit Repair Organizations Act[187] prohibits false or misleading representations and requires disclosure of the "Consumer Credit File Rights Under State and Federal Laws" statement specified in 15 U.S.C. § 1679c. Also, a credit repair company may not demand advance payment. Contracts must be in writing, dated and signed, and a copy must be given to the consumer. The Act also gives consumers certain cancellation rights.

Funeral Services

The FTC's Funeral Rule[188] requires itemized price information and various other disclosures in advertisements of funeral goods and services. In addition, the Rule prohibits a seller of funeral goods or services from:

(a) misrepresenting legal, crematory, and cemetery requirements
(b) embalming for a fee without permission

(c) requiring the purchase of a casket for direct cremation
(d) requiring consumers to buy certain funeral goods or services as a condition for furnishing other funeral goods or services
(e) engaging in other deceptive or unfair practices.

Penalties range up to $41,484 per violation.

Spam

The Controlling the Assault of Nonsolicited Pornography And Marketing Act[189] (CAN-SPAM) mandates a number of disclosures when sending commercial email messages:

(a) The header (To, From, Subject, IP address) must contain accurate disclosures of such information;
(b) A functioning return email address that the recipient may use to request no further messages must be provided;
(c) The message must clearly and conspicuously disclose that it is an advertisement;
(d) The message must include a valid physical postal address, which may be a street address, post office box or a private mailbox registered with a commercial mail receiving agency that is registered with the U.S. Postal Service;
(e) The message must clearly and conspicuously disclose that the recipient has a right to unsubscribe, i.e., a right to opt out of receiving more email messages from the sender;
(f) The message must include a clear and conspicuous explanation of how the recipient can opt out of getting email from the sender in the future.

Any opt-out mechanism that is offered must be capable of processing opt-out requests for at least thirty days after a person receives the message. The sender must honor an opt-out request within ten business days. The sender may not charge a fee or require a recipient to provide personally identifying information (other than an email address) as a condition of opting out. The only things a sender may require in order for a recipient to opt out are that the recipient send a reply email or visit a page on a website to opt out. An opt-out mechanism that is provided on a webpage must be set up in such a way that it requires only a single click on the user's part in order to be effective. Once a person has effectively opted out, the sender may not send more commercial email messages to that person. Nor may the sender sell or transfer the person's email address to others or include it in a mailing list that is sold or given to others, unless the transfer is to a company the sender has retained to help it comply with the CAN-SPAM Act.

Under the FTC's "designated sender" rule, not all contributors, advertisers or senders of a single email message need to be listed in the "From" section of the header, so long as at least one designated sender who assumes responsibility for CAN-SPAM compliance is listed there.

Each individual email violating the CAN-SPAM Act may result in a fine of up to $40,654.

The CAN-SPAM Act applies to all commercial email messages, not just bulk email messages. Even a single commercial email message sent to only one person may be a violation if it does not comply with CAN-SPAM requirements.

The Act applies to both business-to-business commercial messages and business-to-consumer commercial messages. Thus, a wholesaler who emails its price list to retailers must comply with

CAN-SPAM requirements, and a retailer who sends an advertisement to a consumer must comply with CAN-SPAM requirements.

Email messages containing transactional or relationship content are not considered commercial email messages. A transactional or relationship email message is one that does nothing more than one or more of the following:

(a) Facilitates or confirms a commercial transaction to which the recipient has already agreed;
(b) Gives warranty, recall, safety, or security information about a product or service;
(c) Gives information about a change in terms or features or account balance information regarding a membership, subscription, account, loan or other ongoing commercial relationship;
(d) Provides information about an employment relationship or employee benefits;
(e) Delivers goods or services the recipient has already requested or agreed to accept.

An email message does not qualify for this exemption if it is false or misleading. Even transactional and relationship email messages are prohibited from having false or misleading headers or content. Also, both commercial and transactional or relationship email senders must comply with the "designated sender" rule.

An email message that contains both commercial and transactional or relationship content is deemed to be commercial if a reasonable recipient would interpret the subject line as suggesting that the message contains an advertisement or promotion for a product or service. It will also be deemed to be commercial if the transactional or relationship content does not appear mainly at the beginning of the message. Email messages that contain both commercial content and some kind of content other than either commercial, transactional or relationship, are also evaluated using the reasonable recipient standard: If a reasonable recipient would interpret it as primarily a commercial email based on either the subject line or the content of the message, then it is a commercial message.

Solicited email messages (such as an emailed newsletter to which the recipient has subscribed) generally are considered transactional or relationship messages.

An email sender is not permitted to do indirectly what the CAN-SPAM Act prohibits doing directly. Thus, hiring another firm to handle email marketing for a company will not protect the company from liability for CAN-SPAM violations. Both the company that handles the email marketing and the company whose product or service is promoted in the message may be held legally responsible for an email message that violates CAN-SPAM requirements.

Vicarious liability for CAN-SPAM violations is broader than at common law. A seller need not formally hire a person to send email on the seller's behalf in order to be vicariously liable for CAN-SPAM violations. If a seller offers any kind of benefit to another to send a commercial message on the seller's behalf, then the seller may be liable for the sender's CAN-SPAM violations. For example, if the seller offers coupons, discounts, awards, additional entries in a sweepstakes, or the like, in exchange for forwarding a message, the seller may be responsible for the sender's CAN-SPAM compliance. Similarly, a seller may remain responsible for the sender's CAN-SPAM compliance if the seller gives a benefit to the sender in exchange for generating traffic to a website or for any form of referral. Unless the recipient is offered some kind of benefit for forwarding the message, though, merely including a link in an email message that allows the recipient to forward it will not, by itself, make the original sender responsible for the recipient's CAN-SPAM violations in connection with forwarding the message to others.

Many states have enacted laws regulating spam. The CAN-SPAM Act expressly preempts state laws purporting to regulate commercial email messages, but it is subject to some exceptions. State laws that apply to noncommercial email messages, or to both commercial and noncommercial email messages, are not preempted. State laws addressing computer crime or fraud more generally are not preempted, either. Contractual prohibitions against spam (such as in an Internet access provider's Terms of Use) remain enforceable under state law. And state laws prohibiting fraud or deception in commercial email messages (or attachments to them) are not preempted. A state law requiring senders of commercial email messages to make such disclosures as are necessary to prevent a message from being false or misleading might come within this latter exception, but state laws imposing other kinds of disclosure requirements explicitly for commercial email messages alone would be preempted by the CAN-SPAM Act.

The CAN-SPAM Act applies to text messages, too. In addition, a commercial text message may not be sent to a consumer's phone without the consumer's prior express authorization. The message must identify the company and provide an opt-out mechanism that is available for at least thirty days. If a consumer opts out of receiving more messages, then the company must stop sending commercial messages to the consumer within ten days.

At least one court has upheld the constitutionality of the CAN-SPAM Act. Because the First Amendment protects commercial speech, an absolute ban on unsolicited commercial email would most likely be unconstitutional. The CAN-SPAM Act, however, does not impose an absolute prohibition. Commercial speech receives less First Amendment protection than many other kinds of speech do, and false or misleading commercial speech is not constitutionally protected at all. Even truthful commercial speech may be regulated if the regulation furthers a substantial state interest. In *White Buffalo Ventures v. University of Texas at Austin*,[180] the Fifth Circuit Court of Appeals held that blocking unwanted spam is a substantial state interest. So long as a regulation of commercial speech is no more extensive than necessary to further the interest in blocking unwanted spam, it will pass constitutional muster.

In addition to truthfulness and disclosure requirements, the CAN-SPAM Act also provides criminal and civil penalties for certain kinds of conduct in connection with commercial email messages. See Chapter 20.

Unlawful Methods of Advertising

The number of ways to abuse the Internet is limited only by the human imagination, as will be seen in Chapter 20. Some of these methods, insofar as they are pertinent to advertising, are highlighted here.

POP-UP ABUSE

Advertising in pop-up windows is not illegal per se, but barraging consumers with pop-up advertisements as a way of encouraging them to buy pop-up blocking software is an unfair trade practice.

MALVERTISING

Disguising malicious code as a seemingly innocuous advertisement is known as *malvertising*. Disguising a link to a website containing harmful or deceptive content so that it appears to be a link to a harmless website is also a form of malvertising. Malvertising violates the CFAA, the FTC Act and other laws.

DECEPTIVE META TAGS

Subliminal advertising is the placement of images, words or sounds in such a way that viewers are not consciously aware of them. Because research has not confirmed that it has an effect on purchasing decisions, the FTC does not currently treat it as an unfair or deceptive trade practice. If it can be shown to have influenced consumer behavior in a particular case, though, then it may be unlawful. Although the FTC is not prepared to say that subliminal advertising is unfair, the practice may be unlawful if it makes or implies a false or misleading representation. The FTC has taken the position that using hidden meta tags that would convey a false impression to website users if they were able to see them is an unfair or deceptive trade practice. In one case, for example, the FTC charged a company with a violation of the FTC Act for placing the phrase "cancer treatment" in a meta tag for a website featuring unsubstantiated cancer treatment claims for a product that was being sold on the site.

ADWARE AND SPYWARE

The FTC has taken the position that causing adware (software that displays advertising on a computer screen) or spyware (software that tracks a computer user's online activity, usually for the purpose of delivering targeted ads) to be installed on a person's computer without clear and conspicuous disclosure is an unfair or deceptive trade practice. FTC enforcement actions suggest that bundling any program with another software program that is sold to a consumer is an unfair or deceptive trade practice unless the existence and nature of the bundled software is clearly and conspicuously disclosed. Offering spyware detection scans that falsely detect spyware, as part of an effort to sell consumers anti-spyware products, is an unfair and deceptive trade practice.

CLICK FRAUD

Using bots to click on an advertisement in order to boost revenues (or a competitor's advertising costs) under a pay-per-click arrangement is known as click fraud. It is unlawful. Dealing in clickbot software is also a crime.

BAIT AND SWITCH

Advertising a product or service without having any real intention of selling it, all the while planning to sell something different, is known as a "bait and switch" advertising tactic. It is an unfair and deceptive trade practice prohibited by the FTC Act.

SELLING CONFIDENTIAL TELEPHONE NUMBERS TO ADVERTISERS

Selling or offering to sell consumers' confidential telephone numbers to telemarketers or other advertisers is an unfair trade practice.

TELEMARKETING

Even companies that conduct most of their sales online should have a basic understanding of telemarketing laws. These laws may apply to a business even if it never initiates any sales calls. The Telemarketing and Consumer Fraud and Abuse Prevention Act[191] and the FTC's Telemarketing Sales Rule[192] (TSR) implementing it apply to calls a company receives as well as to calls a company initiates. If a business attempts to induce the purchase of a product or service or to solicit a donation during a call, the business is engaged in telemarketing irrespective of who originally placed the call.

TSR Exemptions

Subject to some important exceptions discussed in more detail below, the TSR generally does not apply to:

(a) intrastate calls
(b) unsolicited calls from consumers
(c) calls made in response to a catalog
(d) calls made in response to general media advertising
(e) calls made in response to direct mail advertising
(f) business-to-business calls
(g) common carriers engaging in common carrier activity (e.g., phone companies)
(h) banks, federal savings and loans, federal credit unions
(i) nonprofit, tax-exempt charities telemarketing on their own behalf
(j) securities dealers and brokers that are subject to the jurisdiction of the SEC or the CFTC
(k) insurance sellers, to the extent no state telemarketing law applies.

The foregoing rules are subject to a number of qualifications and exceptions.

UPSELLING

A call from a consumer that would otherwise be exempt loses the exemption to the extent the business engages in upselling during the call. *Upselling* means offering or trying to persuade a caller to purchase a product or service, or to make a donation, different from or additional to the consumer's initial purpose for making the call.

> **Example.** Out of the blue, Hedrick looks up the number for Deluxe Rototillers and places a call to order a front-tine tiller. Since the call is unsolicited, the TSR does not apply. During the call, the company's representative suggests Hedrick should consider buying a rear-tine tiller instead. Rear-tine tillers are more expensive but they are more efficient. This is upselling. The company is now engaged in telemarketing. The TSR applies to the company's attempt to sell the rear-tine tiller.

CONSUMER RESPONSES TO SALES CALLS AND PRERECORDED CALLS

Calls from consumers in response to a sales call or a prerecorded call are not considered unsolicited. Therefore, they may be subject to the TSR.

CATALOGS NOT COVERED BY THE TSR

The exemption for catalog sales applies only if the catalog: (i) contains a written description or illustration of the product or service; (ii) includes the seller's business address; (iii) has more than one page; and (iv) is issued at least annually. Also, the exemption does not apply unless the seller only receives calls initiated by consumers in response to the catalog and does not initiate calls to solicit customers. During the call, the seller may attempt to interest the buyer in other items in the same or a substantially similar catalog, but becomes subject to the TSR if he offers goods or services that are not in the same or a substantially similar catalog.

CALLS ON BEHALF OF EXEMPT ORGANIZATIONS

Companies that engage in telemarketing on behalf of an organization that is exempt from the TSR do not get the benefit of the exemption. A firm hired by a bank to solicit new customers for the bank is an example. A telefunder (a for-profit company that engages in telephone solicitations of donations for charitable organizations) is another example. Some of the TSR requirements for telefunders are slightly different from those for telemarketers generally. Consult the TSR for more information.

CALLS TO EMPLOYEES

The business-to-business exemption does not apply to calls by or to employees of the company. Telemarketers who call a company's employees are subject to the TSR rule.

BUSINESS-TO-BUSINESS SALES OF NONDURABLE OFFICE OR CLEANING SUPPLIES

Business-to-business calls involving retail sales of services or durable goods are not subject to the TSR, but business-to-business calls involving retail sales of nondurable office or cleaning supplies are subject to most TSR requirements. No business-to-business seller, however, is subject to the recordkeeping requirements or the Do-Not-Call Registry provisions of the TSR.

CREDIT REPAIR AND DEBT RELIEF SERVICES

The TSR applies even to calls from consumers in response to general media advertisements if the advertisement relates to credit repair, credit card loss protection, recovery services, advance-fee loans, or debt relief services.

INVESTMENT OPPORTUNITIES

The TSR applies even to calls from consumers in response to general media advertisements if the advertisement relates to investment opportunities.

FRANCHISE AND BUSINESS OPPORTUNITIES

The TSR applies even to calls from consumers in response to general media advertisements if the advertisement relates to franchises or business opportunities that are not covered by the FTC's Franchise Rule or Business Opportunity Rule. Some, but not all, TSR requirements apply to offers of franchise and business opportunities that are subject to these Rules.

PROHIBITED PAYMENT METHODS

Certain kinds of payment methods are prohibited when an order is placed by phone, even if a consumer initiates the call in response to general media or direct mail advertising. The prohibited payment methods are: remotely created payment orders, remotely created checks (electronic checks), cash-to-cash money transfers, and cash reload mechanisms.

CALLS IN RESPONSE TO CERTAIN DIRECT MAIL ADVERTISEMENTS

The TSR applies to calls a consumer makes in response to a direct mail advertisement unless the advertisement discloses: (i) cost and quantity; (ii) any material restrictions, conditions or limitations; and (iii) any "no refund" policy. If the offer includes a prize promotion, credit card loss protection, or a negative option feature, then the mail solicitation must contain additional information specified in the TSR. In the case of direct mail charitable donation solicitations, the exemption applies only if the solicitation contains no material misrepresentations about the nature, purpose or mission of the charitable organization, the tax deductibility of contributions, the purpose for which donations will be used, the percentage or amount of the donation that will go to a charitable organization or program, or any material aspect of a prize promotion or a charitable organization's or telemarketer's affiliations, endorsements or sponsorships.

900-NUMBER OFFERS

Calls relating to the sale of 900-Number services are subject to some of the TSR's provisions.

FACE-TO-FACE INVOLVEMENT

Calls that are part of a transaction that involves a face-to-face sales presentation, either before or after the call, are subject to some TSR provisions but not others.

TSR Requirements

When the TSR applies, it generally imposes the following obligations on a company:

(a) It must disclose any material information about the goods, services or charitable contribution that is the subject of the solicitation;
(b) No false or misleading statements may be made;
(c) It may not call between 9 p.m. and 8 a.m. without the consumer's consent;
(d) It may not block its caller ID from being displayed;
(e) It generally may not abandon outbound calls;
(f) The consumer may not be billed for unauthorized charges;
(g) It may not accept certain forms of payment;
(h) Specified business records must be kept for at least two years;
(i) It generally must refrain from calling people who are on the Do Not Call Registry.

Information is material if it would likely affect a person's choice of goods or services or the person's decision to make a charitable donation. Terms that are deemed material to any offer include:

- Cost
- Quantity
- Restrictions, limitations or conditions
- Any "no refunds" policy

Some kinds of offers require additional disclosures.

Credit card loss protection plan offers must disclose the limits on a consumer's liability under federal law for unauthorized use of a credit card (e.g., $50 if a card is lost or stolen).

Prize promotions must disclose:

(a) the odds of winning
(b) a statement that no purchase is necessary to enter or win
(c) how people can enter without paying any money or buying anything
(d) any material costs or conditions to receive or redeem any prize.

Negative option offers require the following disclosures:

(a) the fact that the customer's account will be charged unless he takes an affirmative action (e.g., canceling) to avoid the charge
(b) the date(s) on which the charge(s) will be submitted for payment
(c) the specific steps the customer must take to avoid the charges.

Debt relief service offers (e.g., an offer of debt consolidation services) must disclose:

(a) a good faith estimate of how long it will take to achieve the represented results
(b) how much money a customer must save before the offeror will make a settlement offer to creditors
(c) the possible consequences if the customer fails to make timely payments to creditors
(d) the customer's rights regarding dedicated accounts if the offeror asks or requires the customer to set aside funds in a dedicated account.

In all cases, the disclosures must be made before collecting credit card or other payment information from the buyer and before the consumer pays for the product or service or makes the donation. They must be clear and conspicuous.

In the case of a call initiated by the seller, or a call in which upselling occurs, the telemarketer must make certain disclosures before making any sales pitch. These include: (a) the seller's identity; (ii) the purpose of the call; (iii) the nature of the goods or services being offered; and (iv) if it is a prize promotion, the fact that no purchase or payment is necessary to enter or win, and that a purchase will not increase the chances of winning. Telefunders must disclose that the purpose of the call is to solicit a donation and must provide the name of the organization on whose behalf they are calling

The Do-Not-Call Registry

Consumers may request to have their telephone numbers placed on a national Do-Not-Call Registry. The FTC maintains the Registry. A company seeking to access it must register and pay a fee. It is at https://telemarketing.donotcall.gov/. Penalties for calling a person who is on the Do-Not-Call Registry are up to $40,654 per call.

The following are not subject to the Do-Not-Call provisions:

(a) political organizations
(b) charities
(c) telephone surveyors
(d) companies with which a consumer has an existing business relationship
(e) business-to-business calls
(f) calls to consumers on behalf of charities (but telefunders must honor a donor's request not to be called on behalf of a particular charitable organization)
(g) calls to consumers who have given signed, written permission to be called.

Calls made in error are sometimes excused, but only if the company has established written Do-Not-Call procedures that meet all requirements and satisfy all conditions set out in the TSR.

The Telephone Consumer Protection Act

The Telephone Consumer Protection Act[193] (TCPA) also addresses the problem of intrusive telemarketing calls. Pursuant to this Act, the FCC has promulgated rules to protect residential telephone subscribers' privacy rights. A telemarketer must maintain a list of all consumers who request not to be called and abide by it, in addition to refraining from calling consumers who are in the National Do-Not-Call Registry. Although not completely banning all of these activities, the TCPA and FCC regulations impose restrictions on the use of automated dialing systems ("robocalling"), artificial or prerecorded voice messages, text messages sent to cell phones, and the use of fax machines to send unsolicited advertisements. For example, unless the consumer gives express, prior, written consent, it is generally unlawful to use an automated dialing system to contact a consumer without including an automated, interactive opt-out mechanism in the call.

The foregoing discussion only covers the main points about telemarketing. A business that plans to engage in telemarketing should review the FTC and FCC regulations in their entirety.

Unlawful Products and Services

The DMCA makes it a crime to traffic in technology that enables others to circumvent technological measures that have been put in place to control access to uses of a copyrighted work. Displaying another person's advertisement for them, or providing a link to a website where they are sold, is a kind of trafficking. Courts are not in agreement as to whether criminal liability may be imposed simply for linking, or whether something more (such as receiving payment for the link) is necessary. The safest course is to check a website's content before linking to it.

Advertising other kinds of illegal commodities and activities is also a crime. This includes but is not limited to advertisements for bootleg recordings, pirated movies, copyright circumvention tools, counterfeit goods, contraband, controlled substances, child pornography, prostitution, gambling, Ponzi schemes, etc. If the product or activity is criminal, then advertising it, sponsoring advertising for it and/or knowingly linking to it usually are, too.

LOTTERIES

Privately operated lotteries are prohibited by both federal and state laws. Exceptions are made for tax-exempt charitable organizations that sponsor gambling events (e.g., bingo or raffles) as fundraisers. It is a criminal offense for anyone else to conduct a lottery. Sweepstakes and prize promotions, on the other hand, generally are legal.

A *lottery* is an arrangement in which a person is required to give money or other consideration for a chance to win a prize. The three characteristics of a lottery are:

- Consideration
- Random chance
- A prize.

Consideration means value of some kind, not necessarily money. If no money or other consideration needs to be given for a chance to win, then it is not a lottery. If a payment or purchase is necessary in order to enter or win a drawing for a prize, then it is a lottery. If a promise to display the sponsor's advertisement on a website is a condition for entering the contest, then value is being given. Therefore, the arrangement may be an illegal lottery. If people are told they must "like" a page in order to qualify for entry into a contest, then value is being given, and the arrangement might be classified as an illegal lottery.

The element of chance also has to be present in order for a promotion to be considered a lottery. If prizes are awarded on the basis of skill (e.g., a "best essay" contest) instead of being awarded randomly, then it is a skill-based contest, not a lottery. To qualify as a skill-based contest, however, objective judging criteria are required. Terms like *best* or *most dazzling* are too subjective to satisfy this requirement. Specifying that the winner will be determined by qualified judges may suffice to transform what would otherwise be a lottery into a skill contest, provided the skilled judges really exist. A "best short fiction" contest, to be judged by the editor of a magazine that regularly publishes short fiction, could qualify as a skill contest.

Sweepstakes are contests that give entrants a chance of winning a prize solely on the basis of chance, usually by means of a random drawing. If money or other consideration is required to enter it, then it is an illegal lottery. If no purchase or other consideration is necessary to enter or win, then it will not be classified as a lottery. A sweepstakes also may be classified as a lottery if a winner must give something of value to collect a prize. This is why sweepstakes and promotions contain a statement like "No Purchase Necessary to Enter or Win."

Promotions that require a product label, receipt or other evidence of a purchase in order to enter or win may be classified as lotteries unless they offer an alternative method for entering that does not require the submission of evidence of a purchase.

Pursuant to FCC and FTC regulations, the material terms and conditions of a promotion must be disclosed. This includes:

- Eligibility
- Prize(s)
- Starting date
- Ending date.

There are also laws and regulations for sweepstakes and promotions at the state level. For example, some states prohibit residents from entering online sweepstakes that are sponsored by manufacturers of alcoholic beverages. Many states require promoters to make specified disclosures, and a number of states impose license and bond requirements. These laws vary considerably from state to state. An e-commerce business will need to comply with the laws of every state from which it plans to accept entries. If a state prohibits promotional offers of the kind that a company advertisers, then the promoter should either avoid sending the offer into that state or display a clear and conspicuous notice that the offer is void in that state. If a contest or promotion involves telephone calls, then it will be necessary to comply with the TSR, along with other legal requirements. The TSR requires specific disclosures, such as the odds of winning a prize, how to participate without buying anything, and the fact that no purchase or payment is required to enter or win. Certain additional disclosures set out in the FTC's 900-Number Rule are required if pay-per-call services are involved.

ALCOHOL

The federal government so far has not acted to prohibit alcohol advertising on the Internet, leaving the matter to voluntary industry self-regulation. Industry associations have established codes for advertisers of alcoholic beverages. These codes reflect a particular concern about advertising that is directed to children. See Chapter 18. Despite the dearth of regulation specific to alcoholic beverage advertisements, they are subject to the FTC Act and other truth in advertising laws of general applicability. Restrictions on sales to underage persons apply to online sales, too.

Some countries ban alcohol advertisements altogether. Others regulate their content. France, for example, imposes strict truth in advertising requirements on advertisements for alcoholic beverages.

TOBACCO

The Public Health Cigarette Smoking Act[194] bans the advertising of cigarettes and little cigars on any medium of communication regulated by the FCC, but so far there is no ban on tobacco advertising on the Internet. Cigarette and smokeless tobacco product advertisements are required to display health warning labels on a rotational basis as specified in administrative regulations. Restrictions on sales to underage persons apply to both in-person and online sales.

To comply with the FTC Act, a claim of "no additives" in a tobacco product must include the following disclosure: "No additives in our tobacco does NOT mean a safer cigarette."

Tobacco advertisements are closely regulated. Additional disclosures beyond those described here exist. Additional information is available from the FTC, the FDA and public health agencies.

MARIJUANA AND OTHER CONTROLLED SUBSTANCES

Although there is a trend toward legalization of marijuana at the state level, federal law prohibits the unauthorized use of the Internet to deliver, distribute or dispense a controlled substance, including but not limited to marijuana. Aiding and abetting the unauthorized use of the Internet to do so is also prohibited, as is knowingly or intentionally using the Internet, or causing the Internet to be used, to advertise the sale of, or to offer to sell, distribute, or dispense controlled substances.

DISCRIMINATION

The federal Civil Rights Act, the Fair Housing Act and other civil rights laws prohibit discrimination in housing, employment, and places of accommodation. Sponsoring discriminatory advertising is also unlawful.

Contributory, Vicarious, and Personal Liability

Criminal laws often make it a crime to aid, abet, solicit or conspire to commit a crime. Civil liability for damages, too, may be imposed on those who facilitate or contribute to wrongdoing. If selling a particular product or service is a crime, then advertising it or sponsoring advertisements for it is usually a crime, too. If foreseeable injury results, then it may result in civil liability for damages, as well.

Linking to advertisements for illegal products or activities may also be a crime. Knowledge of the content virtually assures criminal liability, if it is within a website owner's power to do something about it. For example, if a website owner is asked to display an advertisement for "pirated" copyright-protected works, then proceeding to do so would be acting with knowledge and intent to further a criminal enterprise. On the other hand, if a website owner merely provides a forum where users may post any content they like, and unbeknownst to the website owner somebody posts copyright infringing material, then there should be no criminal liability unless the website owner actually solicited, induced or encouraged the posting of infringing content.

The law does not countenance willful blindness, however. A judge or jury may infer knowledge from circumstantial evidence. Once notice of the content is received, the "lack of knowledge" defense will be difficult or impossible to sustain. Knowledge might be inferred from other kinds of circumstances, too. Complying with the DMCA and implementing the notice-and-take-down mechanism it provides can help build a strong defense against claims of copyright infringement.

CORPORATE OFFICERS, DIRECTORS AND EMPLOYEES

A corporate officer may be held personally liable for violations of the FTC Act if the officer owned, dominated and managed the company and if naming the officer individually is necessary for an enforcement order to be fully effective in preventing the deceptive practices which the FTC has found to have occurred. The FTC is not required to show that a corporate officer intended to defraud consumers in order to hold him personally liable. Individual liability is justified where an executive officer of the company is found to have personally participated in or controlled the challenged acts or practices or if the officer held a control position over employees who committed illegal acts.

Individuals are personally liable for restitution on account of corporate misconduct if they had knowledge that the corporation or its agent(s) engaged in dishonest or fraudulent conduct, that the misrepresentations were the type upon which a reasonable and prudent person would rely, and that consumer injury resulted. The knowledge requirement can be satisfied by showing that the individuals had actual knowledge of a material misrepresentation, were recklessly indifferent to the falsity of a misrepresentation, or were aware of the probability of fraud along with an intentional avoidance of the truth.

ADVERTISING AGENCIES

An advertising agency may be liable for a deceptive advertisement if the agency was an active participant in the preparation of the advertisement and if it knew or should have known that the advertisement was deceptive. An advertising agency will be held to know what claims—express and implied—are conveyed to consumers by their advertisements. An advertising agency does not have to substantiate the claims independently or scientifically reexamine an advertiser's substantiation. It may not ignore obvious shortcomings or facial flaws in an advertiser's substantiation, however

WEB DESIGNERS AND CATALOG MAKERS

Sellers are responsible for claims they make about their products and services. Third parties—such as web designers and catalog marketers—also may be liable for making or disseminating deceptive representations if they participate in the preparation or distribution of the advertising, or know about the deceptive claims.

Wed designers and catalog makers, like advertising agencies, are responsible for reviewing the information used to substantiate advertising claims. They may not simply rely on an advertiser's assurance that the claims are substantiated. In determining whether a designer or catalog maker should be held liable, the FTC looks at the extent of their participation in the preparation of the advertisement and whether they knew or should have known that it included false or deceptive claims.

To protect themselves, catalog marketers should ask for material to back up claims rather than simply repeat what the manufacturer says about the product without question. In writing ad copy, catalogers should only include claims that can be supported.

MEANS AND INSTRUMENTALITIES

Companies may be liable if they provide others with the means and instrumentalities for engaging in deceptive conduct.

AFFILIATE MARKETING

Affiliate marketing is an arrangement in which an online retailer pays a commission to an external website (the affiliate) for traffic or sales generated from its referrals. A company that uses affiliates to drive traffic to its website must monitor the affiliates closely. The FTC has taken enforcement actions against vendors for contracting with affiliates who then used false advertising or other kinds of unfair or deceptive trade practices to steer people to the vendor's website. A business cannot do through a third party what the FTC prohibits it from doing directly.

The FTC requires companies that use affiliates to have reasonable programs in place to train and monitor them. The reasonableness of a training and monitoring program varies depending on the nature and extent of possible harm to consumers. A company that markets potentially harmful drugs, for example, must train and monitor its affiliates more closely than a company that sells clothing. The core elements of any training and monitoring program, however, are the same:

(a) Explain to affiliates what can and cannot be said about the product or service, consistent with the FTC Act and other truth in advertising laws.
(b) Clearly and conspicuously disclose to affiliates that engaging in deceptive advertising practices will result in immediate termination of the affiliate relationship and forfeiture of all monies owed to the affiliate in connection with the affiliate marketing arrangement.
(c) Routinely and regularly monitor affiliate marketing materials, websites, banners, emails, sponsored search terms, and pop-up ads, on at least a monthly basis, to check on what they are saying about the product or service. No advance notice of the time when monitoring will occur should be given to the affiliate, and it should be conducted in a way that does not disclose to the affiliate when the monitoring is occurring.
(d) Promptly investigate any consumer complaint about an affiliate.
(e) Immediately halt the processing of any payments generated by an affiliate that the company knows or should know is engaged in a deceptive marketing practice.
(f) Fully refund, within five business days, any consumer the sale to whom originated from a referral by an affiliate engaging in a deceptive marketing practice.
(g) Terminate affiliates who willfully refuse or repeatedly fail to comply with rules the company has prescribed for affiliates.
(h) Terminate immediately any affiliate that engages in deceptive marketing practices.

A company may be held contributorily liable for the activities of its affiliates only if it induces, encourages, facilitates, knows or has reason to know of the affiliate's activities. Thus, at least one court has held that a company that has no knowledge or reason to know that an affiliate is using keyword advertising in a way that infringes a competitor's trademark cannot be held contributorily liable for it. Of course, if the company comes to acquire such knowledge or a reason to know, then it could be held contributory liability for an affiliate's wrongdoing if it then does nothing about it.

LINK EXCHANGES

There are often situations in which merchants find it mutually beneficial to enter into an arrangement in which one pays the other for the right to include advertising links on the other's website. Entering into a written linking/advertising agreement can be important both in terms of clarifying the parties' expectations and in relation to enforcing rights in the event things do not go as planned. Of course, if a website has specified a procedure for approving links, then that procedure should be used.

Some judgment should be exercised when providing links to other websites. In some cases, providing a link to another website may amount to aiding or facilitating illegal or infringing activity occurring on the linked-to website. Linking to another website normally will not result in liability unless the owner of the linking website knows or should know that the linked-to site contains unlawful content. Lack of actual knowledge about the content of the linked-to site is not necessarily enough to avoid liability, though. The law does not countenance willful blindness.

The fact that illegal activity would be readily apparent from a visit to the website could support a finding that a person should have known about the unlawful content.

International Law

The Undertaking Spam, Spyware and Fraud Enforcement with Enforcers Beyond Borders Act[195] (SAFE WEB Act) is a 2006 amendment to the FTC Act to extend its reach to unfair and deceptive trade practices that are committed in a foreign country and that cause reasonably foreseeable injury in the United States. The purpose of this amendment is to enable the FTC to enforce U.S. anti-fraud laws against individuals and businesses operating in foreign countries. Prior to the enactment of this law, the consumer protection provisions of the FTC Act often could not be enforced against spammers, fraudsters and other miscreants who transmitted offending content into the United States from a location outside of the United States.

The SAFE WEB Act also contains a variety of provisions aimed at facilitating international cooperation among law enforcement agencies for the enforcement of consumer protection laws. It gives the FTC authority to assist other countries in the enforcement of their consumer protection and anti-fraud laws against individuals and businesses located in the United States.

Under the Act, ISPs are immune from liability for making disclosures to the FTC about suspected online fraud or deception.

LAWS OF OTHER COUNTRIES

The United States is not the only country that regulates advertising. Many other countries do, too, and their laws are not always the same as those that have been enacted in the United States. For example, Italy requires government approval of commercial advertising that includes images of works owned by the government (such as Michelangelo's David).

Countries in the EU are very protective of consumers residing there. Website operators and other online service providers located in the EU must comply with laws implementing the Directive on Electronic Commerce. Among other things, this means that if they send unsolicited commercial email messages, then they must regularly check and respect opt-out registers. Their consumer protection laws apply not only to European merchants but also to any foreign merchant that enters into transactions with consumers who are domiciled in a EU country. American companies that sell to European consumers must comply with the applicable European country's advertising and consumer protection laws.

As in the United States, false or misleading advertising is prohibited in EU countries. Further, e-commerce businesses that advertise and/or sell to consumers who are domiciled in the EU must disclose and provide accurate information about the goods and services being offered. At a minimum, this must include:

(a) the main characteristics of the goods or services
(b) price, including taxes
(c) delivery costs
(d) any additional costs of communication
(e) the period for which the offer or the price remains valid
(f) the minimum duration of a purchase contract.

Online auctions generally are exempt from these requirements. At least one European court, however, has interpreted the term very narrowly, holding that an eBay style "auction" is not an auction for purposes of the EU auction exception.

Chapter 16. Disparagement and Defamation

Two common law remedies are potentially available to a company when another business or an individual makes a false statement about the company, its products or its services: defamation and disparagement of trade. The basis of these causes of action is the same: a publication of false information that harms a person or a business. For reasons primarily having to do with the First Amendment, however, the available defenses and remedies are slightly different.

Publication

Publication of either an express or an implied statement of fact is a necessary element of a claim for defamation or trade disparagement. The definition of publication in this context is very broad. Any kind of communication to a third party will suffice. Unlike copyright law, displaying, broadcasting, transmitting via email, or making a statement available for downloading are all forms of publication insofar as defamation and disparagement law are concerned.

The publication need not be to all members of the public. It does not even have to be accessible to a significant portion of the public. A communication of a false statement to even one person via a private email message may qualify. The statement must be communicated to a third party, though.

Falsity

Defamation and disparagement liability exist only for false statements. A true statement about a person may be actionable as an invasion of privacy in some cases, but it is not actionable as defamation.

INNUENDO

When making an assessment of truthfulness, courts consider both the literal aspect of a statement and its innuendo. Even if a statement is technically true, a court may nevertheless impose liability if it is phrased or presented in such a way that a reasonable reader would construe it as implying something false.

> **Example**. John and Bernard participate in a civil rights march. Hillary does not. Bernard issues a statement that he participated in the march. John meets Hillary in an office setting several years later. He then publicly declares that he did not meet Bernard during a march but that he "did meet" Hillary. Technically, John's statement is true. A reasonable reader, however, would construe his statement to mean that Hillary took part in the march and that Bernard is a liar. If Bernard is a

private figure, then John would be at risk of liability for defamation even though his statements are technically true.

Sometimes the positioning of material on a web page can suggest something false even though none of the statements is actually false. Displaying a photograph of an identifiable person directly adjacent to an article about an increase in sexually transmitted diseases might cause a reader to infer that the pictured individual has a sexually transmitted disease. Whether that inference is reasonable or not depends on all the facts and circumstances. If reasonable readers would understand it to mean that the pictured individual has a sexually transmitted disease, then the juxtaposition of the photograph with the text operates as a statement that the pictured individual has a sexually transmitted disease.

To prevail on a truth defense, both the statement and its innuendo must be true.

HYPERBOLE, SARCASM, RHETORIC, AND "PUFFING"

There is no liability for the literal meaning of a hyperbolic, sarcastic or rhetorical statement, or for "puffing," if a reasonable reader understands it to be a hyperbolic, sarcastic or rhetorical statement, or "puffing." (*Puffing* refers to a salesperson's or advertiser's exaggerated expression of an opinion about something, such as "This is the best product on the market!")

The meaning of a statement is assessed by how a reasonable reader would interpret it. The author's intended meaning is not controlling. An author may still incur liability for hyperbolic, sarcastic and rhetorical statements that the author did not intend to be taken literally if a reasonable reader could mistake them for statements of fact.

> **Example**. To drive home the point that she is angry about XYZ Corporation's role in increasing women's cervical cancer rates, Joan blogs that "XYZ Corporation is raping women!" Since corporations are not humans, no reasonable reader would interpret this statement literally. But if Joan were to publish the statement, "The CEO of XYZ Corporation is raping women!" for the same hyperbolic purpose, she might be liable to the CEO for defamation. Although she only intended to use the word 'rape' as a hyperbolic metaphor, a reasonable reader could interpret her statement as meaning that the CEO actually is assaulting women sexually.

If a reasonable reader would not interpret a statement as a factual one, then there can be no liability for defamation. For example, if a person posts the comment, "Oh yeah, like I'm so sure the board of directors of XYZ Corporation is increasing cancer rates in women. Come on!" a reasonable reader would interpret this as sarcasm, not as an allegation that members of the board of XYZ Corporation actually are increasing cancer rates in women. Accordingly, a member of the board of XYZ Corporation would not have a viable defamation claim against the person who posted this comment.

OPINION

Only false statements of fact are actionable as defamation or disparagement. Opinions are not. Again, though, it is not the author's intent that determines whether a statement is factual or not. The question is whether a reasonable reader would interpret it as a factual statement.

Prefacing a factual statement with "I think" or "In my opinion" will not necessarily insulate the speaker from liability. Reasonable readers are likely to interpret a statement of opinion about a factual statement as a factual statement. A reasonable person is likely to interpret the statement, "I think this product that is being marketed as butter is actually oleomargarine" as a representation of fact, not a statement of opinion, for example. Whether a statement that is characterized as an opinion will be treated as an expression of an opinion or as a statement of fact is decided on a case-by-case basis, however. Jurors are instructed to consider all the circumstances surrounding the statement, including the precision with which the statement was made, the likelihood of the author's familiarity with the facts, the reason for making the statement, and so on.

Statements reflecting a necessarily subjective judgment about the quality of a thing are more likely to be perceived as opinions than as statements about objectively verifiable facts. The statement, "Ed Jones is the best candidate for president" is likely to be seen as an opinion, but "In my opinion, Ed Jones accepted a $5 million campaign contribution from Putin Co." is likely to be seen as an allegation of fact.

A person ordinarily will not incur liability for reporting on the person's own emotional response to something. For example, saying, "I tried Brand X and did not like the flavor" or "I get a huge uneasy feeling when I see John Doe hugging young girls," probably will not expose a person to liability. In some jurisdictions, this defense is called the right of fair comment.

Many people think they cannot be held liable for defamation or disparagement if they quote another person's statement, so long as they correctly attribute the statement to that person. Admittedly, there is some logic in this. If *A*'s statement is only that *B* made a particular statement, and if it is, in fact, true that *B* made that statement, then it would be logical to infer that *A*'s statement is true whether *B*'s statement is true or not. Unfortunately, that is not how the law works. Accurately publishing a quotation of someone else's statement may result in liability for defamation or disparagement if that person's statement is false. In many situations, a court may treat a republisher of a false statement the same as the original publisher of the statement.

> **Example**. A newspaper publishes the statement, "John Smith has recently reported on his blog, 'Clyde Jones is a murderer.' This is shocking news." If it turns out Clyde is not really a murderer, then both the newspaper and John Smith might be sued for defamation. The fact that John Smith really did publish the quoted statement on his blog is not a defense.

As always, the determinative question is how a reasonable person interprets what she reads. If the newspaper were to include a statement to the effect that the quoted statement is not true (or not known to be true), then it would not be as likely to be held liable for defamation as a republisher.

Disparagement of Trade

Trade disparagement (sometimes called "commercial disparagement," "trade libel" or "slander of goods") is the publication of a false statement of fact about the quality of a competitor's goods or services, usually for the purpose of diverting sales away from the competitor. The elements of a common law claim are:

(a) publication
(b) of a false statement of fact about another's business, products or services
(c) with knowledge of falsity or reckless disregard for truth or falsity
(d) and intent to cause pecuniary loss
(e) resulting in pecuniary loss ("special damages.")

Some jurisdictions do not require proof of intent to harm, so long as it can be shown that pecuniary loss was a reasonably foreseeable consequence of the publication.

Historically, this tort was reserved exclusively for cases involving disparagement of a company's products. It was subsequently extended to include services, too. It did not cover injury to a company's reputation, however. For that, a defamation claim needed to be asserted. Courts in some states still take this approach. Courts in other jurisdictions, however, have blurred the distinction, treating trade disparagement—whether of goods, services or a company's reputation—as a kind of defamation claim. In any case, damages in trade disparagement cases are limited to provable pecuniary loss, such as loss of business income or customers. General damages for injury to reputation are not recoverable for trade disparagement.

The UDTPA, which many states have adopted, authorizes a business to obtain an injunction against another business for trade disparagement. The elements of a UDTPA claim are:

(a) in the course of the defendant's business, vocation or occupation
(b) the defendant made a false or misleading representation of fact
(c) disparaging the plaintiff's goods, services or business
(d) that is likely to result in damage to the plaintiff.

The first element means, for example, that a business competitor or a reviewer who has been paid to write a review can be sued under UDTPA but unpaid consumer reviewers and commentators cannot. The second element requires only the making of a false or misleading statement. Neither intent to harm nor any actual harm needs to be proven. On the other hand, compensatory damages are not available under this statute. The only remedy is an injunction (and sometimes an award of attorney fees). The statute does not preempt common law claims or claims under other laws for damages, however.

Defamation

Defamation is the publication of a false statement that damages another person's or company's reputation. The elements are:

(a) publication
(b) of a false statement
(c) that is understood to be about a particular person or company
(d) causing damage to reputation or subjection to hatred, contempt or ridicule.

Malice may also need to be proven if the person suing for defamation is a public official or a public figure or if the publication involves a matter of public concern.

Libel is written defamation. Slander is oral defamation.

SUBJECT MATTER

To qualify as defamation, the statement must be about a particular person or company, or understood to be about a particular person or company. Making a false statement about climate change, for example, is not actionable as defamation even though it may contradict statements which climate scientists have made. There is no requirement that a person or company must be explicitly named, however. Providing enough information for a reader to figure out who the subject of the statement is will suffice.

GROUP LIBEL

Group libel refers to the publication of a false statement that injures the reputation of more than one person. Publishing the statement, "All men are rapists" is an example.

Defamation laws penalizing group libel do not violate the First Amendment unless they are either overbroad or content-based.[196] A state does not violate a publisher's First Amendment rights by imposing liability for group libel so long as it does not use defamation law to punish perceived evils other than the making of false statements that are injurious to reputation. A state law selecting particular groups to receive special protections under the state's defamation law—such as a "hate speech" statute calling for enhanced penalties for defaming women and racial minorities, but lesser or no penalty for defaming white males—would be unconstitutional. A statute that imposes a penalty for group libel without excluding or providing special protections for particular groups, on the other hand, would not necessarily violate the First Amendment.

Due to a fear of opening the floodgates to litigation, courts have developed a common law rule that no liability for group libel will be imposed if the defamatory statement is about a very large group. This is only a general rule, however. Liability may still be imposed even if the group is large, if an individual member of the group can demonstrate special application of the defamatory matter to him.

If the statement about a group is understood as applying only to a group collectively and not to each member individually, then an individual member of the group may not sue for defamation. If the group is small, though, then a court may find that a statement about the group necessarily applies to every individual member of it.

Wineries, correspondence schools, trading stamp concerns, and antique dealers are examples of groups that have been deemed to be too large for defamation liability to attach without proof of special application of a statement to a particular member. A fortiori, the group consisting of "all men" is probably too large to give any man a right to sue for defamation when statements like "All men are rapists" are published.

> **Example.** The *Daily Yellow* publishes an article containing the statement, "All men are rapists." So far, it is not at great risk of liability for defamation. The very next statement in the article, however, is: "Al Funniman is a man." Now it is at risk.

Examples of groups courts have deemed small enough to permit an individual member to sue for defamation even though not specifically named include: the jury in a particular case; a specified county commission; a group of coroner's physicians; the occupants of a particular house; the doctors at a particular hospital; "the Fenstermaker family;" a university board. This is not an exhaustive list.

Not all courts are in agreement. For example, some courts have held that a false statement that a particular apartment building is a house of ill repute defames every tenant in the building. Other courts have held that it does not.

When a basis for group libel exists, the fact that the publisher did not intend the statement to include every member of the group is irrelevant. For example, if a writer publishes the false statement, "Teachers employed by Flyover School District No. 16 are adulterers," the fact that the writer only had Alice Cramden and Bob Chickenhatcher in mind when he wrote it is not a defense to a defamation action commenced by Flyover teacher Fred Mertz.

REPUTATION

For defamation liability to attach, it is not enough to show that a statement is false. It must also be shown that it damages a person's or company's reputation. The publication of the statement must be shown to have subjected the person or company to hatred, contempt, or ridicule; decreased good will; or caused others to shun, avoid, or lose confidence in the person. There can be no recovery for defamation if nobody reasonably believes the statement. There also can be no recovery for defamation if the false statement, even if true, would not be injurious to reputation.

Certain kinds of statements are so derogatory that they are presumed to cause damage to reputation. In some states, they are also presumed to be false and malicious. These kinds of statements are said to be *defamatory per se*. Statements in this category effectively shift the burden of proof to the defendant to show that the plaintiff's reputation was not injured.

Categories of statements about a person that courts historically have found to be defamatory per se include:

- Sexually transmitted disease
- Lack of chastity (regarding an unmarried person)
- Crime of moral turpitude
- Poor professional character or standing.

According to some courts, a statement that a married person committed adultery is defamatory per se.

The categories of statements that courts deem defamatory per se are not static. A court may hold that a statement is defamatory per se even though it does not fit into one of the established categories. For statements that are not defamatory per se, the plaintiff must prove that publication of the statement has had a harmful effect on his reputation.

Since damage to reputation must be proven in order to establish a right to recovery for defamation, there can be no recovery if the plaintiff has no good reputation to lose. A person's preexisting bad reputation, therefore, may be asserted as a defense to defamation. For example, a convicted thief may have difficulty proving that a false allegation that he committed a different theft damaged his reputation. On the other hand, there can be liability for making a bad reputation worse. A court is more likely to award reduced or nominal damages than to dismiss a claim for damage to a bad reputation altogether.

INTENT

At common law, intent was a necessary element of a trade disparagement claim. In addition to either knowing a statement was false or acting with reckless disregard for truth or falsity, it had to be shown that the defendant intended the statement to cause pecuniary loss to the plaintiff. Defamation liability, on the other hand, could be premised on either intent or negligence. Today, courts in a number of jurisdictions allow both kinds of claims to be premised on either negligence or intent. In these jurisdictions, it is not necessary to prove the existence of an intent to cause pecuniary loss if it can be shown that pecuniary loss was a reasonably foreseeable consequence of the publication of the false statement.

PUBLIC OFFICIALS AND PUBLIC FIGURES

Although liability generally may be predicated on either negligence or intent, speech about public officials and public figures is at the core of the First Amendment. Accordingly, the U.S. Supreme Court has held that something more than mere negligence needs to be proven before a public official or public figure may prevail on a defamation claim. In these cases, it needs to be shown that the defamatory statement was published with actual malice.

A person publishes a statement with actual malice when one of the following applies:

(a) The person acts with the specific intention of causing defamatory injury;
(b) The person knows the statement is false but publishes it anyway;
(c) The person publishes it with reckless disregard for whether it is true or false.

In the case of statements that are capable of both a defamatory and an innocent interpretation, at least one court has held that something more than knowledge or reckless disregard must be proven. It must be proven that the defendant specifically intended the defamatory meaning

Reckless disregard for the truth means something more than mere negligence. A reporter or publisher may be found to be acting with reckless disregard for the truth if the truth of a matter could easily have been ascertained but no effort at all was made to do so. Publishing a statement that an Internet search would quickly have disclosed to be untrue is an example of acting with reckless disregard for the truth.

A person becomes a public official by seeking or holding political office. A person becomes a public figure by becoming someone in whom the public has an interest. Sports and entertainment celebrities are public figures. The term is not limited to them, though. A person may also become a public figure by voluntarily injecting himself into a public controversy, such as by becoming a vocal advocate with respect to a matter of public concern. It may also occur involuntarily, such as where a person is accused of a crime.

A person who is a public figure solely by virtue of having injected herself into a public controversy is called a *limited public figure*. That is to say, she is a public figure only with respect to the activity giving rise to her status as a public figure. A person who is a public figure only by virtue of publicly advocating for abortion rights, for example, does not become a public figure with respect to her personal shopping habits.

When it is not clear whether a person is a public or private figure with respect to a particular activity or aspect of the person's life, courts tend to prefer characterizing the person as a private person with respect to that activity or aspect of the person's life.

Public officials and public figures (other than limited public figures) must prove actual malice in order to recover damages for defamation even if the defamatory statement is about a matter of private concern. Gossip about a celebrity's personal and romantic relationships is fair game, so long as it is done without actual malice. This is not true of limited public figures. A limited public figure may recover for negligent publication of a false statement about an aspect of her private life that does not relate to the matter of public concern that is the basis for her status as a public figure. It is also not true in some countries other than the United States. Some countries require proof of malice only if the matter is one of public concern. In these countries, a celebrity or other public figure might be able to sue for the publication of a false statement about a matter of private concern, such as personal relationships, without having to prove that the publisher was actuated by malice.

The elements of a cause of action for defamation are different in other countries. In the United States, the person claiming to have been defamed has the burden of proving falsity. In Commonwealth[197] countries, material that is damaging to a person's reputation is presumed to be false, so the burden of proof is on the person who publishes it to prove that it is true. Also, unlike the United States, Commonwealth countries do not require public officials and figures to prove actual malice in order to recover on a defamation claim.

MATTERS OF PUBLIC CONCERN

Defamatory statements involving matters of public concern are not actionable unless actual malice is proven. This is true whether the defamed person is a public figure or a private figure. A private person suing for defamation damages on account of the publication of a false statement about a matter of private concern does not need to prove actual malice. A limited public figure who is suing for defamation on account of the publication of a false statement about a private matter that is outside of the scope of the matter as to which he is a public figure does not need to prove malice, either.

Unfortunately, courts have not given very clear guidance on how to ascertain whether something is a matter of public concern or not. In *Snyder v. Phelps*, for instance, the U.S. Supreme Court declared that something is a matter of public concern if "it can be fairly considered as relating to any matter of political, social, or other concern to the community, or when it is a subject of legitimate news interest; that is, a subject of general interest and of value and concern to the public."[198] A matter of public concern, then, is a matter that is of public concern. Commentators have registered their frustration with the absence of a clear, noncircular standard.[199]

RETRACTIONS

Many states have enacted statutes limiting the amount of damages that may be recovered for defamation if the plaintiff timely demands a retraction and the defendant promptly publishes a retraction in the manner, and within the timeframe, specified in the statute. The retraction statutes of some states only apply to newspapers, television and radio broadcasters, however.

In some states, failure to demand a retraction may prevent the recovery of certain kinds of damages, such as punitive damages.

Failure to publish a retraction after receiving a demand that is accompanied by facts rebutting the false statement may be used as evidence of actual malice.

In some countries, such as the U.K. and Australia, an early offer of an apology and settlement is sometimes a defense if the court determines the settlement offer was reasonable.

DAMAGES

The U.S. Supreme Court has held that for First Amendment reasons, public officials and public figures may not recover punitive damages for defamation. A private figure may recover punitive damages if malice can be proven.

Damages in a trade disparagement case are limited to pecuniary loss. Courts have held that the plaintiff in a defamation case may recover both general damages (at least for presumed injury to a company's business reputation) and any provable special damages, if the defamatory statement was published with actual malice. General (presumed) damages may not be awarded against a media defendant when liability is premised on mere negligence, but may be awarded against a nonmedia defendant if the publication is about a private figure and is a matter of private concern.

PRIVILEGE

Privilege is a defense to defamation. There are two kinds: absolute and qualified.

An absolute privilege exists for

- Statements made in judicial proceedings
- Statements made during legislative debates
- Political speeches and broadcasts
- Top government officials
- Communications between spouses.

Even though false statements made in these contexts may not always be actionable as defamation, there may be other legal penalties for this kind of conduct. A person who makes a false statement under oath in court, for example, may be charged with the crime of perjury.

The privilege in the above-described situations is absolute, meaning the person making the statement cannot be sued for defamation even if the statement is outrageous and even if the person knows it is false.

A qualified privilege exists to make certain kinds of false statements in other contexts. The situations in which a qualified privilege may exist vary from state to state. Some examples of situations in which some (but not all) states recognize a qualified privilege include:

- Statements in governmental reports of official proceedings
- Statements made by lower level government officials
- Testimony given during legislative proceedings
- Statements made in self defense

- Warnings to others about a danger or harm
- Statements communicated by an employer to a former employee's potential new employer
- Statements made in a published review of a movie or book.

A qualified privilege is lost if the person making the statement is acting with malice, hatred, spite or ill will.

When a privilege exists, it carries over to a republication of the statement. The privilege is lost, however, if the republication is itself made with actual malice, hatred, spite or ill will; or if the original statement is republished inaccurately or unfairly. Republishing a snippet of a speech, conversation or testimony out of context in such a way as to create a defamatory misimpression of what the original speaker intended to say is not fair and accurate reporting. A republisher who does this loses the protection of the privilege.

CONSENT

Consent can be a defense to defamation, at least in theory. It is difficult to imagine a scenario in which a person would consent to the publication of a false and defamatory statement of fact about himself, but if that can be proven, it is a defense.

CONTRIBUTORY LIABILITY

At common law, a publisher or republisher of someone else's defamatory statement as if it were fact may be held liable for defamation to the same extent as the person who made the statement originally. The Communications Decency Act[200] (CDA) may provide a defense to contributory and republisher liability for online publishers, however. See Chapter 21.

CRIMINAL DEFAMATION

In several states and countries, defamation is both a crime and a civil wrong. Prosecutions for criminal libel are not as common in the United States as they are in other countries.

Many countries punish defamation quite severely, and not all recognize the distinction between public and private figures in the way the United States does. Germany, Greece, Poland, Switzerland, Belarus, Kazakhstan, the Maldives, Egypt, Zimbabwe and other countries specifically make defamation of a head of state a crime.

Website owners should be careful about traveling to other countries. Before entering a country, they should review the laws of that country to ensure they have not been guilty of transmitting prohibited content into the country via their websites.

Defamation *vs.* Disparagement

Although the trend in the courts is to treat defamation and trade disparagement as equivalent causes of action, they are subject to significantly different First Amendment constraints. Speech about public officials and public figures, and about matters of public concern, is constitutionally protected, at least to some extent, even if it is false and misleading. False or misleading commercial speech, on the other hand, receives no constitutional protection at all. To the extent trade disparagement is commercial speech, liability may be predicated on either negligence or intent, and punitive damages may be awarded in an appropriate case. To the extent it is noncommercial commentary about a public figure (a business entity can be a public figure, by the way) or about a matter of public concern, a showing of malice is necessary and punitive damages may not be awarded.

What is commercial speech? The answer can't be that it is any speech for the publication of which money is spent, or access to which requires the payment of money. If that were the case, then every article in the *New York Times* would be commercial speech. Courts have held to the contrary. Speech soliciting money has been held to be fully protected by the First Amendment, so that is not the defining characteristic of commercial speech, either. Speech that is about commercial subjects (such as business articles and editorials in *Forbes* or the *Wall Street Journal*) receives full constitutional protection, so that is not the criterion. Instead, according to the U.S. Supreme Court, commercial speech is "that which does no more than propose a commercial transaction."[201]

Speech that does nothing more than propose a commercial transaction is certainly one kind of commercial speech, but is it the only kind? The purpose of many advertisements is solely to build name recognition. A billboard displaying nothing more than a pair of golden arches and the slogan, "I'm loving it" seems an awful lot like a commercial advertisement, yet it does not propose any commercial transaction. The statement, "Nine out of ten dentists recommend ABC brand gum for their patients who chew gum" seems like commercial speech even though no transaction is proposed.

In cases decided subsequent to that pronouncement, the U.S. Supreme Court has made it clear that the definition is not that narrow. Instead, the Court determines the scope of the commercial speech doctrine with reference to the rationale for granting constitutional protection to commercial speech at all. The purpose is not to benefit merchants; rather, it is to benefit consumers. The idea is that commercial speech, if truthful, enables consumers to make intelligent and well-informed economic decisions. Commercial speech, then, is not limited to speech that does nothing more than propose a commercial transaction. It may also include speech that informs consumers about available products and services. This definition would be broad enough to reach advertising that does little more than make consumers aware of a brand or remind them that it is an available option. Commercial speech, then, may be described as speech about a company or its products or its services that is presented to consumers for the purpose of inviting or encouraging them to choose to purchase a product or service from the company.

The Court has held that three factors need to be considered when deciding whether a particular presentation is commercial speech:

- Content
- Profit motive
- The advertising form.

In addition, the Court has indicated that merely injecting some political content into what would otherwise clearly be a commercial advertisement will not suffice to elevate it to the status of political speech.

While generalizations in this area are hazardous, it would not be going too far out on a limb to suggest that most speech that fits the common law definition of trade disparagement is probably commercial speech. Defamatory content—such as a false statement that injures a company's reputation—may or may not be commercial speech, depending on whether it originates from a business competitor as part of an effort to divert customers away from the defamed business. The more like a trade disparagement claim a defamation claim is, the more likely it is commercial speech and not truly commentary on a matter of public concern. Of course, each case must be decided on its own facts.

The Lanham Act

Among other things, Section 43(a) of the Lanham Act provides a cause of action for false advertising. The cause of action may be pursued by a business competitor. It does not require a showing of intent to disparage or defame. Lanham Act cases, however, are limited to false or misleading statements that are made "in commercial advertising or promotion." A common law trade disparagement or defamation claim might be available for false statements made in contexts other than commercial advertising or promotion, such as during a news interview. For more information about section 43(a) of the Lanham Act, see Chapter 15.

Chapter 17. Privacy

> Of the desirability—indeed of the necessity—of some ... protection, there can, it is believed, be no doubt. The press is overstepping in every direction the obvious bounds of propriety and of decency. Gossip is no longer the resource of the idle and of the vicious, but has become a trade, which is pursued with industry as well as effrontery.... Triviality destroys at once robustness of thought and delicacy of feeling. No enthusiasm can flourish, no generous impulse can survive under its blighting influence.[202]

The quoted passage was written by Louis Brandeis and Samuel Warren in 1890. George Eastman had just begun marketing his new invention, the Kodak camera. The authors were concerned about the incursions into "sacred precincts" this development, in conjunction with a burgeoning newspaper industry, had wrought. Imagine what they would have to say about what the Internet has wrought.

The common law long ago established a right to privacy in the interest of protecting reputations and human dignity. Although not mentioned explicitly in the Constitution, the Fourth Amendment prohibition against unreasonable searches demonstrates that privacy also was among the rights the Founders believed to be essential to a just society. Since then, numerous statutes and judicial decisions have articulated and refined privacy right protections.

The interest in privacy, of course, conflicts with interests in freedoms of speech and the press. Every law prohibiting the disclosure of information is a limitation on speech and press freedoms. Legislators and courts try to strike a balance between these competing interests.

As a rule, American courts are more inclined to strike the balance in favor of press freedom than courts in other countries are. This is seen most clearly in cases involving celebrities. In America, journalists consider almost every aspect of a famous person's life to be fair game. European countries, by contrast, extend to celebrities most of the same privacy rights that individuals enjoy. Although American courts attach great importance to protecting trade secrets, they do not tend to ascribe great value to personal secrets. Meanwhile, Commonwealth countries broadly prohibit the disclosure of any communication of any kind that any person intended to be held in confidence, except where the information is already publicly available anyway or where disclosure is necessary to protect public safety, health or some other important public interest. American law protects the confidentiality of some kinds of communications, such as those made to a doctor, lawyer or clergyman, but it does not impose a general obligation to respect every individual's desire to keep a personal secret confidential.

Interest in privacy rights in the United States ebbed dramatically after the terror attacks on September 11, 2001. The federal government, with little resistance from judges or the people, greatly increased its own power to intrude on people's privacy. Over a decade and several high-profile data breaches later, a renewed interest in privacy rights has emerged. The concern today, however, is more about the possibility of financial loss due to identity theft than about personal embarrassment or damage to reputation.

Governmental Intrusions on Privacy

Constitutions are enacted to delineate the respective rights and powers of government and the governed. In the United States, privacy is one of the rights of the governed that both federal and state constitutions protect. Though not mentioned explicitly by name in the federal constitution, it is fairly inferred from the amendments to it. The Fourth Amendment protects the privacy of an individual's person, papers, house, and effects. The First Amendment protections of free speech and assembly have been interpreted to include a right to keep one's beliefs and political associations to oneself. The Fifth Amendment prohibits compulsory self-incrimination. This right exists even if a government official has probable cause to believe a crime has been committed.[203] The Fifth Amendment also protects the right to liberty, declaring that the federal government may not deprive a person of it without due process of law. The Fourteenth Amendment contains similar language, applicable to state governments. The Ninth Amendment adds that "[t]he enumeration of certain rights shall not be construed to deny or disparage others retained by the people." This means that when a court is called upon to interpret the meaning of the word *liberty* in the Due Process Clause, it is not limited to only such rights as are specifically enumerated in other Amendments. As one commentator put it:

> [T]he Constitution protects, without specific enumeration, certain essential freedoms of the individual. Labeled peripheral rights, these freedoms are derived from the penumbra or total scope of the constitutional amendments. The penumbral approach incorporates rights not explicitly included in any amendment with the rationale that their existence is vital "in making express guarantees of the various amendments fully meaningful."[204]

Justice Douglas applied this approach in *Griswold v. Connecticut*[205] to determine that doctors have a right of privacy with respect to how they counsel patients about contraceptives. Justice Goldberg, in a separate concurring opinion, opined that the liberty protected in the Due Process Clause is even broader than that. For Goldberg, an unenumerated right may be deserving of protection even if doing so is not necessary to make one of the enumerated rights meaningful. He contended that "the requirements of a free society" are an independent source of protected liberties.[206] Whichever rationale is preferred, later decisions make it clear that government officials may not intrude into certain zones of privacy without a compelling reason for doing so. (A *zone of privacy* is a realm that a reasonable person would expect to be private and in which a person has an actual expectation of privacy, such as a bedroom in one's home.) State constitutions may provide greater protections of privacy than the federal constitution does.

SECTION 1983

Section 1983 (42 U.S.C. § 1983) provides a private cause of action for damages for anyone whose rights under the Constitution and laws of the United States have been violated by a person acting under color of state law, custom or usage. Accordingly, a person whose federally protected privacy rights are violated by a state entity or official may file a lawsuit against the state under Section 1983 for monetary damages, injunctive relief, and sometimes attorney fees. In one widely publicized case, *Robbins v. Lower Merion School District*,[207] students filed suit under Section 1983 against a public school that had remotely activated webcams on students' computers to surreptitiously monitor the students' activities in their own homes.

To be actionable under section 1983, the intrusion must be by a state actor, that is, a person acting in his or her capacity as an agent or representative of a federal, state or municipal governmental entity. Although private entities may be sued under other statutes or under the common law, they generally cannot be sued under Section 1983.

The plaintiff must also prove that the intrusion was into a realm as to which she had both a subjective and an objectively reasonable expectation of privacy.

PRIVACY PROTECTION ACT

The Privacy Protection Act[208] is a federal law that prohibits government officials from searching or seizing any work product or documentary materials held by a "person reasonably believed to have a purpose to disseminate to the public a newspaper, book, broadcast, or other similar form of public communication." An exception exists if the official has probable cause to believe the publisher has committed or is committing a crime to which the materials relate.

ELECTRONIC COMMUNICATIONS PRIVACY ACT

The ECPA protects the privacy of electronic communications, including email and voicemail. All electronically transmitted communications other than oral communications come within its coverage.

Interception of Messages

Title I of the Act prohibits the intentional interception of an electronic communication. It also prohibits the disclosure or use of an electronic communication that is known to have been intercepted in violation of the ECPA.

The prohibition is not absolute. Title III authorizes law enforcement to engage in electronic surveillance pursuant to an electronic surveillance order. An application for an order must state:

(a) the offense allegedly being committed
(b) a detailed showing of probable cause
(c) a showing that normal investigative techniques are not effective in the investigation
(d) the interception point for the communications
(e) the types of conversations to be intercepted
(f) the identity of the person(s) whose communication are to be intercepted

As amended by the USA PATRIOT Act, the ECPA allows the federal government to intercept email messages and monitor Internet activity without a warrant. The FBI may issue National Security Letters (NSLs) with which electronic communication service providers are required to comply.

Seizure of a computer on which email messages are stored might violate Title II but is not an illegal intercept of the messages within the meaning of Title I.

Access to Stored Messages

Title II prohibits unauthorized access to or disclosure of a stored communication. It also bars electronic communication service providers (businesses that provide users with the ability to communicate electronically) and remote computing service providers from disclosing the content of stored electronic communications except under certain circumstances. It applies to both governmental entities and private persons and businesses.

Exceptions exist for disclosures pertaining to a crime or law enforcement and for disclosures made to comply with a warrant, order or other lawful demand from a governmental entity. During the first 180 days that an electronic communication is in storage, disclosure to a government entity is required only if a court has issued a warrant. Thereafter, disclosure by an electronic communication service provider or remote computing service to a government entity pursuant to an administrative subpoena, a court order, a grand jury subpoena, or a warrant is mandatory. In other words, an administrative agency must wait six months before granting itself a subpoena to access stored electronic communications.

Records pertaining to a customer or subscriber of an electronic communication service provider or remote computing service provider must be provided to a government entity only if one or more of the following conditions apply:

(a) The subscriber or customer has consented to the disclosure;
(b) A court has issued a warrant or an order requiring disclosure;
(c) A subpoena has been issued by a court, an administrative agency, or a grand jury;
(d) A government entity formally requests disclosure in connection with a law enforcement investigation into telemarketing fraud, if the customer or subscriber for whom records are sought is engaged in telemarketing.

A subpoena may require disclosure of the subscriber's or customer's name, address, telephone number, subscriber number or identity, any temporarily assigned network addresses, length of service and types of services utilized, telephone connection records, records of session times and durations, and the customer's or subscriber's means and source of payment for the service, including credit card and bank account numbers. When responding to a government entity's request for disclosure in connection with a telemarketing fraud investigation, an electronic communication or remote computing service provider is only obliged to provide the customer's or subscriber's name, address and place of business, unless there is a warrant, court order or subpoena for other kinds of disclosures.

A warrant for stored electronic communications may be issued without prior notice to the customer or subscriber. In the case of a subpoena or a court order other than a warrant, prior notice generally must be given. A court, however, may delay notification for up to ninety days if giving notice sooner would endanger a person's life or safety, jeopardize an investigation, unduly delay a trial, or result in flight from prosecution, destruction or tampering with evidence, or intimidation of a potential witness. A governmental entity that has obtained a subpoena may delay notification for up to ninety days if a supervisory official certifies that earlier notification would have one of these adverse results. Additional ninety-day extensions may be granted by a court or, in the case of an administrative subpoena, by a supervisory official's execution of another "adverse results" certification.

A court order for disclosure of stored communications or other records may be issued only if the governmental entity alleges specific facts establishing reasonable grounds to believe they are relevant and material to an ongoing criminal investigation. A court may modify or quash an order if it determines that compliance would impose an undue burden on the service provider.

Email and other electronic communications that are stored on a third party's server for more than 180 days are considered abandoned. A warrant is required, however, to seize or gain access to email messages that are stored on a user's personal computer, regardless of how long they have been stored there.

Data about individual or group traffic and calling patterns may be obtained without a warrant so long as the actual content of the communication is not accessed.

The USA PATRIOT Act authorizes the FBI to issue National Security Letters (NSLs) to electronic communication service providers allowing the FBI to gain access to subscriber information that is considered relevant to an investigation of terrorism. These are essentially like warrants except that they are issued by the FBI instead of a judge. At least one court has held that an Internet subscriber whose information is turned over to the government has no reasonable expectation of privacy and therefore is not protected by the Fourth Amendment.[209]

Remedies for violations of the ECPA include injunctive or declaratory relief, actual damages, attorney fees and costs. An electronic communication service provider is immune from liability for providing information, facilities or assistance to a government entity pursuant to a warrant, subpoena, court order, or certification, or as otherwise authorized by the ECPA.

PRIVACY ACT OF 1974

The Privacy Act of 1974 gives individuals the rights to:

(a) learn what information the federal government has collected about them
(b) see and obtain copies of the information
(c) correct or amend inaccurate or incomplete information
(d) exercise limited control over disclosure of the information by the government to others.

A private cause of action for damages or injunctive relief is available to enforce these rights.

SHIELD LAWS

When a person fears repercussions for revealing truthful but negative information, a journalist might enter into an agreement to keep the source's identity secret. Shield laws recognize the value of this method of gathering information and attempt to protect journalists from being required to disclose the identities of anonymous sources. In states that have adopted a shield law, a court may not order a journalist to reveal the identity of an anonymous source unless the information is highly relevant and necessary to a legal claim and cannot be obtained from other available sources.

Shield laws vary from state to state and courts vary in their interpretations of them. In many of the states that have shield laws, regular publication is required in order to qualify for the protections the law affords to journalists. Some states limit the protection of shield laws to "journalists," in the traditional sense of newspaper, television and radio reporters. Website owners and bloggers would not be protected in these states. Therefore, website owners and bloggers who promise anonymity to their sources may find it prudent to include in their agreements with such sources a reservation of a right to disclose a source's identity if ordered by a court to do so.

Many countries have no shield laws at all.

IDENTITY THEFT

The FCRA spells out the rights of victims and the responsibilities of business in cases of alleged identity theft. Identity theft victims are entitled to ask businesses for a copy of transaction records—such as applications for credit—relating to the theft of their identity. Victims may authorize law enforcement officers to get the records or ask that the business send a copy of the records directly to a law enforcement officer. The businesses covered by the law must provide copies of these records, free of charge, within thirty days of receiving a written request for them. This means that the law enforcement officials who ask for these records in writing may get them from a business without a subpoena, as long as they have the victim's authorization.

The FTC enforces the FCRA including this requirement, which is set out in Section 609(e). The law applies to any business that has provided credit, goods, or services to, accepted payment from, or otherwise entered into a transaction with someone who is believed to have fraudulently used another person's identification. For example, if a business opened a cell phone account in the victim's name or extended credit to someone misusing the victim's identity, the business may be required to provide the records relating to the transaction to the identity theft victim or to a law enforcement officer acting on that victim's behalf.

The business may require the alleged victim to furnish any or all of the following:

- proof of identity, such as a government-issued ID card
- the same type of information the identity thief used to open the account or the type of information the business is currently requesting from applicants
- a police report
- a completed affidavit.

Victims may use the FTC's Identity Theft Report, available at IdentityTheft.gov, or another affidavit the business accepts. A business may refuse to provide records if it determines in good faith that: (a) it cannot verify the true identity of the person asking for the information; (b) the request for the information is based on a misrepresentation; or (c) the information requested is Internet navigational data or similar information about a person's visit to a website or online service.

A business may not deny disclosure of these records based on the financial privacy provisions of the GLBA. Nevertheless, it may refuse to disclose them if state or another federal law prohibits it from doing so.

FACTA gives consumers a right to place fraud alerts on their credit reports and block credit bureaus from reporting information that is in their files as a result of identity theft.

Non-Governmental Invasions of Privacy

Constitutions protect individuals from governmental intrusions into their privacy. They do not protect individuals from invasions of privacy by nongovernmental organizations or individuals. For those, resort must be had to statutes and the common law.

COMMON LAW CAUSES OF ACTION

There are four kinds of common law causes of action for invasion of privacy:

- Publication of private facts
- False light
- Intrusion
- Misappropriation of personality.

Publication of Private Facts

Liability for invasion of privacy by publication of private facts may be incurred if:

(a) private facts
(b) the disclosure of which would be highly offensive to a reasonable person
(c) are published, i.e., communicated or disclosed to a substantial number of people
(d) intentionally or with knowledge that they are highly personal and that their disclosure would be highly offensive to a reasonable person
(e) resulting in embarrassment, mental anguish or other harm.

All of these conditions must be satisfied before common law liability for publication of private facts may be imposed. This means, for example, that even if a private fact about an individual is not generally known, publication of it is not actionable if disclosing it would not be offensive to a reasonable person.

The facts do not necessarily need to be published in written form. Publishing a photograph of a person qualifies as a publication of "facts" about the person.

PRIVATE FACTS

Private facts are facts that are highly personal and not generally known. Information about a person's sexual organs is an example. Information about disabilities, medical conditions, sexual orientation, sexual exploits, and/or financial condition are also examples of private facts, provided they are not already generally known.

Any fact that is already available to the public is not a private fact. Therefore, unless a person is born on private property and never leaves it, information about a person's face is available to the public. Publishing an image of it without the person's permission might result in liability for misappropriation of personality, but it cannot result in liability for publication of private facts. For the same reason, republishing facts that someone else has already published to the Internet, or in a newspaper or magazine, should not result in liability for publication of a private fact. It might be actionable on some other basis, but not as a publication of private facts. Even if the original publication was an invasion of privacy, the first publication of them destroys their status of private facts. Of course, if the republisher solicited, induced or knowingly facilitated the original publication, then the republisher may be contributorily liable for the original publication.

The *Wonkette* case illustrates the principle. In that case, a former congressional aide sued another former congressional aide for writing about their private sexual relationship on her blog. The former aide also sued Anna Marie Cox of *Wonkette* for mentioning the blog piece on another web site. The court dismissed the "publication of private facts" claim against Cox because her comments were about something that had already been published online. The claim against the congressional aide who originally published the facts may or may not have had merit, but there could be no liability for Cox because the original publication had caused the facts to cease being private.

OFFENSIVENESS

Even if it is clear that a private fact has been published, liability will not attach unless its disclosure would be highly offensive to a reasonable person. Descriptions or depictions of people's sexual organs and activities, toilet practices, addictions, diseases, disabilities, health or financial conditions—to the extent they are not generally known—may be highly offensive to a reasonable person. Photographs of people engaged in sexual activity, or while they are nude or partially nude, or of a woman nursing a baby, or of a woman giving birth are also considered offensive insofar as invasion of privacy liability is concerned. These are not the only kinds of things that could qualify as offensive.

Publishing photographs of military personnel engaged in prisoner abuse has been held to be inoffensive to a reasonable person, and therefore not actionable as a publication of private facts.

Although a wedding may be private, publishing photographs of it is not likely to be considered highly offensive to a reasonable person. Accordingly, a publisher could not be sued for publication of private facts on this basis in the United States. The rule is to the contrary in some other countries. In the United Kingdom, publishing wedding photographs without permission may result in liability for publication of private facts.

Offensiveness is determined by an objective standard. The fact that the subject of the information is offended is not determinative. It must be proven that a reasonable person would find the publication offensive.

REASONABLE EXPECTATION OF PRIVACY

There is no liability for publication of private facts if the subject of the information has no objectively reasonable expectation that the information will remain private. For this reason, publishing information about what someone does in a public place generally should not result in liability for publication of private facts. People generally do not have a reasonable expectation of privacy when they are in public. Publishing a photograph of a couple engaged in amorous activity in their own bedroom could be an actionable publication of a private fact, but publishing a photograph of the same couple engaged in the same activity in a public park would not be.

There are some kinds of public places in which people do have a reasonable expectation of privacy. Public restrooms and changing rooms are examples. Publishing a photograph of a person using a public restroom or undressing in a changing room could be actionable as a publication of a private fact.

If the publication is for commercial or other advantage—such as publishing exclusive nude photographs of a celebrity on a commercial website—there may be liability for appropriation of personality whether or not there is also liability for publication of private facts.

NEWSWORTHINESS

Even if facts are private and their publication would be highly offensive to a reasonable person, there can be no liability for publication of private facts if the information will benefit the public or is a matter of legitimate public interest. Newsworthiness is a defense to a claim of publication of private facts.

Courts have interpreted newsworthiness fairly broadly. In some jurisdictions, the legitimacy of public interest in a particular matter has come to mean something like genuineness. Thus, courts have held that there is a legitimate public interest in nearly every aspect of the private lives of politicians and public figures (e.g., celebrities, movie stars, professional athletes, elected officials, candidates for public office), even those who have unintentionally become public figures (e.g., heroes, arrestees and convicted criminals). Some courts have extended the newsworthiness doctrine to apply to private figures, too. The modern trend is toward viewing all events as newsworthy unless they occur within the confines of a place in which a person has a reasonable expectation of privacy.

Some kinds of events are considered matters of public interest even if they occur in a place in which a person has a reasonable expectation of privacy. Crimes, arrests, police raids, suicides, marriages, divorces, fires, accidents, natural disasters, drug overdoses, rare diseases, the discovery of a person long believed dead, police reports of an escaped animal, and many other things have been found to be matters of legitimate public interest even if they happen in a private home.

Some courts have held that "information concerning interesting phases of human activity" and "all issues about which information is needed or appropriate so that individuals may cope with the exigencies of their period" are matters of legitimate public interest.[210] Under this standard, courts have found things like unusual love relationships, the location and living conditions of a former child prodigy, an Indian rope trick, and the personal characteristics of presidential campaign volunteers to be matters of legitimate public interest.

Courts are more likely to find newsworthiness when the degree of offensiveness is low. They are less likely to find newsworthiness when the degree of offensiveness is high. "The line is to be drawn when the publicity ... becomes a morbid and sensational prying into private lives for its own sake, with which a reasonable member of the public, with decent standards, would say that he had no concern."[211]

The media is allowed to communicate many kinds of facts about the private lives of newsworthy individuals, provided there is a logical connection between the facts and the matter in which the public has a legitimate interest. Thus, for example, a news story about a medical malpractice lawsuit may delve into the professional's marital life and mental health history. In one case, a court held that publication of a photograph of a patient inside a mental hospital is not actionable if the photograph was taken while the patient was walking next to a famous fellow patient, because the public has a legitimate interest in the mental and physical rehabilitation of public figures.

Aspects of a story that are not relevant to a matter of public concern are not within the newsworthiness defense. In *Barber v. Time, Inc.*,[212] a magazine published a story about a woman who was in the hospital for treatment of a rare disease. The court agreed that information about the disease was a matter of public interest and therefore newsworthy, but held that the e patient's name was not. Since the disease was not contagious, there was no public benefit in disclosing her name. The disease was unusual and interesting, but the identity of the person who had it was not of any legitimate interest. The newsworthiness defense gave the magazine the right to publish information about the disease and the fact that someone has it, but it did not give the magazine the right to disclose the identity of the person who has it.

Unfortunately, predictability in this area is difficult because court rulings have not been consistent. For example, the sexual aspects of public officials' lives typically are considered matters of legitimate public interest. In one case, however, the California Court of Appeals ruled that the fact that an elected student body president was a transsexual (born male but underwent a sex change operation) was not a matter of legitimate public interest – despite the fact that it was deemed newsworthy that she was being heralded as the first "female" student body president who had ever been elected. The very next year, however, the same court held that the fact that a public figure (in this case, an otherwise private individual who engaged in a heroic act, namely, protecting President Ford from an assassination attempt) was a gay man was a matter of legitimate public interest.

Newsworthiness can fade with the passage of time. And with the passage of time, it is also sometimes possible for a person who was once a public figure to become an unknown, i.e., to become a private individual again. Due to its virtually unlimited storage capacity and easy searchability, the Internet has created what has been described as "a world without forgetting."[213] Consequently, although it is logically possible, as a practical matter it is likely to be very difficult to prove that a public figure has receded into obscurity.

Facts and information in public court records are public facts. There is an absolute First Amendment privilege to publish information in public court records. Some but not all states extend the privilege to all public records. The privilege does not apply to sealed records.

Intrusion

Intrusion (or "intrusion upon seclusion") means denying a person privacy with respect to a place or forum as to which the person has a reasonable expectation of privacy. This cause of action seeks to compensate individuals for the anguish they suffer when their reasonable expectation of privacy in a place or thing (e.g., their homes, public restrooms, their phone conversations, their mail, or their email) is disturbed. The classic examples are window peeping, eavesdropping, and reading somebody else's mail.

The required elements for an intrusion claim are:

(a) substantial, unauthorized physical intrusion, use of senses to overhear or see, or other investigation or examination
(b) into a place or matter as to which another person has a reasonable expectation of privacy
(c) in a way that is highly offensive to a reasonable person
(d) with intent to intrude or knowledge that the intrusion would be wrong
(e) causing mental anguish or other harm.

Hacking into someone's private email account is an example of intrusion upon seclusion. People generally have a reasonable expectation of privacy in their emails unless they have done something to make them public. Surreptitiously taking a picture of another person might be actionable if the manner of taking the picture would be highly offensive to a reasonable person.

To be actionable, the intrusion must occur at a place or with respect to a matter about which a person has a reasonable expectation of privacy. People have a reasonable expectation of privacy in the contents of their email, for example, and they also have a reasonable expectation of privacy in their dwellings and certain other places, such as restrooms and changing rooms. Copying material from a person's public web site generally would not be an invasion of the website owner's privacy because a website owner cannot reasonably expect anything posted there to remain private.

The purpose of this cause of action is to redress the indignity of the intrusion itself. Neither publication nor disclosure of information to anyone needs to be proven. To be actionable, the intrusion must be substantial and highly offensive to a reasonable person. This means the intrusion must be such as could be expected to cause embarrassment, humiliation or mental anguish to a person of ordinary sensibilities. This is an objective standard, not a subjective one. In a case where an individual sought a remedy for intrusion because Google Maps had photographed his house and posted it to the Internet without his consent, the court denied the claim because no showing was made that this would cause embarrassment or mental anguish to a person of ordinary sensibilities.[214]

False Light

Depicting someone in a *false light* means portraying a person in a false or misleading way. The elements of the common law cause of action are:

(a) publication
(b) of a false or misleading statement or depiction of a person
(c) that would be highly offensive to a reasonable person
(d) with knowledge of falsity or reckless disregard for the false light in which the person would be placed.

Some courts hold that the statement need not be about something that is personal, private or secret. To these courts, it is the portrayal of a person in such a way as to falsely attribute some action, inaction or characteristic to him that is the gravamen of this tort. This interpretation blurs the distinction between invasion of privacy and defamation. As a practical matter, though, classification as either defamation or false light invasion of privacy is really only important with respect to damages. Damages for "false light" invasion of privacy are intended to compensate the victim for the violation of his interest in privacy, the right to be left alone. Damages for defamation are intended to compensate for loss of reputation.

Posting an altered photograph or misinformation about a person to a website in order to cause visitors to the site to have a misimpression about the person would be an example of "false light" invasion of privacy, provided the effect is to cause reasonable people to believe something highly offensive about the person.

Liability for "false light" invasion of privacy may exist even if no factually false information has been communicated. Liability may be predicated entirely on a misleading depiction of a person's character, history, activities or beliefs. Of course, publishing factual text or an unaltered photograph is not as likely to result in "false light" liability as publishing altered text or photoshopped pictures is. It is possible for even an unaltered photograph or news story to portray a person in a false light, though. This can happen if the information conveyed is presented out of context, or in such a way as to create a false impression about the person.

> **Example**. Website *A* truthfully reports that Bob McKinsey was seen engaging in "social intercourse with numerous people at the same time." Website *B* then publishes an article stating that Bob McKinsey "is reported to have been seen engaging in intercourse with numerous people at the same time." Technically, Website *B* has not published a false statement. Nevertheless, a reasonable person probably would understand the word *intercourse*, standing alone, to refer to sexual intercourse. Publishing a claim that a person engaged group sex most likely would be highly offensive to a reasonable person.

The same kind of thing can happen with unaltered photographs.

> **Example**. Bob McKinsey is seen at a picnic reaching for a hamburger bun. A photographer snaps a picture at such an angle that the hamburger buns are not visible, but a woman's derriere is. Publishing such a photograph might be actionable as "false light" invasion of privacy if a reasonable person would interpret the photograph as communicating that Bob McKinsey was reaching out to grab a woman's derriere. Whether a reasonable person really would draw that inference depends on the circumstances. Liability would almost certainly attach, though, if accompanying text suggests, encourages or buttresses a particular interpretation. For example, if the photograph is captioned, "Bob McKinsey really has a thing for 'buns'!" then the risk of liability for "false light" invasion of privacy might increase.

The bottom line is this: Don't try to misrepresent facts through the manipulative or clever use of language or photography.

As with defamation, public officials and public figures cannot sue for false light invasion of privacy with respect to their official acts or duties unless they can prove actual malice, that is, knowing falsity or reckless disregard for the truth.

Misappropriation of Personality

See publicity rights, infra.

Removal Requests

Sometimes a person whose privacy has been invaded will ask the website owner to remove the offending material. Complying with such a request will not necessarily insulate a website owner from liability completely. Refusing to comply, though, may make bad faith intent easier to prove, which greatly increases the chances of being sued and potentially increases the amount of damages that may be awarded.

STATUTORY PRIVACY RIGHTS

Personal Information

The United States has no single, comprehensive law addressing the collection, use or disclosure of personal information. Instead, a variety of federal and state laws impose privacy regulations on particular industries, particular categories of information, and particular methods of collecting, storing, using or sharing information. The closest thing to a national privacy law is the FTC Act. It prohibits unfair or deceptive trade practices and gives the FTC broad authority to bring enforcement actions against businesses that engage in them.

An unfair trade practice is commercial activity as to which all of the following apply:

(a) It causes or is likely to cause substantial injury to consumers
(b) Consumers cannot reasonably avoid the injury themselves
(c) It has no offsetting benefits to consumers or competition.

Disclosing to third parties personally identifying information that a company collects from its customers would seem to come within this definition inasmuch as it could cause substantial injury to a consumer, particularly if it is disclosed either directly to an identity thief or to another person or business who then discloses it to an identity thief. Sales of customer information to advertising firms arguably might have some benefit to consumers or competition in that it enables businesses to reach out to consumers to provide them with information about available products and services. It does not seem likely that this benefit could outweigh the harm that can result from identity theft, though.

Although certain kinds of websites must do so, the FTC so far has not adopted a general rule explicitly requiring all e-commerce businesses to publish a privacy policy, or to give notice to website visitors of the kinds of uses that may be made of personal information that is collected from them, or the kinds of third parties with whom data may be shared. FTC enforcement actions usually focus on requiring companies to comply with their own stated privacy policies, whatever they may be. From the consent orders it has entered into with online companies it has charged with privacy-related violations of the FTC Act, though, some things are clear:

(a) Although publishing a privacy policy is not required of every e-commerce businesses, any company that publishes one on its website must comply with it;
(b) Companies that claim in their privacy policies that they will use personal information collected from consumers only for specified purposes are guilty of engaging in a deceptive trade practice if they use the information for any other purpose;
(c) Companies that claim that they will not share personal information with third parties, or that they will only share information with specified kinds of third parties, are engaging in a deceptive trade practice if they share it with other kinds of third parties;
(d) Companies may not retroactively change their privacy policies without providing existing data subjects an opportunity to opt out of the new privacy practice;
(e) Companies that revise their privacy policies should obtain affirmative express consent before using consumer information in ways that are materially different from the privacy policy that was in effect when the data was collected.

The absence of a rule explicitly stating these things does not mean that businesses may use and share personal information any way they want. The FTC may bring an enforcement action against any business that discloses, uses or shares personal information in a way that causes substantial harm to consumers if it has no offsetting benefits to consumer or competition, irrespective of whether the company has published a privacy policy or not.

Some kinds of information are so sensitive that sharing them with others creates a high risk of causing harm to the subject of the information. If such harm does result, then sharing the information may be deemed an unfair trade practice. The FTC suggests that a business should not share sensitive information about a person with others unless the person has consented to the disclosure of the information. Sensitive information includes:

- Financial information
- Health information
- Information about children
- Geographic location information
- Social Security number.

The FTC Act does not expressly give consumers a general right to review, correct or request deletion of information that an e-commerce business has collected from them. This kind of right only exists with respect to particular kinds of information, such as health information or information collected from children under thirteen years of age.

State laws sometimes impose stricter consumer privacy protection obligations on businesses than the FTC does. California's Online Privacy Protection Act[215] requires online businesses to establish and publish a privacy policy that discloses the kind of information that is collected, the persons with whom it may be shared, how to request changes to the information, and a number of other things. (See discussion of Privacy Policies, infra.) A few other states require at least some kinds of disclosures. Some states, such as Minnesota and Nevada, prohibit ISPs from disclosing private information about their customers without consent. Nearly every state has enacted some version of a deceptive trade practices act similar to the FTC Act.

California's Shine the Light Act[216] gives customers a right to receive an account of how and with whom a company has shared the consumer's personal information in the past year. The right exists only if all of the following conditions exist:

(a) The customer is a California resident;
(b) The information is collected in a consumer transaction, not a business transaction;
(c) The customer has an established business relationship with the company (e.g., has purchased, leased or licensed something or communicated with the company about doing so);
(d) The company has at least twenty employees (full or part time);
(e) The company has disclosed personal information about the customer to one or more third parties within the past calendar year;
(f) The company knows or should know that the third parties used the information for direct marketing;
(g) The customer sends a written, emailed, telephone or faxed request;

(h) The customer has not already made a request under this law during the past year;

(i) The company's privacy policy fails to adopt a policy of not disclosing personal information to third parties for direct marketing purposes unless the customer opts in, or fails to adopt a policy of nondisclosure if the customer opts out.

The account must be provided within thirty days (150 days if the customer uses something other than the company's designated address or other contact method to make the request). It must include (a) a list of the categories of personal information that were shared during the preceding calendar year, and (b) the names and addresses of all recipients, with examples of the products or services they marketed, if known. The name may be a business name; the name of a specific individual is not necessary.

A business that sells to California residents must designate a mailing address, email address, telephone number or facsimile number to which customers may send these requests. In addition, it must do at least one of the following:

(a) Educate employees about customers' rights and how to respond to a customer's request under this law.

(b) Put a link on its home page to a page titled "Your Privacy Rights," or add the words "Your Privacy Rights" to the home page's link to the company's privacy policy. The linked-to page must include the contact information for such requests.

(c) Make the contact information readily available upon request at every place of business in California where the business or its agents regularly have contact with customers.

The statute contains intricate and detailed definitions of third party and personal information. The good news is that a business does not have to worry about complying with this law if it adopts and publishes to its website a privacy policy with an opt-in or opt-out mechanism and notifies the customer of the right to prevent disclosure in the manner described in the privacy policy.

Some states, including California, prohibit businesses from publicly posting, displaying, selling or offering to sell Social Security numbers.

DRIVER'S LICENSE AND MOTOR VEHICLE RECORDS

The Driver's Privacy Protection Act[217] (DPPA) generally prohibits the disclosure or re-disclosure of "highly restricted personal information"—i.e., a person's driver's license or identification card photograph, Social Security number, or medical or disability information—that has been obtained by a state motor vehicle department. This prohibition applies to states and it also applies to persons and businesses who obtain this kind of information from a state motor vehicle department.

Exceptions include:

(a) consent of the data subject

(b) court order

(c) use in connection with a legal proceeding, such as service of process, enforcement of a judgment, investigation in anticipation of litigation

(d) use by an insurance company or self-insured entity in connection with claims investigations, antifraud activities, rating or underwriting
(e) use by an employer or its agent or insurer in relation to a holder of a commercial driver's license required under 4 U.S.C. ch. 313
(f) use by a government agency or officer for a lawful purpose.

Personal information that is not highly restricted (such as name, address, motor vehicle title information, etc.) may be disclosed in any of these circumstances and, in addition, in any of the following circumstances:

(a) verification of the accuracy of personal information submitted by an individual to a business or its agent, employee or contractor
(b) to obtain correct information when an individual has submitted incorrect personal information to a business, if the correct information is needed to prevent fraud or to pursue legal remedies or recover on a debt or enforce a security interest against the individual
(c) matters involving vehicle safety or theft
(d) matters involving driver safety
(e) emissions control compliance
(f) vehicle recalls and the like
(g) disclosures needed to carry out the Automobile Information Disclosure Act,[218] the Anti Car Theft Act,[219] the Clean Air Act[220] or 49 U.S.C. §§ 301, 305, 321–331 (relating to motor vehicles)
(h) performance monitoring of motor vehicles, parts, and dealers
(i) motor vehicle market research
(j) research and statistical purposes, provided personal information is not redisclosed or used to contact individuals
(k) to provide notice to owners of towed or impounded vehicles
(l) private toll transportation facilities
(m) a purpose authorized under the state's laws relating to public safety or the operation of motor vehicles
(n) use by a licensed private investigative agency or security service for one of the above purposes.

A recipient of personal information may disclose or sell the information only for the purposes authorized in the DPPA. Records of every person and entity to whom the recipient rediscloses or resells the information must be kept for five years and made available to the motor vehicle department upon request.

Knowingly obtaining or disclosing personal information from a motor vehicle department record, or making a false representation to obtain the information, is a crime. It may also result in liability for damages, including punitive damages and attorney fees.

COOKIES AND BROWSING ACTIVITY

Tracking cookies and other technologies have enabled a new kind of marketing strategy: behavioral advertising. *Behavioral advertising* is advertising that is tailored to a computer user's browsing activity. It is accomplished by collecting data about the user's search strings, websites visited, and content accessed. This is usually done by placing a tracking cookie in the user's browser. The data that is collected in this way is used to create a profile of the user's interests. Advertisements relevant to those interests are then served to the user.

Historically, the FTC treated information collected for behavioral advertising purposes as nonsensitive information because it does not appear to contain personally identifying information. It reveals a computer user's web surfing behavior, but does not collect a person's name, birth date, etc. The FTC, however, has been expanding its interpretation of the meaning of "personally identifiable information." Enforcement actions and settlement agreements in recent cases indicate that data may be "personally identifiable" if they can reasonably be linked to a particular computer or device, even if not linked to a particular person. It appears that the FTC views static IP addresses, MAC addresses, device identifiers, and the like as personally identifiable information. According to the FTC, failing to disclose that this information is being collected and/or how the collected data is used or shared is an unfair and deceptive trade practice.

In one notable case, the FTC brought an enforcement action against VIZIO, Inc. alleging that VIZIO's tracking and sharing of information about SmartTV users' viewing habits was an unfair and deceptive trade practice. The case ultimately was settled, with VIZIO agreeing to disclose to consumers:

(a) the types of data that will be collected and used
(b) the types of data that will be shared with third parties
(c) the identity or specific categories of persons with whom the data will be shared
(d) all purposes for which the company may share the information.

The settlement requires these disclosures to be displayed separately from the Privacy Policy and Terms of Use. It is not clear if the FTC intends to enforce this particular requirement for every website. In any event, whatever disclosures are necessary must be clearly and prominently displayed.

In addition to making these disclosures, the settlement requires VIZIO to obtain the consumer's affirmative, express consent to the collection and sharing activities and to provide instructions on how to revoke such consent. The FTC's Behavioral Advertising Principles, although described as "voluntary," are consistent with the outcome of this case.

In short, the FTC has come around to the position that a website that uses cookies or other technology to collect information about a user's browsing or viewing activity should give users notice and an opportunity to opt out, at least if sensitive information is collected. (This would include financial information, health information, Social Security number, information about children, or geographic location information.)

Examples of suggested compliance measures that may help forestall an FTC enforcement action against a business that engages in behavioral advertising might include:

(a) prominently displaying a notice on the home page with language like: "We collect, use and share information about your browsing activities and the websites you visit to send you targeted advertisements or to share the information with [identities of persons or specific categories of persons with whom the information is shared] for the purpose of [specify the purposes for sharing the information with such persons]. To opt out of the collection of such information, click here"

(b) providing a 'Click Here' button or textual link that points to an opt-out page
(c) explaining, on the opt-out page, what the specific effects of opting in or out will be
(d) explaining that opting out is browser-specific, so a user must opt-out again if a different browser is used
(e) informing the user of the status of the opt-out after an attempt to exercise the right
(f) displaying the words "Opt out?" on behavioral advertising and formatting the advertisement in such a way that the message "Opt Out of Targeted Ads" is displayed when a user hovers over the ad
(g) linking the displayed message to the opt-out page.

VIDEO PURCHASES AND RENTALS

The Video Privacy Protection Act[221] generally prohibits an audiovisual service provider (e.g., a business that rents or sells videos) from disclosing the audiovisual works a customer rents or purchases unless the customer consents. A business that violates this provision may be sued for damages, punitive damages, attorney fees and other relief. The information may be disclosed, without penalty, with the customer's consent or in response to a warrant or court order.

Consent to disclosure is effective only if it is in writing. Also, it must be informed consent. The consent must be given in a document that is distinct and separate from any document setting out other legal or financial obligations of the consumer. Consent may be given, at the election of the consumer, at the time disclosure is sought or in advance for a set period of time not to exceed two years or until consent is withdrawn by the consumer, whichever occurs sooner. The audiovisual service provider must provide an opportunity, in a clear and conspicuous manner, for the consumer to withdraw on a case-by-case basis or to withdraw from ongoing disclosures, at the consumer's election.

The audiovisual service provider may disclose a customer's name and address alone (i.e., without also disclosing information about the customer's movie selections) if the customer has been offered, in a clear and conspicuous manner, an opportunity to prohibit disclosure, and the disclosure does not identify the title, description or subject matter of any audiovisual material. The subject matter of the materials, however, may be disclosed if the disclosure is for the exclusive purpose of marketing goods and services directly to the consumer.

The Cable Communications Policy Act [222] regulates the collection, protection and disclosure of subscriber data by cable companies.

Email and Other Electronic Communications

The Electronic Communications Privacy Act (ECPA) protects the privacy of email and other electronic communications against invasion by individuals and businesses, as well as against government intrusions.

Title I prohibits the intentional interception of an electronic communication and also prohibits the disclosure or use of an electronic communication that is known to have been intercepted in violation of the ECPA or for the purpose of obstructing justice. A violation of Title I is punishable criminally by a fine and up to five years imprisonment. In a civil suit, the victim may recover the greater of: (a) statutory damages of either \$100 per day for each violation or \$10,000; or (b) actual damages plus any profits the defendant makes from the violation. Punitive damages, attorney fees and costs may also be recovered. Injunctive relief may be available. Unlawfully intercepted communications are not admissible as evidence.

Title II (also known as the Stored Communications Act) prohibits unauthorized access to a stored communication. This includes activity that exceeds the scope of an authorization as well as completely unauthorized activity. In addition, electronic communication service providers may not knowingly disclose the content of a stored communication. A violation of Title II is punishable criminally by a fine and up to two years imprisonment. In a civil suit, a victim may recover compensatory damages, any profits the defendant makes from the violation, punitive damages, attorney fees and costs.

In short, all of the following things are prohibited:

(a) unauthorized interception of another person's electronic communication while in transit
(b) unauthorized use or disclosure of an email message or other electronic communication known to have been unlawfully intercepted, or with the purpose of obstructing justice
(c) unauthorized access to a stored email message or other electronic communication
(d) unauthorized disclosure of a stored email message or other electronic communication by an electronic communication service provider.

This could include accessing, using or disclosing information stored in a cookie.

Under the ECPA, a communication is capable of being intercepted only while it is in transit. Accordingly, accessing email messages residing on a server (such as email messages that have been sent to and received by a mail server but not yet opened by the recipient) does not violate Title I, but might violate Title II.

Of course, an argument may be made that all email messages are stored, even if only briefly. At least one court, however, has held that transient storage of an email communication on its way to the intended recipient is still in transit, and therefore comes within Title I rather than Title II. Once it reaches the server that the recipient will access to retrieve email messages, though, it is no longer in transit. It is then a stored communication. At that point, Title II rather than Title I will apply.

Exceptions to Title I include:

(a) An mail or other electronic communication service provider may intercept, use and disclose electronic messages in the normal course of business while engaged in any activity that is necessarily incident to the rendition of the service or to the protection of the service provider's rights or property.
(b) Anyone may provide information, facilities, and assistance, and may disclose the contents of electronic communications, to law enforcement officers when such officers are exercising lawful authority to intercept electronic communications or to conduct electronic surveillance.
(c) Any person who has information about a lawfully intercepted electronic communication or evidence derived from it may disclose the contents of the communication or such derivative evidence while giving testimony under oath in a federal, state or local government proceeding.
(d) Anyone may intercept a communication to which the person is a party, provided the interception is not for the purpose of committing a crime or tort.

(e) An electronic communication service provider may disclose communications that are sent to it.

(f) Anyone may intercept a communication if the sender or recipient of the communication has given prior consent, provided the interception is not for the purpose of committing a crime or tort.

(g) Anyone may intercept an electronic communication that is made through a system that is configured so that the communication is readily accessible to the general public.

(h) Anyone may intercept an electronic communication the transmission of which is causing harmful interference to any lawfully operating station or consumer electronic equipment, to the extent necessary to identify the source of such interference.

(i) A pen register or a trap and trace device may be used to determine the origin of an electronic communication. This exception does not provide authority for intercepting the content of such a communication, however.

(j) An electronic communication service provider may record the fact that an electronic communication was initiated or completed in order to protect the provider, another provider furnishing service toward the completion of the communication, or a user of that service, from fraudulent, unlawful or abusive use of such service.

(k) An electronic communication service provider may disclose an electronic communication if the sender or recipient of it consents.

(l) An electronic communication service provider may disclose an electronic communication to an employee or agent to forward to its intended destination.

(m) An electronic communication service provider may disclose an electronic communication to a person or business whose facilities are used to forward the communication to its intended destination.

(n) An electronic communication servicer provide may disclose an inadvertently obtained electronic communication to law enforcement if it appears to pertain to the commission of a crime .

Consent may be either express or implied. The burden of proof of consent is on the person who asserts it as a defense.

A person who cooperates with law enforcement in connection with a lawful interception or surveillance operation normally is immune from liability in connection with the interception, provided the person does not disclose the existence of the interception or surveillance or the device used to accomplish it. Disclosure is permitted when required by legal process (e.g., a subpoena) but only if the Attorney General or to the principal prosecuting attorney of the appropriate state or political subdivision thereof is notified. Otherwise, immunity is lost.

Exceptions to Title II:

(a) A user of a communication service may access the user's own communications (messages that were either sent or received by the user;

(b) A user of a communication service, or a third party, may access a stored communication if the communication service provider authorizes it;

(c) Any person may access an electronic communication that is made through a system that is configured so that the communication is readily accessible to the general public;

(d) An electronic communication service provider may disclose a stored electronic communication to the addressee or intended recipient or his agent;
(e) An electronic communication service provider may disclose a stored electronic communication with the consent of either the sender or the intended recipient of it (or the consent of the subscriber, in the case of a remote computing service);
(f) An electronic communication service provider may disclose a stored electronic communication to an employee or agent to forward it to its destination;
(g) An electronic communication service provider may disclose a stored electronic communication to a person whose facilities are used to forward it to its destination;
(h) An electronic communication service provider may disclose a stored electronic communication when necessarily incident to the rendition of its service or to the protection of its property or rights;
(i) A lawfully intercepted communication may be accessed by the person or government entity that lawfully intercepted it;
(j) A person who has lawfully received information from a lawfully intercepted electronic communication may disclose it while giving sworn testimony in a legal proceeding;
(k) An electronic communication service provider may disclose a stored electronic communication as required by a court order or the lawful demand of a governmental entity or official;
(l) An electronic communication service provider may disclose an inadvertently obtained stored electronic communication to a law enforcement agency if it appears to pertain to the commission of a crime;
(m) An electronic communication service provider who has a good faith belief that an emergency involving the possibility of death or serious physical injury to a person requires disclosure without delay may disclose a stored electronic communication;
(n) An electronic communication service provider may disclose a stored electronic communication to the National Center for Missing and Exploited Children in connection with a missing child case.

An electronic communication service provider is immune from liability for providing information, facilities, or assistance with accessing stored communications if it was done pursuant to the terms of a court order, warrant, subpoena, statutory authorization, or certification of a kind contemplated by the ECPA.

The ECPA allows an electronic communication service provider to disclose customer and subscriber records (as distinguished from the contents of stored communications) in the following circumstances:

(a) when required to do so pursuant to a lawful court order or governmental demand
(b) with the customer's or subscriber's consent
(c) when necessarily incident to the rendition of the service or to the protection of the rights or property of the service provider
(d) to a governmental entity, if the provider, in good faith, believes that an emergency involving a danger of death or serious physical injury to any person requires disclosure without delay of information relating to the emergency

(e) to the National Center for Missing and Exploited Children, in connection with a missing child case
(f) to any person other than a governmental entity.

The ECPA also makes the possession, manufacture, sale, advertising or sending of a device knowing that it is primarily useful for the surreptitious interception of communications a crime. Exceptions exist for communication service providers, and those who contract with them or with a government entity, that possess, manufacture, sell or send such a device in the normal course of the business of providing the service. An exception also exists for advertisements of such devices that are sent to a communication service provider or to a governmental entity in the United States.

To reduce the risk of liability, an e-commerce business may find it prudent to include appropriate consent language—including but not limited to consent to the use of cookies—in its Terms of Service or to obtain website users' consent using a clickwrap agreement.

For information about how the ECPA impacts employee privacy, see Chapter 4.

Communications with Professionals

Every state imposes obligations on members of certain professions to refrain from disclosing confidential client communications. These obligations apply to attorneys, accountants, health care providers, psychotherapists, public school administrators, teachers, certain government workers, financial industry workers, and others.

Identity of Alleged Sexual Assault Victim

Several states have enacted laws making it a crime to disclose the identity of an alleged sexual assault victim. It is a defense if the information is obtained from a lawfully obtained public record.

Information Collected From Children

See Chapter 18.

Financial Information

The GLBA is a federal law intended, among other things, to ensure the privacy of financial information. The Safeguards Rule, relating to data security, is discussed in Chapter 13. The Privacy Rule[223] regulates the collection and disclosure of personal financial information. It applies to financial institutions that collect nonpublic personal information from customers or consumers. It also imposes obligations on those who receive customer or consumer personal financial information from a financial institution. It is enforced by the FTC, federal banking agencies, the SEC, the CFTC, and state insurance regulatory agencies.

The Rule distinguishes between "nonpublic personal information," as to which a privacy obligation generally exists, and "publicly available information," as to which a privacy obligation generally does not exist. *Nonpublic personal information* is any personally identifiable information that a financial institution collects about an individual in connection with providing a financial product or service, unless the information is already publicly available by other means.

It includes:

(a) any information an individual provides to get a financial product or service (e.g., name, address, Social Security number, income, and any other information on an application or order form for the product or service)
(b) information obtained from a transaction involving a financial product or service (e.g., account number, payment history, credit or debit card purchases, loan or deposit balances, or the fact that the individual is a customer of the business)
(c) information about an individual that is obtained in the course of providing a financial product or service (e.g., a consumer credit report)
(d) information of a kind that is generally publicly available but which a particular individual has the power to make unavailable to the public and has taken appropriate steps to do so (e.g., an unlisted telephone number).

Publicly available information includes:

(a) federal, state, or local government records that are available to the public (e.g., real estate records like deeds and mortgages; public court documents; articles of incorporation filed with a secretary of state, etc.)
(b) information that appears in widely distributed media (e.g., in telephone books, newspapers, or websites that are available to the general public on an unrestricted basis, even if the site requires a password or fee for access)
(c) information obtained for a purpose other than the financial product or service (e.g., a list of people who respond to an advertisement for a nonfinancial product or service).

A record or list that contains any nonpublic information at all is considered nonpublic information even if some of the information is public.

Example 1. XYZ Lending Co. maintains a list of its borrowers' names, addresses and telephone numbers. The names, addresses and telephone numbers are all publicly available in telephone directories. The fact that these individuals are customers of XYZ Lending Co., however, is nonpublic information. Therefore, XYZ Lending Co.'s customer list is nonpublic information despite the fact that it includes a great deal of publicly available information.

Example 2. Online retailer Amazing.com maintains a list of its credit card customers and a list of subscribers to a newsletter announcing new music CD releases for sale. The first list relates to a financial product or service; the second one does not. Accordingly, the first one is nonpublic information; the second one is not. If Amazing.com merges the two lists into one master list, then all of the contents of the master list would become nonpublic information.

NOTICE OF PRIVACY AND OPT-OUT RIGHTS

Financial institutions must give customers a clear and conspicuous written notice describing their privacy policies and practices. The content and timing of the notice depend on what kind of use will be made of the information that is collected and whether the information relates to a customer or to a consumer who is not a customer. (A *customer* is a person who has an ongoing business relationship with the financial institution. All others are *consumers*. A person with an account at a bank is a customer. A person who applies for a loan is a consumer unless and until she becomes a customer.)

Financial institutions must give all customers a privacy notice at or before the time the customer relationship is established, unless a customer agrees to a different time.

Customers have a right to opt out of having nonpublic information shared with unaffiliated third parties. Financial institutions that share their customers' nonpublic information with unaffiliated third parties must give their customers notice of this right. The notice must also explain how to opt out. The method for opting out must be reasonable, and a reasonable amount of time to opt out must be provided.

Annual notices of the institution's privacy policies and practices must be given to a customer for as long as long as the customer relationship lasts. The annual notice should consist of the institution's full privacy notice, including the notice of the right to opt out of having information shared with others.

In addition to its obligations to customers, financial institutions also have obligations to consumers who are not customers of the financial institution. Financial institutions that share information with unaffiliated third parties also must give consumers who are not customers a privacy notice, including notice of their right to opt out. The notice must be given before information is shared with others. A short form privacy notice may be used for consumers who are not also customers, provided the short form notice explains that the full privacy notice is available upon request, describes a reasonable way for consumers to get the full privacy notice, and contains or is accompanied by an adequate opt-out notice. The annual privacy notice requirement applies only to customers, not to consumers.

The full privacy notice must:

(a) Describe how the business collects, discloses, and protects nonpublic information about consumers and customers, including former customers.

(b) Identify the categories of information collected (e.g., nonpublic information the customer/consumer provides on an application submitted to the business; nonpublic information obtained from a credit reporting agency; etc.)

(c) Identify the categories of information that may be disclosed to unaffiliated third parties

(d) Identify the categories of affiliates and nonaffiliated third parties to whom the information may be disclosed (e.g., financial service providers such as mortgage brokers and insurance companies; nonfinancial companies such as magazine publishers, retailers, direct marketers, nonprofit organizations etc.)

(f) Explain consumers' and customers' right to opt out of disclosures of nonpublic information to others;

(g) Make any disclosures that are required by the FCRA.

(h) State the business's policies and practices with respect to protecting the confidentiality and security of nonpublic information. If access to customer/consumer nonpublic information is restricted to employees who need the information to fulfill orders for products or services, then so state.

(i) Be clear and conspicuous, in plain language, and distinctive in appearance, in a way that is designed to call attention to its significance. Use large, not fine print. Place it on a page that consumers use often and/or place a hyperlink to it directly from a page where transactions are conducted.

(j) Be delivered to each consumer or customer in writing by mail or by personal delivery, or if the consumer/customer agrees, electronically. This requirement may be satisfied by posting the privacy notice on the website and requiring the consumer/customer to acknowledge receiving the notice as a necessary part of obtaining a particular product or service. Annual notices to customers/consumers do not need to be mailed or personally delivered to website users who have agreed to receive notices at the website, provided the e-business does in fact post its full privacy notice continuously in a clear and conspicuous manner on the website.

An opt-out notice may be delivered either as part of the privacy notice or separately from it. If an opt-out notice is required but has not been made part of the privacy notice, then it must be delivered with the privacy notice. An opt-out notice must describe a reasonable means for opting out and provide a reasonable opportunity to do so. Some examples of reasonable means for opting out include providing a toll free telephone number to call for that purpose; providing a form with an 'Opt-out' box that a customer/consumer can check and return; etc. The customer/consumer cannot be required to write a letter as the only means of opting out.

Although the Financial Privacy Rule only requires notice of an opt-out right if nonpublic information may be shared with unaffiliated third parties, the FCRA may require notice of an opt-out right even if nonpublic information will only be shared with affiliates. GLBA notice and opt-out requirements are in addition to any requirements the FCRA may impose. Any such disclosures the FCRA may require must be made part of the privacy policy that is provided to consumers/customers in fulfillment of GLBA requirements.

The statute requires that consumers/customers be given a reasonable opportunity to opt out, but does not specify how much time must be allowed. Waiting thirty days before sharing the consumer's/customer's information with unaffiliated third parties would probably be reasonable, but in some circumstances a shorter period of time might also be reasonable. For a single purchase, requiring a customer to make a decision about whether or not to exercise the opt-out right before completing the transaction may be necessary.

The right to opt out may be exercised at any time even if previously waived, but the consumer or customer does not have a right to make it retroactive. A business must comply as soon as reasonably possible after receiving notice of a consumer's/customer's exercise of the right to opt out.

Example. At the time he orders a money order online from MOsOnline.com, Bob clicks "I Agree" to a clickwrap agreement which provides notice of the opt-out right and states that the customer waives the right and consents to the disclosure of his information to others. The website then collects his personal and financial information and shares it with a payment processing company. The next day, Bob sends an email message to the money order company stating that he is rescinding his consent to the disclosure and instead is exercising his right to opt out.

MOsOnline.com is not guilty of violating Bob's opt-out right unless it makes further disclosures after receiving Bob's email message.

A consumer's decision whether to opt-out or not is effective until the consumer/customer cancels it in writing. The cancellation may also be made electronically, if the consumer/customer has agreed that cancellations may be effected electronically. If a former customer establishes a new customer relationship with a financial institution, then the institution must provide the opt-out notice to the customer again, and the customer must make a new opt-out decision that will apply only to the new relationship.

If a financial institution changes its privacy policy, consumers and customers must be notified and must again be notified of the right to opt out and given an opportunity to do so.

EXCEPTIONS TO THE NOTICE AND OPT-OUT REQUIREMENTS

The customer's/consumer's right to opt out under the Financial Privacy Rule is subject to many exceptions. When these exceptions apply, a company that shares nonpublic information with affiliates or nonaffiliates does not need to provide an opt-out notice; it only needs to give a simplified initial privacy notice (in addition to whatever annual notice may be required). The simplified notice need only describe the company's collection of nonpublic information; state that the company only discloses such information to third parties for joint marketing/service provider purposes or "as permitted by law," as applicable; and describe how the company protects the confidentiality and security of nonpublic information.

The processing/administering exception applies to information sharing that is necessary to process or administer a financial transaction that a consumer has requested or authorized. Examples include: disclosure to a service provider who mails account statements and performs other administrative activities for a consumer's account, or disclosures to creditors listed by a consumer on a credit application to perform a credit check. When this exception applies, the simplified notice need not spell out the specific purposes for which information may be shared, but may simply state that it may be shared "as permitted by law."

A related exception exists for disclosures made in connection with servicing or processing a financial product or service that a customer requests or authorizes; maintaining or servicing a customer's account; or a proposed or actual securitization, secondary market sale (including the sale of servicing rights) or like transactions.

The self-protection/legal-compliance exception allows sharing of information for purposes of self-protection and compliance with legal obligations. When it applies, the simplified notice need not spell out the specific purposes for which information may be shared, but may simply state that it may be shared "as permitted by law."

This exception applies to disclosures made:

(a) to protect the security or confidentiality of records and/or to prevent or protect against actual or potential fraud
(b) to comply with a subpoena or other judicial process
(c) to comply with a summons or other request from authorized government authorities
(d) to comply with a law
(e) to the business's attorney, accountant or auditor

(f) to law enforcement or self-regulatory agencies, to the extent required or permitted by law
(g) to an insurance rate advisory organization
(h) to a person assessing compliance with industry standards
(i) for required institutional risk control
(j) to a credit reporting agency in compliance with FCRA requirements
(k) of information obtained from a credit report in compliance with the FCRA
(l) to a purchaser of a portfolio of consumer loans the business owns
(n) in connection with a merger, transfer, sale or exchange of all or a portion of the business.

The joint marketing/service provider exception allows disclosures for certain service providers and for certain marketing activities. It could cover, for example, a third party that is hired to provide marketing services for the company's products or services or to market financial products jointly for the company and another financial institution, or to do a general analysis of the company's customer transactions. The exception also applies to marketing financial products or services offered through a joint agreement with one or more other financial institutions. A *joint agreement* is a written contract with one or more financial institutions about a joint offering, endorsement, or sponsorship of a financial product or service. A joint agreement will qualify for this exception only if it involves joint marketing with other financial institutions. A joint marketing agreement with a nonfinancial institution would not come within the exception. It only applies to the marketing of financial products or services. Further, a joint marketing/service provider agreement qualifies for the exception only if the agreement expressly prohibits the third party from using or disclosing the information for any purpose other than the one for which it was received.

When the joint marketing/service provider exception applies, the institution must give customers (and any consumer whose information is shared with others) a privacy notice that describes the disclosure. Merely stating that the information may be shared "as permitted by law" will not suffice in this case.

Other exceptions include:

(a) consent
(b) resolution of consumer disputes or inquiries
(c) disclosures to holders of a legal or beneficial interest relating to the consumer
(d) disclosures to attorneys or other persons acting in a fiduciary or representative capacity on behalf of the consumer.

ACCOUNT NUMBERS

Financial institutions may not share account numbers or similar access numbers or codes with unaffiliated third parties for marketing purposes, even if the consumer/customer has not opted out of the disclosure. This rule applies to deposit accounts, credit accounts, and transactions accounts. The FCRA prohibits financial institutions from disclosing an account number to a non-affiliated entity (other than a credit bureau) for telemarketing, email marketing or direct marketing purposes. A transaction account is any account to which a third party may initiate a charge. This provision does not prohibit the sharing of an encrypted account number, if the third party receiving the information has no way to decode it.

The exceptions to the Privacy Rule described above do not apply to the disclosure of account numbers for marketing purposes. For example, a customer cannot give a valid consent to the disclosure of his account number for marketing purposes.

The prohibition applies to the complete marketing transaction, including posting a charge to an account. It does not apply, however, to the disclosure of an account number to the institution's agent or service provider for marketing the institution's own products or services, if the party receiving the information cannot directly initiate charges to the account.

POST-TRANSACTION THIRD PARTY SELLERS

ROSCA makes it unlawful for a merchant to disclose a credit or debit card, bank account, or other financial account number, or to disclose other billing information that is used to charge a customer of the merchant, to any post-transaction third party seller for use in an online sale of any goods or services from the post-transaction third party seller.

It is also unlawful for a post-transaction third party seller to charge or try to charge a consumer's credit or debit card, bank account or other financial account for any goods or services sold in an online transaction without first clearly and conspicuously disclosing all material terms of the transaction to the consumer and receiving the consumer's express informed consent to the charge. Express informed consent means: (a) obtaining from the consumer the full account number of the account to be charged, (b) obtaining from the consumer the consumer's name, address and contact information, and (c) requiring the consumer to perform an additional affirmative action, such as clicking on a confirmation button or checking a box that indicates the consumer's consent to be charged the amount disclosed.

The material terms the third party seller must disclose include:

(a) a description of the goods or services being offered
(b) the fact that the third party seller is not affiliated with the initial merchant, which may include disclosure of the name of the third party seller in a manner that clearly differentiates the third party seller from the initial merchant
(c) the cost of the goods or services.

For purposes of these rules, a post-transaction third party seller is a person who:

(a) sells, or offers for sale, any goods or service on the Internet;
(b) solicits the purchase of such goods or services on the Internet through an initial merchant after the consumer has initiated a transaction with the initial merchant; and
(c) is not (i) the initial merchant, (ii) a subsidiary or corporate affiliate of the initial merchant, or (iii) a successor of an entity described in clause (i) or (ii).

INFORMATION RECEIVED FROM FINANCIAL INSTITUTIONS

Every business that receives nonpublic personal information from a financial institution is subject to certain restrictions on how it may use or disclose the information. These restrictions apply even if the business is not a financial institution.

A business that receives such information from a financial institution under the processing/administering exception or the self-protection/legal compliance exception may only disclose and use the information in the ordinary course of business to carry out the purpose for which it was received. That purpose may include disclosures to other parties in order to carry out activities coming within the ambit of the exception. The information may also be disclosed to affiliates of the originating financial institution and/or affiliates of the business that received the information. Such affiliates are limited in their reuse and redisclosure of the information in the same way as the business receiving it from the financial institution is.

A slightly different rule applies to a business that receives nonpublic information from a financial institution other than pursuant to the processing/administrative or joint marketing/ service provider exceptions. This could include, for example, a business that acquires a financial institution's customer list in order to market its own products or services to those people. In this situation, the business that acquires the information "steps into the shoes" of the financial institution that furnished it. The business may redisclose the information in a way that is consistent with the originating financial institution's privacy policy. If, for example, the originating financial institution's privacy policy says it will not share customer information with nonfinancial institutions, then a business acquiring customer information from it may not share the information with nonfinancial institutions, either.

CREDIT REPORTS

The FCRA imposes additional obligations on any person or business that uses a credit report on a consumer in connection with a credit or insurance transaction. With each written solicitation made to the consumer about the transaction, a notice that the consumer has the right to opt out of receiving prescreened solicitations must be given. The notice must contain a toll free number that the consumer may call to exercise that right. The notice must be clear and conspicuous, easy to understand, and in a type size that is larger than the principal text on the same page. If mailed, it must be no smaller than the principal text on the same page but in no event less than twelve-point type. When the solicitation is sent electronically, the notice must appear on the same page and in close proximity to the principal marketing message; it must be so formatted that it is distinct from other text (e.g., placed inside a border); and it must be in a type style that is distinct from the principal type style used on the same page (such as bolded, italicized, underlined and/or in a contrasting color). The notice must contain nothing more than the above-described content, and it must direct the consumer to the location of a longer notice.

The long notice must be clear, conspicuous, and easy to understand. It must appear in the solicitation and be in a type size that is no smaller than the type size of the principal text on the same page. If sent by regular mail, the type, in any event, must not be smaller than 8–point. It must begin with the heading "PRESCREEN & OPT-OUT NOTICE," in underlined, all-capitals letters. The type style must be different from the principal type style used on the same page, such as bold, italicized, underlined and/or in a contrasting color. It must be set apart from other text on the page, such as by including a blank line above and below the statement, and by indenting both the left and right margins from other text on the page. It must include the following content, and nothing else that would tend to detract from or contradict these statements:

(a) Information contained in the consumer's consumer report was used in connection with the transaction;

(b) The consumer received the offer of credit or insurance because the consumer satisfied the criteria for creditworthiness or insurability under which the consumer was selected for the offer;
(c) If applicable, the credit or insurance may not be extended if, after the consumer responds to the offer, the consumer does not meet the criteria used to select the consumer for the offer or any applicable criteria bearing on creditworthiness or insurability or does not furnish any required collateral;
(d) The consumer has a right to prohibit information contained in the consumer's file with any consumer reporting agency from being used in connection with any credit or insurance transaction that is not initiated by the consumer;
(e) The consumer may exercise the right to opt out by notifying a notification system established under 15 U.S.C. § 1681b(e).

The notice must include the address and toll free telephone number of the appropriate notification system established under 15 U.S.C. § 1681b(e).

A business that uses information in a credit report for credit, insurance, or employment purposes must notify the consumer when an adverse action is taken on the basis of the report. The agency must give consumers an opportunity to dispute entries on their credit reports. The company that reported information to the agency is responsible for investigating any disputed information. If it does not do so, then the credit reporting agency must remove the disputed information from the report.

OTHER REGULATIONS

The GLBA and FCRA are the principal laws pertinent to the privacy of financial information, but they are not the only ones. For example, SEC regulations require securities brokers, dealers, investment companies and investment advisers to maintain the privacy of customer financial information and to furnish them with notices of their privacy policies and practices.

Health and Health Care Information

HIPAA establishes data security and privacy rules for individually identifiable health information that is created or received by a "covered entity," i.e., a health care provider, health plan, or health care clearinghouse. No covered entity may disclose individually identifiable health information unless a specific exemption applies.

HIPAA protects all health information that identifies an individual or that could be used to identify an individual. This includes an individual's past, present or future physical or mental condition; the provision of health care to the individual; and past, present or future payment for the provision of health care to the individual.

The HIPAA Privacy Rule requires appropriate safeguards to protect the privacy of health and health care information, and regulates the uses and disclosures that may be made of such information without patient authorization. Consumer health information may not be disclosed or used for commercial activities besides treatment, payment, health care operations, or other uses and disclosures permitted or required by the HIPAA Privacy Rule, unless the consumer gives prior written permission through a valid HIPAA authorization

A HIPAA authorization must be in plain English, understandable, and include specific terms and descriptions of the uses and disclosures the consumer is authorizing. Subject to some exceptions, the Rule also gives patients rights over their health information, including rights to examine and obtain copies of their health records, and to request corrections. Covered entities are required to create and distribute a privacy policy explaining how individually identifiable health information is collected, used, and shared. Wrongful disclosure of personal health information may result in civil penalties, fines, and in some cases, imprisonment.

HIPAA requirements also apply to any business associate that enters into a contractual arrangement with a covered entity giving the business access to protected health care information. A business that transmits protected health information to a covered entity or to a contractor that is subject to HIPAA requirements is also subject to HIPAA requirements. A business associate may not ask a consumer to sign a HIPAA authorization unless the business associate contract expressly permits the business associate to do so.

A covered entity must secure an agreement from every business or person that is granted access to protected health information that the third party will comply with the same HIPAA obligations with which the covered entity has to comply.

HIPAA provides some protections for whistleblowers. It permits disclosures by an employee of a covered entity when the employee has a good faith belief that disclosure is necessary to protect individual(s) from the covered entity's misconduct. This could include, for example, an employee who discloses protected information in the course of reporting inadequate care and treatment of patients to an appropriate regulatory agency.

Covered entities and their business associates must comply with the FTC Act as well as HIPAA. The FTC Act prohibits companies from engaging in deceptive or unfair acts or practices in or affecting commerce. Among other things, this means that companies must not mislead consumers about what is happening with their health information. A business needs to ensure that any authorization it seeks from a consumer does not create a deceptive or misleading impression. Key facts should be disclosed prominently, not buried in links to a privacy policy, terms of use or the authorization. No inconsistent or contradictory statements should be made. For example, a website should not display a statement that information will never be shared with others if a HIPAA form on the website authorizes disclosure to others.

For information about HIPAA data security requirements, see Chapter 13.

Government Secrets

A number of state and federal laws prohibit the disclosure of certain kinds of things that a government wishes to be kept secret, such as state secrets, troop movements, anti-terror operations, surveillance, intelligence gathering activities, and the details of ongoing criminal investigations. In some cases, the penalty for unauthorized disclosure can be severe. Depending on the circumstances, a website owner or blogger who works with a government source to obtain and publish confidential government information may be charged as a conspirator. Whistleblower statutes sometimes offer some protection, but they often require a person to go through specified government channels that have been established for this purpose rather than going public with the information. A website owner or blogger who has published or who is thinking about publishing information that a government insider has divulged or plans to divulge should retain an attorney.

Contributory Liability

E-commerce businesses should be cautious about allowing their websites or online services to be used by other persons or businesses to collect information from people. Under the theory of contributory liability, a person who facilitates or contributes to another person's commission of an invasion of privacy may be liable for any harm caused by it. Providing a website for another person's invasions of privacy facilitates or contributes to them. Therefore, the website owner may be contributorily liable.

Contributory liability generally will not be imposed unless the facilitator knew or had reason to know of the activity. Actual knowledge or reason to know of a particular invasion of privacy, however, is not required. A website owner may be held liable if he knew the person using the website was engaging in activity that was likely to result in an invasion of privacy. Liability may also attach if a website owner had reason to suspect that such activity was occurring but took deliberate steps to avoid acquiring knowledge of it. The law does not countenance willful blindness.

Privacy Policy

To reduce the likelihood of a charge of engaging in unfair or deceptive trade practices, businesses that wish to reserve the right to collect and/or share a user's personally identifiable information with others should let users of their website know what kinds of information will be collected, how it will be used, whether it will be shared with others, the persons or categories of persons with whom it will be shared and for what purpose. Users should also be informed of their right to opt out and how to do that. Specifically, a Privacy Policy should provide clear explanations of each of the following things:

(a) whether and what kind of information is collected from users of the website
(b) why (for what purpose) the information is collected, and how it will be used
(c) how the information is collected
(d) whether the information collected may be disclosed or shared with others
(e) what kinds of information may be shared with others
(f) for what purpose(s) information will be shared with others
(g) the identity or categories of people or businesses with whom information may be shared
(h) how the website protects data on individuals
(i) a user's right, if any, to access data the website collects on the user
(j) if applicable, a user's right to a reasonable opportunity to review and correct or delete information
(k) the fact that the consumer has a right to opt out of having personal information disclosed or shared with others
(l) how the consumer can exercise the right to opt out
(m) whether and for what purpose cookies or other persistent identifiers are used
(n) any disclosures required by the FTC's COPPA Rule,[224] if applicable
(o) any disclosures required by the GLBA, HIPAA or other laws or regulations
(p) whether the Privacy Policy may be modified and how the customer will be notified of it
(q) the effective date(s).

A link to the privacy policy should be conspicuously displayed both on the home page and wherever else an applicable law may require it to be displayed.

A commercial website owner must take care to ensure that the statements and claims made in the Privacy Policy are truthful and accurate. She must also abide by them. Failure to do either of these things may result in liability to a user. It may also trigger an FTC enforcement action for violating the FTC Act's prohibition against unfair or deceptive trade practices.

Because misleading statements in a privacy policy can result in liability under federal and state laws prohibiting unfair or deceptive trade practices, it is important to word a privacy policy carefully and accurately. Broad generalizations should be avoided if there is even a remote possibility that there could be an exception. For example, a business that wishes to retain the right to share the customer database with the new owner if the business is sold at some point should not make a representation that customer information will "never" be shared with a third party. Adding language to limit the scope of the representation can help reduce the risk of liability. "We will never share your information for direct marketing purposes without your consent" is less risky than "We will never share your information," for example.

The FTC has taken the position that retroactive modifications of a Privacy Policy are an unfair trade practice. A person who used a website prior to the modification of the Privacy Policy cannot be bound by a modification unless he agrees to be bound by the new terms (opts in). A website operator who wants to alter the terms of its Privacy Policy cannot bind previous users to the new terms unless it gives them an opportunity to opt-in.

A Privacy Policy should be conspicuous, easily accessible, and understandable.

COPPA PROVISIONS

The FTC's COPPA Rule requires websites that collect information from children under thirteen years of age to publish a Privacy Policy and specifies its content. See Chapter 18.

STATE LAW REQUIREMENTS

State laws may require the publication of a privacy policy even if information is only collected from adults. California is an example. California's Online Privacy Protection Act requires every operator of a commercial website or online service (including a mobile app) that collects personally identifiable information from a California resident to post a Privacy Policy and to comply with it. In particular, companies that do business with California residents must adopt a Privacy Policy that:

(a) states the categories of information collected (e.g., "If you create a user account, we will collect your contact details. If you purchase an item through our store, we will ask you to provide your physical address and credit card details so we can process your payment.")
(b) identifies the categories of persons or entities with whom information may be shared (e.g., "credit card processors; payment processors")
(c) describes the process by which a user may review and request changes to personally identifiable information
(d) discloses how the website operator responds to "Do Not Track" requests (e.g., "We do not honor 'Do Not Track' requests" or "If you opt out of being tracked, we will ensure

that new data collected about you will not be used by us for targeted advertising purposes")

(e) describes any policy or procedure the operator follows that offers the user a choice not to be tracked

(f) discloses whether third parties may collect personally identifiable information about users through the operator's website or service

(g) describes the process by which the operator notifies consumers of any material changes to the privacy policy

(h) discloses whether the website operator reserves the right to change its privacy policy without notice to the individual user or visitor to the website

(i) states the effective date of the privacy policy

(j) is displayed conspicuously on the website

(k) complies with detailed requirements pertaining to how it is displayed on the website.

The privacy policy may be posted directly on the homepage. Alternatively, an icon or text hyperlink to a separate page on which the privacy policy is posted may be placed on the homepage. The link or policy must be conspicuous and in a distinguishable color. If a text link is used, it must include the word 'PRIVACY' in capital letters in a type size at least as large as the type in the surrounding text.

Under California law, a business has thirty days after being notified of noncompliance to bring itself into compliance. Website operators who fail to post a compliant Privacy Policy, or who fail to abide by it, are subject to civil penalties and injunctions.

The California law adopts a very broad definition of personally identifiable information. It includes any of the following: first and last name; street address; email address; telephone number; Social Security number; drivers license number; height, weight, hair color; birth date; any other identifier that enables physical or online contact with a specific individual; and any other information that is collected online and stored in personally identifiable form.

A few other states also require commercial websites to have a privacy policy.

Of course, state requirements might be avoided by simply refraining from selling to residents of the state. That, however, would mean foregoing sales to many potential customers, including the 39,000,000 people living in California. Compliance with both federal and state requirements enlarges the sales territory for a company's products and services.

European Union

Countries in the EU generally have enacted privacy protections that tend to be stronger than those that have been adopted in the United States.

The Electronic Privacy Directive prohibits the interception or surveillance of communications and related traffic without the user's consent. An exception is provided for interception or surveillance for national security, defense, public safety purposes, or for crime prevention, investigation or prosecution. Member countries have enacted laws implementing this Directive.

The EU's Directive 95/46/EC ("Data Protection Directive") addresses the processing (collection, storage, use, disclosure or destruction) of personal data. It broadly applies to any business, governmental entity, organization or individual that handles personal data. Personal data is defined broadly to include any information that may be used to link data to a particular individual—such as address; credit card number; identification number; or physical, mental, economic, cultural or social attributes. Member states have enacted laws implementing it.

Under this Directive, a data subject has a right to be informed when his personal data is being processed, including information about the purpose of the processing, the recipients of the data, and any other information required to ensure the processing is fair. *Processing* means the performance of an operation on personal data, which may include collection, storage, disclosure, or destruction.

Data may be processed without the data subject's consent only if the processing is necessary for one of the following reasons:

(a) for the performance of a contract to which the data subject is a party
(b) in order to take steps the data subject has requested prior to entering into a contract
(c) to comply with a legal obligation
(d) to protect the vital interests of the data subject
(e) to perform a task that is carried out in the public interest or in the exercise of official authority vested in the data controller
(f) legitimate interests of the data collector or a third party to whom data is disclosed, unless such interests are overridden by the data subject's fundamental rights and freedoms.

A data subject has a right to access all data processed about him, and to demand the correction, deletion or blocking of data that is incomplete, inaccurate or that is not being processed in compliance with the data protection rules.

Personal data may be processed only to the extent relevant and not excessive in relation to the purposes for which they are collected and/or further processed. The data must be accurate and, where necessary, kept up to date.

A business must obtain the subject's explicit consent in order to collect information about a person's race, ethnicity, political opinions, religious beliefs, membership in a union or other organization, physical or mental health, sexual orientation, or criminal record.

A business must notify and obtain a consumer's prior approval before it may sell or share personal data about the consumer. In other words, citizens of EU countries must opt in before a company may share their personal information. A data subject may object at any time to the processing of personal data for the purpose of direct marketing.

The Electronic Privacy Directive of 2002 ("ePrivacy Directive") supplements the Data Protection Directive. It protects both natural persons and legal persons (e.g., corporations). Specifically, it:

(a) prohibits the use of a subscriber's information or data on the location of users unless the character of the information collected and the purpose for which the information will be used is made clear to the subscriber/user beforehand and the subscriber/user is informed of the right to refuse to give consent to such use and is provided an opportunity to exercise the right to opt out
(b) permits the collection and use of data on the location of users only if the data is anonymized, the user consents, or the data is used to provide value-added services
(c) gives subscribers a right to unitemized billing
(d) gives users a right to opt out of calling-line identification.

The ePrivacy Directive also contains provisions that have come to be known as the "Cookie Law". They establish an "opt in" regime for cookies. In particular, cookies may be used only if all of the following conditions are satisfied:

(a) Clear and conspicuous notice of the fact that cookies are used is provided to the user;
(b) The user is informed about the kinds of data that are gathered through the use of cookies and how the data are used;
(c) The user is informed of the right to opt out (disable) cookies and how to do it;
(d) The user consents to the use of cookies.

A website should provide a mechanism by which a user may consent to the use of cookies.

An initial consent to cookies is effective for return visits to the same website by the same user. Also, Directive 2009/136 allows consent to occur through settings, so that separate consent will not need to be obtained for each cookie that is received. Moreover, consent is not required for the use of session cookies that are necessary for the delivery of a service requested by the user, such as cookies that track the contents of a user's shopping cart, to the extent the cookie is actually used for that purpose.

The Cookie Law distinguishes between session and persistent cookies. *Session* cookies are the cookies that serve only to enhance website functionality during a single session. They do not track user activity once the browser window is closed. Examples of session cookies include faceted search filter cookies, user authentication cookies, cookies that enable shopping cart functionality, and cookies used to enable playback of multimedia content. Sites that make exclusive use of session cookies do not require a cookie consent notice.

Persistent cookies are cookies that are used to track user behavior even after they have moved on from the site or closed the browser window. Cookies used by analytics programs and advertising tracking cookies are the most common types of persistent cookies. The Cookie Law does apply to persistent cookies. Most e-commerce websites use both kinds of cookies. A website that uses analytics software, displays advertisements, has affiliate links, uses a single sign-on authentication system, or tracks visitors in any other way, is very likely using persistent cookies.

These rules apply when the business is located in a EU country or when equipment located in a EU country is used to process data. Businesses located outside the EU that use equipment in a EU country to process data also must comply. It appears that a business that transacts online business with a resident of a EU country must comply inasmuch as the business would be using the customer's computer in the processing of data. Under the GDPR (see below), every business that collects or processes personal data on a EU resident must comply, wherever the business is located.

Fines for violating the Cookie Law can be severe.

The ePrivacy Directive also imposes data security requirements. See Chapter 13.

GENERAL DATA PROTECTION REGULATION

The GDPR, adopted in 2016, supersedes the Data Protection Directive and is enforceable beginning on May 25, 2018. Some parts of the old Directive are carried forward. The GDPR explicitly extends the scope of EU data protection law to all foreign companies that collect or process personal data on residents of EU countries; harmonizes data protection laws throughout the EU; and adds stricter compliance provisions. Unlike previous directives, the GDPR is directly binding throughout the EU. Implementing legislation in individual countries is not necessary. Penalties for violations can be severe.

The definition of personal data, under the GDPR, is quite broad. It includes any information relating to an individual, whether it relates to the individual's private, professional or public life. Examples: name, home address, email address, photograph, bank details, posts on social networking websites, medical information, and a computer's IP address. Data controllers have the burden of proof regarding consent, so an opt-in method should be employed. Consent may be withdrawn.

Until data has been anonymized, a data controller may not prevent a data subject from transferring his personal data from one electronic processing system to another. Data controllers must keep records of processing activities showing the purposes of the processing, the categories involved, and the projected time limits.

For information about GDPR data security requirements, see Chapter 13.

DATA EXPORTED FROM THE EUROPEAN UNION

The Directive on Data Protection prohibits the export of personal data about a resident of the EU to countries that do not adequately protect personal data. The fact that EU privacy protections are stronger than those that are in place in the United States could seriously hamper the ability of U.S. companies to do business with European residents. To address this, the EU and the United States entered into a U.S.-EU Safe Harbor Agreement specifying minimum requirements that must be met in order to satisfy EU standards of privacy protection. U.S. companies that complied with these requirements would be deemed to be in compliance with the Directive. A U.S. company could take advantage of this safe harbor by self-certifying compliance to the U.S. Department of Commerce.

In 2015, the European Court of Justice struck down this safe harbor framework. The following year, the U.S. Department of Commerce and the European Commission adopted a new "Privacy Shield'" framework, which is intended to create stronger rights in connection with data transfers. The Privacy Shield imposes more stringent requirements on companies handling data; clear safeguards and transparency obligations pertaining to U.S. government access; effective protection of individual rights; and an annual joint review mechanism.

The most significant stumbling block to EU approval of data transfers into the United States is that U.S. law gives the federal government extremely broad powers to intercept, access and use private information about individuals and businesses. Countries in the EU value the privacy rights of their citizens. In an effort to alleviate EU concerns about violations of privacy rights by the U.S. government, Congress passed a law allowing citizens of ally countries (and organizations, such as the EU) to exercise rights under the Privacy Act of 1974 to the same extent as U.S. citizens can. This law (the Judicial Redress Act of 2015[225]) effectively gives the EU and citizens of ally countries the right to sue the U.S. government for any unlawful disclosure or use of their personal records.

Canada

Canada has enacted a Personal Information Protection and Electronic Documents Act[226] (PIPEDA). Among other things, it requires a company to obtain an individual's consent in order to collect, use or disclose personal information. A business may not make a sale conditional on a consumer's consent except to the extent information is essential to the transaction. Canadian courts have interpreted PIPEDA as applying to any business that collects personal information from Canadian residents. A U.S. business that sells products or services to Canadian residents would be subject to its requirements.

Other Countries

The privacy laws of other countries vary widely. They are too numerous and varied to cover in a book of this size. Companies that do business with residents of other countries should familiarize themselves with the privacy laws of those countries.

Publicity Rights

Every individual has an exclusive right to exploit his or her own identity for commercial or other gain. At common law, appropriating another person's name, voice or likeness for commercial or other gain was considered a form of invasion of privacy. Unlike other kinds of invasion of privacy, though, indignity and offensiveness are not necessary elements of a misappropriation of personality claim. Rather, the gravamen of this kind of complaint is the wrongful exercise of a person's exclusive right to exploit the person's own name, voice or likeness. Because of this, some jurisdictions regard it as being more in the nature of an intellectual property claim than a privacy claim. Other jurisdictions retain its common law treatment as a form of invasion of privacy. Depending on the circumstances, misappropriation of personality may also be a prohibited form of false advertising or unfair competition.

In some jurisdictions, misappropriation of name, voice or likeness is known as appropriation of personality or violation of publicity rights.

The elements of a cause of action for misappropriation of personality are:

(a) unauthorized use
(b) of another person's name, voice, photograph or likeness
(c) for commercial gain or other advantage.

The misappropriation may be effected either by literal reproduction of an individual's name, voice or likeness (such as a photograph or a recording of a person's voice), or by a representation of the individual (such as a drawing of the person or an impersonation of the person's voice). The most common way to incur liability is to use another person's name, likeness or voice in an advertisement without permission, or in a way that suggests endorsement or sponsorship of a product or service. Liability may arise in other ways, too.

A few courts limit the right to those individuals who can prove that their identities already have commercial value—i.e., celebrities and other public figures. The majority of courts, however, hold that the commercial value of a person's identity affects only the amount of damages that may be recovered, not the right to recover.

In most states, the publicity right survives for a specified number of years after the person's death. In a few states, it ends when the person dies.

COMMERCIAL OR OTHER ADVANTAGE

Not every use of a person's name, voice or likeness gives rise to misappropriation liability. Misappropriation liability arises only if the person's name, voice or likeness is used for commercial or other advantage. Liability for misappropriation of personality for commercial advantage may arise, however, even if the person's name, voice or likeness is not used to state or imply sponsorship or endorsement of a particular product or service. Displaying a person's name or likeness on a website whose advertising revenue is tied to the number of hits the site receives, as a way of increasing the number of hits the site receives, is a use for commercial advantage.

Some states limit liability to commercial uses. Other states, like California, prohibit uses for noncommercial kinds of advantage, too. States in the latter category prohibit uses for political advantage, for example. In these states, using a person's name, voice or likeness to state or imply the person's endorsement of a candidate for political office is prohibited in the same way that using the person's name for commercial advantage is.

At least one court has held that using another person's name as a keyword in competitive advertising does not violate the person's exclusive publicity rights.[227] But if the name is also a trademark, then doing this might be a violation of trademark law, in some circumstances. See Chapter 28.

FIRST AMENDMENT DEFENSE

The right of publicity is limited, to some extent, by the First Amendment. The use of a person's name, voice or likeness in connection with reporting on a newsworthy incident is not actionable as misappropriation of personality. For example, a website may publish a photograph of people attending a political rally without violating the privacy or publicity rights of the individual participants depicted in the photograph. A political rally is newsworthy.

In *C.B.C. Distribution and Marketing, Inc. v. Major League Baseball Advanced Media, L.P.*[228] the Eighth Circuit Court of Appeals held that the First Amendment may supersede the right of publicity when a famous person's likeness is used for a commercial purpose other than to endorse a product or service. The case involved a company's use of the likenesses of, and biographical information about, major league baseball players in a fantasy sports game that it marketed to consumers. In ruling against the players, the court found it significant that they were making plenty of money from commercial product endorsements for other companies.

FALSE ADVERTISING AND UNFAIR COMPETITION

The statutory or common law of about half of the states recognize a person's exclusive right to use his name or personality for commercial or other advantage. Even in states that do not recognize such a cause of action, though, publicity rights may be protected under the law of unfair competition. Misappropriation of a person's name, likeness or voice for the purpose of misrepresenting a product or service as being made, sponsored or endorsed by that person is a form of unfair competition.

Publicity rights may also be protected by false advertising law. Using a person's name, voice or likeness in a way that falsely suggests the person's manufacture, sponsorship or endorsement of a product or service may be actionable as false advertising. Celebrities whose names or likenesses have been used in connection with the sale of goods or services without their permission have invoked Section 43(a) to recover damages for violation of their rights of publicity. Use of an imitation of a famous singer's voice may also be actionable under Section 43(a). For more information about false advertising, see Chapter 15.

LICENSES AND PERMISSIONS

Of course, the best way to reduce the risk of liability for misappropriation of personality is to refrain from using other people's names, voices or likenesses for commercial or other advantage. If, however, the decision is made to use another person's name, voice or likeness, then the person's written permission should be obtained. Consent is a defense to misappropriation.

It is also not a bad idea to obtain a person's written permission to use the person's name, voice or likeness if the planned use creates a risk of liability for invasion of privacy.

Children are deemed incapable of giving a valid consent. A parent or legal guardian must give consent on their behalf. Depending on state law, an incompetent, coerced, defrauded or traumatized person also may be incapable of giving consent on her own behalf.

When copying a photograph taken by somebody else, or a drawing made by someone else, it may be necessary to obtain permission from both the photographer/artist and the subject of the photograph/drawing. This is true whether the image is being used for commercial purposes or not. Liability for copyright infringement may attach irrespective of motive. If the copyright is owned by someone other than the photographer/artist, then the permission of both the copyright owner and the subject of the photograph/drawing will be needed.

Permissions should be in writing and signed. This makes it easier to prove that consent was given.

Chapter 18. Children

The chief concern lawmakers have about children's access to the Internet is its potential to expose them to sexually explicit material. That topic is taken up in the next chapter. Lawmakers are also concerned about protecting children from the consequences of their decisions, though. Due to their young age, children do not always have the knowledge and experience needed to exercise sound judgment. They are prone to disclosing more information about themselves while they are online than may be prudent or safe.

Notice of Availability of Parental Controls

The CDA requires providers of interactive online services to give users notice that methods of limiting access to the website by minors are commercially available. The notice must be given at the time the user enters into an agreement for the service (at the time the user clicks the 'I Agree' button to signify assent to the terms of service, for example). It must inform the customer that parental control protections (such as computer hardware, software, or filtering services) are commercially available that may assist the customer in limiting access to material that is harmful to minors. The notice must identify, or provide the customer with access to information identifying, current providers of such protections.

Advertising Directed to Children

DECEPTIVE ADVERTISING

Children may have greater difficulty evaluating advertising claims and understanding the nature of the information provided in an advertisement than adults do. Therefore, when marketing products or services to children, merchants are expected to exercise a higher level of care to avoid misrepresenting a product or its performance. When representations or sales practices are targeted to a specific audience, such as children, the relevant question is whether it is unfair or likely to deceive a reasonable member of that group, not its impact on the average consumer. The Children's Advertising Review Unit of the Council of Better Business Bureaus has published specific guidelines for children's advertising. These guidelines are not a guaranteed safe harbor from a charge of violating the FTC Act or other laws, but compliance with them reduces the risk of such charges.

A similar principle applies in trademark infringement cases. The relevant question in a trademark infringement case is not how likely the average person is to be confused. Rather, likelihood of confusion is gauged in relation to the sophistication of the target audience. For this reason, likelihood of confusion is more likely to be found to exist when a product is marketed to young children.

PRODUCTS NOT AVAILABLE TO CHILDREN

Some states, such as California, prohibit websites from targeting minors with advertisements for products that are not legally available to minors. This includes alcohol, tobacco, firearms, tattoos and lottery tickets.

Alcohol

Restrictions on sales of alcoholic beverages to underage persons apply to every method of ordering—in person, by mail or phone, or online. In addition, laws in California and other states prohibit publishing advertisements for alcoholic beverages that target children. Some attempt to regulate content that could appeal to both children and adults but which may be expected to have a special appeal to children. An Ohio regulation, for example, prohibits liquor licensees from including references to either children or Santa Claus in their advertisements for alcoholic beverages.[229]

Industry associations have established codes for advertisers of alcoholic beverages that reflect a particular concern about advertising directed to children. Currently, they suggest that no more than 28.4% of the audience for an advertisement should consist of people under twenty-one years of age, based on reliable audience data, and that the content should not appeal primarily to people under twenty-one years of age.

Tobacco

Restrictions on sales of tobacco products to underage persons apply to every method of ordering, whether in person, by mail or phone, or online. In addition, laws in some states, such as California, prohibit publishing advertisements for tobacco products that target children.

HOMEWORK HELP LINES AND OTHER 900-NUMBER SERVICES

Under the FTC's 900-Number Rule, advertisements of 900-Number services (i.e., services that are provided by telephone on a pay-per-call or pay-per-minute basis) that are directed primarily to children under eighteen years of age must include a disclosure that persons under eighteen years of age need a parent or guardian's permission to call a pay-per-call or pay-per-minute number.

These kinds of services and the advertisements for them may not be directed to children under twelve years of age at all unless the service is a bona fide educational service. A bona fide educational service is one that provides information or instruction that is related to education, subjects of academic study, or other related areas of school study. The service must be truly educational in nature to meet this exception. A "homework-helper" line, where a child might get help with a homework question or problem, is the kind of service that might be permitted under the rule. On the other hand, a service that is primarily entertainment—but has an incidental educational component—is not allowed under the exception. For example, some services might offer children the opportunity to talk with, or listen to a message from, a popular cartoon character or TV star. These would not be considered bona fide educational services merely because they include some factual information in the program. A quiz program inducing children to call and answer questions in order to receive a prize probably would not be considered a bona fide educational service merely because some of the questions pertain to areas that might be studied in elementary school.

CREDIT CARD OFFERS

Under the Credit CARD Act, no credit card may be issued to a person who is under twenty-one years of age unless: (a) a creditworthy adult over the age of twenty-one co-signs the application; or (b) the applicant submits information demonstrating independent means to repay the obligations that may be incurred using the credit card. An institution of higher education is required to publicly disclose any contract or other agreement it has made with a card issuer or creditor for the purpose of marketing a credit card to college students. The Act also prohibits offering promotional gifts to students on or near the school campus or at a school event to induce them to apply for a card.

Juvenile Perpetrators and Victims of Crime

Some states prohibit the release of information about the identity of a minor who has been accused of a crime, at least when the minor is being tried in juvenile court rather than as an adult. Some states also restrict the release of information about the identity of an alleged victim of a crime when the victim is underage. These kinds of laws vary from state to state.

Content Posted By Minors

A novel law in California gives minors a right to have content they have posted to the Internet erased. Known as the Eraser Law,[230] it requires a website operator or online service (including mobile apps) to permit a minor who resides in California and who is a registered user of the website or service to remove, or to require the website operator or service provider to remove, information that the minor posted. The law applies to websites and services directed to minors. It also applies to any kind of website or service if the operator knows the person is a minor. The law does not apply to general audience websites or services unless the operator knows it is being used by a minor. Also, the law does not require removal of content posted by a third party if the content is anonymized so that the minor cannot be identified. A minor who is paid for content he posts does not have a right to remove it or to have it removed.

When the law applies, a business must comply with the following requirements:

(a) Minors who are registered users must be permitted to remove or to request and obtain removal of content or information that they post;

(b) The privacy policy must give notice to minors who are registered users that they may remove or request and obtain removal of content or information that they post;

(c) The privacy policy must provide clear instructions for how minors may remove or request and obtain the removal of content or information they post;

(d) The privacy policy must provide notice to minors who are registered users that any removal of posted content does not ensure complete or comprehensive removal of the content or information posted (e.g., the content is not visible to other users but remains on the servers in some form).

Capacity to Consent

In most states, contracts entered into by unemancipated minors are voidable at the option of the minor. This means a minor may choose to either abide by the contract (such as keeping and paying for a purchase) or rescind the contract without penalty. Contract provisions requiring a minor to waive this right generally are not enforceable. Depending on the jurisdiction, though, a minor's false representation as to age or as to parental consent may be unlawful.

Contracts to furnish necessities (e.g., food or clothing) to a minor are an exception to the rule that contracts entered into by minors are voidable. These contracts may not be avoided. Typically, they are enforced against the child's parent or another person who is legally responsible for the child's care.

Because a child's consent usually is voidable, it is a good idea for merchants, website operators and service providers to get the consent of a child's parent when the transaction is an important one. For example, because of the potential liability for damages when a child's likeness is used without permission, a website operator may find it prudent to obtain the consent of a child's parent or guardian before using the child's name, voice or likeness for commercial or other advantage.

Educational Websites

Educational website operators that collect information from California students must comply with the Student Online Personal Information Protection Act[231] (SOPIPA). This Act requires protection of the privacy of information collected from students and imposes restrictions on selling, creating a profile, or engaging in targeted advertising using information gathered for K-12 school purposes. It generally prohibits disclosure of information about a student to unauthorized persons, and requires deletion of student data if the school or district requests it. It is subject to some exceptions, such as exceptions allowing disclosures to law enforcement and allowing the use of aggregated and de-identified information, among others. Unlike the federal Family Educational Rights and Privacy Act,[232] SOPIPA imposes liability for violations on website operators, not educational institutions. It also provides a private right of action.

Information Collected from Children Under 13

The Children's Online Privacy Protection Act (COPPA) is a federal statute regulating websites that collect information from children under thirteen years of age. When it applies, a website operator generally must obtain parental consent before collecting personally identifying information from a child under thirteen years of age. A website operator also must maintain the confidentiality, security, and integrity of such information.

COPPA applies whenever:

(a) Information is knowingly collected from a child under the age of thirteen; or
(b) A website or online service is directed to children under thirteen.

Put another way, COPPA applies when a website operator or online service provider either actually knows or should know that information is being collected from a child under the age of thirteen. A person should know that information is being collected from children under the age of thirteen when the website is directed to children under the age of thirteen and the website collects information from visitors to the site.

When COPPA applies, the website or online service must:

(a) post a clear and comprehensive online privacy policy describing its information practices for personal information collected online from children;
(b) give direct notice to parents and obtain verifiable parental consent, with limited exceptions, before collecting personal information online from children;
(c) give parents the option of consenting to the operator's collection and internal use of a child's information but prohibiting the operator from disclosing that information to third parties (unless disclosure is integral to the site or service, in which case this must be made clear to parents);
(d) provide the parent, upon request, an opportunity to review the personal information that is collected from the child, and to have it changed or deleted;
(e) give the parent an opportunity to prevent further use or online collection of a child's personal information;
(f) maintain the confidentiality, security, and integrity of information collected from children, including taking reasonable steps to release such information only to parties capable of maintaining its confidentiality and security;
(g) refrain from conditioning a child's participation in an activity, game or contest on the child's disclosure of more personal information than is reasonably necessary to participate in the activity;
(h) retain personal information collected online from a child for only as long as is necessary to fulfill the purpose for which it was collected; and
(i) delete the information using reasonable measures to protect against its unauthorized access or use.

If a general audience website or service unknowingly collects personal information (such as an email address) from a child under thirteen years of age and later acquires actual knowledge that the person is a child who is under thirteen years of age, it must either delete the child's information immediately or comply with COPPA requirements.

COPPA is enforced by the FTC and other federal and state agencies. As of October 1, 2017, a civil penalty of up to $40,654 may be imposed for each violation.

The FTC has adopted a Rule (the "COPPA Rule") to implement COPPA. It applies to:

(a) operators of commercial websites or online services that are directed to children under thirteen years of age and that collect, use, or disclose personal information from children, either directly or by the integration of an outside service, such as a plug-in or advertising network, that collects personal information from visitors
(b) operators of general audience websites or online services who have actual knowledge that they are collecting, using, or disclosing personal information from children under thirteen
(c) operators of websites or online services (including but not limited to plug-ins and advertising networks) who have actual knowledge that they are collecting personal information from users of another website or online service that is directed to children.

An *operator* is any person who operates a website located on the Internet or an online service and who collects or maintains personal information from or about the users of or visitors to such website or online service, or on whose behalf such information is collected or maintained, or offers products or services for sale through that website or online service, where the website or online service is operated for commercial purposes involving interstate or foreign commerce. The term *operator* does not include platforms for third parties to post their apps for sale. There may be liability, however, for deceptive trade practices if a platform provider misrepresents its level of oversight over websites with child-directed content.

Personal information is "collected or maintained on behalf of an operator" when (a) it is collected or maintained by an agent or service provider of the operator, or (b) the operator benefits by allowing another person to collect personal information directly from users of the website or online service.

An *online service*, for purposes of COPPA, is any service that is available over the Internet, or that connects to the Internet or a wide area network. Examples include services that allow users to play network-connected games, engage in social networking activities, purchase and/or pay for goods or services online, receive online advertisements, or interact with other online content or services. Mobile applications that connect to the Internet, Internet-enabled gaming platforms, voice-over-Internet protocol services, and Internet-enabled location-based services are all online services.

Nonprofits generally are not subject to the COPPA Rule. A nonprofit association or other organization that works for the benefit of for-profit members (such as a professional association), however, is subject to the Rule. Websites operated under contract with and on behalf of the federal government are subject to the Rule, too.

The nationality of a child is not relevant. Domestic websites and online services must comply with COPPA even if they are directed only to children in other countries. Foreign websites and online services must comply with COPPA if they are directed to children.

According to the FTC, knowledge acquired by an employee will not necessarily be imputed to the employer. Also, operators of online chat rooms, discussion forums, and other interactive website and service features, normally are not required to monitor activity on them. COPPA is triggered only if the employer happens to acquire actual knowledge that personal information has been collected or transmitted to the site from a child who is under thirteen. The likelihood of a finding that an employer had actual knowledge may be reduced if the website operator, service provider or advertiser publishes on its website or service some method (such as contact information and/or an online contact form) by which individuals may contact it with COPPA information. Of course, once the website operator or service provider does acquire actual knowledge, then COPPA requirements become applicable.

"DIRECTED TO"

The determination whether a website or service is "directed to children" is made on the basis of consideration of the following factors:

(a) subject matter of the site or service
(b) visual content, the use of animated characters or child-oriented activities and incentives, music or other audio content

(c) age of models
(d) presence of child celebrities or celebrities who appeal to children
(e) language or other characteristics of the website or online service
(f) extent to which advertising promoting or appearing on the website or online service is directed to children
(g) reliable empirical evidence regarding audience composition and/or the intended audience of the site or service.

AGE-SCREENING

COPPA does not require website operators to ask the age of visitors. In fact, a website that is directed at children under thirteen as its primary audience must initially treat all visitors as children under thirteen. It may not screen visitors for age. If children under thirteen are not the primary audience the website or service targets, then visitors may be screened for age. A website or service that targets both children under the age of thirteen and people who are older than thirteen does not primarily target children under thirteen, and therefore may screen visitors for age.

Websites and online services that screen for age must not collect personal information from any visitor prior to collecting age information. They also must prevent the collection, use, or disclosure of personal information from visitors who identify themselves as under thirteen without first complying with the notice and parental consent provisions of the FTC's COPPA Rule.

An operator of a website or online service directed to children may not block children under thirteen from participating in the website or online service, even if s/he does not intend children to be the primary target audience. Age-screening may be used to differentiate between child and adult users for such purposes as offering differing activities or functions depending on the user's age, but children may not be altogether prohibited from participating in a website or service that is directed to children. The operator of a general audience website or service may block children under thirteen from using the website or service.

An operator of a general audience site or service that chooses to screen its users for age in a neutral fashion may rely on the age information its users enter, even if that age information is not accurate. In some circumstances, this may mean that children are able to register on a site, establish an account or purchase a product or service in violation of the operator's Terms of Service. If, however, the operator later determines that a particular user is a child under thirteen, then COPPA notice and parental consent requirements will apply.

The age-screening should be neutral, i.e., designed to obtain accurate age information from users. The best way to do this is to ask visitors to enter their birthdates, and set up the website to calculate their ages from that information. According to the FTC, the placement of a notice on a website or service that children under the age of thirteen may not use the website or service, or that they should ask their parents' permission, encourages children to falsify their age information, so the age-screening would not be neutral The FTC also takes the position that a checkbox next to a statement like, "I am over 12 years old" is not a neutral mechanism, either.

A website operator or service provider that asks users to provide age information, and then fails either to screen out children under thirteen or to obtain parental consent to collecting children's personal information, may be liable for violating COPPA. Accordingly, the FTC recommends using a cookie to prevent children from back-buttoning to enter a different age.

If a general audience website or service unknowingly collects personal information (such as an email address) from a child under thirteen and later acquires actual knowledge that the person is a child under thirteen, it must either delete the child's information immediately or meet COPPA notice and parental consent requirements.

Since COPPA only applies to websites and services that are directed to children or operated by persons who have knowledge that information has been collected from a child under the age of thirteen, a general audience website that is not directed to children may be able to avoid the need to comply with COPPA by implementing measures to prevent the acquisition of knowledge that information from children under thirteen has been collected. Such measures might include, for example, removing age, date of birth, level of education attained, and other age-indicating data collection fields. An operator of a general audience website would also need to ensure that pages directed to children under thirteen, if any, are either removed or modified so that they are not attractive to children under thirteen.

PROTECTED INFORMATION

For purposes of the COPPA Rule, "personal information" includes:

(a) first and last name
(b) home or other physical address, including street name and name of a city or town
(c) online contact information
(d) a screen or user name that functions as online contact information
(e) telephone number
(f) Social Security number
(g) a persistent identifier that can be used to recognize a user over time and across different websites or online services (e.g., a cookie, GUID, an IP address, or the like)
(h) a photograph, video, or audio file containing a child's image or voice, unless the image or sound is modified to make the child unrecognizable (e.g., blurred or redacted)
(i) geolocation information sufficient to identify street name and the name of a city or town
(j) information concerning the child or the parents of the child that the operator collects online from the child and combines with an identifier described above.

A *persistent identifier* is an identifier, such as a customer number held in a cookie, an IP address, a processor or device serial number, or a unique device identifier that can be used to recognize a user over time and across different websites or online services, even where the identifier is not paired with other items of personal information. Accordingly, it will be necessary to disclose in the Privacy Policy and in the direct notice to parents the company's collection, use or disclosure of persistent identifiers. This disclosure is not necessary, however, if the persistent identifiers are collected on or through the website or service solely for the purpose of providing support for the internal operations of the website or service, and no other personal information about the child is collected.

"Support for the internal operations of the website or online service" means activities necessary for the site or service to: maintain or analyze its functioning; perform network communications; authenticate users or personalize content; serve contextual advertising or cap the frequency of advertising; protect the security or integrity of the user, website, or online service; ensure legal or regulatory compliance; or fulfill a request of a child as permitted by the one-time or multiple-contact exception (See below.) It does not include behavioral advertising. The inclusion of personalization within the definition of support for internal operations is intended to permit operators to maintain user-driven preferences, such as game scores or character choices in virtual worlds.

"Online contact information" means an email address, an IM user identifier, a VoIP (Voice over Internet Protocol) identifier, a video chat user identifier, or other substantially similar identifier. A mobile phone number is not online contact information and therefore may not be collected from the child as part of the consent initiation process. However, once the parent is connected via the parent's online contact information, a website operator or online service provider may request the parent's mobile phone number in order to further communicate with him or her.

No personal information may be collected from a child under thirteen without the consent of the child's parent or guardian, nor may it be disclosed or shared without such consent.

COPPA only applies to information collected from children under thirteen. It does not apply to information about children under thirteen that is collected from a different source. For example, it does not apply to information that a parent or guardian provides about a child. Nevertheless, the FTC has stated that it expects operators to keep confidential any information obtained from parents in the course of obtaining parental consent or providing for parental access pursuant to COPPA.

COPPA does not apply to website operators that do not collect information from children under thirteen. Note, however, that COPPA applies even if information is voluntarily provided by a child under the age of thirteen without having been instructed by a website operator or online service provider to do so. For example, if a website allows any user to post comments to the website, then COPPA applies to any comments containing personal information that may be posted by a child who is under thirteen. Passive tracking of a child's personal information through a "persistent identifier" (e.g., a cookie) is also covered, even if the website operator has not actively collected personal information from a child. For these reasons, it is a good idea for nearly every commercial website to comply with the COPPA Rule unless it restricts access to adults using an age verification system.

THE ONE-TIME RESPONSE EXCEPTION

The COPPA Rule provides a limited exception allowing operators to respond to communications they receive from children under thirteen without needing to comply with COPPA's notice to parent and parental consent requirements: the "one-time response" exception. An operator may collect online contact information for the child and the child's parent and may send a response to the child via the child's online contact information without having to send notice to the parent or obtain parental consent. For example, suppose an operator receives a contest entry containing online contact information from a child under thirteen. The operator may let the child know whether the child won or not. A website operator also may respond to a question sent in by a child who is under thirteen.

Unless the operator thereafter complies with COPPA requirements or the multiple-contact or some other exception (see below) applies, the child's online contact information must be deleted from the operator's records promptly after the response is sent. The operator may not recontact the child or disclose the child's online contact information unless COPPA requirements are satisfied. Even if the operator does not respond to the communication, it must still immediately delete the child's personal information from its records unless it complies with COPPA requirements. Additionally, such a communication may give an operator actual knowledge that it has collected personal information from a child under thirteen (e.g., if the child's email address had previously been collected as part of a website registration process). In this circumstance, the operator would need to take steps to ensure that s/he is complying with COPPA, such as obtaining parental consent or immediately deleting any personal information collected from the child.

The one-time response exception only encompasses the online contact information for the child and the child's parent. COPPA requirements must be satisfied if other kinds of information (such as a street address) are collected from the child.

THIRD PARTY COLLECTORS OF INFORMATION

A website or service is not required to disclose to third parties whether it is directed to children or is a general audience website. Disclosing this information will not relieve a website operator or service provider of its obligations under COPPA, either.

A website operator or online service provider is responsible for the information collected from its users regardless of who does the collecting. The operator of a website or online service that is directed to children under thirteen generally must either: (a) provide notice and obtain prior parental consent before collecting or allowing any entity to collect personal information from visitors to the website, and satisfy all other COPPA requirements; or (b) not collect or allow any other entity to collect personal information from visitors to the site or users of the service. The FTC recommends that operators of websites or services directed to children advise third parties of their status and arrange with any third party that collects personal information to provide adequate COPPA protections.

Operators of websites and online services directed to children must be careful about accepting third party advertising. The COPPA Rule holds operators of websites and online services directed to children liable for the collection of information that occurs on or through their sites and services, even if the information is collected by a third party. If, for example, a third party advertiser uses cookies or other persistent identifiers, or collects geolocation or other kinds of information from a child under thirteen who clicks on the advertisement that is displayed on a company's website or service, then the company may be required to provide notice to parents both in its Privacy Policy and in a notice sent directly to parents, and obtain verifiable parental consent, before permitting the advertisement to appear on the website or service.

Advertisers, too, must be careful where they advertise. An advertiser who has actual knowledge that s/he is collecting personal information from users of a website or service that is directed to children must comply with COPPA requirements. Actual knowledge may exist where the website operator or service provider directly communicates the child-directed nature of its content to the advertiser. Actual knowledge may also be acquired in other ways, such as where the advertiser visits the site or service and recognizes that it is directed to children.

Operators of websites or online services must conduct an inquiry into the information collection practices of every third party that may collect information via the website or service. The operator will need to determine each third party's information collection practices so that it can make an informed decision as to whether its presence on the website or service will require the operator to give parents notice and obtain their consent prior to their collection of personal information from children.

According to the FTC, a website operator or online service provider, including an online advertiser, may rely on another website's or service's representation that it is not directed to children. This will not be the case, however, if actual knowledge that the site or service is, in fact, directed to children is acquired.

> **Example**. Website operator assures Advertiser that the website is not directed to children, so Advertiser places advertising on the website. At this point, Advertiser is not necessarily subject to COPPA requirements. Advertiser then visits the site and sees that it is a site in which only children under thirteen normally would have any interest. Now the advertiser may be subject to COPPA requirements.

A website operator may be held responsible for third parties (such as advertisers) with content on their sites, including those whose advertisements appear on the site pursuant to a behavioral advertising program. Therefore, website operators should take steps to ensure that these third party advertisers are not using cookies or other tracking mechanisms to set persistent identifiers for website visitors who are under the age of thirteen.

NOTICE TO PARENTS

The FTC's COPPA Rule requires website operators and service providers to make reasonable efforts, taking into account available technology, to ensure that a parent of a child receives direct notice of the operator's practices with regard to the collection, use, or disclosure of personal information from children under thirteen, including notice of any material changes to practices to which the parent previously consented. This must be done before any personal information is collected from the child (except that the contact information for the child's parent may be collected from a child so that the operator can have a way of knowing where to send the direct notice to parents). There are four situations in which a direct notice is required or appropriate under the Rule:

(a) If an operator seeks to obtain a parent's verifiable consent prior to the collection, use, or disclosure of a child's personal information, the direct notice must (i) state that the operator has collected the parent's online contact information from the child, and, if such is the case, the name of the child or the parent, in order to obtain the parent's consent; (ii) state that the parent's consent is required for the collection, use, or disclosure of such information, and that the operator will not collect, use, or disclose any personal information from the child if the parent does not provide such consent; (iii) set forth the additional items of personal information the operator intends to collect from the child, or the potential opportunities for the disclosure of personal information, should the parent provide consent; (iv) contain a hypertext link to the operator's online notice of its information practices (i.e., its privacy policy); (v) provide the means by which the parent can provide verifiable consent to the collection, use, and disclosure of the information; and (vi) state that if the parent does not provide consent within a reasonable time from the date the direct notice was sent, the operator will delete the parent's online contact information from its records.

(b) If an operator voluntarily seeks to provide notice to a parent of a child's online activities that do not involve the collection, use or disclosure of personal information, the direct notice must (i) state that the operator has collected the parent's online contact information from the child in order to provide notice to, and subsequently update the parent about, a child's participation in a website or online service that does not otherwise collect, use, or disclose children's personal information; (ii) state that the parent's online contact information will not be used or disclosed for any other purpose; (iii) state that the parent may refuse to permit the child's participation in the website or online service and may require the deletion of the parent's online contact information, and how the parent can do so; and (iv) provide a hypertext link to the operator's online notice of its information practices.

(c) If an operator intends to communicate with the child multiple times via the child's online contact information and collects no other information, the direct notice must (i) state that the operator has collected the child's online contact information from the child in order to provide multiple online communications to the child; (ii) state that the operator has collected the parent's online contact information from the child in order to notify the parent that the child has registered to receive multiple online communications from the operator; (iii) state that the online contact information collected from the child will not be used for any other purpose, disclosed, or combined with any other information collected from the child; (iv) state that the parent may refuse to permit further contact with the child and may require the deletion of the parent's and child's online contact information, and describe how the parent may do so; (v) state that if the parent fails to respond to this direct notice, the operator may use the online contact information collected from the child for the purpose stated in the direct notice; and (vi) provide a hypertext link to the operator's online notice of its information practices.

(d) If the operator's purpose for collecting a child's and a parent's name and online contact information is to protect a child's safety and the information is not used or disclosed for any other purpose, the direct notice must (i) state that the operator has collected the name and the online contact information of the child and the parent in order to protect the safety of a child; (ii) state that the information will not be used or disclosed for any purpose unrelated to the child's safety; (iii) state that the parent may refuse to permit the use, and require the deletion, of the information collected, and how the parent may do so; (iv) state that if the parent fails to respond to this direct notice, the operator may use the information for the purpose stated in the direct notice; and (v) provide a hypertext link to the operator's online notice of its information practices.

The "direct notice to parents" requirement may not be satisfied by simply sending parents an email containing a link to the Privacy Policy on the company's website. A link to a privacy policy is required, but it is not enough. The direct notice to parents must contain certain key information within the four corners of the notice itself, depending on the purpose for which the information is being collected.

The direct notice to the parent may be sent by mechanisms other than email, if desired, such as through the device onto which the application is downloaded, if the mechanisms both (a) provide such notice and obtain the parent's consent before any collection of personal information and (b) are reasonably designed to ensure that it is the parent who receives the notice and provides the consent.

VERIFIABLE PARENTAL CONSENT

When COPPA applies, verifiable parental consent[233] generally must be obtained before personal information is collected from a child under thirteen.

Exceptions:

(a) Names and online contact information of the child and the child's parent or guardian may be collected before parental consent is obtained, if the sole purpose of collecting this information is to make it possible to provide notice to a parent and obtain parental consent as required by COPPA. If the operator has not obtained parental consent after a reasonable time from the date of the information collection, the operator must delete the information from its records.

(b) A parent's or guardian's online contact information may be collected before parental consent is obtained if the sole purpose is to provide voluntary notice about the child's participation in a website or online service that does not otherwise collect, use, or disclose children's personal information. Such information may not be used or disclosed for any other purpose and the operator must make reasonable efforts, taking into consideration available technology, to provide a parent with appropriate notice.

(c) A child's name and online contact information may be collected before parental consent is obtained if the sole purpose of collecting the information is to respond directly on a one-time basis to a specific request from the child, and the information is not used to recontact the child or for any other purpose, is not disclosed, and is deleted from the operator's records promptly after responding to the child's request. (This is the one-time contact exception.)

(d) Names and online contact information of the child and the child's parent or guardian may be collected before parental consent is obtained if the purpose is to respond directly more than once to the child's specific request, and the information is not used for any other purpose, is not disclosed, and is not combined with any other information collected from the child. In this situation, however, the operator must provide parents with notice and a means to opt out of allowing the site's future contact of the child. In providing such notice, the operator must make reasonable efforts, taking into consideration available technology, to ensure that the parent receives appropriate notice, and will not be deemed to have made reasonable efforts where the notice to the parent was unable to be delivered. (This is the multiple-contacts exception.)

(e) A child's and a parent's name and online contact information may be collected before parental consent is obtained if the purpose is to protect the safety of a child, and the information is not used or disclosed for any purpose unrelated to the child's safety. In this situation, the operator must make reasonable efforts, taking into consideration available technology, to provide a parent with appropriate notice.

(f) A child's name and online contact information may be collected before parental consent is obtained if the purpose is to (a) protect the security or integrity of the website or online service; (b) take precautions against liability; (c) respond to judicial process; or (d) to the extent permitted under other provisions of law, to provide information to law enforcement agencies or for an investigation on a matter related to public safety.

(g) A persistent identifier may be collected without parental consent if no other personal information is obtained; the identifier is used solely for the purpose of providing support for the internal operations of the website or service; and the persistent identifier is not used or disclosed to contact a specific individual, including through behavioral advertising; to amass a profile on a specific individual; or for any other purpose.

(h) A persistent identifier may be collected without parental consent if no other personal information is obtained and a previous affirmative interaction with the user confirmed the user was not a child (e.g., an age-gated registration process), and this is true even if the operator or service provider has a presence on a third party site (e.g., a social widget or plug-in that is embedded on the site) that the operator or service provider actually knows is a site directed to children.

Parental consent must be obtained not only when personal information is initially collected from a child under thirteen, but also each time a material change is thereafter made to the company's information practices (privacy policy).

Providing required COPPA notices and obtaining verifiable parental consent at the point of purchase may be necessary in the case of a child-oriented application that is designed to collect personal information as soon as it is downloaded. Alternatively, a website may insert a landing page where a parent may receive notice and give consent before a child's download is complete.

Methods of Obtaining Parental Consent

Any method may be used for obtaining parental consent, as long as it is reasonably calculated to ensure that the person providing consent is the child's parent. Acceptable methods include:

(a) Print-and-send, i.e., a form the user prints out for a parent to sign and return via mail, fax, or electronic scan.

(b) Payment card, i.e., requiring the parent, in connection with a monetary transaction, to use a credit card, debit card, or other online payment system that provides notification of each discrete transaction to the primary account holder. Collecting a sixteen-digit credit or debit card number alone is not a satisfactory method of obtaining parental consent unless either: (a) the number is collected in connection with a monetary transaction, or (b) some additional measures are implemented to ensure that the person providing the number is the parent. So long as the notice-to-parent requirement has been met, it is not necessary to ascertain that the credit card account holder is, in fact, the child's parent or guardian.

(c) Phone-in, i.e., having the parent call a toll free telephone number staffed by trained personnel, or having the parent connect to trained personnel via videoconference.

(d) Identification card issued by government (e.g., driver license). This entails verifying a parent's identity by checking a form of government-issued identification against databases of such information. The parent's identification must be promptly deleted after completing the verification. So long as the notice-to-parent requirement has been met, it is not necessary to ascertain that the card holder is, in fact, the child's parent or guardian.

(e) Email-plus, i.e., sending the direct notice to parent in the form of an email to the parent requesting that the parent indicate consent in a return email. This method is acceptable only if the child's personal information will be used solely for internal purposes – that is, the company will not be disclosing the information to third parties or making it publicly available, and will not be providing the child an opportunity to make it publicly available (e.g., through a social networking service, online forums, or personal profiles). If this method is used, then an additional confirming step must be taken after receiving the parent's message (this is the "plus" factor). The confirming step may involve (i) requesting in the initial message to the parent that the parent include a phone or fax number or mailing address in the reply message, so that the company can follow up with a confirming phone call, fax or letter to the parent, or (ii) after a reasonable time delay, sending another message via the parent's online contact information to confirm consent. This confirmatory message should inform the parent that he or she may revoke the consent, and explain how to do that. All of the information that was contained in the direct notice should also be included in this message.

It can be a good idea to offer more than one method of providing parental consent, in case a parent cannot or does not want to use a specified method. For example, the company could offer a print-and-return and/or phone-in method in addition to the credit card or government-issued ID method, for those people who do not like to disclose their credit card or government-issued identification numbers.

A company that has a method of obtaining consent that is not listed above should evaluate it to determine whether it is reasonably calculated to ensure that the person providing consent is the child's parent. Application may be made to the FTC for preapproval.

After notifying and obtaining verifiable consent, it is a good idea to provide the parent with a password or PIN. This way, it will be easier to confirm the parent's identity in future communications.

The child's parent or guardian must be given the following options:

(a) consent to the collection, use, and disclosure of the child's personal information
(b) consent to the collection and use of the child's personal information, but not to disclosure of the information to third parties
(c) refusal of consent to collection, use, and disclosure.

When COPPA applies, an operator must obtain verifiable parental consent to disclosure of the child's information whether the operator will be the one disclosing the information or the child will be the one disclosing it. Verifiable consent must be obtained if the website or service offers an activity that provides a child under thirteen an opportunity to disclose the child's personal information.

Example 1. A website directed to children offers a service that allows children to send a personalized e-card to their friends. If the system allows personal information to be disclosed in the "From" or "Subject" lines of the email header, or in the body of the message, then COPPA requirements must first be satisfied before a child under thirteen may use it.

Example 2. Same as Example 1, except that the web form only collects the recipient's email address and first name, and the child's first name. No other personal information is collected from either the sender or recipient, not even a persistent identifier. The web form does not allow the sender to enter her full name, her email address, or the recipient's full name. It also does not allow the sender to freely type messages either in the subject line of the header or in the body of the message. The recipient's email address is immediately deleted after the message is sent. Now, the one-time contact exception applies, so prior verifiable parental consent is not required.

Example 3. Same as Example 2, except that the recipient's email address is not immediately deleted after the message is sent. In this scenario, the sender's parent's email address must be collected and notice and an opportunity to opt out must be provided to the sender's parent before the e-card is sent. (See "multiple-contacts" exception, infra.)

If an operator that is subject to COPPA collects the email address of a child under thirteen and retains it in retrievable form (e.g., so it can send password reminders), then it must comply with the requirements of the multiple-contact exception, including sending notice to parents and providing parents an opportunity to opt out. Those requirements will not apply, however, if a child's email address is collected solely to authenticate the child's identity for purposes of generating a password reminder, provided all three of the following conditions are met:

(a) No personal information is collected from the child other than the child's email address;
(b) The child cannot disclose any personal information on the website;
(c) The email address is immediately and permanently altered (e.g., through "hashing") so that it can only be used as a password reminder and cannot be reconstructed into its original form or used to contact the child.

The website should explain this process in a clear and conspicuous manner, both at the point of collection and in the privacy policy, so that users and their parents are informed about how the email addresses will be used. This will prevent visitors from mistakenly assuming that the site is improperly collecting and retaining email addresses without any form of parental notice.

The option of consenting to collection and use but not disclosure—option (b), above—need not be offered if disclosure of the information is inherent in the activity to which the parent consents. Note that disclosure, for purposes of the COPPA Rule, includes both a website operator's or service provider's direct release of information to a third party and the child's or another person's disclosure of information using a website or online service. A child's posting of personal information about himself in a chat room, forum or social network is a disclosure of information collected from the child even if the website operator did not solicit the information. A central feature of chat rooms, social media, and similar online services is the sharing of personal information, Therefore, if a parent has given consent for the child to participate in such a service, the operator need not give the parent the option of consenting to the collection and use of information without disclosure (option (b), above). The operator must, however, clearly state its collection, use, and disclosure practices in the direct notice to parent and in its Privacy Policy so that parents can make an informed decision about whether to allow their children to participate in the website or service.

A website operator or online service provider may rely on a third party to obtain parental consent on its behalf, but remains responsible for ensuring compliance with COPPA requirements. A business that takes this approach should ensure that the third party obtains parental consent in a way that is reasonably calculated, in light of available technology, to ensure that the person providing consent is the child's parent. The mere fact that a user has an account with a third party is not sufficient assurance that the person entering the account or password information is the parent, in the absence of other indicia of reliability (e.g., know-ledge-based authentication questions or verification of government identification). The direct notice to parent must still be sent out before the parental consent is obtained, in any event.

A child-directed website may need to provide notice and obtain verifiable parental consent when it puts a third party plug-in on the site. The notice and consent requirements do not apply, however, if the child-directed site does not collect personal information (except for information covered by an exception) and each of the following conditions is met:

(a) The third party operator only collects a persistent identifier and no other personal information
(b) The user affirmatively interacts with the third party operator to trigger the collection
(c) The third-party operator has previously conducted an age-screen of the user, indicating the user is not a child.

This exception does not apply to types of plug-ins where the third party collects more information than a persistent identifier—for example, where the third party also collects user comments or other user-generated content. In addition, a child-directed website cannot rely on this exception to treat particular visitors as adults and track their activities.

Notice and consent requirements also will not be triggered by the inclusion of a plug-in if another exception applies, such as the "support for internal operations" exception.

Schools may act as agents for parents. They may receive the notice to parents and give consent on behalf of parents of children who are enrolled in the school, but only for purposes related to the child's education, not for a commercial or other purpose. Upon the school's request, an operator must provide the school a description of the types of personal information collected; an opportunity to review the child's personal information and/or have the information deleted; and the opportunity to prevent further use or online collection of a child's personal information. As long as the operator limits use of the child's information to the educational context authorized by the school, the operator may presume that the school's authorization is based on the school's having obtained the parent's consent. If, instead of limiting use of a child's personal information to the provision of services to the school, an operator wants to use or disclose children's personal information for its own commercial or other purposes, then it must obtain parental consent. Schools do not have the authority to act on behalf of parents for the purpose of giving consent to the use of children's personal information for commercial or other nonschool-related purposes.

PARENT'S RIGHT TO ACCESS INFORMATION

When a parent exercises his or her right, under COPPA, to access personal information about the child that a website or online service has collected, the operator of the website or online service must use reasonable procedures to confirm that the person requesting the information is the child's parent. This may be accomplished, for example, by assigning a password or PIN to the parent at the time of obtaining verifiable parental consent and then requiring use of the PIN or password to gain access to the child's information. An operator is not required to comply with a parent's request to view it if the operator had already deleted it at the time the request is made.

An operator who follows reasonable procedures in responding to a request for disclosure of a child's personal information will not be liable under any federal or state law for mistakenly releasing a child's personal information to a person other than the parent.

SHARING INFORMATION WITH OTHERS

An operator that collects personal information from a child under thirteen must maintain the confidentiality, security, and integrity of the information collected from children. This includes taking reasonable steps to release the information only to those who are able to maintain its confidentiality, integrity, and security. Before sharing information with a service provider or third party, an operator should determine what the service provider's or third party's policies and practice are for maintaining the confidentiality and security of the data and preventing unauthorized access to or use of the information. Expectations for the treatment of the data should be expressly addressed in any contracts with third parties. In addition, reasonable means, such as periodic monitoring, must be employed to confirm that any third parties with whom the company shares children's personal information maintain the confidentiality and security of that information.

DESTROYING RECORDS

Unlike laws regulating the collection and storage of business, financial and health information, COPPA seeks to limit the amount of information about children under thirteen years of age that website operators and online service providers retain. Website operators and online service providers must delete the information as soon as it is no longer needed for the purpose for which it was collected. A website operator or online service provider is not required to preserve information collected from a child for the sake of responding to a possible request from the child's parent in the future. If the operator or service provider deletes it before a parent asks to see it, then the parent is out of luck. There is no obligation to disclose it if it is deleted before a parent requests it. On the other hand, if a parent makes the request before the information has been deleted, then the operator or service provider must disclose it to the parent as required by COPPA.

Records of information collected from children under thirteen years of age must be destroyed securely.

PRIVACY POLICY

Websites that are subject to the FTC's COPPA Rule must publish a Privacy Policy that contains all of the following information:

(a) the name, address, telephone number, and email address of all operators collecting or maintaining personal information through the website or service (or, after listing all such operators, the contact information for a single one that will handle all inquiries from parents may be provided);
(b) description of the information collected from children, including whether the operator enables children to make their personal information publicly available; how the operator uses such information; and the operator's disclosure practices for such information;
(c) notice that the parent may review or have deleted the child's personal information and refuse to permit its further collection or use, and the procedures for doing so.

The Rule further requires the Privacy Policy to be clearly and understandably written, and it must contain no unrelated, confusing, or contradictory materials. There should be no promotional content in it.

Links to the Privacy Policy must be provided on the home page and on each area of the website where information is collected from children under thirteen. The links must be positioned close to the requests for information in each such area. A link must clearly indicate that it links to the website's Privacy Policy and it must be conspicuous, that is, it must stand out and be noticeable to the site's visitors, such as through the use of a larger font size in a different color on a contrasting background. It must be distinguishable from adjacent links, and it must not be in small print. The links for the policy on collection of data from children under thirteen must take visitors directly to the point in the Privacy Policy where the operator's policies with respect to children are discussed, or it is clearly disclosed at the top of the notice that there is a specific section discussing the operator's information practices with regard to children. Operators should also ensure that the link for the children's portion of the Privacy Policy appears on the home page or screen of any children's area of the site or service, and at each area where personal information is collected from children.

A website that is not currently subject to COPPA should consider having a COPPA-compliant Privacy Policy in place anyway. A child under thirteen years of age could submit personal information at any time (such as a comment or an email communication).

COPPA SAFE HARBOR

The FTC's COPPA Rule allows a person or entity to apply to the FTC for approval of a program that works to ensure that its members are in compliance with COPPA requirements applicable to companies that collect information from children under thirteen years of age. If the program is approved by the FTC, then it becomes a safe harbor. This means that an operator will be deemed to be in compliance with COPPA requirements if it is a participant in such a program, provided the program has been approved by the FTC and the operator is in compliance with its guidelines. More information about safe harbor program criteria and a list of safe harbor programs is posted at the FTC's website, www.ftc.gov/content/safe-harbor-program.

Chapter 19. Sexually Explicit Material

Some kinds of sexually explicit material are protected under the First Amendment. Obscenity and child pornography are not. Possessing or distributing them is a serious crime. Offers to provide child pornography and requests for child pornography are not protected by the First Amendment, either. This is true even if the materials in question do not actually contain any child pornography. Presumably the same would hold true for offers and requests for obscenity.

Obscenity

Federal and state statutes impose severe penalties for the commission of various kinds of acts in connection with obscenity. Attempting, aiding, abetting and conspiring with another to do any of these acts are also crimes. Penalties for most of these offenses may include fines, imprisonment, and registration as a sex offender.

Knowingly producing obscenity with intent to distribute or transmit it via an interactive computer service is prohibited by 18 U.S.C. § 1465. Knowingly distributing or selling obscenity via an interactive computer service is also prohibited. Knowingly transmitting or receiving obscenity via an interactive computer service is prohibited by 18 U.S.C. § 1462. Being in the business of selling, offering or transmitting obscenity is prohibited by 18 U.S.C. § 1466.

Obscenity is not protected by the First Amendment. The U.S. Supreme Court has been very clear about this.[234] The Court has not been quite as forthcoming about what, exactly, obscenity is. Federal statutes do not define it. In *Miller v. California*,[235] the Supreme Court supplied a definition, holding that material is obscene if the average person, applying contemporary community standards, finds that, taken as a whole, it meets all three of the following criteria:

(a) appeals to a prurient interest
(b) describes or depicts sexual activity in a patently offensive way
(c) lacks serious literary, artistic, political, or scientific value.

Prurient interests are erotic, lascivious, abnormal, degrading, shameful, or morbid interests in nudity, sexual activity, or excretion.

Patently offensive material, according to *Miller*, includes any depiction or description that is either (a) a patently offensive representation or description of ultimate sexual acts, normal or perverted, actual or simulated, or (b) a patently offensive representation or description of masturbation, excretory functions, or lewd exhibition of the genitals.

The Court had in mind what is commonly known as "hardcore" pornography. Although the Court expressly declined to create a detailed list of everything that might qualify as obscene, the following itemization may be distilled from the examples they provided:

- Sexual intercourse
- Oral sex
- Anal sex
- Simulated sexual intercourse
- Simulated oral or anal sex
- Masturbation
- Lewd exhibitions of genitals
- Urination
- Defecation.

In *United States v. Twelve 200-Ft. Reels of Film,* the Court upheld the constitutionality of the federal obscenity statute despite the fact that it leaves the terms *obscene* and *indecent* undefined. In response to the argument that the absence of a definition renders the statute unconstitutionally vague and overbroad, the Court wrote, "[W]e are prepared to construe such terms as limiting regulated material to patently offensive representations or descriptions of that specific 'hard core' sexual conduct given as examples in *Miller v. California*.... Of course, Congress could always define other specific 'hard core' conduct."[236] This means that the range of material that may be classified as obscene for constitutional purposes may be larger than the range of material that Congress has chosen to classify as obscene for purposes of federal criminal enforcement. For example, sadomasochistic activity is not mentioned in the *Miller* list, but this does not mean it is not potentially obscene. It just means that it doesn't come within the coverage of the general obscenity statute. If it is specifically mentioned in another federal or state obscenity statute, then it may be considered obscene under that statute.

A state obscenity statute must specify the kinds of portrayals of sexual activity that are deemed patently offensive unless the highest court of the state has issued a constitutionally compliant construction giving specific content to the term.

The third prong of the *Miller* test—literary, artistic, political, or scientific value—is the most doctrinally problematic element of the test. Literary and artistic merit are subjective. Arguably, political and scientific value are, too. Since the *Miller* test assigns the task of determining what has value to "the average person," First Amendment rights are made to depend on whether a majority of people on a jury like or agree with the content. This is at odds with the bedrock First Amendment principle that speech regulation must be content neutral. Nevertheless, "redeeming value" is part of the standard that the highest court in the United States has chosen to adopt. It does not seem likely that the Court will overrule itself on this point at any time in the foreseeable future.

In effect, the Court has handed the ball to juries in local communities to decide the specifics about what kinds of depictions and descriptions they think are offensive and lacking in value. This means that sending material from a liberal community that does not consider it offensive into a community that thinks it is could result in an obscenity conviction. The Internet, of course, is accessible in virtually every community. There is no feasible way to restrict content to specific geographic areas within the United States. Applying *Miller* therefore makes the least tolerant community in the country the arbiter of moral standards for the entire country. Realizing this, some commentators have argued that a nationwide standard should be applied. The Ninth

Circuit Court of Appeals has taken that position.[237] Other circuit courts of appeal do not agree. The Eleventh Circuit Court of Appeals holds that individual members of a local community are the ones who should get to decide what is offensive and lacking in value.[238] The Sixth Circuit, too, has held that the relevant community standards are those of the community into which material is transmitted, not the community from which the material is sent or the nation as a whole.[239]

Fortunately, Americans are not completely at the mercy of the most prudish, least culturally sophisticated people among us. Lack of perceived value is not enough, in and of itself, to render a publication obscene. All three elements of the definition must be present. Since one of those elements requires a depiction of sexual activity, it may safely be assumed that a depiction or description of adult nudity in a way that is not sexually suggestive is constitutionally protected even if it does not have any value. A lewd exhibition of genitals could be considered an obscene sex act, however. Lewd exhibitions of genitals are not necessarily protected by the First Amendment. Even a lewd exhibition of genitals may be constitutionally protected, though, if it has serious literary, artistic, political or scientific value.

Child Pornography

Child pornography is any visual depiction of sexually explicit conduct that is produced with the use of a minor, an image of an identifiable minor, or an image that is indistinguishable from that of a minor. 18 U.S.C. § 2251. The Prosecutorial Remedies and Other Tools to End the Exploitation of Children Today Act[240] (PROTECT Act) prohibits a wide variety of activities in connection with child pornography: advertising, promoting, distributing, presenting, soliciting, selling, possessing, possessing with intent to sell or distribute, reproducing, accessing, transmitting or receiving child pornography are all crimes. 18 U.S.C. §§ 2252, 2252A. It does not matter whether a depiction has been activated for viewing or not. Electronically stored images are considered child pornography if they will yield depictions of child pornography when decrypted and read by a computer. Penalties for violating child pornography laws can be severe.

An *identifiable minor* is a person who is recognizable as an actual person by the person's face, likeness, or other distinguishing characteristic, and who was under the age of eighteen at the time the visual depiction or an image used in the visual depiction was made, altered or modified. A fictional character is not an identifiable minor.

An image is "indistinguishable" from that of a minor if an ordinary person would conclude that the depiction is of an actual minor.

Sexually explicit conduct includes sexual intercourse, oral sex, anal sex, oral-anal sex, bestiality, masturbation, sadistic abuse, masochistic abuse, or lascivious exhibition of the genitals or pubic area of any person.

In the case of images generated by a computer, or that are stored in a digital file, that depict either a minor or an image that is indistinguishable from a minor, sexually explicit conduct includes:

(a) sexual intercourse, oral sex, anal sex, oral-anal sex, bestiality, masturbation, sadistic abuse or masochistic abuse, if any person's genitals or pubic area is visible during any of these activities

(b) lascivious simulated sexual intercourse in which the genitals, breast or pubic area of any person is exhibited
(c) lascivious simulated bestiality, masturbation, sadistic abuse, or masochistic abuse
(d) lascivious exhibition of the genitals or pubic area of any person
(e) simulated lascivious exhibition of the genitals or pubic area of any person.

Any material that comes within the definition of obscenity will also come within the definition of child pornography if any of the participants in the depiction is a minor, i.e., under the age of eighteen. Material does not have to be obscene in order to come within the definition of child pornography, though.

CHILD PORNOGRAPHY USING AN ACTUAL MINOR

Producing child pornography, or being involved in the production of child pornography, is prohibited by 18 U.S.C. § 2251. Penalties are severe, up to and including fines and life imprisonment. The death penalty may be imposed if any person dies during the making of child pornography.

Knowingly transmitting, receiving, distributing, or reproducing for distribution, child pornography that was produced with the use of an actual minor is prohibited by 18 U.S.C. § 2252.

Knowingly possessing, accessing with intent to view, possessing with intent to sell or distribute, or selling child pornography that has been produced with the use of an actual minor is prohibited if any of the following applies:

(a) It has been sent via an instrumentality of interstate commerce (including the Internet);
(b) It was produced with materials that were sent by an instrumentality of interstate commerce
(c) The defendant is within the special maritime and territorial jurisdiction of the United States, on federal land, in a federal building, or in Indian country.

Penalties for sale or possession with intent to sell include a fine and imprisonment for up to twenty years (forty years if the person has a prior sex or pornography conviction). A person with a prior sex or pornography conviction is subject to a mandatory minimum of fifteen years.

Penalties for accessing with intent to view, or possession without intent to sell, are a fine and up to ten years imprisonment The maximum increases to twenty years, with a mandatory minimum of ten years, if the minor is prepubescent or under the age of twelve, or if the defendant has a prior sex or pornography conviction. It is a defense to a charge of accessing with intent to view or possession without intent to sell or distribute that the defendant possessed no more than two items containing such a depiction, did not show it to anyone other than the police, and promptly took steps to either destroy it or report it to the police upon learning of its existence.

CHILD PORNOGRAPHY USING AN IMAGE OF A MINOR

Section 2252 is intended to penalize the direct sexual exploitation of children. It targets people who possess or distribute visual depictions of children that were created while the children were actually involved in sexually explicit activity. A separate statute, 18 U.S.C. § 2252A, was enacted to reach those situations where visual depictions of what appear to be children engaged in sexually explicit activity are created, regardless of whether any children actually engaged in any sexual activity or not. The classic example of a Section 2252A case involves a person photoshopping a photographs of a child's face onto the body of an adult woman who is engaging in sexual activity or lewdly exhibiting genitals.

Section2252A makes all of the following activities unlawful:

(a) knowingly sending, receiving, distributing, or reproducing for distribution child pornography via an instrumentality of interstate commerce (including the Internet)
(b) knowingly possessing, possessing with intent to sell, selling, or accessing with intent to view child pornography in the special maritime and territorial jurisdiction of the United States, on federal land, in a federal building, or in Indian country
(c) knowingly possessing, possessing with intent to sell, selling, or accessing with intent to view child pornography that has been sent via an instrumentality of interstate commerce or that was produced with materials that have been sent via an instrumentality of interstate commerce
(d) knowingly advertising, promoting, presenting or soliciting material in a way that reflects a belief or is intended to cause another person to believe that the material contains a visual depiction of an actual minor engaged in sexually explicit conduct or an obscene depiction of a minor engaging in sexually explicit conduct
(e) knowingly distributing, or producing with intent to distribute, via an instrumentality of interstate commerce, child pornography that is an adapted or modified depiction of an identifiable minor.

It is a defense to the crimes described in paragraphs (a), (b) and (c), above, that everyone in the depiction was an adult at the time. The fact that everyone in the depiction was an adult at the time is not a defense to the crimes described in paragraphs (d) and (e). It is also not a defense to the crimes described in paragraphs (d) and (e) that no minors were used in the production of the depiction.

Violations are punishable by fines and imprisonment. With the exception of possession without intent to sell, accessing with intent to view child pornography, or producing or distributing adapted or modified depictions, there is a mandatory minimum of five years imprisonment. For a person with a prior sex or pornography conviction, the minimum is fifteen years and the maximum is forty years.

Penalties for accessing with intent to view, or possession without intent to sell, are a fine and up to ten years imprisonment The maximum increases to twenty years, with a mandatory minimum of ten years, if the minor is prepubescent or under the age of twelve, or if the defendant has a prior sex or pornography conviction.

It is a defense to a charge of accessing with intent to view or possession without intent to sell or distribute that the defendant possessed no more than two items containing such a depiction, did not show it to anyone other than the police, and promptly took steps to either destroy it or report it to the police upon learning of its existence.

Penalties for producing or distributing adapted or modified depictions include fines and imprisonment up to fifteen years.

More severe criminal penalties are provided for child pornography violations when they are part of a child exploitation enterprise.

A civil action for an injunction and/or monetary damages is also available.

OBSCENE DEPICTION OF A MINOR OR APPARENT MINOR

Knowingly producing obscenity using an actual child is a crime. 18 U.S.C. § 2251.

Under 18 U.S.C. § 1466A, knowingly producing, receiving, distributing, or possessing with intent to distribute a visual depiction of a minor engaging in obscene, sexually explicit conduct is a crime if any of the following conditions apply:

(a) An instrumentality of interstate commerce (including the Internet) was, is or is contemplated to be used in the commission of the act;
(b) An instrumentality of interstate commerce was used to send materials that were used in the production of the obscene material;
(c) A person travels or is transported in interstate or foreign commerce in the course of the commission of the offense;
(d) The offense is committed in the special maritime and territorial jurisdiction of the United States or in any territory or possession of the United States.

Sexually explicit means either of the following:

(a) sexual intercourse, oral sex, anal sex, oral-anal sex, bestiality, masturbation, sadistic or masochistic abuse, or exhibition of the genitals or pubic area of any person
(b) simulated sexual intercourse, oral sex, anal sex, oral-anal sex, bestiality, masturbation, sadistic or masochistic abuse, or lascivious exhibition of a person's genitals or pubic area.

Knowingly producing, receiving, distributing, or possessing with intent to distribute a visual depiction of a minor or what appears to be a minor engaging in sexual intercourse, oral sex, anal sex, oral-anal sex, or graphic bestiality, sadistic or masochistic abuse, under the circumstances described in paragraphs (a) through (d), above, is also a crime, provided the material lacks serious literary, artistic, political or scientific value. A depiction of bestiality, sadistic or masochistic abuse is "graphic" if the genitals or pubic area of any person is visible.

Knowingly possessing a visual depiction of a minor engaging in sexually explicit, obscene conduct, or of a minor or what appears to be a minor engaging in the kinds of conduct described above is also a crime.

The depicted minor need not actually exist. Obscene depictions of fictional children are prohibited, too.

Both criminal penalties and a civil action for an injunction and/or monetary damages are available to enforce this statute. Criminal penalties include fines, imprisonment, and registration as a sex offender. A depiction of a child engaged in sadistic or masochistic activity, or of sexual abuse of an actual child, or for a second violation of the statute, may result in a sentence of life imprisonment.

Although textual and auditory material may be deemed obscene under other statutes, only visual depictions are included within the prohibition of this statute. This includes photographs, audiovisual material, cartoons and artwork.

A person cannot be convicted of simple possession (possession without intent to distribute) if the person has less than three such depictions in his possession. To invoke this defense, the person must do at least one of the following things:

(a) Destroy each such depiction;
(b) Report the matter to a law enforcement agency and give it access to each depiction.

Whichever procedure is followed, it must be done promptly, in good faith, and without retaining or allowing any person other than a law enforcement agency to access a depiction.

Promptly reporting or destroying the material is not a defense to a charge of possession with intent to distribute, distribution, receiving, or production of a prohibited depiction. Nor is it a defense to possession of three or more depictions.

ARTWORK AND DRAWINGS

For purposes of Sections 2251, 2252 and 2252A, child pornography does not include cartoons, drawings, sculptures or paintings. 18 U.S.C. § 2256. By contrast, 18 U.S.C. § 1466A specifically includes cartoons, drawings, paintings and sculpture. The reason for this difference has to do with the different rationales for denying First Amendment protection to child pornography as compared to obscenity. Child pornography is denied constitutional protection because children are harmed in the making of it. That rationale does not exist if no actual children (or images of actual children) are used in the production of it. Obscenity, on the other hand, is outside the realm of First Amendment protection irrespective of whether anybody is harmed in the making of it. Obscenity is denied constitutional protection not because it harms somebody but because a majority of members of the U.S. Supreme Court have not found any value in it. The universe of things that might be obscene is virtually limitless, so long as they are sexual in nature and members of some community somewhere in the United States find them patently offensive, prurient, and without serious literary, artistic, political or scientific value.

Congress expressly excluded cartoons and drawings from the child pornography statute in order to forestall another overbreadth challenge. Children are rarely, if ever, harmed in the drawing of cartoons. So Congress relegated cartoons and other artwork to 18 U.S.C. § 1466A, the statute addressing obscenity depicting a child.

A drawing, cartoon, painting, sculpture or other visual depiction is prohibited under Section 1466A only if it depicts: (a) a minor engaging in obscene sexual conduct; or (b) a minor or what appears to be a minor engaging in one of a variety of enumerated sex-related activities in a way that lacks serious literary, artistic, political or scientific value.

The depiction need not be of any actual living person. It may be an entirely fictional character. In *United States v. Whorley*[241] the Fourth Circuit Court of Appeals upheld the conviction of a Virginia man under the PROTECT Act for downloading Japanese anime cartoons depicting what appeared to be underage fictional characters engaging in sexually explicit conduct.

It is a defense to a charge of possession or transmission of drawings of obscenity involving a minor that the defendant possessed no more than two such images, has not shared them with anyone other than law enforcement, and either (a) took reasonable steps to destroy them or (b) reported and tuned over the images to law enforcement.

Utah and several other states have enacted laws prohibiting drawings or cartoon depictions of children engaged in sexual activity (including lewd exhibitions). State laws vary with respect to such things as whether the cartoon or drawing must depict an actual, living child or not; whether cartoons that are not life-like are permitted or not; and the age of the person or character depicted.

The United States is not the only country with laws against possessing, sending or receiving drawings of minors engaging in sexual activities. In 2008, an Australian appellate court upheld the conviction of an Internet user for possessing drawings of The Simpsons characters engaging in sexual intercourse. Canada, too, has enacted a law prohibiting fictional depictions of children involved in sexual activities. France prohibits making a pornographic drawing that depicts a person under fifteen years of age. A New Zealand court has ruled that country's law against drawings of children engaging in sexual activities extends to anime drawings depicting sex between fantasy creatures. Drawings depicting children engaged in sexual conduct are illegal in England, Wales and Northern Ireland regardless of whether they are realistic or not.

RECORDKEEPING

Anyone who produces an image (photograph, video, or digitally created) of actual human beings engaged in actual or simulated sexually explicit conduct must check each model's ID and keep records of every model's name, date of birth, and any alias or other name the model has ever used. The law establishing this requirement is the Child Protection and Obscenity Enforcement Act[242] (CPOEA). This law also requires the producer to attach a statement to each copy of the image describing where the record is located. For websites, the statement must be posted on every page on which an image depicting human sexual conduct appears.

Failure to comply with CPOEA requirements or a regulation issued pursuant to CPOEA is a crime, as is falsifying a required record or statement. The regulations are specific and detailed. They appear at 28 CFR §§ 75.1–75.9. Violations are punishable by a fine and up to five years imprisonment (ten years for a second violation) for depictions of actual sexual activity; and a fine and up to a year in prison for a depiction of simulated sexual activity.

The CPOEA also makes it a crime for anybody (not just the producer of the image) to knowingly sell, transfer or offer to sell or transfer an image without the required statement attached to it. Unless the seller or transferor is the creator of the image, however, there is no obligation to determine the accuracy of the statement or of the image creator's records.

The Act purports to require the producer to permit the U.S. Attorney General's office to inspect these records, a fine and imprisonment being the punishment for refusal. Whether this requirement is consistent with the Fourth Amendment prohibition against unreasonable searches would seem to be a legitimate question to ask.

The definition of *producer* is very broad. It is not limited to photographers, directors, and those who arrange for the participation of the performers. It also includes those who publish or digitize an existing image, compile or assemble a collection of images, or reproduce or reissue an image intended for commercial distribution. Website operators are expressly included. Thus, a website owner who inserts sexually explicit content—such as a third party banner advertisement containing a sexually explicit image—into the website will need to comply with federal record-keeping requirements.

Excluded from the definition are:

(a) photo processing and digitization services that are not otherwise involved in creating or commercially exploiting the image
(b) distributors (as distinguished from publishers)
(c) ISPs and telecommunications service providers
(d) search engines
(e) hosting, storage, retrieval, transmission, formatting, or translation of a communication with no selection or alteration of content besides removing what is believed to be obscene, "filthy" or objectionable material.

Recordkeeping requirements do not apply to images of adults lewdly exhibiting their genitals if they were created before 2009, provided no other sexual activity is depicted.

For those who qualify for it, an exemption exists for (a) images of adults lewdly exhibiting their genitals, whenever created, that do not also depict sexual activity and (b) images of simulated sexual activity by adults. To qualify for this exemption, a statement must be sent to the Attorney General of the United States certifying that individually identifiable information (name, address and date of birth) regarding all performers is collected and maintained in the regular course of business pursuant to federal and state tax, labor, and other laws, labor agreements, or otherwise pursuant to industry standards. This exemption does not apply to child pornography or images that are marketed (either explicitly or implicitly) as child pornography. It also does not apply to depictions of actual sexual activity between human beings of any age (other than lewd genital exhibitions).

The Tenth Circuit Court of Appeals has held that the provision requiring a publisher who was not involved in arranging for a performer's participation to keep these records is unconstitutional.[243] Whether courts in other circuits or the United States Supreme Court would agree is not known.

Harassment Using Obscenity or Child Pornography

47 U.S.C. § 223 makes it a crime to use the Internet to knowingly make or solicit, and transmit an obscene image, comment, request, suggestion, proposal or communication, or child pornography, with the intent to harass, abuse or threaten someone. It is also a crime to knowingly allow a telecommunications facility to be used for this purpose.

Offering or Providing Obscenity or Pornography to Children

Knowingly sending or trying to send obscenity to a person who is under sixteen years of age is prohibited by 18 U.S.C. § 1470. Penalties include a fine and/or up to ten years imprisonment.

Knowingly offering, sending, distributing or providing to a minor a visual depiction of what is or appears to be a minor engaging in sexual explicit conduct for purposes of inducing the minor to engage in an illegal activity is prohibited by 18 U.S.C. § 2252A.

Knowingly making a commercial communication via the Internet that includes obscenity and is available to a minor under seventeen years of age is prohibited by 47 U.S.C. § 231.

Knowingly producing, soliciting or transmitting child pornography or an obscene request, comment, proposal, suggestion, image or communication to a person who is under eighteen years of age, or using an interactive computer service in a way that makes the material available for a person who is under eighteen years of age to view it is prohibited by 47 U.S.C. § 223. It is also a federal crime to knowingly allow a telecommunications facility to be used for these kinds of activities. Restricting access to such communications by requiring the use of a verified credit card, debit account, adult access code, or adult PIN is a defense. Taking any other good faith, reasonable, effective and appropriate actions to restrict or prevent access by minors is also a defense. Implementation of an effective age verification system is also a defense to claim for damages for the consequences of a minor's access to the website or service.

An employer or principal may be held vicariously liable for an employee's or agent's violation of this law only if the employee or agent was acting within the scope of his employment or agency and the employer knowingly authorized or ratified the conduct or recklessly disregarded it.

State and local laws also prohibit the display of obscenity or child pornography to a minor. Both civil and criminal penalties may be imposed for violation of these laws.

PORNOGRAPHY IN LIBRARIES

Website owners are not required to ensure that pornographic images on their sites are not accessible in libraries. As a condition of receiving federal funds, the Children's Internet Protection Act[244] requires all public libraries to install software that blocks obscene or pornographic images from being viewed on their computers.

Misleading Domain Names and Keywords

Knowingly using a misleading domain name or a misleading keyword or image in meta tags with the intention of deceiving someone into viewing obscenity is prohibited by 18 U.S.C. § 2252B(a). A domain name that indicates the sexual nature of the content (such as "sex" or "porn") is not a violation of this statute. Using a revelatory domain name or a warning notice to alert visitors to the fact that the site contains obscene material does not protect the website operator from criminal liability, though. A website operator may be prosecuted for transmitting, selling, etc. obscenity even if he is completely open and honest about it.

18 U.S.C. §§ 2252B(b) and 2252C prohibit the use of misleading domain names, words, or digital images with the intent to deceive a minor into viewing harmful or obscene material. For purposes of these statutes, "harmful" means material that meets all of the following criteria:

(a) depicts nudity, sexual intercourse, masturbation, physical contact with a person's genitals, excretion, or the condition of human male or female genitals in a state of arousal

(b) taken as a whole, predominantly appeals to the prurient interest of minors

(c) is patently offensive to prevailing standards in the adult community with respect to what is suitable material for minors

(d) lacks serious literary, artistic, political, or scientific value for minors.

A domain name that includes a word that indicates the sexual content of the site (such as "sex" or "porn") is not misleading, and therefore would not violate this law.

PAGEJACKING AND MOUSETRAPPING

Pagejacking is the practice of duplicating legitimate websites and involuntarily diverting Internet users to another website, typically a sexually explicit website. *Mouse trapping* refers to disabling a browser's 'Back' and 'Exit' commands so that a user's efforts to leave the site opens additional windows. The FTC has taken the position that using these methods to force sexually explicit conduct on a user (or to make such content continue to appear) is an unfair or deceptive trade practice.

Harmful Material

The Child Online Protection Act[245] (COPA) does more than outlaw obscenity or child pornography. It makes it a crime to knowingly make any communication for commercial purposes using the World Wide Web that is:

(a) harmful to minors; and
(b) available to a person who is under seventeen years of age.

The definition of "harmful" is broad enough to include obscenity and child pornography, but it also reaches materials that do not come within the meanings of those terms. Material may be harmful to minors even if it consists only of textual matter. Harmful material includes any communication, picture, image, graphic image file, article, recording, writing, or anything else that falls into either of the following categories:

(a) obscenity
(b) a depiction, description or representation of an actual or simulated sex act or sexual contact, an actual or simulated normal or perverted sexual act, or a lewd exhibition of genitals or a postpubescent female breast, in a way that (i) is patently offensive with respect to minors under seventeen years of age; (ii) the average person, applying contemporary community standards, would find, taking the material as a whole and with respect to minors under seventeen years of age, is designed to appeal to, or is designed to pander to, the prurient interest; and (iii) taken as a whole, lacks serious literary, artistic, political, or scientific value for minors under seventeen years of age.

In addition to imprisonment, a fine of $50,000 per day may be imposed for each day that this law is intentionally and knowingly violated. A civil penalty of $50,000 per day may also be imposed.

This statute does not apply to:

(a) telecommunications carriers providing telecommunications services
(b) Internet access providers
(c) businesses providing Internet search tools
(d) persons engaged in the transmission, storage, retrieval, hosting, formatting, or translation (or any combination thereof) of communications made by another person, without selection or alteration of the content of the communication.

COPA also does not apply to noncommercial transmissions, such as material shared for free in chat rooms or via email.

Restricting access by minors to material that is harmful to minors is a defense if one of the following methods is used to restrict access by minors:

(a) requiring the use of a credit card, debit account, adult access code, or adult PIN;
(b) accepting a digital certificate that verifies age;
(c) any other reasonable, technologically feasible measure to restrict access to material by minors.

Information gathered in any of these processes must be protected from disclosure to anyone other than the individual providing it if the individual providing it is over sixteen years of age, or the individual's parent or legal guardian if the individual is less than seventeen years of age.

CONSTITUTIONALITY

The U.S. Supreme Court has declared that obscenity and child pornography are not protected by the First Amendment. Although obscenity and child pornography are not constitutionally protected, the First Amendment does impose limitations on how a government may define these terms. Accordingly, the First Amendment may still be invoked to challenge an obscenity or pornography law, or a law prohibiting "harmful" or "offensive" material, on the grounds that it is either vague or overbroad.

A law is overbroad if it is so worded that it proscribes both protected and unprotected speech. A law is vague if it worded in such an uncertain way that it has a chilling effect on protected speech. The prohibition against vague criminal laws is an aspect of Due Process under the Fifth and Fourteenth Amendments. The idea is that it would be fundamentally unfair to punish a person for a crime without first giving adequate notice of the particular conduct that is proscribed.

Applying these principles the Supreme Court, in *Reno v. ACLU*,[246] struck down a provision of the CDA that prohibited the display of a patently offensive comment, image or other communication in such a way that it could be seen by a minor. The Court held that the phrase *patently offensive*, left undefined, is unconstitutionally vague and overbroad. The term *indecent* is also unconstitutionally vague, if left undefined. Subsequently, in *Ashcroft v. ACLU*,[247] the Court held that the phrase *contemporary community standards* is not so overbroad or vague as to violate the Constitution, even when a statute leaves it undefined. *Ashcroft* did not decide whether other provisions of COPA, as amended after *Reno*, are constitutional.

In 1999, a federal district court granted the American Civil Liberties Union's request for an injunction against enforcement of COPA on the basis that its other provisions are likely to be unconstitutionally vague and overbroad. In 2004, the U.S. Supreme Court issued a decision allowing the injunction against enforcement to stand. Then in 2008, the Third Circuit Court of Appeals, in *ACLU v. Mukasey*,[248] ruled that COPA, even as amended, is unconstitutionally vague and overbroad. The U.S. Supreme Court denied review of that decision. This has left COPA of uncertain constitutional validity in most jurisdictions. Given that the Supreme Court has allowed the injunction against enforcement to stand, attempts to enforce it do not seem likely. Nevertheless, it remains on the books until somebody is successful in securing review and obtaining a ruling on the merits by the Supreme Court.

Although the Supreme Court has approved government regulation of obscenity on the Internet, it has also held that the government does not necessarily have as much power to regulate Internet content as it has to regulate the content of radio and television broadcasts.

A federal court in New York has held that since Internet transmissions of digitized goods are interstate commerce, state regulation of the content of Internet transmissions based on localized community moral standards violates the Commerce Clause because it unduly burdens interstate commerce.[249] Whether the Supreme Court would interpret the Commerce Clause this way remains to be seen.

Immunity from Liability for Censorship

The First Amendment only limits the power of governments to censor the speech of others. No one has a "constitutional right" to publish anything they wish to another person's website. A duty to refrain from preventing or removing another person's publication of content may arise in other ways, though. For example, a contract with a publisher could provide that the author has complete creative control over the content of the work to be created. A commercial website's Terms of Use might make representations about what may and may not be posted, giving rise to a duty, under false advertising laws, to operate the website in a manner consistent with those representations.

To encourage private censorship of user-provided content, the CDA shields providers and users of interactive computer services from liability for restricting access to, or the availability of, any material that the provider or user considers objectionable, even if the material is constitutionally protected. This includes anything the provider or user considers obscene, lewd, lascivious, filthy, excessively violent, harassing, "or otherwise objectionable."

The CDA also shields users and providers from liability for enabling others to use technical means to restrict access to material they find objectionable, or for making those technical means available to people.

Notice of Commercially Available Parental Controls

The CDA requires providers of interactive computer services to give users notice that methods of limiting access to the website by minors are available. The notice must be given at the time the user enters into an agreement for the service, such as at the time the user clicks the 'I Agree' button to signify assent to the terms of service. It must inform the customer that parental control protections (such as computer hardware, software, or filtering services) are commercially available that may assist the customer in limiting access to material that is harmful to minors. The notice must identify, or provide the customer with access to information identifying, current providers of such protections.

Sexually Oriented Email

The CAN-SPAM Act requires email messages containing sexually oriented material to include the warning "SEXUALLY-EXPLICIT" at the beginning of the subject line. In addition, the message must be sent in the electronic equivalent of a brown paper wrapper. When a recipient opens the message, the only things that may be viewable on the recipient's screen are (a) the words "SEXUALLY-EXPLICIT" and (b) the same information that is required in any other commercial email, namely, a disclosure that the message is an advertisement; the sender's physical postal address; and the procedure for how recipients may opt out of receiving messages from the sender in the future.

The message must be composed in such a way that no graphics appear on the screen when the recipient first opens the message. That is to say, it must be constructed in such a way that the recipient has to take some affirmative act, in addition to opening the message, to access sexually explicit content. This affirmative act might be scrolling down, clicking on a link, or the like.

The "brown wrapper" requirement does not apply if the recipient has already given affirmative consent to receive the sender's sexually oriented messages.

Laws of Other Countries

Nearly every country regulates sexually explicit material in some way. Some countries, such as China, have very strict prohibitions against sexually explicit materials and regulate sexuality much more closely than the United States does. In Iran, Mauritania, Nigeria, Saudi Arabia, Sudan, Yemen, for example, homosexuality is a crime punishably by death. Adultery is punishable by death in some countries. Publishing material that depicts, encourages or facilitates these activities may have serious consequences in those countries. Because website content may be used as evidence, people who have published material that may be construed as an admission or advocacy of adultery or homosexuality should avoid traveling to these countries.

Definitions of obscenity and child pornography vary from country to country, as do the penalties for those crimes. As has been seen, the extent to which drawings of fictional characters engaging in sexual activity is permitted varies from country to country, as well.

Chapter 20. Computer Crime and Abuse

Computer crime (sometimes called "cybercrime") is an umbrella term for any crime involving a computer. There are two kinds: (a) using a computer to commit a traditional crime, such as theft, fraud, extortion, stalking, etc.; (b) unlawfully accessing or harming a computer, such as transmitting malicious code or hacking into it. Laws penalizing computer crimes exist on the international, federal and state levels. They often overlap.

The Council of Europe's Convention on Cybercrime is an international treaty to which the United States, most European countries, and several other counties are parties. It seeks to harmonize computer crime laws around the world by requiring member countries to criminalize the knowing and intentional creation or transmission of computer viruses or malware. It also requires member countries to enact laws imposing criminal penalties for computer-related fraud and child pornography offenses. It makes computer crimes extraditable offenses and requires member countries to cooperate in investigations and prosecutions.

In the United States, the CFAA is the principal piece of national cybercrime legislation. It prohibits several kinds of computer crimes and includes an asset forfeiture provision.

The CFAA also authorizes a civil action for damages and/or injunctive relief for any person who is injured by a violation if the defendant's conduct caused any of the following:

(a) economic loss aggregating at least $5,000 in a one-year period
(b) modification or impairment of a medical examination, diagnosis, or treatment
(c) potential modification or impairment of a medical examination, diagnosis or treatment
(d) physical injury
(e) threat to public health or safety
(f) damage affecting a computer used by or for the federal government.

Among other things, damages may include the cost of returning the computer to its previous condition, lost revenue, and other consequential damages caused by an interruption of service.

The CFAA applies to "protected" computers. A *protected computer* is one that is used in interstate or foreign commerce or communication, or that is used by or for the U.S. government or a financial institution. Because it applies to any computer that is used in interstate or foreign commerce or communication, it applies to any computer with an Internet connection. Cell phones that are capable of performing logical and storage functions are considered computers.

When an activity is prohibited by the CFAA, attempting, aiding or abetting, and conspiring to do it are also prohibited.

The FTC Act is another significant piece of legislation. It prohibits "unfair or deceptive trade practices" in interstate or foreign commerce. A *deceptive* trade practice is a representation, omission or conduct that is likely to mislead a consumer acting reasonably in the circumstances, to the consumer's detriment. A trade practice is *unfair* all three of the following criteria apply:

(a) It causes or is likely to cause substantial injury to consumers;
(b) The injury is not reasonably avoidable by the consumers themselves;
(c) The harm outweighs any countervailing benefits to consumers or to competition.

Many of the activities described in this chapter are unfair or deceptive trade practices within the meaning of the FTC Act. The FTC Act is limited to conduct that is committed for a commercial purpose and harmful to consumers. The CFAA is not limited in this way. It applies to both commercial and noncommercial activity, and its protections are not only for consumers but for businesses and governmental entities, too.

Unauthorized Access

The CFAA makes it a crime to intentionally access a nonpublic computer of a federal department or agency without authorization. It is also a crime to knowingly access any protected computer without authorization, or in excess of the authorization given, to obtain information in any of the following categories:

(a) that the U.S. government has determined should not be disclosed without authorization, if it is reasonably believed that the information could be used to the detriment of the United States or to the advantage of a foreign country
(b) from a department or agency of the federal government
(c) in a financial record of a financial institution, a card issuer, or a consumer reporting agency (e.g., a credit bureau)
(d) from any protected computer.

In short, accessing a computer that is connected to the Internet without authorization or in excess of the authorization given is prohibited. This covers what is commonly known as "hacking" but it is broader than that. A hacker is a person who finds and exploits a weakness in a computer system or network to gain access. A person need not find or exploit a weakness in order to exceed an authorization given.

> **Example.** Okra.com restricts access to authorized users. Ike Twister registers with the website and is issued a user name and password. He then shares his user name and password with his wife, Trina, who downloads an okra recipe from the site. Trina has violated the CFAA. Since Ike aided and abetted her commission of the crime, he has violated the CFAA, too.

Intent to gain unauthorized access is a necessary element of this crime. It is not a crime to accidentally gain unauthorized access to a computer. Direct evidence is not required, however. Intent may be proven by circumstantial evidence.

Neither harm nor intent to cause harm is required. People have been convicted of "unauthorized access" crimes even when their sole intention was to illustrate a security vulnerability in the interest of helping a company learn how to better protect itself. Unauthorized access that causes harm is also a crime, and unauthorized access "in furtherance of any criminal or tortious act" are also crimes. Enhanced penalties are provided for them. Supplying false information (such as a fake profile on a social media account) for the purpose of harassing or inflicting emotional distress on another computer user, or hacking into another person's computer to install a virus, are examples of such crimes. If the website only authorizes people who provide truthful profile information to access it, though, then using a fake profile to access the website is a violation of the CFAA even if it is done without any criminal or malicious intent.

Using an anonymous proxy is not illegal per se, but using one for the purpose of bypassing an IP block that was set up to prevent the person from accessing a computer (or to prevent the person from gaining unauthorized access to information residing on the computer) may violate the CFAA.

The CFAA prohibits accessing a computer "in excess of" authorization as well as accessing a computer "without" authorization. A user who rightfully gains access to a computer would be violating the CFAA if she accessed information to which the terms of service prohibit access or used a service offered by the website in a way that the Terms of Use prohibit. If a person is given access to another person's computer for a limited purpose and then uses it for different or additional purposes, then logically it would seem that the person has exceeded the authority given and could be prosecuted under the CFAA. For example, if an employee is given access to a work computer only for work-related purposes and then uses the computer to play fantasy football or engage in some other activity that is not work-related, then the employee would seem to have exceeded the authority given.

Courts are not in agreement on the question whether the CFAA is violated when the use of a computer is authorized but the purpose for which the computer is used is neither expressly authorized nor expressly prohibited. In *International Airport Centers, L.L.C. v. Citrin*[250] the Seventh Circuit Court of Appeals held that access is unauthorized for purposes of the CFAA when an employee accesses the employer's computer for a purpose that is contrary to the employer's interest. The court reasoned that because employees owe an implied duty of loyalty to their employers, an employer cannot reasonably be deemed to have authorized an employee to access the employer's computer for purposes of breaching the duty of loyalty. The Ninth Circuit Court of Appeals rejected this approach. In *LVRC Holdings v. Brekka*,[251] the court held that an authorized user's use of a computer for a purpose that is not expressly prohibited does not violate the CFAA. According to the Ninth Circuit Court of Appeals, CFAA liability cannot be predicated on implied limitations on use. The split among the circuits makes the issue appropriate for Supreme Court review, should a case raising the issue come before it. In the meantime, e-commerce businesses should be very specific, both in their Terms of Use and in their contracts with employees, about the uses of the company's computers and website that are prohibited

Unauthorized access to a stored communication or intercepting an electronic communication while in transit may violate the ECPA. See Chapter 17. Unauthorized access to a computer to steal a trade secret is prohibited by 18 U.S.C. §§ 1831–1832.

Trafficking in Passwords

It is a violation of the CFAA to traffic in passwords or other information that may be used to access a computer without authorization.

Harming a Computer

The CFAA makes it a crime to knowingly cause the transmission of a program, code, command or other content that intentionally causes damage to a protected computer without authorization. The CFAA also makes it a crime to intentionally access a protected computer without authorization and with resulting damage or loss. Both criminal and civil penalties may be imposed for a violation.

Federal and state laws make intentional damage (or "malicious mischief") to government property or communication lines a crime. This could include computers.[252]

State common law causes of action for damages provide remedies for harming a computer, too. The old common law cause of action for trespass to chattels, in particular, has found a new use today as a means of attacking computer crime. Historically developed to make people pay for the loss of value of wrongfully injured livestock, the cause of action for trespass to chattels has since been extended to any kind of tangible personal property. The elements of a claim are:

(a) intentional physical interference with another person's
(b) possessory right in personal property
(c) resulting in injury or damage to the property.

Basically, trespass to chattels means damaging the personal property of another by causing a diminution in its usefulness or value. The injury or damage may include dispossessing a person of the property, but it can also involve acts that diminish the usefulness or value of property without actually dispossessing a person of it. The injury, however, must consist of something more than an affront to a person's dignity.

The measure of damages for trespass to chattels is the diminution in value of the property, including the value of the use of the property, that is caused by the trespass. Since a computer (e.g., a server) is personal property, unauthorized access to it in a way that diminishes its value or usefulness could be actionable as a trespass to chattel.

VIRUSES, WORMS, AND OTHER MALWARE

The CFAA prohibits the unauthorized and knowing transmission of viruses,[253] worms,[254] Trojan horses,[255] logic/time bombs,[256] mousetraps,[257] or other malicious code that causes damage to a computer. Damage to a computer may include damage to files on the computer, hard drives, networks or servers. Under the Convention on Cybercrime, it is an extraditable offense.

SPIDERS, ROBOTS AND SCRAPING

Scraping data from another website, in excess of the authority granted in the Terms of Use, is a violation of the CFAA.[258]

Using spiders and robots to gather ("scrape") information from other websites may also be a form of trespass to chattel, the common law cause of action for damage to property that entitles the victim to an award of compensatory damages. Some courts have held computers, including servers, to be chattel (i.e., personal property) and that sending electrons to make contact with them is physical contact with the property. Increased use of disk space and processing time may suffice as an injury to the property, since those things decrease the value of the property to users.

If the electrons interfere with another person's use or enjoyment of his computer, hard drive, processor, or server, then liability for trespass to chattels should actually be fairly easy to establish. This may happen when access to the server significantly reduces its available memory and processing power.

Robotically and repeatedly performing search functions on a website/server for information may be a kind of trespass to chattel if it has the effect of significantly reducing available memory or processing power. Some courts hold that the cumulative effect if multiple people were to do this at the same time may be considered in determining whether an individual's conduct significantly reduces available memory or processing power.

DENIAL OF SERVICE ATTACKS

A denial of service attack occurs when a person maliciously incapacitates an Internet server by inundating it with sham requests for web pages. This kind of activity may be prosecuted under various laws, such as laws against unauthorized access or harm to a computer, or malicious mischief.

VIRTUAL VANDALISM

Virtual vandalism, the unauthorized alteration of another person's web page, is most often done maliciously for the purpose of embarrassing the website owner. An example would be hacking into a website and changing the hypertext links so that they point to pornographic websites. This kind of activity may be prosecuted under the CFAA and a variety of other criminal laws.

Fraud

Fraud is both an actionable tort and a crime. Unfortunately, the Internet provides an all too convenient vehicle for committing it. With the advent of the Internet, fraud reports have soared. Of these, identity theft is among the most pernicious. Identity theft is a shorthand term for unlawfully acquiring or using someone else's personal information (such as a Social Security number), usually for the purpose of obtaining money, credit or other things of value. It is accomplished in a number of different ways. Numerous criminal and civil anti-fraud laws exist at both the federal and state levels, and both common law and statutory remedies exist.

ACCESSING A COMPUTER WITH FRAUDULENT INTENT

The CFAA makes it a crime to knowingly access a protected computer, without authorization or in excess of authorization given, with intent to defraud. No violation of the CFAA occurs, however, unless the defendant obtains something of value. The thing of value must be either (a) something other than merely the use of the computer, or (b) the use of the computer, where the value of such use is at least $5,000 in a one-year period. In other words, if the only thing obtained through the fraud is the use of another person's computer, then it is not a violation of the CFAA if the value of the use over a one-year period is less than $5,000.

The so-called Nigerian scam is an example of conduct that may violate this provision. The name derives from one of the earliest forms of fraud using email, in which the scammer falsely represents that he is a representative of Nigerian royalty or of a wealthy Nigerian individual who wants to protect money by putting it into an American bank account. The email recipient is promised a large fee or a share of the money for setting up an account in the royal or wealthy person's name in the United States. To demonstrate "good faith," the scammer requires the email recipient to make a deposit of his own money into the account. Once the "good faith deposit" is made, the scammer withdraws it, never to be heard from again. The identity-theft version of the Nigerian scam involves deceiving the email recipient into sharing personal and/or account information with a purported "attorney," "escrow agent" or the like. Variants of the scam abound. If the Terms of Use of an email service provider state that the service may not be used to communicate false information or to commit a crime against another user, then the scammer exceeds the authorized use with the intent to commit fraud and is in violation of the CFAA if anybody falls for the scam. The activity may also violate other laws, as well, including but not necessarily limited to Nigerian laws.

DECEPTIVE TRADE PRACTICES

The FTC Act prohibits unfair or deceptive trade practices. A deceptive trade practice is a representation, omission or conduct that is likely to mislead a consumer acting reasonably in the circumstances, to the consumer's detriment. Comparable laws have been enacted at the state level. These laws are limited to trade practices affecting consumers.

CIRCUMVENTING TICKET SALES CONTROLS

15 U.S.C. § 45c makes it an unfair or deceptive trade practice to circumvent a security measure on a ticket issuer's website or online service that is used to enforce purchasing limits or maintain the integrity of posted ticket purchasing order rules. It is also an unfair or deceptive trade practice to offer or sell an event ticket obtained in this manner.

SPOOFING

Causing an email to appear to have been sent from a source different from the one that actually sent it is known as spoofing. It is accomplished by falsifying the routing information for a message or forging an email header to make it look like it comes from a trusted source. This may violate federal or state fraud laws. It also violates the CAN-SPAM Act, infra.

PHISHING

This is a kind of fraud in which a website is set up to look like it is the official site of a financial institution or a reputable company with the expectation that it will trick people into divulging their account numbers, user names, passwords or other personally identifiable or sensitive information. Fraudsters often use it in combination with spoofing: A spoofed message appearing to be from a bank, credit card company or a reputable company directs the recipient to the phony website. In many cases, the phony website has been set up to look identical or very similar to the reputable company's website. In the typical case, the email message falsely asserts that the recipeent needs to update his account or the information that is on file with the company. The website prompts users to provide their names, account numbers, passwords and/or other identifying information. Upon divulging this information, the "phisher" then proceeds to use it to commit identity theft or to sell it to others. If someone takes the bait and suffers loss as a result, then the "phisher" may be liable for fraud under the CFAA, another statute, or common law.

Sending a spoofed email message is not the only method of directing people to a "phishing" web site. Placing hypertext links to it on other websites is another method, as is using keywords in meta tags to cause the website to turn up in people's search results.

Spear phishing is a kind of phishing that is tailored to a particular targeted individual and involves a person posing as a bank, credit card company or other person or business whom the individual knows or with whom the individual has a business relationship. There are no significant legal differences between spear phishing and other kinds of phishing.

PHARMING

Pharming is similar to phishing. It is the practice of setting up a website that appears to be that of another person or business (such as a bank) and redirecting traffic to this site, the goal being to deceive visitors to the dummy site into divulging their user names, passwords and possibly other personally identifying information. It is accomplished by either implanting software to alter the host file on the victim's computer or exploiting vulnerability in DNS servers. Depending on how it is accomplished, pharming may violate several different anti-fraud laws, and may be actionable at common as fraud or trespass to chattel.

PRETEXTING

Pretexting is the practice of obtaining personal information by impersonating another person. Several laws prohibit it. For example, the FTC's Pretexting Rule, enacted pursuant to the GLBA, makes it unlawful to obtain customer information from financial institutions under false pretenses. The Telephone Records and Privacy Protection Act makes it unlawful to make a false or fraudulent statement to obtain or transfer confidential telephone records. It is similar to the crime of obtaining money or property by false pretenses, which is a theft crime in most jurisdictions.

ONLINE AUCTIONS

Conducting an online auction is not fraudulent or criminal per se. A scheme in which a bidder is required to pay in advance of delivery but is never sent the item might be fraudulent, though, if the person who offered the item for auction never intended to send it. Online auction fraud also may occur where a person makes a false or misleading statement about what is being auctioned or the price or delivery terms.

WIRE FRAUD

Obtaining money or property by making false or fraudulent statements or promises using wire (e.g., accessing the Internet using a telephone land line), radio or television communication is wire fraud. 18 U.S.C. § 1343. Penalties range up to $1,000,000 fine and 30 years imprisonment.

COMMON LAW FRAUD

The elements of a common law action for damages for fraud are:

(a) intentional representation or omission
(b) of a material fact
(c) that is false or misleading
(d) with intent to induce
(e) and that actually does induce
(f) reasonable or justifiable reliance by another person
(g) resulting in economic loss to that person.

Threats

Under the CFAA, it is unlawful to make an extortionate threat to damage a computer, to steal data, or to publicly disclose stolen data. It is also unlawful to request money in relation to damage to a protected computer where the damage was caused to facilitate the extortion.

In addition, 18 U.S.C. § 875 makes it a crime to send a communication containing a

(a) a threat to inflict bodily harm on a person;
(b) a threat to kidnap a person;
(c) a demand for a ransom or reward for the release of a kidnapped person; or
(d) a threat to injure property or reputation or to accuse someone of a crime, for the purpose of extortion.

State laws also make the communication of a threat a crime. Definitions vary, but in general the crime consists of intentionally communicating an expression of a serious intention to commit an illegal act of violence against a particular person or group of persons. In some circumstances, such as where it causes the recipient to suffer emotional distress, communicating a threat may also result in civil liability.

A true threat of bodily harm is not protected by the First Amendment. But a threat transmitted via the Internet may be protected by the First Amendment if the speaker did not act with either the intent to actually carry it out or knowledge that the words used would cause the person at whom it is directed to fear actual harm. The fact that some person subjectively felt threatened, or even that a reasonable person would have felt threatened, is not enough, if the speaker did not have actual intent to do harm or knowledge that the words used would cause the targeted person to fear actual harm. Negligent phrasing is not a crime.

Harassment and Cyberstalking

In most states, it is a crime to stalk or harass another person. In several states, these activities are also actionable as civil wrongs. These laws are usually worded broadly enough that they would cover situations in which an Internet website or blog is used to stalk or harass someone.

Definitions vary from state to state. Typically, they require proof of some unwanted or offensive conduct or contact that is intended to and/or does cause fear or annoyance to a particular person. Many states prohibit harassment only if a threat of physical harm is made. In some states, such as Florida, communications that serve no legitimate purpose other than to cause substantial emotional distress to a specific person qualify as cyberstalking or harassment even if they do not involve a threat of physical harm.

The quickest way to run afoul of online harassment laws is to create a web page for the purpose of being mean to a particular individual. Repeatedly sending emails or posting mean and/or embarrassing content about a person is another way. These are just examples. They are not the only possibilities.

Interstate stalking is a federal offense. 18 U.S.C. § 2261A. It is a crime to use an interactive computer service or an electronic communication service or system (e.g., a website, blog, or email service) to harass, injure, kill, intimidate, or place another person under surveillance with the intent to do so, if it causes such person to be placed in reasonable fear of death or serious bodily injury to himself, an immediate family member, or a spouse or intimate partner; or could reasonably be expected to cause substantial emotional distress to any such person.

Spam

The CAN-SPAM Act imposes a number of disclosure requirements on senders of email messages. It also regulates the sending of sexually explicit email messages. These are discussed in Chapters 15 and 19. The CAN-SPAM Act also seeks to protect the public against unwanted, false or misleading email. In addition to provisions of the Act that are discussed elsewhere in this book, the CAN-SPAM Act makes all of the following kinds of activities crimes:

(a) accessing a computer without authorization and sending multiple commercial email messages through it

(b) using a computer to relay or retransmit multiple commercial email messages with the intent to deceive or mislead recipients or an ISP as to the origin of the messages

(c) accessing a computer without authorization and using it to knowingly relay or retransmit a commercial email message to a recipient who has opted out, or that has false or misleading header information or that fails to include a functional return address or other mechanism for opting out or that fails to make all required disclosures

(d) registering five or more email or online user accounts, or two or more domain names, and sending multiple commercial email messages from two or more accounts or domain names

(e) using scripts or other automated means to register for multiple email accounts or online user accounts from which to send or enable another person to send a commercial email message to a recipient who has opted out, or that has false or misleading header information or that fails to include a functional return address or other mechanism for opting out or that fails to make all required disclosures

(f) falsely representing oneself to be the registrant of five or more IP addresses and sending multiple commercial email messages from them

(g) sending an email message to a recipient who has opted out—or that has false or misleading header information or that fails to include a functional return address or other mechanism for opting out or that fails to make all required disclosures—or providing such an email address to another for sending, knowing the recipient's email address was obtained using automated means either: (i) from a website or service that included a notice that the operator will not give, sell or transfer addresses maintained by the website or service to anyone for the purpose of sending or enabling others to send email messages, or (ii) that generates possible email addresses by combining names, letters or numbers into numerous permutations.

A *commercial* email message is an email message with the primary purpose of advertising or promoting a commercial product or service, including content on a website that is operated for a commercial purpose. Including a reference to a commercial entity or a link to the website of a commercial entity in an electronic mail message does not, by itself, cause the message to be treated as a commercial email message if the primary propose of the message is something other than to advertise or promote a commercial product or service. Transactional and relationship messages are excluded from the definition of a commercial email message.

Transactional and relationship messages are messages the primary purpose of which is to do one or more of the following:

(a) facilitate, complete, or confirm a commercial transaction that the recipient has previously agreed to enter into with the sender
(b) provide warranty information, product recall information, or safety or security information with respect to a commercial product or service used or purchased by the recipient
(c) provide information directly related to an employment relationship or related benefit plan in which the recipient is currently involved, participating, or enrolled
(d) deliver goods or services, including product updates or upgrades, that the recipient is entitled to receive under the terms of a transaction that the recipient has previously agreed to enter into with the sender
(e) give the recipient information about an ongoing commercial relationship involving the ongoing purchase or use by the recipient of products or services offered by the sender, such as a subscription, membership account, or loan, if the information is (i) to notify the recipient of a change in the terms or features, (ii) to notify the recipient of a change in the recipient's standing or status, or (iii) account balance information or other type of account statement, which may be sent at periodic intervals.

It is a crime for a sender of an email message who receives an opt-out request from a recipient to thereafter send a commercial email message to that person if the person used the mechanism the sender provided for opting out. A grace period is provided for the first ten days after the sender receives the opt-out request. After that, neither the sender nor anyone acting on the sender's behalf may send a commercial email message to the person. Assisting in the sending of a message in violation of this provision is also a crime. Finally, it is unlawful for anyone with knowledge of the recipient's opt-out request to sell, lease, exchange, or transfer or release the recipient's email address for any purpose other than to comply with the requirements of the CAN-SPAM Act or other law. It is a defense that the recipient reaffirmed consent to receiving email messages from the sender subsequent to opting out.

Penalties for CAN-SPAM violations can be as high as $40,654 (the amount is adjusted periodically) per email message that violates the Act. It is enforced by the FTC and the U.S. Department of Justice. Although it expressly preempts state laws explicitly governing commercial email messages, exceptions exist for certain kinds of state laws. State laws that apply to noncommercial email messages, or to both commercial and noncommercial email messages, are not preempted. State laws addressing computer crime or fraud more generally are not preempted, either. State laws prohibiting fraud or deception in commercial email messages (or attachments to them) are not preempted. And contractual prohibitions against spam (such as in an Internet access provider's Terms of Use) remain enforceable under state law.

If a relevant service provider's or ISP's Terms of Use prohibit the use of the service to send spam, then violating the Terms of Use in this way may violate the CFAA.[259]

Sending spam may also result in common law liability for damages. An email system is the personal property of an ISP. An ISP may have a cause of action for trespass to chattels if a person uses the service in a manner that is not authorized by the Terms of Use. Thus, if the Terms of Use prohibit the sending of "spam" emails, then using the service to send such emails would expose the user to potential liability for breach of contract. Since a server is personal property, liability to the owner of the server that is used without authorization for the sending of spam might also subject the spammer to liability for trespass to chattels. A spammer who engages in spoofing may be liable for damages for trespass to chattels, fraud, false advertising or possibly even trademark infringement or dilution, if a trademark is involved. Liability for fraud requires proof of economic loss. Economic loss need not be extensive, though. It might consist in the spammer's use of storage space on the email service provider's computer system.

Because the "trespass to chattels" cause of action requires proof of an injury to property, small amounts of spamming that do not make an appreciable impact on a server's operations or disk storage space are not likely to be actionable. Even if common law liability does not exist, however, there may be statutory liability. In addition to the CAN-SPAM Act, a majority of states have enacted anti-spam laws of various kinds.

California and a number of other states have enacted laws requiring any business that advertises via email to California consumers to comply with California laws, including requirements that the advertiser provide a valid return address and inform the recipient of how to opt-out of receiving future email advertisements. Some states prohibit an online seller from sending an email solicitation to a consumer without prior permission. In Virginia, sending unsolicited emails is a felony.

The unauthorized use of a trademark in spam email may be actionable as infringement if it is sent to a substantial number of people and is likely to confuse the recipient about the origin, sponsorship or endorsement of goods or services. If it is a famous mark, the owner of the mark might be able to proceed against the spammer on a dilution theory in some cases.

In the European Union, the ePrivacy Directive establishes an opt-in regime for unsolicited email messages. It generally prohibits the sending of unsolicited email messages for marketing purposes without the recipient's prior consent. Prior consent is not required, however, if the business has an existing customer relationship with the recipient. Prior consent also is not required for marketing similar products or services. Moreover, a business that initially collects address data in the context of the sale of a product or service has the right to use it for commercial purposes provided the customer is given a prior opportunity to opt out of such communications.

HARVESTING EMAIL ADDRESSES

Harvesting email addresses and transmitting them through an email server or service without authorization (or in excess of the authorization given) generally will violate the CFAA.

Spyware

Spyware is a computer program that gathers information about a person without the person's knowledge, or exerts control over a person's computer without the person's knowledge. Adware, system monitors, tracking cookies, Trojans, keyloggers, rootkits, and web beacons are examples. It is principally used for the purposes of tracking and storing an Internet user's movements on the Web, customizing web content and serving up ads targeted to the user. Some, but not all, spyware uses are unfair or deceptive trade practices that violate the FTC Act. Using spyware to alter a consumer's homepage and deliver adware is an example.

A few states include spyware within the meaning of a state statutory prohibition against computer fraud and abuse. The state of Washington, for example, may impose a fine of up to $2,000,000 for planting software that opens when a consumer launches a browser. The statute also prohibits using spyware to harvest personally identifying information or to record keystrokes.

A court may apply the common law cause of action for trespass to chattels to hold people liable for damages for bundling spyware in computer program files. A user's computer is personal property ("chattel.") If including spyware in a program that is distributed to a computer user causes some nontrivial kind of damage to the user's computer, then liability for trespass to chattels may attach. Courts have held that taking up bandwidth on the user's Internet connection, or taking up memory on a user's computer, or causing a user's computer to slow down, or using screen space on a computer monitor, or reducing user productivity due to frustration, are substantial, not merely trivial, kinds of damage for which a computer user may sue.

Cookies

A *cookie* is information transmitted by a third party and saved by the user's web browser. When an Internet user visits a website, the site may place a cookie on the user's web browser so it can recognize the user's device in the future. When the user returns to the site, it can read that cookie to remember the user from her last visit and keep track of her over time. Cookies are used for a variety of purposes: collecting information about the pages a user views and her activities on the site; enabling the website to recognize the user; remembering the user's identity; online shopping carts; tracking a user's activities on the website, customizing the user's browsing experience; delivering targeted advertising to the user.

The use of cookies is not illegal per se in the United States, provided no false or deceptive representations are made. A false or misleading assertion about cookies may violate laws, including the FTC Act's prohibition against unfair or deceptive trade practices. Using cookies to collect information can also raise privacy and data security issues. See Chapters 13 and 17.

Cookie stuffing is an affiliate marketing technique that works like this: A company agrees to pay an affiliate a commission on every sale originating from the affiliate or a referral made by the affiliate. Usually it is anticipated that the affiliate will place an advertisement for the company or one of its products on the affiliate's website with a link to the company's website embedded in it. When a user clicks on the link, a purchase made at the website to which he is directed will be credited to the affiliate. Cookies facilitate this process. Cookie stuffing occurs when an affiliate causes cookies to be installed on the browsers of users who visit websites other than the one on which the affiliate's link appears. That way, anytime the user makes a purchase from the company's website, it will appear as though it resulted from an affiliate's link or referral, and a commission will be deposited to the affiliate's account. At least one court has held that cookie stuffing is a violation of the CFAA.[260]

Pop-up Ads

Requiring a user to pay a fee to prevent pop-up ads from constantly appearing on a website has been held to be an unfair or deceptive method of generating online revenue, violating a state's prohibition against unfair and deceptive trade practices.

Conversion

Conversion, another common law cause of action, is intended to compensate a personal property owner for another person's unlawful exercise of dominion and control over the property. Unlike trespass to chattels, damage to the property is not necessary. Conversion seeks to redress wrongful takings of property, not wrongful damage to property. The elements of a conversion claim are:

(a) exercise of dominion or control
(b) over specifically identifiable personal property
(c) to which another person has a right of immediate possession
(d) after a rightful demand for possession has been made.

The remedy for conversion is a "forced sale" of the property at its full value. This means that the person who is guilty of conversion keeps the property but will be ordered to pay the rightful owner its full value.

Early common law held that conversion only applied to tangible personal property, not to intangibles like intellectual property. This is still the case with respect to copyrights and patents. State common law claims for conversion of patents and copyrights are preempted by federal law. Some, but not all, states allow conversion claims for other kinds of intellectual property. Several states allow recovery for conversion of trade secrets and electronic records (such as customer databases.) And there have been cases in some states where recovery has been allowed for conversion of proprietary information.

Ransomware seems to be a kind of wrong for which the common law cause of action for conversion would be a perfect fit. Ransomware is malware that locks a person out of his own computer files (such as by encrypting them), usually with a demand for payment to regain access. If the computer owner makes a demand to regain possession, then it would seem that all of the necessary elements of a conversion claim would be present. Of course, a lawsuit would require tracking down the person responsible for the ransomware attack. That may be difficult to do.

Property crimes

Many property crime statutes have been enacted at the federal and state level. Common property-related crimes include theft, damage to property, receiving stolen property, and transporting stolen property. This is not an exhaustive list. The language of a particular enactment must be examined carefully to determine whether it applies to digital files. Sometimes legislative history and/or judicial decisions may also need to be consulted.

Slamming

Slamming is the act of changing a person's telephone service, or replacing a person's telephone service with a VoIP service without the person's consent. Under the Communications Act of 1934 and rules promulgated by the FCC, slamming is illegal unless the new company verifies the switch using one of the follow methods:

(a) using an independent third party to verify the customer's oral authorization to switch
(b) obtaining the customer's signature on a letter that indicates, in writing, that the customer wants to switch authorized telephone companies
(c) providing a toll free number that a customer can call to confirm the order to switch authorized telephone companies.

Reporting Computer Crimes

Computer crimes should be reported to local, state, federal and/or international law enforcement agencies, depending on the scope of the crime. In the United States, the federal law enforcement agencies to which reports should be made are as follows:

- Internet fraud or spam: FBI, FTC, U.S. Secret Service
- Internet fraud or child exploitation having a mail nexus: U.S. Postal Inspection Service
- Hacking or password trafficking: FBI, U.S. Secret Service
- Counterfeiting money: U.S. Secret Service
- Child pornography or exploitation (domestic), online harassment, theft of trade secret or economic espionage: FBI
- Child pornography or exploitation (imported), copyright piracy, FBI, ICE
- Counterfeiting: NIPRCC
- Intellectual property crimes: FBI, NIPRCC
- Securities fraud or investment-related spam: SEC
- Internet bomb threats or trafficking in firearms or explosive devices: BATF., FBI
- Incidents related to national security or infrastructure issues: DHS

The NIPRCC (National Intellectual Property Rights Coordination Center) is an online site for reporting intellectual property crimes. It may be accessed at https://www.iprcenter.gov/. In addition, the U.S. Department of Justice maintains a web page for reporting Internet crimes online, the Internet Crime Complaint Center, at https://www.ic3.gov/default.aspx

Chapter 21. User-Provided Content

There are many situations in which one person will be held legally responsible for another person's conduct. When conspirators plan a crime, each participant is responsible for the acts of the individual who carries out the plan. Employers and principals are vicariously liable for acts of their employees and agents, respectively, if committed within the course and scope of the employment or agency. Partners are liable for each other's conduct of partnership business. When a person aids, solicits, encourages or facilitates another person's wrongful act, she may incur contributory liability for it. This should worry anyone who operates an interactive website or online service, such as a website to which users may post company or product reviews or other content. By providing a place for others to publish content, web hosting services, website operators and bloggers risk being held liable for other people's content. The CDA offers some protection, but it is important to understand its limitations.

Publishers, Distributors and Conduits

Historically, the legal standard for contributory liability for another person's publication depended on whether the person sought to be held liable was a publisher, a distributor, or a conduit. Publishers were liable for the third party content they published. Conduits were not liable for materials they transported. Distributors were liable only if they knew or should have known that particular material contained defamatory or other tortious content.

A *conduit* is a service that facilitates communications between other parties but has no legal power to screen or control the content of the communications. Telephone companies are examples. Website operators and hosting services are not conduits if they have the power to monitor and control the content of communications on the sites they own, host or manage. Most website operators and hosting services have this power. They may require their customers and users to comply with the terms of service that they specify. If a website operator violates a hosting service's terms of service, the hosting service may require the operator to remove objectionable content under threat of having the site shut down if it is not removed.

A *distributor* is a person who distributes copies of another person's statement. Unlike a conduit, a distributor has the ability, opportunity and the right to review the content of the publications it distributes. The classic examples are newsstands, libraries, and bookstores. To avoid deputizing distributors as censors, the policy of the law is to refrain from requiring distributors to inspect all the materials that pass through their hands for objectionable content. A distributor will be held liable only if he happens to learn that particular material contains tortious or unlawful content or if he becomes aware of facts that would make it reasonable to conclude that the material probably does contain objectionable content. Web hosting services and some website operators are in this category.

A *publisher* is someone who actually has editorial control over the content of a publication. It is someone who actually prepares the material or reviews or has an opportunity to review it before it makes it way to a distributor or conduit. The classic examples are book and newspaper publishing companies. Because publishers have the legal ability to prevent defamatory or other tortious content from appearing in a publication in the first place, they are held liable for its inclusion even if it is contributed by somebody else. Accordingly, at common law, a publisher of another person's statement generally bears the same legal responsibility for it as if she had been the one who made the statement. Website operators are often in this category.

At common law, the fact that a website owner screened user-provided content for objectionable material prior to its publication to the website could cause her to be classified as a publisher of the content and therefore liable for it. The CDA changed that.

The Communications Decency Act

In *Cubby v. CompuServe, Inc.*[261] a federal district court ruled that CompuServe was a distributor, not a publisher, when it provided subscribers access to a variety of different forums run by third parties. It was held to be a distributor because it did not review the content of posts to the forums before they appeared on the site. A few years later, in *Stratton Oakmont v. Prodigy*,[262] Prodigy was held to be a publisher because it had implemented editorial control measures for the purpose of ensuring its service would be a "family friendly." In particular, Prodigy established and enforced content guidelines and used a software program to screen submissions for objectionable content. Because of this, Prodigy was held liable for defamatory user-provided content.

The outcomes of these cases did not sit well with "family values" legislators who wanted to encourage web service providers to freely review and censor pornographic, profane and blasphemous content in user-provided material. Therefore, when Congress enacted the CDA in 1996, it included a provision titled "Protection for Good Samaritan blocking and screening of offensive material." This provision expressly states that "no provider or user of an interactive computer service shall be treated as the publisher or speaker of any information provided by another information content provider." It further provides that "[n]o cause of action may be brought and no liability may be imposed under any State or local law that is inconsistent with this section."[263]

Section 230 of the CDA has been construed as giving both publishers and distributors immunity from contributory liability for user-provided content.[264] The level of editorial control over user-provided content is irrelevant. CDA immunity may continue to exist even if the service provider or website operator knows or has reason to know of actionable content. The CDA differs in this respect from the DMCA. Under the DMCA, a website owner or web-based service provider who knows or should know that user-provided content infringes a copyright but fails to do anything about it may be held contributorily liable for the infringement. A web hosting service or website owner who knows or should know of defamatory or other actionable user-provided content and fails to remove it generally will not be held contributorily liable for it.

REPUBLISHER IMMUNITY

The CDA grants immunity not only to interactive computer service providers but also to users of interactive computer services when they are acting as publishers of third party content rather than content creators. This means that a user of an interactive web service is immune from liability for republishing content obtained from another website. If a person obtains defamatory information from Website *X* and posts it to Website *Y*, then both the owner of Website *Y* and the user who posted the content on Website *Y* are immune from liability for defamation. Only the original creator of the content on Website *X* would be liable. Interactive website owners are classified as both users and interactive computer service providers. The central idea of the CDA is that only content creators should be held responsible for the content they create; those who publish or republish it should not be held responsible for it.

EXCEPTIONS AND LIMITATIONS

Under the CDA, a website owner or service provider generally is immune from tort liability for user-provided content, but immunity does not exist in the following circumstances:

(a) The website owner or service provider created or co-created the content.
(b) He edits the post in a way that creates new tortious content.
(c) He actively solicits or encourages users to submit tortious content.
(d) He conspires with an information content provider to create or publish tortious content.
(e) An employee of the website owner or service provider posts the content in the course and scope of the employment.
(f) An agent posts the content in the course and scope of the agency.
(g) The conduct is tortious regardless of whether the person doing it is a classified as a publisher, distributor or conduit. Examples include a website operator's false representation about the nature or quality of user-provided content, a website owner's breach of a promise, or an online service provider's failure to warn users of known dangers.
(h) The claim is for infringement of an intellectual property right.
(i) The claim is for violation of the ECPA.
(j) Federal criminal proceedings.

Information Content Providers

Section 230 distinguishes between interactive computer services and information content providers. Information content providers create or supply content. Interactive computer services provide forums for the content provided by information content providers; they do not create the content. An *information content provider* is any person or entity that is responsible, in whole or in part, for the creation or development of information provided through the Internet or any other interactive computer service. Generally, an interactive computer service provider is immune from liability for removing, failing to remove, or editing user-provided content; and the immunity exists even if the provider knows or has notice of the objectionable nature of the content.[265] Content providers, on the other hand, may be liable for the content they create or supply.

An interactive computer service can be any information service, system or access software provider that provides or enables access to a server by multiple users. This language is broad enough to cover most interactive websites, blogs to which users may post comments, forums, listservs, and web hosting services.

An interactive service provider may lose its immunity by so significantly editing user-provided content as to become an information content provider. A court might overlook minor, insignificant edits, but if a service provider's edits have the effect of transforming nontortious content into tortious content, then the service provider may be held liable for the tortious content the service provider adds.

> **Example.** Website owner Ted changes a user's statement from "Bob McKinsey is not a burgler" to "Bob McKinsey is not a burglar." Ted is still an interactive service provider, not an information content provider, because the edit does not materially change the content of the user's statement. Ted then decides to change "Bob McKinsey is not a burglar" to "Bob McKinsey is a burglar." If Bob McKinsey is not a burglar, then Ted's change transforms the user's truthful statement into a false and defamatory one. Now Ted has become an information content provider.

Soliciting or encouraging users to submit objectionable material may result in the loss of Section 230 immunity. By inviting or encouraging a particular kind of content, a website operator is essentially participating in the creation of website content. He therefore becomes an information content provider. For example, although a website owner generally is immune from liability for publishing a nude photograph of a person that a user took without the person's permission, he might incur liability if he specifically invites or encourages users to submit nude photographs of people that were taken without their permission.

A website that invites users to post a discriminatory housing advertisement to the site is an information content provider, and therefore may be contributorily liable if a user accepts the invitation. Thus, an online roommate matching service that asks users to fill out a questionnaire may be contributorily liable for discrimination if the questionnaire asks the user to state a preference with respect to a protected classification such as race.

Soliciting objectionable content or soliciting the gathering of information by illegal means, or making an advance offer to pay for such material, results in a website owner's loss of Section 230 immunity. Merely contracting for or acquiring ownership or publication rights in user-provided content does not result in loss of Section 230 immunity unless the contract specifically seeks or encourages objectionable content. Contractual provisions in a website's Terms of Use to the effect that the website owner has the right to remove or edit user-provided content, or that all user-provided content becomes the property of the website owner, do not automatically have the effect of making the website owner an information content provider whenever users submit content to the site. On the other hand, if a website owner promises to pay users for content, learns that users are obtaining information through illegal means, and then continues to pay them for it anyway, then the website owner and the user are jointly responsible for developing the information and neither one has Section 230 immunity.

Vicarious Liability

Section 230 only offers immunity from contributory liability, not immunity from vicarious liability. *Vicarious liability* refers to the imputation of responsibility for the conduct of another when the other person is essentially an instrumentality of the first person. Employers are held liable for the conduct of their employees within the scope and course of employment. Principals are held liable for the conduct of their agents within the scope and course of the agency. Knowledge of the unlawful activity is not necessary in order for vicarious liability to attach.

Employers and principals are not the only people who may be held vicariously liable for another person's conduct. A court may impose vicarious liability whenever a person has both of the following:

(a) the right and the power to supervise another person's activity
(b) a financial interest in the activity.

A national organization may be held vicariously liable for the activities of a chapter if the national organization has the right to control the activities of the chapter. Parent corporations have been held vicariously liable for the activities of subsidiaries when the requisite elements of control and financial benefit exist.

Receiving a fee for the use of one's property or facilities is not enough, by itself, to support a finding of financial benefit from the conduct if others are charged the same fee to use the property or facilities for lawful conduct. For this reason, web hosting services normally are not held vicariously liable for unlawful activity occurring on hosted websites.

When vicarious liability applies, the conduct of the supervised person is treated as if it were the conduct of the supervisory person, but only to the extent the conduct is either (a) within the course and scope of the supervisory relationship; or (b) known to and either authorized or ratified by the supervising person. Section 230 may be asserted as a defense against an employer's liability for an employee's use of an employer-provided Internet service (or access to Internet service) to engage in conduct that is not within the scope of employment, provided the employer has no knowledge of it and does not authorize or ratify the employee's conduct. An employee's use of an employer-provided Internet account to conduct business on the employer's behalf is within the scope of employment even if the employee proceeds to conduct the business in a tortious way. It is not within the scope of employment if the employee uses the account for personal matters unrelated to the employer's business.

Section 230 does not offer immunity from vicarious liability for the acts of co-conspirators. Each co-conspirator is vicariously liable for the conduct of every other co-conspirator in furtherance of the conspiracy. Accordingly, when a website owner conspires with an information content provider to publish objectionable material, they are both responsible for each other's actions in furtherance of the conspiracy, and Section 230 does not provide a defense.

Bases of Liability Independent of Publisher Status

Although the CDA immunizes a website owner from liability for negligently failing to edit or remove user-provided content, it does not provide immunity from liability for negligent failure to warn people about a known danger the website creates. In *Doe v. Internet Brands, Inc.*[266] the Ninth Circuit Court of Appeals reversed a lower court's Section 230 dismissal of a model's claim against the owner of a website called Model Mayhem. The website provided a networking service for aspiring models, allowing them to post information about themselves so that agents and producers might contact them. The claim alleged that a woman had posted her contact information hoping to get modeling work and that men posing as talent agents contacted her and invited her to what they represented would be an audition. When she showed up, they drugged and raped her, and then sold footage of the crime as pornography. The woman sued the website owner, Internet Brands, Inc., claiming it knew about this scheme and therefore had a common law duty to warn users of the website but didn't. The district court held the claim was barred by Section 230. In reversing that decision and allowing the claim to proceed, the Ninth Circuit Court of Appeals distinguished between liability as a publisher and liability as a person with knowledge of a danger.

Section 230 only provides immunity from liability for publishing. It does not immunize anybody from liability for a tort as to which publication is not an element. The common law duty to warn does not arise from an act of publication; it arises when a person has knowledge of a danger and there is a relationship of a kind that gives rise to a responsibility to disclose the knowledge. A landowner has a common law duty to warn invitees of known dangers. A psychotherapist may have a common law duty to warn a person that her client has expressed a desire to harm or kill the person. As *Internet Brands* illustrates, courts have been expanding the range of relationships to which this duty applies.

Promissory Estoppel

Promissory estoppel is an equitable doctrine that prevents a defendant from objecting to the enforcement of a promise he has made if the promisee relied on the promise to his detriment.

Some courts have held that Section 230 is not a defense to a promissory estoppel claim. Both Craigslist and Yahoo!, for example, have been held liable for user-provided content notwithstanding Section 230 because they promised to remove objectionable material that a customer had asked to be removed and then failed to do so. The customer in each case had relied on the promise to her detriment. Because the companies' promises were not supported by consideration, they normally would not be enforceable. Under the equitable doctrine of promissory estoppel, however, a person may be estopped (prohibited) from denying that a promise the person has made is enforceable, if the promisee relied on the promise to her detriment. Courts that have held Section 230 to be inapplicable to promissory estoppel claims reason that the claim is not against the website operator in his capacity as a publisher. Rather it is a claim against the website operator in his capacity as a promise-maker. The purpose of the CDA is to protect website operators from liability for the content of what they publish, not to enable website operators to make and break promises with impunity.

Other courts have come to the opposite conclusion, holding that Section 230 does immunize web service providers from liability for promissory estoppel with respect to the removal of user-provided content.

The safest course for a website owner to take is to avoid making promises to remove content. Even better, avoid making any statements in the Terms of Use (or elsewhere) about whether and what kind of response to any kind of complaint will be made.

Intellectual Property Claims

Section 230 expressly exempts intellectual property claims from its coverage. It says, "Nothing in this section shall be construed to limit or expand any law pertaining to intellectual property." Accordingly, a web host or website owner may be contributorily liable for a user's infringement of a copyright. The DMCA provides a mechanism for reducing the risk of contributory liability for a user's infringement of a copyright. See Chapter 26.

It is clear that the exemption means the CDA is not a defense to copyright, patent and trademark claims, but it is not completely certain what other kinds of claims are considered intellectual property claims for purposes of the CDA. Some courts hold that the exemption applies to both state and federal law claims. Others hold that it only applies to federal law claims. Accordingly, some courts would hold that it applies to claims for infringement of a federally registered trademark but not to claims of infringement of common law trademarks Other courts would hold that it applies to claims of infringement of either kind of trademark.

Some kinds of user-provided content give rise to both intellectual property and tort claims. Using a trademark to mislead a consumer about the origin, sponsorship or endorsement of a product is not just an infringement of intellectual property; it may also be fraud or false advertising. These claims do not come within the CDA exemption for intellectual property claims. It would seem, then, that the extent to which contributory liability may be avoided depends on the theory of liability under which a claim is brought. If the claim is presented as a fraud, false advertising or unfair competition claim, then Section 230 may be asserted as a defense to contributory liability. If it is prosecuted as trademark infringement, then Section 230 would not provide a defense.

Section 230 would appear to be a defense to a claim brought under the federal Defending Trade Secrets Act, since the Act itself declares that it is not an intellectual property law. It is not clear whether trade secret claims under state law, or claims for violations of publicity or proprietary information rights are within the "intellectual property" exception to the CDA.

ECPA Violations

Section 230 is not a defense to a violation of the ECPA.

Criminal Prosecutions

Section 230 is not a defense to a federal crime.

RESTRICTING ACCESS TO OBJECTIONABLE MATERIAL

Section 230 also immunizes interactive website operators from liability for restricting access to, or the availability of, obscene, lewd, lascivious, filthy, violent, harassing or other material the website operator deems objectionable. This is true whether the material is within a constitutionally unprotected category of speech or not. It also appears to be true even if the restriction breaches an agreement to provide a forum for unrestricted speech.

Other Countries

The CDA is a U.S. law. It is not applicable in other countries. While some other countries have laws that provide similar protections, most do not. In those countries that have not enacted such a law, a website owner or blogger may incur contributory liability for user-contributed content. Courts in other countries can, and have, issued judgments against U.S. companies and individuals on the basis of user-contributed content to a public Internet website that is accessible by citizens of that country.

The SPEECH Act[267] protects Americans from having foreign defamation judgments enforced against them in the United States if Section 230 would have protected them from contributory liability had the lawsuit been brought in the United States. Other kinds of foreign judgments may be enforceable, however.

In some circumstances, online service providers located in EU countries enjoy immunity from liability for third party content under laws enacted pursuant to the Directive on Electronic Commerce. Specifically, ISPs and online service providers in the EU are immune from conduit liability for a third party's transmission of content using the service. The immunity is not available if the provider does not any of the following:

(a) initiates the transmission
(b) selects the receiver of the transmission
(c) selects or modifies the information contained in the transmission.

The provider is also immune from liability for the transient storage of the information, provided it occurs for the sole purpose of carrying out the transmission and is not stored longer than is reasonably necessary for the transmission. Immunity from liability for caching is also provided, if specified conditions are met.

The Directive further immunizes EU web hosting services from liability for the content of the websites they host, if (a) the hosting service does not have actual knowledge of illegal activity or information and, as regards claims for damages, is not aware of facts or circumstances from which the illegal activity or information is apparent; and (b) if the hosting service acquires such knowledge or awareness, it acts expeditiously to remove or disable access to the information.

Unlike in the United States, a service provider in the EU may be held liable for failing to remove content after receiving notice of its illegality, whether or not she has made a promise to do so.

Some countries impose a specific obligation on service providers to monitor and censor user-provided content. China, for example, requires ISPs to monitor and remove user-provided website and email message content that violates Chinese content regulations.

Contractual Limitations of Liability

Because Section 230 immunity does not apply to every situation, a website owner might want to contractually limit its liability for user-provided content in the website's Terms of Use. Of course, the Terms of Use are only binding on users of the website. Not having assented to the Terms of Use, a third party who is damaged by content appearing on the site is not bound by any exclusions or limitations on liability that are set out in the Terms of Use. For this reason, an indemnification clause may be useful. An indemnification clause might require a user of the website to pay a website owner's damages, attorney fees and costs in the event the website owner is sought to be held contributorily liable to any person for content the user provides.

Chapter 22. Other Content Regulations

Although consumer protection is still a principal focus of regulation, lawmakers around the world—and increasingly in the United States—view the Internet as a mechanism of social, political, and moral control. Companies with an online presence, especially those serving an international market, need to be aware of the existence of a diverse array of what is very often ideologically-driven content regulation.

Online Gambling

Two federal statutes prohibit gambling. 28 U.S.C. § 3702 prohibits sports gambling. This includes operating, sponsoring, advertising or promoting sports gambling (taking bets on the outcome of amateur or professional athletic competitions). 18 U.S.C. § 1955 makes owning, operating, financing or supervising an unlawful gambling operation a crime. This includes traditional games of chance such as slot machines and the like, bookmaking, lotteries, numbers games, and selling chances to win.

A gambling operation is unlawful if all of the following conditions apply:

(a) The operation is a violation of the law of a state or political subdivision in which the bet is ether made or received;
(b) At least five people are involved in operating, financing or managing it;
(c) It has been in continuous operation for over thirty days or has gross daily revenue of at least $2,000 in any single day.

This prohibition does not apply to charitable gambling conducted by a 501(c)(3) tax-exempt organization. It also does not apply to savings promotion raffles. A savings promotion raffle is a raffle in which people earn a chance of winning a prize by depositing money into a savings account at a financial institution.

Gambling is not unlawful if all of the following conditions apply:

(a) It occurs entirely within a state or Indian reservation where it is legal;
(b) The website has an age verification system;
(c) The website has data security measures sufficient to verify a person's age and location;
(d) The gambling activity is not illegal under other law.

To be lawful, both the betting establishment and the bettor must be located in a state or reservation where gambling of the kind offered is legal.

Most states prohibit gambling except on Indian reservations. Currently, there are only four states that authorize and license gambling outside of Indian reservations: Delaware,

Pennsylvania, Nevada and New Jersey. Gambling operations are legal in these states only if they are licensed, however.

The kinds of gambling that are authorized in the few states that permit it vary. Typically they include online poker and sometimes other casino games. The Pennsylvania law, which will be fully implemented in 2018, authorizes online poker, satellite casinos, online lotteries, video gaming in truck stops, and fantasy sports. Horse and greyhound racing, and betting involving games of skill are authorized in Nevada. Online casino games of chance are not approved for licensing in Nevada, online poker being the only exception.

The Unlawful Internet Gambling Enforcement Act[268] prohibits gambling businesses (businesses engaged in betting or wagering activities) from knowingly accepting a check, draft, credit card payment or proceeds, EFT proceeds, or funds from a money transmitting business, as payment for a customer's bet or wager in an unlawful gambling activity. For example, a Pennsylvania online gambling website may not accept a credit, debit or EFT payment for a bet from a customer in Utah, where gambling is illegal.

For purposes of this law, the following things are not considered bets or wagers, and therefore may be accepted by an online business:

(a) payment to participate in a contest or game of skill

(b) points or credits that the game sponsor gives to participants for free and that may be redeemed only for participation in games or contests offered by the sponsor

(c) fantasy sports or an educational contest or game not involving any current players on an actual amateur or professional sports team, provided: (i) prizes are announced beforehand and do not depend on the number of participants or the amount of fees paid by participants (i.e., it's not a pool); (ii) winning outcomes reflect the relative knowledge and skill of participants (i.e., it's not purely a game of chance); and (iii) winning outcomes are not based on the score, point spread or performance of a real team or athlete.

Online businesses must comply with federal laws against money laundering.

A bona fide sweepstakes promotion is not a form of unlawful gambling, provided the promoter complies with all applicable licensing, disclosure and other regulatory laws. See Chapter 15.

Racketeer Influenced Corrupt Organizations Act

The Racketeer Influenced Corrupt Organizations Act[269] (RICO) is a United States law providing severe criminal penalties for acts performed as part of an ongoing criminal enterprise. RICO also establishes a private right of action for damages for any person who is damaged in his business or property by a racketeer. Treble damages may be awarded. Many states and some countries have enacted laws similar to it.

Under RICO, a person who has committed more than one predicate act within a ten-year period may be charged with racketeering if the acts relate to an enterprise. Fines and imprisonment for up to twenty years per count are possible, and upon conviction, a person may be required to forfeit everything gained through the racketeering activity.

Acts are related to an enterprise if the actor (a) invested the proceeds of a pattern of racketeering activity into the enterprise; (b) acquired or maintained an interest in, or control of the enterprise through the pattern of racketeering activity; (c) conducted or participated in the affairs of the enterprise through the pattern of racketeering activity; or (d) conspired to do one of these things.

The following crimes are all predicate acts:

- copyright infringement
- fraud
- gambling
- money laundering
- dealing in obscenity
- counterfeiting
- theft
- robbery
- embezzlement
- bribery
- extortion
- kidnapping
- obstruction of justice
- slavery
- racketeering
- murder
- arson
- drug trafficking or dealing in controlled substances
- assisting in bringing in undocumented aliens
- terrorism.

This is not an exhaustive list.

Predicate crimes are related if they have the same or similar purposes, results, participants, victims, or methods of commission, or otherwise are interrelated by distinguishing characteristics and are not isolated events. The criminal acts need not have an economic motive. A pro-life organization has been sued under RICO despite the absence of a financial motive.

Political Speech

TREASON, INSURRECTION AND SEDITION

Treason is a federal crime. Article III of the Constitution defines it as levying war against the United States or adhering to or giving aid and comfort to its enemies. The penalty for treason may include death. Because of the potential threat to First Amendment freedoms this law poses, courts tend to interpret it narrowly. Expressing disagreement with a president's domestic or foreign policy, for example, is not treason.

Insurrection means inciting, engaging in, or giving aid and comfort to a rebellion or insurrection against the authority of the United States or its laws. It is a federal crime. *Sedition* means rebelling or inciting a rebellion against a government. In the United States, it is a federal crime but requires proof of an act or conspiracy to violently overthrow the government. Merely criticizing the government or expressing a belief that different government leaders are needed will not suffice to support a sedition charge. A broader interpretation of this law would violate First Amendment protections of freedom of speech and press.

Other countries are not always as protective of speech freedoms. In India, for example, it is a crime to say or print anything that brings or attempts to bring into hatred or contempt, or excites or attempts to excite disaffection towards government. In many Arab countries, it is a crime to instigate hatred or disrespect against a ruler. China prohibits "incitement of subversion of State power." Several countries interpret their sedition laws broadly as prohibiting the expression of dissatisfaction with the country's government or its policies.

INSULTING ROYALTY OR HEADS OF STATE

"Time and time again, those with the power to censor see criticism of themselves as what needs to be banned."[270]

Americans are often surprised to learn that there is such a thing as a law against saying something unpleasant about a king, queen, or other royalty. Yet *lèse-majesté*, the crime of offending the dignity of a reigning sovereign, is one of the oldest criminal laws the world has known. dating back to Ancient Rome. It is still the law in many countries today. In many places, it has been extended to protect heads of state, as well. Insulting royalty is a crime in such countries as Denmark, the Netherlands, Spain, Cambodia, Jordan, Kuwait, Malaysia, Morocco, Saudi Arabia, and Thailand. In Saudi Arabia, insulting the king is considered an act of terrorism, potentially punishable by death. In Malaysia it is prosecuted as sedition. Thailand's Supreme Court has held that country's *lèse-majesté* law also applies to criticisms and comments that tarnish the reputation of past kings.

Some countries have extended the crime to other government officials. Germany, Greece, Italy, Poland, Turkey, Venezuela and Iran are examples. France prohibits "offending the dignity of the republic," which includes insulting a public servant. Italy and Poland extend the protection to foreign heads of state, too. Iceland makes it a crime to insult a foreign country, its head of state or its representatives. Similarly, Switzerland prohibits insulting foreign heads of state, foreign government officials, and foreign diplomats. Because the Pope is a head of state (Vatican City), insulting the Pope would be a crime in these countries. Prosecutions for insulting the Pope have occurred.

So far, the United States has no *lèse-majesté* law.

SYMBOLS, SLOGANS, SONGS

In the aftermath of World War II, several European countries sought to suppress Nazism legislatively. Germany took the lead. It enacted a law prohibiting the public display or dissemination of the "means of propaganda" of any party that a German court declares to be "unconstitutional." The National Socialist Party (Nazi Party) was and continues to be the primary target. While there is no official list, virtually anything emblematic or close to being emblematic of the National Socialist Party or Nazism is banned: the swastika and all variants of it; the Celtic cross; Sig rune; Wolfsangel; Gauwinkel badge; Sturmabteilung emblem;

Reichskriegsflagge (former German flags); SS motto ("My honor is called loyalty"); the "Heil Hitler" greeting; the "Sieg Heil" greeting;; the Nazi Party anthem.

The ban is not limited to Nazi-related matter. The solar cross (Ku Klux Klan), hammer and sickle (Communist Party), Communist Party flag, ISIS/ISIL flag, the red star, and the People's Protection Unit pennant have also been banned. This is not an exhaustive list.

Like America's obscenity ban, an exception exists for material with redeeming artistic or scientific value. Exceptions also allow the use of otherwise prohibited symbols as bona fide religious symbols, and in teaching materials and reporting about historical events. Literary value is not specifically mentioned, but the ban indicates that artistry, science, and education are not necessarily the only kinds of value that may support an exception. The extent to which the use of banned symbols, greetings, etc. is permitted in fictional writing, comedy sketches, satire, parody, or political speech is uncertain.

Other countries have enacted bans on the display of certain symbols, emblems and the like, too. Austria prohibits the public display of Nazi insignia, symbols, emblems, uniforms, flags, etc., whether the intent is to promote National Socialism or not. Trading in Nazi memorabilia is not prohibited, however. France makes it illegal to publicly display Nazi flags, uniforms and insignia except for the purpose of a historical film or spectacle. Hungary prohibits "symbols of totalitarianism," including the swastika, the SS insignia, the arrow cross, the hammer and sickle, and the red star. Russia, too, prohibits the public display or dissemination of Nazi symbols and things that look like Nazi symbols. In the United States, displaying political symbols of any kind is protected by the First Amendment.

COMPULSORY NATIONALISM

A number of countries enforce nationalism. Although Germany prohibits expressions of reverence for older forms of nationalism, it mandates reverence for symbols of modern Germany. The German Criminal Code makes it unlawful to disparage the country of Germany or its symbols. The United Arab Emirates makes it a crime to use a computer network to "damage national unity." Finland prohibits disparagement of the flag of Finland, including writing on or affixing things to it. France makes it illegal to insult the national flag or the national anthem. Icelandic law makes it illegal to insult the Icelandic flag.

In the United States, federal and state statutes make flag desecration a crime. The First Amendment protects symbolic speech, however, so these laws are unconstitutional.[271]

HISTORICAL BELIEFS

A number of countries prohibit certain beliefs about history. Holocaust denial is a crime in many countries, including Austria, Belgium, the Czech Republic, France, Germany, Greece, Hungary, Israel, Italy, Liechtenstein, Lithuania, Luxemburg, Poland, Romania, Russia, Slovakia, and Switzerland. Some of these laws also prohibit having an incorrect attitude about the Holocaust. Lithuania prohibits condoning or minimizing the significance of the Holocaust. In Germany, Israel and Austria, trying to minimize, excuse or downplay the significance of the Holocaust is a crime. Israel adds that expressing praise or sympathy for Nazi crimes is also a crime. In Russia, denying Nazi crimes, portraying Nazis as heroes, and spreading false information about USSR activities during World War II are all crimes.

A number of countries have extended the ban to other historical events. These countries specify that genocide committed in Communist countries or formerly Communist countries also may not be denied. In some, it is a crime to have the wrong attitude about any war crime, genocide or crime against humanity. The Czech Republic, Hungary, Liechtenstein, Lithuania, Luxemburg, Poland, and Slovakia are examples. Spain's Holocaust denial statute was declared unconstitutional, but trying to justify it remains illegal there.

Some countries, such as Australia, the Netherlands, Portugal and Switzerland, do not explicitly ban denials of atrocities, but prosecute it as hate speech. Germany does both. In Germany, Holocaust denial is a crime and it is also a crime to glorify, justify or approve of the National Socialist rule of arbitrary force.

Political Parties

Membership in the Nazi or Communist parties is banned in Germany, Poland, and some other countries. Some countries forbid membership in any political party that keeps its members' names secret. Various countries have laws that go even further, criminalizing support for or criticism of specified political parties or belief systems. Examples: Germany, Austria, France (no pro-Nazi beliefs allowed); China (no anti-Communist Party beliefs); South Korea (no pro-Communism or pro-North Korea expressions); the Czech Republic (no expressions of sympathy for any movement that seeks to curb people's rights); South Africa (no war propaganda); Spain (no sympathy for terrorism); Russia (no extremism)

China bans a wide array of words, ideas and categories of expression, such as references to democracy, the Free Tibet movement, Taiwan as an independent nation, the Tiananmen Square Massacre, the 2014 Hong Kong protests or the Arab Spring, among other things. Many books, films, social media networks, and websites are banned.

Israel has made it unlawful to call for a boycott against Israel.

In the United States, political beliefs and membership in or support of political parties are currently protected by the First Amendment. Federal laws, however, give government officials broad investigative, surveillance, search and seizure powers to gather intelligence on potential ties between individuals and suspected terrorists, terrorist organizations or residents of other countries. These powers have been used to search and seize the property of members of humanitarian aid, religious and antiwar organizations.

Hate Speech

"Hate speech" is defined differently in different jurisdictions. Broadly speaking, it is any speech that disparages or expresses a negative attitude or sentiment about a person on the basis of membership in a protected class, such as race, color, nationality, ethnic origin, religion, sex, sexual orientation, or disability. Gender identity is beginning to appear in some lists. A handful of countries have added age, language and/or philosophy to the list. Ireland protects travelers from hate speech. South Africa's list includes, among others, pregnancy, marital status, conscience, language and culture.

Prohibitions are enacted to prevent violence, to protect the dignity of members of protected classes, or for both purposes. Depending on the wording of an enactment, incitement of violence or discrimination may or may not be en element of the crime.

In the United States, crimes motivated by bias or prejudice may be punished more severely than other kinds of crimes, but the First Amendment imposes limitations on the direct regulation of speech content. Except in the context of commercial speech, even racist, sexist and other forms of "hate speech" are constitutionally protected so long as they do not contain fighting words (speech inciting imminent unlawful action), a threat of imminent harm, or solicitation to commit a crime, and so long as they do not come within the definition of harassment. Speech that intentionally incites imminent violence is illegal in the United States, as it is in many other countries. It is not protected by the First Amendment.

Many countries have more direct hate speech laws than the United States. Several countries have laws making speech that intentionally incites racial hostility or discrimination a crime even if there is no proof of intent to incite imminent lawless action. A politician in the Netherlands was convicted of hate speech for suggesting there should be fewer Moroccans in the country. Germany once threatened Facebook with criminal prosecution for providing a forum for users to post anti-Semitic comments. Many countries do not require any kind of incitement at all. Laws in these countries ban insults and slurs regardless of their effect or intended effect. Some, such as Finland, prohibit insults, slurs and threats, but allow criticism and expressions of opinions about factual events such as the Holocaust. Others treat Holocaust denial as hate speech.

Germany's hate speech law bans insults and slurs. Satire and artwork are permitted, but they must respect human dignity. Germany's Network Enforcement Act provides for the imposition of fines, potentially in the millions of dollars, on social media and content-sharing websites that persistently fail to remove "illegal" content. Under the law, websites have twenty-four hours to remove "obviously illegal" postings and seven days to remove "illegal" postings that are not obviously so. This law went into effect in 2018.

Article 20(2) of the International Covenant on Civil and Political Rights (ICCPR) requires member countries to prohibit "advocacy of national, racial or religious hatred that constitutes incitement to discrimination, hostility or violence." The United States ratified this treaty subject to the reservation that it is not self-executing. This means that insofar as its application in the United States is concerned, an individual does not have a right to sue, and people may not be criminally prosecuted for violation of the treaty. ICCPR rights are enforceable in the United States only if and to the extent that Congress enacts implementing legislation. Doing that would raise significant constitutional issues. The United States has a strong constitutional tradition of protecting open and robust speech, including uncouth and insulting speech. A statute implementing a prohibition against "hostile" language (as distinguished from language that incites imminent lawless action) would conflict with U.S. Supreme Court decisions interpreting the First Amendment.

Disrespect for the Dead

In some countries, such as Germany, it is a crime to be disrespectful to the dead.

Infliction of Emotional Distress

A growing number of jurisdictions recognize a common law cause of action for intentional infliction of emotional distress. The elements of this cause of action are:

(a) extreme and outrageous conduct
(b) intent to cause, or reckless disregard for the likelihood of causing, emotional distress
(c) causation (actual and proximate)
(d) emotional distress.

Not every affront, insult or annoyance is actionable, however. Mere rudeness is not enough. Instead, the conduct must be so extreme as to "exceed all bounds of that usually tolerated in a civilized community."[272]

The First Amendment may be raised as a defense if the "outrageous conduct" complained of is protected speech, such as criticism of a public official or figure, or commentary on a matter of public concern. There is some authority for the proposition that a public official or public figure may not sue for infliction of emotional distress unless she proves actual malice.

Some states only allow recovery for intentional infliction of emotional distress. A few also allow recovery for negligent infliction of emotional distress. Still others do not recognize the cause of action at all. In these states, emotional distress may be a recoverable element of damage for some other tort (e.g., assault, fraud, etc.) but may not be asserted as an independent basis of liability.

Discrimination

Discrimination in advertising, on the basis of race or membership in certain other protected classes, is prohibited in the United States. Unlike political and religious speech, no showing of a compelling need for a restriction that cannot be accomplished by any less drastic means is required to justify a restriction on commercial speech. To comply with First Amendment requirements, the restriction need only be substantially related to an important government interest. The eradication of discrimination in housing, employment and places of public accommodations is an important government interest. Accordingly, governmental prohibitions against discrimination in housing and employment advertisements, and in advertisements for places of public accommodation, do not violate the Constitution. Such prohibitions exist at both the federal and state levels.

Although not all courts are in agreement, some courts have held that websites, blogs and Internet chat rooms are the legal equivalent of private clubs rather than places of public accommodation. According to these courts, prohibitions against discrimination in public accommodations do not apply to web sites, so a website could offer a chat room specifically for women, or men, or straight people, or gay people, for example. Be aware, however, that at least one court has held that an online video subscription service that offers its service to the public is a place of public accommodation and therefore must provide a closed captioning feature in order to comply with the ADA obligation to make reasonable accommodations for deaf persons.[273]

Whether a particular web site is a place of public accommodation or a private club, it may not host discriminatory advertising or promote discrimination in employment, housing or a public accommodation. Advertising that specifies a preference for applicants on the basis of race, sex, or another protected category is prohibited. Soliciting information about an advertiser's or applicant's preferences regarding these categories for use in an online roommate matching service, housing locator service, job finding service, or the like, is also prohibited, inasmuch as it facilitates and invites others to practice discrimination. Employment discrimination is addressed in Chapter 4.

Violence

Some countries, such as Finland, find certain depictions of violence to be offensive, in much the same way that Americans find depictions of sex to be offensive. In Finland, motion pictures depicting brutal violence are prohibited from being distributed or displayed even if the depiction is a recording of an actual event. An exception exists for material in which a depiction of violence is necessary for artistic or educational purposes. Public displays or exhibitions that glorify criminals, condone crimes or serve no other purpose than to satisfy the public's desire for violence are prohibited in the Philippines.

Very shortly after the September 11, 2001 attacks on the World Trade Center, Congress enacted the USA PATRIOT Act. This law gave the U.S. government sweeping powers to investigate people suspected of being terrorists or members of terrorist organizations, or aiding or supporting terrorists or terrorist organizations. It expired in 2015, but Congress renewed its major provisions that year, in the USA FREEDOM Act.[274] A number of other countries have enacted similar laws. In some cases, merely associating with or expressing support for a suspected terrorist organization is a crime. The laws of several countries are vaguely worded and could easily be applied to reach what would be protected political speech in the United States. In Tunisia, for example, publishing a photograph of a terrorist may be an act of terrorism. In the U.K. it is a crime to possess information that is likely to be of use to a terrorist. Spain's counterterrorism law has been applied to convict puppeteers who staged a show in which al-Qaeda was depicted as a witch that police were hunting.

Although the First Amendment protects freedom of speech in the United States, the U.S. Supreme Court has held that speech directed at inciting imminent lawless action is not protected. Fighting words are not protected, either. State and federal laws criminalize the making of threats of imminent physical violence.

Crimes Against Religion

Several countries, especially in the Middle East, prohibit blasphemy, which under Sharia law means an expression of disrespect for the Islamic religion or Mohammad. Penalties can be severe, up to and including death. Several countries, primarily but not exclusively in the Middle East, have made apostasy and atheism crimes, as well. The penalty may be death.

Middle Eastern countries are not the only places where blasphemy is a crime. It is illegal in Canada, New Zealand, Austria, Brazil, Finland ("blaspheming against God"), Italy (blasphemy against "the Deity"), Thailand (Buddhism) and some states in Australia and the United States. Greek law not only criminalizes blasphemy, but provides an enhanced sentence for "malicious blasphemy."

Many Western countries are folding their old prohibitions against blasphemy into more broadly worded "hate speech" enactments. Ireland, for example, has replaced its blasphemy law with a prohibition against publishing matter that is grossly insulting in relation to matters held sacred by a religion. Switzerland's hate speech regime prohibits mocking a religion or a religious belief. Germany prohibits "defaming" a religious view.

Some countries prohibit witchcraft. In Saudi Arabia, it is punishable by death. Other countries go to the opposite extreme, making religious tolerance mandatory under threat of imprisonment. In Vietnam, for example, it is a crime to "promote division between religious believers and nonbelievers."

Interfering with Abortion or Reproductive Health Services

The Freedom of Access to Clinic Entrances Act provides both criminal penalties and civil liability for intimidating or interfering with another person's attempt to obtain or provide reproductive health services. In *Planned Parenthood v. American Coalition of Life Activists*[275] the Ninth Circuit Court of Appeals ruled that posting Old West style Wanted posters identifying specific doctors known to perform abortions violates this law. The court reasoned that threats are not constitutionally protected, and interpreted the Wanted poster, used in conjunction with the accusation of "crimes against humanity," as an implied threat to inflict harm on doctors who perform abortions.

Fake News

A growing number of countries are making it a crime to publish "fake" or false news. Such laws exist in the Middle East and South Asia, and their adoption is spreading to other parts of the world. Gambia and China have enacted such laws. In Gambia, a person may be sentenced to fifteen years in prison for spreading "false news" about a public official or the government. In China, rumor-mongering is a crime. Rumor-mongering, as defined in Chinese law, means intentionally posting a false rumor that is reposted at least 500 times or viewed at least 5,000 times. Spreading feudal superstitions is also unlawful. Denmark's Media Liability Act requires mass media to act consistently with journalistic ethics, under threat of fines and imprisonment. Germany prohibits malicious gossip. Australia bans publishing material that is capable of deceiving or misleading a voter.

The "fake news" statute in the United States is 18 U.S.C § 1038. It specifies the circumstances under which a person may be fined and imprisoned, potentially for life, for making a false or misleading statement of fact. False or misleading statements on any of the following subjects come within the ban, provided they could reasonably be believed:

- Destruction of an airplane
- Destruction of a motor vehicle
- Drive-by shooting
- Violence at an international airport
- Aircraft parts
- Aiming a laser pointer at an aircraft
- Failure of a commercial motor vehicle to stop for an inspection
- Sale or unauthorized use of a traffic signal preemption transmitter
- Biological weapons
- Chemical weapons
- Nuclear material

- Explosives
- Firearms
- Firearms transfers
- Destruction or tampering with a ship
- Terrorism
- Sabotage of a nuclear facility
- Aircraft hijacking
- Interference with a flight crew
- Bomb or firearm on an airplane.

The statute also makes it a crime, potentially punishable by life imprisonment, to make a false statement about the death, injury, capture, or disappearance of a member of the United States Armed Forces during an armed conflict in which the United States is engaged.

In addition to criminal sanctions, the statute authorizes a civil cause of action for damages for anyone who suffers injury or harm as a result of the statement.

The law does not apply to law enforcement officers.

The common law provides a cause of action for damages for individuals who suffer injury to their reputations as a result of the publication of a false statement. Liability for defamation may be predicated on false statements about the subjects listed above, if they harm a person's reputation. Defamation liability may also be predicated on false statements about subjects other than those enumerated above. See Chapter 16.

Publishing an advertisement that is made to appear as if it is a news article is a deceptive trade practice. It is a violation of the FTC Act unless a disclosure that it is an advertisement is displayed. See Chapter 15.

Glorifying or Condoning Drugs

Some countries prohibit promoting or glorifying the use of controlled substances. France, for example, makes it a crime to present drugs in a positive light or to incite their use. Advocates of drug law reform have been sentenced under this law. The Philippines and some other countries also have laws making it unlawful to express specific viewpoints about drugs.

Negligence

Common law liability may arise not only from intentional wrongdoing, but also from careless acts or omissions, i.e., negligence. This is a broad common law source of liability encompassing any failure to exercise the care that a reasonably prudent person would exercise in similar circumstances.

The four essential elements of any negligence claim are:

(a) duty to exercise the requisite standard of care
(b) breach of the duty
(c) causation (actual and proximate)
(d) damage.

The first element requires two determinations: (i) whether a person owes a duty to another person; and (ii) what the applicable standard of care is. In making these determinations, courts consider the nature of the relationship between the person harmed and the person sought to be held liable; the extent to which harm is reasonably foreseeable from a particular act or omission; and whether it is fair and reasonable to impose liability.

Statutes often impose and define the nature of a person's obligations in particular circumstances. Conduct or inaction that breaches an obligation imposed by a statute is called *negligence per se*. In these kinds of cases, the statute determines the existence of a duty and establishes the appropriate standard of care.

The default duty of care, in the absence of either a statute imposing a specific duty or a relationship between parties that gives rise to one, is to exercise the degree of care that an ordinary, reasonable person would exercise to avoid exposing another person to an unreasonable risk of foreseeable harm. Evidence of the applicable standard of care can take several forms, such as a statute, regulation, industry standard or customary usage of trade. These are not the only ways to establish the applicable standard of care, though.

A negligence claim cannot be predicated on the breach of a contractual duty that causes only economic loss. In such cases, the claim must be pleaded as a breach of contract rather than as a tort.

Courts have held that businesses that collect or maintain personally identifiable information (such as name, address, birth date, etc.) on individuals owe a duty to those individuals to protect the information from being disclosed to third parties without the individual's consent. In one case, the third party recipient of the information used it to track down and kill the individual who was the subject of the data. The court held that the possibility of that happening is a foreseeable risk of releasing an individual's name and address to others. Accordingly, the business that released the information was liable for negligence.[276] On the other hand, an online service provider (such as a social media website) does not owe a duty to underage users to screen adult users to ensure that no pedophiles gain access to the site.[277]

Two kinds of causation must be proven in any negligence case: actual and proximate. Actual causation, also known as *causation in fact*, requires proof that the complained-of injury or damage would not have happened but for the defendant's breach of duty; or proof that the defendant's act or omission materially increased the risk of the complained-of injury occurring. Proximate cause (sometimes called "legal cause") requires that the harm caused by a particular act or omission be reasonably foreseeable. It operates as a limitation on liability for actual causation.

Historically, some sort of physical injury or pecuniary loss had to be proven before a court would allow recovery for negligence. Damages for other kinds of injury (e.g., pain and suffering, mental anguish, emotional distress) were recoverable, but only if some sort of pecuniary loss was first established. This is still the law in several jurisdictions, but some states now permit recovery without proof of pecuniary loss.

The principal defenses to negligence are comparative negligence and assumption of risk. Early common law made any amount of contributory negligence on the plaintiff's part a complete defense to a claim of negligence. Most states have moved away from that approach, considering it too harsh. Instead, most states today apply a comparative negligence principle, under which a defendant's liability may be offset (not eliminated entirely) by the plaintiff's own negligence. Damages are calculated as a proportion of fault, i.e., total damage times the percentage of fault attributable to the defendant.

Assumption of risk is a defense when the plaintiff knew or should have known that her conduct involved a substantial risk of harm but did it anyway. It applies to conduct that is inherently dangerous in which a person participates voluntarily.

MALPRACTICE

Malpractice, also known as "professional negligence," is negligence that is committed by a professional (or a person who holds himself out as one) in the course of providing a professional service. Professionals include doctors, lawyers, accountants and members of certain other professions. They are held to a higher standard of care. The question in these cases is not what a reasonably prudent person would have done under the circumstances, but what a reasonably prudent professional (doctor, lawyer, etc.) would have done under the circumstances. If a reasonably prudent professional in a particular field would not dispense a particular kind of professional advice over the Internet, then a professional in that field who does so may be liable for malpractice if it results in foreseeable harm to a client. Courts have not yet extended professional negligence liability to web designers, web developers, computer programmers, computer geeks, website operators, or business managers. These kinds of service providers may be held liable using a negligence per se or "reasonable person" standard, though.

Professional Ethics

The law imposes certain ethical obligations on certain kinds of professional such as doctors, lawyers, accountants, therapists, and clergy. For these professionals, confidentiality and other obligations exist whether they are spelled out in a contract or not. Members of regulated professions should take steps to ensure their website operations do not violate the rules of professional responsibility applicable to their profession.

Professionals generally must maintain the confidentiality of communications with their clients, patients, parishioners, etc. Consistent with this requirement, professionals should obtain consent before posting information about their clients—or even the names of their clients—to the Internet. This applies to both current and former clients. The First Amendment may provide a defense if the information relates to a former client and is publicly available from open (unsealed) court records.[278]

Professionals should be wary of dispensing professional advice via public websites, forums, discussion groups, social media, etc. Doing so may inadvertently create a professional relationship with a person, causing all obligations attendant to a professional-and-client relationship to become applicable. This includes, for example, the obligations to maintain the confidentiality of communications and to avoid conflicts of interest (including conflicts between future and past clients). Disclaimers of the formation of a professional relationship are not always enforceable.

Professionals need to take care to avoid violating legal prohibitions against unauthorized practice. An attorney providing legal advice to a Facebook friend, or to a visitor to her website, must comply with the ethics rules of the jurisdiction in which she is licensed and also the jurisdiction where the recipient is located. The ethics rules, and sometimes state statutes, prohibit attorneys and certain other professionals from practicing in jurisdictions in which they are not licensed to practice. A professional, therefore, should avoid engaging in online activity that could be construed as the unauthorized practice of law in any jurisdiction where the lawyer is not admitted to practice.

States impose other duties on certain licensed professionals beyond the duty to exercise the requisite standard of care. These obligations may be set out in statutes, in a code of professional responsibility, or both. Attorneys, doctors and other professionals with a presence on the Internet need to ensure that their online dealings, including their websites, comply with these obligations.

Attorneys must avoid communicating with persons who are known to be represented by an attorney. Attorneys must also be cautious in their dealings with unrepresented parties and witnesses in matters they are handling for a client. Using trickery or deceit, such as creating a fake social media account in order to gain access to an adverse party's or witness's private social media account in order to gather information about that party or witness, is an ethical violation. Any publicly viewable information that a social media user publishes online is fair game, though.

A judge's "friending" of an attorney on social media may violate judicial canons of ethics if the attorney may appear in a matter before the judge. Judges are required to maintain neutrality and avoid even the appearance of impropriety.

Product Liability

A manufacturer, distributor or seller of a product may be liable to a consumer if the consumer suffers harm as a result of a defect in the product. Proof of intent to harm or deceive consumers is not necessary. Courts may impose strict liability on manufacturers, distributors and sellers whose products harm consumers.

Digital media may be products, but the expressive content is not. In *James v. Meow Media, Inc.*[279] a court rejected an attempt to hold the creator of violent videogames and movies liable for allegedly desensitizing viewers to violence. The court distinguished between a container of content, which may be a product, and the expression contained within it, which is not.

Conspiracy

A criminal conspiracy exists when two or more people agree to commit a criminal act. Conspiring with others to commit a crime is also a crime. It is punishable, however, only if a step is taken to commit the planned crime. The step need not be a criminal act in itself. Walking into a bank, for example, is not illegal, but walking into a bank with the intent to rob it may qualify as the step toward committing a crime that is needed for a conspiracy conviction.

It is not necessary to personally perform a planned criminal act in order to be convicted of conspiracy. If it is established that an agreement to commit a crime existed and that someone took an action in furtherance of it, then all members of the conspiracy may be found guilty.

It also is not necessary that the crime actually be attempted or completed. For example, if the triggerman enters the bank with the intention of robbing it as planned but immediately leaves the building upon seeing armed guards, he probably could not be convicted of robbery or attempted robbery, but he and his coconspirators might be charged with conspiracy.

The agreement may be express or implied. Mere presence or association with a criminal or with people who are planning a crime is not enough to establish participation in a conspiracy, however. Conspiracy is a specific intent crime, meaning that a person must intend to agree to the commission of a crime and intend the outcome to be achieved. Mere knowledge of a planned crime is not sufficient to prove intent.

If a crime is committed pursuant to a conspiracy, then all participants in the conspiracy may be punished for both the conspiracy and the crime, regardless of who actually performed the actions constituting the crime.

A civil conspiracy occurs when two or more people agree to commit a tort (civil wrong) with the intent of harming another and the commission of the tort does, in fact, result in damage. This could include agreements to engage in unfair competition, interference with a contract, or any other tort. Unlike criminal conspiracies, there cannot be liability for civil conspiracy unless the wrongful act that is the subject of the conspiracy is actually committed and causes damage.

If the existence of a civil conspiracy is established, then all co-conspirators are jointly and severally liable for the actions of every other conspirator.

Liability as a participant in a civil conspiracy may be avoided by withdrawing from it, but only if the other conspirators are informed of it. A withdrawal is effective only with respect to acts committed after the withdrawal. A conspirator will remain liable for any acts committed in furtherance of the conspiracy prior to the withdrawal.

AIDERS, ABETTORS AND ACCESSORIES

Helping or encouraging another person to commit a crime is a crime in itself, as is helping a person conceal evidence or avoid arrest for a crime. A person who helps or encourages another person to commit a crime may be guilty of aiding or abetting a crime. A person who helps another person conceal evidence or avoid arrest for a crime is guilty of being an accessory.

The definitions and rules applicable to these crimes are different in different jurisdictions. At the federal level, a person cannot be convicted of aiding, abetting or being an accessory to a crime unless a crime was actually committed. Proof of intent is also required. For aiders and abettors, it must be proven that the defendant intended to facilitate the crime. For accessories, it must be proven that the defendant intended to hinder the person's apprehension, trial, conviction or punishment.

In some states, liability as an aider or abettor may be avoided by withdrawing before the crime is committed. Among these states, a person seeking to avoid liability this way may be required to notify the perpetrator of the withdrawal and/or notify police before the crime is committed, or make some other bona fide attempt to stop the crime, such as by notifying the potential victim. Even if withdrawal, or attempted withdrawal, does not provide a complete defense in a particular case, evidence of it can sometimes be taken into consideration as a mitigating factor in the sentencing phase.

Solicitation

Solicitation is the crime of asking, demanding or encouraging another person to commit or participate in the commission of a crime which the defendant intends to commit. The crime is complete upon the act of solicitation. Neither an acceptance of the request nor the actual commission of the solicited crime is necessary.

An advertisement for illegal activity may be prosecuted as solicitation. In some cases, it may also violate a specific criminal prohibition. For example, 17 U.S.C. § 1201 (2017) specifically prohibits offers to sell tools for circumventing technological copyright protection measures.

Liability may sometimes be avoided by notifying the other person that the request is withdrawn. In some circumstances, it may be necessary to notify the police, too, in order to prevent criminal activity from occurring as a consequence of the original request. It is too late to withdraw a request after an arrest for solicitation has been made.

Incitement

Incitement means saying things that are intended and likely to produce imminent unlawful action, such as a riot.

Attempt

An attempt to commit a crime may be a crime in itself even if the attempted crime is not ultimately completed. The crime of attempt occurs when a person forms an intention to commit a particular crime and takes a substantial step toward completing it. Both elements must be proven. Merely forming an intention to harm another person is not a crime if no significant effort to act on it is made.

Contempt of Court

Judges are becoming increasingly involved in regulating website content, most often in connection with a family or juvenile court proceeding. Judges are issuing orders directing website owners or bloggers to refrain from posting specified kinds of content and/or to remove specified content. Intentional violation of a court order is contempt of court, punishable by confinement to jail and a fine. As with any order, a court must have personal jurisdiction over a person in order to issue an enforceable order directing the person to do or refrain from doing something.

Website Content as Evidence

Website content is increasingly being used as evidence in court proceedings. Although the rules of evidence prohibit hearsay evidence (unsworn, out-of-court statements) there are many exceptions to that rule. Moreover, the hearsay rule only prohibits the use of an out-of-court statement to prove the truth of the matter asserted. It does not prohibit the use of out-of-court statements as evidence of state of mind, such as motive, intent, ill will, etc. A blog post threatening or revealing animosity toward a particular person, for example, might be used as evidence of ill will, motive or intent to harm the person.

Deleting material from a computer or server does not usually remove all records of it. Also, posting material anonymously or pseudonymously will not necessarily prevent one's identity from being discovered. Law enforcement agencies are generally capable of tracing email messages and Internet postings to the IP addresses from which they were sent.

Courts may issue subpoenas to allow access to computers that may provide evidence of the author or publisher of a web page or blog post. First Amendment arguments have not met with a great deal of success in this area.

Anonymous and Pseudonymous Publishing

Publishing anonymously or pseudonymously will not provide protection from lawsuits. The state or a person who believes he has a legal claim against an anonymous or pseudonymous publisher may initiate a court proceeding against "John Doe" and then ask the court to issue a subpoena to the web hosting service requiring it to reveal the website owner's identity.

Because of the First Amendment freedom of association, anonymous expression is constitutionally protected. The right is not absolute, however. In deciding whether to issue a subpoena to require disclosure of an anonymous website owner's or blogger's identity, a court will weigh the First Amendment interest against the state's interest in disclosure and a party's need for the information in order to redress a claimed injury. In making this determination, the court will take into consideration the relevance of the information, the need for it, and the extent of the injury to associational rights if disclosure is ordered.

It is sometimes possible to fight a subpoena. Failing that, it might be possible to file a motion to prevent further disclosure of one's identity to anyone other than the party who secured the subpoena, such as a motion to seal the record, or to appear in the proceeding without revealing identity. Ultimately, though, if a court is persuaded that at least a prima facie case exists, it will probably issue the subpoena.

Strategic Lawsuits Against Public Participation

Defamation, invasion of privacy, and other kinds of lawsuits seeking damages or injunctions against people for engaging in speech activity can have a chilling effect on the exercise of protected speech and petition rights. In some cases, these kinds of lawsuits are filed for the purpose of inhibiting citizens from exercising their political or legal rights, or to penalize them for doing so.

The hallmark of a strategic lawsuit against public participation (SLAPP) is that it lacks merit and is brought with the goals of obtaining an economic advantage over a citizen party by increasing the cost of litigation to the point that the case will be weakened or abandoned, and of deterring future litigation.[280]

To deter lawsuit abuse, a number of states have enacted anti-SLAPP laws or court rules that provide special procedures and/or remedies for those who are sued for engaging in protected speech or petition activity, such as speech relating to a public official or to a matter of legitimate public concern.

Section 425.16 of the California Code of Civil Procedure is an example. It provides:

> A cause of action against a person arising from any act of that person in furtherance of the person's right of petition or free speech under the United States or California Constitution in connection with a public issue shall be subject to a special motion to strike, unless the court determines that the plaintiff has established that there is a probability that the plaintiff will prevail on the claim.

Some anti-SLAPP statutes or rules provide for an award of attorney fees and costs to the prevailing party. The applicable statute or court rule typically imposes a very short timeframe for asserting anti-SLAPP rights after being served with a SLAPP.

Not all states have enacted anti-SLAPP laws or procedures.

Net Neutrality

Net neutrality is the principle of freedom from content-based interference with network communications or transmissions by network service providers. Interference might be politically motivated, such as censoring portions of a Pearl Jam concert that expresses criticism of George Bush. It could also be commercially motivated, such as where a network service provider charges higher rates for faster delivery of content.

The FCC has jurisdiction over telephone, television, and broadband carriers. Historically, it has maintained a policy favoring neutrality for telephone transmissions but not for television. The leeway that cable television companies have been given to control pricing, terms and programming has had the effect of significantly reducing the volume of independently produced television programming. Net neutrality proponents fear the same thing could happen to broadband unless the FCC adopts and enforces a Net neutrality policy.

The FCC adopted a Net neutrality policy in 2015 and then repealed it in 2017. The repeal has been controversial. As of the writing of this book, the future of Net neutrality is uncertain.

PART IV. INTELLECTUAL PROPERTY

Chapter 23. Copyrights

Copyright issues can come up in e-commerce in one of two ways: (a) use of copyrighted material in website design or content; or (b) an e-commerce business's sale or licensing of copyrighted products, such as digital downloads of music, artwork, photographs and software. An e-commerce business must concern itself both with protecting its own copyrights and with avoiding infringing the copyrights of others.

In the United States, copyright law is almost exclusively federal. Article I, Section 8 of the U.S.. Constitution gives Congress the power to secure exclusive rights to authors. It has done this by enacting the Copyright Act,[281] a compendium of copyright law that has undergone a number of amendments over the years. The first Copyright Act was enacted in 1790. Significant revisions have occurred since then.

Copyright protection exists for any kind of work of creative authorship that is fixed in a tangible medium of expression. This can include nonfiction, fiction, poetry, plays, screenplays, drawings, paintings, graphic art, photographs, architectural designs, music, sound recordings, motion pictures, audiovisual works, computer programs, pantomimes, and choreography.

The purpose or intended use of a work is not relevant to copyright protection; neither are artistic merit or commercial value. The artwork in a business logo, for example, may be protected by copyright, as may an unpublished poem or a doodle on a scratch pad. Email messages are also protected by copyright. Sending a person a letter or an email message does not amount to an "implied gift" of the copyright in the contents of the letter or email message.

A work may be protected by copyright even if there is no copyright notice on it. At one time, omitting the copyright notice could result in copyright protection, but this is no longer true. Works published on or after March 1, 1989 are protected by copyright whether copyright notices appear on them or not. Affixing the words, "All rights reserved" is not necessary to protect the copyright in a work, either. Including these words on a website or blog could be useful in terms of bolstering a denial of an allegation of a grant of a license or authorization to copy or distribute material appearing on the site, but failing to include the notice neither creates a license nor causes copyright protection to be lost.

Registration is not necessary, either. A copyright may exist even if it is not registered with the Copyright Office. A copyright automatically comes into existence when an original work becomes fixed in a tangible medium of expression, even if no application for registration is ever filed. There are substantial benefits to registering a copyright, which are discussed in Chapter 27. Liability for infringement may be incurred, though, even if the work is not registered at the time of the infringement.

As a general rule, then, it should be assumed that everything on the Internet and in email communications is protected by copyright, unless some reason exists to conclude that it is not.

Accordingly, an e-commerce business should adopt a general policy of creating its own website content rather than copying content from other websites (or digitizing other people's offline works for use on a website). If the decision is made to copy and paste something from another website, investigate to determine whether it is indeed protected by copyright. If it is, then investigate further to determine who owns the copyright and then seek a license or permission to use the material.

Subject to some exceptions, a copyright gives its owner the following exclusive rights:

- Reproduction
- Distribution
- Public display
- Public performance
- Digital transmission
- Making derivative works based on the work.

The owner of a copyright in a sound recording has an exclusive right to digitally perform it, but not to publicly perform it by other means. The owner of the copyright in a motion picture has all of the above-listed rights. The "public display" right pertains to each frame in the motion picture. Thus, unauthorized streaming of a clip from a motion picture would infringe both performance and display rights.

There are only five limited circumstances in which a person may copy, publicly display, distribute, publicly perform or modify another person's work without incurring copyright infringement liability:

- Unprotected subject matter
- Public domain
- Fair use
- License or assignment of rights
- Work made for hire.

Using someone else's material can be a violation of other laws, too. If a contract prohibits it, then there may be liability for breach of contract whether it is copyright infringement or not. In some cases, liability may attach even if there is no contract. For example, information may be protected by trade secret, privacy or misappropriation law even though it is not protected by either copyright or a contract. Copyright defenses are not defenses against other kinds of claims.

Co-authorship

As a general rule, if two or more people work together to create a work, then in the absence of an agreement otherwise, they own the copyright jointly, provided they each contribute copyrightable expression.

Whether a work is jointly owned, or whether an element of it is owned separately by the creator of that element, is a question of intent. When two or more people create a work with the intention that their respective contributions will be merged into inseparable or interdependent parts of a unitary whole, then they are joint owners of the resulting work. Otherwise, each one is an individual owner of his or her individual contribution to the work.

> **Example 1**. Bernie is a prolific poet. One day, Elton happens upon one of his poems and says, "Hey, I think I can put music to this." Bernie approves of the idea, so Elton proceeds to create a song using Bernie's poem as the lyric. Since Bernie did not have the intention of creating a song with Elton when he wrote the poem, the copyright in the song is not jointly owned. Instead, Bernie owns the copyright in the lyrics and Elton owns the copyright in the music.

> **Example 2**. Elton asks Bernie to write lyrics for a song Elton is writing. Bernie proceeds to do so. Because they each intended their compositions to be parts of a unitary whole, Elton and Bernie would be joint owners of the copyright in the whole song (both the music and the lyrics).

> **Example 3**. Bernie writes the music and lyrics for a song. Elton comes up with a title for it. In this case, only Bernie would own a copyright in the song. Titles are not copyrightable.

The determination whether the copyright in a work is jointly or individually owned is helped greatly when there is a written agreement evidencing the parties' intention.

Joint creators of a work can enter into assignment agreements. In Example 3, for instance, Bernie could assign part ownership of the copyright to Elton for his contribution of a title to the work.

Owners of the copyright in a joint work are tenants in common. That is to say, they each own an undivided, fractional interest in the copyright. Each joint owner is free to exercise any of the rights of a copyright owner without needing to get the permission of the other joint owners. Each owner may license rights in the work to others. Each joint owner must account to the others, however, for any profits realized from either direct use or licensing of rights in the copyrighted work.

At least one court has held that a joint owner who individually creates a derivative work based on the jointly owned work has sole ownership of the copyright in the derivative work so created. The other joint owners do not have a right to share in the profits from a derivative work that one of the joint owners makes from the co-owned work. The other joint owners may have a right to share in profits attributable to any parts of the original work that are included in the derivative work, but they would not be entitled to share in the profits attributable to the newly created aspects of the derivative work.

Works Made for Hire

The copyright in a work initially belongs to the author. Usually, the person who creates a work is the author. In the case of a work made for hire, however, an employer or a person who specially commissions the work is the author.

A work made for hire is one that is either:

(a) created by an employee in the course of the employment; or
(b) specially commissioned pursuant to an agreement in which the parties expressly agree, in writing, that the work will be considered a work made for hire.

For purposes of this definition, employee status is determined by the law of agency. As a general rule of thumb, the greater the level of control and supervisory power, the more likely the hired party is an employee rather than an independent contractor. But control is not the only consideration. Courts consider several factors to determine whether a person is an employee or an independent contractor, including:

- Source of the tools and instrumentalities for the project
- Location of the work
- Duration of the relationship between the parties
- Right to assign additional projects to the hired person
- Hired person's discretion about when and how long to work
- Skill required
- Method of payment
- Hired person's role in hiring and paying assistants
- Whether the work is part of the regular business of the hiring party
- Whether the hiring party is in business
- Provision of employee benefits
- Tax treatment of the hired party
- The hiring party's right to control the manner and means by which the project is accomplished.

The right to supervise and control the hired person is probably the most significant factor, but no single factor is determinative.

A work created by an employee within the course and scope of employment is automatically a work made for hire even if there is no written agreement to that effect. A specially commissioned work, by contrast, is not a work made for hire unless the agreement between the contractor and the person commissioning the work expressly states that it is a work made for hire and the agreement is signed and in writing.

Because the employer or person specially commissioning a work is treated as the author, the person who actually created a work made for hire will be guilty of infringement if he copies, publicly displays, distributes, publicly performs, or makes derivative works based on it without the employer's permission (or the permission of the person who specially commissioned the work). A prudent content creator, therefore, will want to enter into a licensing agreement instead of a work made for hire agreement. When a work made for hire agreement is unavoidable, the content creator might want to consider including a provision giving him a nonexclusive license to use the work in specified ways (such as the rights to publish a copy of it on his own website and to include a copy of it in his portfolio, for example).

A prudent employer (or person who commissions a work) will want to ensure that the arrangement is properly structured as a work made for hire. In some cases, it may also be prudent to include an assignment of rights that applies if the arrangement is not a valid work made for hire.

A work is not a work made for hire unless it is either created during the course of the employment or created pursuant to the agreement commissioning it. If a writer/artist began creating the work before the employment began or before the agreement was made, then it cannot be a work made for hire. Thus, an author who creates a work and then enters into a contract with a publisher that specifies that the work is a work made for hire will continue to retain ownership of the copyright regardless of what the contract says.

Only the following kinds of specially commissioned works can be made the subject of a work made for hire agreement:

- Contribution to a collective work
- Contribution to a motion picture or other audiovisual work
- Translation
- Supplementary work
- Compilation
- Instructional text
- Test (and/or answer material for a test)
- Atlas.

A supplementary work is one that is prepared as an adjunct to a work by another author. It can include such things as introductions, illustrations, revisions, commentary, forewords, afterwords, maps, charts, tables, annotations, musical arrangements, answer material for tests, bibliographies, appendixes, indexes, etc.

Only copyright protection is acquired by virtue of a work made for hire agreement. Trademark and other intellectual property rights are not. Specific transfers or licenses of those kinds of property need to be made expressly, if at all; they are not implied in a work made for hire arrangement. When hiring someone to create a logo or artwork to be used in connection with marketing a product or service (which may include the website itself), care should be taken to ensure that the contract covers both copyright and trademark rights.

Compilations

A compilation is a collection of data and/or authored works. Examples include: anthologies of short stories, poems, etc.; photograph or artwork collections; catalogs; almanacs; directories; computer databases; and website content.

The selection and arrangement of things to include in a compilation can take some thought and creativity. For this reason, a compilation is considered a work of authorship on the part of the compiler. This means that the editor of a collection of stories may have a protected copyright interest in the collection – specifically, in the selection and arrangement of the elements in a collection – even if none of the works in the collection were authored by him.

Copyright protection for a compilation may exist even if the individual elements included in it are not protected by copyright. The selection of facts, and decisions about how to arrange and present them, may be protected by copyright even though the facts themselves are not. By the same token, the selection and arrangement of a compilation of public domain works may be protected by copyright even if none of the works included in it is.

Since a compilation may be protected by copyright even if its individual components are not, it is risky to copy and paste a data compilation (or a portion of it) from another website.

In the case of a compilation of authored works, it is important to keep in mind that the copyright in the compilation and the copyright(s) in the individual works within it are separate things. The copyright in a compilation exists independently of any copyright in the elements. Merely including a work in a compilation does not have the effect of transferring the copyright in the work to the owner of the copyright in the compilation. An editor may own a copyright in the selection and arrangement aspects of a compilation of short stories, while an author of a story in the collection may own the copyright in the story.

The owner of the copyright in a compilation is presumed to possess the right to reproduce and distribute the works contributed to it only as part of that compilation or a revision of that compilation. Merely owning the copyright in a compilation does not give rise to a right to copy, publicly display or distribute—or to authorize others to copy, publicly display or distribute—an individual story or article that is included in the collection.

The owner of the compilation copyright has an exclusive right to make revisions to the compilation, such as by rearranging the order, adding new stories or information to it, or removing a story or fact from it. The author of a copyrighted work appearing in the compilation, however, has the exclusive right to make derivative works of his copyrighted work. The owner of the copyright in the compilation does not necessarily have the right to alter or modify the content of a copyrighted work that appears in the compilation.

Copyright protection for a compilation does not confer copyright protection on portions of it that would not otherwise receive copyright protection. Owning the copyright in a data compilation does not mean ownership of the data, for example. If something would not be protected by copyright before it was compiled, then it will remain unprotected by copyright after the compilation. Only the manner in which the data is selected, arranged, presented or expressed in a compilation is protected by a copyright in the compilation.

COMPUTER DATABASES

A computer database is a compilation and, as such, is protected by copyright. The owner of a copyright in a computer database does not have a copyright in the data that is compiled within it, though. Only the manner in which the data is selected, arranged, presented or expressed in a compilation is protected by a copyright in a compilation.

The compilation of a computerized database is not protected by copyright unless some creativity goes into the selection or arrangement of the items in the database. The arrangement must not be merely a computer-generated random one or an obvious one, such as a list in alphabetical or numerical order. Creating categories for the organization of data is a sufficiently creative act to warrant copyright protection. If judgment is exercised in selecting the items to include, the selection decision may be protected by copyright. An exercise of judgment as to the words and/or images that are used to communicate information contained in a database may be protected by copyright, provided the information is not merged with the expression of it.

Derivative Works

A derivative work is one that contains elements of a preexisting work but in modified form. Examples of derivative works include: translations, dramatizations, fictionalizations, musical arrangements, screenplays, movie versions of novels, sound recordings of musical compositions, lithographs based on paintings, sculptures based on drawings, drawings based on photographs, abridgements, condensations, adaptations, annotations, revisions, and updated websites. Incorporating copyrighted programming code into another computer program results in the creation of a derivative work. A performance of a song is a derivative work of the song, as is a recording of the performance.

The copyright owner has an exclusive right to make derivative works from the work. No one else may do so without a license or permission from the copyright owner.

A copyright in a derivative work arises only if the person creating it has the right to use the preexisting work Ownership of a copyright in a derivative work only confers rights in the newly created aspects; it does not give the creator of the derivative work any rights in the original work.

Because anyone may freely use works that are in the public domain, derivative works based on public domain works are protected by copyright. The copyright in the derivative work does not confer ownership of a copyright in the original public domain work, though. Other people can make their own derivative works based on the same public domain work. The copyright in a derivative work only protects rights in material that is newly created for the derivative work.

Like any other work, a derivative work does not receive copyright protection unless it involves at least a modicum of creativity and originality. De minimis contributions to, or variations from, the original do not receive copyright protection.

Protectable Subject Matter

To be protected by copyright, a work must have all of the following characteristics:

- In one of the eight categories specified in the Copyright Act
- Fixed in a tangible medium of expression
- Expressive
- Original
- Creative
- Authored by a human.

CATEGORIES OF PROTECTED WORKS

The Copyright Act and regulations implementing it establish categories of works of authorship that may be protected by copyright. The categories are mostly important for registration purposes, but substantive rights sometimes depend on the classification, too. The categories are:

- Literary works
- Musical works (including lyrics)
- Dramatic works (including musical accompaniment)

- Pantomime and choreography
- Pictorial, graphic, and sculptural works
- Motion pictures and audiovisual works
- Sound recordings
- Architectural works.

The first five categories have received federal copyright protection since the time the first Copyright Act was enacted. Federal copyright protection for motion pictures, sound recordings, and architectural works did not come into being until the twentieth century.

Literary works include any kind of readable text, including computer programs. Lyrics receive copyright protection as musical works. Screenplays and scripts fall into the "dramatic works" category, as does the musical accompaniment to a play.

Motion Pictures

The Copyright Act defines a motion picture as "a series of related images which are intrinsically intended to be shown by the use of machines, or devices such as projectors, viewers, or electronic equipment, together with accompanying sounds, if any...."[282] Movies, soundtracks, webinar presentations, slide shows, and videogames are examples. Federal copyright protection for motion pictures began on August 24, 1912.

Because a motion picture is defined as a series of images, a single image accompanied by music, narration, etc. is not a motion picture. The image might be separately protected by copyright as a photograph or visual artwork, but not as a motion picture.

Motion pictures are usually registered as audiovisual works. For registration purposes, an audiovisual work may or may not have an audio element. If it does, then the sound may receive protection as part of the audiovisual work rather than as a sound recording. A preexisting sound recording, however, is treated as a sound recording for copyright purposes.

An audiovisual work may contain within it several different kinds of works in addition to the soundtrack. Elements of an audiovisual work could include a screenplay (which, in turn, may be a derivative work of a novel), musical works, sound recordings, artwork, choreography, production, direction, acting performances, pantomime, and possibly others. Some of these things may be protected by copyright independently of the audiovisual work, if they were created independently of the creation of the audiovisual work and not pursuant to a work made for hire agreement for use in the audiovisual work.

Sound Recordings

Federal copyright protection for sound recordings first came into existence on February 15, 1972. Before then, the performance and production elements of a sound recording were not protected by federal copyright law even if the owner of the copyright in the underlying work had authorized the making of the recording. When Congress amended the Copyright Act to provide copyright protection for sound recordings, sound recordings made before February 15, 1972 did not receive federal copyright protection, but recordings made on or after February 15, 1972 did. The musical or literary works performed on sound recordings, on the other hand, were protected by copyright both before and after 1972. Unauthorized copying of a pre-1972 recording did not infringe a federal copyright in the sound recording, but it could infringe the copyright in the musical composition and/or the lyrics.

State law protection of rights in sound recordings existed before February 15, 1972. Some states, such as California, continue to protect intellectual property rights in sound recordings made before February 15, 1972. California Civil Code Section 980(a) (2), for example, gives the creator of a sound recording fixed before February 15, 1972 exclusive ownership rights. New York courts have established a similar rule as part of the common law of that state.

Although the 1976 Copyright Act expressly preempted state copyright laws, Congress provided that the preemption of state laws protecting exclusive rights in sound recordings would not go into effect until February 15, 2067. Consequently, sound recordings that were made before February 15, 1972 continued to be protected by state intellectual property laws notwithstanding Congress's declaration of an intention to preempt the field.

In October, 2018, Congress enacted legislation establishing protections for the owners of rights in sound recordings that were made before February 15, 1972. Initial rights of ownership of pre-1972 sound recordings are determined by state law, but transfer requirements, the duration of protection, enforcement and remedies are now governed by the Copyright Act.

Some countries began protecting copyrights in sound recordings before the United States did. Sound recordings made in foreign countries may be protected by the copyright laws of those countries irrespective of when the United States began protecting copyrights in sound recordings.

People performing an authorized fixation of a work in a tangible medium may acquire copyright interests of their own if they contribute at least a modicum of creative content. For this reason, a recording artist may acquire a copyright in her authorized performance of a musical work on a recording, and the producer of the authorized recording may acquire a copyright in the production component of the sound recording. A composer may have a copyright interest in the musical work even if the recording is the only medium in which it has ever been fixed. The composer does not lose his copyright in the musical work merely because others have copyright interests in the recording. A copyright in a sound recording of a musical or literary work is separate and distinct from the copyright in the musical or literary work.

A sound recording of a performance of a musical or literary work is a derivative work. Because the owner of the copyright in a work has the exclusive right to make derivative works of it, the owner of the copyright in a musical or literary work has the exclusive right to make sound recordings of it. This right may be licensed to others. A person who makes an unauthorized sound recording of a copyright protected work (such as a song or an oral reading of a book) is guilty of copyright infringement, and acquires no copyright in the recording so made. Of course, if the person has a license to create the sound recording, then doing so is not infringement.

The copyright in a derivative work is distinct from the copyright in the underlying work. Ownership of the copyright in a derivative work only covers rights in the newly created aspects, not the original work itself. For this reason, the producer and performers on an authorized sound recording of a musical work only acquire a copyright in the sound recording. The copyright in the musical composition remains with the owner of the copyright in the musical composition.

It should never be assumed that the owner of the copyright in a sound recording (such as a record company) also owns the copyright in the musical composition. Sometimes this is the case, but sometimes it is not. Singer-songwriters and bands that write their own songs sometimes transfer the copyright in their musical works to a publisher, and recording companies then pursue rights to the song by negotiating with the publisher. This is not always the case, though. Some composers retain the copyrights to their music and work with recording companies directly. And even when a publisher or agent is used, the rights granted vary.

The copyright in a derivative work only protects rights in material that is newly created for the derivative work. Thus, any number of recording companies can independently create recordings of performances of public domain songs, and none would be guilty of infringing the copyright in another person's sound recording for doing so. An unauthorized recording of another sound recording, however, would be an infringement of the copyright in the sound recording, and this would be true even if the musical work that is performed on the sound recording is in the public domain.

For more information about performance rights in sound recordings, see Chapter 33.

Architecture

Copyright protection for architectural designs came into being on December 1, 1990. Both the design for a building (the form, arrangement and composition of spaces) and a depiction of it (blueprint, model or the actual building itself) may receive copyright protection if the building was constructed after November 30, 1990. The design must be fixed in a tangible medium, such as blueprints. The building itself, once constructed, also serves to fix the design in a tangible medium.

Architectural designs that were created before December 1, 1990 do not receive copyright protection if they were published before December 1, 1990, or if they are embodied in a building that was completed before December 1, 1990. An architectural design that was created before December 1, 1990, but was neither published before December 1, 1990 nor embodied in a completed building as of November 30, 1990 is protected by copyright only if a building embodying the design was completed by December 31, 2002. Copyright protection for architectural designs created before, and not published before December 1, 1990, terminated on December 31, 2002 if a building embodying the design had not been completed by then.

The building may be a house, office building, church, gazebo, etc. Designs for bridges, dams, roads and the like are not protected.

Architectural designs are an exception to the general rule that copyright does not protect utilitarian aspects of a work. Some utilitarian elements of an architectural design receive copyright protection. Standard functional features of buildings (doors, windows, etc.), however, do not. Standard configurations are not protected, either. For example, a design consisting of a hallway with multiple rectangular rooms annexed to it is a standard motel configuration. It does not receive copyright protection.

Drawings with architectural designs in them may qualify for copyright protection even if the design does not. Unless a drawing qualifies for protection as an architectural work, however, only the expressive aspects of the drawing receive protection; the idea for the design of the building does not.

PHOTOGRAPHS AND DRAWINGS OF BUILDINGS

Since a building is a medium for the expression of its architectural design, it would seem as if photographing or drawing a picture of a building without permission would infringe a copyright in the architectural design. Congress, however, has created an exemption from copyright infringement liability for photographs and drawings of a building if the building is visible to the public. Copying someone else's photograph or drawing of a building might result in liability for infringement of the copyright in the photograph or drawing, but not for infringement of the copyright in the architecture. The exemption does not extend to the making of three dimensional models or replicas of buildings.

INTERIOR DESIGN

Interior design is not protected by copyright. Therefore, photographing it should not result in liability for infringement. An individual work (such as a painting) does not lose copyright protection by virtue of being made an element of an interior design, however.

MODIFICATIONS OF BUILDINGS

The Copyright Act allows the owner of a building in which architecture is embodied to make or authorize the making of alterations to the building without incurring liability for creating an unauthorized derivative work.

Exclusions from Copyright Protection

Congress has established certain categories of elements of works in which no individual or business may claim a copyright. These exclusions are not the same as the exclusions from First Amendment protection that the Supreme Court has established. A work may be protected by copyright even though it is obscene, for example.

FEDERAL EMBLEMS, NAMES, SLOGANS, AND INSIGNIA

Congress has reserved to the federal government the exclusive right to use certain emblems, insignia, names, slogans and characters. These include such things as: federal department or agency insignia; badges or ID cards; the Red Cross; the Greek Cross; the Red Crescent; the Third Protocol emblem; the 4–H emblem; the great seal of the United States; the official seal of the U.S. President, Vice President, Senate, House of Representatives or Congress; the Golden Eagle insignia; Smokey Bear; and Woodsey Owl. The federal government doesn't really own a copyright on these, but it is a crime for anyone other the federal government and its licensees to make certain kinds of uses of these things.[283]

FEDERAL PUBLICATIONS

Generally, works created by the federal government, or by federal employees within the course and scope of their employment, are not protected by copyright. This includes federal statutes, court decisions, reports prepared by officials or employees of a federal administrative agency, etc. Not every work owned by the federal government is free of copyright, though. The federal government may own copyrights that have been assigned or transferred to it by a person or entity other than the federal government or a federal employee. When this happens, the work is protected by copyright notwithstanding its ownership by the federal government.

Independent contractors normally own the copyrights in works prepared for the federal government unless a contract, statute or regulation provides otherwise.[284]

Works prepared by officers or employees of the U.S. Postal Service, the Corporation for Public Broadcasting, the Public Broadcasting Service (PBS), or National Public Radio (NPR) are not considered works of the U.S. government. Therefore, they may be protected by copyright. Works prepared by officers or employees of the Smithsonian Institution are not considered works of the U.S. government if the author-employee was paid from the Smithsonian trust fund. And the U.S. Secretary of Commerce may secure copyright for a limited term not to exceed five years in any standard reference data prepared or disseminated by the National Technical Information Service pursuant to 15 U.S.C. §§ 1151–1157 (2017). The U.S. Mint also has special protections.

Although U.S. copyright law does not provide copyright protection for works created by the U.S. government, copyright protection for such works may exist outside of the United States.

FIXATION IN A TANGIBLE MEDIUM

To receive copyright protection, a work must be fixed in a tangible medium of expression. Digital files that are stored on a server, a computer's hard drive or a storage device are fixed in a tangible medium. Transmitting an email message entails storage of a digital copy of it. Storage of a copy of a website in a cache also qualifies as fixation in a tangible medium of expression. In short, website content and email messages generally are protected by copyright.

Although copyright protection does not arise until the expression is fixed in a tangible medium, it is the expression, not the medium, which copyright law protects. Once it has been fixed in a tangible medium, copyright protection for the expression continues to exist even if all tangible copies of it are destroyed.

The act of fixing a work in a tangible medium is necessary to the establishment of a protectable copyright, but it is not sufficient. The person who performs the physical act of fixing a creative thought in a tangible medium of expression does not thereby become the owner of the copyright. The creator of expressive content may retain copyright ownership of the content even if he hires or directs another person to perform the act of fixation for him.

Thoughts

Thoughts are not protected by copyright until they are fixed in a tangible medium of expression. Copyright protection is not retroactive to the date of the thought.

Live Performances and Broadcasts

Live performances and broadcasts, extemporaneous speech, unscripted dramatic performances, and musical or comedy improvisation are not protected by copyright unless transcribed or recorded in a tangible medium of expression of some kind. Under the Copyright Act definition of fixation, however, a work consisting of sounds and/or images that are transmitted at the time an authorized recording of them is simultaneously being made is considered "fixed" at the time of transmission. Put another way, if a performance is fixed in a tangible medium by means of simultaneously recording it, then copyright protection commences from the time the recording of the performance began, not from the time it is completed. If a band has hired someone to record their concert, then copyright protection begins when the 'Record' switch is flipped and the band begins performing. Consequently, if both an authorized and an unauthorized recording of a performance are made at the time of the performance, the unauthorized recording is an infringement of the copyright in the authorized recording.

A *bootleg recording* is one that is created by recording a live performance without permission. If the performance is of a musical work that is protected by copyright, then the recording would be an infringing derivative work of the musical work. If no authorized recording of the performance is being made at the time the unauthorized recording is, then under ordinary copyright principles, the maker of the bootleg recording would only be infringing the copyright in the musical work, not the copyright in the performance. This is because a copyright in a performance does not exist until an authorized recording of it has begun. Congress has enacted a special statute to deal with this kind of situation. The Anti-Bootlegging Act[285] (part of the Uruguay Round Agreements Act) declares that anyone who makes, transmits, distributes or reproduces an unauthorized recording of a live musical performance is subject to the same liabilities and criminal penalties as a copyright infringer even if the recording does not actually infringe a copyright in the performance.

EXPRESSION

Copyright only protects expression. It does not protect information, theories or ideas. Information, ideas and theories are not protected by copyright, but the words, sounds or images that are used to communicate them may be. Also, selecting and arranging elements to include in a compilation is considered a form of expression. The selection and arrangement of information and ideas may be protected by copyright even if the information and ideas are not.

Facts and Ideas

Facts and ideas are not protected by copyright, even when they are fixed in a tangible medium of expression. A particular sequence of words that is selected to communicate an idea or a fact may be protected, though. Thus, while the plot or theme of a story is not protected by copyright, the words used to flesh it out may be.

Drawings and diagrams receive copyright protection only for the original artwork and text in them, not the ideas or discoveries they illustrate. An idea for a new game or videogame, the method and procedure for playing the game, and the rules of the game, are not protected by copyright. The text, images, music, sound recordings and/or audiovisual works that are displayed or performed in the course of the game, and any textual matter describing the game, may be protected by copyright, though.

Algorithms, ingredient lists for recipes, blank forms, systems, methods, and processes are all examples of things that do not receive copyright protection because they are ideas.

Craft, stencil, pattern, and how-to works typically contain a mixture of expression, facts and ideas. A project, craft or design is an idea, as is the process for making a thing. The text, artwork and photographs included in a how-to book or article about the project, however, may be protected by copyright, to the extent they are not merged with the idea.

The factual information, methods and procedures included in owner manuals and instructional materials are not protected by copyright. Any unmerged expressive content, such as stylized illustrations, may be protected by copyright, however. The selection and arrangement of information may be protected by copyright, too.

Because an invention is an idea, it does not receive copyright protection no matter how creative or original it is. A person may have a copyright in the particular words used to describe an invention, but not in the idea or invention itself. For that kind of protection, a patent would be needed.

Architectural designs are an exception to the rule that ideas do not receive copyright protection. The design of a building may be protected by copyright.

Themes, Moods and Messages

The overall theme, mood or message of a work is not protected by copyright. The fact that Grace Slick wrote an eerie song referencing drug use, for example, would not give her the exclusive right to compose eerie songs referencing drugs.

Utilitarian Features

Because they represent ideas, the utilitarian features of a work (such as a computer program or a sculpture) generally are not protected by copyright. Utilitarian aspects of a work are functional, not expressive. Useful articles and the utilitarian aspects of designs might be protected by patent law in some cases, but they generally are not protected by copyright law.

The seat, back and legs of a chair are functional. Accordingly, if an artisan makes a sculpture of a chair, other people may freely make sculptures and drawings of articles with seats, backs and legs without fear of liability for copyright infringement. They may not, however, copy the purely expressive, nonutilitarian aspects of the original sculpture, such as the decorative ornamentation on the chair. Similarly, the pattern pieces that are used to create a useful article, such as shapes that may be traced and used to make a sleeve for a dress, generally are not protected by copyright, because they have an intrinsic utilitarian function. Stencils or templates that contain a sufficient amount of original pictorial or graphic artwork or original compilations of such artwork—such as a stencil book that contains original, artistic images of animals, trees, and automobiles—may be protected by copyright, however.

Architectural works are an exception to the general rule that utilitarian features do not receive copyright protection. Some utilitarian features of an architectural design may receive copyright protection.

Fonts, Typefaces, and Calligraphy

Fonts, typefaces, calligraphy and typographic ornamentation generally do not receive copyright protection, no matter how novel or creative they may be. This is because the creative aspect of the character usually cannot be separated from its utilitarian function. On the other hand, if it is possible to separate the pictorial or graphic elements from the utilitarian aspects in a particular case, then the decorative elements may receive copyright protection. A letter drawn in the shape of another object would be an example. And typeface ornamentation that is separable from the typeface characters (such as flourishes, swirls, vector ornaments, scrollwork, borders and frames, wreaths, and the like) may be copyrightable. The ornamentation must involve something more than de minimis creativity, though. The mere use of text effects, such as chalk, neon lighting, beer glass, etc. will not suffice.

Medical, Scientific and Technical Imaging

Medical, scientific and technical images—X-rays, MRIs, mammograms, echocardiography, ultrasound, land surveys generated by echo-sounders, etc.—generally are not protected by copyright. They are utilitarian images and communicate only facts and ideas. Just as a copyright claim may be made in a compilation of data, though, so too a copyright claim may be made in the selection and arrangement of a compilation of medical, scientific or technical images. Also, a work created with one of these technologies may receive copyright protection if it is put to an expressive use, such as the creation of modern art.

Computer Programs

Because ideas are not protected by copyright, only the literal components of a computer program receive copyright protection. The nonliteral aspects (the algorithm, the functions performed, the systems and methods used) do not.

Some courts have held that the sequence, structure and organization (SSO) of a program are protected by copyright. Other courts disagree. The modern trend is to avoid any per se classification of SSO, and to evaluate SSO on a case-by-case basis to determine whether it is an idea, method or process, on one hand, or nonutilitarian expression, on the other.

The source and object code receive copyright protection as a literary work. The same general rules apply. This includes the rule that when an idea is merged with the expression of it, the expression is not protected by copyright. In these situations, the thing is treated as an idea rather than an expression, and therefore not protected by copyright. The more "bare bones" an expression of an idea or information is, the more likely it is that the expression of the idea or information is merged with the idea or information itself, and therefore not protected by copyright.

In general, an aspect of a computer program is not protected by copyright if it is something that is necessary to make the program perform its intended function. The menu command hierarchy is a functional aspect of a program, and therefore is not protected by copyright.

Although using the same algorithm, system or method to perform the same functions as another computer program does not result in liability for copyright infringement, it may result in liability for patent infringement if the software is patented.

Subject vs. Depiction

Unless the scene or subject of a photograph or drawing is itself a copyrighted work, the subject or scene is not protected by copyright. Natural objects and naturally occurring events are facts, not expression. Any number of people may take a photograph of the same tree without infringing each other's copyrights, for example.

Merged Expression

To the extent a work of authorship does nothing more than communicate factual information or an idea, it is not protected by copyright. In these cases, the idea or fact is said to be *merged* with its expression.

> **Example 1**. Every part of the sentence, "The earth is moving through space" is essential to the idea or fact that the earth is moving through space. Since ideas and facts are not protected by copyright, no one can claim ownership of the idea or fact that the earth is moving through space. That being the case, no one can claim an exclusive right to say, "The earth is moving through space."

> **Example 2**. An illustration in a mathematics text consisting of nothing more than a line drawing of a sine function on a Cartesian coordinate graph communicates nothing more than the nature of the sine formula. The drawing and the idea are merged, so the drawing is not protected by copyright. Suppose the artist adds ornamentation to the line to make it look like a rope or a snake. This aspect of the drawing, being unnecessary to communicate the idea of a sine function, is expressive and would be protected by copyright, while the representation of a sine function is not.

Contest rules are another example. They do not receive copyright protection because the idea (the set of rules) is not separable from the expression of the idea.

Any nonfunctional matter that is not essential to the expression of the idea does not merge, and it may be protected by copyright. Illustrations or examples inserted into a set of contest rules in order to help readers understand them better are not necessary elements of the expression of the idea, so they do not merge, and therefore they may be protected by copyright. The words, "like a bat out of hell," in the expression, "The earth is moving through space like a bat out of hell" are not necessary to the communication of the fact or idea that the earth is moving through space, so they do not merge, and therefore may be protected by copyright.

The more "bare bones" the expression of an idea or information is, the more likely it is that the expression of the idea or information is merged with the idea or information itself, and therefore not protected by copyright.

CREATIVITY

Although copyright law, unlike patent law, does not require an author to demonstrate the creation of something novel and unique, a work nevertheless must involve at least a modicum of creativity in order to receive copyright protection.

It is difficult to pinpoint exactly what is required in order to satisfy the creativity requirement. The quality, merit or value of the work is not relevant. What matters is that the author contributes something original and nonobvious.

At one time, courts applied a "sweat of the brow" rule according to which the amount of effort put into a work determined whether it was creative or not. Facts and information could be protected by copyright if the researcher or compiler worked hard to investigate and gather them. That doctrine has been abolished, however. No matter how difficult a research project or fact compilation is, facts and information are not protected by copyright.

Today, creativity is assessed by neither a qualitative nor a quantitative analysis. Unfortunately, that leaves us with no bright-line test for determining whether something is sufficiently creative to warrant copyright protection or not. It is possible, however, to identify certain kinds of things that have been deemed to be too uncreative to receive copyright protection. Examples of things that do not involve a sufficient level of creativity to warrant copyright protection include:

- Titles
- Names
- Short phrases
- *Scènes à faire*
- Jokes and gags
- Blank forms, charts and graphs
- Fact gathering
- Alphabetization
- Consecutive numbering
- Page numbers
- Colorization
- Digitization
- Fonts, typefaces, calligraphy
- Geometric shapes
- Familiar symbols
- Uncreative compilation methods.

Geometric Shapes and Familiar Symbols

A drawing of an unadorned geometric shape, or an arrangement of geometric shapes in an obvious pattern, does not satisfy the creativity requirement. If they are arranged in a nonobvious way, however, the resulting arrangement may be protected by copyright. The same is true of familiar symbols.

Titles and Short Phrases

Courts generally deny copyright protection to titles and short phrases because it is believed that no significant amount of creativity goes into coming up with them. If they are used to market products or services, though, then they may be protected as trademarks.

Characters

Fictional story and cartoon characters are sometimes protected by copyright. In these cases, it is not really the name of the character that is protected by copyright; it is the character's description that is. The use of the same name for a completely different kind of character normally is not a problem. For example, a story about a Vulcan named Mr. Spock who explores the universe aboard a starship could violate a Star Trek copyright. A romance story in which one of the characters is a Philadelphia optometrist named Mr. Spock probably would not.

A character's description receives copyright protection only if it is unique and distinctive. This rule can be easier to state than to apply. Certainly if the character's description is the story, then the character itself may be protected by copyright. *Tarzan of the Apes* is an example. The

Tarzan character is a man who was raised by apes. That is also the story. On the other hand, when a character's description is only an adjunct to a story, more details may be needed before the character description will receive copyright protection. The less unique and developed the character, the less likely it is to be protected by copyright. The more unique and developed a character is, the more likely it is to be protected by copyright.

> **Example**. An alien from another planet who is stranded on earth is such a general description of a character that it probably will not receive copyright protection. As more distinctive features are added— powers of levitation and telepathy, a long neck and a big head, a penchant for saying, "Phone home"—the likelihood that unauthorized use of the character in a different story will be found to infringe a copyright increases.

The author or assignee of a copyright protected work has the exclusive right to make derivative works from it. A new story using unique and distinctive character(s) from a preexisting story is an example of a derivative work. If such a story is created without permission, liability for copyright infringement may be incurred.

The copyright in a motion picture or other work and the copyright in a character appearing within it may be owned by different persons.

Whether a character or character name is protected by copyright or not, it may be protected as a trademark if it is used in connection with the marketing of goods or services. Some fictional characters are protected under both copyright and trademark law.

Scènes à Faire

A *scène à faire* is a stock or standard literary device, typically in a play or other dramatic work. It is a scene or detail that is considered standard in works in a particular genre. Uses of gadgetry in a spy novel, or a male serenading a lady outside her window, are examples. *Scènes à faire* do not receive copyright protection.

In a similar vein, similarities between a scene in one work and a scene in another work do not infringe a copyright in the first work if they follow naturally from the situation. A couple seeking refuge in a church during a storm would be an example.

Stereotypical characters do not receive copyright protection, either. The description of a character as a drunken Irish policeman, for example, is not protected by copyright.

Details that are essential to the description of a particular kind of scene are also considered *scènes à faire*. It has been held, for example, that a movie about the South Bronx featuring drunks, prostitutes, vermin, and junk cars does not infringe the copyright in a previous movie featuring those same things. The court ruled that any movie about the South Bronx would need to feature these things in order to be realistic.

Placing a list of variables at the beginning of the source code is an example of a *scène à faire* in a computer program. The textual content of the list might be protected by copyright, but the practice of listing variables at the beginning is so standard that no one can claim a copyright in this kind of arrangement.

Jokes and Gags

A play, screenplay or other dramatic work may receive copyright protection, but a short joke or gag within it might not.

Blank Forms, Charts and Graphs

The content of a form, graph or chart may receive copyright protection if it is sufficiently creative and original, but the graph, chart or form itself does not.

Fact Gathering

Gathering factual information is not considered a creative act. Selecting which facts to include in a work and how to arrange them may qualify as creative expressions, provided the selection and arrangement are not obvious. Words and images that are used to communicate facts may be protected, to the extent the expression is not merged with the information. Although fact gathering is not protected by copyright, there can be situations in which using information that someone else has gathered may result in liability. See Chapter 31.

Obvious Arrangements

Obvious arrangements are not protected by copyright. Alphabetical, chronological and consecutive numbering arrangements are too obvious to receive copyright protection. A White Pages directory or similar listing generally is not protected by copyright. It may take a lot of work to gather and compile the information, but facts are not protected no matter how much work went into gathering them. The text in a White Pages directory is not protected because it is purely factual information that is merged with the expression of the information. The alphabetical and numerical arrangement of entries in the directory is not protected because it is not a sufficiently creative arrangement. The arrangement of entries in a Yellow Pages directory, on the other hand, may be protected by copyright because at least a modicum of creativity goes into the formulation of categories into which to place directory listings. A page numbering system is not considered sufficiently creative to receive copyright protection.

Photography

The creativity requirement is very easily satisfied in the case of photographs. The mere act of pushing a button on a camera to take a photograph suffices, even if the photographer played no part in designing, manufacturing or selecting the camera; gave no thought at all to angle, lighting, filters, etc.; and had nothing to do with creating the scene depicted in the photograph. A photographer has a copyright in the photographs he takes even if his only contribution to their creation was to push a button on the camera.

On the other hand, no copyright protection exists for a photographer's selection of the angle, distance and lighting employed in a photograph. Decisions about these matters are not deemed to be creative acts.

Restoring an aged or damaged photograph to its original condition is not a sufficiently creative act to warrant copyright protection. Retouching a photograph, on the other hand, may qualify for copyright protection if a substantial amount of new content is added, such as using airbrushing to change the picture. A retouched photograph is a derivative work. Unauthorized derivative works of works that are protected by copyright do not receive copyright protection. Authorized retouching of a photograph may be protected by copyright, as may retouching of public domain photographs.

COLORIZATION AND DIGITIZATION

Colorizing or changing the colors in a photograph or audiovisual work is not a sufficiently creative act to receive copyright protection unless the alteration is unusual. Factors to be considered are: whether and how much creativity went into the selection of colors, how much human involvement there was, and the extent to which overall appearance is affected. Digitization is not a sufficiently creative act to receive copyright protection.

Music

The rule of thumb for musical works is that both the melody and the lyrics of a song are protected by copyright if they are original. Use of either the music alone or the lyrics alone is just as capable of being infringement as use of the words and music together is. Other elements—the beat, rhythm, chord progression, and fills – generally are not protected by copyright.

Song titles and short musical (or lyrical) phrases are not protected by copyright. They may be trademarks, though, if they are used in connection with the marketing of goods or services. "Ziggy Stardust" and "Yellow Submarine" are examples of song titles which, although not protected by copyright, are protected trademarks. Taylor Swift and other popular recording artists have registered a number of their song titles and lyrical phrases as trademarks.

The Copyright Office has taken the position that because a short phrase is not protected by copyright, a series of repetitions of it is not, either. In the Copyright Office's view, a song lyric consisting of multiple repetitions of the phrase, "I love you" would not be protected by copyright because the phrase "I love you" is too short to meet the creativity requirement. It is not clear that the Copyright Office is correct about this. The band Devo's interminable, robotic repetition of the short phrase, "Are we not men? We are Devo" certainly seems to be a creative way of expressing more than what is conveyed by a single iteration of the phrase, much in the same way that Andy Warhol's depiction of identical photographs of the exact same soup can in a pictorial series conveys something more than and different from what a single photograph of the soup can does. There does not appear to be any sound doctrinal basis for declaring either Devo's or Warhol's work to be uncreative. The Copyright Office's opinions are not binding on courts, and it is not certain that all courts would adopt the Copyright Office's position.

CHORD PROGRESSIONS

Chord progressions (sometimes collectively called "harmony") are not protected by copyright. A particular combination of the chord progression with another musical element (such as the melody) may be protected, though.

RHYTHM

The beat or rhythm of a song is not protected by copyright.

ARRANGEMENTS

As a rule of thumb, arrangement parts (such as the bass line) generally are not protected by copyright. An arrangement part may be protected by copyright, however, if it is incorporated into the melody. And a particular combination of arrangement parts, or combination of an arrangement part with a chord progression, may be protected by copyright, if it is sufficiently creative and original. In short, even though the chord progression, harmonies, rhythm accompaniment, musical fill phrases and the like may not be protected by copyright individually, the arrangement, taken as a whole, may be—provided it is not itself merely a copy of a preexisting, copyright-protected arrangement.

A copyright in an arrangement may exist independently of the copyright(s) in the melody and lyrics. For this reason, an original arrangement of a public domain song may be protected by copyright even though the song itself (melody and lyrics) is not. A new arrangement of a copyright-protected musical work, on the other hand, is protected by copyright only if it is either created or authorized by the owner of the copyright in the original musical work. In some situations, the Copyright Act provides a compulsory license to make an arrangement of a musical work. See Chapter 33.

DIGITIZATION

Digitization does not receive copyright protection.

ORIGINALITY

To receive copyright protection, a work must be original, meaning that an author must create the work independently, not by copying another work. Logically, this is simply an aspect of the creativity requirement. Courts, however, treat it as a separate requirement.

Originality is required whether the copied work is protected by copyright or not. Accordingly, neither a work that is created by copying a public domain work nor a work that is created by copying a copyright protected work receives copyright protection.

Because of the originality requirement, the creator of an authorized derivative work only acquires a copyright in the newly created aspects of the derivative work, not in the original work. This can be important when determining whose permission is needed to use a portion of a derivative work. In some cases, permission from both the original and the derivative authors may be necessary. When in doubt, the safest course would be to obtain permission from both.

The creator of an unauthorized derivative work does not acquire a copyright in any aspect of the derivative work. Infringing works do not acquire copyright protection. As a result, copying from an unauthorized derivative work will not result in infringement liability to the author of the derivative work, although it may result in liability to the owner of the copyright in the original work.

Independent Creation

When two or more authors create the same work without either working cooperatively or copying each other, then each is an author and each owns a copyright in the work. If, for example, two musicians write the same song without either of them being aware of the other, then neither of them is guilty of infringement, and each of them may sue others for infringement of the copyright. The two works must truly be created independently, though. If one author copied the other – even subconsciously—then the work that is a copy of the other would not meet the originality requirement and therefore would not receive copyright protection.

Independent creation is a significant issue in the case of musical works because there are typically only a few standard chord progressions in a particular music genre; there are only a limited number of notes in a scale that will harmonize with a chord; and there is a shared pool of common musical techniques and devices (such as an incomplete cadence phrase followed by a complete cadence phrase) that every songwriter draws upon when composing a melody. Add to this the fact that a song may infringe the copyright in another song if the melodies are similar even if the lyrics are completely different, and the possibility that two composers might independently come up with the same or very similar musical compositions is not really all that far-fetched. Be that as it may, courts tend to regard a high degree of similarity between two song melodies as strong circumstantial evidence of copying. If it can be proved that a composer had access to a song (e.g., it was broadcast on a radio station that he could have heard before he wrote his song), then a high degree of similarity between it and a song he later writes may suffice as circumstantial evidence of copying.

It is not necessary to prove intent to infringe in order to prevail on a copyright infringement claim. George Harrison was successfully sued on the basis that he subconsciously copied the melody of the Chiffons' song, "He's So Fine" for his song, "My Sweet Lord," although he was not consciously aware that he was doing it.

The ultimate question is whether the composer of the allegedly infringing composition copied (either consciously or subconsciously) a preexisting song that is protected by copyright. In addition to other kinds of evidence of copying, courts may consider the similarity of the songs. The more similar the melody and/or lyrics, the stronger the circumstantial evidence of copying. The fact that the same rhythm or chord progression is used in both songs will not usually suffice as circumstantial evidence of copying, if the same rhythm or chord progression has been used in a lot of other songs, too. As the arrangement parts, and/or their use together, grow in distinctiveness and originality, however, it becomes less likely that a subsequent song's employment of them is merely coincidental. When the same rhythm accompaniment, chord progression, and arrangement parts are used together in a song with a similar melody or lyrics, the likelihood of a finding of copying, and therefore copyright infringement, increases considerably.

In those rare cases where two authors do independently create identical or very similar works without either one copying the other, they are not joint authors. They are each individual authors of the work, each with protectable copyrights. In this respect, copyrights differ from trademarks. An independently created work may infringe a trademark but it cannot infringe a copyright.

Photographs and Drawings of Other Works

A person who photographs or draws another person's drawing or photograph generally does not have any protected copyright interest in the photograph or drawing so created. Because the taking of a photograph is a means of copying the subject of the photograph, photographing a drawing or other preexisting work that is protected by copyright infringes the copyright owner's exclusive right of reproduction of the work. The maker of an infringing copy of a work acquires no copyright in the infringing copy.

Drawing or photographing existing works would also infringe the copyright owner's exclusive right to make derivative works. A modified version of a copyrighted work would be a derivative work. Only the copyright owner has the right to make derivative works from her work. An infringer acquires no copyright in an unauthorized derivative work.

A drawing of the same subject or scene depicted in a photograph is not a derivative work if it is independently created. For example, the fact that a photographer has taken a picture of the Grand Canyon as seen from a particular angle and distance, and in a particular lighting, does not mean that no one may thereafter make a drawing or painting of the Grand Canyon as seen from the same angle and distance and in the same lighting. What it means is that an artist cannot sit at his desk and try to draw or paint an image of the Grand Canyon using the photograph as a model. If the drawing is created in this manner, then it is a derivative work of the photograph. A copyright in a derivative work arises only if the person creating it has the authority (such as a license from the copyright owner) to use the preexisting work.

Photographing or drawing a copy of public domain material is not infringement. Therefore, such photographs and drawings may be protected by copyright. Owners of the copyrights in such photographs and drawings do not acquire rights in the underlying works, though. The underlying works remain in the public domain.

Although pushing a button on a camera is considered a creative act, courts have held that photographs of other works are not entitled to copyright protection when they involve only slavish copying. Slavishly photographing, scanning or digitizing a preexisting work will not result in the creation of a new copyrightable work if the copy is identical in visual appearance to the original, even if the work in question is in the public domain. An unretouched photograph of the Mona Lisa, for example, normally will not be protected by copyright.

Although photographers and artists do not get copyright protection for slavishly copying other works of authorship, their creations may be protected by copyright to the extent they significantly modify them, so long as such modifications do not infringe a copyright in the underlying work. A photographer who makes a significant modification of a public domain image (rather than simply creating a copy of it) acquires copyright protection for the modification. For example, if a photographer photoshops a mustache into her photograph of the Mona Lisa (which is in the public domain), she may acquire rights in the image she has created of the Mona Lisa with a mustache. A photograph depicting the Mona Lisa painting hanging in a gallery with visitors looking at it would probably be a sufficiently significant modification to earn copyright protection, too. If the underlying work is protected by copyright, however, then no rights in the modification would arise unless the owner of the copyright in the underlying work authorized the modification. As an infringer, the creator of an unauthorized derivative work acquires no rights.

HUMAN AUTHORSHIP

Copyright only protects works that are created by human beings. There is no copyright protection for materials that are created by natural forces, machines, or nonhuman animals. A work, such as a painting, created by a nonhuman animal is not protected by copyright even if a human supplied the tools (paints, brush, etc.) For the same reason, a transcription of the melody a bird sings would not be protected by copyright.

Machine-generated output that is created without any human interaction is not protected by copyright. A human may use a machine to assist in the fixation of a work, and the work that is fixed in a medium of expression as a result may be protected by copyright, but if the machine itself actually creates the output, then it is not.

The configurations and motions of natural objects that are caused by natural forces without human intervention—such as driftwood, the sound of waves crashing, or a cloud pattern in the sky—are not protected by copyright.

Although musical works created by machines, animals or natural forces are not protected by copyright, a human being's exercise of judgment in the selection and arrangement of those sounds may be protected by copyright, provided it is sufficiently original and creative.

Infringement

Infringement occurs when someone without a right or permission to do so exercises one of the exclusive rights of ownership of the copyright in a work (reproduction, distribution, public display, public performance, or the making of a derivative work). It may be direct or indirect. *Direct* infringement refers to an act of infringement (copying, etc.) that is personally committed by the person sought to be held liable for it. *Indirect* infringement refers to situations in which one person commits the act of infringement and another person is held responsible for it. There are three kinds of indirect infringement: vicarious; contributory; and inducement.

DIRECT INFRINGEMENT

To establish direct infringement, the claimant must prove both (a) ownership of a valid copyright, and (b) another person's unauthorized exercise of one of the exclusive rights of copyright ownership.

A person cannot be held liable for direct infringement unless she personally performs the infringing act.

Reproduction

Reproduction, in copyright law, means making a copy (or multiple copies). The copying does not need to be exact. Infringement may occur if it is "substantially similar."

Copying may be proven with direct or circumstantial evidence. Direct evidence might include, for example, the testimony of an eyewitness who actually saw the copying occur. Proof by circumstantial evidence requires a showing of two things: access and similarity.

There must be some evidence of at least potential access to the copyrighted work by the defendant, coupled with a showing that the works are similar. A strong showing on one factor means that the showing on the other factor does not have to be as strong, but there must be at least some amount of evidence to support each. In the absence of direct evidence of copying, a complete lack of evidence of one or the other of these factors should preclude a finding of copying. In rare cases, however, a court may find that the fact that two works are very "strikingly similar" serves as circumstantial evidence of access, as well.

The fame or wide public distribution of a work can provide circumstantial evidence of access, even if there is no direct evidence that the alleged infringer actually viewed or heard the work. In the case of an unpublished or obscure work, some direct evidence of an actual opportunity to see the work may be necessary (such as the fact that the author submitted the work to the person for possible use in a publication, for example).

The similarity may, but does not have to, involve copyrightable elements of the works. If there has been a clear showing of access, then the existence of similar facts, ideas, public domain elements, etc. may help support an inference of copying. For example, even though a mistyped word or other small error in a manuscript is not protectable by copyright, the same error (factual, typographical or grammatical) appearing in two works can provide strong circumstantial evidence of copying.

The ultimate fact that must be proven in order to prevail on claims of infringement of reproduction rights is that copyright-protected expression was copied. If the only thing that can be established is that the defendant copied an idea or an element of a work that is in the public domain, then there can be no liability for copyright infringement. Of course, the fact that the defendant copied ideas or unprotected elements may sometimes support an inference that expressive content was copied as well, but that is not always the case.

Public Display or Performance

Not all displays or performances of copyrighted material are infringement. Only public ones are. Anyone who lawfully acquires a copy of a copyrighted work may display or perform it privately.

A display or performance is public if any of the following is true:

(a) It occurs in a place that is open to the public
(b) A substantial number of people outside of family and social acquaintances gather to view it
(c) It is transmitted or communicated to a place that is open to the public
(d) It is transmitted or communicated to a substantial number of people outside of family and social acquaintances.

An exception to the copyright owner's exclusive right to publicly display a work exists for copies of lawfully purchased works that are displayed to members of the public who are present at the place where the copy is located. This exception does not apply to the performance right.

To qualify as a performance, a transmission must be contemporaneously perceptible. Making and sending a copy of a work in a form that is not contemporaneously perceptible may infringe reproduction and distribution rights, but not performance rights.

As used in copyright law, *public display* is a broad enough term to include transmitting a work electronically via the Internet, emailing it, or uploading it to a website. Sending a work to email subscribers is a public display, at least if the list comprises more than just a small collection of family and friends. For the same reason, displaying a work on an Internet web page is a pubic display even if access is limited to people who pay a fee, or who qualify for membership in a private club. A display does not have to be accessible to all members of the public in order to be considered a public display. Also, a web site is public if it is capable of being accessed by the public, even if nobody has actually visited it. Posting to social media is also considered a public display.

Because public performance of a sound recording is not one of the exclusive rights of the owner of a copyright in a sound recording, publicly performing (playing) a sound recording does not infringe the copyright in the sound recording, although it might infringe the copyright in a musical or literary work that is performed in it. The owner of a copyright in a sound recording does have an exclusive right to publicly perform it by means of digital transmission (such as over the Internet), however.

Distribution

Distribution means an actual transfer of a copy to another person. Offering to distribute a work may qualify as publication, but a majority of courts hold that it does not qualify as distribution. BitTorrent and similar networked file-sharing systems illustrate the point. Merely making files on one's computer available to others to peruse is the legal equivalent of inviting people into one's home. Once there, they may happen upon books and read them. The homeowner could not be sued for copyright infringement in this situation because she has not personally violated any of the copyright owner's exclusive rights. The author's exclusive distribution right is not violated unless the homeowner actually disseminates a copy of the book to the guest. By the same token, inviting someone into a computer is not an act of distribution of a work residing on the computer. A person who accesses a file on the computer and makes a copy of it (downloads it) may be guilty of direct infringement. And depending on the circumstances, the proprietor of the file-sharing network may be indirectly liable for the downloading user's infringement. (See discussion of contributory liability, infra.) The person who made the files on his computer accessible to others, however, would not be liable for direct infringement.[286]

If a person does more than simply make a copyright protected work available, then a risk of indirect infringement liability may arise. Going back to the homeowner analogy, if a homeowner places a copying machine next to the bookshelf and affixes a sign reading, "Feel free to make a copy of anything on the shelf," then she may be secondarily liable for facilitating, inducing or encouraging a houseguest's direct infringement. In the same way, installing file-sharing software on one's computer and allowing other members of the file-sharing network access to files in a folder into which the computer owner has placed copyright protected works for the purpose of sharing them could result in contributory liability if somebody then uses the system to download a copy of a file.

Some courts have ruled to the contrary, holding that merely making a copy available for others to download is indeed enough to constitute distribution. In any event, if the making of a copy to place in the file-sharing folder was not authorized, then doing so would itself be an infringement of the copyright whether or not any distribution occurs.

VICARIOUS INFRINGEMENT

Vicarious infringement refers to the imputation of an infringing act to a person on whose behalf another person committed it. It may be imposed when a person has both of the following:

(a) the right and the power to supervise a direct infringer
(b) a direct financial interest in the infringement.

Knowledge of the infringing activity is not necessary in order for vicarious liability to attach. A person with supervisory power over a person may be held vicariously liable for the person's infringing activity from which she benefits financially even if she had no idea that the person was engaging in infringing activity. An employer may be held vicariously liable when an employee infringes a copyright during the course of the employment. A principal may be held vicariously liable when an agent infringes on the principal's behalf.

In some cases, a person may be held vicariously liable for the infringing activities of an independent contractor. A national organization may be held vicariously liable for the infringing activities of a chapter if the national organization has the right and the ability to control the activities of the chapter. Parent corporations have been held vicariously liable for the infringing activities of subsidiaries when the requisite elements of control and financial benefit exist. An advertiser that sponsors a program may be held vicariously liable for its content if the advertiser has the right to supervise and control the creation of program content.

Supervisory rights and powers may be found to exist if a web host has the right and the power to shut down a hosted website for infringing a copyright. A website owner who has the right to block or cancel the accounts of users who infringe copyrights may be found to possess the requisite level of control. Of course, vicarious liability will not attach unless the supervisory person also derives some financial benefit from the infringing activity. Receiving a fee for the use of one's property or facilities is not enough, by itself, to support a finding of financial benefit from infringing activity if others are charged the same fee to use the property or facilities for noninfringing activities. When that is the case, the financial benefit is derived from the license to use the property, not from infringing activity. Thus, web hosting services normally cannot be held vicariously liable for infringing activity on their clients' websites solely on the basis that they provide a tool that a client might possibly use to commit copyright infringement. In some situations, providing a facility for infringement might support a finding of contributory liability (see below), but in the absence of an additional showing of financial benefit specifically from the infringing activity itself it would not support a finding of vicarious liability.

If the supervisory person has a revenue stream that is enhanced by the infringing activity, then vicarious liability is a possibility. The most obvious examples are profit-sharing arrangements where the supervisory person receives a percentage share of revenues from the infringing activity. But a financial benefit may also be indirect. Increased traffic to a website due to the website's infringing activity may be a financial benefit to the web host if, for example, the web host receives a larger amount of advertising revenue based on the number of hits an advertisement on the hosted website receives.

A commercial website owner derives financial benefit from the content of the website, and also has the right and the power to approve or reject content created or provided by a website designer. Accordingly, a website owner may be vicariously liable for copyright infringement in connection with material that a designer provides or creates for the site.

CONTRIBUTORY INFRINGEMENT

Contributory infringement means knowingly facilitating someone else's act(s) of direct infringement. Doing things such as providing a website on which users are allowed to post infringing content may qualify as contributory infringement if each of the three following elements is established:

(a) Direct infringement occurs
(b) The person sought to be held contributorily liable knows or should know about it
(b) That person materially contributes to the direct infringement.

Unlike vicarious liability, contributory liability may not be imposed unless the person sought to be held responsible either knew or should have known of the unlawful activity. Actual knowledge is not necessary, though. Contributory liability may be imposed if a reasonable person would infer, based on the facts known, that infringing activity is occurring.

A&M Records v. Napster[287] established, among other things, that if an online service provider knows or should know of actual ongoing infringement by a user of the service, and has the right and the ability to stop it, then failure to stop the infringing act may suffice to establish contributory liability for knowingly making a material contribution to the infringing activity.

If a substantial non-infringing use for a facility or mechanism exists, then the mere fact that a person provided the facility or mechanism is not a "material contribution" to the infringement. In *Sony Corp. v. Universal City Studios*[288] the U.S. Supreme Court held that merely providing a mechanism that somebody could use or has used to engage in infringing activity is not enough to qualify as a material contribution to the infringement. There must, in addition, be some affirmative act of solicitation, inducement, encouragement, or assistance to another to use the facility or mechanism to infringe a copyright before contributory liability will be imposed under these circumstances.

In both *Sony* and *Napster*, the copyright owners sued a provider of a means by which people were infringing copyrights. *Sony* involved a distributor of videocassette recording devices. *Napster* involved a provider of a peer-to-peer networking system. The Ninth Circuit Court of Appeals distinguished the cases by explaining that the defendant in *Sony* did not have knowledge of infringing uses, but the defendant in *Napster* did.

INDUCEMENT

In *Metro-Goldwyn-Mayer Studios, Inc. v. Grokster, Ltd.*[289] the U.S. Supreme Court clarified that providing a mechanism that may be used to infringe copyrights, and inducing or encouraging its use for that purpose, may be enough to establish indirect liability for infringement. Failing to remove content upon learning that it infringes a copyright may qualify as "materially contributing" to the infringement if the service provider has the ability and power to remove the content upon learning of it. Inducing or encouraging the users of a peer-to-peer networking system to use it to infringe copyrights also qualifies. Moreover, evidence that a person induced or encouraged infringing activity may also supply the "reason to know" that infringing activity would occur.

The elements of the three kinds of indirect liability are summarized below.

VICARIOUS LIABILITY

- Right and power to control
- Financial benefit

CONTRIBUTORY LIABILITY

- Knowledge (actual or implied) of infringing act
- Material contribution

INDUCEMENT LIABILITY

- providing a mechanism that can be used to infringe copyrights
- fostering or encouraging infringing use.

Congress has enacted some safe harbors to protect website owners, hosts, and other online service providers from contributory liability for infringing activity on the part of users of such services. To qualify for protection, an online service provider needs to comply with the requirements of the DMCA. See Chapter 26.

DEFENSES

General Denial

Denial of the existence of facts necessary to establish that copyright infringement occurred is a defense. This may consist of a denial of the existence of a valid copyright or of a particular plaintiff's entitlement to the particular remedy sought. Asserting that the allegedly infringing work was independently created is an example of this kind of defense.

Fair Use or Public Domain

See Chapters 24 and 25.

Consent

Consent is a defense to infringement. Consent may be manifested in a licensing agreement or in other ways. The defense is lost to the extent the use exceeds the scope of the consent given.

Consent may be express or implied. Implied consent may arise from circumstances that would lead a reasonable person to believe the copyright owner has given permission for what would otherwise be an infringing use. A book containing what the cover describes as "easy-to-use forms" is an example where implied consent to copy for personal use has been given. Distributing copies of the forms to other people, however, would exceed the scope of an implied license to copy forms for one's own use.

The mere act of posting something to the Internet is not tantamount to a grant of an implied license to the whole world to copy and paste it. In some circumstances, however, content posted to an Internet Web site or sent in an email message may carry with it an implied license for certain people to use it in certain ways. It would probably be reasonable for a recipient of an email message to believe he has permission to copy and transmit the text of the message in a responsive email to the sender, so a court would most likely hold that an implied license to do that exists. Similarly, an implied license probably exists for a participant in an online discussion forum (including a Comments section) to copy and paste portions of content that someone else has posted to the same site, for the purpose of referencing the matter to which a responsive comment relates. Forwarding the contents of an email to others without the sender's permission, or copying and pasting a comment on one web site to a different web site, probably would exceed the scope of such implied licenses.

First Sale

The copyright owner's exclusive right to distribute a particular embodiment of a work generally is exhausted upon the first sale or transfer of title to the copy, provided the copy was lawfully made and acquired. The owner of a particular copy that has been lawfully made and acquired is entitled to sell, rent or otherwise dispose of its possession without needing permission from the copyright owner. She may also display it, but only at the place where the copy is located.

The first sale doctrine only applies to the right to distribute the actual lawfully owned copy itself. The copyright owner's other exclusive rights are not exhausted upon the first sale. The first sale doctrine does not give the owner of a lawful copy of a work a right to make additional copies, or to publicly perform, digitally transmit, publicly display, or make derivative works based on the work.

The first sale doctrine only applies to cases in which ownership of a copy has been transferred. It does not apply to cases in which a person is merely in possession of a copy, even if the possession is lawful. Thus, it does not apply to situations in which a person possesses a copy pursuant to a rental or license agreement. Most copies of software are licensed, not sold. In these situations, the buyer's rights are governed by the terms of the rental or licensing agreement rather than the first sale doctrine.

Computer programs and sound recordings of musical works are exceptions to the first sale doctrine. The first sale doctrine does not authorize the commercial exploitation of lawfully acquired copies of sound recordings of musical works or of computer programs. This means, for example, that a lawful purchaser of a music CD may let friends borrow it, but may not exact a fee or derive other commercial advantage from the transaction. Nonprofit libraries and educational institutions may loan or lease copies of sound recordings and computer programs for a noncommercial purpose. A nonprofit school may loan a lawfully made copy of a computer program to faculty, staff, and students, or to another nonprofit educational institution. Nonprofit libraries may loan lawfully made copies of computer programs if a prescribed copyright warning is affixed to them.

The first sale doctrine does apply to copies of most other kinds of works. Thus, the owner of a digital copy or DVD of an audiovisual work may rent it to others for profit without violating copyright law. The lawful owner of a copy of a book or an audiobook may rent it to others for profit without violating copyright law.

A computer program may be rented, leased or loaned if it is embodied in a machine and cannot be copied during the ordinary operation or use of the machine. Thus, renting or loaning a car to others is not copyright infringement even if computerized components are installed in it.

Videogames (i.e., computer programs embodied in or used in conjunction with a limited purpose computer that is designed for playing video games) may be rented, leased or loaned. Computer video games, i.e., games that can be played on a general purpose computer, do not fall into this category. Video games for a Play Station 3 game console, for example, may be rented, leased or loaned, but they may not be rented, leased or loaned if they are in a format that enables them to be installed and run on a PC or other computer.

The owner of a lawfully made and acquired copy of an electronic audiovisual game for use in coin-operated equipment may publicly perform or display the game in coin-operated equipment. A license or permission to display or perform a work of authorship embodied in the game may be required, though, if the copyright in the work of authorship is not owned by the copyright owner of the electronic audiovisual game.

The first sale doctrine is not a defense to a digital transfer of a lawfully acquired digital copy of any kind of work. Digital transfers necessarily involve the making of a copy at the recipient's end. The first sale doctrine only applies to the distribution right, not the reproduction right.

> **Example**. Bob buys a physical copy of the book, *Watership Down* from an online bookseller. At the same time, he purchases a digital copy of it, which he proceeds to download to the hard drive of his computer. After reading it, he offers both versions for sale on a used books website. A buyer sends Bob money to buy both versions.

In this scenario, the first sale doctrine will protect Bob from liability for shipping his physical copy to the buyer. It will also protect Bob from liability for selling the hard drive of his computer with the digital version of the book still stored on it. It will not protect Bob from liability, however, if he delivers his digital copy of the book to the buyer electronically, or if he copies it to a jump drive and then sends the jump drive to the buyer. Copying a digital file to another digital storage device violates the copyright owner's exclusive right to reproduce the work.

DROIT DE SUITE

France and several other counties have laws giving pictorial artists (creators of paintings, drawings, and sculptures) and their heirs a right to a percentage royalty on subsequent sales of their works. This right, called *droit de suite*, typically endures for a period of time after the artist's death.

California is the only jurisdiction in the United States that has enacted a law of this kind. The California Resale Royalty Act[290] (CRRA) requires a 5% royalty to be paid to the artist or the artist's heirs upon any covered resale. It applies only if all of the following conditions exist:

(a) The work is an original painting, drawing, or sculpture;
(b) The seller resides in California or the sale takes place in California;
(c) A profit is made on the sale;
(d) It is sold for at least $1,000 (cash or equivalent value given);
(e) The sale occurs during the artist's lifetime or within twenty years after the artist's death.

The Act does not apply to the artist's initial sale of the work. It also does not apply to resales by art dealers within ten years after the artist's sale to the art dealer, provided all intervening sales have been between art dealers. Nor does it apply to stained glass artistry that was sold as part of the sale of real property to which it is permanently affixed.

The CRRA has been held unconstitutional as applied to sales taking place outside the state of California, on the basis that it imposes an impermissible burden on interstate commerce and is preempted by the first sale doctrine provisions of the Copyright Act. [291]

Statute of Limitations

A copyright infringement action must be commenced within three years from the date of the last infringement. The statute of limitations does not bar an infringement action if the infringement began more than three years prior to the commencement of the lawsuit if the infringement was still going on at some time during the three-year period before the lawsuit is commenced. Damages (and/or profits) may be recovered only for the infringement occurring during the three-year period prior to the commencement of the lawsuit, however.

The statute of limitations may be tolled (suspended) if the claimant had no actual knowledge of the infringing act. Some courts require proof of fraudulent concealment on the defendant's part in order for tolling to apply. Others do not.

The statute of limitations for copyright crimes is five years.

Laches

Laches is an equitable defense that may be available in some copyright cases. It is similar to a statute of limitations defense, in that it may bar a claim if the claimant waits too long to file it in court. Unlike a statute of limitations, though, no fixed time frame for filing claims exists. How much time is "too long" is something that a judge decides on a case-by-case basis.

To prevail on a laches defense, the defendant must prove three things:

(a) unnecessary and unreasonable delay in commencing a lawsuit
(b) reliance on the delay by the defendant
(c) prejudice to the defendant as a result of the delay.

Estoppel

Estoppel is another equitable defense that may be available in some cases. The elements of an estoppel defense are:

(a) knowledge of a fact on the part of the claimant
(b) lack of knowledge of the fact by the defendant
(c) intent to induce the defendant to act upon the claimant's representation or conduct, or conduct that made it reasonable to believe he had that intent
(d) defendant's reliance on claimant's representation or conduct to his detriment.

Abandonment

Abandonment is a defense that may be asserted when a copyright claimant evidences an intention to surrender rights to the copyright in the work, and to allow the public to copy it. Examples include: voluntary dedication to the public domain, such as by placing a notice on a copy of a work that it may be freely copied; knowing failure to take action against widespread infringement; or intentionally destroying the only copy of a videotape of a live broadcast.

Prior to 1989, distributing a copy of a work without a copyright notice affixed to it was considered an abandonment of the copyright. Since the notice is not required for works published after March, 1989, failing to affix it to a work published after 1989 no longer serves as evidence of abandonment.

Copyright Misuse

A court may deny relief to a copyright owner who has engaged in misconduct in connection with obtaining or enforcing the copyright. There are two kinds of copyright misuse:

(a) antitrust violation involving a copyright
(b) use of copyright or copyright law in a way that violates the policy of copyright law.

Examples include:

- Making false or misleading statements to the Copyright Office
- Making spurious threats of infringement litigation
- Unfair dealing with an alleged infringer
- Including an unduly restrictive noncompete clause in a licensing agreement
- Including a provision in a licensing agreement that prohibits the licensee from creating its own original creative works.

The defense does not require proof of any particular injury to the defendant. The relevant consideration is the adverse impact on the public interest.

Copyright misuse does not invalidate the owner's copyright. It merely precludes its enforcement by a particular person during the period of the person's misuse. The defense may not be asserted against a person who has purged himself of the misuse.

Sovereign Immunity

In general, a government may not be sued without its consent. Congress has specifically waived the immunity of the federal government from liability for copyright infringement. The remedies available are limited, but a copyright infringement lawsuit against the federal government may not be dismissed altogether on the basis of sovereign immunity. The Copyright Act asserts that states may be sued for copyright infringement, too. The constitutionality of this provision is unclear, inasmuch as it seems to conflict with the Eleventh Amendment's prohibition against lawsuits against states in federal court.

First Amendment

The First Amendment is a potential defense to copyright infringement in cases where the material in question is a matter of public interest. Footage of the assassination of John F. Kennedy is an example. The scope of the defense is limited, however. Only that amount of copying that is needed to convey the idea is permitted. Unnecessary copying is not protected by the First Amendment. Much fair use jurisprudence is grounded in or at least greatly influenced by First Amendment values. See Chapter 25.

The First Amendment does not protect property interests. It cannot be raised as a defense to a charge of dealing in pirated goods, for example.

Defenses to Vicarious Liability

It is a defense to vicarious liability that no employment or agency relationship existed. It is also a defense that the person sought to be held vicariously liable for another person's infringing activity derived no financial benefit from it. The fact that the employee or agent was engaged in a frolic of his own, i.e., doing things on his own time and/or not within the scope of employment is another possible defense, if the facts support it. The absence of any right or ability to supervise an infringer is also a defense to vicarious liability.

An employer, principal, partner, etc. may assert any defenses that the employee, agent, other partners, etc. may have to a claim of direct infringement, whether the defense is fair use, the statute of limitations, or something else.

Defenses to Contributory Liability

Mere knowledge of the possibility that a product or service can potentially be used in a way that infringes a copyright is not enough to establish that a person should have known it would be used for infringing purposes, if the website, product or service is capable of substantial non-infringing uses. Operating a website or blog that allows user comments, for example, should not expose the site owner to contributory liability merely because it is theoretically possible that someone might use the comments section to upload infringing material. Of course, if an otherwise protected hosting service or website owner learns that infringing material is being published to the site, or if a person claiming copyright ownership makes that assertion to the owner or service provider, then she "knows or should know" about infringing activity, and therefore may be held contributorily liable if she thereafter fails to take appropriate measures within her control to stop it.

In addition to any other defenses that may be available, a person's lack of knowledge or of any reason to know about infringing activity would be a defense to a claim based on contributory negligence. The fact that the defendant did nothing to induce, encourage, facilitate or contribute to the infringement would also be a defense to contributory infringement.

Complying with the requirements of a relevant safe harbor set out in the DMCA is another possible defense to contributory infringement. See Chapter 26.

Innocent Infringement

Innocent infringement generally does not absolve a person of liability for infringement. Good faith, ignorance or a lack of intent to infringe generally are not defenses to copyright infringement. There is one situation where innocent infringement may be a complete defense to infringement, though. If the person named in the copyright notice appearing on copies of the work is not the copyright owner, then the defendant may assert the defense in an infringement action by proving that he was misled by the notice and that he used the work in good faith based on a purported transfer or license from the person named in that notice. This defense, however, is available only if (a) the work was not registered in the name of the copyright owner before the infringement began, and (b) no document executed by the person named in the notice and showing the ownership of the copyright was recorded before the infringement began. In all other situations, innocent infringement is not a defense.

Although not a defense, proof that infringement was not done knowingly may significantly reduce the amount of statutory damages that may be awarded.

Noncommercial Use

The fact that no profit or commercial benefit was gained is not a defense to infringement. It may reduce the amount of damages, and in some situations it may help support a fair use defense, but it is not a stand-alone defense.

REMEDIES

Both civil and criminal remedies are available for the enforcement of copyrights.

Civil liability

At the outset of an infringement proceeding, the plaintiff may request a preliminary injunction against further acts of infringement. To qualify for a preliminary injunction, the plaintiff must prove: (a) ongoing infringement will cause irreparable harm; (b) the infringement claim is likely to succeed on the merits; and (c) the harm to the plaintiff if the injunction is not granted outweighs the harm to the defendant if the injunction is granted. If the delay involved in the process of securing a preliminary injunction will itself cause irreparable injury unless the allegedly infringing activity is immediately restrained, the plaintiff may ask for a temporary restraining order (TRO). A TRO, if granted, lasts only until a decision on the request for a preliminary injunction is made.

If the infringement claim ultimately succeeds, the court may issue a permanent injunction against further acts of infringement by the defendant. A court may issue an injunction even if the infringement was not willful.

In addition to (or in lieu of) a permanent injunction, a court may award actual damages. Actual damages are the out-of-pocket losses and loss of profits the copyright owner has experienced as a result of the infringement. The court may also require the defendant to pay the plaintiff the amount of the profit he has earned from the infringing use. There cannot be a double recovery, however. If lost profits are included as an element of actual damages, they cannot be recovered again in a separate award for lost profits.

In lieu of actual damages and profits, a court may instead award statutory damages in an amount specified by the Copyright Act. No proof of actual damage is necessary if a plaintiff opts for an award of statutory damages. This can be useful in cases where actual damage is negligible or difficult to prove.

The amount of statutory damages that may be awarded ranges from $750 to $30,000, if the infringer had knowledge or notice of the copyright at the time of the infringement. Registration or a proper display of a copyright notice provides notice. If an infringement is willful, the amount may be increased to $150,000. The amount of statutory damages may be reduced to as little as $200, however, if the infringement was innocent, i.e., done without the infringer's notice or knowledge that he was infringing a copyright.[292] Registration, if effected before the infringement begins, can forestall a claim of innocent infringement.

Willful infringement occurs when the defendant either (a) actually knew that his acts infringed a copyright; or (b) acted with deliberate blindness to, or reckless disregard for, the copyright holder's rights. Providing false contact information to a domain name registrar gives rise to a presumption that any copyright infringement effected through the use of the site is willful. Willfulness may also be proven in other ways. A good faith belief that an infringing use was fair use may be a defense to a claim of willfulness, if the belief was objectively reasonable.

Only a single award of statutory damages may be made on account of infringing activity by the same defendant with respect to the same work, no matter how many distinct acts of infringement the defendant committed with respect to that work. A separate award of statutory damages may be made with respect to each work that is infringed.

Statutory damages may not be awarded against nonprofit educational institutions, libraries or public broadcasting entities that had reasonable grounds to believe that the challenged activity was fair use. A person who sues one of these kinds of entities for copyright infringement will need to prove actual damages or lost profits.

Statutory damages may be elected only if the work is registered either before the infringement begins or within three months after the first publication of the work. If the infringement began before the work was registered, and more than three months have gone by since the work was first published, then statutory damages will not be available. Accordingly, it is a good idea to register a copyright either before or within three months after first publishing a work.

Affixing a copyright notice substantially reduces the amount of statutory damages that may be recovered – potentially to as little as $200—if the infringer did not have notice or knowledge of the copyright through other means. And no statutory damages at all may be recovered against an infringer of a work that was distributed without a copyright notice before 1989 unless the infringer had actual knowledge of the copyright. The copyright notice, like registration, gives constructive notice to the entire world that the work is protected by copyright. Therefore, innocent infringement is not available as a basis for reducing the amount of recovery if the copyright notice is affixed to copies of the work. This is one reason why it is a good idea to include the copyright notice on a published work.

When a claimant is entitled to an award of statutory damages and no applicable rule limits the amount, it is up to the court determine the amount. It must be within the range specified in the statute. A copyright claimant has a Seventh Amendment right to a jury trial on this issue. In making this determination, judges and juries typically consider what the actual damages and lost profits are likely to be, and how flagrant the infringing activity was. If the claimant is not likely to have been economically harmed by the infringement, and the infringer did not profit from it, the minimum statutory amount is likely to be awarded.

Attorney fees and costs may be awarded in copyright infringement cases. Timely registration can affect a claimant's eligibility for an award of attorney fees for infringement. Normally, attorney fees may be awarded to either party, on the basis of which party prevails. Attorney fees may be awarded to a copyright infringement claimant, however, only if, in addition to winning the case, the work was registered either before the infringement occurred or within three months after first publication.

A court may, in addition, order the impoundment of infringing copies. The means by which copies are made (such as molds, plates, computers, CD burners, etc.) may also be seized. An impoundment order may be issued even before the proceeding has concluded, but Due Process requires that the defendant be afforded a prompt opportunity for a hearing to challenge the seizure. Under the U.S. Supreme Court's Copyright Rules of Practice, the plaintiff must post a bond in an amount equal to at least twice the value of the impounded items.

At the conclusion of the proceeding, a court may order that infringing copies be either destroyed or turned over the plaintiff.

Criminal Penalties

Willful copyright infringement is a crime. The penalties can be severe. For a first offense, imprisonment for up to five years and a fine of up to $250,000 may be imposed. Imprisonment for up to ten years and a fine of up to $250,000 may be imposed for a second offense. Under the No Electronic Theft Act[293] criminal penalties may be imposed for copyright infringement even if no profit was made.

Fraudulent removal or use of a copyright notice is also a crime, as is the making of a false representation to the Copyright Office in connection with an application for registration. The DMCA makes circumventing copyright protection measures a crime, in some circumstances. It also makes dealing in copyright protection circumvention products unlawful. The DMCA is discussed in Chapter 26.

State Law Claims

State laws may provide a remedy when federal copyright law does not, but only if federal copyright law does not preempt the state law in question.

The Copyright Act expressly preempts a state law claim if both of the following conditions exist:

(a) The state law claim is for the vindication of a right that is equivalent to one of the exclusive rights that the Act protects;

(b) The material is of a kind for which the Copyright Act provides protection.

If the Copyright Act, by its terms, does not provide protection for a particular kind of material, then a state law claim of a right to the material is not preempted. Thus, state law protections of material that is not fixed in a tangible medium of expression, or of ideas, are not preempted by the Copyright Act.

A state law claim that is not simply the equivalent of one of the exclusive rights of copyright ownership—i.e., a claim that seeks to vindicate a different or additional right—is not preempted, either. For this reason, courts generally hold that state law claims for breach of contract of a voluntary copyright licensing agreement are not preempted. On the other hand, enforcement of a contract provision prohibiting acts that would constitute copyright infringement may be deemed preempted, since enforcing such a provision would be the equivalent of enforcing the Copyright Act's prohibition against infringement. This does not mean the licensee is free to breach the contractual prohibition. It simply means that a claim for breach of such a provision must be brought as a copyright infringement claim rather than as a breach of contract claim.

State laws authorizing causes of action for conduct that federal copyright law declares to be fair use are preempted. For example, a state statute authorizing the recovery of damages against a person who reverse engineers a copyrighted software program would be preempted by federal law. People may enter into enforceable contractual waivers of federally protected rights, though.

Therefore, even though a state cannot enact a law prohibiting reverse engineering, a provision in a software licensing contract that prohibits reverse engineering may be enforced.

Moral Rights in Visual Arts

Copyright protects the right of ownership of works of authorship. It does not protect reputational interests. Moral rights legislation seeks to protect the reputations of certain visual artists by giving them the following rights:

- Attribution
- Freedom from false attribution
- Integrity.

European laws have long protected the moral rights of visual artists. Since December 1, 1990, the Visual Artists Rights Act[294] (VARA) protects the moral rights of visual artists in the United States, too.

VARA establishes two kinds of rights: attribution and integrity. Certain visual artists have the right to be identified as the creators of their works and to prevent works not created by them from being attributed to them. The integrity right gives certain visual artists the right to prevent the destruction, distortion, mutilation or other modification of their works. VARA also gives certain visual artists the right to prevent the attribution of a mutilated or modified version of a work to the original artist.

LIMITATIONS ON VARA RIGHTS

VARA rights exist only for the following kinds of visual art works:

- Paintings
- Drawings
- Prints
- Sculptures
- Signed still photographs produced solely for exhibition.

The work must exist in only a single copy, or in a limited edition of no more than 200 copies that are signed and consecutively numbered by the author, or, in the case of a sculpture, in multiple cast, carved, or fabricated sculptures of 200 or fewer that are consecutively numbered by the author and bear the signature or other identifying mark of the author.

If a work does not meet these requirements, it is not protected by VARA. It might be protected by copyright, trademark or other law, but not by VARA.

The following things are specifically excluded from VARA protection:

- posters (as distinguished from prints)
- maps and globes
- technical drawings, diagrams, and models
- applied art

- audiovisual works, such as motion pictures
- books, magazines, newspapers, and other periodicals
- electronic publications
- databases and electronic information services
- advertising, promotional or merchandising items, descriptive works, covering, or packaging materials or containers
- uncopyrighted works
- works made for hire.

Artwork that is not protected by VARA may nevertheless be protected by other law, such as trademark or copyright law. A work must be protected by copyright in order to receive VARA protection, however. The creator of a public domain work does not have VARA rights. An unauthorized painting of a copyrighted photograph is not protected by VARA.

DURATION OF RIGHTS

For works created after December 1, 1990, VARA rights in a work terminate at the end of the calendar year in which the artist dies. VARA rights in collaborative works continue until the end of the calendar year in which the last surviving author dies.

For works created before December 1, 1990, VARA rights last as long as copyright does, but only if the artist was still the owner of title to the work (i.e., had not sold or otherwise transferred title to it) as of December 1, 1990.

TRANSFERABILITY

VARA rights are not transferable. They are independent of copyright. An artist continues to have moral rights even after assigning the copyright to someone else. By the same token, mere ownership of the copyright does not give a person standing to enforce VARA rights. Only the artwork creator has VARA rights.

WAIVER

A visual artist may waive VARA rights. To be enforceable, the waiver must meet all of the following requirements:

(a) It must be in writing;
(b) It must be signed by the artist;
(c) It must expressly waive VARA rights;
(d) It must identify the work;
(e) The uses of the work to which the waiver applies must be specified.

A waiver of VARA rights does not operate as a transfer of copyright in the work unless the agreement expressly provides that it does. A transfer of copyright, or a transfer of a copy in which a copyrighted work is embodied, does not operate as a waiver of VARA rights.

A VARA waiver by one coauthor waives VARA rights for all coauthors.

ENFORCEMENT

VARA rights are only enforceable in a civil proceeding. The Copyright Act does not provide any criminal penalties for violations of VARA rights.

MORAL RIGHTS IN OTHER COUNTRIES

France and several other countries protected the moral rights of artists long before the United States did. In some of these countries, the protections are broader than what VARA provides. There are also countries that do not protect visual artists' moral rights at all.

Chapter 24. The Public Domain

When none of the exclusive rights of the kind that copyright law protects exist, a work is said to be in the public domain. Anyone may use material that is in the public domain.

Material may be in the public domain either because it is a kind of subject matter that copyright law does not protect or because something has happened to cause a copyrighted work to lose its protection. Uncopyrightable subject matter is discussed in Chapter 23.

At one time, it was common for copyright protection to be lost through abandonment or lapse, such as where a copyright owner failed to file a timely renewal, or published a work without a copyright notice on it. Due to changes in the law, that is not likely to happen anymore. Today, most copyrighted works that enter the public domain do so as a result of either the copyright owner's dedication of the work to the public domain or the passage of time.

Congress specifies the term of copyrights, and it has done so numerous times. The validity and duration of a copyright must be determined with reference to the law that was in effect at the time the copyright came into existence, not current law.

It is possible for some elements of a work to be in the public domain while others are not. For example, a sound recording used in an audiovisual work may be protected by copyright even though the audiovisual work is in the public domain. A movie producer's dedication of a film to the public domain will not necessarily result in the screenplay's entry into the public domain, too. A musical work may be protected by copyright even though a sound recording of a performance of it is not. Each copyrighted element of a work must be separately evaluated.

It is not true that anything posted to an Internet website that is freely accessible to the public is in the public domain, and therefore not protected by copyright. Generally, content appearing on a website may not be copied and pasted to another website without permission. Choosing to make a work viewable on one website does not operate as consent to make it viewable on other websites. Publishing material online is not an implied waiver of copyright protection. Since copyright infringement is governed by a strict liability standard, the best strategy is to begin with an assumption that any expressive material that has been published on the Internet is not in the public domain and that permission will be needed to use it.

A number of online public domain depositories exist. These are collections of works that someone believes are in the public domain. Since copyright infringement is a strict liability offense, a good faith belief that a work is in the public domain because it is included in one of these depositories will not prevent liability for infringement. It may be that all or nearly all of the works in these depositories actually are in the public domain, but users are responsible for making their own assessments.

The fact that a work is in the public domain is not a defense to trademark, defamation, misappropriation of information, invasion of privacy, or other kinds of claims.

Dedication to the Public Domain

The owner of the copyright in a work may voluntarily dedicate it to the public domain. That is to say, copyright protection may be voluntarily abandoned. This can be accomplished by including a statement with the work declaring that it is in (or is dedicated to) the public domain. The decision to release a work into the public domain is irrevocable.

Making a work available to the public for free is not the same thing as dedicating it to the public domain. Most freeware and shareware, for example, has not been released into the public domain. They may be used only under the conditions and in the ways specified by the copyright owner.

Only the copyright owner has the power to dedicate a work to the public domain. A licensee's purported dedication of the licensed work to the public domain is of no effect. For the same reason, a person who creates a work pursuant to a work-for-hire agreement can neither dedicate the work to the public domain nor prevent the copyright owner from doing so.

Creative Commons offers a way for copyright owners to arrange to have their works enter the public domain sooner than they normally would. It does this by allowing copyright owners to either dedicate their works to the public domain immediately or, in the alternative, enter into a Founders' Copyright agreement with Creative Commons. This agreement involves the sale of the copyright to Creative Commons for a nominal sum, with an exclusive license back from Creative Commons for fourteen or twenty-eight years.

Duration of Copyrights

GENERAL RULE

The current rule in the United States is that a copyright in a newly created work lasts for the life of the author plus seventy years.

For coauthored works, the copyright lasts for the life of the last surviving author plus seventy years.

The rule is subject to three important exceptions:

- works made for hire
- anonymous or pseudonymous works
- works created or published at an earlier time.

The duration of a copyright is governed by the law of the country in which the copyright came into existence. The United States and many other countries have entered into treaties for the protection and enforcement of foreign copyrights, as well as to achieve greater uniformity in the copyright laws of different countries. There are still variations among countries with respect to certain matters, though, including the duration of a copyright.

WORKS MADE FOR HIRE

The term of a copyright in a newly created work made for hire in the United States is the earlier of (a) (a) 95 years after publication or (b) 120 years after the work was first fixed in a tangible medium.

ANONYMOUS AND PSEUDONYMOUS WORKS

The duration of a U.S. copyright in a newly created work by an anonymous or pseudonymous author is the same as that for a work made for hire, unless the author is identified before the term of the copyright expires. If that happens, then the copyright lasts for the life of the author plus seventy years.

WORKS PUBLISHED OR REGISTERED BEFORE JANUARY 1, 1978

Today, copyright is exclusively a matter of federal law. Prior to 1978, however, federal copyright protection existed only for works that either had been published with a copyright notice or registered with the U.S. Copyright Office. Until a work was published or registered, an author had only common law copyright rights under state law.

The 1976 Copyright Act, which became effective January 1, 1978, preempted the field of copyright, extending federal copyright protection to authors immediately upon the fixation of a work in a tangible medium. With the 1976 Act, publication or registration was no longer a prerequisite for federal copyright protection. In addition, for works created on or after January 1, 1978, the Act replaced the system of renewable fixed-term copyrights with a single term. Initially, the Act set the new single term at the life of the author plus fifty years. The fifty-year period was later extended to seventy years. The term of a copyright in a work that was published or registered before January 1, 1978, however, is not measured this way. The duration or a copyright in a work that was published or registered before January 1, 1978 must be determined by applying the law that was in effect at the time the work was published or registered.

Publication, for purposes of the public domain rules, means either:

(a) an authorized distribution of copies to the public; or
(b) an authorized offer to distribute copies to the public.

Distributing copies of a work without the copyright owner's authorization is not considered a publication of the work, for copyright purposes. Also—and unlike defamation law—the copyright definition does not include distributions to a limited number of people for a limited purpose. Circulating a paper only among one's peers or distributing a report only to the employees of a particular organization, for example, would not qualify as publication for copyright purposes. Nor does broadcasting qualify as publication, for copyright purposes. Only a distribution of copies or an offer to distribute copies does.

Before January 1, 1978, publishing a sound recording of a musical or literary work only had the effect of publishing the sound recording. It did not have the effect of publishing the musical composition or literary work performed on it. Unless it was published as sheet music or in some other way, a musical work remained "unpublished" for copyright purposes despite the release of multiple copies of recordings of performances of the song. For this reason, it was a common practice for publishers and record companies to register musical works as unpublished works in order to secure the benefits of federal registration. Beginning with musical works first published after 1977, distributing copies of a sound recording of a performance of a musical composition is a publication of both the sound recording and the musical and/or literary work performed in it.

Sound Recordings Made Before February 15, 1972

Copyright protection for sound recordings did not begin in the United States until February 15, 1972. Until 2018, sound recordings made in the United States before February 15, 1972 were not protected by federal copyright law, although the musical or literary works in them might be. The Classics Protection and Access Act[295] (CPAA), enacted in October, 2018. provides federal copyright protection for sound recordings made before February 15, 1972. Under this Act, sound recordings published before 1923 will enter the public domain on January 1, 2022. Sound recordings first published between 1923 and 1946 are protected for 100 years. Those first published between 1947 and 1956 are protected for 110 years. Sound recordings first published between 1957 and February 15, 1972 are protected until February 15, 2067. Sound recordings made but not published before February 15, 1972 enter the public domain on February 16, 2067, even if they become published before then. These rules preempt any contrary state laws.

Original and Renewal Terms

The first U.S. copyright law, the Copyright Act of 1790, provided for a term of fourteen years, renewable for another fourteen years. In 1831, Congress extended the original term to twenty-eight years. The Copyright Act of 1909 extended the renewal term to twenty-eight years, as well. Copyright terms were measured from the date of first publication or registration, whichever occurred earlier. If properly renewed, a copyright could have a duration of up to fifty-six years from the earlier of the date of publication or the date of registration.

A copyright had to be renewed during the last year of the original term. Otherwise, it lapsed and the work entered the public domain. If an original registration had not been filed yet, that had to be done before a renewal could be registered.

RENEWAL TERM EXTENSIONS

A series of congressional enactments beginning in 1962 and continuing into the 1970s extended the lengths of renewal terms of copyrights that were in their renewal terms at the time of the enactment. These enactments affected copyrights that had been secured (registered or first published) between September 19, 1906 and December 31, 1918, to the extent they had been timely and properly renewed prior to the enactment in question. The intent was to prevent copyrights from expiring before a new copyright law (ultimately, the Copyright Act of 1976) could be enacted. The effects of these enactments were as follows:

- Copyrights subsisting in their renewal terms on September 19, 1962 were extended to December 31, 1965.
- Copyrights subsisting in their renewal terms on August 28, 1965 were extended to December 31, 1967.
- Copyrights subsisting in their renewal terms on November 16, 1967 were extended to December 31, 1968.
- Copyrights subsisting in their renewal terms on July 23, 1968 were extended to December 31, 1969.

- Copyrights subsisting in their renewal terms on December 16, 1969 were extended to December 31, 1970.
- Copyrights subsisting in their renewal terms on December 17, 1970 were extended to December 31, 1971.
- Copyrights subsisting in their renewal terms on November 24, 1971 were extended to December 31, 1972.
- Copyrights subsisting in their renewal terms on October 25, 1972 were extended to December 31, 1974.
- Copyrights subsisting in their renewal terms on December 31, 1974 were extended to December 31, 1976
- For copyrights subsisting in their renewal terms between December 31, 1976 and December 31, 1977, the duration of the renewal term was extended to forty-seven years.

These extensions only applied to copyrights that still existed on the date of the enactment in question. They did not extend the duration of the original term, nor did they eliminate the requirement of renewing a copyright within the last year of the original term. If a timely renewal had been filed, then these enactments extended the duration of the renewal term in the manner indicated. If a copyright had lapsed due to a failure to timely renew it during the last year of the original term, then it was lost. These enactments did not revive lapsed copyrights.

For those copyrights that were still in existence on January 1, 1978, the Copyright Act of 1976 increased the renewal term from twenty-eight to forty-seven years. This meant that for any copyright that was still in existence on January 1, 1978, the total possible duration of copyright (original + renewal terms) became seventy-five years. The extension applied to any copyrights that were either in their original term on January 1, 1978, or in their renewal term at any time between December 31, 1976 and December 31, 1977, inclusive. The extension also applied to copyrights that were in the last year of their original term between December 31, 1976 and December 31, 1977, inclusive, provided a timely renewal application had been filed.

The Sonny Bono Copyright Term Extension Act of 1998[296] (SBCTEA) added twenty more years to the renewal term, extending the renewal term to sixty-seven years. This extension applied to all renewable copyrights that were still in existence on October 27, 1998.[297]

TYING COPYRIGHT TERMS TO CALENDAR YEARS

Under the 1909 Copyright Act, copyright terms were measured from the date of first publication or registration. The 1976 Copyright Act extended the term of each copyright that was still in existence on January 1, 1978 to the end of the calendar year in which it would otherwise expire. This provision also applies to all copyrights that come into existence on or after January 1, 1978. For example, if a work was first published on April 4, 1970, then the original term would expire on December 31, 1998. The renewal term would begin on January 1, 1999.

An exception exists for works that were first published before March 1, 1989 with a year date in the copyright notice that is earlier than the actual date of publication. In these cases, the renewal term is tied to the year date in the copyright notice, not the actual date of publication.

AUTOMATIC RENEWAL OF CERTAIN PRE-1978 WORKS

1992 amendments to the Copyright Act made renewal automatic for those works that were still in their original term on June 26, 1992, the effective date of the Act. This meant that for works first published or registered between January 1, 1964, and December 31, 1977, inclusive, it was no longer necessary to apply for renewal; it happened automatically.

The elimination of the renewal requirement does not apply retroactively. The Act only eliminates the renewal registration requirement for works that were still in their original term on June 26, 1992. It does not restore the copyright in a work that had already entered the public domain due to failure to renew the copyright before the expiration of the original term.

Although renewal registration is no longer required beginning June 26, 1992, the Act permits any renewable copyright that was still in its original term as of June 26, 1992 to be registered anytime during the renewal period. For works that were in their original terms on June 26, 1992, failure to file a renewal registration prior to the expiration of the original term no longer results in forfeiture of copyright protection, though.

Filing an application to renew a registration during the last year of the original term may not be necessary, but it has some benefits. A renewal registration that is filed during the last year of the original term gives rise to a presumption of validity of the copyright and of the facts set forth in the registration. A renewal registration that is filed during the renewal term does not have that effect.

OWNERSHIP OF THE RENEWAL RIGHT

Even if someone else owns the copyright, the author generally owns the renewal right. When the author dies, the renewal right descends to:

(1) the widow, widower, or children of the author
(2) if no widow, widower or children, then the author's executor
(3) if no will, widow, widower or children, then the author's next of kin.

These rules are subject to some exceptions.

Posthumous Works. A posthumous work is one that was not published during the author's lifetime, i.e., one that has been published, if at all, only after the author died. If the author of a posthumous work did not assign the copyright or exploit any rights in the work during his lifetime, then the owner of the copyright owns the renewal right, too. The owner of the copyright upon an author's death is not necessarily the author's widow, widower, children, executor or nest of kin. Since a copyright is personal property, a copyright owner's will or a state's intestacy laws may provide for a different disposition.

Compilations. The renewal right in a compilation belongs to the owner of the copyright in the compilation. The author of a contribution to a compilation retains the renewal right for his individual contribution, though.

Works Made for Hire, The employer (or person who commissioned the work made for hire) owns the right to renew it. The actual author of the work has no renewal rights, nor do her heirs.

Corporate Works. A corporation owns the renewal right in works originally registered in the corporation's name, even if the work is not a work made for hire. For example, a work created by nonemployee stockholders or directors of the corporation is not a work made for hire, but if the corporation registers a copyright in the work, then the corporation owns the right to renew it. This rule does not apply to situations in which an individual author has assigned or licensed a copyright in a work to the corporation.

TRANSFERS OF THE RENEWAL RIGHT

Copyright law reserves to the author the right to renew the copyright even if he transfers ownership of the copyright to someone else. In addition, the renewal copyright may be conveyed separately from the original copyright. This means that the author may transfer ownership of the original copyright to one person while transferring the right to ownership of the copyright during the renewal term to someone else.

An author's transfer of the original term of a copyright is valid whether the author survives to the beginning of the renewal term or not. A transfer of a renewal copyright that is effected during the original term will not be valid, however, unless the author survives until the commencement of the renewal term. If the author dies during the original term, then the renewal right descends to his heirs, and the author's purported transfer of it to someone else is invalid.

> **Example 1**. William is the author of a book that was published in 1930. In 1945, he transfers the renewal term of the copyright to Orson. William passes away in 1960. Since William was still alive at the time the renewal term began, the transfer is valid, and Orson owns the renewal copyright.

> **Example 2**. Same as Example 1, except that William passes away in 1957. In this situation, Williams' heirs (as defined in the Copyright Act) would inherit the renewal copyright because William was not alive at the time the renewal term began. Orson is out of luck.

> **Example 3**. Same as Example 2, except that William transferred all of his copyright interests (i.e., both the original and the renewal term) to Orson in 1945. In this scenario, Orson would own the copyright for the duration of the original term, but William's heirs would own the renewal right.

A derivative work legitimately created by an assignee or licensee during the original term is subject to the renewal right. If the statutory heirs exercise the renewal right, then the maker of the derivative work will be liable for infringement if he continues to publicly distribute, perform, display or reproduce it after the copyright is renewed. If the original term expires during a time period when copyright renewal is automatic, then the maker of such a derivative work who continues to use it after the end of the original term will not be liable for infringement unless the statutory heirs (or their representative) actually file an application for renewal. (An application for renewal that is filed notwithstanding the fact that renewal is, by law, automatic is called a permissive renewal.) In no event, however, may new derivative works be made during the renewal period without the permission of the owner of the renewal term copyright.

COPYRIGHT NOTICE

Works First Published Before 1978

Works published before 1978 were required to display a copyright notice. Failure to display a copyright notice on a published work would result in loss of copyright protection, causing the work to enter the public domain. Unless a work entered the public domain earlier for some other reason, the date of the first publication without a copyright notice was the date of entry into the public domain.

As of December 31, 1977, any of the following defects would invalidate a copyright notice :

- Absence of an appropriate copyright indicator (the word *Copyright*, the abbreviation *Copr.* or the symbol ©—or, for sound recordings, the symbol ℗).
- Name of the copyright owner omitted. (For sound recordings, a recognizable abbreviation or a generally known alternative designation of the copyright owner was permitted.)
- No year of publication indicated.
- Printed in a language other than English.
- Not positioned or placed in a location authorized by federal regulations.
- Dispersal of the elements of the notice (date, year, and a copyright word or symbol) in such a way that they are not all identified as part of the copyright notice. (But a producer's name appearing anywhere on the label or container of a sound recording was deemed to be "identified" with the notice if no other name appeared in conjunction with the notice.)
- Not visible without tearing the copy apart.
- Illegible.
- So small that a magnifying glass is needed to read it (unless ordinary use of the copy requires magnification, such as microfilm or motion picture film).
- Placement on a detachable tag.
- Placement on a wrapper or container that is normally removed and discarded when the copy is put to use. But the notice could be placed on a container that is designed and expected to remain with the copy, such as an album cover or a CD case.
- Restriction or limitation of the notice exclusively to an element that is not protected by copyright, by virtue of its position on the work, by the use of asterisks, or by other means.
- The person named as copyright owner in the notice had no authority to secure the copyright.
- The year stated in the notice is more than one year after the actual publication date.
- The year stated in the notice is more than one year after the date of copyright registration, in cases where the copyright was secured by registration of an unpublished work rather than by publication.
- The year stated in the notice is more than one year after the first foreign publication date, in cases where the work was first published in a foreign country.

The notice was only required to be displayed on visually perceptible copies of a work. Since an audio recording is not a visually perceptible copy of a musical, dramatic or literary work, the publication of a literary, musical or dramatic work on a phonorecord without the copyright notice, although possibly causing loss of copyright in the sound recording, did not result in loss of copyright in the literary, musical or dramatic work performed in it.

For audiovisual works, the notice could be displayed when the work was performed (such as a notice that is displayed on the screen when a motion picture is played), provided it was displayed near the title, with cast, credits, and similar information, at or near the beginning or end of the work. For works lasting no more than one minute, the notice could also be located on the leader of the film or tape immediately preceding the work. In the case of a copy that was distributed to the public for private use, it was also acceptable for the notice to appear on the container for the copy of the work.

For more detailed information about copyright notice requirements that were in force on a particular date, the federal regulations that were in effect on that date should be consulted.

Works First Published After 1977 and Before March 1, 1989

The copyright notice continued to be required for works first published after 1977 and before March 1, 1989. The requirements for an acceptable notice were similar to those for pre-1978 works, but not exactly the same. Specifically, for works first published between January 1, 1978 and February 28, 1989, inclusive, the requirements for a valid copyright notice were as follows:

(a) legible
(b) not concealed
(c) placed in a position required or allowed by regulations
(d) so located as to give reasonable notice of the claim of copyright
(e) include a name
(f) include a date that is not more than one year after the first publication date
(g) include the additional statement required by federal regulations, if the work consists primarily of U.S. government material.

Additional requirements applicable to notices on visually perceptible copies included:

(i) © symbol, the word Copyright, or the abbreviation, Copr. (℗ for sound recordings)
(ii) the year of first publication
(iii) the name, or an abbreviation or generally known alternative designation, of the copyright owner.

The year of publication was not required to be placed on greeting cards, postcards, stationery, jewelry, dolls, toys, or any useful article, to protect the copyright in a pictorial, graphic, or sculptural work that was reproduced on such item.

Because a dust jacket is removable from a book, placement of a notice on a dust jacket was not adequate to protect the copyright in the book. By the same token, placement of the notice inside the book was not adequate to protect the copyright in dust jacket content.

For compilations and derivative works, the date of publication of the compilation or derivative work was to be used. A single copyright notice applicable to a collective work as a whole was acceptable to indicate copyright protection for all the contributions in the collective work. If, however, the owner of the copyright in the collective work was not the same as the owner of the copyright in an individual contribution, and the individual contribution did not have its own notice, then the contribution could be deemed to have been published with an erroneous notice. This could affect copyright protection for the individual contribution, although it would not affect the copyright in the collective work. A separate contribution to a collective work could bear its own notice of copyright, and its inclusion would not affect the adequacy of the copyright notice on the collective work. A copyright notice on a collective work did not suffice as a notice of copyright for any advertisements contained within it. For those, a separate copyright notice was required.

Federal regulations governed the required location and position of the notice. For books and periodicals, the title page, the page immediately following the title page, either side of the front or the back cover, or the first or the last page of the body of the work were acceptable. For periodicals, additional possibilities included the page containing the masthead; or adjacent to a prominent heading, at or near the front of the issue, containing the title of the periodical and any combination of the volume and issue number and the date of the issue.

For a separate contribution to a collective work, acceptable positions included: under a title appearing at or near the beginning of the contribution; on the first page of the main body of the contribution; immediately following the end of the contribution; or on any of the pages where the contribution appears if the contribution consists of no more than twenty pages, the notice is reproduced prominently, and the application of the notice to the particular contribution is clear.

For works published in machine-readable copies, acceptable positions included: near the title or at the end of the work, on visually perceptible printouts; at the user's terminal upon sign-on; continuous display on the terminal during use; or on a label that is securely affixed to the copies or to a container used as a permanent holder for the copies.

For audiovisual works, the notice was acceptable if it was displayed when the work was performed (e.g., a notice that is displayed on the screen when a motion picture is played), provided the notice was displayed near the title, with cast, credits, and similar information, at or near the beginning or end of the work. For works lasting no more than one minute, the notice could also be located on the leader of the film or tape immediately preceding the work. In the case of a copy that is distributed to the public for private use, it was also acceptable if the notice was on the container for the copy of the work (e.g., DVD case).

For pictorial, graphic or sculptural works that are reproduced in two-dimensional copies, the copyright notice was required to be affixed permanently to the copy. It could be placed on the front or back. Alternatively, it could be placed on any backing, mounting, framing, or other material to which copies were durably attached. For works reproduced in three-dimensional copies, the notice had to be affixed permanently to the copy, and it could be placed on any visible portion of the work; or on any base, mounting, or framing or other material on which the copies were durably attached. If it was impractical to affix a notice to the copies directly or by means of a durable label, a notice was acceptable if it appeared on a tag or durable label attached to the copy so that it would remain with it as it passes through commerce. For works reproduced in copies consisting of sheet-like or strip material bearing multiple or continuous reproductions of the work, such as fabrics or wallpaper, the notice could be applied to the reproduction itself; to the margin, selvage, or reverse side of the material at frequent and regular intervals; or, if the material contained neither a selvage nor a reverse side, to tags or labels attached to the copies and to any spools, reels, or containers housing them in such a way that the notice was visible in commerce.

Federal regulations changed from time to time during this period. The regulations that were in force on the date a work was published without a copyright notice control the determination of the adequacy of a copyright notice and the effect of defects in the notice.

As with pre-1978 works, the publication of a literary, musical or dramatic work on a phonorecord without a copyright notice could cause loss of copyright protection in the sound recording but not loss of copyright in the literary, musical or dramatic work embodied in it. For these kinds of works, only visually perceptible copies need to display a copyright notice.

Omission of a proper copyright notice did not cause a work published during this period to enter the public domain in any of the following circumstances:

(a) It was omitted from only a small number of copies;
(b) It was removed without the copyright owner's authorization;
(c) The publisher had breached an express written agreement to place the notice on copies of the publication;
(d) The copyright owner corrected the problem within five years of discovering it.

"Correcting the problem" meant making a reasonable effort to add the notice to all copies that were distributed to the public in the United Stats after the omission was discovered. In addition, if the work was not yet registered, then the owner had to register it within the five-year curative period.

Some kinds of errors, although not causing a work to enter the public domain, could have other adverse consequences. Publication of a copyright notice erroneously naming the wrong person as the copyright owner could be corrected by registering the work in the name of the actual owner or recording a document executed by the person named in the notice that shows the correct ownership. If this was not done, however, then an innocent infringer who was misled by the notice and obtained an assignment or license from the person named in the notice would have a complete defense against a claim of infringement.

If the only error is that the date indicated in a copyright notice that has been placed on a published work is earlier than the actual date of publication, then the work does not enter the public domain as a result of the error. Instead, the term of copyright is deemed to begin in the copyright year indicated in the notice, not the year of actual publication. A copyright notice that indicates a year later than the actual date of publication does not have this effect. In this situation, the actual year of publication marks the beginning of the copyright term.

A copyright notice containing a date that is more than a year after the actual date of publication is treated as a complete omission of a copyright notice. Subject to the exceptions noted above, such an omission would cause the work to enter the public domain.

Elimination of the Notice Requirement

The Berne Convention for the Protection of Literary and Artistic Works of 1886 provides that copyright enforceability should not be made to depend on compliance with formalities. Many countries were signatories to this treaty prior to 1988. In these countries, omitting a copyright notice does not affect the enforceability of the copyright in the work. The United States did not become a signatory to the Berne Convention until 1988. The Berne Convention Implementation Act[298] became effective on March 1, 1989.

For works first published in the United States on or after March 1, 1989, the copyright notice is optional. Publication without the copyright notice does not cause loss of copyright protection for such works. Elimination of the notice requirement is not retroactive, however. With the exception of certain foreign works that may be restored from the public domain, the entry of a work into the public domain is irreversible.

MANUFACTURING REQUIREMENT

Books, periodicals, lithographs and photoengravings published before July 1, 1986 were required to be manufactured in the United States in order to receive federal copyright protection. This requirement also applied to any illustrations contained in a book or periodical to which the requirement applied, to the extent the illustrations were produced by a photoengraving or lithographic process. The requirement does not apply to works that were first published after June 30, 1986.

The manufacturing requirement never applied to:

- Dramatic works
- Lectures, sermons, addresses
- Musical works
- Maps
- Braille books or periodicals
- Unpublished works
- Works not manufactured by a typesetting, lithographic or photoengraving process
- Pictorial illustrations depicting subjects that are located in a foreign country and that illustrate a scientific work or reproduce a work of art
- Foreign language books by foreign authors that are first published in a foreign country
- English language works published in a foreign country qualifying for ad interim protection.

To register a work to which the manufacturing requirement applies, it is necessary to sign a sworn affidavit of compliance with the manufacturing requirement. Knowingly filing a false affidavit results in forfeiture of the copyright.

Though English language works generally were subject to the manufacturing requirement, foreign language books generally were subject to the manufacturing clause only if they were first published in the United States. If the author was a U.S. national or domiciliary when a foreign language work was first published, however, then the copies had to be manufactured in the United States. If a copy was manufactured abroad, copyright in the United States was lost upon publication, ad interim copyright registration could not be secured, and renewal registration would not be possible.

The manufacturing requirement expired on July 1, 1986.

Ad Interim Registration

Registration of an English language book that was manufactured in a foreign country was permitted if, within thirty days after publication in a foreign country, the author or owner made a request to reserve the copyright, deposited a copy, and filed a statement of the name and nationality of the author and the copyright owner and the date of publication with the U.S. Copyright Office. Doing this gave the applicant ad interim copyright protection which lasted until thirty days after the deposit of the copy with the U.S. Copyright Office.

If the applicant published a U.S. edition in compliance with the manufacturing requirement within the thirty-day period, and applied for interim registration within the thirty-day period, then the work would receive a full twenty-eight-year term of copyright.

For works first published abroad after March 2, 1921, the thirty-day period was later extended to sixty days, and the timeframe for publishing an edition in compliance with manufacturing requirements was lengthened to four months. In 1949, the ad interim registration period was extended to six months and the timeframe for publishing an edition in compliance with manufacturing requirements was lengthened to five years. As with the thirty-day, sixty-day, and fourth-month periods that had been provided for in the earlier versions of the ad interim registration law, publication of a U.S. edition in compliance with the manufacturing requirement during the relevant period qualified the work for registration for a renewable twenty-eight-year term, provided publication and registration occurred during that period. If either compliance with the manufacturing requirement or full registration did not occur within that period, then the work received no federal copyright protection.

Effective September 16, 1955, and pursuant to the Universal Copyright Convention (UCC), works of foreign origin were exempted from the manufacturing requirement if they originated in a country that was a signatory to the UCC and a "UCC notice" consisting of the © symbol accompanied by the name of the copyright proprietor and the year of first publication was properly affixed to published copies of the work. Further, any ad interim protection that had been secured for a work originating in a UCC country was automatically extended to the full term. These provisions did not apply to works of American citizens and domiciliaries that were published abroad or to works that were first published in the United States.

In its final form before it expired, the Act permitted manufacture in either the United States or Canada. Subject to certain limitations such as an exception for books for government, educational, religious or scholarly use, it expressly prohibited importation of certain kinds of foreign-made books and periodicals. At the same time, though, it specified that while a violation of the prohibition against importation (as distinguished from the filing of a false affidavit) could be raised as a complete defense to a claim of infringement, the violation did not affect the validity of the copyright itself.

Transitional provisions in the Copyright Act extended the term of ad interim copyrights subsisting or capable of being secured on December 31, 1977 to the same term as ordinary copyrights that existed on that date. If a work was first published on or after July 1, 1977, and was otherwise eligible for ad interim copyright protection, then registration could be made at any time during the six-month period beginning July 1, 1977, i.e., until December 31, 1977. In other words, the terms of any ad interim copyrights that existed on December 31, 1977, and of any copyrights in works that were first published outside the United States between July 1, 1977 and December 31, 1977, inclusive, that were otherwise eligible for ad interim registration, were made subject to the same rules as to duration as any other copyright that existed on December 31, 1977.

As noted, the manufacturing requirement expired on July 1, 1986.

RESTORATION OF COPYRIGHTS IN FOREIGN WORKS

To comply with international treaties, Congress has provided for the restoration of copyrights in certain foreign works. To be eligible for restoration, each of the following conditions must exist:

(a) At least one author was a citizen or domiciliary of a foreign country that is a signatory to the Agreement on Trade-Related Aspects of Intellectual Property Rights (TRIPS Agreement), the Berne Convention, the World Intellectual Property Organization (WIPO) Copyright Treaty or Performances and Phonograms Treaty, or the subject of a proclamation under 17 U.S.C. § 104A(g); or the work must have been first published in such a country and not published in the United States within thirty days thereafter;
(b) The work is still protected by copyright in its nation of origin;
(c) It is in the public domain in the United States only because of one the following: (i) failure to satisfy a formality (such as registration, renewal, copyright notice, manufacturing requirement); (ii) origination in a country that did not have copyright relations with the United States; or (iii) it is a sound recording that was fixed in a tangible medium before February 15, 1972.

A foreign work is any work that does not fit into any of the following categories:

(a) first published in the United States
(b) first published simultaneously in the United States and in a foreign country that has an applicable treaty with the United States, and whose law provides for a copyright term that is at least as long as what U.S. law provides
(c) first published simultaneously in the United States and a foreign country that does not have an applicable treaty with the United States
(d) first published in a foreign country that does not have an applicable treaty with the United States, but all authors are nationals, domiciliaries, or habitual residents of the United States (or in the case of a motion picture, all authors are legal entities headquartered in the United States)
(e) unpublished work, and all authors are nationals, domiciliaries, or habitual residents of the United States (or in the case of a motion picture, all authors are legal entities headquartered in the United States)
(f) pictorial, graphic, or sculptural work that is incorporated into a building or structure that is located in the United States.

Copyright restoration went into effect on January 1, 1996, for foreign works from countries that were, on that date, members of the World Trade Organization (WTO); adherents to the Berne Convention, the WIPO Copyright Treaty or the WIPO Performances and Phonograms Treaty; or the subject of a proclamation under 17 U.S.C. § 104A(g). Copyright restoration for works from other countries went into effect on the earliest adherence date of the country to one of these treaties or the proclamation date, as applicable.

The duration of a restored copyright is the same as it would have been if it had never entered the public domain.

Pursuant to the Uruguay Round Agreements Act[299] (URAA), copyrights in the described foreign works are automatically restored. No action is required on the part of a copyright owner. An owner of a restored copyright may choose to register the copyright, however.

A person who relied on the public domain status of a foreign work before its copyright was restored is called a *reliance party*. A reliance party is liable for infringement only if (a) the foreign copyright owner filed notice with the U.S. Copyright Office within twenty-four months after the enactment of the URAA (i.e., no later than December 8, 1996), or (b) the foreign copyright owner served notice of intent to enforce the copyright directly on the person. In that event, the person so served may continue to exploit the work for twelve months after receiving the notice.

A reliance party may continue to exploit derivative works that are based on a restored copyright, but must pay reasonable compensation for them.

To be eligible for renewal registration, a foreign work that was first published or registered before 1978 must either have been published with the statutory or UCC notice or made the subject of an ad interim registration, on one hand, or registered as an unpublished work, on the other. In addition, it must have met all statutory requirements to maintain copyright through the full original term and into the renewal term. A work that failed to secure copyright in the United States at the time of first publication, or lost it at any time during the original or renewal terms, is not eligible for renewal registration even if copyright was restored in the United States under the URAA.

WORKS CREATED BUT NOT PUBLISHED OR REGISTERED BEFORE 1978

For works created but not published or registered before January 1, 1978, copyright protection generally lasts for the life of the author (or in the case of joint works, the life of the last surviving author) plus seventy years, or December 31, 2002, whichever is later. If an unpublished work created before January 1, 1978 is published before December 31, 2002, then the term is extended to the life of the author plus seventy years or December 31, 2047, whichever is later.

The copyright in an unpublished work made for hire, or an anonymous or pseudonymous work, that was created before January 1, 1978, lasts for 120 years from the year of creation or ninety-five years from the date of first publication, whichever expires first, but in no event earlier than December 31, 2002. If it is published before December 31, 2002, then the term is extended to December 31, 2047.

If the author of an anonymous or pseudonymous work is identified, and a statement of identity in proper form is timely and properly filed with the Copyright Office before the end of the term of the copyright, then the term of the copyright is governed by the same rules that apply to works created by an identified author.

Before January 1, 1978, distributing copies of a sound recording did not constitute publication of the musical, literary, or dramatic works embodied in it. Accordingly, even though distributing copies of a sound recording during this time period might be considered a publication of the sound recording, it is not considered a publication of the musical, literary, or dramatic works embodied in it. Those works would be deemed "unpublished" despite the publication of the sound recording, unless they had been published in some other way (e.g., sheet music).

PRESUMPTION OF DEATH

There is a rebuttable presumption that at the earlier of ninety-five years after first publication or 120 years after fixation in tangible form, the author has been dead for seventy years. To avoid premature loss of copyright protection, the copyright owner (or the author's estate) must file a statement of living status, or a date of death, with the Copyright Office. This must be done before the earlier of ninety-five years after publication or 120 years after fixation in tangible form. If it is not done within that time period, then the copyright expires.

Works That Are in the Public Domain

A copyrighted work may enter the public domain as a result of a voluntary dedication to the public domain. For all other works, the duration of the copyright is calculated as described below. Note that the first eight provisions do not apply to sound recordings, architectural works and foreign works. These are governed by special rules that are described in the last three provisions.

(I) Works First Published or Registered Before January 1, 1923

Works first published or registered before January 1, 1923 are all in the public domain now.

> **Explanation**: The original copyright term was twenty-eight years. If timely renewed, then the total copyright term was fifty-six years. Many copyrights in works published or registered before January 1, 1923 would have expired before the first statutory extension that occurred on September 19, 1962. Those that were still viable on that date were extended incrementally until the 1976 Act increased the total renewal term to forty-seven years. To qualify for the additional boost up to sixty-seven years, though, the copyright had to continue to be in its renewal term as of October 27, 1998. If the total copyright term had expired on or before December 31, 1997, then it would not qualify for the additional twenty-year extension. Since the total copyright term (original + renewal) under the 1976 Act was seventy-five years, all copyrights secured on or before December 31, 1922 would have expired by December 31, 1997, which was before the effective date of the additional twenty-year boost provided in the SBCTEA of 1998.

(II) Works First Published or Registered Before 1964 and Not Renewed

Works in this category are all in the public domain now. The various extension acts did not eliminate the renewal requirement for works first published or registered before the enactment of the extension in question.

(III) Works First Published or Registered Between 1923 and 1963, and Renewed

Works in this category that were published without a proper copyright notice before March 1989, or that failed to satisfy an applicable manufacturing requirement (which expired on July 1, 1986) are in the public domain. The term of any other copyright in this category is ninety-five years, and they will begin entering the public domain on January 1, 2019.

Explanation: A work published or registered on or after January 1, 1923 would have an original twenty-eight-year term expiring, at the earliest, on January 1, 1951. If renewed, the twenty-eight-year renewal would have been scheduled to expire in 1979, at the earliest. Since all such copyrights would have been in existence on January 1, 1978, however, the 1976 Copyright Act extended the renewal terms of these copyrights to forty-seven years, and changed the expiration date of the renewal term to the last day of the calendar year in which the renewal term was scheduled to end. The earliest any such copyright could have expired, then, would be December 31, 1998. (1923 + 75 = 1998.) Therefore, they all would have been in existence on October 27, 1998, the effective date of the additional twenty-year extension provided by the SBCTEA, so they would all get the ninety-five-year copyright term. Therefore, the earliest such a work could expire would be at the end of the calendar year that is ninety-five years after January 1, 1923. That would be December 31, 2018.

(IV) Works First Published or Registered Between 1964 and 1977

Works in this category that were published without a proper copyright notice before March 1989, or that failed to satisfy an applicable manufacturing requirement (which expired on July 1, 1986) are in the public domain. The term of any other copyright in this category is ninety-five years. These works will not begin to enter the public domain until 2060.

Explanation: The term of a copyright (original + renewal) in works published between 1964 and 1977 is ninety-five years, whether renewal is registered or not. Renewal became automatic as to works in this category in 1992.

(V) Works First Published Between 1978 and 2002 and Created but Not Registered Before 1978

Works in this category that were published before March, 1989 with an omitted or defective copyright notice that was not cured within five years, or that failed to satisfy an applicable manufacturing requirement (which expired on July 1, 1986), are in the public domain. Copyright in most other works in this category lasts for the life of the author plus seventy years or December 31, 2047, whichever is later.

The term of an anonymous or pseudonymous work, a corporation-authored work or a work made for hire in this category is the later of: (a) December 31, 2002; or (b) the earlier of ninety-five years from the date of first publication or 120 years from the date of fixation of the work in a tangible medium of expression. If the date of death of the author is not known, then the term is the earlier of ninety-five years from the date of first publication or 120 years from the date of fixation of the work in a tangible medium of expression.

(VI) Works First Published After 2002 that Were Created but Not Registered Before 1978

Copyright in works created before January 1, 1978 but not published until after December 31, 2002 generally lasts for the later of seventy years after the author's death or December 31, 2002.

For an anonymous or pseudonymous work, a corporation-authored work or a work made for hire, the term is the later of: (a) December 31, 2002; or (b) the earlier of ninety-five years from the date of first publication or 120 years from the date of fixation of the work in a tangible medium of expression. If the date of death of the author is not known, then the term is the earlier of ninety-five years from the date of first publication or 120 years from the date of fixation of the work in a tangible medium of expression.

(VII) Unpublished Works Created but Not Registered Before 1978

Copyrights in works in this category generally last for the life of the author plus seventy years.

For anonymous or pseudonymous works, corporation-authored works and works made for hire, the term is 120 years from the date of fixation of the work in a tangible medium of expression. If the author of an anonymous or pseudonymous work is identified during this period, then the copyright term is the life of the identified author plus seventy years. If the date of death of the author is not known, then the term is 120 years from the date of fixation of the work in a tangible medium of expression.[300]

(VIII) Works Created After 1977

Works in this category that were published before March, 1989 with an omitted or defective copyright notice that was not cured within five years, or that failed to satisfy an applicable manufacturing requirement (which expired on July 1, 1986), are in the public domain.

Copyright in most other works created on or after January 1, 1978 lasts for the life of the author plus seventy years.

For anonymous or pseudonymous works, corporation-authored works and works made for hire, the term is the earlier of ninety-five years from the date of first publication or 120 years from the date of fixation of the work in a tangible medium of expression. If the author of an anonymous or pseudonymous work is identified during this period, then the copyright term is the life of the identified author plus seventy years. If the date of death of the author is not known, then the term is 120 years from the date of fixation of the work in a tangible medium of expression.

(IX) Sound Recordings

Sound recordings published before March 1, 1989 that did not comply with an applicable copyright notice or manufacturing requirement are in the public domain.

Sound recordings first published before 1923 are no longer protected on January 1, 2022..

Sound recordings first published between 1923 and 1946 are protected for 100 years.

Sound recordings first published between 1947 and 1956 are protected for 110 years.

For all other sound recordings first fixed prior to February 15, 1972 lost protection on February 15, 2067.

In all other cases, the following rules apply: Copyrights in sound recordings created after February 14, 1972 and first published before 1978 expire ninety-five years from the date of publication, but in no event earlier than 2068. Copyrights in sound recordings created after 1977 last for the longer of seventy years after the life of the author or 2049; or in the case of a work made for hire, the earlier of ninety-five years after publication or 120 years after creation, but in no event earlier than 2049.

(X) Architectural Works

Copyrights in architectural designs created after November 30, 1990 last for the life of the author plus seventy years. In the case of a work made for hire, the duration is the earlier of 120 years from the date of creation or ninety-five years from the date of publication. (*Publication* can mean either publication of the blueprint or, according to the Copyright Office, construction of multiple copies of the building.) The same rule applies to an architectural design that was created before December 1, 1990, if construction of a building embodying the design is first completed between December 1, 1990 and December 31, 2002, inclusive. In all other cases, architectural works are protected, if at all, only as drawings, and the rules for determining the duration of a copyright in a drawing apply.

(XI) Foreign Works (Works First Published in a Country Other Than the United States)

Published before 1923: in the public domain.

Published between 1923 and 1977, inclusive, and in the public domain in the foreign country as of January 1, 1996: in the public domain.

Published between 1923 and 1977, inclusive, compliant with U.S. formalities and not in the public domain in the foreign country as of January 1, 1996: ninety-five years from the publication date.

Published between 1923 and 1977, inclusive, not compliant with U.S. formalities, but not in the public domain in the foreign country as of January 1, 1996, and not published in the United States within thirty days: ninety-five years from the date of publication.

Published between 1923 and 1977, inclusive, and published in the United States at the same time or less than thirty days thereafter: same as for a domestic work.

Created before 1978, and published between 1978 and 2002, inclusive, in a country that is a signatory to the Berne Convention, WIPO Copyright Treaty, WIPO Performances and Phonograms Treaty, or a WTO member country after the date of enactment of the URAA: Life of the author plus seventy years (or for a work made for hire, ninety-five years from the date of publication) but not earlier than December 31, 2047.

Created before 1978, and published after 2002 in a country that is a signatory to the Berne Convention, WIPO Copyright Treaty, WIPO Performances and Phonograms Treaty, or a WTO member country after the date of enactment of the URAA: Life of the author plus seventy years; for a work made for hire, ninety-five years from the date of publication.

Published between January 1, 1978 and March 1, 1989 without copyright notice, and in the public domain in the foreign country as of January 1, 1996: in the public domain.

Published between January 1, 1978 and March 1, 1989 without copyright notice, not in the public domain in the foreign country as of January 1, 1996, and the country is a signatory to the Berne Convention, WIPO Copyright Treaty, WIPO Performances and Phonograms Treaty, or a WTO member country after the date of enactment of the URAA: Life of the author plus seventy years; for a work made for hire, ninety-five years from the date of publication.

Published between January 1, 1978 and March 1, 1989 with a copyright notice, in a country with which the United States has copyright relations: Life of the author plus seventy years; for a work made for hire, ninety-five years from the date of publication.

Published after March 1, 1989 in a country with which the United States does not have copyright relations: in the public domain. This includes works authored by a resident of, and published in, Afghanistan, Eritrea, Ethiopia, Iran, Iraq, San Marino and possibly other countries.

Published after March 1, 1989 in a country with which the United States has copyright relations: Life of the author plus seventy years; for a work made for hire, ninety-five years from the date of publication.

The foregoing rules pertaining to foreign works are subject to the exceptions and qualifications described below:

A work whose copyright was once owned or administered by the Alien Property Custodian, and whose copyright, if restored, would, as of January 1, 1996, be owned by a government is not protected by U.S. copyright law.

For works published in Algeria, Andorra, Angola, Armenia, Azerbaijan, Belarus, Bhutan, Cambodia, Cape Verde, Comoros, Equatorial Guinea, Grenada, Haiti, Jersey, Jordan, Democratic People's Republic of Korea, Kuwait, Kyrgyzstan, Laos, Malaysia, Micronesia, Mongolia, Montenegro, Nepal, Niue, Oman, Panama, Papua New Guinea, Qatar, Samoa, São Tomé and Príncipe, Saudi Arabia, Solomon Islands, Sudan, Syria, Taiwan, Tajikistan, Tonga, Turkmenistan, United Arab Emirates, Uzbekistan, Vanuatu, Vietnam or Yemen, substitute the date of the country's membership in the WTO or the Berne Convention, whichever is earlier, for January 1, 1996 in the rules described above.

The Ninth Circuit Court of Appeals has held that a work published only in a foreign language in a foreign country, without a copyright notice, between July 1, 1909 and 1978 is an "unpublished" work for purposes of U.S. public domain law until such time as it is published with a copyright notice.[301] Commentators have criticized the decision, and it is not known whether courts in other circuits, or the U.S. Supreme Court, would reach the same conclusion. Jurisdictions within the Ninth Circuit are Alaska, Arizona, California, Hawaii, Idaho, Montana, Nevada, Oregon, Washington, Guam, and the Northern Mariana Islands.

The URAA restored copyright in foreign works published after 1922 that had fallen into the public domain in the United States as of January 1, 1996 because of a failure to comply with U.S. formalities or because the subject matter was not protected by U.S. copyright law (such as pre-1972 sound recordings). For the restoration to apply, at least one of the authors of the work had to be a non-U.S. citizen or resident, the work must not have been published in the United States within thirty days after its first publication abroad, and the work must not have been in the public domain in the country of publication. When restoration applies, a foreign work has a copyright term equivalent to that of a U.S. work that had followed all of the formalities.

Chapter 25. Fair Use

Article I of the Constitution directs Congress to protect copyrights "[t]o promote the progress of science and useful arts..."[302] Congress has invoked this provision as a justification for rejecting a "property rights" rationale for copyright protection, stating that the overarching rationale for copyright laws, instead, is to promote the general public welfare.[303] The U.S. Supreme Court has agreed, asserting that "the sole interest of the United States and the primary object in conferring the monopoly lie in the general benefits derived by the public from the labors of authors."[304] Granting a work's creator an exclusive right to exploit it generally promotes the public welfare by ensuring that artists and inventors will have an incentive to create new things. There may be circumstances, though, in which Congress or the courts determine that a greater public benefit is served by allowing people to use copyright-protected material without having to obtain the owner's permission. In such cases, the infringing use is declared to be "fair use." A person cannot be prosecuted or held liable for damages for making "fair use" of a copyrighted work.

Fair use is an affirmative defense. To rely on it, a defendant must specifically plead it in the answer to the complaint. A person who asserts this defense is essentially acknowledging that infringement may have occurred, but claims the infringement is justified. A person who invokes the fair use defense has the burden of proving it.

The fair use defense is fraught with gray areas. Contrary to popular belief, there is no rule to the effect that a specified number of words in a text or a specified number of notes in a song is fair use. Aside from some narrowly defined safe harbors that Congress has created, the content of the fair use doctrine is fluid, developed by the courts on a case-by-case basis. They apply four broadly worded factors that frequently conflict, with no guidance from Congress about what to do when one factor supports a finding of fair use while another factor does not. For this reason, a federal appeals court judge has called the fair use doctrine "the most troublesome in the whole law of copyright."[305]

Because of this lack of certainty, fair use litigation can be very expensive. Consequently, it is not a good idea to rely on this defense unless one has a firm understanding of its vagaries. When in doubt, obtaining permission from the copyright owner may be a prudent option.

The Four-Factor Test

A use of a copyrighted work may qualify as fair use if, after considering all relevant factors, including but not necessarily limited to the four set out in the Copyright Act, a court determines that an important public policy outweighs the copyright owner's interest in controlling and receiving compensation for his work. 17 U.S.C. § 107 provides:

> [T]he fair use of a copyrighted work, including such use by reproduction in copies or phonorecords or by any other means … for purposes such as criticism, comment, news reporting, teaching (including multiple copies for classroom use), scholarship, or research, is not an infringement of copyright....

The statute directs courts to consider four factors:

- The purpose and character of the use
- The nature of work
- The amount and substantiality of the portion used
- The effect of the use on the market for the work.

The enumerated uses (criticism, commentary, teaching, etc) are not safe harbors. These kinds of uses are likely to be fair use, but they are not always. A court must evaluate the four factors to make a determination in each case.

There is no rule of decision for cases in which some factors support fair use and some do not. Courts decide how much weight to give each factor on an impromptu basis. Also, courts are not limited to these four factors. They may consider any other relevant factors.

PURPOSE AND CHARACTER OF THE USE

Consistent with the language of the statute, the following kinds of uses usually result in a finding that the "purpose and character of the use" factor weighs heavily in favor of fair use:

- Criticism
- Commentary
- News reporting
- Teaching
- Scholarship
- Research
- Charitable uses.

Even for these kinds of uses, however, all four factors must still be considered.

Noncompetitive Purpose

A use is more likely to be deemed fair use if it does not compete against the copyrighted work in the same market. Conversely, a use is less likely to be deemed fair use if it competes in the same market with the original work. This is a principal reason that parodies are usually found to be fair use. A parody usually does not compete in the same market with the original work. Fans of the original work are not likely to be in the market for works that poke fun at it.

Noncommercial Use

Although it is not dispositive of the issue, commercial use is usually less likely to be considered fair use than noncommercial or nonprofit use is. Making copies of a work solely for the purpose of selling or to spare someone the expense of buying a retail copy is highly unlikely to be deemed fair use. At the same time, though,, the fact that only noncommercial use of a work is made does not assure that it is fair use. Courts will consider the other three factors, too.

A use may be commercial even if it there was never any intention to make money from it. If a website has advertising on it and the amount of advertising revenue is tied to the number of hits the website receives, then reproduction of a copyrighted work on the site may be considered a commercial use, since its presence can increase the number of visits to the site and thereby increase advertising revenue. This is true even if the copyrighted work is largely informational and does not advertise any product or service.

Parody is usually fair use even if it is published for a commercial purpose. This is because it is essentially criticism or commentary about the original work itself. Criticism and commentary are at the core of the fair use doctrine. It may be fair use even if a large amount is copied, because the other factors weigh heavily in favor of a finding of fair use. Parody is criticism and commentary, two core "fair use" purposes. It usually has no significant effect on the market for the original work because it does not compete in the market for the work itself. The tendency of a parody to depress sales of the original work because it is critical of the original work is not what is meant by "effect on the market for the work." Copying more than what is needed is not fair use, but how much is needed for an effective parody is difficult to say.

Satire is not as likely to qualify as fair use. A parody targets and mimics the original work to criticize or comment on the work itself. A satire may mimic the original work, too, but not for the purpose of criticizing or commenting on it. A satire may criticize or comment on something else, such as social mores or political institutions, but the purpose of a satire is not to criticize or comment on the work itself. There is a greater need to copy a work, or portions of it to criticize or comment on it than there is to copy a work in connection with criticizing or commenting on something else. In one case, a book using Dr. Seuss characters and style to tell the story of the O. J. Simpson murder trial was held to be satire and therefore not fair use. The court reasoned that the book did not criticize or comment on Dr. Seuss characters., so it was not necessary to copy them to make a point about the O.J. Simpson trial.[306]

Transformative Use

Commercial use does not necessarily rule out a finding of fair use. The fact that a work is sold for money (and therefore commercial) is of less significance in a "fair use" analysis if the work is highly transformative. A transformative use is any use that alters the purpose, meaning or function of a work, or a portion of it. It is any use that makes the work serve a purpose, express a meaning, or function in a way that is different from the purpose, meaning or function of the original work.

The U.S. Supreme Court has held that the more transformative a new work is, the more likely it is to be fair use. In *Campbell v. Acuff-Rose Music*[307] the Court reviewed rap group 2 Live Crew's unauthorized reproduction of the opening musical intro and first line of the Roy Orbison song, "Oh, Pretty Woman" for use in a song they called, "Pretty Woman." The district court denied the copyright owner's infringement claim and the court of appeals reversed. The court of appeals reasoned that the fact that the most distinctive part of the song was copied and that the copied portion helped sell the new work (commercial use) weighed heavily against a finding of fair use.

The U.S. Supreme Court reversed the reversal, holding that 2 Live Crew's use of the song without permission was fair use because the group had transformed the song in such a way that the copied portions communicated a different meaning than the original song did. This, the Court ruled, outweighed the other factors, including the fact that 2 Live Crew had copied the "heart" of the song and that the group's commercial exploitation of Orbison's recording negatively impacted the market for the original.

It is difficult to square this case with those declaring that the most important consideration is the extent to which an infringing work impairs the market for the original work. It is also difficult to square with the Copyright Act's explicit grant of the exclusive right to make derivative works to copyright owners. The Act defines a derivative work as "any form in which a work may be recast, transformed, or adapted."[308] According to the U.S. Supreme Court, though, it seems it is fair use to make a derivative work without the author's permission even if the other fair use factors do not support a finding of fair use, so long as the derivative work has a meaning that is different from the original. Legal scholars debate the correctness of the ruling. Whether the ruling was correct or not, though, it is now the law of the land that the more transformative a use of a work is, the more likely it is to be fair use.

Despite the Supreme Court's ruling, not every transformative use is fair use. For example, in *Warner Bros. Entertainment, Inc. v. RDR Books*[309] a court held that an encyclopedia of terms and lexicons used in Harry Potter novels is not fair use. Although transformative, the court held it was nevertheless an infringing derivative work. A number of other decisions have concluded that the unauthorized use of elements of a preexisting copyrighted work to make a derivative work is not fair use even though the copied elements were used for an entirely different purpose. For example, although parody is generally held to be fair use, courts have held that satire is not. Yet satire, by definition, makes use of elements of a work for a purpose that is entirely different from the original. The purpose of a satire may be to make a reader laugh or to criticize a social or political institution, person or event, but it rarely, if ever, conveys the same meaning or is used for the same purpose as the original. Nevertheless, some courts decline to hold that satire is fair use, at least if the amounts and substantiality of the portions copied are significant.

AESTHETIC IMPRESSION

The Court, in *Campbell*, relied heavily on the parody/satire distinction, viewing 2 Live Crew's production as parody. At the same time, though, the Court eschewed any bright-line test that classifies all parody as fair use and all satire as probable infringement. Although courts have stated that the reason satire does not qualify for fair use is that it does not criticize the work itself but instead uses the work to comment on something else, there are cases where courts, emboldened by the transformative use doctrine announced in *Campbell*, have held that substantial portions of an artist's work may be copied into a new work even though the new work does not serve the purpose of criticizing or commenting on the original work. In *Cariou v. Prince*[310] the Second Circuit Court of Appeals held that an author's incorporation of an entire copyrighted work (as distinguished from merely a portion of it) into a new work may be sufficiently transformative to qualify as fair use even if the new work is not a parody and even if the copying of the original work is not for purposes of criticism or commentary on it. The court determined that the new work—in this case, a copy of a copyrighted photograph with graffiti-like markings drawn on it—created a "different aesthetic" from that imparted by the original work, and therefore was fair use. In so holding, the court expressly rejected the idea that the new work must either criticize or comment on the original in order to be a protected fair use.[311]

It is difficult to reconcile *Cariou* with cases holding that satire is not fair use. Most, if not all, satire creates an aesthetic that is different from the original. An original work may project a somber, philosophical aesthetic. A satire of it most likely will create the opposite aesthetic, humor. It is also difficult to square *Cariou* with the exclusive right of the author to make derivative works. The artist in this case clearly copied substantial elements of the author's work and then modified it. That is what it means to make a derivative work. The Second Circuit's ruling seems to suggest that an author only has an exclusive right to make derivative works that have the same aesthetic as the original.

The potential significance of this ruling is not yet known. How great a difference in aesthetics will qualify as "entirely different"? Since judges are not art experts, will the testimony of an aesthetics expert be necessary in fair use cases? If experts are called to give opinions about aesthetics, what standard relevant to copyright principles should they employ to determine whether a particular work has an "entirely different" aesthetic, on one hand, or only a "partially different" aesthetic, on the other?

The Hon. Pierre Leval, writing in the *Harvard Law Review*, once opined that "[j]udges do not share a consensus on the meaning of fair use." As a result, it has become what he described as "a disorderly basket of exceptions…."[312] This is one more reason why it can be prudent to try to get a copyright owner's permission than to gamble on a court's interpretation and application of the fair use factors.

SEARCHABLE DATABASES

Copying books to a digital format for use in a searchable database can be sufficiently transformative to be fair use. A court has upheld as fair use the maintenance of a database of copyrighted works as part of a plagiarism-checking service, where copies of the works were made solely for comparison purposes. A court has also held that the fair use doctrine means Google Books may make unauthorized copies of over 30,000,000 books, without paying royalties to the authors, so that the company can create a searchable book index that reproduces and displays portions of the books to users in response to their search requests.

An online book search engine that copies the contents of books may publish portions of the contents of the books online for anyone with an Internet connection to access free of charge, without either the service provider or readers having to pay a royalty to authors. A federal circuit court of appeals has decided that making the actual text of books available to everyone free of charge will not significantly reduce the market for the books. Even if it does, though, the court concluded that the value to consumers of being able to find and read the portions of books in which they are interested without having to purchase them outweighed the fact that it would result in depriving authors of compensation for their work.

In reaching this conclusion, the court reasoned that the amount of each book that was actually reproduced and distributed royalty-free to the public in this way was not significant. This conclusion was influenced by Google Books' assertions that only a few "snippets" from a work are reproduced and displayed in response to a search request. According to their website, "a few sentences of your search term in context" are displayed in search results. Full-page and multipage previews reportedly are displayed only if the author or publisher authorizes it. Moreover, Google Books provides a mechanism by which the owner of the copyright in a book may have the book removed from the database.

INLINE LINKING, FRAMING, AND THUMBNAILS

Downloading a copyrighted image, converting it into a thumbnail, and then displaying the thumbnail would infringe a copyright owner's exclusive rights to reproduce, display and make derivative works of the image. On the other hand, merely providing a link to a website where the image is being displayed with the copyright owner's permission would not infringe any of the copyright owner's exclusive rights. No copy is made; providing a link does not "display" anything; and no modification is made to the content of the image.

Inline linking is the placement of a special type of link in the web page coding that enables a viewer of the page to see a file that is hosted on a separate web page without leaving the original web page. In *Perfect 10, Inc. v. Google,*[313] the Ninth Circuit Court of Appeals ruled that providing a hypertext link, whether simple or inline, does not infringe reproduction or display rights. The image a user sees upon clicking a link is displayed as a result of the interaction between the user's system and the server on which the image is stored. The owner of the website providing the link does not "display" the copyrighted material itself.

Causing the linked-to content to appear as thumbnails, on the other hand, does infringe the copyright owner's exclusive right to make derivative works.[314] In *Perfect 10 v. Amazon, Inc.,*[315] the Ninth Circuit Court of Appeals held that making thumbnails solely for inclusion in a searchable index is infringement but it is fair use. The court applied the four-factor test to determine that the public benefit of having a convenient Internet search engine outweighs the negative impact on the market for thumbnail versions of the copyrighted images. Because every application of the four-factor test is case-specific, it cannot be inferred from these cases that everyone may use inline linking to display thumbnail images of other people's images. To the contrary, it seems likely that if Google had not limited its use of the inline-thumbnail technology to an Internet search engine, it could very well have been held liable for copyright infringement.

Framing is the process of causing one website to be displayed in a frame on a screen simultaneously with that of another website. It raises a number of legal issues. If it is likely to create consumer confusion about the origin, sponsorship or endorsement of a product or service, it might constitute trademark infringement. The FTC might consider it a deceptive trade practice. In some cases, it might constitute misappropriation of information or unfair competition, if the conditions for those causes of action exist. Although an argument may be made that it does not infringe a copyright owner's reproduction or display rights, at least one court has held that causing copyrighted content to be displayed within a frame amounts to a modification of the original work, and if unauthorized, it infringes the copyright owner's exclusive right to create derivative works.[316]

Whether a particular kind of link amounts to direct infringement or not, it is clear that linking to a site that contains infringing content, or to a site that facilitates infringing activity, creates a risk of vicarious or contributory liability for the infringement that is occurring there. The DMCA provides some protection for certain website owners who unknowingly link to websites where copyright violations are occurring or being facilitated. For more information about how to qualify for this protection, see Chapter 26.

BIOGRAPHICAL ANCHORS

A short clip of a portion of a band's performance during a recorded television show, in the context of a biography about the band, is sufficiently transformative to be fair use. This conclusion is buttressed by the fact that such use is not likely to cause financial harm to the copyright owner of the recording of the television show. A clip of the entire performance might not be fair use of the musical work the band performed, though.

COPYING PORTIONS OF TEXTBOOKS FOR STUDENTS

Generally, use for an educational purpose is more likely to be deemed fair use than use for other kinds of purposes is. Copying and distributing large amounts of a textbook for use by students, however, is not likely to be fair use. Students are the principal market for a textbook. Making and distributing large portions of it to students decreases students' need to purchase it, thereby diminishing the market for it.

COPYING AUDIO CDS TO MP3 FILES

Making MP3 files of music from an audio CD is not transformative enough to be fair use.

TRANSMITTING RADIO BROADCASTS OVER TELEPHONE LINES

Transmitting or retransmitting radio broadcasts over telephone lines is not, in itself, sufficiently transformative to qualify as fair use.

RETRANSMITTING NEWS FOOTAGE OVER TELEPHONE LINES

Retransmitting copyrighted news footage is not, in itself, a sufficiently transformative use to qualify as fair use.

Comparative Advertising

Although it is a commercial use, use of a work or a portion of it in comparative advertising nevertheless is often deemed fair use.

THE NATURE OF THE WORK

Nonfiction

Use of academic, scholarly, and other factual or practical works is more likely to be fair use than the use of fiction and other kinds of creative works is, but not all infringement of nonfiction works is automatically permitted as fair use. Unauthorized copying and distribution of such a substantial amount that the market for the work is adversely impacted is not likely to be considered fair use even if the work is academic, scholarly or some other kind of nonfiction.

Works With Minimal Creativity or Originality

In general, it may be said that the less creativity or originality there is in the original work, the more likely that use of it is fair use.

Works That Are Difficult to Obtain

When a copy of a work is difficult or impossible to obtain, unauthorized use of it is more likely to be fair use than would otherwise be the case. Of course, this will not be true if an organization is licensed to provide copies at a reasonable cost. Moreover, the fact that a copy of a work is difficult or impossible to obtain does not necessarily mean that every kind of use of it is automatically fair use. The four factors need to be evaluated to make that determination.

Published vs. Unpublished Works

Because the right of first publication is valuable to authors, copying a published work is more likely to be deemed fair use than copying an unpublished work is,

AMOUNT AND SUBSTANTIALITY OF COPYING

As *Cariou* illustrates, copying an entire work may qualify as fair use in some cases. Usually, though, copying an entire work is highly unlikely to be fair use. Copying only a single word or note, by contrast, is not even infringement at all. Stretched between these two extremes is a spectrum along which some amounts of copying are determined to be fair use and some are not. Courts decide that question on a case by case basis. There are no hard-and-fast rules, but a couple of general principles may be gleaned from the cases.

Courts do not apply a numerical test. There is no legal rule that copying up to twenty words of text or four bars of music, or any other specified portion, is automatically fair use. Courts consider the importance of the portion(s) copied, not just the amount. Copying the portion of a work that gives it its popular appeal and commercial success—what courts sometimes call "the heart of the work"—is not as likely to be fair use as copying other elements of a work is. This is true even if the heart of the work comprises only one page in a four hundred page novel, or only a few bars of a song. As *Campbell* illustrates, copying the heart of a work may sometimes be fair use if the purpose of the use is highly transformative. Again, there are no bight-line tests in this area. Each case turns on its own facts and requires an analysis of the four factors.

Courts also examine the purpose to which an infringer puts the portions of the work that she copies. A court is likely to hold that the copying is fair use if only the bare minimum needed for a core "fair use" purpose (criticism, commentary, news reporting, etc.) is copied. The more the use relates to one of these purposes, the larger the amount of copying courts tend to tolerate, even if the copying involves substantial portions of the work. Conversely, copying more than what is needed for a core "fair use" purpose is not as likely to be considered fair use.

EFFECT ON THE MARKET

The effect of the use on the market for the original work is frequently the deciding factor in fair use cases. In many cases, this principle is consistent with the Supreme Court's declaration in *Campbell* that the transformativeness of a new work is the most important factor. The more transformative a new work is, the less likely it is, usually, to adversely affect the market for the original work.

In a similar vein, the "amount and substantiality" factor often helps support a finding of the likely impact on the market for the original work. The smaller the amount of the original work that is copied, and the less substantial the parts copied are, the less likely the copying is to have an adverse effect on the market for the original work.

Both the actual effect of the defendant's conduct on current markets for the work and the projected effect on the market if the conduct were to become widely engaged in by others need to be considered.

The effect on markets of the use of a work that is in direct competition with the copyright owner's work depends on the amount of the work used and whether the defendant's use is commercial or not. The same may be said about making a derivative work in a traditional market, such as making a movie based on another person's novel. Assuming the amount of copied work is substantial and the use is commercial, the effect on the market for the owner's work is likely to be significant. Such uses are not likely to qualify as fair use. Making a derivative work in a nontraditional market may be more likely to be fair use, although courts are not in agreement about this.

If a use is for commercial gain, then the likelihood of a harmful effect on the market(s) for the author's work is presumed. If the use is for a noncommercial purpose, then the likelihood of a harmful impact on the market(s) for the author's work is not presumed; it must be proven. The presumption that a commercial use adversely affects the market for the original work is rebuttable. The best way to rebut it is to show that the work competes in a different market, so that sales of the new work do not detract from sales of the original work.

The absence of a commercial motive or commercial gain does not necessitate a finding of fair use. A finding that an infringing activity adversely affects the market for the original work may prevent a finding of fair use even if the infringer did not profit from the use. For example, making digital downloads available for free on the Internet harms the copyright holders' market for their works, and therefore is not fair use even though no profit is made from the activity.

Although the effect on the market for the original work is arguably the most important consideration, it is still only one of four factors that courts are to consider in every case. It is possible that a court may hold that one or more of the other factors outweighs this consideration in a particular case.

Networked File Exchange Services

Because the practice significantly reduces the market for the original work, using the Internet to exchange copies of copyrighted works with other users is not fair use. For the same reason, providing a service that facilitates such exchanges is not fair use.

Photocopying by Businesses

Photocopying by a for-profit business usually is not fair use, even if the materials are only distributed internally. Similarly, systematic copying and distribution of journal articles to a business's employees is not often fair use.

If there is a ready means to pay for the use of a work and the user is a for-profit venture, using the work without paying for it is not likely to be fair use.

For an annual fee, the Copyright Clearance Center provides a license to copy from any work that is registered with it. This can sometimes be an economical solution for businesses that intend to do a fair amount of copying and distribution of copyrighted material.

Statutory Exemptions

Congress has declared certain kinds of uses to be fair use. When they apply, these exemptions from copyright infringement liability neither require nor permit consideration of the four factors.

THE DIGITAL MILLENNIUM COPYRIGHT ACT

The DMCA is the source of some of the most important statutory exemptions described in this chapter. It also provides a way for online service providers to avoid liability, in some cases, for linking to sites with infringing content and for the infringing content that other people contribute to a website. See Chapter 26.

EPHEMERAL COPIES

A person who has a license or a statutory right to publicly display, perform or transmit a copyrighted work may make a copy of it for use in an authorized transmission or for archival, preservation or security purposes. These kinds of copies are called *ephemeral* copies. The exemption does not authorize further copies to be made. The exemption for ephemeral copies does not apply to audiovisual works.

A person who has lawfully acquired a copy of a sound recording may make a noninteractive transmission of it to a business establishment or in a manner otherwise authorized by a voluntary or statutory license, provided the copyright owner has either authorized the transmission or made a public distribution of the recording. In this situation, too, an ephemeral copy may be made.

A copyright owner who has implemented measures to prevent copying must provide a licensee with the means to make a copy if it is technologically and economically feasible to do so. Otherwise, the licensee may circumvent copyright protection measures and make a copy without incurring liability for a violation of the anti-circumvention provision[317] of the Copyright Act

If an ephemeral copy is made exclusively for archival purposes, then it may be retained indefinitely. Otherwise, it must be destroyed within six months after it was first transmitted to the public. Governmental bodies and nonprofit organizations, however, may make up to thirty copies of a transmission program embodying the performance or display of a work, provided no copies are made from the copies. The governmental body or nonprofit organization may keep one copy indefinitely, for archival purposes. The rest must be destroyed within seven years from the date of the first transmission of the program.

A governmental body or nonprofit organization may make and distribute one copy of a nondramatic musical work of a religious nature (or a sound recording of it) to each transmitting organization that has a right to transmit a performance of the work to the public (pursuant to a license, for example), provided there is no charge for the distribution, and provided the transmitting organization only makes a single transmission of it. The governmental body or nonprofit organization may keep one copy of such a work indefinitely, exclusively for archival purposes. All remaining copies must be destroyed within one year after the first transmission.

A governmental body or nonprofit organization that has a right to transmit a performance for deaf or blind persons may make up to ten copies of the performance, and may allow any governmental body or nonprofit organization that is entitled to transmit such performances to blind or deaf persons to use a copy to do so. The copies must be provided at no charge. All copies must be used solely for transmissions to blind or deaf persons, or for archival preservation or security. No copies may be made from the copies.

TRANSITORY COMMUNICATIONS

The DMCA provides an exemption for digital material transmitted by a service provider who acts only as a data conduit, transmitting digital information from one point on a network to another at someone else's request. It covers acts of transmission, routing, or providing connections for the information, as well as the intermediate and transient copies that are made automatically in the operation of a network. To qualify for this exemption, the following requirements must be met:

(a) The transmission must be initiated by a person other than the provider;
(b) The transmission, routing, provision of connections, or copying must be carried out by an automatic technical process without selection of material by the service provider;
(c) The service provider must not determine the recipients of the material;
(d) Any intermediate copies must not ordinarily be accessible to anyone other than anticipated recipients, and must not be retained for longer than reasonably necessary;
(e) The material must be transmitted with no modification to its content.

SYSTEM CACHING

A service provider may be exempt from liability for damages for copyright infringement due to the intermediate and temporary storage of material on a system or network controlled or operated by or for the service provider if the material is made available online by another person who transmits it through the system or network to another person at that person's request. This exemption is available only if all of the following conditions are satisfied:

(a) The storage occurs automatically;
(b) The material is transmitted to the person without any modification to its content;
(c) The service provider complies with rules concerning the refreshing, reloading, or other up-dating of the material when specified by the person making the material available online in accordance with a generally accepted industry standard data communications protocol for the system or network through which that person makes the material available;
(d) The service provider does not interfere with the ability of technology associated with the material to return to the person making the transmission the information that would have been available to that person if the material had been obtained by subsequent users directly from that person, except in cases where the technology: (i) significantly interferes with the performance of the provider's system or network or with the intermediate storage of the material; (ii) is inconsistent with generally accepted industry standard communications protocols; or (iii) extracts information from the provider's system or network other than the

information that would have been available to the person transmitting the material if the subsequent users had gained access to it directly from that person;

(e) The service provider permits access to the stored material in significant part only to users of its system or network that have met any conditions for access to the material that the person transmitting the material has set, such as payment of a fee or provision of a password, etc.;

(f) Upon notification of infringement, the service provider promptly removes, or disables access to, material that is claimed to be infringing, in cases where (i) the material has previously been removed from the originating site or access to it has been disabled or a court has ordered it removed or access to it disabled, and (ii) the party giving the notification includes in the notification a statement confirming that the material has been removed from the originating site or access to it has been disabled or that a court has ordered that the material be removed from the originating site or that access to the material on the originating site must be disabled;

(g) The service provider has implemented a policy that provides for the termination of subscribers and account holders who are repeat infringers;

(h) The service provider informs subscribers and account holders about the policy;

(i) The service provider accommodates and does not interfere with standard technical measures that are used by copyright owners to identify or protect copyrighted works, and that do not impose substantial costs on service providers or substantial burdens on their systems or networks.

Damages may not be recovered against a service provider who complies with these requirements, although a court may still issue injunctive relief in cases where system caching infringes a copyright.

TRANSITORY DIGITAL NETWORK COMMUNICATIONS

An exemption from copyright liability exists for those who provide users with a connection to the Internet, or make the underlying system of network connections operate. In the absence of an exemption, these service providers might otherwise be liable for contributory infringement simply by reason of providing an Internet connection for the infringer.

An ISP is exempt from liability for damages for copyright infringement for transmitting, routing, or providing connections for, material through a system or network controlled or operated by or for the service provider, or the intermediate and transient storage of that material in the course of such transmitting, routing, or providing connections, if all of the following conditions are satisfied:

(a) The transmission of the material was initiated by someone else;

(b) The transmission, etc. occurs automatically, without selection of material by the service provider;

(c) The service provider does not select the recipients of the material;

(d) No copy of the material made by the service provider in the course of such intermediate or transient storage is maintained on the system or network in a manner ordinarily accessible to anyone other than anticipated recipients, and no such copy is maintained on the system or network in a manner ordinarily accessible to such anticipated recipients for a longer period than is reasonably necessary for the transmission, routing, or provision of connections;

(e) The material is transmitted without modification of its content;

(f) The service provider has implemented a policy that provides for the termination of subscribers and account holders who are repeat infringers;

(g) The service provider informs subscribers and account holders about the policy; and

(h) The service provider accommodates and does not interfere with standard technical measures that are used by copyright owners to identify or protect copyrighted works, and that do not impose substantial costs on service providers or substantial burdens on their systems or networks.

A court may order a service provider to terminate the account(s) of an account holder or subscriber who is using the provider's service to engage in infringing activity. A court may also restrain a service provider from providing access, by taking reasonable steps specified in the order to block access, to a specific, identified, online location outside the United States.

RECEIVING AND DISPLAYING BROADCASTS AND TRANSMISSIONS

An individual may receive and display authorized broadcasts and digital transmissions on a single receiving device such as a television, radio, or networked computer or mobile device, provided people are not charged a fee to watch or hear it. Retransmissions of received broadcasts and transmissions are not protected by this exemption.

This exemption only applies to displaying a received broadcast or transmission. It does not exempt the broadcaster or transmitter from complying with copyright laws. Unauthorized broadcasts and transmissions do not come within the coverage of this exemption.

CERTAIN SECONDARY TRANSMISSIONS

A *secondary transmission* is one that further transmits a received transmission. It is different from a simulcast or multicast in that simulcasts and multicasts occur simultaneously with the primary transmission. A secondary transmission occurs after the primary transmission.

A secondary transmission is exempt from a claim of copyright infringement if it occurs immediately upon receipt of the primary transmission and any of the following conditions apply:

(a) It is transmitted at no charge by the manager of a hotel, apartment building or lodging establishment to guests; the primary transmission is by a broadcast station licensed by the FCC (i.e., not Internet transmissions); and the secondary transmission is within the service area of the broadcast station;

(b) It is transmitted in connection with an online instructional activity of a governmental body or an accredited nonprofit educational institution that meets all the requirements for exemption (See above);

(c) It is transmitted by a carrier that has no control over the content of the primary transmission or the recipients of the secondary transmission, provided the carrier's activities are limited to providing communication channels such as a wires, cables, etc.;

(d) The transmission is by a satellite carrier pursuant to a statutory license;

(e) The transmission is by a governmental body or nonprofit organization, without charge other than for the actual and reasonable costs of maintaining and operating the secondary transmission service;

(f) The transmission is by a cable system with a valid statutory license, provided the transmission is not a violation of FCC rules or regulations; the cable system has complied with accounting and royalty payment requirements; and the primary transmission is not altered in an unauthorized way.

To qualify for any of the above exemptions, the primary transmission must be one that is for reception by the public at large. Even if the primary transmission is only offered to particular people, however, a secondary transmitter may nevertheless be exempt if the primary transmission is by a broadcast station licensed by the FCC; FCC rules, regulations or authorizations require carriage of the signals comprising the secondary transmission; and the secondary transmitter does not alter the primary transmitter's signal.

A different set of rules applies to secondary transmissions of the broadcasts of stations located outside the United States.

PARENTAL CONTROLS

The making imperceptible, by or at the direction of a member of a private household, of limited portions of audio or video content of a motion picture during a performance in or transmitted to that household for private home viewing, from an authorized copy of the motion picture, or the creation or provision of a computer program or other technology that enables such making imperceptible and that is designed and marketed to be used at the direction of a member of a private household for such making imperceptible, is permitted if no fixed copy of the altered version of the motion picture is created by such computer program or other technology.

COMPUTER OPERATIONS

Loading a computer program into a computer's memory is permitted, as is decompilation (converting object code to source code). Distributing copies of it from a website is not covered by this exemption.

REVERSE ENGINEERING

Reverse engineering a computer program is fair use.

COMPULSORY LICENSES FOR COVER VERSIONS OF SONGS

A person who qualifies for a compulsory license to make and distribute copies of a cover version (i.e., her own performance of a musical work) is exempt from liability for infringement of the copyright in the musical work provided she complies with all the conditions and requirements for obtaining and maintaining a compulsory license. The exemption only applies to liability for making and distributing copies. Infringement liability may still arise for publicly performing the work without permission. See Chapter 33.

STATUTORY EXEMPTIONS AND LICENSES FOR SOUND RECORDINGS

Congress has exempted certain kinds of uses of sound recordings from federal copyright protection. It has also created a system of statutory licensing. These provisions do not create immunity from liability for infringement of the copyright in a literary or musical work that is performed in a sound recording. See Chapter 33.

NONSIMULTANEOUS SECONDARY TRANSMISSIONS BY CABLE SYSTEMS

The Copyright Act makes certain nonsimultaneous secondary transmissions by cable systems exempt from infringement liability, provided the cable system complies with detailed conditions specified in the statute and applicable regulations.

PHOTOGRAPHS OF ARTWORK ON USEFUL ARTICLES

A photograph may be taken of a copyrighted work, such as a drawing or painting, that has been incorporated into a useful article, and the photograph may be used in news reports, commentary, and advertising related to the distribution or display of the useful article.

FACULTY AND GRADUATE STUDENTS

When a public or nonprofit institution of higher education is a service provider (e.g., provides access to the Internet, or maintains an informational or commercial website), it is exempt from liability for damages for the infringing activities of an employee on the basis that it transmitted, routed, or provided connections for, or engaged in system caching with respect to, infringing material transmitted at the employee's direction if all of the following conditions apply:

(a) The employee is a faculty member or graduate student at the institution;
(b) The employee is performing a teaching or research function;
(c) The infringing activities do not involve the provision of online access to instructional materials that are or were required or recommended, within the preceding three-year period, for a course the employee taught at the institution;
(d) The institution has not, within the preceding three-year period, received more than two notifications of claimed copyright infringement by the employee (excluding notifications involving a known misrepresentation that content infringed a copyright);
(e) The institution provides to all users of its system or network materials that accurately describe and promote compliance with copyright laws;
(f) The institution has implemented a policy that provides for the termination of subscribers and account holders who are repeat infringers;
(g) The institution informs subscribers and account holders about the policy;
(h) The institution accommodates and does not interfere with standard technical measures used by copyright owners to identify or protect copyrighted works, and that do not impose substantial costs on service providers or substantial burdens on their systems or networks.

If all of these conditions are met, then the employee's knowledge or awareness of his own infringing activities will not be imputed to the institution. This means that the institution may avail itself of the protections of the DMCA, including but not limited to the notice-and-take-down provisions.

This exemption only protects the institution from an award of damages. A court may still issue injunctive relief against the institution if infringing activity is found to have occurred.

ONLINE COURSES OFFERED BY SCHOOLS AND GOVERNMENT

An accredited nonprofit educational institution or a governmental body may display or perform copyrighted works in web-based instructional programs (i.e., programs digitally transmitted over the Internet), provided all of the following conditions are met:

(a) The performance or display is made by, at the direction of, or under the supervision of an instructor as an integral part of a class session offered as a regular part of the systematic mediated instructional activities of a governmental body or an accredited nonprofit educational institution;

(b) It is directly related and of material assistance to the teaching content of the transmission;

(c) The transmission is made solely for, and, to the extent technologically feasible, the reception of such transmission is limited to students officially enrolled in the course, or officers or employees of governmental bodies as a part of their official duties or employment;

(d) The transmitting body or institution has instituted policies regarding copyright; provides materials to faculty, students, and relevant staff members that accurately describe, and promote compliance with, copyright laws; and provides notice to students that materials used in connection with the course may be subject to copyright protection;

(e) The transmitting body or institution applies technological measures that reasonably prevent retention of the work in accessible form by recipients of the transmission from the transmitting body or institution for longer than the class session, and unauthorized further dissemination of the work in accessible form by such recipients to others;

(f) The transmitting body or institution does not engage in conduct that could reasonably be expected to interfere with technological measures used by copyright owners to prevent such retention or unauthorized further dissemination;

(g) The work performed or displayed is not produced or marketed primarily for use in mediated instructional activities that are transmitted digitally;

(h) The performance or display is not given by means of a copy or phonorecord that the transmitting body or institution knew or had reason to believe was illegally made or acquired;

(i) The work performed or displayed is: (i) a performance of a musical or nondramatic literary work; (ii) a performance of a reasonable and limited portion of a dramatic, audiovisual or other kind of work; or (iii) a display of a work in an amount comparable to that which is typically displayed in the course of a live classroom session;

(j) The work performed or displayed is not a textbook, course pack or other material that is typically purchased or acquired by the students in higher education for their independent use and retention or typically purchased or acquired for elementary and secondary students for their possession and independent use.

USE OF MUSIC BY TEACHERS

Nondramatic musical works may be performed in classroom educational activities. This can include Internet transmissions, but only if relevant to the instructional content, and only if the transmission is made by or under the supervision of a teacher as part of a class session offered by a public school or an accredited nonprofit educational institution.

This exemption does not apply to works that are specifically made or marketed for classroom instructional purposes, or to copies of works that were not lawfully obtained.

A webcaster invoking this exception must employ technological measures to prevent recipients of the transmission from retaining the work for longer than the class session, and to prevent unauthorized further dissemination of the work. Also, the webcaster must not do anything that interferes with technological measures used by copyright owners to prevent such retention or unauthorized further dissemination.

RELIGIOUS SERVICES

Performance of a copyrighted musical work or nondramatic literary work, or of a dramatico-musical work of a religious nature, or display of a work, in the course of religious services at a place of worship is fair use. This exemption only covers performances at the place of worship. It does not apply to broadcasts or transmissions of religious services over the Internet.

STATE FAIRS AND AGRICULTURAL OR HORTICULTURAL EXHIBITIONS

In some cases, a governmental body or nonprofit agricultural or horticultural organization is not liable for performing, and is not subject to vicarious or contributory liability for another person's performance of, a nondramatic musical work at an annual agricultural or horticultural fair or exhibition. This exemption, however, only applies to performances at an annual fair. It does not apply to Internet broadcasts or transmissions of them.

FRATERNAL AND VETERANS' ORGANIZATIONS

Performance of a nondramatic literary or musical work in the course of a social function organized and promoted by a nonprofit veterans' organization or a nonprofit fraternal organization to which the general public is not invited is permitted if the proceeds from the performance, after deducting the reasonable costs of producing the performance, are used exclusively for charitable purposes and not for financial gain. This exemption does not apply to the social functions of a college or university fraternity or sorority unless the social function is held solely to raise funds for a specific charitable purpose. It also does not apply to Internet broadcasts or transmissions of the performance.

FACE-TO-FACE EDUCATIONAL ACTIVITIES

Performing or displaying copyrighted works during face-to-face teaching activities at a nonprofit educational institution is permissible. Since they are not conducted face-to-face, online educational activities do not come within this exemption.

FREE, CHARITABLE OR NONPROFIT CONCERTS

Live performances of musical works and nondramatic literary works are permitted if they are free or if all proceeds are used for charitable, religious or educational purposes.

This exemption does not apply to broadcasts or transmissions of the performance.

PERFORMANCES OF NONDRAMATIC LITERARY WORKS FOR BLIND OR DEAF PERSONS

Performances of nondramatic literary works for blind or deaf persons (i.e., reading aloud, communicating with sign language, etc.) may be transmitted to blind or deaf persons, provided the transmission is not for commercial advantage and is made by one of the following:

- Governmental body
- Noncommercial educational broadcast station
- Radio subcarrier authorization
- Cable system.

RECORDING TELEVISION BROADCASTS FOR HOME VIEWING

Videotaping a television broadcast for viewing at a later time is permitted, so long as it is not done for financial gain.[318] The exemption only authorizes copying and displaying a work at the place where the copy is normally kept. It does not authorize the distribution of copies to others. Nor does it authorize public performance or display of the copy. This exemption does not authorize transmitting a home-taped television broadcast from a website, for example.

MUSIC IN RESTAURANTS, BARS AND BUSINESS ESTABLISHMENTS

A restaurant, bar, retail store or other business establishment may play authorized radio, television, cable and satellite broadcasts or transmissions of nondramatic musical works if it does not charge people to see or hear them. The exemption is subject to detailed conditions relating to the size of the establishment and the size and number of screens or speakers that may be employed. The exemption does not authorize the retransmission of music beyond the establishment where it is received.

MUSIC STORES

A retail establishment that is open to the public may "perform" sound recordings of nondramatic musical works (such as by playing a CD or record album) for the sole purpose of promoting sales of sound recordings or devices used to play them, provided it does not charge people to listen to them. This exemption does not authorize transmission beyond the establishment.

RADIO SUBCARRIER TRANSMISSIONS TO BLIND OR DEAF PERSONS

A performance of a dramatic literary work may be transmitted to blind or deaf persons if the work was published at least ten years before the performance, provided the transmission is made by a radio subcarrier authorization and is not for commercial advantage.

LIBRARIES AND ARCHIVES

A number of exemptions apply to libraries. Most of these apply to archives, too.

A library may make and distribute one copy of a work in its collection, provided it is not done for commercial gain; a copyright notice or statement is included; and the collection is either open to the public, or open to both library and nonlibrary researchers doing research in a specialized field.

A library may copy and distribute up to three copies of an unpublished work in its collection, if done solely for the purposes of preservation and security or for deposit for research use in another library or archive. The library may copy it to a digital format, but may not distribute it in digital format. The copies may not be made available to the public in digital format outside the library's premises.

A library may make up to three copies of a published work if it is done solely for the purpose of replacing a copy that is damaged, deteriorating, lost, or stolen, or if the existing format in which the work is stored has become obsolete. This exemption is available only if a replacement cannot be obtained at a fair price. The copies may not be made available to the public in digital format outside the library's premises.

A library may make a copy for a library patron of no more than one contribution to a periodical or collective work, or of a small amount of other kinds of works, if the library reasonably believes it will be used for private study, scholarship or research. A library may make a copy for a library patron of an entire work in its collection, or a copy of a substantial amount of it, if a copy cannot be purchased at a fair price and the library reasonably believes it will be used for private study, scholarship or research. A copyright warning must be posted where orders are placed. Unless specifically authorized by some other exemption, however, a library may not make copies of musical, pictorial, graphic, sculptural or audiovisual works for patrons at their request.

Displaying near its photocopy machine a notice that library materials may be subject to copyright protection will protect a library from contributory liability if an unsupervised patron uses the library's photocopy machine (or other equipment) to infringe a copyrighted work.

A library may copy and lend a limited number of copies of an audiovisual news program if it is not done for commercial gain; its collection is either open to the public or open to both library and nonlibrary researchers doing research in a specialized field; and a copyright notice or a statement that the work may be protected by copyright is included on the copy.

A library may make interlibrary loans of its copies of copyrighted works, so long as the purpose or effect is not to substitute for a subscription to or purchase of the work by the receiving library.

During the last twenty years of any term of copyright of a published work, a library, including a nonprofit educational institution that functions as such, may reproduce, distribute, display, or perform in facsimile or digital form a copy of such work, or portions thereof, for purposes of preservation, scholarship, or research, if the work is not subject to normal commercial exploitation; a copy of the work cannot be obtained at a reasonable price; and the copyright owner has not served notice that it is subject to such exploitation and is available for a reasonable price.

These statutory exemptions are not exclusive. Other kinds of library copying may be permitted under the four-factor fair use standard that courts apply.

The statutory exemptions do not override any licensing agreements or contracts under which a library has obtained a copy of a work. Thus, if a library obtains software under a license, and the license prohibits something which an exemption appears to permit, then the library must abide by the terms of the license agreement. Although it may not be liable for copyright infringement if it fails to do so, it may be liable for breach of the license agreement.

Websites are not libraries, so these exemptions do not apply to them.

GUIDELINES FOR CLASSROOM USE

Agreements on guidelines for the copying of portions of various kinds of works (e.g., books, magazines, newspapers, poems, artwork, musical works, and sound recordings) have been entered into by organizations representing authors, publishers and educators. They provide detailed voluntary guidelines about the amount of a work that may be copied, how often copying may be done, and other matters.

These agreements are probably the source of some of the myths that have grown up around fair use, such as the notion that copying up to 10% of a work is fair use. These guidelines are not binding on anyone who was not a party to devising them, though; nor are they binding on courts. Moreover, they only apply to teachers in nonprofit educational institutions. They do not apply to e-commerce businesses. The guidelines attempt to implement the provision of the Copyright Act that specifically describes making multiple copies for classroom use as a fair use of a copyrighted work. They cannot be carried over and applied in other contexts, such as the Internet. The determination of what amount of copying will be deemed fair use in non-classroom settings depends on different kinds of considerations. It would be a serious mistake to rely on the provisions of these guidelines as a basis for deciding how much of the content of another website's content may be copied.

The Effect of Attribution

Attributing a work to its author or creator is not a defense to an infringement claim. In some cases, though, it can be crucial to the preservation of an otherwise valid fair use defense.

Other Countries

Copyright defenses are not uniform throughout the world. Many countries do not recognize fair use as a defense to copyright infringement

Chapter 26. The Digital Millennium Copyright Act

Congress enacted the Digital Millennium Copyright Act of 1998 (DMCA) to address the application of copyright law to the Internet and digital technology and to implement the 1996 WIPO Copyright Treaty and the Performances and Phonograms Treaty. It attempts to strike a balance between protecting the rights of copyright owners and protecting online service providers from copyright infringement liability. It promotes the first interest primarily by attempting to ensure that the private measures that owners take to protect their copyrights are effecttive. It promotes the second interest primarily by creating safe harbors—statutory provisions that shield online service providers from copyright infringement liability in specified circumstances.

Applicability

The DMCA only applies to works that are protected by federal copyright law. It does not apply to works that are not protected by federal copyright law, such as works that are in the public domain. It also does not apply to trademark rights, rights of privacy, etc. Thus, for example, complying with the DMCA's notice-and-take-down procedure upon receiving notice that website content infringes a trademark, invades someone's privacy or injures a person's reputation will not necessarily protect the website owner from liability for defamation, invasion privacy or trademark infringement. The notice may or may not have that effect in cases of those kinds, but it will not be because of the DMCA.

The DMCA is a U.S. law, so it only protects online service providers in the United States. Its protections do not extent to service providers situated in other countries.

Safe Harbors

The DMCA provides safe harbors for four kinds of online activity:

- hosting user-provided content
- providing information location tools
- caching
- routing and transmission.

Information location tools are things like search engines and hypertext links to other websites.

ELIGIBILITY

To qualify for any of these safe harbors, a person must meet three general requirements, in addition to any other requirements that may apply to a particular safe harbor:

(a) It must be an online service provider;
(b) It must implement a policy of terminating the accounts of repeat infringers;
(c) It must refrain from interfering with copyright protection measures.

"Online Service Provider"

An *online service provider* is "a provider of online services or network access, or the operator of facilities therefore," including "an entity offering the transmission, routing, or providing of connections for digital online communications, between or among points specified by a user, of material of the user's choosing, without modification to the content of the material as sent or received."[319] The definition includes ISPs in the traditional sense and also those who use the Internet to provide an online service to others. Providing information or entertainment to site visitors is a service. There is no requirement that the service must be a paid one, so any website that provides information or entertainment should come within the definition. A website that facilitates the exchange of ideas and information by its users (sites with chat, instant message, user comments, guest bloggers, for example) arguably is providing a service to its users, as well. Web hosting services, email services, file-sharing networks, and search engines are also online services, as are online auction services and sites displaying third-party advertising. One court has observed that "'service provider' is defined so broadly that we have trouble imagining the existence of an online service that would not fall under the definitions...."[320]

Repeat Infringer Termination Policy

To qualify for DMCA immunity, an online service provider must implement a policy of terminating the accounts (or subscriptions, as the case may be) of those persons who use the service to infringe a copyright more than once. The service provider must also inform subscribers and account holders about the repeat infringer policy.

Accommodation of Copyright Protection Measures

To receive DMCA immunity, an online service provider must accommodate, and must not interfere with, any standard technical measures that are used by a copyright owner to identify or protect copyrighted works, if accommodating them does not impose substantial costs on the service provider or substantial burdens on the service provider's system.

USER-PROVIDED CONTENT

At common law, a person may be held liable for another person's wrongful conduct if he aids, abets or facilitates the other person's conduct. This should be a major concern for anyone who hosts or owns a website to which users may post or upload content. By providing a place for the publication of other people's text, images, etc. a hosting service or website owner is facilitating the publication of those things. If one of them infringes a copyright, then the hosing service or website owner may be held liable for it under the common law theory of contributory liability.

Congress enacted Title II of the DMCA to ameliorate this risk. The DMCA attempts to balance the interests of copyright owners against those who provide Internet services—ISP's, search engine services, email service providers, website hosting services, website owners, and bloggers—by granting immunity from contributory liability for copyright infringement to those providers – and only those providers – who comply with the DMCA's provisions.

17 U.S.C. § 512(c) establishes a set of rules collectively known as notice-and-take-down provisions. It provides that a service provider may not be sued for damages for copyright infringement based on the storage, at the direction of a user, of material that resides on a system or network controlled or operated by or for the service provider, if the service provider qualifies for the protections of the Act and complies with specified procedures for dealing with claims of copyright infringement. An injunction may still be sought against a provider who complies with the DMCA, but monetary damages for contributory infringement may not be recovered.

No Direct Financial Benefit

To receive the benefit of immunity from contributory liability for user-provided content, a service provider must meet the general eligibility requirements for all of the safe harbor provisions, and in addition, must not receive a financial benefit directly attributable to the infringing activity. This requirement does not apply to service providers that have neither the right nor the ability to control the content of a site, such as companies that provide telephone lines for a transmission. Because commercial website owners normally do have the ability to control content (such as by removing objectionable content), the "no financial benefit" condition normally applies to them.

No Knowledge of Infringing Content

Eligibility for immunity from contributory liability for user-provided content is lost if the service provider actually knows, at the time the user posts the material, that it infringes a copyright. A website owner who is aware of facts and circumstances making infringing activity apparent does not qualify for this safe harbor, either.

In most cases, an online service provider will not have foreknowledge of the infringing nature of user-provided content because users often share material without first informing the owner what it is they plan to post. In the rare case where a user gives advance notice of what he intends to post, however, and either tells the owner or it is readily apparent that the content intended to be posted infringes a copyright, then the DMCA will not protect the owner who thereafter proceeds to authorize the post.

No Solicitation or Inducement

Even without actual advance knowledge that a particular posting will infringe a copyright, a service provider is not immune from contributory liability for user-provided content if he actively induces, encourages or solicits users of the service to post material to the site that he knows or reasonably should know are likely to be protected by copyright.

Copyright Notifications Agent

Another qualification applicable to this safe harbor is that an online service provider must designate an agent to receive notifications of claimed infringement and let people know who that agent is and where to send notices of claimed infringement. The online service provider must (a) provide the Copyright Office with the name, address, phone number, and email address of the agent, together with any other contact information the Register of Copyrights may deem appropriate; and (b) provide this information to members of the public who visit the website, such as by publishing it to a page that is accessible to the public. The Register of Copyrights may require payment of a fee to designate a copyright notifications agent.

In 2016, the Copyright Office transitioned to an online system for the registration of a designated copyright notifications agent. It is no longer accepting paper forms for this purpose. The Copyright Office maintains a directory of designated agents. A copyright owner or his agent may use the Office's directory of designated agents to find the designated agent of a service provider that is hosting material that is claimed to be infringing, and may use that information to send a notification of claimed infringement to the service provider's designated agent.

Prompt Removal Upon Receiving Notice of Infringing Content

An online service provider must promptly remove or disable access to copyright infringing material or material that is claimed to infringe a copyright upon learning of the infringement or claimed infringement. Otherwise, the DMCA will not insulate the provider from contributory liability for publishing the content. A provider is bound by this requirement, however, only if the notification is in effective form and properly served.

To be effective, a notification must comply with all of the following requirements:

(a) be in writing;
(b) be signed (physically or electronically) by a person who is authorized to act on behalf of the copyright owner;
(c) identify the work in which copyright is claimed, or set out a representative list if multiple works at a single website are covered in a single notification;
(d) identify the material that is claimed to be infringing or to be the subject of infringing activity or provide information reasonably sufficient to permit the service provider to locate the material;
(e) state that the complainant has a good faith belief that use of the material in the manner complained of is not authorized by the copyright owner, its agent, or the law;
(f) provide the complainant's contact information, such as address, telephone number and/or email address;
(g) state that the information in the notification is accurate, and under penalty of perjury, the complaining party is either the copyright owner or authorized to act on behalf of the copyright owner.

A court is not supposed to consider a substantially defective notice when determining whether a service provider knew about infringing activity or had an awareness of facts or circumstances making infringement apparent.

Generally, a notification that does not contain all of the elements required for an effective notification of claimed copyright infringement does not give rise to any obligation on the part of a service provider to remove or disable access to material that is claimed to be infringing a copyright. And a notice that does not substantially comply with the requirements is not to be considered by a court when determining whether a service provider knew about infringing activity or had an awareness of facts or circumstances making infringement apparent.

Apparently concerned that artists, musicians and other creative types might not always follow legal requirement closely, Congress imposed an affirmative obligation on online service providers to help people with their notifications, at least when someone has gotten it almost right. Specifically, the DMCA says that if a notification contains each of these four key elements:

(a) identification of the copyrighted work, or a representative list
(b) identification of the material claimed to be infringing
(c) sufficient information to enable the service provider to locate the material
(d) a statement that the complaining party has a good faith belief that use of the material in the manner complained of is not authorized by the copyright owner, its agent, or the law

then a service provider receiving the notification must promptly try to contact the person or take other reasonable steps to help the person prepare and serve a notification that does substantially comply with the requirements. Otherwise, the attempted notification may be used as evidence against the service provider with respect to the question whether she knew about infringing activity or was aware of facts or circumstances making infringement apparent.

What if a website owner's (or other online service provider's) removal of a user's content would violate an obligation owed to the user? For example, what if a blogger has a contract with a guest blogger to publish the guest blogger's piece for a specified period of time, but the blogger is served with a copyright infringement notification? The DMCA addresses this problem by providing that if a service provider wishes to avoid liability to a subscriber/user for removing or disabling access to the subscriber's/user's material, then upon receiving a notification, the service provider must do the following things in addition to removing the material:

(a) promptly notify the subscriber that it has removed or disabled access to the material
(b) comply with the requirements pertaining to counter notifications, if served with one.

SERVICE ON WEBSITE OWNER *VS.* SERVICE ON HOSTING SERVICE PROVIDER

Should DMCA copyright notifications go to the website owner's notifications agent or the hosting service's notifications agent? The answer depends on what is sought to be accomplished by serving the notice. If the objective is to preserve a claim against the website owner, service should be made on the website owner's designated copyright notifications agent. If the objective is to preserve a claim against the hosting service, it should be served on the hosting service provider's designated copyright notifications agent. To preserve claims against both, service should be made on both.

WhoIs.com is a useful site for determining who provides the hosting service for a website.

COUNTER NOTIFICATIONS

Generally, a service provider may safely remove or disable access to material if it is done in good faith in response to a notification of claimed copyright infringement or if it is based on facts or circumstances from which infringing activity is apparent. The user who provided the content may file a counter notification asserting that the material does not, in fact, infringe a copyright.

A service provider is exempt from liability for removing or disabling access to a content provider's material only if:

(a) The material was removed or access to it was disabled in good faith;
(b) The material was removed or access to it disabled in response to a notification of claimed copyright infringement, or is based on facts or circumstances from which infringing activity is apparent;
(c) The service provider took reasonable steps promptly to notify the content provider that it has removed or disabled access to it;
(d) Upon receipt of an effective counter notification, the service provider promptly provided the person who served the notification of claimed copyright infringement with a copy of the counter notification;
(e) The service provider promptly informed the person who served the notification of infringement that it will replace the removed material or cease disabling access to it in ten business days;
(f) The service provider restored the removed material (or ceased disabling access to it) not less than ten, nor more than fourteen, business days following receipt of the counter notice, unless its designated agent first received notice from the person who submitted the notification of claimed copyright infringement that such person has filed an action seeking a court order to restrain the content provider from engaging in infringing activity relating to the material on the service provider's system or network.

If a service provider complies with all DMCA requirements, then she will be protected from liability to the copyright claimant and also from liability to the content provider.

To be effective, a counter-notification must substantially comply with the following requirements:

(a) be in writing;
(b) be signed (physically or electronically) by the subscriber;
(c) be mailed or transmitted to the service provider's designated agent;
(d) identify the material that has been removed or to which access has been disabled;
(e) identify the location at which the material appeared before it was removed or access to it was disabled;
(f) include a statement under penalty of perjury that the content provider has a good faith belief that the material was removed or disabled as a result of mistake or misidentification of the material to be removed or disabled;
(g) provide the content provider's name, address and phone number;
(h) state that the content provider consents to the jurisdiction of federal district court for the judicial district in which the address is located, or if the address is outside of the United States, for any judicial district in which the service provider may be found, and that the content provider will accept service of process from the person who provided notification of claimed copyright infringement or an agent of such person.

MISREPRESENTATION

Knowingly making false or misleading statements of fact in a notification or counter-notification may result in liability for damages, attorney fees and costs.[321] The DMCA also provides a civil cause of action for the recovery of compensatory damages, including attorney fees and costs, against a person who knowingly misrepresents that material or activity was removed or disabled by mistake or misidentification. Making a false statement in a DMCA notice is also punishable as perjury.

Terms of Use and Copyright Policy

It is a good idea to publish Terms of Use and a Copyright Policy on a website. These should incorporate the described DMCA notice-and-take-down provisions, describe the service provider's policy of terminating the accounts or subscriptions of repeat infringers, and provide contact information for a designated copyright notifications agent. They should also advise users of their rights and responsibilities, describe the service provider's rights and responsibilities, and describe the rights and responsibilities of copyright owners under the DMCA.

The Copyright Policy may be included in the Terms of Use. The Terms of Use is also where an indemnification requirement could be set out as a condition of a person's use of the service.

Finally, it would not be a bad idea to include a clause in the Terms of Use requiring users to post only their own thoughts and words in comments, and to refrain from violating other people's rights when posting comments.

Indemnification Agreement

In addition to designating a DMCA copyright notifications agent and complying with other DMCA requirements, an online service provider may want to consider requiring users and content contributors to agree to indemnify the service provider for any damages, attorney fees and litigation costs incurred in the event the service provider is sued for infringement on account of the user's infringing use of the service.

LINKS AND OTHER INFORMATION LOCATION TOOLS

17 U.S.C. § 512(d) provides qualified immunity from contributory liability for online service providers that provide information location tools (such as online directories, search engines, or hypertext links) to refer, direct or connect users to infringing content on other websites. In addition to satisfying the general eligibility requirements for all of the safe harbor provisions, a website owner must meet also meet two additional eligibility requirements:

(a) no knowledge of infringing activity
(b) either (i) no right or ability to control the infringing activity, or (ii) no direct financial benefit from the infringing activity.

The service provider must promptly remove the content or the link upon learning of the infringing activity.

Courts may have different views about inline linking and framing, but the general rule is that merely providing a hypertext link to another website is not direct infringement of copyrighted material appearing on that website. No copy of the material is made when a link is displayed. Linking to infringing material could potentially result in contributory infringement liability, however. Section 512(d) shields a website owner or service provider from contributory liability for providing links to sites where infringing activity is occurring, but only if:

(a) The provider neither knows nor should know that the material is infringing;
(b) The provider either: (i) has neither the right nor the ability to control the infringing activity, or (ii) receives no direct financial benefit from it;
(c) Upon receiving a proper notification of claimed infringement, the provider promptly takes down or blocks access to the material.

The requirements for Section 512(d) immunity are similar to those for Section 512(c) immunity. A website owner who receives a notice requesting removal of a link to infringing content should handle it in much the same way as a Section 512(c) notice of infringement.

CACHING

Caching is the temporary storage of recently accessed Web content. It generally enhances Internet use by enabling quicker loading of pages. The DMCA protects online service providers from liability for creating cached copies of web pages with copyright protected content.

ROUTING AND TRANSMISSION

The DMCA provides a safe harbor from copyright infringement liability for service providers that operate as nothing more than passive conduits for other people's communications. America Online's service enabling users to create newsgroups for the exchange of files is an example.[322] To qualify, the service must be truly passive. Because most commercial website owners maintain some level of supervisory control over user-provided content, and only a few provide unmoderated, interactive user forums, this safe harbor does not often apply.

Circumvention of Copyright Protection Measures

Because the Internet drastically increased the risk of infringement, copyright owners have come to rely on technological measures to protect copyrighted material and to manage digital rights. The anti-circumvention provisions of Title I are intended to promote and protect the efficacy of these measures. They broadly prohibit the circumvention of technological measures that have been taken to prevent access to, or copying of, a copyrighted work. The DMCA also prohibits making, importing selling or transferring devices or services that are marketed or primarily used to circumvent copyright protection measures. Software designed to crack an encryption mechanism in order to gain access to copyrighted material would be an example of such a device. Knowingly linking to a site that traffics in copyright circumvention devices or services is also prohibited.

Exceptions exist for:

- Law enforcement and government activities
- Nonprofit libraries, archives and schools,
- Reverse engineering by a lawful owner of a copy
- Encryption research
- Protection of minors
- When necessary to protect a persons' privacy
- Security testing.

The exception for nonprofit library, archives and schools applies only if the circumvention is done for the sole purpose of determining whether they wish to obtain authorized access or not.

COPYRIGHT MANAGEMENT INFORMATION

Copyright management information is information about the work, the author, the copyright owner, and if applicable, the performer, writer or director; the terms and conditions for use of the work; and any other information the Register of Copyrights may prescribe.

Tampering with or removing copyright management information is prohibited, as is distributing copies of products that have been tampered with or that have had such information improperly removed from them. Both civil remedies and criminal penalties are available to enforce this provision.

Vessel Hull Designs

Designs do not receive copyright protection. The DMCA, however, provides copyright-like protections for vessel hull designs. A "vessel" is any boat or other vehicle that is designed and capable of steering a course on or through water through its own means of propulsion, and that is capableof carrying and transportaing passenger(s). The hull is the frame or body of the vessel. Protection for vessel hull designs lasts for ten years and is available only for original designs that are embodied in an actual vessel hull. No protection exists for designs that exist only in drawings or models.

Additional Provisions

Title III allows the lawful owner of a copy of a program to make reproductions or adaptations during the maintenance or repair of a computer he owns or leases, or when necessary to use the program in conjunction with a computer that is owned or leased by him. The exemption only permits a copy that is made automatically when a computer is activated.

The remaining provisions of the DMCA address a variety of subjects, such as statutory exemptions, which are discussed elsewhere in this book.

Other Countries

Although the DMCA only protects online service providers in the United States, the European Community Directive on Electronic Commerce provides similar protections for online service providers situated in a EU country. It generally shields them from liability for damages for the storage or reproduction of unlawful materials if the provider is not aware of them. It also shields a provider from liability if he promptly removes or disables access to unlawful materials promptly upon becoming aware of them. Providers have no obligation to monitor users for unlawful activity.

Several other countries around the world have enacted laws shielding online service providers from liability for copyright infringement unless the provider is aware of infringing content and fails to remove or disable access to it. A number of countries have laws establishing notice-and-take-down procedures similar to those of the DMCA. The particulars of these procedures are not identical, however. In Japan and Chile, for example, more things need to happen before an obligation to remove claimed infringing material is triggered.

Chapter 27. Protecting Copyrights

Website owners and online merchants need to be concerned not only about possible liability for infringing the copyright in other people's works, but also about protecting their own works from infringement. Copyright registration and displaying a copyright notice are the principal ways of doing this. Because of the frequency of online copyright infringement—millions of instances per day, by some estimates—copyright owners increasingly are using technology to aid in the prevention of infringement.

Registration

Registration of a copyright is not required but doing so has significant benefits:

- **Evidence of copyright**. A registration certificate provides evidence of the existence of a copyright. This is important both in enforcing a claim and defending against a claim of infringement.
- **Prerequisite to enforcement**. Registration is a prerequisite to filing an infringement claim in court.
- **Presumptions**. The issuance of a registration certificate creates a presumption that the copyright is valid and that the facts stated in the registration are true (ownership, authorship, date).
- **Deterrence of infringement.**
- **Constructive notice.** Registration provides constructive notice of the existence of the copyright, which defeats claims of innocent infringement.
- **Damages**. If a work is timely registered, then statutory damages for infringement may be recovered even if actual damages cannot be proven.
- **Attorney fees**.
- **Seizure of infringing imports**. Registration empowers the U.S. Customs Service to seize infringing copies at the border.

Statutory damages, attorney fees and costs may be awarded if the work was registered either before the infringement occurred or within three months after first publication.

The presumptions of the validity of a copyright and of the facts stated in the registration arise only if the work is registered either (a) before publication, or (b) within five years after publication.

Waiting more than five years after publication to register a copyright does not result in the loss of copyright protection, but it can result in loss of the presumptions. The presumptions are rebuttable. If a copyright is registered, though, then the person challenging it bears the burden of proving that it is invalid, or that someone other than the person named in the registration owns the copyright, or that the copyright came into existence at a time different from what is stated in the registration.

Registration is normally a prerequisite to filing an infringement claim in federal court. If registration has been attempted but the Copyright Office has refused it for some reason, an infringement lawsuit may still be commenced but the claimant must serve notice of the suit on the Copyright Office in addition to serving the other parties to the proceeding. Registration of a foreign work is not required in order to file an infringement claim, but failure to register a foreign work may limit eligibility for statutory damages and attorney fees. Subject to these two qualifications, however, a work must be registered in order to proceed with a copyright infringement claim in court.

There is some case law to the effect that failure to register before filing an infringement suit is "not jurisdictional." This does not mean that registration is not required. It just means that in lieu of dismissing the lawsuit and forever barring any such claim in the future, a court may instead dismiss the lawsuit "without prejudice." This gives a claimant a second chance to file the lawsuit after taking care of getting the work registered. Another filing fee will have to be paid for the second lawsuit, however. Federal court filing fees are substantially higher than copyright registration fees, so it would rarely make sense to file an infringement claim without first registering the copyright. Also, if the statute of limitations runs out between the time the first lawsuit was filed and the time the second one is filed, then the infringement claim will be time-barred. Accordingly, even though registration is not jurisdictional, it still makes a great deal of sense to register the copyright before attempting to enforce it in court.

ELIGIBILITY

The Copyright Act distinguishes between United States and foreign works. Any work that is protected by copyright under U.S. law may be registered in the United States, whether it is classified as a United States work or as a foreign work. (For the kinds of works that receive copyright protection under U.S. law, see Chapter 23.) Unlike a copyright in a United States work, though, the copyright in a foreign work does not need to be registered in the United States in order to file a copyright infringement lawsuit in federal court. U.S. law will be applied in the lawsuit, however. Accordingly, a foreign work must be registered in a timely manner if the claimant wishes to seek an award of statutory damages, attorney fees or costs..

A work is a United States work if any of the following conditions applies:

(a) It is an unpublished work and all the authors are citizens, nationals, domiciliaries, or habitual residents of the United States;

(b) It is an unpublished audiovisual work, and all the authors are legal entities with headquarters in the United States;

(c) It is first published in the United States;

(d) It is first published simultaneously in the United States and a county that is a party to a copyright treaty to which the United States is a party and whose law grants a term of copyright protection that is at least as long as the term provided in the United States;

(e) It is first published simultaneously in the United States and a foreign nation that is not a party to any copyright treaty to which the United States is a party;

(f) It is first published in a foreign nation that is not a party to any copyright treaty to which the United States is a party, and published in the United States within thirty days thereafter and before it is published in a country that is a party to a copyright treaty to which the United States is a party;

(g) It is first published in a foreign nation that is not a party to any copyright treaty to which the United States is a party, and all of the authors of the work are citizens, nationals, domiciliaries, or habitual residents of the United States;

(h) It is an audiovisual work that is first published in a foreign nation that is not a party to any copyright treaty to which the United States is a party, and all of the authors are legal entities with headquarters in the United States;

(i) It is a pictorial, graphic, or sculptural work incorporated in a building or structure that is located in the United States.

All other works are foreign works.

Treaties

Most foreign countries have an applicable treaty with the United States, so most foreign works may be registered in the United States. U.S. law, however, will apply only to works either created or first published (depending on the applicable basis of eligibility) on or after the relevant foreign country entered into the applicable treaty with the United States.

The principal treaties pertinent to U.S. copyright law are:

(a) Buenos Aires Convention, 1910, effective in the United States on July 13, 1914

(b) Universal Copyright Convention, 1952, effective in the United States on September 16, 1955 (the Paris revisions became effective in the United States on July 10, 1974)

(c) Convention for the Protection of Producers of Phonograms Against Unauthorized Duplication of Their Phonograms, 1971, effective in the United States on March 10, 1974

(d) Berne Convention for the Protection of Literary and Artistic Works, 1886, effective in the United States on March 1, 1989

(e) World Intellectual Property Organization (WIPO) Copyright Treaty, 1996, a special agreement under the Berne Convention making changes and adding specific language protecting computer programs and compilations of data or other material, effective in the United States on March 6, 2002

(f) WIPO Performances and Phonograms Treaty, 1996, effective in the United States on May 20, 2002 (covering certain rights for performers and producers of sound recordings)

(g) Agreement on Trade-Related Aspects of Intellectual Property Rights (TRIPS), entered into as part of the WTO, established pursuant to the Marrakesh Agreement of April 15, 1994, which implemented the Uruguay Round Agreements (The effective date of U.S. membership in the WTO is January 1, 1995.)

Unpublished Works

The copyright in any unpublished work may be registered in the United States.

Published Works

Any United States work that is protected by copyright may be registered in the United States. A foreign work may be registered in the United States in any of the following situations:

(a) At least one of the authors is a citizen, national, or domiciliary of the United States at the time of first publication;
(b) At least one of the authors is a citizen, national, domiciliary or sovereign authority of a country that is a party to a copyright treaty to which the United States is a party at the time of first publication;
(c) At least one of the authors is a stateless person at the time of first publication;
(d) It is first published in the United States;
(e) It is first published in a country that is a party to a copyright treaty to which the United States is a party;
(f) It is first published in a country that is not a party to any copyright treaty to which the United States is a party; the publication occurred after September 27, 1998; and the work is thereafter published within thirty days in the United States or in a country that is a party to a copyright treaty to which the United States is a party.

In cases where eligibility depends on nationality and an author is a national of more than one country, the work is eligible if any of the author's nationalities satisfies eligibility requirements. If the work has joint authors, then the work is eligible if any author's nationality satisfies eligibility requirements. In the case of a compilation or derivative work, the relevant nationality is that of the author of the compilation or derivative work, not the authors of individual contributions.

A business entity that has a juridical existence, such as a corporation, is deemed to be a citizen of the state or country in which it is organized. Merely doing business in a country does not make a business entity a national or a domiciliary of that country.

A work that consists of a pictorial, graphic, or sculptural work that is incorporated in a building or structure may be registered in the United States only if the building or structure is located in the United States or in a country that is a party to a copyright treaty to which the United States is a party.

In addition to the categories described above, a work may be protectable and eligible for registration in the United States if the President issues a proclamation: (1) finding that a particular foreign nation extends copyright protection to works by citizens, nationals or domiciliaries of the United States or works that are first published in the United States on substantially the same basis as that on which the foreign nation extends protection to works of its own nationals and domiciliaries and works first published in that nation and (2) extending copyright protection to works of which one or more of the authors is, on the date of first publication, a national, domiciliary, or sovereign authority of that foreign nation, or which was first published in that nation. The President may revise, suspend, or revoke any such proclamation or impose any conditions or limitations on protection under a proclamation.

A work that is first published by the UN, a UN agency, or the Organization of American States, is eligible for protection under the Copyright Act.

THE COPYRIGHT DEFINITION OF PUBLICATION

The meaning of *publication* in copyright law is important for several reasons. The date of publication of a work affects the availability of statutory damages, attorney fees, and the legal presumptions to which registration gives rise. Copyright duration, public domain status, and applicable law can also depend on it. In some cases, it can have a bearing on whether a work is protected by copyright and/or whether it may be registered.

The definition is also of critical importance in the registration process. Unpublished works by the same author may be registered together for one filing fee, using a single application, even if they were created at different times. Published works cannot be registered together if they were published on different dates. And although a copyright in a compilation that includes both published and unpublished works may be registered, the copyright registration will only extend to the editing (selection and arrangement) and to the previously unpublished works in the compilation. It will not serve as a registration of the previously published works within the compilation. The copyrights in published and unpublished works must be registered separately.

Most people think a website is "published" when it goes online. This would be consistent with the defamation and privacy law definitions. The word has a much narrower meaning in copyright law, though.

> Publication is the distribution of copies or phonorecords of a work to the public by sale or other transfer of ownership, or by rental, lease, or lending. The offering to distribute copies or phonorecords to a group of persons for purposes of further distribution, public performance, or public display, constitutes publication. A public performance or display of a work does not of itself constitute publication.[323]

The Act specifically excludes public displays and performances from the meaning of publication. A public performance or display includes, among other things, transmitting or communicating a performance or display of a work to the public "by means of any device or process, whether the members of the public capable of receiving the performance or display receive it in the same place or in separate places and at the same time or at different times."[324] A website that does nothing more than transmit a display or performance of a work (or collections of works) by means of a computer that is connected to other computers electronically, therefore, would appear to be "unpublished" insofar as copyright law is concerned, even after it has gone online.

On the Other Hand . . .

The Copyright Act definition was drafted at a time when most publishing was in print. Sound recordings and audiovisual works were distributed by copying the material onto a record or tape and then distributing physical copies of them. Since radio and television transmissions did not involve making and distributing physical copies, they were called "broadcasts" rather than "publications." By making and distributing physical copies of a recording, a record company could be said to be involved in publishing music. When radio stations received the copies and played them for others to hear, they were engaged in broadcasting, not publishing. The line between the two activities was very clear. The Internet blurred that line. Transmitting electrical signals that cause works to be displayed on a screen would seem to be a display or performance of the work to the public. On the other hand, transmitting code that causes a work to automatically be copied onto a computer when the user executes a particular command arguably is just a new way of distributing copies. Back to the original hand, it is really only the end user's computer that makes the copy, so the end user is really the only one who is making a copy. The transmission, therefore, would not appear to qualify as a distribution of copies, after all. This conundrum has led to some inconsistent results in the courts.

In *NBC Subsidiary (KCNC-TV), Inc. v. Broadcast Information Services*[325] a Colorado court, holding that an Internet transmission is not a publication, adopted the reasoning that a transmission of electrical signals does not involve the making of copies. This is consistent with the legislative history of the 1976 Act. According to House Report 94–1476, "any form of dissemination in which a material object does not change hands ... is not a publication no matter how many people are exposed to the work."[326]

In *Getaped.com, Inc. v. Cangemi,*[327] however, a federal district court in New York held that an Internet transmission of website content is a distribution of the content, and therefore a publication of it. The court reasoned that the ability of any recipient of a transmission to save and copy it makes such transmissions the functional equivalent of a distribution of a physical copy to the recipient. Courts in other jurisdictions have also concluded that posting content to an Internet website is a publication of it for copyright purposes.[328] A few years after *Getaped,* a different New York court ruled that posting content to an Internet website is not publication.[329]

Then, in *Rogers v. Better Business Bureau of Metropolitan Houston, Inc.*[330] a federal district court in Texas ruled that the classification depends on whether end users are authorized to make copies of the content, such as by downloading a copy to a computer or other device. If they are, then the transmission is a publication of the content; if they are not, then it is not.

Copyright Office Guidance

The U.S. Copyright Office has adopted the *Rogers* court' view. According to the Copyright Office, the key is whether the copyright owner authorizes the end user to retain copies of the work or not. The Copyright Office will treat the posting of content to an Internet website as a publication of it if the content is made available to the public in one of the following ways:

(a) with an express authorization to copy
(b) with an implied authorization to copy
(c) as an offer of distribution to intermediaries
(d) as an actual distribution of copies to members of the public.

Express authorization to copy may be literal or may be conveyed by words or symbols that are reasonably interpreted as an express authorization to copy. Making digital files available for purchase on a website, or providing a 'Download Now' or similar button alongside downloadable content are examples.

Implied authorization to copy occurs when a visitor to a website would reasonably believe that permission to distribute content found on the website exists. 'Share' and 'Email' buttons positioned adjacent to displayed content are examples.

Merely displaying content on a website with knowledge that end users have the capability of copying, downloading, and distributing it will not suffice to establish implied authorization.

Authorization to display a work on one's one computer does not imply authorization to copy or distribute it to others.

An offer of distribution to intermediariess means an offer to distribute content to a group of persons for further distribution, public performance or public display. This qualifies as a publication if copies of the work are actually in existence at the time the offer is made. An offer of a motion picture to several movie theaters for showing by them is an example.

Actual distribution of copies of the work to the public is a form of publication, but a mere advertisement or offer that is made directly to consumers is not a publication of the work unless it includes an express or implied authorization to copy.

According to the Copyright Office, then, the following activities are not acts of publication:

(a) streaming
(b) displaying without authorization to copy or distribute to others
(c) displaying with an express or implied prohibition against copying or distribution
(d) using infringing content.

No copyright protection exists for material that infringes a copyright, and no use to which a website owner puts a work without the copyright owner's permission will change its status as either published or unpublished.

The statement, "all rights reserved" might give rise to an implied prohibition against making and distributing copies, as could the copyright owner's employment of technological measures that disable or impair a web browser's print, copy, and/or save capabilities.

Sometime a prohibition may be inferred from its omission from a list of permissions. A copyright owner's express grant of rights to display or perform a work, for example, could imply a denial of permission to make and distribute copies. This is not always the case, though. Courts look at all the facts and circumstances to determine a copyright owner's intent.

The Copyright Office generally will accept an applicant's own determination of whether the work is published or unpublished, unless there are obvious inconsistencies in the application and/or specimen copies provided. The Copyright Office's determination to accept an applicant's classification of a work is not legally binding on a court.

Because of the uncertainty surrounding the classification of website content as published or not, it is a good idea to register the copyright in website content before enabling public access to it. If the content has not been published elsewhere, doing it this way will ensure that the content is classified as "unpublished" at the time of registration, thereby removing doubts about entitlement to statutory damages and so on. Of course, if the material has already been published, then it will be necessary to register it as a published work.

THE APPLICATION FOR REGISTRATION

Claims Not to Make

Most websites contain a mix of elements, only some of which may be registered. To ensure that a registration will cover what it is intended to cover, and that it does not purport to claim copyright in unregistrable content, it is important to identify and state precisely the creative, expressive work(s) in which copyright is claimed. For example, a website is simply the location where copyrightable subject matter is fixed. Therefore, an application for registration should not include a claim of copyright in "the website." Domain names are not registrable, either. Only the creative content uploaded to a website is registrable. It must be specifically identified.

Including a claim for "website layout" also is not recommended. The overall look and feel of a website, the way it is laid out, is not protected by copyright. On the other hand, the selection or arrangement of copyrightable elements on a webpage may be protected by copyright if it is sufficiently creative. The layout (i.e., the size, shape and organization of spaces) of a webpage is not registrable in and of itself, however, regardless of how many elements are used in it. For example, a claim based on the border width for a webpage and demarcated placeholders for blocks of unspecified text or images would not be registrable. By contrast, a claim based on the arrangement of particular text and images may be eligible for registration, but the claim would extend only to the selection and/or arrangement of those particular items. It would not extend to the arrangement of a different set of images and text in the same or a similar way.

Published and unpublished works cannot be registered together. If a copyright for unpublished website content is sought, then previously published works should be expressly excluded. Works that have already been registered or for which an application has already been filed should also be excluded from the claim.

Ownership

The application should correctly identify the owner of the copyright in each element of website content the applicant is seeking to register. Copyright ownership of user-generated content normally remains with the user unless the user has effectively assigned ownership to someone else. Digitally signing an online transfer agreement may meet the "signed writing" requirement for a valid transfer of ownership. Accordingly, if a website's Terms of Use state that the website owner becomes the owner of all the exclusive rights in any works that are lawfully uploaded to the site, and a user indicates acceptance of the Terms of Use, then this may be deemed sufficient as a "signed writing," so that ownership of the copyright in any content the user uploads is effectively transferred to the website owner.[331] A claimant must have a record of the names of the authors who transferred ownership of all the exclusive rights to the claimant in this manner. A transfer from an anonymous or pseudonymous author will not be deemed a valid transfer of ownership for this purpose.

Transferring ownership does not transfer authorship. A website owner may claim ownership of user-generated content that is transferred pursuant to a "click-through" or Terms of Use agreement, but must identify the author of each contribution for which registration is sought.

A licensee should not be listed as the copyright owner unless the licensee has an exclusive license with respect to reproduction and all other rights. A nonexclusive licensee is not a copyright owner. An exclusive licensee of some but not all rights isn't, either.

Perceptible vs. Separately Accessed Elements

There are different ways of registering website content. If it is registered as a collective work, then only those elements of the site that are "perceptible" without downloading or purchasing access to them may be included in the registration. Also, any content that is located on a different website or server cannot be included in the registration. For example, if a website contains music files that users may download and listen to on their computers or devices, those files cannot be included in a collective work registration. They must be registered separately. Similarly, a collective work registration for a website that displays an abstract of a work but requires payment for access to the full article may only include the abstract in the collective work registration. The full article must be registered separately.

Mail vs. Electronic Filing

Copyright registrations may be applied for online or by submitting an application by regular mail, courier or hand delivery. When an application is filed online, deposit copies often may be uploaded online with the application, but may need to be sent by mail, courier or hand delivery in some cases. Electronic registration is cheaper and quicker, but it is not available for all kinds of works.

Effective Date of Registration

An application is not deemed filed until the Copyright Office has received all of the following: (a) a properly completed application; (b) the correct filing fee; and (c) an appropriate deposit. The effective date of registration is the first date by which all three elements have been received by the Copyright Office.

Privacy

All of the information provided in an application is a public record, and it normally cannot be removed after a registration is issued. Some information is not required for registration, and it may be omitted. An applicant may wish to omit a birth date, for example. The entire Rights and Permissions section is optional, too.

Registering Unpublished Website Content

Unpublished content may be registered in one of three ways:

(a) unpublished collection (or a group of unpublished photographs)
(b) collective work
(c) single unpublished work.

UNPUBLISHED COLLECTION

Registering website content as an unpublished collection is advantageous because an unlimited number of works may be registered at the same time using a single application and paying a single fee. This option is available, though, only if all of the following conditions are met:

(a) Each work is unpublished;
(b) At least one author is common to every work;
(c) The claimant of copyright ownership is the same for each work;
(d) The works are assembled in orderly fashion under one title;
(e) The application states that registration of a number of works as an unpublished collection is sought.

The applicant should also expressly state that no claim of authorship is being made in the selection, coordination, or arrangement of works within the website. This will help ensure that the intent is to register the works as an unpublished collection rather than as an unpublished collective work. A special rule applies to photograph collections. See infra.

COLLECTIVE WORK

A *collective work* is a compilation of works. The works may be by the same or different authors and may include unpublished works, published works, or both. The copyright in a collective work, however, only extends to the editing (i.e., the selection, coordination and/or arrangement of the works included in the compilation), and to those previously unpublished, unregistered contributions to the work as to which the compiler is the author or the copyright owner. The copyright in a collective work does not extend to any contribution by a person other than the compiler unless that person has transferred ownership of the copyright to the owner of the copyright in the collective work. Any contributions to a collective work that do not fall into at least one of these categories (such as a previously published or previously registered contribution, or a contribution by a different author who has retained ownership of the copyright in the contributed work) are not covered by a registration of the collective work. An application to register a copyright in a collective work that contains some of these kinds of works may still be filed, but the applicant must indicate in the application that they are excluded from the claim of copyright in the collective work.

If a contributor to a collective work assigns his copyright to the publisher, and the publisher then registers a copyright in the collective work naming itself as the claimant, the publisher's registration will cover the contributor's contribution. The contributor may nevertheless register his contribution to the work, too, if he wishes. The same is true of joint authors. If one of two or more joint authors registers the work naming only himself as the claimant, any joint author(s) may file their own registration(s) of the work, listing themselves as claimants. The requirement that the material must not be previously published still applies, however.

To register website content as a collective work, the applicant must expressly state a claim in the selection, coordination or arrangement of the website content. There may be authorship in the way in which the copyrightable text or digital files are selected or arranged on a particular webpage, or the way in which the pages of the overall website are selected or arranged, such as the manner or hierarchy in which the pages are connected or linked to each other.

To be included in a collective work registration of website content, the content must be perceptible to the user without having to download or purchase access to that specific content. Also, content that is located on a different server or on a different website cannot be included in a collective work registration of a website's content.

Registering as a collective work rather than as an unpublished collection can have an adverse impact on the amount of statutory damages that may be recovered. Although any number of works may be included in a collective work, only one award of statutory damages may be made against a defendant for infringement of the collective work or any work covered by the registration for it. This means that the owner of the copyright in a collective work may have only one recovery of statutory damages against an infringer who has infringed more than one contribution within the collective work. This is not the case with an unpublished collection. A court may make separate awards of statutory damages for each work within an unpublished collection that is infringed.

SINGLE WORK

Website content is often classified as either a collection or a collective work because it contains two or more separate and independent works. Usually, the person who creates the website puts some thought into selecting, coordinating, and arranging them. Registration of website content as a single work may be appropriate, however, if the site displays only one work, or if the applicant is seeking registration for only one of the works on the site.

A single work may combine different kinds of expression. A song may contain music and lyrics; an illustrated story or a photojournal contains text and one or more works of visual art; and so on. This is true even if the authors of the different elements are not the same, provided the elements are created with the intention of producing a unitary whole. If both authors have that intent, then they are joint authors of a single work, even though the work may include elements of different categories of works.

Whether website content is a collective work or a single work depends on the intention of the author(s) and the extent to which the elements can stand on their own as independent works. An element of a website that was created with the intention of being a stand-alone work generally may be considered a single work. If added to a website that has other content, the website as a whole might be considered a collective work. A website with several articles or pieces of artwork by different authors, each of which is capable of standing on its own without the others is probably a collective work. If the same or different authors created content with the intention that the website content be a single unitary whole, then it is a single work. If the website content is a single work, then each contributor of content is a coauthor and a joint owner of the copyright in the entire website, at least initially. If the arrangement is a work made for hire, then the employer or the person commissioning the work is the author.

Registering Published Content

The ways to register published works are:

(a) single published work
(b) contribution to a published work
(c) collective work
(d) group registration.

The Copyright Office also offers an option of registering a "unit of publication," such as a sound recording on a CD and the artwork on the CD case. This option is only available for works that are physically bundled together, however.

Group registration is available only for serial publications and photographs. Some people mistakenly believe that if new content is added to a website on a regular basis, it may be registered as a serial. This is not true. For purposes of copyright law, *serial* means only those works that are issued, or intended to be issued, in successive parts bearing numerical or chronological designations and intended to be continued indefinitely. Unless a website is periodically issued in successive, consecutively numbered volumes or editions, it is not a serial.

Registering Website Updates

A registration only covers works that are in existence at the time the application is filed. It does not cover any works that may be created in the future. To get the benefit of registration for subsequently added material, or for altered versions of existing website content, another application for registration must be filed.

How to claim copyright in newly created or added content depends on how the website content was originally registered. If the website content was registered as a collective work, and individual works have been deleted or added, then a derivative work of the collective work has been created. A new work that is added to the site may be registered individually or the whole website content, as updated, may be registered as a derivative work. Since only one registration can be issued per work, an application must clearly identify the original work as well as the new content for which registration is desired. In addition, the application must expressly exclude the preexisting copyrighted work from the claim of copyright in the derivative work.

If website content was previously registered as a single work, then any additions, deletions, and/or modifications to it will make it a derivative work. If, on the other hand, all previously registered content is removed and replaced with completely new content, then the new content may be registered as a new individual work, not as a derivative work.

If a contribution to a website was previously registered separately from the website content as a whole, and significant changes to the contribution have since been made, then the modified version of the contribution should be registered as a derivative work of the contribution. If the contribution has been completely removed and replaced with a new work, the new work should be registered as an original, not a derivative work.

Generally, only one registration can be issued per work. There are three exceptions:

(a) If a work was previously registered as an unpublished work, the first published edition of the work may also be registered.

(b) An author may separately register a work naming the author as the copyright claimant, even if another registration naming a different individual or legal entity as the copyright claimant for that work has already been issued;

(c) Another registration may be issued for a work if the subsequent applicant alleges that the earlier registration is unauthorized and legally invalid. This is called *adverse claim registration.*

Unless it falls into one of these categories, registration of a derivative work only extends to the newly created elements. If the deposit copy that is submitted contains previously published or registered elements, the applicant should identify and disclaim them in the application for registration of the derivative work.

NEW PUBLISHED CONTENT

The Copyright Act says that "where a work is prepared over a period of time, the portion of [the work] that has been fixed at any particular time constitutes the work as of that time" and "where the work has been prepared in different versions, each version constitutes a separate work."[332] This means that each time more than a de minimis change is made to website content, a new derivative work is created. The fact that a registration of a derivative work does not cover previously published works can present a problem for websites that are updated frequently. The rule means that multiple published works may be registered together only if they were published on the same date. So, for example, a blogger may have to register each blog post separately, since they each have different publication dates.

If the only change to a work is the deletion of some of the content of the original work, then it generally is not necessary to register the work as so altered. The only exception would be if the work in question was registered as a collective work, and registration of a claim in the selection, arrangement and coordination of the revised collective work is desired.

NEW UNPUBLISHED CONTENT

If several changes have been made to an unpublished work over time, there is generally no need to register each version of that work. In most cases, only the most recent or the most complete version need be registered. Registration of an unpublished website that has been updated, modified, or revised from time to time will cover all of the copyrightable material that is submitted for registration, including any unpublished text, photographs, or other content that has been incorporated from prior iterations of the same website. Earlier versions of an unpublished work may be included in the registration of a collection of unpublished works, if desired, provided copies of these versions, as well as the final version, are all included in the deposit. Of course, it should only be necessary to include an earlier version if there is something in the earlier version to protect that is not in the later version.

If the deposit copy contains copyrightable material that appeared in previous versions of the same work there is no need to exclude the preexisting material from the application unless it has been previously published or registered, is in the public domain or is owned by a third party.

To the extent the goal is to file multiple updates in a single application rather than filing a separate application each time a derivative work is created or a new work is added to a website, then posting content in such a way that it is displayed or performed for website visitors as "unpublished" works rather than as a "published" works would be a good strategy.

Computer Programs

A computer program is a literary work. Executable code, nonexecuting text, and comments or data that appear in the source code for a computer program may all be registered. To register a claim in the executable code, use the phrase *computer program* to describe that element. For a claim in the nonexecuting text, use the term *text*.

A computer program and the screen displays it generates generally are considered the same work, so the copyright in them generally may be registered together. If an applicant expressly asserts a claim in a "computer program," the registration will cover the copyrightable expression in the program code and any copyrightable screen displays that may be generated by that code, even if the applicant does not specifically mention the screen displays, and even if the deposit copy does not contain any screen displays. By contrast, if a claim is expressly asserted in "screen displays," the registration will not cover the computer program unless a claim in the "computer program" is also expressly asserted and the deposit includes both the screen displays and the computer program.

Upon publication as a bundled unit, a computer program and its documentation may be registered together on the same application. An unpublished computer program and the documentation for it, however, are separate works and must be registered separately.

Databases

A database is a digital compilation of data (which may be images, sound recordings, text, numbers, etc.) that is arranged in a systematic manner, and is accessible solely by means of an integrated information retrieval program or system that uses a query function to access content. A database is classified according to the kind of material comprising the data.

Registration of an unpublished database covers all copyrightable content in it as of the date the application is received by the Copyright Office, which may include the selection, arrangement and coordination of data files, and/or creation of (or ownership of copyright in) data file(s) that are included in the database. It does not cover any previously published or previously registered material.

Interviews

An interview may be registered as a literary work if it has been fixed in a written transcript, an audio recording, a video recording, or other medium of expression. It may be registered as a work of the performing arts if it was performed or is intended to be performed before an audience, such as a television interview, radio interview, or an onstage interview. Unless it is claimed as a joint work or a work made for hire, or the application includes a transfer statement, it is presumed that the interviewer is the author and owns the copyright in the questions he asks, and the interviewee is the author and owns the copyright in the responses she provides. Accordingly, unless one of these conditions is met, the application should not name only one person as the author, and a claim should not be made in "the entire text" of the interview.

Games

A registration for a game covers all of the copyrightable elements, regardless of whether it is registered as a literary work or as a work of the visual arts.

A videogame is an audiovisual work. It is not, however, a motion picture, even if it portrays motion on the screen. The computer program that makes it run is also a work that may be protected by copyright. If the claimant is the same, copyright in both the computer program and the audiovisual content may be registered at the same time in the same application. It must be made very clear in the application, however, that a claim of copyright is being made in both the audiovisual material and the computer program. A copy of the source code should be included along with the deposit material for the audiovisual content. The computer program for a videogame may be registered separately, if desired.

Sound Recordings

Except when registering a claim in an audiovisual work the SR form (or Sound Recording category) must be used if any of the works for which registration is sought is a sound recording. For example, a person seeking to register both a musical work and the sound recording of a performance of it must use the SR form or select the Sound Recording category.

The same application may be used to register the sound recording and the work performed on it only if the claimant is the same for both works. If the owner of the copyright in the sound recording is different from the owner of the copyright in the musical or literary work, then separate applications need to be filed.

Form SR (Sound Recording category) should not be used unless the applicant is seeking to register a claim to the copyright in the sound recording. If registering a claim in a musical work but not in the sound recording of it, then use the PA form (Performing Art category), even if the deposit copy consists of a sound recording of a performance of the musical work.

Since the Copyright Act excludes the sounds accompanying an audiovisual work from the definition of a sound recording, the SR form (or Sound Recording category) cannot be used to register a claim in the soundtrack of an audiovisual work unless the sound recording was created independently of the audiovisual work and not specifically for the audiovisual work. The PA form (or Performing Art category) must be used to register a claim of copyright in the soundtrack of an audiovisual work if it was created for the audiovisual work.

A special set of rules exists for pre-1972 sound recordings.[333]

Foreign Works

The registration process for foreign works is basically the same as for domestic works. Restored foreign works, however, can only be registered using a paper application submitted on Form GATT. To qualify for a GATT registration, a restored work must have been first published in a foreign country that is now eligible for protection and must not have been published in the United States within thirty days after first publication in that country

Photographs

A group of photographs may be registered together using Form VA. Beginning in 2018, this may be done online without obtaining prior approval from the Registrar. The following conditions apply: (1) All of the works in the group must be photographs. (2) All of the works in the group must be either published or unpublished. Unpublished photographs cannot be registered in the same group with published photographs, and vice versa. (3) No more than 750 photographs may be registered together as a group. (4) All of the photographs must be created by the same author. (5) The copyright claimant(s) for all the photographs must be the same person or entity.

Single Serial Issue

A serial is a work issued or intended to be issued in successive parts bearing numerical or chronological designations and intended to be continued indefinitely. Magazines are examples.

Collections of Unpublished Works

If registering a collection of unpublished works without any claim in the selection, coordination or arrangement of them, it is necessary to inform the Copyright Office that is what you are doing. Provide this information in a cover letter along with the completed paper form. If registering a collection of unpublished works online, this must be stated in the Note to Copyright Office section.

Other Kinds of Works

In all other cases, select the form or category that represents the predominant type of authorship for which registration is sought should be used. When determining what kind of content predominates, do not consider any elements for which registration is not sought. The question is not what kind of material predominates on a website, but what kind of material predominates among the works for which registration is sought.

DEPOSITS

The Copyright Act establishes two deposit requirements: registration and mandatory. The registration deposit requirement necessitates a deposit of copies of works for which copyright registration is sought. The mandatory deposit requirement requires the owner of a copyright or of the exclusive right of publication in a work that is published in the United States to deposit copies with the Copyright Office not later than three months after the date of publication. Fortunately, federal regulations coordinate these in such a way that compliance with the registration deposit requirement will often also satisfy the mandatory deposit requirement.

Mandatory Deposit

The mandatory deposit is the mechanism by which the Library of Congress ensures that copies of all works published in the United States are archived. The requirement applies to all works that are published in the United States, whether copyright registration for them is sought or not. To satisfy the requirement, copies are sent to the Copyright Office. The Copyright Office takes care of the transmittal to the Library of Congress.

The mandatory deposit is not a condition of copyright protection. Failure to comply may result in criminal penalties, however. If the mandatory deposit requirement is not made voluntarily, the Register of Copyrights may make a demand for the provision of copies. If the required deposit is not made within three months after receiving a demand from the Copyright Office, the owner may be subject to a fine of up to $250 per work plus the retail price of a copy of the work. For willful or repeated failure to comply, a fine of $2,500 may be imposed.

The mandatory deposit is only applicable to works that have been published in the United States in either hard copy format or as electronic serials. In addition, regulations exempt certain kinds of works from the requirement simply because the Library of Congress has no interest in archiving them. By either statute or regulation, the mandatory deposit does not apply to any of the following:

(a) unpublished works
(b) works that have only been published in a foreign country, not in the United States
(c) works that have been published exclusively online (except for certain electronic serials, as explained below)
(d) tests and answer material published separately from other works
(e) individually published speeches, sermons, lectures and addresses
(f) works originally published as part of a collective work. The collective work itself may be subject to mandatory deposit, though.

(g) literary, dramatic, and musical works published only in a medium on which a sound recording is fixed (e.g., a music CD). This exception does not apply to audiovisual works. Also, the sound recording itself may be subject to mandatory deposit requirements.
(h) motion picture soundtracks. The motion picture may be subject to mandatory deposit, however.
(i) motion pictures published solely through a license or grant to a nonprofit institution to make a fixation of that program directly from a transmission to the public.
(j) scientific or technical diagrams, models, plans, or designs.
(k) advertising materials, including catalogs.
(l) sculptural works.
(m) jewelry.
(n) dolls, toys, and games.
(o) plaques.
(p) floor coverings, wallpaper and similar commercial wall coverings, textiles and fabrics.
(q) packaging materials.
(r) useful articles.

If the Copyright Acquisitions Division notifies a publisher in writing that a particular title has not been selected for the Library of Congress's collections, that title is exempt from the mandatory deposit requirement. When registering a title that has been exempted from mandatory deposit, the publisher may submit one complete copy in any available format. When submitting an online application, the publisher should cite any notification received in the "Note to the Copyright Office" field and upload a copy of it.

Electronic serials are not subject to the mandatory deposit requirement unless the Copyright Office makes a demand for one. Unpublished works generally are not subject to mandatory deposit, except that the Copyright Office may demand a copy of an audio or audiovisual transmission program (e.g., a webcast series) even if it is unpublished.

In most cases, a copyright owner may satisfy the mandatory deposit requirement by submitting an application to register a work, provided that the owner submits two complete copies of the best edition of the work at that time. This means that when using the online registration system to register a work that has been published in physical form, it will be necessary to mail the required number of physical copies for deposit. Uploading a digital file will not satisfy the requirement of depositing a copy of the "best edition" of the published work if it has been published in physical copies. For more information about the criteria for determining what the best edition of a work is, see Copyright Office Circular 7B. In some cases, only one copy, or identifying material in lieu of an actual copy, may be submitted.

In some circumstances, relief from the mandatory deposit requirement may be requested, such as where compliance would involve undue burden or cost. Requests for special relief must be in writing and signed by the owner of the copyright or the owner of the exclusive right of publication. The Copyright Office may terminate a grant of special relief at any time.

Registration Deposit

Registration deposits are required for the registration of a copyright in any work, whether published or not. A work that is not subject to the mandatory deposit requirement may nevertheless be subject to the registration deposit requirement. They are for the use of the Copyright Office in processing an application for registration of a copyright. The Copyright Office examines them to determine copyrightable authorship, to verify the authorship claimed in the application, and to verify the facts stated in the application. Failing to make a registration deposit will not affect the validity of the copyright, but it will prevent registration. The Copyright Office will not assign a registration date until a proper registration deposit is made.

In some cases, registration and mandatory deposit requirements are the same. When a registration deposit meets the requirements for the mandatory deposit (usually, two complete copies of the best edition), only the registration deposit is necessary. When the requirements are different, separate submissions of copies or identifying material may be needed to register the work and to satisfy the mandatory deposit requirements. For published computer programs, for example, registration may be accomplished with identifying material containing only a selection of the source code for the work, but a mandatory deposit requires two complete copies of the best edition of the published program. In no event may a deposit copy be password-protected or contain any built-in limitations on the period of use.

EXCLUSIVELY ONLINE WORKS

For works that are transmitted exclusively online—i.e., works that are not also distributed in hard copy format—the preferred method of depositing copies is by applying online and uploading them in digital format at that time. The Copyright Office has detailed guidelines regarding acceptable file formats, source code submissions, redaction of trade secrets, and other matters. These are available online and should be followed closely. A less preferred but acceptable method of making a registration deposit for a work that is exclusively available online is by applying online and then submitting files in digital format (e.g., .pdf files on a CD-ROM) by mail, by courier, or by hand delivery. When submitting an online application and delivering the deposit by mail, courier or hand delivery, be sure to attach a shipping slip to the deposit. This enables the Copyright Office to connect the deposit with the application. The online application has an automated process for creating a printable shipping slip.

SPECIAL RELIEF

The Copyright Office may grant special relief from the registration deposit requirements in certain circumstances. The kinds of special relief that may be granted include allowing a deposit of one of the following:

(a) one copy, when two copies are normally required
(b) identifying material, when a copy is normally required
(c) incomplete copies, when complete copies are normally required
(d) a copy that is not the best edition of the work
(e) actual copy of the work, when identifying material is normally required
(f) identifying material that does not comply with copyright regulations.

The Copyright Office may terminate a grant of special relief at any time. This does not affect the validity of any deposit or registration previously made under the grant of special relief.

SPECIAL HANDLING

Special handling is a procedure for expediting the examination and processing of an application. The Copyright Office offers this service for copyright owners and other interested parties who have a compelling reason for the expedited issuance of a certificate of registration (e.g., as a prerequisite for bringing a copyright infringement suit in federal court). A request for special handling may be made at any time before the Copyright Office issues a certificate of registration. If an application is currently pending, the applicant may ask the Office to process the claim on an expedited basis, provided that the applicant pays the special handling fee and provided that there is a compelling reason for the request. For more information about how to request special handling, see the *Compendium of U.S. Copyright Practices*.

FEES

As of April, 2018, the fee for an electronic application generally is $35. The fee for a paper filing generally is $85. There are some exceptions. Check the website for current fees. Filing fees are nonrefundable.

OFFICE ACTIONS

The Copyright Office may contact an applicant if there is a problem with the application, fee, or deposit. The deadline for responding to an email from a registration specialist is twenty calendar days. The deadline for responding to a written communication from the Copyright Office is forty-five calendar days from the date set forth in the reply sheet that is enclosed with the letter.

If an application is filed electronically with a deposit mailed separately, the Copyright Office will notify the applicant electronically if it does not receive the deposit copy(ies) within ninety calendar days. The deadline for submitting the deposit copy(ies) is forty-five calendar days from the date the notification was sent.

It usually takes at least four months after an application is submitted for the Copyright Office to issue a certificate of registration. Certificates are issued on e-filed applications much sooner than on paper filings. A paper application can sometimes take over a year to process.

APPEALS

A denial of registration is appealable. The first appeal, called a *first request for reconsideration*, is an administrative appeal within the Copyright Office. It is commenced by filing a written request for reconsideration along with a statement of the reason(s) the applicant believes the denial of registration was improper. It must be received by the Copyright Office within three months of the date set forth in the refusal. As of January 1, 2018, the filing fee for a first request for reconsideration is $250 per claim. A staff attorney usually responds within four months.

If the first request is denied, a second request for reconsideration may be filed. As of January 1, 2018, the filing fee for a second request for reconsideration is $500 per claim. The second request will be reviewed by the Copyright Review Board. The Board's written decision is a final agency action. Administrative remedies are deemed to have been exhausted once this decision is issued. This means that judicial review may be sought, if desired.

Judicial review is obtained by filing an action against the Register of Copyrights in federal district court. Courts usually apply an "abuse of discretion" standard when reviewing determinations of the Register of Copyrights. They give considerable deference to Register of Copyrights determinations about the registrability of a work.

It is not necessary to appeal a refusal to register in order to institute a copyright infringement action in federal district court. If registration has been refused, though, then a copy of the infringement complaint must be served on the Register as well as the alleged infringer. The Register then has the option of becoming a party to the action with respect to the issue of registrability.

CANCELLATION OF REGISTRATION

The Copyright Office may cancel a registration for any of the following reasons:

(a) The claimed work is not copyrightable subject matter;
(b) The work fails to satisfy requirements for registration;
(c) The application, filing fee, and/or deposit copy(ies) do not satisfy legal requirements, and the Office is unable to correct the defect;
(d) A check for the filing fee was returned for insufficient funds;
(e) The work was registered in the wrong class.

The claimant named in the registration may voluntarily request cancellation of the registration if grounds for cancellation exist.

Once cancelled, a registration cannot be reinstated. If she wishes, the registrant may begin the process anew by filing a new application, filing fee and deposit copies. If a new registration is issued after a cancellation, the effective date will be the date when all elements of the new application are received, not the original effective date.

In some circumstances, a successful litigant in an infringement action may obtain a court order requiring cancellation of a copyright registration. To enhance the enforceability of such an order, it may be a good idea to request that it be worded in such a way as to require a person to effect a "voluntary cancellation" of the registration, rather than simply stating that "the registration shall be cancelled." This way, the court's contempt power may be invoked to enforce the order.

ADVERSE CLAIMS

An application may be filed despite the fact that someone else has already registered a claim in it. A claim registered under these circumstances is called an *adverse claim registration*.

An adverse claim of copyright can arise in two different ways: (a) the Copyright Office receives more than one application from different people to register the exact same work, and the applications contain conflicting statements regarding the authorship and/or ownership of the work, or (b) a person submits an application asserting that another party's claim to copyright is unauthorized or invalid. The Copyright Office does not conduct opposition or adversarial proceedings. Disputes over copyright ownership must be resolved either privately or in court.

A person intending to assert an adverse claim should provide a brief statement in the Note to Copyright Office field or in a cover letter indicating that the exact same work has been registered by another party.

Copyright Notice

Displaying a copyright notice is the most significant copyright protection measure, next to registration. It is no longer mandatory. Doing it has several benefits, however. On a practical level, it helps deter infringement. People may be less likely to infringe when they are aware that someone is claiming a copyright in the work. It can also help establish a defense against future claims of an implied license or dedication of the work to the public domain. It is not conclusive for these purposes, but it can help. Most importantly, it gives people notice that a work is protected by copyright, which can be used to rebut a claim of innocent infringement. The amount of statutory damages that may be recovered against an innocent infringer can be as little as $200. If the infringement is willful – done with knowledge or reason to know the material is protected by copyright – then statutory damages may be as high as $150,000. Including a copyright notice on each page of a website can prevent an infringer from claiming he had neither knowledge nor any reason to know the material was protected by copyright.

The proper format for a copyright notice is:

© [Year of publication] [Copyright owner's name].

"Copyright" or "Copyr." may be used instead of the symbol. The ℗ symbol is used for sound recordings.

The year shown in the copyright notice is the year of publication. If the material on a web page hasn't been published before, the year it was posted to the web page should be used. If it is previously published material, the year that it was previously published should be used. For a website that consists of a compilation of both published and unpublished material, use the date of publication of the website as a whole; and include additional copyright notices for each individual item that was published previously. Whenever a website is updated, the copyright notice should be updated, too. If some of the original material is retained, the notice may indicate a span of years over which modifications to the content were made—e.g., © 2014–2017 John Smith.

"All Rights Reserved"

Displaying the words "All rights reserved" does not have a tremendous amount of legal effect. It can sometimes be useful as evidence of intent, such as where the scope of a license is at issue. It also might operate as a deterrent against infringement in some cases.

Terms of Use and Copyright Policy

Including appropriate Terms of Use and Copyright Policy pages in a website can be a good method of deterring infringement and aiding in the enforcement of copyright and other intellectual property rights. They are not binding, however, unless a user signals assent to them.

CLICKWRAP AGREEMENTS

Clickwrap agreements may be used to secure a user's assent to a website's Terms of Use and/or Copyright Policy before the user is permitted access to the site, or a portion of it.

A clickwrap agreement is neither necessary nor sufficient to establish a claim of infringement. Ownership of a valid copyright, the date of the copyright, and the infringing act are the salient facts in an infringement case. It can help deter infringing acts, though, and it can help defend against a claim of innocent infringement. It can also be useful for protecting forms of intellectual property other than copyright, such as proprietary information.

For more information about clickwrap agreements, see Chapter 9.

Infringement-Tracking Traps

One free way to track careless infringement of a literary work is to plant traps in it. For example, an author could purposely insert a particular spelling, grammatical or punctuation error in a work; or in the case of a database, one fake entry. If someone then proceeds to copy and paste the entire work, the fact that their work contains exactly the same error (or fake entry) can furnish strong circumstantial evidence of copying.

Of course, this method is not foolproof. An astute infringer may catch these errors and correct them. (Most computer users have access to spelling- and grammar-checking tools.) A fake entry in a database compilation may not be quite as easy to detect, however.

Watermarks

To prevent people from downloading and republishing photographs and artwork, owners of copyrights in those kinds of works sometimes superimpose watermarks on them. While not preventing copying altogether, this makes the copied version less useful or valuable. The hope is that an individual who is really interested in displaying the image will pay for an unaltered version of the image. Using watermarks can also make it easier to prove copying.

A digital watermark is digital content that is covertly embedded in a digital file. It can be useful for tracing infringers along the distribution chain and identifying copyright ownership. Because it is not normally visible or audible, potential infringers usually are not aware of its existence.

Technological Controls

Another category of technological measures focuses on preventing copying or certain kinds of access to the copyrighted material or other intellectual property. These measures are commonly known as digital rights management (DRM) measures. Encryption is an example. Password-protecting areas of a website, requiring the use of a product key to access content or install a program, and encoding a digital file in such a way that it cannot be copied or distributed are also examples of DRM.

Technological mechanisms come in various forms. Some work by disabling use of the Print-Screen function for a particular display of content, or by disabling the Print, Copy, Save, Send and/or Download functions for a particular document. Some allow copying but limit the number of copies or prints that can be made, or limit the number of times a user may visit a page or the number of times a user may access a document or the number of devices on which a computer program may be installed. Some regulate the length of time a user may access a site, or a page on a site. Still others simply disable the ability to download or share files. Copy-protection technology vendors abound. ArtistScope, http://artistscope.com/ is one, but there are many others.

Of course, no technological measure is foolproof. A user who cannot deploy the Copy and Save functions on his computer might still copy an image or text that is displayed on his computer screen by taking a photograph of the screen, for example. A person who is prevented from digitally downloading music that is streamed to his computer might still set up a tape recorder next to the computer's speakers and capture the sound that way. And being prevented from copying and pasting text does not prevent a person from simply typing the text into another document. Technological measures do not provide absolute protection against infringement. They can make it less convenient for people to digitally share copyrighted material, though.

SERIAL COPY MANAGEMENT SYSTEM

The Audio Home Recording Act[334] requires makers of digital audio recording devices to include a serial copy management system (SCMS) in their products. The SCMS must be constructed in such a way that copies may be made from originals but copies cannot be made from copies. The Act also requires the makers of such devices to pay 2% of funds received from sales of the devices to the Copyright Office, which distributes the fund to music copyright owners. For purposes of this Act, a computer is not considered a digital audio recording device.[335]

CIRCUMVENTION OF TECHNOLOGICAL MEASURES

Subject to only a few limited exceptions, the DMCA makes it a crime to circumvent a technological copyright protection measure. Trafficking (distributing, offering to distribute or facilitating the distribution of circumvention tools) is also prohibited. A copyright owner may file a civil action against a person who unlawfully circumvents a technological copyright protection measure. Remedies include:

(a) injunction
(b) impoundment of any device or product that was involved in the violation
(c) monetary damages, which may be either actual damages or statutory damages
(d) attorney fees and costs
(e) order for the destruction or remedial modification of any device or product that was involved in the violation.

A court may remit or reduce damages in cases involving innocent violations. Treble damages may be awarded against certain repeat violators.

The DMCA also makes it unlawful to alter or remove, or to knowingly provide false copyright management information with the intent to facilitate or conceal infringement. *Copyright management information* means information such as the author's name, copyright owner's name, and terms and conditions for use of a work. This kind of information typically is distributed with copies of a work, or it is displayed on a web page in close proximity to the work, or a link to it is provided. Violations of this provision also are punishable both civilly and criminally. For more information, see Chapter 26.

Google Alerts and Plagiarism Detectors

Google Alerts, www.google.com/alerts, provides a way to monitor the Internet for possible instances of infringement of website content. It allows a person to set up alerts that notify the person anytime a specified phrase or sentence is used on a website. The system does not differentiate between infringing and noninfringing uses. Nor does it evaluate content for fair use. It is simply a tool for identifying possible infringement.

Several websites offer a means of checking a website for similarity to others. Known as plagiarism detectors, these services typically work by searching the Internet for pages with content that is written in an identical or substantially similar way to another website. Copyscape, www.copyscape.com, is one of the most well-known, but there are others.

Guilds and Registries

A writer's guild, or an author's or musician's registry, may claim to give people a means of proving the date of creation of a work, but this kind of registration does not provide the advantages that registration with the Copyright Office does. For example, it does not give rise to presumptions of ownership or validity. Nor does it satisfy the requirement of registration as a precondition to filing an infringement action. To qualify for the benefits of copyright registration, legal presumptions, and eligibility for court enforcement, the copyright in a work must be registered with the Copyright Office.

"Poor Man's Copyright"

One idea that has been around for a long time is that registration is not necessary if a person simply mails a copy of the work to himself and keeps it sealed upon receipt. Known as a "poor man's copyright," some people claim the procedure provides all the benefits of registration without any of the cost. It would be wonderful if this was true, but it is not. It will still be necessary to register a copyright in order to enforce it in court. Worse, a person employing the "poor man's copyright" method may cheat himself of the opportunity to claim statutory damages and attorney fees because the copyright will not have been timely registered.

Moreover, the person who is the first in time to create a work does not necessarily have a superior claim. The decisive issue in copyright cases is whether somebody copied somebody else's work. If two people independently come up with the identical or a similar work, then they each have copyrights, and neither is guilty of infringing the other's work. By giving constructive notice to the world of the claimed copyright in a work, registration makes independent creation far more difficult to prove.

Other Measures

The examples mentioned in this chapter are merely representative. Many other kinds of technological measures for the protection of intellectual property rights exist. A complete elaboration of all such measures is beyond the scope of this book.

Chapter 28. Trademarks

Trademarks are used to distinguish one business's goods or services from those of others. They communicate information about a company and its products or services, enable consumers to identify the source of a product or service, and distinguish it from competing goods or services. Without one, a company's efforts—through advertising and the development of a good reputation—to foster brand loyalty would be futile. Their existence makes it more likely that consumers will be able to find a company's products and services on the Internet. A well protected trademark that has grown in value can be key to negotiating favorable franchising and licensing terms. For all of these reasons, businesses should take steps to ensure both that they are not infringing other people's trademarks and that they are adequately protecting their own.

Laws regulating trademarks serve two objectives: (a) promotion of fair competition; and (b) protection of consumers from deceptive marketing practices.

Kinds of Trademarks

A trademark can consist of nearly anything that is perceptible—words, phrases, typographical characters, symbols, logos, drawings, photographs, colors, shapes, sounds, motions, scents, textures, product design, packaging, architecture, interior design. If it can be used in commerce to identify the source of goods or services and to distinguish them from the goods or services of others, it could potentially be a trademark.

In the United States, the principal categories of protectable trademarks are:

- standard character ("word mark")
- design
- sound
- shape
- color
- scent
- texture
- motion.

A trademark for services is also known as a *service mark*. A trademark indicating membership in an organization is called a *collective membership mark*. A trademark indicating approval by an organization is called a *certification mark*. There is no special term for a trademark for goods. Such trademarks are simply called *trademarks*. Unless the context otherwise requires, references to trademarks include all of these kinds of trademarks, not just trademarks for goods.

Trademarks can be divided into two broad categories: (a) labels, and (b) trade dress (the packaging or design of the product or of the place where a service is provided).

STANDARD CHARACTERS

Commonly called "word marks," this category is broad enough to cover any letter(s) and/or word(s) in Latin characters; any number(s) in Roman or Arabic numerals; any common punctuation or diacritical marks; and any combination(s) of any of these. Although names and short phrases cannot be copyrighted, they may be used and registered as trademarks.

DESIGNS

A design trademark is a logo, drawing or some other visual graphic. It can incorporate text within it, but a claim in a design trademark is a claim only to the design, not to the standard characters within it. It is not uncommon for a company that uses text in its logo to claim trademark rights in both the text and the design. A trademark consisting of a drawing, photograph or other visual depiction may also qualify for copyright protection in some cases.

SOUNDS

Sounds and sound combinations can receive trademark protection if they are used to identify the source of goods or services. The sound must be nonfunctional, however. A buzzing sound, for example, cannot be used as a trademark for a brand of alarm clocks because buzzing sounds serve the function of waking people up. A combination of sounds that does not qualify for trademark protection might nevertheless qualify for copyright protection if it is original and creative. Conversely, a work may be protected by trademark law even though it is not protected by copyright. For example, a short musical or lyrical phrase, or the title of a song, might be a protected trademark even though it is not protected by copyright.

COLORS

Colors and color combinations can be trademarks. For example, the color brown, as used in connection with parcel delivery services, is a UPS trademark. They are not considered inherently distinctive however. Therefore, in order to claim trademark rights in a color or color combination, it is necessary to establish that it has acquired secondary meaning, i.e., that consumers have come to associate it with a particular business, product or service.

Colors and color combinations receive trademark protection only if they serve no other function than to identify the source of a particular product or service. If the color makes the product more desirable, or helps identify the flavor of a product, then it serves an aesthetic function, and therefore does not receive trademark protection. If the color improves the visibility of a product as to which visibility is an important characteristic (e.g., the blaze orange used in clothing for safety while hunting), then it is not a protectable trademark.

SCENTS, TEXTURES, FLAVORS

Textures, scents and flavors sometimes receive trademark protection. They are not protected, however, if they serve a useful function other than identifying the source of the product. For this reason, a flavor that makes a food or drug product more palatable, or an antiperspirant pleasant to smell, does not get trademark protection. Similarly, because the bumpy texture of a soft drink bottle gives the holder a better grip, it is not protected by trademark. A leather wrapping on a bottle, on the other hand, may be a protected trademark, inasmuch as it serves no useful function other than to identify the source of the product.

The United States Patent and Trademark Office (USPTO) has taken the position that flavors, scents and textures are not inherently distinctive, so proof of secondary meaning is necessary in order to claim trademark rights in them. Some courts, however, hold that a scent may be inherently distinctive if it is used in connection with completely unrelated goods. A citrus scent for biofuels is an example.

Naturally occurring flavors, scents and textures do not receive trademark protection.

In some cases, a flavor or scent that is not a protectable trademark may be generated by a recipe or formula that is protected as a trade secret.

MOTIONS

Motions may be protectable as trademarks. The Peabody Hotels' March of the Peabody Ducks is an example. The registration for this describes it as follows: "The motion elements include the red carpet being rolled out, the appearance of the ducks and uniformed Duckmaster at the elevator door, and the march of the ducks down the red carpet, up the steps, and into the fountain where they begin swimming. The mark also includes the fanfare in reverse sequence." (U. S. Reg. No. 2,710,415.) A hologram is a kind of motion mark. It may be protectable as a trademark if it can be proven that consumers have come to see it as an identifier of the source of goods or services.

Motions generally are considered sufficiently distinctive that proof of secondary meaning is not necessary.

TRADE DRESS

The shape, size, color(s), texture or design of a product or its packaging is called *trade dress*. Sales techniques and the architecture, lighting and/or decor of a place where a service is provided are also kinds of trade dress. If they serve as distinctive source identifiers, then they may be protected trademarks.

Trademark rights cannot be claimed in advantageous functional aspects of a product, service, packaging or presentation. Functional aspects of a website may be patentable in some cases, but they cannot serve as trademarks.

The "look and feel" of a website may qualify as trade dress. An e-commerce business may be exposed to liability for trademark infringement if it copies and uses elements of a competitor's website to create the same (or a confusingly similar) look and feel for its own website. Of course, as in every trademark infringement case, liability will depend on whether distinctiveness and likelihood of confusion can be established.

Sources of Trademark Law

Trademarks are governed by state, federal and international laws. The Lanham Act is the primary source of federal trademark law in the United States. At the state level, common law is the principal source, although many states have enacted statutes to supplement or modify the common law. When international transactions are involved, the trademark laws of countries other than the United States, as applicable, and international law (such as treaties) are also relevant.

Requirements for a Valid Trademark

The four essential requirements for a valid trademark in the United States are:

- Use in commerce
- Nonfunctionality
- Distinctiveness
- No likelihood of confusion.

USE IN COMMERCE

In some countries, trademark rights come into existence by registering the mark with the appropriate government office. In the United States, trademark rights arise through use. Registration can make it easier to enforce a trademark, but a valid trademark may exist and be enforced even if it is unregistered. In the United States, it is not possible to create trademark rights simply by registering a mark with a trademark office. It is necessary to actually use the mark in commerce.

American law distinguishes between a common law trademark and a registered trademark. A *common law trademark* is a trademark that arises through a person's use of it. A *registered trademark* is one that has been registered with a government agency, typically the USPTO. In the United States, all registered trademarks are also common law trademarks, but not all common law trademarks are registered.

Because use in commerce is required, merely having an idea for a brand name, logo, etc. is not enough to give rise to any protectable trademark rights, even if the idea is written down, drawn on paper, or recorded in some other way.

Domain name registration is not sufficient, by itself, to establish trademark rights. The use must be in connection with particular goods or services. Standing alone, a business name, logo, etc. is not a trademark. It can become a trademark only if and when it is used in association with particular goods or services. This might happen when it is affixed to goods or packaging, displayed with goods or services in some other way, or otherwise made known to purchasers in the ordinary course of business in a way that associates the mark with the goods, services or business of the user.

For the same reason, a slogan can be a trademark only if it is used in connection with commerce in goods or services. The fact that an individual has used a particular slogan or catch phrase so often that the public has come to associate it with that individual does not make it a trademark if it hasn't been used in connection with the marketing of particular goods or services.

In the case of a service mark, affixing a label is impractical. For a service mark, therefore, displaying a sign at the place where services are provided, or on letterhead or in advertising material, may suffice as "use in commerce," provided services are also actually rendered.

The use must also be "in commerce," that is to say, an actual sale or transportation of the goods or rendering of a service. Use of the mark in advertising may suffice only if the advertising is significant enough to instill an association between the mark and the product or service in the minds of a substantial number of members of the public. To qualify for federal registration, use of the mark in advertising generally will not suffice at all. On the other hand, use in catalogs, trade show exhibits and instruction manuals accompanying a product have been held to be sufficient to qualify as a use of the mark in commerce, even if presale advertising alone does not.

The use must be substantial, not trivial. It must also be continuous. Sporadic use is not enough. De minimis, inconsequential use (use that is so minimal that it is not likely to come to the attention of a competitor) does not qualify. Purely internal sales or transfers (such as sales limited to employees of the business that is selling the product) do not qualify, either. Shipments of labeled prototypes to a prospective manufacturer do not qualify, but shipments of labeled products to a laboratory for testing might.

The commercial transaction must be bona fide. A sale that is made solely for the purpose of preserving trademark rights is not bona fide. Token use, meaning a single sale bearing no relationship to a plan for commercially exploiting the mark, also does not qualify as bona fide. Multiple sales of the goods or services to consumers normally qualify as bona fide. Sales in a test market do, too.

The use must be visible to others. Retail sales to consumers will suffice for this purpose, as will manufacturer sales to retailers, and the shipment of goods to an independent laboratory for testing (provided the mark is affixed to the goods and clearly visible).

Finally, the use must have the purpose or effect of identifying the source of goods or services. It is not necessary that a mark have the effect of identifying the specific name of the person or business that owns the mark or that manufactures or sells the goods or performs the services. FRESCA, for example, is a valid trademark for soft drinks whether people realize it is owned and manufactured by the Coca-Cola Company or not.

Priority of Use

In the United States, the general rule is that the first to use a trademark in the United States is the one who acquires exclusive rights to use it in the United States.

The use must be in connection with the sale, lease or licensing of a product or service. Presale advertisements and new product announcements do not qualify.

Uses occurring prior to the establishment of a valid trademark are disregarded. This means that if a mark is not inherently distinctive, i.e., if it is merely descriptive, then the first use will not be deemed to occur until after the mark has acquired distinctiveness. A mark that must rely on secondary meaning in order to be distinctive does not come into existence as a trademark until the secondary meaning has become associated with it in consumers' minds.

The date of first use of a mark that is not inherently distinctive can be difficult to establish. Unlike a mark with inherent distinctiveness, it is not the date on which a claimant affixed a mark to goods and sold them, or the date on which person opened a store with the name displayed on it. Since name recognition usually builds up gradually over time, it may not really be possible to identify the precise moment at which a mark acquired distinctiveness. Sometimes the best that can be done is to identify a date by which it had become distinctive, not the actual date on which it did. In that case, the date by which it had become distinctive will be deemed to be the date of first use. This is one reason why selecting an inherently distinctive mark can be advantageous.

Under the Paris Convention, if a citizen of a member country files a trademark application in his own country, and then files an application in another member country within six months, then the priority of both marks is determined by the priority given the mark in connection with the first application.

NONFUNCTIONALITY

Trademark law protects fair competition, not the acquisition of monopoly power. An exclusive right to use a feature of a product that enhances its value is a kind of advantage that could result in the acquisition of monopoly power. For this reason, functional aspects of a product or service, that is to say, features that enhance a product's usefulness, are not given trademark protection.

There are two kinds of functionality: *de facto* and *de jure*. A feature of a product or its packaging is de facto functional when it performs an essential function of the product. It is de jure functional when it serves an advantageous purpose (other than brand distinctiveness) even though it may not be necessary for the essential functions of the product.

> **Example**. A restaurant owner installs a statuette of a clown at each table. The statuette is constructed in such a way that a patron may place an order by speaking to the clown without having to wait for a server to come to the table. Arguably, configuring a restaurant in such a way that customers are able to select food from a menu for consumption on the premises may be trade dress. It does not receive trademark protection, however, because this kind of arrangement serves the essential function of a restaurant. It is de facto functional. Placing an order-taking device on each table, on the other hand, is not essential to the functioning of a restaurant. Restaurant services may be provided without using these devices. Therefore, it is not de facto functional. An order-taking device at a table does give a restaurant an advantage over competing restaurants, though. As such, the feature is de jure functional. Accordingly, this feature does not receive trademark protection, either. The clown face, by contrast, serves no function other than as a brand identifier. Therefore, it could qualify as a trademark.

Although nonfunctionality is required of all kinds of trademarks, it is most likely to be an issue with respect to trade dress. Determining whether trade dress is functional or nonfunctional can be challenging. Color would seem, at first glance, to be a nonfunctional aspect of an outboard boat motor, for example. Certainly it has no de facto functionality in relation to the essential purposes of a boat motor. Nor does the cost of paint vary much by color. An outboard motor will power a boat as efficiently and at about the same cost whether it is painted green or black. In *Brunswick Corp. v. British Seagull Ltd.*,[336] however, a court held that the black color of an outboard boat motor has de jure functionality. Why? Because black is compatible with more boat color schemes than other colors are. Also, black makes motors look smaller. These things give black motors an aesthetic edge in consumer sales that is unrelated to brand loyalty. Trademark protection cannot be afforded to black outboard motors because preventing competitors from using black as the color of their motors would put them at a competitive disadvantage. Sometimes color may qualify as nonfunctional trade dress; sometimes not. Each case must be decided on its own facts.

A feature that is essential to or that improves performance, efficiency (including cost-efficiency), market value or aesthetic value is generally functional, and therefore not protectable as a trademark. In making this determination, a court will consider whether the feature is important to effective competition by others and not practically attainable by using alternative designs or methods.

Trade dress has aesthetic functionality only if each of the following conditions is satisfied:

(a) The product is a kind that is purchased primarily for aesthetic reasons;
(b) The product or package design has significant aesthetic appeal;
(c) There are not a lot of viable alternative designs that would have similar aesthetic appeal.

In some cases, the functional aspects of some products, services or packaging, or the methods of creating them, may be protected as patents or trade secrets.

DISTINCTIVENESS

To receive trademark protection, a mark must be distinctive. This means that it must stand out in such a way that consumers associate it with a particular source of the goods or services. A SHOES label on a box of shoes gives a consumer no idea who made them or where they are from. Such a label does not meet the distinctiveness requirement because it does not serve to associate goods or services with a particular source; it does not do anything to distinguish these shoes from shoes that are made and sold by other companies.

Distinctiveness may be inherent or acquired. An *inherently distinctive* mark is one that requires no further explanation to understand that it could only be used as an identifier of the source of particular goods or services. A very distinctive mark is called a *strong* mark. A mark that is not inherently distinctive but comes to be associated with a particular source through use of the mark is said to have to have *acquired distinctiveness*. A mark that is not inherently distinctive does not receive trademark protection unless it has acquired distinctiveness through use. This is done by showing that consumers associate the mark with a particular source, i.e., that the mark has acquired a *secondary meaning* as a source identifier of a particular product or service.

Not all packaging is inherently distinctive, but it can be. Product design, on the other hand, always requires proof of secondary meaning in order to meet the distinctiveness requirement.

Under the Lanham Act, continuous, exclusive use of a mark for five years is prima facie evidence of secondary meaning. Evidence may be introduced to establish a different period of time.

The Doctrine of Foreign Equivalents

The doctrine of foreign equivalents is the rule that the distinctiveness of foreign words and expressions is to be evaluated after the words have been translated into English.

Categories of Distinctiveness

Abercrombie & Fitch Co. v. Hunting World[337] identifies five categories of distinctiveness. From strongest to weakest, they are:

- Fanciful
- Arbitrary

- Suggestive
- Descriptive
- Generic.

A **fanciful** mark is one that has been invented, and therefore has no other meanings. KODAK, XEROX and MICROSOFT are examples. Fanciful marks are inherently strong. They automatically meet the distinctiveness requirement.

An **arbitrary** mark is one which has not been invented, and which does have at least one existing meaning already, but is used in connection with goods or services to which it bears no reasonable relation. APPLE computers and GORILLA glue are examples of arbitrary marks. Arbitrary marks are also considered inherently distinctive.

A **suggestive** mark is one that implies something about a product or service without directly describing it. It is like a descriptive mark, except that it "requires imagination, thought and perception to reach a conclusion as to the nature of the goods."[338] JAGUAR, as a trademark for automobiles, is an example of a suggestive mark. A jaguar is an animal with the ability to run fast. The word *jaguar,* however, is not simply a synonym for *fast*. Using this word in connection with an automobile, though, could lead a thinking person to infer that the car is fast. For this reason, it is classified as a suggestive mark rather than a descriptive one. Suggestive marks are inherently distinctive.

A **descriptive** mark is one that directly describes a quality or characteristic of the goods or services, such as their origin, properties, ingredients, likely users, or who is selling them. JIFFY LUBE is an example. Self-aggrandizing words, like THE BEST, also fall into the descriptive marks category. Descriptive marks do not get trademark protection unless they are shown to have acquired secondary meaning.

Minor alterations or misspellings of descriptive words will not suffice to transform them into fanciful or arbitrary marks.

A description need not be accurate in order to be classified as a descriptive mark. For example, "The most reliable car in the world" could be a descriptive trademark for Ford automobiles whether or not it is an accurate description of those vehicles. Note, however, that deceptive marks are not protected even if they have secondary meaning.

Descriptiveness is determined by evaluating the mark as a whole, not by examining each part of it individually. Thus, even though *sugar* and *spice,* considered individually, are words that can be descriptive of baked goods, the mark SUGAR & SPICE, taken as a whole, is not.

Product configuration, i.e., the design of the product itself (as distinguished from the packaging) is never considered inherently distinctive. It will always require proof of acquired secondary meaning. Product packaging, on the other hand, is capable of being inherently distinctive. In close or ambiguous cases, courts tend to classify trade dress as a product design rather than product packaging.

Generic marks are common, everyday words that are used to identify a kind of product or service. Because they are inherently incapable of identifying source, they do not receive any trademark protection at all. The best way to determine whether a term is generic or not is to ask whether its significance to the consumer is the product, not the producer. If consumers use the term as a synonym for the product category regardless of manufacturer identity, then it is generic. MILK, TOYS, LUMBER are examples of generic marks.

A mark that would otherwise be a protected trademark can become an unprotected generic term if enough people regularly use it as a generic term for the category of a product rather than as a particular brand of a product within the category. When this happens, trademark protection is said to have been lost through *genericide*. Some examples of marks that have lost trademark protection through genericide include: ASPIRIN, CELLOPHANE, DRY ICE, ESCALATOR, LAUNDROMAT, SHREDDED WHEAT, THERMOS, TRAMPOLINE, and VIDEOTAPE. This is one reason why it is important to police trademarks even after they have been registered, to ensure that people are using it as a brand name and not in a way that could lead to genericide.

A term may be generic for one category of goods or services but not another. For example, APPLE is generic for fruit, but not for computers.

Generic terms are most often nouns, but certain adjectives can also be generic. LIGHT, when used in connection with food or beverage products, is an example. Consumers perceive this as a generic term for any low-calorie food or drink. CUSTOM-BLENDED and TASTY, on the other hand, are considered descriptive, not generic.

Words describing a new product or service, or the characteristics of an existing product or service, may be classified as generic if competitors would have a need to use them to describe competing products or services.

Because of the doctrine of foreign equivalents, a foreign word for a generic term will be considered just as generic as the English word is. VINO, for example, is generic as a trademark for wine because it is simply the Italian word for wine.

LIKELIHOOD OF CONFUSION

A mark receives no protection under trademark law if it is confusingly similar to a mark that is already being used in connection with the same or related goods or services. It does not matter whether the existing mark has been registered or not. Marketing goods or services using a mark that is confusingly similar to a competitor's is both a form of unfair competition and trademark infringement.

The general rule is that likelihood of confusion exists if and only if both of the following conditions exist:

(a) The marks are identical or similar;
(b) Either (i) the goods or services are related in a way that consumers are likely to infer that they come from the same source, or (ii) one of the marks is a famous or well-known one.

Likelihood of confusion is decided on a case-by-case basis. Relevant factors include:

- Similarity in appearance, sound, meaning, and/or commercial impression
- Actual consumer confusion
- Length of concurrent use without actual confusion
- Extent of potential confusion
- Similarity of marketing channels
- Similarity of the goods or services
- Degree of care likely to be exercised by a purchaser of the goods or services
- Fame of the preexisting mark

- Number and nature of similar marks in use on similar goods
- Commercial relationship between the owners of the two marks
- Variety of goods on which a mark is used
- Extent to which the subsequent user of the mark can exclude others
- Any other relevant fact.

These are sometimes referred to as the *du Pont* factors, after the case in which they were enunciated, *In re E. I. du Pont de Nemours & Co.*[339] The Ninth Circuit Court of Appeals has enunciated a somewhat modified set of factors:

- Strength of the mark
- Use of the mark on the same, similar or related goods or services
- Similarity of the marks
- Actual confusion
- Intent (reason for choosing the mark)
- Similarity of marketing/advertising channels
- Purchaser's degree of care
- Product line expansion.

These are sometimes called the *Sleekcraft* factors, after the case in which they were enunciated, *AMF Inc. v. Sleekcraft Boats.*[340]

To these lists may be added:

- Consent agreement, if any
- Seriousness of harm to consumers that may result from confusion.
- Any other relevant factors.

Various kinds of evidence are used to prove likelihood of confusion. Consumer surveys are commonly used, but they are not the only kinds of evidence that may be relevant. Evidence of actual confusion, although not necessary to succeed on a trademark infringement claim, can help establish proof of likelihood of confusion. Conversely, evidence of long use of both marks without actual confusion can be used as evidence that confusion is unlikely.

Even if trade dress is not serving as a trademark, evidence of similarities in trade dress can be used to help establish a claim of likelihood of confusion. The nature and quality of the goods or services can also be relevant.

No proof of intent to infringe is necessary to prevail on a claim of trademark infringement. On the other hand, evidence of bad faith intent to infringe can help establish likelihood of confusion. Doing a trademark search and relying on an attorney's opinion can go a long way toward defending against a claim of bad faith intent. By the same token, disregarding the advice of counsel can be used as evidence of bad faith intent.

The confusion that is relevant to an infringement claim is confusion as to the source, endorsement or sponsorship of particular goods or services. It must be assessed with reference to the target audience. Goods and services for children must be assessed on the basis of whether children are likely to be confused, not whether adults are. If the goods or services are marketed to sophisticated adults, then the relevant question is whether sophisticated adults are likely to be confused, not whether children or unsophisticated adults are.

The confusion must be shown to be likely to affect a substantial number of people, not just a few. Unfortunately, there is no bright-line test for deciding what a "substantial" number is. Different courts determine it in different ways. All courts agree, however, that the proper focus is on the "reasonably prudent consumer," not idiosyncratic or unreasonable ones.

In USPTO proceedings, doubts about likelihood of confusion usually are resolved against the person who is applying for registration of a mark.

Similarity

Marks may be confusingly similar even if they are not identical. Nonidentical marks may be confusingly similar if they look or sound like each other, or have the same or similar meanings, or create similar overall commercial impressions. A mark is similar to another mark if, when used in connection with the same or related goods or services, a substantial number of consumers would mistakenly believe the goods or services are from the same source.

Proof of likelihood of confusion does not require proof that confusion is certain to occur, nor even proof that a particular person or group of persons has, in fact, actually become confused. On the other hand, a purely theoretical possibility of confusion will not suffice. Although there is no bright-line test for similarity, the USPTO has developed guidelines. Largely derived from common law, these help trademark examiners make decisions about whether two marks are so similar as to be likely to cause confusion when used in connection with the same or related goods. They are set out in the *Trademark Manual of Examining Procedure* (TMEP).

Sophistication of the Target Audience

The relevant question in trademark infringement cases is not how likely any random person is to be confused. Confusion is gauged in relation to the sophistication of the target audience. Likelihood of confusion is more likely to be found to exist when a product is marketed to young children, for example.

Distinctiveness

Confusion with a mark is likelier to occur when the mark is strong than when it is weak. The more distinctive a mark is, the more likely a consumer is to associate it with a particular company.

Unitary Consideration

When assessing likelihood of confusion, individual parts of a mark are not considered in isolation. Rather, courts assess the similarity of the entire mark, taken as a whole. For example, even though the word *mars* is wholly contained within the word *marsupial*, it is not very likely that consumers would mistake MARS brand products with MARSUPIAL brand products.

This does mean that individual parts cannot be evaluated separately. An examiner or a court may properly find that BUDWEISER PRIME is confusingly similar to BUDWEISER on the basis of the extreme similarity between the first word of the new mark and the preexisting mark, provided the effect of the addition of the word *prime* on the likelihood of confusion is considered before a final determination is made.

Dominant vs. Peripheral Parts

If the dominant portion of two marks is the same, then the marks may be confusingly similar despite peripheral differences, such as the addition or deletion of word(s) or character(s). For example, MARK LEESML and ML have been deemed confusingly similar, when used on the same or closely related goods or services.

Additions or deletions to marks may suffice to avoid likelihood of confusion if (a) the marks in their entireties convey different commercial impressions, or (b) the matter common to the marks is merely descriptive or diluted. For example, the Trademark Trials and Appeals Board (TTAB) initially found RITZ and THE RITZ KIDS to be confusingly similar, but the Federal Circuit Court of Appeals reversed, holding that they create different commercial impressions. DEER-B-GON and DEER AWAY are deemed sufficiently different because DEER is merely a descriptive term for the product that is being marketed (deer repellent); it has no source-indicating significance.

Third Party Use

The fact that a mark, or a portion of a mark, is used by others in connection with the same or related goods is relevant to show that it is weak and therefore entitled to little, if any, protection. This relates to distinctiveness, but distinctiveness is also relevant to the issue of likelihood of confusion.

Word Marks

Word marks are evaluated for similarity on the basis of appearance, sound, meaning, and commercial impression. Similarity in one of these respects does not automatically result in a finding of likelihood of confusion even if the goods or services are identical. It may be sufficient to support such a finding, but courts and examiners consider all factors, not just one of them in isolation.

Marks that look alike are usually likely to confuse if used with the same or similar goods or services. Homonyms are a good example. The argument that a word has more than one meaning is not extremely persuasive when the same word is used by a competitor as a mark for the same or a similar kind of product. PRUNE COMPUTING, as a mark for computer sales, is likely to be considered confusingly similar to PRUNE COMPUTING as a mark for computer peripherals even though the first claimant may have meant it to refer to a dried plum and the second claimant meant it to connote the act of removing leaves from a plant.

Conversely, marks that look alike are not likely to confuse if used on different goods or services. The more different the goods or services are, the less likely a second use of the same mark is to confuse consumers. A store selling computers under the name APPLE STORE is not likely to be confused with a market selling produce under the same name. Famous or well-known marks are sometimes an exception to this rule, though. (See below.)

TRANSPOSITIONS

Similarity of appearance is sometimes curable by simply changing the order of words, but only if it changes the overall commercial impression. THE WINE SOCIETY OF AMERICA and

AMERICAN WINE SOCIETY are likely to cause confusion. BEST JEWELRY and JEWELERS' BEST, on the other hand, is a transposition the TTAB has found to create different commercial impressions.

HOMOPHONES AND MISSPELLINGS

Homophones (words that sound alike) are usually confusingly similar even if they are spelled differently and have different meanings. The words do not have to sound exactly alike. CUP-A-COLA would probably create confusion with COCA-COLA.

A misspelled version of a word is usually confusingly similar to the correctly spelled version. For example, LITE and LIGHT are usually considered confusingly similar.

The USPTO takes the position that there is no correct pronunciation of a mark. Accordingly, the fact that a mark does not sound exactly like another one when it is pronounced correctly will not necessarily prevent a finding of likelihood of confusion, at least if the two possible pronunciations sound very similar. For example, XCEED was denied registration because it sounded too much like X-SEED, even though an argument could be made that they should be pronounced differently. Likewise, SEYCOS and SEIKO were found to be confusingly similar. Changing the spelling or wording of a mark will not necessarily prevent a finding of likelihood of confusion even if the change also alters the sound.

MEANINGS

Synonyms are often found to be confusingly similar. GAS CITY, for example, has been found to be confusingly similar to GAS TOWN. The average consumer is believed to retain only a general impression of a trademark.

For purposes of comparing meanings, the relevant meaning of a word is the one relating to the goods or services in connection with which the mark is used. PLAYERS, used in connection with shoes, connotes playing sports. The same word used in connection with men's underwear would have a different connotation. PLAYERS as a mark for shoes can coexist with PLAYERS as a mark for men's underwear without confusing consumers.

FOREIGN WORDS

The doctrine of foreign equivalents holds that a mark in a foreign language must be translated into English to assess its distinctiveness or its likelihood of confusion with another mark. When applied in the course of assessing likelihood of confusion, however, the doctrine is limited to only those words that an ordinary American purchaser would stop and translate. For this reason, it only applies to common languages; it does not apply to dead or obscure languages. To the extent Latin is a dead language, the doctrine does not apply to it. The doctrine does apply, however, to Latin terms that are still in use today.

The USPTO normally does not apply the doctrine when both marks are in foreign languages. The average American purchaser may be proficient in one foreign language, but is not likely to be proficient in two. The doctrine might be applied, though, if the words are similar, which often happens when the two languages are Spanish and Italian, for instance.

The USPTO also does not normally apply the doctrine if a foreign phrase has taken on a meaning for Americans that is different from its literal English translation. For example, according to English dictionaries, *cordon bleu* means a skilled chef. The literal translation from French to English, though, would be "blue ribbon." The USPTO would not find BLUE RIBBON similar to CORDON BLEU because in this case the foreign phrase has taken on a whole new meaning to Americans. They are not likely to stop and translate it into English.

It is also possible that Americans may be unlikely to stop and translate a foreign word due to marketplace circumstances or the commercial setting in which the mark is used. TIA MARIA and AUNT MARY mean the same thing, but if TIA MARIA is used in connection with a restaurant that serves Mexican food, then purchasers are not likely to stop and translate it into English. Non-Mexican food products marketed under an AUNT MARY label, therefore, would not be likely to cause confusion with TIA MARIA.

Similarity of marks is just one factor to be considered when determining whether two marks are confusingly similar. The fact that a foreign language mark means exactly the same thing as a preexisting mark when translated into English only shows that they are similar in meaning. All other factors (similarity of appearance, sound or commercial impression; relatedness of goods or services; etc.) must be considered in order to determine whether they are confusingly so.

DOCTRINE OF LEGAL EQUIVALENTS

Under the doctrine of legal equivalents, a word and a visual depiction of it may be considered to be similar in meaning. Thus, a silhouette of a lion's head has been held to be confusingly similar to the word LION. The overall commercial impression must still be considered, however. A visual depiction that is so highly stylized or abstract that it is not likely to cause an association with the word mark might not be deemed confusingly similar.

FAMILIES OF MARKS

When a mark owner employs a common root element in a family of marks, consumers may come to associate the root element with other goods or services on which the mark owner uses it, so that if a new brand name using the same root element appears on the market, the consumer is likely to assume it comes from the same source. The "Mc" in McDONALD'S is an example.

FONTS AND COLORS ("STYLIZED MARKS")

Generally, the more distinctive the other aspects of a design are, the less important color or font becomes; and the less distinctive the other aspects of a design are, the more important color or font becomes. This is why a depiction of a dog peering into a phonograph is likely to be confused with the RCA Victor logo regardless of the colors used, but a depiction of a blue cross is not likely to be confused with the Red Cross logo. A cross, by itself, is not distinctive. It's the red color that causes people to associate it with the Red Cross organization. A dog peering into a phonograph, in any color, is much more distinctive than a cross.

SURNAMES

Surnames are not trademarks unless they have acquired secondary meaning. A name that is also a word, however, is not considered a surname. It is capable of being inherently distinctive in appropriate circumstances. If, for example, Johnny Bench used BENCH as a trademark for catering services, a court could find that it is inherently distinctive. When the secondary meaning of a surname is an issue, the test is how it is perceived by prospective customers: Are they likely to associate the surname with the person or with the goods/services?

Famous historical surnames, such as Da Vinci, are not considered surnames for purposes of trademark law. They may be registered without proof of secondary meaning.

A surname combined with generic terms is treated as primarily a surname. A surname combined with a nongeneric term is not.

If a surname can be shown to have acquired secondary meaning, trademark remedies may be employed to enforce rights in it. This can impose an unfair burden on those individuals who happen to have been born with the same surname. For example, since JOHNSON'S NURSERY is already registered to a man in Wisconsin, theoretically no other person named Johnson may operate a nursery under his own name. In these kinds of cases, a court may issue a conditional injunction, allowing some limited use of the same name by others, subject to conditions designed to prevent confusion, such as requiring the competitor to display a disclaimer.

Non-trademark use of a personal name, such as the use of one's own name in a mailing address, is not infringement.

Design Marks

Consumers are assumed to retain only general memories of design marks. Accordingly, marks may be confusingly similar even though there are differences between them.

Composite Marks

Composite marks are marks that contain two or more kinds of elements, such as a design with characters. Trademark protection exists only for those elements of a composite mark that could qualify for trademark protection if they stood alone. For example, because the word *bread* in WONDER BREAD is a generic term, it receives no trademark protection when it stands alone. *Wonder* is not generic, so it could receive trademark protection.

For purposes of assessing likelihood of confusion, a mark must be considered in its entirety, with greater weight being given to the dominant feature. A word element is often considered dominant because people are most likely to use the wording contained in a mark to refer to the product or service. Nevertheless, there is no general rule about whether words or designs dominate in composite marks; nor is the dominance of a particular element necessarily dispositive of the issue of similarity.

Parody Marks

Parody marks generally are not likely to cause confusion because the effect of the parody, in most cases, is to create a distinction in the viewer's mind between the actual product or mark, and the joke. This is why LARDASHE is not confusingly similar to JORDACHE. On the other hand, there have been cases where the TTAB has found a parody mark to be likely to confuse. For example, CRACKBERRY was found to be confusingly similar to BLACKBERRY; and LESSBUCKS was found to be confusingly similar to STARBUCKS. The right to use words for the purpose of parody does not necessarily extend to the right to use them as trademarks.

Initial Interest Confusion

A website that attracts visitors by using another firm's trademark (or a very similar one) as its domain name is exploiting what is known as *initial interest confusion*. Some courts hold that initial interest confusion may be sufficient to establish likelihood of confusion even if the consumer is apprised of the true source of the goods upon arrival at the site and before a sale is consummated. To these courts, the use of the mark to lure visitors to the site is infringement even if the homepage of the website disclaims ownership or affiliation with the trademark appearing in its domain name. Not all courts agree.

Relatedness of the Goods or Services

In general, the more similar the goods or services are, the less similar the marks need to be to generate confusion; and the less similar the goods or services are, the more similar the marks have to be to generate confusion. The converse is also true: The more similar the marks are, the less similar the good or services have to be to establish likelihood of confusion; and the less similar the marks are, the more similar the goods will need to be to establish likelihood of confusion.

Using the same or a similar mark on a different but related kind of goods or services can also generate confusion in some cases. This can happen even when the related goods or services are not directly competing. For example, computer peripherals do not compete with computers in the market. People are no less likely to buy a peripheral just because they've already bought a computer, nor are they less likely to buy a computer just because they already have a peripheral. To the contrary, a person who already has a computer is probably more likely to buy a peripheral than she would be if she did not own one. Nevertheless, because the two kinds of goods are related, a consumer could mistakenly believe that both kinds of products emanate from the same source.

A mark that is the same as or similar to an existing trademark generally does not acquire protection as a trademark if the goods or services for which the mark is used are the same as, similar to, or related to the goods or services in connection with which the existing mark is being used. By the same token, an identical or similar mark is not disqualified from trademark protection on the basis of likelihood of confusion if it is used in connection with goods or services that are unrelated to the goods or services that are being marketing under the other trademark. (An exception exists for famous or well-known marks, as discussed infra.)

The reason trademark protection is extended not just to goods or services of the same kind but also to different but related goods and services is that consumers generally expect businesses to expand into related areas. Consequently, using the same mark on related goods can create consumer confusion about the source of the goods or services.

Relatedness is a murky concept. Ultimately, the test is whether average, reasonable consumers are likely to infer that two products or services come from the same source if they are marketed under an identical or similar name.

USPTO CLASSIFICATIONS

The international classification (IC) system the USPTO has created for the processing of trademark registration applications does not determine the relatedness of goods. The fact that two kinds of goods or services are in different IC classes does not necessarily mean they are unrelated, and the fact that two kinds of goods or services are in the same International Class does not necessarily mean they are related in the trademark sense. Umbrellas and whips are both in International Class 18, but a consumer who sees a whip for sale in an adult fantasy shop is not likely to assume it comes from the same company that makes and sells umbrellas.

INDICIA OF RELATEDNESS

Although there is no bright-line test for relatedness, a few general principles can be gleaned from the cases. Most important of these is that consumers are likely to assume a business is expanding its marketing or sponsorship into a new area if the goods are commonly used together, such as computers and peripherals; or pancake mix and syrup. This is not always the case, though. For example, it has been held that beer and the restaurants that serve it are not sufficiently related to cause consumers to mistakenly believe they originate from the same source.

Sometimes the fact that two kinds of goods are commonly sold in the same kind of store (e.g., video games and video game consoles) has helped persuade a court that the goods are related.

The fact that goods are made from the same kinds of materials and use the same technology (e.g., padlocks and flashlights) may be evidence of relatedness in some cases.

Being marketed through the same channels of trade and advertised through the same media can sometimes help establish relatedness.

Goods or services that are commonly the subject of a license, endorsement or sponsorship may sometimes lead to a finding of relatedness. For example, using the mark used by a fashion magazine on a line of clothing could suggest to consumers that the fashion magazine is related to the clothing in the sense that the magazine endorses, sponsors or licenses the use of its name to the clothing distributor.

Promotional goods are almost always considered related goods because consumers generally assume that trademark owners license their marks to promotional goods manufacturers. A consumer who sees the Disney logo imprinted on pens and ashtrays is likely to assume the Disney Company has licensed the use of its logo to the pencil and ashtray manufacturers.

PARODY GOODS

Parody goods generally are not considered related goods because consumers are not likely to assume they come from the same source as the original goods. People generally will not assume that a firm is inclined to make fun of itself, or to license someone else to do so. This is not always true, however.

Consent

A prior registrant's consent or waiver of objections to another person's registration of a confusingly similar mark is not binding on the USPTO. Trademark law does not just protect the proprietary interests of business owners. It is also intended to protect consumers from confusion as to source. The existence of a consent agreement is just one factor to be considered in determining likelihood of confusion. It is not controlling.

An agreement that details the particular reasons why the parties believe no likelihood of confusion exists and describes the arrangements the parties have made to avoid confusing the public (such as restricting each other's market), is given considerable weight. Sometimes, though, even a "naked" consent (one that simply sets out the prior registrant's consent to registration without detailing why there's little likelihood of confusion) will be given weight, so long as other factors do not compel a finding of likelihood of confusion.

Collateral Consequences of Confusion

Greater care must be taken to avoid confusion in the case of medical and pharmaceutical products and services because mistakes in the selection and use of these kinds of goods can result in serious and harmful consequences. As a result, a lesser degree of proof is needed to establish likelihood of confusion in these kinds of cases.

Case-by-Case Determination

The rules of thumb set out above are merely guidelines. There is no per se rule in the area of likelihood of confusion. The USPTO and courts consider all relevant facts.

Famous Marks

An exception to the relatedness requirement exists for famous and well-known marks. Using a famous or well-known mark, whether it is a registered or an unregistered one, may subject a person to liability if it is likely to cause confusion, and this is true whether the mark is used on identical, similar, related, or different goods or services. McDonald's, for example, was able to successfully oppose another firm's registration of McBABY for baby furniture even though furniture is not related to food. This is because the "Mc-" format is widely understood to signify products originating from the McDonald's Corporation. McDonald's Corporation has been quite successful in preventing other companies from marketing goods or services this way. In addition to McBABY, it has blocked McSWEET pickled vegetables, a McSLEEP motel chain, and McCLAIM legal services.

As a general rule, it may be said that the more famous a mark is, the less the degree of similarity that is needed to establish likelihood of confusion. In some cases, a famous mark may receive trademark protection even if no likelihood of confusion exists. (See the discussion of trademark dilution, infra.)

Duration of Trademark Rights

GENERAL RULE

A trademark exists as long as it continues to function as one. Federal registrations are for renewable ten-year terms. Failure to renew a registration results in loss of the benefits of registration, but not necessarily loss of common law trademark rights.

ABANDONMENT

If the owner stops using a mark as a trademark and has no intention of resuming use, the mark is deemed abandoned. Once a mark is abandoned, the exclusive right to use it terminates. A person may become the owner of an abandoned mark by being the first one to use it as a trademark after it is abandoned.

Three continuous years of nonuse gives rise to a presumption of abandonment. The presumption may be rebutted by proof of even minor use during that time, or proof of a plan to resume use.

It is important to distinguish between abandonment of a trademark and abandonment of a trademark registration. A person may abandon a registration in several ways, such as by failing to pursue registration to completion, or failing to timely file a renewal. These things may deprive the owner of the benefits of federal registration, but abandoning a registration does not have the effect of divesting a person or business of ownership of a common law trademark.

GENERICIDE

Another way a mark can cease to function as a trademark is by losing its distinctiveness. This can happen, for example, when a brand name becomes a generic word for a category of products rather than a source identifier.

Infringement

Trademark infringement occurs when a trademark (or something confusingly similar to it) is used in commerce in a way that is likely to cause consumers to be confused about the source, sponsorship or endorsement of particular goods or services. The three possible legal bases for a trademark infringement claim are:

- Section 32 of the Lanham Act[341]
- Section 43(a) of the Lanham Act[342]
- State common law.

A Section 32 claim may be filed only if the mark is federally registered. Section 43(a) and state law claims may be filed whether the mark is federally registered or not. State and federal courts have concurrent jurisdiction to hear Lanham Act claims, but a claim may be brought under the Lanham Act only if the mark is used in interstate or foreign commerce. A federally registered mark is presumptively used in interstate or foreign commerce.

SECTION 32

Section 32 of the Lanham Act is the specific federal prohibition against trademark infringement. To prevail under Section 32, a claimant must prove:

(a) a federally registered mark
(b) a copy, counterfeit or imitation of which
(c) is used in interstate or foreign commerce
(d) in connection with a sale, offer, distribution, or advertising
(e) without the trademark owner's consent
(f) in a way that is likely to cause confusion or deceive consumers.

Of course, to establish the first element, it is necessary to prove that a valid trademark exists, which means that the distinctiveness requirement must be satisfied. Federal registration gives rise to a presumption that the trademark is valid, though.

SECTION 43(a)

Section 43(a) of the Lanham Act prohibits unfair competition by means of false or misleading labeling, packaging or advertising. It is broad enough that it can be used as another avenue of recourse for trademark infringement claims when not all of the requirements for a Section 32 claim are satisfied. For example, it may be used to seek redress for the infringement of a trademark that is not federally registered. This does not mean that Section 43(a) is exclusively for common law trademark infringement claims. In many cases, a claim for infringement of a registered trademark may be brought under either Section 32 or Section 43(a), or both.

To prevail on a claim under Section 43(a), a claimant must prove:

(a) a word, name, symbol, device, trade dress, or combination thereof, or a false designation of origin, or a false or misleading statement of fact
(b) is used in interstate or foreign commerce
(c) in connection with goods or services, or containers for them
(d) in a way that either is likely to cause confusion or deceive as to the origin, sponsorship or endorsement of the goods or services, or likely to confuse or deceive as to a person's affiliation, connection or association with another person, or misrepresents the nature, qualities or geographic origin of goods or services, in advertising.

In cases where Section 43(a) standing is predicated on infringement of a competitor's trade dress, a further showing must be made that the trade dress is nonfunctional.

A Section 43(a) claim may be brought by any person who believes she is likely to be damaged by the false or misleading material. This could include a person who believes the material infringes her trademark because it involves the use of a word or device that is likely to cause confusion or deceive as to the origin, sponsorship or endorsement of goods or services. Unlike Section 32 and state claims, however, likelihood of confusion about the origin of the goods need not be proven if it can be shown that the mark was used in a way that misrepresents the nature or qualities of goods or services.

Infringement can occur in many ways. Explicitly marketing a product or service using a mark that is confusingly similar to another is one way, but implicitly associating another's mark with a different product or service can also result in liability. Positioning a photograph of the Rolex logo in close proximity to other kinds of watches that are offered for sale on a website is an example. Visitors to the site would be likely to mistakenly believe the watches being offered are Rolex watches. Similarly, a photograph of the Ford Motor Company logo on an auto repair service's website might cause visitors to the site to mistakenly believe the repair service is sponsored or endorsed by the Ford Company. Trademark infringement liability may arise in these kinds of scenarios because the "likelihood of confusion" standard is governed not by what a logician would infer, but by what an average consumer would infer.

STATE CLAIMS

A state infringement claim may be brought to enforce rights in a mark whether or not it is registered with the USPTO, and whether or not it is used in interstate or foreign commerce.

To prevail on a common law trademark infringement claim, the claimant must prove:

(a) ownership of a valid trademark
(b) another person's use of the same or a similar mark in commerce as a trademark; and
(c) likelihood of confusion as to origin, sponsorship, endorsement, association or affiliation.

ELEMENTS OF A CLAIM

Infringement is a strict liability tort. Neither intent nor bad faith need be proven in order to prevail on a claim of infringement. Both malicious and innocent infringement are unlawful.

Use in Commerce

If a claim is based on the Lanham Act, liability attaches only if the mark is used in interstate or foreign commerce. This is because the Commerce Clause of the Constitution does not authorize Congress to regulate purely intrastate commerce. The Commerce Clause has been interpreted very broadly, though. For example, a retail sale of goods to a resident of the same state may be considered "interstate commerce" if the buyer directs the retailer to ship to a location in another state. Shipping goods manufactured in one state to another state for sale in that state would also be interstate commerce. An intrastate sale may be considered "interstate commerce" if the customer is an interstate traveler (a resident of another state who is visiting the state where the sale takes place). Advertising in more than one state, or in media that has interstate distribution or is transmitted or broadcast into more than one state (such as an Internet website), or on a billboard near an interstate highway, generally will qualify as "use in interstate commerce." Even sending a product from one state to another for the purpose of registering a trademark for the product could be an example of a qualifying "interstate use."

Some early courts held that use of a competitor's trademark as a keyword in a website's meta tags could not result in liability under the Lanham Act. Being invisible to website users, the trademark cannot operate as a source designator. These courts therefore reasoned that such use was not an infringing use in commerce. Today, the majority view appears to be that such use does indeed constitute use in commerce.[343] Of course, to state a claim for infringement, likelihood of confusion must also be proven. That may be difficult to do in the case of keyword advertising, particularly if the website to which the keyed advertisement links displays a clear and conspicuous disclaimer of ownership, affiliation, sponsorship or endorsement by the trademark owner or of the trademarked goods or services.

Although it has been interpreted broadly, the interstate commerce requirement still exists in Lanham Act cases. If an infringing operation is truly an exclusively intrastate one, then only a state claim may be pursued.

USE IN SOCIAL MEDIA

Using another person's trademark as a user name in social media like Facebook or Twitter is trademark infringement if it is likely to create confusion about the origin or source of goods or implies sponsorship or endorsement from the trademark owner.

Most social media sites have intellectual property policies. Facebook, for example, allows users to register their marks and report alleged infringement. A social medium's definition of infringement may or may not be the same as the legal definition. Social media definitions and policies relating to fair use are not necessarily the same as the legal ones, either.

PALMING OFF

Palming off (or "passing off") occurs when a person infringes a trademark in bad faith, or with intent to deceive consumers about the source of goods or services, by means of using another person's trademark to market goods from a different source. Putting *Chips Ahoy!* brand cookies in Pepperidge Farm packages or sewing Gucci labels on clothing purchased from Goodwill as a way of increasing sales are examples.

A cause of action for palming off arises, at common law and under Section 43(a), when a seller misleads customers into believing that the goods he is selling are a competitor's when they really are not. A seller might be tempted to do this, for example, if his own wares are inferior or if the seller has not yet developed a strong reputation.

REVERSE PALMING OFF

Several states also recognize a cause of action for reverse palming off. This occurs when a company removes another company's trademark from a product before reselling it. Instead of luring customers into a sale by making them believe it was made by someone else, reverse palming off involves concealing the original source of a product.

COUNTERFEITING

Counterfeiting is specific kind of infringement in which an identical mark is used on same or similar goods from a different source by someone without trademark rights.

A counterfeiting claim brought pursuant to the Lanham Act requires proof that the mark is identical to a federally registered mark.

In addition to being actionable as infringement, counterfeiting is a crime.

CONTRIBUTORY INFRINGEMENT

In some cases, a person may be held liable for infringement even if she was not the one who actually performed the infringing act, if she facilitated or contributed in some way to the infringing act. Specifically, a person may be liable for contributory infringement if she does one of the following:

(a) intentionally induces another person to infringe a trademark
(b) continues to supply products to a person whom she knows or has reason to know is mislabeling them
(c) provides a service (such as a website) or some other mechanism over which she has control that enables the infringing activity, with knowledge or reason to know that the infringing activity is occurring there, and fails to stop the infringement from occurring (such as by disabling or suspending the infringer's account).

A lessor or swap meet manager who rents space to a vendor whom he knows is engaging in infringing activity on the premises, but does nothing to stop it, could incur contributory liability for infringement. In the same way, a web hosting service or website operator who knows or has reason to know of third party content infringing a trademark but fails to remove it may incur contributory liability for the infringement.

Knowledge is generally a necessary element of a contributory infringement claim. A person may be held liable for contributory infringement only if he knew or should have known that infringing activity was occurring. Generalized awareness of a theoretical possibility of infringing uses is not enough, however. Knowledge or reason to know of specific instances of actual infringement must be proven. On the other hand, courts do not countenance willful blindness, i.e., deliberately avoiding learning of actual instances of infringement. In short, to prevail on a contributory liability claim, the plaintiff must demonstrate either of two things about the defendant:

- Actual knowledge
- Willful blindness.

Willful blindness means a deliberate failure to investigate, despite having reason to suspect infringement.

Merely being aware that it is possible to use a particular instrumentality to infringe trademarks is not enough to establish knowledge or reason to know, if the instrumentality has substantial legitimate use(s).[344] Liability may attach, however, if in addition to providing the instrumentality or mechanism, the provider actively encourages, solicits or induces infringing uses, or has knowledge or reason to know of specific instances of actual infringement and deliberately fails to either investigate or take action to stop the infringing activity.

Only a person who has direct control over the content of a website may be held contributorily liable for it. *Direct control* means the ability and power to allow or remove content from a site. Website hosting services have been held to have direct control over the sites they host if they have the ability to disable accounts or prevent the transmission of trademark-infringing content in some other way.

Generally, the more involved a web host is with an infringer's web site, the greater the risk of being held liable as a contributory infringer, and the greater the duty to investigate becomes. While policing hosted sites for evidence of possible trademark infringement is not required, web hosts that are directly involved in the development of a site (e.g., by offering advice, or implementing search engine optimization for the site, etc.) should monitor these sites for any indication of possible trademark violations, and remove any hosted page or site that is infringing a trademark. And any web host, no matter how closely connected with a client's business he is, should remove allegedly infringing content immediately upon receiving a notice of infringement. Receiving a notice of infringement establishes actual knowledge of it.

A web host's contract with clients should require clients to obey all trademark laws. It would also be a good idea to include an indemnity clause, i.e., a provision requiring the client to pay any litigation costs and attorney fees incurred by the host in defending against a trademark infringement claim, including defending against contributory infringement claims. The contract should also set forth the client's representations and warranties that she either owns or has appropriate authority under a valid license for the trademarks that are used on the client's site, and that she has all necessary intellectual property rights for all content used.

Of course, a contract between a web host and a webpage client will not immunize either of them from liability to a third party. Therefore, if the web host comes to have any reason to believe a client may be engaging in trademark violations (such as registering and using a domain name that is another company's business name or brand name; or selling products or services using brand names, logos, slogans or product packaging that look or sound confusingly similar to those used by another company) she should immediately notify the client that the site will be taken down if the activity does not cease. If the client persists in the activity after receiving the notice, then the web host should promptly take the site down.

The same kinds of considerations also apply to website owners who feature user-provided content such as products for sale, comments, forums, guest blogs, etc. Although a website owner or blogger might not have a traditional formal contract with subscribers and users, a contract may be formed by requiring users to review and signify assent to Terms of Use by clicking on a 'Yes' or 'I Agree' button or box. The owner of a website may be contributorily liable for another person's use of the website to commit trademark infringement if the owner knew or had reason to know of it, had the power to remove the infringing content (such as by disabling the user's account), and failed to do so.

VICARIOUS INFRINGEMENT

A principal, including an employer, may be vicariously liable for the infringing acts of agents and employees, but only if they are within the scope of employment.

Partners may be vicariously liable for the infringing acts of other partners or the partnership. Even if people do not call themselves partners, a court may find a partnership to exist if all of the following elements are established:

(a) sharing of profits and losses
(b) joint control and management of a business or financial venture
(c) a contribution of some kind by each party, which may be money, property, labor, skill or knowledge
(d) intention to be partners (i.e., intent to do the above things).

Dilution

Dilution means the unauthorized use of a famous mark in way that tarnishes it or weakens its distinctiveness. It is an entirely statutory cause of action, originating in Section 43(c)[345] of the Lanham Act and analogous state statutes.

The elements of a Section 43(c) dilution claim are:

(a) commercial use in interstate commerce
(b) of a famous and distinctive mark, or a mark that is so similar to the famous mark that it gives rise to an association between the marks
(c) beginning after the mark became famous
(d) causing, or likely to cause, blurring or tarnishment, i.e., the association is likely to harm the distinctiveness or reputation of the famous mark.

The use does not need to be on related or competing goods, and it does not have to be likely to cause confusion. No proof of economic loss is required. The purpose of the dilution cause of action is not to protect the public from confusion about the source, sponsorship or endorsement of goods and services. It is to protect a company's investment in the distinctiveness of its trademark. Federal registration is not a precondition to asserting a dilution claim.

The elements of a state cause of action for dilution are usually:

(a) a strong (distinctive) mark
(b) likelihood of dilution.

The analysis of likelihood of dilution under state law is similar to the likelihood of confusion analysis, with courts considering the similarity of the marks, the relatedness of the goods or services, predatory intent, fame of the preexisting mark and the allegedly diluting mark, and consumers' level of sophistication. In some states, only local or regional fame need be proven. Other states require proof of national fame. Some states require "substantial similarity" of the marks.

A few states only require a showing of distinctiveness. The majority rule, however, is that the mark must also be famous. The line between distinctiveness and fame is not always clear. According to the Restatement (3d) of Unfair Competition, the relevant test, for common law trademark dilution purposes, is whether a mark evokes, in the public's mind, an association with a specific source only when used in connection with particular goods or service. If it does, then it is not sufficiently distinctive to be protectable against dilution. This standard approximates the "fame" requirement in the federal statute.

The Lanham Act does not permit a state dilution claim to be predicated on an alleged diluter's use of his own federally registered trademark. A state dilution claim may be brought against a common law trademark owner, though.

FAME

Though not always a required element of a state trademark dilution claim, fame is a required element in a federal dilution claim. The mark must be sufficiently well-known that it retains its significance as a source indicator even outside the context of the goods or services with which it is used. If consumers only associate it with those goods or services, then it is not strong enough to merit federal protection from dilution. This means that only famous or well-known marks qualify for federal legal protection against dilution. The vast majority of marks do not.

Factors federal courts are to consider when determining the fame of a mark include:

- the degree of inherent or acquired distinctiveness
- how widely the mark has been used by its owner
- how long mark has been used
- the duration and extent of advertising and publicity of the mark
- the scope of the geographic area in which the mark has been used
- the channels of trade in which the goods or services are marketed
- the degree of recognition of the mark in the trading areas and the channels of trade used by the trademark owner and the alleged diluter
- the nature and extent of the use of same or similar marks by third parties
- whether the mark is federally registered.

Registration is not required in order to file or prevail on a federal trademark dilution claim. The fact of registration, however, can help provide some evidentiary support for an allegation of fame. No single factor, standing alone, is conclusive of the issue, though.

Some jurisdictions, such as the Second Circuit, require proof that the mark, in addition to being famous, is inherently distinctive. Others do not impose this requirement.

Evidence of fame can include consumer surveys; the quantity of sales of products or services bearing the mark; the amount of advertising expenditures; and/or the length of time these indications of commercial awareness have existed.

BLURRING

Blurring means lessening the strength (fame) of a mark as an identifier of source, reducing its capacity to distinguish and identify goods and services as coming from one source rather than another. Another way to put it is that it involves using a famous mark in a way that makes it less clear that it belongs to its owner. An example would be selling tennis shoes under the ROLEX name. Because people associate that brand name with watches, the likelihood that they would mistakenly believe the shoes are coming from the same source as ROLEX watches may not be great. Nevertheless, the company that makes ROLEX watches has an interest in preserving the public's association of that name with high quality watches, and not with just any product or service. Using it in this way makes it less clear that goods marketed under the ROLEX name originate from the high quality watchmaking company. Relevant factors include:

- Similarity of the marks
- Level of sophistication of consumers of the product or service
- Predatory intent
- The fame of each mark.

TARNISHMENT

Tarnishment means causing a mark to have a negative association in the public's mind. This may occur as a result of the unauthorized use of another person's mark on inferior quality or hazardous goods, or in an unwholesome or unsavory context.

While the terms *unwholesome* and *unsavory* have not been defined with any great precision, it is clear that using a trademark, or a close variation of it, in a sexual context or in a way that implies sexual connotations, would qualify. For example, a court shut down the ADULTS R US website, which sold adult sex toys, because it tarnished the "R US" family of trademarks (TOYS R US, KIDS R US, BABIES R US). Using a trademark or a close variation of it in a way that suggests an association with drugs or crime would probably qualify as tarnishment, too.

At first glance, tarnishment law would seem to provide a way for e-commerce businesses to shut down criticism and bad reviews. Trademark law, however, attempts to promote First Amendment values by shielding those who mention or display a trademark in criticism, commentary, opinion, or parody from trademark liability. Referring to a trademark strictly for these purposes is fair use, so long as the content is not false or misleading.

Remedies

The two basic legal remedies for a victim of trademark infringement are money damages and injunctive relief (a court order requiring a person to stop infringing). In counterfeiting cases, the claimant may elect either treble damages or statutory damages. Willful infringement may also be punishable criminally. Damages for dilution may be recovered only if intent to cause dilution or to trade on the reputation of the famous mark is proven. In all other cases, relief is limited to an injunction.

Compensatory damages compensate the trademark owner for decreased sales as a result of consumer confusion, losses incurred as a result of having to sell at a discount in order to compete with the infringer, and the cost of corrective advertising and other expenses incurred in attempting to clear up the confusion the infringement caused. They also compensate the trademark owner for harm to reputation and diminution of good will. A trademark owner may also seek compensation for the loss of a reasonable royalty that would have accrued from licensing the mark to the defendant.

If an infringer acts willfully or in bad faith (i.e., intended to cause confusion or deception), or engaged in palming off, then a court may order her to turn over the profits she has made by virtue of the infringing use. An innocent infringer is not required to forfeit profits made as a result of the infringing use.

Treble damages may be awarded if the infringement was willful. Intent to infringe is not enough, however. Treble damages will be awarded only if the infringer acted with knowledge that its conduct was unlawful, or if the infringer was recklessly indifferent to the law. Punitive damages are rarely awarded, but are possible if an infringer's conduct is particularly egregious.

In exceptional cases, a court may order the infringer to pay the trademark owner's attorney fees. This might be ordered, for example, in cases where the infringement was willful, deliberate, fraudulent or malicious, or when it involves counterfeiting. Conversely, if the trademark owner filed the case in bad faith, or the court determines the claim is frivolous (i.e., has no reasonable basis in law or fact), then it may order the trademark owner to pay the defendant's attorney fees.

A court may order the prevailing party to pay the other party's costs (filing fee, etc.).

An injunction may be issued if the remedy at law (i.e., money damages) is not adequate. Injunctive relief is usually appropriate in trademark infringement cases because infringement is a continuing wrong, so money damages alone normally are not adequate. Proof of actual damage is not required in order for injunctive relief to be granted. An infringer's voluntary suspension of infringing activities will not prevent a court from issuing an injunction.

When injunctive relief is granted, it may do more than simply prohibit use of the mark. It may also order other things, either in addition to such a prohibition or as alternatives to it. For example, a court might order the infringer to destroy or turn over infringing labels, packaging, and advertisements; or to display a disclaimer; or to notify distributors that it is not affiliated with the trademark owner; or to publish corrective advertising; or to recall products bearing infringing labels.

Violation of an injunction is punishable as contempt of court.

In counterfeiting cases, the trademark owner may ask the court to issue an ex parte seizure order. *Ex parte* means it may be issued without advance notice to the alleged infringer. The person seeking the order must post financial security (usually a bond), notify the United States Attorney, and make the showings necessary for ex parte equitable relief (irreparable harm; likelihood of success on the merits, and so on). The claimant must not publicize the seizure request prior to making it; must show that the alleged infringer is likely to move, hide or destroy the goods if he receives notice of the application for a seizure order; and must provide the court with the location of the items to be seized. A hearing must be held promptly after the ex parte order is issued. A defendant may sue for any damages caused by a wrongful seizure.

SEIZURE OF INFRINGING IMPORTS

In addition to pursuing remedies in court, an aggrieved trademark owner may also ask the U.S. Customs Service to seize counterfeit goods or goods bearing a mark that is confusingly similar to a registered mark. To pursue this course of action, the trademark owner must record the registered mark with the U.S. Customs Service. The Customs Service may, but is not required to, seize goods bearing counterfeit marks that are not federally registered.

CRIMINAL PENALTIES

Intentional or attempted trafficking in goods or services using a counterfeit trademark(s) with knowledge that the mark is counterfeit is a felony crime under the Trademark Counterfeiting Act. It is punishable by up to ten years and a $2,000,000 fine for a first offense; and up to twenty years and a $5,000,000 fine for a subsequent offense.

Many states also have laws making trademark counterfeiting a crime.

Trademark counterfeiting is a predicate act, for RICO purposes.

Defenses

Proof of the nonexistence of an element that is necessary to a claim is a defense to the claim. For example, lack of distinctiveness can be a defense to a Section 32 or state law claim of trademark infringement. Similarly, prior use can be a defense in the United States, inasmuch as the way a person acquires exclusive trademark rights in the United States is by being the first to make substantial use of the mark in commerce. Federal registration does not "wipe out" the trademark rights of those who were making substantial use of the mark prior to another claimant's registration. Preexisting common law trademark rights are limited, however, to the geographic area of trade in which the common law trademark is well-known. The owner of an unregistered common law trademark does not have a right to expand into new geographic areas if someone else has registered the mark with the USPTO.

THE FIRST SALE DOCTRINE

Trademark rights are exhausted in the first sale. This means that after a consumer buys a product with a trademark affixed to it, he can resell the item with or without the trademark affixed to it. For example, if Mary goes to the store and buys a Hasbro game, she can freely resell the game, even inside the box with the Hasbro label on it, at her garage sale.

To qualify for this defense, the subsequent sale must be conducted in a truthful fashion, and in a way that is not likely to confuse the public as to the source of the goods. The first sale doctrine is not available as a defense for a person who buys products from one company and then tries to resell them with another company's label attached to them. For the defense to apply, the goods must be genuine. Resales must comply with the trademark owner's quality control requirements. Resale of repackaged goods is also permitted, but only if the fact of repackaging is disclosed; the repackager's name is disclosed; a disclaimer of the repackager's association with the trademark owner is displayed; and no "undue prominence" is given to the trademark. Also, the repackaging must not lower the quality of the goods. If it does, then the trademark owner may sue the repackager for trademark dilution.

The general rule is that the goods will not qualify for the First Sale defense if they have been modified prior to the resale. In some circumstances, though, resale of repaired or reconditioned goods may qualify for the protection of the First Sale doctrine. If the fact that the goods are used is disclosed, any material information about the repair is disclosed, and the repair or reconditioning is not so extensive that the product cannot really be considered the same anymore, then the product may be resold, with or without the original trademark affixed.

Resales of repaired or modified goods that do not meet these requirements do not qualify for the protection of the first sale doctrine. A resale of a ROLEX watch that has been repaired using non-Rolex parts would be an example of a resale that does not qualify.

A resale of a product that has the effect of voiding a warranty is considered a modification of the product. The first sale doctrine cannot be asserted as a defense with respect to these kinds of sales.

Because of the truthfulness requirement, a reseller who falsely states or implies that she is an authorized reseller, or that she has some other relationship with the trademark owner that really does not exist, would not be protected by the first sale doctrine.

Finally, the First Sale defense is not available to a reseller of gray market goods. *Gray market goods* are goods that are imported into the United States bearing a trademark that is confusingly similar to a U.S. trademark, without the consent of the owner of the U.S. trademark. The U.S. Customs Services may block the importation of goods infringing a federally registered mark. The importer is also liable to the owner of the federally registered mark for infringement. The first sale doctrine cannot be asserted as a defense in this situation because the imported goods are not considered genuine. Even if the trademark affixed to the imported goods was properly registered and legally placed on the goods in the country of origin, the appearance of the mark on the goods in the United States identifies them as originating from the owner of the federally registered mark (the U.S. owner). Since they did not really originate from the U.S. owner, the goods are not genuine. Accordingly, the first sale doctrine will not be available as a defense.

An exception exists when the foreign and domestic trademark owner is the same person or there is common control between the foreign and domestic trademark owners (such as where the foreign trademark owner is a parent or subsidiary corporation of the U.S. trademark owner) and the foreign goods are identical to the domestic goods. If they are not identical, then the foreign goods must bear a label giving notice to consumers that they are not physically identical to the American-made goods. Under Customs Service regulations, the notice must be essentially as follows: "This product is not a product authorized by the U.S. trademark owner for importation and is physically and materially different from the authorized product."

FAIR USE

Nominative Fair Use

Merely referring to a trademark (as distinguished from using it in a way that suggests something untrue about the origin, sponsorship or endorsement of goods or services) is not infringement. Using a trademark this way is called *nominative fair use*. It is also sometimes called "referential" or "trademark fair use." It is a defense toboth infringement and dilution claims. The references to trademarks in this book are examples of nominative fair use.

To qualify for this defense, the referential use must be both truthful and not likely to confuse the public about the source, sponsorship or endorsement of products or services. Thus, a repair service may refer to the brand names of products it repairs or services so long as it does not falsely state or imply that it is authorized by or affiliated with the owner of the trademark in some way. Likewise, a shop may sell brand name replacement parts so long as it does not falsely hold itself out as an "authorized" seller or an "affiliate" of the trademark owner.

Courts impose three conditions on this defense:

(a) The product or service is not readily identifiable without using the trademark;
(b) Only so much of the mark is used as is reasonably necessary to identify the product or service;
(c) The user does not state or imply sponsorship or endorsement by the trademark owner.

The defense is commonly associated with the right to use trademarks in reporting, commentary, criticism, parody, and comparative advertising, but it can also apply in other contexts, too.

Referential use of a mark is also permitted if the trademarked product is a component part of another product or service, so long as the public would not be led to believe that the trademark owner is either the source or sponsor of the other product or service. This is sometimes called *collateral use*. An auto parts dealer selling "reconditioned Ford parts" would be an example (so long as no claim is made or implied that the parts are authorized or approved by Ford).

Because of the nominative fair use defense, an e-commerce business may not have much legal recourse against gripe sites (web sites where people post their complaints about a particular product or service) that target the company, its products, or its service, unless they contain false or misleading content.

The defense may not be available, however, in the case of a dilution claim based on a business competitor's use of the mark in connection with unsavory or unwholesome goods or services, or of an alteration or parody of the mark. This kind of activity falls near the core of the "unfair competition" concept. The First Amendment provides only limited protection for commercial speech; it does not serve as a bar to claims of unfair competition or to trademark violation claims sounding in unfair competition.

COMPARATIVE ADVERTISING

A truthful reference to a competitor's brand name in comparative advertising is nominative fair use. It is not actionable as dilution, either. The Lanham Act expressly provides that there will be no liability for dilution when a famous mark is used in comparative advertising, provided the mark is not altered or parodied.

The right to engage in comparative advertising does not include a right to make false or misleading statements.

LOGOS

The nominative fair use defense applies only if the products or services are not readily identifiable without using the trademark. Arguably, displaying a logo is not necessary inasmuch as a brand may be identified by name instead, so nominative fair use might not be available as a defense. On the other hand, trademark law does not establish a hierarchy of trademark types. There is no reason to believe that word marks are superior to design logo marks for identification purposes, nor is there anything in the law that specifically requires the use of a word mark instead of a design mark for identification purposes. Nevertheless, there is some case law suggesting that the nominative fair use defense only allows the use of so much of a mark as is necessary to identify the product, so that if a mark consists of a combination of a word mark and a design mark, only the word mark may be used. In *New Kids on the Block v. News America Publishing, Inc.*,[346]for example, the Ninth Circuit Court of Appeals intimated that using the word mark COCA-COLA in comparative advertising would be fair use, but using Coca-Cola's distinctive lettering would not be.

Even if a court were to rule that nominative fair use does not apply to the use of logos, there can be no infringement liability unless the kind of use made of a trademark is likely to confuse consumers about the source, sponsorship or endorsement of a product or service. A display of a company's logo in the context of a critique of the company or its products and services, or a news report about them, might not be likely to confuse readers about the source, sponsorship or endorsement of the products or services being discussed. Of course, tarnishment liability may exist even if there is no likelihood of confusion, but the tarnishment statute specifically exempts commentary, criticism and news reporting from its coverage.

If a decision is made to reproduce another company's logo on a website (or in email), then steps should be taken to prevent confusion about the source, affiliation with, or sponsorship or endorsement of products or services. Publishing a conspicuous disclaimer of affiliation, sponsorship or endorsement could be useful for this purpose.

If the visual component of a logo is protected by copyright, then displaying another business's logo on a website would raise copyright issues, too. A website owner who has reason to believe that a particular logo may be protected by copyright, and is not sure whether copyright fair use applies, should seek permission to display it. If that is not feasible, but the reference to the trademark qualifies as trademark fair use, then it might be a good idea to refer to the brand by name rather than displaying the logo.

Descriptive Fair Use

Descriptive use is another kind of fair use defense that is available in trademark infringement and dilution cases. Sellers are allowed to use ordinary words to describe their own goods or services even if those words happen to be part of someone else's trademark. For example, if the owner of the trademark, SWEETARTS, which is a telescoped composite of the words *sweet* and *tart*, were to sue a company for infringement for advertising its product as "sweet and tart," the company could assert the defense of descriptive fair use on the basis that it is merely using ordinary words that accurately describe its product or service. Similarly, a new car dealer who happens to have a sales location in Lincoln, Nebraska could advertise its "Lincoln store" even though someone else owns LINCOLN as a registered mark for sales of Lincoln automobiles.

Using one's own personal name in connection with a business is another example of descriptive fair use. If Samuel Adams decides to go into business using his own name as the name of his business, he could assert the Descriptive Fair Use defense if the beer maker were to sue him for infringement.

The defense is lost if the descriptive term is used as a trademark. A firm advertising "sweet and juicy oranges" could probably prevail using the Descriptive Fair Use defense if sued by the owner of the trademark SWEET 'N JUICY. If, however, it were to start using "Sweet and Juicy" as a brand name for the oranges (in other words, as an identifier of the source of the oranges, such as by using that phrase on labels), then it would lose the protection of the Descriptive Fair Use defense.

Also, the defense is available only if the descriptive use is truthful and in good faith. Using a mark with the intention of confusing consumers about the source of the goods or services, or with the intention of exploiting an existing trademark's reputation, exemplifies bad faith.

Noncommercial Use, Criticism, Commentary and Parody

Criticism, commentary, opinion, and parody are protected by the First Amendment. References to a trademark for these purposes, by persons other than business competitors of the trademark owner, normally are fair use. In fact, any expressive use of a mark for purposes other than competition or commercial exploitation is usually fair use. The Lanham Act prohibits the unauthorized use in commerce of a trademark "in connection with the sale, offering for sale, distribution or advertising of goods and services." State laws vary, but all require a person claiming trademark infringement to prove that the use being made of a mark creates a likelihood of confusion with someone else's goods or services that are being marketed under the same or a similar trademark. For this reason, merely referring to someone else's trademark for a noncommercial purpose is not likely to result in liability for infringement. Trademark infringement liability should be a concern only when someone else's mark or something similar to it is being used to sell, lease, offer or advertise goods or services.

The Lanham Act specifically excludes noncommercial uses of a trademark from the definition of dilution by tarnishment. Accordingly, there should be no need to worry about potential dilution liability for things like an incidental display of trademarks in a photograph of a cityscape, or references to brand names in an unpaid product review.

The likelihood of confusion as to source is a useful guide for deciding whether a use of a mark is a non-expressive, commercial use. The greater the likelihood of confusing consumers about the source of the product, the more likely it is being used for a nonexpressive, commercial purpose.

> **Example**. If I write the statement, "These Doritos brand chips are the best!" on a label and affix it to bags of chips that I offer for sale to the public, consumers are likely to mistakenly believe the chips I'm selling in these bags are Doritos brand chips, that is, the chips made by the company that owns the DORITOS trademark. This would be considered a nonexpressive, commercial use; and I could be sued for infringement. Publishing the same statement ("These Doritos brand chips are the best!") as a snack food review on a website, on the other hand, should not cause any rational reader to become confused about the source of Doritos. A court would almost certainly rule the snack food review is an expressive, noncommercial use. As such, it is fair use, which I could assert as a defense if someone tried to sue me for infringement or dilution.

The Lanham Act expressly exempts news reporting, parody, and commentary from dilution liability, but noncommercial use is a defense to a dilution claim only if the mark is not altered. Using an altered mark, even in a parody, may not be a defense against a dilution claim.

Using a mark to truthfully describe one's background or achievements (such as in an advertisement for expert consulting services) is not considered a commercial use, and will not expose a person to liability for dilution.

A website may be "commercial" if it offers a product or service for sale or lease, displays links to commercial web sites, or if there is advertising on it. A paid product review is considered a form of advertising. Nevertheless, even a commercial website is exempt from dilution liability when it uses an unaltered trademark solely for the purpose of criticism, commentary or parody, so long as the content is not false or misleading.

STATUTE OF LIMITATIONS

There is no specific federal statute of limitations for trademark infringement or dilution claims, so federal courts apply state law to determine the appropriate limitations period.

LACHES

Even in the absence of a statute of limitations, courts have inherent authority ("equity power") to deny relief to a claimant whose unreasonable delay in enforcing rights results in prejudice to the alleged violator. This defense is called *laches*.

Unlike a statute of limitations, there is no fixed number of years that must pass in order for the laches defense to apply. Any unreasonable delay in filing a claim may suffice. Unreasonableness is decided on a case-by-case basis. Although a court might rely on an analogous state statute of limitations as a guideline, it is not bound by any specific statutory period.

Three things must be established in order to prevail on a laches defense:

- Knowledge of the wrongful use of the mark
- Delay in bringing a lawsuit
- Prejudice.

Prejudice, in this context, means the trademark violator changed his position to his detriment during the period of delay. The best example of prejudice would be an infringer's substantial investment in a business on the basis of an assumption that the claimant had no objection to the infringing use.

Laches may be invoked as a defense against the enforcement of a common law or registered trademark, even "incontestable" ones. It may be asserted as a defense to intentional infringement or dilution only if the delay is so prolonged and inexcusable that it is or comes very close to being an abandonment of trademark rights.

ACQUIESCENCE

Acquiescence is an equitable defense that may be asserted when a trademark owner intentionally signals to the violator that the infringing or diluting use is acceptable.

ESTOPPEL

Equitable estoppel is a defense courts devised to bar ("estop") a party to litigation from taking unfair advantage of another by asserting a position in litigation that is inconsistent with one he previously asserted, if the other party detrimentally relied on the previous position. All of the following must be proven in order to prevail on an estoppel defense:

(a) misrepresentation or concealment of a material fact
(b) knowledge of the facts at the time of the representation or concealment
(c) lack of knowledge of those facts on the defendant's part
(d) intent or expectation that the other party will act on the basis of the representation or concealment
(e) detrimental reliance on the misrepresentation or concealment.

UNCLEAN HANDS

A court may use its equity power to deny requested relief to a person with unclean hands, that is, a person who is guilty of misconduct himself, provided the misconduct relates to the claim in some way. Some courts will attempt balance the wrongs, enforcing the rights of a trademark owner with unclean hands if the infringer's misconduct in relation to the mark is substantially worse. Other courts will not make an attempt to balance the wrongs. In some cases, a court might use a finding of "unclean hands" as a basis for granting only partial relief to the trademark owner. The "unclean hands" defense may be asserted even if the mark is registered and "incontestable."

ABANDONMENT

A trademark owner can lose trademark rights through abandonment. This occurs when the trademark owner stops using, a mark and has no intention of resuming use within the reasonably foreseeable future.

A sustained period of nonuse can be evidence of intent not to resume use. There is no precise definition of how long a "sustained period of nonuse" is. For registered marks, though, nonuse for three consecutive years creates a presumption of abandonment.

The period of nonuse must be continuous in order for an abandonment to be found to have occurred. Intermittent periods of nonuse or diminished use do not count The presumption of abandonment of a federally registered mark will not be applicable if the claimant makes at least some use of the mark during the three-year period.

Abandonment is not a defense to an infringement claim if the nonuse is due to circumstances that are beyond the owner's control, provided use is resumed when circumstances change.

Token use (e.g., making a couple of sales to friends just to keep trademark protection alive) is treated the same as nonuse.

An owner's abandonment of all use of a mark results in loss of all trademark rights in the mark. If he continues to use the mark on other goods or services covered by the mark, however, then only the right to use the mark in connection with the goods and services as to which he has failed to use the mark will be deemed abandoned.

It is possible for the geographic scope of a common law trademark to shrink over time. This can happen when the owner ceases using the mark in a particular geographic area. The geographic scope of a common law trademark will not include areas in which the mark is no longer being used, if it is shown that the trademark owner has no intention of resuming use in those areas within the reasonably foreseeable future. In other words, a common law trademark can be deemed abandoned in some parts of the geographic region in which the mark had been protected, yet continue to exist in other areas. This is not the case with federally registered marks. Federally registered marks enjoy nationwide protection even if they are not used in all regions of the country.

For purposes of the abandonment defense, advertising is not considered use of a trademark. A mark may be deemed abandoned despite the fact that the owner continues to advertise goods or services using the mark.

The first person to make substantial use of a mark following another person's abandonment of it acquires trademark rights in it.

Naked Licensing

A trademark owner has an affirmative obligation to supervise the use of the mark by licensees (if any) to make sure they observe consistent standards of quality. Giving another person permission to use one's trademark in whatever way he sees fit, without retaining any control over his use of the mark, is called *naked licensing*. Naked licensing can result in a finding of abandonment of the mark.

FRAUDULENT REGISTRATION

Fraud in procuring or maintaining a trademark registration may be asserted as a defense to an infringement claim, even if the trademark registration has become "incontestable." To establish fraudulent registration, it is necessary to prove each of the following elements:

(a) false or misleading representation to, or concealment of information from, the USPTO
(b) the representation or concealment pertains to a material fact
(c) knowledge of falsity or misleading nature, or reckless disregard for the truth
(d) intent to deceive.

A fact is material if it can be shown that registration or renewal, as the case may be, would not have been granted but for the false or misleading representation, or that it would have been denied if the USPTO had known concealed information. Thus, a false declaration of use with respect to any listed category of goods or services would be material. A misstatement of the date of first use is not material if the applicant's actual first date of use was prior to the date given in the application.

Trademark applicants and renewal registrants have a duty of inquiry with respect to certain kinds of material information, such as whether the claimant is using the mark on the kinds of goods or services listed in the application or registration. Failing to ascertain the truth of essential facts like these can amount to "reckless disregard for the truth."

When fraud is asserted in court as a defense to an infringement claim, proof of both knowledge (or reckless disregard) and intent to deceive is required. Intent is not necessarily a difficult thing to prove, though. There have been cases in which an intent to deceive has been found to exist even though the false statement in question was an honest mistake, or a result of negligence. Other courts disagree, holding that mere negligence is not enough.

Fraud with respect to one item within a class invalidates the registration with respect to all goods and services within that class, but fraud with respect to one class does not invalidate the registration with respect to other classes.

An amendment to correct a materially false or misleading statement of use in an application for registration or renewal of a trademark will not remedy the fraud if the original fraud was intentional.

Fraudulent registration is not only a defense to an infringement claim; it can also be grounds for a tort claim. If a person or business is injured by a fraudulent registration of a trademark, the registrant may be sued for money damages under the Lanham Act.[347]

Proof that a registration or renewal was procured by fraud normally only invalidates the registration; it does not invalidate any underlying common law trademark that may exist. If the fraud is egregious enough, though, it might be possible to assert an "unclean hands" defense against a claim of infringement of the common law mark.

There are some things a trademark applicant can do to minimize the risk of liability for fraudulent registration, to forestall the use of fraudulent registration as a defense, and to avoid the cancellation of a registration on the grounds of fraud:

(a) Before filing, verify that the mark is, in fact, being used on all the goods and services listed in the application, registration, or renewal;
(b) Verify that the use is "in commerce;"
(c) File one application for current uses in connection with specified classes of goods/services, and a separate application for intended uses (i.e., do not include intended uses in a use-based application);
(d) File an amendment as soon as an error is discovered;
(e) Have an attorney review the application and examine the specimens.

INNOCENT INFRINGEMENT

Innocent infringement (using a mark in good faith and without knowledge of another person's exclusive right to use it) is not a defense to direct infringement. Infringement may be actionable even if the infringer did not intend to deceive anyone. Evidence of intent to deceive may be admissible to help establish the element of likelihood of confusion, but likelihood of confusion may be proven in other ways. A person who had no intent to deceive or infringe may still be liable for trademark infringement.

Although it is not a defense, an infringer's good faith intent can greatly reduce the amount of damages that may be recovered. A trademark owner can require an infringer to turn over the profits made from unauthorized use of the mark only if the infringement was in bad faith. Other damages – such as the trademark owner's own loss of earnings – may still be recoverable, however, regardless of whether the infringement was innocent or in bad faith.

Compensatory damages may be recovered against an innocent direct infringer, but not against an innocent contributory infringer. Only injunctive relief may be sought against publishers, broadcasters and hosts of another person's infringing material on the basis of contributory infringement.

Injunctive relief may be sought against those who have direct control over the content of a site at which another person's infringing material has been posted. Good faith is not a defense to a claim for injunctive relief. A court may order a website owner or host to remove infringing content even if the website owner or host neither knew nor should have known of the infringement.

Strategies for Reducing the Risk of Liability

To reduce the risk of liability for trademark violations a business owner, first and foremost, should avoid trying to capitalize on another company's trademark or goodwill. Don't try to fool consumers into thinking products or services are those of another, or that goods or services are authorized, sponsored or endorsed by another person or company when they are not. If claiming to be an "authorized" dealer or repair service for Brand X, for example, have something in writing that provides evidence that such authorization has, in fact been given.

Avoid using someone else's trademark as a keyword in meta tags or keyed advertising. If that is not possible, at least avoid including the trademark in the visible advertisement text. To reduce the likelihood of confusion, display a clear and conspicuous disclaimer of ownership, affiliation, sponsorship or endorsement on the website.

Avoid publishing false or misleading statements. "Puffing" and hyperbolic comparatives—such as, "Our products are the best!"—are fine, but check any factual statements to make sure they are true, and make any disclosures that may be needed to prevent them from being misleading.

Conducting a trademark search and/or obtaining an attorney opinion letter about the availability of a trademark can help generate evidence of good faith and evidence to refute a claim of intent to deceive..

If there is any question about whether an intended use of a trademark is permissible, it may be a good idea to get the trademark owner's permission, preferably in a written licensing agreement. If a trademark includes copyrighted expression, ensuring that the license is also for the use of the copyright would not be a bad idea.

DISCLAIMERS

By reducing the risk of confusion, disclaimers of affiliation with, and of endorsement or sponsorship by, companies identified by trademarks on a website can go a long way toward preventing liability for trademark infringement if they are clear, conspicuous and unambiguous. They do not guarantee freedom from liability. Courts will consider all the facts and circumstances, including intent, actual confusion, similarity of the marks, consumer surveys, etc. There have been cases in which courts have held an infringer liable for infringement despite the placement of a disclaimer on the website. Nevertheless, placing appropriate disclaimers on a website is often an effective strategy for reducing the risk of liability for trademark infringement.

No particular form of words is required for a disclaimer. It should identify trademarks that appear on the website and who owns them, and disclaim any affiliation with, or sponsorship or endorsement by such company. If a trademark is registered, then say so.

A disclaimer is not likely to prevent liability for causing initial interest confusion. A website owner who uses someone else's trademark, or something similar to it, in a domain name as a way of attracting people to the site is not likely to meet with much success arguing that users will see a disclaimer on the website upon visiting it.

Fan site operators should publish disclaimers on their web sites to let visitors know that their sites are not "official" ones, unless the trademark owner actually has authorized calling it an "official" fan site. A link to the trademark owner's site should be provided. This will not necessarily prevent liability in every case, but it can be helpful in terms of defending against a claim that a site misleads visitors into thinking that the site, the statements published on it, or the goods or services offered on it, are offered, endorsed or sponsored by the trademark owner.

Trademark disclaimers will only help protect against claims of trademark violations. They will not protect against claims of copyright infringement, in those cases where a trademark is also protected by copyright. If displaying a trademark infringes a copyright, then one of three options should be considered:

(a) Obtain permissions (license) from the copyright owner;
(b) Invoke copyright fair use, if it clearly applies;
(c) Make referential use of the company's name instead of displaying its logo.

Trademarks as Keywords

A *meta tag* is an unseen element in the coding of a web page. It usually consists of a key word that is inserted for the purpose of improving the searchability of a website. Search engines may scour websites for keywords matching a user's search query. Using a competitor's trademark, or something substantially similar to it, in a meta tag may cause one company's website to appear in the search results when a user searches for another company's website. Doing this may generate initial interest confusion on the part of those who use a search engine to reach the website, and therefore may result in liability for trademark infringement.

As in any kind of trademark infringement case, a fair use defense may be asserted, if available. For example, nominative fair use of another person's trademark in a meta tag will not result in liability for trademark infringement. Thus, when a former Playboy model used the words *Playboy* and *Playmate* in her website's meta tags because they described her work experience, a court held she was not liable for trademark infringement.[348] The court found it important that she was not trying to market goods or services that competed in the same market as those offered by Playboy Enterprises. Using a trademark in a meta tag specifically for the purpose of creating initial interest confusion about the origin, sponsorship or endorsement of goods or services, however, would not be fair use. In some cases, the practice may also result in liability for trademark dilution and/or false advertising.

A *pop-up* or *banner* advertisement is one that appears on a user's screen when the user inputs a command to the computer. Many websites use them to display advertising in a frame when a visitor clicks on a link to the website or visits a website page. Search engines like Google monetize their operations by selling context advertising. Google AdWords is an example. Google allows advertisers to bid on keywords a user might include in a search query. Google then links advertisements and sponsored hyperlinks to the search results page that appears on the user's screen when the user searches for that keyword.[349] This practice is called *keying* or *keyed advertising*.

It has been held that a company that offers keyed advertising (such as Google's AdWords program) does not infringe trademarks even if it sells a keyword consisting of a trademark to a competitor of the trademark owner. A business that purchases from Google the right to use a competitor's trademark as a search keyword for purposes of diverting potential customers of the competitor to the other business, however, might be liable for trademark infringement, depending on the kind of advertisement that is displayed. An adult web site that purchases and uses the keyword *Playboy* and uses it to display in a user's search results a hypertext link or an advertisement with a link to its own webpage may be liable for infringing the Playboy trademark if a user is likely to confuse it for a link to the Playboy website. If, on the other hand, the advertisement contains a conspicuous notice that the website is not the Playboy website and is not affiliated with, sponsored or endorsed by Playboy, then the likelihood of confusing consumers is greatly reduced, thereby reducing the risk of trademark infringement liability. Not all courts agree, however. Some impose infringement liability despite the fact that a disclaimer appears on the website to which a link misleadingly points, holding that a disclaimer comes too late to undo initial interest confusion.

Trademarks in Frames

Framing is a technology that allows a website visitor to simultaneously view another website site in a box on the same screen without leaving the original website. The risk of setting up a website this way is that it could cause visitors to mistakenly believe that the host site is affiliated with the framing site. Depending on the circumstances, this might result in liability for trademark infringement or false advertising. The risk may be avoided by linking to other websites in such a way that the other website opens in its own window. Of course, the risk of liability will still exist if a website states or implies sponsorship, endorsement or affiliation with the linked-to website. To reduce the risk of liability even further, a website could prominently display a disclaimer of affiliation, sponsorship or endorsement by or with the other website.

For information about using trademarks in domain names, see Chapter 29.

Registration

In some countries, registration is required in order to establish a valid trademark. In the United States, a valid, enforceable trademark may exist without being registered. Nevertheless, federal registration in the United States has significant benefits:

- **Enforcement.** Registered trademarks enjoy the benefit of several legal presumptions, including presumptions of the ownership of a valid trademark; an exclusive right to use it nationally; the date of first use; nonfunctionality; and distinctiveness.
- **Defense**. Ownership of a registered trademark makes it very easy to defend against claims of infringement. Although not conclusive, the presumption of an exclusive right to use the mark nationally can be very beneficial, especially as against an unregistered mark that does not enjoy the benefit of the presumption.
- **Deterrence**. People are not as likely to infringe if a trademark search discloses that someone else is already using the mark.
- **Constructive notice**. Registration serves as constructive notice of the existence and ownership of the trademark. This makes it easier to prove that any infringement of the mark is willful. It is also important with respect to the rights of transferees of trademark rights.

- **Right to sue in federal court**. Federal registration gives a trademark claimant the right to sue in federal court.
- **Treble damages and attorney fees**. Because registration provides constructive notice, infringers are deemed to know of the existence of the mark and of the owner's exclusive right to use it. This allows a federal court to triple the award of actual damages, and to make an award of attorney fees, too.
- **Preventing importation**. A federal registration may be filed with the U.S. Customs Service to prevent importation of goods with infringing marks on them. It also allows seizure of infringing foreign goods.
- **Incontestability.** After five years of continuous use and registration, certain reasons may no longer be asserted as grounds for cancellation of a registered mark.
- **Protection from cybersquatters**. Cybersquatters acquire domain names containing, or similar to, other people's trademarks, and then demand money from the trademark owner for it. The owner of a registered mark can place a hold on the use of the domain name until a court or arbitrator decides who has the right to use the domain name.
- **National scope**. Federal registration presumptively extends the geographic scope of a trademark to the entire United States. If more than one business is using the trademark, the first to register will be able to expand into new regions of the country while the owner of the unregistered mark will be limited to the geographic region in which it was being used before the other company registered it. If the owner of the unregistered mark is unable to prove use prior to the other's registration of it, he will have to stop using the mark altogether.
- **Protection of investment**. It can take a substantial investment of time and money to establish a reputation and a well-known trademark associated with it. The investment can be lost in an instant if a competitor secures a valid registration first.
- **Retention of customers**. Being forced to change a business or brand name as a result of a competitor's prior registration of a confusingly similar name can result in a company's loss of customers to the competitor.
- **Savings on packaging, advertising and promotional costs**. Undertaking the trademark search and registration process before investing too heavily in signage, labels, advertising and other marketing materials can save a company a lot of money if it is discovered during this process that the mark is already being used or is not enforceable for some other reason.
- **Basis for foreign registration**. Registration in the United States can provide the basis for registration in many other countries, as well.

FEDERAL *vs.* STATE REGISTRATION

Trademarks may be registered with the federal government, a state government, or both. State registration provides some but not all of the above-described benefits of federal registration. Most significantly, state registration only gives the registrant a presumptive right to use the mark throughout the state, not throughout the country. A federal registration gives the registrant a presumptive right to use it anywhere in the country. Obtaining a federal registration makes it unnecessary to register the mark in each individual state where the mark is used.

GEOGRAPHIC SCOPE

Trademarks are territorial. The owner's exclusive right to use one is limited to the geographic area in which it has been used plus any other geographic area in which people have come to associate it with the owner's goods or services. The geographic area in which a mark is used, together with the geographic regions to which reputation and goodwill have spread, is called the *area of trade*. Trademark rights exist within the area of trade, but not beyond it.

The priority of use rule is also subject to a geographic qualification. A common law trademark arises only within the geographic area of trade. Thus, if John has started a landscaping service using the mark HANDSCAPE serving the Phoenix, Arizona area, Jane will not be infringing John's mark if she subsequently uses the same mark in connection with a landscaping business serving the Chicago area, provided John's business reputation has not yet spread to Chicago. Each is considered to have first priority of use with respect to the mark within their respective geographic areas.

Federal registration presumptively extends the geographic scope of a trademark to the borders of the entire country.

Concurrent Use Applications

Courts have equitable power to allow concurrent use of the same or similar marks in a way that is not likely to cause confusion, such as by limiting the geographic scope of the sales territory of one or both owners. This can be an option where, for example, a business has a federally registered trademark that is the same as or confusingly similar to an unregistered mark and the owner of the unregistered mark is able to prove prior use. In this situation, depending on the circumstances, the USPTO or a court might declare that the common law trademark owner has the exclusive right to use the mark in a specified area of trade, while the owner of the registered mark has the exclusive right to use it everywhere else. Businesses may also stipulate to this kind of arrangement as a way of settling trademark disputes.

To register a mark for a specified geographic area instead of one with nationwide scope, a concurrent use application should be filed.

A concurrent use registration is allowed only if the applicant used the mark prior to the date another party registered it, and then only if registration of both marks is not likely to cause confusion. There must be either a judicial or TTAB determination of concurrent rights to use the same mark. Filing a concurrent use application initiates a TTAB concurrent use proceeding.

USE *vs*. INTENT TO USE

Trademark applications may be based on either use or intent to use. If an intent-to-use application is filed, then actual use of the mark in commerce must begin within six months (plus any extensions that are granted) after the application is filed. Evidence of use must be submitted during that same time period.

Under the Lanham Act, the filing of an intent-to-use application is constructive use of the mark. This means that if the applicant files sufficient evidence of use within the allotted time, then the date of use will relate back to the date the application was filed. That is to say, the trademark will be treated as if it was first being used on the date the original application was filed. If the applicant does not properly file such evidence during the allotted time, then the application will be rejected and the benefit of the intent-to-use rules is lost.

PRINCIPAL *vs.* SUPPLEMENTAL REGISTERS

The USPTO offers two kinds of registration. The Principal Register is for marks that currently meet all requirements for registration as a trademark. The Supplemental Register is for things that do not currently meet all requirements for federal registration as a trademark but could potentially qualify in the future.

The most common reason for placement on the Supplemental Register is failure to satisfy the distinctiveness requirement. A mark that is not inherently distinctive would go on the Supplemental Register if it has not yet acquired secondary meaning. Being on the Supplemental Register essentially notifies the world that a mark does not currently qualify for federal trademark protection but someone is working on it. The owner of a mark that is on the Supplemental Register may apply to have it listed on the Principal Register once it has acquired distinctiveness.

A mark that creates a likelihood of confusion with a previously registered mark is not even potentially registrable. Therefore, it may not be included on either the Principal or the Supplemental Register. Because the USPTO may refuse a registration on the basis that it is confusingly similar to a mark on either register, getting a mark on the Supplemental Register can help deter others from trying to register it. This could be important if, for example, a company needs to work on building secondary meaning before a mark will qualify for registration on the Principal Register.

Inclusion on the Supplemental Register does not create a presumption of validity, ownership, or right to use the mark, is not deemed to be constructive notice or use of the mark, and does not give the claimant a right to block importation.

Registration of a mark on either the Supplemental or the Principal Register gives the owner the right to use the ® symbol.

The remainder of this chapter addresses the requirements for inclusion on the Principal Register.

EXCLUSIONS FROM REGISTRATION

Invalid Trademark

Only a valid trademark may be registered. This is true of intent-to-use applications, too. The requirement of use in commerce still applies in such cases. An intent-to-use application just gives an applicant more time to use and furnish evidence of use in commerce.

Before approving an application for registration of a trademark, the USPTO will attempt to determine whether it is confusingly similar to an existing one. Doubts about likelihood of confusion are resolved against the applicant. A mark that is identical to an existing one or very similar to an existing one may be registered as a trademark for unrelated goods or services, though.

In rare cases, the USPTO may allow concurrent use of an identical or similar mark for the same or related goods, subject to conditions and limitations on use to ensure there will be no confusion among consumers as to the source of the goods or services. The USPTO will not do this, however, unless it is convinced that it can be done without confusing consumers.

Wholly Intrastate Commerce

The Commerce Clause of the federal constitution only authorizes Congress to regulate interstate and foreign commerce. Therefore, only those trademarks that are used in interstate or foreign commerce can be registered. Use in interstate commerce is only a federal registration requirement. It does not affect the validity or enforceability of a common law trademark. A wholly intrastate trademark may be registered with a state trademark office. It may also be enforced as a common law trademark.

Living Person's Name, Signature, or Portrait

The USPTO will not allow the registration of a living person's name, signature or portrait without the person's consent. The rule applies not only to full names, but also surnames, first names, shortened names, nicknames, pseudonyms and titles. BARACK'S JOCKS, for example, was refused registration because consumers would associate Barack with Barack Obama, a famous person who had not given his consent to the use.

This rule only applies to situations in which the public would recognize and understand the name, signature or portrait as identifying a particular living individual who is likely to be associated with the goods or services, either because the person is publicly connected with the business or industry in which the mark is used, or because the person is so famous or well-known that the public would reasonably assume a connection.

The fact that a name is used by more than one person does not negate the consent requirement if the mark identifies, to the relevant public, a famous person or a person who is publicly connected with the business or industry.

When consent is required, it must be in writing, and signed. The writing must specifically give consent to the registration of the name, signature or portrait as a trademark. Merely consenting to the use of the mark will not suffice as consent to registration. Consent is presumed if the person whose name or likeness is used in a mark is the one who signs his name to the application for registration.

The validity of a consent signed by a minor child is determined by the law of the state of the child's domicile. If the child can enter into binding contracts, and can sue and be sued, under the laws of that state, then a consent signed by her is valid for the purposes of federal trademark registration. If not, then the consent will need to be signed by a parent or legal guardian.

Consent sometimes may be inferred from an individual's actions. The owner of a company bearing the owner's name may be deemed to have consented to this use of his name. The consent will remain intact even if the business is later sold to a person with a different name, at least if the owner has agreed to relinquish "all rights" to the name to the new owner. It is important to remember, however, that consent to use is not the same thing as consent to register. A person could agree to license the use of his name to another person without at the same time agreeing that the person can register the name. An agreement for the sale of a business should specify exactly which trademark and trademark-related rights are being transferred.

The rule against registration of a name without consent does not bar registration of names that only coincidentally happen to be names of real persons. A connection between the person and the business or industry must exist in the public's mind, or the name must be so famous or well-known that the public could interpret its use on a product as indicating that person's connection to or endorsement of the product. The fact that the Tom James Company has registered the mark TOM JAMES in connection with the sale of clothing does not mean that the author of this book has the right to have the registration cancelled because he did not consent to it. The public is not likely to associate book authorship with clothing sales.

Dead U.S. President's Name, Signature or Portrait

The name, signature or portrait of a dead U.S. President may not be registered as a trademark if the President's spouse is still living and has not consented to the registration. The surviving spouse's consent is required even if another person has or had the same name as the President. For example, if former president Bill Clinton dies, it will be necessary to obtain Hillary's consent in order to register his name, signature or likeness as a trademark, even though a lot of people are named Bill Clinton. The consent must be in writing, and signed.

Flags, Coats of Arms, Insignias, etc.

Flags, coats of arms, insignias, etc. of a governmental unit—whether national, state or municipal—cannot be registered as trademarks.

A mark containing a flag pattern, on the other hand, is registrable if:

(a) The flag pattern is used to form a letter, number, or design;
(b) The flag is substantially obscured by words or other design elements;
(c) It is in a shape that is not normal for a flag;
(d) It uses different colors than the governmental flag does;
(e) A significant feature of the flag is missing or changed.

A mark may include other kinds of patriotic symbols, such as the American eagle, provided it does not create an impression of affiliation with or sponsorship by the federal government.

Designations of certain private organizations also may not be registered. Congress has granted exclusive rights to specified organizations to use certain words, symbols and other designations. The American Legion, Boy Scouts, Girl Scouts and Little League are examples.

Federally Protected Slogans, Words and Symbols

The federal government prohibits the registration of certain words, slogans and symbols, for reasons usually (but not always) having to do with protecting the government's proprietary interest in intellectual property. In some cases, unauthorized use has been made a criminal offense. In any event, the USPTO will deny registration to a mark that employs such a slogan, word or symbol. Smokey Bear, the words *Olympic* and *Copyright*, the Red Cross symbol, and the slogan, "Give a Hoot, Don't Pollute" are examples.

False Association with a Person, Institution, Belief, or National Symbol

Marks falsely suggesting a connection to a person, whether living or dead, are not registrable. Marks falsely suggesting a connection to an institution, a belief, or a national symbol also are not registrable.

This rule will apply when each of the following conditions exists:

(a) The element for which trademark registration is sought is the same as or similar to a person, institution, belief or national symbol;
(b) The public would recognize it as such;
(c) There is no connection between the person, institution, etc. and the goods or services;
(d) The name or symbol is famous or well-known.

The rule against using a dead person's name or likeness does not apply to the use of the name or likeness of a historical figure who has been dead for a long time. Incorporating a drawing of Paul Revere into a company's logo is permissible, for instance.

Geographic Names

The names of countries, states, cities, counties, mountains, rivers, or any other geographic region cannot be registered with the USPTO unless acquired secondary meaning can be shown. The same is true of drawings and maps of them.

This rule is subject to three exceptions:

- Planetary and extraterrestrial terms
- Remote, obscure places
- Uses that are obviously not indicative of geographic source.

These kinds of uses are considered inherently distinctive.

Primarily geographical terms that are deceptively misdescriptive words are not registrable under any circumstances. A geographic misdescription is deceptive if a consumer is likely to mistakenly believe it is connected with that location. SAN ANTONIO SALSA, for example, would be deceptively misdescriptive, and therefore unregistrable, if it is actually made in New York City and not San Antonio. A consumer could reasonably believe it to have been made in San Antonio. By contrast, no reasonable consumer would believe that someone is making salsa in Antarctica. For this reason, ANTARCTIC SALSA would be classified as a fancifully misdescriptive mark, not a deceptively descriptive one. As such, it is inherently distinctive.

Deceptive Marks

The USPTO will not register any mark it determines to be materially deceptive. A mark is materially deceptive if (a) it falsely describes the good or services, or their origin, and (b) the deception is likely to influence a consumer's purchasing decision. A materially deceptive mark cannot be registered even if it has acquired secondary meaning.

Misspellings of Unregistrable Marks

A mark that could not be registered if spelled correctly cannot be made registrable by misspelling it.

Disparaging Marks

The Lanham Act purports to prohibit the registration of any mark that disparages (i.e., brings into disrepute or contempt) any living or dead person, institution, belief or national symbol. In *Matal v. Tam*,[350] the Asian American band, The Slants, sought to register their band name as a trademark. The USPTO refused registration on the basis that it disparaged Asian American people. The U.S. Supreme Court reversed, holding that registered trademarks are private speech, not government speech. As such, they are protected by the First Amendment. The prohibition against registering "disparaging" trademarks violates the First Amendment right of freedom of speech.

Immoral or Scandalous Marks

Federal registration will be denied to a mark that is "immoral" or "scandalous."[351] The USPTO and courts have defined these terms in a variety of ways, such as "shocking to the sense of propriety, offensive to the conscience or moral feelings or calling out for condemnation" or "vulgar" or "lacking in taste, indelicate, morally crude." Profanity, depictions and references to sexual organs and acts, and sometimes nudity, often fall into the category of "scandalous or immoral."

A mark will be rejected on this basis only if a substantial portion of the general public would consider it to be immoral or scandalous in the context of the relevant marketplace. Thus, the determination whether something is immoral or scandalous may vary depending both on the kinds of goods or services it is used to market, and on the segment of the population to which it is marketed. In addition, what is considered immoral or scandalous can change over time. A nineteenth century society member and a politically correct twenty-first century college student would consider many things immoral or scandalous that a person who grew up in the 1960s or 1970s might not.

If a term has both an immoral meaning and an innocent one, the USPTO sometimes ignores the immoral one. Thus, BIG PECKER and PUSSY POWER REVOLUTION are registered trademarks for wine and women's clothing, respectively. *Pussy* can mean cat; and *pecker* can mean a bird's bill. BIG TITS, on the other hand, was refused registration.

A trademark that is denied federal registration may still be enforced as a common law trademark if it otherwise meets all requirements for a valid, enforceable trademark in the jurisdiction in which it is used.

The continuing validity of the Lanham Act's prohibition against immoral or scandalous content is uncertain, in view of the U.S. Supreme Court's ruling in *Tam*. An argument might also be made that the provision is unconstitutionally vague or overbroad.

Title of a Single Book or Movie

The title of a single book or movie generally cannot be registered as a trademark. It may be possible to register a trademark in a recurring word or phrase that appears in every title in a series, though. In that situation, the public may associate the title with the same source. THE MAGIC SCHOOL BUS series of books is an example.

REGISTRATION DISCLAIMERS

It is possible to register a mark without receiving the benefits of trademark registration for every aspect or element of it. This can happen either by omitting a particular claim or by disclaiming trademark rights in a particular aspect or element of a mark. Appropriate disclaimers in a registration application sometimes help prevent registration denials or delays.

DILUTION

The USPTO will not take the initiative to deny registration on the basis that a mark is likely to dilute an existing mark. A third party may file an opposition or cancellation proceeding objecting to registration on the basis that the mark dilutes an existing mark, though. The USPTO may deny registration if a third party claims and proves dilution. Moreover, a person may commence a proceeding to cancel a trademark on the basis that it dilutes an existing mark. The proceeding must be commenced within five years after the registration of the mark that is claimed to dilute the existing mark.

TRADEMARK SEARCHES

A trademark search is not legally required prior to filing an application for registration. A prudent businessperson, however, will perform a trademark search during the process of selecting business and product names. Even if a trademark search was not completed at the time a company began using a mark, doing one prior to applying for registration is a good idea. The USPTO will conduct a search when it reviews applications, but the search it performs will be limited to federal registrations and applications. It will not detect unregistered common law trademarks or trademarks that have been registered at the state but not the federal level. The time and expense involved in filing and processing a trademark application can be high. It can take even longer and cost more if an opposition is filed. Even an unopposed application can take a year or more to make its way through the USPTO examination process. That is a lot of time to waste if the mark turns out to be unregistrable for a reason that could have been discovered during a pre-application trademark search.

The USPTO will not issue an advisory opinion as to the registrability of a trademark. It is up to the applicant to conduct his or her own search before applying for registration.

APPLICATIONS

Applications for registration may be filed electronically or by regular mail. Electronic filing is quicker and significantly less expensive than filing by mail. The Trademark Office's electronic filing system is called TEAS (Trademark Electronic Application System). It may be accessed at www.uspto.gov/ Those without an Internet connection may access TEAS at any Patent and Trademark Resource Center throughout the United States.

Filing Date

All applications are assigned a filing date. If filed electronically, the filing date is the date the transmission reaches the USPTO server, in Eastern Standard Time. The filing date of a paper application is the date the USPTO receives the application. The filing date is important because an earlier filed application usually is given priority for processing. The priority created by having the earlier filing date is not conclusive. If the owner of a later filed application can establish earlier use of the mark, he may file an opposition to the registration of the earlier filed application. Doing that does not accelerate the processing of the later filed application, however.

Ensuring an application is complete is also important. The USPTO may refuse to assign a filing date to an incomplete application.

Under the Paris Convention, if a person files applications to register trademarks in two different countries within six months of each other, then both marks will be assigned the filing date of the earliest one.

Filing Basis

There are three possible bases for a trademark application:

- Use
- Intent to use
- Foreign registration.

An applicant who files an application on the basis of intent to use must actually begin using the mark within six months after receipt of a notice of allowance. The USPTO may grant an extension if it is requested before the six-month period expires. An application to register a mark on the Supplemental Register may not be based on intent to use.

The basis for a pending application may be changed by filing an amendment. It cannot be changed after a registration certificate has issued.

Essential Elements

A use-based application must include:

- Ownership information
- Filing basis
- Categories of goods or services on which the mark has been used
- Description of the goods or services
- Drawing of the mark
- Declaration of use
- Declaration of no known superior claims
- Specimen showing use in commerce
- Signature
- Filing fee.

An intent-to-use application must include:

- Ownership information
- Filing basis
- Categories of goods or services on which the mark is intended to be used
- Description of the goods or services
- Drawing of the mark
- Declaration of bona fide intent to use
- Declaration of no known superior claims
- Signature
- Filing fee.

A declaration of use and a specimen of use must be filed within six months (plus any requested extensions that are granted) of an intent-to-use filing.

Privacy

Any information submitted to the USPTO is accessible by members of the public. Persons who do not want the public to have access to address information should use a PO Box address for correspondence with the USPTO, and list the PO Box address, not a physical address, on the application. A telephone number is optional. If one is listed on an application, it will be available to the public.

Categories of Goods and Services

The categories of goods and/or services for which trademark protection is sought must be specified. There may be more than one, and both goods and services may be specified on the same application. The application must adequately describe the goods and services. The USPTO's *Acceptable Identification of Goods and Services Manual* lists acceptable identifications of goods and services.

Drawing

Every application must include an image or depiction of the mark. The USPTO calls all such images and depictions "drawings" even when the mark consists entirely of typewritten text. The drawing will become part of the USPTO's searchable database. It will also be published in the Official Gazette and will appear on the registration certificate. Do not include the ™, ℠ or ® symbol in the drawing.

There are three categories of drawings:

- Standard character (for word marks)
- Sound (for sound marks)
- Special form (for design and all other kinds of marks).

Specimen

At least one specimen of use is required. It should exhibit the mark's actual use in commerce. For goods, the specimen could be a photograph of the mark as it appears on actual goods, or on a label, tag or packaging. Merely providing a link to a website where the mark is displayed on goods being offered for sale is not an adequate specimen, but a screenshot of such a website page might be. To qualify, the mark must be displayed on or in close proximity to a picture or a text description of the goods, and the goods must be offered for sale at the site. A website that merely advertises the goods without providing a way to order them from the site will not suffice. For digital downloads, an applicant may submit a screenshot that shows use of the mark on an Internet website, provided the file is downloadable from the site. If the website simply advertises the file without providing a way to download it, the specimen will not be unacceptable.

Business cards, advertisements, brochures, leaflets, and the like are not adequate specimens of use in connection with goods, but they can suffice as specimens of use in connection with services. The specimen for a service mark application must indicate, either expressly or by natural implication, the kind of service in connection with which the mark is being used. A service provider's business card may suffice if it states the kinds of services provided. A screenshot of a website page on which a service is advertised should qualify, too.

Additional Information

Additional information may need to be included in an application in some cases. This could include:

- Translation of foreign words used in the mark
- Transliteration
- Prior registration
- Concurrent use
- Claim of acquired distinctiveness
- Consent to use of a person's name or likeness
- Disclaimers of unregistrable aspects of a trademark.

The basis for any claim of secondary meaning in a mark that is not inherently distinctive must be provided in the application.

A *unitary* mark is one that creates a commercial impression separate and apart from any unregistrable component. This happens when "the elements are so merged together that they cannot be divided to be regarded as separable elements."[352] BLACK MAGIC is an example. Even if *black* is descriptive of the goods in question, using it with *magic* yields a noun phrase that has a different and distinct meaning of its own. A disclaimer of the unregistrable part of a unitary mark is not necessary.

Filing Fees

The filing fee for an application varies depending on the type of application—paper, TEAS, TEAS RF (reduced fee) or TEAS Plus—and the number of International Classes of goods or services selected. As of July, 2017, the filing fee was $225 per International Class for electronic filing and $600 for paper filings. Current fees are posted at the USPTO website.

EXAMINATION

An examining attorney will review the application using the TMEP, search the USPTO database of existing registrations and applications, and decide whether it is registrable or not. The examination process can take months. The status of an application can be checked using the USPTO's Trademark Status and Document Retrieval system (TSDR) at www.uspto.gov.

OFFICE ACTIONS

An office action is a communication from the USPTO in regard to a pending application. It may be a request for more information or it may be a notice of a deficiency or problem with the application. The time limit for responding to an office action is six months.

An applicant who receives a final office action determining that the mark is not eligible for registration has three options:

- File a request for reconsideration
- Appeal to the TTAB
- Abandon the application.

The USPTO may consider an application abandoned if the applicant fails to timely respond to an office action. If that happens, a petition for reactivation may be filed with the Commissioner for Trademarks. The petition must be filed within sixty days. If the application is not reactivated, then it will be necessary to start the application process over from scratch, including paying the filing fee again.

A denial of registration is not a determination that the applicant has no trademark rights. A common law trademark may exist even if the USPTO refuses to register it. Similarly, abandoning a registration is not the same thing as abandoning the mark itself. An applicant who abandons a registration application may still have a valid common law trademark.

APPEALS

An appeal of an examiner's decision to the TTAB is called an *ex parte proceeding*. A TTAB decision may be appealed to the Court of Appeals for the Federal Circuit.

PUBLICATION FOR OPPOSITION

If the application for registration of the mark survives the examining attorney's examination, it will be published in the USPTO's *Official Gazette*. The purpose of publication is to give members of the public (including those with competing claims to the same mark) an opportunity to object to the registration.

OPPOSITION PROCEEDINGS

Anyone who believes registration may damage her interests may object to it by filing an opposition with the TTAB. The deadline for filing an opposition is thirty days from the date of first publication in the *Official Gazette,* unless an extension is requested and granted. The filing fee is $300 per class. An opposition initiates a legal proceeding. TTAB decisions in opposition proceedings may be appealed to the Federal Circuit Court of Appeals.

NOTICE OF ALLOWANCE

If the application for registration survives the examination process and opposition proceedings (if any), then the USPTO will issue a Notice of Allowance.

At any time before a Notice of Allowance is issued, an intent-to-use applicant may file an Amendment to Allege Use. This has the effect of converting an intent-to-use application into one based on use. Specimens of use must be submitted along with the amendment. If an Amendment to Allege Use is not filed before the Notice of Allowance is issued, then the applicant will need to file a Statement of Use. The USPTO has a combined Statement of Use/Amendment to Allege Use form for these purposes.

An intent-to-use applicant has up to six months after receiving a Notice of Allowance to file a Declaration of Use and the required specimens of use. An extension of up to six additional months may be requested, and additional six-month extensions may be requested thereafter. In no event, however, may the total time for filing the Statement of Use and specimen(s) be extended more than three years (thirty-six months) beyond the date the Notice of Allowance was received. Extensions are granted only for good cause shown. Extensions must be requested during either the initial six-month period or an extension of it. An extension may not be requested after the time period has lapsed.

CERTIFICATE OF REGISTRATION

In the case of an application based on use, the USPTO will issue a registration certificate shortly after the Notice of Allowance is sent. The registration certificate for an intent-to-use application will be issued only after a proper and timely Statement of Use and specimen(s) are received in the USPTO office.

CONSEQUENCES OF REGISTRATION

Registration on the Principal Register has the following effects:

(a) The registered owner has the right to use the ® symbol. A common law trademark owner may only use the ™ and ℠ symbols.
(b) A registration certificate is prima facie evidence of the ownership and validity of the trademark, and of the registrant's exclusive right to use it anywhere in the United States.
(c) The burden of proof shifts to the defendant, in an infringement or dilution lawsuit filed by a registered trademark owner, to prove the trademark is invalid, indistinctive or likely to confuse, that someone else owns it, or that use began at a different time.
(d) It may establish the registrant's prior use with respect to goods and services listed in the registration.
(e) It provides constructive notice of the registrant's claim of ownership. This prevents another person from asserting innocent infringement or good faith if such person's use began after the date the registrant applied for registration.

(f) It gives the registrant the right to sue in federal court for infringement or dilution.
(g) It gives the registrant the right to use the U.S. Customs Service to prevent counterfeit or infringing imports from entering the United States.
(h) The registrant has a right to file a Declaration of Incontestability after five years.
(i) It provides a basis for registration in other countries, if desired.

Unless it is cancelled, a registered mark is presumed to have been in use nationwide as of the date the application was filed, not just from the time the registration certificate is issued. Once a registration certificate is issued, it establishes nationwide constructive use as of the filing date of the application, conferring right of priority, on or in connection with the goods or services listed in the registration, except as those who can prove prior use.

Registration on the Supplemental Register has the following effects:

(a) The registered owner has the right to use the ® symbol;
(b) The registered owner has the right to apply to have the mark listed on the Principal Register, provided the owner can show that the mark has come to qualify for inclusion on the Principal Register, such as by acquiring secondary meaning.

Except for the right to use the ® symbol, registration on the Supplemental Register does not give the owner the benefits that registration on the Principal Register does. It does not give the registrant an exclusive right to use the mark; and it does not create presumptions of ownership, validity, distinctiveness, exclusive right to use, etc.

Rebuttal of Trademark Presumptions

Registration establishes only a presumption of first use. It is rebuttable by proving that another person was already using it as a trademark before the registrant applied for registration, and that the previous mark has not been abandoned.

Rebuttal may be necessary where the owner of a common law trademark asserts prior use as a basis for opposition to or cancellation of somebody else's registration of an identical or similar mark. The issue may also be raised in a state or federal court proceeding against the registered owner, in which a common law trademark owner alleges trademark infringement or dilution, or a trademark-related cause of action such as false advertising.

To prevail against a registered owner, a common law trademark owner will need to prove the elements of a trademark infringement, dilution or trademark-related cause of action without the benefit of presumptions. This means evidentiary proof will be required as to the fact and dates of use of the common law trademark, its distinctiveness, and so on. Evidence will also be needed to rebut the presumptions to which the other party's registration of the mark gives rise.

A challenge to a registered mark that is based on prior use may be asserted even after the registered mark has become "incontestable."

Although registration does not extinguish preexisting common law marks (provided they are proven), it does "freeze" a common law mark to the geographic area in which it was being used at the time of the registration. If a prior user of a common law mark cannot establish that the registrant's use is in the same area of trade, the USPTO or a court may issue a concurrent use order dividing sales territories between the parties.

Famous Marks

Normally, the protection afforded by registration extends only to the categories of goods and services listed in the registration, and sometimes to good or services that are related to them. The owner of a famous or well-known mark, however, may have an exclusive right to use it in connection with other, completely unrelated goods and services, too.

If a mark, or the construction of a mark, is widely understood as referring to a product originating from the same source as products bearing the famous mark, then the scope of trademark protection for the mark extends to that product, too, even if it is not in the same category or a category related to the one(s) for which the famous mark is registered.

The reason for this rule has to do with the "no likelihood of confusion" requirement for trademark protection. If a mark is so famous or well-known that consumers are likely to think a product originates from the owner of the famous or well-known mark even if it's in a category that is unrelated to the one for which the famous mark is registered, then marketing the product under that name will likely cause confusion among consumers about the source of the product. For example, since the Coca-Cola Company uses its stylized logo on a wide variety of products, consumers are likely to mistakenly believe that virtually anything with that logo on it comes from the Coca-Cola Company.

Famous or well-known marks also enjoy a broader geographic scope of protection than other kind of marks. The owner of a famous or well-known mark has superior rights to use the mark even if it is not registered, and even if another person used or registered the mark in a particular country before the famous mark was used or registered in that country (provided it is famous or well-known there).

Fame is assessed with reference to the country in which trademark protection is sought. For example, if the Coca-Cola Company has not registered or used its trademark in the Congo, but wants to prevent others from using the Coca-Cola brand to sell soft drinks there, then it would need to establish that the name is famous in Uganda, not that it is famous in the United States or some other country. It might accomplish this, for example, by advertising heavily in the Congo.

CANCELLATION OF REGISTRATION

The USPTO and any person claiming to be injured by a registration may file a petition to cancel the registration at any time. The grounds for a cancellation proceeding are limited if a Declaration of Incontestability has been filed.

Preserving Trademark Rights

Registration goes a long way toward protecting trademark rights, but it is not the only thing a trademark owner must do to preserve rights in the mark. Even the owner of a registered mark may lose the exclusive right to use it if adequate steps are not taken to preserve it. This includes:

- Maintaining the registration
- Using an appropriate trademark symbol
- Using the mark

- Using the mark properly, to prevent genericide
- Policing other people's use of the mark.

RENEWAL AND MAINTENANCE OF REGISTRATION

The term of a registration is ten years. It may be renewed for additional ten-year terms any number of times. In addition, the registrant must file an Affidavit of Use or Excusable Nonuse (also called a "Section 8 affidavit") between the fifth and sixth years of the first term. A filing fee is required. Failure to timely and properly file an Affidavit of Use or Excusable Nonuse, or to remit the filing fee, may result in cancellation of the registration before the end of the first term.

In rare cases, failure to use a mark may be excused if it is clear from the circumstances that the nonuse was not due to an intention to abandon the mark. A lack of consumer demand for the product or service is not an acceptable excuse for nonuse. The USPTO construes excusable nonuse very narrowly. Nevertheless, a trademark owner who has a good excuse for failing to use a mark should so indicate on the Declaration of Continued Use or Excusable Nonuse.

Between the ninth and tenth years after registration, another Affidavit of Use or Excusable Nonuse must be filed, this time along with an Application for Renewal. This must be done between every ninth and tenth year after the registration date thereafter. Again, failure to timely file and pay the filing fee may result in cancellation of the registration.

The USPTO will accept a late filing of one of these documents for up to six months after the applicable deadline, but an additional fee must be paid.

If, after the fifth year of registration on the Principal Register, there are no adverse decisions or pending proceedings involving the mark, and it has been in continuous use during that time, the registrant may file a Declaration of Incontestability (also called a "Section 15 declaration"), along with the applicable filing fee. This has the effect of removing some, but not all, grounds for cancellation of registration. Although not a mandatory filing, a Section 15 Declaration can be useful because it makes the rebuttable presumptions of ownership, validity, registration and exclusive right to use irrebuttable.

A Section 15 Declaration does not make a registered trademark absolutely incontestable. There are some exceptions. The following claims and defenses may still be asserted even if a Section 15 Declaration has been filed:

- The mark is (or has become) generic
- The mark is functional
- A prior registration is confusingly similar
- The owner has abandoned the mark
- Fraud in the procurement of the registration
- Fraud in the maintenance of the registration
- Use of the trademark to violate antitrust laws
- Prior use of a common law trademark
- Fair use
- Equitable defenses (e.g., laches, unclean hands)

USING THE ®, ™ AND SM SYMBOLS

The use of trademark symbols is governed by the law of the country in which a mark is used. In the United States, the encircled-R symbol—®—may be used only if the mark is federally registered. It is illegal to use this symbol on anything but a federally registered mark. Further, the mark may be used only in connection with the categories of goods and services listed in the registration. An applicant for federal registration does not acquire a right to use the ® symbol until the registration process is complete. Use of the ® symbol must be discontinued if a registered mark is no longer "live" because the registration has been canceled or abandoned. Unauthorized use of the ® symbol not only violates federal trademark laws; it may also constitute false advertising. In addition, an applicant's use of the symbol while an application for registration is still pending may result in a denial of registration.

The ™ symbol may be used for common law trademarks as well as registered ones. It may be used even if the USPTO has refused registration of the mark, provided that doing so does not violate false advertising, unfair competition laws. The ℠ symbol may be used for service marks.

Use of a trademark symbol is not absolutely necessary. It is highly recommended, though, for several reasons. Most important, it helps identify the mark as a trademark, not just a generic name for the product. Affixing a trademark symbol is not guaranteed to prevent genericide, but it helps. A trademark symbol also puts competitors on notice that someone is claiming an exclusive right to use the mark. This can discourage them from using an identical or confusingly similar term in connection with the same, similar or related goods or services. This is very important in terms of preserving a mark's distinctiveness.

The owner of a registered mark continues to have an exclusive right to use the mark even if he fails to affix the ® symbol. Infringement of a registered mark to which the symbol has not been affixed is still unlawful. In some cases, though, the owner's remedies may be limited if he has not consistently used the ® symbol in connection with the mark.

CONTINUED USE OF THE MARK

Continued use is necessary both for the preservation of the trademark and for the preservation of a federal registration.

GENERICIDE PREVENTION

Exclusive trademark rights come to an end if the mark loses its distinctiveness as a source identifier. It is important, therefore, to be careful not to lose trademark protections through genericide. Here are some things that can be done to help prevent genericide.

Always use the mark as an adjective, not as a noun or verb.

Capitalize the mark, if possible.

Use the word "brand" (e.g., "Scotch brand tape," not "Scotch tape.")

Use the brand name in conjunction with the generic product name (e.g., "Kleenex tissue," not *"Kleenex.")*

Use the mark as a source identifier for several kinds of goods or services.

Display the mark consistently in the same format.

Position the trademark symbol next to the mark, not next to generic words.

Police other people's use of the mark (e.g., make sure licensees, distributors, retailers, franchisees, etc. are referring to the product correctly, in accordance with the above guidelines).

Failure to police trademark rights can be used against a trademark owner as evidence of abandonment of the mark. Actively policing a mark generates evidence of a lack of intention to abandon the mark.

Multinational Trademarks

The geographic scope of a trademark normally is limited to the boundaries of the country in which the mark is legally enforceable as a trademark. In some countries, this means that only marks that are registered in the country are enforceable there. In other countries, it means that only marks that have been used in commerce in the country are enforceable there. The use or registration of a mark in one country does not create any trademark rights in other countries. Registration, too, is only national in scope. For this reason, it is normally either necessary or recommended to file an application for registration in each country in which trademark rights are or may be sought to be enforced.

REGISTRATION OF FOREIGN MARKS IN THE UNITED STATES

If a trademark is registered in a foreign country, it may be registered in the United States on the basis of either use in commerce in the United States or foreign registration. A mark that is already registered in a foreign country may be registered in the United States even if it is not being used in the United States, provided the foreign registration is specified in the application as the filing basis. Like an intent-to-use application, the application must contain a statement of bona fide intent to use it. Unlike an intent-to-use application, U.S. registration of a mark registered in a foreign country may be issued before proof of use in the United States is furnished. If a foreign registrant fails to use the mark in the United States within a reasonable time after registration in the United States, however, the USPTO may cancel the registration on the basis of abandonment. A presumption of abandonment arises if the registrant fails to use the mark in the United States within three years after the registration in the United States. Abandonment may be found to have occurred sooner if there is evidence that the registrant has no intent to use the mark in the United States.

An application based on a foreign registration must include:

- ownership information
- statement of the filing basis
- the categories of goods or services on which the mark is being or is intended to be used
- declaration of a bona fide intention to use the mark in the United States
- declaration of no known superior claims
- copy of the foreign registration
- translation of the foreign registration, if it is not in English
- signature
- filing fee.

An application for registration of a foreign trademark is also known as a Section 66(a) registration, or a "registration for extension of protection." Section 66(a) is the provision of the Trademark Act[353] dealing with the extension of the protection afforded by an international trademark to the United States pursuant to a treaty called the Madrid Protocol.

INTERNATIONAL REGISTRATION

Unfortunately, three is not yet any system in place for the registration of a trademark that will be enforceable anywhere in the world. The Madrid Protocol makes it much easier to apply to register trademarks in multiple countries at one time, though. Pursuant to the Madrid Protocol, an applicant for a national registration may designate on the application any additional countries in which registration is desired, so long as those countries are members of the Madrid Protocol. This kind of registration is known as an *international registration*.

In the United States, this can all be done through the USPTO, thereby obviating the need to file separate applications with the trademark offices of each foreign country in which registration is desired. The USPTO takes care of forwarding the applications to the International Bureau of WIPO. The International Bureau then sends a request for extension of protection to each national office designated in the application.

Each individual country determines whether or not protection for a mark will be granted. The fact that registration has been granted in one country does not mean that another country must approve registration of the mark there. If the trademark office in a designated country does approves a request for extension of protection, though, then the mark is protected in that country to the same extent it would be if it had been registered in that country directly.

The European Union offers a Community trademark. A Community trademark extends protection for a mark to all countries that are members of the EU. An application for a Community trademark may be filed with the Office for Harmonization in the Internal Market. Alternatively, an applicant may apply for a Community trademark by using the Madrid Protocol. In this case, the applicant simply selects the EU as one of the territories in which registration is sought. When filing an application using the Madrid Protocol, the applicant may select registration with the EU as a Community trademark, registration with individual countries, or both.

Belgium, Luxembourg and the Netherlands have a common office for the registration of trademarks, the Benelux Office. Under the Madrid System, protection is requested as if they were a single country (Benelux).

A country may deny the use of its registration system for the registration of a trademark in another country even if both countries have acceded to the Madrid Protocol. For example, the United States may impose a trade embargo prohibiting trademark applicants in the United States from designating Iran on a Madrid Protocol application.

After an application designating one or more foreign countries is filed, additional countries may be designated later, with the filing fees for the additional countries being payable at that time.

Filing Fees

The filing fees for an application for international registration include a service fee to the receiving office and international fees which vary depending on the countries selected and other factors. The international fees must be paid at the time of filing. International fees are substantially higher than the filing fees for U.S. registration. A fee schedule and fee calculator are available at the WIPO website.

Maintaining International Registrations

The term of an international registration is ten years. It is renewable for ten-year terms. Additional filing fees are required for renewals. The term is measured from the date of the international registration, not the date of registration in a particular country. Renewal forms are available from the International Bureau and may be filed online through the WIPO Marks E-Renewal System.

The owner of an international registration must meet the maintenance requirements for the international registration as well as for each of the countries in which the mark is registered or to which the protection of registration has been extended. For a mark registered in a foreign country as to which the protection of an international registration has been extended to the United States, the owner not only must satisfy U.S. requirements for maintaining registrations (continuing use declarations and renewals), but also must satisfy the requirements for maintaining the international registration and the registrations in the other countries where the mark is registered.

Renewal of international registrations is governed by Article 7 of the Madrid Protocol and Rules 29–31 of the Common Regulations under the Madrid Agreement and Protocol. Renewal is through the International Bureau.

MULTINATIONAL TRADEMARK RIGHTS

Like patents, trademarks are territorially limited in scope. To establish and enforce trademark rights in a country, it is necessary to meet the requirements for a valid trademark in that country. In countries like the United States where trademarks come into existence through use in commerce, the commerce must occur domestically. Using a trademark in connection with the sale of goods or services in one country will not suffice to establish trademark rights in another country. Similarly, merely advertising goods for sale in a country will not suffice to establish trademark rights if the country's trademark laws require use in commerce, as United States laws do. "Use in commerce" means actually making a sale of a product or service using the trademark.

Because of the territoriality feature, using a foreign trademark in a country where trademark rights have not yet been established does not infringe the trademark. This is true even if the person using the mark has knowledge of the foreign trademark.

An exception to this rule exists for well-known marks that are used or registered in countries that are signatories to the Paris Convention or the TRIPS Agreement. The Paris Convention established this exception for trademarks in the same or similar goods. The TRIPS Agreement made the exception applicable to the use of trademarks in related goods, as well. It also extended the exception to include service marks.

When the exception for well-known trademarks applies in a particular country that is a signatory to the TRIPS Agreement, the rights of the owner of the well-known mark are superior to the rights of any other claimant, even if the owner of the well-known mark has not established trademark rights in that country and even if someone else has.

> **Example**. The Italian car manufacturer Furori Co. makes and sells a high performance automobile by the same name. Although sales are limited to Europe, the name is well-known in the United States due to media broadcasts of races, articles in automotive magazines, and so on. One day, Michigan-based Ford Motor Co. announces its latest model, the Furori. It sells a number of the cars in the United States and registers the name as a U.S. trademark. Because the United States is a signatory to the Paris Convention and the TRIPS Agreement, it must treat the Furori Co. trademark as superior to Ford Motor Company's rights. Accordingly, Furori Co may sue Ford Motor Co. in the United States for infringement even though Furori Co. has never used or registered its trademark in the United States.

A full discussion of the trademark laws of every country in the world is beyond the scope of this book. Efforts to harmonize global trademark laws are examined in Chapter 34.

Related Sources of Liability

Using another business's trademark or something confusingly similar to it may trigger liability under other laws, in addition to or instead of trademark infringement or dilution. Trademark law overlaps with false advertising and unfair competition laws. For more information on these topics, see Chapters 7 and 15.

Sometimes a name or symbol that does not qualify for trademark or copyright protection may nevertheless be protected by other law. For example, a clever name for a soup might not be protected by copyright law or as a trademark, but appropriating the idea for the name for a competing restaurant's soup might amount to unfair competition in some circumstances.

Chapter 29 Domain Names

Most e-commerce businesses will want to establish a company website. It is possible to engage in e-commerce without one, and many people do. Businesses that sell through Amazon, eBay and Etsy are examples. A business may find it advantageous to establish a web presence of its own, though, either instead of or in addition to using third party online marketplaces. A stand-alone, customizable website gives a business owner space and flexibility to provide more detailed information about products and services; enhanced ability to interact with existing and potential customers and to do things like develop customer lists and engage in email campaigns; and the potential to establish or improve the business's credibility and visibility. Moreover, if all or part of a business involves providing services, then online marketplaces for selling goods may be of little use. To operate a website, it is necessary to have a domain name.

Domain names represent an Internet Protocol (IP) resource, such as a server, a personal computer or a website. Their primary function is to give IP resources with numerical identifiers more easily recognizable, memorable names. They establish a unique identity on the Internet. If a business is fortunate enough to reserve it before anyone else does, a domain name that corresponds to the business's name and/or its trademark(s), products or services will have a significant competitive advantage because it will be easier for Internet users to find the company's products and services online. With over 300,000,000 websites online, that can be important.

The Domain Name System

A domain name is a component of the Uniform Resource Locator (URL) for a web page. To make navigation on the Internet possible, every page on the Web has a unique URL. Here is an example of a URL:

https://www.abcdef.com:443

'https' stands for Hyper Text Transfer Protocol Secure. It is the protocol identifier. Other common protocols are 'http://' (Hyper Text Transfer Protocol); 'ftp://' (File Transfer Protocol); and 'smtp://' (Simple Mail Transfer Protocol). The protocol identifier is not part of a domain name. ':443' in the example is the port number. By default, http uses port 80 and https uses port 443. If a website administrator accepts the default, then there is no need to include the port number in the website's address. The port number is not part of the domain name, either. 'www' stands for World Wide Web. It is a subdomain of the part to the right, signifying that it is the public part of the website (as distinguished from 'ftp,' for example, which might contain files accessible only to the website administrator). The parts that are delimited by dots to the right of it comprise the domain name. In the example, 'abcdef.com' is the domain name.

The hierarchy of domains descends from right to left. The rightmost part identifies the top-level domain (TLD). Each part to the left specifies a subdomain of the part to the right. 'abcdef' is a subdomain of the '.com' domain.' A string of characters appearing to the right of a TLD is called the *post-domain path*. Beginning with a slash mark, this string denotes a location within a website. It is not part of the domain name. In www.abcdef.com/privacypolicy/, the expression, '/privacypolicy/' is a post-domain path. It is not part of the domain name.

All domain names have both a TLD and at least one subdomain, or "second-level" domain name (such as 'abcdef.' in 'www.abcdef.com.') Some have third-level domain names, too. The most widely used TLDs are .com (for commercial enterprises), .org (intended for nonprofits but for-profits are using it, too), .gov (government); .edu (education), .net (network resource). These are called generic TLDs (gTLDs) because they are not specific to any country. There are also country-code TLDs (ccTLDs). Examples: .us (United States); .uk (United Kingdom); .fr (France). The regional TLD .eu denotes the EU. There are a number of other less commonly used TLDs, as well, such as .biz and .blog. A complete list is published at the website of the Internet Assigned Numbers Authority, https://www.iana.org.

While it is possible to create and register new TLDs, doing so requires the payment of thousands of dollars for an evaluation fee. For this reason, most businesses focus on creating and registering unique second-level domain names, not TLDs.

The combination of the second-level domain and the TLD is the part of a domain name that is registrable. In our example, 'abcdef.com' is the part that is registrable.

Registration

The Internet Corporation for Assigned Names and Numbers (ICANN) oversees the name and number systems of the Internet. ICANN accredits domain name registrars, which receive and process applications to register domain names. When a registrar approves an application, it forwards the registration to the appropriate registry. Sometimes called a "network information center," a registry is a company that maintains the database of registered names for a particular TLD. Some registries are also registrars. The registry publishes registrant information using the WHOIS service. Domain name registrant information is accessible to the public using the WHOIS protocol. Domain name registrations, registrars and nameservers may be searched at www.internic.net/whois.html. Domain name searches may be conducted at www.whois.com.

To be registrable, the TLD and second-level domain name combination must be unique, i.e., not already registered. It is only the combination that must be unique, however. The same second-level domain name that has already been registered with one TLD may also be registered with a different TLD. Many domain name registrars have automated database search features that will tell an applicant whether the name sought to be registered is available or not.

Domain names must comply with ICANN naming conventions. They must be formed solely from alphanumeric ASCII characters ('a' to 'z' and '0' to '9'), except that a hyphen is permitted. Hyphens, however, cannot appear at the beginning or end of the domain name. No other special characters, or spaces, are permitted. Domain names must contain between three and sixty-three characters.

Characters are case-insensitive. Thus, if ABC.com has already been registered, then a subsequent attempt to register abc.com would fail because it would not be unique.

Because characters are case-insensitive, care should be taken to avoid confusion. For example, if a therapist locater service were to register the name TherapistFinder.com, the URL will appear as therapistfinder.com. This might convey something different about the kind of professional to whom a site user will be referred than what is intended.

The registered holder of a domain name can create any number of subdomains (third-level domains). For example, the registrant of echionbooks.com could create areas of the website such as blog.echionbooks.com or mail.echionbooks.com. The registrant can also create additional pages with their own URL's that build on the registered domain, such as echionbooks.com/about. Neither subdomains nor individual pages in a website are registrable. Only the combination of a second-level domain with a TLD is registrable.

Transfers of domain names are effected through the domain name registrar.

TRADEMARKS IN DOMAIN NAMES

A domain name may or may not be a trademark. Registration of a domain name does not operate as a registration of a trademark. Registration of a trademark does not operate as a reservation of a domain name. A company seeking to reserve the right to use a particular domain name must register it with a domain name registrar. A company seeking to protect the right to use a particular trademark should register it with the appropriate trademark office.

Because trademarks are geographically limited, the same mark may be owned by different people in different geographic territories. Also, two companies dealing in unrelated goods or services may own the same mark without either being liable for infringement. Infringement only occurs if confusion about the source, sponsorship or endorsement of a product or service is likely. For these reasons, using another person's trademark in a domain name may or may not be trademark infringement. If the use of the domain name is likely to cause consumers to become confused about the source, sponsorship or endorsement of the goods or services offered on the site, then it may be infringement. Otherwise, it is not.

> **Example.** Volkswagen owns the letter combination VW as a trademark for automobiles. Virtual Works, which is not in the automobile business, registers the domain name, vw.net, for its online business transactions. Virtual Works has not infringed the Volkswagen trademark because consumers are not likely to confuse Virtual Works' products and services with automobiles.

On the other hand, using another company's trademark – or something confusingly similar to it—in a domain name as a means of increasing visitors to a website is a form of trademark infringement because it creates initial interest confusion among Internet users. Using trademarks for this purpose is not fair use. It may also result in liability for false advertising.

According to some courts, simply registering a domain name that is confusingly similar to a preexisting trademark and using it to divert consumers from the mark's owner may suffice as "use in connection with goods or services" for purposes of trademark law. Other courts require, in addition, a showing that advertisements for goods or services, or links to commercial websites appear on the website. Most courts agree, however, that a website that is purely a "gripe site" about the company whose name is used in the domain name is protected by the Fair Use doctrine, at least if it is not operated by a competitor and it contains no advertising or links to commercial sites.

Use of a famous or well-known mark as a domain name could potentially subject the domain name owner to liability for dilution, if use of the domain name blurs or tarnishes the mark. Merely using a famous mark in a domain name, however, is not dilution unless the trademark owner can prove that the use blurs or tarnishes the mark.

Using a trademark in a post-domain path is not likely to amount to infringement. The post-domain path is simply a way of organizing pages within a website; it does not indicate a website's source of origin. Consequently, "it is unlikely that the presence of another's trademark in a post-domain path of a URL would ever violate trademark law."[354] Using a trademark as a keyword in keyed advertising that links to the post-domain path, on the other hand, might infringe the trademark owner's rights if doing so creates initial interest confusion. In that case, though, the source of the confusion would be the use of the trademark in a meta tag, not merely its use in a post-domain path.

For more information about trademark law, see Chapter 28.

CYBERSQUATTING

Registering a domain name gives the registrant an exclusive right to use it. Registration is on a first come, first served basis. Knowing this, some enterprising individuals register domain names that they believe someone else will want, then exact fees to relinquish them. This practice is called **cybersquatting.**

The practice can be unfair to trademark owners seeking to establish a website using their trademark as the domain name. A business might take great pains and go to considerable expense protecting its exclusive right to use a particular name and then find itself essentially being extorted for the right to use it. It can also be unfair to a person who wants to establish a website using his own personal names as the domain name, and finds himself being asked to pay a price to do so, by a person who has no interest in the name other than to sell it to a person with that name. Congress enacted the Anticybersquatting Consumer Protection Act[355] (ACPA) to address these problems.

The ACPA prohibits the registration or use of a trademark or trademark-related domain name with bad faith intent to profit from it, and provides a civil cause of action for violations.

To prevail on an ACPA complaint, two things must be proven:

(a) The domain name is identical or confusingly similar to, or dilutive of, the complainant's trademark or is the complainant's personal name;
(b) The domain name was registered or used in bad faith to make a profit at the complainant's expense.

The owner of a mark or personal name need not have registered it with the USPTO or a domain name registrar in order to invoke the protections of the ACPA.

The ACPA has retroactive effect. It applies to all domain names, whenever registered.

A victim of cybersquatting may commence a proceeding against the cybersquatter personally or may initiate an in rem court proceeding. An in rem proceeding is a lawsuit against property rather than a person. It requests a court to issue an order of some kind concerning the property, such as an order declaring that it rightfully belongs to the party initiating the proceeding. It is useful when the identity of the cybersquatter cannot be ascertained, or when the cybersquatter is so situated as to make a court's acquisition of personal jurisdiction problematic, such as where the cybersquatter resides in a foreign country.

The remedies available for a violation of the ACPA are damages; injunction; and attorney fees. The sole remedy that is available with respect to domain names that were registered before November, 1999 is an injunction prohibiting the cybersquatter from using the mark and either cancelling or requiring transfer of the domain name registration. For names that were registered after November 1999, the victim may, in addition, recover damages, profits, and attorney fees. The victim may elect either actual damages or statutory damages. Statutory damages range from $1,000 to $100,000 per domain name. As an alternative to litigation, a person aggrieved by a cybersquatter may commence a UDRP arbitration proceeding. (See Chapter 35.)

Factors relevant to bad faith intent include:

(a) whether the defendant had any intellectual property rights in the domain name at the time of registration
(b) whether the domain name is the defendant's legal name
(c) whether the defendant used the name in connection with a bona fide offering of goods or services before the registration
(d) whether commercial use was made of it
(e) intent to confuse, mislead and divert users into accessing his website, to the detriment of the trademark owner
(f) intent to profit
(g) false representations in connection with the application for registration
(h) acquisition of other domain names that are identical or confusingly similar to other people's trademarks or names
(i) distinctiveness and fame of the mark.

None of these factors, standing alone, is usually determinative. Instead, courts usually consider all of them.

Circumstances that may result in a finding of bad faith include, but are not limited to:

(a) registration by a competitor (especially if the domain name is simply "parked" thereafter, since this suggests that registration was effected with no intent other than to prevent the trademark owner from using the mark as a domain name)
(b) registration of a competitor's trademark
(c) registration with intent to create initial interest confusion with another's trademark
(d) registration with the intent of later selling it to the trademark owner for a profit
(e) offering to sell a registered domain name without ever having used it
(f) past practice of selling domain names without having legitimately used them
(g) false contact information in an application for a domain name
(h) registration of multiple domain names all of which are similar to existing trademarks
(i) registration of a famous or strong mark.

Some courts consider the failure to investigate the status of a trademark before registering it as a domain name probative of bad faith. Others do not.

Indicia of good faith include such things as:

(a) The alleged cybersquatter has trademark rights in the registered name;
(b) The mark is the alleged cybersquatter's personal name;
(c) The alleged cybersquatter has previously used the name in legitimate business activities;
(d) Noncommercial trademark fair use doctrine applies;
(e) The mark is not strong;
(f) The mark is not famous.

The fact that the alleged cybersquatter had a reasonable belief that use of the domain name was fair use or lawful for some other reason is a defense.

In *People for the Ethical Treatment of Animals v. Doughney*,[356] it was held that setting up a parody site using a famous trademark belonging to another person for the domain name may be a violation of the ACPA. Doughney had set up a website called "People Eating Tasty Animals" and registered and used the domain name PETA.org for the site. People for the Ethical Treatment of Animals (PETA) sued under the ACPA. The court analyzed the above factors to find that Doughney had bad faith intent. Although the website was a parody (and therefore arguably fair use), registering and using the mark as a domain name was not a parody. The domain name and URL could be displayed in a user's search engine results without any indication that it is a parody, misleading the user seeking the PETA organization's website into visiting a different website instead. In short, courts are not likely to deem the registration or use of another person's trademark in a domain name to be fair use of the mark.

A fair use defense will be stronger if the domain name contains some clue that it is a parody or a gripe site. A reasonable consumer is not likely to think www.WalMartSucks.com is Wal-Mart's official site. An ACPA violation may be found even in these cases, however, if the website contains no disclaimer of affiliation and the owner of the domain name has a profit motive for using the name, such as where she seeks or accepts payment from the trademark owner to discontinue use of the domain name or to stop using it to for criticism or parody.

Cybersquatting a famous trademark may also be actionable as trademark dilution under the Lanham Act.[357] The elements of a trademark dilution cause of action are not the same as for an ACPA claim. The available defenses and remedies are not the same, either.

Typosquatting

Typosquatting is a kind of cybersquatting in which the squatter registers a domain name that is similar to someone else's trademark but with a typographical error in it. This might be done for a variety of reasons. Knowing that people often make typographical errors, it could be a way of attracting bad spellers and inattentive typists to a competitor's website. Alternatively, it could be a way of getting people to click on a link to a completely unrelated site, such as an advertising site or a site loaded with pay-per-click pop-ups, for example.

For ACPA purposes, the analysis of typosquatting is not really any different from that for cybersquatting. Depending on the content to which the domain name is linked, typosquatting can also implicate other laws, such as the Truth In Domain Names Act, and may be an unfair and deceptive trade practice under the FTC Act.

Personal Names

Personal names may be registered as domain names. Bad faith registration of a living person's personal name as a domain name, however, is prohibited by federal law.[358]

The elements of a claim of bad faith registration of a personal name are:

(a) Domain name registration of a personal name;
(b) The name is identical or confusingly similar to the name of another living person;
(c) Consent has not been given;
(d) Specific intent to profit financially.

An exception exists for copyright owners. A copyright owner may register a personal name as a domain name if it is connected with the work in which the copyright is owned. For example, a rightful assignee of the copyright in a literary work may use the author's name as a domain name.

The only remedies for violation of this statute are an injunction, attorney fees and costs. Damages may not be recovered.

Post-Domain Paths

A domain name is "any alphanumeric designation which is registered with or assigned by any domain name registrar, domain name registry, or other domain name registration authority as part of an electronic address on the Internet."[359] Since registration authorities normally only offer registration for the combination of a second-level domain with a TLD, post-domain paths normally are not registered. Accordingly, the ACPA does not appear to provide a remedy for the use of another person's name or trademark in a post-domain path.

The definition does not specifically limit the term to TLDs and second-level domains, however. Names registered with a domain name registrar are specifically included, but the statute also contemplates other kinds of "domain name registration authority." It could be argued that a website that allows users to claim third-level names and/or post-domain paths (such as www.twitter.com/TonyLaRussa) is a "domain name registration authority." If so, then services like Facebook and Twitter might be considered domain name registration authorities, and therefore within the coverage of the ACPA.

Reverse Domain Name Hijacking

A domain name registrant may recover damages against a person who makes a false or groundless claim of cybersquatting that causes a domain name registrar to cancel or transfer a domain name. To prevail on the claim, the registrant (or former registrant) must prove the alleged reverse domain name hijacker knowingly made a material misstatement or misrepresentation of fact in connection with an allegation of cybersquatting that caused the registrar to cancel or transfer the domain name. Remedies include damages and injunctive relief. Injunctive relief may include an order to the registrar to reactivate the domain name or, if the domain name has been transferred, an order to transfer the domain name back to the registrant.

Conversion of a Domain Name

Some states, such as California, provide a state law cause of action for conversion of a domain name. A person who wrongfully persuades a domain name registrar to transfer someone else's domain name to him, and then refuses to transfer it to the rightful owner after demand is made, may be liable for conversion of the domain name under this kind of law. The ACPA does not preempt state law.

UDRP

In lieu of suing under the ACPA, a victim of cybersquatting may instead initiate an arbitration using the Uniform Domain Name Dispute Resolution Policy (UDRP) system. A UDRP proceeding is quicker and less expensive than an ACPA lawsuit, but damages may not be recovered. Only an order for cancellation or transfer of a domain name registration may be issued. For more information, see Chapter 35.

Registrar Immunity

No domain name registrar may be held liable to a trademark owner or a domain name registrant for refusing to register a domain name or for cancelling a domain name pursuant to a court or UDRP order. A domain name registrar is also immune from liability for trademark infringement or contributory trademark infringement for registering a domain name unless the registrar acted with bad faith intent to profit from it. Injunctive relief may be obtained against a domain name registrar, though.

FALSE INFORMATION IN A DOMAIN NAME REGISTRATION

Under the CAN-SPAM Act, it is a crime to use false information to register for multiple email accounts or domain names.

Misleading Domain Names

Under the Truth in Domain Names Act[360] (part of the PROTECT Act), it is a crime to knowingly use a domain name to mislead a person into visiting a website containing obscene content or to mislead a minor into visiting a website containing harmful material. For more information about what constitutes "harmful material," see Chapter 19.

Chapter 30. Patents

A patent is a grant of an exclusive right to market an invention for a defined period of time. Unlike trademarks, which arise from use, a patent does not come into existence unless and until a governmental body issues one. It is a kind of property and may be transferred or licensed to others In the United States, the federal government has exclusive jurisdiction to issue and regulate patents. The U.S. Patent Office is the issuing agency, and it also develops and implements regulations and examination manuals for the processing of applications. The issuance of a patent gives rise to a rebuttable presumption that the patent is valid and enforceable.

In the United States, there are three principal kinds of patents:

Utility
Design
Plant.[361]

Eligibility for Patent Protection

The five essential requirements for every patent are:

- Protectable subject matter
- Novelty
- Nonobviousness
- Usefulness
- Enablement.

PROTECTABLE SUBJECT MATTER

Both deliberate creations and accidental discoveries are patentable.[362] They must come within the definition of an invention, though, that is, a "useful process, machine, manufacture, or composition of matter, or any new and useful improvement thereof."[363] In all cases, some element of human ingenuity or experimentation is required.

The following kinds of subject matter are not patentable:

- Natural laws
- Naturally occurring phenomena
- Abstract ideas (such as a principle of mathematics)
- Expressive elements of an invention.

Computer programs are sometimes patentable. An algorithm for the performance of mathematical operations only is an abstract idea, and therefore not patentable.[364] An application of a mathematical operation to something nonmathematical, however, might be. An algorithm that performs mathematical operations in the course of transforming something into a different state may be patentable as a process. If an algorithm contains, as one of its steps, the performance of a mathematical operation, the steps in the process may be patented even though the mathematical equation itself cannot be. Thus, a patent may be granted for the use of a particular mathematical equation in conjunction with a specified process (series of steps), but anyone may use the mathematical equation in other ways without infringing the process patent.[365]

A computer program might be patentable as a method if it applies mathematical operations to produce a useful, concrete and tangible result.

With the exception of design patents, the expressive elements of an invention are not protected by patent law. To the extent expression is merged with an idea, the idea is protected, if at all, only by patent law, not copyright law.

NOVELTY

To be patentable, an invention must be something new, that is to say, unique and original. In the United States, this means (a) the invention must not already be in public use, and (b) the applicant must be the first in time to create the invention. In other words, patent rights do not depend on who wins a race to the filing office. It is the date of creation, not the date of filing, that matters.

U.S. law differs substantially from the laws of other countries in this respect. In other countries, the first to file, not the first to create, gets the patent.

To receive a U.S. patent, an invention must not be known or used by others in the United States, or patented or described in a printed publication in any country, at the time the applicant created it. A use in the United States by a person who concealed, suppressed or abandoned the technology does not count, however. As between an inventor who conceals, suppresses or abandons the invention and a later creator of the same invention, the later inventor will get the patent.

Merely maintaining the invention as a trade secret does not necessarily amount to "concealing, suppressing or abandoning" the invention, where the inventor actively exploits the invention commercially.[366] On the other hand, an inventor who makes a secret, commercial use of an invention for more than one year before filing a patent application in the United States forfeits the right to a patent.

NONOBVIOUSNESS

Patents may be granted for inventions that improve or enhance the performance of an existing invention. A patent will not be granted for relatively minor modifications of existing inventions that would be obvious to a person having ordinary skills in the relevant field, however.

In determining nonobviousness, courts must consider three factors:

- Scope and content of the previous art
- Differences between the prior art and the claim at issue
- The meaning of "ordinary skill" in the pertinent art.

(*Art,* as used here, refers to preexisting inventions in the relevant industry.)

In assessing whether the invention would be obvious to someone with ordinary skill in the art, the knowledge possessed by a typical scientist or engineer working within the relevant area is what must be considered.

A principal purpose of the nonobviousness requirement is to ensure that people working in the field are permitted to make routine changes or improvements to existing inventions—such as unrevolutionary substitution of materials, ordinary streamlining of processes, and such—without needing to worry about possible patent infringement liability.

Prior art that is owned by the same entity that owns the new invention at the time the new invention is created is not considered in the nonobviousness analysis. The same rule applies whether the entity owns the prior art or new invention outright or merely has a right to have it assigned to the entity.

ENABLEMENT

A patent will not be granted unless the application describes the invention in sufficient detail to enable a person to actually practice it. If the invention is a machine, then it must be possible for a person to actually build the machine using the description provided in the application. If the invention is a method, then there must be sufficient detail to enable a person to actually use the method.

Utility Patents

About 90% of patents are utility patents. There are four kinds:

- machines
- human-made products
- compositions of matter
- processes.

Method patents, including business method patents, are a kind of process patent.

In addition to the requirements of novelty, originality and nonobviousness, an invention must be shown to serve a useful purpose in order for a utility patent to be issued. This does not mean that it must be an improvement over existing art or even commercially feasible. It simply means that it must be operative and serve something other than a purely ornamental purpose.

At one time, patents for inventions could be denied if the invention could be used in immoral activity, such as gambling. Today, any invention may be patented so long as it has at least one lawful use. The same is true of inventions that facilitate deceptive trade practices. The USPTO and courts are inclined to leave the enforcement of nonpatent laws to other agencies. Still, an invention that has only one use cannot be patented if that use is illegal.

BUSINESS METHODS

Historically, courts held that business methods are not patentable. This is still the rule in many countries, but it is no longer true in the United States. In 1998 the Federal Circuit Court of Appeals held, in *State Street Bank & Trust v. Signature Financial Group,*[367] that business methods are indeed capable of being patented in the United States, provided they meet all of the eligibility requirements (novelty, etc.). In *Bilski v. Kappos*[368] the U.S. Supreme Court affirmed that business methods are not categorically excluded from patentability.

Of course, as with any process patent, a business method is patentable only if it produces a concrete, tangible result.[369] The "tangible result" can include matter or energy, such as electrical signals. For a number of years, courts interpreted this to mean that it must be tied to a machine or the transformation of an article. *Bilski* clarified that is just one way of assessing whether a business method is patentable or not; it is not the only possible way. Specifically, the Court held that a process does not necessarily have to be tied to a machine or the transformation of an article in order to be eligible for a patent.

On the other hand, if a process invention is not tied to a machine or the transformation of an article, it runs the risk of being an unpatentable abstract idea. In *Bilski*, the Court ruled that the claimed invention really just amounted to using mathematical formulae to apply the concept of hedging against the financial risk of price fluctuations to energy markets. As such, it was an abstract idea. Hence, it was not patentable.

The Supreme Court returned to the problem of business method patents again in 2014. In *Alice Corporation v. CLS Bank International*[370] the Court considered the patentability of a method for mitigating settlement risk, i.e., the risk that only one party to an agreed-upon financial exchange will satisfy its obligation. The claim for which patent protection had been granted was the method consisting of the use of a computer that is configured to carry out an exchange of financial obligations between two parties. In other words, it consisted of the idea of using a computer to implement an escrow service. The Court held that because the claims were drawn to an abstract idea—namely, the idea of intermediated settlement—they did not qualify for patent protection. Further, merely requiring generic computer implementation does not transform an abstract idea into a patentable invention.

In reaching its decision, the Court explained that business method patentability requires a two-step analysis:

(1) Does it involve an abstract idea?
(2) If so, does it add something inventive to it, i.e., some "new and useful end"?

The fact that it involves an abstract idea does not necessarily rule out patentability. *Bilski* indicates the "new and useful end" cannot itself be an abstract idea, such as a mathematical formula, or the idea of applying a mathematical formula to the idea. Under *Alice*, an implementation of the idea that is generic, conventional or obvious will not qualify as a "new and useful end," either. The Court deemed the ordinary and customary use of a general purpose digital computer to be a "generic" implementation. A business method claim consisting of the use of a computer "to apply" an abstract idea is not patentable.

Many people have interpreted *Alice* as the death knell of business method patents. Some go further, believing it have put an end to software patents in general.

SOFTWARE PATENTS

Computer programs, to the extent they are patentable and used in e-commerce, are usually utility patents of the business method variety, although that is not necessarily the case.

Algorithms and mathematical formulae are not patentable per se. An invention is not unpatentable merely because it contains an algorithm, though. Patents have been granted for thousands of Internet-related software patents. Search engines, digital file formats, audio software, hyperlinking methods, and e-commerce shopping carts are examples. Processes and methods performed by computer games may also be patented.

A process synthesizing computer software or code with business methodologies or techniques may be patentable as a business method patent. Most e-commerce business method patents relate to financial transaction data processing. Patents have also been granted for processes relating to online purchasing, advertising and marketing

Following the decisions in *Bilski* and *Alice*, efforts to enforce patents on online business method patents are not as likely to succeed as they once were. In addition to the "abstract idea" problem, the novelty and nonobviousness requirements can sometimes present obstacles. In one important case, Soverain Software attempted to enforce patents it had obtained on online shopping cart programs. One of the companies it sued, Newegg, Inc., presented evidence of CompuServe's use of very similar shopping cart technology before Soverain secured its patents. This helped demonstrate that Soverain's shopping cart patents did not satisfy the nonobviousness requirement for patentability.[371] In addition, some business method patents have expired. The patent on Amazon.com's one-click shopping cart method, which allows customers to order online using predefined credit card and shipping address information fields rather than having to reenter this information each time, expired in 2017.

Design Patents

Design patents are granted for the protection of nonutilitarian aspects of the design of an article of manufacture. They must meet the requirements of novelty, originality, and nonobviousness. In addition, the design must be embodied in an article of manufacture and it must be ornamental. A design that serves a useful function cannot be patented. New computer-generated icons and fonts are examples of designs that could qualify for design patent protection.

Plant Patents

A plant patent is for the protection of inventions or discoveries of new, asexually reproduced plant varieties other than tubers.

The Application Process

A patent application is normally to be filed by the inventor. Unlike copyrights, where a work created by an employee for an employer is a work made for hire as to which the employer is deemed the author, an employee who creates an invention in the course of the employment normally continues to be considered the inventor despite the existence of the employment relationship. An employer acquires rights in an employee's invention only if the employer either instructed the employee to create the specific invention in question or has entered into an assignment agreement with the employee. An e-commerce business that wishes to claim patent rights in an employee's invention to the exclusion of the employee's right to claim patent rights should include an invention assignment clause in the employment agreement. Agreements that all of an employee's legal rights for any invention created or discovered in the course of employment are automatically assigned to the employer generally are enforceable.

Even if the inventor has assigned away rights, however, the actual inventor must still be joined in the patent application.

PRELIMINARY STEPS

An inventor should make a written record of his work in the course of creating or discovering the invention. This includes an inventor's log, notebooks, sketches, photographs, source code drafts, and so on—with dated entries. Dated entries are important because they may be used to prove that the inventor was the first in time to create or discover the invention. They can also be useful in cases where "unreasonable delay" is an issue.

Before applying for a patent, it is recommended that a potential applicant perform a patent search. Doing so may reveal prior art demonstrating that the invention is not novel or nonobvious enough to be patentable. Since obtaining a patent can cost thousands of dollars, this can save a prospective applicant a great deal of money. A patent search is also useful because it will be necessary to compare and contrast the invention with prior art as part of the application and examination process.

In most cases, an inventor should engage the services of a patent attorney. Unfortunately, their rates are high relative to other kinds of attorneys, but filing and prosecuting a patent application successfully requires specialized knowledge not only of the applicable field of technology but also of patent law and examining procedures.

PROVISIONAL PATENTS

A provisional patent is a temporary patent that may be issued while an application for a patent is pending. If a patent is granted, then damages may be recovered for infringement occurring between the time the U.S. Patent Office published the application and the time the patent was issued.[372]

REGULAR APPLICATION AND EXAMINATION

Unlike other kinds of intellectual property, a patent comes into being only by means of a grant from a government. The application must provide, along with other information, a description (called a "specification") of the invention that is sufficiently detailed to enable any person skilled in the art to make and use it. The specification must also explain how the invention differs from existing ones similar to it. The application must also include a "claims" section describing the aspects of the invention for which a claim of patent protection is being made. The application must be accompanied by a drawing of the invention, which can include a flow chart, schematic diagram or other methods of exemplifying the process or method sought to be patented. The application must disclose any known and relevant prior art, and must also include an oath or declaration that the applicant is the first inventor of the invention. A nonrefundable filing fee must be paid.

The application will be assigned to a patent examiner, who will search prior art to determine the novelty and nonobviousness of the invention. If the examiner determines it is patentable, a patent will be granted and another fee must be paid. If the examiner denies a patent, the applicant may either resubmit the application with changes that the applicant believes will make the invention patentable, or appeal the decision to the USPTO's Board of Appeals. Further appeal is to the federal court.

A patent application may be denied if the applicant intentionally misrepresents a material fact or fails to disclose known relevant prior art to the USPTO.

The application and examination process is called *prosecution* of the patent. Patent prosecutions take varying amounts of time, but average about eighteen months.

AMERICAN INVENTORS PROTECTION ACT

The American Inventors Protection Act[373] (AIPA) gives the USPTO power to regulate invention promoters, i.e., those who charge inventors money to secure patents for them. The AIPA establishes a "bill of rights" for inventors, and imposes fines and penalties on invention promoters who violate those rights. It also establishes a timeline for patent review, and enhances the ability of patent applicants to challenge administrative denials of their applications.

Term and Maintenance of Patents

The term of utility and plant patents is twenty years from the date the application was filed. The term of a design patent is fourteen years. The term of a utility or plant patent for which the application was filed before June 8, 1995 is twenty years from the date the application was filed or seventeen years from the date the patent was issued, whichever is greater.

After a patent has been in force for a period of time, additional fees must be paid in order to keep it in force.

Infringement

A patent gives the owner of the patent the exclusive right to exploit the invention within the jurisdiction that issued it. Infringement occurs when a person (or business) makes, uses, sells, offers to sell, or imports a patented invention without authority to do so. Neither knowledge nor intent to infringe need be proven in order to prevail on a patent infringement claim. People have a duty to investigate to determine whether an invention is patented before exploiting it

There are two kinds of patent infringement: literal and equivalence. *Literal infringement* occurs when someone makes an unauthorized use of the exact same patented invention. Literal infringement occurs if all elements of a patented claim are used, even if the infringer adds some new elements to it. It does not occur, however, if the alleged infringer omits one or more of the elements. *Equivalence infringement* occurs when, although not all elements of the patented invention are used, substantial equivalents of those elements are used. If an invention performs substantially the same function in substantially the same way as a patented invention, it may be found to be an infringement under the doctrine of equivalents.

A patent owner is not allowed the benefit of the doctrine of equivalents with respect to any element she was obliged to drop from her claim in order to get the USPTO to grant the patent. This principle is known as *file wrapper estoppel.*

Since the patentable claim in a computer software program involves some original process or method, infringement does not occur unless someone actually implements or sells that process or method. If a company deploys someone else's payment processing software on its website, and a patent has been issued for the method or process embodied in it, and that patent is still active, then the company might be liable for patent infringement. If the company instead simply reproduces a copy of the source code on its website, but does not exploit it commercially, then there may possibly be liability for copyright infringement but not for patent infringement.

Selling embodiments of another person's patented software program or selling access to it may result in liability for patent infringement if the seller does not have permission from the patent owner to do so. Lack of knowledge of the existence of a patent is not a defense. Copying or distributing a computer program may result in liability for patent infringement, copyright infringement, or both.

Because patents are territorial, acts occurring in countries where an invention is not patented are not infringement. In the case of a process patent, however, products may not be sold or used or imported into the United States if the patented process was used to make the products in a foreign country, even if the process is only patented in the United States. The Process Patent Amendments Act[374] provides for a number of exceptions and limits the available remedies in such cases, however.

Importing infringing goods into the United States is an act of infringement. Exporting infringing goods is not. Making infringing goods or conducting sales of them in the United States will qualify as infringement, though, even if the goods are made and sold for export. Exporting the components of an infringing product for manufacture abroad may result in indirect infringement liability.

DIRECT AND INDIRECT INFRINGEMENT

Infringement may be direct or indirect. A person incurs direct liability by personally performing the infringing act. *Indirect* liability refers to situations in which a person may be held liable for someone else's infringing act.

Indirect liability may arise either by: (a) actively inducing (aiding and abetting) another person's infringement, or (b) contributing to the infringement by selling:

> a component of a patented machine, manufacture, combination or composition, or a material or apparatus for use in practicing a patented process, constituting a material part of the invention, knowing the same to be especially made or especially adapted for use in an infringement of such patent, and not a staple article or commodity of commerce suitable for substantial non-infringing use....[375]

Designing an infringing device which another person then manufactures is an example of "active inducement." Supplying a device or part that could be put to both infringing and non-infringing uses may also constitute active inducement, if the supplier promotes, through advertising or otherwise, the infringing use. Repairing or maintaining another person's infringing product may also suffice, since these activities enable the infringer to continue the infringement.

Liability for active inducement may be imposed only if two conditions are satisfied: (a) the person knew the invention was patented, and (b) the person intended for someone to make an unauthorized use, manufacture or sale of it.

Selling access codes, keys, passwords or other things that allow unauthorized persons to use and/or copy patented software is an example of an activity that might result in liability for contributory patent infringement.

Contributory liability will not attach unless: (a) the person knows the invention is patented, and (b) the person knows that use of the supplied component will constitute infringement.

REMEDIES

Both injunctive relief and monetary damages are available remedies for patent infringement.

Injunctive relief may include both a preliminary injunction and a permanent injunction. A permanent injunction is not literally permanent. It lasts for the duration of the patent term. To qualify for a permanent injunction, the patentee must establish four things, in addition to patent ownership:

(a) The patentee has suffered irreparable injury due to the infringement;
(b) Money damages ("the remedy at law") are not adequate;
(c) The balance of hardships favors the patentee;
(d) The public interest would not be harmed by the issuance of an injunction.

Recoverable elements of compensatory damage include lost profits and reasonable royalties on sales made by the infringer during the six-year period preceding the lawsuit, with prejudgment interest. The infringer may also be required to compensate the patentee for price erosion occurring due to the decreased profits earned by the patentee because of the profits made on the infringer's sales.

Compensatory damages must be in an amount that is not less than a reasonable royalty, with interest. A patentee who is not able to prove lost profits may recover a reasonable royalty instead.

In exceptional cases of willful infringement, treble damages may be awarded.

The prevailing party may sometimes recover attorney fees, at least if the infringement was willful or if the other party engaged in inequitable conduct or bad faith litigation.

Notice

A person may be ordered to pay damages only for infringing acts that occur after the infringer has either actual or constructive notice of the patent.

Actual notice occurs when the infringer is actually informed of the existence of the patent. It can be effected only by either affirmatively communicating notice of infringement of the patent to the alleged infringer or commencing an infringement lawsuit. An infringer's acquisition of knowledge of the patent through other means does not suffice as actual notice.

Constructive notice is given by placing certain kinds of markings on products that embody a patented invention. The markings should be the words *patented, patent,* or *pat.* followed by the patent number(s) or the URL of a website at which the patented article is associated to one or more patent numbers. The marking must be placed on the product itself, if at all possible. It may be placed on the packaging instead only if it cannot be put on the product for some legitimate reason. In the case of computer programs, it should be placed on any tangible medium on which the program is stored and distributed to users. If a website embodies the software, or provides access to a program or downloadable software covered by the patent, the website should be marked.

Using the words *patent pending* does not have any legal effect. It will not entitle a patentee to damages incurred prior to the issuance of the patent. Since it merely means that a patent has been applied for (not necessarily granted), it should not suffice as constructive notice of the existence of a patent, either.

DEFENSES

Invalidity

Unpatentability is a defense to a patent infringement claim. Any fact or circumstance causing the patent to be invalid is a defense. Grounds for invalidating a patent could include, for example, proof that the invention is not novel or nonobvious, or proof that the patentee failed to meet a deadline or pay a required filing fee.

Derivation

A valid patent may only be issued to the inventor. A person who derives (copies) his invention from someone else cannot be issued a valid patent.

Abandonment

Abandonment of the right to seek a patent prior to the application may also invalidate a patent. This may occur where an inventor unequivocally relinquishes the invention to the public domain, such as by publicly announcing that he will not be seeking a patent for it. Abandonment may also occur during the patent process, such as where the applicant fails to pay a necessary fee or to comply with some other requirement. Of course, in the case of this second kind of abandonment, a patent would not issue, so the better defense to an infringement claim in this situation would be that no patent even exists.

First Inventor of a Business Method

Under the First Inventor Defense Act,[376] the fact that the defendant invented a method of doing business before the plaintiff patented it is a defense to a claim of patent infringement, provided the defendant reduced it to practice at least one year before the filing date of the patent and made commercial use of it in the United States before the filing date.

In other countries, the "first inventor" defense is not limited to business method inventions.

First Sale

A lawful, unrestricted sale of a product embodying a patented invention exhausts the patent rights with respect to that product. A buyer of an automobile embodying several patented technologies, for example, may sell the automobile to another person without having to pay royalties to the patentees.

A patentee may impose restrictions on the use and/or resale of products embodying the invention. Unless a particular restriction violates antitrust or other law, such restrictions are generally enforceable.

The first sale doctrine does not give a buyer a right to make, sell or import new products embodying the invention. A purchaser of a product may repair it but may not reconstruct it.

Experimental Use

Using an invention purely for experimentation is not infringement. Courts, however, have interpreted this defense very narrowly, limiting it to situations in which a person experiments with an invention purely for amusement or out of idle curiosity rather than for a business or commercial purpose. For example, the defense has been held to be unavailable to a nonprofit educational institution that experiments with an invention solely for teaching purposes, since such use furthers the school's business of teaching.[377]

The Hatch-Waxman Act[378] expands the experimental use defense in the case of pharmaceutical drugs. Experimental use of patented pharmaceutical drugs may be made for commercial purposes, even by direct business competitors. A special set of patent provisions has been enacted to coordinate the patent and FDA approval processes.

Statute of Limitations

The statute of limitations for patent infringement is six years. In the case of infringement occurring over a period of time longer than six years, damages may be recovered only for infringement occurring during the six years prior to filing suit.

Laches

When a patentee delays filing suit for a period of time that is unreasonable under the circumstances, he may be denied recovery under the equitable doctrine of laches. Factors that may make a delay reasonable could include things like: negotiations with the infringer; other litigation; illness; lack of financial resources to litigate; a dispute over patent ownership; wartime conditions; the insubstantial nature of the infringement during the period of delay. A desire simply to sit back and let the infringer do all the work of practicing the patent and marketing products embodying it, knowing that the patentee's share of profits that will be awarded in an infringement suit increases over time, is not a valid reason for delay.

Laches will not apply unless it is shown not only that the delay was unreasonable but also that it resulted in prejudice to the infringer. The prejudice may be either economic (such as loss of investment) or evidentiary (such as death of a witness or destruction of records).

Because it is an equitable defense, the infringer's own inequitable conduct will factor into a court's decision about whether to apply it or not.

Laches may be asserted as a defense even if the statute of limitations has not expired yet. If the period of delay is more than six years from the time the patentee learned of the infringement, then the patentee bears the burden of producing evidence that the delay was reasonable; if less than six years, then the claimed infringer bears the burden of proving it was unreasonable. The alleged infringer bears the ultimate burden of persuasion on the issue.

Laches only bars recovery for damages accumulated up to the time the lawsuit is filed. Injunctive relief and future damages may still be awarded even if a laches defense is successful.

Estoppel

If a patentee, through words or conduct, leads a person to believe she does not intend to enforce the patent, or that the person is not infringing it, and the person relies on that representation to her detriment (economic or evidentiary), the patentee may be estopped from later asserting a claim of infringement against the person.

Misuse of Patent

Misuse of patent occurs when a patentee exploits a patent in a way that broadens its lawful scope with anticompetitive effect. Entering into a patent license containing an unlawful tying agreement is an example. In one case, for example, the Morton Salt Company lost patent rights to a patented salt-depositing machine because it required licensees of the machine to use only salt purchased from the Morton Salt Company. Because using a patent to restrain competition in the sale of unpatented products violates the policy of the antitrust laws, courts will not enforce patent rights of a patentee who has used the patent in this way. Other acts that may constitute patent misuse include price-fixing, prohibitions on the manufacture of competing products, conditioning a grant of a license on the acceptance of another license, and calculating royalties on the basis of total sales without regard to the extent to which the patented invention was used.

A patentee may restore the enforceability of a patent by discontinuing the misuse.

Congress has sharply limited the misuse doctrine. Federal law now provides that misuse does not occur merely because the patentee:

(a) gains revenue from acts that would constitute contributory infringement if performed by another;
(b) licenses others to perform acts that would constitute contributory infringement if performed by another;
(c) seeks to enforce the patent;
(d) refuses to license or use the patent; or
(e) enters into a tying agreement.

Entering into a tying agreement involving a patented product may be misuse of patent only if the patentee has market power and the tied goods are unpatented staple articles of commerce.

A patentee's imposition of limitations on the uses to which a product embodying the invention may be put (such as a "single use only" notice on the product label) is not "misuse of patent."

Shop Rights

See Chapter 4.

Untimely Application

Undue delay in enforcing patent rights may bar an infringement claim if the elements of a laches or statute of limitations defense are present. Untimely delay in filing a patent application can also bar an infringement claim. Some kinds of delays between the date of the creation of the inventtion and the date that a patent application is filed may prevent the issuance of a valid patent.

Under the public use doctrine, a patent will not be issued in the United States for an invention that was patented or described in a printed publication in any country, or that was being used by a member of the general public, more than one year prior to the filing of the application.

For purposes of this rule, even a single gift of a single article embodying the invention may qualify as "public use." Experimental uses, however, do not count. Offering an embodiment of an invention to a person to test its functionality is not "public use." An offering for the purpose of testing a product's likely marketplace success is considered a public use, not an experimental use.

A patent also will not be issued in the United States if an embodiment of the invention was offered for sale (or in the language of the Patent Act,[379] it was "on sale") in the United States by anyone more than one year before the application was filed, whether or not any sales actually resulted from it. Offers of sales between related parties, such as for testing or research purposes only, do not count. Offers of sales of inventions that have not yet been reduced to practice (embodied in an article) also do not count, unless there are sufficient diagrams and instructions in place at the time of the offer to enable a person to practice the invention.

An inventor will not receive the benefit of the grace period if he markets the invention, or uses the invention to make products that he markets to the public, more than one year before filing the application, and this is true even if the invention is a process that he has effectively preserved as a trade secret during that time.

A patent also will not be issued in the United States if a foreign patent was applied for more than one year before the filing of the U.S. application and the foreign patent is granted before the U.S. application if filed.

Not all countries offer a grace period or the same kind of grace period as the United States does. Countries that have implemented the European Patent Convention do not offer any grace period at all; disclosure of the invention at any time before the application is filed will bar patentability. In Japan, disclosure of the same invention by a third party at any time before the application filing date will bar patentability, but disclosure by the applicant himself will not bar patentability unless such disclosure occurs more than six months before the application is filed.

Delay can also affect the ability to obtain patent rights in other countries. The United States protects the patent rights of the first person to come up with the invention, but many other countries award the patent to the first person to file an application.

Multinational Patents

Patents, like trademarks, are territorial. This means that in order to obtain an exclusive right to exploit an invention in a particular country, a patent must be obtained in that country.

Some counties prohibit inventors from obtaining patents in foreign countries without the government's permission. The United States is one of those countries. The Invention Secrecy Act[380] requires the inventor of an invention made in the United States to obtain a license from the USPTO before filing an application for a patent in a foreign country. Failure to do so may result in the invalidation of the U.S. patent for the invention. A request for the license may be made expressly or simply by filing an application for a U.S. patent, which is deemed to be both an application for a U.S. patent and an application for a license to apply for a patent in a foreign country. Various federal agencies review the application to determine whether disclosure of the invention may harm national security interests. If the determination is in the affirmative, then the government will issue a secrecy order prohibiting the inventor from filing a foreign patent application and also prohibiting disclosure of the invention. A U.S. patent for the invention will also be denied. An inventor may seek compensation for damages caused by a secrecy order. The USPTO will notify the applicant if a license to file a patent application in a foreign country has been granted or not.

The Patent Cooperation Treaty provides a simplified means for filing patent applications in more than one country. An inventor seeking to patent an invention in more than one country can use an international application, on which any country that is a signatory to the treaty may be named. If the applicant later files national applications in those countries, they will take on the priority date of the international application, provided the national application is filed within thirty months after the international application is filed.

When an international application is filed, the International Searching Authority conducts a prior art search in the designated countries. The USPTO will use the report of this search when a national application is filed in the United States subsequent to the filing of an international application.

Each country specifies its own standards of patentability. Few countries are as receptive to business method patents as the United States is, for example.

Other patent treaties exist in various regions of the world. The European Patent Convention, the Eurasian Patent Convention, the African Intellectual Property Organization treaties, and the African Regional Intellectual Property Organization protocols are examples.

Some treaties are aimed at harmonizing the patent laws of different countries. These are discussed in Chapter 34.

Protection for Unpatented Ideas

In some circumstances, an unpatented idea may be protected by other laws. See Chapter 31.

Chapter 31. Trade Secrets, Information and Ideas

Trade Secrets

Legal protections for trade secrets can be of critical importance to a business for a number of reasons. Other kinds of intellectual property laws generally are not adequate. Since copyrights only protect expression rather than facts and ideas, copyright law provides no protection for things like recipes, formulas, customer lists, and so on. In the case of a secret method, process or other invention, it might be possible to secure a patent, but patent protection only lasts for twenty years. Trade secrets can receive legal protection for much longer than that. The formula for Coca-Cola, for example, has remained a protected trade secret since its creation in 1886. Obtaining a patent also requires public disclosure of how to make the invention. That can severely weaken a company's competitive advantage.

Trade secrets are protected by both federal and state laws. Most state laws originated in the common law, but nearly every state now has enacted the Uniform Trade Secret Act (UTSA). The UTSA codifies much of the common law of trade secrets, while adding some new things to it. While trade secret laws vary from state to state, the general principle set forth in all of them is that it is unlawful to misappropriate another person's trade secret, and doing so may result in liability for damages to the owner of the trade secret.

Patent law complements trade secret law; it does not preempt it. An invention may be protected as a trade secret whether it is patentable or not. Inventors may rely on the protections of trade secret law while a patent application is being processed, provided it remains secret during that time. When a patent is issued, however, the invention can no longer receive protection as a trade secret. The disclosures that must be made in order to obtain a patent make the information "readily ascertainable" to others. Subsequently developed improvements to a patented invention are not protected by the original patent unless they are described in it. They may be protected as trade secrets, though, if in addition to not being described in the patent application, information about the improvement meets the requirements for protection as a trade secret.

Because the secrecy of an invention can give a company a competitive advantage of potentially unlimited duration, a company may prefer to maintain it as a trade secret rather than seeking patent protection for it. There is a certain risk to this approach, however. If another person or business comes up with the same idea independently and proceeds to patent it, then the company that came up with it first but failed to patent it will no longer be able to use or market it without incurring patent infringement liability to the second company. An exception exists for business methods that were in use before another person patents them. In all other cases, though, the issuance of a patent will give its owner the exclusive right to make or use an invention, and this includes the right to exclude prior creators of the same invention who chose to maintain it as a trade secret rather than patenting it.

Of course, if the second company does not create the invention independently—if it misappropriates the first company's trade secret—then it may be liable for misappropriation of a trade secret.

A trade secret can be any kind of information – e.g., a formula, recipe, plan, design, pattern, data compilation, customer list, customer purchasing history, supplier list, financial data, marketing data, personnel information, physical device, method, process, device, computer software, new product ideas, new product launch date, price bids, specifications for how to build or operate a device or service, know-how related to a business, etc.—if all of the following elements are present:

(a) It is secret;
(b) Its secrecy has commercial value, such as giving a business a competitive advantage;
(c) Reasonable measures have been taken to keep it secret.

In determining whether information has commercial value, courts may consider the amount of money and effort that was expended to acquire or develop the information and the amount of money and time it would take for others to acquire or duplicate the information, along with any other evidence of value to a competitor. Merely keeping information about the company secret is not enough. For example, confidential information about a company's financial standing will not qualify as a trade secret unless there is evidence to show that this information is valuable to a competitor.

To qualify as secret, the information must be neither (a) generally known, nor (b) readily ascertainable by a person who can obtain economic value from its disclosure or use (such as a business competitor). For this reason, republishing information that has already been published on a public website will not often result in trade secret liability. This is not always the case, however. If the information has only been published on an obscure site, or if it is quickly taken down after being published, a court may nevertheless treat it as a secret. The critical question is whether the information has become known to someone who can derive economic value from it. Information may be disqualified from trade secret protection if it is known by members of a particular industry, even if it is not known to the public at large.

A person who misappropriates a trade secret may remain liable for it even if the information later becomes generally known. The fact that information may become generally known as a result of a person's act of misappropriation does not negate its status as a trade secret at the time the person misappropriated it. If the rule were otherwise, then people would be permitted to benefit from their own wrongdoing.

Information may be disqualified from trade secret status if it is readily ascertainable by someone who can derive economic value from its disclosure or use, whether or not evidence of actual knowledge exists. Thus, publication of the information in a trade journal, reference materials and the like will disqualify information from trade secret protection. Similarly, information that can be easily obtained through reverse engineering of publicly accessible software is disqualified from trade secret protection. The easier the information is to copy or acquire, the less likely it is to receive trade secret protection.

This principle dovetails with the requirement that a business must take reasonable precautions to protect a trade secret from being accessed or disclosed. This includes physical, procedural, and technical measures. Storing a secret formula in a locked safe is an example of a physical measure. Marking a document as "confidential" or "secret" is another example. Procedural measures are things like requiring employees to sign nondisclosure and noncompete agreements; restricting certain information to only those employees who have a need to know it in order to perform their jobs; nonsolicitation agreements; and nondisclosure agreements with customers, clients, business partners, associates, contractors, consultants, and investors. Technical measures include things like encryption, requiring a password to access a database, and the like.

It is not necessary to take every conceivable precaution to protect secrecy; only "reasonable" measures are required. A court will not require a person to incur significant financial costs as a condition of receiving trade secret protection. In *E.I. du Pont de Nemours, Inc. v. Christopher*,[381] for example, the court rejected the argument that a company should lose trade secret protection by virtue of failing to build a cover to hide a manufacturing plant while it was in the process of being built. Erecting such a structure would have required the company to incur considerable expense.

Programming code may be a trade secret if it has economic value and reasonable efforts have been made to maintain its secrecy. Measures that computer software creators and vendors sometimes employ to protect trade secrets include: nondisclosure covenants in the licensing agreement; nondisclosure covenants with developers and testers; distribution only in executable form; and various kinds of security measures to prevent access to the source code. There have been cases where software licensors have lost trade secret protection by failing to include a nondisclosure covenant in the license agreement, at least where the licensor has done nothing to prevent customers from accessing the programming code.

Unlike noncompete agreements, nondisclosure agreements do not need to be limited to a short period of time. In fact, a nondisclosure agreement that is limited to a short period will undermine a company's claim of having taken "reasonable measures" to protect a trade secret. In one case, for example, a court held that a nondisclosure agreement that only required nondisclosure for a ten-year period was not a reasonable measure to protect a trade secret.

More information about noncompete, nondisclosure and nonsolicitation agreements may be found in Chapter 4.

MISAPPROPRIATION OF TRADE SECRETS

Misappropriation of a trade secret may take three different forms:

(a) obtaining it by improper means
(b) acquiring, disclosing or using it with knowledge or reason to know it was improperly obtained
(c) disclosing or using it without consent, with knowledge or reason to know that it was acquired under circumstances giving rise to a duty to maintain its secrecy.

The third kind, described in paragraph (c), does not require the trade secret to have been obtained by improper means. An employee's use or disclosure in breach of a confidentiality agreement would be an example of this kind of misappropriation. The other three forms require proof that the trade secret was obtained by improper means.

Improper means generally refers to unlawful means. Examples include:

- Breach of nondisclosure agreement
- Inducement to breach a nondisclosure agreement
- Theft
- Bribery
- Fraud
- Electronic espionage
- Violation of a statutory prohibition.

Since the CFAA prohibits accessing a computer without permission, obtaining a trade secret this way would be improper. Violating the ECPA by intercepting an email message would be another example. These are not the only examples that could be given.

Independently creating or developing information that happens to be the subject of another person's trade secret is not improper. Reverse engineering is not an improper means of obtaining information, either, unless it violates a provision in contract.

Accessing publicly available information also is not improper. Moreover, obtaining information by an improper means (such as hacking, breaching a contractual prohibition against reverse engineering, etc.) is not actionable as misappropriation of a trade secret, in any event, unless the information obtained is, in fact, a trade secret.

Remedies for misappropriation of a trade secret include damages, attorney fees, and injunctive relief. An injunction may be issued to enjoin further use or disclosure of the trade secret. Preliminary injunctions and TROs may be issued while litigation is pending. A permanent injunction may be issued at the conclusion of litigation.

Damages may be in an amount that will compensate the business for loss resulting from the misappropriation, or a royalty on any profits the defendant made by using the trade secret. Attorney fees and double damages may be awarded if the misappropriation was willful or malicious.

Assertions of First Amendment protection normally do not succeed as a defense to a claim of trade secret misappropriation. On a rare occasion, a court might be inclined to sustain a First Amendment defense if the trade secret involves a matter of public concern. For example, disclosure that there are toxic chemicals in a food vendor's "secret sauce" probably would be constitutionally protected. On the other hand, use of trade secrets in violation of a confidentiality agreement or in breach of a fiduciary duty (such as the fiduciary duties owed by employees, officers and directors to the employers or organizations they serve) is not protected by the First Amendment.

Consent, express or implied, is a defense. Expiration of the statute of limitations is also a defense. The UTSA provides for a three-year limitations period. Some states have specified lengthier limitations periods, such as five years. Limitations periods generally are measured from the date the plaintiff discovered (or reasonably should have discovered) the misappropriation.

Of course, if a person misappropriates a trade secret in a way that is prohibited in a contract, then there may be liability for breach of contract as well as misappropriation of a trade secret.

Unauthorized use or disclosure of a trade secret may also be a crime. The Economic Espionage Act[382] (EEA) makes the theft or appropriation of a trade secret by fraud, artifice or deception, with intent to harm, or with knowledge that it will cause harm (including financial loss) to its owner or will benefit a foreign government, a federal crime. A violation is punishable by a fine of up to $5,000,000 and up to ten years imprisonment. If done with knowledge or intent to benefit a foreign government, it is punishable by a fine of up to $10,000,000 and fifteen years imprisonment. The Act also provides for civil penalties.

For purposes of the EEA, "appropriating" a trade secret means copying, duplicating, sketching, drawing, photographing, downloading, uploading, altering, destroying, replicating, transmitting, photocopying, delivering, sending, mailing, communicating, or conveying the secret without authorization.

In several states, the unauthorized acquisition, use or disclosure of a trade secret is a crime.

There may be situations in which a business is legally required to disclose a trade secret to a government entity. Fortunately, there are steps that can be taken to prevent further disclosure to the public. Copyright regulations offer ways to submit required deposit copies (which normally are viewable by any member of the public at the Library of Congress) without disclosing trade secret information. FOIA rules giving the public a right to access to records maintained by government agencies contain some exceptions for trade secret material. Similar laws and regulations exist at the state and local level.

Documents filed in court generally may be viewed by the public. A business must take care, therefore, to ensure that pleadings and other documents filed with a court do not disclose a trade secret. The same is true of documents and information a party requests during the discovery phase of litigation. Under court rules and the UTSA, a business may bring a motion to seal a record, or to hold a hearing in camera (without public access), and/or for a protective order. A protective order may either relieve a person from the obligation to comply with a particular discovery request, or it may direct participants in the litigation not to disclose specified information to others without prior court approval.

Before submitting material containing a trade secret to a court, agency or other public entity, a business should carefully research and follow the entity's trade secret protection procedures. If unable to do so, or if no such protection appears to exist in a particular situation, an attorney should be consulted.

Proprietary Information

Sometimes a business invests in acquiring or developing information that it does not intend to keep secret, but as to which it has an economic interest in being the first to disclose. In some circumstances, the common law in some jurisdictions gives certain people the right to prevent or to recover damages for the disclosure of information even if it is not protected by copyright, trademark, trade secret or patent law.

The cause of action for misappropriation of information derives from unfair competition law. It was first expounded in *International News Service v. Associated Press*.[383] In that case, one news service was "scooping" the other by accessing and publishing information the other one gathered before the service that gathered the information had a chance to publish it. The Court held that the news service that had expended effort gathering the information could sue the other news service for appropriating the information to its own use in a way that prevented the first news service from exploiting it commercially. This cause of action is recognized in some jurisdictions but not in others.

Federal copyright and patent laws preempt state misappropriation law to the extent a state law conflicts with, or regulates the same things as, either of these sets of federal laws do. For this reason, states can establish a cause of action for misappropriation of the information but not for misappropriation of the manner of expressing it. Similarly, there can be no state law cause of action for copying a patented invention. Patents are the exclusive province of federal law.

There is no copyright protection for expression when it is the only way of conveying the underlying idea or information. In that situation, the idea is said to have merged with the expression. When that happens, copyright protection vanishes, federal preemption should no longer apply, and liability for a state law misappropriation claim may be possible – provided all the necessary elements of such a claim are established.

The line of demarcation between expression and information is not always clear. In *Barclay's Capital Inc. v. Theflyonthewall.com, Inc.*,[384] a federal court held that a stock advisor's recommendations are expressive, not informational. Therefore, publishing them without permission could be a violation of copyright law, but could not be used as the basis for a state law misappropriation claim because preempted by federal copyright law.

States that recognize this cause of action have adopted differing requirements for recovery. Some only require a showing that a person expended time or value acquiring information; that a competitor used it to his own advantage without compensating the one who acquired it; and that the one who gathered the information suffered damage as a result. Others impose stricter requirements, such as that the information was gathered at a cost; that it is time-sensitive; that the defendant is in direct competition with a product or service offered by the information gatherer; and that allowing others to "free-ride" on the efforts of the information gatherer would threaten the existence or quality of the goods or services the information gatherer offers.

Although traditional common law has not allowed recovery for conversion (basically, theft) of intangibles, some courts have begun to extend the tort of conversion to intangible property, too. For example, a New York court has held that electronic records are legally indistinguishable from paper versions of the same records for purposes of conversion law.[385] This is significant because it could provide a remedy in those cases where information is taken and used without permission but not in a way that would amount to unfair competition. Of course, the elements of a conversion claim would then need to be proven. See Chapter 20.

STRATEGIES FOR REDUCING THE RISK OF LIABILITY

The risk of liability for copyright infringement or misappropriation of information should be a concern for websites that aggregate news stories or that republish content found on other websites. Unfortunately, there is no way to eliminate the risk entirely. Some things can be done to reduce the risk, though.

To reduce the risk of copyright infringement, avoid copying news and informational items verbatim. Use your own words to communicate information found on other websites.

Next, copy only small amounts of material. Copying small amounts of copyrighted content is sometimes permitted as fair use. It is not advisable to rely on this defense alone, though, because there is no quantitative definition of what a small amount is. Copying only a small amount of copyrighted material does not guarantee a successful fair use defense, particularly if the portion copied is the heart of the work.

To reduce the risk of liability for misappropriation of information, refrain from publishing information that still has commercial value for the gatherer of the information. As a rule of thumb, the newer the information is, the greater the risk of liability for misappropriation. Therefore, think twice before republishing information time-sensitive information like stock tips; inside information about businesses that could affect investment decisions; the play-by-play or scores of sporting events as they are occurring, and so on.

The risk of liability for misappropriation of information is greater if using or disclosing the information is in direct competition with the person or business that gathered the information, and disclosure or publication of it impairs the ability of the original information gatherer to commercially exploit it

The risk of liability is also greater if the information gatherer has taken measures to protect the commercial value of the information, such as by requiring payment to access the information. Conversely, if the information gatherer has already published the information on a public web page (i.e., one that is freely accessible, without payment, to anyone with an Internet connection), and the information is not exclusive to that website (i.e., if the same information already appears on other sites), then the risk of liability for misappropriation is low.

The risk of liability for either copyright infringement or misappropriation of information is at its lowest if you use your own words to convey the information (don't just copy and paste text from another site); the information is not "hot news" (i.e., it is already widely available from numerous sources available to the public); and making it available would not diminish the information gatherer's ability to exploit it commercially, such as where she has already published it online for any member of the public to view free of charge.

Of course, the risk of liability is greatly reduced if the information gatherer gives written permission to republish it.

Ideas

We have seen that copyright law does not protect ideas, and patent law only protects ideas that meet strict patentability standards and for which a person has applied and paid what, for many, may be a daunting amount of money. Yet, there may be situations where it would be unfair to allow a person to profit from someone else's idea without compensating the originator of the idea in some way.

If the idea originator entered into a contract under which the idea exploiter is obliged to pay the idea originator for the idea, then the person who exploits the idea may be sued for breach of contract if she does not pay the idea originator as agreed.

Not all contracts need to be express in order to be enforceable. Even in the absence of a written or oral agreement, a contract sometimes may be implied from the conduct of the parties, their course of dealing, and/or customary practices in the trade.

> **Example.** Toymaker Company regularly consults with "idea man" Bob for ideas for new stories with potential toy tie-ins and new designs for toys with potential story tie-ins. If the Company decides to use his idea, they pay Bob a percentage royalty of

> 5%, which is standard in the industry. One day, Bob relates an idea for a new toy with a potential story tie-in to the Company, and the Company decides to use it, but doesn't pay Bob anything. Although the ideas are not patented or copyrighted, and although there is no express agreement between Bob and the Company, Bob may be able to sue the Company for breach of an implied contract based on the parties' course of dealing and customary practices in the trade.

Trade secret law can also provide a remedy for stolen ideas. The common law of trade secrets did not offer much recourse for idea originators because the right to recovery depended on proof that the idea's use in business gave the idea claimant a continuous advantage over competitors. Thus, it could not be invoked by a person who offered an idea to a business but never actually used the idea in a business. Moreover, courts held that the requirement of a "continuous advantage" could not be satisfied if the business with which the idea is shared exploits it in a way that discloses the idea to the public, since the idea would not then be a secret. To qualify as a trade secret, the secrecy of the idea, not the idea itself, must be what gives the business a competitive advantage.

The UTSA, which has been adopted in nearly every state, eliminates the requirement of a showing that the idea claimant used the idea in a way that gave it a continuous advantage over competitors. Under the UTSA, a trade secret must still be something that derives its economic value from not being generally known to others, and some kind of effort must still be made to maintain its secrecy. Now, however, the economic value may be either actual or potential. An idea may be protected as a trade secret even if its originator has not yet had an opportunity to put it to use. Thus, the UTSA protects not just the traditional kind of trade secret, but also any idea that is submitted to a business that decides to exploit the idea—provided, of course, the idea submitter has taken reasonable measures to maintain the secrecy of the idea.

To receive protection as a trade secret, the idea must not be generally known at the time the originator of the idea submits it. The fact that it becomes generally known when the business to which the idea is submitted starts producing it does not negate the fact that it was a trade secret at the time the idea originator submitted it to the business.

> **Example.** Joe submits an idea to a toy manufacturer. The idea is to cut grooves in toy train tracks so the train makes a clattering noise as it travels over them. The idea is not patented, but is not generally known. No one else is making this kind of track, and Joe takes reasonable steps to ensure that the idea is not disclosed to anybody else. The toy manufacturer decides to use the idea. Once the toys are on the market, everybody can easily tell that the grooves in the tracks are what cause the toy trains to making the clattering noises. Other toy makers start making tracks with grooves in them, too. Nobody pays Joe for his great idea.

Under the facts given, neither Joe nor the toy manufacturer could sue for patent infringement because the invention is not patented. Joe could assert a claim for damages against the first manufacturer, however, because the idea of putting grooves in toy train tracks was a trade secret at the time he offered it to the company. Under the UTSA, the fact that it was no longer a secret after it was later disclosed to the public (as a consequence of the toy train tracks having been put on the market) is irrelevant to Joe's claim against the manufacturer, if it was a trade secret at the time he submitted the idea.[386]

Not all courts agree about this. Michigan courts, for example, still impose the common law requirement that an idea must already have acquired value through use before it can attain trade secret status. An idea originator (like Joe, in the Example) would not have a remedy under trade secret law in this jurisdiction unless he had actually put the idea to a value-generating use before submitting it to the alleged misappropriator. Of course, if the idea is necessarily disclosed when put to value-generating use (such as the grooves in the tracks, in the Example), then it would no longer be a secret at the time it is submitted to the alleged misappropriator, so there could be no recovery for misappropriation of a trade secret.[387] As a Pennsylvania court put it: "a product cannot constitute a trade secret when it provides its creator with economic value only when disseminated—or, as here, sold—to third parties."[388] And a South Dakota court has held that the UTSA simply does not apply to new product ideas.[389] Nevertheless, the modern trend in many states is to permit recovery for misappropriation of new product ideas under the UTSA.

In the absence of a viable breach of contract or trade secret claim, resort must be made to common law theories of liability for stealing someone's idea. At one time, these included conversion (which treats an idea as a kind of property); unjust enrichment (quasi-contract); unfair competition; misappropriation of confidential information; fraud (in obtaining access to the secret); interference with prospective business advantage; and breach of fiduciary duty. The UTSA, however, contains a provision stating that the UTSA displaces equivalent common law causes of action. Most, but not all, states have enacted this provision. In those states that have enacted this provisions, claims for conversion, misappropriation of confidential information, unjust enrichment, unfair competition, fraudulently obtaining access to a trade secret, and interference with prospective business advantage are no longer permitted if the interest sought to be vindicated is the same kind of interest that trade secret law protects.

The UTSA does not displace common law claims for breach of contract. Fiduciary duties, including a duty of loyalty, are implied as a matter of law in certain kinds of relationships. Employees owe fiduciary duties to their employer; agents, to their principals; trustees to the beneficiaries; directors and officers, to the corporation; partners, to each other. Courts are not in agreement about the extent to which the UTSA displaces common law claims for breach of fiduciary duty. The clear trend, however, is to hold that the UTSA does not supersede common law causes of action for breach of fiduciary duty except to the extent the cause of action is the equivalent of a cause of action for misappropriation of a trade secret.

Federal patent law does not preempt state laws that protect ideas as trade secrets. This is true even when a state trade secret law extends protection to an unpatentable idea. Unlike patented ideas, though, trade secrets may be exploited by anybody who discovers them in a manner that is not improper. A person who independently discovers an idea, even if by reverse engineering a publicly marketed product, may exploit it without trade secret liability.

Defenses to misappropriation of an idea depend on the theory of liability that is advanced. In every kind of case, however, independent development of the idea is a defense. A person who develops an idea independently, without knowledge that someone else had the same idea, would not be misappropriating anything. This is why some companies segregate mail containing unsolicited ideas so that their product developers and marketers cannot have access to it.

Unless it qualifies as a misappropriation of a trade secret, breach of a contractual or fiduciary obligation, or patent or copyright infringement, a cause of action for "stealing an idea" may be difficult to sustain. Courts in a number of jurisdictions do not recognize a common law tort of misappropriation of an idea that does not fall into one of these categories. An argument could be made that a claim of an exclusive right to exploit an idea on the sole basis that it is novel—that is, a claim to an idea that is not grounded in contract, fiduciary duty, copyright, trademark or trade secret law—is preempted by federal patent law.

According to the Restatement (3d) of Unfair Competition:

> [N]o general rule of law prohibits the appropriation of a competitor's ideas, innovations, or other intangible assets once they become publicly known. In addition, the federal patent and copyright statutes now preempt a considerable portion of the domain in which the common law tort might otherwise apply. The better approach, and the one most likely to achieve an appropriate balance between the competing interests, does not recognize a residual common law tort of misappropriation.[390]

The Restatement takes the position that recovery for misappropriation of an idea (as distinguished from misappropriation of personality, which is discussed in Chapter 17), should be allowed only if at least one of the following applies:

(a) it is a trade secret
(b) the misappropriation breaches an express or implied contract
(c) it can be framed as a cause of action under an intellectual property statute, such as the federal patent law.

While some courts disagree with the Restatement position, it does seem to be the direction in which the law is heading.

For information about the protection of ideas, information and trade secrets in the employment context, see Chapter 4.

Chapter 32. Licenses and Transfers

As with any other property, ownership of intellectual property may be transferred or a right to use it may be granted to another person. A transfer of ownership of intellectual property during the owner's lifetime is called an *assignment*. An assignee acquires all the exclusive rights that the owner had. A *license* is a grant of something less than all of the exclusive rights in property. A person who acquires a right to use property pursuant to a license does not become the owner of the property.

Copyright

There are three mechanisms by which a person other than the creator of a work may acquire rights in it: (a) transfer; (b) license; (c) work made for hire agreement.

TRANSFERS

Transfers of ownership of a copyright may be voluntary or involuntary. Copyrights are potentially subject to seizure by creditors for the satisfaction of unpaid debts, in much the same way that other kinds of property are. A copyright is not subject to seizure by a unit of government.

Upon a copyright owner's death, title to the copyright passes to the heirs of her estate or, if she had a will, then to the beneficiary designated in the will. A transfer of ownership upon a copyright owner's death is called a *transfer by operation of law.*

Voluntary transfers that occur during the owner's lifetime are called *assignments.*

Beginning in 1978, a signed writing is required. The signature may be that of the copyright owner or the owner's authorized agent. Assignments that were effected before 1978 may be either oral or written. No particular formality is required, however. Even after 1977, a written, signed confirmation of an oral assignment may suffice, and an oral assignment that is subsequently confirmed in writing is effective retroactively to the date of the oral assignment. An endorsement of a check may suffice, but only if there is unambiguous indicia that the check is payment for an assignment of the copyright in the work.

In some cases, a written contract for the sale of a business may suffice even if copyrights are not explicitly mentioned, provided transfer of the copyright is clearly what the parties intended. The better practice, of course, is to remove any doubt about the parties' intentions by addressing the transfer of intellectual property, including copyrights, explicitly in the contract.

Recordation

Recording an assignment is not required. Failing to do so does not affect the validity of the transfer, and it is no longer a prerequisite to filing an infringement lawsuit in court. It is strongly recommended, however, as it can help protect an assignee from losing rights to another person to whom the copyright owner might have assigned rights in the same work. It provides strong evidentiary support for the existence and date of the assignment. Also, if the document clearly identifies the work and the work has been registered, then recording an assignment gives the whole world constructive notice of all the facts stated in the assignment.

Under the Copyright Act, a transfer is effective as against a competing claimant of another alleged transfer of the same copyright if it is (a) executed first, and (b) recorded either one month after its execution in the United States (two months, if executed in another country) or before the other alleged transfer is recorded.

A later transferee who gives valuable consideration for the transfer, without notice of the previous transfer, will prevail against a previous transferee if the previous transferee neither recorded the transfer within one month (two months, if executed in another country) nor recorded it before the later transferee did.

> **Example**. Anne assigns the copyright in her article to Bob on May 1, and then executes another assignment to Carol on May 15 and yet another one to Dave on May 25. Dave records his assignment on May 26. Four days later, on May 30, Carol records her assignment. Bob records his assignment on July 15. Both Carol and Dave are bona fide purchasers without notice of the assignment to Bob.

Under the facts given in the Example, Bob will not prevail against Carol or Dave despite the fact that assignment to him preceded the assignments to Carol and Dave, because he did not record his assignment either a month before its execution or before Carol and Dave recorded theirs. As between Carol and Dave, Carol will prevail. Although Dave recorded his assignment before Carol did, the assignment to Carol preceded the one to Dave and Carol recorded it within thirty days of its execution.

The foregoing rule applies to "transfers" of copyrights, as that term is defined in the Copyright Act. As explained below, this includes both outright assignments and grants of exclusive licenses. It also includes grants of security interests in copyrights. It does not include nonexclusive licenses.

LICENSES

Any of the exclusive rights of a copyright owner (reproduction, distribution, public display, public performance, digital transmission, making derivative works) may be licensed to others.

The Copyright Act blurs the distinction between transfers and licenses a bit by referring to grants of exclusive licenses, as well as assignments, as "transfers of copyright ownership":

> A "transfer of copyright ownership" is an assignment, mortgage, exclusive license, or any other conveyance, alienation, or hypothecation of a copyright or of any of the exclusive rights comprised in a copyright, whether or not it is limited in time or place of effect, but not including a nonexclusive license.[391]

In copyright law, then, a grant of an exclusive license to exercise one or more of the rights of copyright ownership (distribution, performance, etc.) transfers "ownership" of that right, which may be subject to terms and conditions that are spelled out in the license agreement. An exclusive license does not transfer ownership of the title to the copyright, however.

The explanation for this rather unusual and confusing language is that Congress wanted to make it possible for exclusive licensees to avail themselves of certain legal benefits of copyright ownership that licensees ordinarily do not possess. This includes the rights to commence a lawsuit against an infringer and to apply for registration of the copyright.

A grant of an exclusive license, then, is not really a transfer of ownership; the licensee is just entitled to be treated like one for purposes of enforcing the copyright. And unless the license agreement provides otherwise, a grant of an "exclusive" license does not include the right to exclude the copyright owner from exercising copyright rights except to the extent of prohibiting the owner from granting licenses to others.[392]

Before 1978, licenses could be oral or written. Exclusive licenses granted after 1977 must be in writing and signed by the copyright owner. An unsigned or oral exclusive license granted after 1977 is not enforceable against the owner. A nonexclusive license may be written or oral, unless a writing is required under the applicable contract law of a state. Even if state law does not require it, though, a written agreement is a good idea. It can help prevent misunderstandings and it facilitates enforcement in the event of breach. It is also important in terms of protecting the licensee in the event the copyright owner transfers the copyright to someone else. A written transfer terminates all prior oral licenses.

Recordation

Recording a license is optional. A license is enforceable between the parties even if it has not been recorded. If the document clearly identifies the work and the work has been registered, though, then recording a license gives the whole world constructive notice of all the facts stated in the license document.

The effect of recordation on nonexclusive licenses is governed by a different set of rules from those that apply to transfers of copyrights. An assignee (or other transferee) takes the transfer subject to any preexisting nonexclusive license that is in writing, even if the license is not recorded. A transferee also takes the transfer subject to any written, nonexclusive licenses that are granted by the original transferor after the transfer but before the transferee records the transfer, if the licensee did not have knowledge of the transfer at the time the license was executed. Any purported grants of nonexclusive licenses by the original transferor after the transferee records the transfer will not be effective as between the transferee and the nonexclusive licensee. This is because recordation gives the whole world constructive notice of the transfer. A person who purchases an interest in property knowing or having reason to know that the person selling it no longer owns it has no recourse against a legitimate buyer of the property.

The rules outlined in the previous paragraph only apply to cases involving written, nonexclusive licenses. They do not apply to conflicts between transferees, as that term is defined in the Copyright Act. For example, they do not apply in cases involving conflicts between an assignee and a mortgagee, or between exclusive licensees. They also do not apply to oral nonexclusive licenses. An oral license is terminated when copyright ownership is transferred.

Divisibility of Rights

The rights that are bundled in a copyright—reproduction, distribution, public display, public performance, digital transmission, making derivative works—may be unbundled and transferred either separately or with other rights. For example, a performance right may be transferred without also transferring a right to make derivative works; distribution rights may be transferred without also transferring the right to make derivative works; and so on.

Terms

The terms of a license agreement are negotiable. Any such agreement, however, should cover at least the following things:

- Subject matter
- The specific rights that are being licensed
- Exclusive vs. nonexclusive
- Duration
- Geographic scope
- Sublicensing
- Assignments and transfers
- Warranty of ownership of copyright
- Indemnification
- Attribution and copyright notice
- Payment
- Termination.

SUBJECT MATTER

A license agreement should specifically describe the work(s) to which the agreement pertains. If rights are being granted to use only a portion of a work, the portion of the work the licensee is authorized to use should be identified.

RIGHTS GRANTED

A licensee has only such rights as are provided for in the license. When entering into a license agreement with a copyright owner, therefore, a licensee should take care to ensure that he is acquiring all the necessary rights that are needed in order to use the copyrighted work in the intended way. For example, if the goal is to display copyrighted text or images on a website, a licensee will want to be sure the agreement specifically includes reproduction, distribution and public display rights. If a right to perform or broadcast a performance of a work is desired, then the license should include public performance rights. If the right to transmit a sound recording over the Internet is desired, then digital transmission ("digital public performance") rights are needed. To make changes to a work, the right to make derivative works is needed. A licensor may find it prudent to limit authorized use to a specific website. If so, the domain name should be identified.

EXCLUSIVE VS. NONEXCLUSIVE

A license may be either exclusive or nonexclusive. A nonexclusive license is gives the licensee permission to use the work but does not give the licensee the right to exclude others from using the work. An exclusive license not only gives the licensee permission to use the work, but also confers the right to exclude everyone else – even the author – from using it. An exclusive licensee of one or more of the exclusive rights of copyright ownership has standing to file an infringement claim and apply for registration of the copyright.

DURATION AND TERMINATION

The term of a license may be perpetual or delimited. An agreement may provide for renewal(s) and may impose conditions on renewal. A contract may be either terminable at will or terminable only for cause. It may also provide notice requirements, such as requirement that a party must provide notice of termination a specified amount of time prior to the termination.

WARRANTY AND INDEMNIFICATION

A prudent licensee will want to include a warranty of copyright ownership in the licensing agreement. This is the licensor's promise to the licensee that the licensor has the legal right to license the use of the work to the licensee. It may include an express representation that the uses authorized by the license agreement do not infringe any copyright.

An *indemnification clause* is one that provides that one party will pay the other for any losses incurred as a result of the indemnifying party's breach of the agreement and/or that party's breach of a warranty contained within the agreement. For example, a licensee may want to require the licensor to indemnify him in the event he is sued for copyright infringement as a result of using the copyright in a way the licensor has purportedly authorized. An indemniftion clause may be made either mutual or applicable to only one of the parties.

SUBLICENSING AND LICENSE TRANSFERS

At common law, a property owner could transfer ownership to others but a licensee did not have the right to sublicense or transfer her license to someone else without the owner's permission. The Copyright Act of 1976 complicated the application of this rule a bit by defining both assignments and exclusive licenses as "transfers of ownership." There are several places in the Act where an exclusive licensee is referred to as the "owner" of the right licensed to him. The addition of this language raises a question whether the Copyright Act changed the common law rule that licenses may not be transferred or sublicensed without the licensor's permission. Some courts have interpreted it that way, concluding that an exclusive licensee now has all the rights of an "owner" with respect to the particular right granted to him, including the right to transfer it to others.[393] Other courts have come to the opposite conclusion, holding that an exclusive licensee is to be treated as an "owner" only for purposes of the authority to apply for registration and to file infringement suits, but is to be treated as a licensee for purposes of the common law rule that licensees may not transfer or sublicense without the owner/licensor's permission.[394] Leading authorities on copyright law are also in disagreement about this issue.[395]

Effect on Other Intellectual Property Rights

A grant of a license to use copyright rights does not confer a license to use a trademark or patent, and vice versa. Accordingly, if a work that is the subject of a copyright license is also a trademark or the subject of a patent (as often happens in the case of computer programs), the copyright licensing agreement should address the question whether and to what extent rights in those properties are also being licensed for use.

> **Example**. Drinking cup seller Homer wants to display Simpsons characters on his website, so he secures a copyright license permitting him to display photographs of Simpsons characters. He then proceeds to display photographs of drinking cups with Simpsons characters on them, offering these cups for sale. Under these circumstances, he might be protected from liability for copyright infringement, but he is not necessarily protected from liability for trademark infringement. Had he wanted to protect himself from both kinds of liability, then he should have secured a license of both copyright and trademark rights in the Simpsons characters.

Copyright is also distinct from the rights of visual artists under VARA. Because VARA rights are not transferable, a copyright license or assignment will not be effective to transfer them even if the agreement purports to do so. VARA rights may be waived, however, provided all requirements for a valid waiver of VARA rights are satisfied. See Chapter 23.

In every intellectual property licensing agreement, the specific kinds of intellectual property and the specific rights in them that are and are not the subject of the agreement should be spelled out very clearly.

FINDING USAGE RIGHTS INFORMATION ONLINE

Many websites provide information about copyrights, licensing and usage rights, either in the Terms of Use or elsewhere on the site. If not, such information usually may be obtained by contacting the website owner. It should not be assumed, however, that a website owner's assertions about copyright ownership are correct. Even an honest website owner may be mistaken about copyright ownership. Not all website owners understand copyright law.

The Copyright Clearance Center, www.copyright.com, can be a useful resource for obtaining permissions to use copyrighted works, provided the work is in their database.

The popular Internet search utility available at www.Google.com allows users to refine a search to limit the results to material with a specific kind(s) of usage right(s). If "Free to Use or Share" is selected, search results will include those works that people are allowed to use or share provided they do not modify them. "Free to Use Share or Modify" should be selected if the right to make a derivative work is sought. Unless otherwise specified, a right to use or share a work does not necessarily include the right to use or share it for commercial purposes. Specify "commercially" in the "Usage Rights" criteria if this right is sought.

When Google indicates that something is "free to use," it only means that it is royalty-free if the user complies with all the terms and conditions of any applicable license agreement. It does not necessarily mean that the material is in the public domain, or that it is not necessary to comply with any licensing terms or conditions.

As Google advises on its website, it only displays results based on the usage rights label a website has assigned to a particular work. It does not warrant the accuracy of the label. A person who uses an image from another website assumes the risk that the website owner may not actually have rights in the image.

In many cases, the licensing agreement for "free to use" material requires the user to properly attribute the work to its creator and/or the copyright owner. A person who fails to comply with this or any other condition set out in the licensing agreement may be liable for copyright infringement. The fact that Google represented it to be "free to use," or that a user thought "free to use" meant it was condition-free is not a defense.

AUTHOR'S RIGHT TO TERMINATE TRANSFERS

The Copyright Act of 1976 gives authors (or their heirs) an inalienable right to terminate transfers (assignments or licenses) of the copyrights in their works under certain circumstances. If an author exercises this right, however, the transferee may nevertheless continue to exploit derivative works produced under the transfer prior to the termination. The terminated transferee may not make new derivative works without permission, though.

> **Example**. Harvey transfers the copyright in his screenplay to Acme Film Studio, which proceeds to make a poorly made film based on it. The film garners gross revenues of about $20. Time-Warner is now interested in using the screenplay. Under certain circumstances, Harvey may take back ownership of the copyright by terminating the transfer to Acme so that he can enter into a more lucrative deal with Time-Warner. If he does so, then Acme may continue to air and sell copies of the film it made but it cannot make a new film based on the screenplay.

Termination must be in writing and served on the transferee in order to be effective. It must comply with Copyright Office regulations and be recorded. It must be served between two and ten years before the effective date of the termination.

The termination right does not apply to works made for hire. Also, the right may not be exercised to terminate a transfer that was made by will.

The specific contours of the termination right vary depending on whether the transfer was made before January 1, 1978 or not.

Pre-1978 Transfers

The author (or his statutory heirs) may terminate a pre-1978 transfer of a renewal term interest to the extent of the thirty-nine-year extension of the renewal term that Congress granted (the nineteen-year extension granted in the 1976 Act plus the twenty-year extension granted in the SBCTEA of 1998). If an author (or his heirs) does not exercise the right with respect to the initial nineteen-year term extension, there is a second opportunity to exercise the right to recapture the twenty-year term extension granted by the SBCTEA. The rights must be exercised within the time periods specified in Sections 304(c) and (d) of the Copyright Act.

Post-1977 Transfers

An author may terminate a post-1977 transfer of a copyright during the five-year period beginning at the end of thirty-five years after the transfer. If the transfer included a transfer of the right of publication, however, the five-year period begins at the earlier of thirty-five years after publication or forty years after the transfer was made

This right belongs only to the author or, if the author is deceased, the statutory heirs specified in the Copyright Act. With the exception of heirs who have a statutory right to terminate as provided in the Copyright Act, a transferee of the copyright from the author does not have a termination right. In the case of a joint work, a termination is effective only if a majority of the joint authors join in it.

Trademarks

LICENSES

One way to reduce the risk of liability for trademark infringement is to acquire a license from the trademark owner. A license agreement may be written, oral, or implied from the parties' conduct and dealings with each other. To avoid misunderstandings and reduce the likelihood of litigation, the better practice is to set out the terms of a license in a written agreement that is signed by each party.

Terms

The terms of a license agreement are negotiable. A well drafted licensing agreement should address at least the following items:

- Identification of the parties
- Identification of the trademarks
- Description of the use that is being authorized
- Geographic scope
- Exclusive vs. nonexclusive
- Sublicensing
- Assignments
- Quality control
- Genericide prevention
- Other trademark protection measures
- Responsibility for enforcing trademark rights against others
- Duration
- Renewal
- Termination
- Indemnification
- Warranties and disclaimers
- Treatment in foreign countries
- Payment.

IDENTIFICATION OF THE PARTIES AND THE TRADEMARKS

The agreement should identify the licensor as the party that controls use of the mark. If the licensor is also the owner of the mark, that should be stated in the agreement. The licensee should be identified as the party who is being authorized to use the mark. The agreement should also identify all persons and entities that will have a right to use the mark. For example, the agreement should address the question whether the licensee's affiliates, subsidiaries, franchisees, etc. will have a right to use the mark, and should specify whether any related companies or third parties will have a right to use the mark.

The trademark(s) should be specifically described and identified. If a mark is registered, the registration number should be included. If an application for registration is pending, that should be stated in the agreement, and any serial number or application number that has been issued should be included, as well.

The agreement should make clear whether any domain names are included in the license.

AUTHORIZED USES

The agreement should state whether the licensee will have a right to use the mark only in certain ways, or only in connection with particular goods or services. From a trademark owner's perspective, it can be a good idea to specify that any use of a licensed mark in a way, or in connection with goods or services, that is not specifically authorized in the license agreement inures to the benefit of the licensor. From a licensee's perspective, the broadest possible license is usually desirable. To prevent misunderstandings, the agreement should state that no rights other than those set out in the agreement are granted.

GEOGRAPHIC SCOPE

The territory in which the licensee is authorized to use the trademark should be specified. If it is a common law trademark, it would be a good idea to conduct a search to determine the available territory. It would also be a good idea to register the trademark, if possible.

EXCLUSIVE VS. NONEXCLUSIVE

The agreement should state whether the licensee will have an exclusive or a nonexclusive right to use the mark. If it is a nonexclusive license, limiting the licensee's use to a specific territory and scope of sales and marketing (advertising) can help prevent consumer confusion about the source of products that use the same brand name.

MARKETING RESTRICTIONS

A license agreement can impose restrictions on such things as choice of customers (if it is a nonexclusive license), sales methods, and whether or not the licensee may advertise and/or sell licensed goods and services on the Internet. If a nonexclusive license is granted, marketing restrictions may be used to prevent the activities of different licensees from overlapping and conflicting with each other.

Restrictions against deceptive or other unlawful kinds of marketing may be included, although they are not necessary inasmuch as the law imposes such requirements anyway. Stating them expressly in the agreement can be useful, though, where there is uncertainty about the licensee's knowledge of the law, or uncertainty about how a court in the applicable jurisdiction will interpret the agreement.

QUALITY CONTROL

Unlike a copyright owner, a trademark licensor has a duty to control the quality of the goods or services offered by a licensee using the trademark. A trademark owner may lose rights in the trademark by entering into a licensing agreement that does not contain quality control provisions or failing to exercise quality control. Granting an unrestricted right to use a mark any way the licensee sees fit, without retaining any supervisory control over the quality of the goods or services, is called *naked licensing*. Failing to actually exercise supervisory control over quality can also result in a finding of naked licensing.

A naked license is not sexy. It can result in a determination that the owner has abandoned the mark. A petition to cancel a registered mark may be granted on the basis that the owner is guilty of naked licensing.

Courts in a few states hold that an actual exercise of supervisory control is not required in order to prevent a finding of naked licensing if the right to control is set out in the agreement. In many states, however, both quality control provisions in the licensing agreement and actual exercise of supervisory control over quality are required if a finding of naked licensing is to be prevented.

A good way to avoid a finding of naked licensing is to include a provision in the licensing agreement giving the licensor a right to periodically inspect operations and samples, and then to actually exercise that right. Further, a licensor should periodically collect records regarding the licensee's advertisements and promotional materials showing use of the trademark.

If a license agreement contains quality control provisions, then a licensee who fails to conform to the requirements set forth in them may be liable to the licensor for breach of contract. If the licensee goes further, and actually markets nonconforming goods or services using the mark, then she may also be liable to the trademark owner for infringement.

On the other hand, a trademark licensor must be careful to avoid exercising too much control over a licensee. Exercising too much control creates a risk that the relationship between the licensor and the licensee may be deemed a franchising relationship. If that happens, then the licensor will need to comply with all federal and state franchising laws and regulations, which can be onerous. In addition, exercising too much control over a licensee may, in some circumstances, be a violation of antitrust laws. See Chapters 5 and 7.

Quality control provisions are imperative not only to protect the licensor, but also to protect the licensee and any future licensees or assignees of the mark. Once a mark is abandoned, it loses its priority of use. The first person to use a mark after it has been abandoned acquires the common law trademark. The licensee of a trademark that is inadvertently abandoned due to naked licensing is at risk of liability for infringement if another person starts using the mark after the naked license was granted but before the naked licensee commences using it.

While there is no "canned" set of required quality control provisions, some commonly used ones include provisions:

- defining the standard of quality
- providing for termination of the license if standards are not met
- specifying the applicable industry or trade standards, or government regulations
- providing manufacturing specifications

- requiring the licensee to submit samples of products for inspection
- giving the licensor a right to inspect the licensee's goods and operations
- defining accepted forms of use of the trademark, including adherence to a separately supplied style manual governing the use of designs, logos, required type faces and colors
- defining procedures for approval of new forms of trademark use, and expressly giving the licensor discretion to refuse to approve such use
- allowing the licensor to terminate the license for cause, including any failure by the licensee to adhere to quality control standards set by the licensor, or failure to follow instructions about the proper use of the mark.

OTHER TRADEMARK PRESERVATION PROVISIONS

Naked licensing is not the only way a trademark owner can lose valuable legal protections when granting others a right to use the mark. To guard against losing rights, a trademark owner should consider including provisions that:

- prohibit the licensee from registering the mark without the licensor's consent
- prohibit the licensee from using or registering a confusingly similar mark
- prohibit alteration or modification of the mark
- stipulate that all use by the licensee shall inure to the benefit of the licensor except as expressly provided otherwise in the agreement
- assign to the licensor all rights in the mark that are acquired by the licensee through use of the mark or otherwise
- disclaim licensee's rights, title or interest in the mark
- protect the mark's distinctiveness
- prevent genericide.

Genericide refers to the process by which a trademark loses its distinctiveness as a brand because it comes to be used as a noun rather than as an identifier of the source or origin of goods. ZIPPER is an example. It was a trademark once; now it is a generic term that anyone may use. A prudent trademark owner will want to include provisions requiring the licensee to follow certain conventions that can reduce the risk of the trademark becoming generic. To this end, the agreement might require the licensee to always use the trade mark as an adjective modifying a noun, and never as a noun standing alone. See Chapter 28.

Protecting distinctiveness could include things like requiring the use of a specified color, font and/or stylization, and prohibiting modification or the addition of new elements to a mark. A licensor might also want to include a requirement that the licensee must always use the appropriate trademark symbol in connection with the mark, i.e., ®, ™ or 'SM'.

SUBLICENSING

The agreement should address the question whether the licensee is permitted to sublicense the mark. It should be stated that in the absence of an express grant of authority, a licensee does not have a right to sublicense a mark he is licensed to use.

Sublicensing can create "naked licensing" problems for a trademark owner. Quality control provisions in the license agreement bind the licensor and the licensee, but a sublicensee is not bound by them because a sublicensee is not a party to the licensor-licensee contract. A mark owner can gain some measure of protection against a claim of failure to maintain quality control by including a provision that any sublicense is subject to the licensor's approval and control. Alternatively, the owner/licensor could simply include a provision prohibiting sublicensing.

TRANSFERABILITY

A license agreement should address whether the licensee may transfer or license rights to someone else or not. To reduce the risk of naked licensing, the agreement should provide that the licensee may not transfer or assign rights to another person without the licensor's consent. Alternatively, the agreement may simply state that transfers are not permitted.

POLICING

The agreement should clarify who will be responsible for policing and enforcing trademark rights. A licensor may wish to retain an exclusive right to register and police the mark(s); prosecute infringers; and recover damages for infringement. Alternatively, the agreement could specify how the licensor and licensee are to share responsibility for these things.

DURATION

The agreement should address whether the license is for a fixed term or of indefinite duration.

A licensor may wish to include a provision giving the licensor the right to terminate the license for the licensee's failure to comply with quality control requirements, improper use of the mark, or bankruptcy.

The parties may also want to address what is to happen to goods bearing a licensed mark if the license agreement is terminated. Will the licensee be allowed to retain and sell remaining inventory after termination? If not, will the licensee be required to destroy goods, packaging, and advertising? Or will he need to turn them over to the licensor instead?

In addition to requiring the licensee to immediately discontinue use of the mark upon termination of the license, the agreement should prohibit the licensee from using marks similar to the licensed mark. The agreement might further provide that the licensee will be required to assign all rights in any new use or stylization of the mark to the licensor.

An agreement might also provide for a phase-out period for a termination, or require a specified period of advance notification for a termination.

RENEWAL

The agreement should address whether the license is renewable or not, and if so, under what conditions and terms.

PAYMENT

Payment may be a flat fee or a percentage royalty in profits earned from the use of the mark. Royalties are customary, but payment terms are negotiable.

INDEMNIFICATION

A licensee may want to include a provision requiring the licensor to indemnify the licensee for any claims of infringement resulting from the licensee's use of the mark. A licensor may want to include a requirement that the licensee defend and indemnify the licensor for any product liability or false advertising claim against the licensee. The agreement may require the licensee to maintain adequate levels of product liability insurance, and may require the licensee to name the licensor as an additional insured on the policy.

WARRANTIES AND DISCLAIMERS

It can be useful to include a disclaimer of any franchise, partnership, agency, employment or other such relationship between the parties. Such a disclaimer is not always controlling, and a few states specifically bar a disclaimer of a franchise relationship from being given effect. Even so, disclaimers often can be useful as evidence of intent.

A licensee may wish to require a provision in the agreement to the effect that the licensor represents and warrants that it owns the trademark and that neither the use nor the licensing of the mark violates the rights of any third party.

Licensee Estoppel

The doctrine of licensee estoppel holds that a trademark licensee will not be permitted to challenge the validity of the licensor's trademark while the license is in effect. Once the license has expired or been terminated, the validity of the trademark may be challenged, but only on the basis of events that occurred after the license expired or was terminated.

Breach

Either party may sue the other for a breach of the agreement. In some cases, a licensee's breach can result in liability for both breach of contract and trademark infringement. Only a trademark owner may sue for infringement. A licensor who breaches an exclusive license agreement by granting a license to the licensee's competitor may be liable for breach of contract but not trademark infringement.

Recordation

Canada, Australia, Brazil, the United Kingdom and some other countries require registration or recordation of trademark licenses. The United States, China, and several other countries permit but do not require it. Even if not required, recording the license in a country can help establish use of the mark in that country, in case that becomes an issue at some time in the future. It also gives constructive notice to the world of the licensee's right to use the mark, which can be important in the event a third party claims exclusive licensing rights. It can also be necessary when engaging in international trade. For example, in China, South Korea, Liberia and some other countries, unrecorded trademarks can be deemed abandoned and monetary penalties may be imposed.

License agreements become publicly accessible documents upon recordation. Accordingly, a license agreement should not be filed "as is" if it contains confidential or sensitive information.

Some jurisdictions permit the filing of a redacted document. Another approach would be to draft the license agreement in such a way that it refers to a document containing the confidential or sensitive information without including that document in the filing.

If the licensee's identity is confidential or secret, and constructive notice of the existence of a license is the only objective, then filing a document that refers to the existence of the license may suffice. Note, however, that this might not suffice as a recordation of the license in those countries that require it. It also might not be accepted as proof of the licensee's authority when a customs official or other third party challenges such authority.

ASSIGNMENTS

An *assignment* is a transfer of ownership of a trademark to another person.

A trademark cannot be transferred unless it exists. Thus, a trademark cannot be assigned to another person before its first use in commerce or after it has been abandoned.

No writing is required to transfer ownership of a common law trademark. A common law trademark may be transferred in a written contract or by oral agreement. It may also be inferred from the parties' conduct. Under the automatic transfer doctrine, the sale of a business is presumed to include the sale of any common law trademark associated with it even if the contract does not specifically mention anything about trademark rights. An assignment of a federally registered mark does require a writing if enforcement under federal laws is being sought.

Assignments in Gross

An assignment in gross is a transfer of a mark separate from the goodwill associated with it. *Goodwill* refers to the expectancy of continued patronage based on the benefit and advantage of an established reputation. Assignments in gross are void and unenforceable.

The purpose of the rule against assignments in gross is to protect the public from confusion about the source of particular goods or services.

The rule can be easier to state than to apply. Courts attempt to interpret and apply the rule in way that will serve its purpose, namely, to protect consumers by preserving the significance of the mark to them.

Conveying both the mark and the physical assets used to produce the goods or render the service associated with the mark is usually deemed sufficient to transfer goodwill with the mark. Such a conveyance, however, will not suffice if the assignee uses the mark on goods or services that are of a fundamentally different nature. Minor alterations are fine, so long as the product is essentially the same before and after the transfer.

Conveying physical assets is not the only way to transfer goodwill along with a mark. If the assignee continues to produce goods of the same nature and quality as the ones previously associated with the trademark, then goodwill may be deemed to have been conveyed along with the mark even if no physical assets were transferred.

For a trademark in goods, the conveyance of a needed trade secret, patent or copyright along with the mark may suffice to establish a transfer of goodwill.

For service marks, continuity of management sometimes suffices to establish a transfer of goodwill. It may not be possible to make a valid assignment of a service mark for a personal service business that is bound up with the mark owner's personal skill (e.g., a medical doctor.)

Since it is not possible for goodwill to exist before use of a mark has been made, trademark transfers prior to use are invalid assignments in gross. In addition, the Lanham Act specifically prohibits assignments of rights in an intent-to-use registration application prior to use.

Because an assignment in gross is void, nonuse of a mark by the original trademark owner after an assignment in gross may result in a finding of abandonment of the mark on the part of the original trademark owner.

Effect of Assignment

If an assignment is valid, the assignee becomes the new owner of the mark and succeeds to all the rights and responsibilities the previous trademark owner had, including but not limited to the duty to police the mark. If it is a federally registered mark, then the assignee must comply with all requirements for maintaining the registration.

The date of first use carries over from the assignor to the assignee. This means an assignee can claim priority of use from the time of the first assignor's use of the mark.

Another effect of an assignment is that it cuts off the original owner's rights in the mark. A trademark owner may be sued for both breach of contract and infringement for continuing to use the mark in commerce after having assigned it to someone else.

An invalid assignment is void. Depending on the circumstances, the reco[oemt of an invalid copyright assignment may have a claim against the purported assignor for fraud or breach of contract but title to the trademark does not pass. Only trademark owners may sue for infringement.

Although an invalid assignment does not pass title to the trademark, a trademark owner may have difficulty enforcing trademark rights if he engaged in unlawful or inequitable conduct in connection with the assignment. Courts of equity may refuse to enforce a right for the benefit a person who has "unclean hands."

Recordation

Recordation of a trademark assignment means filing a record of it with the appropriate government office, i.e., the USPTO, a foreign country's and/or a state's designated office for trademark registrations and recordation.

Recording assignments of federally registered marks with the USPTO is recommended but not required. Failure to record an assignment with the USPTO does not affect the validity of the transfer. An unrecorded assignment still has the effect of transferring all rights in the mark to the assignee.

Even if it is only optional, an assignee who is concerned about protecting and enforcing rights in the trademark may wish to consider doing it. Properly recording an assignment is constructive notice to the entire world that the mark has been assigned to a new owner. That can prevent a subsequent assignee of the same mark from claiming ownership of it.

An unrecorded assignment of a federally registered mark is void as against a subsequent bona fide purchaser who had no knowledge or notice that the mark had already been assigned to someone else. A properly recorded assignment of a federally registered mark is not void as against a subsequent purchaser of the same mark.

To be valid as against a subsequent purchaser, a federal recordation must occur within three months of the assignment or prior to the subsequent purchase.

Proper federal recordation creates a rebuttable presumption that the assignment is valid.

Terms

An assignment contract may be either unilateral or bilateral. A *unilateral* assignment contract is signed by the assignor. A *bilateral* assignment contract is signed by both the assignor and the assignee and contains mutual promises by both parties. Most assignment agreements are bilateral.

An agreement to assign a trademark should clearly identify the assignor, the assignee, and the mark. The registration or application number, if any, should be stated. For an unregistered mark, the mark should be specifically described and the specific goods or services for which the mark has been in use should be identified. It can also be a good idea to specify the date of the assignor's first use of the mark in commerce and the geographic area in which the mark has been used. A statement that the assignor has been using the mark continuously since the date of first use can also sometimes be useful.

Any representations or warranties concerning the mark, such as warranties of validity and ownership, should be stated explicitly. Any warranties that are not intended to apply should be expressly disclaimed.

Sometimes a trademark owner wishes to assign the mark to someone else while reserving a right to use the mark. This may be accomplished by a sale-and-license-back arrangement. Conceptually, the assignment should occur first, since the assignee will not have any rights to license to anybody until they have been assigned to him. It can be useful to create two separate documents: an assignment, which is executed first; and a license, which is executed second.

Other items to consider include: how to handle accrued causes of action for past infringements; a description of any known third party rights that may affect or conflict with the assignee's rights and/or with the use or registration of the mark; whether and what kind of security interest or lien the assignor is reserving in the mark; and, of course, the consideration (payment) for the assignment.

SECURITY INTERESTS AND LIENS

Like any other kind of property, a trademark may be hypothecated or used by its owner as security for a loan, or a creditor may attach it for the satisfaction of a debt in the manner provided by law.

A voluntary grant of a security interest in a trademark does not transfer ownership of the mark. It is essentially only a contingent promise to assign the mark at some time in the future. The contingency is as specified in the grant.

Because it is not an assignment, the rule against assignments in gross does not apply to grants of security interests in trademarks. If the grantor defaults, then an assignment that is made at that time must include a transfer of the goodwill along with the trademark in order to be considered valid. A security interest is not enforceable if, according to its terms, it provides for a transfer of either the mark or the goodwill by itself. In other words, a grant of a security interest that calls for an assignment in gross in the event of default is just as unenforceable as an assignment in gross. For this reason, a lender may wish to include a clause in the security agreement to the effect that goodwill will be transferred along with the trademark in the event of a default. To accomplish this, it might be necessary in some cases to expressly state in the agreement that the lender is also taking a security interest in any needed patent, trade secret, copyright, tangible assets, customer lists, etc.

Perfection and priority of security interests are governed by Article 9 of the U.C.C. or similar law that has been enacted in the relevant state. Typically, a security interest in a trademark is perfected by making a state U.C.C.-1 filing. Recording a lien with the USPTO may be necessary to cut off rights of subsequent bona fide purchasers for value.

BANKRUPTCY

If a trademark owner files for bankruptcy relief, the bankruptcy trustee succeeds to all rights in the debtor's assets, including trademark rights. Thus, a bankruptcy trustee may have a right to transfer a debtor's trademarks to other people.

A trustee's sale of the debtor's business in bankruptcy implicitly includes an assignment of any trademark associated with it, even if the contract of sale is silent about trademarks.

The Bankruptcy Code imposes certain restrictions and limitations on transfers of property, which can include intellectual property such as trademarks. Some of these may apply even before a bankruptcy petition is filed. While bankruptcy law is beyond the scope of this book, it is important to be aware that bankruptcy can have an impact on trademark rights.

Photographs and Artwork

As a rule of thumb, it should be assumed that an image found online is protected by copyright and that permission (a license) to use it is needed. This includes images that are discovered by using Google's search tools, too.

From a licensee's perspective, the best kind of license is a royalty-free license to make both commercial and noncommercial use of the image, and to modify it. A license to make commercial use of the image is essential if the image will be used on an e-commerce website.

Licenses that allow a licensee to make modifications to the image have some advantages, too. With this kind of license, a licensee will be able to crop the image and change its dimensions to fit into desired areas of a website and to make other desired changes to it.

There are several websites that offer images for users to copy and publish on their web sites. Some require the user to pay a royalty; others do not. Popular royalty-free image sites include:

WikiMedia Commons, http://commons.wikimedia.org
Creative Commons, http://search.creativecommons.org
Flickr, http://www.flickr.com/creativecommons/
The Morgue File, http://morguefile.com
Mashable, http://mashable.com/2009/08/04/free-blog-media/

The fact that an image is offered royalty-free does not mean that it is also free of licensing terms and conditions. Be sure to read the license agreement at such sites carefully. Failure to comply with a term of a license agreement pertaining to a copyright protected work is not merely a breach of the license agreement; it is copyright infringement.

Creative Commons is a particularly useful resource. It offers licenses for thousands of images. Contributors retain ownership of the copyright but agree to grant permission to anyone to use the image for specified purposes and on specified conditions. Most of these licenses require attribution of the image to the artist or photographer who created it. Some only allow noncommercial uses; others allow both commercial and noncommercial uses. Some allow modifications to be made to the work; others do not.

Many Creative Commons licenses contain share-alike provision. This means that a person who uses the image must offer it to others under the same terms and conditions. For example, if a royalty-free license contains a "share-alike" provision, then no licensee of it may demand the payment of a royalty from others who want to use it. It is important to read these terms and conditions carefully. Violating a copyright license agreement can be actionable as copyright infringement, not just breach of contract.

Some image licensing websites require payment for the use of their images. Getty Images, iStock, and Shutter Stock are examples. Images at pay sites should not be used without fully complying with all payment and other licensing requirements. Some of these sites may embed tracking information in the images they offer. Copying them without permission or without paying for them can, and often does, result in a cease and desist letter accompanied by a demand for payment of a specified amount for copyright infringement or appropriation of publicity rights. The demand may be accompanied by a threat to sue if the payment is not made. A person or business receiving this kind of letter should consult an attorney.

If an image is not offered with a license at an image repository, and it is not in the public domain, then it will be necessary to contact the copyright owner for permission to use it.

When licensing the right to use a photograph or drawing, care should be taken to ensure that permission is obtained not only from the copyright owner but also from any person who is the subject of the photograph or drawing. In many cases, a photographer or artist will secure a license (often called a "model release") from the subject. The release may authorize the photographer to do things with the photograph – copy it, distribute it, display it, edit it, use it in a compilation, etc. That agreement, however, is only between the photographer/artist and the model. A person's grant of a license to one person to use her photograph does not operate as a license of those rights to the world.

Of course, not every kind of a photograph of a person entails enforceable privacy or publicity rights. The incidental inclusion of a person's image in a newsworthy photograph may not result in liability for invasion of privacy. E-commerce website owners need to be more careful than noncommercial website owners, though, because liability for invasion of privacy or misappropriation of personality is more likely when an image is used for commercial or other advantage than when it is used for noncommercial purposes. See Chapter 17.

Children are deemed incapable of giving a valid consent, so it is necessary for a parent or le-gal guardian to give consent on their behalf. Depending on state law, an incompetent, coerced, defrauded or traumatized person may be incapable of giving consent on her own behalf, too.

If the image includes a trademark, then a trademark license may also be needed. For information about trademark fair use, see Chapter 28.

Music and Sound Recordings

For information about licensing music and sound recordings, see Chapter 33.

Audiovisual Works

It should not be assumed that a license from the owner of a copyright in an audiovisual work will suffice as protection against all copyright infringement claims. Audiovisual works often make use of several separately copyrighted works. A producer may have obtained either an assignment or a license of such copyrights. A license of an audiovisual work might effectively transfer a right to use the production element of the work but will not necessarily be effective to transfer a right to use a separately copyrighted work within it.

In the case of games, a patent license will also be needed, in addition to a copyright license, if the software or other components are patented.

Software

Most "sales" of software are really only sales of a license to use a computer program. Rights and obligations, including authorized and unauthorized uses, are usually governed by a licensing agreement, which may be set out in accompanying documentation or within the program itself.

Software may be programmed in such a way that it cannot be accessed unless the user agrees to the Terms of Use. Clicking on an 'I Accept' or 'I Agree' button in connection with the specified Terms of Use results in a clickwrap agreement, which generally has the same legal effect as a signed, written contract.

The Terms of Use almost always state that the user is only being granted a license, and that only the uses specified in the Terms of Use are authorized. If a use that exceeds the authority granted by the license also violates one of the exclusive rights of copyright owners, then it may be both a breach of contract and copyright infringement. If the software is patented, and the user exploits it commercially in a manner that is not specifically authorized by the patent owner, the user may be liable for patent infringement.

Any of the exclusive rights of a copyright owner (reproduction, distribution, display, performance, making of derivative works) that are not granted by the license remain the exclusive right of the owner. If, as is typically the case, the license agreement specifies the number of copies that may be made (e.g., for backup or personal use), then making more copies than that is a breach of the licensing contract and also infringes the copyright. Similarly, if the license expressly prohibits distribution of the software to others, then doing so is a breach of the license agreement and also copyright infringement.

If the agreement is silent about distribution, this means the copyright owner has chosen to retain the exclusive right of distribution that copyright law affords him. Therefore, distribution of the software without permission would infringe the copyright in the computer program. Similarly, if the agreement is silent about public display of the program, then displaying it (such as by posting the source or object code to a website) without the copyright owner's permission is infringement.

KINDS OF SOFTWARE LICENSES

A *single user license* is one that is intended to give only one person the right to use the software. Some single user licenses allow the user to install it on a specified number of devices. A *concurrent use license* allows more than one person to use the software. The license agreement typically will specify the maximum number of people who are authorized to use it and/or the maximum number of devices on which it may be installed. A *volume* (or "multiuser") licensing arrangement is one in which a number of licenses are sold together, usually at a discount. The individual licenses within the group may or may not be subject to single user limitations. A *site license* is one allowing the use of software on computers at a specific location or within a specific organization.

An *academic license* is one of the foregoing kinds of licenses when it is limited to use by an educational institution and its employees, students, and faculty, or a specified subset thereof. They commonly include restrictions on the purpose for which the software must be used (e.g., nonprofit uses only).

Client access licenses are licenses of server-based programs. Server-based technologies may require additional licensing fees for clients that access the server application. Usually this is charged on a per user basis. Licensing of this sort may require a licensing application or server for the sole purpose of managing the licensing.

An *end user license agreement* (EULA) is any software licensing agreement in which the licensee is a user of the software (as distinguished from a distributor, for example).

A *mass market license* is any standard form contract which the licensee must either accept or decline as-is, without negotiation. Shrinkwrap, clickwrap and browsewrap agreements are typically mass market licenses. A *shrinkwrap license* agreement is one that is included in the packaging of product, such as a computer disk containing a software program. If the packaging so provides, breaking the seal on the package may bind the purchaser to the terms of a license agreement governing the use of the software (or other product). A *clickwrap license* agreement is essentially an online version of a shrinkwrap agreement. It usually involves a website that is set up in such a way that a user must click on a button or link on the website in order to gain access to the particular content or areas on the site. A *browsewrap license* agreement is one that is claimed to be formed simply by a user's continued use of a website that contains a notice that use of the website constitutes consent to the terms of the license to use the site.

In-licensing refers to the process of licensing intellectual property from another person or business. An *outbound license* is a license that is granted to another person or business to use one's own intellectual property. *Cross-licensing* occurs when two businesses each engage in both in-licensing and outbound licensing with the other.

PREEMPTION

The portions of a licensing agreement that purport to impose an obligation on the user to refrain from infringing the copyright in the computer program are preempted by the Copyright Act.

> [A]ll legal or equitable rights that are equivalent to any of the exclusive rights within the general scope of copyright ... in works of authorship that ... come within the subject matter of copyright ... are governed exclusively by this title. Thereafter, no person is entitled to any such right or equivalent right in any such work under the common law or statutes of any State.[396]

At the same time, though, the Copyright Act is clear that "[n]othing in this title annuls or limits any rights or remedies under the common law or statutes of any State with respect to ... subject matter that does not come within the subject matter of copyright...." Nor does it annul or limit state law rights or remedies with respect to "activities violating legal or equitable rights that are not equivalent to any of the exclusive rights within the general scope of copyright...."[397]

What this means is that state law claims for breach of a promise to refrain from infringing a copyright are not enforceable. A person who breaches such a promise may still be sued for infringing a copyright but the claim must be filed under federal copyright law, not state contract law.

States are permitted to enforce legal and equitable rights that are not the equivalent of any of the exclusive rights protected by copyright law. Therefore, to the extent a right set out in a licensing agreement is not the equivalent of a right protected by copyright law, a state or common law breach of contract claim may be pursued.

An agreement not to copy material that is not protected by copyright (such as data) is enforceable under state contract law. This kind of contract does not come within the subject matter of federal copyright law because there is no copyright protection for information, so enforcement of it is not preempted by federal law.

In *ProCD, Inc. v. Zeidenberg*[398] a user of a CD containing a telephone number database made a substantial portion of it available via his website. The vendor of the CD sued for copyright infringement and breach of contract. Because it was merely a list of telephone numbers, it did not meet the originality requirement for copyright protection, so the copyright claims were dismissed. The court held, however, that the shrinkwrap agreement, which prohibited such use, was not preempted, and therefore breach of the agreement was enforceable under state contract law.

OPEN SOURCE SOFTWARE

Open source software is a computer program the source code of which is made available and may be freely copied, distributed and modified by anyone who agrees to the terms of the license. It differs from proprietary software in that proprietary software licenses normally do not authorize modifications of the source code. Open source software licenses do. The purpose of open source software is to promote collaboration and sharing among programmers, the goal being to encourage the development of improvements to software programs.

Terms of open source licenses vary. Typically they require any user who makes a derivative work based on, or incorporating, the software to make the source code available to others on the same terms. If an open source license allows users to make derivative works, then users who create such derivative works must allow others to make derivative works of those derivative works.

Open source licenses may be classified according to how protective of the open source philosophy they are. A strongly protective license is one that requires any derivative works and any software that dynamically links to the licensed work to be treated as derivative works, and to be distributed under the same open source terms as the licensed work is. Under this kind of license, merely including a hyperlink to the work results in a requirement that a program must be made open source, too. A weakly protective license requires derivative works to be open source, but does not require software to be open source merely because it links to the open source program.

Permissive licenses do not require copies of the software or derivatives of it to be distributed as open source software. A permissive license may impose other requirements, though, such as attribution of credit to the original author, a disclaimer of warranties, or the like.

The most common open source license is the GNU General Public License, which falls into the strongly protective category. The Linux operating system is distributed under this license. Examples of weakly protective licenses include the Mozilla Public License and the GNU Lesser Public License. Licenses for Apache versions after 1.0 are examples of permissive licenses, as is the Berkeley Software Distribution License and the MIT License.

Listings and copies of open source licenses may be found at www.opensource.org and www.gnu.org.

If a licensee violates a term of an open source license, the license may automatically terminate if the license agreement so provides. If the license agreement provides for a right to terminate in the event of violation, then it terminates only if the right is exercised. The licensor may also pursue any remedies for copyright infringement and/or breach of contract that may be available.

The Open Source Initiative certifies open source licenses that meet their standards. Among other things, the standards require that the source code must be made available to the licensee; modifications and the making of derivative works must be permitted; distribution of copies and of derivative works must be permitted under the same terms as the original open source license; and the licensor must treat all end users alike. The standards are published at www.opensource.org/docs/osd.

Contrary to popular belief, there is no requirement that open source software must be made available free of charge. There is no generally applicable prohibition against charging a fee for an open source software license.

An e-commerce business that is planning to incorporate open source software into other programs on its website, or to include a link to an open source program in proprietary software that is made available on the site, should carefully read the licensing agreement. Be aware that the meaning of some of the terms in open source license agreements may not always be clear, and they are not always exactly the same meanings as the terms have for the purpose of general copyright law. The term *incorporating* is an example. Depending on the kind of contract, serious consequences may result from "incorporating" an open source program into a proprietary one, including restrictions on how the proprietary software may be distributed thereafter. Unfortunately, some licenses do not clearly define what it means to "incorporate" an open source program into a proprietary one. In most cases, offering visitors an option of downloading and installing open source software for use in conjunction with proprietary software (e.g., an open source plug-in that is to be used in conjunction with proprietary software) probably will not be deemed an act of "incorporating" the open source software into the program. The line between "incorporating" open source software into proprietary software, on one hand, and using open source software "in conjunction with" proprietary software, on the other, is not always clear, though. Obviously, literally copying lines of source code from an open source file and pasting it into the source code of a proprietary program would be an act of "incorporating" it into the program. But what if, instead of copying and pasting, a program is simply designed in such a way that it is inoperable unless a user downloads and installs a particular open source program?

Would this come within the meaning of "incorporating" the open source software? Licensing agreements do not always provide clear answers to questions like these.

One way to resolve an uncertainty about the meaning of a term in a licensing agreement is to ask the licensor for clarification. If this approach is taken, it is probably safe to rely on the answer given, provided it is unequivocal and in writing. Answers to some frequently asked questions about open source licenses are offered on the Open Source Initiative and GNU websites.

Any doubts about whether to use open source software in connection with a website, or about the ramifications of an intended use of it, should be resolved against using it.

PROPRIETARY SOFTWARE

Since the expressive elements of a computer program are protected by copyright, the same general copyright considerations apply when publishing a computer program as when publishing text, drawings or any other kind of work.

In all cases, the owner of a copyright in software who wants to share it with others (either freely or for a price) should have a EULA in place. Samples can be found all over the Internet. In many cases, one of the Open Source templates that can be found online may suffice, although it should be tailored to fit individual needs. It would be a good idea to have an attorney either draft the agreement or review the EULA a client drafts.

Subject to only a few limited exceptions, a contract or agreement is not enforceable unless a person has signaled acceptance of the terms in some way. It does not have to be by means of signing a piece of paper. Acceptance may be signaled in other ways, too. Certain kinds of conduct may implicitly signal acceptance, provided the conduct is widely regarded as an implicit acceptance. For example, when a grocer displays a dollar amount next to an item and a customer brings it to a cash register and tenders the listed amount, the customer is implicitly signaling assent to the price term of an implied sales contract.

An argument might be made that using software that somebody has published online implicitly signals assent to the terms of the license the copyright owner is offering. This might be true, for example, when the licensing agreement is bundled together with the software in a zipped file that the user downloads and then decompresses for use on his computer. It is widely known that a license agreement is normally included when a software program is offered in a zip file. Accordingly, it is possible that a court might find that downloading and decompressing a zip file containing a computer program implicitly signals consent to the license agreement contained within the zip file.

On the other hand, it is also possible that a court might find a particular user was not familiar with that custom, and had no reason to be, so that acceptance of the license was not implied simply by the act of using the software. This is why the better practice is to require a user to take some additional affirmative step to signal acceptance of the terms of the license. Examples would be a radio button a user must click to get access to the software, where the button says, "I agree to the terms of the license." Alternatively, a user could be required to click a box next to the statement, "I agree to the terms and conditions set out in the licensing agreement," where the terms of the agreement are displayed adjacent to the statement. Other variations will work, too, such as a radio button after the license agreement with the words "I accept" on it.

The signaling of acceptance may also be incorporated into the software itself. For example, code can be written in such a way that the first thing to come up on the screen is a query whether the user accepts the terms and conditions of the licensing agreement, and no further operations can be performed unless and until the user clicks on the 'Yes' button.

In all events, the licensing agreement should be made available for the user to read before deciding whether to signal acceptance or not.

Terms

The terms of software licenses vary. Terms that should be included in any software licensing agreement include:

- Statement of ownership
- Description of the software
- Identification of the intellectual property interests claimed
- Description of the rights that are being licensed
- Price (or an indication that it is free)
- Duration
- Exclusive vs. nonexclusive
- Number of allowed users and/or devices
- Permitted and unpermitted uses
- Sharing policy and restrictions
- Limitation of liability
- Disclaimer of warranties.

Other matters that would be prudent to address include:

- Termination and provisions that survive termination
- Indemnification
- DMCA notice and take down provisions
- Forum selection and venue
- Choice of law
- ADR
- Transferability and assignability
- Use of information by third parties
- Nondisclosure
- Technical support
- Training
- Updates and modifications
- Copyright, patent and trademark policies.

Specific prohibitions might include prohibitions against such things as copying, distribution, reverse engineering, export, and so on. It is important to carefully consider the terms to include in a licensing agreement before the software is first offered to the public. Users who have signaled assent to the original license terms normally will not be bound by modifications and additions the proprietor unilaterally makes later.

If a special provision that the average consumer would not typically encounter in a standard software license is included, it would be a good idea to design the program and/or the web site in such a way that the user must separately signal assent to that particular term in addition to signaling assent to the license agreement as a whole. This may help avert future claims that enforcement of that particular contract term would be unfair, unconscionable or the like.

PATENTS AND TRADE SECRETS

If software is patented, then a license will be needed in order to use, make, sell or offer it for sale. A patent license should not be needed to use updates that modify a software program after it was patented, unless another patent has been obtained for the modification. If the information embodied in the modification is protected as a trade secret, however, then it should be made clear in the licensing agreement whether the license also includes a right to use, distribute, etc. any updates that are issued. Even if no patent or trade secret is implicated, software updates will usually contain some expressive content. Accordingly, a software licensing agreement should address the question whether the license applies to the original content only or to both the original content and any updates that are issued. If it covers both original content and updates, then the agreement should further specify what kinds of property rights are being licensed—copyright, patent, trade secret, or a combination of two or more of these.

NONDISCLOSURE AGREEMENTS

Nondisclosure provisions in a software license are important if the software contains proprietary information and/or a trade secret. The provision should detail what information is covered and what is not. The duration of the agreement should be specified.

Website Designer and Developer Agreements

To prevent misunderstandings and to ensure enforceability, agreements with web designers and developers should be in writing and signed. In addition to addressing the price, timeframe and other business concerns, they should also address legal issues, especially copyrights and domain name rights.

In the absence of a valid work made for hire contract or an employment relationship, a person who creates content for a website owns the copyright in the content he creates. This is true even if the website owner owns the domain name and pays for the hosting service. A company that fails to pay a designer after the website is created, and changes the password so that the designer can no longer access the site, may be prosecuted for violating state criminal laws.[399] The designer's ownership of the copyright also means that he alone may make derivative works from these things (modify them). This puts a website owner's rights in any content he later adds to the site at risk,. This would amount to making a derivative work. A person who creates a derivative work without the copyright owner's permission does not acquire a copyright in the content so created. In the absence of an agreement otherwise, a website owner could be infringing the designer's exclusive right to make derivative works if the website owner alters, removes or adds to content the designer created.

To protect rights in new content, and to avoid infringement liability to the designer, a website owner might include provisions in the agreement to the effect that the website owner has a right to make derivative works and that the website owner will be the owner of the copyright in any derivative works she creates.

But what if the website owner, at some point, makes and prints screenshots of the website? In this case, she would be infringing the copyright owner's exclusive right to reproduce a work. Other kinds of uses of website content may violate some of the other exclusive rights of copyright, as well. For this reason, a better solution would be for the website owner to take ownership of the website content.

One way to do this would be for the website owner to make the designer his employee. This will make the creation of web content a work made for hire. The website owner then would automatically be considered the author and copyright owner of the content. A major drawback to structuring the transaction as an employment transaction is that the website owner will be required to withhold and pay payroll taxes and may become subject to worker's compensation and an array of other labor laws. Another drawback is that an employer is vicariously liable for the acts of its employees in the course of employment.

If the designer has other clients, it may make more sense to treat the designer as an independent contractor rather than as an employee, and enter into a work made for hire agreement with the designer as an independent contractor. If the designer creates content as a work made for hire for the website owner, then the website owner will automatically be the copyright owner of the content. There will be no need for an assignment or license of rights from the designer to the website owner if the arrangement is structured this way.

The Copyright Act only allows certain categories of creative contributions to be made the subject of a work made for hire agreement. Illustrations and graphics a designer creates for a website arguably come within the "supplementary work" category. The selection and arrangement of website elements come within the "compilation" category. Because contributed text or artwork must be "supplementary," a work made for hire agreement is not appropriate in cases where the designer creates the entire website including all the text.

If the website is copyrighted as a collective work, then small amounts of text contributed by the designer could be considered contributions to a collective work. In this case, however, the website owner, although owning the copyright in the compilation, would not own the copyright in the designer's contribution, and would be liable to the designer for infringement if she modified the designer's contribution at some time.

Only copyright rights are acquired in a work made for hire arrangement. Trademark and other intellectual property rights are not. When hiring someone to create a logo or image to be used in connection with marketing a product or service (which may include the website itself), the contract should address both copyright and trademark ownership, rights and permissions.

In all events, a website owner should consider including a clause stating that the designer/contributor warrants that the work he creates, obtains or contributes pursuant to the agreement does not infringe copyright(s) or trademark(s). A commercial website owner may be held vicariously liable for infringing content that a designer or other third party provides or creates for the website. An indemnification clause would be a good idea.

The contract should be clear about who is responsible for paying for any third party content (such as software licenses) the designer obtains for the site.

A work made for hire agreement is enforceable only if it is made before the work is created, and it must be in writing and signed. Also, it would be a good idea to expressly state in the contract that the designer is an independent contractor and not an employee.

In cases where a work made for hire arrangement is not feasible (such as where the designer creates most of the content for the site, not just the artwork and arrangement of the site; or the designer has already created some of the artwork), a similar result can be achieved by means of an assignment of the designer's copyright(s) to the website owner. Although not required, it can be a good idea to record the assignment with the Copyright Office.

If a web designer has already created artwork or designs and wants to be able to use them in other projects, then an assignment or work made for hire arrangement will not be feasible with respect to those works. In this situation, the parties may wish to consider including a provision in which the designer grants the website owner a nonexclusive license to use those works. If this approach is taken, then take care to ensure that the agreement is very clear about:

(a) the specific works in which the designer claims ownership
(b) the specific works the designer is licensing
(c) what rights are being licensed to the website owner (reproduction, distribution, public display, public performance, digital transmission, the making of derivative works).

If the designer claims ownership of elements that a website owner may wish to modify (such as the text of one or more of the pages on the site, or the selection and arrangement of website elements, for example), then the website owner will want to make sure the agreement explicitly gives him the right to create derivative works, and addresses the following issues: who will own the copyrights in derivative works and derivative works of derivative works; whether the webpage owner has a right to sublicense the right to make derivative works and who will own the copyright in derivative works created pursuant to a sublicense; whether the license is exclusive or nonexclusive, and so on. Keep in mind that courts do not agree about whether sublicenses of an exclusive copyright right are valid.

Because copyright and trademark are separate and distinct rights, a copyright license is not a grant of permission to use a work, or a portion of a work, as a trademark. By the same token, a trademark assignment or license is not a grant of permission to copy, distribute, publicly display or make derivative works based on the copyright-protected elements of the mark. When appropriate, be sure the contract addresses both copyright and trademark rights.

An agreement may provide for the assignment of some elements and the grant of a license for others. For example, a designer who might want to use drawings and graphics in the design of more than one client's website may want to retain ownership of the copyright and agree only to grant a nonexclusive license to a website owner. She may have less concern about any text she has created for the site, and may even expect the website owner to add to, or alter it, over time. The website owner will have an interest in being able to make changes to the text without acquiring special permission, in writing, from the designer each and every time he wishes to make such a change. Accordingly, it would be reasonable for an agreement to provide that the designer retains ownership of the copyrights in the drawings and graphics she creates, the website owner is granted a nonexclusive license of specified rights to use them, and the designer assigns ownership of the copyright in the text, compilation and everything else to the website owner. If trademarks appear on the website, make sure the contract covers both copyright and trademark rights.

Whether the arrangement is structured as a work made for hire, an assignment or a license, make sure that the contract is clear about what copyright(s) the website owner will own. Ideally, this should include all screens, drawings, graphics, text, content, specific software developed for the site, the "look and feel" of the site, derivative works, compilations, and everything else the designer creates for the site. Remember that the copyright in a compilation is distinct from the copyright in a work within the compilation, so ownership of the copyright in the selection and arrangement of website elements should be explicitly addressed. Even if the copyrights in all the pictures, articles, and other individual elements are owned by the website owner, she may be liable to the designer for infringement if she later removes or adds content, or alters their location or appearance on the website, if the designer owns the compilation copyright in the website.

If it is not possible to negotiate this kind of deal with the designer, then the website owner should at least ensure that the contract grants the website owner an irrevocable, royalty-free license to use the kinds of content the contract specifies the designer will retain. For example, if the designer creates an image for the site and insists on retaining ownership, then the website owner should ensure that the contract provides for a grant of the described license to use the image. If the designer writes a patentable program for the site, then the website owner will want to ensure that the contract also provides for the grant of a patent license. Ideally, the contract should provide that the designer agrees to immediately grant the website owner a nonexclusive, irrevocable, royalty-free patent license. A website owner should strive to retain ownership of all intellectual property that is created for the website, to the fullest extent possible.

The contract should also be clear about who will be responsible for registering the domain name and contracting for web hosting service, as well as what the domain name will be and who owns it, i.e., in whose name it will be registered. A prudent website owner will want to ensure that she is the only one with access to the administrative controls for the domain name at the registrar's site. The password should be changed once the relationship with the designer has concluded.

To avoid misunderstandings, the agreement should be specific about what the designer agrees to do and in what timeframe. The allocation of responsibility for providing content (such as pictures, logos, text, etc.) should be spelled out. The expected functionality of the website should also be made clear to both the web designer and the web developer (if any) —e.g., a functioning online ordering system; integration of payment gateways; the ability to send and receive email; clickwrap agreement(s); chat; search engine optimization (SEO); reporting of statistics on "hits" to the site; speed; bandwidth; browser compatibility; special effects; and so on. The contract may provide for a beta testing period so the website owner can determine if there are any bugs and the designer can have an opportunity to fix them.

The website owner may find it prudent to include a clause in which the designer warrants that all work performed is free of defects, viruses and other kinds of malware, and meets all functionality needs. The length of the warranty period within which the designer or developer will fix problems for free should be specified. In addition, a website owner may want to include a provision requiring the designer or developer to pay all out of pocket expenses that are incurred to make the site functional and free of defects, etc.

A web designer or developer may wish to include limitations of liability in the contract. These could take the form of an "as is" arrangement (no liability) to a limitation of damages to a specified amount.

The agreement should also be clear about who is responsible for expenses such as hosting fees, domain name registration, security certificate, copyright license fees, etc. Of course, the web designer's or developer's fee and the terms of payment should also be specified. The fee or an hourly rate for unanticipated extra work the website owner might ask the designer or developer to do should also be specified. The agreement, and all modifications to it, should be in writing and signed by both parties.

Confidentiality provisions may be necessary if the designer or developer will be working with the website owner's client information, trade secrets, and any other confidential information the designer may come across while building the site.

WEB DEVELOPER AGREEMENTS

Web designers are concerned with the "look and feel" of a website site. Web developers are concerned with its functionality. The same general set of considerations applies to contracts with web developers as applies to contracts with web designers. In addition, when working with a web developer, the website owner should ensure that she has a clear understanding of what the developer can and will do, and that the developer understands the expected functionality of the website and is agreeing to make it happen for the client. The specifications the website must meet in order for the website owner to be obligated to pay for the developer's work should be spelled out very clearly in the contract. A timeframe for the developer to fix any bugs and make any reasonably requested changes should also be specified.

The parties should anticipate that there may be bugs in the website when the developer completes it. Provisions for testing, repairs and maintenance of the website, therefore, should be included in the agreement. Whether, and how much, the client will pay for requested changes should also be addressed.

The contract should also make it clear who will be responsible for contracting for Internet and web hosting service; selecting and registering the domain name (and who will own it, i.e., in whose name it will be registered); and obtaining any needed licenses and permissions from third parties. Most developer agreements assign these responsibilities to the website owner. A prudent website owner will want to ensure that she is the only one with access to the administrative controls for the domain name at the registrar's site. The password should be changed once the relationship with the developer has concluded.

The contract should also address who must pay for obtaining any software and development tools. Usually, the developer agrees to take responsibility for this, but the parties may agree to allocate obligations any way they wish.

Web Hosting Agreements

An e-commerce business should carefully review the terms and conditions set out in any website hosting agreement before selecting a web host, paying particular attention to whether any conditions or restrictions may impair the company's ability to use its web site in the desired way. Are there restrictions against commercial use? What about restrictions against the particular kind of e-commerce activity the company has planned?

The company should also be wary of onerous clauses. For example, some web hosting contracts provide that by using the hosting service, website owners assign their copyrights in website content to the hosting service. It is difficult to imagine a scenario in which it would be a good idea for a website owner to agree to this. Normally, a website owner will want to retain the freedom to make changes to content, to change hosting services, to prevent the content from being sold or licensed to others, and to exercise control over the website content without having to obtain the hosting company's permission. A website owner also will not want to find herself in the position of having to buy back the right to use her own content.

Chapter 33. Music and Sound Recordings

Depending on the nature, format and kinds of uses to which music and sound recordings are sought to be put, a copyright license and/or a trademark license may be needed. Licensing trademark rights in a musical sound mark does not involve any significant issues other than those addressed in Chapter 28. Licensing copyrights in musical works and sound recordings is a little more complicated.

Kinds of licenses

The principal kinds of copyright licenses pertinent to musical works and sound recordings are:

- Folio
- Performance
- Mechanical
- Master use
- Synchronization

A *mechanical* license is a license to make and distribute copies of a musical work. A *master use* license is a license to make and distribute copies of a sound recording. A *performance* license is a license to publicly perform a musical work or sound recording. A *synchronization* license is a license to use music in combination with another work, such as a video. A *folio* license is a license to publish sheet music or the tablature for a musical work.

There are five basic kinds of uses to which music and sound recordings are put on Internet websites:

- Noninteractive streaming
- Interactive streaming
- Distributing copies
- Synchronizing with video
- Publishing sheet music, tablature and/or lyrics.

Noninteractive streaming means the digital transmission of a broadcast or the digital performance of a musical work or sound recording by a website to users over the Internet without a user's involvement in the selection. Internet radio and website background music that plays automatically anytime the site is accessed are examples. *Interactive streaming*, also known as "on demand streaming," refers to the streaming of a recording that a user selects.

When determining what kinds of licenses are needed, it is important to keep in mind that a copyright in a musical work is distinct and different from the copyright in a recorded performance of it.

Musical Works

PUBLISHING SHEET MUSIC, TABLATURE AND LYRICS

Folio licenses are obtained by negotiation with the owner of the copyright in the musical work, or the owner's agent. There is no compulsory or statutory license to publish sheet music, tablature or lyrics.

Songwriters often assign their copyrights to a publisher and the publisher, in return, agrees to pay a portion of the revenue to the songwriter. Sometimes, though, a songwriter will retain ownership of the copyright and enter into a revenue sharing agreement with the publisher. In yet other cases, a song may be self-published or it may not have been published at all.

PERFORMING MUSIC

The owner of the copyright in a musical composition has the exclusive right to perform it in public. Broadcasting or streaming a performance of a song – whether it is live or prerecorded, analog or digital, interactive or noninteractive – is a public performance of it. Unless a "fair use" exception applies (see Chapter 25), a performance license from the owner of the copyright in the musical work is needed.

Performance rights agencies handle licensing of musical works for many songwriters. The principal ones are:

- ASCAP (American Society of Composers, Authors and Publishers)
- BMI (Broadcast Music Incorporated)
- SESAC (Society of European Stage Authors and Composers)
- ACMLA (Association of Composers and Publishers of Latin American Music)
- PRS (Performing Rights Society, U.K.-based).

If a particular song is not in any agency's repertory, then the copyright owner (or her agent) will need to be contacted directly. Moreover, these agencies are usually not an artist's exclusive agent. Accordingly, a person seeking a license to perform a musical work may instead negotiate with the copyright owner directly even if the work is in one of these agencies' repertory.

Performance rights agencies license the right to publicly perform musical works at concerts; in radio or television broadcasts; as background music in bars, restaurants and retail stores; for music-on-hold services; and for transmissions via the Internet. They do not handle folio licenses or mechanical licenses. A performance license does not confer authority to make digital files of the performance available for download on a website, or to sell or give away copies of a CD of the performance. A performance rights licensing agreement does not include the right to make derivative works, such as arrangements, unless the contract so provides.

Dramatic performances (such as plays, musical plays, opera and ballet scores) are not usually authorized by a license issued by one of these agencies, but such licenses sometimes permit nondramatic performances of musical works that have been used in dramatic performances.

A website featuring noninteractive streaming of a musical work will need a performance license for the musical work. A mechanical license is not needed inasmuch as no copies, digital or otherwise, are made and distributed.

Because interactive streaming is functionally similar to both the performance of a musical work and the delivery of a copy of it to the user, both a performance license and a mechanical license may be needed. The performance license may be obtainable through ASCAP or another performance rights agency, but a mechanical license is not.

A compulsory license is one that is established by law when certain conditions are met. There is no compulsory license for performance rights in a musical work. A compulsory license might exist for recording and distributing copies of a musical composition, but not for performing it.

Royalty and Terms

Performance rights licensing agencies set their own rates and terms. Usually, the royalty is calculated as a percentage of the licensee's revenue, but an agency may, in the alternative, offer a blanket license for the use of multiple songs for a specified fee.

ASCAP has established a variety of different rates and terms, depending on whether performance rights are sought for audio or audiovisual transmissions; live or prerecorded transmissions; interactive or noninteractive streaming; the size of the establishment and the potential audience; and other considerations. The ASCAP website has a rate calculator for determining the amount of the royalty. Rates for interactive streaming are typically the greater of a royalty calculated as a percentage of revenue or a per-session royalty, subject to a minimum royalty "floor." It also offers a blanket license option for Internet transmissions of musical works. With a blanket license, a licensee may use any song or combinations of songs in the ASCAP repertory for a single fee. The amount of the fee is tied to a site's traffic and revenue volumes. More information about blanket licenses and the terms and rates for interactive and noninteractive streaming can be found on their website, www.ascap.com.

BMI also has established a variety of different rates and terms for interactive and noninteractive transmissions and other public performances of musical works, depending on whether performance rights are sought for a music services site; a site that sells other things in addition to music; a business site making only incidental use of music; a nonprofit organization site; or a site that makes audiovisual transmissions of music. More information may be found at the BMI website, www.bmi.com.

SESAC, like the other performance rights agencies, licenses musical works for interactive or noninteractive streaming, as well as other kinds of public performances. The royalty rate is calculated on the basis of either aggregate tuning hours or a percentage of revenues.

More information can be found at the SESAC website, www.sesac.com.

MAKING AND DISTRIBUTING COPIES OF A MUSICAL WORK

A mechanical license is needed to make and distribute copies of a performance of a copyrighted musical work, whether the copies are physical or digital downloads. Interactive streaming is functionally equivalent to distributing a copy, albeit only for a limited time, so it arguably requires both a performance license and a mechanical license. A mechanical license is not needed for noninteractive streaming.

The Harry Fox Agency is the primary agency for the mechanical licensing of musical works. It handles licenses to make and distribute physical copies (e.g., CDs) as well as ringtones and digital downloads. It handles both voluntary and compulsory licenses. It does not handle performance rights.

Check the website for current rates, www.harryfox.com.

A person who is interested in obtaining a mechanical license for a musical work is not required to work with the Harry Fox Agency. Licenses may also be obtained in two other ways: negotiation with the copyright owner (or his agent) directly, or by invoking and satisfying the requirements for a compulsory license.

Compulsory Licenses

A compulsory license is a statutory license to make and distribute copies of a musical work. It is a license that the Copyright Act automatically grants to anyone who wants to record and distribute a performance of a song even if the copyright owner does not consent to it—provided certain conditions are met. Basically, it is the right to record and distribute a performance of a cover version of another person's copyrighted musical composition.

The compulsory license only applies to the right to record a musical work and then distribute copies of the recording. It does not include a right to publicly perform the song, such as by noninteractive streaming. A compulsory license also does not confer synchronization rights. A compulsory license does not confer the right to make a music video of a performance of a musical work.

A compulsory license is subject to certain conditions, limitations and exclusions:

(a) There is no compulsory license for dramatic works.
(b) At least one recording authorized by the copyright owner must already have been made. This ensures that songwriters have the first shot at exploiting their works commercially.
(c) No alteration of the basic melody or fundamental character of the work is allowed.
(d) Notice must be sent to the copyright owner before any copies are distributed, and not later than thirty days after the recording is made.
(e) A royalty must be paid.
(f) Periodic accountings are required.
(g) Distribution must be limited to members of the public for their personal use.

A compulsory license does not include a right to make and distribute copies for use in background music systems, jukeboxes, broadcasting, or other public uses.

NOTICE OF INTENTION TO OBTAIN A COMPULSORY LICENSE

A person seeking a compulsory license must serve written notice of intention to obtain a compulsory license on the owner of the copyright in the musical work, or her agent. The notice must be served no later than thirty days after recording a performance of the work, but before copies are distributed.

If Copyright Office records do not identify the copyright owner(s), or do not include an address at which notice can be served, then the notice may instead be filed with the Copyright

Office. In the case of co-owners of a copyright, service on one co-owner is deemed to be service on all co-owners.

A separate notice must be served for each musical work for which a compulsory license is sought.

The notice must be served by mail or by a reputable courier service at the last address of the copyright owner that is shown in the Copyright Office records. If the notice is returned to sender because the copyright owner is no longer at that address or has refused delivery, then the original notice must be filed with the Licensing Division of the Copyright Office along with a brief statement that the notice was sent to the last address for the copyright owner shown by the Copyright Office records but was returned. Appropriate evidence of attempted mailing may be included. No filing fee is required for a notice that is filed under these circumstances.

If the Copyright Office records do not identify the copyright owner or do not provide address information about the copyright owner, then the notice may be served by filing it with the Copyright Office, along with a filing fee. Alternatively, if the copyright owner's address is actually known, then the notice may be served by sending it to that address. If the notice is sent to a person who is not listed as the copyright owner in the Copyright Office's records, or to an address that is not on file with the Copyright Office, the sender assumes all risk that the address is correct. If it is not correct, then the notice will not be deemed to have been properly served.

Although not required, certified or registered mail is recommended. A mailing receipt will establish the date of mailing. This can be critical in the event an issue about the timeliness of a notice is raised. A reputable courier service that provides written documentation showing the first date of attempted delivery will also suffice.

As of October 20, 2016, the filing fee was $75, plus an additional $20 per group of one to ten titles (or $10 per group of 1 to 100 titles, if filing electronically). Fees are subject to change.

A notice is not deemed filed until both the notice (with all required elements included) and the filing fee(s) are received in the Copyright Office. The Copyright Office does not review notices for legal sufficiency.

If a notice identifies more than fifty works, the copyright owner or his agent may demand a copy of the notice and a list of the works be resubmitted in electronic format. The person seeking the compulsory license has thirty days after receiving such a demand to provide these things on magnetic disk or another acceptable medium for electronic storage of data. If the copyright owner's demand authorizes it, the list may be sent via email.

Failure to timely and properly serve a Notice of Intention forecloses the possibility of a compulsory license. Without either a compulsory license or a voluntary (negotiated) license, making and distributing recordings of a copyrighted musical work may result in liability for copyright infringement.

There is no compulsory license to make and distribute copies of a musical work unless a copyright owner is identified in a registration or some other record that has been filed with the Copyright Office.

ARRANGEMENTS

An arrangement of a musical work is a derivative work. If the copyright owner, although retaining ownership of the original work, has authorized another person to make and retain the copyright in an arrangement, then a person seeking to make and distribute copies of a performance of the arrangement will need to secure a license from the owner of the copyright in the arrangement as well as from the owner of the copyright in the original musical work.

A person wishing to make his own arrangement of someone else's copyrighted musical work will need to obtain a license to make a derivative work. To make and distribute copies of a recording of the work as so arranged, a mechanical license for the original elements of the musical work will be needed. Making and distributing an unauthorized derivative work is infringement and does not receive copyright protection.

A compulsory license includes a license to make a new arrangement of a musical work without need for the copyright owner's permission, provided it does not change the basic melody or the fundamental character of the work. Unless the copyright owner agrees, however, a compulsory licensee does not acquire a copyright in the arrangement.

INTERACTIVE STREAMING

Compulsory licensing is intended to apply to reproduction and distribution rights, not performance rights. It clearly authorizes distribution of digital downloads and physical copies and clearly does not include broadcast performances and noninteractive Internet transmissions. Whether it applies to interactive streaming is not as clear. The compulsory license established in the Copyright Act authorizes the making and distribution of physical copies (such as CDs) and "digital phonorecord deliveries," which are defined as:

> [E]ach individual delivery of a phonorecord by digital transmission of a sound recording which results in a specifically identifiable reproduction by or for any transmission recipient of a phonorecord of that sound recording, regardless of whether the digital transmission is also a public performance of the sound recording or any nondramatic musical work embodied therein. A digital phonorecord delivery does not result from a real-time, noninteractive subscription transmission of a sound recording where no reproduction of the sound recording or the musical work embodied therein is made from the inception of the transmission through to its receipt by the transmission recipient in order to make the sound recording audible.[400]

The Code of Federal Regulations clarifies that the copy may be permanent or it may be made available to the recipient for a limited period of time or for a specified number of performances; and that all phonorecords that are made for the purpose of making a digital phonorecord delivery are themselves digital phonorecord deliveries. Unfortunately, this does not really help to clear things up very much.

Music industry representatives once asked the copyright board to rule on whether interactive streaming is a digital phonorecord delivery, and therefore subject to compulsory licensing, or not. The board declined to decide the issue, taking the position that it is a fact question, not a legal question. Subsequently, industry stakeholders reached a settlement agreement. The agreement classifies an interactive stream as an "incidental phonorecord delivery" for purposes of 17 U.S.C. § 115(c)(3)(C) and (D). These provisions relate to compulsory licensing of musical works for digital phonorecord delivery. Unless a court someday rules otherwise, then, it would appear that interactive streaming is subject to compulsory licensing, and the royalty rate for it is the rate applicable to "incidental phonorecord deliveries" as determined by the copyright board in a Chapter 8 proceeding.[401]

Royalties

If the copyright owner is identified in Copyright Office records, then a compulsory licensee must pay a royalty to the copyright owner, but only for any recordings that are made and distributed after Copyright Office records first identified the copyright owner.

The amount of the royalty for copies delivered before January 1, 1998 is $0.0275 per copy or $0.005 per minute of playing time (or fraction thereof), whichever is larger. Royalty payments are due by the twentieth day of the month following the month in which the royalty was earned,

After December 31, 1997, the royalty may be fixed by negotiated agreement between copyright owner(s) and compulsory licensee(s). The agreement may designate nonexclusive agents to negotiate, agree to, pay or receive royalty payments. The agreement may also specify in what year(s) royalty rates will be determined in a Chapter 8 proceeding. (A Chapter 8 proceeding is commenced by filing a petition with the Copyright Royalty Board.)

Instead of specifying that rates and terms will be as provided in a Chapter 8 proceeding, the parties (copyright owner and compulsory licensee) may enter into a voluntary agreement concerning rates and terms of royalties. If they do so, then their agreement, not the rates and terms determined in a Chapter 8 proceeding, governs the rates and terms of royalty payments.

An interested party may commence a Chapter 8 proceeding to determine reasonable royalty rates and terms of royalty payments for compulsory licenses, to go into effect no earlier than January 1 of the second year following the year the petition is filed. Except as noted above, the rates and terms determined by the copyright royalty board are binding on all copyright owners of nondramatic musical works and persons entitled to obtain a compulsory license. Interested parties may submit copies of their voluntary licensing agreements, which the judges may consider when setting reasonable rates for the future. The copyright royalty judges also establish notice and recordkeeping requirements.

PERMANENT DOWNLOADS AND PHYSICAL COPIES

A *permanent* digital download is one that may be retained and accessed by the recipient anytime he chooses. As of October 20, 2016, the royalty rate the Copyright Royalty Board has set for physical copies and permanent digital downloads of nondramatic music is $0.091 per song delivered to a user or $0.0175 per minute of playing time or fraction thereof, whichever is larger. For a ringtone, the rate is $0.24 per ringtone delivered to a user. Accordingly, unless a compulsory licensee has entered into a different agreement with the copyright owner or his agent, a per-song royalty for cover versions of songs that are performed, recorded and delivered to members of the public on physical copies or in permanent digital downloads in the described amounts must be paid. Check with the Copyright Office for current rates.

INTERACTIVE STREAMING AND LIMITED DOWNLOADS

A *limited download* is one that delivers a copy of a sound recording that may only be listened to (a) for a period of less than one month, or for periods of up to one month if renewed, or in the case of a subscription a period of time following the end of the applicable subscription no longer than a subscription renewal period or three months, whichever is shorter, or (b) a specified number of times not to exceed twelve (unless the service, in lieu of retransmitting the same sound recording as another limited download, separately and upon specific request of the end user made through a live network connection, reauthorizes use of another series of twelve or fewer plays, or in the case of a subscription transmission, twelve times after the end of the applicable subscription.

Unless a copyright owner agrees otherwise, a per-song royalty for recorded musical works that are delivered to members of the public by means of interactive streaming or limited digital downloading must be paid. As of October 1, 2016, the royalty is calculated as follows:

(1) Determine the gross annual revenue from sales of interactive streaming and limited downloads of music. Include payments from users for the service and any revenue received by way of sponsorship and commissions as a result of including third party in-stream or in-download advertising as part of the transmission or download, or as a result of placing third party advertising on a relevant page or on a page that directly follows the page leading up to and including the interactive streaming or limited download page or any page that directly follows it. Do not include any revenue from activity to which the promotional royalty rate applies.

(2) Apply 10.5% to the amount calculated in Step 1. (For pre-2008 transmissions, the applicable percentage is 8.5%.)

(3) Determine the minimum royalty specified in 37 CFR § 385.13.

(a) For stand-alone nonportable subscription services offering interactive streaming only, the minimum royalty is the lesser of (i) the aggregate amount of $0.50 per subscriber per month or (ii) one of the following, as applicable: (I) If a record company is the licensee, and a third party service has obtained from the record company the rights to make interactive streams and limited downloads of a sound recording together with the right to reproduce and distribute the musical work embodied therein, 18% of the total amount expensed by the service, including the value of any barter or other nonmonetary consideration provided by the service, for such rights, except that for licensed activity occurring on or before January 1, 2008, it is 14.53% of the amount expensed by the service for such rights for the accounting period; (II) If the relevant service is the licensee and has obtained from a record company the rights to make interactive streams or limited downloads of a sound recording without the right to reproduce and distribute the musical work embodied therein, 22% of the total amount expensed by the service, including the value of any barter or other nonmonetary consideration provided by the service, for such sound recording rights, except that for licensed activity occurring before January 1, 2008, it is 17% of the amount expensed by the service for such sound recording rights for the accounting period.

(b) For other stand-alone nonportable subscription services offering interactive streaming and/or limited downloads, the minimum royalty is the lesser of: (i) the aggregate amount of $0.50 per subscriber per month or (ii) one of the following, as applicable: (I) If a record company is the licensee, and a third party service has obtained from the record company the rights to make interactive streams and limited downloads of a sound recording together with the right to reproduce and distribute the musical work embodied therein, 17.36% of the total amount expensed by the service, including the value of any barter or other nonmonetary consideration provided by the service, for such rights, except that for licensed activity occurring on or before January 1, 2008, it is 14.53% of the amount expensed by the service for such rights for the accounting period; (II) If the relevant service is the licensee and has obtained from a record company the rights to make interactive streams or limited downloads of a sound recording without the right to reproduce and distribute the musical work embodied therein, 21% of the total amount expensed by the service, including the value of any barter or other nonmonetary consideration provided by the service, for such sound recording rights, except that for licensed activity occurring January 1, 2008, it is 17% of the amount expensed by the service for such sound recording rights for the accounting period.

(c) For stand-alone portable interactive streaming or limited download subscription services, the minimum royalty is the lesser of: (i) the aggregate amount of $0.80 per subscriber per month or (ii) one of the following, as applicable: (I) If a record company is the licensee, and a third party service has obtained from the record company the rights to make interactive streams and limited downloads of a sound recording together with the right to reproduce and distribute the musical work embodied therein, 17.36% of the total amount expensed by the service, including the value of any barter or other nonmonetary consideration provided by the service, for such rights, except that for licensed activity occurring on or before January 1, 2008, it is 14.53% of the amount expensed by the service for such rights for the accounting period; (II) If the relevant service is the licensee and has obtained from a record company the rights to make interactive streams or limited downloads of a sound recording without the right to reproduce and distribute the musical work embodied therein, 21% of the total amount expensed by the service, including the value of any barter or other nonmonetary consideration provided by the service, for such sound recording rights, except that for licensed activity occurring January 1, 2008, it is 17% of the amount expensed by the service for such sound recording rights for the accounting period.

(d) For subscription services bundled with other products or services, where the subscription service is not separately priced, the minimum royalty is one of the following, as applicable: (i) If a record company is the licensee, and a third party service has obtained from the record company the rights to make interactive streams and limited downloads of a sound recording together with the right to reproduce and distribute the musical work embodied therein, 17.36% of the total amount expensed by the service, including the value of any barter or other nonmonetary consideration provided by the service, for such rights, except that for licensed activity occurring on or before January 1, 2008, it is 14.53% of the amount expensed by the service for such rights for the accounting period; (ii) If the relevant service is the licensee and has obtained from a record company the rights to make interactive streams or limited downloads of a sound recording without the right to reproduce and distribute the musical work embodied therein, 21% of the total amount expensed by the service, including the value of any barter or other nonmonetary consideration provided by the service, for such sound recording rights, except that for licensed activity occurring January 1, 2008, it is 17% of the amount expensed by the service for such sound recording rights for the accounting period.

(e) For nonsubscription interactive streaming or limited download services, the minimum royalty is one of the following, as applicable: (i) If a record company is the licensee, and a third party service has obtained from the record company the rights to make interactive streams and limited downloads of a sound recording together with the right to reproduce and distribute the musical work embodied therein, 18% of the total amount expensed by the service, including the value of any barter or other nonmonetary consideration provided by the service, for such rights, except that for licensed activity occurring on or before January 1, 2008, it is 14.53% of the amount expensed by the service for such rights for the accounting period; (ii) If the relevant service is the licensee and has obtained from a record company the rights to make interactive streams or limited downloads of a sound recording without the right to reproduce and distribute the musical work embodied therein, 22% of the total amount expensed by the service, including the value of any barter or other nonmonetary consideration provided by the service, for such sound recording rights, except that for licensed activity occurring January 1, 2008, it is 17% of the amount expensed by the service for such sound recording rights for the accounting period.

(4) Determine the "all-in royalty." This is the greater of the percentage royalty calculated in step (2) and the minimum royalty calculated in step (3).

(5) Subtract any performance royalties that have been paid through other means for interactive streaming or partial downloads.

(6) Determine the subscriber-based royalty floor specified in 37 CFR § 385.13

(a) For stand-alone nonportable interactive streaming subscription services, it is the aggregate amount of $0.15 per subscriber per month.

(b) For stand-alone nonportable interactive streaming or limited download subscription services, it is the aggregate amount of $.30 per subscriber per month.

(c) For stand-alone portable interactive streaming or limited download subscription services, it is the aggregate amount of $0.50 per subscriber per month.

(d) For subscription services that are bundled with other products or services, where the subscription service is not separately priced, it is the aggregate of $0.25 per month for each end user who has made at least one play of a licensed work during such month.

(e) There is no subscriber-based royalty floor for nonsubscription interactive streaming or limited download services.

(7) The greater of (5) and (6) is the "Payable Royalty Pool."

(8) Calculate the per-work royalty allocation of the Payable Royalty Pool for each relevant work. This is done by dividing the Payable Royalty Pool by the total number of non-

promotional plays, and then multiplying that fraction by the number of plays a particular song received. Longer songs count as more than one play. For transmissions after October 1, 2010, the first five minutes of a song is considered a "play;" each additional minute is 0.2 "plays." A fraction of a minute is rounded up to the next whole minute. For example, playing a six-minute song one time would count as 1.2 plays of the song; playing a ten-minute song one time would count as two plays of the song.

In the case of an end user who was a subscriber for only a portion of a month, the month must be prorated when computing subscriber-based royalty rates. Months must be deducted on a prorated basis for end users who were covered by a free trial period that is subject to the promotional royalty rate, except that in the case of a bundled subscription service, subscriber-months are instead determined with respect to active subscribers. The product of the total number of subscriber-months for the accounting period and the specified number of cents per subscriber (or active subscriber, as the case may be) is to be used as the subscriber-based component of the minimum or subscriber-based royalty floor, as applicable, for the accounting period.

When streaming and/or partial downloads are bundled with other products or services, the stand-alone published price for end users of each of the other components of the bundle must be deducted when computing gross annual revenue from sales of interactive streaming and limited downloads of music. If there is none, then the average stand-alone published price for end users of the most closely comparable service in the United States is to be used.

Royalty rates are subject to change. Check with the Copyright Office for the latest rates.

A compulsory licensee must maintain accounting records showing how the royalty was calculated for each work. In addition, a statement of account must accompany each monthly royalty payment, and the licensee must provide the copyright owner (or his agent) a CPA-certified annual accounting of royalties earned. Both the monthly and the annual statements of account should be sent by registered or certified mail. The accounting statements must contain information specified by the Register of Copyrights.

If a licensee fails to provide a monthly or annual accounting statement, the copyright owner may give written notice to the licensee that if the default is not cured within thirty days from the date of notice, the compulsory license will be automatically terminated. Thereafter, any further sale or distribution of copies for which royalties have not been made is actionable as copyright infringement.

Background Music, Digital Jukeboxes, and Distributing Lyrics and Tablature

The Harry Fox Agency also handles mechanical licenses for other forms of copying and distribution, such as digital jukeboxes, digital background music, and copying and distribution of lyrics and tablature. The Agency does not handle licensing of Internet radio (noninteractive streaming); print; performance rights; master use; karaoke; or "sampling" rights.

Sound Recordings

A sound recording of a performance of a musical or literary work involves two copyrights: one in the sound recording (the performance and production components) and one in the work that is performed on it. As with licenses for musical and literary works, the kind of license needed depends on the kind of use to which a sound recording is sought to be put.

The first step in licensing a sound recording is to determine who the copyright owner is. As part of their contract with a record company, recording artists, engineers and other contributors to the recording often agree that their contribution(s) will be works made for hire, or they transfer their copyright interests in the sound recording to the record company. That is not always the case, though. Sometimes ownership of the copyright is retained.

The next step is to identify the use(s) to which the recording will be put.

PERFORMING (STREAMING) SOUND RECORDINGS

Copyright protection for sound recordings first began in 1972. It was initially limited to an exclusive right to copy, distribute and make derivative works. There was no exclusive public performance right for sound recordings. So long as they paid a licensing fee for the musical work, radio and television broadcasters could freely play recorded song performances on the air without infringing a copyright.

At the time, this made sense. Radio broadcasts were noninteractive. Listeners had no control over what they played. If they wanted the ability to listen to a particular song at any time they chose, then they had to buy a copy of the recording. Recording artists and record companies made their money from sales of physical copies of their recordings in the form of record albums and cassette tapes. Radio stations provided free advertising for record companies. Since they were getting free advertising, it made no sense for record companies and recording artists to object, much less to expect to be paid a royalty.

The Internet radically changed that model, introducing many new ways of delivering music to listeners. An Internet website can be set up to operate like a traditional radio broadcasting company; or it can be set up to operate like a music store; or it can be set up to operate like a block party where everybody brings their own copies of records to play for each other; or it can be set up to operate like a trading club where people exchange copies of their records with each other; or it can be set up to operate like a pirating operation where people make unauthorized copies of records and either sell or give them away to other people. It also can be set up to do more than one of these things.

Streaming, in particular, created a thorny legal issue. It is like a radio broadcast in that it involves a performance of a sound recording. If a user has some control over which songs to play, though, then it is also like a distribution of a copy. Making songs available for interactive streaming from a website displaces the need to purchase a copy of the recording.

Needless to say, record companies were not happy with this development. They lobbied Congress for a performance right in sound recording copyrights. In 1995, Congress responded by enacting the Digital Performance Right in Sound Recordings Act[402] (DPRA). This law gives the owner of a copyright in a sound recording an exclusive right to digitally perform it. The DMCA refined the DPRA by establishing categories for different kinds of digital transmissions, each with different associated performance rights, statutory licensing requirements, and royalty rates.

The DMCA's elaborate system of statutory licensing represents a compromise between the interests of Internet-based companies and the interests of record companies. In striking this compromise, Congress attempted to implement a system similar to the one for nondigital sound recordings. Like a music store, a distributor of digital downloads or interactive streams must secure the permission of the copyright owner. Like radio and television broadcasts, noninteractive digital transmissions may occur without the permission of the owner of the copyright in the sound recording. An Internet broadcaster may invoke a statutory license instead of negotiating with the copyright owner for permission. Unlike radio and television broadcasts, however, a noninteractive digital transmission may require the payment of a small royalty to the owner of the copyright in the sound recording in some cases.

A website offering interactive streaming or downloads of sound recordings cannot invoke a statutory license. The permission of the owners of the copyrights in the sound recordings must be obtained. Unlike the royalty that is required to be paid in the case of a statutory license, the royalty is arrived at by negotiation between the copyright owner and the website owner.

The only new exclusive right the DPRA establishes for owners of sound recording copyrights is the right to digitally perform (transmit) the recording. It does not give sound recording copyright owners an exclusive right to publicly perform the recording in other ways. As a result, a terrestrial radio station that does an Internet simulcast of its broadcast of a sound recording would need a license (voluntary or statutory) for the Internet simulcast even though no license is needed for the concurrent radio broadcast. To address this anomaly, and to achieve a number of other objectives, Congress has enacted a number of exemptions from liability for various kinds of activities that would otherwise infringe the copyright owner's digital performance right. Of course, no license is needed for a work that is in the public domain.

Live Performances

Generally, unrecorded live performances do not receive copyright protection. Only works that are fixed in a tangible medium do. Congress has established an important exception to this rule, however. If a live performance is being recorded at the same time that it is being transmitted, then the performance is deemed to have been fixed in a tangible medium at the time the transmission was made. This means, for example, that if someone is recording a band's live performance at the time a website simulcasts it, then the website owner is potentially liable for copyright infringement unless he has a license or an exemption applies.

Of course, if the musical work that is being performed live has already been fixed in a tangible medium (e.g., sheet music, digital file, recording tape, etc.), then recording or simulcasting a performance of it without permission could infringe the copyright in the musical work. And an unauthorized, nonexempt transmission of someone else's recording of the live performance would infringe the copyright in the sound recording of the performance.

Civil and criminal penalties may be imposed for the unauthorized recording of a live performance. See Chapter 23.

Mimicking Performances

Because the copyright in a sound recording does not include an exclusive public performance right other than an exclusive right to digitally transmit it, merely mimicking a recording does not infringe the copyright in the recording. A cover band, for example, may perform its own version of a song that it heard being played on a sound recording, and it may even go to great lengths to create a sound that is nearly identical to the sound captured on a previous recording of a song, and this would not violate the rights of the owner of the copyright in the sound recording. Only the actual copying of the sound recording itself (such as by recording the recording or copying and pasting the code from a digital file in which the recording is fixed) counts as infringement of the copyright in a sound recording. There might be liability for infringement of the musical or literary work performed in the recording, but new recordings of new performances that mimic a prior performance do not violate the rights of the owner of a sound recording copyright. No license is needed to mimic performances.

Analog Broadcasts

The federal copyright act does not give the owner of the sound recording copyright an exclusive right to broadcast it by means of analog transmission, i.e., nondigital television and radio broadcasts. A non-Internet-based ("terrestrial"), nonsubscription radio station that does not broadcast via satellite may broadcast a sound recording even if the copy of the sound recording it uses is in digital format.[403] A digital broadcaster (such as an Internet radio station or a webcaster), however, may not transmit a copyrighted sound recording without a license (voluntary or statutory) unless a statutory exemption applies.

RETRANSMISSIONS OF ANALOG BROADCASTS

Retransmission of a nonsubscription, noninteractive terrestrial radio broadcast of a sound recording may infringe the copyright in a sound recording. Congress has exempted such retransmissions from copyright liability only in the following situations:

(a) The radio station's broadcast is not willfully or repeatedly retransmitted more than a radius of 150 miles from the site of the radio broadcast transmitter (or, in the case of a subscription retransmission of a nonsubscription broadcast retransmission, 150 miles from the site of the broadcast retransmitter). The 150-mile limitation does not apply when a nonsubscription broadcast transmission by a radio station is retransmitted on a nonsubscription basis by a terrestrial broadcast station, terrestrial translator, or terrestrial repeater licensed by the FCC. The Copyright Office has also interpreted this exemption as being inapplicable to retransmissions over the Internet. Therefore, be wary of claims that "geofencing" Internet retransmissions of radio broadcasts to an area within a 150-mile radius can be used to avoid exposure to liability for copyright infringement.

(b) The retransmission is of radio station broadcast transmissions that are obtained by the retransmitter over the air; not electronically processed by the retransmitter to deliver separate and discrete signals; and retransmitted only within the local communities served by the retransmitter.

(c) The radio station's broadcast transmission was being retransmitted to cable systems by a satellite carrier on January 1, 1995, and that retransmission was being retransmitted by cable systems as a separate and discrete signal, and the satellite carrier obtains the radio station's broadcast transmission in an analog format, so long as the broadcast transmission being retransmitted embodies the programming of no more than one radio station.

(d) The radio station's broadcast transmission is made by a noncommercial educational broadcast station, consists solely of noncommercial educational and cultural radio programs, and the retransmission is a nonsubscription terrestrial broadcast retransmission.

Simultaneous Retransmissions of Licensed Transmissions

The performance of a sound recording by means of noninteractive digital audio transmission is not an infringement of the copyright in the sound recording if the transmission is a retransmission, including a multichannel video programming distributor, of a transmission by a transmitter licensed to publicly perform the sound recording as part of that transmission, if the retransmission is simultaneous with the licensed transmission and authorized by the transmitter.

Simultaneous Retransmissions to Licensed Interactive Service Users

A retransmission of a digital audio transmission is not an infringement of the copyright in the sound recording if the retransmission is (a) of a transmission by an interactive service licensed to transmit the sound recording to a particular member of the public as part of that transmission, and (b) simultaneous with the licensed transmission, authorized by the transmitter, and limited to that particular member of the public intended by the interactive service to be the recipient of the transmission.

Incidental Transmissions

A transmission of a sound recording by means of noninteractive digital audio transmission is not an infringement of the copyright in the sound recording if it is a transmission incidental to an exempt transmission occurring either before or simultaneously with the exempt transmission, such as a feed received by and then retransmitted by an exempt transmitter, so long as such incidental transmission does not include any subscription transmission directly for reception by members of the public.

Transmissions to a Business Establishment

The performance of a sound recording by means of noninteractive digital transmission is not an infringement of the copyright in the sound recording if the transmission is to a business establishment for use in the ordinary course of its business, provided the business recipient does not retransmit the transmission outside of its premises or the immediately surrounding vicinity, and that the transmission does not exceed the sound recording performance complement.

The sound recording performance complement is the transmission during any three-hour period, on a particular channel used by a transmitting entity, of no more than (a) three different selections of sound recordings from any one phonorecord lawfully distributed for public performance or sale in the United States, if no more than two such selections are transmitted consecutively, or (b) four different selections of sound recordings by the same featured recording artist, or from any set or compilation of phonorecords lawfully distributed together as a unit for public performance or sale in the United States, if no more than three such selections are transmitted consecutively.

Transmissions Within a Business Establishment

The performance of a sound recording by means of noninteractive digital audio transmission is not an infringement of the copyright in the sound recording if the transmission is within a business establishment and confined to its premises or the immediately surrounding vicinity.

Statutory Licenses for Noninteractive Transmissions

The Copyright Act establishes licenses to use certain kinds of copyrighted works, provided the conditions specified in the Act are satisfied. These are called *statutory* licenses because they are provided for by statute; the copyright owner's consent is not required. A compulsory license to record a cover version of a musical work is an example of a statutory license. The Act also establishes statutory licenses for certain noninteractive transmissions of sound recordings.

PREEXISTING DIGITAL TRANSMISSION SERVICES

A preexisting satellite digital radio service has a statutory license to make noninteractive subscription digital audio transmissions of sound recordings, but only if it does not automatically and intentionally cause any device receiving the transmission to switch from one program channel to another. If feasible, the transmission must be accompanied by any information encoded in the recording by or under the authority of the copyright owner of the sound recording that identifies the title, the name of the recording artist, and information about the composer.

In the case of a transmission that is made either by a preexisting satellite digital audio radio service or in the same transmission medium that was used by the service on July 31, 1998, the transmission is subject to statutory licensing if (a) the transmission does not exceed the sound recording performance complement, and (b) the transmitting entity does not cause to be published by means of an advance program schedule or prior announcement the titles of the specific sound recordings or phonorecords embodying such sound recordings to be transmitted.

The sound recording performance complement is the transmission during any three-hour period, on a particular channel used by a transmitting entity, of no more than either:

(a) three different selections of sound recordings from any one phonorecord lawfully distributed for public performance or sale in the United States, if no more than two such selections are transmitted consecutively, or

(b) four different selections of sound recordings by the same featured recording artist, or from any set or compilation of phonorecords lawfully distributed together as a unit for public performance or sale in the United States, if no more than three such selections are transmitted consecutively.

The transmission of selections in excess of the numerical limits from multiple phonorecords nevertheless qualifies as a sound recording performance complement if the programming of the multiple phonorecords was not willfully intended to avoid the prescribed numerical limits.

OTHER NONINTERACTIVE DIGITAL TRANSMISSIONS OF SOUND RECORDINGS

A statutory license may exist for noninteractive digital transmissions of sound recordings that fall into one of the following three categories:

(a) by a service the primary purpose of which is to sell or promote music-related products, services or events
(b) by a new subscription service
(c) by a preexisting subscription service other than in the same transmission medium that was used by such service on July 31, 1998.

These transmissions are subject to statutory licensing if all of the following conditions exist:

(1) The transmission does not exceed the sound recording performance complement, except that this requirement does not apply in the case of a retransmission of a broadcast transmission if the retransmission is made by a transmitting entity that does not have the right or ability to control the programming of the broadcast station making the broadcast transmission, unless:

 (a) the broadcast station makes broadcast transmissions (I) in digital format that regularly exceed the sound recording performance complement, or (II) in analog format, a substantial portion of which, on a weekly basis, exceed the sound recording performance complement; and
 (b) the sound recording copyright owner or its representative has notified the transmitting entity in writing that broadcast transmissions of the copyright owner's sound recordings exceed the sound recording performance complement.

(2) The transmitting entity does not cause to be published, or induce or facilitate the publication, by means of an advance program schedule or prior announcement, the titles of the specific sound recordings to be transmitted, the phonorecords embodying such sound recordings, or, other than for illustrative purposes, the names of the featured recording artists, except that a transmitting entity may make a prior announcement that a particular artist will be featured within an unspecified future time period, and in the case of a retransmission of a broadcast transmission by a transmitting entity that does not have the right or ability to control the programming of the broadcast transmission, the requirement of this clause shall not apply to a prior oral announcement by the broadcast station, or to an advance program schedule published, induced, or facilitated by the broadcast station, if the transmitting entity does not have actual knowledge and has not received written notice from the copyright owner or its representative that the broadcast station publishes or induces or facilitates the publication of such advance program schedule, or if such advance program schedule is a schedule of classical music programming published by the broadcast station in the same manner as published by that broadcast station on or before September 30, 1998.

(3) The transmission:

(a) is not part of an archived program of less than five hours duration;
(b) is not part of an archived program of five hours or greater in duration that is made available for a period exceeding two weeks;
(c) is not part of a continuous program which is of less than three hours duration, or
(d) is not part of an identifiable program in which performances of sound recordings are rendered in a predetermined order, other than an archived or continuous program, that is transmitted at: (I) more than three times in any two-week period that have been publicly announced in advance, in the case of a program of less than one hour in duration, or (II) more than four times in any two-week period that have been publicly announced in advance, in the case of a program of one hour or more in duration, except that the requirement of this subclause shall not apply in the case of a retransmission of a broadcast transmission by a transmitting entity that does not have the right or ability to control the programming of the broadcast transmission, unless the transmitting entity is given notice in writing by the copyright owner of the sound recording that the broadcast station makes broadcast transmissions that regularly violate such requirement.

(4) The transmitting entity does not knowingly perform the sound recording, as part of a service that offers transmissions of visual images contemporaneously with transmissions of sound recordings, in a manner that is likely to cause confusion, to cause mistake, or to deceive, as to the affiliation, connection, or association of the copyright owner or featured recording artist with the transmitting entity or a particular product or service advertised by the transmitting entity, or as to the origin, sponsorship, or approval by the copyright owner or featured recording artist of the activities of the transmitting entity other than the performance of the sound recording itself.

(5) The transmitting entity cooperates to prevent, to the extent feasible without imposing substantial costs or burdens, a transmission recipient or any other person or entity from automatically scanning the transmitting entity's transmissions alone or together with transmissions by other transmitting entities in order to select a particular sound recording to be transmitted to the transmission recipient, except that the requirement of this clause shall not apply to a satellite digital audio service that is in operation, or that is licensed by the FCC, on or before July 31, 1998.

(6) The transmitting entity takes no affirmative steps to cause or induce the making of a copy by the transmission recipient, and if the technology used by the transmitting entity enables the transmitting entity to limit the making by the transmission recipient of copies of the transmission directly in a digital format, the transmitting entity sets such technology to limit such making of copies to the extent permitted by such technology.

(7) Phonorecords of the sound recording have been distributed to the public under the authority of the copyright owner or the copyright owner authorizes the transmitting entity

to transmit the sound recording, and the transmitting entity makes the transmission from a phonorecord lawfully made under the authority of the copyright owner, except that the requirement of this clause does not apply to a retransmission of a broadcast transmission by a transmitting entity that does not have the right or ability to control the programming of the broadcast transmission, unless the transmitting entity is given notice in writing by the copyright owner of the sound recording that the broadcast station makes broadcast transmissions that regularly violate such requirement.

(8) The transmitting entity accommodates and does not interfere with the transmission of technical measures that are widely used by sound recording copyright owners to identify or protect copyrighted works, and that are technically feasible of being transmitted by the transmitting entity without imposing substantial costs on the transmitting entity or resulting in perceptible aural or visual degradation of the digital signal, except that the requirement of this clause does not apply to a satellite digital audio service that is in operation, or that is licensed under the authority of the FCC, on or before July 31, 1998, to the extent that such service has designed, developed, or made commitments to procure equipment or technology that is not compatible with such technical measures before such technical measures are widely adopted by sound recording copyright owners.

(9) The transmitting entity identifies in textual data the sound recording during, but not before, the time it is performed, including the title of the sound recording, the title of the phonorecord embodying such sound recording, if any, and the featured recording artist, in a manner to permit it to be displayed to the transmission recipient by the device or technology intended for receiving the service provided by the transmitting entity, except that the obligation in this clause shall not apply in the case of a retransmission of a broadcast transmission by a transmitting entity that does not have the right or ability to control the programming of the broadcast transmission, or in the case in which devices or technology intended for receiving the service provided by the transmitting entity that have the capability to display such textual data are not common in the marketplace.

EPHEMERAL COPIES

A statutory license to make ephemeral copies also exists, to the extent the copies are needed in connection with the process of making a transmission that is subject to statutory licensing.[404]

ROYALTIES FOR STATUTORY LICENSES

License agreements voluntarily negotiated between owner(s) of sound recording copyrights and persons and entity(ies) desiring to digitally transmit them will be given effect. In the absence of such an agreement, the Copyright Royalty Board sets royalty rates for statutory licenses. The Board also establishes requirements for statutory licensees to give reasonable notice and keep adequate records of their use of a sound recording pursuant to a statutory license.

A receiving agent (person or entity that receives license payments on behalf of sound recording copyright owners) may enter into agreements for the reproduction and transmission of sound recordings by webcasters for a period of not more than eleven years. Once published in the Federal Register, the agreement becomes binding on all copyright owners of sound recordings and other persons entitled to payment, in lieu of any determination by the copyright royalty judges. Any such agreement for commercial webcasters may include provisions for payment of royalties on the basis of a percentage of revenue or expenses, or both, and include a minimum fee. The agreement may include other provisions, too, such as requirements by which copyright owners may receive notice of the use of their sound recordings. Thereafter, the terms of such agreement shall be available, as an option, to any webcaster meeting the eligibility conditions of the agreement.

When a statutory license does not exist, the copyright owner of a sound recording must pay a recording artist who performs on it in accordance with the terms of the contract between the recording artist and the owner of the copyright in the sound recording.

As of October 1, 2016, an agent designated to distribute receipts from a statutory license for a sound recording must distribute them, after costs, as follows:

50% to the owner of the exclusive right to digitally transmit the recording
45% to the recording artist(s) featured on it
2.5% to nonfeatured musicians who perform on it
2.5% to nonfeatured vocalists who perform on it.

Royalties collected under a Section 112 statutory license to make ephemeral copies are distributed to the owner of the copyright in the sound recording.

The royalties to be paid pursuant to a statutory license may not be used as a basis for reducing the amount of any royalty payable to the owner of the copyright in the underlying musical or literary work.

SoundExchange is a sound recording performance rights administrator that collects and disburses statutory license royalty payments from digital transmitters to record companies and recording artists. It only manages licensing of noninteractive digital transmissions of sound recordings. It does not handle licensing for interactive streaming or digital downloads. It also does not manage royalties payable to the owners of copyrights in musical or literary works.

The royalty rate that is set by the Copyright Board for statutory licenses to use sound recordings is adjusted annually. 2016 rates are as follows:

Noncommercial webcasters (owned by a governmental or tax-exempt entity)

(a) offering both subscription and nonsubscription transmissions (CRB): $0.0023 per performance, for any month in which aggregate listener tuning hours are greater than 159,140. A $500 per station or channel minimum annual royalty must be paid annually; monthly per-performance royalties are credited against the annual royalty.
(b) offering only nonsubscription transmissions (WSA[405]): $0.00083 per performance, for any month in which aggregate listener tuning hours are greater than 159,140. A $500 per station or channel minimum annual royalty must be paid annually; monthly per-performance royalties are credited against the annual royalty.
(c) microcaster with less than 44,000 aggregate tuning hours per year (about 120 listener-hours per day): A $500 per station or channel royalty must be paid annually. There

are no per-performance royalties. For an additional $100, a microcaster can get a waiver of the requirement to make monthly reports of use.

(d) educational webcaster: $0.0025 per performance, for any month in which aggregate listener tuning hours are greater than 159,140. A $500 per station or channel minimum royalty must be paid annually; monthly per-performance royalties are credited against the annual royalty. For an additional $100, a noncommercial educational webcaster with less than 55,000 aggregate tuning hours per month can get a waiver of the requirement to make monthly reports of use.

Commercial webcasters

(a) Commercial webcaster (CRB): $0.0023 per performance. A $500 per station or channel (up to $50,000) minimum royalty must be paid annually; monthly per-performance royalties are credited against the annual royalty.

(b) Commercial webcaster not owned or operated by an entity that also owns or operates a terrestrial radio station, if the webcaster elects this rate (WSA): $0.0023 per performance. A $500 per station or channel (up to $50,000) minimum royalty must be paid annually; monthly per-performance royalties are credited against the annual royalty.

(c) Pureplay webcaster (revenues earned primarily through webcasting): $0.0025 per-performance of subscription/syndicated/ bundled transmissions, plus the greater of $0.0014 per-performance or 25% of gross revenues from nonsubscription transmissions. A $25,000 minimum fee must be paid annually.

(d) Small pureplay webcaster [effective 2015, a service may no longer elect this rate]

(e) Small webcaster nonsubscription service (gross annual revenues less than $1,250,000, including gross revenues of affiliates, third party participation revenues, and revenues from a new subscription service; a webcaster selecting this rate must pay the CRB commercial webcaster rate for any subscription service that he offers): Greater of: (i) 10% of the first $250,000 of gross revenues and 12% of all additional gross revenues, or (ii) 7% of expenses. A minimum annual fee of $5,000 must be paid if gross annual revenues are $50,000 or more. Otherwise, the minimum annual fee is $2,000. The "greater of" amount is credited against the minimum annual fee.

(f) Microcaster nonsubscription service (gross annual revenues less than $5,001, including gross revenues of affiliates, third party participation revenues, and revenues from a new subscription service; annual expenses not greater than $10,000; and annual listenership of not more than 18,067 aggregate tuning hours. A webcaster selecting this rate must pay the CRB commercial webcaster rate for any subscription service that he offers): $500 annual fee. There are no per-performance royalties. For an additional $100, a microcaster can get a waiver of the requirement to make monthly reports of use.

(g) Broadcaster nonsubscription webcasts (webcasts by an owner of an AM or FM radio station. Broadcasters must operate subscription-based services under the Commercial Webcaster (CRB) category): $0.0025 per performance. A $500 per station or channel (up to $50,000) minimum royalty must be paid annually; monthly per-performance royalties are credited against the annual royalty.

(h) Small broadcaster nonsubscription webcasts (webcasts with less than 27,777 aggregate tuning hours (about seventy listener-hours per day), by an owner of an AM or FM radio station. Broadcasters must operate subscription-based services under the Commercial Webcaster (CRB) category): $0.0025 per performance. A $500 per station or channel (up to $50,000) minimum royalty must be paid annually; monthly per-performance royalties are credited against the annual royalty. For an additional $100, a small broadcaster can get a waiver of the requirement to make monthly reports of use.

Business background music services (streaming into retail businesses such as bars, restaurants, retail stores, etc.): Royalty of 12% of annual gross proceeds. A $10,000 minimum annual fee is required. Royalty is credited against the minimum annual fee.

Television music services

(a) Stand-alone subscriptions of audio-only digital music programming via residential televisions using cable or satellite television providers: Royalty of $0.0174 per subscriber per month, or 15% of revenue, whichever is greater. A minimum annual fee of $100,000 is required. Royalties are credited against the minimum annual fee.
(b) Bundled subscriptions of audio-only digital music programming via residential televisions using cable or satellite television providers: Royalty of $0.029 per subscriber per month, or 15% of revenue allocated to reflect the objective value of the licensee's service, whichever is greater. A minimum annual fee of $100,000 is required. Royalties are credited against the minimum annual fee.
(c) Audio-only "music channel" services making transmissions via residential televisions using cable or satellite television providers, which were in existence prior to 1998: See 37 CFR § 382, Subpart A; and contact SoundExchange for more information.

SiriusXM Radio: Contact SoundExchange for information.

Rates are subject to change. Check the SoundExchange website for current rates, www.soundexchange.com.

Voluntary Licenses for Noninteractive Transmissions

If no exemption or statutory license applies to a copyright-protected sound recording, use of it will require a license that is voluntarily granted by the copyright owner. To ensure fair competition, Congress has provided that if an owner of a copyright in a sound recording grants an affiliated entity a license to digitally transmit the recording, then it must make a license available, on no less favorable terms, to all bona fide entities that offer similar services. Accordingly, it will behoove a website owner who is seeking a license to review the license agreement the copyright owner has with its affiliated entities, if it has any.

An *affiliated entity* is an entity that engages in noninteractive transmissions and in which the sound recording copyright licensor has a direct or indirect ownership or partnership interest of 5% or more of the outstanding voting or nonvoting stock.

The sound recording copyright owner is not required to offer "no less favorable terms" for promotional transmissions of up to forty-five seconds of the sound recording.

A sound recording copyright owner may establish different terms and conditions than those given to affiliated entities if there are material differences in the scope of the requested license with respect to the type of service, the particular sound recordings licensed, the frequency of use, the number of subscribers served, or the duration.

The "no less favorable terms" requirement does not apply to licenses for interactive transmissions.

Limitations on Exclusive Licenses for Interactive Transmissions

Interactive digital transmissions are not subject to statutory licensing. There are, however, some statutory limitations on a sound recording copyright owners' freedom of contract when licensing interactive streaming rights. These are intended to promote competition and to prevent the monopolization of performance rights in sound recordings, as well as to ensure the existence of more than one outlet for online interactive streaming to consumers. Specifically, the owner of a sound recording copyright may not grant an exclusive license with a duration longer than twelve months if it holds the copyright to more than 1,000 sound recordings. If it holds less than 1,001 copyrights in sound recordings, then the duration of an exclusive license is limited to twenty-four months.

An exclusive licensee is ineligible to receive another exclusive license for the performance of the same sound recording for a period of thirteen months from the time the prior license expires.

The twelve- and twenty-four-month limitations do not apply if (a) the licensor has granted and there remain in effect licenses for the public performance of sound recordings by means of interactive digital audio transmission by at least five different interactive services, if each such license is for a minimum of 10% of the copyrighted sound recordings owned by the licensor that have been licensed to interactive services, but in no event less than fifty sound recordings, or (b) the exclusive license is granted for interactive transmission of up to forty-five seconds of a sound recording and the sole purpose of the performance is to promote the distribution or performance of that sound recording.

DISTRIBUTING COPIES OF A SOUND RECORDING

Making a sound recording available for downloading, or offering physical copies of it from a website, involves a distribution of both a sound recording and the musical or literary work performed in it. If both works are protected by copyright and no exemption applies, then a license is needed for each work. Thus, it is important to ensure that the licensing agreement is clear about which work(s) is/are being licensed, as well as what rights are being granted.

A website owner selling digital downloads or physical copies of music recordings will need a mechanical license for the musical work and a master use license for the sound recording.

The compulsory license provided in 17 U.S.C. § 115 to make and distribute copies of a musical work does not include a right to make and distribute copies of the sound recording. And statutory licenses available under 17 U.S.C. § 114 generally are for streaming, not the distribution of digital downloads or copies. The owner of the sound recording copyright will be liable to the owner of the copyright in the musical work for a third party's transmission of the sound recording with the musical work in it only if the sound recording copyright owner specifically licensed distribution rights in the musical work to the third party. A website that transmits either work without a valid license will be liable in any event.

Statutory licenses generally only pertain to performances and streaming, not to the distribution of copies of a sound recording. In some circumstances, a statutory license exists to make ephemeral copies. These are discussed infra, in connection with licensing performance and digital transmission rights.

There are a number of exemptions and exceptions to the sound recording copyright owner's exclusive rights to make and distribute copies of a sound recording. The general exceptions for public domain works and for recordings that mimic but do not actually copy another sound recording are discussed infra, in connection with licensing performance and digital transmission rights.

Compilations

In addition to securing licenses from both the owners of the copyrights in the sound recordings and the owners of the musical or literary works performed in those recordings, a person seeking to distribute copies of a compilation (such as a "greatest hits" album) may also need the permission of the owner of the copyright in the compilation. Of course, if a particular work is in the public domain or is the subject of an applicable exception or exemption, then a license for that work will not be necessary. The fact that a license is not needed for one work in a compilation, however, does not mean that a license is not necessary for others.

Because the copyright in an individual sound recording that is included in a compilation is separate from the copyright in the compilation, making an individual sound recording that is included in the compilation available for downloading or streaming may infringe the copyrights in the musical work and/or the sound recording even if the compilation owner has granted a license to use the compilation. The owner of the copyright in a collective work is presumed to possess the right to reproduce and distribute the works contributed to it only as part of that collective work or a revision of that collective work. Merely owning the copyright in a compilation does not give rise to a right to copy, perform or distribute—or to authorize others to copy, perform or distribute—an individual song or recording that is included in the collection. Again, license agreements need to be very clear about which works are being licensed.

Copying, distributing, broadcasting or transmitting a single sound recording that appears in a compilation should not require a license from the compilation owner unless the compilation owner also owns the copyright in the sound recording and/or the musical or literary work performed in it.

MUSIC VIDEOS

A person wishing to make a music video by combining a performance of a song with a video will need a synchronization license. Performing rights agencies normally do not handle synchronization licensing. Instead, it is necessary to negotiate a licensing agreement with the owners of the copyrights in the musical composition, the sound recording of it, and the audiovisual work—to the extent the person making the music video is not the owner of the copyright(s) in these elements. Songfile.com provides a synchronization licensing service called eSynch. This service, however, is available only to those who will make noncommercial use of the synchronization. It is ideal for licensing songs that are combined with visual images or videos for free viewing on a personal or business website, or as background music on a website. It cannot be used to license synchronization rights for music videos that are offered for sale. Nor can it be used as a license to upload a music video to a third party website such as YouTube, Vimeo, etc.

Streaming a music video from a website may require a performance license, a mechanical license, and a synchronization license for the musical composition, in addition to any license(s) that are needed for the video.

PODCASTS

A podcast is like a webcast or a radio broadcast, except that it is recorded in a downloadable audio file. Unlike a broadcast or a webcast, the user is provided a copy of the broadcast, which can be listened to on demand.

Because podcasting involves copying, a mechanical license is required. There is some disagreement about whether a podcast also requires a performance license. Mechanical licensing agencies take the position that it is a digital phonorecord delivery, so only a mechanical license is needed. Performing rights organizations take the position that it is also a public performance, so a performance license arguably may be necessary, as well. Clearly, it is a copy, so a mechanical license is needed. Whether it is also a "performance" is debatable. The safest course would be to get both a mechanical and a performance license.

If a sound recording is included in the podcast, then a master use license and a digital performance license for the sound recording will be needed, in addition to the mechanical (and possibly performance) license(s) for the musical work(s).

SoundExchange does not handle licensing of sound recordings for podcasts, because it only licenses recordings to noninteractive services. SoundExchange takes the position that podcasts are interactive transmissions because they are playable on demand.

If a podcast includes images, artwork or video along with musical works and/or sound recordings, then a synchronization license may be needed, too.

SAMPLING

Sampling is the process of reusing a portion of an existing sound recording when making a new sound recording. It is very common in the hip hop and rap genres, and is becoming more common in other genres, too. Dr. Dre reportedly has used over 3,000 "samples" of other artists' recordings in his.

The Copyright Act gives the author (e.g., composer, lyricist, producer) an exclusive right to make and distribute copies of his work unless he transfers the copyright or licenses it to somebody else. It also gives him an exclusive right to make derivative works from it. A derivative work is one that recasts, transforms or adapts a preexisting work. Using part of a musical work in a new musical work would be a recasting, and arguably a transformation, of it. Because the owner of the copyright in a musical work (songwriter or publisher) has an exclusive right to make derivative works (as well as the exclusive right to make and distribute copies of it), unauthorized music sampling would seem to infringe the copyright in the musical work.

The Copyright Act also gives the owner of the copyright in a sound recording the exclusive rights to make and distribute copies of the recording; to make derivative works from the sound recording; and to transmit the recording digitally. Music sampling therefore would seem to infringe the copyright in the sound recording, too.

Contrary to popular belief, purchasing a copy (e.g., a CD or an mp3 file) of a sound recording does not transfer the copyright in the sound recording to the person who bought the CD. Nor does it transfer the copyright in the musical work.

The similarity of the new work and the original work is relevant to the determination whether infringement of a literary or musical work has occurred, but it is not particularly relevant to whether infringement of a sound recording copyright has occurred. A person infringes a copyright in a musical work when he copies it (whether intentionally or subconsciously), and the similarity of the two works can be strong circumstantial evidence of copying. A person who records a new performance of a song, on the other hand, does not violate the copyright in the sound recording unless he copies the actual recording itself. Accordingly, whether the new recording sounds similar, or even identical, to the previous recording is irrelevant. It is the use of the sound recording itself, not the similarity of sounds, that constitutes infringement of a copyright in a sound recording. This is why "sampling" even a de minimis amount of a sound recording is infringement.

Sampling is not per se fair use. Also, there is no de minimis rule with respect to it. Using even a couple of seconds of a sound recording may be infringement. In one case, it was held that sampling that involved only three notes constituted copyright infringement of the sound recording, and this was true even though it probably would not have constituted infringement of the copyright in the musical work.[406] Some kinds of sampling , however, may be permitted as fair use. See Chapter 25.

Licensing for Sampling

The fair use doctrine is fraught with gray areas. It is risky to rely on it as a defense to copyright infringement. It is more prudent to seek license(s) from the copyright owner(s).

To use a clip from a sound recording in a new sound recording of a new musical work, licenses from the owners of the copyrights in the musical work and the sound recordings to make a derivative work may be needed. To make and distribute copies of it, a mechanical license from the owner of the copyright in the musical work and a master use license from the sound recording copyright owner may be needed. To broadcast it (or arrange to have it broadcasted), then a performance license from the owner of the copyright in the musical work may be needed. To transmit it digitally, a license from both the owner of the copyright in the musical work and the owner of the copyright in the sound recording may be needed. To include it in another work (e.g., a music video), then a synchronization licenses may be needed.

The rights to make and distribute copies, and to perform, musical works usually may be licensed through agencies like ASCAP, BMI, SESAC, and Harry Fox. These agencies, however, normally do not handle licenses to make derivative works. Licensing agreements for derivative works need to be negotiated directly with the copyright owner(s).

The rights to make and distribute copies and to make derivative works of sound recordings must be negotiated with the sound recording copyright owner (usually the record company).

A person who obtains a master use license from a record company in order to engage in sampling should take care to ensure that the license includes the right to make derivative works, not just the right to make and distribute copies. A right to reproduce a recording does not necessarily include the right to make derivative works, and vice versa.

PRE-1972 SOUND RECORDINGS

A person may make a noncommercial use of a pre-1972 sound recording that is not being commercially exploited by or under the authority of the rights owner if all of the following apply:

(1) the person makes a good faith, reasonable search for, but does not find, the sound recording either in the Copyright Office's records or on services offering a comprehensive set of sound recordings for sale or streaming;
(2) the person files a notice identifying the sound recordings and the nature of the use in the Copyright Office; and
(3) within 90 days after the notice is indexed into the public records of the Copyright Office, the rights owner does not file a notice opting out of the noncommercial use.

Summary of Licenses Needed

Display lyrics or sheet music: Folio license from the owner of the music copyright.
Noninteractive streaming of a cover version: Performance license from the owner of the music copyright.
Interactive streaming of a cover version: Mechanical and performance licenses from the owner of the music copyright.
Downloads of a cover version: Mechanical license from the owner of the music copyright.
Noninteractive streaming of a recording artist: Performance licenses from the owners of the music copyright and the sound recording copyright.
Interactive streaming of a recording artist: Mechanical and performance licenses from the owner of the music copyright; and performance and master use licenses from the owner of the copyright in the sound recording.
Downloads of a recording artist: Mechanical license from the owner of the music copyright and a master use license from the owner of the sound recording copyright.
Ringtones: Mechanical license from the owner of the music copyright and master use license from the owner of the sound recording copyright.
Music video, podcast, or background music: Mechanical, performance and synchronization licenses from the owner of the music copyright; and performance, master use, and synchronization licenses from the owner of the sound recording copyright.

Summary of How to Get Licenses

Folio: Negotiate with the owner of the music copyright.
Performance of music: ASCAP, BMI, SESAC, or negotiate with the music copyright owner.
Mechanical license to distribute copies of music: Harry Fox Agency, compulsory license, or negotiate with the music copyright owner.

Mechanical license for use of music in a music video or background music: Negotiate with the music copyright owner.
Interactive performance of sound recording: Negotiate with the sound recording copyright owner.
Noninteractive performance of sound recording: SoundExchange, statutory license, or negotiate with the sound recording copyright owner.
Master use license: Negotiate with the owner of the sound recording copyright.
Synchronization license: Negotiate with the owners of the music and sound recording copyrights.

The Musical Works Modernization Act

In October, 2018, the Musical Works Modernization Act[407] (MWMA) was signed into law. It changes the way compulsory licenses to reproduce and distribute nondramatic musical works are obtained. The requirements for obtaining a compulsory license to make and distribute copies nonelectronically (e.g., CDs or other physical copies) remain intact. A person seeking a compulsory license to make and distribute copies of a nondramatic musical work digitally (such as digital downloads or interactive streaming), however may no longer file notices of intention to obtain compulsory licenses with the Copyright Office, even if the copyright owner's identity and/or address are not available. Beginning in 2021, licenses to make and distribute music digitally will be obtained by sending a Notice of License to a mechanical licensing collective (MLC). The MLC will issue blanket licenses. It will also collect and distribute royalties, and identify musical works and their owners for payment. It will establish and maintain a publicly accessible database of musical works and, to the extent known, the identity and location of the copyright owners and the sound recordings in which the musical works are embodied. Operational costs of the MLC will be paid for by digital music providers, in part by means of an administrative assessment. In the interim, digital music providers are shielded from liability for failing to serve a compulsory notice license on a copyright owner, provided they can demonstrate that they engaged in a good faith, commercially reasonable effort to identify and locate the copyright owner. Accured royalties must be paid if and when a copyright owner is located, however. The MWMA also changes the method by which copyright royalty judges set rates.

PART V. DISPUTE RESOLUTION

Chapter 34. Jurisdiction and Conflicts of Laws

Companies that do business online typically engage in transactions with people in other states and countries. If a dispute arises in connection with such transactions, the first question that must be answered is where it will be decided. If a business based in California sells a digital download to a customer in New York who then starts making copies and selling them in breach of the license agreement, is suit to be filed in California, New York, or both? If an Australian company publishes photographs of a British celebrity's wedding to its website, and it is viewed by people in every country, may the celebrity sue for invasion of privacy in the U.K., Australia, or anywhere in the world? The answer will depend on which sovereign state or country has *jurisdiction*, i.e., the authority to exercise power over the parties and over the transaction that is the subject of the dispute.

Once a court has determined that it has jurisdiction, it will then need to decide which laws to apply. In most cases, it will apply the laws of the place where the court sits, but sometimes it will apply a different sovereign's laws. A court in one state will sometimes apply the laws of another state. A court in one country will sometimes apply the laws of another country. The area of law concerned with deciding which laws to apply in interstate and international disputes is called *conflicts of laws.*

Decisions about which laws apply can significantly affect the outcome of a case. Laws differ considerably from country to country. In common law jurisdictions, such as England, Australia and the United States (except Louisiana, which has a civil law system), published judicial decisions have precedential effect, so judges have what might be characterized as the power to "make law." Laws in France, China, Germany, Japan and other civil law jurisdictions are embodied in a statutory code of laws. Religious law has its source in religious documents. Saudi Arabia, Iran, Libya and several other countries, for example, have adopted Islamic law. The substantive content of the laws of the countries in each of these categories of legal systems varies widely both between and within categories. In the United States and other federations, the substantive content also varies between states or provinces.[408]

International trademark infringement cases illustrate the importance of conflicts-of-laws rules. In the United States, it is use in commerce, not registration, that establishes the existence of an enforceable trademark. In many other countries, though, an enforceable trademark comes into being by registration, not use. A company with an unregistered use-based trademark will have enforceable trademark rights if U.S. law is applied but will not have enforceable rights if the law of a country that requires registration is applied.

Conflicts-of-laws determinations can be critical in other kinds of e-commerce disputes, too. For example, the safe havens for online activity that the DMCA, CDA and the First Amendment provide are not available under the laws of all other countries.

Jurisdiction

Jurisdiction refers to the authority to exercise power over a person, property or controversy. *Subject matter jurisdiction* refers to the authority to hear and decide a particular kind of case. *Personal jurisdiction* (sometimes called *in personam* jurisdiction) refers to the authority to exercise power over a person. A court generally must have both kinds of jurisdiction.

The five general justifications, or rationales, for a sovereign's exercise of one or both of these kinds of jurisdiction are:

- Territorial
- Nationality or domicile of the victim ("effects" test)
- Nationality or domicile of the perpetrator
- Protection of the sovereign's interests
- Universal wrong.

The territorial basis of jurisdiction gives a sovereign authority to exercise power when people and things are within its territorial boundaries. The courts of every sovereign generally have this kind of jurisdiction.

The nationality or domicile of the victim principle premises jurisdiction on the effect that something has had on a citizen or domiciliary of the country asserting jurisdiction. The United States has invoked the nationality or domicile of the victim to exercise criminal jurisdiction over foreign terrorists. The United States has also invoked it in its "War On Drugs," as a justification for exercising jurisdiction over foreign nationals who traffic in drugs in other countries, in cases where the drugs eventually make their way into the United States. The principle is embodied in several treaties, such as the Convention on the Prevention and Punishment of Crimes Against Internationally Protected Persons, and the Convention Against Torture and Other Cruel, Inhuman or Degrading Treatment or Punishment.

The nationality or domicile of the perpetrator or other person upon whom an obligation is sought to be imposed is asserted as a basis for the exercise of jurisdiction in some countries. It is more commonly invoked in civil law countries than in common law countries, but its use everywhere is growing. Laws imposing taxes on income earned by citizens as a result of activities conducted in other countries rely on this justification for jurisdiction. Laws authorizing criminal prosecutions of nationals for war crimes and sex offenses committed abroad are examples.

Sometimes jurisdiction is based on a sovereign's desire to protect its own interests, as distinguished from the interests of a citizen. This justification, known as the protective principle, has been applied in the Convention on the Safety of United Nations and Associated Personnel to enable prosecutions of aliens who take hostages or hijack aircraft while outside a sovereign's geographic territory.

The universality principle allows any sovereign to exercise jurisdiction over certain kinds of matters irrespective of where they occur, the nationality or domicile of the perpetrators and victims, or the sovereign's interests. It has been applied as a justification for broad sovereign powers to prosecute any person for crimes against humanity, slavery, piracy, war crimes or crimes against peace.

These principles comprise the possible justifications that a sovereign might have for an exercise of jurisdiction. The fact that one of these principles appears to support an exercise of jurisdiction in a particular case does not mean that a sovereign must exercise jurisdiction, though. It doesn't even mean that it probably will. Every sovereign nation is free to decide whether and when it will choose to exercise jurisdiction. Unfortunately, the only way to determine that is by reviewing the relevant provisions of its constitution, laws, court rules, and the judicial decisions interpreting them.

JURISDICTION IN THE UNITED STATES

The jurisdiction of United States federal courts is governed by the U.S. Constitution and federal laws enacted pursuant to it. State laws govern the jurisdiction of state courts, subject to limitations set out in the U.S. Constitution, such as the Fourteenth Amendment Due Process requirement.

Personal Jurisdiction

There are two kinds of personal jurisdiction: general and specific. *General* personal jurisdiction gives a court authority to adjudicate any kind of claim involving a person. *Specific* personal jurisdiction gives a court authority to adjudicate only such claims as arise out of the transaction or event upon which jurisdiction is premised.

GENERAL PERSONAL JURISDICTION

A court of a state has general personal jurisdiction over persons who are physically present in the state. A corporation is deemed to be physically present in its state of incorporation and also in the state in which its principal place of business is located. Partnerships and LLCs usually are deemed to be physically present in every state in which any partner or member lives.

General personal jurisdiction also may be exercised over a business that maintains continuous and systematic contacts with a state or a resident of the state. Merely conducting sales to residents of a state, however, does not qualify as "continuous and systematic contact." Introducing a product into the stream of commerce in a state does not, either.[409] These things may qualify as a basis for a court's exercise of specific jurisdiction, but not for an exercise of general personal jurisdiction.

SPECIFIC PERSONAL JURISDICTION

Some kinds of contacts a person has with a state are so significant that a court of the state is justified in exercising jurisdiction over the person whether she is physically present in the state or not. To exercise jurisdiction over a nonresident on this basis, a court must have both constitutional and statutory authority.

Long-arm statutes, which have been enacted in every state, specify the circumstances in which a court may exercise jurisdiction over a nonresident. They vary from state to state. California and several other states broadly authorize courts to exercise jurisdiction to the fullest extent allowable under the federal constitution. Others specify the particular circumstances in which jurisdiction over nonresidents may be exercised. Statutes of the latter variety typically authorize courts to exercise jurisdiction over any person who, either directly or through an agent, does any of the following things:

- transacts business in the state
- contracts to supply goods or services in the state
- causes tortious injury by an act or omission in the state
- causes tortious injury in the state by an act or omission outside the state, if the person regularly engages in or solicits business or derives substantial revenue from goods used or consumed or services rendered in the state
- causes injury in the state to a person by breach of warranty in connection with a sale of goods outside the state when he might reasonably have expected the person to use, consume or be affected by the goods in the state, provided he also regularly does or solicits business, or derives substantial revenue from goods used or consumed or services rendered in the state
- causes tortious injury in the state to any person by an act outside the state committed with the purpose of injuring persons, when he might reasonably have expected that some person would be injured thereby in the state
- causes tortious injury to any person by a criminal act, any element of which takes place in the state, which he commits or in the commission of which he is guilty of complicity
- has an interest in, uses, or possesses real property in the state
- contracts to insure any person, property, or risk located within the state at the time of contracting.[410]

Federal courts apply the laws on personal jurisdiction of the state in which the court sits.

A state court's exercise of jurisdiction over nonresidents is also constrained by the federal constitution. The Due Process Clause prohibits a court from exercising jurisdiction over a person if doing so would offend "traditional notions of fair play and substantial justice." In *International Shoe v. Washington*[411] the U.S. Supreme Court held that this means a court may not exercise personal jurisdiction over a nonresident unless he has had such minimum contacts with the state—or has purposefully availed himself of its benefits and protections—that he should reasonably expect to be subject to suit there. As formulated by the Court in *Burger King v. Rudzewicz*,[412] a court's exercise of jurisdiction over a person may offend traditional notions of fair play and substantial justice unless each of the following conditions is satisfied:

(a) At least minimum contacts, i.e., the performance of some act or transaction by which the person purposefully avails himself of the privilege of conducting activities in the state, thereby invoking the benefits and protections of the state's laws and courts;
(b) The claim arises out of those contacts;
(c) The exercise of jurisdiction is reasonable.

Factors relevant to reasonableness include:

- the burden an exercise of jurisdiction would impose on the defendant (travel expenses, etc.)
- the plaintiff's interest in obtaining relief

- the state's interest in the outcome
- the interest of courts in efficiency
- public policy considerations.

International Shoe clarified that "minimum contacts" does not necessarily require either physical presence within the state or continuous, systematic contacts. It may involve such activities as using an agent or maintaining a warehouse in the state, owning property that is located in the state, placing goods in the stream of commerce in the state, selling products to buyers in the state, or displaying or distributing advertisements in the state. Carried to its logical conclusion, *International Shoe* would mean that virtually every website owner would be subject to the jurisdiction of courts everywhere, since Internet website content is transmitted into and may be accessed in nearly every state (and most countries). Such an expansive interpretation would not be reasonable or fair to e-commerce businesses, however. Consequently, courts have been attempting to decide, on a case-by-case basis, what kinds of Internet activity in a state should qualify as justifications for a court's exercise of personal jurisdiction.

Zippo Manufacturing v. Zippo Dot Com[413] drew a distinction between passive and active websites. A *passive* website is one that is operated solely for the purpose of providing information or enhancing brand recognition. No online sales or other business transactions are conducted on it. At least where such a site is accessible to any member of the public, a transmission from it into a state should not be a sufficient contact with the state to establish jurisdiction. In other words, merely transmitting the advertising that appears on a website into a state is not sufficient to establish jurisdiction. This is also true of foreign-based companies that merely transmit advertising into the United States. As discussed infra, if a transmission causes harm to a person in the state, then a court of the state may exercise jurisdiction. Without more, though, the mere act of transmitting advertising into a state is not a sufficient basis for an American court to exercise personal jurisdiction over a nonresident.

An *active* website is one that is used to engage in transactions with users of the site. An active website that a company uses to conduct business with the residents of another state (such as taking orders from customers and/or shipping ordered products to customers in the state) may be a sufficient contact to enable a court of the state in which such a customer resides to exercise jurisdiction over the company.

Zippo recognized that some websites are more "active" than others. An interactive website maintained by a vendor that has only sporadic sales rather than regular sales to customers residing in a particular state, the court suggested, may or may not have sufficient contact with the state to support jurisdiction, depending on the level of interactivity and the commercial nature of the exchange of information. The court then went on to rule that a subscription news service having contracts with 3,000 subscribers and seven ISP's within a particular state is sufficiently "active" to make the exercise of jurisdiction over the service by a court of that state reasonable.

Mink v. AAAA Development LLC[414] held that a website displaying information about products and services along with a printable order form, a telephone number, a mailing address and an email address that could be used for ordering products or services is a passive advertising website. As such, merely transmitting such a website into a state is not a sufficient contact with the state to support jurisdiction. Similarly, in *E-Data v. Micropatent Corp.*,[415] a federal district court ruled that merely transmitting a commercial website from which residents of any state are able to order a product is not, without more, sufficient contact with a state to support jurisdiction. Jurisdiction might exist, however, if sales are actually made to people who order online from the website. According to some courts, jurisdiction might also exist if a passive website also engages in local advertising (advertising specific to a particular state) even if no online orders are placed.

The takeaway from these cases seems to be that either state-specific local advertising or setting up a website in such a way that users can place orders directly from the website (such as by hitting an 'Order Now' button) may make the business amenable to jurisdiction in a state in which a user either orders online or purchases from within a state in which the business advertises locally. Setting a website up in such a way that orders must instead be made by mail, phone or email, without more, might not suffice to confer jurisdiction (although some courts disagree, holding that it can). Of course, if an order is, in fact, placed in one of the latter ways, then the sale that is conducted in that fashion might be a sufficient contact with the state in which the buyer resides to support an exercise of jurisdiction by that state. The basis of jurisdiction in that instance, though, would be the actual sale of a product to a resident of the state, not the transmission of the website into the state.

Unfortunately, there are no bright-line dividers along the "active website" range of the *Zippo* continuum. It might be thought that the placement of an order from a state may suffice for an exercise of jurisdiction by a court in the state into which the product is shipped. At least one court, however, has held that a single order for a product from an online website will not necessarily suffice to support jurisdiction.[416] In another case, a court found that interactivity and the making of two sales to residents of a state were not sufficient, by themselves, to support the exercise of personal jurisdiction by the courts of that state, where the website's Terms of Use called for disputes to be litigated in a different state.[4157]A forum selection clause requiring cases to be heard by courts in State *B* makes it hard to argue that the website owner "purposefully availed" himself of the protections and benefits of the laws and courts of State *A*. The *Zippo* court held that operating an interactive website that accepts orders from 3,000 residents of a state will support jurisdiction. It is not clear where between 1 and 3,000 a court will draw the line between sufficient and insufficient contact. It also is not clear whether different courts will draw the line at the same place. Although a court in one state may conclude that a single order shipped into a state is not enough, a court in another state might conclude that it is.

The only guidance *Zippo* offers is a "sliding scale" test to the effect that the greater the commercial nature and level of interactivity associated with a website, the more likely it is that the website operator has purposefully availed itself of the forum state's jurisdiction, making an exercise of jurisdiction by the forum state reasonable. In cases falling in the gray zone (websites with fewer than 3,000 sales to residents of the state in question), a court must find something more than interactivity. Factors a court may consider include such things as:

(a) transmission of orders for products or services from the website by residents of the forum state
(b) acceptance of payments by credit card or other electronic funds transfers from residents of the forum state
(c) volume of website hits from residents of the forum state
(d) links to other websites that are active within the forum state

(e) operation of a newsgroup or discussion forum that is accessible to residents of the forum state, and the number of residents of the forum state that participate
(f) placement of cookies on computers within the forum state
(g) number of mailing list recipients within the forum state

This is not an exhaustive list.

At least one court has held that the presence of the defendant's server within a state is not enough, by itself, to establish minimum contacts.[418]

Conducting a sale is not the only kind of contact with a resident that might be used to establish jurisdiction. For example, a federal district court in Pennsylvania has ruled that continuous business communications via email between a nonresident and resident of a state may suffice to support a state's exercise of jurisdiction over the nonresident.[419] Actively soliciting buyers or subscribers in a state may also suffice.[420]

Courts apply the *Zippo* sliding scale test in cases involving business transactions and unintentional torts. In cases involving intentional torts, courts apply an effects test to determine whether sufficient "minimum contacts" exist to support a court's exercise of personal jurisdiction over a nonresident. As formulated by the Supreme Court in *Calder v. Jones*[421] three things must be proven in order to establish jurisdiction using the effects test:

- Intentional act
- Knowingly causing harm in the forum state
- Harm expressly aimed at the forum state.

If these three things have occurred, then the person committing the act is deemed to have purposely availed itself of the forum state. Thus, for example, a California court could exercise personal jurisdiction over a nonresident who transmits a defamatory article via the Internet that is read by web users in California and causes damage to the reputation of a California resident. The same would be true of business torts that cause damage to a business in another state.

In *Yahoo! Inc. v. La Ligua Contre le Racisme et l'Antisemitisme*,[422] the Ninth Circuit Court of Appeals held that obtaining a foreign court order against a resident of the forum state requiring the person to do something in the forum state will also satisfy the effects test for jurisdiction. In that case, a French court had determined that Yahoo! was guilty of violating French laws against the publication of Nazi symbols or ideas. The California-based Yahoo! commenced a proceeding in a California court to declare the order unenforceable. The French organizations that had obtained the order moved to dismiss the proceeding on the grounds that the court lacked personal jurisdiction over them. The district court denied the motion. Ultimately, the court of appeals affirmed that part of the decision. The court reasoned that the prospect of being penalized by a court in another jurisdiction for violating that court's order was a kind of harm that could support an exercise of jurisdiction.

When specific jurisdiction is the basis for an exercise of personal jurisdiction, it only gives a court authority to decide claims that are related to the contact that establishes the basis for jurisdiction. Thus, for example, a California-based airline reservations website that sells tickets to a Florida resident could be sued in Florida for failing to deliver them, but not for personal injuries sustained by the buyer while traveling by plane.

CONSENT

Under American law, personal jurisdiction may be conferred upon a court by consent. Minimum contacts may be established by voluntarily consenting to personal jurisdiction. A *forum selection clause* is a provision in a contract stating that both parties agree that the courts of a particular state or country have jurisdiction over the resolution of any disputes arising under the contract. To be enforceable, this kind of clause must have all of the following attributes:

- Reasonable
- Conspicuous
- Cause no undue hardship to the defendant.

Consent to jurisdiction may be express or implied. In some cases, a choice-of-law provision may help support the finding of purposeful availment that is needed to give a court of the state whose law is chosen personal jurisdiction over the parties to the contract even if they did not expressly consent to personal jurisdiction.[423] In every case, though, courts look at the totality of the circumstances. For example, a choice-of-law provision calling for the application of the law of a state to which neither party has any significant connection might not suffice to establish consent to the exercise of personal jurisdiction over the parties by the courts of that state.

To meet Due Process requirements, a forum selection clause must be fair and reasonable.[424] The party challenging the fairness or reasonableness of a forum selection clause bears the burden of proof of unfairness and unreasonableness.

Forum selection clauses are often upheld in the United States. Other countries are not always as hospitable to them.

FORUM NON CONVENIENS

Even if a court has jurisdiction over the parties, it may decline to exercise jurisdiction if a court in a different state also has jurisdiction and is a more suitable forum for the hearing of the case. A motion requesting that a case be heard in a different state with jurisdiction is called a *forum non conveniens* motion. The grounds for a forum non conveniens motion are usually that the parties and/or most of the witnesses and evidence are located in the other state.

In Rem Jurisdiction

The presence of property within a state is another way a court may acquire jurisdiction. This is called *in rem* jurisdiction. A court may exercise in rem jurisdiction over property that is present within the state even without personal jurisdiction over any particular person. The kinds of orders the court may issue, however, are limited to the status of the property itself. For this reason, a court with only in rem jurisdiction may not issue an injunction.

Subject Matter Jurisdiction

In order to exercise jurisdiction, a court must have jurisdiction both over the person and over the kind of dispute that is involved. The latter is called *subject matter* jurisdiction.

Courts with general subject matter jurisdiction have the power to decide any kind of dispute that is not within another court's exclusive jurisdiction. Courts with limited jurisdiction can only decide the kinds of disputes that are specified in a statute or constitution. Federal courts are courts of limited jurisdiction. Their subject matter jurisdiction is defined and limited by the federal constitution. Under Article III, they may only hear and decide controversies arising under federal law (federal question jurisdiction), disputes between citizens of different states or countries (diversity of citizenship jurisdiction), and a limited number of other kinds of disputes. Most state trial courts, by contrast, are courts of general jurisdiction. They may hear and decide any kind of dispute that is not within another court's exclusive jurisdiction. Within each state, there may be specialized courts with limited jurisdiction, such as traffic courts and juvenile courts.

State courts generally have exclusive jurisdiction over the enforcement of state criminal laws. Federal courts generally have jurisdiction over (a) crimes occurring on federal lands; (b) crimes occurring on ships flying the American flag while in foreign waters; (c) crimes involving interstate or foreign commerce that occur aboard ships flying the American flag; (d) crimes committed in foreign countries that are intended to cause harm in the United States, such as cybercrimes; (e) crimes committed on certain tribal reservations, depending on the terms of the agreement between the tribe and the government.

Federal courts generally have exclusive jurisdiction over copyright, patent and bankruptcy cases, and cases in which the United States is a party. A case "arises under" federal law if it seeks a remedy that is expressly provided in the federal law, or asserts a claim that requires construction of a federal statute, or the policy of the federal law requires that federal principles control the disposition of the claim. Since remedies for infringement are provided in the Copyright Act, as are payment rates for compulsory licenses, legal actions for copyright infringement or for payment of a royalty under a compulsory license must be filed in federal court. A claim for breach of a payment term in a voluntary copyright license contract, by contrast, does not "arise under" federal law, so it may be filed in state court. Since it does not require the resolution of a federal question, it must be filed in state court if all parties are citizens of the same state.

When a federal court has federal question jurisdiction, it may also exercise jurisdiction over related state law claims that arise from the same nucleus of operative fact. This kind of subject matter jurisdiction is called *supplemental* jurisdiction. A state law claim for unfair competition—which can include things like false advertising, trademark dilution or infringement, misappropriation of a trade secret, etc.—may be joined with a federal claim for trademark, patent or copyright infringement, for example, if it is based on the same set of facts.

Subject matter jurisdiction cannot be conferred on a court by the consent or agreement of the parties. A court may dismiss a case at any time, with or without a motion for dismissal, if it determines it lacks subject matter jurisdiction.

JURISDICTION IN THE EUROPEAN UNION

In EU countries, jurisdiction is determined in accordance with the Brussels Convention if the defendant is domiciled in a EU country and there is a link between the court and the action or exercising jurisdiction would facilitate "the sound administration of justice." This is true even if the plaintiff is domiciled in a country that is not a member of the EU. If the defendant is not domiciled in a EU country, then jurisdiction is determined in accordance with the laws of the country in which the court sits. A business entity is considered a domiciliary of the country under whose laws it is organized, where its main administrative office is located, or where it has its principal place of business.

The Brussels I Regulation, enacted in 2002, sought to clarify how the Convention is to be applied in the case of online transactions. It provides that a court in a EU country where a consumer resides has jurisdiction over any foreign business or person who pursues commercial or professional activities "by any means" in that country, or whose commercial or professional activities have an effect in the country. The effect can be either intentional or unintentional. Standing alone, however, merely transmitting passive website content into a country does not qualify as commercial or professional activity.

The Brussels I Regulation contains a special provision that is very protective of consumers. In disputes between a merchant and a consumer who resides in the EU, the consumer may sue either in the country where the consumer is domiciled or in the country where the merchant is domiciled. A French consumer who agrees to purchase a product from an American merchant may sue in either France or the United States, for example. A merchant, on the other hand, may only sue a consumer in the EU country in which the consumer is domiciled.

EU countries generally do not recognize the enforceability of forum selection clauses in contracts between a merchant and a consumer. The special consumer provision in Brussels I Regulation cannot be waived. The only forum selection clauses that members of the EU will enforce in consumer contracts are: (a) an agreement made after a dispute has arisen; (b) an agreement to bestow new jurisdiction to a consumer; (c) an agreement between parties located in the same nation to give courts of that nation jurisdiction. In all other cases, the courts of the country in which the consumer resides have jurisdiction.

Forum selection clauses in contracts between merchants, on the other hand, are enforceable in EU countries. In cases involving contracts between merchants that contain no forum selection clause, the courts of the country in which the contract obligations are to be performed have jurisdiction. Thus, in a contract for the sale of goods, courts in the country where the goods have been or should have been delivered would have jurisdiction. In a services contract, courts in the country where the services have been or should have been performed would have jurisdiction.

In tort cases, courts generally determine jurisdiction by applying a "place of the harm" (*lex loci delicti*) test. In a defamation case, for example, a court in a country where the plaintiff feels the embarrassment and humiliation might have jurisdiction. Arguably, other countries might have jurisdiction, as well, to the extent the plaintiff's reputation has been damaged in those countries, too.

In criminal cases, the country where the criminal act was committed normally has jurisdiction. The country where the act was committed is not always obvious, though. It requires an examination of the specific language in the applicable criminal statute. In *In re Pirate Bay*,[425] for example, a Swedish court interpreted its criminal copyright infringement statute as giving a Swedish court jurisdiction over persons who upload infringing content to a website that is transmitted into Sweden and made available for downloading by Swedish users of the website. It did not matter to the court that the actual act of uploading took place in a different country; the determinative question was where the material was "made available." The court did find it important, however, that a server on which the material was made available was located in Sweden.

JURISDICTION IN OTHER COUNTRIES

Not much progress has been made in harmonizing the jurisdiction laws of different countries. Each county has its own set of rules for determining whether and over whom its courts may exercise personal jurisdiction. So far, the United States is the only country that has adopted the "minimum contacts" rules that are applied in contract cases. A number of counties, however, apply something like the effects test in tort cases.

The Hague Convention on Choice of Court Agreements requires courts in signatory countries to enforce forum selection provisions in contracts between merchants, but not necessarily in contracts between a merchant and a consumer. So far, only Mexico, Singapore, and the EU (with the exception of Denmark). have ratified it.

CREDIT CARD TRANSACTIONS

Because a credit card transaction involves multiple parties and multiple contracts, determining which court (or courts) has jurisdiction can be complicated. A court in the state or country in which the card is issued and in which the cardholder resides normally will have jurisdiction over a dispute arising exclusively from the contract between the cardholder and the issuer. A credit card transaction, however, involves additional parties—the merchant, the credit card network, the acquirer. The issuer has a contract with the credit card network; the credit card network has a contract with the acquirer; the acquirer has a contract with the merchant. It is almost always the case that one or more of these parties is located in a different state or country.

In transactions occurring wholly within the United States, questions of personal jurisdiction often can be resolved by referring to the parties' contract. Most American contracts relating to credit card transactions contain forum selection clauses. These clauses generally are enforceable unless shown to be unfair and unreasonable in a particular case. When a contract involves a country or countries other than the United States, however, it may not always be possible to resolve the issue in this manner. Forum selection clauses are not enforceable in some countries.

When it is not possible to resolve issues of personal jurisdiction by enforcing a forum selection clause, and consent to personal jurisdiction either has not been given or is not enforceable, then resort must be had to the common law for resolution of the issue. The question then becomes: May a court exercise personal jurisdiction on the basis of the use of the card (extension of credit) in the forum state or must it be based on the sales contract? If the former, then personal jurisdiction might be premised on the residence of location of the cardholder, merchant or issuer; if the latter, then the rules for determining jurisdiction in sales cases apply.

CYBERSQUATTING CASES

In cybersquatting cases, a lawsuit may be commenced either against the cybersquatter (in personam) or against the domain name (in rem). A court in the United States has in rem jurisdiction to hear a cybersquatting case if the domain name registrar is located in the United States and the plaintiff either is unable to obtain in personam jurisdiction over the person of the cybersquatter, or after due diligence is unable to locate the person. A cybersquatting case based on in rem jurisdiction must be filed in the district where the domain name registrar is located.

Because people can use certain services to register domain names anonymously, it is not always easy to identify and locate a cybersquatter. To establish due diligence, the plaintiff must send notice of the alleged violation to the postal and email addresses on file with the domain name registrar; get an order for publication from the court; and publish notice in the manner ordered by the court.

Because the court does not have personal jurisdiction over a defendant in an in rem proceeding, the only relief that may be granted is an injunction ordering the domain name registration to be cancelled or transferred to the trademark owner. Damages may not be awarded in an in rem proceeding. Of course, if a defendant can be found, and the court acquires personal jurisdiction over him, then the full range of remedies is available (subject to all non-jurisdictionally-based limitations on remedies that would otherwise apply).

Although the ACPA is a federal law, it does not preempt state laws on the same subject, such as state common law claims for domain name conversion. Thus, a federal and state court may have concurrent subject matter jurisdiction over claims involving cybersquatting activity.

CRIMINAL PROSECUTIONS

The principles pertaining to jurisdiction in criminal cases are similar to those that apply in civil cases, but they are not exactly the same. Courts apply the "minimum contacts" framework only to civil cases, not criminal cases.

In the United States, commission of a crime within a state will suffice to give a court of that state jurisdiction. This rule is easy to state but can be difficult to apply.

> **Example.** Digital Downloads is a business owned by Minnesota resident Bob McGee with a principal place of business in Wisconsin. It establishes an online presence using a web hosting service with a server in Nevada. While vacationing in Hawaii, Bob uploads a file containing malicious code and offers it for sale on the website. Joe Newby, a Pennsylvania resident, downloads it while he is traveling on business in California and saves it to his laptop computer. On the flight home, while in Oklahoma airspace, he executes the file, which damages his computer. In which state was Bob's crime committed—Minnesota, Wisconsin, Nevada, Hawaii, Pennsylvania, California, or Oklahoma?

The starting point for answering this question is the specific language of the particular enactment in question. If, as is often the case, the enactment proscribes the act of transmitting something electronically, then the place where the defendant performed the actual act of transmission is the place where the crime was committed. In the Example, Hawaii would have jurisdiction because that is where Bob was when he uploaded the malicious code.

That is just the starting point of the analysis. In *Strassheim v. Milton Daily*[426] the U.S. Supreme Court held that acts performed outside a state nevertheless will provide a basis for an exercise of jurisdiction by a court within the state if the act was performed with the intent to produce detrimental effects within the state and does, in fact, cause such detrimental effects within the state. Known as the *detrimental effects doctrine*, it means that a person who transmits content that harms a computer may be amenable to the criminal jurisdiction of the state in which the harmed computer is located even if the act of transmission was performed in a different state or country.

Every country enforces its own criminal laws and jurisdictional rules within its own geographic borders. A transmission of content into a country that violates the country's criminal laws generally may be prosecuted there even if the sender resides in a different country. Of course, it will still be necessary to secure the person's attendance in court to answer to the charge. That will be difficult to do if the offender is not physically present within the country. Law enforcement officers generally only have the power to make arrests within their own country, unless the country has an extradition treaty with the country in which the offender is physically present.

Pursuant to the Convention on Cybercrime, violations of the CFAA generally are extraditable offenses.

Venue

Venue refers to the most appropriate forum for the hearing or trial of a case. It has nothing to do with the authority of a court to decide a case. Venue rules are applied to determine which of two courts with jurisdiction over the parties and the subject matter should handle it. Decisions about venue usually involve consideration of the location of the parties, witnesses and evidence.

Venue for a cybersquatting proceeding based on in rem jurisdiction is in the district where the domain name registrar is located.

Conflicts of Laws

While conflicts-of-laws rules vary from state to state, it is possible to identify some that are more prevalent than others. Chief among these is that a court will apply the procedural rules of the state in which the court sits. Which state's (or foreign country's) substantive law is applied depends on the kind of case it is.

In tort cases, the traditional rule, historically, has been that the law of the place where the harm occurred should be applied. Today, courts generally hold that the law of the jurisdiction with the most significant relationship to the occurrence and the parties should be applied, and that this requires consideration of more things than just where the harm occurred. Specifically, the following factors must be considered:

(a) place where the harm occurred
(b) place where the conduct causing the harm occurred
(c) the domicile, residence, nationality, place of incorporation and place of business of the parties
(d) the place where the relationship between the parties is centered
(e) the purposes and policies of the forum state's tort law.

For example, in trade libel cases, the harm is to the business entity's reputation, so the "place of the harm" is the place where the business entity is organized. For a corporation, that would the state in which it is incorporated. Historically, that would conclude the issue. It would still conclude the issue in some courts today. In other courts, though, that would just be the starting point of the analysis. Many courts today will make a determination by weighing and evaluating all of the factors, not just the first one.

In contract cases, courts will apply the law of the jurisdiction with the most significant relationship to the claim. In making this determination, they will consider:

(a) the place where the contract was negotiated
(b) the place where the contract was formed
(c) the place of performance
(d) the location of the subject matter of the contract
(e) residence, domicile, nationality, place of incorporation and place of business.

Franchise offers and sales are governed by the law of the state in which an offer or sale of franchise is made. Franchise operations are governed by the law of state in which the franchise is or will be located or where the franchisee is a resident.

When a federal case involves a question of state law, the court generally applies the law of the state in which the federal court is situated, including its conflicts-of-laws principles. This is not always the case, though. Sometimes more than one court could exercise jurisdiction over a matter. In such cases, the court will need to decide whether to apply the laws of the forum state or those of another state that could exercise jurisdiction. Of course, people can enter into agreements about which jurisdiction's laws will apply to their disputes, and usually—but not always—these agreements are enforced. In the absence of an enforceable agreement like this, courts must make these decisions on some other basis.

CHOICE OF LAW AGREEMENTS

In the United States, courts generally enforce contractual provisions specifying the law to be applied to resolve disputes arising under the contract unless enforcement of the provision would be unreasonable and unjust in a particular case. This is true whether the contract is between merchants or between a merchant and a consumer. A court may decline to apply the law of a chosen state if it is contrary to the fundamental policy of a state that has a materially greater interest than the chosen state and is where the contract is to be performed.

GOVERNING LAW IN EUROPEAN UNION CASES

EU member counties are signatories to the Rome I Convention, which established choice-of-law rules. In 2005, the Rome I Regulation displaced the Rome I Convention, but gave individual member countries an option to abide by the older Rome I Convention rather than the Rome I Regulation. In 2008, the European Commission replaced the Rome I Convention with a Community-Wide Regulation, EC No. 593/2008.

In contracts between merchants, contractual choice-of-law provisions generally are enforceable. If an applicable contract between merchants specifies which country's laws are to govern in disputes arising under the contract, then a court in a EU country generally will apply the laws of that country. If the parties have not entered into an agreement containing a choice of law provision, then the law of the country having the closest connection with the contract is to be applied. The country with the closest connection to the contract is generally the country in which the party who is to perform the characteristic performance under the contract habitually resides. *Characteristic performance* refers to the execution of an obligation that characterizes the contract. The obligation to pay money for something is not an obligation that characterizes contracts. The obligation to deliver a particular kind of product or to perform a particular service does. Thus, unless the parties have agreed otherwise, the following choice-of-law rules apply to contracts between merchants:

(a) A contract for the sale of goods is governed by the law of the country in which the seller habitually resides;
(b) A contract for the provision of services is governed by the law of the country in which the service provider habitually resides;
(c) A contract for carriage is governed by the law of the country in which the carrier has its habitual residence;
(d) A contract relating to an in rem right or right of user in immovable property is governed by the law of the country in which the property is located;
(e) A contract relating to intellectual property rights is governed by the law of the country in which the transferor, assignor or licensor habitually resides.

A different rule applies to contracts between a merchant and a consumer. Consumer contracts are governed by the law of the country in which the consumer habitually resides. This special rule only applies to contracts involving a consumer who habitually resides in a EU country. It applies to contracts for goods or services and also to credit contracts relating to a contract for goods or services.

The Rome II Regulation (EC No. 846//2007), enacted by the European Commission in 2007, establishes choice-of-law rules for tort cases. The basic principle is that the law of the place where the wrong occurred should be applied in tort cases. It is unclear where the wrong occurs when a tort (such as defamation) is committed online. It is possible, though, that a European court could hold that an online tort that injures a EU resident's reputation occurs in the EU country in which the person suffering the injury resides.

Conflicts of laws issues in cases involving the rights and obligations of an ISP, web hosting service or other online service provider located in a EU country is governed by laws implementing the Directive on Electronic Commerce. Pursuant to these laws, an online service provider that is established in a EU country need only comply with the laws of the country in which its service is performed, even if its activities affect individuals in other countries. This rule, known as the *country of origin principle,* does not apply to consumer transactions.

International Disputes

Each country establishes its own jurisdictional and conflicts-of-laws principles. As a result, global uniformity does not exist. Nevertheless, it is possible to identify some key concepts that most countries have adopted. These are:

- Comity
- Territoriality
- Nationality.

Comity refers to respect for the laws and institutions of other countries. *Territoriality* is the principle that a country normally is entitled to exercise jurisdiction over people or controversies that are present or arise within the country's territorial boundaries. *Nationality* is the idea that countries have the right to regulate the conduct of their own citizens.

These principles can conflict with each other. Each country makes its own determination how to resolve these conflicts, and not all countries have resolved them in the same way. Sometimes the laws of different countries mesh well. For example, courts in the United States and EU countries have developed a rule that general damages for defamation may be sought in the country in which the statement originates but courts that exercise jurisdiction in other countries may award damages only for the specific harm a defamatory statement is proven to have caused a specific resident of that country (special damages). Treaties, too, have helped establish some uniformity, at least with respect to certain areas of the law, such as copyrights. Unfortunately, there is still a significant lack of uniformity among countries in most areas of the law.

Businesses should be cautious about maintaining servers in other countries. The courts of some countries have held that merely maintaining a server in a country is sufficient to make the company amendable both the laws of that country and to the jurisdiction of the courts of that country. In one case, for example, a German court imposed a criminal sentence on the manager of a business that maintained a server there, on the basis of speech that would be protected by the First Amendment if U.S. law had been applied.

Businesses should also be cautious about using servers in other countries. A criminal prosecution in Denmark for hate speech, for example, was founded on the fact that the person posted the comment on a website that resided on a server that was located in Denmark.

Business may also need to take steps to prevent residents of certain countries from accessing their websites. Some countries, such as Germany, have enacted laws requiring any website that is accessible to citizens of the country to comply with the country's laws.

For these reasons, it is common for businesses that engage in international sales or business transactions to establish separate websites and use different servers in the various countries in which they do business. IBM, for example, has separate websites for each of over 100 countries. A less costly approach would be to create separate websites only for the larger countries to which the company markets. Amazon, for example, has a family of fourteen websites identified by different country codes—www.amazon.cn for China, www.amazon.fr for France, and so on.

The alternative to these approaches is to establish only one website, and then try to structure it in such a way that it complies with the laws of the countries to which the company markets. This might be done by writing content that complies with all laws. Since the laws of different countries can vary considerably, this may not always be feasible. An alternative would be to write the content in a way that complies with the laws of the country to which the company primarily markets, and then include customized provisions for customers in other countries. For example, a company that markets primarily in the United States might write the content of the website in a way that complies with U.S. law, but include a separate Terms of Use (or Privacy Policy, etc.) to which customers in a specific country other than the United States must signify assent. These separate provisions, of course, should be written in the principal language that is spoken by citizens of the country. The same is true of other aspects of a sale—e.g., the form of currency, special taxes, adjusted shipping rates and terms, etc.

INTELLECTUAL PROPERTY TREATIES

Although there is not yet a treaty or convention requiring signatory countries to abide by the same set of conflicts-of-law principles, conflicts of laws in the area of intellectual property have been ameliorated to some extent by treaties requiring or promoting uniformity with respect to certain kinds of legal provisions. Treaties requiring member countries to give citizens of other member countries the same legal protections that are given to their own citizens also help promote uniformity. These treaties do not eliminate conflicts of laws altogether, but they do tend to reduce the frequency with which they occur. Some of these treaties apply to intellectual property rights generally. Others apply only to specific kinds of intellectual property.

The Agreement on Trade Related Aspects of Intellectual Property Rights ("TRIPS Agreement") is an important treaty that brings some uniformity and consistency to international intellectual property law. It requires each member of the WTO to give nationals of other WTO members no less favorable treatment with respect to intellectual property rights than it gives to nationals of any other WTO member state. In addition, any intellectual property right a WTO member state grants to its nationals must be granted to nationals of all other WTO member states, too. It has been added to the General Agreement on Tariffs and Trade (GATT). Ratification of the TRIPS Agreement is required for membership in the WTO. WTO membership is beneficial to countries because it opens up international markets. Consequently, almost every country is a member. The United States is a signatory to the TRIPS Agreement. Congress enacted the URAA to implement it.

The World Intellectual Property Organization (WIPO) is an international agency based in Geneva, Switzerland. Composed of member countries, it facilitates the adoption of intellectual property treaties.

It is important to keep in mind that the requirements of a treaty do not apply to a country that has not acceded to it. For example, some nontreaty South American countries require a trademark notice to display more detailed information than just the ® symbol. Iran requires pharmaceutical products to display the registration number and date along with the registration symbol or mark. Other kinds of requirements exist in other nontreaty countries. Moreover, in some nontreaty countries, intellectual property rights are governed by custom rather than laws.

Copyright

The Berne Convention requires signatory countries to give as much legal protection to the owners of foreign copyrights as it gives to its own citizens and nationals. It also requires a signatory country to recognize the validity of copyrights that are valid under the laws of their country of origin even if they would not be valid under the country's own laws. It requires signatories to abolish formal requirements, such as registration or the display of a copyright notice. It also specifies the minimum kinds of substantive copyright protections each signatory country must enact for the protection of copyright owners. These include the exclusive rights of reproduction, adaptation, translation and public performance, and the moral rights of attribution and integrity. Signatory countries may provide greater rights to copyright owners than these, but they must provide at least these minimum rights. Member countries must apply the law of the country of origin to determine the term of a copyright, but each member country must enact laws providing for a term of at least fifty years.

The TRIPS Agreement requires all member states to comply with the Berne Convention, except Article 6bis. Article 6bis relates to the moral rights of visual artists. Among other things, it also requires member states to protect copyrights in computer programs as literary works and to provide copyright protection for the selection and arrangement of data compilations.

The WIPO Copyright Treaty, like the TRIPS Agreement, calls for the protection of copyrights in computer programs and in the selection and arrangement of data compilations. It also requires protections for distribution and rental rights in computer programs, audiovisual works, and works embodied in sound recordings. And it requires legal protections for technological copyright protection measures and copyright management information. The WIPO Performances and Phonograms Treaty requires protection for both physical and digital reproduction rights in sound recordings. It also requires signatory countries to enact legal protections against the fixation, reproduction, broadcasting and communication to the public of live performances. The United States is a signatory to these treaties.

The Rome Convention applies to broadcasts and recordings of live performances and public performances of sound recordings. The United States—which recognizes an exclusive right to digitally transmit a sound recording, but not an exclusive right to publicly perform a sound recording—is not a signatory to it.

Signatories to the Brussels Satellite Convention, including the United States, must enact laws for the prevention of the misappropriation of satellite signals.

Trademark

The WIPO Trademark Treaty specifies successive ten-year periods for the original and renewal terms of trademarks. It also attempts to harmonize the trademark laws of member countries with respect to other matters, such as protecting both service marks and trademarks, the use of trademark symbols, and application and renewal procedures.

The "no less favorable treatment" requirement in the TRIPS Agreement means that a foreign company may establish trademark rights in the United States under the same conditions that an American business could. In addition, a foreign company may register a trademark in the United States in the same way that an American business can, by filing an application based on either use or intent to use in the United States.

The Paris Convention requires signatory countries to treat domiciliaries of other signatory countries in the same manner as their own domiciliaries with respect to trademark rights. It also allows a trademark applicant to obtain a "priority date" by filing the application in a signatory country. If the applicant files another application in a different signatory country within six months, then the applicant may claim the benefit of the filing date of the earlier filed application. Each signatory country must treat an application that was filed earlier in another signatory country as if it had been filed in the second country on the earlier date, provided the second filing is not more than the specified number of months after the first.

The Madrid Protocol establishes a system for registering trademarks and trademark transfers in more than one country at a time.

Patents

The TRIPS Agreement requires a member state's patent laws to provide for the issuance of patents without regard to whether the grant is in the public interest or not; and to observe certain requirements regarding patentability, including novelty and nonobviousness, and the term of a patent. Detailed provisions relating to a government's issuance of compulsory licenses (more common in countries other than the United States) are also included.

The WIPO Patent Law Treaty is intended to harmonize practices in the intellectual property offices of member countries. Key provisions include:

- Simplified filing requirements
- Harmonization of application forms
- Decreased need for the use of attorneys in administrative matters
- Simplification of ownership transfers
- Possible extension of the priority period
- Enhanced mechanisms to avoid loss of rights.

The treaty has been ratified in the United States, and many of its provisions were implemented by the Patent Law Treaties Implementation Act of 2012. The U.K., Japan and several other countries have also signed on.

The North American Free Trade Agreement requires the United States, Canada and Mexico to commit to certain substantive intellectual property law provisions relating to such things as patent terms, scope of patent rights, and standards of patentability.

The Paris Convention requires signatory countries to treat domiciliaries of other signatory countries in the same manner as their own domiciliaries with respect to patent rights. It also allows a patent applicant to obtain a "priority date" by filing the application in a signatory country. If the applicant files another application in a different signatory country within twelve months, then the applicant may claim the benefit of the filing date of the earlier filed application. Each signatory country must treat an application that was filed earlier in another signatory country as if it had been filed in the second country on the earlier date, provided the second filing is not more than the specified number of months after the first.

The Paris Convention contains some additional protections for inventors, as well. Importantly, information entering the public domain during the twelve-month period will not prejudice the second application. This gives an applicant time to file an application in multiple countries, if desired. Also, the Paris Convention requires patents obtained in different countries to be treated as independent properties. The termination of a patent for an invention in one signatory country will not terminate a patent for the same invention in another signatory country.

Trade Secrets

The TRIPS Agreement includes a requirement obligating member countries to protect rights in trade secrets.

CROSS-BORDER SALES

In an interstate or international sales transaction, conflicts-of-laws issues usually come down to whether a court should apply the law of the jurisdiction where the seller is located or the law of the jurisdiction where the buyer is located. But where are sellers and buyers "located" when a transaction is conducted online? The trend in the United States, Canada and the EU is to identify a person's location with the location of the server from which the person sends a transmission, and to apply the laws of that location. The EU's Directive on Electronic Commerce adopts this approach. Some countries, however, apply the law of the country where the transmission is received.

Commercial law treaties help to reduce conflicts of laws problems by harmonizing the commercial laws of every country that is willing to agree to them. The UN Convention on Contracts for the International Sale of Goods (CISG) is a treaty to which the United States and a number of other countries are parties. It sets out the basic legal principles governing contracts for the sales of goods across international borders. If both parties reside in countries that have acceded to this Convention, then these are the default rules that apply to the contract unless both parties agree to opt out. The UN Convention on the Use of Electronic Communications in International Contracts (ECC) contains a similar provision for parties whose places of business are in different countries. Unlike CISG, this Convention is not limited to sales of goods. It also applies to sales of services, software licenses, and several other kinds of contracts. The ECC applies only if both parties are in countries that have acceded to it. Only a small handful of countries have done so. The United States has not.

Pursuant to the Electronic Commerce Directive, EU countries must enforce electronic contracts on the same terms that they enforce traditional paper contracts.

Foreign Judgments

In theory, legal judgments do not have any force or effect beyond the limits of the sovereignty from which its authority is derived. It is up to each sovereign nation to decide whether to recognize and enforce judgments issued by the courts of other countries.

Pursuant to the Brussels I Regulation, members of the EU have agreed to recognize and enforce judgments issued by courts of other EU countries.

The United States is not a party to any treaty requiring the enforcement of Internet-related judgments issued by courts in other countries. American courts do generally enforce foreign judgments as a matter of comity, but only if each of the following conditions is satisfied:

(a) The foreign court had jurisdiction to enter the judgment;
(b) Process was properly served;
(c) No fraud was involved in the proceeding;
(d) Enforcement of the judgment is not contrary to American public policy.

About half of the states in the United States have enacted a uniform law, the Uniform Foreign Money Judgments Recognition Act (UFMJRA) mandating recognition and enforcement of foreign money judgments under these circumstances. Under the UFMJRA, the foreign judgment must be "conclusive, final and enforceable" in the country of origin. Judgments for taxes, fines and quasi-criminal penalties are not within the scope of the UFMJRA. In addition, the UFMJRA prohibits recognition of a judgment issued by a court system that is not impartial or that dishonors due process, or by a court that did not have personal jurisdiction over the defendant or the subject matter. Recognition of a foreign judgment may also be refused if the defendant did not receive notice of the proceeding.

Significantly, a court may refuse to enforce a foreign judgment if doing so is repugnant to American public policy. The value of freedom of expression that is enshrined in the First Amendment is an example of an American public policy. An American court may refuse to enforce a foreign judgment to the extent enforcement would require an American court to participate in the suppression of protected speech rights in the United States. In *Yahoo, Inc. v. La Ligue Contre Le Racisme et l'Antisemitisme*[427] a federal district court in California considered the question whether an order issued by a court in a foreign country directing an American company to configure its service to block images of Nazi memorabilia from being displayed to residents of France is enforceable in America. The court held that it is not. An American court's obligation to uphold the First Amendment outweighs the principle of comity. The case was appealed. The Eighth Circuit Court of Appeals voted to dismiss the case on procedural grounds, three of the eight judges voting to dismiss on the basis of lack of jurisdiction and three voting to dismiss on the basis that the case was not yet ripe for decision. Although the merits of the case were not necessary to the disposition, some members of the court chose to weigh in on the substantive issue. Some opined that the First Amendment outweighed comity in this case; others argued that it did not. The only conclusion that can safely be drawn from this case is that the First Amendment may outweigh comity in some cases, but it is far from certain that it will do so in every case.

Freedom of expression is not the only American public policy that may serve as grounds for denying recognition to a foreign judgment.

Courts in other countries do not always enforce judgments that have been issued by American courts, either. Some countries have voluntarily adopted a reciprocity policy, enforcing U.S. judgments to the same extent the United States would enforce the same kind of judgment had it been issued in the foreign country under the same set of circumstances. Other countries do not have any kind of reciprocal enforcement policy. Germany and several other European countries, for example, refuse to enforce awards of punitive damages in judgments issued by American courts even though American courts would enforce such judgments if they were issued by courts in those countries.

Within the United States, a judgment issued by a court in one state is generally enforceable in any other state. The Full Faith and Credit Clause in Article VI of the federal constitution requires each state to recognize the validity of the judicial acts of the courts of other states, provided Due Process "minimum contacts" requirements were met. Most states have enacted the Uniform Enforcement of Foreign Judgments Act, which provides a simplified mechanism for enforcing out-of-state judgments.

Foreign Arbitration Awards

The United States and many other countries are signatories to the New York Arbitration Convention. Pursuant to this Convention, arbitration agreements must be enforced if they are in writing. Further, the country in which, or under whose arbitration law, an arbitration award was made has primary jurisdiction over enforcement of the award, and all other signatory countries have secondary jurisdiction. Courts in countries with only secondary jurisdiction must give effect to arbitration awards that are issued in a country with primary jurisdiction; they do not have the power to annual or vacate the award.

REDUCING RISKS

Many countries impose civil and/or criminal liability on persons who transmit certain kinds of content into the country via the Internet or who make certain kinds of uses or conduct certain kinds of transactions using the Internet. This could include things like posting content that is defamatory or an invasion of someone's privacy, pornography, hate speech, insults to royalty, or any of the other kinds of content or conduct that are discussed elsewhere in this book. While the risk of being prosecuted or held liable in other countries for Internet activity cannot be eliminated altogether, there are some things that can be done to reduce the risk.

Some features of website design can help reduce the likelihood of access by residents of countries in which the content is prohibited or actionable. The Terms of Use could prohibit citizens or residents of particular countries from accessing the site, or they could state that the website is only intended for use by residents of specified countries. A clickwrap agreement could require a user to enter a zip code or certify that s/he is or is not a resident of a specified country (ies) as a condition to entering the site. Of course, these methods are not foolproof. Nor is there any certainty that a court in a foreign country would consider such precautions as a defense or as factors to be considered in mitigation of a sentence.

Another method of reducing risk is to avoid traveling to countries whose laws you may have violated. In most countries, a person's physical presence there is a sufficient basis for the exercise of personal jurisdiction by the courts of that country. On the other hand, some foreign criminal statutes do not require physical presence in order to be amenable to the court's jurisdiction. In the absence of an applicable extradition treaty, however, it may be difficult, as a practical matter, for a government to secure a foreign citizen's attendance in court if she is not physically present in the country.

Using forum selection clauses in contracts with online customers may help reduce the risk of being sued by a customer in a different state or country. Choice-of-law provisions can help prevent surprises concerning which laws will be applied to a dispute. Even if the parties have entered into one or both of these kinds of agreements, there must still be a sufficient connection to the selected state for a court to enforce it. A court may also decline to enforce one of these kinds of agreements if it determines that doing so would be unconscionable. See Chapter 9.

Geolocation technologies are another method of reducing the risk of website content being transmitted into a particular region. Geoblocking uses technology to restrict Internet content based on the user's geographical location.

Of course, insurance is another idea to consider.

Chapter 35. Alternatives to Litigation

Litigation is expensive and can extend over a period of years. Fortunately, other methods of resolving disputes are available. These methods often can reduce considerably the expense, delay, invasiveness and uncertainty of litigation. Court rules in a number of jurisdictions require or permit a court to order parties to litigation to attempt resolution of the dispute through a nonjudicial process at some point. Of course, it is not necessary to wait for a court order to try an alternative method of dispute resolution. It may be attempted at any time before trial.

Alternative dispute resolution ("ADR") is an umbrella term for any nonjudicial process for resolving disputes. These processes are administered by private individuals, private organizations, and in some areas, government or community service offices.

ADR methods

The five main categories of ADR are:

- Negotiation
- Mediation
- Arbitration
- Med-Arb (hybrid of arbitration and mediation)
- Expert evaluation.

NEGOTIATION

Negotiation is simply communication between two parties in an attempt to reach an amicable resolution of a dispute between them. It is the oldest ADR method. Even when a case is litigated, negotiations toward a settlement typically take place before and throughout the litigation. In a typical negotiation, both sides begin by making exaggerated demands and offers, and then deploy strategies to put pressure on the other party to make concessions.

Some Internet websites offer automated tools to aid in the negotiation of a settlement. For example, a blind bidding service (sometimes called "automated negotiation") may allow the parties, for a fee, to submit their settlement offers and demands to the service without the other party knowing what the amount is. The parties specify a range of values close to the amount they offer or demand (e.g., 30% of the initial demand). If the program determines that the offer and demand are within the agreed-upon range, then it splits the difference and reports that amount to the parties. Of course, this type of service is most useful when liability is not disputed and the only issue is the amount of damages.

Collaborative law is a type of negotiation in which each party is represented by a trained "collaborative lawyer." If a settlement agreement is not reached, then each attorney must withdraw. New counsel will need to be retained to represent a party in litigation.

MEDIATION

Mediation is a process in which a third party listens to the parties' arguments and concerns, but does not render a decision. Instead, a mediator will attempt to lead the parties in the direction of working out a voluntary agreement resolving the issue(s) between them. This might be done, for example, by suggesting possible ways of resolving the dispute.

Mediation is always nonbinding. There is no "decision" to which the parties could be bound even if they wanted to be. It is also a voluntary process, meaning that either party may end the process simply by saying they no longer want to participate in it. An agreement reached through mediation may be binding on the parties, though, if it is in the form of an enforceable contract.

ARBITRATION

Arbitration is similar to a court proceeding, but less formal. A third party (the arbitrator) receives evidence and hears the arguments of the parties and then renders a decision. In some states, an arbitrator may exercise the subpoena power to demand the production of documents or witnesses. Arbitration proceeds much like a trial does—opening statements, presentation of witnesses and evidence, cross-examination, closing arguments. The decision of an arbitrator may be enforceable under state or federal law, as applicable. Arbitration essentially involves the use of a private "court" and "judge" to render a decision. Because of this, it has many of the same drawbacks as formal litigation does, namely, cost and difficulty of enforcement.

Arbitration may be binding or nonbinding, as agreed by the parties. A decision in a binding arbitration is final. It may not be challenged in court except in narrow circumstances, such as where the arbitrator exceeded the scope of her authority under the arbitration agreement.

Clauses in contracts that call for the resolution of disputes by means of arbitration (or some other ADR process) are generally enforceable. A party seeking to bind another party to such a clause, however, must provide the text of the clause to the other party. Obtaining a person's signature (electronic or otherwise) to a statement that the person "agrees to arbitration clauses" in a contract will not necessarily bind the person to those clauses if the contract document is not shared with that person.

Mandatory arbitration agreements are not invalid per se, but they may be unenforceable if a court determines that enforcement would be unconscionable. Courts examine the circumstances attendant to the formation of a contract to assess unconscionability. If the court finds that a person lacked any meaningful choice about whether to accept or reject a contract term, or that the terms are grossly unfair to the party with less bargaining power, then it may refuse to enforce the contract or term. Factors include: the nature and setting of the transaction; the experience and education of the person claiming unconscionability; whether the contract or term is in fine print; whether high pressure sales tactics were used; and any other consideration relevant to a disparity in the parties' bargaining power. Courts are more likely to make an unconscionability determination with respect to a contractual term when it is in small print and/or buried in a lengthy document than when it is conspicuously displayed in large print in a shorter document.

Mandating arbitration of a kind that is more expensive than others can sometimes lead a court to determine that the clause is unconscionable. For this reason, requiring arbitration by a specific ADR provider may not be a good idea, at least if the provider specified in the contract is more expensive than the American Arbitration Association (AAA), for example.

HYBRID FORMS OF ADR

Med-arb refers to any hybrid ADR process that combines elements of both arbitration and mediation. It can take a variety of different forms. Typically, the third party initially acts as a mediator; then, if resolution cannot be achieved that way, he will proceed to assume the role of an arbitrator.

EXPERT EVALUATION

In lieu of using an arbitrator, mediator, or hybrid of the two, people may choose to retain an expert to evaluate the case and make a recommendation as to how it should be settled. Like an arbitrator, an evaluator will usually receive evidence and arguments from the parties. Unlike an arbitrator, though, the evaluator will not render a decision. Instead, he will evaluate the merits and the value of a claim and make a settlement recommendation. In the course of doing that, an evaluator might offer an opinion about how s/he would rule on the case if s/he were a judge, but neutral evaluations are not binding. A number of organizations maintain databases of experts who provide this service.

Expert evaluations are most productively used in conjunction with one of the other methods of resolving a dispute. For example, it can help expedite a mediation or negotiation process.

Online Dispute Resolution

ADR conducted online rather than face-to-face is called *online dispute resolution*. PayPal and other companies that provide services to facilitate third party sales transactions have established methods for resolving disputes relating to the sale, such as a buyer's claim that an item is defective or not received, or a seller's claim that a buyer failed to pay. In addition, a number of ADR providers offer online services.

Online ADR has a number of advantages over litigation. It is less expensive and quicker. It can decrease acrimony between parties. People who resolve disputes using online ADR may be more willing to continue doing business with each other than they would be if one had sued the other. When parties agree on an ADR provider and the law to be applied, they avoid jurisdictional and conflicts-of-laws problems that can often be difficult (and risky) for courts to resolve.

Crowdjustice is a new form of online arbitration in which members of the online community decide the case. Typically, it involves each party submitting their cases (such as by uploading a video presentation) to the website, at which registered users may vote on who should win, how much money they should get, and the like. Businesses should be cautious about using this form of online dispute resolution unless controls are in place to ensure that the "jury" is not packed primarily with people with a pro-consumer bias. Also be aware that the legal protections that are in place in real courts to ensure that litigants don't get away with presenting scurrilous evidence designed to incite prejudice against the other party rather than to advance a search for truth, and to ensure that jurors follow the law and make findings that are supported by the evidence, might not exist in a Crowdjustice proceeding.

International Arbitration

Several organizations handle the arbitration of international disputes. The International Chamber of Commerce (ICC) maintains an International Court of Arbitration in France. The London Court of International Arbitration (LCIA) and the AAA also handle arbitrations of international disputes. Each of these organizations has it own set of rules. WIPO also provides arbitration services. Arbitration awards in ICC cases must be submitted to the ICC Court for approval. There is no comparable requirement under the LCIA and AAA rules.

The New York Arbitration Convention enables the enforcement of arbitration awards in different countries, provided the arbitration is international.

Disputes between WTO member states over TRIPS Agreement compliance are subject to the WTO Dispute Settlement Understanding, which calls for resolution by a panel established by the Dispute Settlement Body.

A number of e-commerce businesses have established dispute resolution mechanisms that are equipped to resolve both domestic and international disputes.

Chargebacks are essentially a form of ADR. They are discussed in Chapter 11.

Domain Name Dispute Resolution

ICANN requires all domain name registrars to adopt WIPO's UDRP for handling disputes between trademark owners and domain name registrants. If a domain name registrant refuses to transfer a domain name to the trademark owner upon demand, then the trademark owner may file a UDRP arbitration complaint to have the registration canceled. The complaint may be filed with any ICANN-approved ADR provider. UDRP arbitration is usually cheaper, and often more favorable, to trademark claimants than courts are.

ICANN-approved ADR providers include WIPO; the National Arbitration Forum; the International Institute for Conflict Prevention and Resolution (CPR); the Asian Domain Name Dispute Resolution Center; and others. A current list of approved ADR providers is maintained at www.icann.org/udrp/approved-providers.htm

UDRP Rules are available online at: www.icann.org/dndr/udrp/uniform-rules.htm#5biv

When filing a complaint, either a sole panelist or a three-member panel may be requested. The respondent has a right to demand a three-member panel. The complainant normally pays the costs of the arbitration, but if the respondent demands a three-member panel, then costs are divided between the parties.

Normally, arbitration proceedings are conducted by the submission of written documents. Hearings are not held except in unusual cases. The complainant has the burden of proof of the elements of the claim by a preponderance of the evidence. Past UDRP decisions, as well as the judicial decisions of courts of any country, are given precedential effect in UDRP proceedings.

UDRP proceedings are international in scope. They can and often do involve citizens of different countries. Registrars in generic TLDs (.com, .org, .net, etc.) agree to be bound by them. Some country code registrars also agree to abide by the UDRP system. Others have set up their own dispute resolution mechanisms.

UDRP decisions normally are made promptly, typically within two weeks.

The necessary elements of a UDRP claim are:

(a) a domain name that is identical or confusing similar to the complainant's trademark
(b) registrant has no legitimate interest or rights in the domain name
(c) bad faith registration and use of the domain name.

The trademark may be either a registered or a common law mark. It must be a trademark, though. A bad faith registration of a person's surname is not within the purview of a UDRP proceeding unless the surname has acquired secondary meaning as a trademark in the marketplace.

Use of a different TLD extension (.com, .org, etc.) usually has no effect on a determination of confusing similarity. Also, a UDRP panel is not likely to find that merely adding a generic or descriptive word to a trademark will prevent it from being confusingly similar to the trademark.

Since a post-domain path is not part of a domain name, disputes over the use of trademarks or personal names in them are not within the purview of the UDRP process.

A misspelling of a well-known trademark is likely to be considered confusingly similar to the well-known mark. UDRP panels frown on typosquatting.

A UDRP panel typically is more likely to make a finding of confusing similarity than courts are. UDRP panels focus on the similarity of the domain name and the trademark rather than the extent to which consumers are likely to be confused. Thus, a UDRP panel is likely to find a domain name consisting of a trademark and a disparaging word (such as BestBuysucks.com) to be confusingly similar to the trademark, even though a court might not. Some panels cite the fact that that not all Internet users know what the English word *sucks* means as a reason for ruling that adding the word *sucks* to a trademark will not prevent the domain name from being confusingly similar to a trademark. A minority of panels decide the issue as a court would, finding that a domain name formed by adding a derogatory term to a trademark is not confusingly similar to the trademark.

There have been UDRP panels that have acknowledged the importance of protecting protest sites, and distinguish between good faith registrations of domain names for protest sites that are formed by adding a derogatory term to a trademark, on one hand, and bad faith registrations, on the other. To this kind of panel, BestBuySucks.com would probably be registrable by the owner of a protest site unless there is evidence that the name was registered and used in bad faith, e.g., that the registrant tried to make a profit by offering the name for sale to Best Buy for more than the cost of registration.

Although UDRP panels are often more likely than courts to find confusing similarities in domain names, they can also be cognizant of the fact that unlike trademarks, only a limited range of text characters is available for the construction of a domain name. They are also aware of the relative scarcity of domain names. Both the band and the seafood seller may use the trademark ABBA, but only one can use it as a domain name. Website owners do not have as much flexibility in choosing names as business owners have in choosing trademarks. For example, when IMDB sought to disgorge another registrant of the registration of "INDB" as a domain name, a UDRP panel ruled against IMDB. A court, on the other hand, might find the two names confusingly similar for trademark purposes.

The claimant must establish that the registrant has no legitimate interest or rights in the domain name. The existence of a legitimate interest may be established by evidence that the registrant previously used the name in connection with a bona fide offering of goods or services (e.g., goods or services in a different category); or that the registrant is commonly known by the name (e.g., it is his surname or the name of his corporation); or that it is noncommercial or fair use, with no intent to divert consumers or to tarnish the mark. Note, however, that unlike many courts, some panels hold that the use of a mark in a domain name for a site containing criticism of the mark's owner or the goods or services the owner markets under the mark is tarnishment.

It is necessary to establish bad faith on the part of the registrant in order to prevail in a UDRP proceeding. Domain name profiteering—buying a domain name simply for the purpose of selling it to the trademark owner at a higher price—is an example of bad faith. Registering a domain name simply to prevent a business competitor from using it is another example, as is registering and using another company's trademark for the purpose of duping people into visiting one's own website for commercial gain. Some panels regard the offer to sell as being a "use" of the name, for purposes of the "bad faith registration and use of a domain name" requirement. Panels are split as to whether merely holding a domain name registration is, by itself, "use" of it.

UDRP panels do not apply the laws of the United States. Instead, they generally apply and enforce the terms of the UDRP to which a person or company must agree in order to become a domain name registrar. Most countries follow the ICANN's UDRP standards, but some have adopted their own. The United Kingdom has established its own dispute resolution policy for .uk domain names. Australia and Ireland extend UDRP procedures to disputes over registrations of personal names. China shields owners of .cn domain names who have registered for at least two years with an accredited dispute resolution service provider. For the most part, though, the rules that are applied in most UDRP cases, including the factors that are considered to make a determination regarding bad faith, are very similar to those that the ACPA establishes for the protection of trademark owners against cybersquatters.

The only remedy available in a UDRP proceeding is an order to cancel or transfer the domain name registration. No damages or other relief may be awarded. The only remedy available for reverse domain name hijacking (filing a groundless UDRP claim) is declaratory relief, i.e., a declaration about whether the claim is groundless or not.

In the United States, the losing party in a UDRP may challenge the decision by filing suit in federal district court pursuant to the ACPA. This is an original action, not an appeal.

Notes

1. Pub L. 101–336, 104 Stat 327 (codified as amended at 42 U.S.C. §§ 12101–12203)
2. 15 U.S.C. §§ 77b(1) and 78c(a)(10) (2017).
3. SEC v. W.J. Howey Co., 328 U.S. 293 (1946).
4. 17 CFR §§ 230.251–230.346 (2017)
5. An *accredited investor* is one who (a) earned more than $200,000 (or $300,000 together with a spouse) in each of the prior two years, and reasonably expects the same for the current year or (b) has a net worth over $1,000,000, either alone or together with a spouse (excluding the value of the person's primary residence and any loans secured by the residence (up to the value of the residence)).
6. 17 CFR §§ 230.500–230.508 (2017)
7. 17 C.F.R. § 230.144A (2017)
8. 17 CFR. § 230.504 (2017)
9. 17 CFR. § 230.506 (2017)
10. Pub. L. 107–204 (codified as amended in scattered sections of 15 U.S.C., 18 U.S.C., 28 U.S.C. and 29 U.S.C.)
11. Pub. L. 104–67, 109 Stat. 737 (codified as amended in scattered sections of 15 U.S.C.)
12. Pub. L. 105–353, 112 Stat. 3227 (codified as amended in scattered sections of 15 U.S.C.)
13. Note, *Security for Expenses Litigation*, 52 COLUM. L. REV. 267 (1952).
14. Pub. L. 91–596, 84 Stat. 1590 (codified as amended at 29 U.S.C. §§ 651–678)
15. Pub. L. 93–406, 88 Stat. 829 (codified as amended at 29 U.S.C. §§ 1001–1461)
16. Pub. L. 105–19 (codified at 42 U.S.C. §§ 14501–14505)
17. Pub. L. 75–718, 52 Stat. 1060 (codified at 29 U.S.C. §§ 201–219)
18. Pub. L. 110-233, 122 Stat. 881 (codified as amended in scattered sections of 29 U.S.C. and 42 U.S.C.)
19. Pub. L. 91–508, 84 Stat. 1114, Pub. L. 90-321, tit. VI (codified at 15 U.S.C. §§ 1681–1681x)
20. Pub. L. 88–352, 78 Stat. 241 (codified as amended in scattered sections of 5, 28, and 42 U.S.C.)
21. Pub. L. 103–353, 108 Stat. 3149 (codified at 38 U.S.C. §§ 4301–4335)
22. Pub. L. 90-202, 81 Stat 602 (codified as amended at 29 U.S.C. §§ 621–634)
23. Pub. L. 95 555, 92 Stat. 2076 (codified at 42 U.S.C. § 2000e(k))
24. MINN. STAT. § 363A.08 (2017).
25. Pub. L. 88–38, 77 Stat. 56 (codified at 29 U.S.C. § 206)
26. Pub. L. 93–112, 87–355 (codified at 29 U.S.C. §§ 701–796l)
27. Pub. L. 82–540, 86 Stat. 1074 (codified as amended at 38 U.S.C. § 4212)
28. U.S. Equal Employment Opportunity Comm'n, *Enforcement Guidance* 915.002 (2012)
29. No. 2:14–cv-162 (D. Vt. Mar. 19, 2015).
30. 227 F. Supp. 1312 (S.D. Fla. 2002).
31. Pub. L. 100-347, 102 Stat. 646 (codified at 29 U.S.C. §§ 2001–2009)
32. *See, e.g.*, PepsiCo, Inc. v. Redmond, 54 F.3d 1262 (7th Cir. 1995).
33. 61 Cal. App. 4th 881, 72 Cal. Rptr. 2d 73 (1998).
34. *See* Buchanan Capital Markets, LLC v. DeLucca, 41 N.Y.S.3d 229 (1st Dep't 2016).
35. *See, e.g.*, Mattel, Inc. v. MGA Entm't, Inc., 616 F.3d 904 (9th Cir. 2010).
36. Pub. L. 71–798, 46 Stat 1494 (codified as amended at 40 U.S.C. §§ 3141–3148)

37. Pub. L. 89–286, 79 Stat 1084 (codified at 41 U.S.C. §§ 6701–6707)
38. Pub. L. 74–198, 49 Stat. 449 (codified at 29 U.S.C. §§ 151–169)
39. Pub. L. 99–272, 100 Stat. 82 (codified as amended in scattered sections of 26 U.S.C., 29 U.S.C., 42 U.S.C.)
40. Pub. L. 104–191, 110 Stat. 1936 (codified in scattered sections of 29 U.S.C. and 42 U.S.C.)
41. Pub. L. 103–3, 107 Stat. 6 (codified at 29 U.S.C. 2601–2654)
42. The Act also protects public employees.
43. The months worked do not need to be consecutive.
44. Pub. L. 95–572 (codified at 28 U.S.C. § 1875)
45. Migrant and Seasonal Agricultural Worker Protection Act of 1983, Pub. L. 97–470, 96 Stat. 2583 (codified at 29 U.S.C. §§ 1801–1872)
46. Pub. L. 99–603, 100 Stat. 3445 (codified as amended in scattered sections of 8 U.S.C., 20 U.S.C., 31 U.S.C., and 42 U.S.C.)
47. Pub L. 100-379, 102 Stat. 890, (codified at 29 U.S.C. §§ 2101–2109) ("WARN Act")
48. 31 U.S.C. §§ 3729–3733
49. A number of federal and state laws provide whistleblower protections to public employees. These laws are beyond the scope of this book.
50. Stengart v. Loving Care Agency, 990 A.2d 650 (N.J. 2010).
51. Pub. L. 99–508, 100 Stat. 1848 (codified at 18 U.S.C. §§ 2510–2522)
52. Konop v. Hawaiian Airlines, Inc., 236 F.3d 1035 (9th Cir. 2001).
53. *See, e.g.*, Bohach v. City of Reno, 932 F. Supp. 1232, 1237 (D. Nev. 1996).
54. 990 A.2d 650 (N.J. 2010).
55. *Id.*
56. White Cap Industries, Inc. v. Ruppert, 67 P.3d 318 (Nev. 2003).
57. Vizcaino v. Microsoft, 290 F.3d 1043 (9th Cir. 2002).
58. 16 CFR §§ 436.1–436.11 (2018)
59. 16 CFR §§ 437.1–437.10 (2018)
60. 756 F. Supp. 543 (S.D. Fla. 1991).
61. 667 F.2d 670 (8th Cir. 1981).
62. 573 F.3d 947 (10th Cir. 2009).
63. *In re* Doctors Hosp. of Hyde Park, Inc., 373 B.R. 53, 63 (Bankr. N.D. Ill. 2007) (applying New York law).
64. 6 F. Supp. 2d 94, 98 (D. Mass. 1998).
65. 38 Stat. 717 (codified at 15 U.S.C. §§ 41–58)
66. *In re* Koscot Interplanetary, Inc., 86 F.T.C. 1106, 1181 (1975).
67. Pub. L. 73–291, 48 Stat. 881 (codified as amended at 15 U.S.C. §§ 78a–78qq)
68. 15 U.S.C. § 78j(b).
69. 17 C.F.R. § 240.10b-5
70. 17 C.F.R. § 240.10b-5–1
71. 445 U.S. 222 (1980).
72. 521 U.S. 642 (1997).
73. 17 C.F.R. § 240.10b-5–2
74. 574 F.3d 42 (2d Cir. 2009).
75. Pub. L. 104–290, 110 Stat. 3416 (codified as amended in scattered sections of 15 U.S.C.)
76. Sherman Antitrust Act of 1890, 26 Stat. 209 (codified at 15 U.S.C. §§ 1–7)
77. Clayton Antitrust Act of 1914, Pub. L. 63–212, 38 Stat. 730 (codified at 5 U.S.C. §§ 12–29 and 29 U.S.C. §§ 52–53)
78. Trademark Act of 1946, Pub. L. 79–489, 60 Stat 427 (codified at 15 U.S.C. §§ 1051–1141n)
79. 15 U.S.C. § 45. (2018).
80. SEN. REP. NO. 597, 63d Cong., 2d Sess. 13 (1914).

81. Ticketmaster Corp. v. Tickets.com, 54 U.S.P.Q. 2d 1344 (C.D. Cal. 2000).
82. 15 U.S.C. §§ 1 and 2 (2017).
83. United States v. Grinnell, 384 U.S. 563 (1966).
84. 87 F. Supp. 2d 30 (D.C. Cir. 2000).
85. United States v. Colgate, 250 U.S. 300 (1919).
86. Continental TV, Inc. v. GTE Sylvania, Inc., 433 U.S. 36 (1977).
87. U.S. Steel Corp. v. Fortner Enterprises, 429 U.S. 610 (1977).
88. Pub. L 74–692, 49 Stat. 1526 (codified at 15 U.S.C. § 13)
89. 15 U.S.C. § 19 (2017).
90. Reading International Inc. v. Oaktreee Capital Management, 317 F. Supp. 2d 301 (S.D.N.Y. 2003).
91. Pub. L. 94–435, 90 Stat. 1383 (codified at 15 U.S.C. § 18a)
92. Pub. L. 73–66, 48 Stat. 162 (codified as amended in scattered sections of 12 U.S.C.)
93. 70 Stat. 133 (codified as amended at 12 U.S.C. §§ 1841–1848)
94. Financial Services Modernization Act, Pub. L. 106–102, 113 Stat. 1338 (codified as amended in scattered sections of 12 U.S.C. and 15 U.S.C.)
95. Pub. L. 95–128, 91 Stat. 1147 (codified at 12 U.S.C § 2901)
96. Pub. L. 95–213, 91 Stat. 1494 (codified as amended at 15 U.S.C. §§ 78a, 78dd-1 to -3, 78ff, 78m, 78o)
97. Don Silver, *Why Are So Many Internet Start-Ups Failing Today?* Christ Ducker blog, http://www.chrisducker.com/internet-business-failures/ (last visited March 2, 2018).
98. 11 U.S.C. §§ 101–1532 (2017)
99. *Consumer* is a term that appears in many different statutes. While there are some individual differences in how the term is defined, in most cases a consumer is simply a person who purchases something for personal, family or household use, as distinguished from a business purpose.
100. Pub. L. 106–229, 114 Stat. 464 (codified at 15 U.S.C. §§ 7001–7031)
101. Directive on Electronic Commerce: Electronic Commerce Directive 2000/31/EC (EU)
102. *See* Step-Saver Data Sys. v. Wyse Technology, 939 F.2d 91 (3d Cir. 1991).
103. 86 F.3d 1447 (7th Cir. 1996).
104. Feeney v. Dell, Inc., 908 N.E.2d 753 (Mass. 2009).
105. Pub. L. 105–304, 112 Stat. 2860 (codified as amended in scattered sections of 5 U.S.C., 17 U.S.C., 28 U.S.C., 35 U.S.C.)
106. Pub. L. 93–637, 88 Stat. 2183 (codified at 15 U.S.C. §§ 2301–2312)
107 16 CFR §§ 701.1–701.4
108. 16 C.F.R. §§ 702.1–702.3
109. 16 CFR §§ 703.1–703.8
110. Pub. L. 93–495, 88 Stat. 1521 (codified at 15 U.S.C. §§ 1691–1691f)
111. 16 C.F.R. §§ 640.1.–640.6
112. 16 C.F.R. §§ 444.1–444.5
113. Pub. L. 94–240, 90 Stat. 257 (codified at 15 U.S.C. §§ 1667–1667f)
114. 12 CFR § 213
115. Pub. L. 111 345, 124 Stat. 3618 (codified at 15 U.S.C. §§ 8401 8405)
116 Pub. L. 90-321, tit. I, 82 Stat. 146, 146–59 (codified at 15 U.S.C. §§ 1601–1667f)
117. 12 C.F.R. §§ 226.1–226.59
118. Pub. L. 111–24, 123 Stat. 1734 (codified in various sections of Title 16 U.S.C.)
119. 15 U.S.C. § 1643 (2018).
120. Pub. L. 111–203, 124 Stat. 1376 (codified in scattered sections of the U.S. Code)
121. MINN. STAT. § 325G.051, subd. 1(a) (2017). The statute, which was enacted in 1987, requires a merchant who imposes such a surcharge to post a sign and tell purchasers about it orally.
122. Expressions Hair Design v. Schneiderman, 581 U.S. ___, 137 S.Ct. 1144 (2017).

123. Pub L. 93–495 (codified at 15 U.S.C. § 1666–1666j)
124. References in text to *card* include these other mechanisms that serve the same function as a card.
125. Pub. L. 95–630, 92 Stat. 3641 (codified in scattered sections of 12 U.S.C. and 15 U.S.C.)
126. 12 C.F.R. §§ 1005.1–1005
127. Pub. L. 102–242, tit. II, subtit. F, 105 Stat. 2236, 2334–43 (codified at 12 U.S.C. §§ 4301–4313)
128. Uniting and Strengthening America by Providing Appropriate Tools Required to Intercept and Obstruct Terrorism Act of 2001, Pub. L. 107–56, 115 Stat. 272 (codified as amended in scattered sections of 8 U.S.C., 12 U.S.C., 15 U.S.C., 18 U.S.C., 20 U.S.C., 31 U.S.C., 42 U.S.C., 47 U.S.C., 49 U.S.C. and 50 U.S.C.)
129. 209 F.Supp.3d 698 (S.D.N.Y. 2016).
130. Pub. L. 91–508, 84 Stat. 1114 (codified as amended at 12 U.S.C. §§ 1951–1959 and 31 U.S.C. §§ 5311–5332 (2017)
131. Pub. L. 89–487, 80 Stat. 250 (codified as amended at 5 U.S.C. § 552)
132. U.S. Treas. Dep't, Financial Crimes Enforcement Network, FIN-2013–G001, *Application of FinCEN's Regulations to Persons Administering, Exchanging, or Using Virtual Currencies* (2013), retrieved from https://www.fincen.gov/sites/-default/files/shared/FIN-2013–G001.pdf on February 27, 2018.
133. 15 U.S.C. § 1693a (2017).
134. SEC Release No. 81207 (July 25, 2017).
135. 16 C.F.R. §§ 435.1–435.3
136. 16 C.F.R. § 425.1 ("Negative Option Rule")
137. Pub. L. 95–109, 91 Stat 874 (codified as amended at 15 U.S.C. §§ 1692–1692p)
138. 16 C.F.R. §§ 314.1–314.5
139. 45 C.F.R. §§160.101–160.552, 164.102–164.106, 164.500–534
140. Mass. Regs. Code, tit. 201 §§ 17.01–17.05 (2017).
141. *Id.*
142. *Id.*
143. Nev. Rev. Stat. § 603A.215 (2017).
144. Pub. L. 105–277, tit. XIII, 112 Stat. 2681–2728 (codified as amended at 15 U.S.C. §§ 6501–6505)
145. 17 C.F.R. § 210.2–06
146. 16 CFR §§ 682.1–682.5
147. Pub. L. 108–159, 117 Stat. 1952 (codified at 15 U.S.C. § 1681)
148. 16 C.F.R. § 681.1
149. Pub. L. 111–5, tit. XIII, 123 Stat. 115 (codified at 42 U.S.C. §§ 300jj-11 to 300jj-300; 17921–17953)
150. 45 C.F.R. §§ 164.400–414
151. Pub. L. 111–5, 123 Stat. 115 (codified as amended in scattered sections of 16 U.S.C. and 42 U.S.C.)
152. 16 CFR §§ 318.1–318.9
153. Pub. L. 114–113, Division N, tit. I, 129 Stat. 2936 (codified at 6 U.S.C. §§ 1501–1510)
154. Nev. Rev. Stat. § 603A.215 (2017).
155. Other important security standards include the PCI PTS (PIN Transaction Security) and the Payment Application Data Security Standard (PA-DSS). The PTS standards include PIN security requirements, point of interaction modular security requirements, and hardware security module security requirements. Device requirements are for manufacturers to follow in the design, manufacture and transport of a device to the entity that implements it. Merchants and service providers should only use devices or components that are tested and approved by the PCI SSC, which are listed at the www.pcisecuritystandards.org website. The PA-DSS is for software vendors and others who develop payment applications that store, process or transmit cardholder data and/or sensitive authentication data as part of authorization or settlement, when these applications are sold, distributed or licensed to third parties. Most card brands encourage merchants to use payment applications that are tested and approved by the PCI SSC. Validated applications are also listed at www.pcisecuritystandards.org.

156. Directive 95/46/EC (EU)
157. Directive 2002/58/EC (EU)
158. Complete Auto Transit, Inc. v. Brady, 430 U.S. 274 (1977).
159. Pub. L. 105–277, tit. XI, 112 Stat. 2681 (codified at 47 U.S.C. § 151 note)
160. Pub. L. 114–125, 130 Stat. 122
161. National Bellas Hess, Inc. v. Illinois Dep't of Revenue, 386 U.S. 753 (1967). The Commerce Clause "nexus" requirement is different from the Due Process "nexus" requirement. Quill Corp. v. North Dakota, 504 U.S. 298 (1992). For example, advertising in a state may be a sufficient nexus to subject a business to a state's regulatory jurisdiction, as far the Due Process is concerned, but it might not be a sufficient nexus for Commerce Clause purposes.
162. National Bellas Hess, *supra* note 161.
163. Quill, *supra* note 161.
164. Tyler Pipe Industries, Inc. v. Washington State Department of Revenue, 483 U.S. 232 (1987).
165. *See, e.g.*, Ruling of Commissioner, Virginia Dep't of Taxation, No. 00-53 (April 14, 2000); SEAN P. MELVIN, CYBERLAW AND E-COMMERCE REGULATION: AN ENTREPRENEURIAL APPROACH 56–57 (2005).
166. Overstock.com, Inc. and Amazon.com, LLC v. New York State Dep't of Taxation & Fin., 20 N.Y.3d 586, 987 N.E.2d 621 (2013) *cert denied*, 134 S. Ct. 682 (2013).
167. 386 U.S. 753 (1967)
168. 504 U.S. 298 (1992)
169. 151 Ohio St. 3d 278 (2016).
170. 138 S. Ct. 2080 (2018).
171. 129 Cal. App. 4th 1179, 29 Cal. Rptr. 3d 176 (2005).
172. 63 Stat. 884 (codified at 15 U.S.C. §§ 375–378)
173. 15 U.S.C. § 1125 (2018).
174. *Id.*
175. Pub. L. 99–474, 100 Stat. 1213 (codified as 18 U.S.C §1030)
176. 430 U.S. 705, 714 (1977).
177. 471 U.S. 626 (1985).
178. *Id.* at 651.
179. R.J. Reynolds Tobacco Co. v. FDA, 696 F.3d 1205 (D.C. Cir. 2012), *overruled in part by* Am. Meat Inst. v. USDA, 760 F.3d 18 (D.C. Cir. 2014).
180. 81 F.T.C. 23 (1972); *see also* Advertising Substantiation Policy Statement, appended to Thompson Medical Co., 104 F.T.C. 648, 839 (1984), *aff'd*, 791 F.2d 189 (D.C. Cir. 1986), *cert. denied*, 479 U.S. 1086 (1987).
181. Pub. L. 114–258, 130 Stat. 1355 (codified at 15 U.S.C. § 45b)
182. 102 Pub. L. 102–556, 106 Stat. 4181 (codified at 15 U.S.C. §§ 5701–5724)
183 16 CFR §§ 308.1–308.9
184. Pub. L. 101–535, 104 Stat. 2353 (codified as amended at 21 U.S.C. § 343–1)
185. Pub. L. 103–417, 108 Stat. 4325 (codified in scattered sections of 21 U.S.C. and 42 U.S.C.)
186. Pub. L. 105–115, 111 Stat. 2296 (codified in scattered sections of U.S.C.)
187. Pub. L. 90 321, 110 Stat. 3009 (codified as amended at 15 U.S.C. §§ 1679–1679j)
188. 16 CFR §§ 453.1–453.9
189. Pub. L. 108–187, 117 Stat. 2699 (codified at 15 U.S.C. §§ 7701–7713)
190. 420 F.3d 366, 374–78 (5th Cir. 2005).
191. Pub. L. 103–297, 108 Stat. 1545 (codified at 15 U.S.C. §§ 6101–6108)
192. 16 C.F.R. §§ 310.1–310.9
193. Pub. L. 102–243, 105 Stat. 2394 (codified at 47 U.S.C. § 227)
194. Pub. L. 91–222, 84 Stat. 87 (codified as amended at 15 U.S.C. §§ 1331–1339)
195. Pub. L. 109–455, 120 Stat. 3372 (codified at 12 U.S.C. § 3412(e) and in scattered sections of 15 U.S.C.)

196. Beauharnais v. Illinois, 343 U.S. 250 (1952).
197. Commonwealth of Nations (formerly known as the British Commonwealth).
198. 562 U.S. 443, 453 (2011).
199. *See, e.g.*, Clay Calvert, *Defining "Public Concern" after* Snyder v. Phelps: *A Pliable Standard Mingles with News Media Complicity*, 19 VILLANOVA SPORTS & ENT. L. J. 39 (2012); Leslie C. Griffin, Snyder v. Phelps: *Searching for a Legal Standard*, CARDOZO L. REV. DE NOVO 353 (2010), available at https://ssrn.com/abstract=1726607.
200. Pub. L. 104–104, 110 Stat. 137 (codified as amended at 47 U.S.C. § 230)
201. Virginia Pharmacy Bd. v. Virginia Consumer Council, 425 U.S. 748, 762 (1976).
202. Samuel D. Warren & Louis Brandeis, *The Right to Privacy*, 4 HARV. L. REV. 193, 195–196 (1890) (citations omitted).
203. A person may "be forced to surrender a key to a strongbox containing incriminating documents, but not to reveal the combination to his wall safe…." Doe v. United States, 487 U.S. 201, 219 (1988) (Stevens, J., dissenting).
204. Richard Bronner, *Constitutional Law—Right of Privacy—Access to Contraceptive Information*, 17 CASE W. RES. L. REV. 601, 602 (1965) (*quoting* Griswold v. Connecticut, 381 U.S. 479, 483 (1965)).
205. 381 U.S. 479 (1965).
206. *Id.* at 493 (Goldberg, J., concurring).
207. No. 10-CV-00665–JD (E.D. Pa. Feb. 16, 2010)
208. Pub. L. 96–440, 94 Stat 1879 (codified at 42 U.S.C. §§ 2000aa, 2000aa-5 to 2000aa-7)
209. United States v. Perrine, 518 F.3d 1196, 1204 (10th Cir 2008).
210. Campbell v. Seabury Press, 614 F.2d 395, 397 (5th Cir. 1980).
211. Virgil v. Time, Inc., 527 F.2d 1122, 1129 (9th Cir. 1975).
212. 159 S.W.2d 291 (Mo. 1942).
213. Rosen, Jeffrey, *The Web Means the End of Forgetting*, N.Y. TIMES, July 25, 2010, at MM30.
214. Boring v. Google, Inc., 598 F. Supp. 2d 695 (W.D. Pa. 2009).
215. CAL. BUS. & PROF. CODE §§ 22575–22579 (2017)
216. CAL. CIV. CODE § 1798.83 (2018).
217. Pub. L. 103–322, 108 Stat. 1796 (codified at 18 U.S.C. §§ 2721–2725)
218. Pub. L. 85–506, 72 Stat. 326 (codified as amended at 15 U.S.C. 1231–1233)
219. Pub. L. 102–519, 106 Stat. 3384 (codified as amended in scattered sections of 15 U.S.C., 18 U.S.C., 19 U.S.C., and 42 U.S.C.)
220. Pub. L. 88–206, 77 Stat. 392 (codified at 42 U.S.C. §§ 7401–7671q)
221. Pub. L. 100-618, 102 Stat. 3195 (codified at 18 U.S.C. § 2710)
222. Pub. L. 98–549, 98 Stat. 2779 (codified as amended at 47 U.S.C. §§ 551– 573)
223. 16 C.F.R. §§ 313.1–313.18
224. Child Online Privacy Protection Act Rule, 16 CFR §§ 312.1–312.13
225. Pub. L. 114–126, 130 Stat. 282 (codified at 5 U.S.C. § 552a)
226. S.C. 2000, c. 5 (Canada)
227. Habush v. Cannon, 828 N.W.2d 876 (Wis. Ct. App. 2013).
228. 505 F.3d 818 (8th Cir. 2007).
229. OHIO ADMIN. CODE § 4301:1–1–44 (2017).
230. Privacy Rights for California Minors in the Digital World Act of 2015, CAL. BUS. & PROF. CODE §§ 22580–22582 (2018)
231. CAL. BUS & PROF. CODE §§ 22584–22585 (2018)
232. Pub. L. No. 93–380 (codified at 20 U.S.C. § 1232g)
233. As used here, *parental consent* means the consent of a parent or a guardian.
234. Roth v. United States, 354 U.S. 476 (1957).

235. 413 U.S. 15, 24 (1973).
236. 413 U.S. 123, 130 n.7 (1973).
237. United States v. Kilbride, 584 F.3d 1240 (9th Cir. 2009).
238. United States v. Little, 365 Fed. Appx. 159, 2010 WL 357933 (11th Cir. Feb. 8, 2010) (unpublished).
239. United States v. Thomas, 74 F.3d 701 (6th Cir. 1996).
240. Pub. L. 108–21, 117 Stat. 650 (codified at 18 U.S.C. §§1466A, 2251, 2252A and 2423)
241. 550 F.3d 326 (4th Cir. 2008).
242. Child Protection and Obscenity Enforcement Act, Pub. L. 100-690, tit. VII, subtitle N, 102 Stat. 4181 (codified as amended at 18 U.S.C. §§ 2257, 2257A)
243. Sundance Association Inc. v. Reno, 139 F.3d 804 (10th Cir. 1998).
244. Children's Internet Protection Act of 2000, Pub. L. 106–554 (codified as amended at 47 U.S.C. § 254)
245. Child Online Protection Act of 1998, Pub. L. 105–277) (codified as amended at 47 U.S.C. § 231)
246. 521 U.S. 844 (1997).
247. 535 U.S. 564 (2002).
248. 534 F.3d 181 (3d Cir. 2008), *cert. denied*, 555 U.S. 1137 (2009).
249. American Libraries Association v. Pataki, 969 F. Supp. 160, 173 (S.D.N.Y. 1997).
250. 440 F. 3d 418, 420-21 (7th 2006).
251. 581 F.3d 1127, 1135 (9th Cir. 2009).
252. *See, e.g.*, 18 U.S.C. §§ 1361–1362
253. A *virus* is a program that corrupts or deletes data on a computer and is designed to copy itself and spread to other computers. It usually works by attaching itself to an executable file on the targeted computer.
254. A *worm* is a program that installs a back door to a computer allowing the worm owner to control the computer. Like a virus, it is self-replicating. In some cases, worms are programmed to copy themselves in an infinite loop, with the purpose of slowing or shutting down a server or computer.
255. A *Trojan horse* is a program with a false label that appears to be harmless but conceals a malicious function. It is typically used to get information that is stored on a computer (passwords, credit card information, etc.) It is sometimes used to launch a denial of service attack.
256. A *logic/time bomb* is a program that remains dormant until a specified time or until a specified event occurs. When the time comes or the event occurs, it runs in a way that damages the computer, such as by deleting files.
257. *Mousetrapping* software is malware that prevents visitors to a website from leaving it, such as by launching an endless series of pop-up ads or by relaunching the website when the visitor closes it. The FTC regards mousetrapping as an unfair and deceptive trade practice.
258. EF Cultural Travel BV v. Explorica, Inc. 274 F.3d 577 (1st Cir. 2001).
259. America Online, Inc. v. LCGM, Inc., 46 F. Supp. 2d 444 (E.D. Va. 1998).
260. eBay, Inc. v. Digital Point Solutions, Inc., 608 F. Supp. 2d 1156 (N.D. Cal. 2009).
261. 776 F. Supp. 135 (S.D.N.Y. 1991).
262. No. 31063/94, 1995 WL 323710, 23 Media L. Rep. 1794 (N.Y. Sup. Ct. May 24, 1995).
263. 47 U.S.C. § 230 (2017).
264. Barrett v. Rosenthal, 40 Cal. 4th 33, 51 Cal.Rptr.3d 55 (Cal. 2006).
265. Zeran v. America Online, 129 F.3d 327 (4th Cir. 1997).
266. 824 F.3d 846 (9th Cir. 2016).
267. Securing the Protection of Our Enduring and Established Constitutional Heritage Act of 2010, Pub. L. 111–223, 124 Stat. 2480 (codified at 28 U.S.C. § 4101–4105) ("SPEECH Act")
268. Unlawful Internet Gambling Enforcement Act of 2006, Pub. L. 109–347, 120 Stat. 1884 (codified at 31 U.S.C. §§ 5361–5367)
269. Racketeer Influenced and Corrupt Organizations Act of 1970, Pub. L. 91–452, 84 Stat. 922 (codified at 18 U.S.C. §§ 1961–1968)

270. Gregg Lukianoff, Unlearning Liberty: Campus Censorship and the End of American Debate (2012).
271. United States v. Eichman, 496 U.S. 310 (1990).
272. Trerice v. Blue Cross of California, 209 Cal. App. 3d 878, 883, 257 Cal. Rptr. 338 (1989).
273. National Association of the Deaf v. Netflix, Inc., 869 F. Supp. 2d 196 (D. Mass. 2012).
274. Uniting and Strengthening America by Fulfilling Rights and Ensuring Effective Discipline Over Monitoring Act of 2015, Pub. L. 114–23, 129 Stat. 268 (codified in scattered sections of 12 U.S.C., 15 U.S.C., 18 U.S.C. and 50 U.S.C.)
275. 90 F.3d 1058 (9th Cir. 2002).
276. Remsburg v. Docusearch, Inc., 816 A.2d 1001 (N.H. 2003).
277. Doe v. MySpace, Inc., 528 F.3d 413 (5th Cir. 2008).
278. Hunter v. Virginia State Bar, 744 S.E.2d 611 (Va. 2013).
279. 300 F.3d 683, 688 (6th Cir. 2002).
280. United States *ex rel.* Newsham v. Lockheed Missiles & Space Co., 190 F.3d 963, 970–71 (9th Cir. 1999) (*citing* Wilcox v. Superior Court, 33 Cal. Rptr. 2d 446, 449–50 (Cal. Ct. App.1994)).
281. Copyright Act of 1976, Pub. L. 94–553, 90 Stat. 2541 (codified as amended at 17 U.S.C.)
282. 17 U.S.C. § 101 (2017).
283. 18 U.S.C. §§ 701–716 (2017).
284. The Federal Acquisition Regulations and applicable agency regulations, if any, govern contracts entered into by civilian agencies and NASA. The Defense Federal Acquisition Regulation Supplement governs copyright provisions in military contracts.
285. Anti-Bootlegging Act: Uruguay Round Agreements Act, Pub. L. 103–465, tit. V, §§ 512, 513, 108 Stat. 4809 (codified as amended at 17 U.S.C. § 1101 and 18 U.S.C. § 2319A (2006))
286. Atlantic Recording Corp. v. Howell, 554 F. Supp. 2d 976 (D. Ariz. 2008).
287. 239 F.3d 1004 (9th Cir. 2001).
288. 464 U.S. 417 (1984).
289. 545 U.S. 913 (2005).
290. California Resale Royalty Act of 1976, (Cal. Civ. Code §986)
291. Close v. Sothebys, Inc. __F.3d___ (9th Cir. 2018) (slip op.) (*aff'g in part, rev'g in part and remanding,* Estate of Graham v. Sotheby's, Inc., 178 F. Supp. 3d 974 (C.D. Cal. 2016).
292. A court may reduce statutory damages to $0 if the infringer reasonably believed the infringement was fair use, and is either: (a) a nonprofit educational institution, library, or archives, or an employee or agent thereof who was acting within the scope of the employment at the time, and the infringement involved making copies or phonorecords of the work; or (b) a public broadcasting entity which, as a regular part of its nonprofit activities, infringed by performing a published nondramatic literary work or by reproducing a transmission program embodying a performance of such a work.
293 No Electronic Theft Act of 1997, Pub. L. 105–147, 111 Stat. 2678 (codified in scattered sections of 17 U.S.C., 18 U.S.C. and 28 U.S.C.) ("NET Act")
294. Visual Artists Rights Act of 1990, Pub. L. 101–650, tit. VI, 104 Stat. 5128 (codified at 17 U.S.C. § 106A)
295. Pub. L. 115–264 (codified at 17 U.S.C. §§ 301(c) and 1401).
296. Sonny Bono Copyright Term Extension Act of 1998, Pub. L. 105–298, 112 Stat. 2827 (codified as amended in scattered sections of 17 U.S.C.)
297. The U.S. Supreme Court has upheld the constitutionality of congressional extensions of the terms of existing copyrights. Eldred v. Ashcroft, 537 U.S. 186 (2003).
298. Berne Convention Implementation Act of 1988, Pub. L. 100-658, 102 Stat. 2853 (codified as amended at 17 U.S.C. § 116)
299. Uruguay Round Agreements Act of 1994, Pub. L. 103–464, 108 Stat. 4809 (codified as amended in 19 U.S.C. §§ 3501–3556)

300. Unpublished works may still be copyrighted after 120 years, but certification from the Copyright Office that it has no record to indicate whether the person is living or died less than seventy years before is a complete defense to an action for infringement. *See* 17 U.S.C. § 302(e) (2017).
301. Twin Books Corp. v. Walt Disney Co., 83 F.3d 1162 (9th Cir. 1996).
302. U.S. CONST. art. 1, § 8.
303. *See, e.g.*, H.R. No. 2222, 60th Cong., 2nd Sess. (1909).
304. Fox Film Corp. v. Doyal, 286 U.S. 123, 127 (1932).
305. Dellar v. Samuel Goldwyn, 104 F.2d 661, 662 (2nd Cir. 1939).
306. Dr. Seuss Enterprises, L.P. v. Penguin Books USA, Inc., 109 F.3d 1394 (9th Cir. 1997).
307. 510 U.S. 569 (1994).
308. 17 U.S.C. § 101 (2017) (emphasis added).
309. 575 F. Supp. 2d 513 (S.D.N.Y. 2008).
310. 714 F.3d 694 (2d Cir. 2013).
311. The original photograph was taken by Patrick Cariou. A Rastafarian was the subject of the image. Celebrated "appropriation" artist Richard Prince blurred the image a bit and crudely superimposed an electric guitar and violet ovals over the eyes and mouth of the Rastafarian in the photograph.
312. Pierre N. Leval, *Toward a Fair Use Standard*, 103 HARV. L. REV. 1105, 1107 (1990)
313. 416 F. Supp. 2d 828 (C.D. Cal. 2006), *aff'd in part and rev'd in part*, 508 F.3d 1146 (9th Cir. 2007); *see also* Kelly v. Arriba Soft, 280 F.3d 934 (9th Cir. 2002).
314. Perfect 10, Inc. v. Amazon.com, Inc., 508 F.3d 1146 (9th Cir. 2007).
315. 487 F.3d 701, 719 (9th Cir. 2007).
316. Futuredontics Inc. v. Applied Anagramic Inc., 1997 46 USPQ 2d 2005 (C.D. Cal. 1997).
317. 17 U.S.C. § 1201(a) (2017).
318. *See* Sony Corp. v. Universal City Studios, 104 U.S. 774 (1984).
319. 17 U.S.C. § 512(k) (2017).
320. *In re* Aimster, 252 F. Supp. 2d 634, 658 (N.D. Ill. 2002), *aff'd*, 334 F.3d 643 (7th Cir. 2003).
321. 17 U.S.C. § 512 (2017).
322. Ellison v. Robertson, 357 F.3d 1072 (9th Cir. 2004).
323. 17 U.S.C. § 101 (2017).
324. *Id.*
325. 717 F. Supp. 1449, 1451 (D. Colo. 1988).
326. H.R. REP. NO. 94–1476, at 138 (1976), *reprinted in* 1976 U.S.C.C.A.N. at 5754.
327. 188 F. Supp. 2d 398 (S.D.N.Y. 2002).
328. *See, e.g.*, Erickson v. Blake, 839 F. Supp. 2d 1132, 1134 (D. Or. 2012) (describing the posting of a video to YouTube as "publishing" it).
329. McLaren v. Chico's FAS, Inc., No. 10 Civ. 2481 (JSR), 2010 WL 4615772 (S.D.N.Y. Nov. 9, 2010) (unpublished).
330. No. H-10-3741 (S.D. Tex., August 15, 2012) (memorandum opinion).
331. Metropolitan Regional Information Systems v. American Home Realty Network, Inc., 722 F.3d 591 (4th Cir. 2013).
332. 17 U.S.C. § 101 (2017).
333. A schedule-filing procedure, rather than the usual registration requirement, applies to pre-1972 sound recordings. To be eligible to recover statutory damages and/or attorney fees, 17 U.S.C. § 1401(e)(5) (2018) requires a rights owner in a pre-1972 sound recording to file schedules listing their pre-1972 sound recordings with the Copyright Office. Rights owners filing these schedules must include the rights owner's name, the sound recording title, featured artist, and, if known and practicable, the International Standard Recording Code ("ISRC"). Individuals may request timely notification of when rights owners file these schedules. If a digital transmission entity (e.g., website owner who transmits sound recordings digitally

to website users) has filed a valid and timely notice of contact information, a rights owner must send the entity a notice stating that it is not legally authorized to use the pre-1972 sound recording, and identifying the pre-1972 sound recording in a schedule, in order to be eligible for statutory damages and/or attorneys' fees. Statutory damages and attorney fees also are not available unless the use occurs more than ninety days after the information is indexed into the Copyright Office's public records.

334. Audio Home Recording Act of 1992, Pub. L. 102–563, 106 Stat. 4237 (codified as amended at 17 U.S.C. §§ 1001–1010)

335. Recording Industry Association of America v. Diamond Multimedia Systems, 180 F.3d 1072 (9th Cir. 1999).

336. 35 F.3d 1527, 1531 (Fed. Cir. 1994).

337. 537 F.2d 4 (2d Cir. 1976).

338. Stix Prods., Inc. v United Merchants & Manufacturers, Inc., 295 F. Supp. 479, 488 (S.D.N.Y. 1968).

339. 476 F.2d 1357 (C.C.P.A. 1973).

340. 599 F.2d 341, 348–349 (9th Cir. 1979).

341. 15 U.S.C. § 1114 (2017).

342. 15 U.S.C. § 1125(a) (2017).

343. *See* Rescuecom Corp. v. Google, Inc., 562 F.3d 123 (2nd Cir. 2009).

344. Tiffany, Inc. v. eBay, Inc., 574 F. Supp. 2d 4653 (S.D.N.Y. 2008), *aff'd* 600 F.3d 93 (2nd Cir. 2010), *cert denied*, 131 S. Ct. 647 (2010).

345. 15 U.S.C. § 1125(c) (2017).

346. 971 F.2d 302 (9th Cir. 1992).

347. 15 U.S.C. §1120 (2017).

348. Playboy Enterprises, Inc. v. Welles, 279 F.3d 796 (9th Cir. 2002).

349. A related program, Google AdSense, allows website owners to display Google-sponsored advertisements on their websites in return for a payment of a small amount of revenue each time a user clicks on the advertisement on the webpage.

350. 582 U.S. ____, 137 S. Ct. 1744 (2017).

351. 15 U.S.C. § 1052 (2017).

352. U.S. Patent and Trademark Office, *Trademark Manual of Examining Procedures* (TMEP) § 213.05 (2017).

353. Trademark Act of 1946, Pub. L. 79–489, 60 Stat 427 (codified at 15 U.S.C. §§ 1051–1141n) ("Lanham Act")

354. Interactive Products Corp. v. a2z Mobile Office Solution, Inc., 326 F.3d 687, 696 (6th Cir. 2003).

355. Anticybersquatting Consumer Protection Act of 1999, Pub. L. No. 106–113, 113 Stat. 1501A-545 (codified as amended at 15 U.S.C. § 1125(d))

356. 113 F. Supp. 2d 915 (E.D. Va. 2000).

357. Panavision v Toeppen, 945 F. Supp. 1296 (C.D. Cal. 1996).

358. 15 U.S.C. §8131 (2017).

359. 15 U.S.C. § 1127 (2017).

360. Truth in Domain Names Act of 2003, Pub. L. No. 108–21 § 521, 117 Stat. 686 (codified at 18 U.S.C. § 2252B

361. Three other, less common kinds of patents are: "reissue" (issued to correct a previously issued patent); "defensive publication" patents; and "statutory intervention registration" (SIR). Defensive publication patents offered only limited protection and are obsolete now, having been replaced by SIR in 1985–86. In 2011, the America Invents Act repealed statutory provisions relating to SIR. The USPTO no longer issues them.

362. 35 U.S.C. § 100 (2017).

363. 35 U.S.C. § 101 (2017).

364. Gottschalk v. Benson, 409 U.S. 63 (1972).

365. Diamond v. Diehr, 450 U.S. 175 (1981).
366. Dunlop Holdings, Ltd. v. Ram Golf Corp., 524 F.2d 33 (7th Cir. 1975).
367. 149 F.3d 1368 (Fed. Cir. 1998).
368. 561 U.S. 593 (2010).
369. State Street Bank & Trust, *supra* note 367.
370. 573 U.S. ___, 134 S. Ct. 2347 (2014).
371. Soverain Software LLC v. Newegg Inc. 705 F.3d 1333 (Fed. Cir. 2013).
372. 35 U.S.C. § 154 (2017).
373. American Inventors Protection Act of 1999, Pub. L. 106–113, § 4302, 113 Stat. 1501, 1501A–556 (codified as amended in scattered sections of 35 U.S.C.)
374. Process Patent Amendments Act of 1988, Pub. L. No. 100-418, §§ 9001–9007, 102 Stat. 1107, 1563–1567 (codified as amended at 35 U.S.C. §§ 154, 271 and 287)
375. 35 U.S.C. § 271(c) (2017).
376. First Inventor Defense Act of 1999, Pub. L. 106–113, 113 Stat. 1536 (codified at 35 U.S.C. § 273)
377. Madey v. Duke University, 307 F.3d 1351 (Fed. Cir. 2002).
378. Drug Price Competition and Patent Term Restoration Act of 1984, Pub. L. 98–417, 98 Stat. 1585 (codified at 21 U.S.C. §§ 301, 355 and 360cc) ("Hatch-Waxman Act")
379. Patent Act of 1790, as amended, 1 Stat. 109–112 (codified at 35 U.S.C. §§ 1–390)
380. Invention Secrecy Act of 1951, Pub. L. 82–256, 66 Stat. 3 (codified at 35 U.S.C. §§ 181–188)
381. 431 F.2d 1012 (5th Cir. 1970).
382. Economic Espionage Act of 1996, Pub. L. 104–294, 110 Stat. 3488 (codified at 18 U.S.C. § 1831)
383. 248 U.S. 215 (1918).
384. 650 F. 3d 876 (2nd Cir. 2011).
385. Thyroff v. National Mut. Ins. Co., 864 N.E.2d 1272 (N.Y. 2007).
386. *See* Learning Curve Toys, Inc. v. PlayWood Toys, Inc., 342 F.3d 714 (7th Cir. 2003).
387. *See, e.g.,* Stromback v. New Line Cinema, 384 F.3d 283 (6th Cir. 2004) (applying Michigan law).
388. Mainardi v. Prudential Ins. Co., Civ. No. 08–3605, 2009 WL 229757, at *9 (E.D. Pa. Jan. 30, 2009).
389. Daktronics, Inc. v. McAfee, 599 N.W.2d 358, 361 (S.D. 1999).
390. Restatement (3d) Unfair Competition 38, comment b (1995).
391. 17 U.S.C. § 101 (2017).
392. Minder Pictures, Inc. v. John Wiley & Sons, Inc., 795 F.3d 997 (9th Cir. 2015).
393. *See, e.g.,* Traicoff v. Digital Media, Inc., 439 F. Supp. 2d 872 (S.D. Ind. 2006).
394. *See, e.g.,* Cincom Sys. v. Novelis Corp., 581 F.3d 431 (6th Cir. 2009); Gardner v. Nike, Inc., 279 F.3d 774 (9th Cir. 2002).
395. *See, e.g.,* MELVILLE B. NIMMER & DAVID NIMMER, NIMMER ON COPYRIGHT 10.02[B][4][b] (2010); WILLIAM F. PATRY, PATRY ON COPYRIGHT § 5:103 (2013) (calling Gardner v. Nike, *supra* note 394, "one of the most baffling copyright opinions ever" and "decision making run amok"); Aaron Xavier Fellmeth, *Control Without Interest: State Law of Assignment, Federal Preemption, and the Intellectual Property License*, 6 VA. J.L. & TECH. 8, 20–27 (2001); Alice Haemmerli, *Why Doctrine Matters: Patent and Copyright Licensing and the Meaning of Ownership in Federal Context*, 30 COLUM. J.L. & ARTS 1, 14–19 (2006); Peter H. Kang & Jia Ann Yang, Case Note, *Doctrine of Indivisibility Revived?*, 18 SANTA CLARA COMPUTER & HIGH-TECH L.J. 365, 371–73 (2002); *see also* Christopher M. Newman, *An Exclusive License Is Not an Assignment: Disentangling Divisibility and Transferability of Ownership in Copyright*, 74 LA. L.R. 59 (2013).
396. 17 U.S.C. § 301 (2017).
397. *Id.*
398. 86 F.3d 1447 (7th Cir. 1996).
399. *See, e.g.,* State v. Kirby, 161 P.3d 883 (N.M. Ct. App. 2007) (upholding a fraud conviction in these circumstances).

400. 17 U.S.C. § 115 (2017).
401. A Chapter 8 proceeding is one that is heard and decided by the copyright board pursuant to its authority under 17 U.S.C. § 801 to set reasonable royalty rates and other terms for statutory and compulsory licenses.
402. Digital Performance Right in Sound Recordings Act of 1995, Pub. L. 104–39, 109 Stat. 336 (codified at 17 U.S.C. §§ 106, 114, 115)
403. Bonneville International Corp. v. Peters, 153 F. Supp. 2d 763 (E.D. Pa. 2001), *aff'd*, 347 F.3d 485 (3d Cir. 2003).
404. 17 U.S.C. § 112 (2017).
405. Webcaster Settlement Act of 2009, Pub. L. 111–36 (codified at 17 U.S.C. § 114(f)(5))
406. Bridgeport Music, Inc. v. Dimension Films, 410 F.3d 792 (6th Cir. 2005).
407. Pub. L. 115–264 (codified in scattered sections of 17 U.S.C.)
408. The classifications set out in this paragraph are not exact. There is considerable overlap. For example, the United States, which is classified as a common law jurisdiction, has a statutory code of laws, as does each state within it. Statutes can overrule judicial precedents, and judges have the power to "overrule" statutes, if they are unconstitutional. Countries and institutions that apply religious law often codify it and/or empower judges to issue decisions with precedential effect.
409. Goodyear Dunlop Tires Operations, S.A. v. Brown, 564 U.S. 915 (2011).
410. *See, e.g.*, OHIO REV. CODE. § 2307.382 (2003).
411. 326 U.S. 310 (1945).
412. 471 U.S. 462 (1985).
413. 952 F. Supp. 1119 (W.D. Pa. 1997).
414. 190 F.3d 333 (5th Cir. 1999).
415. 989 F. Supp. 173 (D. Conn. 1997).
416. *See* Butler v. Beer Across America, 83 F. Supp. 2d 1261 (N.D. Ala. 2000).
417. Instabook v. Instapublisher.com, 469 F. Supp. 2d 1120 (M.D. Fla. 2006).
418. Pres-Kap, Inc. v. System One, Direct Access, Inc., 636 So.2d 1351 (Fla. Ct. App. 1994).
419 Johnson v. King Media, Inc. Civ. No. 01–2311, 2002 WL 1372363 (E.D. Pa. June 24, 2002).
420. Inset Systems, Inc. v. Instruction Set, 937 F. Supp. 161 (D. Conn. 1996); State v. Granite Resorts, 568 N.W.2d 715 (Minn. Ct. App. 1997).
421. 465 U.S. 783 (1984).
422. 433 F.3d 1199 (9th Cir 2006).
423. Burger King v. Rudzewicz, 471 U.S. 462 (1985).
424. The Bremen v. Zapata Offshore Co., 407 U.S. 1 (1972).
425. No. 13301–06 (Stockholm District Court, April 17, 2009).
426. 221 U.S. 280 (1911).
427. 169 F. Supp. 2d 1181 (N.D. Cal. 2001), *rev'd on other grounds*, 433 F.3d 1199 (9th Cir. 2006).

Bibliography

American Law Institute. *Restatement* (3d) *Unfair Competition*. Philadelphia, Pa.: American Law Institute, 1995.

Asay, Clark D. "Consumer Information Privacy and the Problem(s) of Third-Party Disclosures." *Northwestern Journal of Technology and Intellectual Property* 11(5) 2013: 321–57.

Bargfrede, Allen and Cecily Mak. *Music Law in the Digital Age*. Boston: Berklee Press, 2009.

Barrio, Fernando. "The Consistent Inconsistency in Defining Cyberspace Spatial Boundaries." *Revista Academica Facultad de Derecho de la Universidad La Salle* 4, 2007: 83–100

Basedow, Jurgen and Toshiyuki Kono, eds. *Legal Aspects of Globalization: Conflicts of Laws, Internet, Capital Markets and Insolvency in a Global Economy*. Alphen aan den Rijn, the Netherlands: Kluwer Law International, 2000.

Bellia, Tricia, et al. *Cyberlaw: Problems of Policy and Jurisprudence in the Information Age*. 4th ed., St. Paul, Minn.: West, 2010.

Bettinger, Torsten, ed. *Domain Name Law and Practice: An International Handbook*. Oxford University Press, 2005.

Biegel, Stuart. *Beyond Our Control? Confronting the Limits of Our Legal System in the Age of Cyberspace*. Cambridge, Mass.: MIT Press, 2003

Bigos, Oren. "Jurisdiction Over Cross-Border Wrongs on the Internet." *International and Comparative Law Quarterly* 54(3) 2005: 585.

Bolin, Rebecca. "Opting Out of Spam: A Domain Level Do-Not-Spam Registry." *Yale Law & Policy Review* 24(2) 2006: 399–435.

Borchers, Patrick J. "Tort and Contract Jurisdiction via the Internet: The 'Minimum Contacts' Test and the Brussels Regulation Compared." *Netherlands International Law Review* 50(3) 2003: 401–18.

Bronner, Richard, Note, "Constitutional Law—Right of Privacy—Access to Contraceptive Information," *Case Western Reserve Law Review,* 17, 1965: 601.

Calvert, Clay, "Defining 'Public Concern' After Snyder v. Phelps: A Pliable Standard Mingles with News Media Complicity." *Villanova Sports & Entertainment Law Journal* 19(1) 2012: 39–71.

Chatterjee, Charles. *E-Commerce Law for Business Managers*. Kent, U.K.: Financial World Publishing, 2002

Chen, Cindy. "United States and European Union approaches to Internet Jurisdiction and Their Impact on E-Commerce." *University of Pennsylvania Journal of International Economic Law* 25, 2004: 423–54.

Citron, Danielle K. *Hate Crimes in Cyberspace*. Cambridge, Mass.: Harvard University Press, 2014.

Clarkson, Kenneth W. et al., *West's Business Law: Text and Cases – Legal, Ethical, International, and E-Commerce Environment*, 10th ed. St. Paul, Minn.: Thomson/West, 2005.

Collins, Matthew. *The Law of Defamation and the Internet*. 3rd ed., Oxford University Press: 2010.

Cross, Frank B. and Roger L. Miller, *The Legal Environment of Business: Text and Cases*, 9th ed. Stamford, Conn.: Cengage Learning, 2015.

Darrow, Jonathan J. and Gerald R. Ferrera. "The Search Engine Advertising Market: Lucrative Space or Trademark Liability?" *Texas Intellectual Property Law Journal* 17, 2009: 223–68.

Denicola, Robert C. "The New Law of Ideas." *Harvard Journal of Law & Technology* 28(1) 2014: 195–236.

Edwards, Lilian, ed. *The New Legal Framework for E-Commerce in Europe*. Oxford: Hart, 2005.

Edwards, Lilian and Charlotte Waelde, eds. *Law and the Internet*. 3rd ed., Oxford: Hart, 2010.

Engel, Christoph. "The Role of Law in the Governance of the Internet." *International Review of Law, Computers & Technology* 20, 2006: 201–16.

Estrella Faria, Jose A. "Online Contracting: Legal Certainty for Global Business—The New U.N. Convention on the Use of Electronic Communications in International Contracts." *Uniform Commercial Code Law Journal* 39, 2006: 25.

Fellmeth, Aaron Xavier. "Control Without Interest: State Law of Assignment, Federal Preemption, and the Intellectual Property License." *Virginia Journal of Law & Technology* 6, 2001: 8–27.

Ferrera, Gerald R., et al. *Cyberlaw: Text and Cases*, 3rd ed. Cengage Learning: Boston, Mass.. 2012.

Ficsor, Mihály. *The Law of Copyright and the Internet: The 1996 WIPO Treaties, Their Interpretation and Implementation*. Oxford University Press, 2002.

Fishman, Stephen. *Working with Independent Contractors*. 8th ed., Berkeley, Calif.: Nolo Press, 2014.

Garfinkel, Tara B. "Jurisdiction over Communication Torts: Can You Be Pulled into Another Country's Court System for Making a Defamatory Statement over the Internet—A Comparison of English and U.S. Law." *Transnational Lawyer* 9, 1996: 489–542

Geist, Michael. Is There a There There? Toward Greater Certainty for Internet Jurisdiction, *Berkeley Technology Law Journal* 16(3), 2001: 1345–1406.

Gilden, Michael. "Jurisdiction and the Internet: The 'Real World' Meets Cyberspace." *ILSA Journal of International & Comparative Law* 7, 2000: 149–60

Goldberg, David, et al. *Media Law and Practice*. Oxford University Press: 2009.

Grimmelmann, James. *Internet Law: Cases and Problems*. Oregon City: Semaphore Press, 2016.

Haemmerli, Alice. "Why Doctrine Matters: Patent and Copyright Licensing and the Meaning of Ownership in Federal Context." *Columbia Journal of Law and the Arts* 30(1), 2006: 1–47.

Hayes, Arthur S. *Mass Media Law: The Printing Press to the Internet*. New York: Peter Lang Publishing, 2013.

Hestermeyer, Holger P. "Personal Jurisdiction for Internet Torts: Towards an International Solution." *Northwestern Journal of International Law & Business* 26, 2005: 267.

Hill, Joshua B. and Nancy E. Marion. *Introduction to Cybercrime: Computer Crimes, Laws, and Policing in the 21st Century*. Santa Barbara, Calif.: Praeger, 2016.

Hiller, Janine. and Ronnie Cohen. *Internet Law and Policy*. Upper Saddle River, N.J.: Pearson, 2002.

James, Tom. *Copyright Protection for Websites*. Plymouth, Minn.: Echion, 2017.

_____. *Website Law*. Plymouth, Minn.: Echion, 2017.

Jennings, Lora M. "Finding Legal Certainty for E-Commerce: Traditional Personal Jurisdiction Analysis and the Scope of the Zippo Sliding Scale." *Washburn Law Journal* 44(2), 2005: 381–412.

Jezairian, Sarah K. "Lost in the Virtual Mall: Is Traditional Personal Jurisdiction Analysis Applicable to E-Commerce Cases?" *Arizona Law Review* 42, 2000: 965.

Johnson, David R and David R. Post. "Law and Borders: The Rise of Law in Cyberspace." *Stanford Law Review* 48, 1996: 1367–1404.

Kang, Peter H. and Jia Ann Yang. "Doctrine of Indivisibility Revived?" *Santa Clara Computer & High-tech Law Journal* 18(3), 365–75: (2002)>

Khosrow-pour, Mehdi, ed. *Advanced Topics in Electronic Commerce*. Hershey, Penn.: Idea Group Publishing, 2005.

Kilbey, Ian. "Jurisdiction and Choice of Law Clauses in Internet Contracts. Part One—Package Holidays." *International Travel Law Journal* 2002: 203–206.

Kohn, Al and Bob Kohn. *Kohn on Music Licensing*, 4th ed. Frederick, Md.: Aspen Publishers, 2009.

Kubota, Takashi. *Cyberlaw for Global E-Business: Finance, Payments, and Dispute Resolution*. Hershey, Penn.: Information Science Reference, 2008.

Kunz, Christina L. et al., "Browsewrap Agreements: Validity of Implied Assent in Electronic Form Agreements." *Business Lawyer* 59(1), 2003: 279–312.

Lemley, Mark A. "Intellectual Property and Shrinkwrap Licenses." *Southern California Law Review* 68, 2000: 1239–94.

Lemley, Mark A. et al., *Software and Internet Law*. 4th ed., New York: Wolters Kluwer, 2011.

Leval, Pierre N. "Toward a Fair Use Standard." *Harvard Law Review* 103, 1990: 1105–36.

Love, Michelle. "International Jurisdiction over the Internet: A Case Analysis of *Yahoo! Inc. v. La Ligue contre le Racisme et L'antisemitisme*." *Temple International and Comparative Law Journal* 17(1), 2003: 261.

Maggs, Peter and John Soma. *Internet and Computer Law*, 4th ed. St. Paul, Minn.: West, 2013.

Martin, Trudy S. "Vicarious and Contributory Liability for Internet Host Providers: Combating Copyright Infringement in the United States, Russia and China." *Wisconsin International Law Journal* 27, 2009: 363.

McCarthy, J. Thomas. *McCarthy on Trademarks and Unfair Competition*. St. Paul, Minn.: West, 2002.

_____. *The Rights of Publicity and Privacy*. New York: Clark Boardman, 1992.

McLeod, Kembrew and Peter DiCola. *Creative License: The Law and Culture of Digital Sampling*. Durham, N.C.: Duke University Press, 2011.

Melvin, Sean P. *CyberLaw and E-Commerce Regulation: An Entrepreneurial Approach*. Mason, Ohio: Thomson/South-Western, 2005.

Munir, Abu B. *Internet Banking: Law and Practice*. LexisNexis Butterworths, 2004

Nair, Abhilash. *The Regulation of Internet Pornography: Issues and Challenges*. New York: Routledge, 2018.

Newman, Christopher M. "An Exclusive License Is Not an Assignment: Disentangling Divisibility and Transferability of Ownership in Copyright." *Louisiana Law Review* 74(1), 2013: 59–115.

Nguyen, Xuan-Thao. "Should It Be a Free for All? The Challenge of Extending Trade Dress Protection to the Look and Feel of Websites in the Evolving Internet." *American University Law Review* 49(6), 2000" 1232–77.

Nimmer, Melville D. and David Nimmer. *Nimmer on Copyright*. New York: Matthew Bender, 2013.

Nunziato, Dawn C. *Virtual Freedom: Net Neutrality and Free Speech in the Internet Age*. Stanford, Calif.: Stanford University Press, 2009.

Organisation for Economic Cooperation and Development. *Guidelines for Consumer Protection in the Context of Electronic Commerce*, Paris: OECD, 1999

Packard, Ashley. *Digital Media Law*. 2nd ed., Malden, Mass: Wiley-Blackwell, 2013.

Pappas, Christopher W. "Comparative U.S. and E.U. Approaches to E-Commerce Regulation: Jurisdiction, Electronic Contracts, Electronic Signatures and Taxation." *Denver Journal of International Law and Policy* 31, 2002: 325.

Patry, William F. *Patry on Copyright*. St. Paul, Minn: Thomson/West, 2013.

Pearson, Mark and Mark Polden. *The Journalist's Guide to Media Law: A Handbook for Communicators in a Digital World*. 5th Ed., Crow's Nest, N.S.W.: Allen & Unwin, 2011.

Pember, Don R. and Clay Calvert. *Mass Media Law*. 19th ed., New York: McGraw-Hill, 2015.

Post, David G. "Governing Cyberspace: Law." *Santa Clara Computer High Technology Law Journal* 24(4), 2008: 883–913.

Radin, Margaret et al. *Intellectual Property and the Internet: Cases and Materials*. New York: Foundation Press, 2004.

Reed, C. *Internet Law: Text and Materials*. 2nd ed., Cambridge, U.K.: Cambridge University Press, 2004.

Rosen, Jeffrey. "The Web Means the End of Forgetting." *New York Times Sunday Magazine*, July 25, 2010: MM30.

Rustad, Michael L. *Internet Law in a Nutshell*. St. Paul, Minn.: West, 2009.

_____. Software Licensing, *Cloud Computing Agreements, Open-Source, and Internet Terms of Use: A Practical Approach to Information Age Contracts in a Global Setting*. LexisNexis, 2016.

Rustad, Michael L and Thomas H. Koenig. "Cybertorts and Legal Lag: An Empirical Analysis." *Southern California Interdisciplinary Law Journal* 13, 2008: 77.

Rustad, Michael L. and Sandra R. Paulsson. "Monitoring Employee Email and Internet Usage: Avoiding the Omniscient Electronic Sweatshop: Insights from Europe." *University of Pennsylvania Journal of Labor and Employment Law* 7(4), 2005: 829–904.

Schachter, Madeleine and Joel Kurtz. *Law of Internet Speech*. Durham, N.C.: Carolina Academic Press, 2008.

Schechter, Roger E. and John R. Thomas. *Intellectual Property: The Law of Copyrights, Patents and Trademarks*. St. Paul, Minn.: West, 2003.

Smart, Ursula. *Media and Entertainment Law*. New York: Routledge, 2014.

Solove, Daniel J. *The Future of Reputation: Gossip, Rumor and Privacy on the Internet*. New Haven, Conn.: Yale University Press, 2007.

Spindler, Gerald and Fritjof Börner, eds., *E-Commerce Law in Europe and the USA*. New York: Springer, 2002.

Street, F. Lawrence and Mark P. Grant. *Law of the Internet*. Newark, N.J.: Lexis, 2003.

Tham, Yang-Ming. "Honest to Blog: Balancing the Interests of Public Figures and Anonymous Bloggers in Defamation Lawsuits." *Villanova Sports & Entertainment Law Journal* 17(1), 2010: 229–67.

Towers-Romero, Sandi. *Media and Entertainment Law*. Clifton Park, N.Y.: Delmar Cengage Learning, 2009.

Tushnet, Rebecca. "Power Without Responsibility: Intermediaries and the First Amendment." *George Washington Law Review* 76, 2008: 101–31.

Twomey, David P. and Marianne Moody Jennings. *Business Law*. 4th ed. Stamford, Conn.: Cengage Learning, 2014.

U.S. Copyright Office. *Compendium of U.S. Copyright Office Practices*. 3rd ed. Washington, D.C.: Copyright Office, 2014.

U.S. Patent and Trademark Office. *Trademark Manual of Examining Procedures*. St. Paul, Minn.: Thomson Reuters, 2017.

Uniform Law Commission and American Law Institute. *Uniform Commercial Code*. Philadelphia, Penn.: American Law Institute, 2018.

Waldman, Barry J. "A Unified Approach to Cyber-Libel: Defamation on the Internet: A Suggested Approach." *Richmond Journal of Law and Technology* 6(2), 1999: 9.

Wang, Faye F. *Internet Jurisdiction and Choice of Law: Legal Practices in the EU, US and China*. New York: Cambridge University Press, 2010.

_____. Law of Electronic Commercial Transactions: Contemporary Issues in the EU, US, China, 2d ed. New York: Routledge, 2014.

Warner, Richard, et al. *E-Commerce, the Internet and the Law: Cases and Materials*. St. Paul, Minn.: West, 2006.

Warren, Samuel D. and Louis Brandeis. "The Right to Privacy." *Harvard Law Review* 4(5), 1890: 193–220.

Westby, Jody R. *International Guide to Cybersecurity*. Chicago, Ill.: American Bar Association, 2004.

_____. *International Guide to Privacy*. Chicago, Ill. American Bar Association, 2005.

Zittrain, Jonathan. *The Future of the Internet—And How to Stop It*. New Haven, Conn.: Yale University Press, 2008.

Table of Statutes and Cases

U.S. CONSTITUTION

U.S. CODE SECTIONS

FEDERAL RULES AND REGULATIONS

STATE STATUTES

STATE REGULATIONS

CASES

INDEX

CPSIA information can be obtained
at www.ICGtesting.com
Printed in the USA
LVHW101041220721
693399LV00005B/124

9 781946 397065